New Testament Theology and Ethics

VOLUME TWO

Ben Witherington III

IVP Academic

An imprint of InterVarsity Press
Downers Grove, Illinois

InterVarsity Press
P.O. Box 1400, Downers Grove, IL 60515-1426
ivpress.com
email@ivpress.com

InterVarsity Press® is the book-publishing division of InterVarsity Christian Fellowship/USA®, a movement of students and faculty active on campus at hundreds of universities, colleges and schools of nursing in the United States of America, and a member movement of the International Fellowship of Evangelical Students. For information about local and regional activities, visit intervarsity.org.

Table 4.3, p. 240, is taken from Donald A. Hagner, Encountering the Book of Hebrews, *published by Baker Academic, a division of Baker Publishing Group, ©2002. Used by permission.*

The chart on pp. 390-91 is adapted from Ben Witherington III, The New Testament Story, *©2004, and used by permission of Eerdmans, Grand Rapids, Mich.*

All Scripture quotations, unless otherwise indicated, are the author's translation.

Cover design: Cindy Kiple
Interior design: Beth McGill
Images: axlll/iStockphoto

ISBN 978-0-8308-5134-8 (print)
ISBN 978-0-8308-9984-5 (digital)

Printed in the United States of America ∞

Library of Congress Cataloging-in-Publication Data
Names: Witherington, Ben, III, 1951- author.
Title: New Testament theology and ethics / Ben Witherington III.
Description: Downers Grove : InterVarsity Press, 2016- | Includes index.
Identifiers: LCCN 2015050897 (print) | LCCN 2016001403 (ebook) | ISBN 9780830851331 (v. 1 : pbk. : alk. paper) | ISBN 9780830899838 (eBook)
Subjects: LCSH: Bible. New Testament—Theology. | Ethics in the Bible.
Classification: LCC BS2397 .W58 2016 (print) | LCC BS2397 (ebook) | DDC 230/.0415—dc23
LC record available at http://lccn.loc.gov/2015050897

P	23	22	21	20	19	18	17	16	15	14	13	12	11	10	9	8	7	6	5	4	3	2	1
Y	35	34	33	32	31	30	29	28	27	26	25	24	23	22	21	20	19	18	17	16			

To Nancy and Jerry
whose kindness and sharing of their
Vermont retreat house helped make this possible

And to Dr. Aaron Kuecker,
my former doctoral student who spent many hours
reading and making helpful suggestions and corrections
so that this volume would be a Word on target

Summary of Contents

Contents

Tables

Figures

REWIND

A Brief Synopsis of Volume 1

The first volume of this two-volume work undertook the descriptive task of showing how the various authors of the New Testament, and Jesus as well, did their theologizing and ethicizing. It was emphasized that all, or almost all, of these authors were Jews who became convinced that the eschatological situation changed when Jesus of Nazareth entered the picture. They believed that the long-promised eschatological salvation and royal reign of God upon the earth had broken into human history in the person and through the work of Jesus of Nazareth. This shared conviction shaped how they viewed their symbolic universe and how they had revised their storied world and the theologizing and ethicizing that they did out of that storied world.

Since they were monotheistic Jews (or in the case of Luke and of the author of 2 Peter, perhaps, God-fearers) who still lived in and believed in a collectivistic concept of community that shared this seismic shift in their thinking about God, world, believing community, and other subjects, it is not surprising that the ideological boundaries of this thinking, both theological and ethical, nevertheless remained rather clear. The actual range of acceptable thought was not broad when it came to Jesus and his first followers. The Jesus evangelistic movement in the first century was not a huge or hugely diverse movement, even when the Gentile mission became ascendant in the second half of the century, as it was still largely led by Jews and their coworkers who had rather closely knit social networks throughout the empire and throughout the first century A.D. Theologizing and ethicizing in this social movement were not done in isolation, nor was this a matter of intellectual mavericks creating personal communities or cadres. Rather, a high value was placed on tradition, including the Jesus tradition, and on a shared constellation of beliefs and behaviors.

Jesus and his first followers saw it as crucial to remain faithful to the God of the Old Testament, to remain faithful to the concept of covenant as a way of describing the relationship between God and his people, to remain faithful to the high level of ethical demand within those covenants. In other words, what we do not find in the New Testament is one author who advocates monotheism and another who advocates tritheism, or one author who advocates a rigoristic sexual ethic and another who is libertine, or one author who suggests that its all about belief while another says that "faith without works is dead." Nor do we find one author who says that "the kingdom of God is at hand" and another who says that we are not in the eschatological age. And equally clear is that at the heart of the thinking, believing, and behaving of all these writers is Jesus Christ. He was the change agent, but at the same time he showed the way that eschatological change could be viewed within the context of the Old Testament and early Jewish thought world, such that his followers could conclude, in good sectarian manner, that they were the true, or truest, form of the development of biblical religion, both in terms of orthodoxy and orthopraxy.

The detailed survey of theologizing and ethicizing in the first volume looked not just at the so-called major witnesses (e.g., Paul and the Johannine writers), but at all the materials in the New Testament. Only so could we prepare to see what a theology and ethics of the New Testament might look like, valuing and drawing on all the canonical witnesses. Indeed, I felt it important to do detailed exegetical spade work especially in the portions of the New Testament too often neglected or underplayed in studies of New Testament theology and/or ethics.

Importantly, there emerged a rather clear picture of the interface or interrelationship between theology and ethics as done by Jesus and the writers of the New Testament. I suggested that the concept of the *imago dei* and its renewal in Christ provided us with the necessary bridging concept. By this is meant that all human beings are created in God's image, and after the fall they need to be renewed in that image in order to have an ongoing positive relationship with God. Salvation involves the restoration not merely of relationship between God and humankind, but of human character so that the relationship can be both ongoing and positive rather than sporadic and broken. The aim of salvation is not merely to restart a relationship, but to conform a group of people to the image of God's Son, who is the ultimate image of God ever to grace the earth with his presence.

Salvation, then, involves both belief and behavior, both cognitive content and character. As God is loving, holy, just, and good, so he intends to renovate for himself a people who are loving, holy, just, and good. Ethics is the working out of the saving activity that God's Spirit has been working in and into us, to will and to do. This is why there is so much emphasis in the New Testament on what we would call character or virtue ethics. Salvation thus involves both the divine initiative and the human response, where there is time and opportunity for it. Ethics is not merely gratitude for grace; it is the working out of one's salvation in gracious ways, relying continually on the grace and Spirit of God not merely to renew and sanctify our thinking about God, but also to empower our behaving in Christlike fashion, living out of the new creaturehood that we have in Christ. But new creaturehood or the new birth is but the beginning of salvation. One must go through all three stages of eschatological salvation, including the final conformity to Christ's resurrected image at the eschaton, before salvation is complete.

A Christian is a person who says, "I have been saved, I am being saved, I shall be saved," and that process is neither perfect nor complete until it has reached its terminus. Short of that, infidelity and even apostasy are possible for the Christian. One is not eternally secure until one is securely in eternity. Eschatology undergirds the ethics with stern warnings for Christians who turn back, who make shipwreck of their faith and thus face the wrath to come.

Calling and election, then, are not pillows on which the Christian may rest his or her head; rather, they are ensigns of God's love and initiative, for fallen persons would never love God had he not taken the initiative. Unsurprisingly, election and salvation are viewed by the New Testament writers as collectivistic in character. They happen in Israel in Old Testament times, or in Christ in the New Testament times, and what determines who is a true Jew or a true Christian is not merely grace, but who responds to grace in faith. Salvation, whether initial or final, is by grace, but it is by grace through faith, a faith that the believer must fully and freely exercise without predetermination. Only so could there be a loving response to a loving God. A God who is love made creatures in his image so that they too might love him and their fellow creatures fully, freely, and without predetermination. It must be freely given and freely received, or else we have no proper relationship.

Since salvation involves both belief and behavior, both cognitive and character content, it is unsurprising that we find even in the Pauline corpus the stress on "the obedience that flows forth from faith" or, to put it another way, the law of Christ that all Christians are obligated to keep having been reborn by God's grace. This gracious law involves the teaching of Jesus, those portions of Old Testament teachings that have been reaffirmed in Christ, and the new apostolic teachings that build on these earlier Christian teachings. Discipleship can be summed up as taking up one's cross and following the example of Jesus, as being cocrucified with Christ, as being conformed to the image of God's risen Son. The cross does not merely raise the specter of the death of the old fallen self; it provides the means thereto, for the old person is buried into Christ's death and emerges a new creature in Christ. To put it another way, "We are all baptized by the Holy Spirit into the one body, and all are given the one Spirit from which we (continually must) drink" (see 1 Cor 12:13).

Salvation, however, is but the means to the final end, which is the true worship of God, which is the ensign that the relationship between creature and Creator has been fully restored and made right. All creatures great and small have been made to praise their Maker while they have breath. And so it is that the canon of the New Testament leaves us at its very end with a breathtaking image of final worship when the kingdoms of this world become the kingdoms of our God and of his Christ.

Thus, theology and ethics in and of the New Testament are christocentric, christotelic, christophoric, for as the author of the latest New Testament book says, it is the believer's destination to become "partakers of the divine nature" (2 Pet 1:4), or as Paul would put it, "to be fully conformed to the image of God's Son" (Rom 8:29). In this volume we must explore fully some of these concepts and so discover what a theology and ethics of the New Testament does indeed look like.

PROLEGOMENA

Is New Testament Theology or Ethics Possible?

The Bible tells us not how we should talk to God, but what he says to us; not how we find the way to him, but how he has sought and found the way to us. . . . The Word of God is within the Bible.

KARL BARTH[1]

If one is a student of the scholarly work that has earned the label "New Testament theology," it becomes obvious, after only a little study, that in the modern era New Testament theology, like Old Testament theology, has largely been a Protestant preoccupation until the last ten years or so. The recent study of the subject was set in motion by the landmark work in German by Rudolf Bultmann undertaken between 1948 and 1953 and translated into English in the 1950s and by his German and Swiss successors Hans Conzelmann, Joachim Jeremias, Oscar Cullmann, and Leonhard Goppelt, to mention but a few. As profound and rich as Bultmann's work was, it was overwhelmingly a study of Paul and the Johannine corpus, not the whole of the New Testament by any means. It also had the odd feature of combining a reading of the New Testament through an existentialist lens with a history-of-religions approach to a good deal of the subject matter, not to mention resting on the judgment that Jesus and his teaching were only the presupposition of New Testament theology and not a part of it.[2] Today, few scholars would follow Bultmann's lead in these approaches if the subject is New Testament theology, and rightly so. But a historical approach to the subject

---

[1]Karl Barth, "The Strange New World Within the Bible," in *The Word of God and the Word of Man* (Gloucester, Mass.: Peter Smith), pp. 43, 45.
[2]See the analysis by Frank J. Matera, *New Testament Theology: Exploring Diversity and Unity* (Louisville: Westminster John Knox, 2007), pp. xxi-xxii.

does not require a history of religions approach, as we will see. Frank Matera puts it this way: "Inasmuch as the New Testament communicates its theology through specific narrative and epistolary forms, a theology of the New Testament ought to be a literary and theological analysis of the New Testament writings rather than a history of early Christian thought."[3]

Bultmann's successors fared only a little better, with Jeremias providing a corrective by focusing in his first volume on Jesus, and the others providing more comprehensive approaches than Bultmann undertook.[4] The landmark work of Bultmann also intimated and set a precedent for two notions: (1) New Testament theology is a subject that could and should be treated separately from New Testament ethics (which was seen as a less lofty subject); (2) only certain portions of the New Testament have enough theological ore in them to be worth mining. The present study, in both its focus and emphases, will attempt to overcome and correct both of these presuppositional and methodological deficiencies, which are all too common even in much more recent studies of New Testament theology. Surprisingly, what few of those German and Swiss studies that set the modern discussion in motion were even willing to admit or discuss is that if one talks about New Testament theology or New Testament ethics, one must have some sort of presumption or view about what allows one to undertake such a study, what unifies a subject such as that. In fact, the invisible elephant in the room that such commentators were unwilling to actually discuss was the revealer God who inspired various persons to speak his truth. We have gotten to an odd place indeed when one is not prepared to talk at all about God's possible role in producing books that talk about God!

In other words, before one can do or discover a New Testament theology or ethic, there must be in place a certain way of viewing the New Testament. One must assume that a New Testament theology or ethic exists and can be found in or ferreted out of the diverse texts we call "the New Testament." Unlike the enterprise of looking at the theologies in the New Testament that can be a purely historical and descriptive one that presupposes no faith commitments necessarily, the enterprise undertaken in the present volume presupposes a view of the whole New Testament, namely, that it is in some sense a unity, and more specifically that this unity is given by God. This in

---

[3]Ibid., p. xxvii.
[4]See D. A. Carson, "New Testament Theology," in *Dictionary of the Later New Testament and Its Developments*, ed. R. P. Martin and P. H. Davids (Downers Grove, Ill.: InterVarsity Press, 1997), pp. 796-814.

turn implies a theory about the way God has revealed himself, his will, and his salvation to diverse persons. It also implies a theory of revelation leading to inspiration leading to inscripturation.[5]

I do not intend here to retread all the ground that I have already covered in my book *The Living Word of God*[6] and that I will touch on briefly when I discuss the symbolic universe of the New Testament writers. Here it must suffice to say that in my view, the main issue is not whether we view the Bible, and in this case the New Testament in particular, as God's Word or Scripture, although that is important, but whether the New Testament in fact is, and presents itself as, God's living Word. In my view, the Bible is God's Word whether I believe it or not, know it or not, trust it or not. In short, it is the ontology of the Bible itself that is at issue, not my belief in it or even what I believe about it. This is another way of saying that the New Testament conveys, and claims to convey, the truth about God and his relationships with human beings.

The New Testament makes certain inherent truth claims, and what often happens when we encounter the New Testament with an open heart is that we are "seized by truth"—to borrow the title of an important book by Joel Green.[7] I realize, of course, that whether the Bible functions as Scripture for me depends on how I relate to the Bible, but in my view, that is a second-order question, not the main question. In the rest of this prolegomena I wish to talk more about the New Testament as sacred text, as Word of God, in the context of interacting with Green's book.

THE NEW TESTAMENT AS THE WORD OF GOD: CRITICAL REFLECTIONS ON JOEL B. GREEN'S *SEIZED BY TRUTH*

Green begins his study by pointing out that while it has been something of a mantra in biblical studies that the Bible should be read as we would read any other book, this very approach impedes a reading of the Bible as Scripture.[8]

---

[5]Matera stresses that the descriptive approach to the various New Testament theologies or ethics is insufficient: "For those who ascribe scriptural status to the writings of the New Testament the task of New Testament theology should be bolder. For inasmuch as they identify these writings as Scripture, which bears witness to God's self-revelation, they suppose that these writings possess an inner coherence that is ultimately rooted in God's self-revelation" (*New Testament Theology*, p. xxvii). He then suggests that a New Testament theology should be a work that integrates and relates the various diverse theologies of the New Testament into a unified whole but without harmonizing them. But to do the latter is to create a theology on the basis of the New Testament here and now, not merely uncover one.

[6]Ben Witherington III, *The Living Word of God: Rethinking the Theology of the Bible* (Waco, Tex.: Baylor University Press, 2008).

[7]Joel B. Green, *Seized by Truth: Reading the Bible as Scripture* (Nashville: Abingdon, 2007).

[8]Ibid., p. 2.

Embracing the Bible as a revelation from God, as a coherent whole, as Scripture is a step of faith, and it requires that we attend better to "what we bring with us when we bring ourselves to the task of reading the Bible."[9]

Green stresses that to call the Bible Scripture or the Word of God is to make a theological statement, and it not only draws attention to the origin, role, and aim of these texts in God's self-communication, but also reveals something about the person making the statement. It reveals that person's faith commitments. Nevertheless, it is not the faith commitment that makes the Bible the Word of God or changes information into revelation. Many persons know the Bible well but do not know the God of the Bible. Faith is not required to recognize that the Bible tells the truth about this or that historical or geographical or other sort of factual matter, but to recognize that the Bible is telling the truth about God and the divine human encounter and about the theological interpretation of all of reality requires more than a keen intellect. In short, I am suggesting that the order of things is from the text to faith, not from my faith to the text, for it is the truth in the text that helped form my faith in the first place. The Bible and its truth claims are logically prior to and, as applied by the Holy Spirit, are what prompt or engender anyone's faith response.

In an interesting comparison, Green stresses that whereas paintings are experienced as a whole and at once, texts, by their very nature, are linear, and they reveal their secrets progressively, rather like listening to a sermon.[10] I would insist, however, that with rare exceptions, the New Testament texts that we have were meant to be heard whole in their literary content, exactly like a sermon, and not be taken as sound bites. Is, then, the doing of New Testament theology or ethics a violation of the intended character of how this revelation was meant to be heard, received, and believed? By this I mean, is the extracting of theological or ethical ore from the New Testament working at cross-purposes with how these texts were meant to be heard? I think that the answer to this question can be yes, especially if we take a history-of-ideas sort of approach to New Testament theology and ethics rather than attending to the symbolic universe and narrative thought world in which these ideas are embedded and expressed. Green is right: "Reading the whole text, and reading the text as a whole, together with attention to sequence, thus become nonnegotiable protocols for the competent interpreter."[11]

---

[9]Ibid., p. 3.
[10]Ibid., p. 7.
[11]Ibid., p. 8.

Green goes on to stress that "more necessary than familiarity with ancient peoples, and their cultures, more basic than learning the biblical languages, and more essential than good technique in interpretation are such dispositions and postures as acceptance, devotion, attention and trust. Accordingly, we acknowledge and invite the ongoing work of Scripture's divine author as the One capable and desirous of authoring a community, the church."[12] It appears that he is suggesting a prioritizing of things that I would not entirely agree with. You have to know what and whom you are submitting to before making a viable and vital faith commitment. This in turn requires a certain familiarity with the historical substance of the text. In other words, historical study of the text must not be placed behind faith commitment to the text if we want to both understand and adore our God; rather, it must be seen as an indispensible part of such an undertaking. A deep appreciation of the historical context of the Bible is, at the end of the day, required to properly understand and interpret a great deal of the text.

What the text meant in the first century is still what it means today, though it may have different implications, applications, and significance for us in our time. To say otherwise is to open the door to turning the Bible into God's Ouija board that we use to find the meanings that we deeply wish to be in God's revelation. Instead, the New Testament teaches us in its historical particularity that we must enter its world to understand it through serious study and an act of creative imagination and openness to the otherness of the text. The historical givenness of the text also signals to us like a beacon that the biblical mandates must be lived out specifically and in detail. The New Testament is not serving up insipid platitudes for general consumption regardless of one's level of understanding or faith commitments.

Green is quite right that if we are to discover a New Testament theology or ethics in these texts, a posture of openness and trust is required. We must let these texts shape our thinking and our lives as we seek to understand them. This was put in simple terms by Johannes Bengel long ago: "Apply the whole of yourself to the text [not just your intellectual curiosity], and apply the whole of the text to yourself." But what happens when we do this? Does our posture in relationship to the Bible and our acceptance of it as Scripture somehow change the meaning of the text, at least for us? Here is where I say that the Bible is Scripture whether or not I recognize that it is so, and its truth is resident in the text whether or not I ever receive it or believe it. My posture

---

[12]Ibid., pp. 10-11.

toward or attitude about the matter changes nothing about the Bible itself; it simply changes my degree of openness and receptivity to what is in the text and makes me a better interpreter of the text.

Green suggests that if we accept the premise of historical criticism that "the meaning of texts resides at their historical address," then therefore "historical criticism has no intrinsic need and little room for the theological claim constituted by the joining together of these two collections [the Old Testament and New Testament] as one 'book.'"[13] I see no necessary connection between the acceptance of the historical grounding of meaning in the biblical text and the rejection of theological claims in and about the Old Testament or the New Testament or both as the Word of God. Indeed, one can also stress that since the Bible is loaded with all sorts of theological claims made about God, and even occasionally made about itself (see 2 Tim 3:16), we will not be well served by either historical or theological reductionism when it comes to the meaning of these texts. These texts make both sorts of claims, including making theological claims in their historical givenness.

Part of what Green is driving at is that the Old Testament too must be seen as Christian Scripture, but in what sense? Taking a certain kind of approach to 1 Peter 1:10-12, Green concludes, "What is problematic is the suggestion that this theological pattern is the consequence of reading with a new lens provided by the advent of Christ. What Peter makes clear, actually, is that *this theological pattern is resident already in the Scriptures of Israel themselves.*"[14] Green clarifies his views:

> For me to say that 1 Peter has it that the Spirit of Christ was inspiring the prophets is not anachronistically for me to make the prophets Christian or for me to claim that they use specifically Christian terms. Similarly, for me to say with Jesus in Luke that all the Scriptures have it that the Messiah must suffer and so forth does not mean that I think either that the Old Testament has a "Christian" character or that this character is sitting on top of the Old Testament text. It is rather to say—with [Brevard] Childs, for example—that, say, Isaiah speaks to the same ontological reality to which Jesus in Luke also points or to which Peter points. It is to say that God's character and purpose are already resident in the Scriptures, so that the good news is not alien to those writings even if it has not (always) been apparent to those who read it. So, for example, the "opening of minds" in Luke 24 allows the disciples to see

---

[13]Ibid., p. 35.
[14]Ibid., p. 38 (italics mine).

what Jesus sees in the Scriptures; it does not alter those Scriptures in order that they might say something alien to their nature. It is not, then, that Christians co-opt the Scriptures of Israel as their own. It is that they have found in them the ways of God and, then, their identity with God. So the Scriptures of Israel are not awaiting the advent of Christ so that they might have their revelatory moment (as though their only or primary purpose was to point ahead) but, before the advent of Christ, are already revelatory of the character and ways of God. What we find in, say, Luke and 1 Peter, then, is the theological claim that Israel's Scriptures speak to the same reality of God's character and ways that we find in Christ—though, who would have known this, apart from the work of the Spirit and divine illumination?[15]

We can talk, then, about how these texts foreshadow Christ and even predict the coming of the Son of Man or suffering servant, but it is another matter entirely to suggest that the Old Testament was already speaking in specifically Christian terms, and it is doubtful this is what Peter is actually claiming, nor is Green.

Indeed, as Green will go on to point out, Luke 24 makes evident that without specific enlightenment from Jesus and by means of the Holy Spirit that leads to the opening of the minds of the followers of Jesus, even seeing the prospective character of the Old Testament and its possible reference to the Christ-event would not happen.[16] Why would such pneumatic illumination and study be necessary if the "Christian" character of the Old Testament was there on the surface of the Old Testament text for all to see? What Jesus is pointing to is the teleological character of the Old Testament, pointing forward to something later, something greater than the prophets themselves fully knew or understood or even spoke of. We are not talking here about a surplus of meaning in the text so much as a surplus of fulfillment of the text in the Christ-event.

The prophets themselves were addressing their own age and people, but the larger significance and the ultimate fulfillment of what they spoke would come only in the Christ-event, something of which they only had vague inklings at the time. They knew that they spoke about the future, but they did not have a clear or full understanding of the shape that future would take. As Green, taking issue with the views of some scholars, rightly observes, the Old Testament is not simply a Christian book in advance of the coming of Christ,

---

[15]Joel B. Green, e-mail to the author, September 5, 2008.
[16]Green, *Seized by Truth*, p. 44.

and we do a disservice to our interfaith discussions with our Jewish friends if we claim more about the Old Testament than it claims for itself or, for that matter, than the New Testament writers claim about it.

Does embracing the Bible as a whole as Scripture entail the claim that we must embrace all its stories as "'our own story,' and see the plotline of our lives as continuous with and an ongoing extension of the Biblical narrative"?[17] Of course, in one sense the answer to this is yes, but only in a carefully nuanced way of putting things. We have been inserted into a preexisting story. The story has not been coopted by us, the Christians.

Can we really say, as Green does, "Both of us—God's people then and God's people now—are the church constituted by the Scriptures read in this way"?[18] Green envisions a solidarity and continuity of the primitive church with the church today and at the eschaton, and in one sense this is true; all are Christians submitting to the authority of God's Word. However, different church groups have interpreted that word very differently, indeed have often suggested not only that their way of interpreting the text is the one appropriate one, but also that in fact their church is the only true continuation of the church of the apostles. Green rightly rejects these latter sort of claims and wants to stress the solidarity of all Christians in all generations, so "the text we call the Bible was put together in the first place by the same community that needs to interpret it."[19] The problem that I see with this comes when we ask, "And how is the church universal related to Israel as God's people and to the Hebrew Scriptures of Israel?"

Sometimes the ecclesiocentric way of putting things gets it exactly backwards from how Paul, in Romans 9–11, viewed the matter. There he tells his mostly Gentile audience that they are the wild olive branch being grafted into the true vintage Israelite olive tree, and that although there always has been only one people of God, it is not the Gentile church in all generations, but Israel. A supersessionist approach is basically the kind of argument Paul counters in Romans 9–11 to put arrogant Gentile Christians in their place. Yes, it is true that there always has been only one people of God, and in its current and ongoing phase since the coming of Jesus that people is Jew and Gentile united in Christ, but that does not allow one to then claim that the Old Testament people were simply Christians or that the Hebrew Scriptures

---

[17]Ibid., p. 50.
[18]Ibid.
[19]Ibid., pp. 50-51 (he is quoting Lutheran theologian Robert Jenson).

are simply the church's book. That would be supersessionism, not comple-
tionism. Green, to his credit, is not arguing for such an approach. He is in
fact arguing in the sort of way some canonical theologians such as Brevard
Childs would argue and against some of the things that Francis Watson has
suggested. In other words, some of the ecclesiocentric approaches tend in a
direction that goes against what Paul is insisting on in Romans 9–11.

Christians are indeed indebted to Jews still today, for theirs is the adoption, theirs the covenants, theirs the promises, theirs the Messiah according
to the flesh, as Paul says at the beginning of Romans 9. If asked whether
the Old Testament is still a Jewish book for Jewish persons and if the Jews
in some sense are still the people of God, Paul would have answered yes and
yes. He admits that those who reject Christ are temporarily broken off from
the people of God, but he foresees a day when they can be reintegrated back
into that people, so that "all Israel will be saved" (see Rom 11:25-30). Paul's
bottom-line answer as to whether God has forsaken his first chosen people is
no. It should be ours as well.

One of the claims that Green wants to make at several junctures in his
book is that the Bible is addressed to all God's people in all generations.[20]
In my estimation, this view is questionable, not least because this is actually
historically false. God addresses specific messages to certain specific groups
of his people at specific times and places, precisely because our God is a God
of history who enters and speaks in history through specific persons such as
Amos, Isaiah, and Paul. The fact that I am not personally the addressee of this
or that biblical book does not mean that it cannot speak to me as a latter-day
hearer of this text; however, I am a secondary audience neither foreseen nor
intended by the human authors of Scripture. The fact that God will have
foreseen this and would want me to hear and respond to the Bible in no way
alleviates me of the responsibility of recognizing I am a later overhearer of
this text, not its first intended audience. We gain nothing of Christian value
by denying the specificity of the biblical texts.[21]

For example, the letter of Philemon was not addressed to me or to any

---

[20]See ibid., p. 60, where Green specifically makes this claim about the Old Testament.

[21]Of course, it is true that occasionally the writers of the Old Testament had both their own immediate audience and a more distant one in view (e.g., Ps 102:18: "write it down for a generation
yet to come"). What we learn from this, however, is that in an oral culture one of the reasons
for both speaking and writing something down is that the latter allows the communication to
have a further or additional audience. One this point, Ben Witherington III, *What's in the Word?
Rethinking the Socio-Rhetorical Character of the New Testament* (Waco, Tex.: Baylor University Press,
2009), chap. 1.

modern Western Christian. It was addressed to a first-century leader named "Philemon" and to the church that met in his house. The spiritual continuity that I have with him (we are both Christians) does not provide me with a historical continuity that allows me to ignore the original historical context and its originally intended meaning. The fact that there has been a continual Christian community through all the centuries between Philemon and me does not make my reading or misreading of the text automatically in direct continuity with how Philemon would have heard it. The church has developed over time and developed various different ways of interpreting the text over time. To say that we are in the same position as the original hearers is not true historically. Historical biblical studies does not need to be recast as a theological enterprise that ignores historical particularities in the biblical text. It needs to make room for and do justice to the theologizing and ethicizing done in the text and also to make use of these historical sources for such ongoing purposes.

Green wants to make a case for the ecclesially located interpretation of Scripture; indeed, he wants to argue that "the best interpreters are those actually engaged in communities of biblical interpretation."[22] It is pertinent to ask how we know this. I quite agree that Christians need to meet with other Christians who stand under the Word of God in order to grasp the implications of the text's meaning for faith and life here and now. I have no problem with the interpretation of the Bible in and for the church; indeed, I see it as very important. It has been my experience however, that my non-Christian friends as often help me interpret the Scriptures rightly (as Scriptures) as do my Christian friends. More specifically, I find my times of discussing texts with someone such as Amy-Jill Levine, a Jewish New Testament scholar, more profitable than most of the discussions I have with some of the postcolonialists among Christian interpreters. Why? Because she accepts the historical givenness and meaning of the text and is not interested in coopting it for various modern causes that the Bible does not directly address, and indeed that the biblical authors might even critique if not reject.

Green is aware of the problems, and he fairly addresses how the church can overread the text, just as a historical study of it may underplay, underread, indeed even undercut the theological substance of the text. He is seeking some balance in interpretation between the "thenness" of the text and its current relevance for Christian life. He puts it eloquently:

---

[22]Green, *Seized by Truth*, p. 66.

If some fail to recognize the Bible as "other," others exaggerate the Bible's status as "other" into an insurmountable "distance." If for some the Bible is little more than the dummy sitting in the lap of the talented ventriloquist, for others the Bible has no voice at all. If some are inclined to read the Bible in an opportunistic way so as to relate this or that verse directly to a situation of need today, others find the challenges involved in interpreting biblical materials simply too complex and demanding for the would-be interpreter.[23]

If we accept with Green, as I do, that the Bible provides us with a unitary story of the world and the human dilemma, this does mean that we as Christians must have our lives shaped by this story; indeed, we must become part of the ongoing outworking of the story in space and time.[24] As Green goes on to insist, however, we must do this cautiously and with guidance: "One of the most tragic effects of Bible reading can be that we read our lives into it in such a way that we find divine license for those of our attitudes and practices that are more base than biblical."[25] One of the hedges or protections against such solipsism is in fact a recognition and appreciation of the historical character of the biblical text, such that we realize that interpretation is not about our reading into the text our favorite ideas, but rather is about our being challenged by the text, even when the text seems harsh and alien to us.

Green sets up for us specific keys to engagement with the Bible if we are to interpret it as Christian Scripture: (1) the Old Testament must be interpreted as Christian Scripture, and the New Testament must be seen as incomprehensible without the Old Testament; (2) the church's doctrine provides the rules of engagement in a reading of Scripture—"The question of validity in interpretation for theological readings of Scripture cannot be separated from the question of a particular reading's coherence with classical faith."[26] I have already registered my reservations about the first dictum. I am equally wary of using a later creed or, say, the ecumenical creeds as the guide to the proper reading of, or as the provider of the rules by which we should read, the biblical text. The creeds should be normed by Scripture, but they can expound and further develop ideas found in Scripture.

A Christian reading of the Scriptures does not require a dogma-guided or dogmatically strictured reading of the text. Indeed, such a reading always poses the danger of anachronism and, furthermore, of violating the historical

---

[23]Ibid., p. 70.
[24]Ibid., pp. 72-73.
[25]Ibid., p. 77.
[26]Ibid., p. 81.

meaning of the text. The creeds and confessions should be normed by the meanings of the biblical text, not the other way around.

Furthermore, some ecclesiocentric readings of the text can lead us to forget that early Christianity was about giving away the gospel, about mission to nonbelievers.[27] The gospel was, in the first instance, good news for the lost, not for the community of the found. And frankly, today the church desperately needs to hear from others, outsiders such as Jewish interpreters of the Bible, if it is to hear and heed properly its own Scripture. One must ask, "How does an ecclesially privileged reading of Scripture accord with Jesus' or Paul's (or others') proclamation of the good news and with their dialogues and debates about meaning with non-Christians? How does such an approach to the text really help save or engage the lost or engage other faith groups in meaningful conversation about the Scriptures as sacred texts?"[28]

Green goes on to rightly stress that to read the Bible as Scripture requires humility; it requires that we always ask the question "Are my ways of reading the text, are my interpretive traditions in need of reformation?"[29] He also rightly insists we must have various conversation partners as we discuss and learn from Scripture.[30] This is why he insists that critically responsible interpretation of the Scriptures will be cross-cultural, canonical, historical, communal, global, and hospitable. This is absolutely right, but some of this seems to stand at odds with the two rules enunciated above.

Green goes on to appeal to the necessity of the reading of Scripture being led or informed by the Spirit.[31] He is right about this, and it is precisely here where the discourse becomes more specifically Christian as the Spirit seeks to apply the Word to our lives. We do not absolutely need later dogma or the boundaries of the ecumenical creeds if we already have the Spirit's guidance, and Green is right that accepting the leading of the Spirit implies that we recognize our need for outside help in understanding the biblical text and, beyond that, in doing New Testament theology and ethics on the basis of these texts. This is not to say that the Apostles' Creed, for example, is not

---

[27]Green's view does not necessarily lead to this sort of neglect, but some ecclesiocentric views tend in that direction.

[28]I am not suggesting that Paul, in 1 Corinthians 2 and elsewhere, is wrong that spiritual things are spiritually discerned, but I am suggesting that the Spirit, while especially illuminating the Christian reading, is also involved in illuminating the reading and interpretation of the text by some non-Christians as well, such as Torah-true Jews.

[29]Green, *Seized by Truth*, p. 90.

[30]Ibid., p. 92.

[31]Ibid., p. 94.

a useful and even Spirit-led synopsis of some of what Scripture claims about theological realities. But that is just what it is—a synopsis of what is already in the biblical text, which in its brevity helps clarify some of the essentials.

One of the difficulties I have with Green's approach to Scripture is that he wants to argue that meaning is to be found behind the text, in the text, and in those persons and communities doing the reading of the text, although, to be fair, he does emphasize that the focus should be on the meaning in the text.[32] While I agree that history has meaning, and while I recognize that readers are active and bring things to the text, the only locus of meaning that could be called a "scriptural meaning" is in the biblical text itself and nowhere else. The historical events and background are just that—background, impetus, basis, catalyst, context, but not "the meaning of the Bible." I cannot properly assess the meaning of the Bible without various historical contexts, but the context is not the content, and the meaning of the Bible is in the content of the words in Scripture. Second, while beauty may be in the eyes of the beholder, meaning is not, especially when we are talking about something as crucial as biblical truth. I am not the generator of the meaning of the Bible or of its truth claims. Indeed, it is the height of arrogance for me to think that I should be able to read my meanings into the text and thereby give them some sort of sacred legitimacy. Biblical meaning is not negotiated in an exchange between the text and the reader; rather, it is given by God by means of revelation and encoded into the text itself. This is what inspiration is all about. One can say, however, that meaning is conveyed in a transaction between the text and the reader.

Green rightly places interpretive priority on the meaning in the text itself, but he does not adequately distinguish between the text's meaning and the various significances it may have for this or that reader. While I agree that modern reader-response criticism and other similar approaches are right that the reader of the biblical text is not merely a passive receptacle of the Bible's meaning, I do not agree that this means that the reader has a right to help create the meaning of the biblical text. I am neither God nor the inspired author of any biblical books, and it is not up to me to "make" the text mean something. The text has meaning whether I recognize it or not, whether I engage with it or not, whether I understand it or not, whether I obey it or not.

There are many forms of liberationist readings of the text (e.g., feminist, womanist, Asian, African American) that not only assume as given principles

---

[32]Ibid., p. 106.

a hermeneutic of suspicion that gives license to read against the flow or even against the meaning of the text, but also assume that there is no such thing as objective, unbiased readings of the text. Such approaches stress that all readings come from particular locales and points of view.

Such approaches have problems. First, while it is correct to say there are no purely objective readings of the Bible, and everyone comes from some social location, this does not give license to then assume that the Bible can mean anything and be used for any cause or constructive task of meaning-making. Some readings are more objective than others, but the goal is to help one another get at the inspired meaning of the text, not to validate each other's subjective agendas. Second, all too often a hermeneutic of suspicion leads to a rejection of the meaning of the text and comes at the text without sufficient openness to give it a fair hearing. Too much weight is placed on the reader side of the equation and on the assumption that the reader has superior moral values to those enshrined in the text, with too little placed on the God and revelation side of the equation.[33]

Green argues that "a decision to read a Biblical text as a constituent of the canon of Scripture pre-determines the range of possible readings of the text."[34] By this Green means that certain readings are ruled out if they conflict with the grand narrative of Scripture. I understand this canonical principle, but what I would argue is, for example, that whether or not John 7:53–8:11 is a part of the original inspired text of the Gospel of John does not determine or delimit the meaning of that text. It means what it means whether or not it is an original part of John's Gospel. This then suggests that the canonical principle or even the grand narrative cannot determine the meaning of a particular text, but it can serve as a sort of warning or check that perhaps one has misunderstood the meaning of one or another text if it leads to a contradiction with another sacred text. It is not because a book ended up

---

[33]See Iain Provan, V. Phillips Long, Tremper Longman III, *A Biblical History of Israel* (Louisville: Westminster John Knox, 2003), chaps. 1–2, on the matter of verification versus falsification. The problem with a hermeneutic of suspicion is that it approaches the text not with openness and fairness and in good faith but rather with a "guilty until proven innocent" attitude sometimes mistakenly called "critical thinking." What it actually amounts to is bias against the text, and thus a reading against the grain of the text quite easily ensues and is justified. But if, on the other hand, one demands evidence for rejection or falsification, giving the Bible the same benefit of the doubt that one would give a colleague's work that generally has been recognized by many over a long period of time to be trustworthy, then one ends up working with a much larger and richer body of material in one's analysis of New Testament theology and ethics.

[34]Green, *Seized by Truth*, p. 122.

in the New Testament canon that we can expect its words to be consistent with words in other New Testament documents; rather, it is because all of those documents ultimately come from God and by means of the inspiration of God and speak to the same truths.

Perhaps the most helpful portion of Green's study is where he provides guides for producing a cogent, convincing, and supportable interpretation of this or that sacred text. It must (1) account for the text in its final form without violating the language of the text; (2) account for the text as a whole and be consistent with the whole text without neglecting or masking any portion of it; (3) account for the cultural embeddedness of the language; (4) be ruled by its canonical embeddedness and set within the boundaries of faith; (5) be put into play in transformed lives lived in community. These are useful guides, and I will not repeat my concerns about the fourth one, but here I will simply say that truth is truth whether it is within the canon or outside of it, and what makes it true is not that it is part of a particular collection of early Christian books. It is inspiration and revelation that produces truth, not the later creeds or the later canonization of the material.[35]

Green concludes his study by rightly pleading that we not privilege readings of Scripture that bypass its theology and ethics, prohibit the reader from submitting to the text's inquiry about our lives or "to speak truthfully of the transforming light that shines in the darkness and that the darkness has not overcome," and give too much precedent to the mastery of the text rather than allowing us to be mastered by its message.[36] "We need to recover the freedom to engage with ancient texts as our texts, and with respect and expectancy, as those who thus might embrace Scripture's theological vision and be molded according to its pattern of faith and life."[37] To all of this one can only say, "Amen."

The good news is that Scripture encourages us to study it, to seek to discern its meaning, its patterns, its theology and ethics. This is because Scripture engages us as adults, and it is fair to say, with John Goldingay, "Scripture as a whole is more inclined to seek to persuade us of the truth of things than to expect us to 'believe seven impossible things before breakfast.'"[38] It is time, then, to tease the mind into active thought and see what can be said about a

---

[35]See Witherington, *Living Word of God.*
[36]Green, *Seized by Truth*, p. 157.
[37]Ibid., p. 161.
[38]John Goldingay, *Models for Scripture* (Grand Rapids: Eerdmans, 1994), p. 121.

theology and ethics of the New Testament as a whole.

The journey will not be a short one, but I trust that it will be rewarding and indeed will land us safe on Canaan's side, as the old hymn says. Along the way, we trust that we will find New Testament theology and New Testament ethics and also will do some theologizing and ethicizing on the basis of what we find. If I were asked whether I believe that there is *a* New Testament theology or *a* New Testament ethic and, if so, whether it is possible to find and reconstruct it, my response would be much like that of the person who, when asked "Do you believe in baptism?" responded, "Believe in it? I've seen it!" I have seen New Testament theology and ethics in the text and I have seen them at work in the lives of believers. It is my hope that I will adequately represent what I have seen.

THE PLAN OF THIS BOOK

This treatment of New Testament theology and ethics has a fairly unique perspective, even when compared to other of the more synthetic treatments of the subject. I am convinced that the unity of the New Testament thought world is as much at the level of symbolic universe and narrative substructure as it is at the level of articulation into specific situations. In other words, the analysis of the surface of these texts compared and contrasted will come up with some results but will not show the big picture. This is why I will focus in the early part of the present volume on the shared symbolic universe and narrative thought world of these New Testament writers.

The reader eager to see what I think of Old Testament theology and ethics and their relationship to New Testament theology and ethics or of the relationship of New Testament theology and ethics to biblical or canonical theology and ethics will need to turn to the first and final chapters of the present volume for a treatment on those issues. In my view, biblical and canonical approaches are ex post facto approaches that presuppose the existence of a canon. That is, such approaches analyze the biblical data from a point of view that none of the New Testament writers could have shared (nor did they), since there was as of yet no New Testament canon, and the Old Testament one was still in the process of closure.

I insist on taking an approach to New Testament theology and ethics that does not try to do the analysis while ignoring the historical realities and questions that these texts raise or, even worse, imposing on these texts a later historical or philosophical reality, which actually creates a sense of unreality when we are dealing with New Testament theology and ethics, as if we were dealing with eternal topics in a Gnostic philosophical discourse not well tethered to the particularities of history. This in turn means that I will not be trying to do theology or ethics, or highlight the New Testament theology and ethics, while ignoring exegetical substance and historical particularities. *What I offer in the present volume is the distillation of what can only be called the theology and ethics of Jesus and of the various New Testament writers as it is revealed in detailed exegetical study.*

My goal in this study is, as best I can, to allow the New Testament writers their own say and to articulate their own syntheses of earlier material whether from the Hebrew Scriptures, the teaching of Jesus, earlier apostolic teaching, or elsewhere. Thus, while this volume is indeed about the collective witness to New Testament theology and ethics in the New Testament, including its shared themes, trajectories, and trends, I am focusing on the theology and ethics in the text of the New Testament itself.

I am not trying, for instance, to create an artificial synthesis on the basis of later systematic or canonical categories. Were I to do the latter, I would be creating a New Testament theology or ethic. It would be my synthesis, not that of the writers of the New Testament themselves. Rather, what I am trying to do is let the New Testament writers themselves give us evidence, instances, examples, hints about how they would write such a synthetic work. Since, however, they were not actually undertaking such a task in their situation-specific documents, in allowing them to speak for themselves, we have to be satisfied with partial answers and a certain incompleteness to the picture. We have no systematic theological or ethical treatises in the New Testament, not even in the Sermon on the Mount or in Romans. This is frustrating, but it is the reality of the New Testament text itself. So, once more to be clear, I will be looking at the doing of early Christian theology and ethics in the text by these writers, not trying to force them into some sort of later Procrustean bed, be it dogmatic, systematic or idiomatic.

What all this means is that after the exploration of the symbolic universe and the narrative thought world shared by all these New Testament writers, I will take a census of the consensus of the New Testament writers in an additive approach, with some depiction of how they are synthesizing earlier data along the way. In other words, I will do justice to the theology of Jesus, and then I will consider how the various New Testament writers add to, or reinforce, or delete from such a discussion. I will follow the same procedure with the issue of the ethic of Jesus and then of the New Testament writers.

There is a rationale to this sort of approach: one needs to do justice to the impact of Jesus Christ on the thinking of all these persons, and this includes both the impact of the historical Jesus' person and work and the ongoing impact of the living, ascended Christ on them. Both New Testament theology and ethics are christocentric to the core, and this is precisely what distinguishes them from other early Jewish efforts at doing theology or ethics.

Because of this christological focus, I maintain that what needs to be done with the theology or ethics of any of these writers is first and foremost to examine how they deal with Christology, not how they treat other topics along the way. The reason for this approach is clear: it is the living Christ, both come in the flesh and now reigning from heaven, who has reconfigured their symbolic universe, their narrative thought world, and the very way they articulate theology and ethics, whether they are talking about things such as ecclesiology, eschatology, God the Father or some other topic.

One cannot put the emphasis where the New Testament writers insist on putting it if one starts with something such as protology, or the New Testament writers' views of Israel, or the Mosaic covenant, or eschatology, or a concept of election or predestination found in the Old Testament. Such an approach does not come to grips with the fact that Christ has radically changed the worldview of these writers in a variety of ways, including in the way they view their own sacred texts, which we refer to as the Old Testament.

New Testament theology and ethics are apocalyptic and eschatological in the sense that they reflect the direct divine intervention of God in Christ at a specific point in history, and thus they are not simply a continuation or a completion of Old Testament theology and ethics, though clearly there is a good deal of carryover from the earlier Hebrew thought world, and we can talk about fulfillment as well as completion of various prophecies, rituals, institutions, covenants.

Furthermore, Old Testament theology and ethics, though often foreshadowing those of the New Testament, in many regards have different foci and emphases than we find in the New Testament. The center of thought in that Hebrew thought world is not Jesus Christ; it is Yahweh and his relationship with Israel. The christological glasses with which the New Testament writers view their earlier Jewish sacred texts must not be allowed to beguile us into thinking that they are saying that the Old Testament was written by Christians in a Christian way for the church, in the first instance. No, it was written for pre-Christian Israel in the first place, and as a development and completion of that people came in the church of Jew and Gentile united in Christ, they too continued to listen and to view these sacred texts as their own, though they read them now with a specific sort of christological glasses. Furthermore, they read the text not so much as having a surplus of meaning, but eschatologically and teliologically, by which I mean that they read it in light of the end game, how the story has turned out in Christ and will turn out. Like a movie whose meaning is not unveiled until its climax or conclusion, and then suddenly there is a surprise, an "Aha!" moment, that causes one to reevaluate what has come before and what it really meant, so it is with the theology and ethics of the canon and more specifically the New Testament.

The entire Old Testament is seen in the eschatological age as a prophetic book. It is seen by the New Testament writers as that which prepares for, foreshadows, provides types of, and gives promises and prophecies about the eschatological age inaugurated by the Christ-event, including prophecies and promises about the coming Christ. The before and after of the revelation must be given its due because it was only "when the time had fully come, God sent forth his Son" (Gal 4:4). The promises are not the fulfillment, the antetypes are not the types, and the people who gave the prophecies, though they longed to look into the time and place where they would come to fruition, were told by the Spirit that it was for the eschatological people of God, a later audience, that such things were intended.

The New Testament writers do believe that the preexistent Christ had a role to play in creation and the redemption of Israel prior to the incarnation. They are not suggesting, however, that Abraham was a Christian before his time (he is the prototype of one who was reckoned righteous), nor are they saying that Jesus before the incarnation had previously shown up on planet earth as, say, the angel of the Lord. In fact, the author of Hebrews tells us quite clearly God's Son should never be put into the category of angel. He was always much more than that. The New Testament is entirely, or almost entirely, written by Jews (Luke probably was a God-fearer) who believed that Jew and Gentile united in Christ is the true eschatological people of God, and insofar as it involves Gentiles, they have been grafted into the earlier Jewish heritage, while Jews have not been grafted into a later and different Christian heritage. The good news was for the Jew first, and Jesus was their messiah in the first place. The culmination of revelation in Christ leads to the culmination of the formation of God's people, involving both Jews and Gentiles.

Thus, we must allow the Hebrew Scriptures to speak to us as Christians on their own terms, and when we do that, we discover that they mainly speak about the one we called "the Father," though with some promises and prophecies and "types" that prepare us for the coming of the Son and the coming of the Spirit. A good biblical theology will not try to erase or explain away the dramatic differences between the Old Testament and the New Testament. I will say more about this matter toward the end of this study.

Now, however, it is time for us to begin our odyssey of discovery. A word to the wise: launch out in a large boat with large oars and with all the effort you can muster, for when we are dealing with the ocean that is New Testament theology and ethics, we are dealing with something vast, something deep, something powerful, something beautiful, and something that is, at times, overwhelming and awe-inspiring yet at the same time profoundly reassuring.

1

PRELIMINARY CONSIDERATIONS

From Symbolic Universe to Story to Theology

New Testament Theology is a historical discipline. It is not to be confused with either dogmatics or apologetics: for its purpose is neither to provide scriptural authority for modern doctrinal beliefs nor to make those beliefs appear reasonable and defensible to the unconvinced inquirer. Its purpose is descriptive. We may indeed believe that in the New Testament we have a divine revelation valid for all ages. But that revelation was made in historical events, and those who first thought out the significance of those events did so in relation to the circumstances of their time and with a pastoral concern for particular congregations; even their general statements were made with reference to the particular. . . . The distinction between New Testament theology and other related disciplines is one which has all too often been ignored. Systematic theologians naturally wish their work to be regarded as biblical theology, in the sense that it is in harmony with what they find written in Scripture. But to confound dogmatics with New Testament theology is to assume that the New Testament writers had minds which worked exactly like ours and were interested in the same questions as we are.

G. B. CAIRD[1]

PROLEGOMENA: THE QUESTION OF METHOD

In his magisterial study on New Testament theology (posthumously collected and assembled), G. B. Caird strikes exactly the right note from the outset. New Testament theology, like New Testament ethics, is a particular

---

[1]G. B. Caird, *New Testament Theology*, compl. and ed. L. D. Hurst (Oxford: Oxford University Press, 1994), pp. 1-2.

historical discipline, and it should not be undertaken as if it were an exercise in canonical biblical theology, much less an exercise in systematic or dogmatic theology. The method by which one pursues the matter to a significant degree will determine the outcome of the study.

Generally, there have been two ways to approach New Testament theology: inductively and deductively. Using the inductive approach, one can build a New Testament theology from the bottom up, critically analyzing the individual witnesses and finding congruences and similarities. This is, for example, what one finds at the end of Frank Thielman's volume on New Testament theology or interspersed throughout Howard Marshall's volume. The problem with this approach is that the unity seems small compared to the diversity, leading one to wonder how significant and vital that unity really is. The other approach, the deductive, traditionally is understood to mean that one starts with one's dogmatic or systematic theological categories and slots exegetical data into them piecemeal, in a proof-texting sort of way. This approach has largely fallen by the wayside as our culture has becoming increasingly less Enlightenment oriented in its approach to knowledge and truth. The problem of reductionism when one boils the Bible down to principles, propositions, and themes is well known. Like soup that has been pureed with all its substance filtered out, this results in a bland but palatable outcome that is not very nourishing. Is there another way of doing New Testament theology that neither produces minimal results nor denudes the material of its historical specificity? As it turns out, there is, but before we consider it, I must make a few points clear.

The persistent drive in modernity and postmodernity for "relevance" becomes, unfortunately, a hermeneutical filter by which the theological and ethical substance of the New Testament tends to be read. By this I mean that far too many people these days sort the New Testament by the categories "relevant" or, on the other hand, "obsolete," "outmoded," or "primitive." Sometimes the latter category is characterized by the terms *culturally bound* or *culturally determined*, but such pejorative language presupposes not only a correct knowledge of what will not make sense or work in our own times and culture, but also a criterion of judgment that privileges certain au courant assumptions. A good example of this is certain kinds of special-interest theological readings of the New Testament.

For example, Marxist liberation theology has constantly privileged politicized interpretations of some aspects of New Testament theology and ethics and has deemed other less overtly political readings as "overly spiritualized" or "irrelevant to the current struggle." This approach to the matter tends to assume that the Bible is mainly a tool for supporting current ideologies and to relegate other ideologies to the rubbish bin of historical curiosity. Unfortunately, this whole agenda-driven approach cannot be called a form of historical study of the New Testament. I do not say this because I think that any of us are capable of a value-neutral interpretation of ancient texts. I am also well aware of the special dangers of misuse of a precious or sacred ancient text when one wants to justify one's own thought or actions. The warning of the ancient luminary Werenfels about the Bible is valid: "This is the book in which every one searches for his own opinions, and every one with equal success finds his own opinions."[2]

Subjectivity can and ought to be corrected for by listening to other competent critical interpreters of the New Testament, and thus inherent subjectivity is no excuse for solipcism or anachronistic readings or even for deliberately tendentious uses of ancient texts.[3] Here again Caird is helpful.

> To make the New Testament intelligible is not the same thing as making it credible. The "modern mind" can do what it likes with the teaching of Jesus and the apostles. But it can only have the freedom to do so if the New Testament theologian has first described the material honestly. We are thus involved with the reconstruction of the past, a past accessible to us not by direct scrutiny but only through the interrogation of witnesses. The possibility of conversation depends on the historian's skill in "speaking the same language" as his or her source.[4]

There also must be a certain sympathy with the source material in order to give it a fair hearing and to let it speak for itself. Unfortunately, the modern "hermeneutic of suspicion," filled with self-righteousness about how our modern critical understanding of life is so much superior to the way be-

---

[2]Quoted in ibid., p. 7 ("Hic liber est in quo quaerit sua dogmata quisque, invenit et pariter dogmata quisque sua").

[3]Of course, it is true that in the case of various sorts of postcolonial and other sorts of postmodern readings of the New Testament (e.g., reader-response criticism), an epistemology often is presupposed that gives permission for the assumption that meaning is in the eyes of the active beholder. As I have said earlier, I disagree with this epistemology almost entirely and therefore do not accept the warrant assumed for such tendentious and nonhistorical or even antihistorical readings of the New Testament. For an excellent example of a Marxist sociological reading of Paul, see Neil Elliott, *The Arrogance of Nations: Reading Romans in the Shadow of Empire* (Minneapolis: Fortress, 2008), and my review in *RBL* (March 2009) (http://www.bookreviews.org/pdf/6481_7367.pdf).

[4]Caird, *New Testament Theology*, p. 3.

nighted ancients viewed the world, seldom provides such a sympathetic hearing of the material. As James Moffatt once said, "The essence of the historical mind is the power of putting oneself into a different age and recognizing not simply its differences from the present, but its essential affinities with the present."[5] Is there a way beyond the impasses of subjectivity and modern agendas? I think there is. For a Christian person, there is a recognized indebtedness to the past, especially the biblical witnesses. One treats these witnesses as respected teachers from whom one has learned much, and since the learning has been of benefit, indeed has led one into a personal and saving relationship with God, then "to accept the past as one's own is to commit oneself to a destiny in keeping with it."[6] I quite agree—theology ultimately was intended to lead to doxology and mission.

When Caird set out to do his study of New Testament theology, he remarked on the laziness of analyzing the individual witnesses without undertaking collective comparison of the data. He was right about this, and he was also right that such witness-by-witness analysis results in a certain imbalance caused simply by the fact that the longer and more complex bodies of material (e.g., the Pauline corpus) necessarily get more attention and space, when in fact some of the shorter documents may be just as important (e.g., 1 John).[7] This is precisely why I saw the need for a two-volume study and for a careful and thorough second volume that involves some sort of synthetic approach, since many recent treatments of New Testament theology give the subject insufficient due or attention, settling for presenting New Testament theologies seriatim.

Thus it was that Caird envisioned the conference table or colloquium model whereby all twelve or so of the New Testament writers sat down at table in the presence of a presider who engaged them on various subjects and gave each voice, insofar as it had something to say on that subject, a hearing. This method prevents the monopoly of the verbose or more influential.[8] Of course, Caird realizes that this will appear to be a dialogue with the dead (a problem, as we will see, that Philip Esler also addresses). Yet in another sense, these witnesses are still alive as well, and their living, inspired and inspiring voices can still be heard. Caird provides us with just the right approach to

---

[5]James Moffatt, *The Approach to the New Testament* (London: Hodder & Stoughton, 1921), p. 173.
[6]Caird, *New Testament Theology*, p. 22.
[7]Ibid., pp. 17-18.
[8]Ibid., pp. 18-19.

this entire matter, drawing an analogy with the Jerusalem council in Acts 15, which agreed in essentials about Gentiles and salvation but differed in various particulars.

> Thus the New Testament itself provides a criterion for judging its own unity. The question we must ask is not whether these books all say the same thing, but whether they all bear witness to the same Jesus and through him to the many splendoured wisdom of the one God. If we are persuaded that the second Moses, the son of Man, the friend of sinners, the incarnate *logos*, the firstborn of all creation, the Apostle and High Priest of our calling, the Chief Shepherd, and the Lamb opening the scroll are the same person in whom the one God has achieved and is achieving his mighty work, we shall neither attempt to press all our witnesses into a single mould nor captiously complain that one seems at some points deficient in comparison with another. What we shall do is rejoice that God has seen fit to establish His gospel at the mouth of so many independent witnesses. The music of the New Testament choir is not written to be sung in unison.[9]

Just so, but in fact they are singing the same choral work in many parts and with much improvisation. How do we get at that shared score from which they are all singing?

I suggest that one starts with the symbolic universe that all the New Testament writers lived in and were influenced by. In that universe there were fixed stars such as God, revelation, redemption, messiah, holiness, mighty works (or miracles), to mention but a few things taken for granted by all the authors. All of the New Testament authors were Jews, except perhaps in the singular case of Luke, a God-fearer. Their symbolic universe was formed and shaped by things such as the books we refer to as the Old Testament, other

---

[9]Ibid., p. 24. In addition, Caird provides a good reason why a canonical biblical theology that does not have a sense of progressive revelation and will not allow the Old Testament to speak in its pre-Christian way is problematic. He reminds us that in our efforts to continue to see the Old Testament as Christian Scripture there must not be a going back or reneging on the recognition that these texts were Jewish Scriptures first, written by non-Christians. "It cannot be too often or too emphatically said that, if we read into the text of scripture something that the author himself did not intend, we have no right to claim that we are putting ourselves under the authority of the word of God" (ibid., p. 25). I quite agree with this, and so one must also be wary of certain kinds of *sensus plenior* arguments that read more into the Old Testament than is there. Jesus, for example, was not the angel of the Lord during Old Testament times. Indeed, the writers of the New Testament repudiate an angelomorphic Christology at several points. The revelation before Jesus was partial and piecemeal, as Hebrews 1 tells us. We must accept this as the author of Hebrews does. This means for him a typological but not an allegorical reading of the Old Testament is possible because the former does justice to the before-and-after nature of progressive revelation in various changing historical contexts.

early Jewish literature, the Jesus tradition, apostolic tradition, new prophetic revelation and, to a considerably lesser degree, Greco-Roman thought. Out of that shared symbolic universe was formed their narrative thought world.

Here I am suggesting that the New Testament writers not only held in common certain "big ticket" ideas, but also shared a narrative thought world. All of them were convinced, for example, that history was going somewhere, that God was guiding it and working things together for good, and that they were writing late in the story, trying to get the good news out in time for the final edition to be published before the deadline was reached. These writers stood on tiptoe, utterly convinced that they already lived in the eschatological age and were looking for a consummation devoutly to be wished. The failure to recognize the common narrative thought world presupposed by the various New Testament writers is a significant failure indeed.[10]

Finally, out of that narrative thought world the New Testament writers theologize and ethicize into particular contexts. The commonality lies as much or more at the presuppositional level as at the articulation level. Analyzing only the articulated similarities between the various New Testament witnesses is like analyzing and comparing the tips of what appear to be several different icebergs and noticing their similarities in shape and hue and size, all the while failing to note that all of them are united below the surface of the intellectual ocean in which they are floating. In other words, they are all individual peaks of one, much larger, common mass. The present volume, then, must dwell more at the level of symbolic universe and narrative thought world than at the level of articulation into particular contexts. Of course, there are other ways of doing New Testament theology or ethics, and here it is profitable to review a few good examples of other attempts, but first a couple of more points are crucial.

The unity of thought that exists in the New Testament is not dependent on our ability to reconstruct it on the basis of the ad hoc evidence, the bits and pieces of data, that we have. After all, none of the New Testament documents are systematic or even reasonably complete studies of New Testament

---

[10]Matera recognizes this (New Testament Theology, p. xxx). He suggests that the master story told in the New Testament can be summarized using five categories: (1) humanity in need of salvation; (2) the bringer of salvation; (3) the community of the sanctified; (4) the life of the sanctified; (5) the hope of the sanctified. He sees these categories as corresponding to theological categories such as Christian anthropology and soteriology, Christology, ecclesiology, ethics, and eschatology. The problem I see with this is that there is no discussion of protology and Christ's role in creation, though Matera is right that the New Testament does not focus on a theology of creation. The other problem with this is that eschatology permeates and shapes all the rest.

theology or New Testament ethics. If we call the scholarly efforts at assembling the witnesses in a certain way "New Testament theology," recognizing that it is something scholars after the fact (and after the canon was closed) have synthesized, this at best in a small way demonstrates the larger coherence of thought of these early Christian writers. Just as the history of any given period is much larger and more complex than written history about such a period, so our ability to reconstruct what was the extant unity of the theological and ethical thought world of early Christians pales in comparison to that world itself, and at best such a reconstruction can be only a précis or summation of highlights of that world. The reader needs to keep this steadily in view while working through the present volume. But there is another crucial factor to keep in mind as well. Although we often treat the writers of the New Testament as if they were late Western individualists, they were not, and their work was not written from or for such a point of view. These writings address a very different social world than ours, about which a few comments are in order since it affects the way we look at New Testament theology and ethics.

THE SOCIAL WORLD OF CHRISTIAN BELIEF AND BEHAVIOR

If you were to interview the authors of the New Testament, it seems clear enough that they would deny having their "own" theology or ethics. For example, Paul would be uncomfortable talking about "Pauline" Christology, as if that were something notably distinct from early Christian Christology in general. The writers of the New Testament were not modern Western individualists each seeking to stake out a unique intellectual turf and protect a personal intellectual property. Nor were they looking to make a "new" contribution to a theological or ethical field of research. The New Testament was written in a culture far more group-oriented than ours and in a world where tradition was valued over innovation and what most people wanted in a religion was antiquity and a proven quality of benefit, not something "new" that would be characterized by most as a "superstition," not to mention illicit. On top of all this, we are talking about documents written by pious Jews or, possibly in one or two cases, God-fearers.

The social conditions under which these documents were written by these people, in a world where they were a tiny and suspected minority, are such that there would have been considerable pressure to "get their story straight," and dangerous variations in theology or ethics would have been dealt with severely, and in fact were. A moment's glance at how Paul in the early 50s dealt with severe ethical violations in 1 Corinthians 5–6, counseling expulsion and shunning, or how the elder in the 80s dealt with christological aberration in 1-3 John ought to make clear that although the social boundaries of the community were somewhat porous in this evangelistic sect because they wanted more members, the intellectual or thought-world boundaries were much more tightly drawn that many modern scholars might think. A good clue that this was the case right across the movement is the way various New Testament authors talk about apostasy.

For example, in Hebrews 6 and 10 the author says that someone who commits apostasy cannot be restored, and for such a person there is no more atonement or forgiveness for sins. Or, in 1 John 5 the author talks about "the sin unto death" in the context of speaking about christological and ethical error. Or in the Pastoral Letters we hear about various people who are said to have made shipwreck of their faith. Or in Acts we hear about the consequences of lying about one's resources (Acts 5) and about Simon Magus practicing magic (Acts 8). Equally revealing is the way false teachers are viewed and spoken of in an early document such as Jude, which is recycled at the end of the century in 2 Peter. At the ideational and ideological levels, then, there was considerable concern, and fencing practices were employed to keep the theological and ethical thought world pure, and such practices were engaged in by a wide variety of leaders. All this is a normal part of identity formation for a new sectarian religious group, and it was all the more crucial because this one was highly evangelistic and did not want Gentiles to assume that the Christian faith was much like Greco-Roman religions.

By this I mean that for the most part, beliefs were not the heart of ancient religion, whether Greco-Roman or even the religions that came out of the ancient Near East. Priests, temples, sacrifices, and ritual were the heart of almost all these religions. Orthopraxy rather than orthodoxy was the prime concern, and here, again, praxis refers not primarily to ethics in the normal sense, but rather to religious and ritualistic behavior. As Rodney Stark puts it, Roman religion failed to support the moral order. "The same applied to Greek religion: the Greeks did not regard morality as God-given, but of human origins—'Greek gods do not give laws.'"[11] How very different this was from Jewish religion, including Christianity. Ethical instruction, including

---

[11]Rodney Stark, *Cities of God: The Real Story of How Christianity Became an Urban Movement and Conquered Rome* (San Francisco: HarperSanFrancisco, 2006), p. 88.

laws, was at the heart of what the God of the Bible gave his people. Notice also: "Given that their societies were abundant in profound *written* philosophies, it is remarkable that the traditional Greek and Roman religions had no scriptures. 'They had no written works which established their tenets and doctrines, or provided explanation of their rituals or moral prescription for their adherents.'"[12] It follows from this that it would have been obvious to ancients that Christians cared tremendously about getting their theological and ethical beliefs correct; indeed, they needed to be seen to be "by the book," the book being Scripture, or at least according to the gospel of the apostolic witnesses.

One of the things that made Christianity stand out from many ancient religions then was precisely its insistence on a strong belief system with reasonably clear boundaries. Of course, it shared this with some subdivisions of its religious parent, Judaism, but this was worlds apart from the essence of most pagan religions, which had to do with placating deities and imploring them for things such as health, wealth, wisdom, and the usual things that make for a good life. This is so very clear when one does a detailed study of what the word *salvation* actually means in such religions: healing, rescue, and other this-worldly things.[13] The concern, then, with the thought world and the need for reasonably precise articulation of theology and ethics is an important, I would say crucial, factor in the rise of Christianity in the first century. In order to convert others, one needed to be consistent and clear. And what was abundantly clear was that "for Jews, Christianity added to their religious capital; for Gentiles, Christianity required that they replace their capital."[14] It is therefore all the more remarkable that apparently most of the converts to Christianity were Gentiles not Jews, which may be as much of a commentary on the weakness of paganism in various regards as on the attraction of Christianity.

What, then, prompted conversion and the embracing of this considerable theological and ethical belief system that would make a Christian in Antioch or Corinth or Rome or Jerusalem distinguishable from the myriad of other devotees to other religions? The answers are various and must include the affective conversion as well as the intellectual conversion

---

[12]Ibid., p. 89 (quoting Mary Beard, John North, and Simon Price, *Religions of Rome* [Cambridge: Cambridge University Press, 1998], 1:284).
[13]See the detailed discussion of this in Ben Witherington III, *The Acts of the Apostles: A Socio-Rhetorical Commentary* (Grand Rapids: Eerdmans, 1998), appendix 2.
[14]Stark, *Cities of God*, p. 131.

of persons, and one must talk about the social conversion as well, by which I mean that the communal life of love, self-sacrifice, and sharing surely was a powerful incentive to convert to Christianity. Our concern here is with the intellectual or ideational side of the equation. I am suggesting that the tight social networks of early Christianity make clear that discussions about Christian belief and behavior did not take place in isolated conventicles, but rather much trafficking of ideas took place such that there was clearly enough a large group of core beliefs and behaviors endorsed by all, or nearly all, and a traveling Christian would expect, for example, that much the same things would be said about Jesus as Lord in Antioch as would be said in Rome. We may call this shared thought world with reasonably and recognizably clear boundaries "proto-orthodoxy" and "proto-orthopraxy." The upshot of all this is that the social context of any religion becomes crucial to understanding the meaning of the key terms in its symbolic universe and then grasping its narrative thought world. Words and ideas do not exist in some splendid isolation from social context. Indeed, it is the larger social context and not merely the immediate literary context that provides the necessary clues as to how what was for the most part common or familiar terms were being used by this or that rhetor or writer.

FROM OLD TESTAMENT THEOLOGY AND ETHICS TO NEW TESTAMENT THEOLOGY AND ETHICS: A HISTORICAL PERSPECTIVE

The issue of the interrelationship of the two Testaments and their respective thought worlds, old and new, is a vexed one in many regards. For one thing, the practice of delineating an "Old Testament theology" has overwhelmingly been a Christian enterprise and, more specifically, mostly a Protestant one, given who the major practitioners have been.[15] Even on a cursory glance of what are usually seen to be the major elements of Old Testament theology (e.g., God in relationship to humanity and the world as both creator and redeemer, and God's special relationship with Israel), it is perfectly clear that while there are elements of continuity between Old Testament theology and New Testament theology, there are even more elements of discontinuity. A few illustrations will have to suffice.

---

[15]See W. E. Lemke, "Theology (Old Testament)," in *The Anchor Bible Dictionary*, ed. D. N. Freedman (New York: Doubleday, 1992), 6:469-71; James K. Mead, *Biblical Theology: Issues, Methods, and Themes* (Louisville: Westminster John Knox, 2007).

At the very heart of the New Testament thought world is Jesus Christ, and yet in the Old Testament there is little discussion of messianism in general or a messiah in particular, at least directly. The term *māšiaḥ* hardly ever occurs, and then when it does, as in Isaiah, it is applied to an unexpected party: Cyrus the Persian is called "the anointed one" of God (Is 45:1)! Furthermore, what the New Testament means by "Christ," particularly in its insistence on a crucified and risen messiah, is at variance with what probably the majority of early Jews expected of a redeemer or messiah figure.[16]

This is not to say that there is not plenty of material in the Old Testament that could be and would be used for messianic purposes and the crafting of a messianic worldview, but that is a different matter. Messianic redeemer figures are not at the heart of Old Testament theology; rather, Yahweh is. And here is where we note that for all the interest in the monarchy, in Saul and his successors, and in the later northern kings of Israel, the king was not, properly speaking, a subject that belonged to the discussion of God and to God-talk, for the king, however inspired or exalted or glorious, even David and Solomon, was always viewed as merely mortal. A messiah that had some sort of divine nature and status could never be seen as just another king in the line of David.

I suspect that this is one of the reasons that in Old Testament studies a "history of Israel" approach has often replaced an "Old Testament theology" approach to the material. The discussion of the patriarchs, prophets, judges or kings, while often ethically interesting, does not, properly speaking, fall into the provenance of what Christians mean by theology in the narrow sense of the word, even though there is a narrative thought world generating things like the material we find in the so-called Former Prophets (1-2 Samuel, 1-2 Kings, 1-2 Chronicles). However surprising it may seem, the Old Testament has far more to say about the patriarchs and Israel and human beings in terms of direct discourse than it has to say about Israel's God. Yes, there is a particular focus on the divine-human encounter, but very little direct interest is shown in theologizing in the sense of describing in detail the traits or attributes of God. The portrait of God in the Old Testament has to be assembled largely from indirect evidence or passing remarks, or God's character is repeatedly revealed in and by what God does (see, e.g., Ex 6;

---

[16]There may now be some evidence, in the so-called Gabriel Stone, that some early Jews reflected on the notion of a suffering messiah (perhaps in light of Is 52–53), and certainly *4 Ezra*, from the end of the first century A.D., speaks of a dying Son of Man figure.

Deut 4). It is hard to imagine an entire book in the New Testament that, like the book of Esther, never mentions God directly.

A second illustration of the discontinuity between the Testaments comes when one is examining what is said about the afterlife and the other world. Until we get to the exilic and postexilic writers of the Old Testament, there is precious little discussion of any sort of positive afterlife, much less a discussion of heaven or hell in the Old Testament. The concept of Sheol, or the land of the dead, is miles apart from the prevalent focus in the New Testament not only on eschatology, a future final state on earth that has some analogy in some of the later prophetic material in the Old Testament, but also on a viable other world—heaven and hell or Gehenna. Speaking generally, the New Testament is a much more "otherworldly" collection of writings, whereas the focus in the Old Testament tends to be much more on the present world. Naturally, this affects the theologizing in various ways and respects.

Third, the Old Testament contains not even a nodal or an incipient doctrine of the Trinity, despite the best efforts and allegorizing of various Nicene and post-Nicene church fathers to find such a notion there. There is, however, without question, a clear incorporation of Christ into God-talk in the New Testament, and also the Holy Spirit is portrayed as a person within the scope of the divine being in the New Testament. In other words, we have the raw materials for, and the beginnings of the articulation of, a trinitarian view of God in the New Testament. Old Testament images of God and his royal retinue or court, or God and his elect angels such as the "angel of the Lord," are hardly precursors to such thinking, or at best are rather feeble foreshadowings of such thinking. Typology, when attempted in the New Testament (e.g., Hebrews), seems far more plausible and doing less violence to the meaning and actual substance Old Testament texts than does the later Christian allegorizing of the whole Old Testament.

There was a Copernican revolution in the thinking of the early Jews who became followers of Jesus not only in regard to messiah, but also in regard to God, the end times, and a host of other subjects. There is no way that New Testament theology can be seen as a mere natural development or even just a fulfillment or further progression of the theologizing found in the Old Testament, though indeed there are some strong elements of continuity (the idea of a single deity, the idea of an elect or chosen people with whom God has a special covenantal relationship, the idea of a creator and redeemer God who keeps intervening in world affairs, especially in the life of his people).

Telling is the way God is named in the Old Testament compared to the way God is named in the New Testament. In the Old Testament, we are hard pressed to find much evidence of God being called "Father," much less prayed to as Father, but this is the dominant way God is named and addressed in the New Testament, which is a reflex of the unique relationship that Jesus believed he had with God and could pass on to his followers to a lesser degree, such that they too could address God as "Abba, Father."[17]

More than a little revealing is the way the Old Testament texts are used in the New Testament. The distribution of use of texts is hardly even (the later prophetic books, especially Isaiah, and the Psalms are used the most by far, with some books, such as Esther, not even being mentioned), and most of the texts that are used are used with a christological focus and filter. Jesus is seen, broadly speaking, as the fulfillment of all the institutions of the Old Testament as well as all its future-oriented prophecies. All the promises of God are said to be "yes" in Jesus Christ (2 Cor 1:20). This led to some very creative use of the Old Testament indeed. For example, in Matthew 1 we see the employment of Isaiah 7:14 to explain the awkward fact of the virginal conception. It is the event in the life of Mary that prompted this after-the-fact rereading of the prophecy in a fresh way. The prophecy itself did not prompt the creation of a fictional story of a virginal conception. What we are dealing with is not prophecy "historicized" in such cases, but rather history looking for a prophetic home and backing.

The "fulfillment and completion" mentality with a focus on Christ and the eschatological age or kingdom that he was inaugurating is clear in numerous places in the New Testament. This comports entirely with the mentality that contrasts previous covenants and ministries with the new covenant or with the ministry of Christ (see, e.g., 2 Cor 3:1-18, the ministry of Moses versus the ministry of Paul in Christ; Gal 4, the tale of the Sinai covenant as bracketed by the Abrahamic and new covenants, which are linked; Heb 8, the new covenant making the previous ones obsolete). In other words, while New Testament theology is clearly enough dependent on and using the resources of the Old Testament and Old Testament theology to do its theologizing (for the Old Testament is its sacred text source [see 2 Tim 3:16]), what most stands out about these efforts are the fresh ways the material is

---

[17]See Ben Witherington III, *The Individual Witnesses*, vol. 1 of *The Indelible Image: The Theological and Ethical Thought World of the New Testament* (Downers Grove, Ill.: IVP Academic, 2009), pp. 63-170.

used to serve what can only be called christological and Christian purposes.[18] Although sometimes the larger context of an Old Testament quotation or allusion in the New Testament is presupposed as known, this is far from universally the case. Paul is hardly thinking of the larger context of Old Testament rules about fair treatment of animals when he suggests that ministers have as much right to be paid for their hard work as oxen have a right to eat some of the grain they thresh.

Nevertheless, the dependency of New Testament writers on Old Testament material for their ethicizing often seems clearer and involving less modification than it does for their theologizing. This is particularly clear in the recycling of some of the Ten Commandments and the Shema not only in the Gospels but also in Paul's letters (see, e.g., Rom 12; 1 Cor 8:6). And yet not all of the Ten Commandments are reaffirmed in the New Testament (e.g., the Sabbath commandment), and huge chunks of Mosaic law are seen as no longer applicable—for example, the laws about sacrifice, clean and unclean, and the like no longer apply (on sacrifice, see Hebrews; on clean and unclean, see Mk 7:13-15; Acts 10), and the theology of holy war is entirely replaced in places by a theology of holy peace, so to speak, a theology of peacemaking, nonretaliation, and nonresistance (cf. Mt 5–7 to Rom 12, though see a small foreshadowing in 2 Kings 6:8-23). This is not entirely unexpected, since orthopraxy rather than orthodoxy was to the fore in early Judaism, and early Jewish ethics were easier to use and adapt directly for creating the social ethos of early Jewish Christian communities. Yet even so, modifications were underway almost from the outset when it came to praxis or rituals, particularly the adapting and morphing of Passover ideas and praxis into the Lord's Supper meal, and the adapting of early Jewish water rituals and baptismal practices (particularly John's) to provide the entrance ritual of Christian baptism (see, e.g., Acts 18–19; Heb 6:1-4).

What is clear from a close reading of the New Testament is that the Christian writers of these books seem far more preoccupied with theology proper than were various of the writers of Old Testament books and, for that matter, of contemporary early Jewish writers such as the authors of the Maccabean corpus or Josephus, though clearly Philo has more philosophical and theological bones than some of his early Jewish peers.

---

[18]For a detailed study of the use of the Old Testament in the New Testament, see G. K. Beale and D. A. Carson, eds., *Commentary on the New Testament Use of the Old Testament* (Grand Rapids: Baker Academic, 2007).

How had a focus largely on praxis and ethics in early Judaism been so significantly changed as to shift to a historical person, Jesus, and theologizing about that person and his ramifications for reconceptualizing the rest of theology and ethics? This rather dramatic change in worldview has to be accounted for as a historical phenomena. I suggest that this trajectory was already set in motion by the life, words, and work of Jesus, and particularly by his self-presentation of his messianic self-understanding. All this theologizing about Jesus is explicable and understandable if Jesus himself provided the impetus and some of the initial substance in this direction. It is rather inexplicable if Jesus was some nonmessianic figure who never made any extraordinary claims either directly or indirectly. Especially inexplicable is any attempt to valorize Jesus' shameful crucifixion positively if it was not already believed that he was someone unique, messianic, special.

What all this should tell us is that while the writers of the New Testament are well grounded in and regularly draw from their Hebrew Scriptures to do their theologizing and ethicizing in their Christian worldview, the Old Testament material does not function the same way as it did for various other early Jewish groups that had not affirmed the messiahship of the historical person Jesus of Nazareth. In other words, it is the Christian experience of things, particularly of the life, death, and resurrection appearances of Jesus, and their later worship experiences as well that have caused a rather clear and dramatic reconfiguration of even the basic lineaments of Old Testament thought.

In short, while one can talk about some considerable continuity between the theologizing and ethicizing found in the Old Testament and New Testament, it is the discontinuity that often stands out the most, and this is because of the ongoing effects of the Christ-event on these writers' lives, not only in regard to the memory of the Jesus of history, but also because of the ongoing encounter in worship, vision, and life of the Christ of faith.

When the New Testament writers talk from time to time about a new covenant and a new relationship with God, this is precisely what they mean, not merely a renewed form of some old covenant. One of the clearest proofs of this is that beginning with Jesus and continuing on through the New Testament writers, Israel is generally seen as lost and in need of salvation or redemption from God. Not just the Jewish sinners, but even the saints, such as the pious Nicodemus, are called to conversion (see Jn 3), and when there is a discussion about how one gets into the community of Jesus, it focuses on new birth or new creation, which, call it what you like, is a way of talking about conversion, not merely a continuation or a renewal of a previous relationship that one had with God. One does not use the language previously applied to proselytes to Judaism to all persons unless one is emphasizing the new beginning, the new community, the need to be born anew as the most crucial thing for all persons.

True enough, this can be called "the restoration of Israel" (Lk 24:21), but it is restoration through redemption in Christ. The discussion in Romans 9–11, though complex, makes clear that even a former Pharisee such as Paul is prepared to talk about the temporary breaking off of Jews who do not accept Jesus from the people of God, with the hopes of grafting them back into the people of God eschatologically, but on the same terms and basis on which Gentiles come into the Christian community: by grace through faith in Jesus and by the pure mercy of God. Even Paul does not envision two peoples of God with two sets of promises and prophecies applied to each; rather, his vision is of Jew and Gentile united in Christ (Gal 3:28; Eph 2) both in the present and at the eschaton.

What this means is that early Christianity, largely composed of Jews well into the first century, was a very sectarian group, an offshoot of early Judaism transplanted into new soil rather than simply a natural growth and development or just another form of early Judaism, not least because the earliest followers of Jesus made rather exclusive claims about their views, their Savior, their community as the people of God, and so on. True enough, they saw this not as a replacement or supersessionist theology and ethic, but rather as a completionist theology and ethic. However, once the church became predominantly Gentile, this way of doing theology and ethics inevitably would sound like supersessionism to non-Christian Jews, as it does to this very day, and the praxis of the church would simply reinforce that impression.

To draw this discussion to a conclusion: New Testament theology and ethics have no other major written source of their substance from an earlier era than the materials found in the Old Testament. However—and this is a big "however"—what most colors, determines, and shapes the thought world of the New Testament writers is the new thing that God has been and is doing in Jesus, including a particular focus on both the person and works of Christ, both as the historical Jesus and as the exalted Lord, and a strong and repeated focus on Christ's crucifixion and resurrection.

In some ways, the collections of Jesus' sayings, the early creedal statements, the christological hymns, and the catena of Old Testament quotations seen in a christological light, as written sources, are more determinative of what is being claimed in the New Testament in regard to theology and ethics than simply the materials carried over and reaffirmed from the Old Testament. This reveals the default and starting point of these writers and also explains why I am approaching this material not by beginning with a rehearsal of Old Testament theology and ethics, but by beginning with what we find in the New Testament itself and relating it to its various source materials. New Testament theology and ethics deserve to be studied in their own right, not merely seen as a development, however logical or natural of Old Testament theology and ethics. Indeed, unless we approach the matter that way, it is doubtful that we will be ever able to explain the distinctive character of the material.

A CONCISE REVIEW OF KEY LITERATURE

I have reserved for the present volume a brief review of key literature relevant to the discussion of New Testament because it is easy to get swallowed up by the debate and dialogue of one scholar with another and never actually deal directly with the New Testament texts. I did the latter in the first volume, but here is the place for dialogue and critique of recent efforts of relevance to the study of New Testament theology and ethics.

Here I must list some problems with Kevin Vanhoozer's approach to doctrine and theology, though I have learned much from his work.[19] There are problems with seeing the Bible as a theo-drama. A drama or play, by its nature, while it may mime or depict reality, is not reality. In fact, it is a literary fiction. These problems are only exacerbated if one begins to talk about the "drama" as if it were a one-actor play, the actor being God, to which we simply respond with gratitude or applause as God enters and exits the stage, or if one talks about the drama as if it involved a predetermined script from which none of the actors can or should vary.

Vanhoozer says, for example, "Theology must come to grips with the Bible as performative rather than simply informative discourse. . . . The biblical theo-drama owes its shape to the divine promise that generates the action. . . . God's promise establishes his covenant with Israel. This confirms the evangelical principle that God's speech and action are prior to theology's

---

[19]I am referring to Vanhoozer's seminal work *The Drama of Doctrine: A Canonical-Linguistic Approach to Christian Theology* (Louisville: Westminster John Knox, 2005).

speech and action. Second, the Bible is Scripture—the authoritative word of God—precisely because it is a word for which God assumes the rights and responsibilities of authorship. The church's script is ultimately a matter of divine discourse."[20] In Vanhoozer's view, we need take little account of how and whether Israel responds to God's act of covenanting. God says it, and that settles it. Although I would not deny that God's action is prior to our response or even that God's action enables our response, I would not want to say that God's promise determines how we respond.

Furthermore, God inspires the human biblical authors to speak truthfully about a whole host of subjects, but certainly God is not the sole author of this material, and the way he works with his human authors is, for the most part, by way of inspiration, not dictation. There are not two speakers or two levels of discourse in this material, but only one: the divinely inspired human voice—unless, of course, we are talking about a prophetic oracle. To fail to take into account the human authors involved in the writing of this script or even to minimize their contribution as if it were not substantial is a problem.[21] The Bible is a revelation from God and thus indeed is true information that can produce transformation. This is so, however, not because of the inherently performative character of divine speech; it is so because the truth, in the hands of the Holy Spirit and in the lives of those who are open to it, changes things.

Then, too, the problem with this drama image is that it ignores that there are many actors in the drama of redemption, of which God is only the overwhelmingly most important one. God not merely calls, exhorts, and redeems people; he insists that they participate in their own redemption and indeed in the redemption of others. Doubtless, an omnipotent God could have done it unilaterally and otherwise than God has done it, but God did not take such an approach. Thus, in order to talk about the drama of redemption and be truly biblical, one needs to list all the dramatis personae, even if the actors other than God are dependent on God and play minor roles in comparison to God.

The problem is further exacerbated if one looks at Scripture as the script of the drama, when in fact much, perhaps most, of Scripture describes what God has already done in human history, and only a minority of texts provide a script of what is yet to come. A script for a play is never written after the fact

---

[20]Ibid., p. 64.
[21]See Ben Witherington III, *The Living Word of God: Rethinking the Theology of the Bible* (Waco, Tex.: Baylor University Press, 2008).

on the basis of observing the play; rather, it provides the blueprint for doing the play in the first place. The Gospels and the book Acts do not work prospectively like a script for a play. They work retrospectively, telling us what God has done in Christ when the time had fully come. In other words, they work like biography or historical monograph, not like a script for a drama. In sum, Vanhoozer is using the wrong narratological language or analogy to talk about these things, and by this I mean a language that does not comport with the genre and character of the New Testament documents themselves. It is fine to talk about the Bible informing us of the story of which we are a part and then to say that we improvise our roles on the basis of that story and the instructions and even demands that come with the story, but this is rather less than Vanhoozer wants to assert, it appears.[22]

For my part, then, it seems better to talk about narrative rather than the drama. Narrative can be just as dramatic as drama, often more so. Narratives, even of surprising or unfortunate events, are mostly retrospective in character, just as the first five books of the New Testament are, and the first five-plus books of the Old Testament as well. It is prophecy that is mostly prospective in character. But New Testament prophecy provides us only with a very limited blueprint of a very sketchy sort about the future. You could never deduce your full role in the "drama" from reading Mark 13 or the book of Revelation. You really need the New Testament Letters to help with that.

Vanhoozer tries to make a distinction between drama and narrative in that drama involves speaking and acting, whereas narrative involves just narrating, a form of speaking. This distinction does not work, especially in the setting of first-century culture, where reading was done out loud and where narrating as a storyteller was an action, often a dramatic action if you were a good storyteller. We must envision the Gospel narratives being performed orally with some rhetorical skill, not because they thought it was a play, but because they wanted it to be a rhetorically persuasive and effective communication. Notice in one-man performances of a Gospel like Mark that it involves both words and brief actions and gestures as the narrative comes to life. This is not because it is a play with various actors and parts, but because it is being effectively narrated. A fitting conclusion to this part of the discussion is Richard Burridge's cautionary words as he argues for a narrative

---

[22]I am equally unconvinced by the suggestion of N. T. Wright that we are talking about a drama with a missing act (to be supplied). This again suggests a play with a script rather than a story that is still unfolding and in which various of the characters are still in motion, still improvising their roles.

rather than drama approach to the New Testament: "Some people describe the gospel as 'tragic' or 'dramatic,' without recognising that *they do not contain any of the formal elements required for ancient drama, such as being in verse, using a chorus and actors and so forth. Such 'adjectival' descriptions of a work are really about its* mode; *thus something which is written in the genre of a 'biography' or an 'epistle' may be tragic or dramatic or historical or elegiac in its mode.*"[23]

Frank Thielman

Other sorts of problems attend more traditional efforts at doing New Testament theology, of which Frank Thielman's fine book is an example.[24] Most of what he presents is not "the theology of the New Testament" (despite his book title), but rather samplings of the theologizing of the individual witnesses within the New Testament. This can be seen as theology *in* the New Testament, but not a theology *of* the New Testament. The latter implies a synthetic presentation of the whole in some sense and fashion. His book does not do this except briefly at a few junctures and at the end. This is all too common in such textbooks.

I. Howard Marshall

A good deal more needs to be said about Howard Marshall's important study. Marshall argues that "the aim of students of New Testament theology is to explore the New Testament writers' developing understanding of God and the world, more particularly the world of people and their relationship to one another."[25] This definition is broad enough to cover a lot of approaches, but I want to highlight the word "developing." Marshall is quite right in this, and he is getting at something important. The New Testament itself is not a self-contained theology or ethics textbook; rather, it provides us with samples, examples, and trajectories of thought that can and ought to be pursued further. It is a historically conditioned and occasional document.

Marshall goes on to describe what a good effort at studying New Testament theology would look like: "The initial task of a theology of the New Testament is to make a collection of the theologies that may be presumed to

---

[23]Richard A. Burridge, *Imitating Jesus: An Inclusive Approach of New Testament Ethics* (Grand Rapids: Eerdmans, 2007), p. 24 (italics mine).

[24]Frank Thielman, *Theology of the New Testament: A Canonical and Synthetic Approach* (Grand Rapids: Zondervan, 2005).

[25]I. Howard Marshall, *New Testament Theology: Many Witnesses, One Gospel* (Downers Grove, Ill.: InterVarsity Press, 2004), p. 23.

come to expression in its various documents."[26] But is a theology of the New Testament or of the early church simply a collection of studies of the theologies of different believers brought together within the covers of one book, or must there not be some comparison between them to establish whether the several theologies form a unity, sharing the same basic understanding, however much they may differ in the ways in which they express it or in the details of the content? "It is surely the duty of the New Testament theologian to attempt some comparison of the outlooks of the writers in order to ascertain how far there is such an entity as *the* theology of the New Testament, and if so what this entity might be."[27] I agree with this conclusion, and this certainly describes a good deal of the task undertaken in the present volume along with the parallel task of seeing what New Testament ethics might look like.

One of the most helpful aspects of Marshall's work is that he understands that even if one is doing a synthetic look at New Testament theology or New Testament ethics, this does not mean that one strips all the context away from these various documents, leaving us with a pile of similar ideas or concepts. He therefore clusters the synthetic discussion appropriately. For example, he compares the Synoptic theologies to one another and to Acts because of their use of the same material in various ways, or their use of the same methodology in handling the source material. He also compares the Johannine material because it seems to arise from the same ethos and sources. This genre-sensitive and source-sensitive approach is what is needed in a synthetic approach to either New Testament theology or New Testament ethics. I intend to follow his lead in some of this at the appropriate juncture in my discussion.

Philip Esler

To his credit, we find something quite different and creative going on in Philip Esler's work.[28] Esler is fully committed to a belief that there must be a historical investigation of what messages New Testament writers conveyed in their works. By this he means that a systematic theology approach, or even a "theo-drama" approach that denudes the theological discussion of its historical givenness, is a nonstarter for him. One of the great merits of Esler's work is not merely that it provides a social analytical way of looking at New

---

[26]Ibid., p. 29. The task that Marshall identifies I undertook in the first volume of the present study.
[27]Ibid.
[28]Philip Esler, *New Testament Theology: Communion and Community* (Minneapolis: Fortress, 2005).

Testament thought, but that he rightly stresses that belief and behavior are as intertwined as feelings and thinking, and so there are cognitive, evaluative, and emotive dimensions to belonging to a group such as "the body of Christ." Thus he rightly stresses,

> Just as there is a lot more to social identity than group beliefs, so too there is much more to being a Christian than holding this belief (*vere Deus vere homo*). First, there are other beliefs that are important, such as how the cosmos and human beings originated, the manner in which they should interact, and the ultimate destiny for the cosmos and humanity. Second, and perhaps more important, there are behavioral patterns that are presented as Christian. . . . These patterns include a relationship with God expressed in prayer and ways of relating to other people. Third, for some Christians, there is the continuous annual cycle of Christian liturgy. Fourth, there are the emotional and evaluative dimensions of being a Christian.[29]

Esler rightly objects to the reductionism and strip mining of texts in the service of a theological cause. He puts it this way: "The whole process is like a mining operation. Areas with a rich lode of the right ore (passages containing the theological concepts prioritized by the exegete) are dynamited and excavated (the act of exegesis) and the minerals separated (the act of interpreting the exegetical results) from the rock (the text under discussion), thus leaving nasty scars on the landscape (the text) and desolate heaps of tailings (the remnants of texts thought irrelevant)."[30]

In contrast to the usual approach, Esler sets out what he identifies as an interpersonal approach to New Testament theology and ethics. By this he means that contemporary believers are part of an ongoing living people of God and can have communion and community and indeed communication with the previous members of this community, which includes having a dialogue with the various New Testament witnesses. Writings have the effect of maintaining personal presence (not just the presence of ideas) over a distance of time or space or both.

One of the merits of Esler's approach is that he rejects an atheological approach to New Testament theology and ethics. He especially deplores "the advocacy of a theological perspective adopted in advance of the historical interpretation of the Bible," and he is equally adamant in opposing "ascribing to history an inadequate function."[31] In this case, he is rightly critiquing not

---

[29]Ibid., p. 5.
[30]Ibid., pp. 6-7.
[31]Ibid., p. 36.

merely dogmatism but certain canonical approaches to "biblical" theology, including some of the efforts of Francis Watson. In contrast to this, Esler offers an approach to theology that "finds in its *ecclesiology* the principles of interpretation and meaning."[32]

One of the more crucial things that Esler is opposing is any and all forms of the disembodied approach to the text of the New Testament. For example, he argues,

> There is a personal dimension to the works of the Old and New Testaments that I find impossible to ignore. This attitude makes me unsympathetic, for example, to claims that the intentions of the those who composed these works are of no consequence, that once they were published they became entirely disconnected from their authors, or that when we read them we are at complete liberty to impute or create meaning rather than attending carefully to the meanings these works conveyed to their original audiences.[33]

If God is being in relationship, something that connotes not instability or flux but rather communion of a plurality in unity, then Esler suggests that perhaps a relational model of doing theology and ethics is more in keeping with the nature of God. It is interesting how he uses the "I-Thou" concepts of the Jewish mystic Martin Buber to talk about the plurality within the Godhead.[34]

> What Christianity needed was a conception of God that avoided Greek monism but also the radical gulf between God and the material world espoused by Gnostics. The answer came from pastoral theologians such as Ignatius of Antioch and Irenaeus who approached the being of God through the experience of the ecclesial community, of *ecclesial being*, especially as it was embodied in eucharistic practice.[35]

Such theologians argued that since God was a relational being, one could not talk about God without the concept of communion.

Equally, however, because human beings are created in the image of God in precisely this same way, their personhood involves being in relationship, and this means that both humans and God are interactive creatures and their beings are beings in relationship, not in isolation. Communion between the persons of the Trinity does not involve absorption, any more than relationship

---

[32]Ibid.
[33]Ibid., p. 39.
[34]See ibid., pp. 59-61.
[35]Ibid., p. 61.

between humans need mean a lost of identity or individuality. Communion involves union without uniformity or singularity. Indeed, communion and union are only possible between distinguishable persons. Ethics in the light of this involves, among other things, behaving according to what we already are in relationship to God and each other. It also involves living in accord with the paradigmatic story of Jesus.

Esler also makes a distinction between literary and nonliterary texts and believes that the New Testament documents fall into the latter category. If by this he means that they are not texts created mainly for purely literary purposes (i.e., created as "literature"), he is right. They mainly have didactic and practical purposes. This does not mean that these texts do not have some literary qualities to them, but it does mean that we need to take seriously their oral and aural character and their practical nature. This is all the more the case when we are studying the theology or ethics of these documents. None of them were written primarily to entertain or for aesthetic purposes; rather, they were intended to instruct, persuade, illuminate, exhort, even transform.

In essence, Esler wants us to read the New Testament in communion with the saints, which means not merely paying attention to previous lines of interpretation and theological development, but interpreting the text as a part of the living body of Christ and so being amenable to its judgments, suggestions, urgings. Unfortunately, Esler gives only a small sample of how this seems to work at the interpretive level (looking at 1 Cor 10–14). Only at the end of the book do we find a brief discussion of a whole New Testament book, Romans, and here it finally becomes clearer how one can have a dialogue with the dead, in this case Paul.

Stressing the oral, nonliterary character of New Testament documents that links them closely to the notion of authorial intentionality (since they are specific words spoken into specific situations, not abstract poetry or the like), Esler says that Paul's voice can be heard in his words, and that since Paul is still alive in the presence of the Lord, he is not a dead author, but a living one. The notion of the communion of the saints means not only that we must speak no ill of the dead, but also that we must respect them and their intentions as still living and still having a living voice through their writings. Thus, detailed contextual exegesis is necessary to actually hear that voice correctly. I agree with most of this, and I quite agree that detailed contextual study of New Testament documents can yield an understanding of these authors' meanings as well as some of their intentions.

G. B. Caird

Oddly enough, Esler's theory about the "living dead," Paul and other saints still speaking today, provides a nice segue to dealing with G. B. Caird's volume on New Testament theology, which in fact was composed in its present form by L. D. Hurst, after Caird's death, based on draft chapters, fragments, hints, notes, related articles, and Hurst's own expansions, hopefully in keeping with Caird's thought.[36] In a few ways, this is the most intriguing and creative of the volumes reviewed. Caird sees the New Testament writers as being like an apostolic council meeting, the members sitting around a table discussing crucial theological matters and hammering out their understanding of their unity, all the while allowing considerable diversity. In some ways, this is like my image of the choir singing the same the piece of music but in varying parts. The difference is that the choir image indicates a context of doxology, praise to our Maker, whereas Caird's image suggests human dialogue or debate.

In one special respect I disagree with how Caird decided to handle the material. Thankfully, he rejected Bultmann's idea that Jesus is merely the presupposition of New Testament theology, but his idea that Jesus should be treated last instead of as the catalyst for much of the New Testament seems to be a critical mistake. I agree with Caird that Bultmann was responsible for a good deal of what has been wrong with New Testament theology discussions over the last seventy-plus years, especially the denuding of such discussion from their historical context in various ways. But to his credit, Bultmann's good synthetic mind was able to show that figures such as Paul did have a comprehensive and coherent thought world that led to a coherent presentation of theologizing and ethicizing into particular situations.

What none of these writers whose work I have briefly reviewed does, however, is deal with the underpinnings of the thought world expressed in these New Testament works. They are content to deal with the surface phenomena as we have it, not exploring the foundations of New Testament thought. I will address this issue in the next chapter.

---

[36]Caird, *New Testament Theology*.

2

THE SYMBOLIC UNIVERSE
OF JESUS AND THE
NEW TESTAMENT WRITERS

*Theology . . . is for the sociology of knowledge a kind of knowledge that is
the product of systematic reflection upon a symbolic universe, and indeed
of reflection that serves to maintain that universe when it is in some kind
of jeopardy, as for example from the threats of doubt, of disagreement, of
competing symbolic universes.*

NORMAN PETERSEN[1]

WHAT IS THE SYMBOLIC UNIVERSE OF JESUS
AND THE NEW TESTAMENT WRITERS?

When I talk about a symbolic universe, I am referring to the fixed furniture
in our mind from which we furnish our narrative thought world. Concepts
such as God, sin, salvation, Israel, faith, heaven, hell, love, forgiveness, adultery, and truth, are examples of the mental furniture to which I am referring.
I am specifically interested in the theological and ethical part of the mental
furniture, not all parts of it. There is not world and time enough to deal with
all the clutter in the mental attic of the early Christians who spoke and wrote
material that made its way into the New Testament. To put it concisely, I am
suggesting that all the New Testament writers shared the same basic early
Jewish Christian symbolic universe. This is not always evident, as they articulate their symbolic universe in different narrative forms, have different
urgencies and agendas, speak to different audiences, and use different forms
of argumentation and persuasion.

---

[1]Norman R. Petersen, *Rediscovering Paul: Philemon and the Sociology of Paul's Narrative World* (Philadelphia: Fortress, 1985), pp. 29-30.

There are, then, various reasons why the surface phenomena of, say, the letter of James appear different from that of the letter to the Galatians. Yet the truth is that these two very different short documents share a common symbolic universe. For example, in both documents we find the following: (1) "God" always refers to the Father, the one called "Yahweh" in the Old Testament. It does not mean, for example, Baal in one of these documents and Yahweh in the other. The two writers share a common theological symbolic universe at the most fundamental level. (2) When the two writers think of the concepts of both faith/trust and obedience, they think of Abraham. This means that they think in very specifically Jewish ways about what faith means. Again the symbolic universe is the same, but the way it is formed into narrative thought and exposition differs. (3) Perhaps most importantly, the Lord Jesus Christ is the whole reason why these authors are writing these documents and addressing these specific communities. Paul and James share at the most fundamental level a christological understanding of God and salvation and salvation history. Much of this is below-the-surface phenomena that we find in these documents. The commonality and unity are not immediately evident, and so it is possible to mistake different uses of the Abraham story for different purposes and emphases as some sort of theological tension or contradiction when it is not. Both authors believe in the priority of grace and faith, both believe faith works, and both believe in the obedience that flows forth from faith—the "obedience of faith." "Justification," if we want to use that anachronistic term, in neither Paul's nor James's narrative thought world stands alone. Paul did not believe that "justification" was the be-all and end-all of salvation. He also believed sanctification was necessary to salvation, and one aspect of that was working out one's salvation with fear and trembling by means of obedience and good deeds. Indeed, justification for Paul has to do only with conversion or initial salvation, or new creation. The whole of salvation cannot and should not be subsumed under the banner of justification, even in Pauline theology. Real faith works, and real salvation that goes beyond conversion necessarily involves obedience and deeds. This is as true for Paul as it is for James.

I have chosen this particular initial example—perhaps the most controversial example I could choose from the New Testament on the issue of faith and obedience ("works")—precisely because it needs to be stressed that the analysis of New Testament theology and ethics too often has been approached with the wrong sort of atomistic presuppositions. Having taken into account the symbolic universe shared by all the New Testament writers, one suddenly realizes that there is a much more profound unity to New Testament theology and ethics than previously imagined, even though it requires some probing to see this underground shared foundation on which all New Testament writers and speakers stand.

The only partial exception to this rule is Jesus himself. Since Jesus does not speak to us from after the Christ-event of death and resurrection, and since he is addressing non-Christian Jews (including his disciples, who are just beginning to head in the right direction), the foundation on which he stands, his symbolic universe, looks a bit different. I will need to say much more about this in due course. But even so, Jesus sees himself as the straw that stirs the drink. He is the game-changing performer. He is the kingdom-bringer. He is the Son of Man savior figure meant to establish dominion on earth forever. The events that will change the aeons and history as well stand before him, whereas for all the New Testament authors these first eschatological events stand behind them, and they have the benefit of hindsight and retrospective analysis.

When dealing specifically with a devout person's religious symbolic universe, which is our concern in this project, we are dealing with something that, though not impervious to change, requires a Copernican revolution in one's thinking to change in significant ways. By this I mean that it requires what most ancients thought was difficult if not impossible: conversion of the imagination to a new paradigm, not just individual new ideas. The writers of the New Testament share a paradigm shift in their religious thinking, some a more radical shift than others, and none more radical than Paul. One of the clearest signs of whether we are dealing with a seismic shift or with a more modest change is the degree to which a person continues trying to put the new things into the old Procrustean bed or paradigm. A good example of this is the persons we often call "Judaizers"—hardline Jewish Christians who insisted that all persons must become like them to be saved and so must keep the Mosaic law in detail, even if they are Gentiles.

Take, for example, how they are portrayed by Luke in Acts 15:1. Luke says that these folks went up to Antioch from Jerusalem and taught the Christian believers, "Unless you are circumcised according to the custom taught by Moses, you cannot be saved." This is expanded and clarified in Acts 15:5: "The Gentiles must be circumcised and required to obey the law of Moses." Here are people who are not conjuring with a dramatic paradigm shift. For them, not only is Jesus the Jewish messiah, but also one must become a Jew, become Jewish, to get the real benefit of Jesus, even if one is a Gentile. Jesus becomes the factor that completes the old paradigm, and a drastic rethinking of the symbolic universe is not required.

Say what you will about Paul, he could see that the implications of Jesus were far more radical than that, particularly the implications of Jesus' death and resurrection. It appears that some of the Judaizers thought that the coming of the messiah, though it did involve the coming of the end times, did not mean the coming of a new covenant in which there was more discontinuity than continuity with the past and with previous covenants. Either they thought that Jeremiah 31 was merely about a renewal of the old covenant (perhaps especially the Mosaic one) or they did not think that that particular prophecy yet applied. Paul begged to differ. A new covenant implied a new vision of God's people united in Christ and no longer defined by ethnic, social or gender particularities (see Gal 3:28). Somewhere in between was the view of James that although Gentiles did not need to be circumcised or keep food and other Levitical laws, they did need to avoid pagan idolatry and immorality, which was at the heart of the Ten Commandments (see the decree in Acts 15). It may be that James thought that Jewish Christians needed to remain true to Torah, unlike Paul, who saw Torah observance as a blessed option for Jewish Christians, even a missional tactic at times (see 1 Cor 9), but not required even of Jewish Christians.

What needs to be noticed here is that some of these differences have to do with ways of thinking about orthopraxy ("How, then, shall we live?"), and some have to do with orthodoxy ("What shall we believe?"). I see no evidence of any significant number of early Christians who did not think that Jesus' death and resurrection were crucial to salvation and changed some things quite drastically. It is just that some had not worked out all the implications of the Christ-event to the degree Paul had done. Some had a more converted or changed symbolic universe than others. But we have no New Testament writers who represent the extreme Judaizing point of view—not James, not the author of Matthew, not Jude, not anyone. To the contrary, all of these New Testament writers share to a great degree a common symbolic universe that has a christologically reformed shape, affecting everything—their view of God, people, world, and eschatological matters. The form of the world was passing away, and the new had already come. All the New Testament writers are convinced of this, and they stand on tiptoe waiting for what is next, especially when Christ returns. They are looking forward, not dwelling on or in the past. The model that I offer for consideration when it comes to the symbolic universe involves circles—intersecting circles (see fig. 2.1).

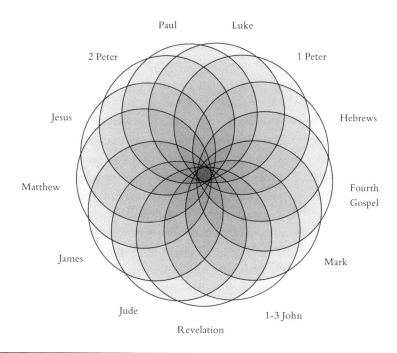

Figure 2.1. Thought World of the New Testament

This is a form of Venn diagram. In this particular form we are dealing with multiple intersecting circles. All of the circles share a considerable amount of overlap in the center. And notice that the outer limits of all the thought worlds indicate that no one of these witnesses is dramatically out of sync with the others; were that not so, the larger circle of the thought world would have a bulge in one direction, ruining the concentric and basically well-rounded shape of the larger shared thought world. Because all of the witnesses as we have them are speaking into specific situations, the place where a particular circle is located in the configuration of the whole differs from the other circles. For example, the less Hellenized witnesses who are basically addressing Jewish Christians appear mostly on the bottom left side of the diagram, from Matthew down to 1-3 John. Jesus is found here as well, although he is addressing Jews on the way to becoming Jewish Christians. Those more in the Pauline orbit, and more clearly focusing on a largely Gentile audience, appear in the upper right side of the model, from Paul down to Mark, though interestingly the authors of Hebrews and 1 Peter share the Pauline perspective but are addressing Hellenized Jewish Christians in Rome and Asia respectively. The identity of the audience of the Fourth Gospel, though debatable, seems to be Diaspora Jewish Christians by and large. In the case of 2 Peter we have an encyclical to the whole church that reflects influence from both the more Jewish Christian and the more Pauline sides of the model. Paul and 2 Peter are at the top of the diagram for a good reason. In them we have the more universalizable form of the New Testament thought world, a form that could be addressed to Jews or Gentiles equally well.

All the authors of this material share the Old Testament, which, prior to their Christian faith, formed and furnished their religious symbolic universe. This is one of the main reasons why there is so much overlap between Jesus and his followers. They share a universe of discourse, although they have a difference in time frame that affects the perspective on that universe. But there is Jesus material and also events in Jesus' story that are shared by these various witnesses as well. The overlap is not caused simply by the sharing of a common sacred text; they also share a common faith in Jesus and the Christ-event.

If we inquire as to how we know what is at the heart of their symbolic universe, we can derive an important clue by examining the rituals of the group, by which I mean baptism and the Lord's Supper. Social historians remind us of a crucial point: rituals and ceremonies depict and encode at least some of the major values of the community that practices these exercises. We can learn much about the belief and behavior structure that is at the heart of early Judaism and early Christianity by asking questions such as these: What is depicted and said about rituals such as circumcision and baptism, on the one hand, and about ceremonies such as Passover and the Lord's Supper, on the other? What values are inculcated by these procedures? For example, it is no accident that both circumcision and Passover are associated with group-founding events: the inauguration of the Abrahamic covenant and the exodus Sinai events respectively. Nor is it an accident that Christian baptism is associated with aspects of Jesus' death and the cleansing from sin, and that the Lord's Supper is also associated with Jesus' death and resurrection. What we see from rituals such as baptism is that the Christians believe in change happening in connection with the embracing of the death and resurrection of Jesus. Equally, we see from their Lord's Supper ritual their belief that a new covenant has begun with Jesus.

Rituals and ceremonies are a form of symbolic proclamation, the Word made visible, of the community's most sacred beliefs and values. In the cases of Judaism and Christianity, these sorts of rituals and ceremonies are linked to historical and historic events, events that led to the foundation of the community in the first place. They are not, in the first instance, symbols of generic religious experiences. They have to do with historic covenanting acts and foundational redemption events. In this regard, they are quite different from various sorts of Greco-Roman religious rituals and ceremonies, including the rites of Isis or the Tauroboleum, or the Dionysian rites, or the mystery rituals. There is a difference between how rituals and ceremonies function in historically founded and grounded religions and in mythologically grounded ones. But what happens when a meal, or some sort of ceremony involving eating and drinking, becomes the central symbol of a faith? I say "central" advisedly, as boundary rituals are one thing, central ceremonies and symbols another.[2] The latter especially allude to the central values and beliefs of a sect or religious group.

Meals, perhaps more than any other social event in antiquity, encoded the values of a society, or if it was a sectarian meal, of the sect itself. Although we might be prone to calling them "rules of etiquette," something that Ms. Manners might expostulate on, in antiquity the rules and taboos that applied to meals were serious business. They dictated who would be invited to a meal, where they would sit, what they would eat, and the like. Such meals had pecking orders, with the elite guests reclining on the best couches and getting the best food, and the less prominent guests further from the head couches and the host of the dinner. As Mary Douglas puts it, "If food is treated as a code, the messages it encodes will be found in the pattern of social relations being expressed. The message is about different degrees of hierarchy, inclusion and exclusion, boundaries and transactions across boundaries. . . . Food categories therefore encode social events."[3]

I suggest, then, that we learn a lot about the symbolic universe of the early Christians from examining their rituals, and from this we discover that ev-

---

[2]Sadly, many people treat the Lord's Supper as a boundary ritual, which it never was intended to be.

[3]Mary Douglas, "Deciphering a Meal," in *Implicit Meanings: Selected Essays in Anthropology* (London: Routledge & Kegan Paul, 1975), p. 249.

eryone seems to have assumed that the death and resurrection of Jesus were at the heart of their faith and thought world. It was a given that theology, ethics, and praxis would be done in the light of those central christological realities. Few were actually arguing about or contesting this approach, and when a test or false teaching did arise that touched the christological core of the faith, such as we see in 2–3 John or Jude or 2 Peter, the response was swift and decisive. No challenge to the core values in the symbolic universe was to be allowed. People who did not believe that Jesus was the Christ who came in the flesh, died in the flesh, and rose again in the flesh or who did not believe in conversion or the new eschatology and new covenant would quickly find themselves no longer within the bounded circle of the Christian symbolic universe. The same applied to the rather rigorous ethical code of this community. Sometimes, of course, people had to be told that they were out of bounds, and no doubt some were put out of bounds as well. But the fact that we see this boundary-defining kind of behavior in a plethora of the New Testament witnesses, including Jesus himself according to our earliest Gospel, Mark, makes evident that getting the thought world straight was crucial when it came to a variety of theological and ethical and practical subjects.

In other words, there was already an incipient sense and form of what would come to be called orthodoxy and orthopraxy in the New Testament era itself, and it was shared in various significant ways by the authors of these documents. This is not because history is written by the "winners"; it is because this group of writers represented the full spectrum of the acceptable symbolic universe, and there were no whole Christian communities that represented markedly dissenting voices at this point in time when it came to the core values at the heart of the symbolic universe. There were, for example, no Q communities that focused only on the sayings of Jesus and not his death and resurrection, or Gnostic communities that tried to transmute and syncretize the Jewish substance of the gospel with Greco-Roman philosophy and other ideas. The latter development would come later in the second century, and the former does not appear to have happened at all.

If we ask the more particular question of how Jesus' symbolic universe differs from that of his post-Easter followers, several things should be said in response. Jesus' symbolic universe focuses on the Father, his dominion and his divine saving eschatological activity happening in and through Jesus' own ministry. Jesus does have various important things to say about himself, but this is not at the absolute center of his thought world, nor is it emphasized as much as these other things just mentioned. Jesus was an early Jew, and of course he does not look back on his own death and resurrection as central to human history in the way his followers do. This is a matter of temporal perspective but also emphasis.

There is also the further issue that Jesus says a lot about Jewish ritual and religious matters (such as the issues of *corban* and of gleaning on the Sabbath) that simply do not come up in later Christian discussions, or at least in discussions referred or alluded to in New Testament documents, so far as we can tell. It is not improbable that Jerusalem Jewish Christians continued to talk about these things, but their discussions do not appear in the New Testament. And this brings us to a crucial point. We can reconstruct the symbolic universe of any of these figures only with the New Testament evidence that we have, and our evidence is quite clearly incomplete. We would love to know what Jesus thought about later issues—for instance, the later discussions of spiritual gifts such as speaking in tongues, or ethical issues such as whether his followers should eat meat offered to idols. Alas, there are many such issues that Jesus does not address, due in part to the overwhelmingly Jewish context of his ministry. So much of the rest of the New Testament assumes and addresses a broader audience, or at least an audience no longer (or never) within the orbit of non-Christian Judaism.

We do well, then, to consider at this juncture a rather extended glossary of terms, referring to staple items in the symbolic universe, that the witnesses listed above would have shared and indeed have taken for granted. This glossary differs some from that of other early Jewish groups due to the Jesus factor, but there are notable overlaps with other early Jewish communities, such as the one of Qumran.

GLOSSARY OF TERMS SIGNIFICANT IN THE SYMBOLIC UNIVERSE OF JESUS AND THE NEW TESTAMENT WRITERS

God

The most fundamental term in any monotheistic religious symbolic universe is, of course, *God*. What is meant by the term *God* in the New Testament? The answer may not be as self-evident as Christians today might think. The term never refers to "God in three persons, blessed Trinity," as the famous hymn has it. It refers either to God the Father (the one identified as Yahweh in the Old Testament) or to Jesus the Son, in some seven cases. The Holy Spirit is not called *theos* in the New Testament, though the Spirit certainly is seen as part of the Godhead. And here we encounter a difficulty in discussing the symbolic universe of the New Testament: a glossary of mere terms will not cover the gamut of thought. This is why we need to ask how the thought is put together in the narratives and logic of the discourses found in the New Testament.

Why is it that it is the Father who is overwhelmingly designated as God in the New Testament? This requires a two-part answer. All the writers are either Jews or God-fearers (in Luke's case, perhaps) who assume and subsume the basic Jewish lexicon into their own symbolic universe. Only one person is called "God," properly speaking, in that early Jewish thought world, and it is Yahweh.

But the second part to the answer is more telling. Why is the term *Father* used so frequently of the Jewish God? Indeed, why is it used some 140 times in the Fourth Gospel alone especially in view of the dearth of such usage in the Old Testament and in early Judaism? Here we find one of those instances where Jesus' own articulation of his thought world has changed the discourse of his followers. It is Jesus' use of *Abba* that seems to have prompted his followers to use the term of intimacy so frequently.[4] Here Jesus' followers are not being original but rather are following the paradigm provided by their master teacher. It is Jesus himself who spurred the Copernican revolution in their thinking about God, as can be seen by the frequent use of the "Father" language in the New Testament.

Even as early as within about twenty years of Jesus' death we find in 1 Corinthians 8:4-6 a christological reformulation of the Shema (Deut 6:4-5), the Jewish faith statement about God being one. Christians here are said to believe in one God, the Father, and one Lord, Jesus Christ, whereas the Shema referred the terms *God* and *Lord* to the same person. When change happens in the symbolic universe, even with as creative a thinker as Paul, it manifests itself through the modification of the existing faith statements, in this case the Shema. The old is not simply abandoned, it is transformed to incorporate the new.[5]

Assumed throughout the New Testament is that God is the creator and

---

[4]I explored this at some length in the first volume of the present study. See Ben Witherington III, *The Individual Witnesses*, vol. 1 of *The Indelible Image: The Theological and Ethical Thought World of the New Testament* (Downers Grove, Ill.: IVP Academic, 2009), pp. 63-170.

[5]Richard Bauckham has done very helpful work on this matter. See, for example, his seminal essays in *Jesus and the God of Israel: God Crucified and Other Studies on the New Testament's Christology of Divine Identity* (Grand Rapids: Eerdmans, 2008), especially those in the first half of the volume.

sustainer of the universe and indeed also is the one who saves people, intervening in human affairs. God plays a role from creation to new creation and in between as well. God is not in any way envisioned as a watchmaker deity who wound up the universe and then watched it tick away, leaving it alone. To the contrary, the God of the New Testament, as was true in the Old Testament, is the one who continues to come down and meddle in human affairs continuously through both natural and supernatural means. We can see this in the New Testament writers when they talk about the dominion of God coming on earth as in heaven. Dominion in this way of thinking does not merely refer to God's reign in the abstract over his creation; it refers to the will of God being eschatologically enacted on earth in a world gone wrong, enacted through Jesus, and angels, and followers of Jesus. It involves an interactive model of God and world (preferring the term *interactive* to *interventionist* because the latter makes God seem like an occasional intruder in his own universe).

The New Testament writers also assume that God is at the beginning of the end of his dealings with his creatures. By this I mean all these writers are convinced that the eschatological events and things are in play in their lifetimes. And this leads to an important point. Do they see themselves as at the endpoint of proper discussion of God?

Although certainly the Father, the Son, and the Spirit are seen in various places and ways as God and as currently active in human history in the New Testament, we are still a long way from the reflections at Nicea or Chalcedon, much less from the later confessions. If we discuss the subject of "a trinitarian reading of the Bible," we will have to define what we mean by "Trinity." Is it the later, more refined and specified and defined term of creedal or confessional orthodoxy that we have in mind? Or do we mean by it the somewhat primitive and initial trajectories that we find pushing in this direction in the New Testament?

If we mean the latter, then we do not look for a discussion of *homoousios* in the New Testament in the same way we find such a discussion at Nicea. In other words, the later discussions can be said to be on a trajectory from the New Testament and in various ways to be consistent with what the New Testament says, but we cannot anachronistically claim that all of that later teaching is found *in* the New Testament. We cannot claim, then, that it is all part of "New Testament theology" any more than we can claim that the later discussions about no postbaptismal sins are already found in the New

Testament. And if we say that an orthodox doctrine of God should be based on both the New Testament and later church tradition, what then happens to *sola scriptura* as the measuring rod of truth and orthodoxy? These matters are too little discussed. Even if we say that orthodoxy is "what the New Testament teaches and necessarily implies," this still does not match up fully with the scope of the robust statements in the later creeds, statements about, for instance, the impassable God. There are some things in the later creeds and confessions that the New Testament seems to neither state nor imply. Indeed, there are some ideas that seem to be at odds with what the New Testament states about such matters (for instance, about the impassable nature of God).

Jesus

This may seem redundant at first, but the name *Jesus* in the New Testament refers to a human being. And in fact it always, with one possible exception, refers in the New Testament to the same human being, Jesus of Nazareth, even though the name *Yeshua/Joshua* was exceedingly common in that era.[6] If ever there was a clear proof that all the New Testament writers are circulating in the same lexical neighborhood, this is it. Whenever the name *Jesus* shows up in the New Testament, and it does in almost all twenty-seven books, it refers to Jesus of Nazareth. This is proof positive, if any were needed, that all these writers are believing Christians.

How had an obscure manual laborer from Nazareth become a household name, on the tip of every New Testament writer's pen, indeed so familiar and common that there is seldom any effort to explain to the audience who is meant? Furthermore, we very frequently find the name combined with the title *Christ* as if it were a second name; rarely do we have "Jesus the Christ," but rather a preference for "Jesus Christ." And this is true from the very earliest New Testament documents (Paul's letters) right to the end of the canon in its latest document (see 2 Pet 3:18). Not only did all the New Testament writers share an understanding of who this person Jesus was historically, but also they believed profound theological things about him, and this was encapsulated in part by the word *Christ* or by a word such as *Lord*. Jesus was the Jewish messiah, but as we see in 2 Peter 3:18, this was taken to also mean, or be closely associated with the idea, that he was the only savior for the world in general as well. In other words, all the New Testament writers share a particular brand of messianic thinking, a brand that focuses on one

---

[6]The partial exception is found in Acts 13:6, but this man's name is *Bar-Jesus* ("son of Jesus").

historical figure who has already lived, died, and was believed to have been risen from the grave. This is so very different from early Jewish messianic prophecy, which essentially was forward-looking and occasionally fixated on a particular person such as Bar Kokhba but more often was indefinite, as we see at Qumran. In short, the New Testament writers think that the messiah has already come—and gone! But they also believed that he would be back again. This was indeed a very particular—many Jews would have said very peculiar—kind of Jewish messianism. It was peculiar because of who Jesus was, where he came from, what he did, and especially because of how his life came to an end, since the vast majority of early Jews did not seem to be expecting a crucified messiah. But this brings us to the cross.

The Cross / Tree

Paul, in a moment of painful honesty, tells us that the initial general reaction to the preaching of a crucified messiah was rejection and ridicule. He puts it this way: "But we preach Christ crucified: a stumbling block to Jews and foolishness to Gentiles" (1 Cor 1:23). Notice: it is not merely "Christ died," or even "Christ killed," or even "Christ martyred," but "Christ crucified." This was indeed a shameful message, but it was one dwelt on and explained in numerous different ways in the New Testament. The Gospels can rightly be identified as passion narratives with long introductions, as each of them spends one-third or more of its account on the events of Jesus' last week, leading up to the crucifixion and its sequel. Acts repeatedly returns to this theme in numerous speeches. Paul's letters repeatedly resound with the message of Christ crucified and risen. We find profound meditation on the death of Christ in 1 Peter, in Hebrews, and in Revelation, where the slain Lamb is also the Lion of Judah. Yes indeed, the New Testament writers, from the least to the greatest, shared not merely a general Jewish religious vocabulary, but a specifically christologically reconfigured one, reconfigured by the actual course of events in the life of Jesus, which changed the form of messianic expectations and the expression of messianic theology.

So familiar was this sort of discussion in early Christianity that all one had to do was talk about the cross or the tree, and immediately the audience knew which tree, which cross, which crucifixion was alluded to, in a Roman Empire full of crosses and executions. Notice the use of "tree" language (without further explanation) in the earliest layers of the kerygma in some of the early sermons of Acts (Acts 5:30; 10:39; 13:29; cf. Gal 3:13). We seldom feel the impact of this abrasive and offensive language and message today as it would have been felt in the first century. To the outsider, it must have seemed as if Christians were masochistic, glorying in their shame. So far as we can tell, only Jesus' followers saw something redemptive or atoning in human crucifixion and, in particular, in Jesus' crucifixion.

The Substitutionary Sacrifice of a Human Being

The idea of human sacrifice was basically abhorrent to early Jews, unless one meant by that the notion of an honorable martyrological death, such as the Maccabees experienced on the battlefield (see 2 Macc 7). Even so, such deaths were seen, in the main, not as sin offerings but rather as substitutionary sacrifices necessary to save the nation. When a Jew needed to offer a sacrifice for sin or atonement, it was always an animal that would be chosen, not a human being. Even the story of Isaac involved God intervening and substituting an animal so that Isaac would not need to be sacrificed. There is something very new, then, about the early Christian way of conceptualizing the death of Jesus on the cross as a substitutionary sacrifice for sin, and indeed even a ransom for the many, as Jesus himself called it (Mk 10:45). Many theological images and ideas were applied to the death of Jesus, but most of them included the notion that somehow Jesus' death helped reconcile God and humankind and took care of the sin problem, though the specifics were not always clear (cf. 1 Tim 2:5-6; 1 Pet 1:2-10). Yet we find such ideas in various forms in all four Gospels, sporadically in Acts, replete in Paul's letters, profoundly discussed in 1 Peter, Hebrews, and Revelation, and not absent from the other epistolary literature either, even though it is very ad hoc in character.

Jesus never was seen by these earliest Christians as just a teacher/sage or just a miracle-worker. There was something about his very life, his very nature, his death, and his resurrection that was seen as theologically and ethically so profound that it reoriented a worldview. Paul states emphatically that if Jesus did not die and rise again, then Christian faith is in vain, and we are "still in our sins" (1 Cor 15:17). This last phrase is telling. It suggests that atonement was made and sinners were transformed not just by the death of Jesus, but by his death and resurrection and the benefits that accrued from these events. Substitutionary human sacrifice (followed by vindication in the form of resurrection) proved to be the unexpected but necessary and sufficient means of human redemption. In 1 Tim 2:5 we have it in formulaic terms in yet another christological modification of the Shema: "For there is one God and one mediator between God and humankind, Christ Jesus himself being human, who gave himself as a ransom for all." If it was one for all, then it must also be once for all time, making all other sacrifices superfluous. It was left to a Pauline coworker to spin this out more fully in his homily to the Hebrews and to rightly see what the implications of this would be for how the Mosaic covenant and its laws must now be viewed. A better covenant, with a better mediator, a better sacrifice, and a better outcome had appeared, eclipsing all that came before and making unnecessary any successors or subsequent similar efforts at redemption.

In an extraordinary tour de force, John of Patmos stressed not only that Jesus was the slain Lamb of God, but also thay he remained the slain Lamb standing in glory in heaven, applying the benefits of his death from there in heaven to believers everywhere, just as the author of Hebrews' high priest is said to do in that document. There is a compatibility to the way the cross is viewed by the various New Testament writers, and none of them are suggesting that the death of Jesus on the cross is not of prime significance for Christian thought. This idea is so deeply entrenched in the early Christian symbolic universe that not even the odium of severe shame associated with crucifixion could prevent Christians from proclaiming it far and wide. In the non-Christian catacombs we see a pagan reaction to this in a depiction of a donkey on a cross with a soldier kneeling and worshiping it, with the inscription saying that the soldier worships his God. But at least the graffito had gotten it right. Christians did indeed worship Jesus as God, and that included worshiping the crucified Jesus as divine even though he died in that hideous manner. What sort of profound conviction could have led Jews to believe in a God who not merely suffers but dies for his people?

Sin/Transgression

In a monotheistic honor-shame culture, the concept and indeed the sense of sin are omnipresent. Sin in such a society is a violation of God's will, plan, law, commandments. And there were various gradations of sin: accidental sin, sins of anger, sins of ignorance, sins with a high hand and so on. Paul later made the distinction clear between sin and transgression, the latter being a willful violation of a known law. Paul saw the effect of the law on fallen people as turning sin into transgression and making it exceedingly sinful. This was not the intent or purpose of the law but nonetheless was its effect.

The whole discussion of sin was not merely a moral discussion; it was also a ritual and theological discussion, for there were rituals for dealing with sin, in particular sacrifices, hopefully atoning ones. Sin was always a sin against God and so was inherently a theological problem. There was also ritual impurity as well as moral impurity to contend with, and the two were intertwined in that world. The author of Hebrews stated rather emphatically that the Mosaic sacrifices dealt only with externals and could not give the sinner a clean conscience, but only a fresh start with God and others. This was contrasted with the once-for-all sacrifice of Christ (Heb 9).

Not surprisingly, there was also discussion of the relationship of sickness and sin, and Jesus had several things to say on the subject, not the least of which was that one could not make a one-to-one correlation between sickness and sin (i.e., one could not assume a person's illness resulted from personal or parental sin [see Jn 9:1-2]). This association was hardly a surprise, since the original sin in the Genesis story was said to have prompted the penalty of death.

Humanity, in the view of all the New Testament writers, had a sin problem, an incurable sin problem until Jesus came along, and somehow Jesus' death on the cross made a decisive difference in the battle against sin. The retrospective way that New Testament writers thought about this matter is clear: if Jesus' death atoned for sins once and for all, then the previous sacrifices must have been of only temporal or temporary benefit at best. Some New Testament writers went as far as to say that before the death of Jesus there had been no atonement at all for deliberate premeditated sin (see Acts 13; Heb 9), and that this was one of the distinctive benefits of Jesus' death that showed that it eclipsed what previous and other sorts of sacrifices had accomplished or could accomplish. Just as the effects of sin had been extensive and intensive on fallen human beings, so the atonement of Jesus was seen as having an extensive (once for all persons and for all time) and intensive effect (even cleansing the heart or conscience). As E. P. Sanders once put the matter, New Testament writers were reasoning from solution to plight, and the plight was grave.[7] But this was not merely the woe of a private individual, for sin was most often an interpersonal matter from the beginning (see the story of Cain and Abel in Gen 4). Sin destroyed relationships and thus communion and community.

If we ask the question of why Jesus not only offered forgiveness of sins but

---

[7]See E. P. Sanders, *Paul and Palestinian Judaism: A Comparison of Patterns of Religion* (London: SCM Press, 1977).

also performed healings and exorcisms, the answer would have seemed rather obvious to people in Jesus' world: he was attacking all of the effects of sin and its sources as well. He was attacking the whole nexus of things that bewitched, bothered, and bewildered humankind and alienated them from God. Sin was not merely a violation of God's will; it was that which estranged human beings from God and made it impossible for them to relate properly to their deity. Sin, then, was viewed as something more than mere error or mistake; it was seen as an affront to a holy God, and assault on God's principles and plan, a rejection of God's rule, a corruption of God's image in humankind—in short, an intolerable violation of God's character by the image of God. This in turn meant that only God could set this situation right, since all human beings had sinned and kept falling short of God's glory. It can be no accident that Jesus' healings and exorcisms are intended to reintegrate people back into their religious community. Sin, disease, and uncleanness alienated people not only from their God but also from their own community.

The Risen Lord

Early Christians did not much talk about resurrection in the abstract. The discussion always seems to center on what happened to Jesus beyond death and, as a subdominant theme, what would happen to those who followed him in regard to resurrection. With the phrase "risen Lord" a title is linked to a particular event, the resurrection of Jesus. It was at the resurrection that Jesus assumed the role of Lord. This is what the early christological hymn tells us so clearly in Philippians 2:5-11. And here is where we begin to see the importance not just of doing word studies, however valuable, of the key terms in the symbolic universe and also their limitations. As it turns out, it is how these terms are combined into a coherent narrative or discourse that makes so much difference. But here the point is to focus on what can be said about the ideas themselves.

I can find no discussion about a risen messiah in early Judaism prior to the coming of Jesus.[8] Resurrection of the righteous or the wicked was often enough discussed as something that would happen in the messianic age or when the messiah came, but that subject has now been postponed in our New Testament writers' thought world until the discussion of the "second com-

---

[8]There is now a possible but very debatable exception to this rule in the so-called Gabriel Stone, which may mention a messianic figured who "lived" or "came to life," but even if this is the correct reading of the Semitic script, its meaning is ambiguous.

ing," and instead resurrection is discussed as something that has happened already to a particular individual named "Jesus" that allowed him to assume a variety of exalted roles, including being Lord of both believers and the world (though the latter is oblivious to the fact), and even to be Lord over the powers and principalities.

When the title *kyrios* is applied by numerous New Testament authors to Jesus, what is happening is not merely the transferal of an elite human title to a manual laborer, which would be surprising enough in the stratified world of first-century culture, especially when applied to one who claimed that he came to be a servant and not a human lord, but the application of the "name that is above all names," the name of God in the LXX, to Jesus. If the earliest Christian confession was "Jesus is Lord" (see 1 Cor 12:3), then something highly exalted was believed to be the case about Jesus. He was rightly called by the names previously reserved for Yahweh, and those names were believed to connote something about his nature.

If we are looking for the reagent that caused the seismic shift in these writers' symbolic universes, some of it must be the theological and ethical reflection that arose out of the devotional life of the earliest Christians, which involved worshiping Jesus, praying to Jesus, baptizing people in the name of Jesus, celebrating the death of Jesus until he comes in a sacred meal, and the like. Larry Hurtado stresses that devotion to Jesus, worshiping him as God, "began so early that no trace is left of any stages of development; it is also taken for granted as uncontroversial among Christian circles in the Pauline letters. . . . Indeed, important data such as the *maranatha* formula . . . and the lack of indication that the devotional life of the Pauline churches constitutes any major innovation in previous Christian practice, combine to make it necessary to attribute the origins of the cultic reverence of Christ to Aramaic-speaking and Greek-speaking circles, and to the first years of the Christian movement (the 30s)."[9] Indeed, I suggest that it must be traced ultimately back to the encounters with the risen Jesus that prompted the first Christian worship acts (see Mt 28:9; John 20:28). The Copernican revolution in thinking sprung from experiences that these followers of Jesus could not deny but the import of which they had to explain.

Monotheistic Jews pray to God, and yet as the aforementioned Aramaic *maranatha* prayer, "Come, O Lord," intimates, Jesus himself is the object of a

---

[9]Larry Hurtado, *Lord Jesus Christ: Devotion to Jesus in Earliest Christianity* (Grand Rapids: Eerdmans, 2003), p. 136.

prayer for him to return. And yet, as a close examinations of Acts 2–4 shows, it is not as if the earliest Christians are starting a new cultus centered on Jesus. To the contrary, they continue to worship in the temple, and they incorporate their prayers to Jesus and worship of Jesus into their worship of the God of the Old Testament. Their hermeneutical move amounts to incorporating the new into the old pattern, but thereby the old symbolic universe is necessarily transformed, as 1 Corinthians 8:4-6 makes perfectly evident. If we ask why and how a crucified and totally shamed man subsequently became the object of prayer, praise, devotion, and proclamation by the very first Christians, the answer surely must be that the disciples had encountered him alive beyond the grave. Events and the experience of them transform habits of the heart, beliefs of the soul, even the religious symbolic universe of the mind. The nexus of connection between events, the appearances of Jesus following his resurrection, and certain new beliefs about Jesus is especially close at this juncture. In regard to the theological reinterpretation of the cross in light of the resurrection, it is now seen as something redemptive as well, not an unholy shame.

The New/True People of God

One's concept of God's people is crucial to how one addresses such people. If we think that only Jews and proselytes to Judaism can be counted as God's people, then that is one understanding of things. But if we think that Jew and Gentile united by faith in Christ are God's people, then we have an entirely different view of things. The dilemma for the Jewish Christians who wrote the New Testament was that they certainly wanted to see themselves as true and loyal Jews, but also they knew that things had changed in their world-view. They knew, for example, that they were in a rather distinct minority, even among Jews, and even with considerable Jewish converts who believed that Jesus of Nazareth was the Jewish messiah. They badly wanted to suggest that they were the righteous remnant of Israel, just as the Qumranites had viewed themselves, and they wanted to preserve their Jewish heritage to one degree or another, depending on the individual. Yet at least some of them knew that there were traditions that in the eschatological covenant situation God would be no respecter of persons, that he would be impartial in calling all to salvation while not neglecting his previous promises to Torah-true Jews. How in the world was this to be sorted out? The idea of there being two Israels, or two true peoples of God, was a nonstarter. So what would the eschatological people of God look like?

Even if one agreed that in Christ there was neither Jew nor Gentile when it came to the matter of salvation, the question then involved on what basis Gentiles could be included in what was basically still a Jewish monotheistic religion grounded in the Old Testament. Here, though all agreed that Jews and Gentiles could be part of the new people of God, the question of how those two groups would relate to each other in the new community was answered differently by various parties. All agreed that Gentiles could become Christians by grace and faith. But how should they live thereafter? Would they be required to keep Torah, or at least the Noachic commandments, or the like?

The Pharisaic Judaizing Christians in Jerusalem insisted on circumcision and full compliance with the law for full integration into the community. James insisted that Gentiles cease and desist from idolatry and immorality, particularly avoiding the things that went on in pagan temples, while Jewish Christians should still keep Torah. But Paul, ever the more radical of the bunch, insisted that since all are now saved by grace through faith in Christ, when Jews and Gentiles meet and dine together, there should be compromises of love and understanding but not of principles. By this he meant that those Gentile Christians who had no scruples about eating nonkosher meat should not cause their more scrupulous Jewish Christian brothers and sisters to stumble by insisting on doing things their way when they met together. Paul, unlike James, did not think that even Jewish Christians like himself were required to keep the Mosaic covenant any longer. It was a blessed option perhaps, assumed pro tempore for the sake of witness to Jews, but not an obligation.

In other words, only Paul saw a way forward that would prevent there being two churches, one largely Jewish and Torah-observant and one largely Gentile and not Torah-observant. In his mind, the new covenant required submission of all not to Moses' law but to the law of Christ, which at its heart was the law of love also found in the Old Testament. Therefore sacrifices of praxis not principle were possible and needed on both sides to bind together the people of God into one body. In Paul's view, Jewish Christians could do as they like when they met only with fellow Jews, but when they met with Gentiles, they did not need to insist on doing things according to Moses. This meant that Paul assumed that they, like the apostle himself, no longer saw such rituals and rules as a matter of conscience, but in fact many continued to view things that way. Peter did not seem to be one of them, nor did Barnabas, but they could be shamed into retreating from full fellowship with Gentiles in a Gentile manner by the Judaizers from Jerusalem, as Galatians 1–2 makes plain.

Paul could and did call in 1 Corinthians for his largely Gentile audience to be understanding of the Jewish Christians for whom food was still a matter of conscience, and he urged them not to make such people stumble by compelling them to violate their own scruples. It cannot have been easy for Paul to model being the Jew to the Jew and the Gentile to the Gentile without appearing to be self-contradictory to both sides. But this overlooks that for Paul there was a huge part of ethics dictated no longer by Mosaic requirements but rather by the law of Christ, the law of love, the law of self-sacrifice, which makes compromise possible on nonessential things.

In sum, the writers of the New Testament agreed that "people of God" or even "assembly of God" would refer to any group made up of devotees of Jesus Christ. However, the basis for meeting, eating, and sharing things together, the basis for living together as a family of faith, was not agreed upon by all the writers of the New Testament. Some must have seen the new covenant as a renewed form of the Mosaic one, but Paul saw it differently.

The issue among these writers was not the basis of conversion, but sanctification. How should they live together as a holy people? What role should the old Mosaic rules play in making it such a united and holy people? Paul, Peter, and James were in agreement that Gentiles had to forsake their pagan past both in its theological and ethical implications, as it involved idolatry and immorality. This did not mean that all Gentile ethics were incompatible with the gospel, nor did it mean all pagan theological insights were incongruent with God's revelation of the divine character in the Old Testament and in the gospel, but it did mean that much had to be critically sifted and the chaff left behind.

It is important to emphasize, however, that none of the New Testament writers believed that there were two peoples of God, one involving non-Christian Jews, one involving Christian Jews and Gentiles. Only Paul, in Romans 9–11, seems to have thought through all this to the end, understanding it to mean that those Jews who now rejected Jesus were temporarily broken off from God's people but could be grafted back in again. Others, like James, apparently did not say such things, but the very fact that he agreed that even devout Jews needed Jesus and needed to be evangelized implied that they were lost, as Jesus himself had said. All seem to have agreed that in Christ came the fulfillment of God's promises to Israel, and in Christ one would obtain the inheritance of Abraham. If the promises of God were "yes" and "amen" in Jesus and were being realized in his people, then it followed that one had to join that people to receive the benefit of those promises. Some New Testament writers worked out the implications of these things more clearly and fully than others.

The Eschatological Spirit and the Spirit's Gifts

One of the more notable facts about the writers of the New Testament, and indeed about Jesus himself, is their belief that they live at the beginning of the eschatological age, the age when the fullness of the Spirit would come on God's people, and not only would there be new prophecies to be fulfilled, but also many old ones would come to pass. Whether we think of the scene in John 20 where Jesus breathes on the disciples and says, "Receive the Holy Spirit," or the story of Pentecost as told in Acts 2 (which only begins the telling of the falling of the Spirit on various persons in Acts), or the proclamation of Paul in 1 Corinthians 12 that no one can say "Jesus is Lord" without the prompting of the Holy Spirit, or the word of Peter in 1 Peter 1:10-12 that it was the Spirit of Christ that prompted the Old Testament prophets to speak of his own era, or the confession of John of Patmos that his visions came to him when he was "in the Spirit" (Rev 1:10), the New Testament writers see themselves as living in exciting, propitious, pneumatic, and teleological times. There are, of course, other ways to express this same sense of finality, a sense that God's promises and prophecies of yore were finally coming to pass. Paul can speak of "when the time had fully come" (Gal 4:4), but at the heart of the matter is the outpouring of the eschatological Spirit, who inaugurates the end times. Were any of these writers to be magically transported to the present day and hear the question "When will the end times begin?" they would laugh and explain that the end times began two millennia ago.

It is precisely because of the presence and power of the Spirit coming upon and dwelling in Jesus and his followers that miracles of all sorts are recorded, new teaching and prophecies are inspired, and a new covenant is said to be possible and inaugurated between God and his people. Although the writers of the New Testament do not fully grasp the radical implications of all this, they celebrate it nonetheless. They live in an age of new revelation, new inspiration, new healing, renewal of the people of God, and in fact God is said to be present with them always in the Spirit and indeed sometimes in a christological form as Immanuel—Christ in you, the hope of glory. No longer is there but sporadic or intermittent contact with God or occasional empowerment by the Spirit; God has come to stay with his people.

Yet even with all this eschatological hope and joy permeating the New Testament, there is still the realism in these documents that the end of the end has not yet come, that Jesus must return to complete the fulfillment of things, and no one knew when exactly that return would transpire, whether sooner or later. Although the writers believed that "the appointed time has been shortened" and "the present form of this world is passing away" (1 Cor 7:29, 31), and so they conjured with the live possibility that Jesus could come back soon, what they did not do, unlike many moderns, is let expectation degenerate into prognostication and calculation. They lived in hope and without four-colored charts locking God into a timetable.

It seems that all the New Testament writers believed that God had revealed enough about the future to give them hope and anticipation, but not so much that they did not have to have faith and exercise their trust in the Almighty. The Spirit reassured them that all manner of things would be well, but alas, the Spirit did not tell them when all manner of things would be resolved. And so they looked forward with longing and anticipation all the more when some of their members were persecuted, prosecuted or executed. Then especially the future hope, the hope for what was not yet, was lifted high like a bright torch in the midst of the pitch blackness of a dark night. Soon and very soon, God would vindicate his people, but that final justice must be left in God's hands.

In the meantime, the Holy Spirit was seen as the counselor, the advocate of Christ, the inspirer, the reassurer, the sanctifier, the one who produces the fruit of a good character in the believer, producing love, joy, peace, patience, kindness, goodness, self-control, and so much more. The Spirit produced a plethora of viable spiritual gifts as well, though interestingly, new prophecy needed to be sifted in a way and to a degree that Old Testament prophecy did not, because, as Paul intimates in Romans 12, prophecy sometimes could be given that went beyond the pale, beyond the measure of faith and inspiration of the speaker. But what is most interesting about how the New Testament writers view the age of the Spirit is that they see it mainly as a time for the fulfillment of old prophecies rather than the generation of new ones. Some may be surprised that we have only one book of prophecy in the New Testament—the last one, Revelation—though certainly some of the early New Testament documents contain prophetic portions. But this is not a surprise in view of the way the writers viewed their age. There were, after all, many promises and prophecies of God from the sacred Scriptures that had not yet been fulfilled. What need could there be for a vast number of new prophecies in such a situation?

No, more time needed to be spent correlating the Word and current pneumatic experience than on generating whole new prophecies. Even the prophecies of Jesus about the events leading up to the demise of the temple in A.D. 70 were viewed as being about their own day, their own time, the first generation of the new age. Jesus said only a few enigmatic things about the cosmic events that would follow the fall of the temple, when the Son of Man returned. He left behind no signs on the earth that could be read as directly signaling the timing of the great and terrible Day of the Lord. And so it was that the earliest Christians, including all the writers of the New Testament, turned to their sacred Scriptures for illumination of their situation. This brings us to another crucial part of the symbolic universe, indeed one of the two main tributaries or fonts of that universe shared by all the New Testament writers: the Hebrew Scriptures.

The Sacred Scriptures

To a significant extent, the New Testament writers and Jesus himself shared a symbolic worldview because they shared the Hebrew Scriptures. All of the New Testament writers were either Jews who knew Torah or God-fearers, like Luke, who at least knew the LXX quite well. The importance of this can hardly be overestimated. The people of the Spirit were also the people of the Word and, indeed, of the Book. In an oral culture (which is largely an illiterate culture) sacred texts have an even more exalted function than we might imagine in a text-saturated and highly literate age. And it is no accident that all these writers lived at the time when the Old Testament canon was coming to closure about what books were in or out. The debates about books such as Esther, which does not directly mention God, or the late wisdom writing of Ecclesiastes are not reflected in the pages of the New Testament. Our writers largely stick with the undisputed sacred texts, only occasionally foraying into noncanonical material such as we find in the use of Enochian material in Jude or of material from Wisdom of Solomon in various places in the New Testament, including in its earliest documents, the Pauline corpus.

It is notable how much focus is on the so-called Latter Prophets, particularly the apocalyptic ones, Daniel and Zechariah. But the most frequently cited source in the New Testament is in fact Isaiah (especially Is 40–61), followed by some of the royal psalms. By one count, there are some 250 clear citations from Isaiah, not to mention the many allusions to or echoes of that grand text in Revelation and elsewhere. No wonder some church fathers called Isaiah the "Fifth Gospel." It is a telling revelation of the urgencies of New Testament writers to note which portions of Isaiah are not drawn on in their books. Isaiah 2–4; 14–21; 23–24; 26; 30–34; 36–39; 46–48; 63 do not show up in citations. Among the Gospels, Isaiah is most used in Matthew and Luke, and among the letters, we find it most in Romans, 1 Corinthians, and 1 Peter, but again this is based on a count of clear citations or partial citations. There are over fifty allusions to Isaiah in Revelation with few citations. One could argue that Isaiah is the subtext of a good portion of Revelation, and in a similar manner Psalm 110:1 seems to serve not merely as a subtext but as a cited text used as a banner waved by various of the earliest Christians when they wanted to indicate how highly exalted Christ is.

In order to get a picture of how much the symbolic universe of the New Testament writers is informed by their shared dependence on and use of the Old Testament, here I will spell out the use of the Psalms in the New Testament in some detail. Since I am limiting myself to direct citations, this is quite literally the tip of the proverbial iceberg.[10]

1. Acts 4:25-26/Ps 2:1-2—Psalm spoken by Holy Spirit through David; royal psalm; applied to Christ and his encounter with Pilate and Herod.

2. Rev 11:17-18/Ps 2:1-2—Refers to God, who brings wrath.

3. Acts 13:33/Ps 2:7 (with Is 55:3; Ps 16:10)—Used of Christ as God's Son, who did not decay.

4. Heb 1:5; 5:5/Ps 2:7—Jesus as God's Son.

5. Rev 2:26-27; 12:5; 19:15/Ps 2:8-9—In Revelation 2 it appears to apply to the saints who will be conquerors and rule; in Revelation 12; 19 it applies to Jesus.

6. Eph 4:26/Ps 4:4—Ethical exhortation to the Ephesians.

7. Rom 3:13/Ps 5:9 (with Ps 14:1-3; 53:1-3; Eccles 7:20; Ps 140:3; Is 59:7-8; Ps 26:1)—To describe all of world's Jews and Gentiles and sinners; their condition is as the psalmist said ("as it is written"); this seems to be a testimonia.

---

[10]For a view of how vast is the use of the Old Testament in the New Testament, see G. K. Beale and D. A. Carson, eds., *Commentary on the New Testament Use of the Old Testament* (Grand Rapids: Baker Academic, 2007).

8. Mt 7:23/Lk 13:27/Ps 6:8a—Jesus quotes the psalm of himself instead of the psalmist, but this is just using biblical language to describe one's experience.

9. Mt 21:16/Ps 8:2—Jesus interprets infant's praise of himself (in the psalm, praise of God).

10. Heb 2:6-8/Ps 8:4-6—Testified of Jesus; he is the "son of man."

11. 1 Cor 15:27/Eph 1:22/Ps 8:6—Of Jesus in the future.

12. Rom 3:14/Ps 10:7—See number 7 above.

13. Rom 3:10-12/Ps 14:1-3—See number 7 above.

14. Acts 2:25-28, 31/Ps 16:8-11—Of Christ (in the psalm, of God).

15. Acts 2:31/Ps 16:10—See number 14 above.

16. Rom 15:9/Ps 18:49/2 Sam 22:50 (with Deut 32:43; Ps 117:1; Is 11:10)—A testimonia about Gentiles; catchword *ethnē*.

17. Rom 10:18/Ps 19:4 (with Is 53:1; Deut 32:31; Is 65:1-2)—Testimonia, theme: those who heard the message and who received it, Jews and Gentiles (possibly *laos/ethnē* as a catchword).

18. Rev 16:7; 19:2/Ps 19:9—Use of an Old Testament catchphrase to express something true of God's nature always.

19. Mt 27:46/Mk 15:34/Ps 22:1—Jesus laments from the cross (in the psalm, the psalmist laments).

   Mt 27:39/Mk 15:29/Lk 23:35/Ps 22:7-8—Two robbers die with Jesus.

   Mt 27:43/Ps 22:8—Chief priest questions Jesus; He said, "I am the Son."

   1 Pet 5:8/Ps 22:13—Satan as a lion roaring, looking for someone to devour; not a quotation.

   Jn 19:28/Ps 22:16; cf. Ps 69:21—"I am thirsty."

   Mt 27:35/Mk 15:24/Ps 22:18—Cast lots for clothes.

   2 Tim 4:17/Ps 22:21—Used by Paul of himself, delivered from lion's mouth; use of scriptural language; not fulfillment.

   Heb 2:12, 17; Ps 22:22—As if Jesus is speaking the psalm; "declare name to brethren."

20. Rev 7:17/Ps 23:1-2—Jesus as shepherd who leads them by still waters.

21. 1 Cor 10:26/Ps 24:1; 50:12—Here, because the earth is the Lord's, all food is acceptable to eat.

22. Lk 23:26/Ps 31:5—Jesus commends himself into God's hands, speaking David's words of himself.

23. Rom 4:7-8/Ps 32:1-2—Proof text for justification by faith.

24. Rev 5:9; 14:3/Ps 33:3-8—Use of the phrase "new song."

25. 1 Pet 2:3/Ps 34:8—Use of biblical language to describe Christian experience.

26. 1 Pet 3:10-12/Ps 34:12-16—Ethical exhortation by quoting the psalm.

27. Jn 19:36/Ps 34:20—These things happen so that Scripture would be fulfilled; "Not one of his bones will be broken."

28. Jn 15:25/Ps 35:19—This is to fulfill what is written; "They hated me without a reason."

29. Rom 3:18/Ps 36:1—See number 7 above.

30. Mt 5:5/Ps 37:11—Beatitude of Jesus; "the meek will inherit the land" in the psalm.

31. Heb 10:5-7, 8-11/Ps 40:6-8—Quoted as if the words of Christ.

32. Jn 13:18/Ps 41:9—"This is to fulfill the Scripture, 'He who shared my bread lifted up his heel against me.'"

33. Mt 26:38/Mk 14:34/Ps 42:5, 6/Ps 43:5—Jesus quotes, "My soul is overwhelmed with sorrow."

34. Rom 8:36/Ps 44:22—"As it is written"; Paul quotes the psalm of his own experience of suffering; use of scriptural language.

35. Heb 1:8-9/Ps 45:6-7—(Quoted with Ps 2:7; 2 Sam. 7:14; Deut 32:43; Ps 104:4; Ps. 102:25-27; 110:1) Testimonium about Christ in Hebrews; God speaks of "Son"; "Your throne, O God, will last forever."

36. Mt 5:35/Ps 48:2—The earth is God's footstool; use of the psalm to speak of a truth about God.

37. 1 Cor 10:26/Ps 50:12; cf. Ps 24:1—See number 21 above.

38. Mt 5:33/Heb 13:15/Ps 50:14, 23—The Matthew text is a quotation; the Hebrews text encourages the offering of a sacrifice of prayer.

39. Rom 3:4/Ps 51:4—"As it is written"; God is true and right, as the psalmist says.

40. Rom 3:10-12/Ps 53:1-2—See number 7 above.

41. 1 Pet 5:7/Ps 55:22—ethical exhortation; "Cast all your anxiety" on God.

42. Eph 4:8/Ps 68:18—Used of Christ when he ascended.

43. Jn 15:25/Ps 69:4—Royal psalm; see number 28 above.

44. Jn 2:17/Rom 15:3/Ps 69:9—"It is written"; disciples remembered; "Zeal for my house" used of temple cleansing.

45. Mt 27:34, 48/Mk 15: 23, 36/Lk 23:36/Jn 19:28/Ps 69:21—Vinegar offered for thirst; fulfillment.

46. Rom 11:9, 10/Ps 69:22-23—Used of apostate Israel due to their reaction to Christ (in the psalm, used of enemies of the psalmist).

47. Acts 1:20/Ps 69:25 (with Ps 109:8)—Used of Judas being replaced (in the psalm, used of enemies of the psalmist); "it is written in the book of Psalms"; example of midrash pesher?

48. Rev 3:5; 17:8; 20:12; 21:27/Ps 69:28—Those blotted out of the book of life (in the psalm, used of enemies).

49. Rev 14:10/Ps 75:8—Those who worship the beast drink the wine of wrath (in the psalm, all the wicked drink it).

50. Mt 13:35/Ps 78:2—"I will open my mouth in parables"; in Matthew, it is the fulfillment of what a prophet, rather than psalmist, said (all of Psalms treated as written prophecy).

51. Jn 6:31/Ps 78:24; 105:40—"As it is written, 'He gave them bread from heaven to eat.'"

52. Jn 10:34/Ps 82:6—Jesus quotes, "Is it not written in your law, 'I have said you are Gods'?"

53. Rev 3:9; 15:4/Ps 86:8-10—In Jesus' words "I will make them come and worship at your feet," "your" refers to saints (in the psalm, to God).

54. Acts 2:30/Ps 89:3-4—David was a prophet and knew that God would place someone on the throne, a descendant; in Acts, Peter says that the psalm text speaks of Christ.

55. Heb 1:5/Ps 89:26-27/2 Sam 7:14 —"I will be his Father." In Hebrews, spoken of Christ (in the psalm, of David).

56. Rev 1:5/Ps 89:27—In Revelation, Jesus as firstborn from the dead, ruler

of earth's kings (in the psalm, David is firstborn, most exalted king on earth).

57. 2 Pet 3:8/Ps 90:4—In the psalm, for God, one thousand years are as a day; 2 Peter adds the converse.

58. Mt 4:6/Lk 4:10-11/Ps 91:11-12—The devil quotes Scripture; he commands angels to guard (in the psalm, used of any believer).

59. Lk 10:19/Ps 91:13—Authority to trample snakes and overcome enemies given to Jesus' disciples (in the psalm, to believers in general).

60. 1 Cor 3:20/Ps 94:11 —"As it is written, 'The Lord knows the thoughts of the wise'" (in the psalm, the thoughts of humankind).

61. Rom 11:1-2/Ps 94:14—God will not reject; use of scriptural language to speak of Israel.

62. Heb 4:7/Ps 95:7-8—"Through David he said. . . ."

63. Heb 3:7-11/Ps 95:7-11—Quotation applied to the church rather than Israel: "Today if you hear my voice. . . ."

64. Heb 4:3/Ps 95:11—Believers who do not enter rest (in the psalm, wilderness generation did not enter rest).

65. Heb 1:6/Ps 97:7—Christ worshiped by angels (in the psalm, Yahweh worshiped).

66. Heb 1:10-12/Ps 102:25-27—See number 35 above.

67. Jas 5:11/Ps 103:8 (cf. Ps 111:4)—God is full of compassion and mercy; simple allusion.

68. Heb 1:7/Ps 104:4—See number 35 above.

69. John 6:31/Ps 105:40 (cf. Ps 78:24)—See number 51 above.

70. Rom 1:23/Ps 106:20—Allusion to exchanging glory of God for the image of a bull.

71. Acts 1:20/Ps 109:8—See number 47 above.

72. Mt 27:39/Mk 15:29/Ps 109:25—Taunting by Christ's adversaries described in language of psalmist's taunters.

73. Mk 12:31 par.; 14:62; 16:19/Acts 2:34-35/1 Cor 15:25/Eph 1:20/Col 3:1/Heb 1:13; 8:1; 10:12-13; 12:2/Ps 110:1—Most frequently used psalm verse for christological purposes and in all types of New Testament mate-

rial; "sits at the right hand" presumably refers to king in the psalm, seen as prince regent, next to God, who is the real king.

74. Heb 5:6; 7:17, 27/Ps 110:4—"You are a priest after the order of Melchizedek"; unique to Hebrews, applied to Christ.

75. 2 Cor 9:9/Ps 112:9—"He has scattered abroad his gifts to the poor"; quotation used of Christians, whom God takes care of.

76. Rev 9:20/Ps 115:4-7—Allusion to psalm text (not a quotation) regarding idols and what they are made of.

77. Rev 11:18; 19:5/Ps 115:13—Saints, small and great, who revere the Name; use of scriptural language.

78. 2 Cor 4:13/Ps 116:10—Use of "it is written" formula to quote "I believed, and so I spoke" from the psalm; Paul says, "We also believe, and so we speak."

79. Rom 15:11/Ps 117:1—See number 16 above.

80. Heb 13:6/Ps 118:6—Quotation of psalm preceded by allusion to Deut 31:6; direct analogy.

81. Mk 12:10 par./Acts 4:11/1 Pet 2:7 (with Is 28:16; Is 8:14)/Ps 118:22-23—Testimonia using catchword "stone" ('eben).

82. Mk 11:9-10 par./Jn 12:13/Ps 118:25-26—"Blessed is he who comes in the name of the Lord."

83. Mt 23:39/Lk 13:35; 19:38/Ps 118:26—Jesus uses the psalm verse of himself.

84. Acts 7:46/Ps 132:5—Allusion to David's desire to build a temple for God.

85. Acts 2:30/Ps 132:11—Simple allusion.

86. Rev 9:20/Ps 135:15-17—See number 76 above.

87. Rev 18:6/Ps 137:8—Allusion, but in reference to Rome.

88. Lk 19:44/Ps 137:9—Jesus uses psalm text to refer to Jerusalem's children (in the psalm, refers to enemies' children).

89. Rom 3:13/Ps 140:3—See number 7 above.

90. Rom 3:10/Gal 2:16/Ps 143:2—Use of scriptural language to speak of something else.

91. Acts 4:24/14:15/Rev 10:6/Ps 146:6—Allusion to God making everything.

Roughly speaking, there seem to be four or five basic ways that New Testament writers used the Old Testament, and almost all of these uses serve the cause of making the point that Jesus is the Messiah or that the church is the fulfillment of God's people and plan of salvation. In other words, the Old Testament is read through christocentric or ecclesiocentric glasses. The boldness of the hermeneutical move is much clearer when material from Psalms or even the Prophets is cited to make some point about Jesus' birth, life, death, resurrection, or his current roles in heaven or future roles at the eschaton.[11]

In my view, the christological interpretation goes back to Jesus in various ways, but also more broadly back to early Jewish messianic readings of the Old Testament. The church simply followed the example of Jesus and other early Jews who were messianically minded. Luke 24 (cf. Lk 4:16-22) suggests that the risen Jesus taught his followers to interpret the Old Testament christologically, but it is believable that he even did some of this before his crucifixion, since he had a messianic self-understanding.

What is especially notable about all this is how far from Gnosticism and Marcionism these writers are. They live in a symbolic world that is deeply grounded in the Old Testament as well other key facets of early Judaism. They share a profound Jewish creation theology and are happy to use not merely the prophetic portions of the Old Testament, but other portions as well as they characterize the new age that they are experiencing. Time and again they see it as important to stress the necessity that these Old Testament promises and prophecies be fulfilled, and they were and are being fulfilled in Christ and in his people, not elsewhere. Their reading of the Old Testament is at once christocentric and ecclesiocentric, and thus pneumatic exegesis, midrash, and homiletical use of the Old Testament is frequent. This tells us how desperately they wanted to show that all these new things were not unforeseen, were not out of line with previous revelation from God, were not a departure but rather were a fulfillment of God's good plans and intentions manifested in various previous eras, revelations, and ways.

---

[11]See Matthew Black, "The Christological Use of the Old Testament in the New Testament," *NTS* 18 (1971–1972): 1-14; J. C. McCullough, "Some Recent Developments in Research on the Epistle to the Hebrews, Part II," *IBS* 3 (1981): 28-45, especially pp. 28-35.

In short, the writers of the New Testament were Jews or Jewish adherents before they were Christians, and they saw what happened in Jesus and what was happening in the Spirit as the fulfillment of all their Jewish hopes and dreams, the fulfillment of their sacred texts and covenants. Once one realizes that this is true about Jesus and of the authors of all twenty-seven New Testament books, one sees immediately why a document such as the *Gospel of Thomas* or a truncated canon such as that of Marcion, which casts aspersions on the God of the Old Testament and his previous revelations, would have been seen as totally out of line with the ethos of the early Christian movement. However much there may be of anti-Pharisaism and anti-Saducceanism in the New Testament at various places, there certainly is no anti-Semitism in this book. The debate between the writers of the New Testament, or even Jesus, and other forms of early Judaism is an in-house debate or, later, a next-door neighbor debate, not a debate between Jews and non-Jews. Gnostics and Marcionites are not even on the horizon of this discussion or debate. It will be useful at this juncture, because of the extreme importance of the Bible in funding the thought world of the earliest Christians, to take a brief look at their view of the living Word of God as oral proclamation, as text, and as person, Jesus.[12]

A CLOSER LOOK: THE LIVING WORD OF GOD

Ancient peoples did not think that words, especially divine words, were mere ciphers or sounds. They believed that words partook of the character and quality of the one who spoke them, and that this was especially true of God's words. And not surprisingly, in an oral culture a premium was put on the oral word. The living voice generally was preferred, except when it came to holy words spoken to unholy people. Then there might well be a preference for a mediated conveyance of God's word, a reading or proclaiming of his word by a spokesperson—a prophet, priest, or king or, for the Christian community, an apostle, prophet, or elder. As the author of Hebrews says, the Israelites at Sinai heard "such a voice speaking words that those who heard it begged that no further word be spoken to them" (Heb 12:19). When the living Word was proclaimed by a living voice, whether of God directly or through God's messenger or emissary, things were likely to happen. All of this helps us to begin to understand the use of the expression "Word of God" in the New Testament.

---

[12]This material appears in more detailed form in Ben Witherington III, *The Living Word of God: Rethinking the Theology of the Bible* (Waco, Tex.: Baylor University Press, 2008).

By general consensus among New Testament scholars (such nearly universal agreement is rare in the guild), 1 Thessalonians is one of the first, if not the very first, of the New Testament documents to be written. And from near the very beginning of this discourse we hear about "the Word of God." In 1 Thessalonians 2:13 we read, "When you received the Word of God, which you heard from us, you accepted it not as the word of humans, but as it actually is, the Word of God." This verse deserves some unpacking. In the first place, Paul equates the message he proclaimed to the residents of Thessalonica with "the Word of God." Clearly, this phrase refers to an oral proclamation that was heard. Whatever else Paul's message may have contained, surely it contained the good news about Jesus and perhaps also some quoting and exegeting of some Old Testament texts.

Then Paul makes a remarkable statement. The Thessalonians received this proclamation as it actually was: not merely the words of human beings, cooked up or contrived by mere mortals, but as a word from God, indeed as "the Word of God" to and for them. Clearly enough, we see already in Paul's words here at least one expression of a theology of God's Word. God's Word, though spoken in human language, should never be confused with mere human speech or even mere human words about God, however accurate. Rather, we are talking about divine speech that changes human lives. But then Paul adds another remarkable phrase: "which is (still) at work in you who believe." The Word of God is seen as something living and active and, having taken up residence in the life of Paul's converts, still in the process of working on and in them.

The implications of these statements are enormous and include the following: (1) Paul believes that he adequately and accurately speaks God's oral Word and has the authority to do so. (2) From the context it becomes quite clear that this does not simply mean that he is a good reader of Old Testament texts, though certainly he sees the Old Testament as God's Word written down. (3) What must be included in the phrase "Word of God" here is what later came to be called "the gospel," the good news of and about Jesus Christ. This was the heart and soul of Paul's message wherever he proclaimed it in the empire. (4) In and through these words that Paul proclaimed, God was speaking, and it should never be seen as merely the words of human beings. A profound theology of revelation and a clear conception of Paul being an inspired person who could truthfully convey God's message of salvation are presupposed. Ancients had little trouble believing in the idea of divine revelation. It is moderns who have trouble with the idea.

Another early Pauline text of relevance to this discussion is 1 Corinthians 14:36-37, where Paul asks his audience if the Word of God originated with them or if they were the only ones whom it had reached. Of course, he is not talking about the Corinthians having received a shipment of Bibles from the Gideons! He is talking about their having heard and received the oral proclamation of God's Word from Paul and others. But what Paul goes on to say is more than a little important: "If any think that they are prophets or are spiritually gifted, let them acknowledge that what I am writing is the Lord's command" (1 Cor 14:37). Here, finally, we have a reference to a text being "the Lord's command" and not just any text. In this case, the reference is to Paul's own letter written to the Corinthians. Here indeed is the nodal idea of an inspired text being God's Word, in this case involving some imperatives.

But it is not only Paul who has this concept that the Word of God is an oral proclamation that includes telling the story about Jesus and that it is a living and active thing. We see this in various places in the book of Acts. Several texts deserve brief mention. First, Acts 4:31 reports that the Holy Spirit of God filled all who were present (men and women), and that they all "spoke the Word of God boldly." In this text we begin to see the connection, already obvious in various Old Testament prophetic texts (e.g., Is 61:1, where the Spirit of God prompts the preaching of the good news), that it is the Holy Spirit, not merely the human spirit, who inspires the speaking of God's Word. Here already the concept of prophetic inspiration and revelation is transferred to the followers of Jesus, apparently to all of them, and all on this occasion and in this place are prompted to speak God's Word boldly. Again, we are not talking about preaching from a text or preaching a text, but rather about an oral proclamation of a late word from God.

So much is the Word of God (in this case, the proclamation about Jesus) seen as a living thing in Acts that we have texts such as Acts 6:7, where we hear how the Word of God itself grew and spread. This is not merely a personification of an abstract idea. The author believes that God's Word is alive, and when it is heard and received, it changes human lives and takes up residence in them, and so this verse goes on to report that "the number of the disciples in Jerusalem increased." Note also Acts 12:24, where it is said that God's Word grew and spread.

We see this same sort of concept of the Word of God in the book of Hebrews. Hebrews 4:12-13 is worth quoting in full: "For the Word of God is living and active. Sharper than any two-edged sword, it penetrates even to the dividing of the soul and spirit, joints and marrow; it judges the thoughts and attitudes of the heart. Nothing in all of creation is hidden from God's sight." Here again the subject of the phrase "Word of God" is an oral proclamation. The focus is not on the after-the-fact literary residue of that proclamation, as is perfectly clear because the author speaks of it sinking into the inner being of the listener. But even more remarkable is the fact that here the "Word of God" inside the believer is said to be analogous to God's eyes; it penetrates the innermost being of a person and judges the thoughts of their heart or mind, laying everything bare. The author, however, is not the originator of these ideas. We can fruitfully compare what is said here with Psalm 139, where the focus is on the work of God's presence or Spirit. What is said in Psalm 139 about the Spirit is said here about the living and active Word. These two things are seen as going and working together.

Another relevant text is 1 Peter 1:23, which speaks of believers being born anew by "the living and abiding Word of God." This certainly can refer to the oral proclamation, but "living" may also convey the sense of life-giving, as it does, for example, in the phrase "living bread" in John 6:51. And we may compare this to 1 Peter 1:3, which speaks of a living hope, which surely means more than merely an extant hope. Or we may consider 1 Peter 2:4-5, which speaks of believers as living stones of the new spiritual house of God. When we hear the phrase "the living Word of God," we are meant to think of something that is actually God's Word and, as such, has life-giving potential. Normally, the phrase also connotes an oral proclamation of God's Word in some form.

Notice that thus far I have said nothing about the other use of the phrase "Word of God" in the New Testament to refer to Jesus himself (Jn 1) or about the concept that the written Old Testament is the Word of God as well. But now I can make some remarks about these other uses of the phrase. The Logos theology of the prologue to John's Gospel is often thought to be distinctive of that book, but we may well see it also in 1 John 1:1-2, where we hear of "the word of life," which seems to be synonymous with both Jesus (who could be touched) and the message about Jesus as God's incarnate Word. Similarly, in Revelation 19:13 the name of God's Son is said to be "the Word of God." We have seen some hints already of the notion that texts could be the Word of God as well, and now we must turn to more evidence of this by looking in detail at 2 Timothy 3:16 and some texts in Hebrews.

Because of the enormous significance of 2 Timothy 3:16-17, I must go into considerably more detailed explanation of these verses. Indeed, entire theories about the nature of God's Word and of inspiration have been derived from these verses. Here, clearly enough, the subject matter is a written text, in this case what Christians now refer to as the Old Testament. The Old Testament was the Bible of the earliest Christians because, of course, the New Testament had not yet been written, collected, or canonized. Indeed, even the Old Testament canon, or list of included books, was not completely settled before the waning decades of the first century A.D. or perhaps in the second century. Here we must make an important distinction between "the Bible" as one form that God's Word took, the written form, and the "Word of God," which is a much broader category. The Word of God in the first instance refers to inspired and powerful spoken words. The earliest Christians were neither without a Scripture (the Old Testament) nor without the living voice, the oral Word of God, which, in their view, now included Christian proclamation, especially the good news about Jesus.

It is interesting that the New Testament writers tend to say more about the inspiration of the Old Testament than do the Old Testament writers themselves. For example, in Mark 12:36 Jesus tells his audience that "David, in the Holy Spirit, said . . . ," and then a portion of a psalm is quoted. Or in Acts 1:16 we hear that the Holy Spirit, through the mouth of David, predicted what would happen to Judas. We may compare 2 Peter 1:21, where it is said that "persons moved by the Holy Spirit spoke from God." We therefore are not surprised to hear about the inspiration of Old Testament figures in the New Testament, but 2 Timothy 3:16-17 goes a step beyond that in talking about an inspired text itself. It appears that the inspiration of persons who could write could entail the inspiration of particular texts, though apparently no one would claim that everything that they ever said or wrote was the inspired Word of God.

Surely, 2 Timothy 3:16-17 is the most famous text in that letter, cited over one hundred times in the patristic literature. There are, however, various ways to translate it, and each one causes a variable in its meaning. It could read, for instance, "Every *graphē* [i.e., Scripture] is God-breathed and profitable/useful . . . so that/with the result that the person of God is ready, equipped for good works." Usually, when *pas* is used with a noun without the definite article, it means "every" rather than "all." Thus, the meaning seems likely to be "every Scripture" or perhaps "every passage of Scripture." Paul does use *graphē* in the singular to refer to the whole of Scripture in Romans 11:2, but there we have the definite article (cf. Gal 3:22). Of course, this means that "all Scripture" is included, but the emphasis would be on each one being God-breathed. Paul does not envision any part of Scripture that is not God-breathed. It is also possible to read the verse to mean "Every inspired Scripture is useful," but against this view is that it is more natural to take the two qualifying adjectives as relating to the noun in the same way as in 1 Timothy 4:4.

A further issue is what to make of the adjective *theopneustos*. Its literal meaning is "God-breathed," and it is used in pagan literature—for example, in reference to the *Sibylline Oracles* (see *Sib. Or.* 5:308, 407; Plutarch, *Pyth. orac.* 7; Ps.-Phoc. 121), and in the papyri (*SIG* 95; *CMRDM* 2.A8). We may compare, for example, an aretology to Isis written in Macedonia that reads at one point, "This encomium is written not only by the hand of a man, but also by the mind of a god" (line 14).[13] Greek words with the *-tos* ending tend to be passive rather than active, so we should take this to mean not "every Scripture is inspiring" but rather "every Scripture is inspired." What is meant is that God speaks through these words. God breathed life and meaning and truth into them all (see, similarly, Num 24:2; Hos 9:7; cf. 2 Pet 1:21; Josephus, *Ag. Ap.* 1.37-39; Philo, *Moses* 2.292; *Spec. Laws.* 1.65; 4.49).

Note that we are not given an explanation of how that works. This text by itself does not explicate a theory of inspiration or its nature. Does the Spirit lift the mind of the writer to see, understand, and write, or is it a matter of mechanical dictation? These questions are not answered here. What is suggested is that whatever the process, the product is God's Word, telling God's truth.

The emphasis here is on God's Word being good or profitable as a source of teaching about God and human beings and their ways, as a means of refuting false arguments or errors and offering positive "proofs" and rebuking sin, and as a means of offering constructive wisdom and teaching on how to live a life pleasing to God. It will be seen, then, that the Old Testament is viewed here largely as a source for ethical instruction and exhortation, which is unsurprising, given the emphasis in this letter. There is no emphasis here on it being a sourcebook for Christian theology, which would come more from the Christian kerygma and Christian tradition. We may also want to consult other places where Paul speaks about the nature of the Old Testament Scriptures, such as Romans 15:3-4 and 1 Corinthians 10:11, which confirm that Paul thinks that what we refer to as the Old Testament is quite suitable for Christian instruction, especially for training in righteousness and other ethical matters.

There is debate about 2 Timothy 3:17 as to whether we should see it as a purpose or result clause. Is it the purpose of Scripture to fit a person of God for ready service, or does that happen as the result and effect of Scripture? Probably, this is a result clause. The result of learning Scripture is that one is equipped. It seems likely also that since this is directed specifically to Timothy here, "person of God" in this verse refers to a minister of some sort. Paul then would be talking about equipping the minister by means of studying the Scriptures.

---

[13]The full text is cited in G. H. R. Horsley and S. Llewelyn, eds., *New Documents Illustrating Early Christianity* (North Ryde, NSW: The Ancient History Documentary Research Centre, Macquarie University, 1981–), 1:10-11.

Using the rhetorical device of *gradatio*, Paul brings the list of what Scripture is useful for to a climax and conclusion with the phrase "training in righteousness." Here, "righteousness" surely has an ethical rather than a forensic sense, in keeping with the ethical focus of the rest of what Scripture is said to be useful for. John Chrysostom puts it this way: "This is why the exhortation of the Scripture is given: that the man of God may be rendered complete by it. Without this he cannot grow to maturity" (*Hom. 2 Tim.* 9) Clearly, with this text, we are well on the way to a full-blown theology of inspired written texts being God's Word, being God-breathed. What is interesting is that neither Paul nor the author of Hebrews views the Old Testament as an example of what God once said, relegating the revelation and speaking to the past. No, it still has the life and power and truth of God in it, and it still speaks in and to the present.

Especially striking are the formula quotations in Hebrews. These are the ways that the author of Hebrews introduces Old Testament quotations in his quotation-filled sermon. Most striking in the sermon is that God the Father, Jesus Christ, and the Holy Spirit are said to be the speakers of various Old Testament texts. A few examples must suffice. As the author introduces a quotation from Deuteronomy 32:43 at Hebrews 1:6, he uses the phrase "when God brings his firstborn into the world, he says . . ." (note the present tense of the verb *say*). But in Hebrews 2:11-12, in introducing a quotation from Psalm 22:22, he writes, "So Jesus is not ashamed to call them brothers and sisters. He says . . ." (cf. Heb 10:5). Christ is depicted as speaking an Old Testament text. And on multiple occasions we see in Hebrews "As the Holy Spirit says" used to introduce various Old Testament quotations (see Heb 3:7; 10:16).

Two things stand out about this. It seems clear enough that the author already has the beginnings of a trinitarian theology. What Scripture says, God says, and the God who is said to be speaking these Old Testament texts is Father, Son, or Spirit. However, we do not yet have a text in which all three of them are said to speak one particular passage of Scripture. Equally telling is that the present-tense verb keeps cropping up. The Old Testament is not just for God's original chosen people; it is viewed as a text that speaks directly and pertinently to Christians in the present. Furthermore, it is seen as speaking about a host of subjects, including God's Son, not just about ethics. The author of Hebrews takes up stories from the Old Testament, laws, and covenants as well as ethical material in order to convey the living Word of God about Jesus and Christian life to the audience.

Then too, the author enunciates a hermeneutic of progressive revelation from the very beginning of the book. He says that God revealed himself in various times and ways, or partially and piecemeal in the past, but now God has revealed himself fully and finally in the person of his Son (Heb 1:1-2). Clearly, the incarnate Word is seen as the most crucial revelation of God, with earlier revelations functioning to prepare for, foreshadow, or foretell of it. But this by no means causes him to suggest that the Old Testament ceases to be God's Word when the incarnate Word appears. To the contrary, Jesus specifically and the Christ-event in general are seen as the hermeneutical keys to understanding the Old Testament, but also the Old Testament is understood as crucial to understanding the Christ-event. There is some sort of symbiotic relationship between Word written, Word proclaimed, and Word incarnate envisioned.

One more text is of direct relevance to this discussion, particularly in regard to the issue of inspiration and revelation. In 2 Peter 1:20-21 we read, "Above all, you must understand that no prophecy of Scripture came about by the prophet's own interpretation. For prophecy never had its origin in the human will, but prophets, though human, spoke from God as they were carried along by the Holy Spirit." It is indeed normally about prophets and prophecy that we hear about the notion of inspiration, and this text seems to add a bit more to the discussion than does 2 Timothy 3:16.

Here we have a contrast between prophecy that made it into Scripture and other prophecies. The author says that whatever may be the case about other prophecies, in regard to Old Testament prophecy it cannot be a matter of purely private or individual interpretation or explanation. That is, the author sees a meaning in the prophecy itself that makes a claim on the listener, and the listener is not to "determine the meaning" of the text but rather to discover it. Indeed, he even means that it was not up to the prophet to interpret it or add his own interpretation to it. The prophet was constrained by the source of the information to speak another's words and meaning—God's. This is made clearer in what follows in 2 Peter 1:21, which speaks about the origins of true prophecy and insists that it does not originate as a matter of human will or ingenuity. To the contrary, the Holy Spirit is the one who inspires the prophet. In fact, the text literally says that the prophet is carried along or forcefully moved by the Spirit to say what is said. The prophet is so led by the Spirit that the prophet's words can be said to be God's Word, originating from a divine source.

Much more could be said along these lines, but this must suffice as this excursus comes to a close. The living Word of God is seen as an oral message, an incarnate person, and finally as a text, in particular the text of the Old Testament. Its life, power, and truth are a derived life, power, and truth if we are talking about the oral or written Word. The source is God, who inspires, speaks, and empowers the words with qualities that reflect the divine character. It is right to assert that Paul thinks that what he says, God is saying. It is right to assert that both Paul and the author of Hebrews think that what the Old Testament says, God says. These same writers think that what Jesus says, God says. Indeed, the author of Hebrews is audacious enough to suggest that the preexistent Christ actually spoke some of the Old Testament texts into existence. It is also right to say that the emphatic center and focus of the proclamation of "the Word of God" by early Christians were Jesus and the Christ-event in general. It is also right to say that some New Testament writers even reached the point of being able to talk about Jesus being the Word of God incarnate, come in the flesh, such that when Jesus spoke on earth, he spoke not merely *for* God but *as* God, and indeed he spoke about himself. In this case, the message and the messenger are one.

C. S. Lewis once said that when the author of a play comes out on the stage, the play is over. The authors of the Johannine literature, but also the other New Testament writers, believed that when Jesus came, history, particularly salvation history, had reached its zenith; they were now in the eschatological era when all the promises and prophecies of God were coming true in and through Jesus and his followers. Jesus was seen as the climax of revelation and as the climactic revelation. He was seen as God's Word, God's purpose, God's salvation, God's being come in person. What was previously predicated of Wisdom (Prov 3:8; Wisdom of Solomon) and of Torah (Sirach) is now predicated of a historical person, Jesus, or of the returning, exalted Christ (Rev 19:13).

Summary

A great deal more could be said about the symbolic universe that the New Testament writers share, but this must suffice for now, as I have shown more than adequately that these writers share a universe of discourse out of which they tell their stories, offer their logic, do their theologizing and ethicizing, and draw their conclusions. Obviously, there are many other elements in this shared symbolic universe that I have not explicated here—for example, the shared conviction about the goodness of all God's creation, or the God-ordained nature of marriage, or that human beings are created in the image of God, or that angels and demons aplenty are part of the world. We have looked only at a representative sampling of those elements taken for granted in the early Christian symbolic universe. Much of this universe lurks beneath the surface of the New Testament texts and must be uncovered to be understood, but when we take the time to do such exploration, we discover a vast foundation on which all these writers stand.

We have no final New Testament era figure who gathers together all the theologizing and ethicizing that goes on in these documents and tells us what a New Testament theology and ethics, properly synthesized and presented, ought to look like. But in a sense, this ought not to worry us, as we can see how much the particular articulations of theology and ethics in the various documents are done from the same or very similar starting point, with similar assumptions about reality, truth, God, sacred texts, the eschatological situation, and so on. The New Testament is a profoundly Jewish document, operating on Jewish premises and assumptions and with a Jewish thought world, albeit one significantly modified by the Christ-event and its fallout. In order to understand this world, we must, through an act of creative imagination, enter into it rather than require it to conform to our thought world.

When all is said and done, a theology and/or ethics stripped of its first-century context is not simply like a picture removed from its frame, for we lose not just its original framework and setting for interpretation, but its incarnational character and nature of the theologizing and ethicizing done into specific contexts for specific purposes. One way to begin to properly enter into the New Testament's thought world is to examine the stories that the New Testament writers share and tell. To this task we now turn.

3

THE NARRATIVE THOUGHT WORLD
OF JESUS AND THE
NEW TESTAMENT WRITERS

On the one hand, this universe will be seen to have a different form from theology, for it has the form of a narrative, or at least of a drama that Paul represents in narrative form—as a story about what God and Christ have done, are doing, and will do in connection with the earthly sphere of the other actors in the story. Paul's theologizing refers to this story and provides argumentative elaborations of it, and for this reason we will often have to work through his theologizing to the symbolic universe it presupposes. . . . Paradoxically, although theological knowledge is about the knowledge we find in symbolic universes, Paul's theologizing is more important for us than his theology because his theologizing takes place as a form of social relations between himself and other actors in the sphere of their social universe. His theologizing is a means of securing certain kinds of behavior from the other actors by appealing to their shared symbolic universe.

NORMAN PETERSEN[1]

The unity of New Testament theology is grounded in the implied master story to which these writings witness.

FRANK MATERA[2]

---

[1]Norman R. Petersen, *Rediscovering Paul: Philemon and the Sociology of Paul's Narrative World* (Philadelphia: Fortress, 1985), p. 30. I would add to this that we have only the theologizing of Paul in his letters; we do not have a theology in the abstract, as Paul wrote no textbooks that we know of.
[2]Frank J. Matera, *New Testament Theology: Exploring Diversity and Unity* (Louisville: Westminster John Knox, 2007), p. 427.

There is something else besides the symbolic universe that the writers of the New Testament share. That universe is drawn up in the context of narratological thinking about life and more specifically about religious life. From the Gospel narratives, to the book of Acts, to the stories on which Paul relies, to the narrative visions of John of Patmos, a storied world is imaged forth by these writers, a storied world that they share, though they tell the communal stories somewhat differently depending on the occasion, the audience, and other considerations.

Lest we think that narratological readings of the Bible are something new, Joel Green reminds us that even Israel's first credo took the form of a narrative: "A wandering Aramean was my ancestor . . ." (Deut 26:5-10). Story is the primary means by which the meaning of God and the divine human encounter is conveyed from the very first chapter of Genesis.[3] In other words, the Bible itself encourages both the conveying and the reading of its theology and ethics in the context of a narrative. But, as James Dunn has asked, how do we analyze the narratives in and of the sacred text without engaging in a flight from history, by which he means the historical events that stand behind the text?[4] I agree with Green that an unfortunate choice has often been foisted on students of the Bible: either story or history, either historicity or creativity. But such an either/or is unnecessary. Why not a both/and approach, and particularly one that recognizes the historical character and embeddedness of the grand narrative of the Bible?[5] As Green goes on to point out, recent studies of historical narratives have noticed that they need not be seen as attempts to create significance through imposing a narrative order and interpretive framework on the messiness of historical events but rather as efforts to recognize thematic and causal ties between events in the real world.[6] Green stresses,

> Narrative is less about chronicling events and more about drawing out their significance and inviting response. To put it differently, "narrative" is not just "story" but also "action." Indeed, narration is a particular telling of a story to a particular audience in a particular situation in order to get a particular end. Narrative then is an exercise in influence.[7]

---

[3]Joel B. Green, *Seized by Truth: Reading the Bible as Scripture* (Nashville: Abingdon, 2007), p. 165.
[4]J. D. G. Dunn, *Jesus Remembered*, vol. 1 of *Christianity in the Making* (Grand Rapids: Eerdmans, 2003), p. 94.
[5]Green, *Seized by Truth*, p. 166.
[6]Ibid., p. 167.
[7]Ibid., p. 168.

He is right that the focus of narrative is not so much on answering the question "Did this happen?" as though the audience were skeptical about the historical substance of the account, but rather on answering the question "What does this mean, and what does it call me to do?" That is, narrative focuses on answering theological and ethical questions that are the implications of the divine-human encounter. The reader is invited to enter into such an encounter, become a part of the ever flowing stream of God's people, and believe and behave in different ways.

When we turn to the New Testament itself, we must admit from the outset that many of its stories are drawn right from the Old Testament, but there are the fresh experiences that the followers of Jesus had with him and then after his time on earth, and these experiences too become the subject of narratological thinking and storytelling. Without question, eschatological thinking, thinking that history has purpose, direction, and a goal, lends itself quite naturally to narratological thinking about matters of the faith. For one thing, eschatological thinking is forward-looking, believing that there will be a resolution to the human dilemma in space and time, not merely in another world. Thus there is a storied world behind the thinking of Jesus and his followers, but also a storied world in front of their thinking as well, so to speak.

At first glance, this may not seem as apparent when one is dealing with letters or sermons, but as we will see, not only do the theologizing and ethicizing done in such documents presuppose a storied world shared between author and audience, but also from time to time those stories are allowed to surface in the discourse, are reshaped and retold for the occasion, and serve as a manner of making theological and ethical points. At this juncture, we must work through some examples from our sources.

THE NARRATIVE THOUGHT WORLD OF JESUS

It was G. B. Caird who said that Jesus was the starting point and goal of New Testament theology.[8] He meant this in several ways. For one thing, in the thought world of the earliest Christians there is continuity between the Jesus of history and the Christ of faith, and between Jesus and the risen Lord. Caird put it this way: "Without the Jesus of history the Christ of faith becomes a Docetic figure, a figment of pious imagination who, like Alice's Cheshire

---

[8]G. B. Caird, *New Testament Theology*, compl. and ed. L. D. Hurst (Oxford: Oxford University Press, 1994), p. 346.

cat, ultimately disappears from view."[9] Unfortunately, that happens all too regularly in volumes on New Testament theology, which is why I am starting this part of the discussion with an examination of Jesus' narrative thought world, which most certainly influenced that of his earliest followers, who, like him, were Torah-loving Jews.

It was Caird's view (and I think he is right) that human experience is the point at which theology is grounded in history. It was the experiencing of the risen Lord or the experiencing of conversion to Christ that led to the Copernican revolution in the thinking of those Jews who became Christians after Easter. Later, it was the worshiping of Christ that led to rethinking his significance and how to tell his story.[10] These sorts of things caused the earliest Christians to go back and reevaluate what the historical Jesus had said and done, and particularly to reevaluate his own teaching. What sort of worldview had undergirded and been articulated in Jesus' teaching?

Without question, Jesus was one of the great sages of all time, and that included being a great storyteller. Whether we consider his original parables or his creative handling of Old Testament stories, he was quite the improviser, to say the least. He lived out of and spoke into a rich storied world, and he told his own and others' tales in light of the dawning eschatological realities. Not surprisingly, his storied world is populated chiefly by Old Testament figures and stories, alluded to, retold, and recycled in various ways, but also his storied world involves the spinning out of new tales, often in the form of parables or visionary remarks (e.g., "I saw Satan fall like lightning from the sky" [Lk 10:18]). The function of Jesus' discourse was not merely to inform but also to transform, and that transformation was to involve not merely the audience's symbolic universe but also its behavior, in relationship to God as well as in relationship to each other. In other words, there was both a theological and an ethical thrust to Jesus' teaching. The stories were meant to transform not only the religious imagination of the audience but also their praxis, giving them samples and examples of how to believe and behave in the light of the inbreaking dominion of God.

If there is a difference in thrust in the way Jesus articulated his eschatological worldview from that of his predecessor John the Baptizer, it is that Jesus, even in his more apocalyptic sayings, tended to emphasize the good news

---

[9]Ibid., 347.

[10]On which, see Larry Hurtado, *Lord Jesus Christ: Devotion to Jesus in Earliest Christianity* (Grand Rapids: Eerdmans, 2003).

about the coming of the dominion on earth. "The object of winnowing is not to collect enough chaff to have a glorious bonfire; it is to gather the wheat into the granary; the bonfire is purely incidental."[11] Thus, Jesus set about to rescue the perishing and to free Israel from its various forms of bondage. In this, Jesus is not trying to be Israel, any more than the Twelve were set up initially to be Israel. All of them were trying to free Israel through a mission of preaching, teaching, and healing. There was, however, urgency and corporate focus to what they did. "The disciples were not evangelistic preachers sent out to save individual souls for some unearthly paradise. They were couriers proclaiming a national emergency and conducting a referendum on a question of national survival."[12] The storm of judgment was looming on the horizon for the Jewish faith centered on temple, territory, and Torah. God was intervening in Jesus and his followers before this disaster happened, just as he had already intervened through John the Baptizer. It is this context of social unrest and sense of impending doom that we must keep in view when considering the way Jesus articulates his thought world and the urgency with which he stresses certain things.

This line of discussion raises the issue of the relationship of Jesus to Israel. I suggest that Jesus presents himself not as Israel but rather as the Son of Man, and as the Son of Man, he is Adam gone right. That is, the scope of his messianic ministry is much broader than fulfilling the promise of being the ultimate Son of David restoring Israel and its reign in the Holy Land. That is a part of what Jesus is about, but only a part. The temptation scenes make clear that something more wide-ranging and more cosmic is at stake, for Jesus is tempted as Son of God, not as Israel or Son of David. The issue is what sort of Son of God was Jesus to be. Was it one that comported with his being the true Son of Man of Danielic prophecy or not?

Of course, Jesus spoke to a different audience than did his later Christian followers. Every single one of the New Testament documents is written for Christians, even if in some cases written for Christians to use in some form with outsiders. Jesus, on the other hand, was addressing Jews, even when he was addressing his disciples, and so he was able to presuppose the storied world of the Old Testament as something that he and his audience shared. This perhaps explains why Jesus is able to simply allude to figures such as the queen of the South (Mt 12:41-42 par.), or Noah (Mt 24:36-41), or a widow

---

[11]Caird, *New Testament Theology*, p. 360.
[12]Ibid., p. 361.

in Zarephath (Lk 4:26) and expect the audience to know who he meant.

It is no surprise that many of the figures from the past that Jesus speaks of are associated with judgments past and future, including both the queen of the South and Noah. According to Matthew 12:38-40 (cf. Mt 16:1-4; Lk 11:29-32), the only "sign" that a wicked generation would get out of Jesus was the sign of Jonah, that reluctant crisis-intervention specialist called upon to warn the people Nineveh of impending disaster if they did not repent. Jonah 3:4 says that the Ninevites were warned that if they did not repent, destruction would fall upon them within forty days. Jesus offers a similar warning in Mark 13, except that the clock is set to forty years. Luke, in his relating of this sort of teaching, makes it all the more explicit that Jesus means the destruction of Jerusalem by human armies, namely, Roman armies (Lk 19:41-44; 21:20-24; 23:27-31).

It is interesting, however, that most of the stories that Jesus told were of his own making, stories about contemporaries and contemporary things, such as the coming of God's eschatological saving activity. As we read through even just the narrative parables, we find anonymous human figures providing examples of various sorts. Only the parable of the rich man and Lazarus presents a story about a named individual human being (Lk 16:19-31). Even more interesting is the fact that God is portrayed as an actor in various of these parables; he is the owner of the vineyard in the parable of the wicked tenants (Mk 12:1-11), and the forgiving Father in the parable of the prodigal son (Lk 15:11-32). Most importantly, we discover that Jesus provides an example of how to do theology and ethics in story form, for these stories are about both divine activity and human responses of various sorts.

There is also a dark edge to the stories that Jesus tells when it comes to the evaluation of his own people. By this I mean that they are portrayed as lost (see Lk 15), and their leaders as those who reject God's emissaries the prophets and even his Son (Mt 23:29-39). The eschatological situation is portrayed as drastic, with all sorts of unexpected persons trying to race through the narrow gate into the kingdom, while the invited guests have snubbed the host and either refused to come or have come late and without the appropriate attire. Pious Jews are going away from temple prayer unjustified while tax collectors are being accepted. There is some sort of drastic reversal of normal expectations happening as the dominion breaks into human history, and it does not bode well for the faithful elder brothers of the family, it would appear. God is busy vindicating the oppressed, liberating the lost, enfranchising the least and last, and changing the guest list at the messianic banquet. These are stories about the upsetting of a highly stratified world, about the changing of the guard, about new occasions teaching new duties, about both judgment and redemption catching Jews by surprise, and perhaps most of all about the need for repentance by one and all as God's divine saving activity is happening in their midst, and yet many are blind to it.

The storied world that Jesus tells of has not only a dark edge but also a strangeness. Good shepherds do not leave ninety-nine sheep to rescue one straggler. People do not plant a weed such as a mustard bush, as it only attracts the wrong sort of birds and attention. God is not like an unjust judge who has to be forced into vindicating a persistent widow. We could go on. Jesus is offering new perspectives on old images and ideas, and in some cases new perspectives on new vistas and horizons that are coming into view.

N. T. Wright rightly senses what is going on in Jesus' ministry when he says,

> The crucial element in his prophetic activity was the story, both implicit and explicit, that he was telling and acting out. It was Israel's story reaching its climax: the long-awaiting moment has arrived! . . . To say "the kingdom of God is at hand" makes sense only when the hearers know "the story thus far" and are waiting for it to be completed.[13]

And precisely because Jesus is operating in the Jewish ethos of ʾ*ereṣ yiśrāʾēl* ("land of Israel"), he can presuppose a storied world context that most of the writers of the New Testament cannot presuppose. This may well explain why indeed we find no parables outside the Gospels. It is because we are no longer speaking into Jesus' specific world, a world where sapiential Jewish thinking with an eschatological twist made sense.

In its own context, then, how would Jesus' articulation of his vision in stories have been heard? Again Wright helps us:

> It would clearly *both* challenge some prevailing assumptions within that Jewish context *and* retain a special focus which would be characteristic only of Jesus' career, not the work of his post-Easter followers. It must be set within Judaism, but as a challenge; it must be the presupposition for the church, but not the blueprint.[14]

---

[13]N. T. Wright, *Jesus and the Victory of God*, vol. 2 of *Christian Origins and the Question of God* (Minneapolis: Fortress, 1996), p. 226.
[14]Ibid.

Just so, and this means that it is crucial to get the balance right between continuity and discontinuity when it comes to assessing the storied world of Jesus and of his post-Easter followers. And again, the point of the parables is to reorder the thinking of Jews: "The parables offer not only information, but challenge; they are stories designed to evoke fresh praxis, to reorder the symbolic world, to break open current understandings and inculcate fresh ones."[15]

A good example to examine closely is the parable of the sower in Mark 4:1-9. Here, as Wright observes, we have the revolutionary notion that Jesus is the person who is bringing the story of Israel to a climax in his own ministry. "If we fail to see how profoundly subversive, how almost suicidally dangerous, such a claim was," it is because we have tended to turn Jesus' counterorder wisdom speech into innocuous sermon illustrations.[16] It is right to say that when we are dealing with the narrative parables, we need to follow the narrative logic of the story, not assume that these are thinly veiled allegories of history in detail. At the same time, there are allegorical elements in Jesus' parables, and especially perhaps this one. Modern distinctions between parable and allegory are not all that helpful when it comes to ancient Jewish storytelling.[17] Who, then, is the sower in this parable? Along with most commentators, I agree that it is Jesus, assuming a divine role here of planting God's Word about the dominion in surprising as well as familiar places.

There are some surprising results of following this narrative logic. For one thing, Jesus is not sanguine that most of those who hear him will respond positively in the long term. He is unlike the naïve and overly optimistic preacher of today. But what is perhaps most telling about this parable is that Jesus expects rejection and ephemeral positive responses. He expects too much competition to allow his message to grow in the hearts of many. He expects absolute, hard-hearted rejection. And yes, in the good soil he expects good, long-lasting results.

This is an odd message for a person who saw himself in a messianic light, as one who had come to rescue Israel from disaster. In a sense, it is a message about the end of one thought world and the unexpected beginnings of another out of the ashes of the first one. In Jesus' view, his world is hell-bent, not heaven bound, and he, like John the Baptizer, is here to try to rescue a

---

[15]Ibid., p. 229.

[16]Ibid., p. 235.

[17]On which, see Ben Witherington III, *Jesus the Sage: The Pilgrimage of Wisdom* (Minneapolis: Fortress, 1994); *Jesus the Seer: The Progress of Prophecy* (Peabody, Mass.: Hendrickson, 1999).

few of the perishing before the dark night of judgment falls. This parable differs considerably from the one in Mark 12:1-11 about the wicked tenants, as that is a commentary on Jewish leadership in the vineyard, not about the state of the Jewish vineyard in general. But both parables presuppose that things are coming to a climax, and that God's last-ditch efforts to rescue his people are culminating in the ministry of Jesus, who seeks to reclaim God's land, his vineyard, before it produces nothing but the grapes of wrath.

Along with Wright, I think that the aforementioned parables in Mark 4 and Mark 12 would have been seen as echoing or alluding to Isaiah 5–6. In this light, there can be no question but that the vineyard is Israel, and Jesus sees himself as fulfilling a prophetic role like that of Isaiah, dealing with hard-of-hearing Israel. But what is most telling when we closely read Isaiah 5–6 and then think of these two parables of Jesus is that already in Isaiah the theme of impending judgment and the exile of God's Jewish people is clear. In this context, the use of parables reflects and indeed presupposes the hard-heartedness of the audience and their refusal to listen. They will not hear and understand unless they turn or repent. Listen to some of Isaiah's Song of the Vineyard: "What more could have been done for my vineyard than I have done for it? When I looked for good grapes, why did it yield only bad? Now I will tell you what I am going to do to my vineyard: I will take away its hedge, and it will be destroyed; I will break down its wall and it will be trampled" (Is 5:4-5). The song is a lament that goes on to bemoan the injustice and bloodshed in Israel.

Here is where I say that this all comports nicely with Jesus' prediction of the demise of the temple and Jerusalem in Mark 13. In Jesus' view, as his prophetic sign-act in the temple showed, this temple was the temple of doom, one that God would judge within a generation. And indeed, exactly one biblical generation after Jesus died in A.D. 30 the temple fell in Jerusalem to the Romans. Jesus was no false prophet any more than Isaiah was in regard to the demise of Jerusalem and exile in his own era. In light of all this, it is interesting that the later Christian followers of Jesus not only continued to evangelize Jews and see God as promising them much, but also, as a text such as Romans 9–11 shows, continued to believe that God, though he might temporarily break off Jews from his people who did not accept Jesus as their messiah, would not replace an unresponsive Jewish people with a more responsive Gentile one. This is surprising only to those who do not know the regular pattern in the Old Testament prophetic oracles of redemption of Israel after and indeed as a result of judgment on Israel (see, e.g., Hosea, Amos and, of course, Isaiah). Perhaps most radically and paradoxically, Jesus was suggesting in Mark 4 that God's radical rescue of his people would come not by means of military action or a warrior-messiah but rather through the call and response of Jesus' preaching of the good news.

This brings us to the other seed parables in Mark 4. Jesus seems to think that there will be some "seedy" characters, indeed some characters that Jews would consider "for the birds" (cf. Dan 4:20-22) in the dominion, to the surprise of the long-time dwellers there. Hence, Jesus tells the parable of the mustard seed—a seed that no Jewish farmer would ever plant in a garden. The parable of the mustard seed is a parable of contrast between small beginnings and large, if noxious and surprising, outcomes, but it is also a parable that tells us what sort of persons were going to end up in the vineyard: the wild birds from afar, which should probably be seen as an allusion to Gentiles.

The parable of the seed growing secretly tells us something about the method by which the dominion is coming: secretly, under the radar, without a lot of human effort and certainly without violence.[18] This parable can be fruitfully compared to the parable of the leaven in the dough (Mt 13:33 // Lk 13:20-21) in that both suggest a sort of automatic process, one without human aid that produces the result. The hiddenness theme is also evident in parables of the pearl of great price and the treasure in the field (Mt 13:44-46). There are apocalyptic overtones to all these parables as they emerge from a world of opacity, of secrets that require teasing the brain into active thought to figure out, of God producing a crop and a harvest or a treasure as if by sleight of hand. The harvest theme is a dead giveaway that Jesus believed that the eschatological scenario was already in play. And here precisely is where I differ strongly with Wright. These are not parables about return from exile. If anything, they are parables about the surprising presence of God's saving activity in the midst of occupation and oppression in the Holy Land, a very different message indeed. Jesus did not come to meet the audience's messianic expectations; he came to meet their needs. But ultimately, that task could be consummated only through a sacrifice on a cross and its sequel. Redemption would not come on the cheap or even just by a spiritual revival of good preaching accompanied by some miracles. The sin problem would not be dealt with or overcome by those means alone. And this brings us to another crucial point.

---

[18]See the discussion in Wright, *Jesus and the Victory of God*, pp. 240-41.

Did Jesus tell stories about himself? One could argue that Jesus appears in some of the parables. For example, in Mark 4 he seems to be the sower and in Mark 12 it seems clear enough that he is the Son who is rejected, killed, and thrown out of the vineyard. We could perhaps also suggest that in the parables of the lost sheep he is the shepherd, or in the parable of the lost coin he is the woman seeking the coin (see Lk 15:3-10). But these parables in the main are not about the king Jesus; they are about the coming of the kingdom of God.

When Jesus referred to himself, he chose a phrase that we do not find in any of the parables: the "Son of Man." A close examination of his use of this term shows that at least a good bit of the time he is alluding to the story of that enigmatic "one like a son of man" in Daniel 7:13-14, the one who would be given a kingdom by God and would rule and judge the earth forever. This is especially clear in a saying such as that in Mark 14:62, but it is also in evidence in other Son of Man sayings, even in the Johannine tradition (see Jn 1:51; 3:13; 8:28). Jesus, it appears, exegeted his own career, purpose, existence, and importance out of various Old Testament stories, and I suggest that this influenced the various christological hymns that his earliest follow-ers created after Easter. The link between the proclaimer and becoming the one proclaimed becomes clearer when we realize that Jesus also exegeted himself out of the story of Wisdom. This is especially clear in various places in Matthew 11, especially Matthew 11:19, where Jesus calls himself Wisdom directly. Then too we must point to a text such as Mark 12:35-37, where Jesus cleverly intimates in his interpretation of Psalm 110 that the messiah is in fact not just David's son, but even greater than that, he is David's lord; and in either case he is alluding to himself here. Jesus himself, then, provided the catalyst for interpreting and exegeting his significance out of the prophetic and Wisdom literature of early Judaism.[19]

Jesus is not merely telling a story or carrying a story already in play for-ward to its logical climax. This becomes quite clear in, for example, his "yoke" saying (Mt 11:28-30), where it is Jesus' yoke that his disciples are to take upon themselves with rigor and vigor, not the yoke of the Mosaic law. The Mosaic law, having been fulfilled in the Christ-event, would not provide the ethical script for all Christian conduct going forward; rather, the law of Christ would do so. Of course, this would be confusing because some

---

[19]For a full-dress presentation of Jesus' self-understanding, see Ben Witherington III, *The Christol-ogy of Jesus* (Minneapolis: Fortress, 1990).

elements of the Mosaic law would be renewed or reaffirmed or intensified by Christ—for example, the Great Commandment—and thus would be part of the binding contract known as the new covenant. But Christ's followers would do these things because they were part of Christ's yoke, which he commanded his disciples to take up, called, paradoxically, a light burden. They would not merely continue the story of obedience (and disobedience) of Israel to Moses' law.

However subversive or paradoxical the later Christian message may have seemed or have been, and however much they may have relied on Jesus' message, even his message about himself, Christian preachers did not by and large follow Jesus' methodology of preaching. They told the story straight. Partly, this had to do with ethos and social context, since most audiences outside Israel were not well schooled in Jewish sapiential literature. Partly also, however, this had to do with the change in symbolic universe from before to after the death and resurrection of Jesus. The proclaimer had become the universally proclaimed, and this because of the way his life turned out. Apparently, it was felt that the message about a crucified and risen messiah was paradoxical enough in itself, and required enough explaining in itself, that an evangelistic religion needed to tell the story in a clear and straightforward way. While some of the themes of the "good news" song and part of the tune remained the same, the lyrics needed to be less enigmatic and more singularly focused on Jesus himself and his redemptive work.

Here is where I suggest that we can see the modulation of the tune and lyrics best by considering some of the hymn fragments found in Paul's storied arsenal, and to these we soon will turn, but we will approach this by looking at the broader contours of Paul's storied world first, and there we will see overlap with Jesus' storied world, especially in regard to "Abba" and "kingdom" language. Paul provides us with the earliest post-Easter examples of the modulations of the tune that Jesus sang.

The Narrative Thought World of Paul

Because Israel's story speaks of a creator god who claims all people, all lands, as his own, Paul is able to reach out from within that story and address Jew and Gentile alike. He thus claims that the story of Jesus fulfills the purpose for which the creator god called Abraham in the first place. Although his telling of the story subverted the narrative world of his Jewish contemporaries, his claim was that it actually reinstated the true sense of the covenant promises.

What had made the difference, clearly, was Jesus; or, more fully, Jesus and the divine spirit. Paul's theology can, I suggest, be plotted most accurately and fully on the basis that it represents his rethinking, in the light of Jesus and the divine spirit, of the fundamental Jewish beliefs: monotheism (of the creational and covenantal sort), election, and eschatology. This theology was integrated with the rethought narrative world at every point.[20]

Here, N. T. Wright orients us in the right direction insofar as we seek to answer the question of how Paul dealt with his Jewish thought world once he became a Christian. However, we need also to inquire about the things Paul derived from his more proximate Christians sources, such as Jerusalem Christians such as Peter, James the brother of Jesus, and John. I will speak to the latter issue first.

Early Christian Prayers and Confessions in the Pauline Letters

The logical place to start is by examining Aramaic material found in our sources, as this material surely must go back to Palestinian Christianity and perhaps back to the earliest Jewish Christian community of all in Jerusalem. Thus we begin by looking at use of the term *Abba* in two places in Paul's letters, Romans 8:15 and Galatians 4:6. In both texts we are told that it is the Holy Spirit in the life of the Christian believer who prompts the invocation of or cry to God as Abba. It thus appears that Paul is linking the use of *Abba* to a form of ecstatic utterance, or at least he sees it as an example of the Spirit speaking through the believer.

Yet Paul is addressing non–Palestinian Christians who are doing this praying, certainly including some Gentiles (see, e.g., Rom 10:13; Gal 2:8), and it is very probable that these non-Palestinan non-Jewish Christians did not know Aramaic. Notice too that Romans 8:15 indicates that *Abba* is the common cry or prayer of both Paul and his audience, suggesting its widespread use, even in Rome, where most Christians likely were Gentiles.

The use of *Abba* is seen as the sign that the speaker is an heir of God, a joint heir with Christ, a child of God. I suggest that the reference to being joint heirs with Christ has to do with the fact that Paul knows that Jesus prayed "Abba" and is suggesting that just as this was the cry of the Son who is the heir, so also it is the cry of the sons and daughters who are joint heirs.[21] We

---

[20]N. T. Wright, *The New Testament and the People of God*, vol. 1 of *Christian Origins and the Question of God* (Minneapolis: Fortress, 1992), p. 407.

[21]At this juncture, the reader should review the discussion about Jesus and the use of *Abba* in the first volume of this work. See Ben Witherington III, *The Individual Witnesses*, vol. 1 of *The Indel-*

discover that Jesus and Paul talk about the Father in the same way. This part of the symbolic world remains unchanged from Jesus to Paul, even to the extent of seeing "Abba" as the proper way to address God in prayer.

It is also possible that these texts, especially Romans 8:15, suggest that the Holy Spirit prompts glossolalia in the form of non-Aramaic speakers addressing God in Aramaic. In fact, Galatians 4:6 indicates that it is the Spirit who is crying "Abba! Father!"[22] and this is what Romans 8:16 suggests as well. Romans 8:26 may also be about this same phenomenon ("the Spirit intercedes with sighs too deep for words"). In any case, these texts speak of a depth of communication with God that suggests a deeply felt intimacy between God and the one who prays. The earliest Christian worship not only was heartfelt, but also was Spirit-inspired and probably involved charismatic utterances "in other tongues." Especially the Romans text suggests that it was Jesus, by example and through his mediatorship ("joint heirs"), that initiated the believer into this sort of filial relationship with God and this sort of prayer language, though now it is the Spirit who enables the believer to pray in this fashion.

The next Aramaic phrase is found in 1 Corinthians 16:22. Here again we seem to have some sort of prayer language in Aramaic. There is debate over whether the original phrase involved just the *maranatha* phrase or whether it was originally *anathema maranatha* in view of the first part of the verse. However, if, as many think, Revelation 22:20 is a translation and further example of the *maranatha* phrase, then it seems that *maranatha* stood alone in the prayer (cf. Jude 14). How the key phrase should be translated is partly determined by whether we divide it as *maran atha* or as *marana tha*. Does the phrase mean "Our Lord has/is come" or "Our Lord, come"? In view of the parallels in Revelation 22:20 and Jude 14, it probably is the latter.

The term *mare* means "lord," but it is hardly plausible that here it merely means "master" or "respected sir." One does not pray to a deceased rabbi or revered master teacher to come. Here the term must mean more than "lord," more like "Lord" with the implication of divinity of some sort. This prayer has not only christological but also eschatological significance, reflecting a

ible Image: The Theological and Ethical Thought World of the New Testament (Downers Grove, Ill.: IVP Academic, 2009), pp. 96-100.
[22]Note, however, that *Abba* is clearly translated as "Father" here, which may suggest that the Gentiles in the audience were told the meaning of this word early on, and in mixed congregations the translation became part of the form of address. It could also be that the translation is not part of the prayer, but in each case is simply Paul's translation of the invocation for his audiences.

belief not only in Jesus as Lord, but also as a Lord who would return. At a very early date, then, Jewish Christians prayed to Jesus as Lord, but this was not only the language of prayer, but also the language of the earliest confession.

If we ask how it was that early Jewish Christians came to address Jesus not merely as "lord" but rather as "Lord," we must consider the confessional fragments found in Philippians 2:11 especially, and also 1 Corinthians 12:3 and Romans 10:9. The confession "Jesus is Lord" was one of the early Christian confessions, perhaps the earliest, and Philippians 2:11 especially helps us to see what it meant. It meant Jesus is the risen Lord, which is to say that this was a brief summary of the story of the risen Jesus, a way of alluding to the whole tale in a shorthand fashion. The title "Lord" was appropriate only after Jesus had completed his earthly work, including being obedient even unto death on the cross. The hymn in Philippians 2:6-11 tells us that the name was bestowed on Jesus by God as a result of the successful completion of his mission. I will say much more about this hymn shortly, but we should note that the name being bestowed on Jesus was God's Old Testament (LXX) name, *kyrios* ("Lord"), the divine name, which is a name above all others. In other words, the earliest confession of Christians was a very high christological one indeed that reflected the church's response to the Easter experiences.

In the second text, 1 Corinthians 12:3, we get a contrast between saying "Anathema Jesus" and "Jesus is Lord." Paul, writing this letter only a little over two decades after Jesus' death, speaks of the confession as something that would be familiar to his Corinthian converts, something that they themselves probably had confessed at conversion. It is the Holy Spirit who prompts and guides the believer to make a true confession. Only someone with the Holy Spirit in his or her life can do so. Again we have clear evidence that it was only a very high christological assertion that got one recognized as a Christian, at least in the Pauline communities.

There were, of course, many gods and lords in the Greco-Roman world, as Paul acknowledges in 1 Corinthians 8:5, but the confession of Jesus as Lord was something different. All the Greek and Roman gods or heroes being called *kyrios* were either mythological figures or legendary figures from hoary antiquity, whereas Jesus was a historical figure about whom many still had living memory. It is also true that during the first century A.D., beginning with Augustus, many emperors were being divinized, not just after their deaths but during their lives as well. By the end of the century, Domitian felt comfortable insisting that he be called *deus et dominus noster* ("God and our Lord"). Thus, it is possible that the Christian confession was in part an attempt to distinguish the worship of Jesus from emperor worship and other forms of pagan worship. In terms of the Christian storied world, Jesus is seen as the reality of which the emperor is merely the parody.[23]

This particular co-opting of the emperor's rhetoric or story may also in part explain formulations such as "the Lord Jesus Christ," which bears a certain resemblance to "Imperator Caesar Augustus." Notice how in 1 Corinthians 12:3 the confession of Jesus is connected with its opposite, cursing Jesus. I suspect that various scholars are right who have suggested that it was not in the first place the study of the Old Testament by early Christians or even the study of Jesus' teachings that prompted this confession but rather the experiences of the risen, and later of the ascended, Lord. Certainly the *maranatha* confession implies the heavenly position of Christ and his divine ability in due course to come.

The third text is Romans 10:9, which clearly is given in a confessional context. This text is important in several regards. First, confessing that Jesus is Lord and believing that God raised him from the dead are paralleled. This strongly suggests that the confessional formula entailed the proposition "Jesus is the risen Lord." Second, not just heartfelt belief but confessing with one's lips is, in Paul's view, instrumental to being saved. Here again we note that the earliest post-Easter christological discussions seem to have focused on Jesus as Lord. Notice too that here the connection between the story of the risen Jesus is clearly connected to the confession of him as Lord. This was to become the most paradigmatic of all stories in Paul's storied world.

Romans 10:9 leads us to examine briefly another text widely regarded as reflecting a primitive confessional formula: Romans 1:3-4.[24] Here we find two parallel phrases being applied to Jesus: (1) he was born of the family of David according to the flesh; (2) he was appointed or installed Son of God in power according to the Spirit of holiness by resurrection from the dead. The result of these two facts is a third one: he is "Jesus Christ our Lord." What is important here is that the story of Jesus' human origins is linked with the story of his divine vindication. This reminds us once more, if we needed a

---

[23]As N. T. Wright likes to put it.
[24]For a fuller discussion of this important text, see Ben Witherington III, *Paul's Narrative Thought World: The Tapestry of Tragedy and Triumph* (Louisville: Westminster John Knox, 1994), pp. 117-19. It is interesting that Paul, Mark, and the speeches of Acts reflect no knowledge that Jesus was born in Bethlehem, and yet all of these sources know of and affirm the claim that he was of Davidic descent.

reminder, that in Paul's storied world, as in Jesus' storied world, God is deeply involved, and the interaction between the human and the divine on the stage of human history is profound.

Several exegetical notes are necessary at this point. First, the phrase "in power" likely modifies "Son of God," not "appointed." Second, the key participle *horisthentos* most likely means "appointed, installed," not "declared." Third, it is possible to interpret the preposition *ek* to mean either "by" or "from the time of" (= "since"). Finally, it is possible to see three clauses here rather than two: (1) "his Son born of the seed of David according to the flesh"; (2) "appointed Son of God in power according to the Spirit of holiness"; (3) "since the resurrection of the dead, Jesus Christ our Lord." If so, the confession has three parts, having to do first with what Jesus was in himself by physical birth, and then as a result of the work of God's Spirit in his life after death, and finally what he has been to and for believers ever since the resurrection, namely, their Lord.[25]

It is clear enough that Paul is not saying that Jesus became the Son of God at the resurrection, but rather that he became the Son of God in power at that point, having previously been Son of God in weakness. The way the beginning of Romans 1:3 is phrased also suggests that Paul saw Jesus as God's Son already at the point of his physical birth; it was the Son who was born of David's seed. Whether or not one accepts the suggested threefold division of the confession, it seems clear enough that the text is indicating that Jesus assumed the role of Lord over his followers since (and probably because of) his resurrection from the dead. In other words, much of Pauline Christology can only be properly explicated in a story or narratival form, as we are dealing not with abstract ideas but rather with events in which a real historical person was involved.

A good deal more could be said about the early prayers and confessions of the first Jewish Christians, but I must summarize here the import of this material for a discussion of the storied world of Paul and other of the earliest Christians. (1) It was considered appropriate to pray to or confess Jesus in the same way God was prayed to or confessed. (2) It was considered appropriate to call Jesus, at least after his resurrection, by the title used in the Old Testament of God, *kyrios*. This title denoted a relationship between the believer and Jesus that formerly Jewish believers had recognized as appropriate only

---

[25]For the details on this exegesis, see Ben Witherington III and Darlene Hyatt, *Paul's Letter to the Romans: A Socio-Rhetorical Commentary* (Grand Rapids: Eerdmans, 2004).

to describe the relationship of God and the believer. (3) It was believed that Jesus assumed after his resurrection and ascension a lordship role that he had not previously undertaken; (4) Closely parallel to this last point is the assumption that Jesus was installed (in heaven) as Son of God in power by means of the Spirit and after the resurrection. (5) It was believed that Jesus as Lord would return at some point, and this was prayed for. (6) It was believed that Christians were enabled to be in a relationship to God the Father of the same sort of intimacy that Jesus as a human being had while on earth, such that the Spirit prompted Christians to call God "Abba" as Jesus had done and to recognize their filial relationship to God that also made them heirs, joint heirs with Christ. (7) It was the Holy Spirit who was said to enable believers to offer prayers from the heart to God and true confessions from the heart about Jesus to the world. But early Christians not only prayed and confessed, they also sang the story of Jesus. We must now consider these hymn fragments found in a variety of places in the New Testament.

A CLOSER LOOK: THE CHRIST HYMNS SUNG BY PAUL AND OTHERS

Well before the time of Jesus, early Jews were already singing the praises of God's Wisdom and Word as encapsulated in Torah, as can be seen even in the canonical psalms (e.g., Pss 1; 119). This praise developed considerably during the intertestamental time to include the praise of the personification of Wisdom, as is especially seen in texts such as Wisdom of Solomon 7–8.[26] Thus, with regard to the New Testament hymn fragments, we are dealing not with creations out of nothing but rather with songs that drew on several sources for their material: (1) the Old Testament song book, the Psalms; (2) Wisdom literature, particularly Wisdom hymns; (3) early Christian material about the life, death, and exaltation of Jesus. The story about Jesus was articulated in song long before there were written Gospels, and while it is fair to say that it was not necessarily born in song, it certainly was amplified and proclaimed in song. What I would stress just on the basis of the three points about sources listed above is the creativity in handling Israel's stories and the new Jesus stories and blending them together in various ways. A new storied world was in the process of being born, and we see it in these hymnic texts.

To a large extent, christological storytelling grew out of early Christian experiences of the risen Lord both individually and in corporate worship, as well as out of early Christian reflection upon the Gospel stories and Jesus' traditions. Lest we make too sharp a distinction between the before and after (Easter) factors affect-

---

[26]See Witherington, *Jesus the Sage*, pp. 249-94, and the literature cited there.

ing christological storytelling, we should remember that the earliest christological prayers, confessions, and hymns were in all likelihood first formulated by some of those who had been a part of Jesus' ministry before Easter and could compare and relate the before-and-after factors that affected their reflection and reenvisioning of their Jewish thought world. In general, the material in the hymns about Jesus' death and resurrection seems to draw on the early Gospel source material, whereas the material about the Son's preexistence and incarnation draws on the Wisdom literature, and finally the material about Jesus' exaltation and roles at the right hand of God tends to draw on the psalms.

It will be seen from close scrutiny of what follows that the early christological stories in song had a characteristic V-pattern chronicling the preexistence, earthly existence, and postexistence of the Son. In short, they were exercises in narrative Christology tracing the full career of the Son, not just his earthly ministry. What this fuller presentation of Christ involved was discussing his role in creation as well as redemption. That we find these hymn fragments in a variety of sources (Pauline letters, Hebrews, the Gospel of John) shows, as Martin Hengel stressed, that there was a much more unified structure to early christological thinking done in a variety of Christian communities than some New Testament scholars are willing to recognize. More to the point for our purposes here, we find a clear window into the narrative thought world and symbolic universe of the earliest Christians that demonstrates beyond a shadow of a doubt the enormous amount of shared thought about Jesus and other things of these believers, however little or much they articulated it or exposited about it as they theologized and ethicized into specific situations.[27]

Philippians 2:6-11. The first hymn for consideration is found in Philippians 2:6-11. This is in some respects the fullest manifestation of the hymnic structure, with all three portions of the V-pattern or, perhaps better said, U-pattern manifested.[28] It is characteristic of these hymns that they tend to skip directly from the birth to the death of Christ, focusing on the moments of especial soteriological and christological importance during Jesus' earthly sojourn (cf., e.g., Rev 12). We will start with a fresh translation.

Part I

Who, being in the form of God,

did not consider having equality with God something to take advantage of,

but stripped/emptied himself,

---

[27]Martin Hengel, "Christological Titles in Early Christianity," in *The Messiah: Developments in Earliest Judaism and Christianity*, ed. James H. Charlesworth (Minneapolis: Fortress, 1992), p. 443.

[28]A *U* better represents the notion that Christ came and stayed on earth for a while; he did not merely touch down and then immediately reascend into heaven, as a *V* might suggest.

taking the form of a servant,

being born in the likeness of human beings,

and being found in appearance like a human being,

humbled himself, being obedient to the point of death,

even death on the cross.

Part II

That is why God has highly exalted him

and gave him the name, the one above all names,

in order that at the name of Jesus

all knees will bend—those in heaven, on earth, and under the earth—

and all tongues confess publicly that Jesus Christ is LORD

unto the glory of God the Father.

First, this hymn is not likely an attempt to contrast Christ with Adam, the latter being the disobedient one who grasped at divinity, the former being the obedient one who did not. That interpretation is largely based on a dubious rendering of the key term *harpagmos* as "grasp." Nothing is said here about Jesus making a choice on earth parallel to Adam's choice in the garden; rather, the choice to be a servant was made by the Son in heaven before his human nature was assumed. The language of the "last Adam," or about Christ beginning a new race, or about Christ being the firstfruits of a new creation by means of resurrection is entirely absent here. Furthermore, an early Jewish Christian person, being thoroughly monotheistic, would not likely have thought it appropriate to call a human being such as Adam, even the last Adam, *kyrios*. The contrast between being in the form of God and becoming in the form of human beings would make little sense if what was being contrasted was two stages in the life of a mere mortal. It is not Adam's tale that is being retold and reformed here; rather, it is the story of God's Wisdom come in the flesh, God's preexistent Son come in person.

The term *morphē* always signifies an outward form that truly and fully expresses the real being that underlies it. As applied to Christ, this means not that he merely appeared to have the form of God, but rather that he had a form that truly manifested the very nature and being of God. This is the reason the further phrase says what it does: Christ had equality with God. He had by right and nature what God had. In this matter it is useful to compare the parallel text in 2 Corinthians 8:9, where too the preexistent Christ is said to humble himself and become poor for our sake. What is so important for our purposes is that we are being told that the Son of God is part of both the story of God and the story of humankind. He is not merely the mediator between these two stories; he is an active participant in both stories.

The word *harpagmos* has been the subject of endless debate. Does it refer to something that a person has and clutches, or does it refer to something that a person desires and tries to seize or grab? The "clutching" interpretation is nearer the mark, but the most probable way to read the word is that it refers to not taking advantage of something that one rightfully already has. The contrast then between Philippians 2:6b and Philippians 2:7a becomes clear. Christ did not see being equal with God as something that he had to take advantage of; instead, he stripped himself, which likely means that he set aside his rightful divine prerogatives or perhaps his glory in order to be fully and truly human. This need not mean that he set aside his divine nature, but only that he did not draw on his rightful divine prerogatives while on earth. He took on limitations of time, space, knowledge, and perhaps power while on earth. But in fact, Christ went even further, identifying with the lowest sort of human, a slave, a person without any rights. When it says that he "humbled" himself, the term *tapeinoō* has almost its literal secular sense, that he became like a slave, one who must serve all others, one who is obedient even unto death.

The exaltation part of the hymn alludes to Isaiah 45:21-25, which says that only God is God and Savior, and that one should bow only to God. Christ now is given God's very name and deserves such homage. N. T. Wright calls this "christological monotheism," a form of monotheism that wishes to assert the divinity of Christ without taking away from the glory of the Father and without denying that there is only one true God.[29] Nevertheless, when you change the story, it is clear enough that your symbolic world has changed, and something fundamental and basic has changed in the way you view God and the world of reality.

The hymn, then, is divided into two major parts, speaking of what Christ chooses to do (Phil 2:6-8) and what God has done for him as result of what he did (Phil 2:9-11). In this hymn Christ is portrayed not just as a wise man who makes good choices and is rewarded by God in the end, but rather as God's very Wisdom who comes to earth is rejected and yet is exalted by God in the end. Read in light of Wisdom of Solomom 1–11, or the more general profile of Wisdom, or some of the material in Sirach 3; 11, the text makes good sense. Already here we see a rather explicit christological affirmation of the divinity of Christ both before and after his earthly career, and presumably during that career as well, since the text does not that say he gave up his divinity to become human. We will see that some of these other hymns are no less explicit in their christological affirmations.

---

[29]See N. T. Wright, *The Climax of the Covenant: Christ and the Law in Pauline Theology* (Edinburgh: T & T Clark, 1991), p. 116.

Colossians 1:15-20. The next hymn is found in Colossians 1:15-20 and focuses a good deal more on Christ's role in the work of creation and very little on his role since the resurrection. What we discover about the quotations of these hymns is that Paul and others have adopted and adapted them to serve the specific purposes of the document in which a particular hymn is found. This is the way they theologize out of the shared Christian thought world into specific situations.

Part I

Who is the image of the invisible God,

firstborn of all creation,

because in him were created all things,

in the heavens and upon the earth,

the seen and the unseen,

whether thrones or dominions

or sovereignties or powers.

Everything [created] through him was also created for him.

And he is before everything, and everything coheres in him.

And he is the head of the body, the church.

Part II

Who is the beginning (source),

the firstborn from the dead,

in order that he might take precedence in all things.

Because in him is pleased to dwell all the *plērōma*,

and through him is reconciled everything for him,

making peace through the blood of his cross,

whether things on earth or in the heavens.

This hymn has a rather clear parallel structure in the two stanzas, especially at the beginning of each one. The first stanza is deeply indebted to Wisdom of Solomon 6:22–8:1. It is rather clear that the author of this hymn has simply taken various ideas and phrases that were applied to Wisdom in the Wisdom of Solomon and applied them to the story of Christ's preexistence, though with certain subtle modifications. Philippians 2 and Colossians 1 contain the most similar content of the hymn fragments, though there is no "servant" discussion in Colossians 1, and there is more distinctively non-Pauline vocabulary in the Colossians hymn. It is interesting that the nadir of the V pattern in this hymn is not Christ's incarnation or death, but rather the body or church, though Paul goes on to refer to making peace through the blood of the cross. Here, as in the Philippians hymn, Christ's being the image of God means that he is the exact likeness or representation of God, so much so that it is said that the fullness of God dwells in Christ.

The "firstborn" terminology is found in each stanza, but in neither case should the reference to birth be taken literally. In the first stanza the Christ is said to be the author of all creation, so the term *prōtotokos* probably refers not to his being created but rather to his existence prior to all of creation and his precedence and supremacy over it, just as he also precedes all other in the resurrection of the dead. Colossians 1:16 in fact stresses that Christ created even the supernatural powers and principalities, all of which began as good creatures, as did the human race, but then fell and so, with humans, are said to need reconciliation to God through Christ. The *Christus victor* idea, or Christ as both creator of and later triumphant over the spiritual beings, is alluded to here.

It seems that the idea of incarnation is already implied in this hymn as it was in the Philippians hymn, for the author is saying that the person who hung the stars and created the powers is the same person who died on the cross and was the first to experience resurrection and became the reconciler of all things. This is not unthinkable, for already in Sirach 24 we find the idea of the incarnation of Wisdom on earth in the Torah. The new development here is simply the notion of an incarnation of, and in, a person. Thus, it is untrue to say that we find the notion of incarnation for the first time in John 1, as it is already at least implicit in Philippians 2 and Colossians 1.

Colossians 2:9 provides the proper commentary on the idea of *plērōma* in this hymn, which says that the whole "fullness" dwells in Christ bodily. This comment is perhaps polemical and meant to counter the idea of there being a variety of intermediaries between God and humankind, each possessing a bit of the divine within. Both here and in Philippians 2 there is a note of universalism at the end of the hymn. In Philippians 2 it is said all will bend the knee to Christ, but this may mean that some will do so willingly and some will be forced to recognize the Christ's position. Here too the meaning may be that in the end some will experience the *shalom* or peace of being reconciled to God, while others will simply be pacified, but in either case all hostilities against God and God's people will cease when the work of salvation is complete. One should compare Wisdom of Solomon 5:1-10 on all of this. The Colossian hymn emphasizes the cosmic role of Christ in creation and thus implies his divine status even before he became the Savior of all higher beings.

1 Timothy 3:16. Our next hymn fragment, 1 Timothy 3:16, also is found in the Pauline corpus, in one of its latest parts, and is indeed brief, saying nothing explicitly about preexistence but rather speaking about the Christ's role on earth and beyond. It reads as follows:

Who was revealed in flesh,
vindicated by the Spirit,
seen by angels,
proclaimed among the nations,
believed in throughout the world,
taken up in glory.

The first two lines remind us of the statements about Christ in Romans 1:3-4, but most of the ideas in this hymn fragment can be found in 1 Peter 3:18-22 as well.

It is not surprising that all the verbs in this particular hymn fragment in 1 Timothy 3:16 are in the passive tense, as we have already seen that in the second stanza of the hymn in Philippians 2 we hear of what God does to and for Christ, and the present fragment is decidedly a second stanza, though the verb "revealed" in all likelihood presumes the preexistence of the one revealed.

It is unclear whether this hymn manifests a clear chronological order, but probably it does as follows: (1) the first clause alludes to preexistence and speaks of incarnation; (2) the second refers to Jesus' resurrection by the Holy Spirit (cf. Rom 1:3-4); (3) the third phrase refers to Christ's ascent to heaven, during which, according to the early tradition found in 1 Peter 3:19-20, he preached to the spirits (i.e., angels) in prison (see also 2 Pet 2:4; Jude 6; the reference is to the sinning angels referred to in Gen 6); (4) once exalted to God's side, Christ was first preached to the nations and then (5) believed on in the world; (6) this resulted in glory for the Son (compare how the hymn in Phil 2 finishes on the note of glory). This hymn once again stresses the universal scope of Christ's work, but it is also for the first time stresses the role that believers play in finishing the task of spreading salvation to the world. The allusion to Christ's preexistence and glory are the primary portions of the hymn that hint at the divinity of Christ. As we will see, glory is at the heart of the next hymn fragment.

Hebrews 1:2b-4. At this point, I am going to take a brief detour from Paul's narrative thought world in order to demonstrate that he is not the inventor or only expositor of this christological story and its thought world. Others articulated this same story in equally profound ways, and this strongly makes the point that I have already insisted on: there is a large, shared symbolic universe and narrative thought world in early Christianity that undergirds the articulated theologies and ethicizing found in these documents. Only in the case of the material in Hebrews could we argue that it may reflect the influence of Paul.

The hymnic material in Hebrews 1:2b-4 includes the entire V-pattern speaking of the preexistence, earthly existence, and postexistence of the Son. In the preexistence portion of the hymn God is the actor, but thereafter Christ is the initiator of the action. A basic translation is as follows:

Whom he appointed heir of all things,

through whom also he made the aeons [= universe];

who, being the radiance of glory,

and the exact representation of his being,

upholding all things by his powerful word;

having made purification for sins,

he sat down on the right hand of the Majesty on high,

having become as much better than the angels as he has,

(He) has inherited a more excellent name in comparison to them.

The hymn fragment occurs, as is true of the one found in John 1, as part of the prologue of the document meant to make clear that God's revelation in his Son was full, final, and definitive in a way that previous revelations were not, and that no other beings, including angels, can compare to God's Son. The Son has more glory, a more excellent name and nature (being the exact representation of God), and he alone has made purification for sins—a major issue in this homily. In Greek this fragment is part of one long sentence that stretches from Hebrews 1:1 to Hebrews 1:4 and involves alliteration and rhythm not evident in English translations. The the author of Hebrews mainly calls Jesus "the Son," but in the hymn fragment Jesus is called by no title, and it is striking that in none of the hymn fragments under consideration here is Jesus called "the Son." Sonship Christology seems to have arisen from some other source or quarter. Various Old Testament texts are being drawn on to compose this hymn (see, e.g., Deut 32:43; Ps 2; 45:6-7; 104:4; 110:1), but it is also clear enough that the author is steeped in later Wisdom material such as that found in Wisdom of Solomon 7–8 and is saying of the Son and his glory what previously had been said of God's Wisdom.[30]

The hymn begins with the affirmation that God had a plan for the redeemer to also be the inheritor of all things and, furthermore, to be the agent through whom God created the universe. The theme of the Son as both aid in creation and inheritor of all things is by now familiar. It is the similarity of motifs and concepts in all of these hymns that shows the existence of a core set of beliefs about Christ that was widely shared in early Jewish Christianity and was propagated through

---

[30]It is true that Psalm 2 includes a sonship motif, but our author's sonship Christology can hardly be mainly attributed to or drawn from that brief reference.

the use of this hymnic material in various parts of the Diaspora by Paul and others. Not only is the Christ involved in the beginning and end of all things, but also he is the one upholding the universe by the word of his power. This is not dissimilar to the notion that in him all things cohere or hold together (see Col 1:17). In other words, the author does not see the universe as being like a watch that God wound up and left to run on its own.

In terms of christological story, Hebrews 1:3a is very important. Here we find two key terms, *apaugasma* and *charaktēr*. The first term can be taken as active or passive in sense, but in view of the background in Wisdom of Solomon 7:25-26, it is likely to be active and to mean "effulgence" rather than just "reflection." The difference is that a reflection is like a shadow, but not directly connected to the light source, whereas effulgence suggests a beam coming forth from that light source. The normal referent of the second term is a stamp or the impression that a signet ring leaves on wax or that a stamping device would make on a coin. The meaning seems to be that the redeemer bears the exact likeness of God's nature. This material is remarkably close to what we have already seen in Colossians 1:15-17, though with rearranged clauses.

The author does not want to lead his audience to call the redeemer "the Father," but he does want to make clear that the redeemer is divine, is God's final self expression and exact representation and thus higher than any angel in nature. The Son is not merely an act or power of God; he is a person who is the spitting image of the Father and so is to be worshiped as no mere angel should be. It may be right, as many have concluded, that this hymn is a rejoinder to those who wished to see Christ as some sort of special angelic being, but it is also possible that the author is stressing that the new covenant is superior to the one that was mediated by angels, the Mosaic covenant (cf. Acts 7:53; Gal 3:19; *Jub.* 1:29), because this one is mediated by a divine being, not merely a supernatural one. It is striking that the author withholds the human name of the redeemer until Hebrews 2:9, perhaps because he understood that the redeemer was, properly speaking, not Jesus until he took on a human nature.

Various scholars have noted closeness between this hymn and the one in Philippians 2 on the matter of Christ's obedience. In Philippians, however, it is discussed as an aspect of his relationship to the Father, whereas here it is discussed in relationship to the way it benefits the Christian community. The discussion of purification followed by the sitting down of the Son at God's right hand requires a knowledge of sacrificial practices in antiquity. The author's point is that the purification made by the Son was once for all time and thus required no repetition. Whereas other priests had to stand and repeatedly offer sacrifices, this priest did the job in such a definitive and final way that he could sit down thereafter (see Heb 10:11-15). Here the author may be drawing on Sirach 24:10, where it is said of Wisdom that she ministered before God in the earthly temple. The author's own distinctive christological thrusts can be seen and are served here as well, for he wishes to say that Christ is the believers' heavenly high priest even now, and that he is a forever priest, since he is an eternal being. The author is combining various christological insights at the end of this hymn, in particular combining the preexistent Wisdom Christology with the enthronement of the Son at or after the resurrection Christology.

The end of the hymn stresses God's endorsement of what the Son has done. Not only is he given the favored right-hand seat, the side of honor and power next to a ruler, but also he is given a divine or throne name. This theme of receiving a name is found also in Philippians 2, though here in Hebrews 1 we are not told explicitly what the name is, only that it is a higher name than angels could have. Notice, however, that here it is a matter of inheriting a better name. The concept of a messianic figure not being called such until he has completed his work is found elsewhere in *Testament of Levi* 4:2-3 and *3 Enoch* 12:15. The influence of *1 Enoch* 42 is also possible at the end of this hymn for, in that text Wisdom takes her seat among, but as one superior to, the angels when she returns from earth to heaven.

This christological hymn shows how a variety of rich traditions can be drawn on and blended together to present a striking and divine image of God's Son as an eternal being who bears God's exact likeness. It is another example of christological monotheism, which perhaps receives its ultimate expression in our final hymn text, the prologue in John 1. Equally importantly, it shows how the story of Christ could absorb and transform and transcend other earlier stories.

John 1. There are at least four stanzas to the hymn material in John 1, and most scholars see this material as the apex of the expression of incarnational thinking about Christ in the canon, though we have noted that the idea of incarnation was likely present in Philippians 2, Colossians 1, and Hebrews 1, if not also in 1 Timothy. Thus, what we find in this hymn is not a radical departure from what we have already seen in the christological hymns, but rather is a further development thereof. There are several major themes in this hymn, including (1) the preexistent Word *(logos);* (2) the Word and creation; (3) the response of those created (rejection); (4) incarnation and revelation; (5) the response of the faithful community ("we have seen his glory"). The first two stages of the V-pattern, preexistence and earthly existence, are the focus of this hymn. Like the hymn in Hebrews 1, the

material in John 1 is used to establish at the outset the character and career of the
main character of the book. The author of the Fourth Gospel is, however, concerned about where the Word is going as well as where he came from, and indeed
especially in this Gospel it is made evident that one cannot truly understand the
Christ and his character unless one knows about his divine origins and destiny. In
all probability, John 1:6-9, concerning John the Baptizer, is not an original part of
the hymn, and so it likely originally read as follows:

> In the beginning was the Word,
> and the Word was with God,
> and the Word was God.
> He was with God in the beginning.
>
> Through him all things were made.
> Without him nothing came to be.
> In him was life,
> and this life was the light of humankind.
> The light shines in the darkness,
> and the darkness has not overcome/understood it.
>
> He was in the world,
> and though the world was made by him,
> it did not recognize/respond to him.
> To his own he came,
> yet his own did not receive him.
> But all those who did accept him
> he empowered to become children of God.
> [Jn 1:12b-13 is the author's explanatory insertion about how one
>   becomes such a child.]
>
> And the Word became flesh
> and dwelt among us.
> And we beheld his glory,
> the glory of the only begotten Son of the Father,
> full of grace and truth.

It has often been noted that this hymn is indebted to Genesis 1, but less frequently has it been recognized that what this hymn is most indebted to is the
sapiential interpretation of Genesis 1 found in texts such as Proverbs 3 or Proverbs
8:1–9:6. It must also be kept in mind that Torah and Wisdom are seen as interrelated, the former being the consummate expression on earth of the latter, according to Wisdom literature (see Sir 24). We also should recall the interplay of

Wisdom and Word in the Wisdom of Solomon. The two terms are used in parallel in Wisdom of Solomon 9:1-2, in Wisdom of Solomon 9:10 it is Wisdom that is said to be sent from God's throne by God, and in Wisdom of Solomon 18:15 we hear that God's "all-powerful Word leaped from heaven, from the royal throne into the midst of the land." At the very end of this hymn we learn, however, that the Son or Word eclipses this Torah. Interestingly, in Sirach 24:8 Wisdom is said to "tent" in Israel in Torah. In other words, what has been previously said about Torah as the repository of Wisdom is now being said of Christ. That phrases are being used in this hymn that were familiar in early Judaism can be seen by examining 1QS XI, 11: "All things come to pass by his knowledge. He establishes all things by his design, and without him nothing is done [or 'made']." The phrase "full of grace and truth" in John 1:17 is reminiscent of the Colossian idea of Christ being the *plērōma* or "fullness" of God, another hint that all of these hymns likely came out of the same sort of situation in life.

The very first verse of the prologue is in some ways the most important verse of that text and indeed of the whole Fourth Gospel. The author wants to make clear from the outset that the deeds and words of Jesus, God's Word and Son, are the deeds and words of a divine being, and not of a created supernatural being either, for he existed prior to all creation. That he is said to be *monogenēs* (Jn 1:14, 18) may mean that he is the unique Son, but more probably it means that like produces like, and that the Son has come forth from the Father having the same nature, not like those other distinct beings who were made by the Father and the Word. Jesus, then, is seen as the natural Son of God, whereas others are the adopted sons and-daughters of God through the new birth.

The Word is said to be involved in the whole scope of the divine work. Nothing was created and nothing is saved without him. Light and life are benefits of both the creation and the recreation that comes from and through the Word. There is great irony in what is said in the third stanza: the creatures rejected the one who created them when they rejected his offer of salvation. In fact, the real statement of the incar- nation does not come until John 1:14, where we are told that the Word took on flesh, or reached the human stage. The point is that the Word became more than he was before, not less, adding a human to his divine nature. There is no "emptying" lan- guage here. As Ernst Käsemann once asserted, in this whole Gospel Jesus bestrides the stage of history like a God, and there is truth to this claim.

Although the stay of the Word on earth was of limited duration so that only some saw his glory, all have an opportunity to benefit from the Word's coming, all can received grace and truth at any time by believing. Truth in the Fourth Gospel always refers to saving truth, not just accurate information. Moses and Torah gave accurate information about God's will and plan, but the Word gave the ability to perform God's will and truly understand that plan. Although it is a bit of an overstatement, E. D. Freed was basically right when he remarked, "It may not be going too far to say that the writer of the logos verses in John has scarcely done more than add the technical term logos to a Christology which had already been formulated by Paul and others."[31]

Summary. I must now draw this discussion of the hymns to a close. It appears that the creators of these various hymns were concerned to make clear that the subject being discussed was a person, not merely a divine attribute or power of God. In each of these hymns in one way or another, whether through reference to death on a cross or making purification for sins, or by reference to flesh, the author makes clear that he is talking about a real human figure who acted on the stage of history. In other words, here was an attempt to guard against these hymns being understood as mere myth-making.

When Jewish Christians composed these hymns, they sought and found exalted language from their Jewish heritage that they believed gave adequate expression to their faith in Christ. They found particularly appropriate the using of earlier hymnic material praising God's Wisdom found in places such as Proverbs 8–9, Sirach 24, and Wisdom of Solomon 7–9 to praise Christ. It seems probable that these hymns were composed in Greek, especially in view of their indebtedness to Wisdom of Solomon, which may mean that they arose in the Diaspora, but this is by no means necessarily the case, not least because there were already Greek-speaking Christians who were part of the earliest Jerusalem church, if we are to believe Acts 6–7. In any case, there is no reason to see any of these hymns as reflecting late Gentile thinking about Jesus.

The hymns are thoroughly Jewish in their concepts and phrases, and even in the V-pattern they are indebted to earlier Jewish literature about Wisdom. The earliest Christians were groping for a way to adequately praise the divine Christ and at the same time not relinquish a belief in the one true God. The early Jewish discussion of the relationship between God and God's Wisdom facilitated this sort of christological development, and this surely transpired well before the Gospels were written. This in turn reminds us, as we return to the discussion of Paul's storied world, that Paul was not a unique innovator of this sort of complex theological storytelling. Other had gone before him and stood beside him and were doing the same sorts of theologizing.

---

[31]E. D. Freed, "Theological Prelude and the Prologue of John's Gospel," *SJT* 32 (1979): 266.

The Narratological Approach to Paul's Thought in Contemporary Scholarship
Of the many ways to examine Paul's storied world, one of the more fruitful ones is to observe how he handles Old Testament stories. Occasionally Paul will retell some of these stories, and occasionally they bubble up to the surface in a relatively full form (see, e.g., 1 Cor 10; Gal 4), but by and large they function as the presupposition, the subtext of what we actually find in Paul's letters. Like a tune always playing in Paul's head that occasionally we hear the apostle humming or singing, Paul's storied world provides the music, the harmony, the inspiration of and for his life and thought processes. Just as we might overlook the revealing tune a companion was humming as we walked and talked, so in the past many have overlooked this important and revealing dimension of the apostle's thought world. This oversight is now being remedied by a variety of scholars. Because it is more controversial to some to treat Paul's thought as essentially narratological in shape than it is to treat Jesus' thought that way, I need to interact briefly with some of the scholars who have pioneered this approach to Paul's thought and who have led us away from the old deductive, systematic theology sorts of approaches.

Before I discuss the substance and major exponents of the narratological trend in Pauline studies, I must emphasize that this approach to Paul's thought, like this approach to Jesus' thought, does not arise out of the postmodern interest in story and the logic and discourse of narratives, though that is surely in some cases a contributing factor. To the contrary, it arises to a substantial degree out of the recognition that Paul was an ancient person. He was not a post-Enlightenment theologian or ethicist or philosopher, and the attempt to reduce his letters to such categories is anachronistic. This is not to say that Paul did not use ancient Greek forms of syllogistic logic from time to time (see, e.g., 1 Cor 15:12-19), but by and large Paul's logic is a narrative one. It has to do with stories about Adam, Abraham, Moses, Israel, Christ, himself, and Christians. Unless one has a sense of the scope and dimensions of the drama out of which Paul lives and thinks, it is difficult to understand how the individual parts or details of his thought world fit together.

Prior to the rise of narratological studies of Paul, it often had been suggested by Pauline scholars that Paul's thought is essentially ad hoc, essentially a response to a situation in the life of some church that he finds he must address. Because this approach still prevails in many quarters, it is necessary to justify briefly the narratological approach to Paul's thought by interaction with its chief exponents.

The narratological approach to Paul's letters suggests that it is only partially correct to focus on the way the social situation prompts Paul to say what he does. This approach is significantly misleading if taken to be the key to making sense of Paul's thought world. The situations that Paul addresses prompt or cause him to articulate his thoughts in one way or another, but those thoughts by and large have arisen as a result of his deep and profound reflection on his preexisting symbolic universe and the narratives that mold all his thought.

The Paul encountered in the extant letters had been a mature Christian for many years before they were written. Even in the case of the earliest of these letters, perhaps Galatians or 1 Thessalonians, Paul had been a Christian for more than a decade and had undergone an incredible diversity of experiences, many of them difficult and dangerous, during that time. Whatever development of Paul's thought that may have taken place, it appears for the most part to have taken place before any of the extant letters were written. Even in the crucial matter of Christology there is precious little development that can be traced in Paul's later letters, apart perhaps for more emphasis on the role of Christ in relationship to the cosmos. Thus, a narratological approach to Paul's thought emphasizes that the contingent situations that Paul faced affected how and when he articulated different aspects of his thought but did not determine that thought.

Norman Petersen is close to the mark: "Paul integrates his social instructions within a symbolic universe [and storied world] rather than a social one, for the consequences of compliance or noncompliance are not determined socially, that is by social actors, but eschatologically by the Lord. In this respect, therefore the force of Paul's instructions is derived from the symbolic universe which makes them nonnegotiable and gives them the status of commands."[32] These comments are about Pauline ethics, but Petersen rightly goes on to add that for Paul, "theology is a form of systematic reflection upon prior knowledge"[33] I would add the qualifier "most of the time." One must also add to this remark that Paul's storehouse of knowledge involves certain paradigmatic stories. One of the main implications of the narratological approach to Paul's thought for such a study can be stated here. The distinction between a coherent core and a contingent fringe of Paul's thought is not a very useful model for understanding the apostle. Contingency has to do with the mode or manner of Paul's expression, not, for the most part, the matter expressed.

---

[32]Petersen, *Rediscovering Paul*, p. 135.
[33]Ibid., p. 202.

The narratological approach to Paul's letters is one of the more recent trends in Pauline studies, and so there are few full-dress attempts to read Paul's thought this way. We can see something of a narratological approach to the whole study of New Testament material in N. T. Wright's *New Testament and the People of God*, where he says that "human writing is best conceived as . . . the telling of stories which bring worldviews into articulation."[34] This in itself would not necessarily signal that Wright sees a narrative substructure to Paul's or other New Testament writers' thought, but he goes on to say, following Petersen, that each of Paul's letters has a narrative world that is presupposed by the text. Then, going even further, Wright asks, "What were the stories which give narrative depth to Paul's worldview, which formed an irreducible part of his symbolic universe?"[35] and then he stresses that "it is arguable that we can only understand the more limited narrative worlds of the different letters if we locate them at their appropriate points within this overall story-world, and indeed within the symbolic universe that accompanies it."[36]

Wright then gives a brief sketch of his reading of Paul's narrative thought world, with a promise that he intends to elucidate it more fully in the fourth volume of his series *Christian Origins and the Question of God*. The stress in Wright's reading of Paul's thought world is that it is a thoroughly Jewish thought world without any significant indebtedness to Greco-Roman thought, and that Israel is at the heart of the story, though there is an intriguing twist to the story that most early Jews would have found unexpected: it is in and through Jesus of Nazareth that the role of Abraham in relationship to the world and the promises to Abraham are fulfilled. The "*story of Jesus*, interpreted precisely within the wider Jewish narrative world, was the hinge upon which Paul's rereading of that larger story [of Israel] turned."[37] Wright's analysis is a work in progress, so it remains to be seen how he will more carefully elucidate the Pauline data.

A fuller version of this sort of approach to Paul surfaces in two works by Richard Hays, *The Faith of Jesus Christ* and *Echoes of Scripture in the Letters of Paul*.[38] The burden of Hays's earlier work is to establish that a story about

---

[34]Wright, *New Testament and the People of God*, p. 65.

[35]Ibid., p. 404.

[36]Ibid., p. 405.

[37]Ibid., p. 407.

[38]Richard B. Hays, *The Faith of Jesus Christ: An Investigation of the Narrative Substructure of Galatians 3:1–4:11* (SBLDS 56; Chico, Calif.: Scholars Press, 1983); *Echoes of Scripture in the Letters of Paul*

Jesus is foundational for Paul's theological and ethical formulations in his letters.[39] The story that Hays has in mind includes not only the earthly existence of Jesus and his death and resurrection but also his preexistence, such that the Christ story follows a decided V-pattern of preexistence, earthly existence, and exaltation to God's right hand after or by means of resurrection. Hays also stresses that because Paul's language is "highly allusive and . . . depends heavily on the foundational language of story, we must also reckon with another possible implication: perhaps Paul's language is less univocal and more 'poetic' than the Western theological tradition has usually supposed."[40] We saw something of the poetic character of Paul's thought in my earlier discussion of Paul's handling of the hymn material.

Hays's *Echoes of Scripture in the Letters of Paul* is a study in intertextuality, which is to say that he is interested how the larger context of various passages in the Hebrew Scriptures are alluded to and depended upon in Paul's letters. The focus is on Paul as an exegete and on his hermeneutical moves as he contextualizes and contemporizes the Old Testament text for his own audience. In short, there is actually less discussion here of the broader narrative substructure of Paul's thought and more of the way the stories in the Old Testament shape Paul's discourse. This serves as a nice complementary study to his earlier work, which focused on the story of Jesus himself. More recently, Ross Wagner, a former doctoral student of Hays, followed this intertextual echo approach with illuminating results.[41]

Stephen Fowl has focused in a more concentrated fashion on the way Paul's own presupposed narrative about the Christ shapes his ethics.[42] The stress on the imitation of Christ is seen to be grounded in the foundational story of the Christ. Yet Fowl also points out how the Old Testament stories, such as the story of the suffering servant and the story of Abraham, provide not merely a substructure or foundation but exemplars for Christians to follow.[43] In my book *Paul's Narrative Thought World* I present a full-scale proposal along these

---

(New Haven: Yale University Press, 1989). The former volume is a revision of Hays's doctoral dissertation, and the latter is the much celebrated sequel.

[39]See Hays, *Faith of Jesus Christ*, p. 256.

[40]Ibid., p. 265.

[41]See J. Ross Wagner, *Heralds of the Good News: Isaiah and Paul "in Concert" in the Letter to the Romans* (NovTSup 101; Leiden: Brill, 2002). See also J. Ross Wagner, C. Kavin Rowe, and A. Katherine Grieb, eds., *The Word Leaps the Gap: Essays on Scripture and Theology in Honor of Richard B. Hays* (Grand Rapids: Eerdmans, 2008).

[42]See Stephen E. Fowl, *The Story of Christ in the Ethics of Paul: An Analysis of the Function of the Hymnic Material in the Pauline Corpus* (JSNTSup 36; Sheffield: JSOT Press, 1990).

[43]Ibid., pp. 61-63, 94.

lines, and so a précis of that volume's results is in order.[44] I did not come to a narratological study of Paul as a result of postmodern interest in narrative. Indeed, to the contrary, my interest in this subject arose in part because of my own literary background as a writer and a student of English literature, and also because of the influence of a little book that my doctoral supervisor, C. K. Barrett, wrote some time ago entitled *From First Adam to Last*.[45]

This brings up an important point. Not all narratological studies of Paul's thought start with the same premises or take the same approach to this subject. The works of Hays and Wagner are chiefly what are known as studies in intertextuality, where echoes of the Old Testament texts are listened for in Paul's own texts. The approach that I take is of a broader nature than intertexual studies in that some of the narrative substructure of Paul's thought comes not from a text, such as the Old Testament, but from Christian oral tradition that he has inherited and passed along (see, e.g., 1 Cor 15:3-8). I am interested in all the formative narratives that shape Paul's thought world, whether or not these narratives can be found in the Old Testament. This sort of approach is closer to some of what we find in Wright's important work and in Hays's earliest work.

Five Stories That Shaped Paul's Worldview

Here, in summary form, are the formative narratives that I see Paul grounded in, reflecting on, and using. They are five interwoven stories comprising one large drama: (1) the story of God, the one who existed before all worlds and made them; (2) the story of the world gone wrong in Adam; (3) the story of God's people in that world, from Abraham to Moses and beyond; (4) the story of the Jewish messiah, the Christ, which arises out of the story of both humankind and of Israel, but in fact arises out of the larger story of God as creator and redeemer; (5) the story of Christians, including Paul himself, which arises out of the second, third, and fourth stories.

The stories of Christ and Christians are in various ways closely knit together such that they begin to tell the tale of how the world is being set right again. Christ's story is the center in the middle of this narrative tapestry or, to put it another way, the hinge, the crucial turning point, bringing to a climax the previous stories and determining how the rest of the story will play out

---

[44]Ben Witherington III, *Paul's Narrative Thought World: The Tapestry of Tragedy and Triumph* (Louisville: Westminster John Knox, 1994).

[45]C. K. Barrett, *From First Adam to Last: A Study in Pauline Theology* (London: Adam & Charles Black, 1962).

and turn out. The story of God's own people in effect contracts to that of the Christ, the seed of Abraham, when he comes, but it expands again to include Christ's followers. Let us consider briefly each story in turn. In a study on Paul the storyteller, some storytelling and getting the story straight are in order.

The story of God. It may come as something of a surprise to some, but Paul does not spend a good deal of time on "theology" proper in his letters. By this I mean that he does not spend nearly as much time as we might expect discussing the one whom he calls "God the Father." Of course, this is partly because for Paul, Christ is part of the story of God. In fact, Christ is the most crucial part for someone such as Paul, who is concerned about the salvation of the world and not merely with abstract or philosophical reflections on the creator God of the sort we sometimes find in, for example, the writings of Philo. The soteriological and eschatological urgencies dictate in large measure the way Paul deals with the story of God.

What, then, do we know from Paul about God's own story? First, Paul has a clear understanding that God created the world, created it good, created human beings in that world, and made them male and female in the divine image (see Rom 1:19-20; 1 Cor 11:8-12). As 1 Corinthians 11:12 says, "All things come from God." Paul is no advocate of two divinities or powers in heaven, no advocate of ontological dualism with two gods, one good and one evil, fighting it out for control of the universe. Nor does he make the mistake, as did the later Gnostics, of divorcing God from the creation by making God and spirit good but matter and the material universe evil or tainted. He is firmly committed to monotheism, as his adoption and modification of the Shema (the credo of Israel: "Hear, O Israel, the Lord our God, the Lord is one") in 1 Corinthians 8:5-6 shows. It is just that Paul's understanding of Christ and his activities have caused a reevaluation of what or whom is included in or meant by the terms *God* and *Lord*.

But for Paul, it is not just a matter of "In the beginning, God. . . ." As Paul asserts in 1 Corinthians 15:28, when all is said and done and when Christ has completed all his tasks after the second coming, "then the Son himself will also be subjected to the one who put all things in subjection under him, so that God may be all in all" (cf. Eph 1:22). Nor is it just a matter for Paul of God the Father having a role at the beginning and at the end of the drama, with Christ and the Spirit doing everything in between. William Paley's watchmaker God, who starts things going, winds up the clock, and then lets it tick on its own, is not the God of the apostle Paul.

Paul's God is continually involved in the work of creating and sustaining. For example, Paul stresses that it was God who raised Jesus from the dead (1 Cor 15:15); Jesus did not raise himself. This event in space and time shows that for Paul, God is still working, indeed continually so. Furthermore, the Father is the one who answers prayer, the one whom the believer and the Spirit within prompting the believer seeks to provide succor or salvation, comfort or consolation (Rom 8:15). Galatians 4:6 informs us that God is the one who sent the Spirit of his Son into our hearts so that we might cry out, "Abba!" We also learn that it is God who was in Christ reconciling the world to himself (2 Cor 5:18-19). Notice the stress that ultimately, even redemption and reconciliation come from God, not just from Christ: "All this is from God, who reconciles us to himself through Christ and has given us the ministry of reconciliation" (2 Cor 5:18).

When Paul reflects on his own story as well, he stresses that it was God who had set him apart before his birth and called him by grace and was pleased to reveal his Son in him (Gal 1:15-16). Much more could be said along these lines, but this will have to suffice. Paul, in the vast majority of the cases in his letters, uses the term *theos* for God the Father, not for Christ or the Trinity, though occasionally, as we will see shortly (see below on Rom 9:5), Paul is quite willing to use the term *theos* of Christ. In Paul's view, God the Father has always been the instigator and sustainer and redeemer and is no absentee landlord in a universe that he has left to its own devices. Not only is God continuing to create, sustain, and redeem, but also he is busy judging, goading and guiding, and answering prayers. The story of the Christ and of the Spirit (the Spirit "of God" or "of the Lord" [see 2 Cor 3:17-18]) is to some extent a subset of the story of the Father. This needs to be borne carefully in mind. Paul believed that he had not given up monotheism when he became a Christian. He believed that his understanding of what monotheism entailed had simply been broadened through his conversion.

The story of humankind. The story of humankind is, in Paul's view, the story of three universals. All live in this present age and are subject to its spiritual and even supernatural wickedness and problems. Indeed, even the creation itself experiences the fall (Rom 8:19-22). All live in bondage to sin, so none can be justified by their works (Rom 3:23-25). All are subject to death. Outside of Christ, one experiences the unholy trinity of the world, the flesh, and the devil, and that trinity rules in a human being's life. There is only lostness outside of Christ and a complete inability to save oneself.

But how did humankind come to be in such a drastic and dark state of affairs if God had in fact created all things good? Paul's answer is to tell the story of Adam. It is interesting that Paul says little about original righteousness or the prefallen condition. He focuses on the world as he finds it since Adam, the world whose form is passing away (1 Cor 7:31), and Adam is brought into the discussion only to explain the present malaise (Rom 5:12-21; 2 Cor 11:3). Of course, Paul knows the story of man created from the dust and given a natural life-animating principle (1 Cor 15:47-48) and the story of being created in the image of God, with Eve originally coming forth from Adam but man coming forth from woman ever since (1 Cor 11:7-12). Paul says no more about this precisely because his audience no longer lives in that world. They live in a world of dark shadows of disease, decay, death, and the devil. To be sure, humankind is not as bad as it could be; the mirror image has been bent or broken but not entirely shattered or lost. The point, however, is that humankind has fallen and cannot get up on its own. For Paul, salvation is not a human self-help program.

What is of prime importance to Paul about the story of Adam and Eve is the effect that they have had on the rest of the race. Paul mainly holds Adam responsible for the fall (Rom 5:12; 1 Cor 15:21-22), and as for Eve, she was deceived (2 Cor 11:3). Paul believes that the story of Adam and Eve is more than a personal tragedy; their story is representative and affects those who come forth after them. The original couple not only committed the original sin but also passed on both the inclination and the determination to go and do likewise. Paul concludes, "Just as sin came into the world through one man, and death came through sin, so death spread to all because all have sinned" (Rom 5:12). The progeny are like the parents in their tragedy.

One of Paul's most creative moves in telling the story of human falleness is found in Romans 7:7-13. He tells the story in the midst of commenting on the law. Paul apparently thought that the original sin was a violation of the tenth commandment, the one against coveting. In Romans 7:7-13 Paul is dealing with the paradox that while God's commandments certainly are good, human beings would not have known what transgression amounts to had there not been commandments: "I would not have known what it is to covet if the law had not said, 'You shall not covet'" (Rom 7:7).

For dramatic purposes, Paul has chosen to retell the tale of Adam in the first person and to personify sin as the snake. One can then read Romans 7:8-11 as follows: "But the serpent [sin], seizing an opportunity in the commandment, produced in me all kinds of covetousness. . . . But I [Adam] was once alive apart from the law, but when the commandment came, sin sprang to life and I died, and the very commandment that promised life proved to be death to me. For sin [the serpent], seizing an opportunity in the commandment, deceived me and through it killed me." Here is the now familiar primeval tale of life apart from sin, then comes a commandment, deception, disobedience, and ensuing death.

There are strong reasons for such a reading of Romans 7:7-13: (1) In Romans 7:7-8 there is reference to one specific commandment, referred to as *the* commandment in Romans 7:8, and Adam was given only one. (2) In Romans 7:9 Paul says, "I was living once apart from the law," but certainly the only persons Paul believed to have lived both before or apart from any law are Adam and Eve. (3) In Romans 7:11 sin is personified as a living thing that seized an opportunity and deceived a human being. This surely is the tale of Eve and Adam and the snake. (4) The verb used in Romans 7:11 for "deceive" *(exapataō)* is the same one used in 2 Corinthians 11:3 to speak directly about Eve being deceived in the garden. (5) In Romans 7:7 Paul says that sin was not known except through the commandment. But everyone since Adam has had personal or experiential knowledge of sin. The view that best makes sense of all the nuances of Romans 7:7-13 is that Paul is reflecting back on the primeval story of Adam and how human sin and fallenness began.

If Romans 7:7-13, which involves past-tense verbs, is about Adam, then whose story is told in Romans 7:14-25, where we find present-tense verbs? I suggest that it is a dramatic presentation of the present fallenness of all humanity, who followed in Adam's footsteps, with perhaps the story told primarily from the point of view of a Jewish person outside of Christ or even a person at the point of conversion and under conviction of sin, recognizing his bondage. Paul has prepared for this discussion earlier in Romans 5:12, where he explained that not only did sin enter the world through Adam, but also all his progeny went on to sin as well, both Jews and Gentiles. Indeed, as Romans 2:9 says, judgment for sin will begin with the household of God (to borrow a phrase from 1 Pet 4:17). Romans 5:17 says that sin and death came to reign over all humankind, and Romans 6:17 says those outside Christ are slaves to sin, unable to avoid sin or escape its bondage.

I must stress once again that the context of Romans 7:14-25 is a discussion of the law. Notice the important statements that prepare for this section in Romans 7:5-6, where Paul speaks of what believers were in the past in the

flesh, and what they have now been made in Christ (Rom 7:6). Believers
have been released from the law, as the analogy with the death of the husband
makes clear. One is no longer under its jurisdiction, no longer obligated to
it. Notice too how in Romans 8:8-9 Paul uses the phrase "in the flesh," just
as he did in Romans 7:5-6, to characterize what was true of a person before
becoming a Christian. Yet the person described in Romans 7:14-25 is said to
be fleshly and sold under sin (Rom 7:14) and cries out for deliverance. This
is not a person who is free in Christ.

I have discussed elsewhere in detail the identity of the "I" in Romans
7:14-25, considering all of the major options, and only two make sense of the
context of Romans 7:14-25.[46] Paul may be discussing the Jew who knows
and strives to obey the law, but the Jew as now seen by Paul with twenty-
twenty hindsight and Christian insight. This person knows that the law of
God is good but, being led by a fallen nature, does what he or she ought not
to do. The other possibility is that Paul is describing the plight of any person
outside of Christ who is under conviction, having heard God's Word, in particular his law, and yet is still in the bondage to sin. It must be kept in mind
that earlier, in Romans 2:14-15, Paul had said that the essence of what the
law requires is written on Gentile hearts. Thus, Romans 7:14-25 would describe the person under conviction of sin and crying out for redemption, and
Romans 8:1-15 would be the response of God to this cry and the description
of the transformation that happens once one is in Christ.

Notice that Romans 8:1-10 makes clear not only that the verdict of no
condemnation has been pronounced, but also that the Spirit has entered the
believer's life and has set that person free from the bondage to sin. The spirit
of such slavery has been replaced by the spirit of adoption, and what this Spirit
prompts the person to say is not "Who will deliver me from the body of this
death?" but rather "Abba! Father!" (contrast Rom 7:24 and Rom 8:15). Paul
is not saying that believers instantly become perfect or are no longer tempted
to sin after conversion. The point is that although the temptation to sin remains, it no longer reigns. But, having taken a journey through Romans 7–8,
I have given a preview of coming attractions. I have gotten ahead of the story
and shown where it is leading. The next crucial story after the story of Adam
in Paul's narrative thought world is the story of Abraham.

The story of God's people. It comes as something of a shock that Paul, the
former Pharisee, devotes a great deal of time and space to the discussion

---

[46]See Witherington and Hyatt, *Paul's Letter to the Romans.*

of Abraham and his story (see Rom 4; 9:6-15; 11:1; Gal 3:6-18; 4:21-31) and gives Moses far less ink. For Paul, Abraham is the critical example of faith prior to the coming of Christ. Galatians 3:8 puts it this way: "And the scripture, foreseeing that God would justify the Gentiles by faith, declared the gospel beforehand to Abraham." Abraham is the prototype or, as Fowl has put it, exemplar of Christian faith because he heard the first preaching of the good news about justification by faith and responded appropriately.[47] Abraham thus is seen as the ancestor of both Jew and Gentile. Even Gentiles share the faith of Abraham (Rom 4:16) and become, with Jewish Christians, his heirs and the beneficiary of the promises given to him through Christ (Gal 3:14).

As is true with all the stories of the Hebrew Scriptures, Paul looks at the story of Abraham through christological and, to a lesser degree, ecclesiological glasses. The elements in the stories that he stresses are those most germane for his Christian audience. Yet what Paul omits from his discussion (e.g., the sacrifice of Isaac, the destruction of Sodom and Gomorrah, the entertaining of angels, the blessing by Melchizedek) is as telling as what he includes. Paul's concern is to show that Abraham is a paradigm and a paragon of faith, and that the promises to him are fulfilled in his seed Christ and by that means to those who are in Christ. In part, this means that one of the most crucial aspects of the Abraham material is its chronology.

It is crucial not only that Abraham is already promised many offspring in Genesis 12:2-3, but also that God's covenant with him is already initiated in Genesis 15. The most crucial remark is "And he believed God, and it was reckoned to him as righteousness" (Gen 15:6). All of this transpires prior to any discussion about circumcision as a covenant sign, which appears in Genesis 17. Note also that the discussion of Hagar and Sarah does not show up until after Genesis 15:6 (see Gen 16; 21:8-21). This order of events allows Paul to appeal to God's original dealings with Abraham over against any later institution of circumcision, whether Abrahamic or Mosaic. This leads to conclusions such as the one in Romans 4:11-12: circumcision is only the seal or sign of a righteousness or right standing that Abraham had already obtained through faith in God. Paul also sees this order of events as implying that Abraham can be the father of Gentile believers as well as Jewish ones, for like them, he believed without having already been circumcised, and he was accepted on this basis (see Rom 4:1). He is the forefather of all believers not

---

[47]One could even argue that Abraham received credit for righteousness after and as a result of believing the promise.

according to the flesh, but rather on the basis of faith. This can also lead to a further corollary. Not all of Abraham's physical descendants are true children of God, true Israelites, for it is not the children of the flesh but rather those of the promise who are true descendants (Rom 9:6-7).

The paradigmatic character of Abraham comes to the fore in a text such as Romans 4:23-24. Abraham is Exhibit A of relating to God on the proper basis of eschatological faith: "Now the words 'it was reckoned to him' were not written for his sake alone, but for ours also. It will be reckoned to us who believe in him who raised Jesus our Lord from the dead."[48] It needs to be stressed that this is not just any story but rather a scriptural story, and as such, it provides a normative model for the people of the Book. Abraham is not merely analogous to Christians; he is their scriptural model or prototype.[49]

The story of Abraham takes a surprising turn in Galatians 3:16, where, in a tour de force argument, Paul maintains that the term "seed" in the Abraham story refers in particular to Christ. Wright is correct to repeatedly stress the twists in the tale that Paul administers to his foundational Jewish stories.[50] Genesis 17:6-7 seems to lie in the background here. It is this version of the promise to Abraham that refers to the fact that kings will come from Abraham, and it is this version that also says that the covenant is between God and Abraham and his offspring. Romans 9:6-7 shows that Paul knows quite well that "seed" is a collective noun, but the larger context of Genesis 17 has provided Paul with the legitimate opportunity to talk about the most important Jewish king who was to be the descendant of Abraham. We learn from this discussion that Paul sees the risen Christ as, like God, an inclusive personality, one in whom many can abide or dwell. Christ is the seed, and believers in Christ are also that seed if they are in him. They become heirs through being in the seed who is Christ. "Seed," then, in Galatians 3:16 has both a particular and a collective sense (Christ and those in him), just as it did in the case of Abraham (Isaac and subsequent descendants are promised). This means that if Galatians 3 is read carefully in light of the larger context of Genesis 17, if one hears the intertextual echo, then Paul in the end is not guilty of exegetical legerdemain here.

---

[48]Here, Paul uses "Jesus" rather than "Christ" probably to punctuate that it was a human being who was raised by God, albeit a very special and unique one.

[49]See Fowl, Story of Christ, p. 94. Notice too that it is Abraham's faith that is reckoned as his righteousness. Nothing is said about Christ's righteousness being imputed to him. On this subject, see Witherington, Individual Witnesses, pp. 218-31.

[50]Wright, New Testament and the People of God, pp. 405-9.

Of crucial importance for understanding Paul's narrative thought world is the connection mapped out between the Abrahamic and new covenants in Galatians 3–4. The Abrahamic covenant is seen as being fulfilled in Christ, and thus the covenant that he began is the consummation of the Abrahamic one. Both covenants involved both the circumcised and the uncircumcised. From Paul's perspective, circumcision is not the essential thing; faith is, for Genesis 15 precedes Genesis 17. Both covenants involve children given by the grace of God, both involve an everlasting covenant, and both have to do with the fact that in this context all the nations of the earth will be blessed (see Gen 17:6).

In terms of the narrative flow of Paul's thought, the cost of closely linking the Abrahamic and the new covenant is high. It means that for Paul, the Mosaic covenant must be seen as an interim arrangement, a parenthesis between the promises given to Abraham and the promises fulfilled in Christ. This would not mean that the law was a bad thing, just a temporary one, a temporary guardian or child minder to keep God's people in line until the Messiah came.

When Paul thinks of Adam, he thinks of the entire story of sin and fall, and when he thinks of Abraham, he thinks of a faith-based covenant and the promises that went with it, but when he thinks of Moses, he thinks of the law, and in particular the law as something given pro tempore. Nowhere is this more evident than in Galatians 3–4, although Romans suggests the same thing.[51] Because Paul thinks christologically about the timeline of salvation history, when Christ came, the situation in regard to the law and God's people also changed: "But when the fullness of time had come, God sent forth his Son, born under the law, in order to redeem those under the law, so that we might receive adoption as children" (Gal 4:4-5). The Mosaic law is seen neither as opposed to the promises nor as annulling the Abrahamic covenant (Gal 3:17-21); it simply was given for different times and purposes.

Paul perhaps makes clearest his views on the Mosaic covenant in 2 Corinthians 3. This is a retelling of the story of Moses' visit to Mount Sinai, and without a knowledge of this story, one will not understand the nuances of Paul's interpretive moves here. This chapter of 2 Corinthians can also be said to be a tale of two ministries of two called servants of God (Moses and Paul)

---

[51]For a more detailed substantiation of this line of argument, see Ben Witherington III, *Grace in Galatia: A Commentary on St. Paul's Letter to the Galatians* (Grand Rapids: Eerdmans, 1998), pp. 197-341.

that leads to comments on two covenants, the Mosaic one and the new one. This tale clearly is not about the Hebrew Scriptures itself, and Paul is not suggesting that we adopt a particular hermeneutic here—spiritual versus literal—in the interpretation of the text. Nor is Paul pitting the written word (here written in stone because the Decalogue is meant) against the Spirit or even the spoken word. Rather, he is comparing and contrasting ministries and the covenants on behalf of which these two ministries were undertaken.

Moses ascended Mount Sinai and came back down with the Decalogue, trailing clouds of glory. The Decalogue, like the law as a whole, is seen by Paul as holy, just, good, and even spiritual (Rom 7:12, 14). Paul in no way disputes that the law came attended with splendor. The fact is, however, that its glory or splendor and that of Moses have been eclipsed by the greater splendor of Christ and the new covenant. Thus, not only is the glory on Moses' face being annulled, but also the Mosaic covenant itself (2 Cor 3:11). Unfortunately, although the intent and purpose was otherwise, the direct effect of the law on fallen human beings was death-dealing rather than life-giving. The problem with the law was that it could not give life, it could not enable one to obey it, which meant that it could not but condemn fallen human behavior over and over again. What was to be done about this?

The crucial verb in 2 Corinthians 3:7, 11, 13, 14 is *katargeō*. Twenty-one of the twenty-seven New Testament occurrences of this verb are found in the Pauline corpus, and in other Pauline texts the word always refers to something replaced, invalidated, abolished, not merely something that is faded. The deliberate contrast between the ministry of life and that of death in 2 Corinthians 3 strongly suggests that we must interpret the verb similarly here. The coming of the glorious Christ has put even former glories in the shade, in effect making them obsolete. Paul's argument is grounded in his reading of the way salvation history has progressed. It is not about human attitudes or approaches toward the law, nor is the law itself seen as defective. The defect lies in fallen human beings. The effect of the law on such fallen ones is contrasted with the effect of the Spirit on them. The written code kills, the Spirit gives life. Galatians 3:19 makes clear that a change of guides or guardians was needed. The law was only until Christ came.

The story of Christ. Thus once again, as was true when Moses came on the scene, the story of humankind takes a decisive new turn when Christ comes on the scene. Yet Christ himself came on the scene, like Moses coming down from the mountain, trailing clouds of glory. Ironically enough, though, Christ chose to leave his glory behind in order to fully take on the human form, indeed the form of a servant among human beings. The story of the Christ, the plot of his career, is most ably and nobly summed up in the christological hymn material found in Philippians 2:5-11, which we have already had occasion to explore earlier.

Here it is important to stress that Philippians 2:5 deliberately draws a parallel between the frame of mind and decision-making of the preexistent Son of God and that of Christians. This exalted piece of theological discourse has an ethical function meant to produce the imitation of Christ in and by believers. Christ deliberately stepped down, he deliberately did not draw on his divine prerogatives, he deliberately took a lower place, he deliberately submitted even to death on the cross. Of course, the analogy drawn here between the behavior of Christ and that of Christians is just that—an analogy. But it is a potent one. The essence of the analogy is that believers ought to follow Christ's self-sacrificial life style so that others may benefit. The first half of the hymn has a paraenetic thrust. It may also be that the second half hints that God will do for the believer what he has already done for Christ: provide a resurrection, saying, "Come up higher, brother or sister" and the like. The crucified conqueror's story is to be recapitulated in the life of his followers, as Paul himself was in various ways experiencing. It is in this same letter Paul says, "I want to know Christ and the power of his resurrection and the sharing in common of his sufferings by becoming like him in his death, if somehow I might attain the resurrection of the dead" (Phil 3:10-11). Paul mentions this not least because he sees himself as modeling Christ so that his converts will do likewise. This is made very clear in Philippians 3:17, where Paul pleads directly, "Brothers and sisters join in imitating me" (cf. 1 Cor 11:1). The context must be remembered, however. This is not hubris; it is the modeling that a good teacher was expected to do. Paul is not claiming to be *the* pattern, but only a good example of how one follows the pattern.

Paul assumes that the gift of right standing with God is the platform or basis for exhorting his charges to Christlikeness and promising them the completion of the process if they remain faithful to the end. To "gain Christ" (Phil 3:8) is not merely to gain right standing with God; it is to gain full Christlikeness at the resurrection (Phil 3:10-11).

It is thus the human career of Christ, beginning with the taking on the form of a servant and continuing on through death and resurrection, that is said to be analogous to the plot of the story of Christians. Christ not only stripped himself but also shunned any rightful human accolades or dignity, taking on the form of a servant or slave. How very differently he lived than did most ancient persons, caught up in honor challenges and striving for more public recognition. Yet in the end he was honored.

Christ's story is the crucial hinge story in the whole human drama, as Wright stresses, which indicates how the story will end.[52] Paul is able to retell this story in many other creative forms (see, e.g., Col 1:15-20), but its essence is the same in each case. It is about a preexistent divine Son of God, who stooped to conquer. The means of triumph was not only taking on the form of a servant, but also dying a slave's death on the cross and then being vindicated by God through the resurrection (see Rom 1:3-4). And this story has a sequel involving the return of Christ to earth. This in turn means that the follower of Christ must live between the advents, keeping one eye on each horizon. There is an "already and not yet" character to the story of Christ and so also to the story of his followers. As I draw to a close this discussion of Paul's narrative thought world, the thought world that undergirds and guides all of his exegesis, ethical remarks, and theologizing, we will look briefly at Paul's telling of the story of Christians.

Paul is interested in the entire story of humankind from beginning to end. When he reaches the climax of the story, the story of Christ, it is notable that he focuses overwhelmingly on the end of the Christ story, the death and resurrection, though the coming and true humanity also are emphasized. Paul's gospel about Christ is a passion and resurrection narrative with a short introduction. Yet he does not neglect the cosmic origins and ends of the story, not least because the latter has direct effect on the believer's story now. If it is true that Christ has led supernatural captivity captive (Eph 4:8), and believers are no longer in the thrall of demons (though they may still be pestered or persecuted by such foes), then Christians need to know this and not live as those without hope or help.

The story of Paul and Christians. The story of humankind was narrowed down to the story of Israel in the persons of Abraham and Moses and their successors, which in turn was further narrowed down to the story of Jewish messiah, the Christ, and thereafter the story widens again to embrace the story of those who are in the Christ, and of course this includes Paul himself, who believed that his own story had been radically changed through an encounter with Christ on the road to Damascus.

---

[52]Wright, *New Testament and the People of God*, pp. 406-7.

A much neglected text in the study of Paul's conversion is 2 Corinthians 4, particularly 2 Corinthians 4:6. Here we find a partial citation of Genesis 1 that refers to God making light to shine out of darkness. Paul wishes to connect the text, however, with the fact that "Christ has shone in our hearts to give the light of the knowledge of the glory of God in the face of Christ." Paul is saying that conversion is the beginning of a whole new world for the convert, who becomes a new creature or part of a new creation. This new world of illumination dawned on Paul when he saw the risen Lord on the road to Damascus or, as he puts it here, saw the very presence, the very glory of God in the shape of the face of Jesus. The new creation, then, is very much like the first one, a matter of God "calling into being the things that do not exist" (Rom 4:17). This implies a radical departure from the past, a truly new and fresh start. The emphasis is on discontinuity with the past. It may be in part that Paul is envisioning here his story in terms of the story of the first Adam (see above), but it is clear enough that he envisions it even more in terms of the story of the last Adam, the one who gave up much and took the form of a servant.

This is very much how Paul sees himself, as is clear from an autobiographical text such as Philippians 3:4-10, and it is no accident that Paul tells his own tale here with echoes of the way he had told the story of Christ in Philippians 2. Paul's status and standing and prerogatives in Judaism were considerable, and he was advancing in it well beyond his peers, as he tells us in Galatians 1. He was on the way up, not on the way to becoming a servant among human beings. Yet as a Christian, Paul is prepared to count all of that as in the loss column in comparison to the surpassing privilege of knowing and being known by Christ and being conformed to his image. Thus Paul, in a text such as Galatians 6:15, is clearly able to distinguish between the things that once mattered greatly to him, such as whether one was circumcised or not (cf. Phil 3:5), and the things that now matter, namely, the new creation. As Richard Longenecker has rightly stressed, Paul is not just talking about re-creation, but rather about a new creation with an emphasis on the word *new*.[53] This comports with the fact that Paul is not simply talking about a renewed covenant either, but rather about a new one that eclipses, brings to closure, and in various senses fulfills or completes the old ones and the whole process of God's covenanting with his people.

Paul, in 2 Corinthians 5:17, describes the fact that a person in Christ is a

---

[53]Richard N. Longenecker, *Galatians* (WBC 41; Dallas: Word, 1990), p. 296.

new creature. Among other things, this dramatically changed Paul's view of Jesus. Whereas formerly he evaluated Jesus from a fallen and worldly point of view, he certainly does so no longer (2 Cor 5:16). Yet it would be a mistake to think that Paul sees conversion as involving only a transvaluation of values and attitudes about various matters. He believes that conversion also entails a change in one's spiritual makeup. One's life becomes christoform in shape.

It is no accident that one of Paul's favorite descriptions of himself is as servant (Rom 1:1; Phil 1:1). Paul's story is analogous to that of Christ and is modeled on it. But this is not just a matter of imitating Christ; it is also a matter of being conformed to the image of Christ by God. Thus, in 2 Corinthians 1:5 Paul speaks of suffering the sufferings of Christ. In Paul's view, the trajectory of his own life is much like that of his Master. Paul's hope is to be completely conformed to Christ's image by means of obtaining a resurrection like his. In addition, Paul does not just draw on the pattern of Christ's life for his ethical and theological exhortations; from time to time he also draws on Christ's actual teachings for these purposes (see Rom 12–15; 1 Cor 7).

It appears quite likely, in view of 1 Corinthians 15:8-9, that what was being said about Paul is that his transformation from persecutor of the church to apostle of Christ was something that happened with unnatural haste. Early Jews were accustomed to persons becoming proselytes to Judaism gradually, after first having been inquirers or God-fearers for a period of time. Paul, by contrast, seems to have had a sudden change of character. Ancient persons were suspicious of claims about people changing their nature or character, for character was seen as innate, something that one was born with, and then manifested over the course of one's life. It therefore is not surprising if some were calling Paul an *ektrōma* and therefore unfit to be or be called an apostle of Jesus due to his persecuting activities (1 Cor 15:8-9). An *ektrōma* was a miscarriage perhaps due to having a stillborn or an abortion—in short, a child rushed prematurely into the world. The image is connected here by Paul with his being last to see the risen Lord. The implication seems to be that had this not happened quickly, it might not have happened at all.

It is not clear whether Paul just means that people saw his conversion as something that happened too suddenly, with ungodly haste, or that they also saw his sudden adoption of an apostolic role as too hasty. It may also be that Paul means that the appearance he received from the Lord happened out of due season, indeed apparently well after the other appearances (to judge from Acts), and so had it not happened as it did, out of due season, it would not have happened at all. In any case, it is clear that both Paul saw himself as unworthy to be an apostle, and his critics saw him the same way. But it was not a matter of worth or works, it was a matter of grace.

Being born a new creature in midlife is no easy thing, as it means giving up much that one has worked for and loved. In one sense, it means dying to one's past and being born again. Paul spoke for himself and other Christians when he says in Romans 6:2-4 that conversion means being buried with Christ in baptism, being baptized into his death, and so beginning to be put into the story of Christ. The heart of the creed for Paul was that Christ died for our sins according to the Scriptures, was buried, and was raised on the third day (1 Cor 15:3-5). Interestingly, this becomes the heart of his description by means of analogy of what happens and will happen to Christians in Romans 6:2-4: just as Christ died for sins, so believers die to sin; just as Christ was buried, so believers have been buried with Christ in his death; just as Christ has been raised, so believers can now walk in the Spirit, walk in newness of life and look forward to their own bodily resurrection. Of a similar sort is what is said in Colossians 2:6-11. When Paul refers to "the circumcision of Christ" in Colossians 2:11, is he referring just to what happened to him or also to what happens to the believer in Christ? The believer is raised together with Christ "through faith in the effective working of God, who raised him from the dead" (Col 2:12). Christ's story is efficacious for the believer when by analogy it is recapitulated in that believer such that he or she goes from being dead in trespasses to being made alive in him. What Christ has done *for* the believer on the cross and in the resurrection is the basis of what he later does *in* the believer. Christians experience Christlikeness in the Spirit only because Christ himself first experienced death and resurrection.

The story of Paul's life and of the lives of other Christians does not stop at the point of right standing by grace through faith, although as a text such as Galatians 2:15-21 makes clear, that is the crucial beginning point.[54] One must go on to work out one's salvation with fear and trembling, going on to grow in grace and in holiness. One must consciously choose to walk in the Spirit and not indulge the works of the flesh (Gal 5). One must have a sense of the already, but also of the not yet, of one's Christian existence, suspended between new birth and new body, between inner renewal and outer decay.

Two crucial things remain to be said about the Christian's story. First, one should not expect to be exempt from suffering in this life, since Christ and his

---

[54]See Witherington, *Grace in Galatia*, pp.169-94.

apostles were not; second, one must have a clear vision that Christ's history is the believer's destiny. This is precisely what Paul has in mind when he talks about the believers being the latter fruit of a crop of resurrection persons of which Christ was the firstfruits (1 Cor 15:20-23). This is also what he has in mind when he speaks of believers being destined in advance to be conformed to the glorious resurrected image of God's Son (Rom 8:29). The moral conforming is happening now, the physical conforming will happen later.

Thus, Paul himself sees his life as a pilgrimage toward resurrection: "I want to know Christ and the power of his resurrection and the sharing of his sufferings by becoming like him in his death, if somehow I may attain the resurrection of the dead" (Phil 3:10-11). Paul knows that this latter event will not happen before the Lord returns. This means that the present is a time for striving and pressing on toward the goal. Every Christian, like Paul, should have the honesty to admit "not that I have already obtained this or have already reached the goal; but I press on to make it my own, because Christ Jesus has made me his own" (Phil 3:12). This sounds neither like eternal security nor like eternal optimism of the wrong sort, but rather reflects a quiet confidence that one is headed toward the desired goal, but there are miles to go before one sleeps in the Lord, and so one must make every effort to press onward.

The mark on and of the Christian is the mark of Christ. The believer belongs to Christ and imitates the Master and is spiritually conformed to the image of the Master. This involves tragedy and triumph, sorrow and joy. Paul would have heartily endorsed these words of William Penn as a description of the Christlike life: "No pain, no palm; no gall, no glory; no cross, no crown"—and indeed, no final resolution until the author of all these stories brings down the curtain on the human drama in the person of his Son when he returns. Then the human story, the story of Israel, the story of Christians will be finally and fully gathered up into the story of Christ, and every knee shall bow and every tongue confess, whether willingly or unwillingly, that Jesus Christ is Lord, and the glory will be to the Father, whose story began this discussion.

Summary. This retelling of Paul's fundamental stories leads to the conclusion that there is still much to be learned about the historical Paul from such an analysis. For now, it is sufficient to say that Paul lived in and out of a storied world, and his thought cannot be understood apart from these foundational narratives. Not surprisingly, the one story by which Paul exegetes all the others is the story of Christ, which is not a story in the Old Testament but rather a retelling of the kerygma of the early church. This is one reason why, in the end, intertextual studies will not alone suffice to plumb the depths of Paul's thought world.

I also doubt that we can confine Paul's thought world to the story of Israel or insist that Israel's story is the central one for him. Paul spends next to no time on the story of David, and the Davidic character of Christ and much more time on the Adam/last Adam tandem. He spends more time on Abraham than on Moses, which is to say on the forefather of Israel, but not on Israel proper as it came forth from Egypt and became a people called Israel at Sinai. When Paul does focus on Moses and the law in Galatians and in 2 Corinthians 3, the discussion is more about obsolescence than fulfillment, more about the newness of the new ministry than its continuity with the old, more about the surpassing glory than the fading glory. For Paul, all humankind stands not between Sinai and the promised land but rather between Adam and the eschatological Adam and must live out of the story of one or the other of these Adams and their respective stories. The center of Paul's story is christological, not ecclesiological or Israelological. It appears, then, that my reading of Paul's narrative thought world will differ somewhat from Wright's, but we must wait to see how Wright culminates his study of Paul's narrative thought world in his forthcoming work. For now, it must be said that he needs to heed the strong stress on christocentric universalism in Paul's thought rather than on the Israelological or Israelocentric character of that thought.

About Paul as a person, this portion of our study has only confirmed that Paul saw his own identity defined primarily in relationship to Christ and his people, and he made it his personal goal to be conformed to Christ's image. This is the sort of action we would expect of an ancient person looking for a paradigm to follow and a community to be a part of in order to understand one's own place in the world. An identity was shaped and established not by how a person stood out from the crowd and models, but rather by how that person followed them.

Paul's Hermeneutics of the Old Testament

We cannot understand Paul the exegete, or for that matter Paul the ethicist or theologian, unless we have clearly in mind the sort of synopsis of Paul's narrative thought world briefly presented here. These stories are sacred stories taken from the Hebrew Scriptures and from the Christian tradition. Yet the old, old stories have been reconfigured in the light of the Christ story. Paul's hermeneutic is both christocentric in terms of its guiding force and aim and ecclesiocentric in terms of its scope and application. Christ is the hermeneutical key to a right reading of the Scriptures, and the church is the primary audience for hearing this rereading. Thus, Paul reads the sacred traditions through the eyes of the Christ primarily for the sake of the Christian community and its edification. A few illustrations of Paul's use of the Old Testament stories for Christian purposes is in order.

Of course, Paul sees all of the Hebrew Scriptures, including the law, as God's Word and therefore as profitable for learning and teaching. Even the ritual law has lessons for the Christian (see 1 Cor 9:8-9). Paul believed that it was crucial to know where God's people were in the working out of the story of salvation history—that is, beyond the era of the law and under the reign of Christ—if they are to properly understand the significance of Scripture for them. They are not under the Mosaic covenant, but they are under the guidance of the Scriptures, which are fulfilled in the messianic age. More often than we might realize, Paul the pastor is busy using and applying the text in creative ways rather than simply interpreting the text. In other words, he is engaging in what has been called a "pesher," or contemporizing of the text, a skill that he may have learned in part while he was a Pharisee.

In his magisterial study of the intertextual echoes of the Hebrew Scriptures in Paul's letters, Richard Hays has shown in detail that even when Paul is not formally quoting Scripture, he often is alluding to it, relying on echoes to conjure up the larger whole of the particular Old Testament context.[55] If we take into account not only the formal quotations but also the allusions to the Old Testament, we quickly discover what a crucial role Scripture played in forming Paul's thought world and symbolic universe. However, this mental furniture underwent some drastic rearrangement and reconception when Paul accepted the story of the one who was crucified and risen.

There is indeed a sense in which Paul sees the whole of the Hebrew Scriptures as a giant repository of largely prophetic texts that have some key lessons to teach Christians. Even seemingly unpromising texts such as Deuteronomy 25:4 can, in the hands of the master applier of the Word, be seen to teach us something about God's ways with his new covenant people (see 1 Cor 9:8-12). The principle of analogy brings the text to life again and again because Paul assumes that it is the same God, operating in the same ways, in his own day as in Old Testament times. The form of the community has changed, but the character of God and God's ways with humankind have

---

[55]See Hays, *Echoes of Scripture*.

not. Yet we must be able to distinguish, as Paul himself does, between the original meaning of the text and its larger significance and relevance to the eschatological community of God's people in Christ.

As a representative example of Paul's use of the principle of analogy and the rhetorical device known as *synkrisis* or historical comparison, let us consider for a moment the typological use of Scripture in 1 Corinthians 10:1-13. Paul believes fervently that the things reported of God's people in Old Testament times really happened and are not cunningly devised fables, and furthermore he believes that at least part of the reason various of these things happened and were recorded in Scripture is that they are "types" for the Christian community. There is a strong sense in which Paul would claim that the Hebrew Scriptures are the book of and for Jews and Gentiles united in Christ, intended especially for the instruction, edification, and exhortation of that eschatological community. This is because he sees the whole as, to some degree, a prophetic corpus. It was, of course, the Scripture for those who came before Christ as well, but Paul believes that he now lives in an age when the true implications and significance of these texts can more fully be seen, as was never fully the case before that time.

The fundamental idea behind typology is that since God's character never changes, God acts in similar ways in differing ages of history and, perhaps more importantly, provides persons and events that foreshadow other later persons and events in salvation history. In other words, it is not an ahistorical reading of the text but rather one that compares what has happened before to God's people and what is happening now. Cognizance of both stories is crucial if analogy is to be drawn. There is also the sense, as we have noted, that all that has come before Christ was preparatory and pointing forward to what has been happening since Christ appeared.

Typology as we find it in 1 Corinthians 10 does not involve a point-by-point comparison in all matters. For example, Paul does not believe that the Corinthians have yet perished in the spiritual desert of the pagan world; indeed, the whole point of his proffering the analogy is to prevent them from doing so. However, Paul does entertain the possibility that some of his converts may yet end up like the wilderness-wandering generation of Israelites. Paul wishes to use the Old Testament to show Christians how they should and should not live in view of God's consistent judging of idolatry among his people. Notice how Paul begins 1 Corinthians 10 with reference to "our ancestors." The story of the Israelites is "our" story because in Paul's view,

Jew and Gentile united in Christ is the continuation and true development of the Old Testament people of God.

Paul's way of handling this text works two ways. He will interpret the Old Testament events in a Christian and christological manner, and he will interpret contemporary events in light of the Old Testament stories. In other words, he will move in both directions at once: from experience to text and from text to contemporary experience. When Paul says that "the rock was Christ" (1 Cor 10:4), note that he does not say either that "the rock is Christ" or that "the rock signifies Christ." In Paul's view, it is appropriate to read the Old Testament in the light of his knowledge of how these texts were interpreted in Jewish sapiential literature, where it was argued that Wisdom was the rock that provided water for thirsty Israel in the desert (Wis 11). Paul believes that Christ, who is the Wisdom of God, was in fact spiritually present, as the preexistent one, with Israel and providing them with benefits. This is not an interpretive or a hermeneutical move so much as a theological reflection on what was believed to be actually the case during the Old Testament times.

The very reason this analogy works so well in Paul's view is that both his present audience and the one referred to in the Old Testament text had benefits from Christ. Yet those benefits did not spare the Israelites from judgment, any more than partaking of the Christian sacraments would spare Corinthian Christians who were attending idol feasts from being judged by God. Notice how in 1 Corinthians 10:1-4 Paul, using deliberately Christianized language, stresses that all the Israelites partook of the so-called Mosaic sacraments. Paul knows full well that the Red Sea crossing was no baptismal rite (1 Cor 10:2), for he knows that the Israelites went across on dry ground, nor is he suggesting that the partaking of manna had the same sacramental character as the Lord's Supper. His point is simply this: the Israelites had the same general sort of spiritual benefits (note 1 Cor 10:3: food spiritually provided) from the same God, and it did not save them from judgment.

We may pause to ask here in what sense the rock or the food or the drink that the Israelites had was "spiritual." I suggest that the term is chosen to indicate the source of this sustenance: it came from God, who is Spirit. Paul also may be assuming that spiritual people like himself should be able to discern the deeper spiritual lessons to be drawn from such analogies. The food was no more figurative or allegorical than the Corinthians' sacraments. However, the spiritual significance of that reality needed to be seen.

Because it reveals something of how Paul views the Old Testament text, 1 Corinthians 10:11 is important. He says that these things happened as a warning to himself and his audience, "upon whom the ends of the ages have come." Paul believed that he lived in the eschatological age when one would see the significance and the beginning of the completion of the divine designs for humankind. The goals toward which history had been pressing had in his day begun to be realized.

If we grant Paul his theological assumptions that (1) the preexistent Christ had a hand in the affairs of the Israelites, and (2) Paul and his converts were living in the eschatological age when all the promises and prophecies and paradigms were coming to pass and to fruition, and (3) the Scriptures were written for God's people and perhaps especially for the eschatological gathering of God's people, then what Paul does with this text makes very good sense. It is not a matter of exegetical legerdemain or hermeneutical hocus pocus; rather, it is a matter of having the right eschatological and christological and ecclesiological perspectives to see the new significance of these historic texts for Paul's own audience.

When Paul seeks to do typology, he announces his intentions so that the audience will see how he is proceeding by analogy. Likewise, when he uses another major hermeneutical technique, allegorizing a nonallegorical text, he announces his intentions. We see this clearly in Galatians 4:21–5:1, where in the midst of the discussion Paul says straightforwardly, "Now this is an allegory" (Gal 4:24). We need to keep in mind that the verb *allēgoreō* can mean either "to speak allegorically" or "to interpret allegorically," and so one must be able to distinguish between (1) a text created as an allegory, (2) an allegorizing of elements or portions of a text, and (3) allegorical interpretation of a nonallegorical text. Surely, Paul is well aware that he is doing a creative allegorical interpretation of a text that is not in itself an allegory, and in fact he is also allegorizing only certain elements in the text. Again this falls into the category of hermeneutics rather than exegesis, a distinction too often overlooked.

Whereas typology is more firmly grounded in the actual characteristics of the type and antetype displayed in the narratives, and it is normally persons or events rather than things that are set up as types or antetypes, in allegory persons, places, and things all can take on symbolic or secondary connotations. I suspect that if asked, Paul would freely admit that Hagar was not a "type" of either Mount Sinai or the present Jerusalem. Only the concept of bondage or slavery binds them together, and it is this linkage that allegorizing the text brings to light. Paul is not doing exegesis here at all but presupposes a basic understanding of the story and then creatively uses elements of the story for pastoral hermeneutics and application. This falls into the category of a pastoral or homiletical use of a text and should not be evaluated as a bizarre attempt at contextual exegesis. Paul's allegorizing of the historical narrative is perhaps closest to what we find at Qumran (see CD VI, 3-11, where Num 21:18 is similarly allegorized). In both cases contemporary events outside the text (e.g., in Paul's case, the presence of Jewish agitators in Galatia) lead to creative handlings of the text.

At this point, I must call upon Richard Hays as a dialogue partner as I attempt to assess Paul's exegetical and hermeneutical techniques. Hays argues that Paul believes in the concept of a *sensus plenior*, that the text has a deeper or latent or even metaphorical meaning that can be liberated or ferreted out by a creative "spiritual" handling of the text.[56] I suggest that this confuses the issues of meaning and significance or application.

To a large extent, Hays reaches his conclusion on the basis of a certain reading of 2 Corinthians 3, which he takes to reveal Paul's hermeneutics. Christians are freed from the bondage to a circumscribed reading of the old covenant and are empowered to read it with freedom, indeed even with reckless abandon. This conclusion comes from a fundamental misreading of the contrast between letter and Spirit by Hays. Paul is not saying that one sort of interpretive move in handling the Old Testament is death-dealing, while another, more free-wheeling one is life-giving. Paul is saying that the effect of the law, even the Ten Commandments, on fallen persons is condemnation, is death-dealing. By contrast, the effect of the Spirit on fallen persons is that it gives life.

Paul says much the same thing elsewhere in Romans and Galatians about the effect of the law on fallen persons (see, e.g., Gal 3:21). Not exegesis or hermeneutics but spiritual experience is the issue here. Victor Furnish sees this quite clearly: "The description Paul gives of the *new covenant* does not so much reflect his hermeneutical perspective on the law or scripture in general as it does his eschatological perspective on God's redemptive work in history."[57] Paul is offering a tale of two ministries and two covenants, not a discussion of two ways of reading or two kinds of attitudes toward the Old Testament or the law. Paul the exegete is a second-order issue to Paul the sto-

---

[56]Ibid., p. 154.
[57]Victor P. Furnish, *II Corinthians* (AB 32A; Garden City, N.Y.: Doubleday, 1984), p. 200.

ryteller. Paul thinks that these stories are coming true by the power of God, and so the primary thing is always spiritual experience, not spiritual exegesis or hermeneutics.

What about a text such as Galatians 3:8? Here clearly Paul personifies Scripture as a prophetic book. Scripture saw in advance that God will set right the Gentiles by faith and so "prepreached" the gospel to Abraham. The point here again is not about a deeper meaning in the Old Testament text. The point is that Paul actually believes that Abraham heard the essence of the gospel message of acceptability to God through faith reckoned as righteousness and responded positively. This is not anachronism, but rather analogy. In particular it is an argument, such as we find in 1 Corinthians 10, based on analogous experience. Salvation-historical experience shared in common by Abraham and by Paul's converts is the point. The only anachronism is calling this message that Abraham heard and responded to "the gospel." The gospel message is not "hidden in Old Testament Scripture"; rather, it is in plain sight as a message once given to Abraham.

Let us consider another of Hays's key texts, Romans 10:5-10. Here Hays has more of a case, to be sure. But is Paul really arguing that there is a concealed or hidden meaning in Deuteronomy 30:11-14? To the contrary, he is arguing that there is a revealed meaning in the text, not behind or beneath it. Just as the word was near to them, it is all the more near to the eschatological community of faith. The phrase "the word is near you, in your mouth and in your heart" provides Paul an opportunity to talk about the word of faith that he preaches and that those in his audience believe in their hearts and confess. Here, Paul clearly is using the pesher technique of contemporizing the text. He believes that the phrase had meaning in its original setting, but now he will use these scriptural words to speak about something that is true of his preaching and the Christian's experience.

The personified "righteousness from faith" in Romans 10:6 has caused no end of debate. Whoever or whatever this is, it cannot be Moses, for it is contrasted with Moses, who wrote concerning the righteousness that comes from the law: "Moses *writes* concerning legal righteousness . . . *but* the righteousness from faith *says* . . ." (Rom 10:5-6). This may be a reference to Christ and the way he spoke the gospel, using Old Testament phrases, when he was on earth.[58] Alternatively, this may refer to the Christian oral tradition about

---

[58]See Romans 3–4, where it is argued that God has shown forth his righteousness in a new way in Christ, the paradigmatic example of faith and faithfulness.

righteousness from faith and the way it uses the Old Testament text to make its points. Still another possibility is that the abstract concept "righteousness from faith" has been personified (just as elsewhere Paul has personified Scripture) and is speaking the inspired word of God for today using Old Testament phrases. This personification is in fact the personification of what Paul calls the gospel, the oral message summarized in places such as Galatians 2:15-21. This last option seems most likely here.

In any event, we must be able to distinguish between a contemporizing use of scriptural phrases, as here, and a theory about how Paul believed the Old Testament text had a hidden or deeper meaning. The meaning of the text is one thing, how it is used hermeneutically is another. It is hermeneutics when one is seeing a further significance of the text for some application today that goes beyond its original meaning. This, I submit, is what Paul is doing here. It therefore is unwarranted to conclude from such pastoral uses of the text that "Paul's readings of Scripture are not constrained by a historical scrupulousness about the original meaning of the text. Eschatological meaning subsumes original sense."[59] I would say that eschatological application extends original meaning and application, following the principle of analogy.

Yet in the end, I must agree with Hays that Paul's hermeneutic is narratologically oriented, which explains the importance of typology for Paul. "Paul reads Scripture under the conviction that its story prefigures the climactic realities of his own time."[60] In other words, Paul, unlike Philo, is basically not an allegorist looking for some abstract eternal truth of philosophical profundity buried in a narrative. Paul thinks in terms of historical progressions and the breaking into space and time of God's divine saving activity. The narratives in Paul's thought world are founded and grounded in God and in history, and this of course includes the narratives about Christ and Christians. Typology is the technique of one who has a profound belief in the historical substance of what he speaks and a profound belief in the God who is sovereign over history and relates in a consistent way to his people age after age.

Paul's allusive handling of Scripture shows repeatedly that he believed that one needed to know the whole story to appreciate the parts. As an exegete and applier of the text, Paul was creative, using typology and even allegorizing to relate the Scriptures to the situations of his converts. Yet it

---

[59]Hays, *Echoes of Scripture*, p. 156.
[60]Ibid., p. 161.

would be a mistake to see him as an early predecessor of Augustine or others who were constantly looking for a *sensus plenior*, a deeper or hidden sense to Scripture. Paul, to the contrary, believed that he lived in an age when the hidden had been brought to light and the meaning and truth of Scripture had been made plain. He believed that he lived in the eschatological age, when the ends and goals and aims of all the ages were coming to fruition through Christ and his body. What Paul was looking for was new ways to apply the old meaning to his converts, and it is his hermeneutical creativity that helps him find these ways.

Paul's reads Scripture with a historical and narratological consciousness dictating how he views the befores and afters in the story. He is not Philo, looking for abstract or eternal Platonic ideals in the midst of the maze of historical particulars. For Paul, history and experience are the realms that Scripture speaks of and to again and again. One needs to look into history and into the sacred story, not beyond or behind it, to find the meaning and purpose of life and the explanation for what transpires.

Paul's hermeneutic was christologically determined and focused, the Christ-event being the lens through which all must be seen and understood. Yet it was ecclesiologically directed. It was also eschatologically generated, as Paul sees himself living in the age when the prophetic and the promissory come to pass. The story that summed up all that came before and encompassed all that was to follow was the story of Christ. It was the key that unlocked all the secrets, the key that opened the door, setting the prisoners free from fallenness, from slavery to the powers of darkness, from servitude to the law. Paul believed that the story had reached its climax, and he was living in the denouement. He believed that the story was being replicated in his own experience, and that it was calling him to the imitation of Christ. But was Paul some sort of anomaly, or did other New Testament writers also do theology and ethics in a narratological mode? We must turn to Hebrews next to begin to answer this question, but let us remind ourselves once more of the stories that Paul most used and emphasized in articulating his symbolic universe. They are five interwoven stories comprising one large drama: (1) the story of God, the one who existed before all worlds and made them; (2) the story of the world gone wrong in Adam; (3) the story of God's people in that world, from Abraham to Moses and beyond; (4) the story of the Jewish messiah, the Christ, which arises out of the story of both humankind and of Israel, but in fact arises out of the larger story of God as creator and redeemer; (5) the story of Christians, including Paul himself, which arises out of the second, third, and fourth stories.

The Narrative Thought World of the Author of Hebrews

> Entering the world of the letter to the Hebrews after a close study of Paul is a bit like listening to Monteverdi after listening to Bach. We are clearly in the same world, but the texture is different, the allusions are different, the whole flavor is changed.[61]

I have demonstrated elsewhere that the author of Hebrews very likely was part of the Pauline circle of evangelists and coworkers and indeed may even have been Apollos.[62] Whoever he was, he was as formidable a thinker as Paul himself, and he shows some indebtedness to Pauline thought at points, but he has made such concepts and readings of the Christian story his own and given them his own focus and emphases. He is no mere imitator, and nothing about his homily can be said to be derivative in any way. For one thing, he wants to retell the story of Israel differently than Paul does and emphasize much different aspects of it. The tabernacle, Moses, Melchizedek, the priesthood in general, and much more play roles in this author's Christian thought world in ways that they do not in Paul's.

Furthermore, the author of Hebrews is indebted to some different Jewish sources of material than Paul is—for example, the end of Sirach. As Wright shows, Sirach 44:1–50:21 is profitably compared to Hebrews 11–12, except that in Sirach the list of heroes culminates when the history of the world and of Israel climaxes in the worship of Yaweh in the Jerusalem temple, especially in the spectacular ministry of the high priest Simon ben Onias. "This is where Israel's history has been leading: a great high priest, magnificently robed, splendid in his liturgical operations, coming out of the sanctuary after the worship to bless the people."[63]

Strikingly, this is echoed in Hebrews. Now, however, Jesus is the great high priest, the holy of holies is the heavenly sanctuary, and the sacrifice was Jesus himself; and when he comes forth from that heavenly sanctuary, it will be to save those who eagerly await him. The story that Jesus ben Sira was telling is subverted by the story that the author of Hebrews is telling such that

---

[61]Wright, *New Testament and the People of God*, p. 409.
[62]See Ben Witherington III, *Letters and Homilies for Jewish Christians: A Socio-Rhetorical Commentary on Hebrews, James, and Jude* (Downers Grove, Ill.: IVP Academic, 2007).
[63]Wright, *New Testament and the People of God*, p. 410.

Jesus of Nazareth becomes the focus of worship, the creator of a new sort of worship that is not tied to an earthly sanctuary, be it the ancient tabernacle or the temple in Jerusalem. The true worship of the true God now is both facilitated by and directed toward Jesus. I need to unpack this some by exploring a few elements of the narrative thought world that makes Hebrews stand apart from Paul and other New Testament writers.

When I spoke of the christological hymn fragment in Hebrews 1 earlier in this chapter, I dealt with how the author chooses to present the story of the preexistent Son of God, who is indeed properly called "God" and has various of the divine attributes and the trajectory of his story, including his making purification for sins and then returning to heaven. Here it will be useful to deal with Hebrews 4:14–5:9, a passage that talks about his humanity and its necessity in order that he could be a human priest, indeed the believer's high priest now and forever.

First, in Hebrews 4:14 we hear about Christ's journey to heaven, which is described as a "passing through the heavens," perhaps echoing the idea of the high priest passing through the curtains into the holy of holies. More pertinently, early Jewish listeners would think of the earlier experiences of Enoch (see Gen 5:24; cf. *1 En.* 14–19; 70–71) or Elijah perhaps (2 Kings 2:11) or of the post–Old Testament traditions about the ascension of Isaiah (*Ascen. Isa.* 6–7). We may also notice that the phrase "great high priest" is not unprecedented (used of Simon in 1 Macc 13:42; and the high priest is often called a "great priest" in the LXX [e.g., Lev 21:10; Num 35:25-28; Zech 6:11]). But the author of Hebrews means something special by the appellation; he is referring to one of a whole different ilk and priestly line. The audience members are urged to "hold fast" to their confession already given about this great high priest. Although his methodology is more subtle, the author's argument is not different in thrust from Paul's: you already have in Christ all that you might look or long for from Old Testament religion.

One thing that the author makes clear here is that "Christ's full humanness and his sinlessness are not contradictory. Being sinful is not intrinsic or necessary to being fully human, nor, to state the opposite, is being sinless an obstacle to full humanness."[64] It is a modern notion that sinning makes one more human or approachable, a notion not shared by the author of Hebrews or other early Jews. There was in early Judaism, in any case, the notion

---

[64]Donald Hagner, *Encountering the Book of Hebrews: An Exposition* (Grand Rapids: Baker Academic, 2004), p. 78.

of a righteous messiah who would come (see *Pss. Sol.* 17:36). The phrase
"tested in every respect/way" probably means not that Jesus endured every
basic temptation that humans undergo, but rather that he underwent the full
gamut of types of temptation that we experience. He therefore is able to sympathize with his fellow human beings' struggles and weaknesses.

The phrase *kath' homoiotēta* in Hebrews 4:15 could mean that Jesus was
tested "according to the likeness of our temptations" or "according to his
likeness to us." The point in either case is that he has experienced all the sorts
of temptations that we have, and being like us, he therefore understands what
we go through. The final clause in Hebrews 4:15, *chōris hamartias*, means
literally "without sin." There has been some controversy about the meaning of this. Christ went through the same sort of temptations as we do but
emerged unscathed. In view of Hebrews 7:26, this assertion of sinlessness applies to Jesus not just in heaven and as a result of his death, but in fact before
it, when he offered a pure and unblemished sacrifice. He was not only a high
priest without sin, but also a sacrifice without sin, so that he did not have to
die for himself, but could offer the perfect and full sacrifice that brings final
atonement.

In regard to the exhortations in these two verses, "hold on firmly" to the
confession (Heb 4:14) and "draw near" to the throne of grace (Heb 4:16), the
second verb, *proserchōmetha* (cf. Heb 7:25; 10:22; 11:6; 12:18-22), is almost
a technical term for the liturgical work of the priest drawing near to the altar
or of worshipers drawing near to God (cf., in the LXX, Lev 9:7; 21:17, 21;
22:3; Num 18:3). It is a mirror opposite of the warned against "shrinking
back" or "turning away" (Heb 3:12; 6:6; 10:38-39). Although the audience
may feel alienated from the macroculture at the moment, or even from the
Jewish subculture, the author is stressing that they are right where they need
to be, in the center of God's will, having already arrived at the doorstep of
Zion, and are in the process of "entering into" God's blessed rest and eternal
salvation. Now is no time to look back with longing or to shrink back from
the finish line. The author, in order to justify the use of the image of high
priest applied to Jesus, must resort to the novel idea that Jesus is a priest after
the order of Melchizedek, which is not a hereditary priesthood but rather a
forever one. This comports nicely with the way the author will insist that Jesus' sacrifice is once for all time as well. The story of priesthood and sacrifice
has been tailored to fit the specific theological points that the author wants
to make about Jesus.

It would not be at all obvious to the audience that Jesus was a high priest. Jewish Christians would have queried such an assertion on the basis of Jesus' genealogy and the geographical locale and character of his ministry, not to mention the incident in the temple in Jerusalem when Jesus overturned the tables of the money changers. Jesus went through none of the following, which normally accompanied investing someone with the office of high priest: taking a purification bath, donning sacred vestments, being anointed with oil, offering sacrifices, and especially going into the holy of holies on the Day of Atonement (cf. Ex 28:41; 29; Lev 8). Thus, rhetorically speaking, the author of Hebrews must exercise no little amount of persuasion (off and on in the entire section between Heb 4:14 and the end of Heb 10) to make a convincing case that Jesus was a priest at all, much less a high priest. One could say that he does so by a tour de force argument whereby in essence he argues that Jesus was a high priest on a whole different level: in heaven, not on earth. Although Jesus offers himself as the sacrifice while on earth, he assumes the mantle of full-fledged priest in heaven.

We do not know where the author of Hebrews got the ideas that he shares here, though perhaps there are some parallels with the Qumranite concept of a priest/king or priest/messiah. For the Hasmonaens and later the Sadducees, Melchizedek was the prototype of their priestly-kingly view of rulers; for the Pharisees, he was to be identified with Shem and to be demoted for his irreverence from any continuing priestly succession; for Philo, he was mainly the manifestation of the eternal Logos; for Josephus, he was a Canaanite chieftain who became God's priest at Jerusalem due to his piety; and most importantly, for the Qumran community (11Q13), he was a heavenly and eschatological figure, even perhaps an archangel redeemer who exercised certain priestly characteristics in atoning for sin. In view of the Qumran finds, it is easy to see how the author might be able to argue for the superiority of Christ over the Levitical priesthood on the basis of a connection to the order of Melchizedek, since there were some Jews who viewed him as a heavenly redeemer figure.[65]

But in fact, one need look no further than the Old Testament example of the king-priest Melchizedek, which probably is the source of our author's thought. Jesus will be presented here as both royal Son and priest after the order and fashion of Melchizedek, but greater. Whatever the source of the ideas, the author has made them his own and turned them into a unique and

---

[65]See Joseph A. Fitzmyer, "Further Light on Melchizedek from Qumran Cave 11," *JBL* 86 (1967): 41.

specific commentary on Jesus, with elements such as the self-sacrifice that could only have come from his knowledge of Jesus' own story.

Obviously, the most fundamental requirement for Christ to be a priest is that he had to be a human being. Angels may play the role of messengers or even warriors, but they are not mediators because they do not partake of a human nature. Priests, then, are a different sort of intermediary than angels, not least because they primarily represent human beings to God, whereas angels do the reverse. The priest's most basic role is said to be offering gifts and sacrifices to God (a stock phrase, and so we should not differentiate between the two terms [see 1 Kings 8:64; cf. Heb 8:3]), and in due course one hears about the special form that takes with the high priest (Heb 9:7, 25).

It is not expected that a priest be perfect and without sin, though it is expected that he be cleansed, forgiven, and shriven of sin when he takes up his holy tasks. But one of those tasks is in fact offering sacrifices for himself and his own sins, as well as for the sins of others. On the one hand, it is a good thing that the priest is weak and knows his own shortcomings, as he is better able to identify and empathize with other weak mortals, but on the other hand, his weakness is not a strength in another respect: he must sacrifice for his own sins. Hebrews 5:2 contains the only New Testament occurrence of the verb *metriopatheō*, literally "to moderate the pathos," indicating control of one's deeper emotions. The issue here is not sympathy but rather the ability to control one's anger with ignorant or spiritually wayward people. Whereas the ordinary priest controls his anger, Jesus is said to actively sympathize with his fellow humans.

In the Old Testament sacrifices for sin were efficacious if offered for sins of ignorance or sins committed unwittingly or unintentionally (see Lev 4:13; Ezek 45:20). These sins are viewed differently from sins committed intentionally or willfully, or as the Old Testament puts it, "with a high hand" (Num 15:30-31). Acts 13:39 states clearly that through Christ's death, atonement is now possible for intentional sins that were not covered under Old Testament law. This is one of the reasons why the author of Hebrews will emphasize that Christian believers have a very merciful high priest. He will also stress, in making clear the mercy of Christ, that in the Old Testament deliberate sin was viewed less mercifully (see Heb 6:4-8; 10:26-31; 12:17). Thus, when the author speaks of how gently Jesus deals with his audience, there is an implicit contrast with other priests and earlier sacrificial systems. The great extent of this mercy is further demonstrated by the fact that Jesus, unlike all other priests, was not a sinner. At Hebrews 7:26-27 the author will make much of the fact that Jesus is unlike other high priests because he, being "holy, blameless, unstained," had no need to sacrifice for his own sins. Jesus was the one person for whom Jesus did not have to die as an atonement for sin.

At Hebrews 5:4 the author will make the further point that priesthood is not an office and an honor earned but rather is granted by God, who "calls" priests. Aaron is singled out as the example (cf. Ex 28:1) of this process of divine selection, and the author totally ignores the fact that in Herod's temple there was a whole series of high priests who were not divinely chosen, to say the least, but rather were appointed by human rulers, involving a political process. Indeed, the control over who became high priest was one of the most vital and volatile political issues that a procurator had to supervise without appearing to interfere or control.

According to Hebrews 5:5, Jesus met the essential requirement of being selected by God, not being self-selected, to be priest. Here, Psalm 2:7 comes to the fore, as it did in Hebrews 1:5, only this time the issue is God selecting the Son to be a priest rather than for a different sort of royal role. The author moves on to consider another psalm again as well, this time Psalm 110, and it is fair to say that he reads Psalm 110:4 in light of Psalm 110:1; and in fact it is Psalm 110:1 that links his reading of Psalm 2:7 to that of Psalm 110:4. The logic of Hebrews 5:5 and Hebrews 5:6, which involve the quoting of phrases from Psalm 2:7 and Psalm 110:4 is this: because the Son has been exalted to rule from God's right hand, he is in the place and condition where he can be the perfect heavenly high priest, a forever high priest always in the inner sanctum, right in the presence of God forever. His exalted sonship role allows him to play the role of heavenly high priest.

Perhaps surprisingly and suddenly, in Hebrews 5:7 the author seems to turn to the Gethsemane scene of Christ struggling to obey God's will. The description is full of pathos and meant to evoke the deeper emotions of the audience. Presumably, part of what is going on here is a demonstration of how Christ can identify with the audience in their own struggles and in their own pressure-packed situations that may lead to their suffering and death. Actually, here we have another dimension of the priestly portrait of Jesus, for prayers were something that the priest was supposed to offer to God, for himself and for others.

Here we note that although *eulabeia* can mean "piety" or "devotion" in a general sense both here in Hebrews 5:7 and in Hebrews 12:28 (the only two New Testament occurrences of the term), it is used in the context of talking about Christ's priestly service. Thus, it suggests the attitude of reverence appropriate to priestly service. In any case, *eulabeia*, since it carries the connotation of a pious attitude such as godly fear, is not the term to indicate ordinary fear (when the author wanted to talk about deliverance from the fear of death, he used *phobos* [Heb 2:15]). It is thus far-fetched to think that this refers to Jesus' fear of death.

Much debate has surrounded what the author means here in saying that "he was *heard* because of his reverence"[66] when he had been pleading to be spared from death. This verse has been debated since the times of the church fathers and is still debated today. Perhaps the author means that when Jesus said to his Father, "Nevertheless, your will be done," that part of the prayer was heard. This may be correct, but the author then would be assuming that his audience knows the fuller Gethsemane story beyond his dramatic characterization of it here and knows about the "nevertheless" remark.

This sermon called "Hebrews" likely was written before any Gospel account of the Gethsemane episode was set down in writing, and so it is interesting to compare this to, for example, the accounts in Matthew 26:36-46 and Luke 22:43-44 (found only in some manuscripts of Luke), which in some respects most resemble what we have here in Hebrews 5:7 in terms of the pathos expressed: "And being in anguish, he prayed more earnestly, and his sweat was like drops of blood falling to the ground" (Lk 22:44). Possibly, this Western text of Luke 22 is drawing on some traditions also known to the author of Hebrews. They could reflect an early authentic tradition, one even known to him, but one that was not originally part of any canonical Gospel.

If one draws this conclusion, what do these traditions add to our understanding of the Gethsemane story? First, they increase the emphasis on the humanity of Jesus and his great distress in the garden. An angel appears to him and strengthens him so that he can survive the test (cf. Mk 1:13). Second, they show that Jesus is a man of prayer dependent on the Father for help. Third, the text speaks not of Jesus having bloody sweat but rather of his sweat being like, or presumably being the size of, blood droplets. Fourth, we

---

[66]Some have even translated this as "he was heard and delivered from fear of death," but this translation labors under the difficulty that words with the *eulab-* root indicate reverence not abject fear, such as a fear of death.

are told that Jesus was in anguish, which is compatible with the picture of Jesus praying for the cup to be taken from him. In other words, rhetorically speaking, this Lukan text serves much the same set of purposes as does the brief telling of the Gethsemane moment of testing here in Hebrews. Jesus was tempted to bail out, but he passed the test.

Thus, this brief vignette from the life of Jesus serves to illustrate the point made in Hebrews 4:15 about his being tempted/tested in every respect like us, save without sin, and his ability to identify with human struggles to remain faithful and obedient to God. The scenario envisioned here involves multiple prayers, not merely a cry of anguish. If we ask why the author chose to use this episode from the life of Jesus, the answer is likely to be because it provides a paradigm for the audience to follow in their own trials, suffering, and possibility of facing a martyr's death. Here is simply another way that Jesus is seen as their pioneer or trailblazer. One can also point to the material in the Maccabean literature where earnest prayer is described as involving loud cries and tears (2 Macc 11:6; 3 Macc 1:16; 5:7, 25). However, this material simply reflects that this is the way early Jews did indeed entreat God in a crisis situation. It need not suggest any literary dependence between this material and that in Hebrews, although I would not rule out the author of Hebrews knowing the Maccabean literature.

Hebrews 5:8-9 says that Jesus learned obedience through his suffering (noting the neat aural play on words here with *emathen* ["he learned"] and *epathen* ["he suffered"]), and that he was made complete; that is, he is fully equipped and enabled to play the role of heavenly high priest and thus a source of salvation, he himself having been the perfect sacrifice that makes atonement for sin, and can be the basis of interceding with the Father in heaven. We should compare Hebrews 2:10 on the issue of perfection, and here in fact we are talking about a sort of completion of ministerial training, his preparation to be high priest in heaven. Instead of a "trial sermon," he had a trial sacrifice—of himself! Notice that in Leviticus 4:5; 8:33; 16:32; 21:10 and Numbers 3:3 the appropriate translation of this "perfection" *(teleioō)* terminology used of priests in the LXX is "consecrate." Jesus was "consecrated" to the ministry of being heavenly high priest by his suffering and death. In this sense, he was made holy, set apart, complete, perfect through suffering. It is not a statement about his moral condition.

Notice also the proviso in Hebrews 5:9: Jesus is the source of salvation for all who obey him. The author is not satisfied to say that Jesus is our high priest; he wants to make clear that Jesus eclipses all previous ones, and one of the ways the author accomplishes this is to make clear that unlike ordinary high priests, Jesus is actually the source of salvation, and the salvation that he offers is eternal (only here in the New Testament do we have the phrase "eternal salvation"), not the temporary expedient of short-term atonement by one sacrifice after another. The "how much more" or "can you top this?" motif in the earlier comparison with Moses (see Heb 3) is carried out here as well, not only in the two ways just mentioned but also by means of stressing that Jesus was of a greater priestly order than Aaron's, namely, that of Melchizedek—a theme to which our author will not return until Hebrews 7. Here the author is content to say that Jesus exceeds the high priestly job description and surpasses all rivals and comparisons. Through his death he became fully qualified to be appointed a priest, and God did so, assigning him a forever priesthood (Heb 5:6). Nobody before or since has been assigned a job quite like that.

What is so remarkable about all of this is that the author of Hebrews creatively combines the Old Testament stories about the role of priests, and perhaps also even here the descriptions in Sirach 44–50, with the story of Jesus' Gethsemane experience in order to make clear the suitability of Jesus to be our high priest forever after the order of Melchizedek. The Gospel story is fitted nicely into the larger story that the author wishes to tell about Jesus and his impact and significance. Typological use of the Old Testament, combined with the notions that the climax of revelation comes in God's Son and that his human story is a crucial part of how he came to be our heavenly high priest, melds into a single fluid presentation.

When we think of the author's narrative thought world, we cannot simply think of his revising Old Testament stories, when in fact it is his story of Christ that causes him to revise how he views all Old Testament institutions and stories, even the stories of the Old Testament patriarchs, prophets, and heroes. And it should be stressed that the author does not try to suggest that there is a heavenly climax to this story. As is also the case in the thought of other New Testament writers, here the climax comes when Jesus returns from heaven to bestow eternal salvation, a consummation and theophany described at the climax of the discourse in Hebrews 12 and contrasted with the theophany at Sinai, which Moses and the people of Israel endured and did not enjoy. This is a truly remarkable example of bold storytelling, subverting and revising old stories, especially when one takes into account that this is written to Jewish Christians in Rome who are thinking about going back to being non-Christian Jews.[67] Despite dwelling a lot on what is true now in heaven, the author agrees with and ends with the usual eschatological climax to the story found in many places elsewhere in the New Testament. He is not into providing alternate endings to the story of Christ and his people and their salvation.

If we compare this material with what we find in the Jesus material and in Paul's letters, we see that a pattern has emerged involving the following: (1) focus on Christ; (2) christological or christotelic interpretation of the Old Testament, a rereading not only of the prophetic material but also even of the priestly material in light of the Christ-event; (3) a focus on both the humanity and the divinity of Christ; (4) a belief that Christ the Messiah has brought in the beginning of the eschatological realities called "kingdom" or "salvation," or both; (5) an expansion of monotheistic ideas now to include Christ; (6) a belief that the eschatological Spirit has been bestowed, among other benefits, by the exalted Christ on his people; (6) the people of God are viewed as Jew and Gentile united in Christ, and in this people is found both the culmination of the mission of Israel and the completion of its formation as a people.

We will hear of more on this last point when we turn to Luke-Acts next, but here it is important to stress that at the heart of New Testament theology is indeed Christology. This is what most distinguishes these documents from other early Jewish documents and at the same time most makes clear that these authors share a common, Christ-focused worldview that has changed the way they view their own storied world and the stories from the Hebrew Scriptures that they learned while growing up.

THE NARRATIVE THOUGHT WORLD OF LUKE–ACTS

> The idea that history is story is widely held among critics from a number of disciplines, including history, although it is fair to say that it is not a prevailing idea, especially among historians. . . . History as it happened is something that can only be grasped by telling stories about it. History in the strict sense is a story about events, not the events themselves, or even a verbal representation of them, since it is impossible to represent the enormous mass of "events" we perceive even in a given day.[68]

---

[67]On all this, see Witherington, *Letters and Homilies for Jewish Christians*, pp. 17-33.
[68]Petersen, *Rediscovering Paul*, p. 10.

Luke was no ordinary storyteller, and we are fortunate to have two volumes of his work in the New Testament, which make up about one-third of that corpus. In fact, Luke was a master storyteller and a master editor of his sources as well, as even a cursory examination of his handling of the material that he derived from Mark makes clear. And from Luke we receive the widest vista when it comes to telling the story of the rise and spread of the good news, as Luke situates the story clearly in the larger context of God's saving activities in the world and for his people. For good reason, Luke has been called "the theologian of salvation history."[69]

It must be stressed from the outset that Luke is operating differently than the other Gospel writers are, as he is offering a two-volume historical monograph indebted not only to biblical history but also to ancient Hellenistic historians in terms of methodology and approach. He does not give us a biography of Jesus in his first volume any more than he gives us a biography of the apostles in the second one. His focus is on the narration of the "things which have happened among us" (Lk 1:1) and what they mean. One would not know that Luke's Gospel was going to be about Jesus at all from the first column or so of the document, for there we have a brief prologue in which Jesus is not mentioned, and then we are introduced to the story of Zechariah and Elizabeth and the divine intervention that happened in their lives. Luke feels that he must get a running start before engaging in telling stories about Jesus and his family and followers. In other words, the story is ongoing by the time we get to Jesus, and indeed it has been going on for quite some time before we get to the ministry of Jesus.

Luke conveys this sense of continuity with the past in a very different way than does Matthew, who begins with a genealogy. Luke, by contrast, begins by indicating his historian's approach and then tells of the sequence of events that led up to the angelic visitation to Mary. Divine intervention—salvation history—is already in process when Mary is called upon by God's messenger. God has a plan, a long-term plan, and it is working itself out through various historical persons and processes. At a few points along the way Luke will show how the macrohistory of the empire interfaces with the microhistory of salvation history that happens in particular places involving particular persons at particular times, but by and large he is content to tell the story of

---

[69]For a detailed study of Luke as a Hellenistic historian, see Ben Witherington III, *The Acts of the Apostles: A Socio-Rhetorical Commentary* (Grand Rapids: Eerdmans, 1998), especially the introduction.

the good news spreading from Galilee to Jerusalem, and then from Jerusalem heading west to the that whole part of the empire. Instead of synchronisms or the use of formula quotations, Luke will establish contact with the longer sweep of biblical history by means of allusion, echo, and occasional Scripture quotation.

For instance, in the story of Zechariah and Elizabeth, Luke intends for us to hear echoes of the stories about the birth of Samuel and the beginnings of the Israelite monarchy.[70] A new king is coming, and preceding him will be a new herald whose mother had an experience like the one Hannah had (see 1 Sam 1–2). So as N. T. Wright observes, John the Baptizer will play Samuel to Jesus' David, and the climax of their interaction comes when Samuel anoints David and the Spirit of God comes mightily upon him (1 Sam 16:13) and when John baptizes Jesus and once more the Spirit comes down mightily and remains on Jesus. "The story of salvation continues in parallel. David's anointing is followed, in the narrative of 1 Samuel, by his taking on Goliath single-handed, as the representative of Israel. Jesus' anointing is followed at once by his battle with Satan."[71] The game's afoot, and the king is abroad in his land, though in incognito at first. We would be remiss not to also hear repeated echoes of the story of Abraham and Sarah in the Lukan birth narratives, especially in the poignant story of Elizabeth and her plight, except in this tale Elizabeth must be her own Abraham, as her husband is struck dumb for lack of faith and trust in the angelic announcement, in contrast to Mary's response.

The point of such parallels is to suggest not recapitulation of an old story but rather foreshadowing and climax to the story of salvation history. It suggests a God who operates with his people following a consistent and persistent plan and pattern, and Luke is all about displaying the patterns of salvation history, including many parallels between his Gospel and his Acts volume, as we will see momentarily. Yet it would be a mistake to think that Luke's storytelling is simply like that found in Hebrews. Luke is not merely doing typology and saying that this later person/action is better than that older one. Luke is saying that this is the climax and fulfillment of a long historical process only dimly foreshadowed before.

Luke, more than the other two Synoptic writers, wants to stress that Jesus is the savior of the world (Lk 2:10-11), and his coming proves to be the real-

---

[70]See Wright, *New Testament and the People of God*, p. 379.
[71]Ibid., p. 380.

ity of which the emperor's coming and "good news" is only a parody. Luke therefore has no interest either in simply saying that Jesus will save his own people or that he will lead the revolt that will throw off the yoke of Rome and liberate God's oppressed people. This is because there is no need either to ghettoize the gospel or to politicize it, as God is directly intervening in Jesus and will go on doing so. Wright puts it this way:

> The End has happened in Calvary, Easter, and Pentecost; one need no longer fight for it, since it has already happened. At the same time, the End is yet to come, with the return of Jesus (Acts 1.11). . . . If this double End enables Luke to avoid the false antithesis of the ghetto and the sword, it also enables him to avoid the bland triumphalism of Eusebius, who in turn subverts Luke's story by combining the story of the kingdom of Israel's god with the story of the kingdom of Constantine.[72]

Luke is not interested in merely telling how the story of Israel and their Davidic monarch came to climactic fulfillment, though that is part of his aim. It is clear not only from Luke 1–2 but also from Luke 3 that this story has a more universal scope than that. This is why the genealogy in Luke 3 traces Jesus back to Adam and from there even to God. Jesus is son of Adam and son of God. This affects the way one can and should read the Son of Man material in Luke's Gospel, which, like Mark, he chooses to use as the main way of revealing who Jesus was during his ministry.

In Luke 4 as well, something remarkable happens. God's dealings with Israel, including "this present generation," are coming to a climax as Isaiah had foreseen. It therefore is no accident that Jesus will cite Isaiah 61:1-2 and then go on to say to those who have rejected the idea that it was being fulfilled in their hearing that he, like former northern prophets Elijah and Elisha, was not accepted in his own region by his own folks. And so healing and blessing ended up going to someone from Sidon or from Syria, neither of whom were Jews. Luke prepares us for a large rejection of Jesus by Jews and then a turning to Gentiles already in Luke 4. This will play itself out in Acts in the motif of "to the Jews first, and if and when they reject the good news, then to the Gentiles," which is said to characterize Paul's missionary work (see, e.g., Acts 13–14). The story of the good news continues on the larger stage of world history, as is revealed in Acts. This is not because the Jewish story or appeal to Jews has been left behind; it is because the Jewish story has been

---

[72]Ibid., p. 382.

taken up into a larger story of world redemption in the hands of Luke. It is not surprising that Luke made this rhetorical move with his presentation, since he seems to be writing for his patron Theophilus, a high-status Gentile new convert to Christianity.

It is interesting that in the plotting of the narratives in Luke and Acts there is a paradigmatic speech in each volume that sets in motion the mission of the good news: the speech of Jesus in Nazareth in Luke 4, and the speech of Peter in Acts 2 in Jerusalem. Over and over again, the living Word of God changes things either by transforming or scandalizing the audience. It is no accident that Luke presents as much speech material in Acts as he does in his Gospel. In fact, in Acts we find remarkable parallelism between the speeches and deeds of Peter, the apostle to the Jews, and Paul, the apostle to the Gentiles:[73]

Peter	Paul
2:22-29	13:26-41
3:1-10	14:8-11
4:8	13:9
5:15	19:12
8:17	19:6
8:18-24	13:6-11
9:36-41	20:9-12
12:6-11	16:25-41

These parallels are interesting and telling, reassuring Theophilus that God is no respecter of persons and is doing the same sort of saving work with Gentiles as with Jews. But one could also note the parallels between the trials of Jesus (before Judeans, and then the hearing with the Galilean king, and then before Pilate) and the trials of Paul. Paul, like Jesus, is repeatedly said to be innocent of any crime. Just as the centurion beneath the cross in Luke's Gospel proclaims Jesus a righteous man, so too at one of Paul's trials the judge says that he can find no crime that Paul has committed. The gospel, then, is not presented as a challenge to the social authority of emperor and empire, nor preaching the good news as a violation of Roman law. Thus, Christianity is not a religion of and for felons or just for the least, the last, and the lost, though certainly it is for them as well. Jesus was crucified out of ignorance, say the speeches in Acts, and Paul's incarceration in Philippi (and elsewhere) is wrong, since he is a Roman citizen.

---

[73]I owe this list to James Dunn. See Witherington, *Acts of the Apostles*, pp. 72-73.

However, it is more than an emphasis on the social benefits and political expediency that prompts Luke to tell the story of salvation history the way that he does. The crucial theme of God's plan and Scripture fulfillment had to be emphasized in order to show that the "Way" of Jesus was no innovation, but rather was intended by God all along. God's plan was to spread the good news involving Jesus from Galilee to Samaria and from Samaria to Jerusalem and Judea during the lifetime of Jesus (as chronicled in Luke's Gospel), and then to show how the good news spread in and around Jerusalem (Acts 1:1–6:7), to Judea and Samaria (Acts 6:7–9:31), and to Gentiles (Acts 9:32–12:24), which paves the way for it spreading to Asia (Acts 12:24–16:5), Europe (Acts 16:5–19:20), and finally Rome (Acts 19:20–28) at the heart of the empire.

One of the interesting ways Luke gives a sense of motion and growth to his story, particularly in Acts, is by short summary statements of change and growth (see Acts 6:7; 9:31; 12:24; 16:5; 19:20) that divide his second book into panels of a sort. Notice especially the remarkable language in Acts 6:7 and Acts 12:24 about how the Word of God grew, it being viewed as a living thing. This is neither a mere recapitulation of an Old Testament story nor even merely the fulfillment of the hopes and dreams of Israel, though it entails that as well. The former stories have been fulfilled, filled out more fully, extended, stretched, brought to a climax, and then in Acts even gone beyond. For Luke, as for the other New Testament writers, the story of Christ is the linchpin or hinge of the whole story of Israel and, even more, of the whole human drama. Salvation is of the Jews, but it is good news for all peoples.

One of the notable parallels between Luke's Gospel and Acts is the references to the eschatological Spirit being at work. In the Gospel the locus of this is primarily Jesus (see Lk 3:22; 4:1, 14, 18), and in Acts the locus is Jesus' followers and those who become his followers beginning in Acts 2. For good reason, Luke has been called the "theologian of the Holy Spirit," and his second volume is actually better titled "Acts of the Holy Spirit." For Luke, this makes clear that he thinks that he lives in the eschatological age, when the dominion of God's saving reign is already breaking into human history but is yet to be completed. Like all the New Testament writers, he has a sense of eschatological "already and not yet," and it is simply untrue that he ignores the "not yet" dimension of things, for he speaks of the return of Christ in both volumes (cf. Luke 17:22-36; Acts 1:11). Yet operating as a historian, he must place his focus on the past and the present, not the future, and rightly so. Luke's work is not a book of prophecies, but rather is a writing of salvation history.

It speaks volumes that the Synoptic Gospel writers share so much common material about Jesus and his exploits. This is because they believe much the same things about Jesus and what he said and did. Each of these writers, in his own way, seeks to set the story straight about Jesus, especially about the end and import of his life, and each of these three documents can be understood as a passion narrative with a long introduction. In fact, all four Gospels are this way because ancient people believed that how a person died most revealed that person's character, and how Jesus died was shameful and shocking.

The storytellers had to explain how Jesus could indeed be the Jewish messiah, and even the savior of the world, in spite of the fact that he died on a Roman cross. This required a great deal of explanation. Hence, all four evangelists spend almost one-third of their storytelling on the last week of Jesus' life, showing how it was a fulfillment of Scripture, of God's divine plan for his Son. Since this was an outcome not expected by most early Jews when they thought of their messiah, much less by Gentiles looking for a savior, much of the story had to be devoted to explaining such a thing. Furthermore, it was needful to show that Jesus was vindicated beyond the crucifixion, so the cross did not have the last word about him, and his story carried on.

All four evangelists agreed that the story of Easter had to be told or else the story would hemorrhage and die, coming to an abrupt, untimely, one could even say ungodly, end, with Jesus lamenting, "My God, my God, why have you forsaken me?" All four agreed that the resurrection of Jesus involved, indeed necessarily entailed, an empty tomb, for resurrection meant something miraculous that happened to a human body. Indeed, all four told recognizably the same story about the same Jesus, who was baptized by John, had a brief ministry involving preaching, teaching, and healing, and then they chronicled the demise and rise of this man.

But it was not just the evangelists for whom the Christ tale, at least in summary form, was the hinge and basis for a reordering of the way one viewed the story of God, Israel, and the world. Peter stood up on that first Pentecost and said,

> People of Israel, listen to this: Jesus of Nazareth was a man accredited by God to you by miracles, wonders, and signs, which God did among you through him, as you yourselves know. This man was handed over to you by God's set purpose and foreknowledge; and you, with the help of wicked people, put him

to death by nailing him to the cross. But God raised him from the dead, free-
ing him from the agony of death. . . . God has raised this Jesus to life, and we
are all witnesses of this fact. Exalted to the right hand of God, he has received
from the Father the promised Holy Spirit and has poured out what you now
see and hear. . . . Therefore let all Israel be assured that God has made this
Jesus, whom you crucified, both Lord and Christ. (Acts 2:22-36)

Some such summary of the life and work of Jesus as this was repeated in-
numerable times across the empire in the first century, was expanded into full
Gospels, and was the basis for preaching and teaching by Paul, Peter, James,
Jude, the Beloved Disciple, John of Patmos, and many others.[74] The Christ
story was what set apart the followers of Jesus, and it became the basis of
the reordering of their symbolic universe and their narrative thought world.
And to be sure, because it was such a surprising, unexpected and, in various
respects, problematic story, they felt a need to get the story straight, and they
did so. This story was shared by all the writers of the New Testament and was
a font to which they returned again and again to draw living water.

THE NARRATIVE THOUGHT WORLD OF MATTHEW AND JOHN

> [Ernst] Käsemann describes John's portrait of Jesus memorably as, "God strid-
> ing across the earth."[75]

> Matthew did not write his Gospel without forethought: he was a historian-
> biographer and interpreter, not just a storyteller.[76]

Both Matthew and John approach telling the story of Jesus differently than
does either Mark or Luke in this respect: they intend to emphasize in two different ways that Jesus is both a sage and the Wisdom of God come in person.
Matthew's presentation focuses on Jesus as son of David like unto but greater
than Solomon, and so there is a strongly Jewish flavor to the presentation.
John chooses a broader approach: Jesus is the Logos of God come in the flesh,
Wisdom incarnate, so to speak. The former presentation would work better
with more traditional and less Hellenized Jews who lived in a world where
scribes and Pharisees abounded, namely, in Galilee. But the Fourth Gospel is
written for Hellenized Jews who live in a largely Gentile environment. The

---

[74]As was noted some time ago by C. H. Dodd in his classic study *The Apostolic Preaching and Its Developments: Three Lectures with an Appendix on Eschatology and History* (New York: Harper, 1936).
[75]Richard A. Burridge, *Imitating Jesus: An Inclusive Approach to New Testament Ethics* (Grand Rapids:
Eerdmans, 2007), p. 305.
[76]Craig Keener, *A Commentary on the Gospel of Matthew* (Grand Rapids: Eerdmans, 1999), pp. 23-24.

latter's ethos was not one in which demons were a regular concern nor Jewish parables a regular teaching technique. There was a need for greater clarity about the identity of Jesus in that Asian environment, whereas in the former environment the true Jewishness and messianic character of Jesus had to be demonstrated. Nevertheless, the same basic story and narrative thought world are drawn on to present Jesus.

The Gospel of John has greater scope than Matthew's Gospel. It begins with a retelling of the story of creation in Genesis 1, but it is Genesis as filtered through the Wisdom interpretations found in places such as Proverbs 3; 8–9 or the Wisdom of Solomon. Jesus is presented as the Wisdom who was the cocreator with the Father before the space-time continuum existed. The story of the historical Jesus is suddenly viewed through a lens of much wider angle.

There is a further difference. Although both John and Matthew share a sapiential approach to writing, the focus in John is more personally on Jesus as Wisdom, as is clear from Jesus' "I am" statements (e.g., "I am the way, and the truth, and the life" [Jn 14:6]), whereas the focus in Matthew is on wise teaching for life, which is more in accord with traditional Jewish Wisdom literature. Bear in mind that there are few real "parables" in the Fourth Gospel, whereas parables, aphorisms, riddles, and proverbs proliferate in Matthew. Both books offer something of a counterorder sort of wisdom, and both rely primarily on revelatory wisdom, the wisdom that comes not from examining nature or human nature but rather from above.

Focusing on Matthew for a moment, we note that one thing that distinguishes this Gospel from John is that it is the work of a careful scribe who has taken over some 95 percent of the material that he found in Mark and reaudienced it for his Jewish Christian listeners in Galilee. This contrasts with the eyewitness approach of John's Gospel, where the author is not following a tradition carefully but rather is writing up his memoirs in his own manner and style. Matthew stands in the scribal tradition that wants to correlate things carefully with the Old Testament text and show fulfillment of prophecies and the like, thus stressing continuity with the Jewish past, but this is far less of a concern in John. The greater concern in the latter document is how wisdom involving and focusing on Jesus could be conveyed to an audience of highly Hellenized Jews in the Diaspora.

The author of Matthew sees himself as standing not primarily in the mold of latter rabbinic scribes doing midrash on the Old Testament but rather in the mold of the older sapiential scribes described in Sirach 39:1-3: "He seeks out the wisdom of all the ancients, and is concerned with prophecies; he preserves the sayings of the famous and the subtleties of parables; he seeks out the hidden meaning of proverbs." In Matthew the focus is on Jesus' teaching being the culmination and fulfillment of all older wisdom. In John the focus is on Jesus offering new wisdom, new revelation, repeatedly. This is not to say that Matthew has no concern for the new as well, as Matthew 13:52 shows, but the larger issue is continuity with older Jewish wisdom and fulfillment and extension of Torah wisdom. Matthew skillfully weaves together the old and the new to portray Jesus as both sage and Wisdom, as both the revealer of God and Immanuel. John takes this a step further by revealing Jesus as the Logos, the Word of God, which preexisted all of creation. One other interesting fact is that Matthew seems to have seen himself as a scribe, not a sage, and so as a conserver and combiner of the past wisdom. The Beloved Disciple, if also responsible for 1-3 John (as is likely), is a sage himself, conveying Christian wisdom for life. He follows in the footsteps of Jesus; he does not merely stand in his shadow.

Without question, the gestalt of these two books differs in part because they were meant to serve different purposes. If we take John 20:31 seriously, it seems that the stories in the Fourth Gospel were meant to be winsome tools to be used in spreading the good news in order that people may believe in Jesus. This contrasts with the apparent purpose and function of Matthew's Gospel, which is as a training or teaching manual for Jewish Christians being socialized into the Jewish Christian ethos in Galilee and being taught how to distinguish themselves from other groups, such as the Pharisees. The difference of social context (Galilee versus Ephesus or Asia Minor) explains in part why the story is told differently, but the difference in purpose also comes into play. The Jewishness of Jesus must be stressed in the Galilean context, whereas the more universal character of Jesus and his wisdom must be stressed in Asia Minor. In Galilee one hears about Jesus being greater than Moses and greater than Solomon and the like. In Asia Minor one hears about Jesus being greater than the emperor, as being the one who deserves to be called "my Lord and my God" (Jn 20:28), usurping the claims of Domitian.

Most important for our purposes, despite all these differences, is this: the basic outline of the story of Jesus is the same in both Matthew and John. There is a Galilean ministry involving teaching and miracles, there is a final fateful trip up to Jerusalem, and there is a long focus on the last week of Jesus' life, including the triumphal entry, the final meal(s) with the disciples, the betrayal, the trial(s), the crucifixion and the resurrection and resurrection appearances. Some parts of the story simply could not be left out. It is quite telling that John feels that he must include the story of the cleansing of the temple, as all three Synoptic writers do, even though he feels free to push it forward to near the beginning of Jesus' ministry so that it supports his theme of Jesus replacing or fulfilling the institutions of Judaism with himself (i.e., he is the Passover lamb; he is the temple where God resides on earth; he is the light, life, bread and liberation that other Jewish festivals celebrate, and so on). The basic template of storytelling is the same in these two Gospels: an account of Jesus' origins, his relationship with John the Baptizer, the Galilean ministry, the final week of his life, and its outcome. Within that larger script are implemented various ways to tell the story.

Matthew wants to focus on Jesus as the royal son of David like unto but greater than Solo0mon. John wants to insist that Jesus is both the Word/Wisdom of God and the Jewish source of salvation for the world (Jn 3:16), since salvation is "of the Jews" (Jn 4:22). Especially when we compare what Jesus says about himself in a chapter such as Matthew 11 and in the "I am" discourses in John, we recognize that it is the same Jesus, who is and conveys God's Wisdom. But John's Gospel is not a rewrite or variation on a Synoptic theme; it is a taking of the basic score about the life of Jesus and composing a whole new oratorio. What Matthew and John show us is the limits of the possible while still trying to present Jesus within a sapiential framework and while being faithful to the basic Jesus story. These are two different portraits of Jesus, but in both we recognize the same wise person, the same divine person who can be called "Immanuel," God's Wisdom come in the flesh.

THE NARRATIVE THOUGHT WORLD OF MARK

> A strong argument can easily be made that Mark—whoever he may have been (and we have no other sure work from his hand)—is the most original narrative writer in history, an apparently effortless sovereign of all the skills and arts of durably convincing storytelling.[77]

Mark's Gospel, as far as we can tell, was the first attempt to narrate in written form at length the story of Jesus, and to some extent it seems to have

---

[77]Reynolds Price, *Three Gospels* (New York: Scribner, 1997), p. 17.

provided the template for the presentations by Matthew and Luke. Those two authors chose to do much more than just replicate the Mark outline, but they did follow the skeletal chronological outline that Mark sets up, often in detail. This is especially the case with the Matthean use of some 95 percent of Mark, whereas Luke takes over only a bit more than half of the Markan material. But more telling than the amount of common material is that neither Matthew nor Luke chose to tell the story in the apocalyptic fashion that Mark did. If Matthew was indebted to sapiential ways of looking at narrative, Mark resonates far more with the material found in Daniel or Zechariah.

Mark's biographical portrayal of Jesus and his ministry is both dark and stark. There are commands to silence interspersed with moments of disclosure of Jesus' identity. The disclosure moments punctuate the narrative at its outset (at the baptism of Jesus), at the climax of the first half of the Gospel (Caesarea Philippi) on the Mount of Transfiguration, where Jesus, Elijah and Moses appear to Peter, James and John, at the Jewish trial, at the crucifixion, and indeed at the empty tomb as well. Ched Myers, in a helpful study, shows how apocalyptic is the approach of Mark in the unveiling of the secret of Jesus' true identity. The audience lives in a benighted world and condition, lacking faith and understanding unless there is revelation from on high.[78]

Baptism	Transfiguration	Crucifixion
heavens rent	garments turn white	sanctuary veil rent
voice from heaven	voice from cloud	Jesus' great voice
"You are my beloved Son"	"This is my beloved Son"	"Truly this man is the son of God"
John the Baptizer as Elijah	Jesus appears with Elijah	"Is he calling Elijah"

As Myers points out on the basis of this chart, these disclosure moments are meant to focus the audience's attention on the identity of Jesus. This is not a surprise in an ancient biography, but it is surprising that there is a "messianic secret" motif involved here. Apparently, Mark is telling us that the narrative can go forward, and Jesus can be understood, only if there is periodic revelation of his identity from on high. Clearly, this is not something that "flesh and blood" could deduce on its own, however sagacious one might be. We perhaps can distinquish between the more apocalyptic moments that involve

---

[78]See Ched Myers, *Binding the Strong Man: A Political Reading of Mark's Story of Jesus* (Maryknoll, N.Y.: Orbis, 1988), pp. 390-91.

a vision at the baptism and the transfiguration and the disclosure moments, but both point to a world, and indeed a group of disciples, that are in the dark about who Jesus is. Thus, the entire first half of the narrative of Mark involves the raising of "who" and "why" questions about Jesus (cf. Mk 1:27; 2:7, 16, 24; 4:41 (especially); 6:2; 7:5), and the "who" question is not answered until Caesarea Philippi (Mk 8:27-30), even for the disciples themselves. And only at that juncture does Jesus reveal in a fourfold manner in three straight chapters (Mk 8:31; 9:31; 10:32) that he is the man born to suffer many things and be killed and rise again; or as Mark 10:45 puts it, he is the one who has come to be a servant and give his life as a ransom for the many. In this sort of narrative plotting, then, the passion and Easter narratives, which take up Mark 11–16, are the chronicling of the accomplishment of the mission set out in the passion predictions in Mark 8–10.

This whole structure in turn suggests that Mark is telling his audience that until they answer the "who" question about Jesus, they cannot possibly understand why he had to die and rise again. Thus, the Caesarea Philippi and the transfiguration stories become crucial at the heart of the narrative because there is repeated effort to make clear to the disciples precisely who Jesus is before the passion events ensue. With knowledge is supposed to come power and responsibility, but it is no accident that when push comes to shove, Jesus envisions a fulfillment of the apocalyptic sayings in Zechariah not only about the striking of the shepherd, but also about the scattering of the sheep (Mk 14:27), and Mark most emphatically presents a tale of woe of how the Twelve betrayed, denied, or deserted Jesus in his hour of need, fulfilling this very prophecy that all would fall away. We have here a failure of monumental proportions, and restoration comes only at and after Easter when Jesus appears to his disciples, going before them into Galilee and revealing himself there.

One thing certainly held in common in all four Gospel portrayals of the last week of Jesus' earthly life before Easter is the need for a full explanation of why Jesus' demise happened as it did. There is a sense of urgency in providing scriptural support for all this, even down to when Jesus on the cross says, "I thirst." This is partly caused by the disconnect that would be felt in talking about a crucified messiah, never mind a crucified God. It was caused partly because this outcome was, though not unforeshadowed or unannounced, unprecedented and unexpected even by the closest disciples. Few if any had talked about a crucified messiah in those terms before, Isaiah 53 not being interpreted that way in early Judaism as far as we can tell. When one believes, as many ancients did, that how a person dies most reveals that person's character, then certainly the death of Jesus required major explanation, especially if one wanted to claim that it somehow unexpectedly atoned for the sins of the world.[79] Mark set the other evangelist storytellers a benchmark, making clear that a full explanation of that last week, especially its salvific import, was crucial to making a good case for the good news, especially in a world that viewed crucifixion in no redeeming light at all, indeed as the most shameful of all ways to die.

I have said very little about the theologizing and ethicizing done out of the core narrative about Jesus' life. I am talking about the powerful and extensive shared story that all four evangelists felt compelled to tell in their various ways and with their varying emphases. But the Christ story is a huge block of common material that they shared; and not only did the evangelists share it, but also in the oral culture in which they lived, long before it was written down by Mark, it was being summarized and epitomized by teachers and preachers in various places and ways, as Acts makes clear. C. H. Dodd, some seventy-five years ago, was correct to emphasize the apostolic preaching of the good news and its carrying forth of the story, as we find in certain summaries in Acts and in some of the epistolary literature in the New Testament.[80] There is a good reason why Luke, in his prologue (Lk 1:1-4), tells us that he had been listening to preachers and eyewitnesses tell this tale for a long time. He had! And he did not need to rely purely on Mark in order to know the story, get it straight and give an orderly account of it. Mark was only one teller of the common tale shared and highly valued by all early Christians in many places.

And this brings us to a point where we can draw a crucial conclusion. Too often the study of "New Testament theology" has been viewed as a matter of assembling the disparate pieces of a complex jigsaw puzzle or, to use another metaphor, winnowing a large pile of contingent chaff to get at the coherent kernels, the core, the substance shared by New Testament writers and then attempting to synthesize these nuggets. What this whole process ignores is that these writers are operating out of a fundamental unity that in fact makes them Christians and sets them apart from non-Christian Jews.

---

[79]Mark, since he takes a more apocalyptic or revelatory approach to the christological storytelling, not surprisingly focuses on materials from Daniel and Zechariah and some messianic psalms in bringing forward the Old Testament stories in order to exegete the Christ-event and explain its peculiarities.

[80]Dodd, *Apostolic Preaching.*

The writers of the New Testament share a common story and belief system, a common symbolic universe and narrative thought world, out of which they do their theologizing and ethicizing into particular situations. The unity primarily exists in that shared narrative thought world and highly Jewish symbolic universe. There is, of course, also some unity of theological and ethical expression, of articulation of that thought world, but that is less profound or vast in scope than their shared commitment to the Old Testament and its stories, to the story of Jesus and of his earliest disciples, and the like.

To be sure, we occasionally get glimpses of how true it is to speak of a large shared unity of thought world. For example, Paul tells us in the early 50s that he passed on to his Corinthians the very narrative that he himself had received as sacred story about the death, burial, resurrection and appearances of Jesus (1 Cor 15:1-4). He does not need to mention this more than in passing because his audience has already learned this story, has heard it on repeated occasions and indeed has embraced it.

We must keep in mind that the whole of the New Testament is addressed to those who already are Christians and have already heard their story told in many ways and on many occasions. The narrative thought world, including the way the Christ story has reconfigured the Jewish thought world, is simply presupposed as a baseline assumption, a fundamental unity, from which all such Christian discourse should begin. And when the Christ story is challenged in any crucial way, the response is swift and particular: to not believe that Jesus Christ has come in the flesh, has died, has come forth in glory and has been seen and touched and known beyond his death is already marked as false teaching in a sermon such as 1 John. We do not need to wait until the second century to find out that the early Christians had a sense of the boundaries of their thought world and recognized when someone had misrepresented the Christ story. The unity behind, beneath and undergirding these New Testament texts certainly is more vast than the unity that can be shown from comparing and contrasting the articulation of theology and ethics on the basis of the shared narrative thought world, and yet, as we will see, that outward visible edge of the unity as expressed by various authors is impressive and substantive as well.

THE NARRATIVE THOUGHT WORLD OF 1–2 PETER

1 Peter

For all its Pauline echoes, however, 1 Peter also has close affinities with the synoptic tradition and to a lesser extent with the Gospel of John, Hebrews, and

James. There are remarkable convergences with Peter's speeches in Acts. Since 1 Peter resonates with such a wide spectrum of early Christian witnesses, some scholars have suggested, only half jokingly, that its author knew the whole New Testament! . . . Part of 1 Peter's enduring appeal stems from the breadth and depth of common tradition on which it draws and its appropriation of the earlier, apostolic consensus in giving authority to its distinctive voice.[81]

As much as or more than any other New Testament text, 1 Peter is a meditation on suffering, trying to steel the audience for what they have endured and would endure. The rhetorical strategy of the author for dealing with this pastoral problem is to remind them of the story of the suffering servant of Isaiah (and Psalms) and the particular embodiment of that story in Jesus' own story, and then to suggest that the audience is called to the imitation of those stories, should it come to that. But there is so much more to say about the tradition and narrative-rich Petrine legacy.

It has been said that Christianity in the first century was a social world in the making.[82] This is true, and we want to know what sort of social world was being constructed by the external evangelistic program, the good news storytelling, and the internal ordering of Christian communities based in house churches. Was it an ordering that baptized various forms of the social status quo and called it good? Was the aim to make clear that Christianity was not a revolutionary new religious sect in the Roman Empire? Was it an attempt to extend largely Jewish values and beliefs to a wider audience? And what role was 1 Peter meant to play in this social constructing of a "new world" or at least a new Christian society and subculture?

Often missed in such a sociological study of 1 Peter is the fact that the author is also busily constructing a rhetorical world, a world of advice and consent, of persuasion of dissuasion, where certain beliefs and behaviors are inculcated not merely for social reasons but also for theological or ideological ones. When we analyze 1 Peter as rhetoric, what do we learn about the aims and purposes of this document, broadly speaking? Is it meant to steel the audience for persecution by persuading them about the value of Christlikeness? Is there some considerable rhetorical exigence or problem that this discourse is meant to overcome? And what do we make of the intertextual echoes in

---

[81]Carl Holladay, *A Critical Introduction to the New Testament: Interpreting the Message and Meaning of Jesus Christ* (Nashville: Abingdon, 2005), p. 485.

[82]See John H. Elliott, *A Home for the Homeless: A Sociological Exegesis of 1 Peter, Its Situation and Strategy* (Philadelphia: Fortress, 1981), p. 2.

this document, not only of the Old Testament but also of material from the rhetoric of Jesus, of James and of Paul?

Where was the author placed geographically, socially, temporally and rhetorically that he would have known all of the material mentioned by Carl Holladay in the quotation that began this section, and does such evidence provide clues to the authorship of this document? Could 1 Peter really be the masterpiece and last grand act of the great apostle who had known both the persons and the rhetoric of Jesus, James and Paul and now was making their contributions serviceable for his own audience? Was the author at the font from which the apostolic tributaries flowed forth and so in touch with the origins of Jewish and Gentile Christianity and its leaders, or was he at the place where all those tributaries came back together at the end of the first century and the beginning of the second? For now, it is interesting to note that although 2 Peter is a composite document deeply indebted to its predecessors, this characterizes 1 Peter as well, though in a very different way. The Petrine legacy in the canon is tradition rich and not story-impaired either.

Commentators have often stressed that 1 Peter is more of a theocentric than christocentric discourse, but if we ask what has caused the reconfiguration of Peter's thought world, certainly what he thinks about Christ has caused the shift. He operates with a christocentric or christotelic[83] hermeneutic when it comes to his handling of the Old Testament (see, e.g., 1 Pet 1:10-12), which is by no means unique to this book in the New Testament (cf. Lk 24:25-26, 45-47), and not only does the teaching of Christ echo in his words, and the figure of Christ entirely shape his theology of sacrifice and atonement, but also Christ provides the ethical pattern set forth for his audience to emulate. And this brings us to a further critical point. The longer I work with the New Testament, the less satisfied I am to see theology and ethics divided from one another as if they were discrete subjects. By this I mean that the figure and pattern of Christ binds the two together and grounds both the indicative (what Christ was and did) and the imperative (what his followers should do and be). In one sense, the ethics of 1 Peter is just a playing out of what it means to be like and to follow Christ. Believers participate in the sufferings of Christ in some sense and also look forward to an exaltation like Christ's, and the V-pattern (humbling self and being exalted) is repeated in the life of the disciple (see 1 Pet 4:13; 5:1-6).

---

[83]I borrow this term from Richard Hays. It refers to how Scripture is seen as pointing to or having Christ as its goal or fulfillment.

In 1 Peter the christological language, indeed the whole theological language set, is suffused with the eschatological and apocalyptic worldview of the author. It therefore is no surprise that Jesus' second coming is referred to in 1 Peter as a "revealing" or "unveiling," with the same language being applied to the day of judgment that comes at and with and by means of the return of Christ (cf. 1 Pet 1:3-7, 13 with 1 Pet 1:8; 4:13; 5:4). Christ is exalted, having entered heaven, and so now is hidden, but one day he will be revealed, at which juncture believers will see him once more (1 Pet 1:8; 4:13). Interestingly, Peter is even prepared to call the first coming of Christ an "appearance" (1 Pet 1:20). It was that appearing that set the eschatological clock ticking, and the author lives in the exciting atmosphere of expectation about the return of Christ, possibly his near return, although expectation never degenerates into calculation in 1 Peter. In some ways, this is no surprise, since we find much the same sort of orientation in Mark's articulation of things, and Mark is dependent to a degree on Peter's telling of the Christ story.[84]

We must be satisfied here with examining two ways that Peter articulates his narrative thought world. The first involves the reevaluation of the meaning of Old Testament texts in the light of the Christ-event, and the second involves a brief comparison of Peter's speeches in Acts and what we find in 1 Peter. The latter provides us with one more piece of evidence, if we needed it, that shows how even such different figures as Peter and Luke share the same narrative thought world, and Luke has a concern to articulate that world in a way that is faithful to how Peter actually preached.

1 Peter's christological use of the Old Testament. Let us closely consider how Peter uses the Old Testament in 1 Peter 2:6. First, he quotes the Old Testament there and in part confirms what he has said in 1 Peter 2:4-5, but he goes on to advance his argument (not just proof-texting his point) using Old Testament phrases after that. Sometimes Peter, like other New Testament writers, uses the Old Testament to mean things that probably were not the main point that the Old Testament writer had in mind. In 1 Peter 2:6 we have a quotation from Isaiah 28:16 LXX (cf. Rom 9:33). The phrase "in him" is not found in the MT, but only in some LXX versions. Peter cites the version that makes the christological point clearest. During the whole course of this argument Peter seems to have in mind Jesus' own words about "the stone that the builders rejected" (cf. Mark 12:10-11; 13:1-2; 14:58). Notably, Mark, Peter's interpreter, highlights Jesus' use of

---

[84]On which, see Ben Witherington III, *The Gospel of Mark: A Socio-Rhetorical Commentary* (Grand Rapids: Eerdmans, 2002).

these terms near the end of his Gospel. I am inclined to agree with the suggestion that Peter learned how to handle texts in these christological and ecclesiological manners from observing the praxis of Jesus himself.

It is quite striking that the quotation here is introduced by a unique phrase that literally reads "for it says in writing." But of course, Peter is not talking about just any kind of writing; he is talking about the Old Testament. Is Peter implying that because it is in writing it has more authority? This depends on his theology of sacred texts, but I think the answer to this question is yes. In an oral culture texts, especially religious texts, take on an even more sacral aura then they do in our culture of endless texts.

The quotation refers to God laying a stone in Zion, which is synonymous for Jerusalem in general and more often indicates the city of God, the place of his indwelling or his sanctuary, the temple hill being called "Mount Zion" (cf. Pss 20; 48; 74). Here the usage makes sense because Christians look forward to a new Jerusalem. They *are* the new temple, but they expect a new Zion (cf. Rev 14:1).

By etymology, the Greek word in question, *akrogōniaios*, means "extreme" *(akro)* "corner" *(gonias)*, and so certainly "cornerstone" is a possible meaning here. But is it a bottom corner, like a modern cornerstone (for which there is little ancient evidence), or a "top corner"? I suggest that *akrogōniaios* probably indicates a stone designed for the top corner of a wall, not a capstone of an arch, but it could be the latter. This interpretation has the advantage of matching up with the Scripture citation in 1 Peter 2:7 and means that there is not a different sort of stone in view when one compares Psalm 118:22 and Isaiah 28:16. This interpretation also has the advantage of matching up with *Testament of Solomon* 22:7-9; 23:1-4, which speaks of Solomon's erection of a temple in which "there was a great corner stone *[lithos akrogōniaios]* that I wished to put at the head of the corner *[kephalēn gōnias]*." The stone, then, is set on the pinnacle of the temple at the top and juncture of the two walls.

It would be impossible to stumble on a capstone or a head of the corner stone unless it is envisioned as being on the ground and not yet in place in the building, which is why various commentators think that a cornerstone is meant.[85] Also, a foundation stone that is below ground is not likely in view. We are talking not about the foundation here but rather about a special stone around which the rest of the edifice is built, which could be either a corner-

---

[85]Unless, of course, one was standing on the pinnacle of the temple, as Jesus is envisioned as doing in the temptation stories (see Mt 4:5; Lk 4:9).

stone, a keystone or a head of the corner stone, which is clearly referred to in the second part of the quotation. So, Christians are viewed as being built into the community that is vitally linked to and designed around Christ. Christ is the elect and precious one, or one held in honor, who makes it possible for believers who are "in Christ" to be elect and precious to God. Indeed, 1 Peter 2:7 even refers to honor that comes to the one who believes in Jesus. It is interesting to contrast the discussion here with that at Qumran, where the Qumran community itself is characterized as the "precious cornerstone" by way of this very same text from Isaiah 28 (1QS VIII, 7; cf. 1QH[a] XIV, 26).

The quotation itself also says that those who believe in Jesus will not be "put to shame." This is an Old Testament idiomatic expression referring to being condemned by God at the last judgment, the ultimate disgrace that one can undergo, which results in shame rather than honor for the person involved. Believers share in the honor that belongs to Christ. But to unbelievers, those who build the edifice of their life rejecting the key or crucial stone, Christ, it becomes a stone that they stumble over—that is, they sin (just as walking implies obeying in Old Testament). Christ is said to be a rock that is a stumbling block. The Greek term here is *skandalon*, from which we get the English word *scandalous*. Here it refers to that which occasions sin or stumbling, generally an obstacle in the way of the sinner. The irony is that these builders rejected the very one whom God selected and made into the head of the corner. Far from being a cast off, he was the one of chief importance, the head of it all, particularly in the matter of salvation.

Peter is developing his argument here by drawing on two other "stone" passages, Isaiah 8:14; Psalm 118:22. Notice that both Romans 9:33 and our text here are closer to the MT than to the LXX, perhaps because the LXX leaves out the notion of offense or scandal. There was another reason to follow the MT for several of these texts: in the LXX of Isaiah 28:16 there is reference to the stone in question being sunk in the foundations, and therefore being something that one could not likely trip over. This has led some to suggest that here Peter is following a catena of "stone" texts that he and Paul shared. This is possible, but it is also possible that Peter, in Rome, had read Romans or knew of its argument, especially since Romans had been available to that community for some years, since about A.D. 57 or 58. In favor of the testimonia view is Ramsey Michael's point: "If Peter were using Paul [here], it is unlikely he would separate out two quotations that Paul had so carefully integrated into one. Moreover, his middle quotation, Psalm 117[118]:22, is not found in Paul's epistles . . . but (within the NT) only in 1 Peter and the Gospels (cf. Mark 12:10 // Matt 21:42 // Luke 20:17; cf. the paraphrase attributed to Peter in Acts 4:11)."[86]

In 1 Peter 2:9 Christians are seen as a chosen race, a holy people for God's possession—Exhibit A, revealing the mighty acts of God. Indeed, they are chosen for the specific purpose of proclaiming God's mighty acts. What has happened to believers has happened so that these acts might be proclaimed and thus God be glorified. Redemption is for the believer's succor, but it is also for God's glory. God is the one who called persons from the darkness of sin and spiritual blindness into his marvelous and everlasting light. There is nothing here about an old Israel that is being replaced by a new one. To the contrary, Peter's view is that the one people of God have kept going all along, only now their true expression is found in Jew and Gentile united in Christ. This is more of an eschatological completionist schema than a replacement schema.[87] There certainly is neither any anti-Jewish sentiment in this discourse nor even any polemic against the synagogue, but here Exodus 19:6 is being appropriated and applied to the community of Christ. Here, as in Hebrews, Christ and his people are seen as bringing to completion the mission of Israel and the people of God.

One phrase calls for close scrutiny in 1 Peter 2:9. Is *basileion hierateuma* an adjective and a noun or two nouns? Does it mean (1) royal priesthood; (2) house of the king, body of priests; (3) a priesthood in service of the king; (4) a kingdom of priests; (5) a group of kings, a body of priests? In favor of option 4 is the Old Testament background, Exodus 19:6 as translated in the LXX. The Hebrew reads "a kingdom of priests," but the LXX translates it as two substantives, two nouns in apposition to one another: kings and priests. It may seem odd to stick two nouns side by side, but if the LXX could do it, so could Peter. If option 4 is the correct rendering, it implies not that believers are kings, but rather that they are priests in service of the king. Against option 5 we may argue that there is no precedent for the word *basileion* meaning a "group of kings."

Against option 1 and option 3 we must argue (a) if *basileion* were an adjective, it normally would follow its noun as *eklektos* follows *genos* and

---

[86]J. Ramsey Michaels, *1 Peter* (WBC 49; Waco, Tex.: Word, 1988), p. 94.

[87]It is true that on my reading, 1 Peter by and large is not addressing Gentiles. As I have said, however, it is quite likely that some God-fearers came into Peter's churches through evangelism of Jews, as was true with other apostolic work. Thus, Peter is thinking of true Israel as Jew and Gentile united in Christ the living stone.

hagios follows *ethnos*; (b) in the only other use of *basileion* in the New Testament (Lk 7:25) it means "palace" or "king's house," and is not an adjective, and in parallel Hellenistic literature it is normally a noun (see 2 Macc 2:17; Philo, *Sobriety* 661; *Abraham* 56); (c) what precedes this in 1 Peter 2:5, a reference to a "spiritual house," may suggest a parallel here: "king's house." Thus, perhaps we should see this as two nouns in apposition, and if so, option 2, "house of the king, body of priests," is the best translation. If the LXX and Hebrew background is in view, as the other terms in the list may suggest, perhaps we should translate "a kingdom of priests" or even "a royal priesthood" because the other four honorific phrases here involve a noun and a modifier. If the latter, it is simply affirming that all believers are priests; if the former, it stresses that believers are both collectively God's house and his priests.

Notice the contrast in 1 Peter 2:10: "You who were once not a people are now a people." Here Edward Selwyn urges,

> What Peter's words conveyed to people so placed was that they now once again belonged to a community which claimed their loyalty; and it was something which could give all their instincts of patriotism full satisfaction. In short, the term connotes in Greek, community. In the mixed society of the Roman Empire, where freedom of association was suspect and subject to restrictive laws, as in modern despotic states, this sense of community must have worn very thin, and produced a widespread feeling of homelessness.[88]

These words from Hosea originally referred to Jews, and there is no reason why they cannot refer primarily to Jewish Christians here either.

Notice also the "now" in this text. Peter emphasizes both what God has now done and what he will yet do. To be a people, a community, means that believers have experienced the mercy of God. Many commentators think that 1 Peter 2:10 could not have been spoken of Jews, that Peter can only be talking about Gentiles here who are now included in God's new chosen race. But that notion overlooks that in Peter's view, when Jews have rejected Christ, they at least temporarily cease to be part of the people of God (cf. Rom 11). Here Peter is referencing Hosea 1:6-10 and probably Hosea 2:23 as well, and these texts certainly were being applied to Jews in their context, as they likely are here as well. What we have seen in this section of the discourse is a tour de force use of the Old Testament as a basis for argumentation, loaded with

[88]Edward G. Selwyn, *The First Epistle of Peter: The Greek Text, with Introduction, Notes and Essays*, 2nd ed. (London: Macmillan, 1947), p. 101.

allusions and partial quotations tailored to fit the context here, and as such, it rivals what we find in Romans 9–11 and the use of the Scripture there.

For Peter, it was essential to ground his argument in such a way that he could say, as he does in 1 Peter 2:6, "For it is contained in Scripture that. . . ." For him, this is the final and irrefutable authority that clinches the arguments and makes the case. No audience would be more likely to pronounce the amen to that theology of the Word than Jewish Christians who also knew and resonated with these very texts. But how poignant must these texts have been for Peter himself, who was called "Cephas" (Jn 1:42), but also a "stumbling block" (*skandalon*) on the same occasion when he confessed Jesus as the Christ (Mt 16:23). One can understand his wrestling with these very texts to understand not only Jesus' identity but also his own. This argument is brought to a close by a reminder to the audience that they have a high calling, they are a temple, and indeed they are a royal priesthood, and as such, they are God's option in their own pagan environment, and so they must live in a fashion that makes them good witnesses, good neighbors, good people.

1 Peter's connection with Peter's speeches in Acts. On a close reading of Acts and 1 Peter, it becomes apparent almost from the very beginning of the latter that there is some connection between the speeches of Peter in the two works. In 1 Peter 1:2 we hear about the elect who had been chosen according to the foreknowledge of God, and the only other reference to *prognōsis* in the New Testament comes in Acts 2:23, where we hear about "this Jesus delivered up according to the foreknowledge and plan of God." Were this the only correspondence, it might pass as a coincidence.[89] But in fact, as we work through 1 Peter, we discover many other correspondences, always with the speeches of Peter in Acts, not with Acts in general or speeches in Acts in general.

Elsewhere I have dealt at length with the speeches in Acts, including Peter's speeches.[90] These speeches present the largest challenge to the student trying to evaluate the historical substance of the book of Acts, since in many cases Luke could not have been present to hear these speeches, and in all, or nearly all, cases we have only summaries of speeches, not a transcript of whole speeches. These speeches make up some 365 verses of Acts, about one-third of the whole book. The goal of a good Hellenistic historian was to present the major points of a speech, not just the singular main point, and to do so in a style and form that comported with Peter and his own ethos. Luke has made

---

[89]See John H. Elliott, *1 Peter* (AB 37B; New York: Doubleday, 2000), p. 376.
[90]Witherington, *Acts of the Apostles*, pp. 116-23.

his source material his own, but precisely because there are correspondences between the Petrine speeches in Acts and the diction in 1 Peter, it becomes clear that he must have been rather faithful to those sources and their style and substance. I have made the case elsewhere that Luke was a careful Hellenistic historian following the conventions of predecessors such as Thucydides and Polybius.[91] This result will be assumed here, not argued for. One of the important conclusions of that study was that since Luke believed that the early Christian movement was in one sense created and carried along by evangelism, the spreading of the Word (see, e.g., Acts 6:7), he spent disproportionately more time on speeches in his work than did his Hellenistic predecessors. There are in fact some longer speeches in Polybius and Thucydides than in Acts, but far less in number or percentage of the entire verbiage of the work.

We have eight speeches by Peter, all of them in the first half of Acts (Acts 1; 2; 3; 4; 5; 10; 11; 15), and there are a further nine speeches by Paul (Acts 13; 14; 17; 20; 22; 23; 24; 26; 28), and thus we see that Paul is, in a way, depicted as picking up where the trail of Peter goes cold. These two are given by far the most space for speeches in Acts, the next closest being the one long speech by Stephen in Acts 7 and two speeches by James in Acts 15; 21.

What is especially interesting about the place where Peter's speeches stop is that this is the juncture where Peter apparently went to the very places listed in 1 Peter 1:1-2. The correspondences between 1 Peter and these speeches, as we are now about to see, suggest that Peter continued to preach in the same fashion and using the same subject matter as he had earlier. Three important impressions stand out from reading through Peter's speeches in Acts: (1) Peter is always addressing Jews or, in one case, God-fearers, such as Cornelius, and there are no representative speeches to pagan Gentiles; (2) in the paradigmatic speech at Pentecost in Acts 2, which sets the tone for all that follows in Acts, Peter uses the Old Testament in much the same Jewish and messianic ways that we find him using it in 1 Peter; (3) the rough Semitic style and primitive doctrine in these speeches (e.g., especially Acts 10:34-43) comport with both what we know of Peter elsewhere in the Gospels, in Paul's letters and in 1 Peter.

Edward Selwyn, over sixty years ago, pointed out in detail the correspondences between the speeches of Peter in Acts and 1 Peter.[92] Let us review that data here.

---

[91]Ibid., pp. 1-65.
[92]Selwyn, *First Epistle of Peter*, pp. 33-36.

Acts 2:14-40. The reference to the Spirit that Christ sends falling on the church as the signal of the eschatological age being in process should be compared to what is said about prophets in 1 Peter 1:10-12. In this speech Christ's death is said to take place according to God's counsel and foreknowledge (cf. 1 Pet 1:20; see also 1 Pet 1:2). The statement that Christ was not left in Hades and his flesh saw no corruption but rather he was raised from the dead (Acts 2:27, 31) should be compared to 1 Peter 3:18; 4:6. Notice how Christ's resurrection and ascension are closely linked in Acts 2:32-36, and we can compare 1 Peter 1:21; 3:22. According to Acts 2:38, the purpose of baptism is remission of sins, which should be compared to 1 Peter 3:21. The universality of grace promised in Acts 2:39 becomes a theme that runs through 1 Peter (see especially 1 Pet 1:10-12; 2:9-10).

Acts 3:11-26. Here we have the references to Jesus as God's servant (Acts 3:13, 26; 4:27-30), which seems clearly enough to echo Isaiah 40–55, a source text used christologically that certainly crops up in 1 Peter with some regularity. Particularly, the language that Peter uses about the death and vindication of Jesus seems to echo Isaiah 53. Equally interesting and telling is the theme of *agnoia* found in Acts 3:17 (cf. 1 Pet 1:14). What is especially telling about this is that the ignorance in the Acts passage is predicated of Jews, as is probably the case in 1 Peter 1:14. The various general parallels between these speeches and 1 Peter provide support for seeing a close parallel on the ignorance issue. Notice also the parallel references to the second coming in Acts 3:20 and 1 Peter 1:7, 13; 4:13, and to the rejection and slander of believers (cf. Acts 3:23 and 1 Pet 2:7, 10). Further notice the parallel reference to the inevitable nature of Christ's suffering (cf. Acts 3:18 and 1 Pet 1:11, 20).

Acts 4:9-12. This is only a brief speech, but notice the use of the Old Testament "stone" material here in Acts 4:9-12 and in 1 Peter 2:7, in both cases drawing on Psalm 118:22.

Acts 5:29-32. Here and in Acts 10:39 the cross is called a *zylon*, "tree" (cf. 1 Pet 2:24 and Acts 13:29). This undoubtedly echoes Deuteronomy 21:23. In Acts 5:32 the disciples are said to be witnesses of *tōn rēmatōn*, "these things," where "things" refers to actions or events or even words (cf. 1 Pet 1:25).

Acts 10:9-16, 34-43. Notice the use of *prosōpolēmptēs* in Acts 10:34, and see in 1 Peter 1:17 the use of *aprosōpolēmptōs*. One can also compare the phrase "the judge of the living and the dead," used of Christ in Acts 10:42, and what is said in 1 Peter 4:5.

Acts 15:7-11. Compare the emphasis on God's choice in Acts 15:7 and in 1 Peter 1:1; 2:9, and on the cleansing power of faith in Acts 15:9 and 1 Peter 1:22.

In addition to the foregoing correspondences, it is striking that we have the reference to the name *christianos* in Acts 11:26; 26:28 and in 1 Peter 4:16. This name arises when Christians live in a predominantly Gentile environment.

After reviewing this evidence, Selwyn concludes,

> Few would suggest that the parallels of thought and phrase between the speeches and 1 Peter are based upon St. Luke's reading of the Epistles: for in both documents they clearly belong to their contexts, and the doctrinal issues in the speeches, notably the idea of Christ as *pais Theou*, are obviously original and not deductions from the Epistle. On the other hand, they are what might be expected if both alike are utterances of the same mind, given on different occasions. The connexion, that is to say, is not literary but historical: the common ground lies in the mind of St. Peter who gave, and was known to have given, teaching along these lines and to a great extent in these terms.[93]

Though in strong agreement with Selwyn, I would phrase things a bit differently. The evidence considered here is sufficient to say that the implied author of 1 Peter certainly reflects various of the speech traits and thematic interests of the Peter who speaks in the sermons in Acts. The issue is how to explain this. Carl Holladay suggests that the author of 1 Peter wrote so late in the New Testament era that he knew various other New Testament works. This is not impossible, but this could even be true at a time well before the ninth decade of the first century; it depends on the dating of the other New Testament books. But in fact what neither Holladay nor others have been able to show is a literary relationship between 1 Peter and Acts or with various of Paul's letters or the Synoptics. It seems instead to be more on the level of oral tradition or familiarity of the author with some of this material directly, by which I mean that the author of 1 Peter knew some of the people who wrote these books—for example Paul and Mark, and perhaps the author of Hebrews.

Here is where the issue of social location comes into play. The author of 1 Peter is in Babylon (i.e., Rome). Whether he is Peter or some later figure writing in Peter's name, he is a Christian who could have had access to Christian documents written in or sent to Rome, such as Romans, Hebrews,

---

[93]Ibid., p. 36.

Mark and perhaps even Acts (to judge from Acts 28, where the narrative breaks off). In my view, the correspondences between 1 Peter and the Petrine speeches in Acts are too subtle and convincing to be the work of a mere copier or imitator who decided to mimic the Petrine style of the speeches when he wrote 1 Peter.

It is a far better and more economical thesis, and one that avoids the serious problems of seeing 1 Peter as a pseudepigraph and therefore a deceptive work, to suggest that the Peter who was a disciple of Jesus and knew his teaching, was an associate of James and knew some of his teaching, was an associate of Paul and knew some of his teaching, and had Mark, the author of the earliest Gospel, as a coworker in Rome is responsible for 1 Peter. Furthermore, we must consider the possibility that Luke too finished in Rome and perhaps had access to Peter while he was there during the period of Paul's house arrest in Rome in the years A.D. 60–62. If so, then Peter is the source of the summaries of his own sermons in Acts, and it therefore is no surprise that 1 Peter sounds like some of that sermonic material. This is not because Luke is a good imitator and editor; it is because he, though certainly a good editor, had in the case of Peter's sermons a good eyewitness and original preacher source (just as he claims in Luke 1:1-4), the man called "Cephas." Although all roads may not lead to Rome, all these rabbit trails and echoes of other Christian sources in 1 Peter eventually lead back to the historical figure of Peter himself. He is the best candidate, perhaps with the help of Silvanus, for the authorship of 1 Peter, just as he is the one who spoke of these things on many occasions to Jews in Jerusalem and elsewhere during the first decade of the life of the church and beyond.

Parallels between Paul's letters and 1 Peter. This brings us to a further crucial point. We could also go on to note the various parallels between Paul's letters and 1 Peter, including the use of the phrase "in Christ." Not only did the New Testament writers share a common thought world grounded in their shared sacred text, the Old Testament, but also they exchanged information, shared stories, built up the new Christian thought world together. This involved not merely a social world in the making, but a Christian thought world in the making. The fact that there are so many similarities in the way the Old Testament is used and the way the Christ story is articulated among so many of these witnesses suggests a movement with considerable social networks and obvious dialogue. The unity is not limited to just the obvious shared ideas that lie on the surface of various of these New Testament texts.

Here we do well to remember what Paul tells us in Galatians 2. He says that he set his gospel before the pillar apostles so that he would not be running in vain. He says that he received the right hand of fellowship from these pillars, and that his mission to Gentiles was recognized and endorsed. Whatever differences of praxis that would and did arise between Paul and some Judaizers from Jerusalem (some men from James, but not James or Peter or John in particular), it did not have to do with the articulation of the gospel, the story of Christ, nor have we any reason to think it had to do with the christological and ecclesiological way the Old Testament was now being read. Acts 15 shows that James was just as busy offering such readings as was Paul or Peter or any other early Christian writer. Within the many and divergent articulations of theology and ethics in the New Testament there was a considerable unity of narrative thought such that wherever one went in the empire and spent time with Christians, the gospel and its new way of reading the Old Testament was shared in common.

2 Peter

And this brings us to just a few comments about 2 Peter. This letter is a composite document assembled probably in the last decade of the first century A.D. It is indebted to 1 Peter and an otherwise unknown Petrine fragment recounting his reaction to the transfiguration. It is indebted to Jude, and it is indebted to Paul. The editor of this material is not an innovator, nor does he seek to be. He is a collector and consolidator of earlier Christian traditions. But what 2 Peter shows is that he assumes that the earlier traditions are not in any way discordant. He assumes that they work very well together to address his own Christian audience. He assumes that they all have their own stories straight, and indeed they are all telling the same Christian story, unlike the false teachers whom he is doing polemics against. The apostolic tradition is already in play and a living reality in his discourse. This attention to and dependency on shared sacred tradition should in no way surprise us, since the author, like all the other New Testament authors, except perhaps Luke, is a Jew. But it tells us a great deal about the early Christian movement that so much material was shared, including, of course, both the Old Testament and the gospel. It then comes as less of a surprise that all of these writers articulate their theology and ethics in ways that are harmonious with, and sometimes even identical with, what we find in other New Testament writings. Christianity was, after all, a fledgling minority movement in the first century A.D. regarded by many as a pernicious religious superstition, not a licit religion. Under such circumstances, it is no surprise that these Christians hung together in the way they thought, taught and preached, lest they hang separately, and of course they did that together as well.

THE NARRATIVE THOUGHT WORLD OF REVELATION

> Those first ancient auditors of the Apocalypse came together not merely to be informed but to be transformed, to undergo a collective change in consciousness.[94]

We could spend some brief time on the narrative thought worlds of James, Jude and 1-3 John, but it is so allusive that in James we have bare references to Job and Elijah and a little more about Abraham, in 1 John we have a passing reference to Cain, and in Jude we have colorful references to a group of the bad boys of the Pentateuch coupled with references to extracanonical traditions about Enoch and Moses. But in all cases these stories are taken for granted as shared with the audiences, known to the Jewish audiences, and so there was no need at all for elaboration. Furthermore, in each case the names arise or are alluded to in order to make ethical points, not theological ones. The issue is praxis and behavior, not primarily the thought world in each case. In addition, of course, there are allusions to and echoes of Jesus' teachings, particularly in James. But in these more paraenetic discourses the thought world is not much in play or articulated, and this is even less the case in the brief personal letters of 2–3 John. Thus, this brings us to the very rich and complex last volume in the canon, the book of Revelation.

Revelation is different from all of the rest of the New Testament, providing us with a book of apocalyptic prophecy within an epistolary framework. The narrative thought world of this book is more extensive than many New Testament books, especially in regard to the future of Christ's story and the story of the world and of his people.

One of the interesting features of John's narrative thought world is that clearly his is a Scripture-saturated mind. There are literally hundreds of allusions, echoes or partial quotations of the Old Testament in this book, but they are used in the service of a christological vision of the present and the future. Once again the Christ story reconfigures how the Old Testament is viewed and, more importantly, how it is used. John believes that he knows how all those prophecies in the Old Testament will be fulfilled and by whom, and the answer is through and in Christ and his people. A unique feature of John's visionary rhetoric is that he recounts the story not only of what is and will

---

[94]Allen Dwight Callahan, "The Language of the Apocalypse," *HTR* 88 (1995): 460.

transpire on earth, but also of what is transpiring in heaven. As G. B. Caird suggested, John gives us a glimpse into control central, into the heavenly court, where we find the divine situation room and learn of how God is and will manage the crisis of sin and evil on the earth by bringing both temporal and eternal judgments and acts of redemption to those on earth, though ultimately the real solution to the human dilemma has been provided already by the slain Lamb and the Word of God. John also will recount how what is currently "up there" will some day be "out there" when Christ returns and the new heaven and new earth follow. The other world and the afterlife effect a corporate merger.

We should not be led astray by the hyperbolic, bizarre, and sometimes even mythological images to assume that John's revelation is not referential and is not intended to speak about the future. That assumption is false. John believes in a literal return of Christ in space and time, and there is no reason to doubt that he also believes in a series of redemptive judgments that will fall upon the earth prior to that consummation. The overall message is that God is in his heaven and all will be right with the world because God's divine reign will come fully on earth when Jesus returns, and before then, God will already be dealing with rescuing his people and judging their oppressors. There is a strong stress on the sovereignty of God over the historical process, including the future. No one should see this as ephemeral idealist rhetoric, the ancient equivalent of insubstantial comfort food. John is quite in earnest about the coming judgments and redemption wrought by God.

The arc of the narrative that John tells pretty much begins and ends with the story of a Christ who is Alpha and Omega, and so the one who is present in the beginning and at the end, but is born of a woman at a particular point in time and is snatched back up into heaven just when Satan had thought he was going to snuff out his life for good. This story is juxtaposed to the story of the threefold fall of Satan, who tries to do away with this Incarnate One but ends up falling not only from grace and heaven to earth but also into the pit and thence into the lake of fire. But between the fall from heaven and the fall into the pit Satan chases the woman, the emblem of God's people. She is protected on the earth, not raptured into heaven, as Revelation 12 makes clear.

John's story has not only more scope than most of the tellings of the story in the New Testament, but also more texture and depth. For example, John is concerned to contrast the evil empire with the godly one. So we hear about the emperor under the figure of Mr. 666, and there is his imperial cult apparatus under the figure of the false prophet/priest and the land beast. The emperor and empire are as one in the image of the beast with multiple horns and wounded head. In addition, we have a tale of two cities, not Jerusalem versus Rome, but rather Rome the harlot versus the new Jerusalem, which will come down from heaven. Despite all the stress on three sets of seven judgments that takes up the largest single bit of the plot, John has an expansive vision of saved Jews and myriads of Gentiles, of 144,000 of the Jewish saints saved, but also the Gentile ones, of Old Testament saints and New Testament apostles being foundational to the heavenly city not made with human hands. The political nature of this coded rhetoric far outstrips the allusions we find from time to time to the emperor cult in Paul's writings and elsewhere in the New Testament. This book certainly is not mainly about pie in the sky by and by; it is about justice and redemption being done upon the earth. It is not the ancient equivalent of escapist fiction.

John believes in the interface between the material universe and a spiritual one, between earth and heaven. Thus, he does not believe that human history is a self-contained homogenous process where the normal lines of historical cause and effect apply in all cases. Divine governance is a perpetual condition, and divine intervention is a regular occurrence. For John, the most important events in human history have already happened: the death of the Lamb and his resurrection and exaltation to the right hand of God the Father. John believes that the end of history has already broken into space and time, and so his is an eschatological perspective, not an ordinary salvation-historical perspective. God's eschatological judgment on history, not a normal chronicling of history, is going on here, and of course it is future history that is being prophesied and commented on in this book. In this telling of the story history receives its final meaning from what is yet to come. The comfort for the suffering audience comes mainly not from the reassurance that they will go to be with the Lord, though surely that is believed and spoken of, and not even from the promise that God will judge their oppressors before the end; rather, it comes from the vision of the end itself, which involves new heaven and new earth and the final elimination of sin, suffering, sorrow, disease, decay and death, and evil as well. John's focus is not on the meaning of history but rather on the meaning of suffering and the response of God to it, showing that God remains sovereign even in this vale of tears.

Like Luke, John of Patmos believes that the story of the church is a continuation of the story of Jesus in various senses. Thus, for example, in Revelation 12:1–14:20 and Revelation 15:2-4 we have the story of God's people in the present (and future) in conflict with evil and dealing with suffering, and the pattern of Jesus' suffering is replicated in the saints who are martyred and end up under the altar in heaven (Rev 6:9-11). John believes that there is one continuous history of God's people from the patriarchs to the consummation, but obviously the nature of that people changes, becoming Jew and Gentile united in Christ once the Lamb is slain and then exalted on high. There is no separate history for Israel and the church, but only one ongoing tale.

The macrostory of God's people helps give perspective on the trials and tribulations of the particular churches that John is addressing in Revelation 2–3. Their travails are set against the backdrop of those of God's people before and after them. What we learn of the story of John's churches is that they have existed for a considerable period of time and have had various ups and downs, various temptations and triumphs, and they are ongoing. Some of these churches are doing better than others, but John tells them the cautionary tale in Revelation 12 to remind them that they have protection from obliteration, but they need to be vigilant as well. If the two lampstands in Revelation 11 are two of these churches, then there is the reassurance that "if anyone tries to harm them, fire comes from their mouths and devours their enemies" (Rev 11:5). Fire-breathing churches is a rather fierce image of the church's ability to endure through persecution, prosecution, and execution.

The intersections of the stories of Christ, the church, and the known world's empire are various, and much is woven together. But not surprisingly, it is the Lamb who is also the Lion who is also the Lord who has the first and last words about both his church and his world, as Revelation 21–22 make clear. This story is only foreshadowed and alluded to in the little apocalypse in Mark 13 (and its Synoptic parallels), but what John says here is consonant with what we find there, and for that matter with what we find in 1 Corinthians 15 and 2 Thessalonians 2. The shared eschatological and christological worldview of all the New Testament writers is presented to us in detail and in "hi-def" in Revelation. Jesus too, in his discussions of a future coming of the dominion involving a messianic banquet, the patriarchs, himself and his converts, suggests that he envisions a future millennial messianic kingdom on earth not unlike what Revelation 20 has in mind—a not uncommon view held by early Jews, such as Pharisees and Qumranites, who subscribed to an eschatological afterlife view.

SUMMARY

We have by no means covered the entire shared narrative thought world spoken of or alluded to in the various New Testament books and in the teaching of Jesus. A great deal more could be said. My goal in this chapter was to present a representative sampling to show the depth and scope of this narrative thought world and also the degree to which it is shared by all these writers and with Jesus as well. Monotheistic, messianic, eschatological thinking characterized the thought world of all these early Jews. They believed that they lived in the age of the fulfillment of prophecy, the climax of history, the arrival of final redemption and judgment that would begin with the household of God. It was not only John of Patmos who held this perspective; he is but the most obvious example of this sort of thinking, bringing it to its fullest and most vivid expression. The revision of monotheism in a christological light characterizes all of this literature's narrative thought, even beginning with Jesus himself.

Here I should reiterate some of the salient conclusions drawn earlier in this chapter. If we compare all this material, a pattern emerges involving (1) focus on Christ; (2) christological or christotelic interpretation of the Old Testament, a rereading not only of the prophetic material but even of the priestly material in light of the Christ-event; (3) a focus on both the humanity and the divinity of Christ; (4) a belief that Jesus Christ, the Messiah, has brought in the beginning of the eschatological realities called "kingdom" or "salvation" or both; (5) an expansion of monotheistic ideas now to include Christ; (6) a belief that the eschatological Spirit has been bestowed, among other benefits, by the exalted Christ on his people, and the people of God are viewed as Jew and Gentile united in Christ. In this people we find both the culmination of the mission of Israel and the completion of its formation as a people. Here it is important to stress that at the heart of New Testament theology is indeed Christology. This is what most distinguishes these documents from other early Jewish documents and at the same time most makes clear that these authors are sharing a common Christ-focused worldview that has changed the way they view their own storied world and the stories from the Hebrew Scriptures that they learned growing up.

It remains for us to examine at some length what the articulation of New Testament theology and ethics growing out of this narrative thought world looks like as a synthetic whole. It is time now to hear how the early Christian choir sings together their good news oratorio.

4

THE NEW TESTAMENT
CONSENSUS ON CHRIST

Early Christians such as Paul did take over the story contained in the Scriptures, understanding it in the light of their history, and they did see their experience as the next stage in the story. Paul, however, does not so much tell a story in his letters as rather comment on the story and its implications for his readers. It is important that the story be told correctly and not given a different kind of spin, as was happening in the Jewish understanding of it that led on a trajectory to a rabbinic Judaism that denied the Messiah had come.

I. HOWARD MARSHALL[1]

In spite of the varied viewpoints and differing circumstances, one hears a symphony, not a cacophony. The divine conductor, the Holy Spirit, has orchestrated a most remarkable composition. In these "27 documents that changed the world" we hear the Master's voice. Whether through Evangelists who faithfully transmit the sayings or deeds of Jesus or through apostolic letters and tracts, before us lies one coherent message. Jesus Christ, Son of God, Savior, has become one with us in order to redeem and recreate a fallen humanity and world.

LARRY R. HELYER[2]

---

[1]I. Howard Marshall, *New Testament Theology: Many Witnesses, One Gospel* (Downers Grove, Ill.: InterVarsity Press, 2004), p. 423.

[2]Larry R. Helyer, *The Witness of Jesus, Paul, and John: An Exploration in Biblical Theology* (Downers Grove, Ill.: IVP Academic, 2008), p. 403. There is some irony to this, Helyer's final conclusion of his study, since throughout he has labored to demonstrate that the kingdom of God or, put another way, salvation history is the major theme that unites the canon, including the so-called major witnesses of the New Testament—Jesus, Paul, and John. But of course, although Jesus Christ is indeed what unifies the New Testament, he is not the focus of the Old Testament, and hence comes the need to look for a broader and more abstract theme to unify all of biblical theology.

In this chapter and the next few the goal is to examine what can be said about a consensus, or set of shared beliefs, when it comes to New Testament theology. I will take the same approach in the following chapters in regard to New Testament ethics. This in turn will lead to some discussions about the interface between theology and ethics in the New Testament, about traditions and trajectories grounded in the Old Testament but leading into the New Testament, and finally a discussion of biblical theology. What I am striving for here is not just to identify the shared ideas or commonalities of the various New Testament witnesses about some subject. Although certainly I am interested in the consistent and repeated core stories and ideas, I am taking an additive approach to the material, indicating also what this or that writer adds to the discussion without gainsaying the consistent or repeated core teachings. Keep in mind the image of the oratorio: I am analyzing the various parts of the score to see not only the main notes that this or that singer sings in unison with others, but also where they offer a solo that further enriches the composition without violating the spirit or tenor of the masterpiece as a whole.

It will be clear from the preceding discussion in this volume that in my view we must begin with Christology when we approach New Testament theology, for it is the straw that stirs the drink, it is the ideational cluster that causes the reconfiguration of thoughts about God, God's people, humankind in general, salvation and eschatology, to mention but a few subjects. I propose in this section to take an additive approach, building up the synthetic portrait of New Testament theology by assembling the key singers of this complex oratorio and asking each one to perform his role, looking for doubling and dissonance along the way as well as creative soloing. What must be considered first is the main theme of the whole masterpiece: the focus on the Master, Jesus the Christ. This is not a study of Handel's oratorio *Messiah*, but it is a study of the New Testament's doxological and hymnic treatment of the same subject.

Along the way, we will begin to see how other important subjects are closely bound together with the christological visions of the various New Testament authors. How they view the law, eschatology, community, Israel, soteriology, and many other subjects is affected by their christological perspectives on Jesus. We will sample some of this correlative material as well in this chapter and see how the New Testament writers themselves began to work out a synthesis, while working out of a christological consensus on these matters. Sometimes in more complex material, such as we find in Revelation, a more detailed sampling and discussion is in order, and at other times that will not be necessary. In all cases, however, we are left with a profound impression of how all things theological and ethical are colored by the christologically reshaped worldview of these authors.

JESUS CHRIST, THE ALPHA AND OMEGA OF NEW TESTAMENT THEOLOGY

We begin with a simple chart of which books call Jesus what. This is a key clue to the shared ideational system or symbolic universe and also to some of the shared narrative thought world when it gets articulated in particular texts for particular circumstances.

Table 4.1. Distribution of New Testament Titles for Jesus

	"Christ"	"Lord"	"Son of God"	"Son of Man"
Matthew	X	X	X	X
Mark	X	X	X	X
Luke	X	X	X	X
John	X	X	X	X
Acts	X	X	X	X
Romans	X	X	X	
1 Corinthians	X	X	X	
2 Corinthians	X	X	X	
Galatians	X	X	X	
Ephesians	X	X	X	
Philippians	X	X	X	
Colossians	X	X	X	
1 Thessalonians	X	X	X	
2 Thessalonians	X	X	X	
1 Timothy	X	X	X	
2 Timothy	X	X	X	
Titus	X	X	X	
Philemon	X	X		
Hebrews	X	X	X	X
James	X	X		
1 Peter	X	X		
2 Peter	X	X	X	
1 John	X	X		
2 John	X	X		
3 John				
Jude	X	X	X	
Revelation	X	X	X	X

What do we make of this? The most notable thing is that with the exception of 3 John, two or more of these titles occur in every New Testament book in reference to the same person, Jesus of Nazareth. One could argue that the use of "Son" differs from the use of "Son of God," but in practice the two are interchangeable in the sense that both refer to Jesus. The most frequent combination phrase that occurs in the vast majority of these books is not "Jesus the Christ" but rather "Jesus Christ," as if the title "Christ" had become a second name.

Not infrequently we find in some of the New Testament letters the combination "Lord Jesus Christ," but never "Jesus Lord Christ" or "Christ Lord Jesus." Sometimes we find "Christ Jesus" or "Christ Jesus the Lord." In other words, there is an understanding that "Lord" and "Christ" are actually titles, so there is a definite effort to avoid simply putting two titles together if the human name "Jesus" is also going to be used. The most obvious variation of pattern is that all the Gospel writers all use "Son of Man" with frequency, but this title virtually disappears in the rest of the New Testament, and even its occurrences in Hebrews and Revelation, since they are parts of a Daniel 7 allusion, probably do not count. That leaves one bare reference in Acts outside the Gospels.

It has been argued that the use of the "last Adam" language by Paul in Romans and 1 Corinthians as applied to Jesus is his equivalent term for "Son of Man," and this may be so, but it is hard to see why Adam would be thought to be a more generic symbol or idea than Son of Man by a largely Gentile audience. Perhaps the latter was seen as too bland or apparently vacuous, whereas Adam suggested a particular individual person. In any case, Adam is a primordial figure, the Son of Man an eschatological one.

Even with all the variations that we find, the chart of terms/titles is significant because it leads to some important points. First, even allowing for individual nuances in individual documents, we see that the consistency of use of at least two or three of these titles throughout these books (again, with the exception of 3 John) and always applied to the same person, Jesus of Nazareth, indicates that we are dealing here with the very heart of the shared symbol system. Other than the term "God" itself, no other theologically pregnant term comes even close in frequency of occurrence in the New Testament. Second, there are 1,368 occurrences of "God" in the New Testament, at least seven of which actually refer to Christ, and several hundred more references to the "Father" (16 times as "heavenly Father," 63 times as "our Father," and an amazing 73 times as "the Father of our Lord Jesus Christ"). There are 301 occurrences of "Son of God" (or "Son") referring to Jesus, a further 340 occasions where Jesus is called both "Lord" and "Christ" within a few words, a further 550 occurrences of "Jesus Christ," a further 381 times Jesus is called just "Lord" (sometimes in a more mundane sense), and, depending on what we count, 300 or more occurrences of "Son of Man" applied to Jesus, usually on his own lips. Contrast this with the notion that something like the kingdom of God is the unifying theme of the New Testament, a phrase that occurs frequently in the Synoptics, occasionally in John, a handful of times in Paul and rarely elsewhere in the New Testament, even allowing for variant forms of the phrase.

Just by sheer statistical word count, it is simply wrong to say that the New Testament is more patrocentric than christocentric. Both categories are part of the theocentrism of these documents, but the christological language is more frequent and dominant, to such a degree that often when the Father is brought into the discussion, it is as the Father of Jesus, or as "our Father," with whom the Christian has a relationship because of Jesus. What is especially stunning about this is that all the writers of the New Testament, perhaps with the exceptions of Luke and the final editor of 2 Peter, are Jews. And yet they do not primarily talk about Yahweh in the same way we find God discussed in the Old Testament. There has been a definite shift in the ideational center of the thought world in a christocentric direction such that even the Father and the Spirit are viewed for the most part through the category of or in relationship to the Son. The attempts to resist this conclusion must be rejected. These conclusions do not make the New Testament a christomonistic document by any means, but they absolutely do show where the center of gravity or, to use the oratorio analogy, the dominant theme of the musical masterpiece, is. The focus is not primarily on the Father or Spirit or salvation or eschatology or prophecy or the kingdom, but on Jesus. And this brings us to our third point.

By the time the New Testament documents were written, probably in the fifty-year span of A.D. 49–99, enough water had gone under the bridge that the authors had to know that they were a sectarian offshoot of Judaism, and many of them understood that they were on the way to establishing a new religion, since the large majority of Jews rejected the worship of Jesus as Lord or Son of God. There is surprisingly little attempt to redefine the word *Israel* in the New Testament to refer to Christians (whether Jewish or Gentile) rather than non-Christian Jews (Gal 6:16 is possibly a rare exception, but not certainly, since it could just refer to the Judaizers or more broadly to Jewish Christians). There is some effort in various books to say that Christian Jews are the true Jews, the real righteous remnant, but already in our earliest New Testament documents, the letters of Paul, we see "in Christ" used as a community-identifying label (also in 1 Peter).

In other words, at least in some quarters there was already a sense of at least one degree of separation from the ancestral faith when the New Testament documents began to appear. And frankly, the New Testament, though very Jewish, is also very sectarian. Belief in Jesus as Christ, Lord, the Son of God and the like is the sine qua non of salvation in book after book of the New Testament. The New Testament itself is christological to the core, on page after page, and although this is implicitly trinitarian, the focus rarely is on the Three in One but rather is on the One, the Righteous One, the only Begotten One, who provides access to the Three. We certainly can call parts of the New Testament "proto-Trinitarian," but we cannot accurately call it "proto-Christological." In other words, whatever our theological predilections or preferences, we must allow the focus of the New Testament to be what it is.

I suspect that one of the reasons why this is not recognized more clearly or is resisted by some is that it is too monolithically sectarian for some modern tastes, it involves too much focus on what distinguishes Christianity from Judaism and other religions. Yet I emphasize that we must let the early Christian thought world be what it was: it had narrower boundaries of thought with less diversity than often is imagined, and clearly it had a more singular focus on Jesus than often is allowed. Orthodoxy, at least christological orthodoxy, was already present in large measure in the first century, and that was the yardstick by which much of Christian life, both theological and ethical, was measured even in Paul's day before the fall of the temple. This being the case, we need to some degree to reiterate and reexamine the Christology of the New Testament from a slightly different angle that will reinforce what I have just suggested. This will then allow us to consider the development of some of the other common elements in New Testament theologizing.

Scholars in recent years have been understandably wary of overfocusing on Christ when studying New Testament theology, since there are so many other important subjects to cover as well, not the least of which is the broader subject of the shared eschatology of the Christian movement. However, it is undeniable that what early Christians thought, believed, knew and experienced when it came to Jesus is at the epicenter of their thought world, and it set them apart from both other early Jews and Gentiles. So much was this the case that engagement with the message of the good news was practically equated with encounter with the risen Lord. Listen, for example, to the prologue of 1 John: "That which was from the beginning, which we have heard, which we have seen with our eyes, which we have looked at and our hands have touched—this we proclaim concerning the Word of life. The life appeared, we have seen it and testify to it, and we proclaim to you the eternal life which was with the Father and has appeared to us" (1 Jn 1:1-2). Here we have a case where the message is the medium, so to speak, rather than vice versa; it conveys what it reports. There is not a single New Testament book that does not mention, directly or indirectly, that Jesus of Nazareth is the Christ, or Lord, or Son of God, or some other significant attribution.[3]

How very different this sounds from the general tenor of most non-Christian early Jewish literature. Even taking into account recent revelations from various early Jewish sources, including the Qumran material and the so-called Gabriel Stone, it is fair to say that messianism is hardly the dominant focus of conversation in much, if any, of this material. This stands in dramatic contrast to what we find in the New Testament, where Christ and Christology appear as subjects on almost every page of these Christian texts. Obviously, some historical explanation is required for this fact, given that all the New Testament documents, with the possible exception of Luke-Acts and perhaps 2 Peter, were written by Jews.

Furthermore, there is the more particular point made by Raymond Brown that "in all Jewish history before A.D. 130 (and then dubiously), we have no evidence that any living Jew was ever referred to as the Messiah except Jesus of Nazareth."[4] To this we may add the point made by John Collins that no living Jew of the period other than Jesus was ever identified with the Danielic Son of Man figure.[5] Again, these facts require some explanation, and they

---

[3]The exception to this, perhaps, is 3 John, although "the Name" in 3 John 7 may actually allude to Jesus.

[4]Raymond E. Brown, *An Introduction to New Testament Christology* (Mahwah, N.J.: Paulist Press, 1994), p. 73. Again, the Gabriel Stone may be the singular exception to this verdict, but the jury is still out.

[5]John J. Collins, *The Scepter and the Star: The Messiahs of the Dead Sea Scrolls and Other Ancient Literature* (New York: Doubleday, 1995), pp. 208-9.

serve to drive us to the very nub of the matter.

What do we make of the fact that Jesus is both the basis and the focus of New Testament thought? Should we conclude that this is yet another example of the enthusiasms of a group of religious zealots exaggerating the importance of their founder? Or is there some sort of historical warrant and explanation for such a focus?

After some preliminary considerations about the story of Jesus, we must focus first on our earliest window into New Testament Christology, the letters of Paul. What we will discover is that there is already a fully developed ideational system of theology and ethics that could be articulated with finesse into a variety of contexts. Paul was articulate, but he certainly did not invent all these ideas about Jesus, as is shown by the fact that almost every one of them can be found elsewhere in the New Testament, often in places where there is no likelihood of Paul's influence on the writer. The proper conclusion to draw is that there was a broad and deep ideational system at the heart of which was Jesus, and it was shared by the most literate and articulate of the early Christians whose writings we find in the New Testament. I do not have space here to demonstrate this for every single New Testament book, but I will deal with a representative sample of the witnesses and show how they focus on Jesus as someone more than merely mortal in one way or another, indeed as Savior and Lord and Messiah.

Jesus Christ as the Basis of New Testament Thought

Insofar as we can talk about "New Testament thought," and not merely the thoughts of New Testament writers, there is very little reason to object to the proposition that Jesus is the basis of much of the worldview projected and reflected by the New Testament writers.[6] Even more skeptical New Testament scholars such as Rudolf Bultmann were well aware of the enormous impact of Jesus on the theologizing of the New Testament writers. Whether one examines the way the New Testament writers talk about God the Father or about the Spirit or about soteriology or about eschatology or about ecclesiology, the impact is clear. I have shown in another context that it is inadequate to argue that the "Father" language used for God in the New Testament is simply a development of that usage in earlier Judaism. To the contrary, God is

---

[6]Some of this material appears in another form in Ben Witherington III, "Jesus as the Alpha and Omega of New Testament Thought," in *Contours of Christology in the New Testament*, ed. Richard N. Longenecker (MNTS; Grand Rapids: Eerdmans, 2005), pp. 25-46.

called the "Father" of Jesus Christ and "Abba" in the New Testament in ways that are not claimed in other early Jewish literature.[7] To put it another way, patrology is viewed through christological spectacles in various parts of the New Testament. The same can be said in regard to pneumatology. The Spirit is the one promised by Christ or by God through Christ, or is sent by him, or is even called the "Spirit of Jesus Christ" (Phil 1:19) in the New Testament. There is no real analogy to this in early Jewish literature that I know of, nor is there one in the Hebrew Scriptures for that matter. The writers of the New Testament apparently felt it incumbent upon them to speak in these new and fresh christological ways.

When we consider the issue of soteriology, we see that the focus is not merely on the person of Jesus but rather on a specific event in his life: his death and ensuing resurrection. So much is this the case that one can hardly speak of alternative theories of salvation in the New Testament, if by that one means theories that do not in some way involve Christ and his death and resurrection. Even if we were tempted to be skeptical about finding the pieces of the meteor called the Christ-event at this great a remove, we certainly can examine the enormous impact or crater made by the Christ-event on these early Jews' thinking about God, the Spirit, salvation and a host of other issues.

Consider for a moment the issue of eschatology. Just as it is very doubtful that Jews before Jesus were conjuring with the possibility of a crucified messiah,[8] it is equally implausible that they expected a resurrected one, as an isolated event in human history, rather than the final resurrection of the righteous.[9] And yet Paul, our earliest New Testament writer, speaks of Jesus' resurrection as the firstfruits of the general resurrection. In other words,

---

[7]See the critique of Marianne Meye Thompson's *The Promise of the Father* in Ben Witherington III and Laura M. Ice, *The Shadow of the Almighty: Father, Son, and Spirit in Biblical Perspective* (Grand Rapids: Eerdmans, 2002), pp. 1-42.

[8]For a discussion of the fragments found at Qumran that might be thought to point in this direction, see Ben Witherington III, *The Many Faces of the Christ: The Christologies of the New Testament and Beyond* (New York: Crossroad, 1998), pp. 20-21. The evidence from *4 Ezra* is from too late in the first century to be germane to a discussion about Jesus and his own setting. Only the evidence from the Gabriel Stone may be an early example of mention of a messiah who dies, but absolutely nothing is said there, any more than in *4 Ezra*, about a messiah suffering crucifixion.

[9]Again, the Gabriel Stone may allude to an imperative from the angel Gabriel that commands some sort of messianic figure to "live" (*ḥāyâ*), but by no means is this clear, as the stone at this point is blurry and missing some letters, and this requires creative reconstruction such as that advocated by Israel Knohl, "The Messiah Son of Joseph: 'Gabriel's Revelation' and the Birth of a New Messianic Model," *BAR* 34, no. 5 (2008): 58-62.

the eschatology that formerly spoke about the resurrection of the righteous, or perhaps of all, is now modified to speak in a firstfruits/latter fruits way, with one particular historical individual, Jesus, being said to be the firstfruits of the resurrection. One could also point to the way that final judgment, whether one thinks of the book of Revelation or Mark 14:62 or 2 Corinthians 5:10, is now seen as focusing on or involving Christ as the judge or implementer of judgment.

The ecclesiological language also has been altered under the impact of the Christ-event. This is the case in obvious ways such as Paul's use of "body of Christ" language or the reference to Jesus' community in Matthew 16:18, but also even more elaborate conversations about Israel in Romans 9–11 or passing references to the twelve tribes in the Dispersion (Jas 1:1) or the exiles in the Dispersion (1 Pet 1:1) have been affected by the Christ-event and by the new vision that God's people are Jew and Gentile united in Christ. It is a matter not just of transferring language from one community to the other, but of transfiguring the language itself such that Christ defines the terms. In all of these instances, and in many more, Christ or the Christ-event is the catalyst for new ways of expressing one's faith about matters pertaining to deity, soteriology, eschatology and ecclesiology. When a group of people can be said to be "in Christ" when previously they would never have been called this whether they were religious groups of Jews or Gentiles or some mixture thereof, clearly the thought world and the symbol system and the narrative have taken a dramatically new turn. Indeed, one can speak of an epistemic shift so significant that all of reality is now viewed through the Christ-event, and discussions of it are rendered through a christological form of discourse.

It hardly needs to be said that Christ is the focus of the Gospels. Even a cursory examination of the word usage reveals this fact. For example, Jesus is the subject of one-fourth of the verbs in Mark (24.4 percent), and another one-fifth of the verbs in this earliest Gospel occur on his lips. The next closest figure is the one-eighth of all verbs that refer to the disciples individually or corporately. In Matthew and Luke Jesus also dominates the narrative, being the subject of 17.2 percent of all the verbs in Matthew and 17.9 percent in Luke. It is also interesting that while 20.2 percent of Mark's verbs focus on Jesus' teaching (including parables), in Matthew it is 42.5 percent and in Luke 36.8 percent. In the Gospel of John over one-fifth of the verbs (20.2 percent) have Jesus as the subject, and in addition over one-third of the Johannine verbs occur in the teaching or discourse material by Jesus (34 percent). Of this material, almost 10 percent is self-referential.

"All together then, over half the verbs are taken up with Jesus' deeds or words, performed by him or spoken by him (55.3%). . . . Thus the Fourth Gospel occupies a middle position between Mark and Matthew/Luke: despite all John's different 'feel' and discourse material, he places less teaching on Jesus' lips than Matthew and Luke do, and gives Jesus more prominence in his narrative than they have."[10] What is most remarkable about this is that even when we are dealing with a historical monograph rather than an ancient biography (which Mark, Matthew and John are), a monograph that is not focusing on the personality or character of the one known as Jesus but rather is telling the story of salvation history, Jesus still dominates the story line in Luke's Gospel. And interestingly, this focus on or preoccupation with Jesus can be seen in the very earliest New Testament documents. This was not an ideological change that gradually developed and increased and only appears in Gospels; it is already obvious in Paul's thought.

THE CHRISTOLOGICAL CONSENSUS OF THE NEW TESTAMENT DOCUMENTS

Paul's Letters: The Narratological Shape of Paul's Christology Revisited

It is not just the Gospels where Christ is so evidently the focus of thought. For example, we discover that the term *christos* is used in Paul's letters some 270 times, or on average more than two times on every single page of these letters.[11] To this we may add the nearly 200 times Paul uses the term *kyrios* in these same documents. But there are other, more effective ways to demonstrate the centrality of Christ throughout the Pauline corpus—for example, by considering how Paul's storied world is reshaped around the Christ-event, and how Paul's hermeneutic in handling the Old Testament, the law, God, eschatology, Adam and a plethora of other subjects changed once he began to look at such things through the eyes of Christ. It will be worthwhile to concentrate on the Pauline material in the rest of this section of the discussion because his letters provide us with the earliest literary witness to how early Christian thinking focused on the person and work of Christ.

Paul's thought revolved around the Son, whom he called with great regu-

---

[10]Richard A. Burridge, *What Are the Gospels? A Comparison with Graeco-Roman Biography* (Cambridge: Cambridge University Press, 1992), p. 223. All these statistics are from this same volume (see pp. 196-97).

[11]I am counting by the number of pages in the Pauline portion of the Greek New Testament, not in a translation.

larity "Jesus Christ."[12] There are particular landmark human figures in the story of God's people with whom Paul chooses to compare and contrast Christ (Adam, Abraham, Moses), but he also says quite a lot about Christ's relationship to the Father and to the Holy Spirit, though without fully articulating a description of the Trinity. The former comparisons are only natural because Paul thought of Christ as a truly human figure, but the latter ones are equally important, for Paul thought of Christ as divine, as part of the story of God, without violating his own vision of monotheism. In other words, Christology was a form of theology for Paul (without his thought being christomonistic in approach), but it also had much to do with anthropology.

By way of reminder, I have spoken of a fourfold narrative that gives Paul's Christology its essential shape and contours.[13] There is, of course, first of all the story of Christ himself. This story involves telling about the one who was in the very form of God (Phil 2:6) but set aside his divine prerogatives and status in order to take the status of a human, indeed even a slave among humans, and died a slave's death on a cross, and because of this God highly exalted him. Much of this story of Christ Paul seems to have derived from his reflection on and elaboration of early Christian hymns, including the notions of the Christ as God's Wisdom, and from his experience on the road to Damascus, and also from the apostolic traditions that he received from the pillar apostles (see Gal 1–2).[14] Paul, however, does not think that the story of Christ ends with Christ's exaltation to the right hand of God, for he goes on to relate how Christ has an ongoing role in heaven, and how he will come again as a judge and triumphant Lord. Furthermore, for Paul, Christ's exalted state does not merely recapitulate his preexistent state.

For Paul, the christological hymn in Philippians 2:6-11 indicates that it is the career of Christ that determined how he should be confessed.[15] Jesus is given the throne name of God ("Lord") precisely because God exalted him as a result of his finished work on earth. We must take seriously the "therefore" in Philippians 2:9, which indicates that since his death and because of his

---

[12]In fact, some 270 of 531 total uses of "Christ" in the New Testament occur in the Pauline corpus.

[13]See Ben Witherington III, *The Individual Witnesses*, vol. 1 of *The Indelible Image: The Theological and Ethical Thought World of the New Testament* (Downers Grove, Ill.: IVP Academic, 2009), pp. 182-203.

[14]On these, see pp. 90-100 above.

[15]For another form of this argument, see Ben Witherington III, "Christology," in *Dictionary of Paul and His Letters*, ed. Gerald F. Hawthorne and Ralph P. Martin (Downers Grove, Ill.: InterVarsity Press, 1993), pp. 100-115.

prior life and death as God's and humankind's servant, Jesus has received this name. The end result of this process is that Christ has now assumed the role of Lord and is functioning as Lord over all.[16] In other words, the acclamation of Christ as Lord means that Jesus is the risen Lord (the Lord since the resurrection), but the term "Lord" is not viewed as merely honorific. A phrase that occurs with regularity in Paul's letters is "the Lord, Jesus Christ." If we compare this to the emperor's throne name, "Imperator, Caesar Augustus," it suggests that Paul could use "Christ" not only as a name but also as a title, such that Christ's name rivals and surpasses that of the emperor.[17] In Paul's view, Christ is now functioning as Lord reigning from heaven.[18] It appears from a text such as 1 Corinthians 15:28 that Paul believes that after Christ's work is done (which involves completing the job of placing everything under the divine dominion at and after the parousia), the lordship over everything and everyone (even the Son) will be returned to the Father.[19] In all of this it is clear that one must ask what point on the time or career line of the Christ one is talking about if one is going to discover which titles are then appropriate to predicate of Christ. Christological titles are predicated to a significant degree on the basis of function or task being undertaken at the time.

A good example of what I have just discussed can be seen in the few times that Paul uses *christos* as something other than a mere second name for Jesus.[20] As an actual title, *christos* describes the roles assumed during the Son's earthly career climaxing in the cross. This is why Paul can resolve "to know nothing but Christ, and him crucified" (1 Cor 2:2). This last striking and paradoxical affirmation is crucial for Paul in various ways. It shows that he, like other

---

[16]It is right to stress that Paul often uses this title to enforce paraenetic material or practical advice or in ethical instruction. For example, Paul advises in 1 Corinthians 7 that Christians are free to marry but that such marriages should take place "in the Lord" (see 1 Cor 7:39).

[17]Another thing that points in the direction of Paul's sensitivity to Christ as a title is that he never simply combines the two titles "Lord" and "Christ" ("Lord Christ").

[18]Eduard Schweizer (*Jesus Christ: The Man from Nazareth and the Exalted Lord* [Macon, Ga.: Mercer University Press, 1987], pp. 15-18) rightly points out that since the contrast to "Jesus is Lord" is "Jesus be cursed" (1 Cor 12:3), it becomes clear that the acclamation "Jesus is Lord" mainly refers to his lordship over the church, over those who confess and submit to him. Pointing also to Romans 1:3-4, Schweizer adds, "His human existence was a preliminary stage in which he was the designated, but not yet ruling king. Again, resurrection is installation to lordship over the church" (ibid., p. 17).

[19]It therefore is correct to say that Christ's lordship looks to the ultimate lordship and reign of God the Father.

[20]In general it can be said, as is noted by Werner Kramer (*Christ, Lord, Son of God*, trans. Brian Hardy [Naperville, Ill.: Allenson], p. 186), that Paul tends to use familiar titles for Christ repeatedly because his addressees would naturally be expected to assent to such formulae.

early Jews, saw the Christ as a human being, one who could be killed. It also shows that the actual story of Jesus has caused Paul to reevaluate what it meant to be the Jewish messiah, for it is probable that Paul was no different from other early Jews in that he did not expect a crucified messiah.

Paul is not content to use *christos* in the ways he found it used in his sources; rather, he also puts it to new and sometimes paradoxical uses. For most early Jews, the phrase "Christ crucified" would be not merely a paradox, but a contradiction in terms. How could the Anointed One of God, God's most blessed, at the same time be cursed by God, as would be apparent from such a hideous death (read in the light of Deut 21:23)? If the story of Jesus was merely read in the light of Scripture, it was possible to conclude that Jesus was not the Christ. But if the starting point was God's action through Jesus, and one then read the Old Testament in light of the recent events in the life of Jesus, another conclusion was possible. In short, the primary story for Paul is the story of the historical figure Jesus, and it is this story that is seen as the key to all other stories, including all the ones found in the Hebrew Scriptures. Paul, of course, did not always use the term *christos* in a purely historical manner, as is shown by the way he can use it even to speak of the Son during his preexistence or even after his death and resurrection (see, e.g., 1 Cor 10:4).[21] All of this makes clear that it is crucial to understand the Pauline titles for Christ within the story line and narrative framework that Paul presents to us.

A second, larger story, that of Israel, also informs Paul's discussion of the Christ. For example, we are told in Galatians 4:4 that Jesus was born not only of a woman but also under the law, which probably goes beyond simply saying that he was a Jew, though it does include that notion. For Paul, this entailed God's sending of the Son to be the human Jesus, sending him to redeem those under the law. In other words, Jesus was specifically sent to redeem Israel. This, of course, presupposes the lostness of Israel. After all, it was to Israel that a messiah had been promised in the first place (Rom 9:4-5), and it was to Israel that a messiah would spread his benefits to others.

We must take seriously Romans 1:16 and the whole discussion in Romans 9–11. Salvation and the messiah who brings it are for Israel first, but also for

---

[21]I am assuming that when Paul says that "the rock was Christ," he means that Christ actually existed during Old Testament times and aided God's people then, but that he did so in the same fashion God the Father did, from heaven. In other words, in 1 Corinthians 10:4 Paul is not discussing an earlier incarnation of the Christ on earth as a rock!

Gentiles. Messiah, in Paul's view, brings the story of Israel to its proper conclusion and climax. It is also well to keep in mind that for Paul, "sonship" was another way of speaking of the Jewish royal character of Jesus, who, Paul is happy to affirm, was born in the line of David (Rom 1:3-4), even though this is not a major emphasis in Paul's letters, and seems in Romans 1 rather to be a quotation of a confessional statement of early Jewish Christians. Paul's use of "Son" also shows that he understands the relational significance of the term; it implies a special relationship with the Father. All the same, he uses this title far less often than he does *christos* or *kyrios*.

A third and yet larger story into which the stories of Christ and of Israel fit is that of a world gone wrong. For Paul, the world clearly is a fallen place (see Rom 1; 8) and, for that matter, is living on borrowed time, for the current form of this world is passing away (1 Cor 7:31; Gal 1:4). The fact of the world's gradual demise makes decisions about crucial issues in this life all the more critical. The world is hell-bent, headed for destruction, but longs for liberation. This is true not just of human beings, but also, in Paul's view, of creation as a whole (see Rom 8:20-22). But it is not just that the world has fallen and cannot get up or is gradually decaying; the problem is also that there is active personal evil abroad in the universe. In other words, there are demons and Satan to reckon with, who are part of the present evil age (see 1 Cor 10:20-21; 2 Cor 2:11; 4:4). This is the dark backdrop against which the story of Christ and God's people, both old and new, is played out.

Fourth, and transcending yet involved in all of the stories just mentioned of Christ, of Israel and of the world, is the story of God. This is the story of the interrelationship of Father, Son and Holy Spirit, and this story also informs Paul's Christology in important ways. For example, in the christological hymn in Colossians 1:15-20 (cf. 2 Cor 4:4) we are informed that the Son played an important role in the creation of all things and beings, even human beings. The role of redeemer that Christ plays is part of the story of God's attempt to win back that which God had created in the first place. Creation and re-creation are undertaken not by different actors in the drama but rather by the same one, though in multiple personal forms.

Furthermore, the incarnation is seen by Paul as part of the story of God. The story of the subduing and reconciling of the powers and principalities is also part of this larger story of God, but it is Christ who undertakes these tasks for the Father and in the service of redeeming humankind (1 Cor 15:24).

Whether or not one thinks that Paul wrote Colossians (and most scholars, including me, still do), the elements of this broad christological vision are already evident in 1 Corinthians 15:24-26. For Paul, the big picture involves not just "In the beginning, God . . ." but also "In the end, God. . . ." The difference is that the eschatological action is undertaken by God in Christ or, perhaps better said, God as Christ, which leads us to look more specifically at Christ's divinity in Pauline thinking.[22]

Christ as God in Paul's letters. First, it must be said that this issue cannot be narrowed down to whether or not Paul called Jesus *theos* ("God"). In the christological hymn in Philippians 2 Christ is called "Lord," which was one of God's names or titles in the LXX, and so even if we were to confine ourselves to titles, there are other titles that Paul uses of Jesus suggesting that he saw him as divine in some sense. One must assume that the hymnic material that Paul adopted and adapted he also endorsed, and thus it tells us something about his own views as well as the views of those early Christians from whom he borrowed this material. Eduard Schweizer has said that to a large extent Paul's importance lies in the way he brought together a wide variety of material (hymns, creeds, confessions, Old Testament formulae and catenae, doxologies and his own formulations) and focused them by his understanding of Christ's death and resurrection.[23] There is a large measure of truth in this, but Paul's letters are not just a repository of earlier Christian fragments that have now been focused. Paul's narratological approach to Christology provides him with a large framework in which many truths can be expressed and understood, and through it all Paul has made his source material his own so that we can rightly speak of Pauline Christology.

The evidence is also augmented by instances where Jesus is referred to as God's Wisdom and/or his agent in creation (1 Cor 1:24, 30; 8:6; Col 1:15-17). For example, the role Wisdom played in Wisdom of Solomon of providing water in the wilderness to God's people is said in 1 Corinthians 10:4 to be undertaken by the preexistent Christ. Paul is grounding the story of Christ not so much in the story of Israel as in the archetypal story of God's Wisdom. It seems likely that the sapiential ideas found in 1 Corinthians 1:24, 30; 8:6 blossomed into Paul's concept of the cosmic Christ: not only Lord

---

[22]As my former doctoral student Aaron Kuecker has put it, Christ is like a radioactive isotope at the core of some reality that changes everything it touches or affects.

[23]Schweizer, *Jesus Christ*, p. 27.

over land and universe, but also involved in its creation. The full flower of this sort of thinking is seen in texts such as Colossians 1:15-20, which we have already had occasion to examine. In that hymn Christ is said to be the image of the invisible God, the firstborn of creation and the means and goal of creation, just as Wisdom is in Wisdom of Solomon 7:25-26. The point is that Paul is quite happy to attribute divine attributes to Christ, so one must actually ask whether or not he would have gone so far as to call Jesus Christ "God." I have already suggested that Philippians 2:6-7 says as much; Jesus had the status of being equal to God, and the divine prerogatives he could have taken advantage of.[24]

Another crucial text is the much debated Romans 9:5. Before dealing with the particulars of this text, I must set the discussion in the larger context of the use of *theos* in the New Testament in general. Murray Harris has shown in detail that the term *theos* is not used of the Trinity but reflects early Jewish Christian ways of thinking. In particular, *theos* is used in the vast majority of cases for the one whom Jews called "Yahweh" and some early Jews and early Jewish Christians called "Father." Indeed, *theos* is almost a proper name for the Father in some texts. Occasionally, however, the term *theos* is used in the New Testament of Christ in his preincarnate, incarnate or postincarnate states.[25] The texts that Harris has in mind are Romans 9:5; Titus 2:13; Hebrews 1:8; John 1:1; 20:28; 2 Peter 1:1. We must now examine the first of these, noting here the scope of documents in which we find such an attribution. Not just Pauline communities, but also Petrine and Johannine ones, called Jesus "God." One could argue that in these seven examples we see clear evidence of the ideational unity of earliest Christianity such that even the term *God* has come to have fresh christological meaning in all these communities.

Romans 9:5 comes at the beginning of Paul's discussion of the advantages that the nation Israel has. The sentence poses a problem in regard to its proper punctuation. The argument turns on whether the verse should be read as the NRSV has it, ". . . comes the Messiah, who is over all, God blessed forever," or with the NRSV marginal reading, ". . . comes the Messiah, who is God over

---

[24]The "divine" language would have been all the more striking in Paul's day because the language here that Paul or his source is coopting was also being said of the emperor, that he was divine but humbled himself to be a public servant. But the deity whom Paul has in mind performs his public service by dying on the cross and producing peace with God and between humans, whereas the Roman one performs his public service by erecting a few more crosses and so creating a very different sort of peace, the *pax Romana*.

[25]See Murray J. Harris, *Jesus as God: The New Testament Use of* Theos *in Reference to Jesus* (Grand Rapids: Baker, 1992), pp. 298-99.

all, blessed forever," or with the NEB rendering, ". . . sprang the Messiah. May God, supreme over all, be blessed forever." In the NEB Romans 9:5b becomes a separate sentence from Romans 9:5a, or at least a separate clause. The JB, NIV and NKJV support the first of these readings, which makes *theos* a qualification of "Christ." Both the grammar and the context favor one of the first two readings.

Notice that Romans 9:5a has the phrase *ho christos to kata sarka*. As the parallel in Romans 1:3-4 suggests, we would expect a parallel following clause telling us about what Christ was according to some other category. The language "according the the flesh" suggests an attempt to disclose one aspect of the truth, and it sets up the anticipation that more will be said; otherwise, the phrase is unnatural. Furthermore, the Greek expression *ho ōn*, translated "who is," is normally a way to introduce a relative clause, and here the parallel in 2 Corinthians 11:31 is clear enough (where we find "who is blessed forever" expressed using *ho ōn*).

The NEB translation unjustifiably fragmentizes things by starting an invocation with the word *theos* ("May God be blessed . . ."), but grammatically this is very difficult. Why should a participle agreeing with "Messiah" first be separated from the term and then be given the form of a wish with a different person (God rather than Christ) as the subject? This is most uncalled for. Furthermore, although Paul is offering a doxology of sorts here, elsewhere his doxologies always are attached to some antecedent subject; and also, the Hebrew and LXX doxologies, in form and word order, tend to be "blessed be God," not "God blessed." There is, then, a very high probability that Paul calls Christ "God" here in a doxological statement that shows the degree to which Paul is willing to qualify his monotheistic remarks, something already evident in statements such as 1 Corinthians 8:6. There is a certain naturalness to speaking of the Messiah as someone blessed forever (by the Father), since he is the Anointed One.

As for the meaning of the use of *theos* here, Harris makes an important distinction between the examples such as here and in John 1, where we have *theos* without the definite article, and the other texts mentioned previously, where the article is present. The word *theos* without the article is a generic reference indicating that Christ belongs to the class or category of being called "God" or "Deity." When the article is present, the titular aspect seems to come to the fore.[26]

---

[26]See Harris, *Jesus as God*, p. 298.

Thus far we have noticed that Paul predicates both divine attributes and divine titles or names to Christ (Wisdom, Lord, God), but he uses other language that makes equally clear that he sees christological language as "God" language. For example, one of the most prevalent phrases throughout the Pauline corpus is *en christō* ("in Christ"). As C. F. D. Moule has noted, although some of this usage means no more than that one is a Christian, in numerous examples it is actually being used to say something about the Christian's condition or religious location. Only of an omnipresent being can one suggest that in some sense *that* being is the place where and the person in whom believers dwell.[27]

Here a caveat needs to be put into the discussion. Paul's thought was not christomonistic, but sometimes New Testament scholars have overreacted to the emphasis on Christology in Paul's thought by claiming that Paul's thought is essentially theocentric rather than christocentric. It can be pointed out that

> God the Father is the initiator of the story for Paul, as he is for all New Testament writers: the gospel is the gospel of God (Rom 1:1). God the Father is the creator of the universe (1 Cor 8:6), and human beings are made in his image (1 Cor 11:7). He expects their worship and their willing obedience to his way of life for them (cf. Rom 1:21). He is living and active, by contrast with the idols worshiped by the Gentiles (1 Thess 1:9). He will judge the world for its sinfulness (Rom 2:5); his wrath is already being revealed in a way in which human sin leads to human misery (Rom 1:18). He has been active in the story of Israel, the nation called to be his people. . . . And now he is active in initiating and effecting salvation. He is faithful to the people who he has called and who have responded to his call (1 Cor 1:9; 1 Thess 5:24; cf. Phil 1:6).[28]

All of this is undeniable, but it is equally undeniable, as I have been noting, that for Paul, the subject "Christ" falls properly within the scope of the topic "God." So much is this so that the reason God is called "Father" in Paul's letters, and that Paul says that Christians can say, "Abba! Father!" is primarily because he is the Father of the Lord Jesus Christ. That is, the way the Father is viewed has been reconfigured because of the way the Son is viewed, not the other way around. This tells us much about what the driving force is in Paul's thought world. That which causes rethinking about the other elements

---

[27]See C. F. D. Moule, *The Origin of Christology* (Cambridge: Cambridge University Press, 1977), pp. 62-65.

[28]Marshall, *New Testament Theology*, p. 424.

in the thought world is the Christ-event, the Christ story.

The picture that I have been drawing can be further enlarged by examining what Paul says about Christ's relationship to the Spirit. It is old news that Paul closely identifies Christ and the Spirit. For example, in 1 Corinthians 15:45 Christ is said to be "a life-giving spirit," and in Romans 1:3-4 it is made clear that without Jesus' resurrection the Spirit would never have come to believers in the first place, but also that it was through the Spirit's power that Jesus was enabled to be Son of God in power. "Being in Christ" is often simply another way of speaking about being in the Spirit, as is shown by the following: (1) believers are righteous in Christ (Phil 3:8-9) but also in the Spirit (Rom 14:17); (2) believers have life in Christ (Col 3:4) but also in the Spirit (Rom 8:11); (3) believers have hope in Christ for the life to come (1 Cor 15:19) and in the power of the Spirit to give them eternal life (Gal 6:8); (4) believers are sanctified in Christ (1 Cor 1:2) but also in the Spirit (Rom 15:16); (5) believers are sealed both in Christ (Eph 1:13) and in the Spirit (Eph 4:30). Although in 2 Corinthians 3:17 it is unlikely that Paul is simply equating the Lord and the Spirit, and rather more likely that in the text he is dealing with (Ex 34) "the Lord" means "the Spirit," the verse does show the close connection between the two in Paul's mind. Notice that in Romans 8:8-9 the Spirit of Christ = the Spirit of God = the Spirit of the Lord. Of course, Paul does distinguish the two as well: only Christ came in the flesh, died on the cross and rose again. Christ sent the Spirit to believers on earth while he in his resurrected body remained in heaven. The point of all this, however, is that this identity in function and effect between the Spirit and Christ surely at least implies the deity of Christ. From an Old Testament perspective, it is only God who can send or be a life-giving Spirit. In sum, in the church age Christ and the Spirit are not one but two in identity, but often they are one in function and effect because the Spirit is Christ's agent on earth.

Pauline Christology involves not only the divinity of Christ, but also his humanity. The references to Jesus as Son of David, last Adam or human being have to do with aspects of Jesus' tasks on earth as a human being, as does the term "Messiah." It must be stressed that Paul does not use the phrase "Son of Man" at all, and the phrase "Son of God" is relational in character and seems to have been kept for exceptional use at the climax of certain key statements about Christ's work as a human being and also as more than human. We will consider the "Son of God" phrase first as a transition to a discussion of Christ's humanity.

In Romans 1:3-9 we are informed that the Son is the theme of Paul's gospel, and elsewhere he is the content of what God revealed to and in Paul in his experience of the road to Damascus (Gal 1:16). In statements such as Romans 5:10; 8:32; Galatians 2:20; Colossians 1:13-14 Paul emphasizes the supreme value of Christ's death by stressing that it was God's Son, the one who stood closest to God, who died on the cross. The humanness is thereby stressed. It is the Son who is descended from David as well as come forth from God (Rom 1:3-4), and he is also said to become Son of God in power since the resurrection. In other words, he is Son not just on earth but also in heaven beyond death. If we take the sequence of Colossians 1:13-15 seriously, it also suggests that Paul has no problem calling the preincarnate one the "beloved Son," for whom or through whom all things were created. The term "Son" and the phrase "Son of God," perhaps more than any other similar term or title except perhaps "Christ," bind together the narrative of the career of the Redeemer in Paul's thought and stress Christ's unique relationship with the Father, which in turn allows him to have a unique relationship with God's people.

Christ as human in Paul's Letters. It is no accident that when Paul discusses Jesus' humanity in various ways, he stresses his Jewishness. For example, in Galatians 4:4 Jesus is not merely said to be born of woman, but also said to be born under the law. His appearance in this world came in the form of a normal birth from a human Jewish mother. This text implies nothing peculiar or unusual about his birth. Notice too that Paul stresses that Jesus was born under the law to redeem those under the law; in other words, his ministry was directed to Israel.[29] In Paul's thought there is an interesting paradox: salvation is of God, but it could come to human beings only in and through a human being, the man Jesus Christ, in fact a particular sort of human being, a Jew. For Paul, the heart of the matter is that salvation comes in the form of Christ crucified and risen, which in turn means that the humanness of the Savior is a necessity as well as his more than humanness.

There are various texts that stress that the Son was born in human likeness, ranging from Philippians 2:7 to Romans 8:3. Probably the carefully worded phrase "in the likeness of sinful flesh" in the latter text is meant to indicate

---

[29]This fact, coupled with the fact that Paul is the missionary to the Gentiles, may go some way in explaining why Paul does not say more about Jesus' earthly ministry: Jesus' ministry was to a largely different audience than his own.

that Jesus did not look any different from any other human being, but Paul wishes to avoid saying that Jesus was a sinner or was born with a sinful nature. This comports with what we find elsewhere in the metaphorical statement that Jesus was the paschal lamb (1 Cor 5:7), who had to be unblemished and spotless to be an appropriate sacrificial offering to God. In other words, like Adam, Jesus was born with an unfallen nature that had a capacity to sin, but unlike Adam, he was obedient to God even unto death (see Phil 2:8) and so in due course became an unblemished sacrifice.[30] It is interesting that the only other event besides Jesus' death that he did as a human being that Paul mentions is his participation in the Last Supper. Jesus was one who broke bread, poured wine and shared in fellowship with his disciples, but even here Paul is interested not just in these mundane facts but rather in their soteriological import. He only mentions events in the life of Jesus that are of prime theological weight.

By far the most common term that Paul uses for Jesus is "Christ," usually as a name, but occasionally as a title, as in Romans 9:5. For most Jews, it appears that *māšiah* was a term referring to an especially anointed and singled-out human being, usually a king or sometimes a priest. It therefore is no surprise that in the context where Paul mentions Jesus' messianic character there is stress on his humanity: he is born of the seed of David (Rom 1:3-4). Thus, for Paul, the use of "Christ" probably especially stresses the humanness of the messiah. This also is clearly implied in the phrase "Christ crucified" (1 Cor 1:23). Of course, the story of Jesus brought about a redefinition of Paul's understanding of the Davidic messiah in various ways, but it did not cause Paul to drop the Davidic terminology or categories altogether.

Paul says very little about Jesus' humanity in general; the subject of anthropology does not intrigue him when applied to Christ, except insofar as it

---

[30]One of the problems in dealing with the christological material in Philippians 2 is the tendency to either overestimate or underestimate the degree to which the image of Christ as the last Adam is guiding what Paul says here. In general, the parallels are confined to what is said by way of contrast: (1) unlike Adam, Christ was equal to God and had divine prerogatives; (2) also unlike Adam, Christ was obedient even unto death. The hymn focuses on choices made by Christ, both before and during his earthly career, as a model for choices that Christians must make, and thus the conclusion that Christ's preexistence and incarnation are not referred to here is incorrect. The text does not say that Christ was merely like God in some one particular respect; rather, it says that he had the status and condition such that he was equal to God. For a discussion of this hymn and how it functions rhetorically, see Ben Witherington III, *Friendship and Finances in Philippi: The Letter of Paul to the Philippians* (NTC; Valley Forge, Penn.: Trinity Press International, 1994), pp. 57-74.

has christological significance. This is seen because of what we have already noted about Paul's presentation of Christ's humanity, and it can be further noticed when we examine Paul's presentation of Christ as the last Adam. This concept comes up in more than one Pauline letter, and so obviously it was of some importance to Paul. When Paul thought of Jesus' true human-ness, he thought in terms of a comparison with the first human being.[31] In fact, he thought typologically on this subject.

In Romans 5, in the midst of his comparison and contrast between Adam and Christ, Paul says in Romans 5:15 that just as death came by "the one" Adam, so God's grace and the gift that accompanied it (righteousness [Rom 5:17]) came by "the one" Jesus. This point is reiterated in 1 Corinthians 15:21, but here the last half of the statement speaks of resurrection coming through a human being. In the later and disputed Paulines, in particular in 1 Timothy 2:5, these notions are further developed when we hear about Christ as the one mediator between God and human beings, and again he is said to be "the human being Christ," but there is more emphasis here on Jesus being both God and human being, standing at once on both sides of the fence in order to experience and know and represent both sides of things. Why all this stress on grace, righteousness, reconciliation, and even resur-rection coming by a human being? Presumably, part of the answer is that sin was a human problem that had to be resolved for humankind by and through a human being. Although sometimes it has been stressed that the efficacy of salvation was due to Jesus' divinity, Paul in fact emphasizes the opposite. If Jesus had not been human, humans would never have received God's grace. God, of course, apart from an incarnation, is not subject to death, and thus for one who stresses Christ crucified, there must also be a stress on Christ's humanity.

The "last Adam" motif in 1 Corinthians 15:21-23, 44-49 deserves a more extended comment. Here, the responsibility for sin and its consequences is placed squarely on Adam's shoulders. It is interesting that in this context Psalm 8:6 is applied to Jesus (in 1 Cor 15:27), which suggests to some that "last Adam" is Paul's substitute for the phrase "Son of Man." Adam and Christ are seen to be both like and unlike each other. Both were truly human, both are representative heads of a human race, and both had a dramatic effect on their physical/spiritual progeny. However, in some ways the differences out-

---

[31]Indeed, this may partially explain Paul's use of the phrase "in the likeness of sinful flesh" in Romans 8:3.

weigh the similarities. The powerful effect of Adam's act on humanity was death (1 Cor 15:21), whereas Christ's act produced life in the very specific form of resurrection from death, a far greater and more surprising effect. The parallelism here is not perfect, for although all did indeed die in Adam, Paul does not seem to think that all will rise in Christ. For example, in both 1 Corinthians 15 and 1 Thessalonians 4:16 Paul makes it quite clear that elsewhere when he speaks of resurrection, it is of those who are in Christ. This impression is strengthened by 1 Corinthians 15:23, where Paul speaks of the resurrection of those who belong to Christ.[32]

We can devise a chart showing how Paul compares Adam and Christ in 1 Corinthians 15:44-49.

Table 4.2. Adam and Christ in 1 Corinthians 15:44-49

	Adam	Christ
1 Cor 15:45	the first Adam	the last Adam
1 Cor 15:45	a living being	a life-giving spirit
1 Cor 15:47	the human being	the second human being
1 Cor 15:47-48	from earth's dust	from heaven

Paul relies on the concept of representative headship. In one sense, Adam sinned for all humankind, and so the human race died in and because of him. To put it another way, because humankind's representative sinned, the whole race felt the effects. Adam is a corporate head of a body of people who are affected when he acts for all (cf. Rom 5:12 with Col 1:14).

The second key to understanding the Adam/Christ analogy or typology is that salvation comes only "in Christ." A person must be in Christ to receive the benefits of Christ's work, and the person who is in him both dies to sin and rises to newness of life, becoming a new creature (cf. Rom 6:3-4 with 2 Cor 5:17). The idea of representative headship when applied to Christ, the last Adam, means that Christ performed deeds that subsequently shaped that race. He died in a believer's place as his or her corporate head, just as Adam sinned for and in the place of humankind. Calling Jesus "the last Adam" or

---

[32]In Acts 24:15 the Pauline speech mentions a resurrection of the just and of the unjust. Although 1 Corinthians 15 does not deny the existence of the latter, it does not associate the two resurrections, and one could argue that even in Acts 24 there is no point in mentioning both a resurrection of the just and also of the unjust unless some sort of distinction is being implied; otherwise, one could have just spoken of the resurrection of all humankind without markers of moral distinction. Interestingly, early Pharisaism seems to have distinguished the resurrection of the righteous from the fate of the rest of the dead, and so, apparently, does Jesus (see John 5:24-29: all are raised, but some rise to positive new life, and others do not).

"the second human being" involves an eschatological claim: Christ, as the firstfruits of the new creation, is the beginning as well as the progenitor of a new race. Yet paradoxically, in another sense he is the end and goal of the human race, bringing in the last age, the end of God's plan, which means the new creation.

There is a further difference between Adam and Christ. Adam was strictly an earth creature, made from the earth and returned to dust. His body and life were natural and physical. Insofar as humankind is indebted to him, humankind is also earthly, physical, contingent, fallen and has only a natural life in the body. Christ, by contrast, was from heaven and of heaven in that he was a life-giving Spirit.

Several points of importance come out of this analogy. Christ is not merely living like Adam but rather is a life-giving spirit, whereas Adam in fact gave us death. Paul also likely means not that Christ had no body in heaven, but that he lived in the spiritual realm and was the one who dispensed the Spirit and thus life. Equally, for Paul, the phrase "a spiritual body" indicates not a body made out of immaterial substance but rather a body totally empowered by the Spirit. It is interesting that Paul, in contrast to Philo, does not see the Adam of Genesis 1 as the model or ideal human; rather, in Paul's thought it is the last, not the first, founder of the race who is seen as the ideal human being.

Turning back to Romans 5:12-18 for a moment, we notice that not only death, but also sin, entered the world through Adam. In fact, death enters the picture because of sin, so that for Paul, human death at least is not a natural phenomenon but rather is a consequence of evil in the world. It appears that Paul accepted Genesis 1–3 as a straightforward historical account, but as always, his concern is with its theological and soteriological significance. It is interesting that Paul takes a both/and approach to sin. Whatever believers may have inherited from Adam, whatever effect his sin had on the race, Paul believes nevertheless that each individual, personally responsible for sin, digs his or her own grave. God has not unjustly punished any with death simply because of original sin, though of course it is true that none of the race would be dying if Adam had not done what he did. Thus, we have an interesting dualism. On the one hand, Paul can say in Romans 5:15, "many died by the tresspass of one man," or through Adam death reigned, but on the other hand, he can also insist on personal responsibility. It is similar when we come to discuss salvation. Salvation clearly is from God in Christ and happens to those in Christ because of what the one man, Christ, did for us, especially on the cross. Yet it is also true that the individual does not automatically get this benefit; it must be appropriated by faith, which includes the faith response of confessing Jesus as Lord (Rom 10:9-10).

In Paul's view, God's antidote in Christ for sin is not merely an equal and opposite reaction to the trespass. The gift is far greater than the trespass and can affect far more in the believer than the trespass could (Rom 5:15). Whereas the death penalty followed just one sin, grace came after very many sins and quite apart from what humans deserved. Romans 5:17 makes apparent that the life lived in Christ is not merely more powerful than the death Adam passed on to humankind; instead, it is of an entirely different order, coming from heaven, the Spirit, from the realm that transcends and transforms nature and can even overcome death. But none of this comes to pass without the christological facts that make it possible. In particular, for Paul, it is Christ's righteousness, which includes his sinlessness and obedience even unto death, that made possible the undoing of all that Adam's disobedience and sin inflicted upon the human race. In Paul's thought, salvation is not a self-help program; rather it is a gift available only because of the finished work of Christ.

Christ, the center of Pauline thought. One way to demonstrate the importance and centrality of Christology for Paul is to examine the impact that it had on other areas of his thinking, of which I will briefly discuss four: eschatology, soteriology, ecclesiology and God. The encounter of Christ on the road to Damascus caused a Copernican revolution in Paul's thinking about all these matters and much more.[33] First, Paul's eschatological outlook most certainly changed when he encountered Christ on the road to Damascus. There is little or no evidence that early Jews expected two comings of a messiah, yet that is precisely what both Paul and the other early Jewish Christians who prayed *maranatha* believed. This bifurcation of the Christ-event affected how Paul viewed the future and the life of believers. For Paul, because Christ had already come in the "fullness of time" (Gal 4:4), the eschatological age could be said to have already dawned, though it was not yet completed. Redemption was already available in part—now in the spirit, but later in the body as well when Christ returned. In other words, redemption had yet to be completed.

---

[33]See Seyoon Kim, *The Origin of Paul's Gospel* (Grand Rapids: Eerdmans, 1982).

The coming of the eschatological age had relativized everything, such that the form and institutions of this world, though still extant, were already passing away (1 Cor 7:31) and should not be adhered or clung to in some sort of ultimate fashion. Powers and principalities still existed and menaced the world, but they could not separate believers from God's love. Colossians 2:15 in fact makes clear that Christ had disarmed the powers and principalities insofar as their being able to dominate or rule believers was concerned. Further, the inner life of believers had indeed changed. A believer was now a new creature, part of a new creation begun by the last Adam (2 Cor 5:17), a new creature that had righteousness and joy and peace in the Holy Spirit. This was a major part of what it meant in Paul's mind that the kingdom had already come (Rom 14:17). The full redemption of the body at resurrection was yet to come, so that not only the world but also the believer's very existence was in an "already and not yet" state of eschatological affairs, which had been initiated by Christ's coming and would be brought to consummation only when he returned.

There is little or no early Jewish evidence that a resurrection of the messiah, much less an isolated resurrection of the messiah apart from other believers, was expected in the midst of history, yet on the basis of the life and story of Jesus, this is precisely what Paul proclaimed. It must be understood that for a Pharisee such as Paul, resurrection was perhaps the clearest piece of evidence that the eschaton had arrived.[34] Again, it was what happened to Christ that made Paul rethink and reshape his eschatology. Paul managed to continue to see resurrection as a unified thing by using the concept of Christ being only the firstfruits of the resurrection of all believers.

Paul's concept of salvation was equally reshaped because of what he came to believe about Christ, in particular about his death and resurrection. I see no evidence suggesting that early Jews were expecting a crucified messiah, and unless new finds from Qumran change the picture, Paul seems to have been the first to reflect in depth on such a subject. In fact, Paul tells us that this message of a crucified messiah was a scandalous one in the eyes of Jews (1 Cor 1:23). The message here is deliberately paradoxical: to the factionalized Corinthians Paul depicts a Christ who on the surface appears to create more divisions than he heals, being a stumbling block to Jews and a scandal

---

[34]"Paul sees the Christian reality from the perspective of the risen Lord, the one whom God raised from the dead" (Earl J. Richard, *Jesus, One and Many: The Christological Concept of New Testament Authors* [Wilmington, DE: Michael Glazier, 1988], p. 326).

to Gentiles. Deuteronomy 21:23 does not speak directly to the matter of crucifixion, much less crucifixion of God's Anointed One, and could not have generated such a belief. Nor is there any early first-century evidence that Isaiah 53 was understood to refer to a crucified messiah (though see the later *Tg. Isa.* 53). Because of the bifurcation of the Christ-event, salvation also came in more than one stage or part. Paul speaks of large numbers of Gentiles already being saved, but God had not completed his plan for saving Jews yet (see Rom 11). Already a believer had right standing with God and even peace (Rom 5:1), but the same believer was not yet fully sanctified and glorified, as is clear from the ongoing tension between flesh and the Holy Spirit in the believer's life (Gal 5:16-26).

Without a doubt, Paul's thinking about God's people was changed because of the coming of Jesus. This is especially so in regard to the issue of the basis for inclusion in God's people. In Paul's view, God's people were Jews and Gentiles united in Christ (Gal 3:28), and perhaps they could even be called "the Israel of God" (Gal 6:16), or at least Jewish Christians could be. Neither heredity nor obedience to Torah could secure one a place in true Israel or in God's coming kingdom (see Rom 3:23–4:8). In Christ the law, at least as a basis of obtaining or maintaining right standing with God, was at an end (Rom 10:4). Paul also states clearly in Romans 14:14 that it was no longer necessary for him or other Jewish and Gentile Christians to continue to keep the laws of clean and unclean. This means that in Paul's mind the Christ-event had changed the very basis of fellowship among God's people and also the badges or markers of identity that singled out God's people.

If Torah, temple, and territory were three of the great pillars or landmarks of early Judaism, in Christ these landmarks had undergone a remarkable transformation. We already examined a bit about Paul's view of the law, but an examination of what he says about sacrifice and temple also reveals a radically different view of things. For one thing, Christ is seen as the paschal lamb who was sacrificed once for all, thus making any further such literal sacrifices unnecessary and not even useful (1 Cor 5:7). Henceforth, only the sacrifice of presenting one's self wholly to God in devotion and for service was required (Rom 12:1-4). It is also Paul's belief that the new temple is, on the one hand, comprised of Jew and Gentile united in Christ as the body in which the Holy Spirit dwells (1 Cor 6:19), and, on the other hand, the individual believer's body (1 Cor 3:16-17).

It is also notable that the territorial doctrine of Israel nowhere comes up for discussion in the Pauline letters, even though Paul wrote when such a doctrine was still a critical part of Israel's hope, before A.D. 70. It is possible that Paul made room for such an idea as feasible when Christ returned and "all Israel" was saved (Rom 11:23-26); however, it is remarkable that in the list of things that Paul says God promised Israel according to the flesh (Rom 9:4-5), nowhere is land mentioned (unless the vague reference to the promises involves such an idea). It appears that the territorial doctrine also was transformed by Paul's understanding of the Christ-event such that he could speak of an inheritance (Col 1:12) or possibly even a commonwealth or citizenship in heaven (Phil 3:20).

We have already seen evidence of how Paul's christological monotheism changed his thinking about God, but further evidence certainly can be produced. Notice, for instance, that in 2 Corinthians 5:10 and 1 Thessalonians 5:4-10 it is not Yahweh but Christ who will come to judge the world, and this is not because the Father decided to send someone less than divine to accomplish this task. Paul is quite happy to speak about Christ assuming a variety of functions previously predicated only of Yahweh in the Old Testament. Although Paul certainly did not articulate a full trinitarian theology, the raw stuff of trinitarian thinking surfaces repeatedly in his letters, especially in doxological texts, when Paul is thinking about whom he worships, or in prayer texts (see 2 Cor 13:14; 1 Thess 1:2-5). Paul invoked blessing only in God's name, but now God had three names by which the Lord could be called. Much more could be said along these lines, but this is sufficient to make the point that already at the earliest stages of articulation of New Testament thought Christ is the basis, center, focus, starting point, goal, catalyst for the way the Jewish thought world is reconfigured in various ways. As we will see, this is no less true of Christians writing after Paul in the first century A.D.[35]

Although I have been speaking about Christ as the basis and focus of New Testament thought, we need to keep steadily in view that early Christianity did not solely, perhaps even not primarily, involve an intellectual revolution.

---

[35]See Gordon D. Fee, *Pauline Christology: An Exegetical-Theological Study* (Peabody, Mass.: Hendrickson, 2007). Fee's fine, detailed study, helpful in many ways, takes a much more traditional route in analyzing Pauline Christology than I have taken here. However, Fee claims that intertestamental Wisdom literature and the Wisdom persona had no influence on Paul's christological thinking, a decidedly minority position at this juncture in the discussion. Fee's conclusion is reached partly because he does not read Paul's thought narratologically, but also because he denies that a similar story is told of Wisdom in Wisdom of Solomon 11 after the first verse of that chapter, thus denying any connection between Wisdom of Solomon 11 and 1 Corinthians 10, where Paul says that the rock was Christ. This I find astounding and unconvincing.

There is something not quite right with treating this subject as a matter of abstract thought. By and large, the earliest Christians were not philosophers or highly educated people, nor were most of them wealthy persons of leisure who had time for contemplation or dialogue with the great minds of the age. It is a mistake to see even the authors of the New Testament as being akin to modern scholars, persons with doctoral degrees devoted to the life of the mind and the flexing of their intellectual muscles. What we are dealing with here is a group of people who had had profound religious experiences that they interpreted as encounters with a living Lord, Jesus. To be sure, some of their leaders, such as Paul or the author of Hebrews or the Beloved Disciple, could match wits with many of the great minds of their age, but it was the religious experiences of Christ that they held in common and the shared communities formed out of those experiences that provided the matrix for reflection about the meaning of the Christ-event.

Even more to the point, these communities were worshiping communities, and probably all of the New Testament writers derived much of their orientation about these matters from the context of worship, which generated hymns, creeds, confessions and other source material that often was christologically focused. More attention needs to be paid to the social setting, namely, worship in house churches, which produced the orientation and reflection on the one seen as the living Lord. Perhaps it would even be in order to reflect on household worship in the Greco-Roman world in general. Here it must suffice to say that Christ is indeed the basis and focus of New Testament thought because he was believed and experienced to be the basis and focus of early Christian life, both worship life and daily life. At the bottom of the christological well lie deep waters of religious experience of which we have by no means plumbed the depths, even two thousand years after the death of Christ.

Having started with the earliest exponent of this thought world, the apostle Paul, let us consider how others built upon this foundation or developed other aspects of this thought world independently. We will be considering the question of compatibility and harmony, not least because we have no evidence at all of flat-out contradictions between various groups of early Christians over issues such as whether or not Jesus was the risen Lord. As the oratorio continued to be composed and one voice after another was added to the choir, was there consonance or dissonance when they sang together about "this same Jesus of Nazareth"? As this chapter continues, we will be examining materials where there seems to have been not merely some kinship with the Pauline thought world, but some actual influence by Paul on these writers, especially in regard to Christology and the interrelated soteriological, eschatological, and ecclesiological concepts. To refresh the reader's memory, here again is the Venn diagram from chapter 2 about the New Testament writers, showing where the closer associations of thought world were amidst the diversity (see fig. 4.1).

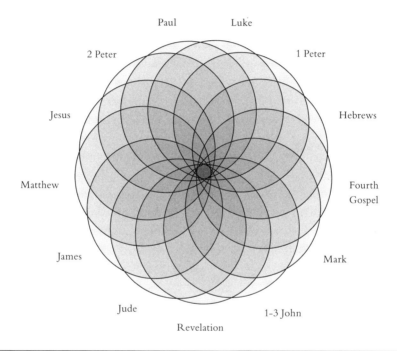

Figure 4.1. Thought World of the New Testament

In a sense, we will be working our way around the circle in this diagram, pointing out the connections between the writers' various ways of articulating a Christian thought world.

Hebrews: Jesus as the Perfection of the Old Covenant

At first glance, it seems that we are in a very different thought world when it comes to examining the Christology of Hebrews compared to that of Paul. Although Paul mentions in passing that Christ is the Passover sacrifice for

Christians, he says nothing about Christ being our high priest. Paul spends no time drawing intricate analogies between the Levitical system, including the tabernacle, and the death of Christ on the cross and his role in heaven thereafter. Thus, it is true that Hebrews contains a value-added dimension. The author does not simply repeat the same themes that we find in Paul's writings, though certainly what he adds to the discussion is not discordant with what we have already heard from Paul. Just as much as Paul, this author stresses both the divinity and the humanity of Jesus; indeed, perhaps in some ways he stresses both things more than Paul does. Jesus clearly is called "God" at several places in Hebrews, and Jesus' humanness is stressed at length to build the case that he is a priest (and also a sacrifice). Paul alludes to the story of the Last Supper in 1 Corinthians 11, but the author of Hebrews actually seems to retell the story of the garden of Gethsemane in Hebrews 5:7-10. What is interesting is that neither of them tells any prepassion stories about Jesus (other than that he was born a Jew and thus born under the law, as Gal 4:4 puts it).

Sometimes it has been suggested that the author of Hebrews takes a much more otherworldly view of Christ than Paul does, neglecting Christ's future role at the eschaton. This is wrong. It is true enough that the author of Hebrews emphasizes Christ's current roles in heaven for the believer. This comports with his use of epideictic rhetoric that focuses on what is true now in the present. But he does not neglect the future return of Christ for judgment and salvation (see Heb 9:28; 10:25), and indeed his rhetoric climaxes with a presentation in Hebrews 12 of the final Christophany on earth at the end, which is contrasted with the theophany at Sinai. The typological exegesis found in Hebrews is already present in a passage such as 1 Corinthians 10.

Furthermore, right from the outset of his discourse the author of Hebrews stresses, at least as much as Paul does, the divine sonship of Jesus (Heb 1:1-4), and, like Paul, he can use the term *christos* as a virtual second name for Jesus (see, e.g., Heb 9:14). "The Christ" as a name pattern recurs throughout the New Testament, and this should have been a tip-off to scholars long ago that we are dealing with a movement that has a considerable shared thought world and a coherent way of expressing it that would make instant sense to insiders, but not necessarily to outsiders.

After all, the New Testament is written entirely in Greek, and the Greek word *christos* had no specific religious significance in the Greco-Roman world; indeed, it could be used as an adjective referring to anointing or smearing with oil in the most mundane of senses or ways. If used as a noun, the expression "anointed one" would have been as opaque as apocalyptic visions to someone with no knowledge of the Old Testament or early Jewish ways of talking about their messiah. And yet throughout the New Testament, including in documents written especially for Gentiles, it is simply assumed without explanation that this term will make sense to the audience. Why? Because there was a shared theological and ethical basis to this movement that especially involved theological and ethical reflection on the Christ story.

One of the problems with studying Christology in isolation from other related topics is that these ideas are interrelated and integrated by means of the story of Christ. So, for instance, who Jesus is thought to be is very much dependent on what he is thought to have done and what happened to him at the end of his life. Atonement theology, for example, should not be severed from Christology, since the death of Jesus and its theological valorization have everything to do with how one views Christ himself. Nowhere is this clearer than in Hebrews, and in various ways what is said in this discourse can be understood as a considerable expansion on what Paul had already said in places such as Romans 3; 5.

Paul most certainly had a concept of penal substitutionary atonement as one image of the significance of the death of Jesus. Jesus' death not only cleansed the sinner but also set aside the enmity of God against sin, propitiating God. It effected reconciliation of two estranged parties; indeed, it made peace through the blood of the cross. Of course, Paul can talk about redemption (using a slavery metaphor) or payment (using an accounting metaphor) and also other models that were compatible ways of describing the significance of that death. The author of Hebrews agrees with all of that and takes things a step further, clarifying certain things that were only implied in Paul's articulation of the matter.

In a helpful summary of the way Paul and the author of Hebrews share a common theological and ethical vision of many things, Frank Matera, following L. D. Hurst, provides us with no fewer than twenty-six points of ideational overlap between Paul and Hebrews: (1) a similar view of the incarnation; (2) Christ's humiliation; (3) Christ's obedience; (4) Christ's offering for us; (5) Christ viewed as an *apolytrōsis* ("redemption") for sin; (6) Christ's intercession for us; (7) the superiority of the new covenant; (8) Christ's inheritance of the exalted name; (9) a reference to signs and wonders; (10) the depiction of Christ as our brother; (11) the emphasis on

Abraham as our example of faith; (12) the negative example of the generation that wandered in the wilderness; (13) the portrayal of the Christian life as a race; (14) conversion as enlightenment; (15) the use of similar Old Testament passages; (16) Christ's death as the defeat of demonic powers; (17) Christ's death as expiation (and, I would add, propitiation); (18) waiting for Christ's return; (19) a Pauline-like ending to the document; (20) righteousness by faith; (21) Christians described as descendants of Abraham; (22) Paul's insistence on Abraham hearing the good news in advance, and the author of Hebrews saying Abraham saw the promise from afar; (23) the rebuke that some believers are suited only for milk, not meat; (24) the use of *teleios* to refer to maturity; (25) Christian teaching referred to as a *themelios* ("foundation"); (26) the nature of stewards as faithful.[36] This is a helpful list, and while it may suggest various things about the author of Hebrews' indebtedness to Pauline ideas and letters, more importantly it suggests that he shared a common thought world and followed many similar lines of thought based on the same faith in the human and yet divine, once incarnate, but now exalted Son of God. The indebtedness reflects agreement particularly on the christological essentials and their ethical implications, as most of this list has to do with Christ.

Fundamental for the author of Hebrews is that Jesus needed to be truly and fully human, and yet without sin to be either the perfect sacrifice or the perfect high priest or both. Unlike the authors of the First and Third Gospels he does not try to explain how this could be (i.e., by means of a virginal conception) but he clearly assumes it is the case that Jesus is sinless and pure. This allows him to say the following sorts of things about Jesus' death including that it was a propitiatory sacrifice. We will consider for a moment what the author says in detail at Hebrews 9:6-15, as we take a closer look at some of the author's real contributions to New Testament theology.

A CLOSER LOOK: ATONEMENT AND COVENANTAL THEOLOGY IN HEBREWS

In Hebrews 9:5 we hear of the "cherubim of glory," called such because the Shekinah glory of God (his very presence) was understood to reside over the *hilastērion*. The function of the cherubim was to support the invisible presence of

---

[36]Frank J. Matera, *New Testament Theology: Exploring Diversity and Unity* (Louisville: Westminster John Knox, 2007), p. 254. Matera is drawing on L. D. Hurst, *The Epistle to the Hebrews: Its Background of Thought* (SNTSMS 65; Cambridge: Cambridge University Press, 1990), p. 107.

God. The Greek word *hilastērion* translates the Hebrew word *kappōret* and means "place of propitiation" or, more broadly, "place of atonement" (cf. Ex 25:17, 21 LXX; Rom 3:25). As a result, since God's wrath is assuaged at this location, it becomes a place from which his mercy can flow thereafter. Hence, it has been translated as "mercy seat." Here I do not have space to debate the propitiation/expiation controversy, which I have already addressed in part. The noun *hilastērion* occurs in the New Testament only here in Hebrews 9:5 and in Romans 3:25, but we have the cognate verb *hilaskomai* in Hebrews 2:17 (cf. Lk 18:13). In Hebrews 9:5 the author says that this is not the place to speak in detail about these things, which shows that the description that he offers serves as a foil for his description of Christ's work.

Hebrews 9:6 speaks of the continual activity of the priests, and surely this refers to their activity in the outer court. By contrast, the second tent was entered only once a year, only by the high priest and only with blood to make propitiation on the Day of Atonement for his and others' sins, and then only for sins of ignorance. The author's point is to indicate the limited access to God under the old regime and the limited atonement available under it. Notice in Hebrews 9:7 the author's continued fondness (cf. Heb 4:15; 6:10; 7:20; 9:18, 22) for the emphatic double negative: it is "not without blood" that the high priest enters the holy of holies once a year. What is most interesting about the author's presentation of the priest's role is that what is said here is guided by what he has said and wants to say about the high priestly ministry of Christ. Even what the ancient high priest did was of help only for inadvertent sins (cf. Num 15:22, 30; Heb 10:26), although some early Jewish traditions do read Leviticus 16:5, 9, 16 to mean that even voluntary sins were atoned for on the Day of Atonement (see Philo, *Spec. Laws* 2.196). Later traditions even held that if someone said, "I will sin and the Day of Atonement will effect atonement," then "the Day of Atonement effects no atonement" (*m. Yoma* 8:9; cf. *Jub.* 5:17-19).

The author turns to stating his argument about the nature of Christ's work, and he will do it in various ways in the section Hebrews 9:11–10:18. Note that several key *dia* clauses help explain what the author is intending, and an understanding of them is crucial to the argument. In general, these *dia* clauses have to do with the instrumentality "through" which Christ accomplished his mission (through eternal spirit, through his own blood, and so on). He is the high priest of the good things that have come. Hebrews 9:11 says that Christ went through "the better and more perfect tent, the one not made with human hands *[cheiropoiētos]*," which implies that the Mosaic one had some greatness and perfection to it. The word *cheiropoïetos* occurs twice in this section (cf. Heb 9:24). It may be that this reflects the author's knowledge of some saying of Jesus about such a temple (cf. Mk 14:58; Acts 7:48; 17:24). The author, while acknowledging the goodness of the old tabernacle, wants to stress that we now have a better and more perfect one that does not suffer from the flaws of one made by human hands. In fact, Hebrews 9:11 says that Jesus "arrived as high priest," making clear that Jesus did not seize priestly prerogatives even though he was not of a priestly line.

The second part of Hebrews 9:11 makes clear that the author is not talking about a tent that is part of the material creation. The proper understanding of Hebrews 9:12 is important, for here we have one of those crucial *dia* clauses. We are told that Jesus entered the heavenly sanctuary not through the blood of goats and bulls but rather *through* his own blood, and when he entered it, it was once for all time. The point of this is: (1) shed blood is the means or the prerequisite for him to be able to enter that most holy place, as was also true for the high priest on earth; (2) it was his own blood, not the blood of others, that qualified him to enter this heavenly holy place; (3) such was the efficacy of his shed blood that he could enter once for all time, having made final and effective atonement. By this death and this entering he found or obtained eternal redemption all by himself.

The word *lytrōsis* derives from *lytron*, which means "ransom" (cf. Mk 10:45), and was used of buying back slaves (Lev 25:48; cf. *lytron* in Ex 21:30) or deliverance from oppressive powers (Lk 1:68; 2:38; *T. Jos.* 8:1), and thus its basic connotation is redemption, originally the buying back of slaves, but it could also be used to speak of liberation from prison or from sin. Hebrews 9:12 is the only place this noun occurs in Hebrews, but its cognate *apolytrōsis* occurs in Hebrews 9:15; 11:35 (cf. Rom 3:24; Eph 1:7; Col 1:14; cf. *lytroomai* in Tit 2:14; 1 Pet 1:18), and the sense of the term is "redemption," often connoting release from prison or slavery (cf. *Let. Aris.* 12:33; Josephus, *Ant.* 12.27). The redemption is eternal not only because of its eternal effect but also because of the nature of the one who procured it and how he did so. thus, it is qualitatively, not just quantitatively, different from the redemption that came by means of the earthly tabernacle system. In this passage the author will go on to allow that that system did in fact provide ritual or material or cultic cleansing for uncleanness and sins of ignorance, and so in a sense the criticism here is less severe than the criticism from Qumran of the Herodian temple (see 1QpHab XII, 8-9; cf. *T. Mos.* 6:1; we perhaps find critique of this temple also in *Sib. Or.* 4.8-39).

Notice that Hebrews 9:13-14 contains one of those a fortiori, or "how much more," arguments that the author likes so well. If the blood of bulls and goats and the ashes of the red heifer (which, when mixed with water, were used to make ritually pure the unclean or common; see Num 19, where it is specifically stated to be a ritual for ceremonial impurity) are able to make possible the purity of the flesh, how much more the blood of Christ will even purify our consciences from dead works and for the worship of the living God. The author does not dispute that the former ritual is effective in the outer and material sphere for ceremonial cleansing. This is not a polemic against the Old Testament institutions, however obsolescent they may be.

The phrase "from dead works," which, when attached to "our conscience," surely rules out the idea that the author means by this "meaningless outward Jewish rituals." Rather, it means here what it meant in Hebrews 6:1: sinful acts that are death-dealing, not life-giving. This is why in Hebrews 6:1 these works are associated with repentance and here with conscience. They must, by definition, amount to something that is not merely useless but in fact defiles the conscience and requires repentance. Thus, the author does not use the expression "dead works" to refer to the same thing as Paul does when he speaks of works of the law. Christ's sacrifice is accepted not least because it is perfect or, as it says in Hebrews 9:14, "unblemished." The author is not the only one concerned about heart piety in early Judaism; one could equally well refer to Philo's remark that "genuine worship is that of the soul bringing simple reality as its only sacrifice; all that is mere display, fed by lavish expenditure on externals is counterfeit" (*Worse* 21). But in fact our author is more concerned about the effect of Christ's work on the inner self of the believer than about the sincerity of the worship itself.

One more point should be stressed. In Hebrews 9:12 the phrase "through his own blood" does not likely mean "with his own blood," as though he actually carried his blood to heaven and finished the work of atonement there. The word *ephapax* ("once for all time") indicates an act of atonement in time that is unique, final and definitive, not continued in heaven. Thus, there is no warrant here for the idea of the atonement happening in two acts, for after all, the analogy with the human practice in the tabernacle is not perfect but rather is selective. Nor is there warrant for the idea that Christ continually re-presents his blood to the Father and so in this fashion pleads for us, or that we as priests are called to continually offer up Christ in such fashion.

At this juncture a chart from the work of Donald Hagner will help us to see some of the comparisons that the author of Hebrews is making.[37]

Table 4.3. New Covenant/Order and Old Covenant/Order in Hebrews

New Covenant/Order	Old Covenant/Order
the good things are already here (9:11, 23-24)	shadows, copies (8:5; 9:23; 10:1)
greater and more perfect tent (9:11, 14)	man-made tent (9:1, 11, 24)
entered the holy place once for all (9:12, 25-28; 10:1-3, 10-14)	entered every day or year (7:27; 9:7; 10:1)
through his own blood (9:12; 10:4-10)	through the blood of goats and bulls (9:12, 18-22)
obtained eternal redemption and purifies conscience (9:12-15)	obtained ritual/outward cleansing (9:9-13; 10:2, 11)
the consummation of the ages (9:26)	until the time of the reformation (9:10)

This brings us to an important point. The author of the Hebrews makes explicit what is implicit elsewhere in the New Testament: the earliest Christians believed that Christ inaugurated a new covenant based on a perfect sacrifice that made obsolescent the old covenant with its laws and sacrifices. The author recognizes that the Mosaic covenant and its practices continue, but he sees them as passing away. Like Paul in his argument about the Mosaic law and circumcision in Galatians 3–4 or his comparison and contrast of the ministries of the Mosaic and new covenants in 2 Corinthians 3, the author of Hebrews believes not only that he lives in the age of the eschatological fulfillment of things, but also that this means that previous ways of relating to God, though good, are inadequate. Whether we identify this as a completionist/fulfillment schema or a supersessionist one, the effect is the same. Christ is viewed as the final, definitive revelation of God and God's will, the final and definitive sacrifice once for all time that makes all such previous sacrifices and rituals redundant, and final and definitive savior of all who believe in him.

This teleological sense of having arrived at the endgame is woven into the warp and woof of the fabric of New Testament thought, and the author of Hebrews is just the clearest exponent of it. He believes this not because God has replaced one people of God with another, but rather because Jew and Gentile united in Christ is seen as the continuation of the one true people of God. This is why Jesus is the climax of the hall of faith and is called the "pioneer and perfecter" of faith—the ultimate exemplar of good Jewish faith in

---

[37]Donald A. Hagner, *Encountering the Book of Hebrews: An Exposition* (EBS; Grand Rapids: Baker Academic, 2002), p. 122.

God (see Heb 11:1–12:2). There is no separation of the old era from the new one, the old people from the new people of God; rather, there is continuity between the two, with Christ himself linking them. The author does not use the clever Pauline image of Christ being the seed of Abraham who links Christians to Abraham, but his argument in Hebrews 11 has much the same effect here and is consonant with such an idea.

And not only does the author of Hebrews make the link between Jews in the past and present Christian Jews the clearest one made by any New Testament writer, but also he most clearly and distinctively links the historical Jesus with the ascended and exalted Christ, and he does this by a remarkable idea. He paints a picture of earth (specifically Jerusalem) being the outer court of the temple, and heaven being the inner sanctum.[38] Jesus the priest offers himself as a sacrifice in the outer court, and then after death and resurrection he enters into the inner sanctum and applies the blood and intercedes for God's people. The rhetorical conceit even goes so far in Hebrews 10:19-25 as to suggest that the body of Christ is the veil that was rent in the temple thereby giving an all-access pass to Christ's followers into the very presence of God, in part now, but also in death even more so when believers, like Christ, who blazed the trail before them, are made perfect through suffering death and enter into the perfect realm (see Heb 2:10: 12:23).

More is said on the subject of perfection in Hebrews than in any other book in the New Testament, and this again reminds us that the author has his own "solos" when it comes to singing in the New Testament choir; indeed, he has several of them. One of the more interesting solos that he sings is about how even Christ was made perfect through suffering (cf. Heb 2:10; 5:9; 7:28; 9:11). Since the author also is the clearest exponent in the New Testament of the sinlessness of Christ, it is also clear that he is talking not in moral terms but rather in terms of completion. Mortality stands over against eternity. The temporal stands over against the permanent. In order to enter the land of perfection/completion, one must either die or be taken up into heaven. In this sense, Christ was made perfect through suffering and provided the martyr's paradigm thereafter. But there is another sense in which Christ was made perfect through suffering: he perfectly or completely finished or fulfilled what God had sent him to earth to do, namely, make purification for sins, as Hebrews 1:2-4 suggests. One suspects that so much is said about the humanity, mortality and sinlessness of Christ in

---

[38]That this is a rhetorical conceit for the author is made clear when he says in Hebrews 13:12-13 that Christ died outside the camp (i.e., outside the city walls of Jerusalem).

this discourse because it supports the paradigmatic story line of Jesus being a high priest forever after the order of Melchizedek. And indeed, the author is singing solo on that theme, which we should consider briefly.

Jesus was not, as the author of Hebrews knew, of the Zadokite or Levite or Aaronite line of priests. To our knowledge, he never served in any capacity in the temple, unless one counts his teaching at the age of twelve (Lk 2:41-52) or his prophetic sign-act against the buyers and sellers (Mk 11:15-17 par.), neither of which qualifies as regular Jewish priestly duties. How, then, could Jesus be said to be a priest at all? In a tour de force performance, the author argues that the person being referred to in Psalm 110:1-2 is Christ, and that therefore the story in Genesis about Melchizedek is a foreshadowing of the truth about Jesus himself. Is this somehow incompatible with a presentation of Jesus as the Messiah, or as the preexistent Son of God, or indeed as divine? Obviously, the author of Hebrews does not think so, since he draws on all these story lines in his presentation. These ideas about Christ as priest and sacrifice are compatible with the more traditional images of Jesus, but they add something new, even a new way of seeing the relationship of the historical Jesus and the exalted Christ. Not only are they the same person, they are the same person performing two stages of the same priestly mission.

There are many voices in the New Testament choir who, when it comes to singing the gospel oratorio, are basically "seconding"—a musical term that refers to singing in unison on the major choral parts of the oratorio. There are also soloists who have there own distinct parts that add to the oratorio richness, texture, color, and new ideas. The author of the Hebrews, like Paul, is one of the soloists. He could be contrasted with the author of 2 Peter, who is basically repeating or seconding what others have said, though he has a brief cameo solo in 2 Peter 1 presenting us with the eyewitness story of what Peter saw on the Mount of Transfiguration. This brings up an important point. If even the least original or creative of the New Testament writers has something to add to the ensemble, then it is a mistake to see any of them as merely time markers or page turners for the pianist. They too are performing their parts in the gospel oratorio, and their importance should not be minimized simply because their "original" or solo contribution is minimal.

The Gospel of Mark: The Secret Son of Man
Mark's Gospel is important for a host of reasons, not the least of which is that it is the earliest Gospel, and its author ostensibly has connections with both

Peter and Paul. We have been examining the earliest signs of unity among the New Testament writers, in this case in the writers probably connected with Paul, who likely was the earliest Christian writer.

Mark's is the Gospel nearest to the font, the ultimate source of all Christian thinking about Jesus, the touchstone—Jesus himself. Mark makes clear that Jesus' own preferred terminology for himself was "Son of Man," conjuring up the story in Daniel 7. And as is the case with that "one like a son of man" (Dan 7:13), it requires a revelation and some explanation to understand what he is about and who he really is.

When I think of Mark's contribution to the Christ story that all the New Testament authors are telling, I think of a basso profundo, singing low and in minor keys, providing the undercurrent and undergirding for the whole oratorio. "Son of Man" is the bass line, the touchstone about which Jesus himself was prepared to sing. But what a secret agent he was, this Son of Man! He was dark and stark, and only revelations from above made clear to a few who he was during his ministry. Otherwise, most folks thought that he was a prophet or miracle-worker at most. They were not looking for a messianic figure who called himself "Son of Man." They were not humming the Daniel 7 tune when Jesus came to town.

In two respects, there is an interesting and unexpected harmonic convergence between Mark's portrait of Jesus and that found in Hebrews. The author of Hebrews speaks of Christ being a priest forever, based on Psalm 110:1-2. Jesus Christ is the same yesterday, today and forever. The story in Daniel 7 speaks of "a son of man" who will rule in a kingdom forever—not that he will have a family line that will rule forever, but he himself will rule forever. And this is to happen after he descends from heaven and the judgment seats are set up. Mark 14:62 echoes this scene quite clearly and makes evident that it is viewed as an event happening on earth, with the Son of Man descending for the event as the eschatological judge. One of the interesting things about Mark's Gospel is that although its structure is set up to highlight the epiphanies that reveal that Jesus is the Christ or the Son of God,[39] Mark spends most of his time stressing that Jesus called himself "the Son of Man," in the third person no less. We do find a reference to Jesus as Son of Man in Hebrews 2:5-8, but there it is connected with the more generic language about human beings in Psalm 8. We may likewise compare Revelation 1:13, where there is an allusion to Daniel 7 and also the

---

[39]On this subject, see Witherington, *Individual Witnesses*, pp. 603-40.

image of "one like a son of man" is combined with that of the Ancient of Days. We may also compare Acts 7:56, where Stephen refers to the exalted Christ in heaven as the standing "Son of Man." This seems to reflect the Daniel 7 background as well.

My point is this: Mark is dealing with a theme, Jesus as Son of Man, that gets very little play outside the Gospels. And even in the case of the Stephen example we are dealing with a Jewish context where apocalyptic images were familiar, not a Gentile context at all. It appears that John of Patmos likewise is dealing with a largely Jewish audience that had some understanding of apocalyptic prophecy. The example from Hebrews is more generic, but note again that the audience is Jewish Christian. However, when the audience of some New Testament writer is largely Gentile, this "Son of Man" title or imagery basically disappears altogether. This brings us to the important conclusion that even when we are talking about shared Christology among the New Testament writers, there were some constraints caused by the nature of the audience that brought about adaptation of how Jesus was referred to. It could be argued that Paul, instead of employing "the Son of Man" (which he never uses of Jesus), chose to use sparingly the alternate image of Jesus as the last Adam (see Rom 5; 1 Cor 15). There may be something to this suggestion, as we will soon see.

Also especially interesting about the "Son of Man" image is that although it is prevalent in the Synoptics, it is much less to the fore in John (some seven or so examples) and is not the dominant christological image there that it is in Mark. On the one hand, this tells us that we are dealing with something that certainly goes back to Jesus himself and his own self-designation; on the other hand, it tells us that early Christians, to make points about Jesus, were not afraid to use terminology and story lines different from the ones he used.

Does this make the "Son of Man" story line a dead end? Obviously not, since it is retold three times over at length in the Synoptics, and it is clear from John that it was possible to tell the gospel story effectively without much using this notion. Here is where a certain amount of finesse is necessary to understand what is going on in the christological storytelling. There were some ways of telling the gospel that better suited a Jewish audience familiar with apocalyptic ideas and images, and there were some ways of telling it better suited to a Gentile or even pagan audience that had little or no contact with Torah or synagogue.

The images of Jesus as Son of Man and as Son of God are not contradictory; they are complimentary, but they need not both be used. Would we not lose the divine side of the equation if the only emphasis was on Jesus as Son of Man? As it turns out, the answer to this question is no. The "son of man" in Daniel 7 is given a forever kingdom, and he is expected to personally rule it forever. He is the climax and end of the story of how beastly empires would be one day replaced by a human and humane one in the person of the human and yet divine "son of man." Thus, while "Son of Man" could emphasize the humanity of Jesus, as in Hebrews 2, it also could convey divine overtones.[40] The Jesus story was profound and complex enough that many images and ideas could be used to express the truth about him. As Eduard Schweizer observed, Jesus was the man who fit no one formula.

Thus, we need not talk about dueling Christologies in early Christianity. There was a kaleidoscope of images, ideas and story lines that could be applied to Jesus, and by the end of the New Testament period a multitude of them were being used, as is clear from what we find in the book of Revelation, which still in the 90s is adding new terms, ideas, and images to the glossary of Christ.

Never in the New Testament do we find direct contradictions of one source by another in regard to the theological significance of Jesus. By this I mean, for example, that we do not find Mark telling us that Jesus was the Son of Man, and another writer saying, "No, wait, he was not the Son of Man, he was the Son of God." We see instead an augmentative process and sometimes perhaps a substitutionary process (if the "Son of Man" image is too vague for the audience, use the "last Adam" image), but not a corrective process. The singers in the New Testament choir are not like dueling banjos; they are more like multiple voices in a massed ensemble, each one singing a portion and stressing a part in a large, harmonious oratorio. The more voices, the more complex the harmonies can be and are. But still, all of them are singing recognizably the same song: the good news about Jesus and its implications.

Here it will be useful to do a little profiling, Markan style. What things does Mark actually say about who the Son of Man is and what he can do?

---

[40]The "son of man" can be seen as representative of the holy ones later in Daniel, but this does not forestall the conclusion that he could also be seen as divine, since the former idea is a development of the human side of the "son of man" imagery but does not exclude other dimensions of the story line. This is true not least because in the ancient Near East kings, the people's representatives, often were viewed as divine in some sense, a son of some god or gods.

1. Jesus alone is called "Son of Man" in Mark's Gospel, and Jesus persistently and insistently refers to himself this way throughout the book, even at the trial in Mark 14.

2. The phrase "Son of Man" does not occur at all in Mark 1. Jesus is introduced by way of the more familiar images of Jesus as the Christ or the Son of God in Mark 1:1 and at the baptismal scene in Mark 1:9-11, and he is called the "Holy One of God" by demons (Mk 1:24). Not until the healing of the paralytic in Mark 2 is Jesus called "Son of Man," and it is Jesus himself who introduces the nomenclature into the story. It is possible, however, to take Mark 2:10 ("but that you may know that the Son of Man has authority on earth to forgive sin") as a parenthetical interpretive comment by Mark himself, and some have even suggested that this is true also of Mark 2:28 ("so the Son of Man is Lord even of the sabbath"). If this is true of either of these cases, it means that Mark himself chooses to especially highlight this way of referring to Jesus, and what he is telling us is that Jesus has divine power and authority not only to forgive sins but also to say what is and is not appropriate behavior on the Sabbath. In other words, the expression "Son of Man" connotes for Mark not a mere mortal, a mere human being, but rather something christological and something divine as well.

3. Confirmation that we are on the right track in saying that "Son of Man" connotes something divine to Mark is found in both Mark 13:26-27 and Mark 14:62, where we hear about the theophany of the Son of Man coming on the clouds to judge the world, a role played by Yahweh in the Day of the Lord passages in the Old Testament (see, e.g., Amos 5:16-27). Notice that in Mark 13:27 he is said to have personal angels that he can send out to gather the elect, as God was to do.

4. The humanity of the Son of Man is emphasized in the threefold passion and resurrection predictions, which always involve the "Son of Man," in Mark 8:31; 9:31; 10:33-34. Notice too Mark 9:12, which reprises this theme. Especially interesting is Mark 9:9, where Peter, James, and John are ordered not to discuss the transfiguration "until the Son of Man has risen from the dead." The disciples did not understand what this order means, presumably because they were looking not for an isolated resurrection of one individual, Jesus, all by himself but rather for a resurrection of the righteous. But then again, in all likelihood they were not looking for a suffering and executed Messiah either. The importance of Mark 9:9 is that Jesus stands alone as the Son of Man raised from the dead. This implies something distinct about Jesus that sets him apart from other righteous persons who might one day be raised. It implies something about how God the Father viewed Jesus and his impor-

tance. Presumably, this is why the Father says to the three disciples, "This is my Son, whom I love. Listen to him" (Mk 9:7).

5. The phrase "Son of Man" is used in the most profound theological reflection on his impending death in Mark's Gospel: "For even the Son of Man did not come to be served but to serve, and to give his life as a ransom for many" (Mk 10:45). Here we have a theology of atonement enunciated, and it is connected with the fact that Jesus is the Son of Man and came to die.

6. Unlike in John 9, no one confesses Jesus to be the Son of Man in Mark's Gospel, despite the fact that he is portrayed as such throughout the book.

7. For Mark, then, it was appropriate to use the phrase "Son of Man" to refer to Jesus' earthly ministry in various of its facets, particularly in his divine authority to pronounce forgiveness of sins (without offering a sacrifice first) or change the Sabbath rules (see Mk 7:15-19). It was especially appropriate terminology to refer to his coming atoning death and isolated resurrection. And finally, it was also appropriate to refer to the return of Christ for final judgment. In other words, the whole tale of Jesus could be told under the banner or title "Son of Man." It linked the human and yet divine dimensions of Jesus' character quite nicely, as was foreshadowed in Daniel 7 itself.

These seven points bring us to an important conclusion. Even in our earliest and most primitive of Gospels, we do not find a portrait of Jesus as a merely extraordinary human being, a prophet or a messiah figure empowered by God. There is already a divine dimension to the portrayal of Jesus worked into the mix by the use of the echoes of Daniel 7 developed in direct application to Jesus himself during his ministry and thereafter. Though certainly the divine Christology is more explicit in Matthew and especially in John, it is untrue to say that it is not evident in Mark as well, because it is. The earliest evangelist is not out of synch with the portrayal of Jesus found in Paul's writings or in Hebrews. He does, however, find another way to tell the story by emphasizing the "son of man" apocalyptic material from Daniel.

To be sure, Mark indicates that the identity of Jesus is a secret to most people in Jesus' life until it is revealed to them. Nevertheless, the messianic character of Jesus shines through, including in the way he is said to provide a king's ransom for the many (Mk 10:45). The "son of man" figure in Daniel 7 is portrayed as the once and future king, indeed as the final great ruler over a kingdom who eclipses all the previous emperors and world empires. The Son of Man is the one who rules for (and as) God in God's dominion forever and ever, and only an eternal person could do that. The contrast with 2 Samuel 7 could hardly be more clear. Jesus is not merely Son of David; indeed, there is actually a critique of that messianic tradition in Mark 12:35-37. Rather, Jesus is David's Lord, being a divine figure called "Son of Man." And as such, he is a more universal figure, one that Mark's probably largely Gentile audience could relate to. He will be ruler of God's world, not merely king of Israel.

1 Peter: The Suffering Messiah

The echoes of earlier Pauline, or just earlier Christian, ways of talking about Jesus are found in abundance in 1 Peter. Jesus is called "Jesus Christ" repeatedly, as if that were his name, and we even see the Pauline phrase "in Christ" (1 Pet 3:16; 5:10). He is also called "the Lord Jesus Christ," which we have already seen in Paul's writings as well. Peter speaks confidently about the resurrection of Jesus from the dead (1 Pet 1:3) and his return, which is said to be when he will be "revealed" (1 Pet 1:8, 13), the same sort of apocalyptic language found in texts as varied as 2 Thessalonians 2:8 and Mark's Gospel. There are small new nuances to the discussion when the Spirit who inspired Old Testament prophecy is called "the Spirit of Christ" (1 Pet 1:11). The author seems to know well the V-pattern of the early christological hymns such as we find in Philippians 2, Colossians 1 and Hebrews 1 ("He was chosen before the creation of the world, but was revealed in these last times for your sake" [1 Pet 1:20]), and also he reflects the early Jewish Christian tendency to mostly use the term *God* to refer to the Father ("Through him you believe in God, who raised him from the dead and glorified him, and so your faith and hope are in God" [1 Pet 1:21]).

But the term or concept that appears most frequently with "Christ" in this discourse is "suffering." Peter's contribution to the oratorio is to present Christ in light of the Isaianic concept of the suffering servant of Isaiah 52–53. He is not the only one to think this way about Jesus, as texts such as Mark 10:45 probably show, and Acts 8 definitely shows, but in some ways his presentation is the most profound. And not surprisingly, since suffering is to the fore when Christ comes up, Peter reinforces earlier tendencies to see Jesus as the sacrificial lamb of God, or Passover lamb, which were already present in Paul and in Hebrews.

The reason that suffering is to the fore is that the audience itself is suffering or faces suffering, and Peter believes that the Christ story provides a story line and paradigm that show them how to respond to such suffering in their own lives. Here we do well to look in more detail at what is said on this in 1 Peter 1, but we must remember that Paul had already talked about suffering as Christ suffered, indeed about sharing in the fellowship of Christ's sufferings, so Peter is doing nothing novel here, but rather is further spinning out a certain early Christian trajectory of thought. And Peter's theology of suffering needs to be examined in the larger context of his Christology, so a brief survey of the christological contours of this letter is in order here.

Elsewhere I have dealt at length with the Christology of 1 Peter, and here I can only review a few things that were stressed there.[41] Commentators have often stressed that 1 Peter is more of a theocentric than christocentric discourse, but if we ask what has caused the reconfiguration of Peter's thought world, certainly what he thinks about Christ has caused the shift. He operates with a christocentric or christotelic[42] hermeneutic when it comes to his handling of the Old Testament (see, e.g., 1 Pet 1:10-12), which is by no means unique to this book in the New Testament (cf. Lk 24:25-26, 45-47), and not only does the teaching of Christ echo in his words, and the figure of Christ entirely shape his theology of sacrifice and atonement, but also Christ provides the ethical pattern set forth for his audience to emulate. And this brings us to a further critical point. The longer I work with the New Testament, the less satisfied I am to see theology and ethics divided from one another as if they were discrete subjects. By this I mean that the figure and pattern of Christ binds the two together and grounds both the indicative (what Christ was and did) and the imperative (what his followers should do and be). In one sense, the ethics of 1 Peter is just a playing out of what it means to be like and to follow Christ. Believers participate in the sufferings of Christ in some sense and also look forward to an exaltation like Christ's, and the V-pattern (humbling self and being exalted) is repeated in the life of the disciple (see 1 Pet 4:13; 5:1-6).

Let us consider several of the features of the Christology of 1 Peter. Many have noted the use of the Pauline phrase "in Christ" in 1 Peter 3:16; 5:10, 14, but less often observed is that this phrase is used in spite of the fact that the term *christianos* also appears in this document (see 1 Pet 4:14-16). This latter

---

[41]See Witherington, *Many Faces of the Christ*, especially pp. 207-13.

[42]I borrow this term from Richard Hays. It refers to how Scripture is seen as pointing to or having Christ as its goal or fulfillment.

term appears originally to have been a pejorative one applied to Christians by outsiders (see Acts 11:26), but "in Christ" seems to come from Paul and is still the preferred self-designation of Peter. This is telling.

Discipleship happens "in Christ," which does not mean merely in the context of Christ's body of followers, but in the context of one's relationship to and emulation of Christ. That the term *christianos* is not the preferred self-designation but rather is a term spoken of in the context of Christian public witness and consequent suffering is all the more striking because in 1 Peter we have the expression "Jesus Christ" (with "Christ" now almost a second name) some eight times, and even more tellingly just the term "Christ" as a name used an additional twelve times in this discourse. To this we may add the use of the phrase "Lord Jesus Christ" once in 1 Peter. Clearly, the author knows that *christos* is a title, but just as clearly he is comfortable using it as a virtual name for Jesus. So wrapped up in the identity of Jesus is his Jewish messianic role for the author that the two cannot be completely separated. It therefore is no surprise that nowhere in the New Testament is there a more profound reflection on how Christ should be seen as the fulfillment of Isaiah 53 than here in 1 Peter. In all of this Peter sounds much like Paul, except that he stresses even more the theological implications of suffering for what one believes.

It is a huge oversight that a recent volume dedicated entirely to the topic of Isaiah 53 and Christian origins treats the use of Isaiah 53 in 1 Peter as if it deserves scant mention. This is all the more strange when one of its contributors, David Sapp, warns, "Allusions to the Hebrew text of Isaiah 53:10-11 in the above New Testament passages [Mt 20:28; Mk 10:45; 14:24; Acts 3:13; Rom 5:15, 19; Phil 2:7; 1 John 3:5a] would call into question the view that atonement theology based on Isaiah 53 arose in a late stage of New Testament teaching *represented by 1 Peter 2:24*."[43] Indeed, what would call such thinking even more into question is that 1 Peter was written probably right at the end of Paul's lifetime, in the mid-60s, and formulated by Peter himself. Here is a person in direct contact with both Jesus and his original teaching. Even if Petrine authorship was only likely rather than very probable (as I think it is), it could hardly fail to be important to the discussion of Isaiah 53 and Christian origins that Isaiah 53 makes a large imprint on the thinking of the author of 1 Peter about Jesus. If I am right about this, the import is great, for it means

---

[43]David A. Sapp, "The LXX, 1QIsa, and MT Versions of Isaiah 53 and the Christian Doctrine of Atonement," in *Jesus and the Suffering Servant: Isaiah 53 and Christian Origins,* ed. William H. Bellinger and William R. Farmer (Harrisburg, Penn.: Trinity Press, 1998), p. 187 (italics added).

that what we are dealing with in 1 Peter to some degree is a reflection of the Christology of Jesus himself, how he viewed himself and his life mission and death.[44] Acts 3 provides confirmation for this conclusion, for there too Peter reflects on a Christology of the suffering servant.

If we reflect on the use of the *kyrios* ("Lord") language in 1 Peter, we discover the interesting phenomenon, also known from Paul's letters, wherein this title is applied to both Christ and God with equal ease, and in some texts it is actually difficult to decipher which is meant (see 1 Pet 1:25; 2:3; 3:12), though twice "Lord" is used as a clear-cut form of address for Jesus, including in a variation on the primitive (Pauline?) Christian confession formula "Jesus is Lord" or "Jesus Christ is Lord" (see Rom 10:9; Phil 2:11), except here it is "Christ is Lord" (see 1 Pet 3:15). "Christ" is used more frequently than "Lord" in this discourse, which may be a small indicator not only of the primitive character of the Christology here but also of the Jewish character of the audience, for whom Jesus being the fulfillment of early Jewish messianic expectations was of paramount importance.

In 1 Peter the christological language, indeed the whole theological language set, is suffused with the eschatological and apocalyptic worldview of our author. It is therefore no surprise that Jesus' second coming is referred to in 1 Peter as a "revealing" or "unveiling," with the same language being applied to the day of judgment that comes with and by means of the return of Christ (cf. 1 Pet 1:3-7, 13 with 1 Pet 1:5; 4:13; 5:4). Christ is exalted, having entered heaven, and so now is hidden, but one day he will be revealed, at which juncture believers will see him once more (1 Pet 1:8; 4:13). Interestingly, Peter is even prepared to call the first coming of Christ an "appearance" (1 Pet 1:20). It was that appearing that set the eschatological clock ticking, and the author lives in the exciting atmosphere of expectation about the return of Christ, possibly his near return, though expectation never degenerates into calculation in 1 Peter.

The evidence that Peter views Jesus as in some sense divine is by no means limited to his use of divine titles such as "Lord" for Christ. There is also the evidence that Peter possibly speaks about the preexistence of Christ in the reference to the pretemporal choosing of Christ (1 Pet 1:19). We must remember that 1 Peter 1:20 is a discussion about a person, a person chosen in advance, not merely about a preexistent plan or purpose. Paul Achtemeier suggests that 1 Peter 1:11 refers to the idea of Christ being present with the

---

[44]See Ben Witherington III, *The Christology of Jesus* (Minneapolis: Fortress, 1990).

Old Testament prophets and inspiring them and supports the idea by showing how common it was in the early postapostolic era.[45] What gives this some plausibility is that in this ad hoc document Peter has little to say about the Holy Spirit (contrast Acts 2), though certainly he has a robust pneumatology (see 1 Pet 1:2, 12; 4:14) that includes an understanding of the sanctifying work of the Spirit in and after conversion, a Spirit of glory that is said to rest on the believer.

Christology and atonement in 1 Peter. Much has been and should be made about the intersection of Christology and atonement thought in 1 Peter. In 1 Peter 1:19 we hear about the precious blood of Jesus "as of a lamb" chosen before all worlds as a sacrifice for sin, a possible allusion to Isaiah 53:7. The sprinkled and thus atoning blood of Jesus has already been mentioned in 1 Peter 1:2 with allusion to Exodus 24:3-8. To this must be added 1 Peter 2:24, where Christ is said to be the bearer or carrier of sin for others in his body, and thus the scapegoat concept is applied to Jesus. It cannot be stressed enough that Peter envisions the sacrifice of Christ as both substitutionary and penal in character. It is a death endured as a punishment for sins, and it is a death undertaken in our stead or place. Thus, 1 Peter 2:21 can speak of Jesus suffering "for you" (the audience). Christ carries the consequences of those sins to the cross on behalf of others and does away with those consequences (cf. 1 Peter 4:1; 2:24; 3:18). Christ's death is once for all time and all persons, and he is the representative sacrifice and simply the representative for all sinners as a result (1 Pet 3:18-22).

While the death of Jesus is likely viewed in the light of Isaiah 53 as a crucial eschatological turning point, so also is the resurrection of Jesus, for it is by the raising of Jesus that God gave Christians both new birth and a living hope (1 Pet 1:3). It is by the resurrection and not by magical means that baptism is said to save (1 Pet 3:21). And interestingly enough, it is the resurrection of Jesus that leads to believers placing their faith and hope in God the Father (1 Pet 1:21). Ramsey Michaels puts it this way

> If the cross is the basis of Christian ethics [for Peter], the resurrection is the basis of Christian experience. . . . It is quite apparent that Peter's interpretation

---

[45]Paul J. Achtemeier, "Suffering Servant and Suffering Christ in 1 Peter," in *The Future of Christology: Essays in Honor of Leander E. Keck*, ed. Abraham J. Malherbe and Wayne A. Meeks (Minneapolis: Fortress, 1993), pp. 186-87. Note that the phrase "chosen according to the foreknowledge" in 1 Peter 1:2 in reference to human beings by no means necessarily implies the preexistence of human beings in general. Foreknowing happens pretemporally, but the clause does not tell us when the choosing happened.

of the death and resurrection of Jesus Christ in relation to Christian experience is neither a perfect carbon copy nor a pale shadow of Paul's interpretation of these saving events. It is a theology of Christian salvation in its own right, worthy of attention alongside of the other major witnesses of the New Testament canon to the meaning and significance of Christ's saving work.[46]

To this we must add that there is a narrative arc to Peter's Christology that reflects the early Christian pattern found in Philippians 2:5-11 charting the career of a Christ who was preexistent, existed on earth, was exalted and will come again to judge "the quick and the dead." The possible use of creedal fragments in 1 Peter 1:20; 2:21-24; 3:18-22 point us in this direction.[47] And clearly, from texts such as 1 Peter 4:1 no one could claim that the Christology of Peter is Docetic in the least. Not only are Christ's sufferings in the body just as real the sufferings of the audience, but also there is a sense in which the audience's visceral sufferings participate in those of Christ.

There are some distinctive Christological ideas in 1 Peter that show the author's creativity. The image of Jesus as the shepherd of the sheep is, of course, not novel,[48] but the notion of Jesus being the "overseer," the chief shepherd and guardian of the flock (1 Pet 2:25), relating him to the under-shepherds and elders, is an interesting and pregnant idea and image. Equally, the image of the risen and exalted Jesus as the living stone, with disciples being a copy of that stone—a chip off the old block, so to speak—is striking. The notion of the stone that the builders rejected becoming the head of the corner provides us with an interesting combination of ideas from Isaiah 53 and from Psalms. In my view, it is no accident that Peter is portrayed as using Psalm 118:22 in Acts 4:11, just as we see it used in 1 Peter 2:4-8 as well. This is because the summaries of speeches in Acts have been carefully crafted by Luke after interviewing the eyewitnesses and early preachers of the Word, including probably Peter.

Theology proper and its ecclesiological implications. The detailed discussion of the theology of 1 Peter by Ralph Martin is a good foundation for evaluating the larger significance of this theology and its contribution to the wider realm of New Testament thought, and I will draw on his work briefly here in the rest of this section.[49] Martin is quite right to stress that

---

[46]J. Ramsey Michaels, *1 Peter* (WBC 49; Waco, Tex.: Word, 1988), p. lxxii.

[47]See Earl Richard, "The Functional Christology of First Peter," in *Perspectives on First Peter*, ed. Charles H. Talbert (Macon, Ga.: Mercer University Press, 1986), pp. 127-33.

[48]On which, see pp. 283-88 below.

[49]Ralph P. Martin, "1 Peter," in Andrew Chester and Ralph P. Martin, *The Theology of the Letters*

1 Peter has a strong theocentric flavor. God is portrayed from the outset as the Father of the Lord Jesus Christ (1 Pet 1:3) and right to the end as the one from whom grace ultimately comes (1 Pet 5:12). The term *theos* refers to God the Father in this discourse, not Jesus the Son. This in itself should be seen as one more piece of evidence that the author and the audience share a Jewish background as well as a Christian foreground. God is depicted as the one who raised Jesus from the dead (1 Pet 1:3; 3:21), enthroned him at the right hand and crowned him with glory (1 Pet 1:21; 3:21).

Repeatedly in this discourse we hear about how God has called the audience to follow Christ, who also was called by God to a vocation of suffering (1 Pet 2:20-21), and to reverence or "fear" God throughout and by means of every aspect of their lives (1 Pet 2:17). Jesus is indeed the Christ, the Elect One of God, and human beings become part of the chosen only by being "in Christ" (1 Pet 1:2; 2:4, 7). The theology of election is christocentric and corporate, and nothing is said about lost individuals being destined to be "in Christ." The means of entry is described as involving both grace and a faithful response to it. Even mere true belief in God is now said to come about through Christ (1 Pet 1:21; 5:14). God is depicted as the Father who protects and looks after his children, all the while judging their works (1 Pet 1:17; 2:25), but this is done in tandem with Christ, who is also the overseer and shepherd of the flock. The christological reformulation of monotheism is in full evidence in 1 Peter, but this does not lead to the eclipse of traditional Jewish God-talk about the Father.

It would be a mistake not to discuss Peter's rather robust ecclesiology, which has its distinctive elements. The audience members are not merely actual resident aliens and sojourners in Asia Minor; they also have an inherent alien and alienated character just because they are Christians. Unlike in Hebrews, here the author reflects little on the journey or pilgrimage notion as a description of the Christian life (cf. Heb 11), and it is fair to say that this discourse is eschatologically focused to such a degree that we would not expect much language about heaven, much less of dying and going to heaven. It is, instead, resisting the devil while enduring suffering, with one eye on the horizon for the future return of Christ, on which our author exhorts the audience to focus. To that end, he talks about the audience being built into a holy building, indeed being the house of God and also priests within it (1 Pet 2:4-10), instead of talking

---

of James, Peter, and Jude (NTT; Cambridge: Cambridge University Press, 1994), pp. 87-133, especially pp. 104-33.

about the "assembly" or "assemblies" *(ekklēsiai)*. Here he departs from Paul in an important way. And here an important point needs to be stressed.

Peter is suggesting that his converts need not be looking for a home, heavenly or otherwise. They need to get on with *being* a home, a house of God, a hospitable place for all sorts of people, including especially the suffering ones. The audience members are, like Christ, living stones being shaped and fitted into the household of God (again a reference to the Father). This reinforces the discourse's insistent paraenetic thrust, calling the audience to a holy life, but it also gives them a sense of well-being, of having arrived, of being called to a priesthood of all believers. Peter is equally comfortable talking about the worldwide brotherhood and using "family" language to describe believers. These two images—household of God and brotherhood—coinhere ideologically (families live in and make up households), and this comports with the actual social praxis of the early church, which met in people's homes and not in churches or synagogues or other purpose-built buildings. Rather, the audience is God's purpose-built dwelling place that is constantly under construction. Like all other facets of Peter's thinking, his ecclesiology has been galvanized and transformed by what he believes to be true of Christ—the mediator, the model, the mentor, the shepherd, the overseer, the living stone, the head of the corner, the head of the household.

Although he lived in the shade of towering figures such as Paul and was indebted to significant leaders such as James, Peter cast his own distinctive theological shadow, of which we have still not taken the full measure. We must do so, for no one more profoundly reflects on the sufferings of the Christ or Christians in the New Testament than does Peter, and no one is likely to be more directly indebted to the teaching and impact of the Christ himself than he is. As such, he needs to be appreciated as the living link to the living stone. And that is no small contribution to early Christianity. We have been looking at some samples of how Christology in one form or another is the center of the New Testament thought world, but there are, of course, other theological concepts that are prominently featured as entailed within a Christian view of Christ, and we see some of that in Luke-Acts.

Luke–Acts: Jesus as the Hinge of History

If there is a case to be made for one of the New Testament writers being both a Gentile and an ancient Greco-Roman historian, that case must be made for Luke.[50] These factors seem to have affected Luke's christological perspective, but it also appears likely that we must add to the discussion of Luke's Christology the probability that Luke's audience was also largely Gentile. We may see these factors coming into play when Christ is designated savior of both Jews and Gentiles in Luke-Acts (see, e.g., Lk 2:11, 30-32), but there are other ways these factors affect Luke's presentation of Jesus. For example, it has been widely noted that Luke deals with his christological titles with some historical sensitivity. Thus, for example, while Luke himself calls Jesus "Lord" in the narrative framework of his Gospel in the full Christian sense of the term (see Lk 7:13), he is careful to avoid placing such a full Christian usage on the lips of his characters in the Gospel narrative (see below).[51] These factors need to be taken into account as we examine the christological material in Luke-Acts.

There was a time when it was thought of Acts as it has been thought of Mark, that at most one could find a rudimentary Christology here. In more recent years numerous scholars have shown Luke to be a masterful theologian as well as a historian, even though he does present various examples of primitive christological reflection, especially in Acts. I will begin my discussion of Lukan Christology with Acts for the very good reason that Luke seeks to avoid reading later Christian theology back into the life of Jesus in his first volume.

Christology in Acts: Jesus as the exalted Lord. Certain things immediately stand out when one examines Acts in comparison to Luke's Gospel. For instance, we may contrast the plentiful use of the phrase "Son of Man" in the Gospel with the singular use of the term in Acts 7:56. Yet even the single reference to "Son of Man" in Acts is significant because it is the only use of this expression outside the Gospels other than when Psalm 8 is quoted in Hebrews (Heb 2:6) and when Daniel 7 is referenced in Revelation (Rev 1:13; 14:14), and here the use is not titular but rather involves an analogy ("one like a son of man"). Clearly enough, there were various titles or terms with a Jewish and/or Old Testament background that soon fell into disuse once the gospel was increasingly shared with Gentiles, and the expression "Son of Man" seems to have been a victim of this process. It is interesting that in Acts

---

[50]This section appears in a more extended form in Witherington, *Many Faces of the Christ.*

[51]Unfortunately, the important study of Luke's narrative Christology by C. Kavin Rowe appeared too late to be incorporated into this study, but see now his *Early Narrative Christology: The Lord in the Gospel of Luke* (Grand Rapids: Baker Academic, 2009).

7:56 there are differences in the way the phrase is used compared to what we find in Luke's Gospel.

First, in Luke's Gospel the Son of Man and glory are discussed purely in future terms, unlike the case here in Acts. Second, here the Son of Man is standing, not merely seated, at the right hand of God. Clearly, both here and in Luke's future "Son of Man" sayings in his Gospel, Daniel 7 lies in the background. Here we see the way the time frame affects the christological expression. Stephen speaks believing that Jesus is already ascended and at God's right hand, for the church exists in the era after Jesus' resurrection and ascension. In other words, the image in Acts 7:56 would be out of place in the Gospel unless Jesus was speaking of someone other than himself when he referred to the future coming of the Son of Man. This is but one example showing that Luke uses christological terms and titles with a clear historical perspective on the differences between the pre- and postresurrection situation and the pre- and postresurrection community of Jesus' followers. From a historian's point of view, the resurrection has decisively changed things for and about Jesus, and so too for and about the community that spoke of him.

It is in fact an integral part of Luke's very spatial and temporal approach to things, including Christology, that at the end of Luke's Gospel (Lk 24) and throughout Acts he employs an exaltation Christology: Jesus is up there in heaven, exalted to the right hand of God. It is no accident that both the Gospel and Acts include the ascension, which makes clear Christ's bodily absence. This too is a reflection of Luke's attempt to think historically about what happened to Jesus and his body. Jesus, then, in Luke's view, left nothing behind but his followers. This is also why the sending of the Spirit is so crucial in the Lukan scheme of things. If Jesus is absent, the church must have some source of divine power and direction, and the Spirit provides both.

Thoughts on the ascension. Probably too much has been made of the fact that only Luke gives us a doctrine of the ascension, for certainly it is alluded to in Hebrews, and it may well be referenced in John's Gospel in statements about Jesus returning or ascending to the Father (see, e.g., Jn 3:13; 6:62; 13:1; 16:10, 28; 20:17), and texts such as John 20:17 suggest that this has some bearing on Mary and others clinging to Jesus' body. The notion may also be implied in the christological hymns that refer to Christ's exaltation to God's right hand, and more to the point, texts such as 1 Corinthians 15 not only assert a bodily resurrection of Jesus but also a definite limited period of time after Easter when Jesus appeared in the body to his followers, after which Jesus bodily presence on earth ceased. In other words, although only Luke articulates the notion of the ascension, it seems to be presupposed in other New Testament sources and so probably is not conjured up by Luke as a sort of theologoumenon or nonhistorical theological idea. To the contrary, the christological hymns, which are early, assume a descending and ascending Christ, a notion found in Ephesians 4:8 as well when Paul applies Psalm 68:18 to Christ. For a Gentile audience, the ascension of Jesus would have reminded them of ancient heroic figures who were approved by the gods and taken up into heaven.

It is right to stress that for Luke the ascension implies a sort of absentee role for Christ in heaven, with the Spirit now acting on earth as Christ's agent. Texts such as Acts 2:33; 3:21; 9:3; 22:6; 26:13 stress that Christ is in heaven, even if he appears to some on earth such as to Stephen or Paul (see, e.g., Acts 7:55-56; 9:4-5; 23:11). In almost all instances in Acts it is by the Spirit or an angel that God acts on earth (see Acts 8:26, 29, 39; 11:28; 12:7; 13:4; 15:28; 16:6; 20:23; 21:11; 27:23). Notice as a corollary of this that we do not find an "in Christ" or corporate Christ theology in Luke-Acts as we do in Paul's letters, nor is there any ongoing Immanuel sort of Christology in Acts such as we find at the beginning and end of Matthew's Gospel. In other words, Luke's Christology seems simpler and more primitive than what we find in Paul's letters or in the incorporation theology in the Fourth Gospel.

The historical perspective of Luke. The historical perspective of Luke is in full evidence if we compare and contrast the use of "Lord" in Acts and in Luke's Gospel. Luke calls Jesus "Lord" in the narrative portions of both his volumes (cf. Lk 7:13 with Acts 23:11) in a way the other Synoptic writers refrain from doing in the narrative sections of their Gospels. It also appears that Jesus even calls himself "Lord" obliquely once in Luke 19:31-34, but this usage is found in the other Synoptics as well and may mean little more than "master" or "owner." However, no other being calls Jesus "Lord" in Luke's Gospel except by divine inspiration (Lk 1:43, 76) or unless the term is found on the lips of an angel (Lk 2:11). Once we get past the resurrection of Jesus, various people can and do call Jesus "Lord" in the ordinary course of things (cf. Lk 24:34 with Acts 10:36-38).

The same sort of phenomenon can be found in the use of "sonship" language. In the Gospel of Luke, Jesus is called "Son" by other than human voices (Lk 1:32, 35; 3:22; 4:3, 9; 8:28), but in Acts Paul clearly calls him this openly (Acts 9:20; 13:33). Then too, words about Jesus as savior or as one who saves are found only on superhuman lips in the Gospel (Lk 2:11, 30; 3:6), but after the resurrection and ascension such talk is an essential part of the church's confession (Acts 4:12; 5:31; 13:23). Luke is supremely conscious of the difference that the resurrection made in terms of what Jesus did and what he could become for his followers. He could not have truly fulfilled his christological role, nor could his followers have confessed him as Christ, had he not risen from the dead. The resurrection is, for Luke, the watershed event for both Christology and ecclesiology.

It is not entirely surprising that in Luke's two volumes, which are so firmly grounded in historical considerations, no clear "preexistence" language is applied to Christ, though some texts might imply the notion. It is interesting, however, that Acts 2:31 implies that David saw Jesus' resurrection coming in the future but says nothing about David seeing or foreseeing Jesus himself. In any event, Christ's preexistence (which does not deal with his historical manifestation) is not a subject that Luke chooses to debate or even to address. Luke's concern is with Jesus from his birth to his present and ongoing exaltation in and reigning from heaven as Lord over all. He also refers to Christ as the coming judge (Acts 3:20-21; 17:31), though this is not a central concern of his in either of his volumes. Notice the focus of Peter's description in Acts 2:22-36, where the whole scope of Jesus' ministry is chronicled from birth as a man (Acts 2:22) to his exaltation and coronation (Acts 2:33-36).

The humanness of Jesus is stressed in Acts by the repeated reference to Jesus being "of Nazareth" (e.g., Acts 3:6; 4:10), just as it was stressed in Luke's Gospel. Notice that often this is stressed in conjunction with the name "Jesus Christ," not just "Jesus." In various ways, Acts 10:36-43 is one of the more important texts in Acts for christological discussion, for here not only do we see the exalted Christ, the one who is Lord over all, but also in the same text we find the so-called "low" christological notion of God being with Jesus and anointing him with the Spirit and power while he was on earth. The point is that Luke wishes to stress Jesus' humanness but at the same time reveal his divine roles.

Luke is also concerned to reveal Jesus as the Davidic Messiah and Son of God, a connection made by way of Psalm 2:7, among other texts. Acts 2:30 and Acts 13:33 bring to the fore a "Messianic figure, God's Son of Davidic descent who rules over Israel in the latter days."[52] This is not a major image in Acts, but it is significant in that it makes clear that Luke has no desire to portray Jesus as simply a man or a generic savior, but rather as a Jew and, indeed, the Jewish messiah. This comports with the use of the Isaianic material in Acts (Acts 3:13; 4:27-30), which reveals that Jesus is the servant of whom the prophet spoke. It is material such as this that gives no aid to those who think that Luke is simply inserting a Christology of his own throughout Acts rather than trying to present a variety of Christologies that he found in his sources. This likely also explains why we find both the titular and nominal use of "Christ" in various of the early Petrine speeches in Acts.[53] Luke does not iron out all the divergencies that he finds in the sources that he uses in Acts, and this is why some primitive material can still be found in Acts.

It often has often asserted on the basis of texts such as Acts 2:36 (where it is said that God has made Jesus "Lord and Christ") that Luke is adoptionist in his Christology. This overlooks that Luke is operating in a historical and narratological mode and discusses such things from a functional perspective. The issue for Luke is not who is Jesus before and after the resurrection, for it is "this same Jesus" in both cases, but rather what roles or functions he assumes after Easter that he could not, or could not fully, assume before Easter. Luke's point is that only as the exalted one could Jesus truly assume the tasks of Lord over all and be the Messiah and Savior for all. In other words, Luke is not given to ontological speculation; rather, such texts are about roles and functions and what tasks Jesus did when.

True, there is not a great deal of reflection on the atoning nature of Christ's death in Luke-Acts, but certainly there is some. One form that this takes is found on the lips of Paul in the problematic text Acts 20:28, which probably reads "the blood of his own," referring to Christ's blood. Another form that this takes is in the discussion about Christ suffering in order to release people from their sins or to provide forgiveness (cf. Acts 13:38 with Acts 2:38). This is not an insignificant theme, for as David Moessner has stressed, "It is, how-

---

[52]Eduard Schweizer, "The Concept of the Davidic 'Son of God' in Acts and Its Old Testament Background," in *Studies in Luke-Acts: Essays Presented in Honor of Paul Schubert*, ed. Leander E. Keck and J. Louis Martyn (Philadelphia: Fortress, 1980), p. 191.

[53]See Stephen S. Smalley, "The Christology of Acts Again," in *Christ and Spirit in the New Testament: Edited by Barnabas Lindars and Stephen S. Smalley in Honour of Charles Francis Digby Moule* (Cambridge: Cambridge University Press, 1973), pp. 79-84; "The Christology of Acts," *ExpTim* 73 (1961–1962): 358-62.

ever, the suffering or death of Jesus that is the fulfillment of Scripture tied most closely to 'the plan of God' which results in the release of sins."[54]

Kyrios Christos *in Acts.* Before turning to some of the distinctive and interesting christological elements in Luke's Gospel, we do well to look more closely at two of the key titles in Acts: *kyrios* and *christos.* The former is by far the most frequently used title in Luke-Acts, occurring almost twice as often as *christos.* In fact, out of a total of 717 instances in the New Testament, the majority of references to Christ as *kyrios* occur either in Luke-Acts (210 times) or in the Pauline letters (275 times). The basic concept that Luke has of *kyrios* seems to be one who exercises dominion over the world, particularly over human lives and events. In other words, the term is always used relationally, for if one is to be a lord, one must have subjects.

The term *kyrios* occurs in Acts 104 times, of which only eighteen are references to God the Father and forty-seven definitely refer to Jesus, with most of the rest referring either to Jesus or God, though it is not always clear which is meant in some of these texts. A clear reference to Jesus is evident in some texts because *kyrios* is combined with the name "Jesus" (Acts 1:21; 4:33; 8:16; 15:11; 16:31; 19:5, 13, 17; 20:24, 25; 21:13) or the name "Jesus Christ" (Acts 11:17; 15:26; 28:31). It is also clear that where *theos* and *kyrios* are combined, it is not Jesus that is being discussed (Acts 2:39; 3:22). In Acts 2:34, which draws on Psalm 110:1, both God and Jesus are called "Lord." It would be wrong to conclude from such a text that Luke sees Christ as only the believer's Lord, for Acts 10:36 makes such an assertion impossible.

Probably when we encounter various Old Testament phrases such as "day of the Lord" (Acts 2:20), "angel of the Lord" (Acts 5:19; 12:11, 23), "fear of the Lord" (Acts 9:31) or "hand of the Lord" (13:11), it is proper to assume that God rather than Jesus is meant. There are, however, two probable exceptions to this rule. In view of Christianity being called "the Way" in Acts, it is probable that "the way of the Lord" in Acts 18:25 involves a reference to Christ. Then too, "the Word of the Lord" appears to refer to the Word about or from Jesus (cf. Acts 8:25; 13:44, 49; 15:35-36). In any case, it is important not to underestimate the significance of transferring the term *kyrios* from God the Father to Jesus. "In using *kyrios* of both Yahweh and Jesus in his writings Luke continues the sense of the title already being used in the

---

[54]David P. Moessner, "The 'Script' of the Scriptures in Acts," in *History, Literature and Society in the Book of Acts,* ed. Ben Witherington III (Cambridge: Cambridge University Press, 1996), p. 249.

early Christian community, which in some sense regarded Jesus as on a level with Yahweh."[55] Luke does not directly call Jesus "God," but he stands in the tradition of those who found it appropriate to worship Jesus as the Lord and so as divine. He is well aware that the early church's confession was that Jesus is the risen Lord (Acts 10:46; 11:16; 16:31; 20:21). It is to Jesus the risen and exalted Lord that one must turn to be saved (Acts 5:14; 9:35; 11:17) and to whom a believer must remain faithful (Acts 20:19), and Jesus as Lord commissions people for ministry (Acts 20:24).

Luke, even within Acts, seems conscious that as time went on, the "Lord" terminology was used of Christ more and more frequently. It is striking that the vast majority of references where God, not Jesus, is called "Lord" are found in Acts 1–10 (Acts 2:39; 3:19, 22; 4:26; 7:31; 10:4, 33) or on the lips of Jews or proselytes to Judaism. The further one gets into Acts, the more Christians speak for themselves, and when they do, "Lord" almost always means "Christ." After the council in Acts 15, only one text seems clearly to use *kyrios* of God rather than of Christ, Acts 17:24. Luke does not shy away from the paradox of speaking of a risen Lord (Lk 24:34); indeed, it is said to be the resurrection that makes him Lord in some sense (Acts 2:36). What this suggests is that Luke uses the term sometimes to indicate when Jesus began to function as Lord, and sometimes as simply the Christian way of referring to Christ in Luke's Gentile environment.

More univocal is Luke's use of *christos* in Acts. The term occurs some twenty-six times, and in every case, not surprisingly, it refers to Jesus. Texts such as Acts 3:18 or Acts 4:26, which have the qualifier "his," make clear that Luke knows the root meaning of the term *christos* and also understands the term's relational character. If one is "the Christ," one must have been anointed by someone else, namely, God. Hence, in Acts Jesus is God's Christ or anointed one, but the believers' (and all other creatures') Lord. The full phrase "our Lord Jesus Christ" (Acts 15:26) implies both of these relationships. Luke makes explicit in two places that being a Christian involves confessing Jesus as "the Christ" (Acts 9:22; 17:22). It is in the witness to the synagogue that this issue is pressed.

By way of generalization, we may say that "Christ" mainly functions as a name when the audience is Gentile but can serve as a title when the audience is Jewish (although texts such as Acts 2:38; 4:10; 8:12; 10:48; 15:26

---

[55]Joseph A. Fitzmyer, *The Gospel According to Luke (I-IX)* (AB 28; Garden City, N.Y.: Doubleday, 1981), p. 203.

make evident that this is not always so). What was critical for Jews to confess is that Jesus is the Christ, the Jewish messiah (Acts 5:22; 7:3), whereas for Gentiles what was paramount was confessing Jesus as Lord (Acts 15:23-26). Luke can also stress that it was God's plan for the Christ to suffer (Acts 17:2-3) and be raised (Acts 2:31, citing Ps 16:10). Finally, baptism in the name of Jesus Christ is seen as the characteristic entrance ritual for Christians (cf. Acts 2:38; 10:48).

Christology in Luke's Gospel: Jesus the spirited messiah. Turning to the Christology of the Gospel, we see that "Savior," though certainly not the most common title, is a unique one in terms of the usage in the Synoptic Gospels (cf. Lk 1:47; 2:11; Acts 5:31; 13:23).[56] This title is found elsewhere in the Gospels only at John 4:42. This term was a common one in the Greek-speaking world, but it is uncommon in the New Testament except in Luke-Acts and in the Pastoral Letters (cf. 1 Tim 1:1; 2:3; 4:10; Tit 1:3; 2:10; 3:4 using the term of God, and 2 Tim 1:10; Tit 1:4; 2:13; 3:6 using it of Christ).[57] For instance, we find it on an inscription about Julius Caesar dating to A.D. 48, where he is called "God manifest and the common savior of human life." Thus Luke, at the inception of his Gospel (here at Lk 2:11) wants to stress who the real savior is to his Gentile audience. As Luke uses the title, it refers to Jesus right from his birth and relates to the Old Testament promises of salvation (cf. Acts 13:23). In Acts 4:12 he argues that salvation is found in no other name (such as the name of the emperor). Some of this emphasis may reflect Luke's use of the LXX, for God is called "savior" *(sōtēr)* fairly often in the LXX (see, e.g., Is 45:15).

It is interesting that Luke alone among the Synoptic writers combines the title "Christ/Messiah" with reference to Jesus' suffering (Lk 24:26, 46; cf. Acts 3:18; 17:3; 26:23). In view of the fact that such an idea probably was not found in early Judaism, and Luke himself does not overly stress the point, the idea likely goes back to Jesus in the form of the Son of Man suffering.[58] Notice Luke's careful use of *christos* mostly in the titular sense in his Gospel

---

[56]It appears probable that Luke's more primitive Christology, in comparison to Matthew's, results in part from his historiographical perspective and from his attempt to Hellenize the narrative somewhat for his Gentile audience. It is not clear whether Luke's Gospel was written before or after Matthew's, or even whether the date makes a difference in the christological presentation.

[57]This is one more piece of evidence that Luke may well have been the one who wrote the Pastoral Letters, perhaps at Paul's behest.

[58]"Servant" language is occasionally applied to Jesus in Acts (Acts 3:13, 26; 4:27, 30), and in a few places the "suffering servant" notion seems to be in the background; certainly Acts 3:13 alludes to Isaiah 53:12. It is not, however, a major motif.

(Lk 2:11, 26; 3:15; 4:41; 9:20; 20:41; 22:67), but more often as a title in Acts (Acts 2:38; 3:6; 4:10, 33; 8:12).

At the climax of Luke's Gospel comes a rather clear repudiation of the idea that when Jesus is called "king," it has some sort of political connotation. In Luke's Gospel, as in Mark's, the title on the cross is "King of the Jews"; thus, Jesus is crucified for insurrection. Ironically, Jesus shows his kingship in weakness by suffering. The soldiers mock Jesus, assuming that "king" indicates a political ruler (Lk 23:37), but the thief on the cross understands that Jesus' kingdom is not of this world (Lk 23:42). Thus, in his passion narrative Luke juxtaposes the two different attitudes toward kings and ruling. Notably, it is only in Luke that Jesus is praised as king as he enters the city on Palm Sunday (Lk 19:38), and it is also only in Luke that at the Last Supper Jesus explains that in his realm servanthood, not lording it over people, is the way leaders should act, and he is conferring this sort of leadership role and kingdom on his disciples (Lk 22:25-30). We may compare this to Acts 17:7, where again we find controversy over a misunderstanding about Jesus. The early Christian proclaimers are heard to have proclaimed a king other than Caesar, which is both true and false in different ways. In other words, the irony and sense of double meaning found in the Gospel passages about Jesus as king are seen in this Acts passage as well.

In regard to the use of "sonship "language in his Gospel, Luke is exercised to show that Jesus is God's Son not by adoption or by obedience but rather by birth, hence the emphasis on the virginal conception in Luke's birth narrative. Luke 1:32-35 states plainly the truth that Jesus is born God's Son. Luke is happy to refer to Jesus as "Son of God," "Son of the Most High," or "my [God's] Son." It is probable that "Son" is not exactly synonymous in Luke's mind with "king" or "messiah," though it includes such a notion. In the Old Testament, however, the phrase "Son of God" is never directly used of the coming Davidic messiah (but see 2 Sam 7). For Luke, "Son" implies a unique relationship between Jesus and the one whom he calls "Father," as the birth narrative makes clear (see, e.g., Lk 2:49), even though Jesus' disciples may also address God in this fashion (see Lk 11:2). Texts such as Luke 6:35 make evident that the sonship of believers is not on a par with that of Jesus. This is apparent also from Acts, where "Son of God" is something that Christ is confessed to be uniquely (Acts 9:20; cf. Acts 8:37 in the Western text).[59]

---

[59]See Rudolf Schnackenburg, *Jesus in the Gospels: A Biblical Christology*, trans. O. C. Dean Jr. (Lou-

The use of "Son of Man" in Luke's Gospel is very much the same as what we have found in Mark's Gospel: "Son of Man" is used to describe the earthly ministry, the suffering and also the future coming and judging activities of Christ.[60] Luke always uses the definite article before the phrase "Son of Man." It appears that Luke finds this title important, for in his Gospel we find at least three cases where Luke uses the phrase but it is not found in the parallel (cf. Lk 6:22 with Mt 5:11; Lk 9:22 with Mt 16:21; Lk 12:8 with Mt 10:32), and in each of these cases the phrase is on Jesus' lips, as is true in all its other uses in this Gospel.

There are other titles or terms applied to Jesus that are found only in Luke's Gospel and are used only during Jesus' ministry, such as "doctor" (Lk 4:23), but these do not amount to major motifs in Luke's christological presentation. If, however, one couples the "doctor" language with the abundant language and discussion of healing in Luke-Acts, it can be seen that this is a more important subject for Luke than for the other Synoptists.

Perhaps a further piece of evidence pointing to the primitive character of the Christology in Luke-Acts is that more than many New Testament writers, Luke places notable emphasis on Jesus as a prophet, indeed perhaps as the great prophet like unto Moses whom God would raise up. As such, Jesus is seen as the last great eschatological and messianic prophet or, to put it the other way around, a prophetic messiah. Perhaps the easiest point of entry into this form of christological thinking is Acts 2:22-24, where we read about "Jesus of Nazareth, a man attested to you by God with mighty works and wonders and signs which God did through him in your midst. . . . This Jesus you crucified. . . . But God raised him up." This must be compared to Deuteronomy 34:10-11: "There has not arisen a prophet since in Israel like Moses, whom the LORD knew face to face, none like him for all the signs and wonders which the LORD sent him to do." This prophecy is given in the context of a statement about Joshua (in Greek, "Jesus") that he was "full of the spirit of wisdom, for Moses had laid his hands upon him" (Deut 34:9). In early Judaism it was not believed that Joshua completely fulfilled what Deuteronomy 34:10-12 predicted, and so an eschatological fulfillment in a latter-day Moses/Joshua figure was looked for (see 4Q175 1-5; Jn 1:21; 4:19; 6:14). In Acts 2:22-24, cited

---

isville: Westminster John Knox, 1995), pp. 152-53.

[60]Although Luke uses "Son of Man" less often than does, for instance, Matthew when the parousia is in view, Luke does not omit the idea (see, e.g., Lk 21:27-28).

above (cf. Acts 3:20), the deeds of Jesus during his ministry couple with his being "raised up" (in a nonmetaphorical sense) by God is seen as clear evidence that the prophecy in Deuteronomy has come to fulfillment in Jesus. Once one recognizes that this is one of the ways Luke is portraying Jesus, it is possible to go back to his Gospel and make sense of a variety of other pieces of data.

For example, like Joshua, Jesus is said not only to have received the Spirit bodily (Lk 3:22) but also to have been "full of the Spirit" when tempted (Lk 4:1), and that he began his preaching "in the power of the Spirit" (Lk 4:14). The paradigmatic sermon in Jesus' hometown (see Lk 4:16-30), which sets the agenda for what follows in the Gospel, depicts Jesus as reading from Isaiah and claiming not only that he understands prophecy but also that he fulfills it (Lk 4:21). Jesus is the one anointed by God with the Holy Spirit and power (Acts 10:38; cf. Acts 4:27) to prophesy great things, do mighty works and even bring to fulfillment God's eschatological promises. Luke-Acts is written with the understanding that something fundamental is being revealed about Jesus' prophetic character in Luke 4. Indeed, he calls himself "prophet" at Luke 4:24. Near the end of the speech in Luke 4 Jesus compares himself to Elijah and Elisha in his deeds (Lk 4:25-27).

Notice too how in Luke 7 this comparison is fully fleshed out, for there Jesus heals a Gentile centurion through Jews interceding for him (Lk 7:1-10), just as Elisha had healed a foreigner in like fashion through the intercession of a Jewish girl (2 Kings 5:1-14); and then, just as Elijah had raised a widow's son from the dead (1 Kings 17:17-24), Jesus raises the widow of Nain's son (Lk 7:11-15), after which the response to such deeds is that a "great prophet whom God raised up" is in their midst, and through him "God is visiting his people" (Lk 7:16). It is precisely at this juncture that Jesus sends word to John the Baptizer that "the poor have good news preached to them," fulfilling the prophecy announced in Luke 4.

Equally important to the discussion of this christological theme in Luke-Acts is Luke 13:33-34. The lament over Jerusalem that begins in Luke 13:34 is Q material also found in Matthew 23:37-39. But Luke has prefaced this with a statement from Jesus found only in this Gospel: "Yet today and to-morrow and the next day I must be on my way, because it is impossible for a prophet to be killed outside of Jerusalem" (Luke 13:33). Here Jesus is not merely identified as a prophet; he calls himself a "prophet" as he nears the climax of his ministry, and he looks to suffer a prophet's fate. This theme becomes even more explicit in Acts when, in his speech in Acts 7, Stephen, himself a prophetic and visionary figure, speaks of a twofold sending of Moses to God's people, first in weakness and then in power, with two offers of salvation to God's people (Acts 7:23-43). Those who reject Moses after the second offer of salvation and the great signs and wonders that he worked are themselves to be rejected by God. Stephen especially makes the connection with Jesus crystal clear when he says, "This is the Moses who said to the Israelites, 'God will raise up for you a prophet from your brothers as he raised me up' " (Acts 7:37).

But as it turns out, Jesus is not just a prophet; he is the one in the church age who sends the Spirit of inspiration and prophecy to Christians so that they can offer prophetic witness as well. Thus, as Luke Timothy Johnson says, "the power active in their prophetic witness is the Spirit of Jesus (Acts 2:33; 3:13; 4:10; 13:30-33),"[61] or perhaps better said, the Spirit Jesus sent.[62] This image, then, of Jesus as the eschatological or Mosaic prophet who is also therefore the prophetic Messiah is an important one for Luke, and it serves to bind his christological presentation in Luke-Acts together to some degree. Luke stresses that Jesus is not only prophet but also messiah throughout his earthly career and beyond (at birth [Lk 2:11; cf. Lk 1:35]; during the ministry [Lk 4:21, 41; 7:20-23; 9:20]; at his death [Lk 24:26, 46; Acts 3:18; 17:3; 26:23]; at the resurrection he becomes both Lord and Messiah [Acts 2:36]; as such, he is the object of the proclamation [Acts 5:42; 8:5; 9:22; 18:5, 28]; and he will come again as the Messiah one day [Acts 3:20; cf. Acts 1:11]). It is understandable why Luke might highlight this theme if indeed he was writing to Gentiles, since among them there was great respect for and interest in prophecy, including especially Jewish prophecy.[63]

---

[61]Luke Timothy Johnson, *The Gospel of Luke* (SP 3; Collegeville, Minn.: Liturgical Press, 1991), p. 18; see also pp. 19-20. Throughout this section on Jesus as prophet I am indebted to Johnson's discussion.

[62]This comports with Luke's major emphasis throughout his two volumes that it is the Spirit who brings salvation as well as its announcement. Jesus and his disciples must be full of the Spirit to perform their ministries. Jesus himself provides the paradigm of the person anointed, appointed, and empowered by the Spirit. It is not, however, true to say that Jesus is the only Spirit-filled and Spirit-driven person during his life. That would overlook Mary, Anna, Simeon, John the Baptizer, and others, though the Spirit seems to fall on them, as it did on the Old Testament prophets, sporadically. Luke's view of the Spirit, like his view of prophets and prophecy, owes much to the Old Testament presentation of these matters.

[63]Consider, for example, the famous story of Josephus saving his own life by prophesying that his captor, Vespasian, would become emperor, which in fact did happen.

Another way Jesus is depicted in Luke's Gospel, likely meant to get the attention of Gentiles, is as a sage. We see this image especially at the beginning and end of Luke's Gospel. Thus, in Luke 2:46-48 we find the boy Jesus astounding the Jewish teachers with both his questions and answers and overall understanding, and after this episode Luke stresses that Jesus grew in wisdom and stature (Lk 2:52). The alert reader is thus prepared for what follows in, for example, Luke 6; 8; 10–18, where Jesus is revealed as a great sage who offers sapiential speech in the form of beatitudes and woes, aphorisms and parables, and riddles and pronouncements but never prefaces his teaching with the prophetic formula "Thus says Yahweh" or with a citation of human authorities that he was following, instead choosing simply to speak on his own authority in a metaphorical way.

As he draws his Gospel to a close, Luke portrays Jesus as the ideal wise man, like a Socrates who with perfect self-control and freedom from fear goes to his death and is proclaimed a righteous man by an independent unbiased Gentile witness (Lk 23:47). It is also part of this portrayal that Luke turns the Last Supper into something of a farewell address at a Greco-Roman banquet and a handing over of authority to his successors (Lk 22:29-30).[64]

In summing up, I note two major factors that seem to affect Luke's christological presentation. The first is Luke's historical consciousness, which causes him to be careful about what titles and ideas he predicates of Jesus at what point. He avoids having ordinary persons or disciples call Jesus "Lord" during the ministry, but he finds this characteristic of Christians after the resurrection. Second, it is important to Luke to distinguish who Jesus is and what he is called. The titles often seem to have more to do with what particular roles, functions or tasks that Jesus assumes at particular points in time (e.g., after his baptism or after his resurrection) than to do with ontology, though there are exceptions to this. Jesus is God's Son from birth in Luke's presentation, but Jesus is not in any full sense Lord until he completes his earthly mission, dies and is raised and exalted by God so that he may take on such roles. It is also true that although Jesus is Son from birth, he is not called this by a group of his followers until some time later. Luke is aware of the disparity between truth's presentation and the recognition of that truth.

Most of these titles indicate relationships as well as authority: Jesus is God's Christ or Anointed One or God's Son, but the believers' Lord and Savior. In

---

[64]See Luke Timothy Johnson, "Luke-Acts, Book of," in *Anchor Bible Dictionary*, ed. David Noel Freedman (New York: Doubleday, 1992), 4:414.

general, what Jesus is in relationship to God is constant from first to last, but what Jesus is in relationship to other human beings, in particular believers, changes along the way depending on a variety of factors, such as whether or not Jesus is yet raised from the dead. The phrase "Son of Man" seems to bridge the ontological and functional titles and refer to both who Jesus is (the human being who represents God's people) and what he does (exercise dominion and power, bring in a kingdom). Luke is cautious to make clear that "Christ" was not merely a second name for Jesus. In both Luke and Acts he uses the term with the article to indicate this fact, though also he increasingly uses it as a name as Acts develops.

Reginald Fuller offers a useful summary of what we find in Luke-Acts. He stresses that at birth Jesus is destined (and, I would add, made able by nature and pedigree, being Son of God and Son of David) to be Messiah for God's people. At baptism he is invested as the eschatological prophet and equipped for ministry with the Holy Spirit. At death he is king and suffering messiah, though the latter is not revealed until after the resurrection, and it is revealed by Jesus himself (Lk 24). Yet Jesus does not completely fulfill any of the major titles ("Lord," "Son of Man," "Savior," "Son of God") until he is exalted to the right hand of God the Father and can truly and fully offer inspiration and salvation by the Spirit, whom he sends to those who accept him on earth. Then he assumes these roles openly and fully.[65] This is Luke's portrait of the Christ.

I have reviewed this data at some length and stressed how Luke's historical perspective affects his presentation of the data. There is a sense of "before and after" to his presentation. But what is most striking about it is that Luke uses the same terminology as do the other Synoptic writers and with essentially the same meaning as well. In other words, the shared ideational system remains intact even when processed through a historical point of view. This, I believe, shows more than most anything else could show that the New Testament writers felt compelled to present the story of Christ in a way that comported with other such tellings that they knew were going on in their era. There was, to use modern language, a sense of orthodoxy, when it came to what one should and should not say about Jesus. There were ideational boundaries to the symbol system and the narrative thought world within which one still had some room for creativity, some room to maneuver. But

---

[65]See Reginald H. Fuller and Pheme Perkins, *Who Is This Christ? Gospel Christology and Contemporary Faith* (Philadelphia: Fortress, 1983), pp. 81-95, especially pp. 93-95.

since the primary function of my discussion in this second volume is to address the unity of the thought, I can conclude with the following remarks.

I doubt that any other of the other Gospel writers would have objected to any of the ways Luke portrayed Jesus, even though they would not have been operating with the same broad historical approach. Luke uses the same titles and with the same content, and although the author of the Fourth Gospel will want to say more about, for instance, the preexistent Logos, he would not have gainsaid what Luke has asserted, but simply would add to it. Instead of a historical perspective, the Fourth Gospel brings a cosmic one, with the V-pattern brought in to link the eternal and temporal phases of the Son of God's career.

Again, I want to stress, addition is not done by subtraction in such cases. Addition assumes the rightness not only of what one is adding to the discussion, but also of the foundation to which one is doing the adding. And certainly there is no evolutionary spiral of Christology in the New Testament anyway, since the early christological hymn material in Philippians 2, Colossians 1 and Hebrews 1 shows that an exalted view of Jesus as God already existed long before John 1 was ever penned. What John 1 does do is make clearer the cosmic scope of the Son's work and salvation's plan. I will say more on this shortly, but first we must consider the sapiential material in Matthew, which in its own way paved the way for seeing Jesus as a cosmic figure, like Wisdom.

Matthew: The Gospel for Jewish Christians

A variety of New Testament writings stress how Jesus fulfills the need that Jews had for a messiah. Paul famously puts it this way: "But when the time had fully come, God sent forth his Son, born of woman, born under the law, to redeem those under the law, so that we might receive adoption as sons" (Gal 4:4). To a largely Gentile audience he stresses that Jesus was a son of David according to the flesh (Rom 1:3; cf. Rom 9:5). Of course, it was a hard sell to convince a Greco-Roman world, often noted for its anti-Semitism, that the Savior of the world was a Jew. Paul knew this. But Matthew was speaking to a very different audience, one that apparently needed to know and understand and embrace Jesus as a Jew who fulfilled all the hopes and dreams of Israel.

Writing to Jewish Christians under fire, probably in Galilee, perhaps in Antioch, Matthew crafts a brilliant portrayal of Jesus as Immanuel, God's

Wisdom come in the flesh, as the greatest sage of all, even greater than Solomon, as king of the Jews who inaugurates a kingdom that had many unexpected features and participants, a kingdom with laws that look more demanding than Moses was and sometimes different from Moses' requirements. But in regard to the issue of Israel and the law, does Matthew's Gospel present a divergent perspective on this subject compared to what we find elsewhere in the New Testament? Much depends on how one views Matthew's audience. If it is Jewish Christians, that is one thing. If it is an audience of converts from paganism along with some Jews, that would be another thing altogether. I have argued at length elsewhere for the audience being Jewish Christians in Galilee.[66]

Part of the problem in viewing Matthew theologically comes from a certain assumption about the views of Paul about Israel and the supposed widely divergent view of Israel presented elsewhere in the New Testament, perhaps especially in Matthew. So the examination of Matthew gives us a good chance to walk through this minefield and see if some of these theories blow up or can pass through successfully.

Israel and the law in Matthew and in the New Testament. Let me first say something about Paul and Israel. G. B. Caird puts it this way:

> Paul's theology, even at its most universalist, is deeply rooted in his Jewish past. Though the Jews have no advantage in being entrusted with the Law unless they keep it, it is a great advantage to have been "entrusted with the oracles of God"—i.e., the Old Testament interpreted as God's plan of salvation (Rom. 3:2). When Paul contrasts the old humanity of Adam with the new humanity of Christ, Adam's history is entirely a *Jewish* history which includes Moses and the Torah (Rom. 5:12-21). Though "in Christ there is neither Jew nor Greek" (Gal. 3:27; Col. 3:10), nevertheless Gentile Christians are "grafted, like branches from a wild olive, onto a Jewish olive tree" (Rom. 11:17). It is not enough for Paul to prove that Jew and Gentile are equally children of God; he must prove that they are equally children of Abraham (Gal. 3:7; Rom. 4:11-12).[67]

Furthermore, "the whole argument of Romans 9–11 is designed to persuade Gentile Christians that God has not written Israel off," and by "Israel" is meant ethnic Israel, non-Christian Israel, in these three chapters.[68]

---

[66]See the introduction in Ben Witherington III, *Matthew* (SHBC; Macon, Ga.: Smyth & Helwys, 2006).

[67]G. B. Caird, *New Testament Theology*, compl. and ed. L. D. Hurst (Oxford: Oxford University Press, 1994), p. 53.

[68]Ibid.

What comes to light upon closer inspection of what Paul says is that he, like other New Testament writers, holds to a remnant theology, and in his view the righteous remnant when he wrote Romans was Jews who believed in Jesus. They provided the continuity with the righteous remnant all the way back to the patriarch Abraham. But what is remarkable is Paul's belief that there is still a future for non-Christian Jews as well, for when Christ comes back, "all Israel will be saved" (Rom 11:26), by which is meant a large number of Jews who are currently broken off from the people of God.

This is consistent with Paul's stance in Romans 1:16 that the gospel is for Jews first, and also for the Gentiles. God has not forsaken his first chosen people, nor is the church called "Israel" in Romans 9–11. It is possible that there is a different use of "Israel" in Galatians 6:16, but even there, "the Israel of God" seems to refer to Jews and not Gentiles, perhaps more specifically Jews who believe in Jesus who are currently giving Paul so much trouble. But we must not forget that Paul is operating with a concept of Israel that is described as follows by the apostle himself: "For not all who are from Israel are Israel" (Rom 9:6). What Paul adds to the discussion is the notion spoken of in Romans 11 about the temporary breaking off from the people of God of those Jews who reject Jesus. He believes in one continuous people of God in continuity with the patriarchs, but what now decides who is in and who is out is faith in Christ and the mercy of God. There are not two peoples of God in Paul's theology.

Not surprisingly, since Luke is the sometime companion of Paul, Luke provides a narratological version of the good news to the Jew first and also to the Gentiles not only in his Gospel but also in Acts. In Acts, Paul and others go to the synagogue first wherever they go, and even in Acts 28 Paul is still conversing with Jews and trying to convince them about Jesus, though it appears to be a hard sell. In Acts it is clear enough, by the minority of Jews who join the largely Gentile churches of Paul, that Luke too believes that God has not forsaken his first chosen people. But what about the law and this new community of Jew and Gentile united in Christ? Since the proper way to regard this, in Paul's and Luke's view, is that Gentiles are now joining the community of "true Jews," then we should not talk about supersessionism in the case of either of these authors. But it is equally clear that both of them believe that Gentiles join this community by grace and through faith in Christ, not by means of keeping a certain modicum of the Torah. The matter in Acts 15 is not about Jewish food laws; rather, it is about staying away from pagan temples, where idolatry and immorality transpire in the context of a meal. There were Pharisaic Jewish Christians (see Acts 15:1-4), of course, who did not agree with James's compromise with Paul and Peter on this matter. The issue, then, became this: were even Jewish Christians required to keep Torah in order to be good Jews? Paul's answer was no (see 1 Cor 9), but some Jewish Christians in the Holy Land said yes to this question, and even James may be one of them (see Acts 21:20-26). The question then becomes, Where on this spectrum of views did Matthew and his community stand when it came to Israel, the law and the followers of Jesus?

First, we note that Jesus himself says that during the time of his ministry he is sent only to the lost sheep of Israel, and he instructs his disciples to "go nowhere among the Gentiles or Samaritans" during this period of time (see Mt 10:5-6; 15:24). This is not to say that Jesus would not minister to a Gentile who came to him. This surely is the point of the story in Matthew 8:5-13, and note especially Jesus' remark "I have not found anyone in Israel with such great faith," which must be tantamount to "any Jew in the Holy Land," since this man is speaking to Jesus in Capernaum. Jesus, in Matthew's Gospel, is offering the good news to the Jew first, just as Paul later says is proper. And it is clear enough that Jesus too operates with a remnant concept, which is focused on response to his gospel. The Galilean Jewish cities that reject Jesus will be judged on the day of judgment (Mt 11:20-24; cf. Mt 23 on Pharisees who reject Jesus). True Jews are those who accept and follow Jesus.

But what is the Matthean Jesus' view of Torah? In Mark's Gospel it seems clear enough that Jesus is portrayed as having the authority to change the rules of the game to some extent in view of the eschatological saving activity that is transpiring. He is Lord of the Sabbath, and he can forgive sins. The parenthetical comment of Mark at Mark 7:19 makes clear that in Mark's estimation Jesus thought that at least some of the purity laws in regard to food were obsolete.

The Matthean Jesus, however, says that he has come not to abolish the law and the prophets but rather to fulfill them. Indeed, he adds that not one stroke will disappear from the law, not one vowel point or breathing mark, until all is accomplished (Mt 5:17-18). Of course, this is said in the context of the Sermon on the Mount, where there is not merely an intensification of Torah but also some variance from Moses' teachings at key points. What, then, does the saying in Matthew 5:17-18 mean? The key verb in Matthew 5:17, *katalyō*, means "to annul, set aside," and it is applied to the law and the prophets, not just the law. This verb must be seen as the direct opposite of the verb in the following sentence, *plēroō*, which refers to fulfilling these things—that is, fulfilling their intention, their promises, fulfilling the will of God expressed in this earlier teaching. "Fulfill" is a terminology often used of prophecy, and it has a teleological sense. It hints that the Old Testament was pointing to something greater than and beyond its scope that was only promised or prophesied before but now is being realized. As Matthew constantly reminds us, this is what the whole of Jesus' life and ministry is about— the fulfillment of prophecy—and all of God's word is seen as prophetic in a certain sense. By fulfilling the law, Jesus was demonstrating its truth, and so certainly he was not abolishing it in the sense of declaring it false. This brings us to another point.

Fulfilling something is not the same as obeying it now and forever. If it is fulfilled in the new eschatological situation, then its purpose has been accomplished, the sense and intent have been brought to pass. This in turn means that it is no longer applicable carte blanche, but only as reaffirmed by Jesus as part of the new eschatological situation, the new covenant. But since only some of the law and the prophets was fulfilled during the ministry of Jesus, this meant that some of it was yet to be fulfilled and applied. Thus, in the meantime, it could be reaffirmed and reapplied, at least with Jews. The law is not lost or erased as the eschatological salvation and new covenant breaks in, but there are parts that no longer apply because they have been fulfilled in or by Christ, specifically, as Hebrews was to stress, the whole Levitical system. A truth does not become less true just because it is a timely truth as opposed to a timeless one. In short, even in Matthew's Gospel there are some things that are applicable to only one stage or covenant period in the life of God's people.

It appears likely that Matthew's community is a community of Torah-observant Jewish Christians. However, they read the Scriptures eschatologically and messianically, as Jesus did. This being the case, they saw no need to observe all the things that they believed Jesus had already fulfilled. Those things were accomplished and did not need repeating. For example, we do not find disciples being urged to go up to Jerusalem and offer sacrifices for sin or purification. There is a period of transition while the Old covenant is becoming fulfilled, and thus obsolescent, and the new one is being established (see 2 Cor 4:1-12), and even Jewish Christians in Matthew's community know this. In the meantime, they honor the Torah and seek to live good Jewish lives so as to be good witnesses to their surrounding Jewish neighbors. What is not clear from Matthew is whether this community thought like the Judaizers mentioned in Galatians and in Acts 15:1-4. It would seem not, since they take this eschatological approach to the changing situation and the way it affects observance of the law. The law, as reaffirmed, amplified, intensified, interpreted, and augmented by Jesus, was what was to be kept, but now as part of a different covenant—the new one inaugurated by Jesus' sacrificial death (see Mt 26:28).

To sum up, some Jewish Christians felt that they must be Torah-observant and keep the Mosaic law as it was. Others believed that such Jewish observance was a blessed option, not an obligation. Still others saw their keeping of the "law of Christ" as the proper way to honor the law and the prophets. It is likely that none of the principles and writers of the New Testament, whether James, Peter, the Beloved Disciple, or Paul (all of whom were Jews), thought that Jewish Christians should be required to "live like a Gentile" in order to have fellowship with them. As it works out in 1 Corinthians 8–10, Paul is asking Gentiles to compromise in order to have fellowship with their Jewish Christian brothers and sisters who still have scruples about nonkosher food and the like. And of course, a scrupulous Jewish Christian could dine with a Gentile and thereafter do a purification rite if that was thought to be necessary.

In short, there is a spectrum of opinion in regard to the keeping of the law in the New Testament insofar as how Christians should and must live. The pragmatic missionary attitude of "to the Jew I will be as a Jew" was something that Paul was happy with, but others would have seen it as radical. It is interesting, however, that the hardline Judaizing view that Gentiles must be circumcised and become Jews, taking on the yoke of Mosaic law in order to be Christians, is mentioned in the New Testament but is nowhere endorsed by any of the writers of the New Testament, not even in the portrayals of Jesus by the evangelists, not even in Matthew, if my reading of Matthew 5 offered above is correct. And this brings us to an important point.

It is instructive to compare Mark's portrayal of Jesus to Matthew's because some 95 percent of Mark is recycled and reaudienced in Matthew, and also to compare Luke's usage with both of these because of the numerous similarities between the presentations of the Synoptic writers. As Howard Marshall

stresses, the high degree of verbal similarity in the common material shared
between Mark, Matthew, and Luke, coupled with the large number of passages
found in all three of these Gospels, speaks volumes about the degree of shared
perspective that these evangelists have on Jesus. All of these Gospel writers
view Jesus as the Christ, the Son of God, the Son of Man, the Son of David,
which is to say that there is a high degree of overlap in their Christologies.[69]
Scholars tend sometimes to overlook this because often they are fascinated by,
and fixated on trying to explain, the differences between the accounts.

Matthew and "the church." One way that Matthew has often been thought
to stand out from the other Gospels is in its references to the community
(ekklēsia) of Jesus in Matthew 16:18; 18:17. But in fact the former of these
texts, and perhaps the latter as well, is talking about a future community of
Jesus' disciples. Even in Matthew there is no description of community meetings of Jesus' followers in the various cities or villages that he frequented.
Jesus has a group of close disciples in all these Gospels, but "we hear nothing
of people forming themselves into distinct communities in their own towns
and villages. . . . The Evangelists cannot be accused of reading the life of the
church into the pre-Easter period. Here we have a sharp distinction between
before and after Easter."[70] There is little "ecclesiology" proper to be found at
all in the Gospels, and none that is not proleptic, and this speaks well of their
avoidance of anachronism.

If we want to find discussions of Christian communities in the New Testament, we must look to Acts, the epistolary literature, and Revelation. And
this again brings up a crucial point. The Gospels must be handled very carefully when we are asking and answering the question about Christian theology. It can, to some degree, be found in the way materials are edited and
presented and arranged, but it requires careful study, and above all it is a mistake to read the Gospels as a transcript of later Christian community life. For
example, when the blind man is cast out of the synagogue in John 9, it ought
not to immediately be assumed that this refers to later tensions between the
community of the Beloved Disciple and the synagogue in Asia Minor near
the end of the first century. There is no reason why some of Jesus' disciples
or potential disciples might not have been treated rudely during his ministry.
He was a controversial figure by all accounts and stirred up strong feelings in
many who encountered him and his disciples.

---

[69]Marshall, *New Testament Theology*, p. 185.
[70]Ibid., p. 195.

What we certainly can gather from all four Gospels is that the Jesus story is being interpreted by means of and in light of the Old Testament to one degree or another, and all of these writers assume not only a shared corpus of sacred texts, but also that this corpus can be read prophetically and messianically. It was Jesus himself who set this process in motion during his ministry, but it was clearly accelerated by the way his life came to an abrupt end. Especially the last week of Jesus' life required explanation by means of Scripture so that people would know that this was what God intended to happen; and as Matthew's Gospel shows, the beginning of Jesus' life, particularly its original and unusual features, also required some scriptural support. No New Testament writer is doubting or denying that Jesus set the fulfillment of Scriptures in motion, the eschatological age being inaugurated.

The Spirit and the disciples in Matthew and in the other Synoptic Gospels. One of the clearest signs that the evangelists, including Matthew, have a sense of time and timing and the desire to avoid anachronism or false harmonization of things from before and after Easter is that the Holy Spirit rarely comes up when the subject is Jesus and his disciples. To be sure, the Spirit is mentioned as inspiring prophecy, just as it had always done in the history of God's people, and that included inspiring the written oracles of God called "the scriptures" (see Mk 12:36 par.) as well as inspiring living prophets or prophetesses such as Elizabeth or Anna. The Spirit also is mentioned in the Gopels as descending upon Jesus at his baptism and resting on him, and it is God's Spirit who enables Jesus to perform miracles and to preach (Mt 12:18; Lk 4:18). The Holy Spirit also, in both Matthew and Luke, is seen as the agency through which Mary became impregnated. Luke is interesting in that he alone talks about some being filled with the Spirit and thus inspired to speak or empowered to do something (Lk 1:15, 41, 67; 4:1), but this idea is present also in texts such as Ephesians 5:18, where again the subject is not conversion or sanctification but rather empowerment or inspiration for some ministry.

And in the Synoptics it is John the Baptizer, not Jesus, who speaks of Jesus baptizing people with the Spirit (and with fire, according to Matthew and Luke) at some undisclosed point in the future, a promise only fulfilled after Easter (see Acts 11:16; cf. Lk 24; Acts 1–2). The Spirit is promised to the disciples in Luke 24 and John 14–17 but not dispensed, probably not even in John 20:19-23, where we see a prophetic sign-act. In Luke 11:13 we read that Jesus will give the Spirit to those who ask the Father, but by contrast Matthew has at this point a reference to "good things" (Mt 7:11). If we look at Luke and Acts together, we can understand why some scholars have dubbed Luke the "theologian of the Holy Spirit." But even Luke does not portray Jesus' disciples as having the Holy Spirit indwelling them prior to Pentecost.

And this brings up a crucial point. To judge from both Acts and Pauline texts such as 1 Corinthians 12, a person could not be a Christian without the Holy Spirit, could not even truly confess Jesus was Lord without the Holy Spirit. Therefore, the first disciples of Jesus are not portrayed in any of these Gospels as full-fledged Christians who could fully understand Jesus and his significance. They are simply followers of Jesus on the way to becoming Christians. And here we have reached a crucial insight. The disciples are not portrayed as paradigms for Christian behavior in the Gospels, not even in Matthew or John. Indeed, they are portrayed as those of little or no faith, those who understand little or nothing, those who even when they do step out on faith sink quickly (even Peter), those who deny even though they swear never to do so, and those who even when they correctly confess some part of the truth quickly reveal their failure to understand the most crucial things—for example, why Jesus needed to die and rise again.

The reason this frank portrayal of the disciples even in Matthew and John is so impressive is that these are the wisdom Gospels, and it was widely believed in early Judaism that one could behave wisely if one knew wisdom. However, the wisdom that Jesus most often refers to is not nature wisdom (though there is some of that in Mt 5–7) but rather wisdom that must be revealed from above, not from nature or human instruction. This is a wisdom that comes only from above for the disciples when God's Spirit descends and conveys it, providing the correct interpretation of the death and resurrection of Jesus, among other things. We therefore should not expect to find a full-fledged theology of the Holy Spirit in the Gospels, although John 14–17 offers much. For such a theology we have to turn to Acts, and here is Marshall's summary of the view of the Spirit in that book:

> Reception of the Spirit is evidently the sine qua non of being a Christian and is the clear mark that God has accepted recipients into his people (Acts 15:8). It follows inescapably that the Spirit is not only the agent of mission but also the mark of belonging to Christ. There is a tension in that some individuals are said to be full of the Spirit (Acts 6:3, 5, 8; 7:55; 11:24) in a way that might suggest there are degrees of possession, . . . and there is the phenomenon of "filling" people who already have the Spirit for specific tasks (Acts 2:4/4:8;

9:17/13:9). Evidently the baptism of the Spirit is a permanent endowment of believers, a mark of belonging to the new covenant, and is common to them all. . . . Nor is it correct to argue that the baptism with the Spirit is a later experience that tends to be detached from the initial act of belief in Christ.[71]

We would never have guessed that all of this was what early Christians believed if we only had the Gospels themselves, and the reason is that they are chronicles of the period before there were any Christians, not transcripts of later Christian community life. If we consider just the Gospel of Matthew for a moment, we note that there is no mention of the bestowal of the Spirit on anyone other than Jesus in the narrative, and even the Great Commission (Mt 28:18-20), though it mentions baptism in the name of the Father, Son, and Spirit, does not mention the bestowal of the Spirit in general on disciples. In Matthew there is particular emphasis not only at Jesus' baptism but also in Matthew 12:15-21, where Isaiah 42:1-4 is cited about the Spirit of the Lord resting on Jesus; he, not others, is the bearer of the Spirit during his ministry. It therefore is no surprise that not only does Matthew 12:28 say that Jesus casts out demons by God's Spirit, but also Matthew 12:30-31 indicates that blasphemy against the Spirit is committed by identifying the work of Jesus as work of the devil. The idea here is that it is by the Spirit within him that Jesus has performed exorcisms, not by his being the Son of Man. In other words, the Spirit is so much isolated to being in Jesus and not in others that blasphemy of the Spirit could be committed in regard to the ministry of Jesus only if it involved a criticism of the divine power and work that came through Jesus himself. Nothing similar is said about the disciples in this Gospel or, for that matter, in the others. The power and the authority of the disciples are entirely dependent on Christ; they do their deeds in the name of Jesus, even the exorcisms that the Twelve perform when sent out on mission by Jesus. They are two stages removed from the power source, unlike Jesus. He alone is the bearer of the Spirit, as opposed to some who occasionally were inspired by the Spirit to speak.

And this leads us to another important point. It is hard to doubt that the community of Matthew believed that the promise about Jesus baptizing people with the Spirit had transpired. Yet of this we see nothing in the Gospel of Matthew. What should we conclude from this? We should conclude that

---

[71]Ibid., p. 201.

Matthew's community had more resources, both oral and, probably, written, than just this Gospel, which was written specifically for them. They knew, either from oral or written sources, about what happened after the ascension of Jesus and at the Pentecost event, and they knew of the Spirit from their own experience.

We must not conceive of these different evangelists' communities as isolated conventicles ignorant of what was said or done in other Christian communities. To the contrary, the high degree of traveling and intercommunication indicated in Acts must be taken as characteristic of at least many of the leaders of this movement, especially as it increasingly sought to fulfill the missionary mandate. And with traveling came communication, sharing of traditions, documents and other things. I suggest that crucial communities, such as the ones in Jerusalem, Capernaum, Damascus, Antioch, Ephesus, Philippi, Corinth, Rome (and others as well) became both repositories of various early Christian documents and sites where these were regularly copied and disseminated.

In principle, all of the books of the New Testament, with the possible exception of the two latest ones, Revelation and 2 Peter, could have been shared by all the major Christian communities by A.D. 90 or so. Especially with the dying out of the apostles there would have been a strong impetus to collect and disseminate these documents, in particular, apparently, the Gospels and Acts and Paul's letters, but also the letters of 1 Peter, Jude and James, to judge from 2 Peter.

My point is this: there was already something that could be identified as early Christian theology and ethics in the first century, both proto-orthodoxy and proto-orthopraxy. Although this theology and ethics were not quite coterminous with what we today may call "New Testament theology" and "New Testament ethics," they likely were close, especially if these foundational apostolic documents were shared as widely in the New Testament era as I have suggested.

Were the Synoptic Gospels Written for All Christians?

This brings us to Richard Bauckham's important discussion in *The Gospel for All Christians*.[72] Bauckham argues that these Gospels were written not just for one local congregation but rather to be disseminated widely across

---

[72]See Richard Bauckham, "For Whom Were Gospels Written?" in *The Gospel for All Christians: Rethinking the Gospel Audiences*, ed. Richard Bauckham (Grand Rapids: Eerdmans, 2001), pp. 9-48.

the empire. I am not prepared to go quite so far as to say that these Gospels were not in the first instance written for particular communities. This seems especially clear in Luke's case, where an individual named "Theophilus" is mentioned, probably Luke's patron. But it does make sense to say that although in the first instance these Gospels were written to be used by the local Christian community, these communities were all evangelistic as far as we know, and so these Gospels may well have been written with one eye on the larger audience (cf. Jn 20:31: "written so that you might begin to believe") and certainly were meant to be used to train those who did evangelism.

This being the case, I see it as likely that these documents were copied early and often and were widely circulated. Indeed, at least by the early second century the four canonical Gospels were being circulated together, hence the four titles—"According to Mark" and so forth—to distinguish each one. One of the first codices in wide use probably was a collection of these four Gospels bound together.[73] Although there was no New Testament as a whole in the New Testament era, it was likely already being assembled toward the close of the first century, at least in regard to a collection of Gospels and of Pauline letters (see 2 Pet 3:15-16). This brings us to the Gospel of John.

The Gospel of John: A Unique Tradition Among the Evangelists

One of the problems in presenting a unified picture of Christ and of other matters theological and ethical is the differences between the Fourth Gospel and the Synoptics. In fact, some have seen contradictory images of Christ and his teaching and the history involved in the Fourth Gospel when compared to the Synoptics. Thus, it is of theological as well as historical importance to consider some of these issues here.

Most scholars conclude that the Fourth Gospel is an independent testimony to the life of Jesus, a conclusion with which I agree, but even those who see the Fourth Gospel this way often also think that this Gospel writer was aware of other Gospels, perhaps particularly Mark. With the exception of the episode of the cleansing of the temple being moved forward in Jesus' ministry (Jn 2:13-22), the Johannine chronology, particularly the Johannine passion narrative, seems to have about the same shape and order as the Markan one.

---

[73]On this matter, see Ben Witherington III, *The Gospel of Mark: A Socio-Rhetorical Commentary* (Grand Rapids: Eerdmans, 2002), pp. 1-62.

However, more than the issue of the evangelist's possible knowledge of previous Gospels is raised by a close reading of the Fourth Gospel. One wonders if the author of the Fourth Gospel wrote assuming that his audience already knew one or more of the Synoptics. I am on record as having argued that the Fourth Gospel was written not as a tract to be handed out for evangelism but rather as a tool for Christian evangelists to draw on as they bore witness.[74] The writer of the Fourth Gospel may well have known that these evangelists did indeed already know at least the Markan outline, if not Mark itself.

This Fourth Gospel, then, would in part become a supplement to the Synoptics, meant to fill in certain gaps: (1) the issue of the ongoing Judean ministry of Jesus resulting in Judean disciples such as Mary, Martha, and Lazarus and his close relationship with them; (2) the relationship of several of his disciples with the ministry of John the Baptizer; (3) Jesus' relationship with his mother and brothers; (4) his in-house teaching of the disciples in discourse rather than parable form; (5) the extended nature of Jesus' ministry, which this Gospel suggests could have involved at least two or more years (see the mention in Jn 7:2 of the Feast of Tabernacles); (6) the almost entire absence of parables and the complete absence of exorcisms in this Gospel. This last item surely seems intentional. This may well be because the author of the Fourth Gospel assumes his audience's knowledge of those aspects of the Galilean ministry but wishes to focus on the Judean teaching, relationships and miracles.

Seeing the Fourth Gospel as, in part, an intended supplement and not a substitute for any of the Synoptics makes good sense. The author knows that there are other traditions about Jesus, and he even says that "Jesus performed many other signs in the presence of his disciples, which are not recorded in this book" (Jn 20:30). Notice that he does not say that they are "not recorded at all." In addition, there is the author's comment in John 21:25: "Jesus did many other things as well; if every one of them were written down, I suppose that even the whole world would not have room for the books that would be written." This comment is odd if the author believes that no other Gospels have already been written. More likely it implies that already multiple Gospels have been written, and he and his fellow Christians in the audience know it, and he has written a further one for a specific purpose: to supplement the others. Clearly too, this final verse implies that Jesus did many things, surely over several years, too many to be included in any one Gospel.

---

[74]Ben Witherington III, *John's Wisdom: A Commentary on the Fourth Gospel* (Louisville, Ky.: Westminster John Knox, 1995), p. 11.

Another thing of importance is that the Fourth Gospel presents Jesus and his life and teachings in a sapiential manner. Unlike the Matthean sapiential portrait of Jesus, which is more traditional, showing Jesus to be a sage, this author chooses to present Jesus as offering discourses like those that Wisdom speaks in Proverbs 8–9 or in the Wisdom of Solomon. Thus, the fact that a wisdom approach is taken in John does not in itself completely explain the differences between the Johannine Jesus and the Synoptic Jesus; there is another factor involved: John's Gospel takes a more personal, eyewitness kind of approach to the material. Thus, there is more freedom in the way the material is handled. In other words, the author is not following a particular tradition, such as the Synoptic way of presenting the teaching of Jesus; rather, he is creating his own tradition from scratch. Bearing these things in mind, we can now consider whether the Johannine Jesus and Gospel present a deliberately divergent Gospel that disagrees with or even contradicts the earlier ones.

Do John's differences from the Synoptics constitute disagreements? Some scholars seem to have difficulty distinguishing between difference and disagreement. By this I mean that when, for example, John 1:45-49 speaks of a disciple named "Nathanael," and there is no disciple by this name listed in Mark 3:13-19, some scholars assume that there must be a contradiction here. Nathanael is presented as one of the first disciples, apparently, to come into the fold. Is this a contradiction with the Markan account?

First, the Fourth Gospel is not interested in the Twelve as "12." They receive little mention as a group in this Gospel. This is understandable if this Gospel was written by a Judean who was not part of the Twelve. Second, Jesus certainly had more followers than the Twelve even in Galilee, even if we are counting only the male disciples. Apparently, some were itinerant and some were not. Thus we cannot really say that John contradicts the Synoptics at this point, not least because some of these disciples may well have had more than one name or, like Peter, a name and a nickname.

More substantive is the complaint that John 1:42 presents a very different telling of the story of how, or at least when, Simon came to be called "Cephas" or "Peter" than we find in Matthew. First, we must remember that Mark does not have Jesus' words to Peter found in Matthew 16:17-19. Instead, Mark merely makes passing mention in the list of the Twelve as follows: "Simon (to whom he gave the name Peter)" (Mk 3:16). In John, Simon seems to have gotten his nickname at the outset of the ministry (Jn 1:42), but in Matthew it appears to come at the Caesarea Philippi incident (Mt 16:13-20), something that the parallel account in Mark does not suggest (Mk 8:27-30). How can we explain these differences, especially if the author of the Fourth Gospel knew Mark and Matthew?

Looking closely at John 1:42, we see that Simon "will be called [*klēthēsē*] Cephas" (future tense). This suggests that this was to happen at some point in the future, and it is right for us to ask who would do this calling. Would it be Jesus? If so, then the Caesarea episode in Matthew 16:13-20 reveals when he was directly called "Cephas," the rock. Mark 3:16 does not tell us when and where Jesus gave Simon the name "Cephas." That this naming is historical cannot be doubted, since we find Simon called "Peter" by Paul in his earliest letter (Gal 1–2). But what this discussion brings to light is that the author of the Fourth Gospel probably did not get his information about this naming from Mark. His account with the direct naming by Jesus sounds more like Matthew's account. Should we assume that he knew Matthew's Gospel as well and chose to tell the story differently? This certainly is possible. It is clear enough the author of the Fourth Gospel exercised more freedom in editing, arranging, and phrasing his material than did the Synoptic writers.[75]

If, however, the author of this material is indeed the Beloved Disciple, who was on occasion closely associated with Peter himself, then we can imagine a scenario in which Peter told the Beloved Disciple that although Jesus had hinted at the outset that someday he would be called "Cephas," this in fact did not happen until Caesarea Philippi when he got his special commission in regard to Jesus' later community. And sure enough, Acts shows that it is when there is such a community after Pentecost that this man is predominantly called "Petros" or "Cephas" (even in 1 Pet 1:1). What this discussion shows is that the differences between the Gospels may have varied and complex explanations that do not necessarily require the conclusion that they flatly disagree on something.

What we certainly cannot conclude from reading the Fourth Gospel after the Synoptics is that its author was intentionally trying to correct previous tellings of certain key events and stories. Rather, if we look at a story such as the feeding of the five thousand, told in all four Gospels as the same story, we see the degree of freedom in regard to the arranging and relating of the

---

[75]See Craig Blomberg, *The Historical Reliability of John's Gospel: Issues and Commentary* (Downers Grove, Ill.: InterVarsity Press, 2001).

particulars that the author of the Fourth Gospel felt he had in telling his version of the story. The historical question that ought to be asked is this: did he operate like a Jewish scribe doing midrash, who presupposes an earlier fixed text known to the community and so feels free to creatively edit and arrange and present the story to draw out some fresh points?

Does the Beloved Disciple, and the Christian audience for whom he is writing, know that there is a long-established Gospel tradition, and therefore he can feel free to recast the material in a sapiential way and rearrange it to make his own points? This is entirely possible, but it would require that his audience also know one or more of these earlier Gospels so that they would know what he was doing, namely, offering a colorful "Impressionist" painting of Jesus that presupposes the earlier, more "Rockwellian" portraits. John 20–21 suggests that he knows and does presuppose one or more earlier Gospels. It is also possible, however, that the author simply decided that regardless of what others have done (and so in a manner different from Luke, who operates with one eye on the earlier tradition, as Lk 1:1-4 says), he would give his own independent testimony and tell the story in his own way. Either way, his work must be assessed on the basis of what he was trying to accomplish. If he was not trying to do the same thing that his predecessors did, then this must be taken into account before anyone decides that he was contradicting earlier accounts. *Contradiction* is a word that can be applied only if we have multiple accounts of the same incident, all the accounts trying to tell the same story in the same way, and clear disagreements among them (e.g., if we had a story where one Last Supper account had "This is my body broken for you," and another account had "This is the bread of haste shared with you"). The well-known difference in the placement of the story of the temple cleansing in John as opposed to the Synoptics falls well within the parameters of the sort of latitude that I am suggesting. John's placement of the story is theological rather than chronological, and since this is so, the Beloved Disciple's chronology should not be faulted.

Is John's Logos Christology compatible with Synoptic Christology? The same sort of logic needs to be applied when we are dealing with theological matters in John versus what we find in the Synoptics. Does the Logos Christology go beyond what we find in the Synoptics? Indeed it does. Similar ideas can be found in other christological hymn passages such as Philippians 2:5-11 and Hebrews 1:2-4, but not in the Synoptics. Does, then, this divine Christology contradict what we find in the Synoptics? No, it does not. Addition is not the same as subtraction or substitution, and a close look at the Fourth Gospel shows a Synoptic-like emphasis on Jesus as Son of Man and Son of God. Furthermore, the Son of Man theology even in the Synoptics suggests something more than mortal about Jesus, as we have seen earlier in this study.[76] We need to stop drawing too drastic a contrast between the theology of the Synoptics and the theology of John. Difference does not necessarily connote disagreement or contradiction.

So a better question to ask is this: what does the Fourth Gospel add to the theological conversation, especially about Jesus? Much can be said, but here a list must suffice. (1) The Logos Christology firmly grounds the story of Jesus in eternity, prior to and indeed after his human life. It makes clear not only his preexistence but also that he is properly called *theos*. (2) This same Gospel suggests that the whole of the ministry of Jesus needs to be read in light of the Logos hymn. In this Gospel, one cannot understand who Jesus is unless one understands where he has come from and where he is going. Thus, time and again in this Gospel people misidentify or underestimate Jesus. They think that they know him to be the son of Joseph, when really he is the only begotten Son of God. (3) The sapiential portrait of Jesus, especially in the discourse material and in the "I am" sayings, suggests that in Jesus, God's Wisdom is embodied to such a degree that one need never look elsewhere for light and life. Indeed, as Jesus says, "No one comes to the Father except by me" (Jn 14:6). (4) We learn a good deal about Jesus' relationship with the Father, in terms of both its intimacy and of Jesus' dependency on the Father for guidance and direction during the ministry. (5) Equally, since the Synoptics are Holy Spirit deficient, we learn a good deal more about the relationship between Jesus and the coming Spirit, whom he will send to his followers. The Spirit is the agent of Jesus, just as Jesus is the agent or advocate of the Father in this Gospel. We begin to see how trinitarian theology ought to be developed, but this was already implicit in places in Matthew (see Mt 1–2; 11; 28). (6) In the Gospel we also learn a good deal about anthropology that we might not have guessed from reading the Synoptics. In the Fourth Gospel human beings are not viewed as children of God simply because they are human beings created in God's image. One has to become a son or daughter of God through the new birth and so become an adopted child of God. This is made plain at the outset (Jn 1:12-13). We also learn later in this Gospel

---

[76]See pp. 111, 242-48 above.

that without the Spirit's enlightenment, a person would not understand the teaching of Jesus, among other things. (7) We learn that Jesus' brothers (and sisters?) did not follow him, were not his disciples during the ministry (Jn 7:2-5). This is part of the larger pattern in which "his own" received/understood him not (Jn 1:11), as can also be said of various other Jews and Jewish officials. The rejection motif is strong from the outset of this Gospel, but it is by no means universal. There are, after all, still disciples of Jesus, both male and female, all of them Jews, when we get to the end of this Gospel. (8) Some scholars suggest that we learn some things about sacramental theology from this Gospel, but I doubt that. John 3 is not a discussion of baptism at all, and in John 13 there is no discussion of the elements of the Lord's Supper, and it may be doubted that John 6:50-51 adds anything to such a discussion. Jesus is talking in a metaphorical way about taking himself into their lives or inner beings. He is no more talking about the sacraments than he is talking about cannibalism. (9) There is a clear and interesting coordination of eschatological ideas about "my hour" with the discussion about the death of Jesus. The death of Jesus is seen as prime time, when God brings to pass eschatological redemption, for Jesus is the Lamb of God who takes away the sins of the world, as we already learned in John 1:29. In addition, in this Gospel Jesus' death is presented as the first stage of the exaltation of Jesus; when he is lifted up on the cross, he is already on the way up to the Father. Not only the resurrection, but also the ascension and glorification of Jesus, are reflecting light back on his death. Furthermore, the lifting up of Jesus proves to be a witness to God's fulfilling his salvation plan like the lifting up of the serpent in the desert. (10) The tangibility and embodied condition of the risen Jesus are given further stress in this Gospel, even to the point of stressing the continuity with the corpse of Jesus in that the risen Jesus still bears the marks of the nails and spear wound. This makes as clear as it could be that it is this same Jesus in his same body who has been raised from the dead. At the same time, the "lack of recognition" motif is found in the Mary Magdalene story in John 20, as it is also in the Emmaus story in Luke 24. (11) The author clearly and cleverly combines the Son of Man story with the story of Wisdom/Logos, so that it is the Son of Man who not only comes down from heaven for salvation (and later judgment), but also goes back up to heaven at the ascension. This is not an unnatural development, since in the Synoptics, as in Daniel 7, there is reference to the Son of Man coming to earth for judgment. (12) For the first time in a Gospel we hear, however briefly, about grace and truth in tandem. Certainly there is a theology of grace and of truth implicit in all these canonical Gospels, but only John contains explicit reference to this and to the fact that Jesus is the one who is full of grace and truth, just as he is the embodiment of God's wisdom. I will save comments about Johannine ethics in this Gospel for a subsequent chapter.

We do find in the Fourth Gospel a boldness at the end of the New Testament era and a strong attempt to make perfectly clear the larger theological significance of the Christ-event and Jesus' story. The canvas is broad and it stretches from eternity to eternity, but without evacuating Jesus of his human significance or character. The Johannine Jesus is not merely one who appears to be human; he still gets hungry, thirsty, and tired in this Gospel, and he dies just like all other humans. There is no Docetic Christ here. He is both fully human and fully divine because redemption could not be accomplished if he were not both. But the volume certainly is turned up on the "divine" channel of the two speakers in the Fourth Gospel.

If the Synoptic writers are the Gospel choir who often sing in unison and with minor theme-and-variation twists and occasional unique bits, the Fourth Evangelist is the dominant voice in the choir singing one solo after another in his own style and way, but without being out of synch or harmony with the other members of this choir. Sometimes he finds his own pace and rhythm and certainly adds new themes and stories to the oratorio, but when he gets to the passion narrative, there is considerable doubling, reinforcing and amplifying what the other choir members are also saying about the last week of Jesus' life before his crucifixion. But what of that other Johannine voice, John of Patmos? What does his theological tune and tone add to this musical masterpiece?

Revelation: Jesus as Slain Lamb and Roaring Lion

Revelation is presented from the outset as a "revelation of Jesus Christ" that, among other things, reminds us that John's Christology is the heart of the matter for him when it comes to theology. It is Christ's vision that John conveys, and the vision is about Christ, in whose hands is the scroll that is to be unsealed and all the truths to be revealed. Christ is the one who sets in motion the eschatological judgments and provides the final redemption. It thus behooves us to consider carefully John's reflections on the Christ, as that is a key to understanding the work as a whole.

There are a plethora of primitive ideas and images and also some highly polished ones about Christ in this book.[77] Since Revelation is a document meant to address Christians in physical and spiritual danger, we should not be surprised if it concentrates on images and ideas of Christ that would be helpful to address that situation. It thus is natural for the author to stress the sovereignty of God, the power of Christ, Christ's judgment of the wicked for the saints and the like. In short, it is natural for the author to stress forensic images of Christ as both judge and one who redeems the faithful from judgment (as the Lamb of God). It comes as no surprise that no "gentle Jesus, meek and mild" appears in this book, but instead one who sits on the judgment seat with his Father, one who rides forth in judgment with a sword proceeding from his mouth, one who even can be seen as a lamb and a lion at the same time. Here is a mighty and fearsome Christ indeed, with most of the emphasis on what Christ in heaven now is (an exalted Lord) or will be for believers when he returns. In Revelation, then, there is little attention to the ministry of Jesus or to the merely human side of him except by way of emphasizing his death and its benefits.

A rapid survey of the various titles applied to Christ in Revelation reveals the following: "Christ" only appears seven times, "Son of God" once, "Son of Man" twice (but in each case as part of an analogy, not a title), "Logos/Word" once, but "Lord" twenty-three times (and it is also used interchangably of God and of Christ) and "Lamb" twenty-eight times. In this work none of the merely human titles of Jesus, such as "teacher," "rabbi," "servant," "prophet," or "man," are used. It is equally interesting that some of the more Hellenistic titles, such as "Savior" or "God," are also notably absent. In other words, in terms of terminology and titles, this book is very different from John's Gospel, where "Son of God" and "Son of Man" dominate the landscape, and from the New Testament Letters, where "Christ" and "Son of God" are prominent. The extreme Jewishness of this document and its different christological terms is enough to make one suspect that it was not written by the same person who wrote the Johannine Gospel or the Johannine Letters or both, a suspicion that is only reinforced when one notes the very different sort of Greek in this document compared to the rest of the Johannine corpus. This document has a very high Christology stressing Christ's heavenly exaltation and roles since and because of his death and resurrection.

---

[77]What follows here is found in a somewhat different form in Witherington, *Many Faces of the Christ.* The terms *Savior* and *God* are common in imperial inscriptions from all over the empire, especially in the province of Asia where this Gospel likely originated and these titles had already long been used of kings in that region and elsewhere in Alexander's old empire.

The christological tone for the book is set in the first chapter with the first christological vision of John of Patmos. The book begins with the assertion that it is "the revelation of Jesus Christ," and it probably is no accident that only in this chapter do we find the title "Jesus Christ" (three times). "The first Christian readers would need to be led from Jesus Christ to the Lamb, the name which dominates the second part of the book."[78] Jesus is the faithful witness, the firstborn from the dead, the ruler of the kings of the earth (Rev 1:5), and also the one who will come on the clouds in the future for judgment (Rev 1:7). Revelation 1:5 also mentions Jesus' redemptive death and blood. It is also in this chapter that we have the first of only two references in this book to Jesus as one like a Son of Man, except here his garb makes clear his divinity. What is interesting about this is that the author begins here a trend that will continue throughout the work of applying Old Testament images and names formerly used of Yahweh to Christ or to both the Father and Christ. Whereas it was the Ancient of days in Daniel 7 who has such raiment, here it is Christ who is both divine and one like a Son of Man (Rev 1:13). It is not clear whether the person referred to as Alpha and Omega in Revelation 1:8 is God or Christ (cf. Rev 21:6), though probably it is God, but more clearly at Revelation 1:17-18 Christ is referred to as the First and Last (and at Rev 22:13 he is the Alpha and Omega), the one who was dead but is now alive forever and has in his hands the keys of Death and Hades and also holds the churches in the palm of his hand, something that a Christian under fire might find comforting. From this lofty christological height the book never descends.

Christ and the Father as Alpha and Omega. It is worthwhile considering for a moment the significance of calling both God and Christ "the Alpha and Omega." Richard Bauckham likely is correct in suggesting that it conveys the idea that the person in question "precedes and originates all things, as their Creator, and he will bring all things to their eschatological fulfillment. The titles cannot mean anything else when they are used of Christ in 22:13."[79] Furthermore, it needs to be stressed that when Jesus is called "the First and the Last," this seems to be grounded in Isaiah 44:6; 48:12, where it is a divine self-designation of Yahweh. Not only so, but also it

---

[78]Donald Guthrie, "The Christology of Revelation," in *Jesus of Nazareth, Lord and Christ: Essays on the Historical Jesus and New Testament Christology*, ed. Joel B. Green and Max Turner (Grand Rapids: Eerdmans, 1994), p. 398.

[79]Richard Bauckham, *The Theology of the Book of Revelation* (NTT; Cambridge: Cambridge University Press, 1993), p. 55. In the next few paragraphs I will echo and amplify various of Bauckham's arguments with which I am in agreement.

is used in a context where it aids in stressing the exclusive monotheistic proposition "Besides me there is no God." Here in Revelation, "First and Last" probably does not mean anything very different from what "Alpha and Omega" means.

This interpretation comports with Revelation 3:14, where Christ is called "the origin *[archē]* of God's creation," which likely does not mean that he is the first created being or the firstborn from the dead (for which other terminology is used) but rather is another way of saying about Christ what is said clearly in Revelation 22:13. In other words, Christ, as in the Logos hymn in John 1, is seen as preceding all things and is in part the source or creator of all things, along with the Father. Hearing that he is the Omega or Last, we probably should think of Christ's assumption of the role of the coming final judge on the eschatological Day of Lord (see Rev 19).

Bauckham concludes about this "First and Last"/"Alpha and Omega" language that "as a way of stating unambiguously that Jesus belongs to the fullness of the eternal being of God, this surpasses anything in the [rest of the] New Testament."[80] It therefore is no surprise that in Revelation, perhaps more than in any other New Testament book, Jesus is the object of worship and adoration, which in this same book is said to be inappropriate of mere angelic supernatural beings (see Rev 19:10; 22:8-9). This whole development makes Revelation in some ways the perfect book to conclude the canon, showing the full development of the divine side of the christological question without neglecting the human side. In this respect, Revelation is much like Hebrews in emphasizing the exalted Christ and his heavenly roles in the present.

Because Jesus is included in John of Patmos's definition of God, he is seen as a very appropriate object of worship. In Revelation 5 we are introduced to the image of Christ as the Lamb, which is to become the dominant image in the book thereafter. Notice, for example, how in Revelation 5:8 the Lamb, who has triumphed through his death and resurrection, is the focus of the circle of worship in heaven that includes the worship of the living creatures and the elders, the representatives of all kinds of creatures, both animal and human (see Rev 5:6; 7:17).[81] It is precisely as slain lamb that this Lamb conquers and then judges with righteous wrath (Rev 6:16). The worship of the

---

[80]Ibid., p. 57.

[81]Even as the Lamb, Christ is seen not as weak but rather as powerful and fully capable of overthrowing enemies, not unlike the lamb symbol in *Testament of Joseph*. There is perhaps some indebtedness of John to the author of this work, for in *Testament of Joseph* 19:8-9 we hear of the twofold messiah, who is presented as both lion and lamb.

Lamb is not somehow separate from or distinct from the worship of God, but rather is seen as a part of it in Revelation 5:13. If a doxology is a clear indication of the object of worship, then the one offered to Christ alone in Revelation 1:5-6 surely indicates that he is being approached as deity. This doxology should be compared to two other such doxologies offered to Christ alone at 2 Timothy 4:18 and 2 Peter 3:18, which suggests that the practices described in Revelation of worshiping Christ were not somehow an aberration, but rather were a widespread practice in a variety of Christian communities.[82]

It is perhaps right to note that John of Patmos does not, unlike the case in the Fourth Gospel, choose to use the concept of the Wisdom of God to be able to include Christ in the Godhead. Indebtedness to Wisdom of Solomon does seem to be apparent at one crucial point, however (Rev 19:11-16), where the conquering warrior is called "the Word of God" (Rev 19:13). To this we must compare Wisdom of Solomon 18:16-18, where the Word leaps from heaven carrying a sharp sword.

John stresses that Christ shares the names, the throne, the work, and the worship of God. It is true that for Christians, because Christ functioned as God—as creator, redeemer, present Lord, and coming future judge—he thus was worshiped, but to say this is probably to say too little. John believes that only God can perform what Christ performs, and thus there is at least an implicit assertion of Christ's divine nature in all this material. Consider what it means to say that the slaughtered Lamb is seen on the throne and is worshiped for his overcoming, through death and resurrection, the powers of this world. It surely must include the notion that God was in Christ reconciling the world to himself, but more to the point, the way God rules the world is by and in the slaughtered and exalted Lamb. Christ's suffering and death are seen as the act of an eternal being, thus having eternal efficacy and making evident how God has chosen to overcome evil and rule the world. Only God saves, and he has done this as the Lamb. What is especially remarkable about all this is that, as Larry Hurtado says, the author is not self-consciously engaged in doctrinal development or explication, but rather is trying to urge perseverance in Christian faith and worship despite persecution.[83] That the worship of Christ is so strongly emphasized suggests to Hurtado that the high

---

[82]Does it say anything to us that these three texts perhaps were addressed to Christians in Asia Minor in areas where emperor worship was prevalent?

[83]Larry Hurtado, *Lord Jesus Christ: Devotion to Jesus in Earliest Christianity* (Grand Rapids: Eerdmans, 2003), p. 590.

Christology arises in part out of the worship experience of these Christians, including their visionary experiences.

The one who is called "the ruler of God's creation" in Revelation 3:14 is also in that same chapter called "the one who holds the key of David" (Rev 3:7), and thus he is the Jewish messiah. Just because John thinks that he is more than the Jewish messiah does not mean that he leaves behind this notion as unimportant. In Revelation 5:5 Jesus is seen as "the Lion of the tribe of Judah" and also "the Root of David." The Lamb image also is thoroughly Jewish, and a slaughtered lamb is the ultimate symbol of atonement for sins in a Jewish context. But John has transformed this image to speak not only of a lamb slain, but also of something else that no early Jew who was not a Christian spoke of: a lamb once slain but now glorified and powerful. Here the story of Jesus has transformed this Jewish image into something unexpected, paradoxical, new. It is no surprise that the slain Lamb image arises repeatedly in a document written to Christians who are being persecuted. They too are lambs for the slaughter, but, like Jesus, in the end they will have victory over death and their human tormentors.

Another image transferred from God to Christ is the image of Jesus being the one who has the book of life and who opens the scrolls that disclose God's future plan and will. Only he, it is said in Revelation 5, is worthy enough to open not only the scroll but also all the seals upon it. Here we see the notion of Christ as the implementer of divine justice upon the earth. The concept of redemptive judgment may seem foreign to us, but it is a prevalent concept in the Old Testament, especially in Joshua and Judges. The core idea is that God redeems his oppressed people by judging their enemies, hence "redemptive judgment." Thus, our author is not saying anything novel by predicating both judgment and redemption of his deity; the only novelty is that Christ is said to be assuming these divine roles. He is both the savior of the saved and the judge of the wicked. Notice how the end result of the battle of good and evil will be, and indeed in John's view already is, "the kingdom of the world has become the kingdom of our Lord and of his Christ, and he will reign forever and ever" (Rev 11:15). Here, "Lord" refers to God rather than Christ, and "Christ" is used in its titular and Jewish sense. The author is not guilty of Christomonism, though he clearly includes Christ within his description of God alongside the Father. This way of putting things in Revelation 11:15 suggests that the author was in touch with the earliest Jewish Christian ways of confessing their monotheism, such as we have already seen in 1 Corinthians 8:6.[84]

Thus, the Lamb will triumph and one day invite his own to a wedding feast (Rev 19:9). He also will come as the pale rider, the grim reaper or executioner spoken of in Revelation 19. The Lamb is also the Lion. As Christ, he will reign for a thousand years with his martyrs (Rev 20:4-6). This may refer to his present reign in heaven with the martyrs already there, but in view of the discussion of resurrection in Revelation 20, it probably refers to a future reign on earth at the close of the age. Christ is the one who began and will bring to a close God's plan for humanity.

We are told in Revelation 21 that Christ and the Lord God (here the Father) will be the temple and glory of God's people, and they will dwell together forever, beyond disease, decay, death, sin, suffering, sorrow, tears, and torment. For now, our author sees Christ as one who stands at the door of human hearts and knocks, but one day he will burst on the human scene as the ravaging Lion destroying or at least judging the wicked and thereby rescuing the righteous. Thus, believers are urged at the close of the book to plead for him to come—the one who is the Daystar dawning on history's horizon. Both horizontal and vertical eschatology fuse in the final vision of things such that heaven and earth in effect merge. The new Jerusalem descends from above, making a new earth to go along with a new heaven. The one who lies at the center of this vision, indeed the one who turns this vision into reality, is, according to John, none other than Jesus, who is at once Lamb, Lion, and Lord. We should have expected this christocentric and theocentric conclusion in view of the fact that we were told at the outset of the book that this is "the revelation of (and about) Jesus Christ."

It is useful to ask at this point in what way or ways John of Patmos seems indebted to the Christology that we find in the other Johannine documents. In some ways this is an easy question to answer. We may point to texts such as Revelation 7:17, where we see Christ as shepherd leading his people to springs of living water. This parallels what we find in John 10:1-30 (cf. Jn 21:15-17), where Jesus states that he is the good shepherd. On the other hand, when we try to examine the way the author uses the term *logos* in the form "the Word of God" in Revelation 19:13 compared to what we find in John 1, the context is very different. Here the Word, as in Wisdom of Solomon, is involved in judgment, but in John 1 the image is used to speak of a role in creation and redemption. Or again we may explore the similarities between

---

[84]On this text, see pp. 115-16 above.

the Lamb in John 1:29, 32 and in Revelation, but it is immediately notable that a different Greek term for *lamb* is used in each (*amnos* in the Gospel, *arnion* in Revelation). In the Gospel the Lamb is seen as a purely redemptive one who takes away sin, whereas in Revelation the Lamb's role involves both redemption and judgment. In John 10:7 Jesus is said to be the gate, while in Revelation 3:20 he stands outside it and knocks. In the Fourth Gospel "Son of Man" is an important title with a cluster of key ideas surrounding it; in Revelation it is simply part of an allusion to the analogy found in Daniel 7.

The overall impression left is that John of Patmos knows Johannine Christology, but he is not interested in slavishly imitating it or simply passing it along. Rather, he deliberately varies or modifies what he knows of Johannine Christology to suit the message he wants to convey. There is, on the whole, a much more varied scope of images and ideas that come into play in Revelation than in the other Johannine documents, but then the other documents are not apocalyptic literature and do not use pictographic language. What all parts of the Johannine corpus do share in common is a strong emphasis on the importance of Jesus' death and an equally strong stress on both the true humanity and the divinity of Christ. It is repeatedly the Christ of glory, the exalted one, who appears in these documents, even in the account of the ministry in the Fourth Gospel. These documents have no problem with using the various names and titles of God for Jesus Christ, nor do they have any problem with offering worship to Christ as God. All of them seem prepared to redefine Jewish monotheism to accommodate what they wish to say about Christ. Thus, we may say that certainly some of the highest Christology to be found in the New Testament is in Revelation, but this is not surprising if this document comes from the same circles that produced the Gospel of John.[85]

It is no accident that at the inception of this remarkable book John says that when he was in a pneumatic state, he first heard something and then saw something (Rev 1:10-11). Although this book is mostly a visionary work, it has its aural and oracular dimensions, and the visionary material is set within the context of the interpreting oracles. But even more telling is that these visions are set within a larger story about redemption and judgment, and more specifically how that story will be brought to a climax. The teleological and eschatological presentation of the visions is always pointing us forward to the climax. It is clear enough that John thinks of story as the overarching

---

[85]For the debate about how Christian and christological the book of Revelation is, see Eduard Lohse, "Wie christlich ist die Offenbarung des Johannes?" *NTS* 34 (1988): 321-38.

paradigm into which he can slot both epistolary elements and apocalyptic visions. One could almost read Revelation as a sequel to Luke-Acts, in a different vein and genre of course, but nonetheless continuing and completing the story of salvation history.

In Revelation 1:17-20 the revealer is the exalted Christ, who identifies himself as one who was once dead but is now alive. In short, he speaks appropriately according to the time in which John lives. There is nothing here to suggest that sayings of the risen Lord that would be appropriate to place on the lips of the historical Jesus were conveyed in this way. Indeed, a saying such as Revelation 1:17b-20 would not have been appropriate if found on Jesus' lips before he died. The same may be said about the oracle in Revelation 16:15, "Behold, I am coming like a thief . . ." (cf. Rev 22:7, 12-14), an oracle that is appropriate on the lips of the exalted Christ but different from those found on the lips of the historical Jesus, who speaks in the third person of a future coming of the Son of Man. We could also point to other examples of oracular speech in Revelation 13:9-10; 14:13; 18:21-24 (words of an angel); 19:9; 21:3-4, 5-8; 22:18-20, and certainly we should note how there is a concentration of such oracles at the beginning and end of the book, making clear the prophetic character of the work.

To such oracles we could add the clearly demarcated prophetic character of the oracles to the seven churches in Revelation 2–3, all of which have a shared prophetic pattern involving (1) introductory commissioning word, (2) middle portion, and (3) double conclusion involving a call for vigilance and a saying about conquering. In each case, John is commanded to write to each of these churches, which due to his exile is "a functional equivalent to the sending of prophetic messengers in the Old Testament."[86]

Notice that in each case there is a citation formula, "thus says" *(tade legei)*, after which the exalted Christ speaks. Of course, the content of each oracle after the citation formula in the central or middle "I know" part varies according to the situation of each church. The exhortative nature of the central section of these prophecies is clear, and the often strongly negative tone reminds us that Christian prophets and seers such as John saw themselves having a role similar to Old Testament prophets as "guardians and preservers of Christian behavior, beliefs, and customs."[87] They too could be prosecu-

---

[86]David E. Aune, *Prophecy in Early Christianity and the Ancient Meditarranean World* (Grand Rapids: Eerdmans, 1983), p. 275.
[87]Ibid., p. 277.

tors of the covenant lawsuit, only in this case it is the new covenant lawsuit. We may conjecture that there must have been a dearth of leadership in these churches that in turn necessitated prophetic intervention by John. Prophets and seers could be seen as crisis intervention specialists, especially when there was a power or leadership vacuum. As guardian of the true belief, behavior, and praxis, John feels strongly enough about the inspired nature of his revelation to insist at the end of the work that it should not be subtracted from or supplemented, much less ignored or distorted.

Theology in Revelation 11. It is time to consider a specific sample of visionary material from Revelation in order to get a sense of its character. Scrutiny will be given to two consecutive sections: Revelation 11, which presents the tale of the two witnesses, and Revelation 12, the story of the woman and the dragon. It is possible, though debated, to see Revelation 11 as a continuation of Revelation 10. In any case, there is no debate about the indebtedness of Revelation 11 to Ezekiel 40–48.

In the vision John is given a staff and told to rise and measure the temple of God and its surroundings. There have been at least four basic suggestions as to what this measuring means: (1) It is the preliminary to rebuilding and restoring the temple. This certainly is true in the case of Ezekiel 40–48, and it is understandable how a Jewish Christian prophet after A.D. 70 who is in exile might see himself as being in the same position as Ezekiel. How, then, would this square with the fact that John seems to see the church as the new temple of God such that any restoration of the old temple would be superfluous? (2) The temple is being sized up for destruction. This makes especially good sense if this book was written in the 60s rather than, as is usually thought, the 90s and if the author was familiar with the Jesus tradition on this subject (see Mk 13). On the whole, the arguments for a date in the 60s are unconvincing. (3) The measurements are taken to indicate the parts to be protected from physical harm. This does not seem to fit with the theme found earlier in Revelation of partial judgments even on God's people. (4) Measuring refers to protection from spiritual rather than physical harm.

One clue to unraveling this mystery is found at Revelation 11:14, where one discovers that what is recounted as happening to the temple and to its worshipers (the latter being a point against this being a retrospective remark about A.D. 70) is said to be the second woe, not the last woe. Notice that this event is clearly identified as happening in Jerusalem, for there is mention of the place where the Lord was crucified.

We must now broach the subject of the two witnesses in Revelation 11:3. Whoever they are supposed to represent, it is clear enough that they are presented here as being at least like Moses and Elijah, the two witnesses who stood with Jesus on the Mount of Transfiguration according to the Synoptic tradition (Mk 9:2-10 par). Notice that these witnesses bring the fire-breathing word of God to earth, including plagues and the like, but also they are taken back up into heaven. If this is a prophecy of Jerusalem's fall, why has it been placed in this locale in Revelation and identified as the second woe? If this is a prophecy about the final preservation of the Jewish people, why are the witnesses identified with the figure used in the letters to identify the church? A more probable explanation is that this is about the universal church and its task of witnessing, or more specifically about the churches at Smyrna and Philadelphia, which were undergoing persecution and perhaps enduring instances of martyrdom as John wrote. This would explain why the number *two* is used of the witnesses here rather than the earlier *seven* of all the churches that John is addressing.

Some have seen here an allusion to Deuteronomy 19:15, where it is said that the verification of the truth of anything requires the validating testimony of two witnesses. However, if John believed this still to be true, it would seem to imply that he needed a second witness to validate his own testimony—something that this prophet apparently sees no need for. His words appear to have independent authority for the seven churches, and he expects them to go unchallenged. It surely is easier to see here a reference to two of John's churches undergoing persecution. This fits with the reference in Revelation 11:4 to lampstands (cf. Rev 2–3). If John could cast his own role in the light of the prophet Ezekiel, there is no reason why he could not cast the role of two of his churches in the light of the experiences of Elijah and Moses.[88] The implication is that not only John's life, but also that of his churches, bears prophetic witness to God's revelation or truth. On this view, the idea of outward harm and even physical death is meant to suggest that even such extreme persecution cannot harm such witnesses spiritually.

The two witnesses are called "olive trees" (Rev. 11:4), for they carry within them the fuel needed to light their candlesticks. The reference to Daniel's three and a half years suggests that the church will go through such persecution, not be raptured out of it. One must also see the reference to

---

[88]See David E. Aune, *Revelation 1–5* (WBC 52; Dallas: Word, 1997), p. 600.

Sodom and Egypt as a statement about the spiritual status of Jerusalem, a city occupied and trampled underfoot by Gentiles in the last decade of the first century. In other words, it is a place of oppression, slavery, and immorality. Burial for the bodies of the witnesses is disallowed, an act seen in the ancient Near East as one of the worst indignities or crimes that could be perpetrated (cf. *Pss. Sol.* 2:27).

Again, Ezekiel is drawn upon in Revelation 11:11 to speak of the resurrection of the two witnesses, possibly alluding to the resurrection of the martyrs that will be referred to in Revelation 20:2. According to Revelation 11:13, once the witnesses were vindicated by being taken to heaven, judgment fell upon a tenth part of the unholy city during a supernaturally induced upheaval, and seven thousand people are killed. Perhaps not coincidentally, this would have been about a tenth of the nonfestival season population of Jerusalem. The upshot of this is that John is suggesting that Jews, symbolized by Jerusalem, are the persecuting agents troubling the churches in this case. Here we have a coded message of great relevance to the present and future situation of at least two of John's churches, offering them future hope of vindication despite present difficulties.

Theology in Revelation 12. Of a similar sort and with a similar point is the much controverted revelation about the woman and the dragon in Revelation 12. Here is a classic case where the author has drawn on various sources, including pagan myths, to make a Christian point. One gets the feeling in apocalyptic, especially when the audience is largely Gentile, that any and all sources are fair game for raw material as long as they can be Christianized. Adela Yarbro Collins has given a book-length treatment of this material, demonstrating that the story line in this chapter is based in part on the ancient combat myth, probably in its Babylonian form.[89] The myth in its basic form involves a dragon threatening the reigning gods or the supreme god. Sometimes in these myths the supreme god is even killed, which results in the dragon reigning in chaos for a time. Finally, the dragon is defeated by the god who had ruled before or one of his allies.

Perhaps the closest form of the myth to the text of Revelation is the Greek version that involves the birth of the god Apollo from the goddess Leto. One form of this tale speaks of the great dragon Python who pursued Leto because he learned that she would bear a child who would kill him. Leto was carried

---

[89]Adela Yarbro Collins, *The Combat Myth in the Book of Revelation* (HDR 9; Missoula, Mont.: Scholars Press, 1976).

off to Poseidon, the god of the sea, who placed her on a remote island and then sank the island beneath the sea for good measure. After a vain search, Python went away to Parnassus, and Leto's island was brought back up to the surface of the sea. When the infant was born, he immediately gained full strength, and thus within four days Apollo went and slew Python at Mount Parnassus.

An even more primitive version of this story, this one from Babylonia, speaks of war between Tiamat, the seven-headed sea monster, and the gods of heaven. Tiamat's flaunting of these gods was ended by Marduk, a young god of light, who hewed the sea monster in pieces. In the war with Tiamat a third of the stars were thrown from the sky. Interestingly, Marduk's mother is portrayed in similar fashion to the way the woman is portrayed in Revelation 12. We may also point to the Egyptian story about Osiris, whose wife, Isis, gives birth to the sun god, Horus. Isis is portrayed with the sun on her head. The dragon Typhon is portrayed as red in color (but sometimes is represented as a crocodile or a serpent). In this Egyptian myth the dragon slays Osiris and pursues Isis, who is about to give birth. In a miraculous manner she does give birth and escapes to an island in a papyrus boat. The son, Horus, eventually overcomes the dragon, which is destroyed through fire (cf. Rev 20:1-3, 7-10).

Clearly, the parallels between these various myths and the visionary materials found in Revelation 12 are too striking to be accidental and, in most forms, too early to have been derived from Revelation. Rather, John has freely drawn on elements of these myths, adding certain components to conform the tale to the Christian story about the Savior. It is probable that John's audience was familiar with one form, if not more, of this myth and so would recognize what the seer was doing. The implication in part would be that in Christ all the primal myths and the truths that they enshrine come true. He proves to be the archetype of which all these others are mere types or fictional copies.

Yet, there is a further and more ominous undercurrent here, for various emperors saw these myths as being about themselves (the emperor being the incarnation of divine Apollo, for example). It is probable that the woman in Revelation 12 is portrayed as the Queen of Heaven. On Roman coins the emperor and his wife were portrayed as the sun and the moon. Roma, the patron goddess, was represented as the queen of the gods and mother of the savior, the emperor. Here, then, in Revelation 12 we find a counterclaim. Jesus, the male child, is the real conqueror, not the emperor, and the woman from whom he comes, either the people of God or Mary, is the real Queen of Heaven, the real mother of the Savior, instead of Roma. This is an antiestablishment story borrowing from classical myths but also grounded in the story of Jesus and in the Hebrew Scriptures (e.g., in Dan 7).

One of the keys to understanding this and other texts in Revelation is the notion of the intertwined nature of things heavenly and earthly. Thus, I must disagree with G. B. Caird that John is simply describing earthly realities and struggles using mythical or heavenly symbols.[90] Instead, John believed that he was describing supernatural as well as earthly realities, though freely describing these things using metaphorical and mythical language. It is not that John is describing a sort of heavenly parallel universe to earth so that war in heaven mirrors war on earth. Rather, in his view, there is but one struggle, both heavenly and earthly, both supernatural and natural, both divine and human, and these forces interact with each other.

Revelation 12 begins by reporting that the seer saw a great portent or sign in the heavens, the normal place where such portents were expected to appear (see, e.g., Mt 2:1-2). We hear of a woman clothed with the sun, with the moon under her feet, and wearing a crown with twelve stars. Some have suggested that this crown might represent the constellations or, more to the point, the twelve signs of the zodiac. If so, the point would seem to be that in this woman lies the whole destiny or fate of the race, drawing on the notion that stars controlled one's future. Although possibly there is a reference to Mary here, more probably there is not, for two reasons. First, Revelation 12:17 mentions the rest of the woman's offspring. This is unlikely to be a reference to Jesus' actual brothers and sisters. It is far more likely to refer to Christ's brothers and sisters in the faith who are being addressed in this book, perhaps especially those facing or even enduring persecution. Second, the echoes of Isaiah 66:6-9 here are loud and clear, which means echoes of the mother Zion tradition. Notice how in Galatians 4:26 Paul refers to the new heavenly Jerusalem as "our mother." What is likely in view here is the community of God's people portrayed as a woman (cf. Rev 21:9-14). There is an implied continuity between the Old Testament and New Testament people of God, at least in the sense that Jesus came forth from the Jewish people of God, and his brothers and sisters did likewise.

---

[90]G. B. Caird, *A Commentary on the Revelation of St. John the Divine* (repr., Peabody, Mass.: Hendrickson, 1987), pp. 147-50.

The woman is depicted as being in anguish to give birth. The red or fiery (or bloody) dragon is said to be a second portent in the sky or heavens. That he has ten horns suggests one of awesome strength, and clearly the imagery of Daniel 7–8 is drawn on here, though in Daniel the reference is to beastly empires and their rulers. That the dragon has seven crowns may suggest that he has usurped all power, but notice that in Greek his crowns are called *diadēmata*, whereas mother Zion's crown is called a *stephanos* (the laurel wreath crown of those who are victors). The twelve stars in the woman's crown are likely to refer to the twelve tribes of Israel and thus are a symbol that one is dealing with a community, the whole people of God.

It is clear that this apocalyptic vision involves more than just predictive prophecy, for it describes an event that had already transpired: the birth of the male child or savior. Revelation 12:4b depicts the dragon as almost hovering in front of the woman, who is about to give birth, so that it can devour the child as soon as it is born. Drawing on Psalm 2, the author depicts the male child as destined to be a shepherd who would rule the nations with an iron hand or, as the text says, an iron rod (Rev 12:5). The image conveys his absolute power over the nations and perhaps also his power to judge.

The text goes on to say that at the crucial moment the child was seized by God and carried off to God and his throne. John has skipped from the Savior's birth to his death, ascension, and exaltation. The point for Christians under pressure or persecution is that what the powers of darkness may have seen as the end of Jesus and as intended for evil, God used for good, indeed used to give the male child more power over the forces of darkness. What might have been thought to diminish the power of the male child actually further empowered him. By being taken away from earth by God, he was enthroned in heaven.

In Revelation 12:6 the woman flees into the desert, and since this woman represents the people of God, we are meant to hear echoes of the exodus here (note how exodus imagery crops up again in Rev 12:13-15). There in the desert this woman is nurtured, just as the Israelites were by God during their period of wandering in the wilderness. It is not said here that the church is raptured into heaven; rather, it is protected while on earth from the wrath of the dragon. The woman is put in a place prepared by God and made to stay there a definite period of time, Daniel's three and a half years (1,260 days). In view of Revelation 13:5 and Revelation 11:1-13, what probably is in view here is the great tribulation, during which Satan is viewed as trying to crush the church out of existence.

At Revelation 12:7 the scene shifts to war in heaven. We might expect this war to be waged by Christ against the dragon, but instead Michael, the archangel, leads the fighting for the saints. Here again this author is adopting and adapting traditional material. In *Testament of Daniel* 6:2 Michael is seen as a mediator between God and humankind. In the canonical book of Daniel, Michael is seen as the guardian angel of Israel, fighting against the angelic leaders of the Gentile nations (Dan 10:13-15; 12:1). Here in Revelation 12 his task is to take on the adversary of the people of God. In general, Michael prevails, and the devil and his minions are cast down to earth. There is in fact a threefold fall of Satan in Revelation: from heaven to earth (Rev 12:9), from earth to the abyss (Rev 20:2), and from the abyss to the lake of fire (Rev 20:10).

Satan is seen not just as a prosecuting attorney or the accuser of the people of God; he has lost his role in the heavenly court, and now, in Revelation 12:9, he is seen as the deceiver of the whole *oikoumenē*, a term used to identify the civilized or human world. At Revelation 12:10 a loud voice is heard in heaven proclaiming that salvation, kingship and power come when Satan is cast down to earth. The "our brothers" in that verse may well be those who have already been martyred (cf. Rev 6:9-11). Because of the atoning death of the Lamb and the word of his testimony, the accuser is no longer allowed to accuse. The author seems to suggest that the casting down of Satan took place at the death of Christ or immediately thereafter, when the benefits of his death began to accrue for God's people. Revelation 12:12 makes clear that as a result of Christ's death, Satan's days are numbered, and he knows it. Some have seen John 12:27-33 as a useful commentary on this text or the saying of Jesus in Luke 10:18 about seeing Satan fall like lightning from the sky as a possible source of some of this imagery.

Notice, however, that Satan is not prevented from pursuing the woman, but she is aided in her flight by being given the wings of eagles (cf. Ex 19:4). Revelation 12:15 says that Satan produces a river to flush the woman out of the wilderness or desert, another possible allusion to the exodus/Sinai events. Since in the primal myth the sea monster is the evil one, it is not surprising that here water is his modus operandi for trying to do in the woman. Yet, unable to destroy the church collectively, Satan contents himself with attacking individual Christians, the ones keeping God's commandments and bearing the testimony of Christ. The section concludes with the sea monster or dragon standing next to his native element, the sea (often a symbol of chaos and the locus of evil things and creatures in the Hebrew tradition).

These two chapters offer a rich intertextual feast, with echoes of both biblical and nonbiblical texts, both Jewish and Gentile traditions. The author hears oracles and songs and sees visions, but he chooses to relate these visions in language that his Hellenized readers can understand and apply to themselves. The language is definitely referential, though it is also symbolic and metaphorical and even mythic in character. It cannot be taken literally, but it must be taken seriously, for the author believes that he is depicting in apocalyptic language some truths and realities that his audience needs to know about. This is not merely heavenly language with an earthly meaning; rather, it is apocalyptic language about the interplay of heaven and earth, time and eternity, history and the supernatural. If we turn to Revelation 19–22, we see that the author can indeed offer predictions about the future in apocalyptic form as well as descriptions of the past and present in that same visionary form. Both the eschatological as well as the otherworldly dimensions and the horizontal as well as the vertical dimensions of this author's vision of the final solution are prominent throughout.

So, then, should we see the inscribing of such visions as we find in Revelation 12 into a literary work that we call "Revelation" as a prophetic activity in and of itself? Surely, it need not be, because one could use a scribe to accomplish that aim. It is unlikely that we should see Revelation as a purely literary exercise unlike various of the pseudonymous apocalypses, and the presence of actual prophecy (not merely of the ex eventu variety) raises again the question of this work's actual genre. I suggest that we recognize this as a work of apocalyptic prophecy by a known and named author, John.

It is best to stick with the phrase "apocalyptic prophecy" when it comes to the book of Revelation. It stands firmly in the prophetic tradition in its later Jewish and early Christian apocalyptic forms, and it has rightly stood the test of time, being one of the great masterpieces of early Christian literature. It is promulgated not on the basis of a supposed connection with dead Jewish saints, but rather on the basis of a connection with the living Lamb, Lion, Lord. H. B. Swete put things well when he observed,

> The Apocalypse of John is in many ways a new departure. (1) The Jewish
> apocalypses are without exception pseudepigraphic; the Christian apocalypse

bears the author's name. This abandonment of a long-established tradition is significant; by it John claims for himself the position of a prophet who, conscious that he draws his inspiration from Christ or His angel and not at second hand, has no need to seek shelter under the name of a Biblical saint. (2) How hard it is to determine the date and provenance of Jewish apocalypses is clear from the wide differences which divide the best scholars on these points. . . . The Apocalypse of John, on the contrary, makes no secret of its origin and destination; it is the work of a Christian undergoing exile in one of the islands of the Aegean; and it is addressed to the Christian congregations in seven of the chief cities of the adjacent continent. . . . Whatever view may be taken of his indebtedness to Jewish sources, there can be no doubt that he has produced a book which, taken as a whole, is profoundly Christian, and widely removed from the field in which Jewish apocalyptic occupied itself. The narrow sphere of Jewish national hopes has been exchanged for the life and aims of a society whose field is the world and whose goal is the conquest of the human race. The Jewish Messiah, an uncertain and unrealized idea, has given place to the historical, personal Christ, and the Christ of the Christian apocalypse is already victorious, ascended, and glorified.[91]

A final word is in order about the nature of the book of Revelation. John Collins, in his landmark study on the apocalyptic imagination, says this: "The language of the apocalypses is not descriptive, referential, newspaper language but the expressive language of poetry, which uses symbols and imagery to articulate a sense or feeling about the world. Their abiding value does not lie in the pseudo-information they provide about cosmology or future history, but in their affirmation of a transcendent world."[92] Collins is right in some of what he affirms but is wrong in much of what he denies, at least insofar as it applies to the book of Revelation. He is wrong in the first place because the book of Revelation is indeed a work of prophecy, apocalyptic prophecy to be sure, but nonetheless prophecy, and not the pseudo-prophecy of the ex eventu sort that one finds in pseudonymous apocalypses. As prophecy, this material in Revelation is meant to be referential whether or not we can ferret out what the references are or agree with them. To take but one example, Babylon is quite clearly Rome in the book of Revelation. What one can say, however, is that this highly imagaic and poetic language uses

[91]H. B. Swete, *The Apocalypse of St. John: The Greek Text with Introduction, Notes, and Indices* (New York: Macmillan, 1906), pp. xxviii-xxix.

[92]John J. Collins, *The Apocalyptic Imagination: An Introduction to the Jewish Matrix of Christianity* (New York: Crossroad, 1984), p 214.

universal metaphors and symbols and so is capable of being used to interpret a variety of historical persons and events.

Nor is it the case that Revelation is purely about the transcendent. It is about providing a transcendent perspective on the interface between the transcendent realm and the historical realm, showing the underlying and overarching supernatural forces at work in human history, guiding and goading human beings and human institutions. There is indeed in this work a passionate concern about how history will ultimately turn out, and the earliest recorded reflections by second- and third-century Christian commentators certainly took the book as referential and historically focused in nature. For example, it was assumed that Revelation 20 was indeed speaking about a millennial kingdom of Christ coming upon the earth at or near the end of human history (see, e.g., the commentary of Victorinus of Pettau).

Thus, whatever our level of discomfort or comfort with this fact, due attention must be given to the referential nature of John's symbols. He seems to have fervently believed that justice and redemption would neither be finally accomplished nor be seen to be accomplished unless such matters were finalized in space and time, when "the kingdom of this world has become the kingdom of our Lord and of his Christ" (Rev 11:15). None of us is in the position to say that John was wrong about the climax of human history, for thus far we have not arrived at this climax in some two thousand years of church history. The language of imminence in this work is a clarion call to be prepared for that end, whenever it may come. The church is called to be the church expectant, the church prepared for "what will yet come." Like the saints under the altar in Revelation 6:9-11, it is more appropriate for the church to cry out, "How long, O Lord?" than to simply wish to join those saints in their present location. By this I mean that the book of Revelation does not encourage us to have a purely otherworldly view of eternal life, does not encourage us to focus on heaven rather than history as the final goal or terminus of Christian life, does not encourage us to abandon the eschatology of the earliest Christians such as Paul. The saints in heaven are impatient for the end of history and final vindication; they are not basking in everlasting peace, believing that they have reached the end.

Thus, the book of Revelation has much to tell us about "what was, and is, and is to come." It is our job to have ears capable of hearing what John says on all of these matters. If we do so, we will learn that God's yes to life is louder than evil and death's no to it, that justice and redemption one day will prevail on earth, and that this is indeed good news coming in the form of a "revelation from Jesus Christ," which is to say, coming from one who both experienced death and triumphed over it. It is Christ who knows what is above and beyond our present mundane historical concerns and situation. He alone is worthy and able to reveal such profound truths.

John's mixed-genre approach as a picture of the whole New Testament. The book of Revelation is a remarkable hybrid of ad hoc letters, apocalyptic visions, and narrative storytelling, with the subject being Christ's redemptive judgment of the world. Its synthetic nature and power show that a combination of theological materials could take place in a mixed-genre work and with good result. This gives us good hope about our abilities to synthesize New Testament theological discussion into a reasonable whole. But a caution is in order: the visions arise out of or are a form of genuine Christian experience, and the theologizing is done out of this experience and into specific situations of the seven churches in need of comfort and confrontation, compassion and counseling, information and transformation. John, standing at the end of the New Testament period, would not have expected that a proper New Testament theology could be written unless it was the fruit of such genuine Christian experience and worship. Doxology is the presupposition for theology in this case. John, in a sense, sums up much of what has come before him, both in the Old Testament and in the Jesus tradition, but he enfolds it all into a larger fresh whole as a revelation of Jesus Christ, and so there are some fresh and new insights into the one he calls "Alpha and Omega," going beyond but not against what has come before.

The earlier parts of the New Testament comprised narratives, letters or discourses, and some prophecies, and John has woven them all into one climactic piece that serves both literarily and theologically as an appropriate climax to the New Testament era and its canon-to-be. John does not see the myriads of christological images that he uses as dueling or contesting images but rather as appropriate ways of describing the man who neither fits one formula nor can be painted in one single icon, nor whose significance can be exhausted by the singing of one oratorio. Thus, in a sense Revelation, by its very scope and complexity, becomes an invitation to go deeper, explore theology further, exalt Christ higher and in even bolder images, all the while the church expectant eagerly awaits his return.

It is easy enough to see why later church fathers saw the career trajectory of the V-pattern as a clue as to where to hang the different christological hats that Jesus would be asked to wear. There would be some titles more appropriate to his preexistence ("Logos," "only begotten Son," "Wisdom"), some more appropriate to refer to his earthly ministry ("Root of Jesse," "Son of Man," "Messiah," and indeed the very name "Jesus"), some more appropriate to use of his risen status ("risen Lord," "Savior," "firstborn from the dead"), some more appropriate to his exalted status and roles ("heavenly high priest," "Alpha and Omega"), and some more appropriate to his return, final judgment and rule in the kingdom (interestingly enough, "Son of Man" comes up here again). The beginning of the integration of the images can be seen in places such as Revelation. It was left up to the church fathers to continue to pursue the hints and leads left to them in the New Testament texts.

5

THE NEW TESTAMENT CONSENSUS ON GOD THE FATHER

The Bible's witness to God's existence is so fundamental that every state-
ment made about God necessarily assumes and affirms divine reality. . . .
[However, there are] crucial differences between the Old and New Tes-
tament's language about God, causing us immediately to confront the
matter of New Testament theology's distinct understanding of God.

JAMES K. MEAD[1]

Although the New Testament writers share, to a remarkable degree, a common understanding and focus on Jesus, they are not christomonistic, focusing on Christ alone in their theologizing. Indeed, they also have quite a lot to say about the one whom Jesus called "Abba." And when they thought about God in those terms, they were thinking through their Christology to their understanding of God.

The Father was in the first instance the Father of Jesus, and in the second instance the Father of Jesus' followers. This surely must have struck many early Jews as odd, if not heretical. In the view of non-Christian Jews, God was simply the Father and God of Jews. God's special relationship was with Jews, and anyone else who wanted in on that relationship had to become a Jew. There was no notion that one had to "come to the Father through Jesus the Son" in early Jewish thought, even if it took the more generic form of coming to the Father through the Jewish messiah. This was something distinctive about early Christian thought. And, as I have demonstrated at length

---

[1]James K. Mead, *Biblical Theology: Issues, Methods, and Themes* (Louisville: Westminster John Knox, 2007), p. 172.

elsewhere, "Father" language was seldom used in early Judaism for God and nowhere in its prayer language.[2] The change in the prayer language came from Jesus himself, whom his followers patterned themselves after.

In the discussion that follows I attempt to examine the most salient and crucial aspects of the God-talk of the New Testament writers, not only the aspects that show how their Christology and eschatological mindsets have modified the earlier vision of the God of Israel, but also some of those aspects that are reaffirmed and in some cases amplified from what we find in the Old Testament.

GOD'S WILL AND THE SALVATION-HISTORICAL PLAN

There are many dimensions to the discussion of God the Father (whether or not in a particular text he is called "Father") in the New Testament, and perhaps it will be helpful to speak broadly first of how God the Father was viewed. What roles and functions was he believed to have played in the story of creation and redemption? One place to start this discussion is with the writer who thinks historically about all such subjects, Luke.

One of the most interesting and telling features of Luke's theological understanding is the historical scope that he brings to the discussion. Luke informs us that God has had a plan since before the beginning of time that is revealed in Scripture and is fulfilled, and is being fulfilled, by Christ and the Spirit. What is interesting is not merely the ways in which the portrayal of Peter in Acts mirrors various of the themes in 1 Peter, or how the one Christian speech of Paul in Acts 20 to the Ephesian elders sounds very much like the Paul who wrote various letters to Christians, but how both Peter and Paul are presented as exponents of the larger schema that Luke outlines of salvation history, a schema found in miniature in the christological hymn fragments in Philippians 2 and Colossians 1 and alluded to, as we have seen, in 1 Peter 2.

G. B. Caird argues, "Luke held a well-rounded theology, which, since he attributed it to Peter and to Paul, *he must have believed to be the common theology of the early Church.*"[3] Caird summarizes that Lukan/common theology as follows:

---

[2]See Ben Witherington III, *The Individual Witnesses*, vol. 1 of *The Indelible Image: The Theological and Ethical Thought World of the New Testament* (Downers Grove, Ill.: IVP Academic, 2009), pp. 96-100; Ben Witherington III and Laura M. Ice, *The Shadow of the Almighty: Father, Son, and Spirit in Biblical Perspective* (Grand Rapids: Eerdmans, 2002), pp. 1-50.

[3]G. B. Caird, *New Testament Theology*, compl. and ed. L. D. Hurst (Oxford: Oxford University Press, 1994), p. 30 (italics mine).

1. The gospel story and its sequel (Acts) were events in which God was personally present and active.

2. The human characters in the story were actors in a drama with a pre-ordained plot of such power and flexibility that not only their obedience but their disobedience contributed to its fulfillment.

3. This plot was God's plan of salvation for Israel and through Israel for the world.

4. The plan of salvation was present in outline or in explicit promise in every part of the Old Testament.

5. This way of reading the Old Testament originated with Jesus who had understood God's plan from the beginning and had conducted his ministry in conformity with it.

6. In light of the events in which God's plan had been put into operation the risen Jesus explained the scriptural necessity which they had previously failed to understand.

7. Jesus' interpretation of the Old Testament had much in it that was offensive to his opponents and much that was puzzling to his friends, but it rested on theological convictions already held by pious Jews before his coming.[4]

This is an interesting list indeed, but it has some notable lacunae. It certainly conveys the historical sweep of Luke's storytelling about salvation, but it does not convey either the centrality or cruciality of Christ to this story line, nor does it convey the teleological and eschatological character of the story line, involving the frequent mention of the second coming throughout the New Testament corpus, including in Luke-Acts. What this outline does aptly convey is the sense of the scope of the story about salvation that Luke is telling, a sense of scope shared with other New Testament writers such as Paul and Peter, though they at most only summarize the plot line or allude to it in passing, assuming that the audience basically knows the gospel story, even in its wider cosmic scope.

It is not quite accurate, however, to call Luke a chronicler of universal history. He tells little or no story of creation and fall. He presupposes such a history, to be sure, but he is a theologian of salvation history, which is a particular story, and he provides synchronisms with the macrostory of the

---

[4]Ibid.

empire and its local governance of the Holy Land at places such Luke 3:1-2. It is true, however, as Hans Frei suggests, that "far from seeking, like Homer, merely to make us forget our own reality for a few hours [by telling an enthralling tale], it seeks to overcome our reality: we are to fit our own life into its world, feel ourselves to be elements in its structure of universal history"[5] The "it" to which Frei refers is the biblical story, but his point about seeking to overcome existing paradigms and worldviews certainly could be applied to Luke. He sees Christians as those who have turned the world upside down, especially when it comes to what amounts to salvation, how one obtains it, and what its implications are.

One good point of comparison, noted by Caird, is that when the Paul of Acts speaks about revealing the whole counsel of the Father God about the aforementioned sorts of salvation issues (see Acts 20:27), one certainly could argue that we find this same kind of exposition in Ephesians 1–3. God's hidden salvation plan is revealed in Christ, a plan to unite Jews and Gentiles into one people. Indeed, "all things" in the universe are to be brought into a unity in Christ, according to the breathtaking rhetoric of Ephesians 1. It is not just that the secret plan of God has been revealed in Christ; it has been put into operation in Christ and is still being executed by Christ.

As Caird points out, Paul trots out the full glossary of apocalyptic terms to refer to this plan or story line that God is pursuing. It is God's secret plan/design *(mystērion)*, will *(thelēma)*, purpose *(prothesis)*, wisdom *(sophia)*, even God's good pleasure *(eudokia)*.[6] And that good pleasure is to implement his love for the world in such a fashion that his saving reign or dominion comes throughout the earth.

What is perhaps most interesting about the way Luke unveils this plan or purpose of God is that it is something that involves God even using or overcoming the ignorance and hostility of Jesus' opponents to accomplish his divine ends. We see this in, for instance, the theme of ignorance in regard to why Jews crucified their own messiah (see, e.g., Acts 3:17; 13:27). God, in Luke's vision, is capable of working all things together for good, even using the wrath of ignorant and wicked persons to glorify his name. This is little different from what Paul suggests in Romans 8:28-39, and we hear echoes of the same in 1 Peter 1.

---

[5]Hans Frei, *The Eclipse of Biblical Narrative: A Study in Eighteenth and Nineteenth Century Hermeneutics* (New Haven: Yale University Press, 1974), p. 3.
[6]Caird, *New Testament Theology*, p. 41.

Yet this theme of the plan/will/purpose of God is a complex one, and it is clear enough that often the language, while certainly conveying the idea that God is sovereign and purposeful in the way he relates to human beings and human history, especially in regard to the way he planned for Christ to do and be certain things when he came to earth (see 1 Pet 1), in the end does not amount to predetermination. As Luke and other Gospel writers say repeatedly, it was "necessary" *(dei)* that the Christ suffer many things and die (see Mk 8:31 par.; cf. Lk 24:26). But this necessity is not a necessity of predetermination; rather, it is a necessity if there is to be a certain outcome. God had devised no other way that salvation could be accomplished. It was necessary in the sense that otherwise no salvation would be available.

This did not mean that Jesus had no choice in the matter, or that he could not have chosen otherwise when he wrestled with doing God's will in the garden of Gethsemane. Luke is emphatic about this, having Jesus say, "Father, if you are willing, let this cup pass from me. Nevertheless, not my will, but yours, be done" (Lk 22:42). Jesus is depicted by Luke as freely submitting to God's will. Jesus recognizes that his own desire and will are in some ways different from the Father's, and he wishes to submit to the Father's will in this situation. There is neither compulsion nor predetermination in evidence here, yet it is necessary that God's will be done if the world is to be saved.

We may compare this discussion with what we find in Revelation, as Caird himself notes. There are, to be sure, some divinely determined events in human history, what may be called "acts of God." These, for example, are the three sets of seven judgments that come down from heaven upon some inhabitants of the earth. These earthly things happen because Christ in heaven has unsealed the seals. Yet in this book there is also clearly a sense of the permissive will of God, which is not identical with God's directive will—the seven-headed monster is merely allowed to make war on God's people (Rev 13:7). But there is more. Human beings can frustrate God's plan and design for their lives. A person's name can be written in the book of life (Rev 17:8; 21:27), but lest we mistake this for determinism, the name of a person who commits apostasy can be erased from that book as well (Rev 3:5).[7] This means that a person is only provisionally in that book until the end of all things or the end of that person's life.

In short, God is the most powerful and important participant in the human

---

[7]Ibid., p. 48.

story, and he has a will, a plan, and he takes action in regard to this plan. There certainly is such a thing as divine intervention, as all the writers of the New Testament suggest. This is why prayer is both necessary and can be effective if one asks according to the will of God. But at the same time, God is not the only participant in the human story, not the only one who has a will, not the only one who can decide outcomes, even eternal outcomes. This is why there are warnings like the one in Revelation 3:5, and it is also why Christians are urged to pray for God's will to be done on earth. This is not asking for the obvious or inevitable, if we are referring to the present; it is asking for divine intervention.

In other words, for the writers of the New Testament, including even Luke, who most uses the "necessity" language in both his volumes, the old mystery about the relationship between divine sovereignty and unpredetermined human choice is not resolved by simply affirming either end of this spectrum of possibilities. Both are affirmed, and reassurance is given that there is only one almighty player in the game of life, and God alone can bring about his eschatological will and dominion on earth, his will for the salvation of human beings. In the New Testament salvation is never viewed as a human self-help program, or even a "with a little help from above" program; rather, it is viewed as a divine plan that God is implementing whether or not this or that individual responds to it, and so the initiative is with God, and only the response is left to human beings. This does not mean that apostasy is impossible for someone who first responds and is changed by God and then later has a change of mind, as Revelation 3:5 makes clear. There is a mystery in all of this, but all the New Testament writers want to make clear that the author of and chief character in the story is God. Luke-Acts, then, is in some key respects more theocentric than christocentric, or, better said, its christo-centrism is a part of the larger theological vision.

GOD AS FATHER IN THE NEW TESTAMENT

It is a telling and moving fact that Jesus and Paul both refer to God as "Abba." Hardly anything could be a clearer clue that Paul knew the essential and distinctive teaching of Jesus than his use of *Abba* in Galatians and Romans. What Paul adds to the conversation is that it is the indwelling Spirit within the believer's life that prompts the cry "Abba!" indeed authorizes and insti-gates it, giving the believer holy boldness in addressing God. We should take note that the use of "Father" language in the New Testament for God has nothing to do with ancient anthropological patriarchy, nor does it have to do with any sort of regular calling of God "Father" in the Old Testament or "Abba" in New Testament times. In particular, to the best of our knowledge, God is nowhere prayed to as Abba outside the New Testament.

As far as we can tell, early Christians called God "Father" for one reason: he was believed to be the Father of Jesus Christ in a very special and particular sense. Whether it was expressed by saying that Jesus is the only begotten of God or by talking of his virginal conception or in some other way, it was believed that Jesus was God's Son in a way that others could claim neither by nature nor by merit. At most, believers could only be identified as God's adopted sons and daughters.

This line of thought is even taken to the point in John 1 where we are told that God's human creatures are not by virtue of being humans (made in God's image) God's children. They only become God's children by being born again (Jn 1:12-13). And one has to wonder if this whole discussion of new birth is something of a development of what Jesus said when he insisted, "Unless you turn and become like children, you will not enter the dominion of God" (Mt 18:3). But I digress. The real children of God, by virtue of their relationship with Jesus, have permission to call God what Jesus called him, "Abba," and for the same reason. It took a miracle for them to be in this relationship with God, a new birth, just as it took a miraculous conception for Jesus to be in that relationship with God as a human being. It will be worth demonstrating how the "Father" language used in the New Testament is quite specifically linked to Jesus' relationship to God, just as the "Abba" parallels between the speech of Jesus and Paul already suggested.

In Romans 15:6; 2 Corinthians 1:3; Ephesians 1:3; Colossians 1:3; 1 Peter 1:3 is the phrase "the Father of our Lord Jesus Christ." What is interesting about this phrase is that it always shows up in invocations or prayers to God himself. In other words, it is part of the prayer life of Peter and Paul and so of early Christians. When we put this together with the "Abba" material discussed in the first volume in the present study,[8] we discover that Christians view God as the Father of Jesus in the first instance, and as their Father only derivatively and through having a personal relationship with Abba through Jesus and through the Spirit. We can see how Jesus in fact invited his followers into such a relationship with God by teaching them to pray "Abba" as

---

[8]See Witherington, *Individual Witnesses*, pp. 96-100.

he did (Mt 6:9; Lk 11:2), and also there is the tradition in John 20:17 where Jesus commissions Mary Magdalene to go and tell the male disciples, "I am returning to my Father and your Father, to my God and your God." How gracious this is after they had betrayed, denied or deserted him. Christians held on to this treasured privilege and nurtured their use of the language without forgetting who gave them the permission and possibility of using such language of God.

There is another whole group of Pauline texts that simply punctuates what has just been said. Paul offers grace to his converts from God "our Father" and the Lord Jesus Christ as well (Rom 1:7; 1 Cor 1:3; 2 Cor 1:2; Eph 1:2; Phil 1:2; Col 1:2; 2 Thess 1:1; Philem 3; see also 2 Thess 2:16). And here something crucial comes to light. Just as when the Beloved Disciple thinks of the nature or character of God he primarily thinks of love (see Jn 3:16; 1 Jn 4:8), so when Paul thinks of this same Father God he primarily thinks of his graciousness, especially expressed in the gift of his Son.

Neither Jesus nor Paul primarily thinks of the sovereignty of God when thinking of God's character, though certainly they believe that God is almighty. To them, the Father connotes, above all else, grace and love, which is why Paul leads with the idea of grace at the beginning of almost all his letters in association with a clear statement of whom it comes from. It is not just Paul sending greetings, it is God sending grace to them.

In addition to all this we find over one hundred verses in the New Testament where God is simply called "the Father" in a wide variety of contexts, and these simply confirm what I have just suggested. Early Christians called God "Father" with great liberality, and in all sorts of contexts and ways, but they never forgot the rock from which they were hewn, they never forgot that they came to the Father through Jesus the Son. Nowhere is this any clearer than in the Fourth Gospel, where there are over 140 or so examples of God being called "Father," and almost all of them either directly or contextually use this appellation for God because of his special relationship with Jesus. It becomes especially clear in the Fourth Gospel how Christology is the hinge on which all the "God" language turns in the New Testament.[9]

---

[9]An interesting but odd footnote to this discussion is that God is not called "the Father" or "our Father" or "the Father of our Lord Jesus Christ" anywhere in the book of Revelation. This borders on being bizarre if one wants to insist that the Fourth Gospel and Revelation have the same author, which I reject. A person's "God" language, especially personal prayer language, does not change that much from one document to the next.

The Primacy of Eschatology over Protology
in the New Testament

There is actually not that much stress on what has been called "protology," the emphasis on God as the creator of the universe or discussion about his original creation design. It is often assumed and occasionally expressed (e.g., Jn 1:1-5; Heb 1:2), and it is reflected in Revelation 4 by the fact that all creatures worship God. But mainly, creation is only the back story to the story that is being told in the New Testament, the prequel. The focus in the New Testament is not looking back in longing or in dread but rather in looking forward to the climax of human history. In other words, the orientation of all the New Testament writers is on eschatology, "in the end, God," not on protology, "in the beginning, God." Of course, there is some discussion of a creation order when Jesus discusses marriage and divorce and compares the original intent with the Mosaic legislation, which took into account fallen human behavior and hard hearts (see Mk 10:2-12 par.). But when Jesus talks about the kingdom in Matthew 19:10-12, he introduces a whole new possibility of being a eunuch (i.e., single) for the sake of the kingdom of God.

Recognizing the kingdom or eschatological orientation of the New Testament becomes all the more critical when we get to the subject of anthropology, which I will address when we get to ethics in the next chapter. I stress this here because it makes all the difference when one comes to a reading of a text such as 1 Corinthians 11. The emphasis here is not primarily on what men and women are by way of the creation order, but rather on what they now are in Christ, which does not simply involve a reaffirmation of what is sometimes understood as the creation order. The trajectory of the argument hinges on the little word "nevertheless" *(plēn)* in 1 Corinthians 11:11: "In the Lord, nevertheless, woman is not independent of man, nor is man of woman." The reason why creation, even a reaffirmation of creation, is not enough is that the fall so marred human beings that drastic intervention was required.

Salvation is not just creation renewed, and even if it were, it would not involve patriarchy in the modern sense. Man, to be complete, required woman. That is clear from the creation story. She was the crown of creation, the creation that God saw to be very good. If this tells us anything, it is that woman, not man, is the apex of creation because there seems to be an ascending order of creation, climaxing with woman. And when we learn in Genesis 3 that the fall is when things went south, when to love and cherish was turned into the curse to desire and to dominate ("Your desire will be for your husband, and he will lord it over you" [Gen 3:16]), then redemption, whatever else it would entail, would have to reestablish some mutuality and equality of things, not a domination of one sex by the other, either way. And this is exactly what Paul says. Woman and man are not independent of one another; they are interdependent creatures, with neither one being more important than the other. Headship in the order of redemption, then, looks like head servant, taking the lead in sacrificing, not like head knocker. The eschatological perspective on all of this is quite clear in the New Testament. The focus is on the final state of affairs breaking into human history, and this relativizes all worldly institutions, including marriage, for "the form of this world is passing away" (1 Cor 7:31). I will say more on this in due course.

GOD AS ONE WHO ANSWERS PRAYER

When Jews thought of their creator God, they also believed that God intervenes in human history and sustains the universe in existence. They also believed that God responds to prayer. Their vision of God was not that of William Paley's watchmaker God, who wound up the world and then left it to its own devices. Not surprisingly, this absentee landlord vision of God is not that of the New Testament writers either. Above all, God is depicted as an answerer of prayer and the giver of every good and perfect gift (Mt 6:5-6; Jas 1:17). This is a God deeply involved in the everyday life of the world and especially of his people, and one who works all things together for good for those who love him (Rom 8:28). What is notable in the New Testament is that many of the former functions of Yahweh are now predicated either of Jesus alone (e.g., he will come to judge the world [Mt 25:31-32; Mk 13:26-27]) or of both the Father and the Son (see the discussion of this collaboration in Jn 14–17). The author of Hebrews keeps the Father busy by making Jesus the heavenly intercessor and the Father the one who answers the prayers.

But of course Jesus too responds to prayer and intervenes in lives, often offering visions of guidance and comfort and change (see Acts 9; 22; 26; Rev 1–5). The New Testament writers see it as a divine team effort, this work of redemption and judgment and eventual restoration of all creation. This is why it is sometimes difficult to distinguish who is performing what function among Father, Son, and Spirit. If in Revelation both the Son and the Father can twice be called the "Alpha and Omega" (when in Isaiah it was only Yahweh), then it seems clear that we are well beyond the notions of adoptionist Christology by the end of the first century, if indeed that ever was a school of thought. The divine being involves several persons, so much so that the Son is not only the one through whom all things were made, but also the one for whom all things were made, the one who inherits all things, and the one whom every tongue will eventually confess as "Lord," the LXX name for Yahweh.

THE FATHER, ELECTION, AND SALVATION

God the Father and Election

What is basically not predicated of the Son or the Spirit is, as we saw at the outset of this subsection, "the divine plan." And that includes the concept of election. Scholars have long noticed that there is a theocentric bent to Romans in particular among Paul's letters, and one has to wonder why. My answer is that from the start of Romans Paul is concerned about making clear that the God of Israel, the God of the Old Testament, has not abandoned his Jewish people. This is why in Romans 1 we hear not only about "the good news of God" but also about the gospel being for "the Jew first and also the Gentile" (Rom 1:1, 16). This prepares for the discussion in Romans 9–11. And so at this juncture it is in order to explore the issue of the Father and election. Jesus is never said to be the elector, though sometimes he is portrayed as the Elect One of God. Here we are in the provenance of something that can be said specifically about the Father in the New Testament.

It is understandable that Paul would associate election with the first person of the Trinity for the very good reason that election was going on long before there was a human being named "Jesus." Election is something that comes up as a feature of the relationship between Yahweh and his people Israel in various ways in the Old Testament. Thus, it is natural to continue to talk about election in relationship to the Father rather than the Son when the subject is the elector or chooser. One of the problems in using the word *election* is that it is so closely associated with the word *salvation* in modern Protestant thinking that the two often are assumed to be almost synonymous. But even a moment's study of the Old Testament ideas about salvation will make very clear that later Christian ideas about salvation are not a good place to start for understanding the Old Testament concept of election.

Put succinctly, in the Old Testament there is little or no concept of eternal salvation, let alone eternal security. Furthermore, election in the Old Testament is corporate and does not guarantee the salvation (in the Christian sense) of particular individuals. How could it be otherwise when from an early Christian point of view the Savior had not even showed up yet on the planet, nor brought about atonement for sins through his death, nor made available the benefits of his death to anyone? That a different view of election is in play in the Old Testament becomes quite clear when the generation of the wilderness wandering, all of whom are considered God's chosen people, undergo a severe pruning or judgment by God, and only two of their people make it into the promised land, leaving a "righteous remnant" of two. Paul retells this story in a revealing way in 1 Corinthians 10 to warn his Corinthian converts against the dangers of apostasy. Election had to do with the large mass of chosen people, says Paul, and did not guarantee salvation to all of them. Behavior affected the outcome in each individual case.

Is there a selection within the election process resulting in the salvation of the righteous remnant? Or is more than selection the determining factor in such issues, and one must ask, "Selected for what?" When we ask the question about "selected" for what, we must remember that Israel was chosen in the first place to be the torchbearer for the one true God. They were chosen to be a light to the nations. Being chosen for some particular historical purpose does not guarantee the individual chosen ones that they will be eternally saved come what may and behave as they will. Thus, there is often a distinction made in the modern discussion between election for particular historical purposes (e.g., Cyrus the Persian was chosen as God's "anointed one" [Is 45:1] to set God's exiled people free) and election for eternal salvation. This discussion is based on a certain kind of reading of Romans 8–11 and God's role as described in those chapters. With this as a backdrop, we need to turn to those chapters.

Let us start with Romans 8:28-39. This discussion is not about how a person becomes saved or becomes a Christian. It is a word of assurance given to those who are already Christians about their future or destiny. They are reassured that no outside forces can rip them out of the hands of God as they journey through the travails of life, making progress toward the dominion and glorification. Neither circumstances, nor angelic beings, nor other human beings, nor any other things in creation can separate believers from the love of God. God's undying love is clear here, and this theme will continue throughout Romans 9–11, making evident that the answer to the question "Has God forsaken/given up on his first chosen people, even those who have now rejected Jesus" is an emphatic no.

What exactly is going on in Romans 8:28-39? Divided Christians in Rome, largely Gentile, but some Jews, are reassured that for those who love

God, namely, for Christians, God works all things together for good for those who are called "according to choice/purpose." A common English translation in Romans 8:28 is "according to his purpose," but in fact that is not what the Greek indicates. There is no pronominal adjective in the text here, and the choice/purpose here could be either God's or the believer's. Either is possible because in the context both are actively involved in this process: God is working, and the believer is loving God. There is no sense that one of the participants in the process is active and the other merely passive. And there can be no disputing that Paul is speaking about God's providence here, how an almighty God can work things together for good for Christians. God is not merely a participant in the process; rather, he is the one capable of controlling the process or weaving all things together for good. That much is clear. This does not make "all things" inherently good in themselves, nor does it make them all destined by God, but nothing is beyond God's power to work and weave together for good; he is the dominant participant in all such matters. Paul is not talking about God's sovereignty in some abstract way. Here the point is that God is almighty to save, providential in rescue, powerful in working for the good. The discussion is not about whether God is the first cause of all things that happen. By "all things," we may assume that Paul gives us a list beginning at Romans 8:31 of what he has in mind. Even sufferings and hardship, which Christians are not exempt from simply because they are Christians, can be worked together for good for those who are called.

Here is where we note that the word *prothesis* in Romans 8:28 could mean "choice," "purpose," "plan," or even "resolve." Some of the early Greek fathers, such as Origen, Theodoret, and particularly John Chrysostom, all of whom knew Paul's Greek as their native tongue, took the key phrase in this verse to mean "called by their choice" or "called according to their own choice." Here is the way Chrysostom puts it: "For if the calling alone were sufficient, how is it that all were not saved? [Note that we could ask the same about the electing]. Hence [Paul] says it is not the calling alone, but the purpose of those called too, that works for salvation, for the calling was not forced upon them, nor compulsory. All then were called, but all did not obey the call."[10] By this Chrysostom means not only that they did not feel compelled to respond, but also that they were not predetermined to do so.

---

[10]See the broader discussion in Ben Witherington III and Darlene Hyatt, *Paul's Letter to the Romans: A Socio-Rhetorical Commentary* (Grand Rapids: Eerdmans, 2004), pp. 226-27.

It is possible to counter and point to Romans 9:11, which speaks of "God's purpose *[prothesis]* in election." However, the context is different. Here in Romans 8 the discussion is about Christians, but there in Romans 9 it is about the patriarchs and how they were chosen to be bearers of light and witnesses for God. Here the issue is God working life together for good for Christians, but there the discussion is about the initial choice by God of these patriarchs for specific historical purposes. The chief difference between the two texts is that in Romans 8 the issue is about what God is currently doing in the lives of those who have for some time been lovers of God. This is not the context for Romans 9:11.

This conclusion becomes all the more clearly correct when we get to Romans 8:29, which begins with *hous* ("whom"), the "whom" in question being those who are already Christians. The discussion in Romans 8:29-30 is not about how one becomes a Christian; rather, it is about how God works in and for the lives of those who already are Christians. More specifically, Paul is largely painting a picture of the future for those already Christian while reminding them a bit about their past.

What Paul is not discussing is how God chose some out of a mass of unredeemed humanity to become Christians in the first place. Before Augustine, most of the church fathers were quite clear about this. Gerald Bray, in summing up the Greek fathers' view of Romans 8, says this:

> Apart from Augustine, who embraced it wholeheartedly, most of the Fathers found it somewhat puzzling to accept the apostle's teaching at face value. They did not want to deny that the world was planned and ordered by God, but neither did they want to suggest that there were some people that God had predestined to damnation. *They were convinced that predestination did not remove human free will. God's call to salvation was generally understood to be universal. The fact that not all responded was their fault entirely and the result of a deliberate choice on their part. . . . Only Augustine, and then only in his later writings, was prepared to accept the full implications of divine predestination.*"[11]

The Greek word *hoti* at the outset of Romans 8:29 clearly connects the preceding verse to what follows, and this means that Romans 8:29-30 explains why all things work together for good for those who love God and have responded to his call. This working together happens because all along God had a salvation plan for believers: they needed to be set right or justified,

---

[11]Gerald Bray, ed., *Romans* (ACCS/NT 6; Downers Grove, Ill.: InterVarsity Press, 1998), pp. 233, 244 (italics mine).

they needed to be sanctified, they needed to be glorified, and in general they needed to be conformed to the image of God's Son, Jesus. Those believers whom God knew in advance he also destined in advance to these outcomes. The crucial issue here is what "knowing" means. Some have argued that "knowing" here has the Old Testamental sense of a relationship established, experienced and acknowledged, an intimate relationship, as in "Adam knew Eve." That sort or degree of intimacy is assumed by some to be in mind here. The problem is that one cannot have intimacy in, or the experience of, a relationship before the relationship exists, and one certainly cannot have intimacy in or the experience of a relationship before the other person even exists! One can, however, know something in advance without yet experiencing it, and surely this is what Paul has in mind here (cf. Acts 26:5; 2 Pet 3:17).

Thus, God the Father is depicted in Romans 8 as having a game plan, a salvation plan for getting believers to the finish line intact, come hell or Noachic high waters. No outside power, degree of suffering, temptation or circumstance can rip the believer out of the firm grasp of the Father. God is working things together for good in every stage of the relationship that he has with believers, once that relationship is established. This is a great reassurance indeed. In other words, this text is about what God is prepared to do to help believers persevere and reach the finish line. Here the entire emphasis is on what God is prepared to do, but elsewhere Paul will stress the human side of what is necessary (e.g., Phil 2:12: "Work out your salvation with fear and trembling"). Here there is no need for such a discussion.

As Paul Achtemeier says, Paul's use of the terms *foreknow* and *predestine* "do not refer in the first instance to some limitation on our freedom, nor do they refer to some arbitrary decision by God that some creatures are to be denied all chance of salvation. They simply point to the fact that God knows the end to which he will bring his creation, namely redemption, and that destiny is firmly set in his purposes."[12] Note that when Paul gets around to discussing the human response to divine initiatives, he does allow that an individual can opt out of the covenantal relationship, can commit apostasy. The one factor not listed among the things that cannot separate a believer from the love of God in Christ is one's self, and that this factor is important is evident in the discussion in Romans 9–11, where various Jews rejected their messiah and then were broken off from the people of God, at least temporarily. Clearly, Paul's view of

---

[12]Paul J. Achtemeier, *Romans* (IBC; Atlanta: John Knox, 1985), p. 144.

election and salvation and foreknowledge is rather more like that of other early
Jews and not very much like Augustine's or Calvin's later views. This brings us
to Romans 9–11 and the role of God as described therein.

As I have shown at length elsewhere, Paul's discussion about election and
foreknowledge should be set in the context of early Jewish discussions of the
same, in particular the context of Pharisaic discussions of the same, since
Paul was a Pharisee before be became a Christian. Here a remark by Josephus
about Pharisaic beliefs is apposite. He tells us that Pharisees stood somewhere
between the highly deterministic theology of the Essenes, who said that God
destined all things in advance, and the Sadducees, who said that there was no
such thing as foreordination of things. The Pharisees took the middle ground
in the discussion. Here is Josephus's summary: "While the Pharisees hold that
all things are brought about by destiny, they do not deprive the human will
of its own impulse to do them, it having pleased God that there should be a
cooperation and that to the deliberation (of God) about destiny, humans, in
the case of the one who wills, should assent, with virtue or wickedness" (*Ant.*
18.1-3). Elsewhere he adds that Pharisees ascribe all things to God, except
that to do right or wrong lies mainly in the hands of human beings, with God
as a auxiliary force aiding their efforts (*J.W.* 2.8-14).

When considering the flow of the argument in Romans 9–11, we need
to keep steadily in view several key points. In Paul's discussion of God and a
righteous remnant of Israel, the point is not to distinguish a saved group of
Israelites from a damned or permanently lost one, for as Paul will go on to
say, even those Jews currently broken off are broken off only temporally and
temporarily perhaps. They could be regrafted in if they respond to the Messiah when he comes again. The remnant process is described to make clear
how God works to create a people for his purposes. Israel was chosen or created not primarily for its own benefit but rather to be a light to the nations. In
Paul's view, Israel's salvation, or anyone else's for that matter, is not complete
until the eschaton, and if we are talking about particular individuals, the
outcome is not predetermined.

Until then, while the believer may have assurance of his or her conversion and current saved status, that assurance always stands under the proviso
that one must persevere until the end of life, which is possible only by means
of God's grace through faith and by the obedience of faith, which involves
working out one's salvation with fear and trembling (while God works within
to will and to do). Paul believes that even the saved person can commit an

act of apostasy, a dramatic act of willful rejection and rebellion against God's work in one's life. One is not eternally secure until one is securely in eternity and has experienced the full conformity to Jesus' image in the body at the resurrection. Salvation involves resurrection in the end, not just spiritual renewal or conversion or sanctification in the present.

Since all have sinned and fallen short of God's glory, God owes salvation to no one. It is all about mercy and grace. This even includes Israel, who has rejected the Messiah. Salvation is not the same as election for historical purposes. Salvation is by grace and through faith initially and involves individuals of course. Election is largely seen as a corporate thing and takes place "in Israel" or "in Christ." In Ephesians 1 Christ is seen as the Elect One of God, the one God chose from before the foundation of the world to be the Savior. Christians are elect only if they are in Christ, and that happens by grace and through faith.

Indeed, when Paul wants to describe the actual process of getting saved in Romans 9–11, he does not talk about election; rather, he talks about preaching and the human response to it. "'The word is near you; it is in your heart,' that is, the word of faith we are proclaiming: That if you confess with your mouth, 'Jesus is Lord' and believe in your heart that God raised him from the dead, you will be saved. For it is with your heart that you believe and are set right/justified, and it is with your mouth that you confess and are saved. . . . For 'Everyone who calls on the name of the Lord will be saved.'" (Rom 10:8-10, 13).

What is most interesting about this passage is that having told his audience that justification is all about what God does in Romans 8:28-30, here he turns around and says that being set right requires first that one believe in one's heart and then confess with one's lips and so be saved. There is then this chain of things leading to actual salvation that does not begin with God's election. It goes like this: preaching the good news leads to hearing, hearing the good news leads (in some cases) to believing, believing to calling on God, calling on the name of the Lord (in this case, Jesus) and believing that God raised him from the dead to being saved or set right. In short, Romans 8:28-30, on further review, is only meant to tell half the story, and indeed its main stress there is on what God does for Christians who love him. The main stress in Romans 10 is on how one gets saved in the first place.

Thus, when Paul wants to talk about how one gets saved, he talks more about human response to preaching. When he wants to reassure distressed

Christians about reaching the final salvation finish line, he talks more about the work of God on their behalf. And when he talks about election, he talks about it as a corporate thing that happens in Israel or in Christ and has mainly to do with historical purposes; and even when salvation enters the picture in such a discussion, the salvation of particular individuals is not guaranteed at the outset or at conversion.

Is God Unjust to Israel?

Achtemeier stresses about Romans 9–11, Paul

> is not writing about the fate of each individual. He is making a statement about how God dealt with Israel, and continues to deal with it, even when it rejects his Son; namely he deals with it in mercy, even when it deserves wrath. That is why one so badly distorts Paul's point if one assumes these verses tell me about my fate, or anyone else's fate, before God: damned or saved. Rather, what these verses tell me is that the same gracious purpose at work in the election of Israel is now at work in a new chosen people to whom I can now belong, by that same gracious purpose of God. The passage then is about the enlargement of God's mercy to include Gentiles, not about the narrow and predetermined fate of each individual.[13]

In regard to the character of God, the issue is whether or not God is unjust. Has God reneged on his promises to Israel? Paul's answer is that God is not unjust, and even more, God has actually found a way to be merciful to both wayward Jews and wayward Gentiles and to make sure that salvation is a matter of mercy and grace for one and all.

Of particular interest is the end of the discussion about God's justice and mercy in Romans 11. Here Paul, having told Gentiles that they have no ground for boasting since they are like wild olive branches grafted into the preexisting native olive tree of Israel in order for them to be part of the saved people of God at all, turns around and says that God had broken off the non-believing Jews in order to graft the Gentiles in. But also the breaking off of unbelieving Jews was in order to regraft those same Jews back in when the redeemer returns from heavenly Zion and turns away the impiety of Jacob. Then and then only, at the resurrection, will "all Israel will be saved," and then and then only will every knee bow and every tongue confess that Jesus is Lord (cf. Phil 2:10-11). If we follow the whole convoluted argument from

---

[13]Ibid., p. 255.

the beginning of Romans 9 to the end of Romans 11, what we clearly see
is that Paul is thinking eschatologically. He is seeing the whole process of
salvation from its end, and that final salvific end does not come until Jesus
returns and the dead in Christ are raised. Short of that, individuals can be
chosen, and then opt out, and then be grafted back in again so far as salvation
is concerned.

God's honor is saved by the stress on the fact that God did not renege on
his promises to his people, whether they responded to them appropriately or
not. God kept on loving, kept on calling, kept on chiding, kept on saving,
kept on having mercy, kept on being true to his Word. Indeed, through an
eschatological miracle he even found a way to save and have mercy on the lost
Israelites at the end when Jesus returns and they finally recognize their messiah. The emphasis is on the graciousness of God throughout these chapters,
not on his sovereignty or predetermination of some to be saved and others
to be lost. There is a difference. Salvation is not a unilateral thing. God, of
course, is the initiator, the sustainer, the enabler, the one without whom it
would be impossible, the one whose grace makes it possible, but there is the
issue of human response, not just once at conversion but on an ongoing basis
until it is time to go and be with the Lord in heaven or until Jesus returns,
which ever comes first.

This picture of the loving and merciful God the Father comports well
with what Paul says elsewhere about God's character. For example, when in
2 Corinthians 5:18-19 Paul says that God was in Christ reconciling the world
to himself, God is depicted not as sending Jesus to sort out the preordained
saved from the lost, but rather as wanting the whole world reconciled to himself if possible. That at least is God's intent and the purpose for sending Jesus
in the first place. God is said to be making his appeal to the world through
Paul his ambassador, and the message is good news, not bad news.

This image of a God who cares about the world as a whole and who sent
Jesus to save the world comports nicely with the later Paulines and makes
it more probable that we could attribute them to Paul. Quite clear in this
regard is 1 Timothy 2:3-6: "This is good and pleases God our Savior, who
wants all people to be saved and come to a knowledge of the truth. For there
is one God and one mediator between God and human beings, Christ Jesus,
himself human who gave himself as a ransom for all." Here it is interesting
that it is God the Father who probably is called "Savior," and his saving intent
is made clear in the fact that Jesus died as a ransom for all, not just the elect.

Notice that it is not just a case of God's desire that all be saved; he put a plan in motion to make that outcome possible. Clearly enough, this passage will have nothing to do with the notion that God limits the atonement's efficacy to the elect.

The Difference Between Salvation and Election

Another verse of interest that confirms the distinction made earlier between election and salvation in Paul's thought is 2 Timothy 2:10, where Paul says that he endures all things for the sake of the elect so "that they too may obtain the salvation that is in Christ Jesus, with eternal glory." Here "the elect" could refer to Israel, who are not yet saved, once again demonstrating that even for Paul, election is one thing, salvation another. But even if it refers to Christians who are converted, election is seen as different from final salvation, which is viewed as future here.

Equally interesting is Titus 3:5-7, where a distinction is made between salvation in the present and the "hope of eternal life," which is seen as future and part of something inherited later. Once again God is viewed as the Savior (Tit 1:3), and his will is implemented by Christ and then by other emissaries such as Paul who spread his word. No distinction is made between the will of God and the will of Christ or expressed in Christ, or between some supposed hidden will of God and the revealed will of God to save the world in Christ. God the Father, as it turns out, is not just sending the Son or cheering him on; rather, this is a "hands on" God who is intimately involved in the salvation of the world, reconciling the world to himself.

Perhaps above all of this, God is viewed throughout the New Testament as the appropriate object of worship. He is the one to whom glory is to be given (this is why to predicate of the Son his own glory not only implies his divinity but also that he is worthy of worship because he manifests the divine presence [see Phil 2:11]), and as Revelation 4 makes quite clear, every sort of creature and all creatures are supposed to worship this God. In part this is a response for God's many good gifts, but God is to be worshiped simply for who God is, not just for his benefits. In 1 John we learn that God is both light and love (1 Jn 1:5; 4:8, 16). What is interesting about this characterization is that these are noun ascriptions, not adjectives. In other words, we hear a good deal about God being just and fair and holy and almighty as an attribute, but when we are told that God is love and light, this is a character description, not merely a description of how God behaves or even just of an isolated facet of the divine being. There is something fundamental about calling God "light." Among other things, it refers to his purity, but in a Johannine context it also means that God is the revelation. This goes beyond what we find in Revelation 1:1, where we learn that God even gives Jesus the revelation that he then reveals to his human seers. God is the source of Jesus' revelations.

GOD IS LOVE

What Does It Mean to Say That God Is Love?

But what does it mean to say that God is love? Let us take in the whole context of 1 John 4:7-12:

> Beloved, let us love one another, for love comes from God. Everyone who loves has been born of God and knows God. Whoever does not love does not know God, because God is love. This is how God showed his love among us: he sent his only begotten Son into the world so that we might live through him. This is love: not that we loved God, but that he loved us and sent his Son as an atoning sacrifice for our sins. Beloved, since God so loved us, we also ought to love one another. No one has ever seen God; but if we love one another, God lives within us, and his love is made complete in us.

This requires a detailed unpacking, but it is clear from the outset that our author is not saying that "love is our God," unlike what our culture might suggest.

Here, for the third time in this sermon, the author speaks about brotherly/sisterly love and also its connection with God's love (on love as a sign of walking in the light, see 1 Jn 2:7-11; on love as a form of righteousness and a mark of being a child of God, see 1 Jn 3:10-18). The author begins 1 John 4:7 by calling the audience *agapētoi* ("beloved"), which is followed by the verb *agapōmen* ("let us love"), by the noun *agapē* ("love"), and by the participle *agapōn* ("loving"). This probably is the most "love-filled" verse in the Bible! "Love constitutes the foundation of the author's thinking about God and Christian community."[14]

The ability for Christians to love one another comes from God, for "love is of God," and God has an unending supply, however short our human supply may run. "Anyone who enters into a real relationship with a loving God can be transformed into a loving person."[15] The author is saying more than just that we love in gratitude for the fact that God first loved us. In fact, he will also say that if we are sharing such love, "we know God" in the process of loving. Lov-

[14]William Loader, *The Johannine Epistles* (London: Epworth, 1992), p. 51.
[15]Stephen S. Smalley, *1, 2, 3 John* (WBC 51; Waco, Tex.: Word, 1984), p. 238.

ing is a way of getting to know God or of getting to know better what God is really like. By contrast, the author says in 1 John 4:8, those who do not love know nothing of God. It needs to be stressed that the author is not suggesting that being loving is in itself a sufficient sign that someone is born of God. "Human love, however noble and however highly motivated, falls short if it refuses to include the Father and the Son as supreme objects of its affection. It falls short of the divine pattern, and by itself cannot save a man; it cannot be put in the balance to compensate for the sin of rejecting God."[16]

The subject of love, being godly and godlike and of God's love, has come up before in this discourse, but it will be dealt with more thoroughly here as the main portion of the sermon draws to a close. If we ask why love is emphasized so much in 1 John, the answer surely must be, at least in part, that the author is trying to heal the wounds of schism and to get the remaining faithful Christians to redouble their efforts to create true Christian community. They must pull together after the crisis of schism. This brotherly/sisterly love, if exhibited and expressed, will shore up the boundaries and heal the wounds of the community. The author does not speak to the issue of loving the world or non-Christians, although some of the things that he says could be applied by extension to that relationship.

In Greek literature before New Testament times the verb *agapaō* ("to love") has nowhere near the importance or even the connotations that it has in the New Testament.[17] How can we explain the usage in the New Testament? C. H. Dodd puts it this way:

> The noun is scarcely found in non-Biblical Greek. The verb generally has such meanings as "to be content with," "to like," "to esteem," "to prefer." It is a comparatively cool and colourless word. It is this word, with its noun, that the translators of the Old Testament used by preference for the love of God to man and man's response, and by doing so they began to fill it with the distinctive content for which paganism, even in its highest forms, had no proper expression. In the New Testament this fresh content is enlarged and intensified through meditation upon the meaning of the death of Christ.[18]

---

[16]I. Howard Marshall, *The Epistles of John* (NICNT; Grand Rapids: Eerdmans, 1978), p. 212.

[17]Within the huge body of literature on this subject, see especially Anders Nygren, *Agape and Eros*, trans. Philip S. Watson (Philadelphia: Westminster, 1953); Ceslas Spicq, *Agape in the New Testament*, trans. Maria Aquinas McNamara and Mary Honoria Richter, 3 vols. (St. Louis: Herder, 1963-1966); Victor P. Furnish, *The Love Command in the New Testament* (Nashville: Abingdon, 1972).

[18]C. H. Dodd, *The Johannine Epistles* (MNTC; London: Hodder & Stoughton, 1946), pp. 111-12.

It is interesting, in addition, that when pagan religious writers do speak of a god loving, they usually use the word *eros*, which normally refers to sexual desire and sexual love. This is precisely what the New Testament writers do not want to say about God's love for humankind or God's character. From the Jewish point of view, a deity is not merely a human being writ large and having a whole lot more power and life. The God of the Bible is the creator God, who is wholly other and is not a being who takes cues from human behavior. God is the definition of what goodness, truth, life, light, love, and holiness mean. God does not conform to human definitions of these things.

Thus it was the usage of the term in the LXX (which was for many early Christians their only Bible, especially in the Diaspora) that explains in part the New Testament usage. But in addition there was the story of Jesus, which filled the term with new meaning as well. In fact, the Christ-event led to a more robust and personal definition of God. Here we learn that "God is love," which is in fact the second attempt at defining God in this discourse, the first coming at 1 John 1:5, "God is light," and we may also rightly compare John 4:24, where Jesus tell us that "God is spirit," a statement about God's metaphysical nature. The two other predications are about God's character.

We may be inclined to take the statement "God is love" to mean that God is loving and so is defined by his loving activities, and although that is true, the statement seems to mean something more. God not merely possesses or expresses love; *love* is a term that seems to embrace all that God is.

Nevertheless, God is not really being defined here by an abstraction, nor is it a claim that the reverse of this statement is true ("love is God"). What may be meant by "God is love" is in part, as Dodd says,

> If the characteristic divine activity is that of loving, then God must be personal, for we cannot be loved by an abstraction, or by anything less than a person. . . . But to say "God is love" implies that *all* his activity is loving activity. If he creates, he creates in love; if he rules, he rules in love; if he judges, he judges in love. All that he does is the expression of his nature, which is—to love.[19]

One more thing: the definition of love proceeds from God and works its way down to us—"not that we loved God but that God loved us and sent his Son" (1 Jn 4:10).

Exhibit A of the loving character of God, paradoxically enough, is that he sent his Son to die for a sinful and ungrateful world. As applied to Jesus,

---

[19]Ibid., pp. 109-10.

monogenēs is found only in Johannine literature, four times in the Fourth Gospel (Jn 1:14, 18; 3:16, 18) and once here in 1 John 4:9. One can translate this word "only born" or, less probably, "only begotten," but in any case the distinction is with those who are adopted as sons and daughters of God when we are comparing Jesus' status to that of believers. It is a term sometimes used in the LXX to translate the Hebrew word *yāhîd*, which means "single" or "only" (e.g., Judg 11:34). The term also can mean "unique" or "one of a kind." The term is used of only children (Lk 7:12; 8:42; 9:38; Heb 11:17), stressing that they are someone's only natural offspring. If one places stress on the second part of the word, from *genos*, it indicates derivation or kind rather than birth. It is not all that helpful or correct to insist on the word referring only to derivation and not to source as well, since derivation implies source, even if the emphasis here is on derivation. We can say that the word does not focus on "begetting" or the process or means of derivation.

In 1 John 4:9-10 it is stressed first that Jesus was sent so that we might have life through him, and second that God sent his Son as a sacrifice of atonement to propitiate divine anger about sin. If God is love, then it is hardly a surprise that God is supremely and righteously angry with our sinning, for it destroys the love relationships that we have with God and with each other. Here we have statements akin to what we find in John 3:16-17. Love and life are the polar opposites of hate and death, and yet the substitutionary and atoning death of Jesus is the prime example of God's love for us.

Substitutionary Atonement and Propitiation

C. H. Dodd championed the view that *hilasmos/hilastērion* need not indicate or imply propitiation, but he cannot be said to have had the better of the argument, and more to the point, to leave out propitiation is to misunderstand the nature of God's character, including God's love. Expiation is of course included in this term, the cleansing from sin and from its effect guilt and sometimes expiation is even emphasized in this term in the LXX (Lev 25:9; Num 5:8; Ps 129:4 [130:4 MT]; Ezek 44:27). But there can be no expiation unless God's demand for righteousness and justice is also satisfied. James Denney put it this way:

> So far from finding any kind of contrast between love and propitiation, the apostle can convey no idea of love to anyone except by pointing to propitiation—love is what is manifested there. . . . For him to say "God is love" is

exactly the same as to say "God has in His Son made atonement for the sin of the world." If the propitiatory death of Jesus is eliminated from the love of God, it might be unfair to say that the love of God is robbed of all meaning, but it is certainly robbed of its apostolic meaning. It has no longer that meaning which goes deeper than sin, sorrow, and death, and which recreates life in the adoring joy, wonder, and purity of the first Epistle of John.[20]

Denney means, I take it, that propitiation shows the great depths of God's love, for in effect God assuaged his own wrath against sin by setting up his Son as a sin offering. Here we also note that there is no definite article before *hilasmos* in 1 John 4:10, which means that the emphasis is on an atoning sacrifice for all sins, emphasizing the quality of the act.

Again in 1 John 4:10 it is stressed that it is not that we have first generated this love that creates community in Christ, but rather God has loved us, and so "our loving is a participation in the loving which first came to us and enabled us to love."[21] Having said all of this, the author rounds off this subsection by ending in 1 John 4:11 where he began, with the command to the beloved ones to love one another, except that now the context, the content and the character have been made much clearer through its linkage to the character and actions of God, especially God's actions in and through his Son. Thus, this verse is yet another example of amplification, since the author has already said this in similar terms in 1 John 3:16 and has referred to the sacrifice of Christ there to do so as well. This way of ending this short section on love is something of a surprise because we might have expected the author to say that since God has loved us in this way, we should reciprocate such love to God. But in fact the author is more concerned about the spreading of God's love throughout the community—intravenously, so to speak. In any case, we probably are meant to hear an echo of what Jesus has said in John 13:34, where brotherly/sisterly love is grounded in Jesus' love for his followers. John Painter puts it this way:

God's love is definitive, primary, and the source of all love. In arguing this way the author implies . . . that human love is seen to be derivative and responsive. This implies that human love continually needs to be redefined and corrected by divine love because human love in the world has the potential to be corrupted."[22]

---

[20]James Denney, *The Death of Christ*, ed. R. V. G. Tasker (London: Tyndale, 1951), p. 152.
[21]Loader, *Johannine Epistles*, p. 53.
[22]John Painter, *1, 2, and 3 John* (SP 18; Collegeville, Minn.: Liturgical Press, 2002), p. 270.

Who Shall See God?

In 1 John 4:12-16 we have another subsection in this Johannine sermon, one that mainly reiterates themes already discussed in more detail. However, 1 John 4:12 begins with a bold claim that distinguishes biblical religion from its competitors: "No one at any time has seen *[tetheatai]* God." The verb *theaomai* here has the sense of to gaze on someone or something and contemplate it, referring to physical sight and reflection. No amount of gazing or hard stares has ever enabled a person to detect the presence of the invisible God in some location. This idea can be said to go back to Exodus 33:20, which speaks of no mortal being able to see God and live (cf. Deut 4:12; Jn 5:37; Sir 43:31; Josephus, *J.W.* 7.346). In 1 John 4:12 "God" surely must refer to the Father, not the Son, not least because the author has claimed, and will do so again in a moment, to have seen the Son, whom he regards as God. Remember the climax of the prologue to the Fourth Gospel: "No one has ever seen God; God's one and only Son has made him known" (Jn 1:18). The Father, then, has manifested himself in a person (Jesus) but also as love, which dwells in the believer and in the Christian community.

An eschatological promise is made by Jesus in Matthew 5:8 that the pure in heart shall one day see God, and perhaps more pertinent to the present discourse, in John 14:9 Jesus says that whoever has seen him has in effect seen the Father. What by implication is being dismissed here is the mystical ascent to some sort of beatific vision of God, not least because such ascent is not necessary. God has already come to us and appeared in the person of his Son, and God's glory is even visible in that appearance, as John 1:14 stresses. Howard Marshall puts the matter this way:

> John turns his back on mystical experience as the high point of religion. Not for him the retreat from the world of men into the privacy of a vision of God. On the contrary, it is only when a person loves his fellow-Christians . . . that he fully experiences the love of God in his own heart and knows the presence of God with him. . . . We cannot find God by withdrawing from the world and its obligation to love one another; but equally we cannot find God merely by trying to love one another.[23]

It is in fact more a matter of God coming and finding the lost.

The author stresses that instead of physically seeing the Father, if we fulfill the commandment to love one another, we know and experience the presence

---

[23]Marshall, *Epistles of John*, pp. 217-18.

of God in our midst, and God's love is thereby made complete, or brought to perfect expression, or had its full intended effect (cf. 1 Jn 2:5 with 1 Jn 4:17). Alfred Plummer puts it this way: "Let us love one another, and then we may be sure that He is not only *with* us but *in* us, and not merely *in* us but *abides*."[24] The circuit of God's love is brought to completion when we love each other. If we take the several statements about perfect or complete love together (1 Jn 2:5; 4:12, 17-18), the net effect is this: "Obedience, active love, confidence, these three point to the same fact. Where the one is, the other is. The source of all is the full development of the divine gift of love."[25]

Is there anything like this in Paul's letters? Yes, Romans 5:1-11 is quite like it. Notice in Romans 5:5 it is God who poured his love into believers' hearts, and in Roman 5:8 it is God who demonstrated his love for us by sending his Son to die for those who were still sinners. The focus is on reconciliation with God in Romans 5 and on reconciliation and love between believers in 1 John 4, but despite this, much the same emphasis is made about God's love. The emphasis in Romans 5 also makes clear that God's love is expressed for those who were estranged, for sinners, for the ungodly, indeed for God's enemies. Note that this has nothing to do with the concept of covenant love, a love that God previously had promised to give to his people. Salvation has to do with self-sacrificial love in the truest possible of senses, a love that is not promised to be requited, a love that has not already been contracted for, even a love of the unloving and unlovely.

Yet another trait of God, related to God being love, is God's perfection. The context of Matthew 5:48 makes clear that what is in view is not an ontological quality (such as purity or holiness) but rather a characteristic of how God behaves. Matthew 5:48 says that disciples are to be perfect even as the heavenly Father is perfect. The context indicates that this refers to loving indiscriminately as does God, who makes his blessings to shower down on the righteous and the unrighteous. Note that in this context there is also the exhortation to love one's enemies, which again has nothing to do with the reciprocity cycle involved in covenant love. Notice especially Matthew 5:46: "If you love those who love you, what reward will you get?"

GOD'S IMPARTIALITY

Another of God's traits is impartiality (see, e.g., 1 Sam 12), which comes up

---

[24]Alfred Plummer, *The Epistles of St. John* (Grand Rapids: Baker, 1980), p. 103.
[25]B. F. Westcott, *The Epistles of St. John* (Grand Rapids: Eerdmans, 1966), p. 153.

in various places in the New Testament. For example, in Romans 2:11 Paul bluntly says, in the context of talking about final judgment and final reward, "God does not show partiality/favoritism," a rather surprising dictum from someone who believes that Jews are God's chosen people. The issue here is not just the ancient one of "showing" or "giving" face to someone, though that seems to be implied. The issue is justice. But Paul is not talking about what could be called "front-end" partiality, or partiality shown in this life. Paul is talking about "back-end" partiality, whether God will judge Gentiles any differently than Jews when it comes to rewards and punishments at the final judgment. The background to this sort of discussion of partiality surely is Deuteronomy 10:17, which indicates that God will condemn wickedness wherever he finds it, within or outside of Israel (see also Ps 81:2 LXX [82:2 MT]).[26]

Equally interesting is Acts 10:34-35, which involves front-end partiality. Here Peter says, "I now realize how true it is that God does not show favoritism but accepts those from every nation who fear him and do what is right." And James exhorts his audience not to show favoritism "as believers in our glorious Lord Jesus Christ" but rather to care for the needy and not just show face to the rich (Jas 2:1-8, 14-17). The way this is put suggests that belief in Christ is the basis of knowing that favoritism is wrong, which probably implies that James is thinking of the example that Christ set in such a matter. God is no respecter of persons, and so Christians likewise should not play favorites.

GOD IS SPIRIT

God's nature, as described in John 4:24, is spirit. This seems to be an ontological statement, not merely one about God's personality or character or actions. Note in this verse that Jesus does not say that God is "a spirit" or "the Spirit" (cf. Jn 3:6, 8, 34); rather, he is commenting on the character of God as spirit—immaterial, invisible and yet the greatest reality of all. What is interesting about this comment in John 4:24 is that it connects God's nature with the nature of proper worship: in spirit and in truth. The emphasis from the context seems to be that worship should not be linked to particular physical locations as somehow more appropriate than others; rather, it should be characterized by a particular spiritual approach. It must be genuine, wholehearted

---

[26]For an interesting discussion of this subject, see Jouette M. Bassler, *Divine Impartiality: Paul and a Theological Axiom* (SBLDS 59; Chico, Calif.: Scholars Press, 1982).

and involving true devotion, not just ritualistic or religious actions. It is possible that Jesus is also reaffirming here the opposition to "graven images" or deities found in the Mosaic code. Genuine worship of the God who is spirit does not involve talismans, totems, idols, requirements of particular physical objects or particular locations.

God's Will

A good place to find ascriptions of the character of God is in doxologies and benedictions. For example, Romans 15:32 speaks of God's will directing Paul's life, and Romans 15:33 speaks of God as "the God of peace," whom Paul believes can be with all of his addressees. This is a remarkable set of ascriptions. It includes the idea of God's omnipresence, or at least omnipresence with all his people. It characterizes God as someone who is proactive for peace, creating the conditions and ethos that make for peace between God and humankind and among humans. But then too we learn of the purposive nature of God: he has a will for human lives, including Paul's, which might allow or preclude Paul coming to the Romans. Not a lot is said about the "will of God" in the New Testament, so it will be worthwhile to review briefly the twenty-two instances of that phrase. Here is the list: Mark 3:35; Romans 1:10; 8:27; 12:2; 15:32; 1 Corinthians 1:1; 2 Corinthians 1:1; 8:5; Ephesians 1:1; 6:6; Colossians 1:1; 4:12; 1 Thessalonians 4:3; 5:18; 2 Timothy 1:1; Hebrews 10:36; 1 Peter 2:15; 3:17; 4:2, 19; 5:2; 1 John 2:17.[27]

A glance at this list reveals that it is Paul and Peter who are most interested in this subject in the New Testament, and it is hardly mentioned by anyone else. We have one reference predicated of Jesus in Mark and a general one in 1 John, but otherwise all the references are in Paul's writings and 1 Peter. In the example in Mark, Jesus is talking about "doing the will of God" or human behavior. Doing the will of God makes someone a brother or sister of Jesus, who himself is all about doing the will of God on earth (see, e.g., the Lord's Prayer and Jesus' prayer in the garden of Gethsemane). What is interesting about the discussion in the Gospel is that human cooperation is involved if God's will is to be fully done on earth. So, for example, Jesus must submit to God's will and give up his own in the garden of Gethsemane.

In other places in the New Testament the phrase "will of God" refers to something that God directs, permits, or does. In Romans 1:10 Paul says that

---

[27]Of course, there are closely related concepts implying that God has a specific will—for example, the concept of "necessity" discussed earler. See pp. 313-14 above.

he prays that "by God's will" the way may be opened for him to come to Rome, much the same sense of the phrase as in Romans 15:32. In Romans 8:27 we hear that even the Spirit dances to the tune of God's will; the Spirit intercedes for the saints in accordance with God's will. Romans 12:2 is a crucial verse for the anthropological side of the discussion of God's will. Those who present themselves to God as a living sacrifice and are not conformed to the mold of the world experience a transformation of the mind and thus are able to figure out, to test, and approve what God's will is in a particular circumstance—what is good and pleasing to God, and what is his perfect or complete will. This last phrase, unique in the New Testament, suggests that there is both a proximate and a more complete doing of God's will, and Paul wants his audience to strive for the latter, for that will be truly good and pleasing to God.

Paul affirms in 1 Corinthians 1:1; 2 Corinthians 1:1; Ephesians 1:1; Colossians 1:1; 2 Timothy 1:1 that he is an apostle according to the will of God. It did not happen by accident or merely because he claimed to be or said so. In 2 Corinthians 8:5 we have an interesting comment about the Macedonian churches, which are said to have given themselves first to God and then to Paul "in keeping with God's will." God's will, it turns out, is something that humans must voluntarily submit to, and it is not always done on earth as it is in heaven. God had a will in regard to the relationship between Paul and his converts in Macedonian. Equally interesting is Ephesians 6:6, where the service of slaves to their masters can be said to be doing the will of God from the heart. Indeed, they are exhorted to do it wholeheartedly. This does not suggest that Paul thinks that slavery is God's will, but obedience and service can be God's will even in a fallen world filled with imperfect situations. Colossians 4:12 mentions a prayer for converts to stand firm in the will of God. The latter's content is assumed to be known, and it is equally assumed that the converts must freely submit to and persevere in this known will of God for their lives. Notice the "stand firm in all the will of God" emphasis. This seems to suggest that one could stand firm in a part of it and not all of it, hence the exhortation to make one's submission to God's will comprehensive.

In most of the New Testament when the will of God has as its content some sort of ethical thrust, the audience is usually assumed to know what is meant. Thus, 1 Thessalonians 4:3 is a help. It tells us that sanctification is God's will for disciples, and in this case what is meant is sexually moral behavior. In the same letter, 1 Thessalonians 5:18 is interesting as it relates to prayer. Christians are to give thanks "in all circumstances," and this is said to be God's will. Notice that it does not say that the believer should thank God *for* all circumstances, as if everything came from God the good and the bad, but rather *in* all circumstances.

Hebrews 10:36 is another example of an ethical use of the phrase "the will of God." Here we have an entreaty to persevere despite pressure and persecution. Being faithful to the faith to the end, even while enduring opposition, is said to be doing the will of God. God wants his converts to make it to the finish line. That is his will for them. But it is not just up to God, as this verse makes clear. It also involves the perseverance of human beings if God's will is to be done in their individual lives. Of a similar ethical ilk is 1 Peter 2:15, which says that it is God's will that believers do the good and so silence the idle chatter of pagans about Christians. Also, in 1 Peter 4:2 a contrast is made between living according to the will of God and living according to human lusts. Also important is 1 Peter 3:17 because it makes evident that God could will for a Christian to suffer for a good cause. But it would not be God's will for a Christian to suffer doing ill rather than doing well. By this is meant that God would not will them to do ill, whether they suffered for it or not, but God does will them to do good even if it entails suffering. In short, the suffering of believers is not against God's will if it is done for some noble or Christian purpose or reason. This is made all the more clear in 1 Peter 4:19: "For those who suffer according to God's will should submit themselves to their faithful Creator and continue to do good." Notice the reference to God being faithful to the believer even in the midst of suffering, and how the believer must continue to do good even if suffering.

In 1 Peter 5:2 the issue of God's will for leaders in the church arises. They are to serve as overseers of God's flock not because they must or under compulsion but rather because they are willing, just as God wills or wants them to be. Here we have crossed into that gray area between willing and wanting. Of course, what God wills God wants to happen. But a verse such as this one makes clear that God's desire is not the only factor in determining whether something happens or not. The overseers must freely, without compulsion or predetermination, serve as the leaders God wants them to be. This exhortation would be unnecessary if there was no possibility of their not complying with God's will.

Rounding out this discussion is 1 John 2:17. Here we have a great promise.

Whereas the world and its lusts pass away, whoever does the will of God lives forever. Here again we see the essentially ethical thrust of the phrase. It is all about doing God's will. One's behavior is said to have an effect on whether or not one lives forever. What strikes me greatly in studying all these examples is how very different this sounds from, for example, a Muslim saying "as God wills" or even Robert E. Lee saying "God's will" at Gettysburg as he ordered Pickett's charge. There is nothing fatalistic about any of these examples, nothing to suggest that God's will is predetermined to happen in all circumstances. Indeed, in many of these examples it is suggested that human behavior affects whether God's will gets done at all, at least by the person in question and in his or her life. The stress in most of these discussions is, however, on human behavior that conforms to God's will. One suspects that Paul so strongly stresses his calling to ministry as being according to God's will because many did not accept that he was a genuine apostle. The other most striking thing about the phrase "the will of God" as used here is that most of the time Paul or Peter or the Beloved Disciple assumes that the audience knows already what is meant by the phrase, so that its content, even in regard to behavior, need not be spelled out in detail.

And this brings us to a further point. When modern people talk about knowing the will of God, typically they are talking about what God's purpose or calling is for their life, at least at a particular juncture—what they should do or be or become or what course of life or calling or vocation they should pursue. Very little of the New Testament discussion has anything to do with this seeking of direction in regard to a life's calling. The Pauline references at the beginning of various of his letters suggest that a person can indeed be called to do or be something "according to the will of God," but we find no one seeking guidance about this in the New Testament. What we hear about is the will of God for those who are already Christians, and most of the time it has to do with them living a good Christian life in general—praying, worshiping, submitting to God, living morally upright lives, persevering in the faith to the end. But what about a text such as Ephesians 1:3-14, where we learn so much about God's work and will and character? Does this tell us something more or different about the will of God than what we have just noted? We need to look at this theocentric text more closely and in detail here.

THE FATHER'S ELECTION OF THE SON
Beginning at Ephesians 1:4 and in several places in this discourse, Paul talks

about the concept of election. The key phrase to understanding what he means by this concept is "in him" or "in Christ." When Paul says that believers were chosen before the foundation of the world "in him" (i.e., Christ), he does not mean that believers preexisted or even merely that God's salvation plan preexisted, though the latter is true. He means that Christ preexisted the creation of the universe, and by God's choosing of him (who is the Elect One), those who would come to be in him were chosen in the person of their agent or redeemer. God, because of his great love, destined those who believe for the adoption as sons and daughters. This freely given love is stressed in Ephesians 1:5. This happens only through Christ and according to God's good pleasure. Paul says that "we were graced with this grace" in the Christ the beloved and for the sake of God's praise (Eph 1:6).

The concept of election and destination here is a corporate one. If one is in Christ, one is elect and destined. Paul is talking not about the pretemporal electing or choosing of individual humans outside of Christ to be in Christ, but rather about the election of Christ and what is destined to happen to those, whoever they may be, who are in Christ.[28] The concept here is not radically different from the concept of the election of Israel. During the Old Testament era, if one was in Israel, one was a part of God's chosen people, but if one had no such connection, one was not elect. Individual persons within Israel could opt out by means of apostasy, and others could be grafted in (see the story of Ruth). These concepts of election were then applied to Christ, who as a divine person could incorporate into himself various others. Christ becomes the locus of election and salvation because in Paul's thinking the story of the people of God is whittled down to the story of Jesus the Anointed One and then built back up in the risen Christ thereafter.[29] When Paul speaks of how a lost person gets "into Christ," he speaks on the more mundane level

---

[28]Contrast this with what we find at Qumran, where the fate of both the righteous, who will be elected, and the wicked, who will be condemned, is determined prior to creation of the universe (CD-A II, 7; 1QS III, 15-17). Ernest Best aptly observes that predestination is a concept dealing with God's purpose from all eternity rather than being about individual salvation (*A Critical and Exegetical Commentary on Ephesians* [ICC; Edinburgh: T & T Clark, 1998], pp. 119-20). Pheme Perkins also rightly notes the total lack of discussion of the predestination of the wicked here ("The Letter to the Ephesians," in *The New Interpreter's Bible*, ed. Leander E. Keck [Nashville: Abingdon, 1994–2004], 11:373). Ephesians depicts election not as that which divides the human race but rather as that which unites it in Christ, hence the strong contrast with the Qumran language about the election and salvation of the few righteous in contrast to the majority of the race (see Perkins, "Letter to the Ephesians," p. 377).

[29]See Ben Witherington III, *Paul's Narrative Thought World: The Tapestry of Tragedy and Triumph* (Louisville: Westminster John Knox, 1994), pp. 245-337.

of preaching, hearing, responding in faith, not of God's prechoosing of our choices for us. This doctrine of corporate election in Christ is meant as a comfort for those who already believe, reassuring them that by God's grace and their perseverance in the faith they can and will make the eschatological goal or finish line.[30]

This approach to the matter also comports with the ecclesiocentric focus of Ephesians. The Christology found already in Colossians 1:15-20 is here used in service of an explanation of the benefits that believers have in Christ.[31] It is possible that Jesus' baptismal scene is in mind at Ephesians 1:6-7, for here Christ is called "the beloved," and at Jesus' baptism there is also the language of washing away of sins (cf. Mt 3:11-17). The word *apolytrōsis* (Eph 1:7; cf. Dan 4:34 lxx) can refer to a buying back or ransoming of a slave. Paul says nothing of a ransom paid to Satan, as God owes Satan nothing. Christ is redeeming the lost person from the bondage of sin by paying the price for that sin.[32] Redemption is only had "in him." This redemption terminology, then, is metaphorical, as is shown by the equation with forgiveness of sins. Forgiveness comes to the believer out of the riches of God's grace, not because she or he merits it. This grace is said to overflow to Gentiles as well as to Jews, and it comes about by the revelation of the secret, the *mystērion* (Eph 1:9), which here refers to God's plan to reconcile all things, all peoples, all worlds in Christ.

The revelation of the secret comes in preaching, but the preaching comes about only because God has first done something in human history through the death and resurrection of Jesus. It is therefore quite unlike other religions that may have had purely other worldly mysteries in view. This open secret is about what God has accomplished in Christ in space and time. Christ was sent for the administration or ministry[33] in the fullness of time (Eph 1:10; cf. Gal 4:4-5; as an apocalyptic concept, see 2 Esd 4:37; *2 Bar.* 40:3; 1QpHab

---

[30]For a helpful study of Paul's and the other New Testament authors' conceptions of election and perseverance, see I. Howard Marshall, *Kept by the Power of God: A Study of Perseverance and Falling Away* (London: Epworth, 1969).

[31]Paul is not talking about the personal preexistence of believers in heaven. What is being discussed is our election in the preexistent Christ, by which is meant that believers are chosen in him, and believers were in God's plan from the beginning, the plan God enacted in Christ.

[32]One suspects, although Paul does not say so, that if he was pressed with the question "Ransom paid to whom?" the answer would be "God," because only God is owed something when one of his children sins, for all sinning is done against God and his standards.

[33]The word *oikonomia* refers to the management or administration of something or to the basis of such administration, namely, a plan. Whereas in Colossians 1:25 it refers to a plan or stewardship administered by Paul, here God is the one who does the administering and has a plan.

VII, 13-14), summing up under one head, all things in himself. The idea of the fullness of time connotes not merely that the right and ripe time has come, thus bringing a long-awaited event or process; it also conveys the notion of the starting of a whole new set of circumstances at the precise time God chose to begin it. The word *anakephalaioō* (Eph 1:10) can simply mean "to sum up," but in view of the way Paul is going to use the term "head" *(kephalē)* of Christ in Ephesians 1:22, it is much more likely that he is playing on the literal meaning of the term, "to bring together under or in one head." This bringing together or summing up in Christ involves things in heaven and on earth. This would be puzzling were there not things in heaven that needed this unifying work. What we learn from a section such as this one in Ephesians is that the division of labor between Father and Son and the roles that they play are not strict, as this is a cooperative effort to save the lost. Still, distinctions can be made. Only the Son comes to earth and administers the salvation plan.

Ephesians 1:11 reiterates the theme of Ephesians 1:4 that believers were chosen "in him." The constant refrain of "in him" must be kept steadily in view throughout this eulogy. Christ carries out the intention of God's good will. Ephesians 1:12 says that believers, as redeemed, are redeemed for the purpose of God's glorious praise. This is the ultimate aim of humanity: to live for the praise of God, to let all that we are and all that we do be doxology, a giving of glory to God. The catechismal formulation puts it well in saying that the chief end of humankind is to love God and enjoy God forever. It was in Christ that the good news was heard, the word of truth about God's plan, good will and intention. It was "in him" that believers believed and thus in him were affixed with the seal, the promised Holy Spirit.

The seal here is not likely baptism, since Paul nowhere mentions baptism in this passage, but rather the Holy Spirit. The function of a seal in antiquity was to authenticate a document, but here this term could also refer to the branding of a slave. In that way, one would know to whom the servant belonged. In view of the word "ownership" or "acquisition" *(peripoiēsis)* in Ephesians 1:14, it likely has the latter meaning here. The point is not the protection or eternal security of the person in question but rather the identification of who belongs to Christ.

This Spirit is also the pledge of our inheritance. The term *arrabōn* (Eph 1:14) means "down payment, first installment, deposit"; here it does not simply mean "guarantee," although that idea is not excluded. It is the first installment and thus surety that God plans to complete his work of salvation in the believer. The Spirit, then, is a foretaste, not merely a foreshadowing, down payment, or pledge, of the eternal inheritance. "Although Ephesians depicts the gifts of salvation as fully present in the lives of believers, the designation 'pledge' suggests a future perfection to this experience."[34] The benefits that Christians already enjoy are but a foreshadowing of the blessings yet to come, a fact that should stimulate even more praise to the ultimate benefactor. "Despite their minority status in the world of first-century C.E. Asia Minor, Christians found themselves at the center of God's cosmic design because they belonged to the risen Lord, who is exalted over all the heavenly powers. Benefits that humans might expect to receive from 'the heavens' have been conferred by God in Christ."[35] Yet still, all believers await the acquisition of full redemption or, perhaps better said, God's full redemption of his possession, the church. Even in Ephesians there is a "not yet" dimension to salvation. Here, then, we have a discussion on God's will that focuses more on what God is doing to implement that saving will and purpose in the universe. It nicely rounds out the discussion of the will of God, showing that sometimes it can have a more anthropocentric and ethical focus, sometimes a more theocentric and theological one, as here. These two things are not at odds with one another but rather are the two sides of the one concept.

The Perfections of God

In the epistolary doxologies and benedictions, as we had already begun to note, we learn more about the way New Testament writers viewed God the Father. For example, in Romans 16:26-27 we hear of the eternal God, the only wise God. This comports with 1 John 3:20, a reminder that God knows everything, even what is in human hearts. The threefold benediction in 2 Corinthians 13:14 not only speaks of the grace of Jesus and the fellowship of the Spirit, but also stresses the love of God, which Paul wishes will be with all the audience. It is clear enough from texts such as Romans 5:1-11 and this benediction and others (see Eph 6:23) that Paul stressed that God the Father is, above all else, a loving God, just as the author of 1 John did. That love is especially expressed in the work of redemption now and in the future.

But so is *shalom*, "peace." Part of establishing peace between God and human beings is saving and sanctifying them. Thus, 1 Thessalonians 5:23-24

---

[34]Perkins, "Letter to the Ephesians," p. 376.
[35]Ibid.

says, "May God, the God of peace, sanctify you through and through. May your whole spirit, life and body be kept blameless at the coming of our Lord Jesus Christ. The one who calls you is faithful, and he will do it." This brings in the important note that God is proactively working to get Christians perfected and in the right condition for when Jesus returns. Paul wants the audience to trust and be assured that God is sanctifying them and is faithful and will continue to do so. Of a very similar nature is the doxology in Jude 24-25: "To him who is able to keep you from falling and to present you before his glorious presence without fault and with great joy, to the only God our Savior be glory, majesty, power, and authority, through Jesus Christ our Lord, before all ages, now and ever more." Here again we have the promise of God's ongoing work in and for believers. God is the one who is sanctifying and preparing them for being in the direct presence of God forever. The mention of God's glory, power and authority brings in familiar ascriptions to the God of the Bible, who is all-knowing, all-good, all-powerful, all-present and so on.

In regard to God being all-knowing and all-wise, we have the marvelous paean of praise in Romans 11:33-36: "O the depth of the riches of the wisdom and knowledge of God. How unsearchable his judgments, his paths past tracing out. . . . For from him and through him and to him are all things." There are no limitations to this deity. All the "omni's" are summed up in this God. All things are known to him and ultimately come from him. It therefore is important to stress that although human choice and limited freedom certainly are affirmed in the New Testament, at the same time there is great emphasis on the magnificence of God and that God is almighty, particularly almighty to save. God is constantly at work in the human sphere and process, working all things together for good for those who love him. Nor are humans seen as equal partners with God in such matters. To the contrary, God is the dominant and most powerful actor even on the stage of human history, even when it comes to the most important human matter or choice of all, salvation. There is, then, a mystery or tension between God's almighty working out of his purposes and human freedom that is not resolved on either side of the conundrum in the New Testament. But equally, it is clear that God is the dominant player in this story. God, however, does not merely act from afar; God comes in person, and not merely in the person of the Son, but also in the person of the Holy Spirit, and it is to the Spirit we must turn in the next chapter.

6

THE NEW TESTAMENT CONSENSUS ON THE PERSON OF THE HOLY SPIRIT

Nothing in the New Testament authorizes biblical theologians to work backward from the New to the Old and pour a developed Christology or Trinitarian theology into every messianic reference or every text about the [S]pirit. But these New Testament references do reveal that their authors were working in the other direction, affirming that God's [S]pirit was still at work in Israel and that what was true of Yahweh in the Old Testament was true of Jesus in the New.

JAMES K. MEAD[1]

It is an odd fact, at least for a Christian, but nonetheless a fact, that the Old Testament says about as little about the Holy Spirit as it says about the Christ. In fact, the expression "Holy Spirit" occurs only once in the Old Testament, at Psalm 51:11: "take not your Holy Spirit from me." Most, if not almost all, of the references to the Spirit in the Old Testament involve not the third person of the Trinity but rather God's own spirit or living presence. But on the vast majority of pages in the New Testament we have references to the Holy Spirit, who is distinguished with regularity from both God the Father and Jesus. We can account for some of this because the New Testament writers believed that they lived in the age of the fulfillment of prophecy, which is to say the eschatological age, and this would include the prophecy of Joel 2:28-32, which the apostle Peter claims was fulfilled at Pentecost in A.D. 30 (Acts 2:16-21).

---

[1]James K. Mead, *Biblical Theology: Issues, Methods, and Themes* (Louisville: Westminster John Knox, 2007), p. 175. I have capitalized "Spirit" in the quotation because here Mead is in fact talking about the Holy Spirit from a New Testament point of view.

This last text brings up an important difference between the Gospels and the rest of the New Testament. In the Gospels, Jesus alone seems to be the primary locus of the Spirit, and in fact the Spirit is not mentioned all that frequently in the Synoptics, and especially not apart from Jesus; but once one turns the page to Acts, the Spirit is all over the place. This reflects the strong sense of early Christians that they had been empowered, enlightened, gifted by God's eschatological Spirit in a way that was not true of disciples prior to the death of Jesus.

It is true that most New Testament texts focus on the function of the Holy Spirit rather than on the Spirit's personhood, but there are more than enough texts in both Paul's letters and in the Gospel of John where the Spirit is treated as a person, not merely a power, presence, or force. As I have argued elsewhere, what is notable about the New Testament when read against the backdrop of early Jewish literature is the discontinuity with that earlier literature.[2] The new thing involves treating the Spirit as a person and, in some texts, as the personal agent of Jesus Christ. One of the things that makes analyzing the New Testament data about the Spirit easier than analyzing the New Testament data about Christ is that one does not have to deal with the issue of the Spirit having a human as well as a divine nature.

God's Spirit, the Human Spirit, and Unclean Spirits

A distinction is made in the New Testament between the human spirit of a normal person and the Holy Spirit when the Spirit enters and empowers a person's life. This distinction between God's spirit and the human spirit can already be seen, at least in a limited way, in Psalm 51:10-11, which talks about God putting a steadfast human spirit within the psalmist and not taking away God's Holy Spirit from him. By far the most common use of the term *rûaḥ* ("spirit, breath, wind") in the prophetic books of the Old Testament is to refer to God's Spirit inspiring, revealing, and uplifting various of the prophets.

In language much like what we find in Revelation, Ezekiel speaks about how "the spirit lifted me up and brought me into the inner court" (Ezek 43:5). This is the language of transportation in a vision, and what is meant is that God's spirit gave the prophet a visual glimpse of what was happening in that far-off location by means of that vision. The spirit here in Ezekiel is simply the inspiring presence of God, who gives vision and revelation to Ezekiel.

---

[2]Ben Witherington III and Laura M. Ice, *The Shadow of the Almighty: Father, Son, and Spirit in Biblical Perspective* (Grand Rapids: Eerdmans, 2002), pp. 101-47.

It is notable also that in the Old Testament the spirit comes on selected believers in the Old Testament, particularly prophetic and sometimes priestly or royal figures and, interestingly, even on the artisans who build the tabernacle, a trend that continues into intertestamental and later Jewish literature (see Sir 48:24; 2 Esdras 14:22; *Jub.* 40:5; *1 En.* 71:11; Philo, *Dreams* 2.252; Josephus, *Ant.* 10.239). At Qumran we find a fair number of references to the spirit as endowing or inspiring a priest or prophet like Moses (e.g., 1QS IX, 10-11; 11Q13 II, 18; *T. Levi* 18). The spirit in such literature is the spirit who inspires prophecy for the most part, and we see some of this in the New Testament, but we also find much more that is distinctive.

I have alluded to the scarcity of references to the Holy Spirit in the Synoptics, particularly Mark, where after the first chapter (Mk 1:8, 10, 12) the author shows little interest in the Holy Spirit. We have mention of blasphemy against the Spirit (Mk 3:29), a brief reference to David being inspired by the Spirit (Mk 12:36), and the reference to Jesus' disciples in the future speaking under the prompting of the Spirit (Mk 13:11). What is noteworthy about the Mark 3:29 reference is that Jesus speaks of the Spirit as a person—one cannot blaspheme a force or mere power, but only God. It is an act of sacrilege. In the same saying the close link between Jesus and the Spirit is very evident. To say that Jesus acted under demonic influence or had an unclean spirit is not just an affront to Jesus; it is an assault on the Spirit within him by whom he performed his miracles and exorcisms. Yet, it was already made clear in the Markan baptism scene that Jesus is not the Spirit, for the Spirit comes upon him there and empowers him and then the Spirit engages in a personal act—driving Jesus out into the wilderness (Mk 1:9-12).

Theological consequences follow from Jesus enunciating the idea that the Spirit is a person to be reckoned with in a personal way, a person who has not just power but also a will and purpose. It is, in a sense, unfortunate that in both Hebrew and Greek the word for *spirit* is also the word for *breath* or *wind*—impersonal forces. This in turn must have been partly what prompted some through the ages to see the Spirit as an "it," a force or a power. The language and imagery of baptism used by John the Baptizer in Mark 1 also suggests something quantifiable, not a person.

Baptism with the Spirit is said to be analogous to baptism with water. It is understandable, then, how even Christians have come to treat the Spirit as being like a substance or power that one could get more of. The language of "filling" or "pouring," as in Joel 2:28, contributes to this confusion as well, a confusion that Jesus seems to have wanted to sort out. But if the Spirit is a personal presence and not just a power or spiritual substance, then one can no more have a little bit of the Spirit in one's life than one can be a little bit pregnant. Either the Spirit as a person is in one's life or not. Punctuating this point is Mark 13:11, which says that the Spirit will give the disciples the words that they need or will speak through them when they must bear witness. This presumes an intelligent being who can communicate, albeit through a human vessel. Just as an unclean spirit can speak through the demoniac (Mk 5:7-9), so the Holy Spirit can speak through the disciple. In both cases we are dealing with personal beings, not mere forces. Demons, like angels, are beings, and so is the Holy Spirit. Equally clear is the Q saying in Matthew 12:32 // Luke 12:10, where the Holy Spirit is paralleled with the Son of Man and again the Spirit is treated as a person who can be blasphemed, indeed treated as a divine person. Submission to the Spirit within a believer, not getting more of the Spirit, is the key to a more "spiritual" and sanctified life.

THE HOLY SPIRIT IN MATTHEW

The first reference to the Holy Spirit in Matthew, significantly enough, speaks about the virginal conception of Jesus within Mary. Matthew 1:18 stresses that the Holy Spirit was the means by which Mary came to be pregnant, though it is not clear who it was that "found Mary to be with child by means of the Holy Spirit."[3] Of course, Joseph did discover that she was pregnant, but the story implies that he did not know that she had conceived by means of the Holy Spirit. The importance of this reference is that it indicates the creative power of the Spirit, who is able to generate something out of very little or nothing. In other words, the Spirit is seen here as God at work, as in the story in Genesis 1. According to Matthew 1:20, an angel confirms to Joseph that he ought not to refuse to take Mary as his wife, for her pregnancy happened through the agency of the Holy Spirit.

The next reference to the Holy Spirit comes in Matthew 3:11, where the one who comes after John is said to baptize in/with the Holy Spirit and fire. Scholars have debated what the reference to fire implies, but Matthew at least seems to understand it to refer to judgment, in view of Matthew 3:12. It is possible, then, to read Matthew 3:11 to mean that Jesus will baptize some with the Spirit and some with fire or to take both agencies to refer to the

---

[3]Some of the material in this section occurs in another form in Witherington and Ice, *Shadow of the Almighty*.

same action, in which case it refers to a baptism by fire through the Holy Spirit, which could be said to be purgative but also redemptive (burning up the chaff but gathering in the grain).

At Matthew 3:16, in the story about the baptism of Jesus, the "Spirit of God" is said to be seen by Jesus descending and landing upon him like a dove.[4] Matthew stresses in a way that Mark did not that the Spirit did not just come down upon Jesus, but in fact landed and remained on him (cf. Jn 1:33). The Spirit's action is seen to be more gentle in Matthew than in Mark. For example, in Mark 1:12 the Spirit is said to "drive" Jesus out into the wilderness, whereas in Matthew 4:1 Jesus is said to be "led" by the Spirit into the wilderness. The act of leading is normally seen to be an activity of a personal agency, and so Matthew, like Jesus and Mark before him, stresses the personal nature of the Spirit.

A few interpreters of Matthew 5:3 have thought Jesus was referring to those who were impoverished due to their lack of the Holy Spirit, but this is an unlikely interpretation for several reasons. The parallel in Luke, as is well known, mentions only poverty with no reference to "spirit," but more importantly, this is not the normal way Matthew refers to the Holy Spirit. He uses either "Holy Spirit" or "Spirit of God." Furthermore, the Holy Spirit is nowhere else a subject for discussion in the Sermon on the Mount material that Matthew derived from Q. As was the case in Mark, Matthew 10:1 refers to the authority/power that Jesus bestows on the Twelve to cast out demons, and he also refers to the curing of diseases with this power (contrast Mark 3:15; 6:7), but nothing is said of the Holy Spirit being the agency of these mighty works.

Matthew has moved the discussion in Mark 13 about disciples appearing before various hostile authorities back into a setting where it appears to refer to activities during the ministry of Jesus. Matthew 10:16-23 deals with a variety of possible scenarios, but crucial for our purpose is the reassurance that "the Spirit of your Father" will be speaking through them when they have to testify before Jewish or Gentile authorities (Mt 10:20). Here is the first reference we have found to "the Spirit of your Father." This could be taken to indicate simply the presence of God the Father within the disciple, but since Matthew's Markan source refers to the Holy Spirit (Mk 13:11), and since elsewhere in Matthew he does not use "the Spirit" language in an impersonal

---

[4]The Markan parallel simply has "the Spirit" and makes no mention of the Spirit alighting on Jesus (Mk 1:10).

way as it is used in the Old Testament, we probably should see a Jewish Christian usage here. The emphasis, then, would be on the Father as the one who sends or gives the Spirit to the disciples so that they may utter testimony.

Matthew 12:18-21 quotes Isaiah 42:1-4, including the line where God says of his servant, "I will put my spirit upon him." For Matthew, of course, this refers to Jesus, but I would stress that since this a direct quotation of the Old Testament, it should not surprise us that the reference is to the spirit of God in an impersonal way. This is not Matthew's normal way of speaking about the Spirit, whom he does indeed see as a person, but since he was quoting Isaiah, he was constrained by his source.

The discussion about Beelzebul and blasphemy that follows in Matthew 12 is interesting for the variety of ways the Spirit is referred to in a short span of verses. Matthew 12:28 offers the "If I by the Spirit of God cast out . . ." saying, but Matthew 12:31 refers simply to "the Spirit," who may be blasphemed against (contrast Mk 3:29, which refers to the Holy Spirit). In the very next verse, however, we have a reference to the Holy Spirit. There are, then, four different ways the Spirit is referred to in this chapter, but only in the quotation from Isaiah is the reference to the presence or Spirit of Yahweh. In the other references, an entity clearly personal and distinguishable from the Son of Man is referred to. The variety of usage likely reflects to some degree Matthew's faithfulness to what he found in his sources (in this case, Isaiah, Mark and Q), but since at Matthew 12:31 he alters the Markan usage, it cannot simply be explained in that way.

It is a remarkable fact that after four references to the Spirit in Matthew 12, we have none in Matthew 13–21. The next reference to the Spirit occurs at Matthew 22:43. Here the Greek literally says, "How is it that David in spirit calls him Lord, saying . . . ?" This may be taken to mean "by the Spirit," referring to inspired speech, but it is striking that we find this same phrase *(en pneumati)* in Revelation 1:10, which we might call an Old Testament or Jewish way of referring to God's spirit. The spirit is seen to be the atmosphere or sphere that one enters (note that it is not the reverse being claimed, that the Spirit was in the speaker) that leads to inspired speech or a vision. The Spirit, then, seems to be referred to in an impersonal fashion, but this is not entirely surprising, since Jesus is talking about David's experience in Old Testament times, and he is about to quote a passage from the Old Testament (Ps 110:1). There are no further references, personal or impersonal, to the Holy Spirit in Matthew until the very end of this Gospel at Matthew 28:19. In essence, this means that we find only one passing reference, rooted in the Old Testament, to the Spirit between Matthew 13 and Matthew 28:18.

Matthew 28:19, however, is something quite different from what we find in Matthew 22:43 or, for that matter, anywhere else in this Gospel. Here, not only is the Spirit called the "Holy Spirit" and referred to in a personal way, but also the Spirit is clearly said, along with the Father and the Son, to be part of the divine name.

The noun "name" *(onoma)* in Matthew 28:19 is in the singular. There is one God, who has a name of a tripersonal nature. Matthew reports Jesus mandating that baptism be performed using this tripersonal name. Here indeed we see the beginnings of explicitly trinitarian expression about God. It is no accident that Matthew portrays Jesus speaking in this way after Easter and as the risen Lord, who has been bequeathed all authority, power, and, for that matter, divine knowledge by the Father. He is now able to reveal the full name of God, which is to say the full identity of God: Father, Son, and Holy Spirit (not merely the Spirit or presence of the Father or the Son). We may be sure that early Christians would not have baptized persons into a name that was viewed as less than divine, but Matthew here reveals the sort of Christian speech that his own community must have used for baptism. He does not anachronistically predicate such speech of Jesus or others prior to the resurrection. Indeed, the disciples do not speak of the Holy Spirit at all during Jesus' ministry in either Mark's or Matthew's Gospel. We must turn now to Luke's Gospel and see if indeed he deserves to be called the "theologian of the Holy Spirit."

THE HOLY SPIRIT IN LUKE–ACTS

We have observed that in Mark and Matthew there is no promise of the Holy Spirit or dispensing of the Spirit by Jesus, but in Luke the picture changes considerably. For example, in Luke 11:13 Jesus says that the heavenly Father will give the Holy Spirit to those who ask, and in Luke 24:49 the risen Jesus urges the disciples quite pointedly to stay in Jerusalem until they receive power from on high that is called "what my Father promised." Interestingly enough, the place bearing heaviest reference to the Holy Spirit in Luke's Gospel is the birth narrative, where clearly he is not drawing on Mark or Q. Thus, a prima facie case can be mounted, quite apart from the book of Acts, that Luke does wish to stress the work of the Holy Spirit.

Perhaps most remarkable about this is that Luke, ever the historian, chooses to refer to the Spirit in the Old Testament manner in his Gospel, speaking of a power or a presence or a force or something that fills a person. Very little in his Gospel could be said to reflect the personal nature of the Spirit (but see below). By contrast, in Acts the Holy Spirit is seen to be an actor in the drama, so much so that he is one of the persons who hands down the Jerusalem decree in Acts 15. Acts 15:28 reads, "For it has seemed good to the Holy Spirit and to us to impose on you no further burden than these necessary things." Or again in Acts 16:6 the Holy Spirit forbids Paul to speak the Word in Asia on his second missionary journey. In this same text we see the further Christian stress on the connection between Christ and the Spirit. Thus, at Acts 16:7 the Holy Spirit is called the "Spirit of Jesus." Luke knows that the more personal nature of the Spirit is a Christian concern and emphasis, and so he largely avoids anachronism in his treatment of what the characters in his Gospel narrative say about the Spirit.[5]

Let us consider the treatment of the Holy Spirit in Luke 1–2.[6] The narrative in Luke begins with the story of John the Baptizer's parents and the miraculous conception of John. In the midst of promising this child born out of due season, the angel says to Zechariah that John will be "filled with the Holy Spirit" (Lk 1:15). It is not clear whether we should see the reference to John having "the spirit and power of Elijah" (Lk 1:17) as also a reference to the Holy Spirit. Since, however, John is seen as an Elijah figure in Luke's Gospel, and since Elisha once asked for a double portion of Elijah's spirit (2 Kings 2:9), it seems likely that Luke 1:17 does not refer to the Holy Spirit.

The next reference to the Holy Spirit in Luke's Gospel is perhaps the most famous one, found at Luke 1:35. Mary is told by the angel that she will be miraculously impregnated, for "the Holy Spirit will come upon you, and the power of the Most High will overshadow you." We may take this as two ways of referring to the same thing. The power of the Most High is the same as the Holy Spirit that will both come upon Mary and protect her as God's power works within her. Equally rooted in the Old Testament is the reference in this birth narrative to the Spirit filling a person to speak or sing in an inspired fashion. We see this at Luke 1:41 when Elizabeth is filled with the Spirit and proclaims to Mary that she is most blessed among all women, and

---

[5]This is very much like the way Luke handles the christological matter of Jesus being called "Lord." He may be called "Lord" in the narrative framework of the Gospel but not in the speech material (see, e.g., Lk 7:13). Luke is sensitive to the issue of historical anachronism.
[6]See Joel B. Green, *The Theology of the Gospel of Luke* (NTT; Cambridge: Cambridge University Press, 1995), pp. 41-47.

in Luke 1:67 the same sort of filling is said to happen to Zechariah. Perhaps a bit more personal is the description of Simeon, of whom it is said the Spirit rested on him (Lk 2:25), and that he is guided by the Spirit (Lk 2:27), and that the Holy Spirit had revealed to him he would not see death until he saw the Messiah (Lk 2:26).

In Luke 3:16 Luke, like Matthew, has John speak of the one following him baptizing people with/in the Holy Spirit and fire. The one new note in the Lukan form of the story about the baptism of Jesus is the reference to the Spirit descending on Jesus in "bodily form" like a dove (Lk 3:22). This in turn leads to the uniquely Lukan statement that Jesus returned from the Jordan "full of the Holy Spirit" (Lk 4:1), a Spirit who leads Jesus while he is in the wilderness.[7] Thus, Luke wishes to stress that Jesus was not abandoned by the presence of God while undergoing temptation and testing. Again, at the end of the temptation scene, we hear that Jesus returned to Galilee filled with the power of the Spirit (Lk 4:14), a note found in neither Mark nor Matthew. All of this prepares us for the uniquely Lukan citation of Isaiah 61:1-2, which Jesus uses to declare that the Spirit of the Lord (i.e., Yahweh) is upon him prompting and empowering both his preaching and his miracle-working.

The next reference to the Holy Spirit comes at Luke 10:21, which is uniquely Lukan, as a comparison with the parallel in Matthew 11:25-27 will show. Jesus rejoiced in the Holy Spirit[8] that God had unveiled the hidden things to him.[9] Luke also has the blasphemy against the Holy Spirit contrast with the blasphemy of the Son of Man, which he combines with the promise that the Spirit will teach the disciples what to say when they are hauled before authorities (Lk 12:10-12). The likely background to this saying is Isaiah 63:10, which refers to the rebellion of the wilderness generation grieving

---

[7]Notice the difference from Matthew 4:1, which says that the Spirit led Jesus into the wilderness, and from Mark 1:12, which says that the Spirit drove Jesus into the wilderness.

[8]Some valuable witnesses, including $\mathfrak{P}$45, have simply "rejoiced in spirit," perhaps meaning Jesus' own human spirit here, but the word "holy" is well attested in some key witnesses and probably is original here.

[9]The pattern of Luke adding references to the Holy Spirit compared to what he found in his source seems clear, but it is interesting that in his recounting of the Beelzebul controversy there is no reference to the Spirit, unlike in Matthew and Mark (see Lk 11:14-23). It is also notable that at Luke 20:42 David speaks on his own when the quotation of Psalm 110:1 is mentioned, with no reference to his being inspired by the Spirit, unlike in the Synoptic parallels. One can contrast Mark 13:11, with its reference to the Spirit being the one providing words for the disciples, with Luke 21:15, where Jesus says about the messianic woes that his disciples must endure them, and when they are confronted, "I will give you mouth and wisdom."

God's Holy Spirit.[10] One can compare Luke's reference to the teaching of
the Holy Spirit with Mark, who says more bluntly that the Spirit will do
the talking (Mk 13:11), and Matthew, who refers to the Spirit of the Father
speaking through them (Mt 10:20). In other words, Luke emphasizes the
Spirit instructing the disciples rather than just taking over the disciples and
speaking through them. In all three cases the personal agency and nature of
the Spirit are stressed.

References to the Spirit in the rest of this Gospel are quite scarce until
Luke 24. Here I would simply stress that Luke's report that Jesus claimed
that he would send the Spirit promised by the Father (Lk 24:49). Thus, Luke
ends his Gospel with a stress on the connection between the Spirit and Jesus.
Throughout his Gospel the disciples are never said to be full of the Spirit,
but Jesus, John, Elizabeth, Zechariah, and Simeon are so characterized, and
promises are made to the disciples about receiving the Spirit in a way that
distinguishes Luke's account from Matthew's and Mark's. More often than
not thus far, Luke places more emphasis on the activity or power of the Spirit
rather than on the Spirit as personal agent, though the latter is not entirely
absent. None of the Synoptic Gospels have any significant amount of discussion about the Holy Spirit. It is not a topic discoursed on by Jesus or others.
The audience is simply assumed to know what is meant when the phrase
"Holy Spirit" or "Spirit of God" or the like is used. We do well at this juncture to consider Luke's handling of this matter in Acts.

It has been said that the book of Acts should be called "Acts of the Holy
Spirit" rather than "Acts of the Apostles," and there can be little doubt that
God the Spirit is seen as the primary agency of action in this book. Sometimes, as in Acts 2:1-4; 10:44-48, the Spirit simply invades the human sphere
and falls upon people before they even know what has happened to them,
changing their lives in dramatic fashion. It is no accident that the book of
Acts begins with a retrospective that includes the reminder that even Jesus,
even the risen Jesus, operated on the basis of the Holy Spirit, for it says that
Jesus was taken up "after giving instructions through the Holy Spirit to the
apostles whom he had chosen" (Acts 1:2). The instruction to remain in Jerusalem and await the promise of the Father is mentioned twice (Lk 24:49; Acts

---

[10]In general, Second and Third Isaiah seem to be the primary sources from the Old Testament for
Jesus and the Synoptic evangelists when they are looking for ideas and phrases to describe the work
of the Spirit. There are, however, plenty of echoes of the extracanonical early Jewish literature
as well.

1:4). An explicit connection is made by the risen Jesus between the prophecy of John and the baptism with the Holy Spirit (Acts 1:5). Bear in mind that John the Baptizer spoke of baptism with Spirit and with fire (Lk 3:16), and indeed this is how Luke describes the Pentecost event, which involves both tongues of fire and a filling with the Holy Spirit (Acts 2:3-4).

In some ways, Acts 1:8 is the most important mention of the Holy Spirit in the introduction to Acts, for it involves yet another reiteration of Jesus' promise to his disciples "You will receive power when the Holy Spirit has come upon you." What is most significant about this verse is that it does not simply equate the Spirit with the power of God in some impersonal way. Yet the emphasis on the powerful Spirit is a consistent Lukan emphasis. The Spirit is seen as the personal agent who will supply the power that the disciples so badly need. This power will enable them to be witnesses throughout the Mediterranean crescent.

THE HOLY SPIRIT AT PENTECOST

In Peter's speech before the 120 believers, the Spirit is once again spoken of in a personal manner. It was the Holy Spirit, speaking through David, who foretold what would happen to Judas (Acts 1:16). Throughout Acts the Spirit is indeed seen as the Spirit of prophecy, but also as the Spirit who empowers the disciples to work miracles.

The account of Pentecost has been analyzed and overanalyzed, but for our purposes only a few points are necessary. The sudden coming of the Spirit is described by analogies; it is aptly said to come like a violent wind (remember that *pneuma* is the word for both "wind" and "spirit"). Again, the divided tongues are said to be like fire. These analogies describe the impression left on the disciples when the Spirit fell upon them. The description is given in rather impersonal terms not least because it is influenced by Old Testament prophecies, such as the one cited in Acts 2:17-21 (citing Joel 2:28-32), which speak of a pouring out of the Spirit as if it were a substance like water. We must bear this in mind because in Acts 1:2, 16 Luke has already made clear the personal nature of the Spirit. When he adopts and adapts language from the Old Testament to describe the work of the Spirit, it tends to involve impersonal language. Acts 2:4 is an interesting example of the mixture of personal and impersonal language of the Spirit. On the one hand, the Spirit is said to be the person who gave the disciples the ability to speak in other languages; on the other hand, they are said to be "filled with the Spirit," which is impersonal and metaphorical language drawn from the Old Testament that refers to inspiration prior to prophetic speaking. Notice that it is said that the Spirit filled them all. This was not merely an endowment for a few leaders.

Luke certainly wishes to leave Theophilus with the impression that the falling of the Spirit on the believers had a dramatic and overwhelming effect. Thus, the analogy with being drunk is not a surprising one (Acts 2:13, 15). The disciples are acting in an abnormal manner and are surprisingly loquacious, even in foreign languages. Peter explains the phenomenon by citing Joel 2:28-32. The disciples are simply Spirit-empowered and Spirit-enabled persons, just like Jesus, through whom God performed deeds of power, wonders and signs (Acts 2:22). Notice how Luke puts the matter. God acted through Jesus, and in light of the portrayal of Jesus in Luke's Gospel, this surely must refer to the fact that Jesus acted on the basis of the power of the Spirit within him, once the Spirit had come upon him at his baptism. In other words, Acts 2:22 probably should be seen as evidence that Luke was prepared to call the Spirit "God," for it is by being filled with the Spirit that Jesus is enabled to do and say all that he does during the ministry (cf. Lk 3:22; 4:1, 14, 18).

At Acts 2:33 we learn that it was when Jesus was exalted to the right hand of God that he then received the "promise of the Holy Spirit" from the Father and then in turn poured it out on the disciples, motivating them to speak. The connection between Christ and the Spirit and the Father is close here. All three are in heaven together, and the sending of the Spirit is handed over from the Father to the Son. There is an implicit trintarianism here, for the assumption is that Father, Son, and Spirit are part of the divine identity, are together in heaven, and are working together to enable God's people to spread the Gospel. If one compares and takes Acts 2:17 together with Acts 2:33, Jesus would seem to be called "God" here.

At Acts 2:38 we learn that someone who is to receive "the gift of the Spirit" must repent and also be baptized and receive forgiveness for sins.[11] The promised Spirit is said to be for the immediately present Jews, for their offspring, and for all those who are far off (Diaspora Jews?), indeed for everyone whom God calls (Acts 2:39). Speaking in an Old Testamental vein, Peter goes on to urge his fellow Jews to repent so that "times of refreshing may come from the presence of the Lord" (Acts 3:19). The Spirit's coming is

---

[11]Notice that although the Spirit is promised by the Father, this is not something owed to human beings. This is still a gift even though its giving has been prophesied or promised.

associated with the renewal and refreshment and life sent from the very presence of God or, put another way, conveyed by the coming of God's presence in the person of the Spirit. It is no less than God and God's presence that come when the Spirit comes on a person.

In Acts 4:8 Peter is depicted as a Spirit-filled person who is inspired to speak boldly to the Jewish authorities. The Jewish leaders had asked by what power or authority he was doing what he was doing, and Luke leaves us in no doubt that it is by the power and authority of the Spirit. The Spirit inspires not merely boldness (see Acts 4:13) but also educated and articulate discourse. The personal agency of the Spirit is again stressed at Acts 4:25, where once more we find a somewhat familiar phrase (cf. Acts 1:16) "Sovereign Lord [i.e., God the Father], who made heaven and earth, the sea and everything in them, it is you who said by the Holy Spirit through our ancestor David. . . ." This is again intriguing because it speaks of God working through or by the Spirit and through the human agency of David as well. The Father speaks by the Spirit and through the human agent. Again we begin to see an implicitly trinitarian way of thinking about the way God operates.

Acts 5 contains the remarkable story about Ananias and Sapphira, who are accused by Peter of "lying to the Holy Spirit" (Acts 5:3). Here again the Spirit is seen as a person who can be spoken to. At Acts 5:9 it is said to be "the Spirit of the Lord" whom this couple had put to the test. Notice the close connection between the Spirit and God (or possibly "Lord" here refers to Christ). To put the Spirit of the Lord to the test is to put God to the test. The Spirit clearly is not seen as someone or something less than God. It is possible that the phrase here indicates the Spirit which the Lord sent and now resides in Peter and others. Acts 5:32 adds a reference to the Spirit acting as a personal witness alongside of the disciples in the testimony about Jesus, and it also is said that the Spirit is given by God to those who obey him. This suggests perhaps that "Lord" in Acts 5:9 refers to God rather than Christ.

THE HOLY SPIRIT IN THE LIFE AND WORK OF THE DISCIPLES

One of the essential criteria for selecting seven new leaders from among the early church disciples is, according to Acts 6:3, that they must be "full of the Spirit and of wisdom." This may be an example of hendiadys, in which case the meaning would be "full of the Spirit, who conveys wisdom." At Acts 6:5 we are told that the first person chosen, Stephen, is full of faith and of the Holy Spirit. He is also said at Acts 6:8 to be full of grace and power and

thereby enabled to perform great wonders and signs among the people. Here
we get a fuller glimpse of what the Spirit bequeaths. The Spirit not only inspires prophetic speech, but also conveys wisdom, faith, grace, and the power
to perform miracles. Those who opposed Stephen's evangelizing were unable
to "withstand the wisdom and Spirit with which he spoke" (Acts 6:10). They
were only able to commit libel by suggesting that Stephen was blaspheming.
This is a significant juncture in the story when many Jews are about to turn
against the gospel, and the alert reader who remembers from Luke's Gospel
what was said about blasphemy against the Holy Spirit (see above) will realize
the gravity of this situation for God's people. Again, at the end of his speech
at Acts 7:55, Stephen is said to be filled with the Spirit, and on this occasion the Spirit inspires a vision, for Stephen sees the Son of Man standing in
heaven. Thus, the Spirit inspires not only words but also visions.

Acts 8 recounts a new stage in the missionary work of the church marked
by outreach to the Samaritans. Philip, however, does not convey the Spirit
to these people. Instead, it is when Peter and John come down that there is
prayer that the Samaritans might receive the Holy Spirit (Acts 8:15-16). Luke
explains that as of yet they had received water baptism but had not yet received the Holy Spirit. The reference to prayer here is important and should
be compared to Acts 1:24–2:1. This reference makes evident that even the
chief apostles could not dispense the Spirit at will from their own personal
supply, as it were; rather, they must ask God to give it to others.

Notice that Simon Magus asks these apostles not for the Spirit but rather
for the power to convey the Spirit (Acts 8:19), and he is peremptorily turned
down. The Spirit is said to be given through the laying on of hands, but this
is only after prayer (Acts 8:15-18). This story is important because it shows
that Luke does not necessarily associate the reception of the Spirit with the
reception of water baptism. Indeed, the two are clearly distinguished in time
and nature here, just as in Luke's Gospel there is a distinction between the
reception of John's baptism and the reception of the Spirit through the action of Jesus. Yet on some occasions the reception of water and Spirit can be
nearly coincident in time, as was the case with Jesus himself and apparently
also the Ethiopian eunuch (cf. Lk 3:21-22; Acts 8:26-40).[12] However, we are
told quite explicitly by Luke that the baptism of Jesus with water came first,
and then, when Jesus was praying, the heavens were opened, and the Spirit

---

[12]On the relationship of water and Spirit baptisms, see Ben Witheringtom III, *Troubled Waters: The
Real New Testament Theology of Baptism* (Waco, Tex.: Baylor University Press, 2007).

came down (Lk 3:21-22). The sequence is close, but the water baptism does not convey the Spirit. The Spirit comes in response to prayer, as in Acts 8:15. Acts 8:39 ends this chapter by portraying Philip as a latter-day prophetic figure like Elijah for whom the Spirit even provides transportation. The Spirit "snatched Philip away," and the next thing he knew, he was at Azotus (cf. 1 Kings 18:46).

The next reference to the Holy Spirit occurs in the story of Saul's conversion. Ananias is sent on a mission by Jesus to Saul so that he might regain his sight and "be filled with the Holy Spirit" (Acts 9:17). Saul's baptism is also mentioned at Acts 9:18, but Luke says nothing about what the connection, if any, between being filled with the Spirit and being baptized in water might be. We may surmise that Luke believes that if one has the Spirit, water baptism should not be withheld (cf. Acts 10:44-48). The text is more naturally read to suggest a connection between a regaining of sight and the filling with the Spirit rather than a connection with baptism.

The summary statement in Acts 9:31 is interesting. The church in the Holy Land is said to be living in the fear of the Lord (i.e., God) and in the comfort of the Spirit. Notice the parallelism. The Spirit is not simply identified with God the Father but is clearly implied to be personal in nature, capable of comforting believers. This theme of the personal nature of the Spirit is continued in Acts 10:19, which reports that the Spirit spoke to Peter after his vision, alerting him to the arrival of Cornelius's emissaries (also in Peter's recounting of the issue at Acts 11:12). This can be seen in Peter's speech where he briefly rehearses the story of Jesus, and at Acts 10:38 he tells how God anointed Jesus "with the Holy Spirit and with power." This may be an example of hendiadys, but in light of the personal approach to the Spirit in this chapter, the two things probably should be distinguished. The Spirit is not simply impersonal divine power, but certainly the Spirit can and does convey power to Jesus and others.

Acts 10:44 speaks of the Holy Spirit falling on all of Cornelius's family who heard the preaching. Peter recognizes that this event has transpired because he hears them speaking in tongues and praising God. Baptism should not be withheld from those who have already received the Spirit. We have thus seen the order of water then Spirit in Acts 8, and of Spirit then water in Acts 10. We can only conclude that Luke is not suggesting that one particular order of things is normative. For Luke, the sine qua non of Christian experience is receiving the Spirit, not being baptized, as seems clear from the case of Apollos in Acts 18:24-28. Perhaps the most important comment of Peter about the Cornelius episode is that found in Acts 11:15, where he stresses that it was the same Spirit who fell on these Gentiles as fell on the Jews earlier in Acts 2:1-4, and it happened to these Gentiles just as it happened then, unexpectedly and at the divine initiative. The contrast between water and Spirit baptism in Acts 11:16 is also interesting. John the Baptizer offered the former, but Peter says that Jesus promised the latter.[13] Notice too at Acts 11:17 that it is said to be God who gives the gift of the Spirit to those who believed in Christ. We begin to see a close connection between preaching, believing in Jesus, and receiving the Spirit.

Barnabas is an important figure in Luke's narrative even before Acts 11:22-26 (cf. Acts 4:36-37; 9:26-27), but in Acts 11 he becomes even more important. The description of him as "full of the Holy Spirit and of faith" (Acts 11:24) is the same as that of Stephen in Acts 6:5 except that the terms are reversed. The close connection between having the Spirit and having faith is stressed. Equally interesting in this text is the reference to Agabus, the Christian prophet who "predicted by the Spirit that there would be a severe famine" (Acts 11:28). The Spirit is again seen as the Spirit of prophecy. Agabus reappears at Acts 21:10, this time in Caesarea rather than in Antioch, and as he performs the symbolic gesture of binding Paul, he remarks, "Thus says the Holy Spirit: 'This is the way the Jews in Jerusalem will bind the man. . . .'" (Acts 21:11). There can be little doubt from this last reference that the Spirit is seen as God, for here the standard prophetic formula "Thus says the Lord" is modified to "Thus says the Holy Spirit."

We find another example of the Holy Spirit speaking at Acts 13:2, here commanding that Paul and Barnabas be set apart for a missionary venture. Notice that it is said that this speaking transpires while the church is worshiping and fasting. Presumably, we are meant to think that a prophet spoke these words prompted by the Spirit. It is also stated quite clearly that it is the Holy Spirit who sends these men out. Thus, we see the Spirit acting like a person in two ways here: speaking and sending others out. Yet we also hear of Paul being filled with the Spirit and given spiritual sight or insight into Elymas (Acts 13:9-10). This phrase about being filled with the Spirit, often compounded with something else, is very common in Luke-Acts, and we find another

---

[13]This is doubly interesting because at Luke 3:16 we have a saying of John, but here Peter speaks of a saying of Jesus. Perhaps we are meant to think that what John said was later repeated by Jesus to the disciples. If so, Luke does not record such an event in his Gospel, but we do find it at Acts 1:5.

example in the summary remark in Acts 13:52, where the disciples are said to be full of joy and the Holy Spirit.

At the crucial council in Jerusalem recorded in Acts 15, Peter remarks about Gentiles, "And God, who knows the human heart, testified to them by giving them the Holy Spirit" (Acts 15:8). Thus, the Spirit is seen as a divine seal of approval indicating to one and all that they are acceptable. As we have already noted, it is also the Holy Spirit who helps make the final ruling about Gentile Christians and their activities (Acts 15:28) and who forbids Paul to go into Bithynia (Acts 16:7),[14] and we may have a reference to Apollos as boiling over in the Spirit in (Acts 18:25), though it is possible that a less literal translation like "with burning enthusiasm" (NRSV) captures the gist of the text at this point.

The discussion between Paul and "some disciples" in Acts 19:1-7 is an intriguing and disputed one. It appears on the whole that Luke is referring to disciples of John the Baptizer who, prior to meeting Paul, had not even heard about the Holy Spirit. In other words, they are not Christian disciples who sometime after they accepted Christ were baptized in/by the Spirit. This is why Paul must go through the entire process of conversion and initiation with them, first baptizing them and then laying hands on them so that they receive the Holy Spirit. They stand in contrast with Apollos at Acts 18:24-28, who knows the way of the Lord, preaches Christ with zeal, but needs further instruction about Christian baptism.

Paul's famous Miletus speech (Acts 20:18-35) includes a reference to the Holy Spirit testifying to him in every city that imprisonment and persecutions await him in Jerusalem (Acts 20:23). This presumably alludes to the testimonies of prophets to him about what is yet to come (see, e.g., Acts 21:4).[15] Notice too at Acts 20:28 that Paul says that it is the Holy Spirit who has made these Ephesian elders into overseers of the flock in that region. This comports with what was said in Acts 13:2, that Paul and Barnabas were set apart

---

[14]Here, for the first and only time, the Holy Spirit is called "the Spirit of Jesus." This comports with the general pattern of Lukan divine speech in Acts. In general, the further the story gets away from Jerusalem, the more specifically Christian and the less specifically non-Christian Jewish the diction becomes. See Ben Witherington III, *The Acts of the Apostles: A Socio-Rhetorical Commentary* (Grand Rapids: Eerdmans, 1998), pp. 147-53.

[15]The phraseology is interesting at Acts 21:4: "Through the Spirit they told Paul not to go on to Jerusalem." This presumably means "by means of the Spirit," which in turn would seem to indicate when they were in an ecstatic state or being prompted by the Spirit. The odd thing about this is that Paul ignores these warnings of the Spirit, if such they were, believing that God wants him to go to Jerusalem.

as missionaries by the direction of the Holy Spirit. The Holy Spirit also casts a decisive vote in regard to the decree in Acts 15. Luke's ecclesiology seems remarkably pneumatic rather than early catholic. Luke is not even concerned to record what happened to most of the Twelve or how they related to or influenced their successors. The warning from Agabus recorded in Acts 21:11 does not deter Paul either, and it is interesting that the congregation that he is with does not simply take the prophecy as an indication that Paul should not go to Jerusalem. Indeed, they say at Acts 21:14, "The will of the Lord be done." Perhaps we are to think that the Spirit is just warning Paul that things will get difficult for him when he goes to Jerusalem. It is intriguing that in the chapters about the legal wrangling over Paul and about the sea voyage that the Holy Spirit (no references in Acts 21:12–28:25) is not referred to, not even in the recounting of Paul's conversion in Acts 22 (see Acts 22:14-16; cf. Acts 9:17-19; 26:19-20).

The final reference to the Spirit in Acts comes at Acts 28:25, where Paul says that it was the Holy Spirit who spoke to Israel in the Isaianic prophecies, in this case in Isaiah 6:9-10. This is interesting because here not only does Luke confirm the relationship of the Spirit to the inspired text of the Hebrew Scriptures, but also he stresses that the same Holy Spirit who has been speaking to Christians in the events recounted in this book also spoke to the Jewish ancestors. In other words, the coming of the Spirit on Elizabeth or Mary or the church was not the beginning of the story of the Holy Spirit. The Spirit as a personal being has a history with God's people. The Spirit is not merely a power or a force. We do well to remember this conclusion when we come to the Pauline material and also to John's Gospel, to which we turn next.

By way of reminder: What I am striving for here is not just to identify the shared ideas or commonalities of the various New Testament witnesses, in this case about the Holy Spirit. I am interested in the consistent and repeated core ideas, but I am taking an additive approach to the material, indicating also what this or that writer adds to the discussion without gainsaying the consistent or repeated core teachings.

The Paraclete as Agent and Advocate in John's Gospel

The first reference to the Holy Spirit in John's Gospel comes in the evangelist's distinctive recounting of John the Baptizer's testimony about Jesus. John says that he saw the Spirit descend and remain on Jesus and was informed by God that the one on whom he saw the Spirit descend is to baptize others with the Holy Spirit (Jn 1:32-33). There is an emphasis in this account on the Spirit remaining on Jesus.

The second reference to the Spirit comes in the dialogue with Nicodemus in John 3, Jesus says, "No one can enter the dominion of God without being born of water and of Spirit" (Jn 3:5). Jesus goes on to say that flesh is born of the flesh, and the Spirit gives birth to spirit (Jn 3:6). I have argued at length elsewhere that here "water" has nothing to do with water baptism, but rather is a metaphorical way to refer to physical birth, a birth "out of water" to be contrasted with spiritual birth, which is a birth "out of Spirit."[16] Water and Spirit are seen as the mediums or agencies by which such a birth transpires. Those born of the Spirit know where things come from and where they go. That is, they know that this spiritual birth comes from God, just as Jesus comes from God. John 4:24 refers to God being spirit, but this is indeed a discussion about the Father's divine nature, not about the person called the "Holy Spirit." Humans must learn to worship with their whole being and in truth, in authentic fashion. Nor is it clear that John 6:63 is about the Holy Spirit. Spirit is opposed to flesh, and the former is said to give life. But is it the spirit of God or the Holy Spirit that is meant? The second half of the verse claims that Jesus' words are spirit and life. This supports the conclusion that Jesus is not talking about the Holy Spirit here. The commentary of the evangelist at John 7:39 indicates that Jesus spoke about the Spirit, but only elliptically (in terms of rivers of living water flowing out of a person). More important is the comment that follows in that verse saying that believers were to receive the Spirit, but "as yet there was no Spirit because Jesus was not yet glorified." The Synoptic and Johannine evangelists agree that the Spirit was not dispensed to the disciples prior to the death of Jesus. It rested on Jesus, but not on his disciples during the ministry. They also agree that Jesus offered little or no public teaching on the Spirit during his ministry, apart perhaps from a promise that the Spirit would be coming.[17]

We come now to the discussion of the Spirit in the farewell discourses. There are some five "Paraclete" sayings in John's Gospel, all in the farewell discourses (14:16-17, 26; 15:26; 16:7-11, 12-15). The one whom Jesus promises to send to the disciples or have the Father send to them (cf. Jn 14:26 with

---

[16]See Ben Witherington III, *John's Wisdom: A Commentary on the Fourth Gospel* (Louisville: Westminster John Knox, 1995), pp. 94-97.

[17]The discourse with Nicodemus is a private one, just as the discussions about the Spirit in the Farewell Discourse are private discussions with a few disciples.

Jn 15:26) is called a *paraklētos* or, to be more specific, "another *paraklētos*." There is an implied comparison between Jesus and the Spirit. They are persons who have the same agenda, function and power. Does the term in question mean "counselor," "comforter," or "advocate"? An examination of the passages in the farewell discourses about the Spirit suggests that the Spirit has a threefold task: (1) to indwell the believer and convey the divine presence and peace, including Jesus' presence, to the believer (Jn 14:17-20, 27); (2) to teach and lead the believer into all truth and to testify to the believer about and on behalf of Jesus (Jn 14:26; 15:26); (3) to enable the disciples to testify about Jesus to the world and by means of the Spirit's guidance to convict the world about sin, righteousness, and judgment (Jn 15:26-27; 16:8-11). The Spirit is clearly seen as Jesus' agent, just as Jesus is seen as the agent of the Father on earth (see Jn 16:13-15). It is also true that judicial language is used of the Spirit's role in these discourses. This strongly favors the translation of *paraklētos* as "advocate."

Jesus is the advocate of the Father, and the Spirit is the advocate of the Son. It is the task of an advocate to speak on behalf of and as a representative of the sender. The advocate is the authorized legal agent of the sender. For our purpose, it is crucial to stress that only a personal being can be an advocate, and the comparison with the Son's role further reinforces the conclusion that the author of the Fourth Gospel sees the Spirit in personal and divine terms, distinguishable from the Father and the Son, yet working in concert with them as part of the divine identity. The Spirit is Jesus' surrogate on earth after the Son returns to the Father. The Spirit will equip the disciples with the presence of Jesus, the understanding of Jesus' teaching, and the power to convict and convert the world, as well as with the perseverance to endure persecution. The ultimate goal of the Spirit is the salvation of the individual through sanctification in the truth, and through such persons the salvation of at least some in the dark world.

This brings us to the final reference to the Spirit in the Fourth Gospel. The risen Jesus breathes on the disciples and says, "Receive the Holy Spirit" (Jn 20:22). Is this the Johannine version of Pentecost, as some have thought? Such a suggestion seems unlikely, not least because the disciples, in the Johannine way of telling the tale, are no different a week later. They are still frightened and hiding behind locked doors. They are not showing any signs of the effects of the Spirit mentioned in the farewell discourses. They do not yet set out on their missionary work. Thus, we must see Jesus' act as a prophetic sign–act promising the Spirit after he returns to the Father (which is what the farewell discourses said must happen before the other Advocate could come). The Fourth Gospel therefore agrees with the Synoptics that the Spirit was not given prior to Jesus' departure from this earth. But the farewell discourses do enrich our understanding of the Spirit as Jesus' "secret agent" on earth. What we also find in the Fourth Gospel is very little use of impersonal language to speak about this most personal of beings—the one who dwells within the believer and who acts for and like the Son.

THE HOLY SPIRIT IN THE PAULINE CORPUS

The evidence of the Pauline corpus is our earliest window on what was thought about the Holy Spirit at the beginning of church history. It is important to stress at the outset, however, that mention of the Spirit is so frequent in Paul's letters that it is quite impossible to present all the results of analyzing the more than one hundred occurrences. Paul uses the full name "Holy Spirit" sixteen or seventeen times, "his Spirit/Spirit of God" sixteen times, and "Spirit of Christ/his Son" three times (Rom 8:9; Gal 4:6; Phil 1:19), but the term *pneuma* occurs some 145 times in his letters, and in the vast majority of cases the Holy Spirit is meant.[18] In contrast to the author of Luke-Acts, Paul never speaks of being "filled with the Holy Spirit."[19] The primary way Paul expresses the initial receiving of the Spirit is either to talk about God giving his Spirit, placing it within a person (Rom 5:5; 2 Cor 1:22; 5:5; Eph 1:7; 1 Thess 4:8; 2 Tim 1:7), or to talk about the supplying of the Spirit (Gal 3:5; Phil 1:19), or he may speak of believers receiving the Spirit (Rom 8:15; 1 Cor 2:12; 2 Cor 11:4; Gal 3:2, 14) or of their simply having the Spirit (Rom 8:9; 1 Cor 2:16; 7:40).[20] It is interesting that Paul tends to avoid images for the Spirit that imply an impersonal power (e.g., water, oil,

---

[18]Gordon D. Fee, *God's Empowering Presence: The Holy Spirit in the Letters of Paul* (Peabody, Mass.: Hendrickson, 1994), pp. 14-15.

[19]Ephesians 5:18-19 may be thought to be an exception to this rule, but it is not. Being drunk with wine is opposed to being full/filled in spirit. The verb *plērousthe* in Ephesians 5:18 is a present passive, meaning "let yourselves be filled" (ongoing action). The author does not say "become filled." It is not a matter of receiving the Spirit or receiving a second dose of the Spirit but rather of being filled with the Spirit, who already dwells within the believer. The idea is of the Spirit penetrating one's whole being, inspiring one to sing various kinds of songs. Furthermore, the verb *plēroō* with the preposition *en* means "be filled by means of the Spirit," not be "full of the Spirit," as if the Spirit were the content of the filling. When one is fully inspired by the Spirit, one is led to sing songs, hymns, and spiritual songs. See Ben Witherington III, *Paul's Narrative Thought World: The Tapestry of Tragedy and Triumph* (Louisville: Westminster John Knox, 1994), p. 285.

[20]See Fee, *God's Empowering Presence*, p. 830.

wind, fire). We must concentrate in the first instance on Paul's stress on the
personal nature of the Holy Spirit.

Many times in the Pauline corpus "Spirit" or "Holy Spirit" is coupled
with verbs that indicate a personal agency is involved. For example, the Spirit
cries out from within us (Gal 4:6), has desires that oppose "the flesh" (Gal
5:17), leads us in God's ways (Rom 8:14; Gal 5:18), and bears witness with
our human spirits (Rom 8:16). The Spirit intercedes for us (Rom 8:26-27),
helps us when we are weak (Rom 8:26), strengthens believers (Eph 3:16), and
is grieved by human sinfulness (Eph 4:30). In addition, the Spirit searches all
things (1 Cor 2:10), even searching and knowing God's mind (1 Cor 2:11).
The Spirit dwells among and within believers (Rom 8:11; 1 Cor 3:16; 2 Tim
1:14), and the Spirit teaches the gospel to believers (1 Cor 2:13).

Another clear clue that Paul sees the Spirit as a person is that he predicates
the same activity of the Spirit as he does of Christ or of God. For example, in
1 Corinthians 12:6-11 God is said to produce a variety of activities in various
people, but notice that the Spirit is also said to produce these activities (1 Cor
12:11). Or again, in Romans 8:26 it is said that the Spirit intercedes for believers, and only a few verses later Christ is said to do so (Rom 8:34).[21]

At times, scholars have become confused about how Paul views the relationship between the Spirit and Christ because often he predicates the same
thing of both persons. We have life in Christ, but also in the Spirit (cf. Col
3:4 with Rom 8:11); joy in Christ, but also in the Spirit (cf. Phil 4:4 with
Rom 14:17); righteousness from Christ, but also from the Spirit (cf. Phil
3:8-9 with Rom 14:17). It is, however, a serious mistake to think that Paul
simply identified the Spirit with Christ or simply saw the Spirit as a noncor-
poreal manifestation of Christ—Christ's Spirit, so to speak, or the form in
which Christ now comes to believers after his glorification. No, Paul knows
quite well that Christ is the one who died and rose again, not the Holy Spirit,
and he is perfectly capable of distinguishing the two even when referring to
the current life of the believer. For instance, the Christian is meant to follow
the example of the "faithfulness of Jesus Christ" and have faith in Christ, but
Paul says nothing of following the example of the "faithfulness of the Spirit."
This is because Christ, in a way that is untrue of the Spirit, was a historical
figure who could set such a paradigm for other historical persons to follow.
Christ had a story that his followers could live out of and into, but the Spirit

does not.[22] It is quite true that Paul does reflect on the close working relationship between Christ and the Spirit, especially in the life of the believer, but it is simply untrue that he views the Spirit in strictly christological terms.

Against that latter conclusion Gordon Fee rightly points out the following: (1) Only three times does Paul refer to the Spirit of Christ. Paul primarily concentrates on the Spirit's relationship to the Father. In particular, it is the Father who sends the Spirit into believer's lives (e.g., 2 Cor 1:22; 5:5; Gal 4:6; 1 Thess 4:8). (2) The phrase "Spirit of God" or "Spirit of Christ" refers to the activity of God or Christ that is being conveyed to the believer by the Spirit. It is not an indication of some sort of ontological equation of Father or Son with the Spirit. (3) In particular, in the three places where Paul refers to the Spirit of Christ, he is referring to the work of Christ in some manner. (4) The point of phrases such as "Spirit of God" or "Spirit of Christ" is to distinguish this Spirit from other sorts of spirits or, to put it the other way around, to identify this Spirit through the Spirit's relationship to the Father or to Christ. Notice how in Romans 8:9-11 the Spirit of God is absolutely identified with the Spirit of Christ. It is one and the same Spirit. The difference is that now the Spirit carries on the work of Christ as well as the work of God. Or again, notice how in 1 Corinthians 2:12-16 to have the Spirit of God is the same as having the mind of Christ (or at least the former is the means to the latter). It is true that "Christ and his work give definition to the Spirit and his work in the Christian life";[23] it is not true that Christ and the Spirit are simply equated, even at the level of Christian experience. This brings us to the main text that has tended to cause the misunderstanding that "Christ = Spirit" in Paul's thought, 2 Corinthians 3:17-18.

To begin with, 2 Corinthians 3:17-18 is alluding to Exodus 34:34. What we have here is an imaginative application of an Old Testament text. A proper expansive rendering of the key text goes as follows: "Now the term 'Lord' here [in this text] means the Spirit, and where the Spirit of the Lord is, there is freedom." Notice how the Spirit and the Lord are actually distinguished in the second half of this key text. Two other texts, 1 Corinthians 6:17; 15:45, are also wrongly thought to suggest a "Spirit Christology." The former text is about spiritual union between the believer and Christ. Paul says, "Anyone united to the Lord becomes one spirit with him." Here "spirit" should not be capitalized, and most recent translations do not do so (e.g., the NRSV).

---

[22]See ibid., especially pp. 831-45.
[23]Ibid., p. 837. I am following Fee's lead throughout this portion of this chapter.

Paul is not saying that being united to the Lord can simply be equated with being united to the Spirit without remainder. Indeed, the Spirit does not come up for discussion here at all. There is instead a contrast between the physical union with the prostitute and the spiritual union with Christ.[24] The latter text is more difficult because it refers to the last Adam as a "life-giving spirit." The context here is a contrast with the first Adam, who was a living, breathing human being. Paul is referring to the risen Christ and what he became as a result of the resurrection. The background to the discussion here is found in 1 Corinthians 15:21-22, where Paul has said that all will be made alive through Christ because resurrection has come on the human scene through him and his experience. This is contrasted with how death came through the first Adam.

The issue in 1 Corinthians 15:45 is soteriological, not christological. Paul will go on to speak about a spiritual body that can be contrasted with the physical body. Christ, as the one who already has the resurrection or spiritual body, is the one who gives life to those who are in him. The parallelism with the first Adam is what has dictated the phrase "life-giving spirit" (as opposed to the living *psyche* that describes the first Adam).

> Paul makes a play on this language. The one who will "breathe" new life into these mortal bodies—with life-giving *pneuma* (as in Ezek 37:14) and thus make them immortal—is none other than the Risen Christ. . . . The concern . . . therefore, is not christological, as though Christ and the Spirit were somehow now interchangable terms for Paul. Indeed, he does not intend to say that Christ became *the* life-giving Spirit, but a life-giving spirit.[25]

One further possibility is worth pondering. Sometimes the word *pneuma* ("spirit") is used in the New Testament to simply refer to a supernatural being other than the Holy Spirit, such as an angel or a demon. The term apparently could be used in a generic sense to refer to any sort of supernatural being, even including a divine being such as Christ. We see this generic use of *pneuma* in texts such as Hebrews 1:14 and 1 Peter 3:19, in the former referring to angels, in the latter to demons or fallen angels. That latter text also stresses that Christ was made alive in the spirit after he died. Once one has

---

[24]Paul perhaps could have said that it is the Spirit who produces such a union between the believer and Christ, but even if this was what he meant, he would not be identifying Christ and the Spirit. The Spirit would be the means and Christ would be the end or object of the union or relationship. See below on 1 Corinthians 12.

[25]Fee, *God's Empowering Presence*, pp. 266-67.

passed into the spiritual realm, it appears that one could be called a "spirit." Perhaps Paul is using the term in this broader, more generic way in 1 Corinthians 15:45.

Having said all of this, I must also stress that Paul does indeed believe that the Spirit and Christ have a close relationship with each other and work closely together. For example, in Romans 8:26-34 Paul says that both Christ and the Spirit intercede for us, but the Spirit does so on earth from within the life of the believer, while Christ is in heaven interceding from there. When Paul uses the language of "indwelling," he can almost identify the function of Christ and the Spirit. Romans 8:9-10 refers to our having the Spirit of Christ, while Ephesians 3:16-17 actually refers to Christ within the believer. Had Paul worked out the nuances, he might have suggested that the Spirit conveys to the believer the very presence of Christ, even though Christ remains in heaven at the right hand of God.[26] "Thus when Paul in Galatians 2:20 . . . speaks of Christ as living in him, he almost certainly means 'Christ lives in me *by his Spirit.*'"[27] Paul will go on to stress immediately after Galatians 2:20-21 that the primary question about the Galatians (as about himself) is whether or not they had received the Spirit (Gal 3:2). For Paul as for Luke, the presence of the Spirit is the sine qua non of the Christian existence. The means of Christian existence is the presence of the Spirit, and the end or focus of that existence is Christ and his example.

This last point is made especially clearly in 1 Corinthians 12:13. In that text Paul says that by the one Spirit "we were all baptized into one body . . . and we were all made to drink of one Spirit." Notice the stress here on the one Spirit. Paul is making clear that there are not many spirits with which Christians have to deal. It is this one Spirit who joins a person to the body of Christ and provides the spiritual sustenance one needs thereafter to survive as a Christian. It is the one true Spirit of God who also prompts the true confession of Jesus as Lord by the believer (1 Cor 12:3).[28] There is no such thing as a true Christian whose life does not have the Holy Spirit.

Paul is at least functionally trinitarian in his thinking on these matters. We may illustrate this last point by looking at several key texts. The way one worships says a lot about a one's faith. In 2 Corinthians 13:13 we find

---

[26]See ibid., p. 838.

[27]Ibid.

[28]Notice how in 1 Corinthians 12:3 the Spirit is called both the "Spirit of God" and the "Holy Spirit."

a remarkable benediction: "The grace of the Lord Jesus Christ, the love of God, and the communion of the Holy Spirit be with you all." Here we see once more the dramatic effect that the death and resurrection of Jesus and the giving of the Holy Spirit had on a monotheistic Jew's understand of God.[29] The grace, love, and communion to which Paul refers are gifts of God. Yet each person of the Godhead can be said to make his own contribution to the life of the believer.

In fact, Paul finds it quite natural to speak in a trinitarian fashion. Notice, for example, how in 1 Corinthians 12:4-6 he refers to a variety of gifts, services and activities but one and the same Spirit, one and the same Lord, and one God involved. Or again notice when Paul gives thanks to God in 2 Thessalonians 2:13-15 that he does so because God chose them, the Spirit sanctified them, and they look forward to obtaining the glory of the Lord Jesus Christ. Ephesians 4:4-6 also comes readily to mind, where we hear of one Spirit, one Lord and one God and Father of all. Even if this is by a later Paulinist, it is clearly in the spirit of the functional trinitarianism that we find in Paul's earlier letters (cf. Rom 8:3-4; 1 Cor 2:4-5; 1 Thess 1:4-5).[30] It is therefore fully warranted to conclude that Paul sees the Holy Spirit not only as part of the divine identity but also as much more than an impersonal force or power. The Spirit is a teacher, a sanctifier, a guider, one who has desires for the believer, and one who produces gifts and fruit in the believer. To the activities of the Spirit in the life of the believer we now turn, having carefully demonstrated the personal and divine character of the Spirit in Paul's thinking.[31]

To judge by current discussion in the church, one might assume that Paul focuses his discussion on the gifts of the Spirit almost singularly and only occasionally refers to the fruit of the Spirit (once at Gal 5:22-23?). This conclusion is unjustified, not least because all of Paul's letters are occasional in nature, and if the Corinthians had not been struggling with the issue of spiritual gifts and their proper expression, we might not even have the discussion found in 1 Corinthians 12–14. With occasional letters, it is hard to know where the emphasis lies in Paul's thought world. What can be said

---

[29]See pp. 115-16 above on 1 Corinthians 8:6.

[30]See Fee, *God's Empowering Presence*, pp. 841-42.

[31]To a large extent, Fee is countering the efforts of various scholars, particularly James Dunn (*Jesus and the Spirit: A Study of the Religious and Charismatic Experience of Jesus and the First Christians as Reflected in the New Testament* [Grand Rapids: Eerdmans 1997]), who tend to talk about a Spirit Christology or all too often reduce the Spirit to an impersonal force or power.

with some certainty is that Paul is concerned with the character of his converts in all of his letters, and the fruit of the Spirit has to do with character traits and their manifestation in Christian living. Paul's belief that the way one exercises one's spiritual gifts should be normed by the fruit of the Spirit is shown quite clearly by the fact that he interrupts the discussion of the gifts in 1 Corinthians 12–14 to discourse at length on the chief fruit of the Spirit, love, and how love is the manner and means that should dictate how gifts are exercised. Accordingly, we will consider briefly what Paul says about the fruit of the Spirit first.

It is quite clear that the Spirit in question in Galatians 5:16-25 is the Holy Spirit. Paul is in the midst of a discussion about the tug of war between the Spirit and the flesh in the life of the believer. The Spirit is trying to pull and guide the believer in the direction of a more Christlike character. The believer who walks by the Spirit will not indulge the desires of the flesh, but the believer must continually submit to the guidance of the Spirit. A common observation that nonetheless needs emphasis is that Paul refers not to "fruits" of the Spirit but rather to "fruit." The implication is that he expects all of these traits to be manifest at some point and in some way in the normal Christian life. Paul is talking about certain character traits that should manifest themselves in interpersonal behavior. Paul discourses on individual aspects of this fruit in numerous places in his letters. For example, at Romans 5:5 he speaks of the love of God, which has been poured into the believer's heart by the Spirit. This reminds us that when Paul is speaking of the fruit of the Spirit, he is talking not about natural character traits but rather about something supernatural produced in the believer that may have little or nothing to do with one's natural inclinations or traits. The discourse on love in 1 Corinthians 13 sometimes has been said to involve a character description of Christ (particularly 1 Cor 13:4-7), and there can be little doubt that Paul sees the Spirit's work as conforming a Christian to the image of Christ.

The joy that Paul refers to in Galatians 5:22 is not a product of circumstances or temporary pleasures; it is a result of the internal work of the Spirit within a person (cf. Rom 14:17). It can even exist in the midst of suffering because it knows that eventually God will fulfill his promises (Rom 5:2-11). The peace that Paul refers to in Galatians 5:22 is chiefly peace with God wrought by Christ's death (cf. Col 3:15), but it also involves peace between believers and between believers and their neighbors. It is the polar opposite of a divisive spirit or a spirit of disorder and dissension (see Rom 15:33; 1 Cor 14:33). Patience involves having a slow fuse, not being quick to anger. It also involves a willingness to bear wrong in love (1 Cor 13:4).[32]

There are other traits that Paul refers to, but these are sufficient to show that Paul has in mind dispositions that should result in certain kinds of behaviors. Specifically, the fruit of the Spirit fosters fellowship and concord between believers, thus uniting the body of Christ. By contrast, sin is divisive and produce disorder and chaos in the community. Paul believes that God is already working into the believer, by means of the Holy Spirit, those virtues that Paul then expects and explains must be worked out in human relationships. If Christians walk in the Spirit, they will not merely avoid the indulgences of the flesh, they will model the character of Christ. This is an important point. The Spirit's work points toward Christ and seeks to shape Christians in Christ's image. We do not hear Paul speaking about focusing on the Spirit or having faith in the Spirit or following the example of the Spirit. The Spirit points away from himself to Christ. The Christian faith is meant to be christocentric, not pneumatocentric. The Spirit is God and Christ's agent in the believer. Bearing this is mind, we turn briefly to a discussion of the gifts of the Spirit in 1 Corinthians 12–14.

When Paul talks about the gifts of the Spirit, it is quite clear that he thinks very differently about them than he does about the fruit of the Spirit. About the latter, he expects all Christians to manifest all the fruit in one way or another, but as for the gifts, he is quite clear that they are parceled out differently to different persons by the Spirit. The rhetorical questions in 1 Corinthians 12:29-30 must be taken with absolute seriousness. Each question in the Greek begins with the word "not." The only appropriate response to each question is no. Paul is saying, for example, "Not all speak in tongues, do they?" He then expects no to be the answer to each of these questions. Not all prophesy, not all speak in tongues, not all perform miracles. Thus, gifts are distributed throughout the body for the common good. This in turn makes it necessary for Christians to rely on one another if the full complement of gifts are to be exercised in the body.

In this discussion 1 Corinthians 12:11 is a crucial verse. It tells us that all spiritual gifts are allotted and activated by the Holy Spirit, not some other source, and it is the Spirit who chooses which gift to allot to which person. It could hardly be clearer that Paul views the Spirit as a rational being capable of

---

[32]On this, see Witherington, *Paul's Narrative Thought World*, pp. 295-300.

making rational choices. It is also notable that Paul ranks the intelligible gifts highly, specifically gifts of preaching, prophecy, and teaching, ahead of gifts of healing or wonder working or speaking in tongues (1 Cor 12:28-31). In 1 Corinthians 14:1 he will urge pursuit of the gift of prophecy. Presumably, what he means by this is that one can petition the Spirit for some particular gift, but the Spirit will decide who gets what and when. Paul clearly believes that God is a God of order, and that gifts are given to enhance, not detract, from order in the body. Paul does not dismiss the gift of tongues; indeed, he says that he has and exercises this gift (1 Cor 14:18). But this angelic prayer language, he believes, should not be spoken in worship unless there is an interpreter to make it possible for all to benefit from the experience. One gets the impression that the majority of spiritual gifts are speech gifts that aid in the proclamation of the truth of the gospel in one way or another, though some gifts also focus on physical injuries and illnesses, and in the case of tongues there is a focus on enhancing the prayer and praise life of the individual Christian. The communal or more social gifts are stressed. It is interesting that Paul speaks in 1 Corinthians 14:16-17 of the apologetic value of a gift such as prophecy, but in the main the focus of most spiritual gifts (apart perhaps from the gift of evangelism or preaching) seems to be the building up of the body of Christ and its internal life.

What we have seen thus far in the New Testament is the emphasis on both the personal nature and the activities of the Holy Spirit. It is not possible to derive a pneumatic or Spirit Christology from these texts, as if Christ and the Spirit were one and the same person, but it is clear enough that authors such as Luke, Paul and the author of the Fourth Gospel do wish to stress how closely the Spirit and Christ, or the Spirit and God, or all three, work together.

It is important to stress, as 1 Corinthians 12 makes clear, that the juncture at which a believer gets the Holy Spirit in his or her life is the juncture at which that believer is spiritually united to the body of Christ through baptism by the Spirit. Reception of the Spirit and "joining the church" (to use an anachronistic phrase) happen at the same time. The Spirit is not received after conversion, nor is more of the Spirit received subsequent to conversion and being ingrafted into the body of Christ. Indeed, one cannot even truly confess "Jesus is Lord" from the heart without the prompting of the Spirit (1 Cor 12:3). The Spirit can more fully get hold of this or that aspect of a believer's life over time (renovating the mind, the heart, the will, the emotions), but the believer does not get more of the Spirit after being joined to the body of Christ. Obedience and openness to the Spirit who dwells already within are what leads to being "filled by the Spirit" for various and sundry spiritual pursuits, including praising God.

THE HOLY SPIRIT IN THE GENERAL EPISTLES AND REVELATION

Some documents in the New Testament make little or no mention of the Spirit. For example, in James and 2–3 John there are no references to the Spirit, and in Jude there is just one reference to praying in the Spirit (Jude 20), which may correlate with what Paul is talking about in Romans 8:15 when he speaks of the Spirit-led cry "Abba! Father!"[33] There is but one important passage in 1 Peter and one in 2 Peter about the Holy Spirit, and both have to do with the fact that the Spirit inspires prophetic speech. In 2 Peter 1:20-21 we read, "No prophecy of scripture is a matter of one's own interpretation, because no prophecy came by human will, but men and women moved by the Holy Spirit spoke from God." This text is interesting not least because it suggests that the source of the utterance is God the Father, but the motivator or inspirer who moved the person to speak at all was the Holy Spirit. The author does not believe that there is a significant human contribution other than men and women being mouthpieces. It is significant that the author mentions male and female prophets *(anthrōpoi)*, and here we may hear an echo of Joel 2:28 and perhaps also a memory of the inaugural Christian message given by Peter in Acts 2:14-36.

Even more significant is 1 Peter 1:10-12, which speaks of Old Testament prophets searching about the person and the time God had in mind when there was reference to sufferings and glory destined for the messiah. They were told that they were serving a later generation of believers, not their own generation, with such prophecies. The author of 1 Peter clearly believes in predictive prophecy. He calls the inspirer of such prophecy "the Spirit of Christ within them" (1 Pet 1:11). This phrase likely indicates the same Spirit referred to in 1 Peter 1:12: the Holy Spirit sent from heaven, who spoke the good news through human emissaries who brought the message to Peter's audience. Why, then, does the author refer to the Holy Spirit as the "Spirit of Christ"? Is he advocating a Spirit or pneumatic Christology? That is possible, but a more likely explanation is as follows: (1) the author believes that the same Holy Spirit who inspires Christian speakers in his era also inspired the

---

[33]On which, see pp. 113-14 above.

Old Testament prophets in their day; (2) he believes that since it was Christ who sent the Holy Spirit to believers in this era, the preexistent Christ may have been responsible for sending the Spirit before to inspire the prophets of old; (3) therefore the "Spirit of Christ" is the Spirit who came from Christ and inspires speech and prophecy about Christ in every era of human history. One further reason for not identifying Christ and Spirit in this text is that the author refers to the sufferings that Christ is destined to endure, something that he would not wish to predicate of the Spirit.

The book of Hebrews does not have a plethora of references to the Holy Spirit, but the ones present are significant. In Hebrews 2:4 we apparently hear something of an intertextual echo of 1 Corinthians 12:11. Here, however, we are told that it is God who distributes the gifts of the Holy Spirit and who does so as part of the testimony about the great salvation first declared by the Lord. The implicit trinitarianism of Hebrews 2:3-4 needs to be recognized. Jesus is the Lord (having already been said in Heb 1 to be the preexistent Son), who first declared that eschatological salvation had come, to which God the Father added his testimony by signs and wonders and by gifts of the Holy Spirit.

The second reference to the Holy Spirit comes at Hebrews 3:7, where we are told that it is the Holy Spirit who "says" what we find in Psalm 95:7-11. From a Christian perspective, the Holy Spirit is the Spirit of prophecy in all ages, even though these early Christians believed that the Spirit was not given as a permanent possession prior to the time of Jesus. We see this very same phenomenon at Hebrews 10:16-17, where the Spirit is the one speaking, offering the material found in Jeremiah 31:33-34.

Hebrews 6:4 is a crucial text when the issue of the perseverance of believers comes up. We are told that a person who has shared in the Holy Spirit but then turns away cannot be restored again to repentance. It is also said that such a person has been enlightened, has tasted of the heavenly gift, and has tasted the goodness of God's word and of the powers of the age to come. A more complete description of a Christian person is hard to imagine. For this author, as for Paul and others in the New Testament, having shared in the Holy Spirit is the sine qua non for declaring a person to be a Christian. Notice that the author does not speak of having a share of the Holy Spirit, as if the Spirit were a substance that could be parceled out to various people, but literally says, "having become a participator of the Holy Spirit." One takes part *in*, rather than takes a part *of*, the life in the Spirit.

As is well known, the author of Hebrews engages in quite a lot of typological exegesis of Old Testament texts and institutions. At Hebrews 9:8, during the course of explaining about the tabernacle and the priest's role, he refers to the fact that the way into the eternal sanctuary had not yet been disclosed while the first tabernacle was still standing. He adds that it is the Holy Spirit who indicates by the existence of the tabernacle that the ultimate state of affairs had not yet come to pass. This appears to mean that the Holy Spirit was the one who inspired the words of the Scriptures about the instructions for the high priest and for making atonement. The Spirit knew in advance that a greater tabernacle was to come, and by the limitations of the first tabernacle and its continued existence there was an indicator that more was yet to come. The first tabernacle was but an antetype of the true sanctuary and was less perfect in nature and in effect (dealing only with unintentional sins) than the one that was to come. Here again we see the Christian notion that the third person of the divine identity preexisted and was active in Israel's history. At Hebrews 10:29 we find the interesting phrase "Spirit of grace." This may be a reference to the Holy Spirit, who was being outraged by the rejection of Christ and his atoning death by some. Notice the predication of the personal emotion "outrage" to the Spirit.

The last document to consider is the last book of the New Testament, Revelation. Here we are embedded in the world of apocalyptic where there are always some surprises. In terms of basic perspective, John seems to vary little from other New Testament writers. He believes that the Holy Spirit is God or Christ's agent or representative on earth, since both the Father and the Son are now in heaven. This is why, for instance, it is both the Spirit and the bride who bid Christ the bridegroom to return to earth at the close of the book (Rev 22:17). The Spirit speaks with and through the church and from the church's perspective.

John, heavily influenced as he is by the Old Testament, finds some creative ways to talk about the Holy Spirit. As Richard Bauckham suggests, it appears likely that his use of the seven spirits of the seven churches image is indebted to Zechariah 4:1-14. Indeed, Bauckham stresses, "It seems to have been the key Old Testament passage for John's understanding of the role of the Spirit in the divine activity in the world."[34] The vision is intended to teach Zerubbabel that it is by God's spirit that things will truly be accomplished (Zech

---

[34]Richard Bauckham, *The Theology of the Book of Revelation* (NTT; Cambridge: Cambridge University Press, 1993), p. 110.

4:6). The image chosen is of seven lamps with seven lips (Zech 4:2), but in a change of the metaphor, Zechariah also speaks of the seven eyes of the Lord, which range throughout the whole earth (Zech 4:10). As Bauckham notes, one of the main questions that Revelation seeks to answer for its audiences is how God's plan will be worked out on earth, given the beastly empire and seemingly irresistible evil and power of it. John's answer is the same as Zechariah's: the Spirit of God will accomplish it. But there is more to the vision in Zechariah than is immediately evident on the surface. It is likely that John would have connected the seven lamps with the seven branched lampstand that stood in the temple (see Ex 25:31-40). Thus, it is no surprise that in John's vision he sees the seven lamps that he identifies as the seven spirits burning before the throne of God (= the mercy seat of God in the holy of holies). But we must remember that the heavenly sanctuary was seen as the model for the earthly one, and in fact Exodus 40:25 speaks directly of the seven lamps that burned before the Lord in the earthly tabernacle.

If we have any doubts that the seven spirits belong to the divine identity, Revelation 1:4-5 offers a trinitarian blessing that includes the seven spirits before the throne. But the seven spirits are associated closely not only with God but also with Christ, for in Revelation 5:6 the Lamb is said to have seven eyes that are the seven spirits of God sent out into all the earth (echoing Zech 4:10b). As Bauckham observes, the "eyes of Yahweh" indicate not only that God knows all that happens on earth, but also that he is able to act powerfully on the basis of this knowledge wherever he chooses. Thus, "the seven Spirits are the presence and power of God on earth bringing about God's kingdom by implementing the Lamb's victory throughout the world."[35] But there is more to the seven spirits than just being a force or a power. John indicates by this bifurcation of the Spirit that each of his seven churches has full measure of the Holy Spirit; none are short changed in terms of the power or presence or revelation of God. And as elsewhere in the New Testament where we have seen the Spirit having a role of intercession for believers,[36] so here the seven spirits represent the Spirit interceding before the throne of God on behalf of these persecuted churches. Only persons, not forces, can so intercede.[37] But

---

[35]Ibid., p. 113. I disagree, however, with Bauckham's further conclusion that the Spirit is then seen as the divine power that is now the Spirit of Christ or the manner of Christ's presence on earth. It seems clear to me that in fact the Spirit is seen as a person distinguishable from Christ, as the final presentation of the Spirit and the bride speaking in Revelation 22:17 suggests.

[36]See pp. 368-71 above.

[37]We should also keep in mind that the generic term *spirit*, whether referring to Christ or to some

the Spirit does not only represent the church to God; the Spirit also represents Christ to the church, serving as Christ's agent, as Revelation 5:6 suggests.

Apart from the discussion of the seven spirits, there are fourteen references to the Holy Spirit in Revelation, all having to do with the Spirit being the source of John's prophecy. Without question, the dominant image of the Spirit in this book is as the Spirit of prophecy, which is no surprise in light of how Jewish this work is. It is perhaps possible to make a distinction between the seven spirits that say something about the Spirit's mission to the world (see Rev 5:6) and the other references to the Holy Spirit that focus on the activity of the Spirit within and addressing the church. In just one of these fourteen references, Revelation 19:10, there is actually some question about whether the Holy Spirit is meant. There an angel upbraids John for trying to worship him and concludes by saying that the testimony to Jesus is "the spirit of prophecy." It is not clear to me that this is anything other than a metaphorical use of the term *pneuma* meaning something like the "essence" or "focus" or "gist" of prophecy.

Four of the other thirteen references refer to the actual moment of inspiration when John received a vision through the Spirit. Thus, in Revelation 1:10 and Revelation 4:2 we are told that he was "in the Spirit," and two other times that the angel carried him away by means of the Spirit (Rev 17:3; 21:10 [cf. Ezek 3:12-14]). The way this is described suggests an ecstatic and overpowering experience of some sort that had a visionary component. As Bauckham notes, these four references are strategically placed so as to make clear that the whole of John's visionary experiences came through the agency of the Holy Spirit. But Bauckham appears also to be correct that the "Spirit does not give the content of the revelation, but the visionary experience which enables John to receive the revelation."[38] The revelation comes from God or Christ but by means of the agency of the Spirit. As we have seen in Revelation 22:17, the Spirit is able to speak for himself (see also Rev 14:13). John is quite capable of distinguishing the Spirit from Christ, and it would be a mistake to see the Spirit as simply the mouthpiece of either God or Christ. The Spirit is seen as a distinguishable personal entity, working on earth in close consort with God and Christ in heaven.

---

other supernatural being such as an angel or demon (see pp. 348-50 above), refers in such cases to a personal entity, not a mere force or power. This is true here in Revelation 1 as well.

[38]Bauckham, *Theology of the Book of Revelation*, p. 116. Here and throughout this section I am indebted to Bauckham's insights.

The book of Revelation provides yet one more example of how Old Testamental images and ideas affected early Christian portrayal of the Spirit. This did not, however, prevent them from emphasizing in various ways the personal nature of the divine Spirit, nor did it prevent them from making appropriate distinctions between the Spirit and Christ or God. The book of Revelation is in some ways the most explicitly trinitarian of all New Testament books, and it shows where the discussion of the Spirit could and would be furthered in the postcanonical period.

CONCLUSIONS FOR CHAPTERS 4–6: GOD-TALK IN THE NEW TESTAMENT

One of the immediate impressions one gets from working through all the references to Son, Father, and Spirit in the New Testament is that there is a lot of commonality in this material, and not just between the Synoptic Gospels. For one thing, all of the writers of the New Testament know perfectly well that Father, Son, and Spirit should all be treated as persons and referred to in a personal way, even though the evangelists dutifully report that the impersonal way of referring to the Spirit continued during the period of Jesus' ministry and was only countered by Jesus himself.

The second major impression that comes from examining this material is how much more often the New Testament writers refer not only to the Messiah/Christ but also to the Holy Spirit than other early Jewish documents do. The writers of the New Testament are under the conviction that not only has the Messiah come, but so also has the eschatological Spirit, and furthermore that these two persons have led to a different way of relating to the God of the Old Testament, including calling him "Abba," as Jesus did. The "God" language has changed for all these writers, and they all are Jews, with the possible exceptions of Luke and the author of 2 Peter. I submit that when the "God" language has changed as much as we find in the New Testament in comparison to other early Jewish documents, then certainly a major change has occurred in the symbolic universe of these writers. They even view God very differently. God can be spoken of in three different personal ways, and these persons can be distinguished, not only in function but also in other ways. The language of "Father, Son, Spirit" is not interchangeable. For example, it was not the Father or the Spirit who came in the flesh or died on the cross, and it was not the Son who came down at Pentecost.

Also notable is that we see no evidence that the New Testament writers took dramatically incompatible views of the Father, the Son, or the Spirit. There are differences in emphasis, nuance, and stress, but nothing like the differences that arose later between orthodox Christians and Gnostic Christians in the late second century and the third century when it came to talking about God. This is not a surprise, since all the writers of the New Testament are monotheists deeply indebted to Jewish monotheism and not indebted, or very little indebted, to Platonic or other sorts of Greek speculations about God. Christianity is a sectarian development of early Judaism, not a syncretistic combination of Judaism with some other extant forms of Semitic or Greco-Roman religion. Of course, the Judaism that Christianity grew out of was to some degree Hellenized, and this too is reflected in the New Testament (e.g., Luke-Acts and Hebrews), but nevertheless none of the New Testament books look like foreign bodies in an otherwise rather homogeneous collection. For example, we find no evidence of pantheism in the New Testament, unlike in the later *Gospel of Thomas* ("Cleave the wood, and I am there" [*Gos. Thom.* 77]). The ideational boundaries of early Christianity when it comes to God-talk are rather clear and narrow and Jewish, and perhaps equally importantly they are viewed as fulfilling Old Testament ideas and texts and so are seen as within the Jewish orbit of ideas, symbols, and narrative thought world.

If we ask what it was that caused the seismic shift in the thinking of these early Jews such that they do not simply sound like Philo or Josephus or the Qumranites, the answer must be the Christ-event and its sequel at that Pentecost celebration in A.D. 30. The impact of Jesus—his life, death, teachings, resurrection, and sending of the Spirit—indeed changed things dramatically for these early Jews. Their theological expression reflected their experiences, including the experiences of the risen Jesus, and those experiences were profound and led to the worship of Jesus already within the Jerusalem community of Jesus' followers after Easter. They believed not only that Jesus had come, but also that the eschatological age of fulfillment had come, and they had personally received the promised Holy Spirit into their lives. The new and final covenantal arrangement between God and his people had begun, and this meant also the inflowing of Gentiles into God's people. The only question was "On what basis?"

All of this also changed these writer's views of the future, both proximate and more remote. So we must explore New Testament eschatology as represented in the various witnesses, but first we must deal with perhaps the most crucial concept, outside of the God-talk, in the New Testament: the concept of salvation. Here already we can stress that the "God" language itself suggests that the three persons of the Godhead worked together as a team in the matter of salvation. The Father had a will and a plan, the Son actualized and made possible the implementation of the plan, the Spirit implemented the plan both outside of (convicting and convincing the world of sin) and within the believer. This plan was that saved human beings be conformed to the image of the Son and so glorify God as they were originally intended and created to do. The aim and end of salvation is glorification both in the sense of believers being conformed to the image of Christ and in the sense that they will be prompted to do what they were created to do: praise their Maker while they have breath. The New Testament writers are already doing doxology when we catch up with them in these documents, for theologizing and ethicizing to the glory of God is doxology. We now must more fully explore the salvific side of things, which made possible this praise.

7

THE NEW TESTAMENT CONSENSUS ON SALVATION AND THE END OF ALL THINGS

The salvation Jesus proclaims during his earthly ministry is a present reality that already affects people "today." . . . It restores them to health and releases them from Satan's bondage; it offers forgiveness and effects a reversal of fortunes. It is also a future reality that will not be fully experienced until the final manifestation of God's Kingdom.

FRANK J. MATERA[1]

SALVATION IN THE NEW TESTAMENT: CONVERSION, SANCTIFICATION, GLORIFICATION

Mention the word *conversion* to most modern persons, and they think of a conversion experience: "I got saved" = "I converted to some religion." This is understandable in a highly individualistic culture, but salvation looked very different in antiquity, and the context of the New Testament discussion is crucial. Salvation is not viewed in the New Testament as a one-time prepackaged event for an individual with an all-expenses-paid trip to heaven guaranteed therein. Salvation has to be understood in the context of the way ancient people viewed human personality and change. To say that the Jesus movement was a conversionist sect would be true, but what were people being converted from and to? Some preliminary remarks are in order.

Gender, generation, and geography provided the major clues to identity and personality in antiquity. People assumed that these three factors affected, indeed largely determined, human personality. Ancient people did not believe that personality developed over time or with education and aging. They believed that a person was born with a certain personality and was stuck with

---

[1]Frank J. Matera, *New Testament Theology: Exploring Diversity and Unity* (Louisville: Westminster John Knox, 2007), p. 71.

it thereafter. Of course, it was understood that there were exceptions to the rule. There were such things as deviants or outcasts. There were those who were not true Romans or true Jews. I submit that Paul, and Jesus before him, were in the process of deconstructing some of the basic assumptions about human beings based on gender, generation, and geography. This is in fact precisely how texts such as Romans 2:28-29 and Mark 10:13 function. In other words, both Jesus and Paul believed that radical change via the new birth could happen to a person, overcoming the stereotypes and stigmas about gender, generation, and geography. A person could start over, indeed should start over (2 Cor 5:17; Gal 3:28), but must be ready to be rejected by a world that would go on judging people on the basis of gender, generation, and geography. One must be ready to be despised and rejected as a deviant. Such was the nature of one's life as a member of a conversionist sect.

What must be stressed about this change, however, is that conversion did not make person a radical individualist. It was not a matter of leaving a group and a group mentality and becoming a "lone ranger." To the contrary, it was a matter of joining a new family or community or body of people from which one derived essential aspects of one's new identity.

There was, however, another crucial aspect to this change. The change agent was seen to be a particular person, Jesus Christ, and personality in the group of his followers henceforth would be modeled on Christ himself. In some sense, the followers of Jesus would be incorporated into a spiritual reality that involved direct union with Christ, so becoming his body. Indeed, they would take Christ into their very beings, as the continued celebration of the Lord's Supper would stress. They would be in Christ, and Christ would be in them. In other words, salvation involved, so to speak, a close encounter of the first order with a particular person, not some particular process or ritual or even one specific form of experience that all needed to go through in order to be "saved."

The story of Christ would not just be recapitulated in the life of believers, but in a sense they would become a part of the continuation of Christ's story by being his body on the earth. Even statements such as "Saul, Saul, why do you persecute me," spoken by the heavenly Christ to Saul the persecutor of Christians (Acts 9:4) in a vision, could make sense in this context. Saul was not merely persecuting Christ's followers, he was in fact persecuting the Jewish messiah himself thereby. Thus we need to stress that conversion or salvation, though it was something that could happen to an individual or a family or a group of people, was always conversion into a new community, a new body of believers. A new creature in Christ became part of an ongoing creation known as the community of Christ. And salvation involved far more than a spiritual change of orientation in someone's life. Indeed, for most ancient persons, the term *salvation* indicated things such as being rescued, healed, redeemed from bondage and the like. It did not refer just to some spiritual change or change of religious thinking or orientation in a person's life. Perhaps the place to begin exploring this issue is by considering the use of "salvation" language by the one real salvation historian in the New Testament, Luke.

Although it will seem strange to almost all moderns, it is true that very little of ancient religion, particularly pagan religion but also Jewish religion, had to do with attempts to be or become "saved" or to obtain eternal life in some form. The salvation that most ancients sought was from disease, disaster, death in this lifetime, and the redemption that they most cried out for was from some social bondage such as slavery, not some internal personal bondage called "sin." The questions that the ancients asked of the Pythia at Delphi had to do with being kept safe in childbirth or on a journey or being protected from some danger or disease. Ancient peoples were not looking for a personality transplant or transformation, on the whole. As Ramsay Mac-Mullen points out, the chief business of even the healing cults among the ancient religions was to make the sick well or to protect the well from harm or curses and the like.[2] Paul, it will be remembered, wrote all of his letters in this sort of Greco-Roman context, and he provides us with our earliest New Testament documents. In that world, "'savior' . . . or 'salvation' had to do with health or other matters of this earth, not of the soul for life eternal."[3] In fact, one could say pretty much the same thing about religion in the preexilic period of Israel's existence. It would be hard to overemphasize this point. The most that the majority of pagans hoped for was to be immortalized in someone's memories, memoirs, poetry, epitaphs and the like, and the most that the patriarchs hoped for was to be gathered to their fathers and have their lives and legacy carried on through their children.

Assurances of immortality for the living, much less insistence on everlasting life beginning here and now before one died, is very difficult to find in

---

[2]Ramsay MacMullen, *Paganism in the Roman Empire* (New Haven: Yale University Press, 1981), p. 49.

[3]Ibid., p. 57.

Greco-Roman literature. Indeed, it would be hard to name one deity on Mount Olympus to whom one and all would turn in order to be saved from extinction in the afterlife. This was not the job of these gods. Even dramatic initiation rites into the mysteries promised immediate results in the here and now—for example, a restoration of fertility as one bathed in the blood of a bull. These were initiation rites, and for the most part they could not be called "conversion experiences," though doubtless extra votive offerings would be given to the god if the results desired transpired. Even some of the new religions on the rise in the first century A.D., such as the emperor cult, though they were all about worshiping and honoring the emperor, could not be said to entail people being "converted" to the emperor or "saved" by him in any spiritual or afterlife kind of way. The salvation that the emperor was offering was a stable and pacified world order with safety where business as usual could go on. It seems to me that Luke is writing his two-volume work with one eye on this larger context and wishes to make clear that the salvation being offered in Christ was not of the same ilk as what the emperor was offering.[4]

Christianity was and would be viewed for a long time in the Roman Empire as yet another Eastern religion, like the worship of Isis, for example, which was imported into the western part of the Empire from its eastern provinces. What new thing did Christianity offer that one could not find in the worship of Isis or even in early Judaism? Well, the worship of Isis was said to bring many benefits, but all of them were this-worldly. For instance, when Isis promises "new life" to a supplicant, it is not everlasting life or even life beyond the grave but rather a forestalling or averting of death and therefore more of the life that one already had.[5] This could take the form of Isis providing cures for diseases or rescue from danger. It is interesting that the main god of healing in the Greco-Roman world is called by the same term used for Jesus in Luke-Acts, *sōtēr* ("savior"). It will not be a surprise, then, that healing is part of what Luke predicates of Jesus when he casts him as the Savior of the world.

There are a few hints that some pagans were interested in the afterlife and believed that a religion could help them have a better afterlife. Cicero,

---

[4]Although, he may have seen the new Christian faith as in competition with the emperor cult for devotees.
[5]See Ben Witherington III, *The Acts of the Apostles: A Socio-Rhetorical Commentary* (Grand Rapids: Eerdmans, 1998), pp. 824-25.

for example, speaks of the Eleusinian mysteries as providing joy in this life and shows how to die with better hopes in the next life (*Leg.* 2.36). But even in this case nothing is said about repentance or mortification of sins here that leads to benefits in the afterlife. Almost all ancient religion was seen as a means of obtaining some benefit in this life, not merely in the life to come.

What does Luke say to Theophilus about salvation in a context like this? For one thing, he is prepared to use the terms *save* and *salvation* in the mundane senses in which they were used in the larger context. So, for example, *sōtēria* ("salvation") in Acts 27:34 refers to safety, not Christian conversion (note the NET translation: "survival"). There are also cases in Luke-Acts where *sōzō* ("save") means "heal" (e.g., Acts 4:9). Even the phrase in Luke's Gospel "your faith has saved you" often means "you have been healed through your trust in me" (Lk 8:48; 18:42). The same can be said about a text such as Luke 6:9, where Jesus is asking if it is lawful to heal on the Sabbath. Of course, there are also more pregnant uses of the word *save*. In Luke 7:50, for example, no physical healing is involved, but a woman's sins are said to be forgiven, and so Jesus says, "Your faith has saved you." New creation in Christ could have both spiritual and physical dimensions.

In light of the speech of Jesus in Luke 4:18-21, where Isaiah 61:1-2; 58:6 are cited, it is fair to say that Luke sees healing as part of the Christian program of salvation now that the eschatological age is here, the age of the fulfillment of the ancient prophecies and promises. One can say that healing is seen as a viable aspect of salvation received in and from Jesus but not always as a needed or necessary consequence of that salvation. Some who were healed by Jesus were not necessarily saved in the more profound sense, and some who were saved and had sins forgiven were not necessarily physically healed (see, e.g., Acts 10:34-38). This means that we cannot simply presume that Luke loads all the meanings of "save" into any one example. And definitely there is an emphasis on salvation involving conversion especially in Acts. Yet this Christian salvation does not promise exemption from future suffering or danger or imprisonment (see Acts 14:19; 16:16-40).

Here is a good place to say something about Paul's own conversion as told by Luke. Exhibit A of what a conversion looked like, at least from Luke's perspective, is the conversion of Saul of Tarsus, a tale told three times over in Acts.

A CLOSER LOOK: THE TRIPLE ANATOMY OF SAUL'S CONVERSION

Luke presents three renditions of Saul's conversion story.[6]

Acts 9:1ff.	Acts 22:1ff.	Acts 26:1ff
third person	first person	first person
Luke's summary from talking with Paul	In Hebrew/Aramaic; Paul's Greek summary given to Luke?	Spoken by Paul to Festus and Agrippa (Luke present).
Letters from the high priest to synagogues to bring Christians back to Jerusalem (9:1-2).	Letters from the high priest and council to bring back Christians to Jerusalem for punishment (22:5).	Authorization from the chief priests to imprison saints (26:10).
Light from heaven flashed about him (9:3).	At noon, great light from heaven shone about me (22:6).	At midday, I saw light from heaven, brighter than the sun, shining about me and those with me (26:13).
He fell to the ground and heard a voice (9:4).	I fell to the ground and heard a voice (22:7).	We all fell to the ground, and I heard a voice speaking in Hebrew (26:14).
"Saul, Saul, why do you persecute me?" "Who are you, sir?" "I am Jesus, whom you are persecuting" (9:4-5).	Same as 9:4-5 (22:7-8).	Same as 9:4-5 except, "It hurts you to kick against the goads" and "The Lord said, 'I am Jesus, whom you are persecuting" (26:14-15).
"Rise and enter the city, and you will be told what to do" (9:6).	"What shall I do, sir?" "Rise, and go into Damascus, and there you will be told all that is appointed for you to do" (22:10).	"Rise and stand on your feet; for I have appeared to you for this purpose, to appoint you to serve and bear witness to the things in which you have seen me and to those in which I will appear to you, delivering you from the people and from the Gentiles—to whom I send you to open their eyes, that they may turn from darkness to light and from the power of Satan to God, that they may receive forgiveness of sins and a place among those who are sanctified by faith in me" (26:16-18).

[6]The following chart is adapted from Ben Witherington III, *The New Testament Story* (Grand Rapids: Eerdmans, 2004), pp. 157-58.

Those traveling with him stood speechless, hearing the voice but seeing no one (9:7).	Those with me saw the light but did not hear the voice of the one who was speaking to me (22:9).	
Saul arose from the ground; when his eyes were opened, he could see nothing; they led him by the hand to Damascus; for three days he was without sight and neither ate nor drank (9:8-9).	I could not see because of the brightness of the light; I was led by the hand by those who were with me and came into Damascus (22:11).	
Ananias had a vision of Christ, who instructed him concerning Saul (9:10-16).	Ananias (no vision of Christ mentioned) came to me and said, "Brother Saul, receive your sight" (22:12-13).	
Ananias went to Saul, laid hands on him, and said, "Brother Saul, the Lord Jesus, who appeared on the road by which you came, has sent me that you may regain your sight and be filled with the Holy Spirit" (9:17).	Ananias said, "The God of our fathers appointed you to know his will, to see the Just One, and to hear a voice from his mouth; for you will be a witness for him to all people of what you have seen and heard" (22:14-15).	
Something like scales fell from Saul's eyes, and he regained his sight; then he arose and was baptized (9:18).	Ananias said, "And now why do you wait? Rise and be baptized, and wash away your sins, calling on his name" (22:16).	
Saul took food and was strengthened (9:19).		"I was not disobedient to the heavenly vision" (26:19).

Since I have analyzed the similarities and differences in these three accounts elsewhere, here we will focus on the implications of the story in regard to the matter of the opening event of salvation: conversion, and in this case Saul's conversion. I agree with C. K. Barrett's view: "This was a radical change of religious direction, and it was accompanied by as radical a change of action: the active persecutor became an even more active preacher and evangelist. If such radical changes do not amount to conversion it is hard to know what would do so."[7] One can say that Paul moved ideologically from being a Pharisaic Jew to being a Christian Jew, but the seeds of separation, and being part of a new hybrid entity that would be rejected by most Jews, were already planted in this initial crisis event in the life of Saul.

Early Christianity was, at least in some of its prominent forms, enough of a radical departure from early Judaism in regard to Torah, temple, territory, messiah, Holy Spirit, and some other things that it is impossible not to speak of a conversion in Saul's case. However, his was not a conversion from being Jewish to being Christian. This was a conversion from being a Pharisaic Jew to being a Christian one. This is different from being a partially Christianized Pharisaic Jew, such as we see in Acts 15:1-2. And it would be Paul who, more clearly than most others, saw the implications of this. He knew that this meant leaving certain things behind. No one who can go on to say that as a follower of Jesus he was capable of being the Jew to the Jew and the Gentile to the Gentile so that by all means he might save some (1 Cor 9:20-21) is still simply a Jew as he was before. Rather, he can distinguish himself from most Jews and from much of Judaism, thus furthering the sectarian split off of the Christian group of Jews.

Early Christianity proved to be an unexpected development of Jewish messianism and one that was largely rejected by the synagogue. In calling Jews to worship a crucified Jewish manual laborer from Nazareth who clearly was a human being, there was a challenge to go beyond or further develop early Jewish monotheism, just as there was a challenge to transcend certain aspects of ethnic and social distinctiveness (in regard to circumcision, purity and food laws, temple piety and pilgrimages). This surely stretched all normal definitions of Judaism past the breaking point. Alan Segal was right to subtitle his important study of Paul *The Apostolate and Apostasy of Saul the Pharisee*.[8] Of course, Paul and Luke did not see the matter that way; they saw Christianity as the completion or most true development of Old Testament religion and faith, but as far as we can tell, most early Jews disagreed with this conclusion.

---

[7]C. K. Barrett, *A Critical and Exegetical Commentary on the Acts of the Apostles* (2 vols.; ICC; Edinburgh: T & T Clark, 1994), 1:442. An in-depth analysis of this material can be found in my commentary *The Acts of the Apostles: A Socio-Rhetorical Commentary* (Grand Rapids:Eerdmans, 1998), pp. 307-14.

[8]Alan Segal, *Paul the Convert: The Apostolate and Apostasy of Saul the Pharisee* (New Haven: Yale University Press, 1990).

Saul's conversion involved an event that led to a process at the end of which it could be said that Saul had become a follower of Jesus. Notice immediately that Saul's name does not change on the road to Damascus; that change happens on the mission field years later, according to Acts 13:9, and in response to having to interact with Gentiles. By A.D. 49, when Paul begins to write letters, he always and everywhere calls himself by that name, not by his Hebrew name, nor does he anywhere relate the change of name to his conversion any more than Luke did. So, change there was at the conversion, but it did not involve a renaming by Jesus or by Paul himself. In fact, Richard Bauckham has even argued that since *saulus* in Latin means "to walk like a harlot," *Paulus* was the chosen Latinized version of *Saul*, probably not a new name at all.

The experience of Saul on Damascus road is depicted as, in a limited sense, a shared experience. His companions saw a light and heard a sound, but the human figure and the audible intelligible voice only Paul heard and saw, and it blinded him but apparently did not have this effect on his companions. What happened to Saul on that day must be called a visionary experience, and that is precisely how Paul himself describes it: an event in which God was pleased "to reveal his Son in me" (Gal. 1:16). This was to present a problem, for Jesus had already ascended to heaven, and so Paul's resurrection appearance story was different from that of the earlier eyewitnesses of the risen Lord. Yet Paul clearly ranks his experience with theirs in his list of appearances of the risen Christ in 1 Corinthians 15:5-8.

The appearance of Jesus that Paul received was last and was the strangest and most unexpected of all. Some apparently saw it as bogus as well, or else Paul probably would not have had to defend his conversion and call to be an apostle so vigorously while admitting that he was like an *ektrōma*, someone hastened into the world of Christian life and service in an unseemly fashion, as one abnormally or prematurely born (1 Cor 15:8).

It is to Luke's credit that he indicates that Saul's conversion was not completed in that instance on the road to Damascus. He was led into Damascus, and it was some days before he was cured of his blindness, arose and was baptized, and received the Holy Spirit. This ensuing set of events after the event on the road to Damascus is seen as part of the process called the "conversion of Saul." But there can be no doubt that a radical change was wrought in him.

When Paul chooses to talk about conversion, he says this: "Therefore, if anyone is in Christ, there is a new creature/creation. The old is gone, the new is here!" (2 Cor 5:17). Notice Paul does not say "the old is passing away" but rather "the old has passed away." This is the language of radical change. But interestingly enough, conversion is seen by one after another of the New Testament writers as only the beginning of the change, as often they are apt to speak of salvation as something to be fully obtained in the future. There are many accounts of conversion in Acts and elsewhere in the New Testament, and what Paul refers to as becoming a "new creature/creation" the writer of the Fourth Gospel speaks of as being "born again" or "born from above," which means much the same even though the imagery differs. But it is telling that none of these New Testament writers think that the matter is complete as a result of conversion. It is, instead, more of a work in progress. This is quite different from pagan rituals where there was believed to be wrought some miraculous change in health or virility or the like. Pagans saw such initiation rituals as one-time events, and of course they hoped for enduring results, but they did not speak of that initiation as the beginning of a process of salvation that would only culminate much later.

To put it another way, the New Testament writers no more believed in completely realized salvation in the here and now than they believed in completely realized eschatology in the here and now (on which, see below). Conversion is the doorway into salvation, and then there is a process of sanctification that also is a part of salvation, and finally there is the last act of salvation, which entails full conformity to the image of Christ, according to Paul, and this comes about only by means of resurrection, such that one's body is as eternally saved as the rest of one's person. A Christian could say, "I have been saved, I am being saved, and I will be saved." I need to put some flesh on these bare bones and provide some evidence for the assertion that this is how the writers of the New Testament viewed the matter. Since there is little dispute that the writers of the New Testament saw conversion as initial salvation, as did Jesus (see, e.g., Lk 19:1-10, where Jesus speaks of his mission as seeking and saving the lost, and he says that salvation came to Zacchaeus's house that day, as evidenced by his repentance and giving back various funds), we need not dwell on those sorts of passages. Texts such as Romans 1:16 (proclamation leads to salvation of Jews or Gentiles), Romans 10:10 (conversion and confession lead to salvation), and 2 Corinthians 6:2 ("now is the day of salvation") are too common to dwell on here.

In Romans 13:11 Paul speaks of salvation as something that is coming in the future. It is nearer now than it was in the past, but still it lies in the future.

In 2 Corinthians 7:10 Paul, addressing his recalcitrant converts in Corinth, speaks of bringing them to fresh repentance by way of a godly sorrow that "leads to salvation." They had already been converted, but beyond that, Paul wanted them to be "saved to the uttermost." Philippians 2:12 is the well-known verse where Paul exhorts Christians in Philippi to work out their salvation with fear and trembling as God works in their midst to will and to do. Here salvation is seen as something that the audience must participate in or work out, as God is working it in. In common parlance, he is talking about the process of sanctification, which is synergistic, involving effort both by God and by believers.

In 1 Thessalonians 5:8 Paul speaks of the hope of salvation, here seen as neither in the past nor in process but rather as something in the future. Similarly, in 1 Thessalonians 5:9 Paul contrasts suffering wrath in the future with obtaining salvation in the future. Here we should compare 2 Timothy 2:10, where Paul says that he endures various things so that his converts may obtain the salvation and the glory that are in Christ. Hebrews 1:14 speaks of believers inheriting salvation in the future, and in Hebrews 9:28 salvation is something that believers await and is linked to the return of Christ. In 1 Peter 1:5 we hear of a salvation ready to be revealed in the last time, and 1 Peter 1:9 speaks of the salvation of the believers' life as the "end" or goal of their current Christian faith. Salvation according to 1 Peter 2:2 is something that new Christians need to grow into or toward.

Of course, it is also perfectly clear that none of the New Testament writers see salvation as just some sort of self-help program. As Revelation 12:10; 19:1 make clear, salvation is of and belongs to God, and Ephesians 2:8 says that salvation is by grace and through faith. But what is striking is that in the New Testament salvation can and must be spoken of as having past, present and future dimensions, with its present dimension least frequently called "salvation." And it would be a truncated discussion of salvation indeed if we talked only about the present benefits of salvation (e.g., forgiveness of sins; renovation of the mind, will, emotions, spirit; empowerment and enlightenment; reception of the Spirit).

Human salvation is viewed by all the New Testament writers as part of the larger program of God's eschatological work. And indeed salvation is not viewed as inevitable even for the saints or the "elect." This is why we have sayings such as the Pauline one in 2 Timothy 2:10: "Therefore I endure all things for the sake of the elect, that they may obtain the salvation that is in

Christ Jesus with eternal glory." Or in Titus 3:6-7 Paul speaks of being saved and set right through the cleansing of rebirth and renewal by means of the Spirit so that believers might "become heirs with the hope of eternal life."

Before we go on to explore other aspects of eschatology, it will be useful to make one more crucial point: God's desire and intent are that all persons be saved, even though God knows that not all persons will be saved. This is clear not only from a renowned text such as John 3:16, but also from a Pauline one such as 1 Timothy 2:3-5, which speaks of God our Savior desiring that all people be saved and come to a knowledge of the truth, and which adds that Christ died as a ransom for all. Acts 2:21 puts it this way: whoever entreats or calls upon the name of the Lord will be saved (cf. Rom 10:13). Human salvation, as it turns out, is only the beginning of the reclamation project and the restoration of perfect communion between the creator God and his creation. Salvation leads to eternal life in a new heaven and a new earth.[9]

Eschatology in the New Testament

If there is a high degree of congruity in the God-talk in the New Testament, the same can be said about the discussion of the future. And for all of these writers, the key to the future, like the key to the present, is Christ. Thus, a whole series of eschatological events are tagged or linked or seen as the consequence of the second coming, or the coming of the Son of Man, or the parousia, or the glorious appearing—a variety of terms or phrases used to refer to the same eschatological event.

Christology not only has reshaped these writers' visions of the past, including the extant Holy Scriptures, and the present, but also it has reshaped their vision of the future. So much is this the case that a writer such as Paul links the return of hard-hearted Israel to the fold to the return of the redeemer from Zion who will turn back the impiety of Jacob, and a writer such as John of Patmos stresses that Christians must leave justice in the hands of the returning rider on the white horse rather than trying to take things and weapons into their own hands when they are persecuted, prosecuted, and even executed. It is true that all the New Testament authors are convinced that they already live in the eschatological age as a result of the christological events that have already transpired, but they also believe that they live

---

[9]I have already discussed at length what the New Testament has to say about the atoning death of Jesus as the necessary objective means of salvation, so I will not repeat that material here. See pp. 236-39, 332-33 above.

between the times, between the already and the not yet of the coming saving divine reign of God on earth—the "dominion," as Jesus preferred to call it—and so they urged disciples to pray for it. It therefore will be useful for us to look in some detail at the eschatological framework of the thinking of the New Testament writers and to compare and contrast some of the differing features in their writings.

What we are going to discover, however, is an essential harmony when it comes to the vision of the future: all of these writers believe that Jesus is coming back, and that his return will bring about the conclusion of human history as we know it without bringing about "the end of the world." A whole variety of these writers affirm that there will be both final judgment and final redemption, that there will be resurrection of the dead, that God is not done with Jews or Israel yet, that the final destiny of believers is not somewhere out there but is in the new heaven and new earth, which will entail numerous further events (e.g., the messianic banquet, the enthronement of the twelve judging Israel, death being overthrown, the kingdoms of this world being subjected to God's dominion), all of which Jesus will trigger, bring about, or be involved with. And there is enough overlap in the various witnesses of the New Testament on these matters that it is possible to see coherence on such subjects even when they do not all talk about all these subjects or discuss them in the exact same terms. Let us start with the two dominant witnesses whom we need to come to grips with, Jesus and Paul.[10]

Eschatological Commonalities Between Jesus and Paul

In some ways it is unsurprising that both Jesus and Paul believed in things such as the future coming of God's reign on earth, the resurrection of the dead, a final day of judgment and redemption, and a future time in which Israel would be saved, redeemed, ransomed, renewed, and a new community of God would be formed. To one degree or another, all of these beliefs can be found at Qumran or elsewhere in early Judaism, particularly in Pharisaism, and one thing that is clear about Jesus is that he agreed with the Pharisees on various theological matters, including resurrection. However, if we ask about what beliefs Jesus and Paul seem to have shared that were not found, or at least rarely found, elsewhere in early Judaism, there would be at least two: (1) a belief in a dying and rising messiah; (2) a belief in an agent of God who would

---

[10]For an extended treatment of this topic, see Ben Witherington III, *Jesus, Paul, and the End of the World: A Comparative Study in New Testament Eschatology* (Downers Grove, Ill.: InterVarsity Press, 1992).

assume the role of God on the day of judgment, judging the world. Jesus speaks of this as the Son of Man coming to judge (Mk 14:62), and Paul speaks of it as Christ coming to judge (e.g., Rom 2:16; 2 Cor 5:10). Agreement, even on these matters, will seem less remarkable when we remember that in all likelihood Paul got some of his thinking on such matters from the Jesus tradition.

What is especially intriguing, as I have demonstrated at length elsewhere,[11] is that both Jesus and Paul distinguish between the dominion of God, Israel, and the community of Jesus' followers. Perhaps for both Jesus and Paul the community of Jesus' followers is seen as the legitimate, or a legitimate, development of Israel (cf. Mt 16; Rom 9–11). Neither Paul nor Jesus simply equates the term *ekklēsia/qāhāl* with the term *Israel* without qualification. For both Paul and Jesus the dominion of God is something that is happening in the midst of God's people; God is establishing his saving reign or rule over his people and they need to repent, but neither of them identifies the "kingdom" with Israel without remainder. And for both Paul and Jesus there is a future dimension to the dominion such that these two men can talk about inheriting, entering or obtaining this dominion.[12] These future dominion sayings make especially clear that the community of Jesus cannot be equated with the dominion. The community already exists in the present, whereas the dominion is yet to arrive, and so Jesus' disciples still pray for its advent and look forward to entering it. When the dominion is spoken of as a realm, it is never spoken of in the present tense. When it is spoken of in the present tense, the reference is to an activity—the divine saving reign of God breaking into the life of a person or of a group of persons.

Another thing that Jesus and Paul seem to share is a clear and profound sense of the lostness of most of Israel and also a conviction that God has not given up on Israel. We see this very clearly in Romans 9–11 and equally clearly in Matthew's Gospel, with its stress on Jesus having come for the lost sheep of Israel (Mt 10:6; 15:24). Both men, then, believed that there was something seriously wrong in and with Israel that required repentance and redemption, seeking and saving. Just as Jesus sent his disciples out to Israel two by two to announce the good news, so Paul began his mission in numerous places by starting in the synagogues of the Diaspora. At no point does either Jesus or Paul think that there might be two peoples of God. For Paul, the one people of God is Jew and Gentile united in Christ, but at the same

---

[11]Ibid.

[12]See ibid., pp. 51-74.

time, God is not finished with non-Christian Jews.

It would be a mistake to think that Paul got all of his best theological ideas from Jesus. This would be overstating the indebtedness. Paul was a creative thinker, and his idea that first the full number of Gentiles must be saved and only then all Israel will be saved is something that he did not get from perusing the teachings of the historical Jesus. Nor is there any reason to think that Paul's teaching about the future resurrection of Jesus' followers and the meeting with Christ in the air when he returns (1 Thess 4:13-18) was something he simply derived from Jesus. After all, Paul was a prophet who believed that he received revelations directly from God (called "mysteries" [see, e.g., Eph 3:3]).[13]

Nevertheless, the dominant, indeed overwhelming, impression of a meticulous examination of the eschatological teaching of Jesus and Paul is that Albert Schweitzer was correct when he said, "Paul shares with Jesus the eschatological worldview and the eschatological expectation. . . . The only difference is the hour in the world clock in the two cases. To use another figure, both are looking toward the same mountain range, but whereas Jesus sees it as lying before Him, Paul already stands upon it, and its first slopes are already behind him."[14] There is in fact an "already" dimension to Jesus' teaching about the dominion of God; he is bringing it in through his ministry of preaching, teaching and healing. Neither Jesus nor Paul is purely future-oriented in regard to eschatology, but there is a difference in emphasis between them. One always gets the feeling that for Paul the most crucial eschatological events, the death and resurrection of Jesus, lie in the past, whereas for Jesus the most crucial ones lie in the future. Paul can speak of the form of this world passing away and the time until the end being shortened by the Christ-event, which had already happened (see 1 Cor 7:29-31). Jesus saw such things as in the future.

It is also telling that for both Jesus and Paul the ultimate future will happen in this world, not in heaven. Jesus barely discusses heaven (but see Lk 16:19-31; 23:43), and Paul, in 2 Corinthians 5:1-5, calls it a state of nakedness before God, which he would rather avoid by going directly from this body to the resurrection body without death and the intermediate state. For

---

[13]See Ben Witherington III, *Jesus the Seer: The Progress of Prophecy* (Peabody, Mass.: Hendrickson, 1999), 301-16.

[14]Albert Schweitzer, *The Mysticism of Paul the Apostle*, trans. William Montgomery (New York: Henry Holt, 1931), p. 113.

both Jesus and Paul redemption reaches its consummation only when resurrection is experienced here on earth. Neither of these early Jews had an essentially otherworldly view of eternal life or salvation.

One of the more revealing parallels between the teachings of Jesus and of
Paul is what I call "the thief in the night" motif. Both men use this metaphor to talk about the second coming, or return, of the Son of Man. They
use it because they want to emphasize the unknown time of this return (see
Mk 13:32; cf. Mt 25:1-15; 1 Thess 4–5) and its sudden and unexpected inbreaking. Both Jesus and Paul envision the saints going through whatever
tribulation there may be that precedes the return of Christ as well (cf. Mk
13; 2 Thess 2). Neither man engages in speculation about the timing of the
second coming; indeed, the metaphor of the thief in the night is meant to
discourage such speculation.

Otherworldly Versus This-Worldly Eschatologies in the New Testament

Some have thought that although the summary just offered here about the
teaching of Jesus and Paul may well be correct or mostly correct, there are
other New Testament writers who begged to differ and focused on an otherworldly resolution or solution to the human dilemma. The chief of these
is thought to be the author of Hebrews, perhaps coupled with the author of
the Fourth Gospel and maybe the author of Revelation, who certainly has a
great deal to say about life in heaven and elsewhere in the other realm. In fact,
only the Fourth Gospel says little about the afterlife or future eschatology,
but even there some things are said along the way. Let us consider first what
is said in Hebrews, which often is viewed as having a strongly, if not entirely,
otherworldly eschatological perspective.

In Hebrews. It has long been realized that there is a good deal of what may
be called "realized eschatology" in the book of Hebrews. This is perhaps
especially clear in the peroration in Hebrews 12:18-29. But it is not the case
that even here the author has completely exchanged all future eschatology
for realized eschatology. We need to bear in mind that epideictic rhetoric is
the rhetoric of what is true in the present; by and large, it is not by nature
past- or future-oriented. In keeping with that fact, we should not expect
much discussion of future eschatology in this sermon. The fact that there is
some at regular intervals in the homily is telling and reveals that the author
very much affirms such future eschatology, though it is not the focus of his
present rhetorical piece.

I will now deliberately work through the eschatological material in this document from back to front, from peroration to exordium, to make clear that the future eschatology becomes more abundant and more evident the further one goes in the discourse, especially so in Hebrews 10–12, and the fact that the peroration especially emphasizes the final eschatology theophany involving God and Christ is crucial, revealing the author's hand quite clearly. When one considers this and remembers the restraints that the author was under as he was offering an epideictic discourse that must focus on present truths, there is no reason in the end to read his use of "heavenly Zion" language any differently from what one finds in Galatians 4 or especially Revelation 21–22.

Various things need to be kept in mind in evaluating the eschatology of Hebrews. These things are most easily made clear by way of a list of events unresolved or still to come: (1) The new Jerusalem, the heavenly city, is clearly described as "the city that is yet to come" (Heb 13:14). Notice that it does not say "the heavenly city to which we, when we die, will go" (though the author probably believes that to be true as well). (2) The final shaking of heaven and earth has yet to transpire (Heb 12:26 says that it is promised but not yet delivered). (3) Believers in the present are in the process of "receiving" (*paralambanontes*, present participle) a kingdom (Heb 12:28), but they have not yet received the consummation of this kingdom. (4) The believers have come "to" Mount Zion, but they have not yet entered it. This is because it is spatially near but not yet here to be entered by those still on earth, such as the audience (Heb 12:22). (5) The author refers to a grace of God yet to come and to a seeing of God yet to come, which the audience, were they to commit apostasy, could miss out on (Heb 12:14-15). (6) Hebrews 11:35 is a reminder that forward-looking believers still have rewards and promises yet to be received, including "a better resurrection." (7) Hebrews 11:39-40 is a reminder that none of the Old Testament saints received what was promised, but God had planned things so that they would be made perfect "together with us." But when is that to transpire? If we see in Hebrews 12:18-29 a proleptic portrayal of the final theophany when God the judge and Jesus the mediator descend with the heavenly city, it is only then when the angels, the spirits of the deceased, and the living believers will reach such a consummation. (8) Hebrews 11:16 says that God has prepared a better and heavenly place for the Old Testament saints. Notice the word "prepared." It implies that they have not yet received it, nor are they there yet, not least because they will do so in tandem with New Testament saints. (9) The unshakeable kingdom comes down from heaven and replaces the present shakeable created order after the last judgment falls on that order (Heb 12:27-28). It does not follow from this that we are to see this city or kingdom as immaterial in character. (10) Notice the language of Hebrews 10:34. Current material possessions will be replaced not by no possessions but rather by better and lasting ones. (11) The warning about future judgment that will befall those who fall into the hands of the living God if they have rejected the gospel (Heb 10:26-31) is reinforced by the closing image of the peroration, which warns, "For our God is a consuming fire" (Heb 12:29; cf. Heb 10:27). (12) In Hebrews 7:19; 10:22; 12:22 the descriptor of the present position of believers is that they can draw near to God and to the holy city. They are not said to enter it, and indeed there is not even any discussion of deceased believers entering it when they die, though surely this is implied in several places in the sermon. My point is that in this sermon the emphasis is never on following Jesus into heaven. (13) Jesus is seated at the right hand of God, as is often stated in this discourse using Psalm 110:1, but notice also how Hebrews 10:13 stresses that in that posture he is still awaiting for his enemies to be made his footstool. (14) Especially crucial is Hebrews 9:28, which stresses that Jesus will come a second time to finish the salvific work appointed to him, not to bear sin as he did the first time he came but rather to bring salvation to those who are awaiting him. This verse is especially important because it makes clear that however realized some of the author's eschatology may be, he still sees the consummation of human salvation as awaiting the parousia of Christ. (15) The author emphasizes that resurrection from out of the realm of the dead and eternal judgment are two of the first things that Christians were taught, and they should need no reminder of such teaching (Heb 6:2). This explains in part why the author feels no need to stress future eschatology, though certainly he affirms it. (16) The great promise of entering the divine rest is yet to be fulfilled, remaining a promise (Heb 4:1). This is why at Hebrews 4:11 the author encourages the audience to strive to enter this rest. He draws an analogy with those who failed to enter the promised land and its rest (Heb 3:18-19). (17) The fine balance of his eschatology, featuring events both present and future, is seen in a verse such as Hebrews 3:14: "We have come to share in Christ, if we hold firmly to the end the confidence we had at first." (18) When the author speaks of the future, he does not speak of entering heaven as the end of the eschatological process. To the contrary, he speaks in much the same way as other early Jews did about "the world to come" (Heb 2:5). This world to come, country to come, city to come, Savior to come, kingdom that is coming, final judgment to come all transpires outside of heaven and within a transformed or entirely new and permanent material realm where resurrection is possible and serves as a prelude to final judgment on earth. (19) The coming cataclysm is described in the language of Psalm 102:25-27 in Hebrews 1:11-12. The present order will wear out like a garment and be rolled up like a robe. But notice that the text does not suggest that the material realm called a "garment" will be replaced by something immaterial. To the contrary, it is said that "like a garment they will be changed" (Heb 1:12). We can compare this to Hebrews 12:27, which speaks of the shakeable things being removed. That final sifting process is not said to leave us only with heaven; rather, it is said to leave us with that which will be permanent—a better garment, an eternal kingdom that the resurrected can enter and a Mount Zion city that believers may approach now but will enter only when Jesus the mediator returns. Jesus is, after all, said in the christological hymn that begins this discourse to be the "heir of all things" (Heb 1:2), and this requires that there actually be some "things" left for him to inherit, and not just "the spirits of righteous persons made perfect." Indeed, those spirits are said to await the real consummation until "we" can all partake of it together. This implies that they do not yet experience that full consummation even though apparently they are in heaven now.

Early Jews who had a fully formed eschatology (such as Pharisees, those at Qumran, John the Baptizer and Jesus) expected a consummation "down here," not merely "out there," and it is wrong to see the author of Hebrews as an exponent of purely or primarily otherworldly afterlife thinking. To the contrary, what he is emphasizing is the present role of Christ in the heavenly sanctuary and its benefits for those on earth. Otherworldly Christology, not otherworldly soteriology, is his focus.

It is no accident that in the one place where Christ is clearly presented as the example that Christians should follow, Hebrews 12:1-3, the analogy drawn is between the race that Jesus (notice the emphasis on the human name) ran faithfully and true while on earth even unto the finish line of death and the same race that he would have his audience run faithfully to the end of life. The author does not say what happens when the spiritual athlete crosses the finish line. He does not draw an analogy between Christ experiencing heavenly life as the reward and believers doing so. Indeed, whenever he speaks of the reward for believers, he talks about what will yet happen at the consummation, when Jesus returns and the dead are raised. This is quite clear in Hebrews 11–12. Perhaps, then, it is time to stop suggesting that the author has an "overrealized" or mostly "otherworldly" eschatology. He, like other early Jewish Christians, believed that what is now "up there" will one day be "out there" or, better said, "down here" when Jesus returns. And then there will be no more need to speak of drawing near to the heavenly city. Then it will be a matter of entering it once and for all and enjoying the eternal kingdom "on earth as it is in heaven."

In Revelation. It is relatively easy to dispel the notion that the book of Revelation has in mind an otherworldly conclusion to the human dilemma. For one thing, the book ends with the return of Christ, a millennium on earth preceded and followed by an event of resurrection, and a new heaven and a new earth as the heavenly Jerusalem descends with Christ to planet earth and Christ and God reign forever there with God's people. In addition, even much earlier in the book texts such as Revelation 6:9-11 make evident that the saints who are in heaven are unsatisfied and find no resolution of their legitimate concerns about justice in heaven.[15] Indeed, one could argue that one of the major concerns of John of Patmos is to demonstrate to persecuted and prosecuted Christians that justice will finally be done by God on the earth. He is not talking about heavenly compensation for earthly abuse. He reassures his audience that God will take care of the problem in space and time on earth. The seals, the bowls and the trumpets signal temporal judgments, and the return of Christ in Revelation 19 likewise envisions a historical conclusion to the matters of justice and redemption. The fact that the author has a robust view of what goes on in heaven does not cause him to neglect the fact that he wants to proclaim an eschatological conclusion to human history in which various Old Testament prophecies, especially the Isaianic ones, are fulfilled on earth.

In the Gospel of John. But what about the Gospel of John? Is it an exception to the overwhelmingly future-oriented focus of the New Testament when it comes to the conclusion of everlasting life? First, it must be admitted that the focus of the Gospel of John is on what is true now, both in this life and in heaven. Clearly, there is not the same amount of interest in future eschatology in this Gospel as in the others or, for that matter, in Revelation. It is one of the better reasons to doubt that the author of Revelation was the author of the composition we know as the Fourth Gospel. Furthermore, in the farewell

---

[15]See Ben Witherington III, *Revelation* (NCamBC; Cambridge: Cambridge University Press, 2003), 134-36.

discourses in John 14–17 Jesus says things such as "My Father's house has plenty of rooms; if that were not so, would I have told you that I am going there to prepare a place for you? And if I go and prepare a place for you, I will come back and take you to be with me, so that you may also be where I am" (Jn 14:2-3). Clearly enough this is a promise about heaven and about being in heaven with God and Christ. And it is in this same Gospel that Jesus says so very clearly to Pilate, "My kingdom is not of this world. If it were, my servants would fight to prevent my arrest by the Jewish leaders. But now, my kingdom is from another place" (Jn 18:36). Notice that Jesus does not say, "My kingdom is not *in* this world." Jesus is talking about the character of his kingdom and its source; it is from another realm and comes down from above, but it is manifested in this world.

Having recognized and fully granted that there is a strong sense and proclamation in the Fourth Gospel about the other world, we would be wrong to say that this Gospel completely neglects the future, and not just the proximate future when the Spirit will come and descend on the disciples after Jesus departs to heaven. No, there are some sayings in the Fourth Gospel that show that this evangelist also knows of the future eschatology of Jesus and is happy to refer to it.

For example, in the discussion between Jesus and Nicodemus, Jesus tells Nicodemus emphatically that unless he is born of water and the Spirit, he will not enter the kingdom of God in the future (Jn 3:5). Jesus had just said the same thing (Jn 3:3), except there he said that no one will see the kingdom of God without being born again or from above. The importance of this teaching is that it comports with the pronouncements of Jesus in the Synoptics about entering the kingdom in the future. The language here does not seem to have a different nuance to what it has in the Synoptics. But this is not all.

We also can point to a text such as John 5:28, where Jesus says, "For a time is coming when all who are in their graves will hear his voice and come out; those who have done what is good will rise to live, and those who have done what is evil will rise to be condemned." We could back up to John 5:25, where Jesus says, "A time is coming when the dead will hear the voice of the Son of God, and those who hear will live." The former of these two verses makes clear that Jesus is not just talking about the spiritually dead. The spiritually dead are not dwelling in graves. Notice that it is the Son who calls the dead out of their graves, and there is a resurrection to everlasting life, but there is also a resurrection to condemnation. This is very similar to what we hear about the two resurrections in Revelation 20. Back one verse further, at

John 5:24, Jesus promises that those who hear his word and believe in the one who sent him will have everlasting life and will not be judged in the future. It seems clear from this important passage that the author believes (1) in the future judgment of the living and the dead; (2) in the future resurrection of the dead; (3) that it is Jesus who summons the dead, which presumes his return to earth to do so, since elsewhere this Gospel is emphatic about Jesus returning to the heavenly Father after his death and resurrection. Thus, there may be little future eschatology in the Fourth Gospel, but nevertheless there is some, although this evangelist places more emphasis on the other world that exists now and to which the dead followers of Jesus will go. It therefore is wrong to say that this Gospel offers us a different theology of everlasting life and a different view of the everlasting dwelling place. It does not stick out like a sore thumb compared to the rest of the New Testament on this issue, despite the claims of some scholars.

The "End of the World" in New Testament Eschatology

Another interesting topic to address at this juncture is what the New Testament writers say about whether the world or physical universal is eternal or will come to an end. Oddly enough, New Testament scholars seldom discuss this particular subject. In fact, they avoid it like the plague. They do sometimes talk about the destruction of the temple being the end of *a* world—the temple-centered religion of early Judaism—but they seldom talk about the end of *the* world.

In Romans 8. Perhaps a good place to begin this discussion is Romans 8. Paul, in the course of talking about the future resurrection of believers, adds this: "I consider that our present sufferings are not worth comparing with the glory that will be revealed in us. The creation waits in eager expectation for the children of God to be revealed. For the creation was subjected to frustration not by its own choice, but by the will of the one who subjected it, in hope that the creation itself will be liberated from its bondage to decay and brought into the freedom and glory of the children of God" (Rom 8:18-21). When Paul refers to the "glory that will be revealed in us," he is talking about the future glorious resurrection body (see 1 Cor 15:35-50) that believers will receive when Christ returns and raises the dead. Then he tells us that the rest of creation is eagerly awaiting not only human liberation but also its own liberation, being set free from the bondage of disease, decay and death. In some ways this reflection is unsurprising because Paul and the other New Testament writers are remarkably indebted to Isaiah in their vision of the future, and here we could point to Isaiah 60–66 in particular, where there is a considerable vision of the renewal and restoration not only of God's creatures but also of creation itself. What good would renewed persons be on an old worn-out earth? There is, then, a certain solidarity between the human creature and the rest of creation. But is this a vision of renewal, or replacement, or some of both? Is it about the end of one world and the beginning of another? Is the new heaven and the new earth just a renewed and improved old heaven and earth? Paul, in 1 Corinthians 15:25-28, tells us that after the return of Christ the last enemy to be put under his feet is death itself, which is seen not as something natural but rather as the penalty or wages of sin, a penalty that both humans and the rest of creation had to endure after the fall. But what texts such as 1 Corinthians 15 and Romans 8 suggest is not a total replacement of former creatures and creation with all new creatures and creation. Indeed, the doctrine of resurrection enunciated in 1 Corinthians 15 implies both continuity and discontinuity between the old and new person in Christ, and so one would expect the same to be true with the rest of creation.

In Hebrews. The author of Hebrews, a writer indebted to Paul, seems to have an opinion on this very subject: "But now he has promised, 'Once more I will shake not only the earth but also the heavens' [Hag 2:6]. The words 'once more' indicate the removing of what can be shaken—that is, created things—so that what cannot be shaken may remain. Therefore, since we are receiving a kingdom which cannot be shaken, let us be thankful" (Heb 12:26-28). These verses deserve a more detailed discussion.

Hebrews 12:26 mentions God's voice shaking the earth, likely alluding to the earthquakes connected with the Sinai events. Then, in that same verse, Haggai 2:6 LXX is quoted quite closely and followed by the usual midrashic running commentary on certain key words. What needs to be stressed about this quotation is that it has nothing to do with the disappearance of the material universe. Here the author's key hermeneutical move is to take the words *eti hapax* ("once more") to refer to a future and indeed final eschatological shaking of the earth but also even of heaven, after which the only things left are the unshakeable things. Only once more will there be an earth-shaking theophany where God sorts things out with his people. Like someone winnowing grain such that the chaff is sifted out from the wheat but nonetheless the wheat remains, God is said to sort out the material creation. All the rest, the shakeable part, of the created order will be removed. Clearly, the author does not believe in the eternality of this earth or even of the heavens. He sees it as all part of the created order, which will undergo "change" *(metathesis)*,

not disappear altogether. Bear in mind what he said about the final conflagration earlier mentioned in the quotation in Hebrews 1:10-12. It will be
useful to quote the whole verse from Haggai, which surely was in the author's
mind: "The Lord Almighty says, 'In a little while I will once more shake the
heavens and the earth, the sea and the dry land. I will shake all nations, and
the Desired of all nations will come, and I will fill this house with glory. . . .
The glory of this present house will be greater than the glory of the former
house,' says the Lord Almighty. 'And in this place I will grant peace'" (Hag
2:6-9 LXX).

There could hardly be a more appropriate quotation, for the following
reasons: (1) it could be seen by a Christian writer as alluding to the second coming of Jesus; (2) it refers to a replacement of former glory with
greater glory, part of the message of Hebrews throughout the discourse;
(3) the "shake-up" involves not the complete dissolution of the material
realm but rather the sorting of all things and putting them right; (4) the new
and glorious dwelling place of God will be where God grants *shalom*, final
wholeness for his people. This is why we have the language in our passage
about all being joined together, Old Testament and New Testament saints,
and all being perfected together.

To be sure, the author envisions the replacement of the temporal and the
temporary by the permanent and eternal that comes down from heaven, but
he is not envisioning the replacement of the material realm with a nonmaterial realm simply called "heaven" any more than Paul was when he used
similar language (1 Cor 7:31; cf. 1 John 2:8, 17; Rev 21:1). The heavenly
city involves persons like Jesus who have a resurrection body and those who
have received, at his coming, a better resurrection. What he envisions is not
less solid or material; rather, it is more so, more permanent, an unshakeable
kingdom on earth as it once was in heaven but has come down and is in
the process of being received but has not yet reached its consummate state.
To this one can add that the shaking of the earth, and indeed earthquakes,
were regularly associated with theophanies, and especially with the coming Yom Yahweh, the Day of the Lord (Is 13:1-22; 34:1-17; Ezek 7:1-27;
30:1-9; Joel 2:1-11), and more generally with the end times (2 Esdras 6:16;
10:26; *2 Bar.* 32:1; *Sib. Or.* 3:675). "The text does not suggest that God
destroys a lower realm and preserves a higher one . . . both heaven and earth
are shaken."[16]

---

[16]Craig Koester, *Hebrews* (AB 36; New York: Doubleday, 2001), p. 547.

Thus, the author must end with the warning that the audience be careful to receive this kingdom. They are in the process of "receiving" (*paralam̄ ban-ontes*, participle in the present tense [Heb 12:28]) this kingdom but have not fully done so, and if they pull out before the end, there will be hell to pay, literally. Here is the only mention of receiving a kingdom, but it is an unshakeable one that comes as a gift that should prompt the believer's gratitude, worshiping with reverence in a fashion acceptable to God. We probably hear echoes of Daniel 7:18-22 here, which is significant because there the kingdom is given to the saints once the Ancient of Days or "one like a son of man" comes down for final judgment theophany in favor of the saints and against the beastly nations, and they finally possess this kingdom—on earth, not in heaven. At the end of Hebrews 12 the theophany involves believers worshiping with a sense of awe about all this, and the author has attempted to reinculcate that sense of awe by the imagaic discussion that has just preceded.

These reflections near the end of the discourse in Hebrews reinforce what was said by way of quotation of Psalm 102:25-27 in Hebrews 1:10-12, where an analogy is drawn between an old garment that will wear out and be rolled up and the foundations of the earth and heavens that will wear out one day, unlike the eternal nature of God. The psalmist, of course, is referring to creation as it now exists, subject to decay and death, not to the new creation, which is not denied or referred to here. The point of comparison is between an eternal God and his temporal and contingent creation, which is subject to aging and obsolescence.

In 2 Peter 3. Here we must also certainly look at 2 Peter 3 in some detail because it provides us with the most extended discussion about "the end of the world" in the New Testament. Beginning with 2 Peter 3:5, the author starts to reply to the quoted scoffers, giving a response both about the delay of the parousia and its reasons, but also about the falseness of supposing that nothing ever has changed and so nothing ever will change in this world as far as divine intervention is concerned. It is possible that the false teachers' belief in fact was not "no divine intervention" but rather "no divine judgment" in human history. After all, how could they deny intervention altogether without denying the incarnation of Christ? These verses posit a connection, as do other New Testament texts, between the destiny and fate of humans and the destiny and fate of the physical earth (see Rom 8). In a sense, redemption and judgment involve all creation, not just the creature, though clearly the focus is on the latter. The author accuses the opponents of wishful thinking (2 Pet

3:5) and also probably deliberately ignoring (not just overlooking) various Old Testament texts and events. Clearly, 2 Peter 3:5 is a reference to creation, and here much has been made of the use of Genesis 1:2—the creation of the world out of *mabbûl*, or the primeval chaos waters over which the Spirit hovered. Apparently, this *mabbûl* was then assumed to become the heavenly ocean, the waters above the firmament from which God pulled the plugs when he let down the rains that led to the flood. The goal here in 2 Peter is not to teach cosmology, except in general to make the following four points, though the focus clearly is on human judgment (2 Pet 3:7) and its attendant circumstances.

1. God created the earth, bringing forth land by separating the waters (above) from the waters (below). In this sense, the earth could be said to be created by water. The reference to "out of water" (2 Pet 3:5) probably means "out of the original chaos," *mabbûl* (Gen 1:2).

2. God caused the earth to experience an initial destruction at the flood. Clearly, the author sees it as a worldwide cataclysm, not a local flood.

3. All of creation was made and remade by God's Word.

4. The final judgment will entail another worldwide cataclysm, but this time by fire. In 2 Peter 3:5 there is a deliberate contrast between the old (then) world and the present world, and then the author will go on to talk about the new heavens and new earth. The point of this all is to contradict the opponents' charge, that nothing changes, by saying, "God has started and changed things before, and he will do so, again. It is the same God and his same divine fiat that caused the first creation and will cause, by the same word, the final conflagration." Although 2 Peter 3:6 suggests a worldwide flood, it is not clear that it necessitates the view that the author thought that God made a whole new world after the flood. It is not clear what the antecedents of *di hōn* ("through which things") at the beginning of this verse are, but probably this refers to water and God's Word, the proximate and ultimate cause of these things. The notion of a whole new world would hardly comport with the Genesis story. Rather, it is a whole new *human* world, with all its organization and facets, that begins again after the flood. Thus, the word *kosmos* is used somewhat similarly to what we find in 2 Peter 2:5, where it specifies the world of godless people that is washed away. Richard Bauckham observes,

> We may therefore concede that in 3:6 his emphasis is on the Flood as a universal judgment on sinful men and women. But he evidently

conceives this judgment as having been executed by means of a cosmic catastrophe which affected the heavens as well as the earth. . . .

The idea of the destruction of the antediluvian world need not be taken to mean total annihilation. Rather, just as it was created by being brought out of the primeval ocean, so it was destroyed when it was once again submerged in the primeval ocean. The ordered world . . . reverted to chaos.

The author of 2 Peter (no doubt following his Jewish apocalyptic source) seems to envisage world history in three great periods, divided by two great cataclysms: the world before the Flood, the present world which will end in the eschatological conflagration (v. 7), and the new world to come (v. 13).[17]

The author proceeds to argue in 2 Peter 3:7 that the world has been preserved, kept, stored up for fire, a fire that will come on judgment day, when ungodly people will be destroyed (cf. Is 30:30; Nah 1:6; Zeph 1:18; 3:8). The perfect participle of the verb *thēsaurizō* occurs here, which means "to store up" and is the source of our word *thesaurus*—a storehouse of information. It is not said at this point that the known world will be annihilated, but rather that it will be destroyed, and 2 Peter 3:10 depicts the world collapsing, falling apart, and the melting of the stars, and the dissolving of the heavens, not unlike what would happen if the earth was absorbed back into our sun and our part of the universe collapsed. However, this does not mean that nothing would be left out of which the new heavens and earth would and could be made. Obviously, there are numerous Old Testament texts that use "fire" to speak of the fate of the wicked (Deut 32:22; Ps 97:3; Is 66:15-16). Stoics taught that such a conflagration was periodic and natural unlike our text. Thus,

the essential element in most Jewish and Christian references to the eschatological conflagration is the destruction of the wicked by the fire of divine judgment; this idea, which differs from the Zoroastrian fire of purification and from the Stoic idea of a natural, deterministic cycle of destruction and renewal, is fundamentally Jewish and biblical. The author of 2 Peter, who is really interested in the conflagration as judgment on the wicked . . . , follows this Jewish tradition. If he was aware of the pagan parallels, he is unlikely to have been very concerned with them.[18]

---

[17]Richard Bauckham, *2 Peter and Jude* (WBC 50; Waco, Tex.: Word, 1983), p. 299.
[18]Ibid., p. 301.

The idea that the world has been kept until that judgment day may imply that the world will not end until then. Until then, the world will be preserved. Note that in 2 Peter 3:7 the verb *tēreō* ("to keep"), applied earlier to bad angels and false teachers (2 Pet 2:4, 9), is now applied to "the present heavens and earth": they are kept, reserved, set aside until judgment day and will undergo a similar judgment and destruction as the bad angels and ungodly humans. It is interesting that Josephus tells us that early Jews sometimes attributed to Adam himself the notion of a dual cataclysm by water and by fire (*Ant.* 1.70). Later Zoroastrian or even Stoic speculations that involve the idea of a repeated restoration of the earth through fire need not enter into the discussion here. We may also quote from the Jewish *Sibylline Oracles*: "For stars from heaven shall fall into all the seas, and all the souls of human beings shall gnash their teeth. Burned both by sulphur stream and force of fire in ravenous soil, and ashes hide all things. And then the world shall be bereft of all the elements—air, earth, sea, light, sky, days, nights; and no longer in the air shall fly birds without number, nor shall living things which swim in the sea swim any longer, nor heavy cargo ship pass over the waves, nor straight-cutting plow carve the field" (*Sib. Or.* 2:251-252; cf. *1 En.* 83:3-5).

In 2 Peter 3:8-9 the author contrasts his readers with the false teachers, but it is particularly telling that he thinks that at least some in his audience may share the doubts about the parousia expressed by the false teachers. Although they may well fully ignore Old Testament prophecy and examples and the changes that the universe has already undergone, his readers must not let several other factors escape their notice. For instance, he refers to what Psalm 89:4 LXX (90:4 MT) says: "For a thousand years in your sight are like a day that has just gone by." Note that only the second half of the sentence in 2 Peter 3:8 corresponds to this. The first half has "one day is as a thousand years." In some ways it would be easier if we had only the "thousand years is as one day" part of the sentence to cope with. The general drift is clear enough. God's time is not the same as human time. If this is what is meant, then it is saying that in eternity a different time clock operates than in created time. This might lead to the conclusion that ever since Christ brought eternity and the eschatological things into time, we are operating on a different clock (i.e., the last days in the eschatological age are days according to God's clock, not ours). One must not use normal human reckoning to assess them, our author would be suggesting. However, it may be that what these words mean is that God's view of human time is not the same as our view of it, in which case the author is simply saying that one needs to see things from God's perspective. Not only does God see time from a different perspective (a thousand years would seem but a day to the eternal Being), but also he sees time with an intensity that we lack (one day can seem like a thousand years to God). Bauckham remarks,

> In the first place, God, who determines the time of the Parousia, does so from a different perspective on time from that of men and women. He is not limited by a human life span, but surveys the whole course of human history, so that, as the psalmist observed (Ps 90:4), periods which by human standards are of great length may be from his perspective very short. Those who complain of the delay of the Parousia, impatient to see it in their own lifetime, are limiting the divine strategy in history to the short-term expectations to which transient human beings are accustomed. But God's purpose transcends such expectations. Thus the false teachers' accusation, that it is now too late for the Parousia to be expected, is based on their own evaluation of "lateness," not necessarily on God's.[19]

The problem with this view is that 2 Peter 3:8 does not have just "a thousand years is as a day"; it also adds the converse, suggesting that for God, one day could be one thousand times longer than we reckon one day. Therefore, in God's sight time is both contractible and expandable, depending on what God desires and intends. Here we may compare *2 Baruch* 48:13: "With you [the Lord] the hours are like the ages, and the days like generations." This is not simply a remark about time's relativity. In its original context the saying in Psalm 90:4 means that God is eternal and we are transient. Our whole life span is but a blink of an eye for God. If that were meant in 2 Peter 3:8, we would have expected "a thousand years are as one day" but not "one day is as a thousand years." It is interesting that later Christians, taking their cue from this text's use of the psalm, came to the conclusion that each day of creation presaged a thousand years, so that the world would last six thousand years, and this would be followed by the return of Christ and a sabbath of one thousand years for the saints (see *Barn.* 15:4-7; Justin, *Dial.* 81.3-4; Irenaeus, *Haer.* 5.28.3). Of this, the author of 2 Peter says nothing, as he is not interested in speculations about the timing of the end. But there can be no doubt that most of the earliest Christian interpreters of Revelation 20 and of 2 Peter 3:8 were premillenialists when it came to their theology about the return of Christ and his reign upon the earth.

---

[19]Ibid., p. 321.

Therefore, I conclude that the author of 2 Peter is saying, "You must see things from God's broader perspective. For God, human time until the end is expandable or contractible, depending on various considerations. The time of the end is in God's hands, and he has chosen to expand the interval due to his long suffering or patience, giving us time to amend our lives and repent so that we will not perish." Notice that the Qumranites also wrestled with what appeared to be a delay in the coming of the Yom Yahweh (1QpHab VII, 6-14). Further, it is telling that texts such as *Jubilees* 4:30 and *2 Enoch* 33 also seem to have connected the number 1,000 with the numbers of days of creation to calculate how long human history would last. Finally, it is good to keep steadily in mind that this author has simply drawn an analogy: for God, one day is *like* a thousand years, and vice versa. Analogies compare two unlike things that in some particular way are the same or similar. The question to be asked is this: in what way is one day like a thousand for God, and the converse?

In 2 Peter 3:9 we have the verb *bradynō*, which means "is slow in effecting," "is delayed or late," or "is negligent about." Since, however, the problem is lateness (i.e., the parousia is late and overdue), not slowness, the latter two translations better suit the context. But how can God be late for the messianic banquet of which he is the host and scheduler? In this verse, then, the author is denying that God is late or overdue (or slow). Lateness presupposes a knowledge of when the end should have happened, definitely, and the author is going on to point out that no human has that sort of inside information. Thus, we have here the rebuttal to the scoffers' skepticism in 2 Peter 3:4 in the form of a "not . . . but" style of argumentation.

The promise referred to in 2 Peter 3:9 is the promise of the parousia (cf. 2 Pet 3:4). And the "some" who think that God is late are the false teachers. The second part of 2 Peter 3:9 is important because it says that God's forbearance or lateness is deliberate. He is showing patience to the believers. The last part of 2 Peter 3:9 must not be separated from the second part. Obviously, the Old Testament concept of God giving time for repentance and amending of life is in view here (cf. Ex 34:6-7; Num 14:18; Neh 9:17; Ps 86:15). But it is these Christians being addressed to whom God is giving time to straighten up, not just anyone. God shows patience "to you," says the text. Therefore, the last part of the verse must mean that God desires that no Christians should perish, but that all should repent and be saved. This in turn presupposes that it is indeed possible for Christians to apostasize and then be judged by God.

Of course, elsewhere in the New Testament (see Acts 17:30-31; Rom 11:32; 1 Tim 2:4; cf. Ezek 18:23, 32; 33:11) we find the thought that God wants all to come to know Christ, but that is not the point here. The focus here is more narrowly on Christians who stand in danger of perishing if they do not forsake the false teachers' ways and repent. Thus, 2 Peter 3:9 states that God has expanded the time until the end to give them an opportunity to repent, for that is God's compassionate character (see Jon 4:2; Joel 2:12-13; *1 En.* 60:5; *2 Bar.* 11:13; 12:4; 21:20-21). The corollary of this is found in 2 Peter 3:12, where it is suggested that by living in a godly way, believers might hasten the parousia. This is not to suggest that believers can force God's hand, but rather that if they do amend their lives, this may shorten the time until the end. The length of time is flexible in God's hands for a host of reasons, but of course God knows when it will finally come.

For humans and from a human perspective, however, 2 Peter 3:10 expresses the fact that "that day will come suddenly," unexpectedly, so far as its timing is concerned. Notice the emphatic position of the verb "will come" *(hēxei)* in the Greek text, where it is the first word in the sentence. That day will break in like a burglar. The "thief" image in this verse is a common one in the New Testament, sometimes used to speak of the timing of Christ's coming, and sometimes of the timing of the day of Christ, both of which are simultaneous and come together. This teaching clearly goes back to Jesus and his parable in Matthew 24:43-44 // Luke 12:39-40. It is used in all sorts of strands of New Testament teaching, both early and late (1 Thess 5:2; 2 Pet 3:10; Rev 3:3; 16:15). It may be said to be a governing metaphor for Pauline and other Christian theological reflections on the parousia chronology.[20] If the coming is as a thief, it cannot be calculated, and therefore it could happen soon (or later). One therefore can argue that there is a consistent view of parousia chronology throughout the New Testament era. It is constantly used to correct eschatologies that are overrealized, underrealized, or nonrealized. The second coming will burst in upon humankind suddenly, and it will not be a quiet affair.

At that time, the heavens will pass away with a loud noise or with a rushing, crackling sound (perhaps the sound of burning). The word *roizēdon* is onomatopoeic; it sounds like snoring, hissing, roaring, or whizzing by. After the heavens are destroyed, the *stoicheia* will fall apart, being burned up. These *stoicheia* are either the elements of the universe (earth, air, fire, water) or

---

[20]See Witherington, *Jesus, Paul, and the End of the World.*

perhaps the heavenly bodies. The author probably has Malachi 3:19 LXX (4:1 ET) in view, "for the day of the Lord is coming burning like an oven," possibly coupled with Isaiah 34:4 LXX, "all the powers of the heavens will melt" (Codex B), texts alluded to also in *2 Clement* 16:3. One can also compare the Greco-Roman ideas about the world/universe going up in flames at the end of things (Cicero, *Nat. d.* 2.46.118). The point is that here the author has expressed himself in ways both the Jewish and the Gentile Christians in the audience could relate to: the stars will fall from the sky in the conflagration, fire in heaven and on earth.

The last part of 2 Peter 3:10 contains a difficult textual problem. Bauckham does his best to sort this out, and here I can only give his conclusions. The word *heurethēsetai* (literally, "will be found"), being a very difficult reading, is likely original. Textual emendations or deletions are a last-ditch desperation move, the tactic of a frustrated exegete, and the variant readings are easier and cannot explain how *heurethēsetai* arose. Bauckham chooses to interpret *heurethēsetai* as the settled text and provides a plausible explanation: the earth and human beings' works "will be found out" ("by God" is implied in this use of the so-called divine passive). The point is that neither the earth nor human deeds will escape God's judgment (cf. 1 Sam 26:18; *Pss. Sol.* 17:10).[21] They too will be found out and dealt with. Perhaps here the author still has in mind Psalm 90, which says, "We are consumed by your anger. . . . You have set our iniquities before you, our secret sins in the light of your presence. All our days pass away under your wrath; we finish our years with a moan" (Ps 90:7-9). The author probably is talking about the dissolution of the heavenly bodies, involving stars falling to earth, and the fire then strips bare and exposes the earth but does not cause it to dissolve or disappear. There is, then, some continuity with the new heaven and the new earth envisioned.

Christians are called upon to go on waiting but to realize that their godly lives, because God can expand or contract the time until the end, may even have the effect of hastening the end (cf. 2 Esd 4:38-39; Acts 3:19-20; *2 Clem.* 12:6–13:1; and in the Jewish tradition there was the notion that God would send the messiah or fulfill his promises for the end times sooner if Israel would truly repent or keep the law [*b. Sanh.* 97b; 98a]). In another age, Augustine conjectured that if all Christians remained celibate and chaste, God would have to return or else Christians would die out. He apparently either

---

[21]Bauckham, *2 Peter and Jude*, pp. 322-23.

forgot or ignored that Christianity is mainly propagated by evangelism, not marriage.

The phrase "the coming of the day of God" in 2 Peter 3:12 is unusual (cf. Jer 46:10; Rev 16:14). It is most unlikely that the author distinguished this from the the Day of the Lord. When that day comes, it will be the cause of the heavens being set on fire (cf. Mal 4:1 [3:19 LXX]) and the heavenly bodies melting (cf. Is 34:4 LXX: "all the powers of the heavens will melt" [Codex B]). This involves extreme heat that no one could survive without protection from God. It is difficult to say how much of this the author intended to be taken literally and how much is simply eschatological and metaphorical language used to describe the very real and coming event of the parousia, which will involve real redemption and judgment. What is clear is that the author, like the rest of the New Testament writers, has a linear rather than a cyclical view of things: the world is heading for an eschatological conclusion wrought by the hand of God.

In view of the language of "new heavens and new earth" that follows in 2 Peter 3:13 (cf. *1 En.* 72:1; Rev 21:1), it is likely that this author believed in a real and physical transformation of the earth and its setting. It is worth noting, however, that this is an earth-centered perspective. Yes, stars will fall, and the earth will burn, and the heavens surrounding the earth will collapse, but even all this does not necessarily imply the destruction of the whole universe, but only the part that needed to undergo judgment.[22] We are waiting for a new heaven and a new earth. Here the vision of Isaiah lies in the background (Is 65:17-25; 66:15-16, 22-24). The author envisions a time when God's justice will finally be done on earth, when righteousness will find a home here on earth (cf. Gen 18:19; Lev 19:15; Ps 9:8; 11:7; Is 9:7; 11:4-5; Mt 5:6; Rom 14:17). There certainly is nothing here of a purely otherworldly piety or otherworldly resolution of all human problems. The author stands with the earlier Christian witnesses in his eschatology. Thus, he has rounded off his final argument, ending on a positive note. Especially noteworthy about this presentation is that it shows that the vibrant future eschatology is still being affirmed and reflected on even at the end of the first century A.D. by the author of 2 Peter.

In Revelation 21–22. What, then, is to be made of the conclusion of the

---

[22]That is, the author seems to be advocating renovation in some form rather than absolute annihilation. See Gale Z. Heide, "What Is New about the New Heaven and the New Earth? A Theology of Creation from Revelation 21 and 2 Peter 3," *JETS* 40 (1997): 37-56.

canon's last book, Revelation 21:1–22:5? Just like Paul, the author of Hebrews, and the author of 2 Peter, John of Patmos draws on the font of Isaiah
to explain the ultimate future of believers. If one follows the logic of the
argument of Revelation 19–22, it seems clear enough that the new heaven
and the new earth come about not by natural renewal processes but rather
by a miracle that transpires when Christ and the heavenly Jerusalem come
down and there is a corporate merger of heaven and earth. The world of
contingency and mortality is replaced by the world of everlasting life, which
involves not only new creatures but also a whole new creation for them to
live in. And it could not be otherwise, for God himself has come down to
dwell forever with his people—Immanuel—and thus the conditions must be
compatible with the holy and immortal presence of God. The trick is to get
the elements of continuity and discontinuity in balance between the old and
the new. Life goes on, life in embodied states goes on, an earth and a heaven
continue to exist, human community goes on, but disease, decay, death, sin,
suffering, and sorrow do not go on. One of the clearest symbols in Revelation 21–22 of the continuity between old and new is the reference to the trees
that have healing in their leaves (Rev 22:2). Why would one need this in the
new creation with a resurrection body? Why indeed, except of course that
since the new persons are also the old persons, there needs to be the healing
of the memories of things gone wrong in the old life in the old earth.

John is not being novel in his presentation, except for the christological
element, with Jesus Christ as the bridegroom. We may wish to compare
speculation about the new Jerusalem in Zechariah 12:1–13:6; Tobit 14:4-7;
2 Esdras 8:52; 10:2-7; *Apocalypse of Daniel* 5:4-13; *1 Enoch* 85–90; *Sibylline
Oracles* 3:552-731; 5:362-433. Notice that in John's vision there is no more
temple, as the division between God and his people, between the sacred and
the profane, is destroyed once and for all. Probably Ezekiel 28, where the
holy mountain is coupled with images of Eden, lies in the background here as
well. But without the temple, John clearly is not just recapitulating the vision
of Ezekiel. Instead, he is superseding it, for Christ has broken down the barriers and divisions between God and humankind. True human community
can be created only when God comes down and dwells with his people, not
by any attempts of humans to build up a city, in Babel-like fashion.

Not only will no temple building be needed, but also no sun or moon will
be needed, for God can be the Shekinah glory light of his people. The image
of the river flowing from the throne (Rev 22:1) also makes clear that God is

the source of his people's ongoing life as well—pure life, clean life, refreshing life, restorative life. As far as the curse was found, so far too will the renewal or making new of all things go. Not only will God's face be seen, but also his character will be fully stamped on each one who beholds it, and finally we will have come home to an everlasting home, a final resting place.

Eugene Peterson, as much as anyone else, has seen clearly the implications of John's concluding vision in Revelation. He says this:

> The biblical heaven is not a nice environment far removed from the stress of hard city life. It is the invasion of the city by the City. We enter heaven not by escaping what we don't like, but by the sanctification of the place in which God has placed us.
>
> There is not so much as a hint of escapism in St. John's heaven. This is not a long (eternal) weekend away from the responsibilities of employment and citizenship, but the intensification and healing of them.[23]

Peterson goes on to stress that the holiness that the heavenly Jerusalem possesses is expressed in its beauty and symmetry, its light, life-giving fruit and fertility. Peterson notes that this holiness "is perfectly proportioned wholeness."[24] It is

> a holiness that is neither cramped or distorted, but spacious; an illumination that goes beyond the minimum of showing what is true by showing it extravagantly beautiful; a nourishment that is the healthy feeding of our lives, not the frivolous adornment of them. . . . There is an implicit rejection in the visions of versions of holiness that are squinty and contorted, versions of truth that are dull and drab, and versions of growth that are decorative or effete.[25]

The holiness of the holy city has to do with love and community and the best family reunion ever. It is the opposite of a tourniquet mentality that, rather than giving joy, kills it by stressing what must be given up rather than what can be had. Holiness and newness as depicted in the New Testament are about the deepest hopes and longings of humankind being met in Christ and in his sanctifying and redeeming actions involving both creatures and creation. Just as John's vision does not involve the exchanging of earthly pleasures for heavenly boredom and asceticism, so also it does not entail a disembodied shadowy existence. The new creation is precisely that—a new

---

[23]Eugene H. Peterson, *Reversed Thunder: The Revelation of John and the Praying Imagination* (San Francisco: HarperSanFrancisco, 1988), p. 174.
[24]Ibid., p. 177.
[25]Ibid., p. 183.

creation involving persons in resurrection bodies and an earth that has been renewed and made permanent. As it turns out, God, according to John's vision, is the ultimate ecologist.

Summary

As I bring this representative theological discussion of eschatology to a close, I can say with some assurance that no New Testament writer envisions an otherworldly conclusion to the human dilemma and existence. It is the afterlife, rather than the other world, where the emphasis lies, and so much is this the case that in the end heaven has to come down; the heavenly Jerusalem has to descend, and there has to be a new earth to go along with the new heaven, and the kingdom has to come on earth, not merely in heaven. Only then will justice and mercy, judgment and redemption, love and holiness be fully done or exhibited on the earth as in heaven.

It appears unlikely that any New Testament writer sees a mere replacement of the old with the new creation. There are telltale signs and hints of continuity between the old and new, even in Revelation 21–22. But no New Testament writer has given up on his theology of God as creator and of creation as good and renewable. The eschatological framework shared by all the New Testament involves a big, bold, and beautiful vision of the end, but it also involves a telling insistence that there will also be judgment and eternal consequences for those who will not own or respond positively to God. None of the New Testament writers are universalists in this respect, but at the same time, none of them emphasize the lost or the losing, nor do they show any relish in talking about those who end up outside the new Jerusalem.

When faith one day becomes sight, and we know as we are known, perhaps we will understand God's chosen ways of justice and mercy, holiness and love. For now, we must say that all of this theology, and especially the truth that God intends to set the world right in all respects, has clear implications for ethics. In the following chapters we must consider what the consensus of New Testament writers seems to be about ethics. We will discover that far from doing ethics in the abstract, they do it out of their storied world and theological reflections. The imperative grew out of the indicative: as God is holy, so his people must be; as God is love, so his people must be; as God is merciful and just, so his people must be. In this way, the indelible image of God in us becomes a true reflection of God's character.

8

NEW TESTAMENT ETHICS: PRELIMINARY CONSIDERATIONS

Even drama is too static an understanding of theological ethics. Ethics cannot be simply about rehearsing and repeating the same script and story over and over again, albeit on a fresh stage with new players. . . . The Bible is not so much a script that the church learns and performs as it is a training school that shapes the habits and practices of a community.

SAMUEL WELLS[1]

Ethics is theological: Ethics is not about using power, restoring former glory, or fulfilling individual freedom: it is about imitating God, following Christ, being formed by the Spirit to become friends with God.

SAMUEL WELLS[2]

THE PLACE OF ETHICS IN NEW TESTAMENT THEOLOGY

It is sad but true to say that New Testament ethics has been the stepchild of New Testament studies throughout the twentieth century and into the twenty-first. There are a variety of reasons for this in the scholarly world. One is the disparaging remarks made about New Testament ethics by various highly influential New Testament scholars. When someone complains that what we have in large portions of the New Testament is "bourgeois" ethics (e.g., in the Pastoral Letters), or an ethical miscellany cobbled together from Greco-Roman and Jewish ethics, or a baptizing of various forms of the status

---

[1]Samuel Wells, *Improvisation: The Drama of Christian Ethics* (Grand Rapids: Brazos Press, 2004), p. 12.
[2]Ibid., pp. 30-31.

quo, the contempt for what is being urged in the New Testament is not far beneath the surface of the discourse.

But there is another reason why New Testament ethics has suffered both abuse and neglect, and it is theological. In some forms of Reformed theology, ethics is an afterthought. Reformed theology is all about God's sovereignty and grace and divine salvation, and there is an almost allergic reaction to the notion that the ethics of the New Testament have something to do with theology, have something to do with human salvation, because of course ethics is almost exclusively about human behavior, not God's behavior. Even a Reformed scholar who emphasizes ethics as an essential act of gratitude in response to grace has failed to do justice to the inherent and necessary connection between theology and ethics in the New Testament. For example, salvation has to do with both theology and ethics in the New Testament. And there is a crucial epistemological issue to consider: how exactly can one "know" a truth in the biblical sense without living into and out of that truth? In the Bible understanding often comes from doing or experiencing. Belief and behavior are not meant to be separated from one another into two hermetically sealed containers. The obedience that flows from faith is also the obedience which reassures, strengthens and more fully forms faith.

And there is a third issue. Modern Christian scholars are overwhelmingly non-Jewish in background, whether they be Protestant, Catholic or Orthodox scholars. As such, they do not reflect the orientation and ethos of early Judaism, unlike the way most New Testament writers do. By this I mean that early Judaism was primarily about orthopraxy, not orthodoxy. It was overwhelmingly about behavior, whether ritualized or simply moral behavior. It was seeking to answer the question "How may we live faithfully and appropriately in response to God?" It is true that the New Testament is more theological in character than many other early Jewish documents, but it is not true that ethics is just an afterthought in this New Testament literature. Indeed, ethics is often at the heart of what is going on in many if not most of the New Testament documents.

For example, as theological in character as Galatians is, the function of all the language is to prevent a certain kind of behavior that the audience is considering: getting oneself circumcised and keeping the Mosaic law. Or to take another example, the sermon called "Hebrews" has long exhortation sections interspersed between the textual exposition sections of the discourse, the exposition leading to the punch line of exhortation. The author is trying to prevent the audience from going AWOL, committing apostasy. This is also the agenda of several other New Testament documents, including 1 John and Revelation. Had we been paying more attention to the imperatives in the New Testament all along, we would have realized that ethics is just the logical implication and real-life working out of the theology in a person's or community's life.

And this brings us to another crucial preliminary observation. It is not merely that the imperative is built or based on the indicative, though that is true. It is that the imperative presupposes the work of the living God within the very inner being of the community and its individuals, such that God is commanding what he is already enabling by the divine saving action in the audience's midst.

Ethics is not merely the response of a grateful heart to what God has done for someone or for a community. Ethics is the necessary outworking of what God has worked in the community and its individual members. Ethics is not an optional added extra if one wishes to be saved to the uttermost. Nor is ethics is an optional added extra if one wishes to please God. Nor is ethics merely the fruit that a good tree bears. Christian ethics does indeed have to do with human behavior, the chosen behavior of a person saved and empowered by grace to respond to God's commands and emulate the behavior of exemplars such as Christ and his apostles. There is, then, a middle term between the action of God and the ethical response of God's child or community, and that is the experience of God's action within the community and its individuals, an experience wrought by the Holy Spirit. I will say more about this as the chapter develops.

THE SHARED MORAL VISION OF THE NEW TESTAMENT WRITERS

The Bible is replete with reminders that "without vision the people perish," and this is especially the case when it comes to ethical or moral vision. Believing, in the sense of notional assent to a set of ideas, somehow seems to come much easier than behaving or understanding how one ought to behave. And let us be clear about the order of things when it comes to theology and ethics: it is true that the New Testament writers believe that "obedience is a consequence [and gift] of salvation, not its condition. The Holy Spirit is not a theological abstraction but the manifestation of God's presence in the community, making everything new. Those who respond to the gospel have entered the sphere of the Spirit's power, where they find themselves changed and empowered for obedience."[3] Indeed, one can say that the Spirit is characterized as a sort of GPS device, giving guidance and direction on the fly, such that even a figure such as James can say, "It seemed good to the Holy Spirit and to us . . ." (Acts 15:28). The Spirit not merely empowers, energizes and enables the believer; the Spirit leads the believer into all truth, and into "the paths of righteousness for his name's sake."

What is too seldom noted about the shared moral vision of the New Testament writers (and note that I do not say "visions") is that it is grounded in the first instance in story and experience—the story of Christ himself and the experience of Christ by means of the work of the Spirit. The construction of a Christian ethic is not an abstract intellectual exercise; rather, it is a response to the work of God in the midst of God's people. And what they are most responding to is Christ and his story as it has impacted them.[4]

Consider, for example, what is going on in Romans 12:9-21; 13:8-10. Scholars often have noted echoes of the Sermon on the Mount in this material, including echoes of the Beatitudes. Paul has imbibed and embodied this teaching and has made it his own, and he is prepared to reapply it to a different situation. And we note his stress on how love is the fulfilling of the law, even of various of the Ten Commandments. This is not an independent reflection on the Old Testament law but rather one that reflects a variety of things that Jesus said, including about what is the greatest of the commandments. What is especially interesting, however, is the phrase "the other law" in Romans 13:8. What other law? This seems likely to be a reference to the law of Christ, to which Paul refers elsewhere (1 Cor 9:21; Gal 6:2), a law that is, as it turns out, composed of three elements: (1) emulating the pattern of Christ's life; (2) the obedience of faith, which includes obeying Christ's teachings (including his reaffirmation of some Old Testament teachings) as reapplied to the Christian community; (3) obeying the new apostolic teaching, which amplifies and expands upon the example and teaching of Christ. All of this presupposes and is grounded in the story of Christ. It presupposes that the audience is already well familiar with that story and with the essential teachings of Jesus such that even with a new audience that Paul has

---

[3]Richard B. Hays, *The Moral Vision of the New Testament: Community, Cross, New Creation* (San Francisco: HarperSanFrancisco, 1996), p. 45.

[4]Here Hays and I differ some. He talks about focal images that unite New Testament ethics: community, cross, and new creation (see Hays, *Moral Vision of the New Testament*, p. 5). But what unites those three things is Christ, who died on the cross, formed a community, and rose again and thereby made possible new creation in the lives of those who responded to him in faith.

not addressed before, as is the case with the audience in Rome, he does not have to engage in the hard sell even when commanding nonviolence and no retaliation, two of the stand-out or distinctive planks in the ethical platform of the historical Jesus. This is remarkable, and it shows what I have already stressed.

The early Christian community was a small, rather closely knit, and socially linked community across the empire. It shared a considerable amount of common teaching of both an ethical and theological sort. This is part of what made a Christian community in any given locale recognizably different from other faith communities. The unity of the ethics in the New Testament is not a contrived unity, something that modern scholars produce miraculously, like pulling a rabbit out of a hat by demonstrating the compatibility and coherence of the New Testament ethics as a modern exercise. On the contrary, the unity arises out of the coherence of these communities when it comes to the shared ideological and narratological framework in which they did their theologizing and ethicizing.

There was much that these communities had in common and indeed took largely for granted, so great was the impact crater of the Christ-event (person, works, teachings) on so many of them. We honestly do not absolutely need focal images to unite New Testament ethics, though they can be helpful to some degree. There is a focal person behind it all as both the exemplar and the provider of examples, as both the teacher and the teaching. Ultimately, New Testament ethics is about the imitation of Christ, in various of the possible meanings of that phrase.

This is why the metaphor of walking is so crucial not just in early Jewish ethics in general but in the New Testament in particular. Walking presupposes that one is going somewhere. Walking presupposes that one has a sense of direction, a roadmap, a guide. Walking assumes that there is a plot or plan or a course to follow. And when the Christian begins walking, he or she is supposed to be following in the footsteps of Christ—taking up a cross, denying self and following Jesus. This is the heart of the matter, and the rest is an amplification and commentary on that journey.

A journey involves drama, but a journey is no play or play acting. It involves not only following the map and directions provided, but also often doing some improvisation, about which I will say more later. The life of Jesus is seen as the map, and the law of Christ is the directions for how to follow it. There are many things in the daily walk not shown on the map, and many things not referred to in the directions given. Life is more detailed and involved than a map or set of directions can show or account for. Unlike a drama, which has a climax perhaps and an end, a journey has a goal, and that goal, as is clearly stated by Jesus, Paul and other New Testament figures, is not heaven but rather the dominion of God here on earth.

Inheriting, entering, obtaining that dominion is the goal. It is what Jesus taught us to pray for, and what we seek to obtain in due course. Indeed, it is said to be the inheritance of Christ's followers, not surprisingly since they are children of a king who will rule there forever. John Updike puts it this way:

> This Kingdom is the hope and pain of Christianity; it is attained against the grain, through the denial of instinct and social wisdom and through faith in the unseen [see Heb 11]. Using natural metaphors as effortlessly as an author quoting his own works, Jesus disclaims Nature and its rules of survival. Nature's way, obvious and broad, leads to death; this other way is narrow and difficult: "Come in by the narrow gate. . . ."
>
> Christ's preaching threatens men, the virtuous even more than the wicked, with a radical transformation of values whereby the rich and pious are damned and harlots and tax collectors are rather more acceptable. The poor, ignorant, and childish are more acceptable yet.[5]

Jesus set out a vision of this journey's end called "kingdom" in his beatitudes, a vision expounded on in many ways in the New Testament and most beautifully in the end of the book of Revelation, where we are told about how the kingdoms of this world become the kingdom of our God and of his Christ, with the vision of the descending heavenly city and the merger of heaven and earth when Christ returns, the dead are raised, justice is done, and everlasting peace and salvation are established upon the earth in the new creation.

The Beatitudes are eschatological blessings for believers, things that will apply when one reaches the kingdom goal and the kingdom of God comes on earth as it is in heaven. And here is the good news: the dominion will be theirs, they will inherit the earth, they will be comforted, they will be filled with righteousness, they will be shown mercy, and most of all, they will see God and be called "children of God," being like him (cf. 1 Cor 13:12; Rev 21). Their present condition, however, seems to be the opposite of all this. They are poor in spirit, they are mourning, meek, persecuted, and yet they

---

[5]John Updike, "The Gospel According to Saint Matthew," in *Incarnation: Contemporary Writers on the New Testament*, ed. Alfred Corn (New York: Viking Press, 1990), pp. 8-9.

are in a blessed moral condition because they are pure in heart, merciful, indeed even peacemakers. As Matthew 5:12 suggests, though the reward will be great in the kingdom, the travail on the journey may be great. It will be a rough ride into the kingdom and not like one on a roller coaster, for which the course is preordained and one is strapped into the seat so that reaching the goal is inevitable. Why not? Because the human behavior of the disciples affects the outcome for them. Ethics is not just about attitude or gratitude; it is about a necessary walking in the right direction, having heard the clarion call of Jesus to "walk this way." And the clearer the image we have of Jesus and his character in our mind's eye, the more clearly we may be able to discern how to emulate his character and behavior.

It is likely that Jesus' own moral vision of how one must be and behave in order to enter the dominion is derived from his own call narrative of sorts, the one in whose light he exegetes his own ministry, Isaiah 61:1-7:

> The Spirit of the Sovereign LORD is upon me, because the LORD has anointed me to preach good news to the poor. He sent me to bind up the brokenhearted, to proclaim freedom for the captives and release for the prisoners, to proclaim the year of the LORD's favor and the day of the vengeance of God, to comfort all who mourn, and provide for those who grieve in Zion, to bestow on them a crown of beauty instead of ashes, the oil of gladness instead of mourning, and a garment of praise instead of a spirit of despair. . . . Instead of their shame my people will receive a double portion, and instead of disgrace they will rejoice in their inheritance.

Jesus' ministry was the inauguration of the kingdom on earth, the divine saving reign of God upon the earth, where God's will is at last done for one and all. But as the Beatitudes make very clear, entering, obtaining or inheriting all that is promised still lies in the future. So the disciples of Jesus live between the times. They live between the beginning and the consummation of the dominion of God upon the earth. The journey has begun, but it is nowhere near done.

A further element to Jesus' recitation from Isaiah 61 and his proclamation that it was being fulfilled in the audience's hearing requires notice and reflection. This text alludes to what will happen in the Jubilee Year, the year in which debts are forgiven, land is allowed to go fallow, slaves are set free or allowed to return to their point or family of origin. In other words, it was a season when the usual rules of the road, indeed the very laws of Moses, did not apply in various cases. It is no surprise that Jesus would use such language to characterize the inbreaking of the divine saving reign or dominion of God if he wanted to stress the element of newness and discontinuity with the way things had previously been done as far as behavior and praxis were concerned. Jesus' ministry inaugurates the eschatological Jubilee Year.

Let us reflect on Leviticus 25 for a moment. Basically, this is a text proclaiming a sabbatical year for the land and for the people of the land. The land itself is keeping a sort of sabbath in the Jubilee Year, and this was meant as a reminder to God's people that they did not own the land, but rather that it belonged to God and they were actually just sojourners and foreigners in the land, however long they may have lived there. The Jubilee Year was the fiftieth year after seven cycles of seven years. However, it was not just a year of rest for the land; it was a year of redemption or emancipation for slaves as well as for houses (people could get their homes back after they had been sold out from under them) and of emancipation for all sorts of people from debts as well. Redemption and pardon characterized this year. This script of the Jubilee is in part the source of Jesus' moral vision, as Luke 4 tells the tale. Among other things, it explains (1) why Jesus thought that healing was especially appropriate on the Sabbath: it was the right day to give people "rest" from what ails them; (2) why Jesus pronounced the remission of debts and forgiveness of sins; (3) why Jesus went about setting captives free (e.g., those possessed by demons); 4) the close analogy between the celebration of the Feast of Pentecost and the Jubilee celebration, because Pentecost was the celebration after seven weeks of harvest.

Suddenly we can see a connection between Jesus' inaugural sermon and what happened in Acts 2 and the inaugural sermon there by Peter. In Luke 4 Jesus says that the Spirit has fallen on him and empowered and inspired him to proclaim the Jubilee Year and to begin to enact it. In Acts 2 Peter proclaims that the Spirit has now fallen on the whole community of Jesus' followers, and they must now go forth to continue and emulate the ministry of Christ. The pouring out of the Spirit on all flesh is seen as the clearest sign that the eschatological age is now in full swing, and the ethical import of this can hardly be missed. Now the disciples are empowered not only for mission but also for obedience to God, for walking in a holy way that is pleasing to the Lord, for they are filled with God's Holy Spirit. The ethics of the kingdom now becomes a live possibility for them, not just a utopian dream that only Jesus could live out. They are pilgrims empowered to pray, praise, proclaim, and walk as Jesus walked, heading for the kingdom goal.

When Paul wants to talk about what is needed for the journey into the dominion, having exhorted his audience about fulfilling the new law by means of loving, he says, "And do this understanding the present time. . . . Let us put aside the deeds of darkness and put on the armor of light. Let us behave decently, as in the daytime [not in nighttime behavior]. . . . Clothe yourselves with the Lord Jesus Christ, and do not think about how to gratify the desires of the flesh" (Rom 13:11-14). I submit that for Paul to be able to exhort a congregation he never visited to "clothe yourselves with the Lord," they must already know what that looks like, they must know what that means. The author and the audience must share the same road map and set of directions when it comes to walking in the light and reaching the kingdom goal, and Paul must be counting on the Holy Spirit to illumine and empower such a venture. In short, they must already share the same moral vision.

If we ask who cast this new moral vision focused on a kingdom goal, the answer is, of course, Jesus, from the very beginning of his ministry when he spoke about the kingdom being at hand (Mk 1:15). The king has come, but his followers still await the consummation of his kingdom. In the meantime, they are not on a crusade but rather on a pilgrimage to the holy city, sharing with those they meet along the way about what is coming and what has already come of the Christ-event. Failure to walk in the light, failure to put on one's protective under armor before traveling, can lead to a failure to reach the goal.[6]

Reading a moral map and understanding and following directions carefully requires moral discernment. Indeed, it requires having the mind of Christ and thinking as he thought and also bearing in mind his own pilgrimage. This is why Paul first says, "Have this mind in yourself that was also in Christ Jesus," and then proceeds to retell the story of the V-pattern of Christ's career in Philippians 2:5-11. He does this in order to encourage the audience to also take a self-sacrificial approach to life. Always before the audience is held up an image of self-sacrificial love and its rewards and benefits.

Jesus insisted on close listening with two good ears to understand his moral teaching, but Paul insists that the renewal of the mind is also necessary "so that you may discern what is the will of God—what is good and acceptable and perfect" (Rom 12:2). One might argue that since we have a huge quan-

---

[6]The reason for the imperatives given to new creatures in Christ is that even new creatures can act in old ways. They may have fled their old temptations, lifestyle, and behaviors but left a forwarding address.

tity of commandments already in God's Word, there is no need for a process of moral discernment, that ethics is about obeying the script of the Scripture. But no, New Testament ethics is not just about that, not least because so many of the decisions that a Christian must make along the journey have no direct analog in the directions in the New Testament. Indeed, most of life's mundane decisions are not scripted or ordered in the New Testament. This is why improvisation is necessary, and moral discernment is required in many situations in life, even in the case of the most sheltered of Christian lives.

It needs to be said at this time that one's assessment of the moral vision of the New Testament certainly is affected by how one views the relationship of the New Testament to the Old Testament or, more particularly, the relationship of the new covenant to all previous biblical covenants. It is perfectly clear from a close reading of the Sermon on the Mount and the ethical teachings of Paul that the new covenant is not just a renewal of one or more old covenants, not even the Mosaic one.[7] Indeed, there are various provisions of the New Testament, such as the proscription against oaths, the eschewing of violence altogether, the practice of nonresistance, the loving of enemies, and the nullifying of the belief that one can be defiled by a food that enters one's mouth, that make impossible the notion that the new covenant is just the new and improved version of an older covenant. When the eschatological kingdom comes, we study war no more, and there are other things that fall into abeyance as well. A Christian approach to war cannot appeal to the various pieces of legislation or moral examples found in the Old Testament unless one or another of them is found renewed or reaffirmed by some New Testament writer or Jesus.

Thus, New Testament ethics, on a variety of subjects, will overlap with Old Testament ethics, in some cases dismissing or intensifying some provision of Old Testament ethics, and in some cases simply replacing it with a very different ethical principle or practice. Some allowable oaths are replaced by no oaths at all. Some forms of food laws are replaced by no required food laws per se. Some Sabbath requirements are replaced by no Sabbath observance being required of any Christian. Some use of violence is replaced by no use of violence by Christians to resolve their problems. The new covenant

---

[7]There is a considerable difference between the renewal of a covenant and its fulfillment. In Galatians 3–4 Paul certainly argues for the fulfillment of the promises to Abraham in Christ and thus, in a sense, the fulfillment of the Abrahamic covenant in the new one. Fulfillment, however, means completion, not reiteration. The new covenant completes the old order of things, the old prophecies and promises, and then sets out on a new course with a new map.

is just that—a new covenant, not just the old covenant part two. And it is not only certain ritual practices that are said to be obsolete or replaced; it is also some of the ethical principles that are replaced and seen as outmoded now that the kingdom is coming with observation. Jesus was the caster of a moral vision, and some of the vision that he cast was indeed something new altogether.

LEVELS OF MORAL DISCOURSE

Unfortunately, besides the neglect or disparagement of New Testament ethics, one of the other negative things that has happened to New Testament ethical material is the decontexualizing of the material and the failure to see its usual ad hoc nature. All too often it has been treated rather flatly or uniformly. These things ought not to be. New Testament ethics is just as much a word on target for certain Christian audiences as the theologizing that we find in these same documents. And in fact, when we have material that is repeated in more than one document (e.g., the household codes), we begin to discover that there are trajectories of change in some of this material, just as there are levels of discourse. Let me explain what I mean by these two concepts (levels of discourse and trajectories of change), for in fact they are intertwined.

Anyone who has any sensibility about wanting to make an effective communication with a particular audience and persuade them of something, especially if the issue is exhortation and application, must (1) understand the nature of the relationship between the author and the audience; (2) be able to gauge the level and character of the communication so that it will be not merely understood but also received as persuasive; (3) speak to the place that the conversation has been able to develop thus far. For example, if we compare what Paul says in Colossians, Ephesians, and Philemon about slavery, a reasonably clear trajectory of change can be mapped out that, not incidentally or accidentally, parallels the level of discourse that Paul is offering in the given document.

Colossians, not unlike Romans, is what can be called "first-order moral discourse," and that affects the ethical remarks in these letters just as much as their theologizing. First-order discourse is what one is able and willing to say to an audience the first time one addresses them and begins the dialogue. An effective rhetorician will start with the audience where they are and in the course of dialogue and discussion try to move the audience to where the speaker thinks they ought to be. Not everything can be and should be attempted or discussed in one's opening salvo, and this is particularly the case when one wants an audience to change their long-accepted and deeply ingrained behavior patterns.

Paul's letter to the Colossians was written to a congregation that Paul did not convert and apparently had not yet even visited. It seems to have been one of Paul's coworkers who planted the church in Colossae.[8] Paul addresses his audience knowing that there already exists in Colossae, and among the church members there, a patriarchal cultural structure and also a domination system, slavery. His interest is in household management within Christian homes, particularly as it affects Christian congregations, not in general. In his opening salvo Paul starts with the household structure in which women, slaves, and minors are in a decidedly inferior and subordinate position in the household compared to the male head of the household, and he begins to bring Christian ethical concerns to bear on these preexisting relationships, thus ameliorating already at the outset some of the harsher dimensions of those fallen relationships. Paul is bold, but he is not stupid. He does not try to push the conversation further than the traffic will bear in an opening conversation.

Thus, in Colossians 3–4 Paul talks about household relationships being lived out in ways that are more pleasing to the Lord or fitting in the Lord. When Paul turns to exhorting the head of the household, which is unusual in ancient discussions of household management,[9] he restricts the power and way of relating to the subordinate members of the family: the husband must love his wife and not be harsh with her, he must not embitter his children so that they get discouraged, and most of all he must treat his slaves as persons, giving them what is right and fair (even though in Roman law slaves were "living property," meaning that they had no rights). Herein we see only the beginning of the process of putting the leaven of the gospel into these fallen situations.

The next level of discourse, "second-order moral discourse," can be seen in Ephesians, a circular homily that went to the church in Ephesus and probably to the Colossians and other nearby Pauline churches. Here Paul is able to push the envelope a bit further than we find in Colossians. For example,

---

[8]For a fuller form of what follows here, see Ben Witherington III, *The Letters to Philemon, the Colossians, and the Ephesians: A Socio-Rhetorical Commentary on the Captivity Epistles* (Grand Rapids: Eerdmans, 2007), pp. 1-50.

[9]For parallel examples of pagan household codes, see Ben Witherington III, *Women in the Earliest Churches* (SNTSMS 59; Cambridge: Cambridge University Press, 1988).

at the introduction to the household code at Ephesians 5:21, Paul exhorts all Christians to submit to one another out of reverence to Christ. Suddenly, it is not just the customarily subordinate persons in that society who are doing the submitting—wives, children, slaves; now even the men are submitting to their fellow Christians and serving them. This self-sacrificial and serving ethic is something that Jesus himself enunciated: he did not come to be served, but to serve and to give his life as a ransom for the many (Mk 10:45). Paul takes up this theme in Philippians 2:5-11 by showing how the coming of the Son into the world is an example, in fact the example par excellence, of one stripping oneself of prerogatives and taking on the very form and approach of a slave, serving others. Instead of domineering and causing others to submit, Jesus stepped down and served others, setting his followers an example of freely chosen submission and service of others.

But it is not just in the introduction to the household code in Ephesians 5–6 that we find that the trajectory of change has moved on further from Colossians. Other remarks show this as well. The husband is not merely to love his wife; he is to love her in the same self-sacrificial way Christ loved the church and gave up his very life for it. In regard to the husband's relationship with his children, he is charged with the task of bringing them up in the Christian faith and ethical practices. In Ephesians, this task is not left for the wife to do. Astonishingly, in Ephesians 6:9 Paul says to slave owners, "Treat your slaves in the same manner." In the same manner as what? In the same manner as the slaves are to serve their masters, wholeheartedly, serving as though they were serving the Lord himself. In other words, the master must serve and respect servants and do it wholeheartedly. And then we also have the warning not to threaten or abuse the slaves, backed with the sanction that the masters themselves have a Master in heaven who is all-seeing and all-knowing. Most remarkably, Paul spends more time exhorting the head of the household than the rest of the household combined, attenuating his power, Christianizing his thinking, restricting his privileges, calling him to love and self-sacrificially serve. This goes well beyond Greco-Roman household management advice.

Finally, if we turn to Philemon, we have what can be called "third-order moral discourse," the sort of discourse that one could and would have with an intimate. Here one no longer needs to hold anything in reserve; one can speak frankly, and Paul does. He calls for Philemon to manumit his wayward runaway slave, Onesimus, rather than punish him, insists that Philemon treat Onesimus "no longer as a slave, but more than a slave, a brother in Christ," and urges Philemon to treat and receive Onesimus as he would treat the apostle himself.

And just in case Philemon had not figured out that Paul was as serious as a heart attack about what he was urging, Paul reminds him that he owes him his very spiritual life, and that he hopes to come to him soon (to make sure that Philemon follows through on what Paul is now persuading him to do). Here indeed we see how far the ethical discussion of slavery could and would go in an early Christian Pauline context. Paul is not afraid to imply that treating someone as a sibling is incompatible with having someone as a slave. This comports with what Paul says in 1 Corinthians 7:21, where he states that a slave who is offered freedom should take it. As the levels of moral discourse progress from initial discussion to talking with an intimate, one can see the trajectory of change enunciated over time when the same person is treating the same subject with some portion of the same audience (it appears that Philemon was part of the church in Colossae).

It is unfortunate that we do not have more examples of all three levels of discourse offered on the same or a similar subject to the same audience at various points in their relationship. But these examples tells us something important: especially with ethical remarks we need to ask not only about the position taken but also about the direction of the remarks. Where are these remarks heading? Do they stand out from the usual advice of that social world, and if so, in what way? In what way can they be seen as examples, if they can, of attempts to bring about change in the status quo? The same sorts of questions can be asked when we compare the teaching of Jesus to that of other early Jewish teachers in a variety of subjects. When we do so, we discover that although Jesus is conventional in some regards, clearly enough in various of his ethical teachings he is moving well beyond and challenging the existing status quo. But we will see and know this only if we do our homework and study Jesus in his proper social context. These are the sorts of questions we need to ask of the ethical texts found in the New Testament.

MATTERS OF CONSCIENCE AND THE BODY OF CHRIST IN NEW TESTAMENT ETHICS

Leaving aside for a moment the obvious direct commandments of the New Testament that order behavior in both general and specific ways, we note that there are many indications that we also have help in forming the Christian conscience and faculty of moral discernment so that one can make moral judgments for oneself or so that a community can collectively make such judgments, particularly in matters for which there is no specific teaching or commandment in the New Testament. Let us consider the discussion in a couple of Pauline texts: Romans 14:5-6; 1 Corinthians 8–10.

Romans 14:5-6 is remarkable as a pronouncement made by a former Pharisee. Formerly a strict Sabbatarian and follower of ritual purity codes (see Phil 3:6), Paul now says,

> Some consider one day more sacred than another; others consider every day alike. All should be fully persuaded in their own minds. Those who regard one day as special do so to the Lord. Those who eat meat do so to the Lord, for they give thanks to God; and those who abstain do so to the Lord and give thanks to God.

This discussion should be compared to the more lengthy one in 1 Corinthians 8–10 about eating meat sacrificed to idols and going to pagan temple feasts. But here the context is about the divisions between Jewish and Gentile Christians in Rome over issues such as the Sabbath and food. Paul says to them that about such things "all should be fully persuaded in their own minds."

As we might say, it is a matter of individual conscience, and as Paul was to stress more clearly in 1 Corinthians 8–10, whatever a person cannot do in good conscience is sin, at least for that person—a violation of one's faith and conscience. Clearly enough, Paul thinks that keeping the food laws or keeping the Sabbath is no longer required of the followers of Jesus. The eschatological age has broken in, and new occasions teach new duties. What is also remarkable about the discussion in both these Pauline texts is that although Paul largely agrees with the Gentiles that observing such food laws and Sabbatarian practice is no longer required of the followers of Jesus, even the Jewish ones, he nonetheless seeks to protect those whom he calls the "weaker" (in conscience) brothers and sisters, those who, in his view, have too many scruples about food and Sabbath and the like.

In 1 Corinthians 8–10 Paul is trying to raise the consciousness of the self-centered, more elite Gentile Christians in Corinth that they have an obligation not to cause their Jewish brothers and sisters with more scruples to stumble about eating meat that had been sacrificed to idols. The conscience of others, however overly scrupulous it might be, must not be violated by trying to cajole them into eating something that they do not feel comfortable eating. Paul views the overly scrupulous conscience as a weaker conscience, not a stronger one, but out of love he does not want the weaker in faith to be led into sin.

In this circumstance, what is and is not Christian ethical behavior depends on how sensitive one's own conscience is about such matters. And one gets the sense that there are many such matters that Paul would consider *adiaphora*, or "things indifferent," in themselves: what one wears or eats or when one observes a holy day. They become ethically charged matters when questions such as these are asked: "If I do such and such a thing, will it cause my brother or sister to stumble?" "Am I standing on my own rights and conscience without discerning the effects of my actions on those who are not equally convinced about this form of behavior?" "What sort of behavior in this matter builds up the body of Christ and what sort rips it asunder?" In other words, in these kinds of matters the ethic of love for the other, especially within the body of Christ, and the need to do good to and honor the other becomes the principle guide as to what is and is not ethical behavior in such situations where a difference of opinion and conscience exists over a matter that is actually *adiaphora* now that the dominion is breaking into the human sphere.

At the very heart of the ethic of Jesus and of his followers who wrote New Testament books was the ethic of love—wholehearted love of God and love of neighbor as self, but also love of enemy. Love, according to Romans 13:8, is the one debt constantly owed by the believer to others. What is interesting about all the emphasis on love in so many places in the New Testament (see, e.g., Mt 5–7; John 3; Rom 12–13; 1 John 4–5) is that love has a concrete face, and it is fleshed out by quite specific enjoinders and commandments of various sorts. Love is not allowed to be some sort of fuzzy guiding principle that each person is allowed to define on his or her own terms.

Although there is plenty of room for moral discernment in the Christian ethic, there are so many imperatives in the New Testament that make clear what love ought to look like, even tough love with the recalcitrant (see 1 Cor 5), that we do not hear the modern refrain in the New Testament "What is the loving thing to do?" as if this question could be asked while ignoring things such as the vice list in 1 Corinthians 6:9-10, which tells us what sort of behaviors, if persisted in, will keep even Christians out of the kingdom, or while ignoring the commandments from the Decalogue that are reiterated in Romans 13:9-10. As Paul says in that context, the essence of the Decalogue insofar as it involves interpersonal behavior is "love does no wrong to the neighbor," and the Decalogue shows more specifically what sort of things count as wrongs.

What we should discern from all of this is that there are both ethical principles and ethical practices, and forms of behavior that are considered right or wrong in all situations, and then there are other forms of behavior that become right or wrong depending on their effect on the neighbor or the fellow member of the body of Christ. One cannot simply look at the map or reread the directions in all cases. One needs, so to speak, an indwelling GPS device, a sense of moral direction in the many instances where there is no commandment specified in the new covenant. And this calls for a sense of and a knack for proper and holy ethical improvisation, which requires more explanation at this juncture.[10]

CHRISTIAN ETHICS: PERFORMANCE OR JOURNEY?

Mention improvisation, and most people will think of something spontaneous like free-form musical experimentation such as one finds in jazz music. This clearly is not what Samuel Wells has in mind in his book *Improvisation: The Drama of Christian Ethics*. As Wells says, ethics presupposes a context, and an understanding of context presupposes narrative. Whose story are we supposed to be living out of and into? We have already seen in the preceding section of this discussion that Paul is encouraging his converts to do some improvising so that the conscience of a weaker brother or sister is not violated and so that the building up of the community and the love of the other is the goal of all actions.

Wells reasons that the Christian story is drama, and therefore ethics is a form of performance of the drama.[11] In this he sounds remarkably like Kevin Vanhoozer, except that Vanhoozer is speaking about doctrine.[12] The problem that I have with the approach of both of these scholars is that drama is the wrong analogy, and so performance is not what behaving ethically is about. It is about pilgrimage, not performance; odyssey or journey, not drama. It is more like *Pilgrim's Progress* than Archibald MacLeish's *J.B.*

---

[10]Discerning the difference between a nonnegotiable and *adiaphora* can be difficult if (1) one is barely biblically literate; (2) one makes the mistake of assuming that the ethics of the old covenant are still binding on all Christians; (3) one reads into the New Testament ethic things that are not there (e.g., a ban on chewing tobacco). I suggest that one start by taking the explicit commandments in the New Testament at face value as nonnegotiables unless one sees evidence of a trajectory of change in several instances of a discussion of the same subject and the levels of moral discourse are of several sorts.

[11]See Wells, *Improvisation*, pp. 59-70.

[12]I am referring to Kevin Vanhoozer, *The Drama of Doctrine: A Canonical-Linguistic Approach to Christian Theology* (Louisville: Westminster John Knox, 2005).

The Christian life is not a play, and we are not performing a preordained part or script.[13]

Wells recognizes some of the problems with this model of ethics as performance of a script. He lists two problems: (1) A script might be assumed to provide a comprehensive version of life in which all questions and eventualities are covered. Clearly enough, this is not what we have in the New Testament when it comes to ethics, as anyone who has argued about the issue of abortion on the basis of New Testament principles rather than specific commandments has to admit. (2) The notion of performance of a script gives the impression that the Bible includes or encompasses the whole of the church's story and how it should be lived out. If only that were true! But as Acts 28 reminds us, we have been plopped down in the city of humankind with no resolution to the story yet in sight. We are all still "waiting for Godot" or, in this case, for Jesus to come back and resolve various matters. It is for this very reason that I have used the analogy with the roadmap (or even treasure map) and its directions when thinking of the New Testament and ethics.

A roadmap, even with attendant directions, is not like a full script of a drama where every entrance and exit, every speech and action, is prescripted. Wells also rightly points out that a script suggests that there was a time when God's people did get it right, a golden age, so to speak, and we should simply retrace their steps. This ignores the many tales of failure, sin, loss and tragedy that we have in the Bible; and more to the point, often such tales are told about people who in their better moments are ethical paradigms—Peter, for example. Furthermore, a script and performance model of Christian ethics risks the danger of having no genuine engagement with the world, no clear response in the present to unexpected twists and turns in life.[14] To this I would add that the drama/script/performance model has a sense of artificiality to it. A play is, after all, about acting, not so much about being. But Christian ethics certainly is not about acting or pretending to be someone or something that one is not. Instead, it is about walking—walking as yourself with your own name, in a particular direction, following the map, the directions, and yes, the internal GPS device.

And this brings us to Wells's helpful concept of improvisation. "When improvisers are trained to work in the theater, they are schooled in a tradition

---

[13]To his credit, Vanhoozer does talk a good deal about improvisation, but he still wants to hold on to the notion of a script in most cases.

[14]See Wells, *Improvisation*, pp. 62-63.

so thoroughly that they learn to act from habit in ways that are appropriate to the circumstance. This is exactly the goal of theological ethics."[15] So, then, we are talking about the ingrained habits of the heart, providing a natural tracking device or guidance system when the road forward is covered with underbrush or it is not clear which turn to take. Wells goes on to ward off misconceptions of his term *improvisation*. "One misapprehension is that improvisation is about being original."[16] No, improvisation presumes a detailed knowledge of the situation and the circumstances and an ability to react to the unexpected in an appropriate manner—or to use drama terminology, to act in character rather than out of character.

It is interesting that the author of Hebrews, who uses the pilgrimage model at length when describing the Christian life and provides a long list of examples of folks in the hall of faith in Hebrews 11 that one should consider and reflect on, finishes that hall by telling the audience that Jesus is the pioneer and perfecter or trailblazer and finisher of faith, and therefore the Christian is said to be one who must be "looking to Jesus" and following him and the trail he blazed into glory (Heb 12:1-2). He is finally the ultimate paradigm of what faith and faithfulness look like, and he, as the lead runner, is the one whom we should be trotting along behind and on the same right track as well.

This model of Christian ethics is rather different from the drama/script/performance model. The improvisation that Wells is rightly talking about does not necessarily involve being original, clever, or witty; it involves faithfully reacting to situations and circumstances that, though unexpected, are not uncommon, and it calls for improvisation within the parameters of good Christian character. Think of the analogy of a runner in a long-distance race with a crowded field of competitors. The runner is constantly bumped and jostled, knocked off balance or slightly off course by the regular jockeying for position, the attempts to pass slower runners, and so on. Thus, the runner must develop coping skills to maintain balance, to avoid stepping on someone else's foot and so twist an ankle, to avoid falling or running outside the lane lines. The Christian ethical journey or race is much the same, and fortunately many have gone before us, showing us the way, particularly the ultimate trailblazer, Jesus. Improvisation in a race involves, to a great extent, watching others successfully navigate around obstacles and following their examples.

It is no accident that Paul tells his Corinthian converts that no tempta-

---

[15]Ibid., p. 65.
[16]Ibid., p. 67.

tion has overcome them that is not common to humanity, and that with such trials God can provide an adequate means of escape. Their journey is no more arduous than that of the exodus generation that wandered in the wilderness, but also no less perilous (1 Cor 10). Improvisation is not merely for the elite who are clever; it is for any and every Christian who would but embrace it. When the map and the directions do not specify, what does one do? The answer is faithful and in-character improvisation. As clichéd as it might sound, it involves asking, "What would Jesus do?" for we are indeed living out of and emulating his story, his journey, his pilgrimage from gall to glory, from disgrace to grace, from death to resurrection. In short, New Testament ethics involves living out of the very heart of the New Testament thought world—the narrative of and about Jesus, which includes his words as well as his deeds.

Wells is also right that the sort of improvisation he is talking about is not the isolated performance of a gifted individual—say, a Robin Williams type improvising in spontaneous stream of consciousness. It is more like the ensemble playing of a group of jazz musicians who inwardly know where the boundaries are, when to rise and fall, when to speed up and slow down, when to play sharps and when flats, when to be loud and when soft, and they know this because of years of interactive playing with other improvisers. One is creating a response to life not de novo or by oneself but rather in community as a fellow traveler with all the other travelers singing the pilgrimage songs, the songs of Zion, together and in harmony. Harmonizing requires listening intently to the other improvisers and fitting in. It requires restraint of one's own natural individualistic self-expression and creativity. It requires channeling one's efforts and energies in the same direction in which the others are going.

I would add to Wells's reflections that what allows one to successfully improvise in unexpected situations such that the improvisation is in accord with Christian ethics is that one has first internalized deeply the Scriptures, especially the story of Jesus, such that the almost instinctive reaction will flow right out of and in accord with the story that one has internalized and seeks to live by, the map and directions one has memorized and seeks to follow.

But alas, true improvisation becomes difficult and dangerous and is not for beginners if they are biblically illiterate. If you have not carefully studied the map, learned its contours, looked at the examples of those who have traveled this way before you, including especially Jesus, and read and reread the directions so that you do not need to keep looking them up, then you are not ready for prime time, you are not ready for "A Night at the Improv." You are not prepared for the unexpected crises that come along the way. In short, especially younger Christians need the community of faith to model how to do the improvisation. Let me illustrate what I mean.

On September 11, 2001, many people came unglued, including many Christians, and indeed even many clergy. One pastor on the West Coast launched a tirade the following Sunday. He got into the pulpit and said words to this effect: "I am an American first, and a Christian second. Bomb them back into the stone age." When challenged on this by more than one parishioner, he did not listen, and he suggested that perhaps they were not patriotic enough. Three things are most interesting about this. First, this pastor certainly never paused to ask, "What would Jesus do in this situation?" My hunch is that Jesus would be right there at Ground Zero, running into buildings and rescuing people, binding up the wounds and helping the healing process, not figuring out the coordinates and trajectories involved in a successful retaliation. Second, a crisis will reveal what your real values are, what your real internal GPS tracking device is, what your real default mode is. For this pastor, it was not Christianity that he had most deeply internalized, it was nationalism. Third, accordingly, the advice that he gave his congregation, besides being a direct contradiction of texts such as Romans 12:17-21, was in fact unethical. Love had given way to hate, unrighteous anger had fueled his response, and he sounded nothing like Jesus in the pulpit on that day. Indeed, he had simply revealed his own idolatry. In all likelihood, his problem was not that he did not know what the New Testament says about revenge, but rather that he had not embodied and internalized it and let it change his natural inclinations. So when he sought to improvise on the spot during a crisis, his improvisation, unfortunately, was unChristian. I will have more to say about good and bad improvisation later.

At this juncture it is time to stop the ground-clearing exercises and get down to cases. The point that I wish to make in concluding this chapter is simply this: New Testament ethics is not a mundane subject, and the ethics found in the New Testament is not a mere rehashing of conventional ethics, whether Jewish or Greco-Roman. There is borrowing, and influences can be detected, but no influence is more dominating in the New Testament than that of Jesus and his own ethic, and we can see this in witnesses as diverse as the reflections on suffering love in 1 Peter and on how to live wisely in community in James, or the ethic of love enunciated by Paul or by the elder in 1 John.

Just as Jesus' teaching needs to be considered in any discussion of New Testament theology, so too Jesus' teaching needs to be considered in any discussion of New Testament ethics. At least four writers, the four evangelists, thought that the ethics of Jesus was relevant to the Christians whom they addressed. As it turns out, they were not alone; the other New Testament writers thought so as well to one degree or another. Even a remarkable work such as Revelation, which has much to say about future judgment and Christ's role in it, uses all its thunder and lightning as a way of reinforcing that the Christian audiences need to be prepared to forgo retaliation, to suffer martyrdom, to get back to their first love, to leave justice and vindication in the hands of the one who can unseal the seals.

9

The Ethics of Jesus and Its Influence on the New Testament Writers

The foundation [of Jesus' ethic] is the radicalization of the love commandment, which Jesus extends to love for one's enemies. In light of the in-breaking of the kingdom of God this love will clearly illuminate the signs of the incomprehensible mercy of God in the midst of this world.

Richard Burridge[1]

What did Jesus think that it meant to be a disciple of his? According to the Gospels, perhaps especially the Synoptic Gospels, it was all about following Jesus and emulating him. It was all about leaving other occupations and preoccupations behind and coming with Jesus as he did ministry across Galilee, Samaria, and Judea. But at some point, Jesus let his disciples know that discipleship means more than just following him around and imitating his behavior. At some point, he told them that those who want to be his disciples must take up their own crosses, deny themselves, and follow him.

Herein lies a call to follow the story of Jesus to the bitter end. You do not take up a cross unless you are a condemned person. The story of the Master was to become the story of the disciple. And interestingly enough, few of the original Christians understood this more clearly than Peter and Paul—Peter with his reflections on being a suffering servant and a holy person, Paul with his reflections on having been crucified with Christ or filling up the sufferings of Christ. The ethic of Jesus is all about self-sacrifice, not merely denying one's self something in particular, but actually denying oneself, ceding one's

---

[1]Richard A. Burridge, *Imitating Jesus: An Inclusive Approach to New Testament Ethics* (Grand Rapids: Eerdmans, 2007), p. 55.

life to Christ. His story becomes our story, and it is indeed a story of death and deliverance beyond death and self-sacrifice. Jesus came not to be served, but rather to serve and to give his life as ransom for the many (Mk 10:45).

When you enunciate an ethic that valorizes taking up a cross and being a servant or slave of others, you are articulating an ethic that stands foursquare against the dominant ethic of the Greco-Roman world, which saw crucifixion as the most shameful way to die and saw being a slave as beneath the dignity of honorable persons. Acting in slavish fashion was considered shameful indeed. Not surprisingly in that world, humility, stepping down and serving others and being self-effacing, was not seen as a virtue. In the ethic of Jesus it is not just a reversal of fortune that happens when the last, least, and lost become the first, most, and found; it is also reversal of cultural expectations and a transvaluation of values and virtues when a crucified manual laborer from Nazareth becomes the savior of the world and models servanthood and self-sacrificial, other-loving grace. Jesus' ethic was not merely countercultural; in some aspects it was counterintuitive, and it made his ministry, and that of his followers, stand out in various respects. It demanded a response then, and it still does today.

In a remarkable and fascinating study, Jewish biblical scholar David Flusser recounts his journey with the study of Jesus through the years and how he became convinced that Jesus was indeed a messianic figure. Indeed, Flusser came to believe that Jesus' radical ethic about loving enemies had enormous importance even today as a force that could change the world. He came to admire the Mennonites as those whom he could identify as people closely following the ethic of Jesus, and he once said, "If the Christians would be Mennonites, then my [book on Jesus] would be a Christian book."[2] This shows that even for those outside the church community, this ethic of Jesus remains compelling, demanding, beckoning. It will bear close scrutiny.

REVISITING THE ETHICS OF THE KINGDOM

When you believe you have come to set the world on fire, you usually have no time to provide a detailed explanation. You are in a hurry, and things must be done rather quickly. The dominion of God is breaking in, and the breathless nature of the situation is conveyed well by the earliest Gospel writer, Mark, who uses the adverb *immediately* about forty times to give a sense of the pace

---

[2]David Flusser, *The Sage from Galilee: Rediscovering Jesus' Genius* (Grand Rapids: Eerdmans, 2007), p. xix.

of things. Mark's Gospel is not, to borrow Eugene Peterson's phrase, about "a long obedience in the same direction." It is about "hurry up and repent" because the divine redemptive judgment is coming soon to a theater near you. With that sort of eschatological mindset, what sort of ethics can be and should be done?

Albert Schweitzer had an answer: interim ethics. Actually, Schweitzer assumed that it had to be an ethic for an assumed short period of time. But Jesus does not assume that there is very little future in his future. What he assumes is that the future has already begun to happen, and thus we are all on the clock, but no one knows when the clock will run out of ticks. There is a sense of urgency, but not immediate emergency. Jesus' ethic is eschatological in flavor, assuming that the kingdom is already coming, but it is not the ethic of a doomsday prophet who thinks that time will run out soon and very soon. Jesus' ethic is one of great expectations but no specific prognostications. Schweitzer, then, was wrong about the ethic of Jesus. An eschatological ethic need not presuppose a near-horizon scenario. In fact, one can say that it is as much the eschatological "already" that dictates the ethic of Jesus as the sanction of the "not yet" coming judgment and final salvation. Like a pendulum between the eschatological "already" and the "not yet," Jesus offers wise teaching on how to live between what is and is to come. Jesus came not just to end old things, but also to start new things.

The coming of the final divine saving activity on earth changed many things. One of those things is the nature of God's community, according to Jesus. Whatever concepts had existed before based on gender, generation and geography were replaced with the more complex notion that whoever does the will of God is Jesus' brother, sister, mother (Mk 3:31-35). In Jesus' view, the family of faith, not the physical family, is the primary unit of true community, something that one might leave one's physical family to become a part of.

We should note that this is not a concept of a righteous remnant per se. The Twelve, or even the wider circle of disciples, were not seen as an alternative Israel. The Twelve were not called to be Israel but rather to free and, later at the eschaton, to judge the tribes of Israel. Faith in Jesus and in his teaching and attempting to emulate and follow him bound these disciples together. To be sure, all of them were Jews. The good news was for Jews first. But it was not only for Jews, even in Jesus' day. Jesus was perfectly willing to commend the faith of a Syrophoenician woman or a Gentile centurion when it outshone that of his inner circle. It was, even with Jesus, all about faith and doing the eschatological will of God. What I must do in what follows is give a taste of the distinctive and also the characteristic flavors of Jesus' ethic.[3]

The Ethics of Marriage, Divorce, Children, and Singleness

It was radical enough to suggest that the family of faithful followers of Jesus was the primary family. But Jesus did not stop there. He redefined how one should look at marriage, family, and singleness in a Jewish context. Here we do well to reflect in a bit of detail on Mark 10 // Matthew 19 and consider the "family values" and other ethical codes as enunciated by Jesus.[4]

The material in roughly the first half of Mark 10 deals with family matters, including marriage, divorce, children, and the effect of discipleship on family obligations and family possessions. The net effect of Jesus' teachings on these matters is to make clear that the cost of discipleship and of living by dominion principles is high, indeed too high for some (such as the rich man) to accept. The setting of this teaching material (note the emphasis on teaching at the end of Mk 10:1) is the region of Judea and "across the Jordan." It is not completely clear whether Mark is describing already Jesus' final journey up from Galilee to Judea or instead some sort of ministry in Judea and Perea that he has not highlighted elsewhere. At the least, the point seems to be that Jesus continues to feel free to reach out to those beyond the Holy Land as well as those within it.

The narrative begins in Mark 10:2 with Jesus being confronted with a group of Pharisees who are seeking to hear his opinion as to whether it is legally permitted for a man to divorce his wife. But the questioning is done for the purpose of trapping Jesus in what he will say. In other words, Jesus is being put to the test. Thus, in a sense it need not be the case that the Pharisees were confronting Jesus with a live possibility in this setting. Like the Sadducees questioning Jesus about the woman who married a bevy of brothers in sequence, the question here could have been hypothetical and posed to flush out Jesus' real thoughts on the matter. There is evidence from this era

---

[3]We cannot really tell how unique some of this material is, since we do not have an exhaustive knowledge of either those sages who came before Jesus or those who came after him. It therefore is better to speak of what seems to characterize Jesus' teaching, what seems to be distinctive about it.

[4]For more exegetical detail, see Ben Witherington III, *The Gospel of Mark: A Socio-Rhetorical Commentary* (Grand Rapids: Eerdmans, 2001); *Matthew* (SHBC; Macon, Ga.: Smith & Helwys, 2006).

of a more strict attitude toward divorce than that espoused by, for example, Shammai or Hillel, both of whom agreed that there were grounds for divorce based on either a lenient or a strict reading of material found in Deuteronomy 24 (cf. CD-A IV). According to David Daube, this passage follows a traditional pattern of early Jewish debating in which there is a question by an opponent (Mk 10:2), a public response sufficient to silence the inquisitor but that states only part of the truth (Mk 10:5-9), and a private explanation given to one's followers in a fuller way (Mk 10:10-12).[5]

There has been much discussion among scholars about the differences between the Matthean and Markan forms of this debate. In Matthew the question has to do with what legitimate causes there are for divorce (with the privilege of divorce itself simply assumed), and the response of Jesus in Matthew 19 takes into account that there is at least one exception to the no divorce rule, whereas in Mark nothing is said about an exception. In Mark the discussion is about the legitimacy of divorce itself, not the grounds for divorce. In view of 1 Corinthians 7:10-11, it seems reasonably clear that Mark is closer than Matthew in form to the original teaching of Jesus on this matter. As early as the 50s it was clear to Paul that Jesus' teaching was that two (believing) people joined together by God should not divorce. This, to say the least, was a radical teaching, even within early Jewish circles, and so we need to consider Mark 10 in some more detail.

First, separation of a married couple without divorce was basically not a legal possibility in early Judaism.[6] Second, it seems clear that Matthew has emended his Markan source here to make it more apt for his own more Jewish Christian audience. Third, divorce in Jesus' setting was almost without exception a male privilege. Thus, there is some merit to Elisabeth Schüssler Fiorenza's remarks:

> Divorce is necessary because of the male's *hardness of heart,* that is, because of men's patriarchal mind-set and reality. . . . However, Jesus insists, God did not intend patriarchy but created persons as male and female human beings. It is not woman who is given into the power of man in order to continue "his" house and family line, but it is man who shall sever connections with his own patriarchal family and "the two persons shall become one *sarx*." . . . The passage is best translated as "The two persons—man and woman—enter

---

[5]David Daube, *The New Testament and Rabbinic Judaism* (London: Athlone Press, 1956), pp. 141-43.
[6]See Ben Witherington III, *Women in the Ministry of Jesus: A Study of Jesus' Attitudes to Women and Their Roles as Reflected in His Earthly Life* (SNTSMS 51; Cambridge: Cambridge University Press, 1984), pp. 2-6.

into a common human life and social relationship because they are created as equals."[7]

In Mark 10:3 Jesus asks, "What did Moses command you?" Jesus does not dispute the authority of Mosaic law, but he sees it as concessionary in nature, introduced because of human weakness or hard-heartedness. The Pharisees respond that Moses permitted a man to write a bill of divorce and to divorce. Jesus in turn rejoins that Moses wrote this commandment for them because of their hardening of the spiritual arteries. This raises an interesting hermeneutical issue: what force should divine laws have that originally were written, in Jesus' view, as concessions to human fallenness? It appears that in Jesus' view, he was prepared to appeal to God's original prefall intentions for marriage over against the Mosaic requirements of Deuteronomy 24:1-4. Specifically, a bill of divorce was required to be given to the woman in order to make clear that she was no longer married. Jesus seems to suggest that the Mosaic provision was meant to limit a problem, not to license a practice that in essence goes against God's original intentions for marriage.[8]

In the Markan form of the discussion Jesus goes immediately from the remark on hard-heartedness to a partial quotation of Genesis 1:27; 5:2; 2:24 (Mk 10:6-7). The creation order is that from the beginning of creation God made human beings male and female. Because of this duality of the sexes, a man will leave his father and mother and cleave to his wife. In Mark 10:8 Jesus says that the two will become one flesh.[9] "The implication is that the one flesh union becomes more constitutive of a man and a woman's being than their uniqueness. Only two can become one, and when they do they are no longer two."[10] This is not to say that the marriage could not be broken up by some third party. Notice that the text says "what [i.e., the union] God has joined together, let no one put asunder" (Mk 10:9). The verb *chōrizō* actually means "to separate" and is used in the Greek papyri to mean "to divorce." Could Jesus be suggesting to officials that they should not grant a legal divorce in such a situation? More clearly, here Jesus is talking only about faithful Jews whom God has joined together. He says nothing about pagan

---

[7]Elisabeth Schüssler Fiorenza, *In Memory of Her: A Feminist Theological Reconstruction of Christian Origins* (New York: Crossroad, 1985), p. 143.

[8]Exodus 21:10-11 does not seem to discuss the same matter, for the issue there seems to be polygamy and whether there is still a duty to the first wife after a man takes another.

[9]The Hebrew of Genesis 2:24 simply says "they will become one flesh." It is the LXX where "the two" first appears, which makes clear that monogamy is the goal.

[10]Witherington, *Women in the Ministry of Jesus*, p. 26.

marriages, nor does he suggest that God joins all marriages together, for he objected to relationships such as that of Herod Antipas and Herodias. The qualifiers that Jesus makes in his remarks must be taken seriously.

Jesus' argument, then, seems to be as follows. In creation God made two distinct but complementary human genders. God then also brought the two complimentary genders together in marriage. No third party is allowed into this relationship. Anyone who seeks to divide those who share such a marriage and one-flesh union attacks not only the marriage and the two united in that marriage but also God who brought them together as well. Both the Creator and the creational order undergird marriage. If a man and a woman so joined together do divorce, they must not remarry anyone else, for to do so would be adultery. Jesus recognizes the reality of divorce, but he does not think that this legitimizes remarriage if the original couple were joined together by God in the first place.

Mark 10:11 is a teaching apparently independently attested in Luke 16:18a. Mark seems to have added to the original form of the teaching the phrase *ep' autēn*, which can be translated either "against her" or "with her." Early Jews apparently never spoke of a man committing adultery against his own wife, and thus the phrase in question could be translated "with her" (i.e., with the second woman). Thus, Mark 10:11 could mean "Whoever divorces his wife and marries another commits adultery with the other." This makes good sense because adultery is, by definition, an act committed by a married person with a third party. But there are good reasons to favor the translation "against her." Certainly, the verse reflects the spirit of Jesus' views, for only Jesus, or someone as radical as he was, was likely to go against the grain of patriarchy to the degree of defining adultery not as an act committed against another man who has a wife but rather in terms of infidelity either against one's own wife or with another's wife. What is interesting about this verse is not only its strictness, for Jesus seems to assume that the first one-flesh union is still in force even after the divorce, hence the second marriage is seen as an act of adultery, but also, against the normal use of the term in antiquity, it is the man who is labeled as an adulterer.

One could argue that Mark 10:12 is Mark's adaptation of Jesus' radical teaching on divorce to a Greco-Roman setting, since Jewish women basically did not have the power or legal permission to divorce their husbands in Jesus' locale and era. Josephus says, "For it is (only) the man who is permitted by us to do this, and not even a divorced woman may marry again on her own initiative unless her former husband consents" (*Ant.* 15.259). Yet there is some evidence that some Jewish women in Palestine could both write out the bill of divorce and even pronounce the divorce formula. Some Jewish women of high rank, such as Herodias, did divorce their husbands, but this could be seen as the exception that proves the general rule (for the social elite often did not play by the normal rules).[11] This raises the possibility that Mark 10:12 is Jesus' own comment on the famous case of Herodias (see also Lk 13:31-32). Donald Juel's conclusion about this whole passage is apt:

> [Jesus'] forbidding of divorce is clearly a statement about the status of women in society. They are to be safeguarded as vulnerable members of society. That also explains the passage about Jesus and the children who were both vulnerable members of society. Crucial to their survival has always been economic support. Easy divorce of women with young children means abrogating responsibility for caring for the most important members of society at a time of maximum vulnerability. The community that forms around Jesus will be an alternative community.[12]

The narrative about Jesus and children begins in Mark 10:13 with the remark that "they" (perhaps parents) were bringing *paidia*, a word usually referring to young children (cf. Jn 16:21 with *Gos. Thom.* 22; but in Mark 5:39-42 it refers to a twelve-year-old), so that he might touch them, presumably to bless them (see Gen 48:14). But the disciples scolded or rebuked those bringing the children. This may reflect a typical ancient attitude that young children were less important than adults, and that important teachers should not be bothered by them. Some early Jewish texts stress the immaturity of children (see *m. 'Abot* 3:11; 4:20).

This action of the disciples causes Jesus to be indignant with them, and in essence he rebukes the rebukers. They had not remembered the lesson about receiving the little ones in Jesus' name (Mk 9:36-37). He says, "Permit the young children to come to me, and do not hinder them, for *tōn . . . toioutōn* is the dominion of God" (Mk 10:14). The Greek phrase quoted here seems to indicate "these children who are brought to Jesus and those others who are of this sort." It is fair to say that it is quite impossible to make the primary reference of *tōn . . . toioutōn* a comparison with other individuals. In other words, this text cannot simply be referring to those adults who are childlike to the

---

[11]For additional evidence in favor of seeing this as Jesus' teaching about a famously scandalous situation see ibid., p. 149 n. 144.

[12]Donald H. Juel, *The Gospel of Mark* (IBT; Nashville: Abingdon, 1999), pp. 131-32.

exclusion of those who are actually young children being brought to Jesus. It can refer to the young children and those adults who come to Jesus in child-like fashion. Notice that Jesus says nothing about building or accomplishing the dominion or making it happen, but only of receiving or entering it. Jesus is not romanticizing children or childhood as a time of innocence. His point is that children are content to be led somewhere and receive something as a gift, and this is the proper way for all persons to receive the dominion or divine saving activity of God.

After this saying there is appended an additional one from Jesus found in Mark and Luke (cf. Mt 18:3): "Truly, I say to you, unless you receive the dominion as a child, you shall not enter it" (Mk 10:15; Lk 18:17). Notice how this saying suggests both a present ("receive") and a future dimension ("enter") to God's dominion. This is unlikely to mean "unless you receive the dominion during childhood," but possibly it means "unless you receive the dominion in like fashion to which you should receive a little child, uncon-ditionally and with open arms," as Jesus did. Notice that Jesus gives a warm embrace to children in Mark 9:36; 10:16. This novel suggestion intimates that we are to treat the dominion as if it were a child.

The usual reading of the aphorism, however, is that Jesus means that we should receive the dominion in the same fashion that children receive it. This is a more probable reading in view of Mark 10:13-14, 16, which recount how Jesus received children, verses that speak to the issue of the place of children in the dominion. The point, then, is that the dominion is made up of children and those like them, not that the dominion is like a child in some manner. Perhaps making the child's behavior a model for adult behavior was so counterintuitive in Jesus' setting that the strong assertion of Jesus' personal authority ("Truly, I say to you . . .") was required to back it up. In context, there is a notable contrast between the ease with which children enter the dominion of God and the difficulty with which rich adults do so.

The pericope closes in Mark 10:16 with an action by Jesus that indicates clear acceptance of the children and of the intentions of those who brought them. Jesus goes beyond touching the children to hugging them. Thus, it can be said that Jesus uses the smallest member of the physical family as a model for members of the family of faith and gives children a place in the kingdom. The evidence of Jesus' positive attitude toward children, their place in the kingdom, and how they might serve as models for disciples and be served by disciples seems to imply a positive estimation of a woman's role as childbearer and mother (as well as a positive estimation of the father's role). Of course, this text is also a parade example demonstrating Jesus' great concern for and compassion on the weak and most vulnerable members of society. Ched Myers rightly asks,

> Why should not the child represent an actual class of exploited *persons*, as does every other subject of Jesus' advocacy in Mark? . . . [Mark is] concerned to unmask the realities of domination within community and even within kindred relationships. Indeed, from the narrative world of Mark we have cause to suspect that all is not well for the child in first-century Palestinian society. For where do we meet children in the Gospel? In every case, it is in situations of sickness and oppression: the synagogue ruler's daughter (5:21ff.), the Syrophoenician's daughter (7:24ff.), the deaf dumb son (9:14ff.). . . . The social signification of such a consistent narrative portrait suggests that Mark understands the child as victim.[13]

Indeed, the two Markan passages reviewed here show Jesus to be the protector of both women and children, the most vulnerable members of society. In the first instance he protects women by forbidding divorce, thus giving them more social and economic security; in the second instance he protects children by showing them to be valid and valuable members of God's dominion who should be welcomed with open arms.

But what did Jesus think of single persons? Here we have to turn to Matthew 19:10-12, the Matthean supplement to this passage on marriage, divorce and children. In the Matthean presentation of things the disciples are upset by Jesus' teaching, which essentially amounted to a proscription against divorce, taking away male privilege, and so Jesus offers them an alternative by speaking of eunuchs: some are born eunuchs, some are made eunuchs by others, and some make themselves eunuchs for the sake of the dominion of God.

Several things are stunning and radical about this teaching. Eunuchs, according to Old Testament law, were not allowed to participate fully in temple worship. Most Jews would have seen persons as cursed or blighted by God because they were unable to fulfill the mandate of the creation order to be fruitful and multiply. But Jesus does not hesitate to use the term *eunuch* to refer to single persons in general, perhaps thinking of Isaiah 56:4-5: "To the eunuchs who keep my sabbaths, who choose what pleases me, and hold fast to my covenant, to them I will give within my temple and within its walls

---

[13]Ched Myers, *Binding the Strong Man: A Political Reading of Mark's Story of Jesus* (Maryknoll, N.Y.: Orbis, 1988), p. 268.

a memorial and a name better than sons and daughters. I will give them an everlasting name that will endure forever." The prophet is envisioning an eschatological time when the earlier strictures will no longer apply, and eunuchs can be included in the full worship of God. This too could be seen as part of the Jubilee Year vision of Jesus.

But here in Matthew 19:10-12 Jesus is simply making the point that remaining single for the sake of the kingdom is a good thing, pleasing to God. Notice the phrase "to whom it is given." This sort of phrase will crop up again in 1 Corinthians 7, where Paul talks about having a grace gift, a *charisma*, to remain single for the sake of the kingdom or to be married in the Lord. Thus, two options are presented to the disciples of Jesus: either fidelity in a heterosexual monogamous marriage brought about by God or celibacy in singleness. It is assumed that a disciple will have the gift for one or the other of these conditions. What is new here is the stress on the goodness of singleness. At the very least, Jesus is enunciating a teaching highly unusual in early Judaism. The upshot of such teaching on singleness was to give women more possible roles in society, roles other than wife or mother. The dominion was coming, and new occasions teach new relationships and arrangements and new duties as well.

THE ETHICS OF WEALTH AND ETERNAL LIFE

Jesus and the Rich Young Man in Mark 10:17-31

Although the issue of entering God's dominion has just been broached in the passage about children, it can be said that Mark 10:17-31, which seems to be a single unit, distills Jesus' essential teaching about entrance into the realm of God's divine saving activity. The unit has something of a concentric structure, as Myers points out:

A   Question about eternal life
B   Rich man cannot leave possessions and follow
C   Jesus' explanation, disciples' reaction (twice)
B' Disciples have left possessions and followed
A' Answer to question about eternal life[14]

The story begins with Jesus continuing his trek up to Jerusalem when a man runs up to him, falls on his knees, and calls Jesus "Good Teacher." This form of address seems unparalleled either in the Hebrew Scriptures or in early Jewish literature. Only God was called "good" in the ultimate sense in early

---

[14]Ibid., p. 272.

Judaism. It is hard to say whether the man's address to Jesus is flattery or a sincere remark. It may be that a Near Eastern custom is at the root of this interchange, for if the remark is flattery, then the man is setting up a reciprocity exchange in which he expects a flattering remark in return. If so, Jesus quickly dashes the man's hopes. Notice also the form of the question asked: "What must I do to inherit eternal life?" (Mk 10:17). Mark 10:18 may well be Jesus' attempt to make clear to the inquirer that human achievement cannot make a person good, and only God was categorically good. Perhaps we are meant to think that this man believed that he and Jesus were good men because of their deeds, and notice how Jesus responded in terms of deeds. Mark 10:18 is a rebuke to the idea that human beings can be called good because of their deeds, or that the ultimate good in life (eternal life) can be had by doing. It is interesting that in the Greek word order "me" is in an emphatic position in Jesus' response (literally, "Why me do you call good?").

At Mark 10:19 Jesus lists some of the commandments. Perhaps most significant is what he does not list: the Sabbath commandment. This deliberate omission may reflect Jesus' view that now that the eschatological age was dawning, keeping a particular day as the Sabbath was no longer obligatory, for now all days would be holy unto the Lord. The reference to defrauding may well be given in place of the commandment about coveting because Jesus is dealing with a wealthy person who might not covet another's goods but nonetheless might engage in defrauding as a matter of normal business (cf Mal 3:5 LXX). The man replies that he has kept these commandments since his youth, perhaps meaning since the time of his becoming a "son of the commandments" at adolescence, when he assumed the full yoke of adult obedience (see *m. Nid.* 5:6).

Mark 10:21 provides a tender moment, reporting that Jesus looked straight at the man and loved him—the only time in this Gospel Jesus is specifically said to love someone. There was perhaps an earnestness about him that Jesus saw as salutary. But Jesus apparently knows that there is one major obstacle to the man offering total devotion to God: his many possessions. Thus, Jesus tell the man that he lacks one thing and commands him to sell whatever he has and give to the poor.[15] Instead of such possessions the man is to have treasure in heaven and to come and follow Jesus. It appears that the man had thought that as long as he lived a good life and obeyed the major commandments, he was in good shape as far as eternal life is concerned. But keeping com-

---

[15]Jesus does not tell him to give "all" to the poor, though that may be implied (cf. Lk 18:22).

mandments can lead to a false sense of security, a sense that God owes one something. There is no substitute for obedience when God calls one to do something more than obey the Ten Commandments. Mark is making clear that the demands of discipleship to Jesus go beyond the demands of the Mosaic law. The ultimate test of obedience is seen as the willingness to assume the yoke of discipleship to Jesus.

There may have been many early Jews in the position of Saul of Tarsus, who claimed that in regard to obedience to the law he was "blameless" (see Phil 3:6), which must mean having committed no willful violations of a known Mosaic law, so he could not be accused of being a lawbreaker. Perhaps this man who came to Jesus fell into the same category. But not having broken a known law and being innocent or faultless are two different things. It is yet another thing also to talk about being righteous, for it is to a higher righteousness that Jesus calls this man.

In Judaism almsgiving was one of the three pillar virtues, but it presupposes that one has some assets from which to share. What Jesus says amounts to a rejection of conventional Jewish piety that said it was alright to be wealthy as long as one was also generous. Notice the examples from somewhat later Jewish literature where rabbis forbade selling all of one's property, so that one would not be reduced to poverty and dependency on others (*m. ʿArak.* 8:4; *b. Ketub.* 50a). Jesus clearly is enunciating a new Jewish ethic here, and it is not surprising that the man is said to have looked gloomy when he heard about it. The bar had just been raised on what amounted to being a good or godly person, much less being a disciple of Jesus. The man leaves saddened, and it is only at this juncture in the story that we are told that he has many possessions. Notice that Mark does not call him a "rich young ruler."

Mark 10:23 is important and must be translated carefully: "With what difficulty will those who have wealth enter the dominion of God." Jesus does not say that entry is impossible. Mark 10:24 says something a bit different: "Children, how difficult it is to enter the dominion of God."[16] The disciples are addressed as children in spiritual knowledge. Jesus intimates that it is difficult for anyone to get into the dominion, but it is particularly difficult for the wealthy. Jesus' metaphor in Mark 10:25 about the camel going through the eye of the needle has some precedents in early Judaism in which we find phrases about an elephant going through the eye of a needle. This aphorism

---

[16]This is the only place in the Synoptic Gospels where the disciples are called "children" (cf. Jn 21:5).

is not to be rationalized by some reference to a nonexistent needle gate in the city of Jerusalem. Some later scribes actually altered *kamēlos* ("camel") to *kamilos* ("rope") in hopes of making a deliberately hyperbolic remark seem less outlandish. Jesus, however, is deliberately contrasting the largest animal and the smallest hole that an early Jew in Israel would likely think of. The point is that salvation is not obtainable through even strenuous human effort, trying to squeeze into God's dominion. For once, the disciples understand this implication of Jesus rather clearly and so they ask, "Then who can be saved?" (Mk 10:26). This verse suggests that the disciples had the same vision of salvation through human obedience or effort that the young man had. Jesus then indicates that salvation, though impossible for humans by means of mere human effort, is possible for God (Mk 10:27), who can give it to humans as a gift.

But obviously, Peter still does not understand, for in Mark 10:28 he points to all the sacrifices that he and other disciples have made to follow Jesus. Jesus replies that no such sacrifice goes without its reward, though the reward is not salvation itself but rather family and nurture within the dominion of God (Mk 10:29-30). Getting into the dominion means accepting a free gift. There may be a bit of deliberate irony here in that Jesus may be alluding to the fact that the disciples would have to get their food and shelter from many others who would take them in as family and offer them hospitality as they traveled. It is most unlikely that Jesus is enunciating here a get-rich-quick-through-Christian-sacrifice schema. The list of persons and things that Jesus offers is quite revealing about ancient social values: relatives and basic property (house and land) were the very basis of survival and existence. To cut one's self off from all family and property was to endanger one's very existence.

It is worth pointing out that this new family of faith is both affirming of gender equality (made up equally of brothers and sisters, fathers and mothers) and inclusive of children and others of the "least among you." Notice too that with the blessings of the family of faith and Christian hospitality come also persecution, something that Mark's Roman audience probably could relate to. It is indeed possible that Mark has added the phrase "with persecutions" (Mk 10:30) to the original saying of Jesus in order to contemporize the text, just as the phrase "for the sake of the gospel" (Mk 10:29) may be an addition. In any event, the renunciations that Jesus is referring to do not mean that he is offering an ethic of asceticism. Poverty here is seen as serving justice and perhaps evangelism, not private asceticism.

Mark 10:30 bears witness to traditional Jewish "two age" theology, the age to come being the eschatological age. Jesus is bringing in a foretaste of such an age, inaugurating the age to come in the midst of this age. Nevertheless, the chief blessing of the age to come, eternal life, apparently is to be had only in the future. Mark 10:31 seems to be an isolated saying that simply was attached here, though it suits the discussion on wealth. The verse deals with the matter of reversal of status and standing and so also a reversal of human expectations. Many of the first will be last in the dominion, and many now considered least, last and lost will be first in the dominion. "While the call to become part of Jesus' group of disciples seems, at times, to be a call to be part of his mission, here it also seems to be an essential condition for eternal life."[17]

What we have discovered in this examination is that Jesus' kingdom ethic relates to everyday matters of importance to all—marriage, divorce, singleness, children, wealth, land, the most basic aspects of normal early Jewish life. Jesus is not shy about making radical pronouncements about singleness or wealth. In fact, Jesus has a great deal to say about the dangers of wealth, however uncomfortable it may be for us to hear his teaching on this matter.[18]

In the aphorism cited above, Jesus warned that it is quite difficult for a rich person to get into the kingdom. The point is not just that all things are possible for God, but also that wealth can be an enormous impediment to being a genuine follower of Jesus, as the story related shows. It can create an idolatrous situation where one places ultimate trust and faith and sense of security in one's wealth rather than in God, even though one appears to be very devout, keeping all the central Mosaic commandments. Notice that the commandments cited in this story do not include the commandments in Leviticus about how to treat the poor.

In a related story, Jesus explains in the parable of the rich fool what happens to a person who does not reckon with either God or mortality and instead puts hope and trust in bigger barns, more resources, and the like, counting on a comfortable retirement and the leisure to eat, drink, and be merry (Lk 12:16-21). Here it will be good to take some time to look at two other Lukan parables in the context of the entirety of Luke 16, since it gives us many clues as to Jesus' view of money and wealth.

---

[17]John Painter, *Mark's Gospel* (NTR; London: Routledge, 1997), p. 140.
[18]I address this topic in depth in *Jesus and Money* (Grand Rapids: Brazos, 2010).

Jesus' Teaching on Wealth in Luke 16

Luke 16:1 makes clear from the outset that the teaching in this chapter is for disciples. The scenario that is set up in Luke 16:2 is that a rich man has an estate manager, whom someone has charged with squandering the owner's property. That this is not merely an allegation seems clear from Luke 16:8, where the manager is called "dishonest." It is possible that something is going on in this parable that is not apparent on the surface. The rich man has various people in his debt. What we are not told is whether what was loaned was loaned without interest or with interest, and in view of the rich man's admiration for his manager's shrewdness, we may expect that he had loaned things with interest.

J. D. M. Derrett suggests that what the manager did was remove the interest involved in these transactions and got the debtors to pay off the principle.[19] Of course, various Old Testament texts warned against usury (see Ex 22:24; Lev 23:36-37; Deut 15:7-8; 23:20-21), so possibly the manager did something biblical for a change, treating the debtors according to biblical principles and thereby winning friends among these debtors, which might be needed if indeed he got fired. In regard to Derrett's suggestion, one would have to speculate that there was a variable rate of interest, for one person ends up paying 50 percent of what he originally owed, and the other 80 percent. This too is possible, since interest sometimes was charged according to what the lender may have thought the borrower could eventually afford to pay.

Notice that the manager has to ask these persons what they owed. Would it really be the case that he did not already know this if he had originally brokered the deal and had a commission riding on that debt? It seems unlikely. What the owner had asked for was to see the manager's records or accounts or to hear a report about them (Lk 16:2). The manager's job was to manage the estate, not to lend things without the owner's initiative. The manager was not the original lender and was not working on commission. He was a hired hand. The debt was owed directly to the rich man with interest, and the manager was only a collection agent in this case.

The desperation of the manager is also clear. He has been told he can never be the manager again, and so his acts of desperation are to secure his future by making friends with those who might be his future employers. We get a glimpse into the manager's state of mind in Luke 16:3-4. He tells himself he is not strong enough to do hard manual labor (such as digging), and he

---

[19]See J. D. M. Derrett, *Law in the New Testament* (London: Darton, Longman & Todd, 1970), pp. 48-77.

is too proud or, better said, too ashamed to beg. Thus, he devises a strategy to be welcomed into other persons' homes, those who would be grateful for his help with debt relief and presumably give him a job. One man owes a hundred jugs of olive oil, another a hundred containers of wheat. Clearly, the debt is owed to the owner, not to the manager, who acts as the middle man (note Lk 16:5: "How much do you owe my master?"). Notice also the reference in Luke 16:6 to paying a bill quickly. This was not a barter situation. The man is presented with a bill and expected to pay in coin, not in kind. The going rate for a hundred "baths" of oil was about one thousand denarii, or just over three years' wages for a day laborer, whereas the going rate for a hundred containers of wheat (perhaps about one thousand bushels from one hundred acres) was about twenty-five hundred to three thousand denarii, or about eight to nine years' wages, a very substantial sum indeed.

At Luke 16:8 we are told that the manager not only was dishonest but also was shrewd. Presumably, this means he was formerly dishonest, since we are not likely to think of this transaction as being dishonest. Had this transaction been dishonest, the owner at least should have been upset. This verse also suggests that there is something to be learned from the behavior of this steward, for we are told that the children of this age are shrewder in dealing with their own kind than the children of light are. But what is the lesson the disciples are to learn here?

Luke 16:9 says that the lesson has to do with making friends by means of reducing someone else's debt so that one will be welcomed into eternal tents. Actually, what it says is "make friends by means of unrighteous mammon." This phrase seems to refer to the fact that there is an alluring quality to money that prompts humans, especially greedy ones, to act in unrighteous ways. Had Jesus thought that money was inherently evil, he would not be teaching lessons about its proper and improper uses. What this parable seems to be teaching is that the disciples should be opportunistic and generous to "debtors," and that there will be a reward in the eternal habitations if one behaves in that fashion. In other words, it teaches the same lesson as Luke 12:33, which speaks of selling one's possessions and giving to the poor and so storing up for oneself treasure in heaven.

The saying in Luke 16:10-11 seems to follow on from the parable rather well. Here we also seem to get a clearer picture of Jesus' view of money. Jesus draws a contrast between the "true wealth" and "dishonest mammon." Jesus seems to mean, first, that money is not the true wealth, and second, that money is inherently tainted, it is too much of a temptation for fallen human beings not to use it dishonestly. We also have a "from the lesser to the greater" type of sapiential argument. Whoever is faithful in the smallest things is also likely to be faithful in much, and the converse is also true in regard to dishonesty. Like so many aphorisms and proverbs, these statements are meant to be seen not as universal truths but rather as reflecting things that are usually or normally true.

Luke 16:12 takes things a step further. It suggests that the litmus test of trustworthiness is what one does with someone else's resources. In an honor-shame culture where being shamed was worse than being poor, one was more concerned with one's reputation and thus more with how one handled other people's property than how one handled one's own. The second half of this saying suggests that even what is "your own" is in fact something given to you. This is ambiguous, but probably it reflects Jesus' general view of material creation that it all belongs to God, and so even what we might count as "our own" is in fact given to us by God. We are merely stewards of what properly belongs to God.

Luke 16:13 is the well-known Q aphorism (cf. Mt 6:24) about being unable to serve two masters, God and mammon. Here money is seen not as a potential resource or litmus test of character but rather as a potential master. It is interesting that in Jesus' day and social context slaves sometimes could have more than one owner. In such a case, one's service undoubtedly would be less than fully satisfactory to one or the other of the masters. True service requires an undivided loyalty and an exclusive sort of love for one's genuine master (see Ex 21:5). More to the point, a lord who is not lord of all is not really lord at all, for the very nature of lordship is something all-encompassing, at least when one is talking about God.

Mammon cannot be a true lord, and if one tries to serve it, one cannot be a true servant, not least because mammon is only a thing, not a person with whom one can have a servant-lord relationship. It can only be a distorted lordship and a distorted servitude. Some early Jews were able to warn about being "enslaved to lucre" (see Josephus, *Ant.* 4.238), and Jesus is one such sage. Notice the teaching about the love of money in 1 Timothy 6:10, which comports with the warnings here. Luke's audience may have known a saying, quite similar to the one in Luke 16:13, of Demophilus: "It is impossible for the same person to be a lover of money and a lover of god."

Luke 16:14-15 records the reaction of some Pharisees to this teaching and

Jesus' further response. We are told that some avaricious Pharisees heard all this teaching and literally "turned up their noses" (*exemyktērizon*) at Jesus, a gesture of contempt. Luke does not say or suggest that all Pharisees were avaricious, but clearly the teaching of Jesus had pricked the conscience of some who held other views of wealth. It is fair to say that the Jesus movement and the Pharisaic movement were dueling holiness movements, and both of them grounded themselves to a significant extent in wisdom material. These Pharisees perhaps had taken the simplistic approach to some of the teaching in Proverbs and had assumed that wealth was simply a blessing from God and was not a danger or a temptation. Indeed, they may even have assumed that it was a reward from God for their righteous behavior.

Jesus clearly had counterorder and counterintuitive ideas about the matter. He says that these Pharisees are the ones vindicating themselves before human beings. But he warns that God knows their hearts, and what humans may commend, God may condemn. Avarice or greed is a serious sin in Jesus' view. The audience should be playing to an "audience of One," seeking divine approval of their conduct, not playing to the crowd and assuming that the public's view of money justifies their conduct.

Luke 16:16, a Q saying found also in Matthew 11:12-13 in the reverse order, may at first seem unrelated to what comes before, but actually it explains Jesus' hermeneutics rather well. Jesus comes at all of his ethics, including his views of money and marriage, from a sense of the eschatological moment and situation. John the Baptizer is seen as a watershed figure bringing to a climax the age of the law and the prophets, for he is the eschatological Elijah who comes before the end times. What is only implicit in the Matthean form of this material is made explicit in Luke (who probably is giving us the later form of this material). Luke says rather clearly that the law and the prophets were until John, but from that time on, the dominion is preached. In the Lukan scheme of things John is a transitional figure who has one foot in the old era, bringing it to a close, and one foot in the new era, an Elijah figure preparing the way and serving as precursor to the Messiah.

The second half of Luke 16:16 is much debated. Does it mean that people are pressing or forcing their way into the dominion, or that with the preaching people are being pressed and persuaded to enter it (NET: "everyone is urged to enter it")? Those inclined to the latter view draw an analogy with Luke 14:23. Much depends on whether one takes the verb "to force" as having a more active or a more passive sense (the Greek verb, *biazetai*, is a present middle indicative). Is the dominion somehow suffering violence? This is possible if one is thinking about the violent reaction to John the Baptizer and his beheading and possibly about the rejection and reactions that Jesus' is receiving from some, especially as he draws closer to Jerusalem. Are we meant to see those trying to force their way into the dominion as zealots prepared to use force, or perhaps see the crowds that are pressing Jesus at every turn? These too are possibilities. Perhaps more important than figuring out this deliberately enigmatic wisdom saying is what Luke adds in Luke 16:17.

What Luke seems to be anxious about is making clear that although the eschatological time has come, and the era of the law and prophets is passing away, this does not mean that a lawless time has arrived. It is easier for heaven and earth to pass away than for one stroke of the letter of the law simply to be dropped or dismissed. To the contrary, it is an eschatological time when the law and the prophets are being fulfilled as the dominion comes in and through Jesus (see, e.g., Lk 24:44), and this means not a legally easier time but rather a time of even more intensified ethical demands.

This becomes clear in the very next verse, Luke 16:18, where, as an example of the legal situation as the dominion dawns, Luke quotes Jesus' view of divorce, which is "stricter" than required by Moses in the law. This is the only place in Luke's Gospel where Jesus' view on divorce is discussed, and as in Mark 10, the essential teaching is "no divorce." So much is this the case, that if a man divorces and remarries, he is committing adultery because in God's eyes the first marriage's one-flesh union is still in effect and thus is being violated. This rule applies even if one has not been married before but marries a divorced woman. Adultery is still being committed in that situation against the woman's first marital partner. This verse is all that Luke needed to add to make clear that the end of an era and the beginning of the eschatological times does not mean the end of God's ethical demands on his people. To the contrary, the demands are in various ways intensified, whether one is talking about money or marriage. In Luke's Gospel the cost of discipleship is clearly depicted as being very high indeed.

The theme of riches and their consequences continues in Luke 16:19-31, which presents the well-known parable of the rich man and Lazarus. Besides being the only parable of Jesus having a named individual, it is also one of the very few places where we learn something about what Jesus thinks about the afterlife, in particular Hades.

The parable of the rich man and Lazarus may well reflect the fact that Jesus is drawing elements of a familiar story but then making the story his own to make his own points. The story of Setme and his son Si-Osiris likely was extant before the time of Jesus. The story tells of an Egyptian who was allowed to return from the dead (reincarnated in the child Si-Osiris) to deal with an Ethiopian magician who was besting Egypt's finest magicians. Before he returned to the land of the dead, he and his father observed two funerals, one of a rich man and one of a poor man, the former buried in sumptuous fashion, the latter buried without ceremony. Setme declared that he would rather have the lot of the rich man, but his son corrects him and says that he would do better to wish for the fate of the poor man. In order to justify this view, he takes his father on a tour of seven halls of the other world. The rich man is shown being tormented, whereas the pauper is elevated to a high rank near Osiris. The son then explains to the father the fate of those whose bad deeds outweighed their good ones, such as the rich man, and the fate of those whose good deeds outweighed their bad ones, such as the pauper.

There were also some seven Jewish versions of this same story, which focused on the reversal of fortunes of the rich man and the poor man in the afterlife. In *y. Sanh.* 23c and *y. Ḥag.* 77d is recorded the story of a rich tax collector and a poor Torah scholar who experience these reversal of fortunes in the afterlife. Most interesting is the description of the fate of the tax collector, whose torment in hell is that he continually tries to drink from a river but is unable to do so. The story goes on to say that the rich man had his reward in this life, a nice funeral, because he had done one good deed in his life, whereas the poor man had a poor funeral because he had committed one sin in this life but was rewarded in the next for his many good deeds. The principle here is that the basically righteous are punished in this life for their few sins, and the basically wicked are rewarded in this life for their few good deeds, but there is total reversal in the next life. Bearing this in mind, we are ready to examine the parable in Luke.

Luke 16:19 begins by building up a clear picture of a rich man who is self-indulgent, wearing royal purple robes and fine linen and feasting sumptuously every day. He lived like a king (see Prov 31:22). In fact, it is not impossible that Jesus is alluding to King Herod Antipas, who had five brothers when this parable was told (cf. Lk 16:28). The contrast with Lazarus described in Luke 16:20 is dramatic: he is a poor man with body sores, and he lies at the gate of the rich man's house. In other words, he was readily visible to the rich man on a daily basis, but the rich man did nothing to help him. Instead, though the poor man longed even for the scraps and leftovers from the rich man's feast, he was unable to obtain any, and the scavenging dogs, which may have gotten some, even came and licked the poor man's sores, adding insult to injury. Not surprisingly, the poor man soon died. He was carried by angels to Abraham's bosom (in Jewish estimation, the spot of highest honor in heaven [see *b. Qidd.* 72ab]), presumably in the highest level of heaven, in paradise. The image conveys the notion that he is right beside Abraham and is now his "bosom" friend, his intimate. Notice that it is not said that the poor man even received a proper burial.

It is said, however, in Luke 16:22 that the rich man died and was buried. Luke 16:23 adds that the man was in Hades and was being tormented. He looks up and sees Abraham far away with Lazarus "in his bosom." Thus, in Luke 16:24 the rich man calls upon "father Abraham" (making clear that the rich man is a Jew) and asks him to send Lazarus to him with "cool" fingers (dipped in water) to touch his tongue, which is on fire, because he is in agony, being engulfed in flames. In other words, the rich man, even in Hades, thinks that he can still treat the poor man like a servant or someone beneath him on the social ladder.

Abraham, however, in Luke 16:25 breaks it gently to the rich man (calling him "child," since he himself had been addressed as "father") that he received his good things during his earthly life, just as Lazarus in like manner had received evil things. But now, things are reversed: the poor man is comforted, and the rich man is in agony, and there can be no relief. Luke 16:26 makes very clear that there can be no reversal of the reversal once one dies and is in the afterlife. There is no shuttle service from Hades to Abraham's place. There is a great chasm fixed by God between the two otherworldly destinations.

His own fate sealed, the rich man then lobbies Abraham in Luke 16:27-28 to send Lazarus back from the dead to his father's house to warn his five brothers so that they will not end up in Hades like the rich man. But Abraham refuses this request as well, saying that they have Moses and the prophets, and they should listen to them. In Luke 16:30 the rich man makes one last plea; he thinks that his brothers will not repent unless someone comes back from the dead and warns them. In the final verse, Luke 16:31, Abraham says that if they were not persuaded by Moses and the prophets, they will not be convinced if someone rises from the dead.

This parable suggests many things, not the least of which is that one's behavior in this life matters eternally, a point that not only Jesus but also various of the New Testament writers will stress. There is such a thing as moral apostasy as well as theological apostasy. It may also suggest that Jesus believed, as did some other Jews, that eternal punishment and reward begins right after death. However, since this is a parable, the idea should not be pressed too hard, not least because elsewhere Jesus talks about resurrection, final judgment on the earth when the Son of Man returns, and other eschatological concepts that see resolution of justice issues accomplished in space and time.

More important in this chapter is the focus on the problems of wealth and how indeed it is true that it is hard for a rich person to enter the kingdom of God. Jesus' sympathies clearly are with the pious poor. In the parable's present setting, Jesus is seen as critiquing the older sapiential assumptions of the Pharisees (those encapsulated in Proverbs about wealth being a sign of God's blessing and to be enjoyed) and offering instead wisdom that has passed through the crucible of eschatological thinking and believes in the reversal of the injustices experienced in this life. Wealth and poverty are no good guides of how God evaluates a person in this life, and those who will ignore the Word of God will also ignore the work of God as well.

What we have seen in the ethics of Jesus thus far examined is a radical ethic that assumes that things change when the eschatological saving reign of God finally breaks into human history. The verities assumed to be true about marriage, family, children, land, wealth, and the good life in general are challenged in a variety of ways by Jesus' ethic. Discipleship makes considerable demands on all of these aspects of normal life; indeed, it urges serious sacrifices in order to pursue the path into the dominion of God. The gate into the dominion is not narrow just for a rich person; it is narrow for any disciple for a variety of reasons, yet God can make entrance possible, even for a formerly rich person. Since Jesus was not reluctant to comment on the much debated subject of wealth and money in general, we will not be surprised if he also comments about taxes and tributes and toll money. To this aspect of his ethic we now must turn.

Rendering unto Caesar: Matthew 22:15-22

In Matthew 22:15-22 we have another episode in the ongoing road show "Stump the Sage." The attempt is made once more to trap Jesus in his own words. The question raised here surely is a Judean one, since only Judea was directly ruled by Caesar by means of his infamous provincial governor Pontius Pilate. Since entrapment is the name of the game, the question asked must be seen as malicious, not a sincere attempt to find the truth. The question asked is whether it is permitted under Mosaic law to pay the census head tax to Caesar using one of Caesar's coins, in this case the silver denarius. If Jesus simply said, "Yes, pay it," he would be exposed as a traitor to the Jewish cause, at least in the minds of some Jews. If he simply said, "No, do not pay it," he could be branded as a revolutionary who was guilty of treason or sedition.

Notice that Jesus has to ask for a denarius, which implies that he has none on his person. This fact might make a favorable impression on the crowd watching this minidrama. It is not clear from the context whether it was the Herodians or the Pharisees who had the coin (the former is more likely because they were open and official collaborators with Rome). This may mean that what Jesus' saying implies is that if "they" were going to use Caesar's money (and influence), then "they" had to pay the price. We must bear in mind that the emperor controlled the production of gold and silver coins in the empire. In the final analysis, they were quite literally his. What makes this discussion especially pointed and poignant is that the required poll tax rendered unto Caesar is what had sparked the revolution of Judas the Galilean in A.D. 6 (Josephus, *J.W.* 2.118). Thus, we are dealing with a loaded question here, and Jesus' deft handling of it suggests that he is no Zealot revolutionary in the sense that Judas was. Jews had to use the Caesar coin to pay the tribute, and Jesus does not seem to oppose their doing so.

The most intriguing aspect of the discussion comes when Jesus asks whose image is on the coin and what the inscription says, knowing full well what the answer is. This possibly suggests that Jesus could not read Latin. During Jesus' ministry Tiberius was the emperor, and the coin in question read "Tiberius Caesar, son of divine Augustus" on one side and "Pontifex Maximus" (high priest) on the other. In other words, the coin indicated that Caesar was the highest religious official in the empire. Jesus does not explicitly recognize this authority, but neither does he reject it, and to judge from Romans 13:1-7 and 1 Peter 2:13-17, Paul and Peter did not interpret Jesus' teachings on this matter to suggest a rejection of human governing authorities in general. Jesus did have issues with corrupt officials such as Herod Antipas, whom he called "that fox" (Lk 13:32), but note that when questioned by Pontius Pilate, Jesus, the record suggests, indicated that Pilate had authority that ultimately came from God, otherwise he would have no power over Jesus to do what he ultimately did. Jesus' kingdom, though in this world, was not of this world, and so it did not attempt to dethrone or usurp the authority of Caesar by force (see Jn 18:28-40).

What all of this suggests is that Jesus was not a theocrat, and his preaching of the dominion coming should not be read that way. By this I mean that Jesus did not try to establish a theocracy on earth that would have ruled out human kings and the like ruling in the Holy Land. In fact, this very saying suggests that Jesus opposed attempts to reestablish a theocracy. To the contrary, Jews, including his followers, should pay the tribute money. But there is another dimension to Jesus' enigmatic reply.

When Jesus suggests that the audience render unto God what is God's, he is implicitly suggesting that Caesar did not deserve divine honors, only God does. In other words, Jesus the monotheist recognizes only the God of the Bible's claims to be God, not the emperor. This is why the emperor is distinguished from God. Some things were appropriately rendered to Caesar, namely, his tribute money, but divine honors and acclaim were not included. God's divine claims are higher, prior and preclude Caesar from legitimately claiming divine honors. Furthermore, Jesus believed in the biblical theology of the psalmist that the earth is the Lord's and the fullness thereof (see Ps 24:1). Thus, there is a sense in which not even the tribute money belongs to Caesar, strictly speaking. Indeed, in Matthew 24 Jesus will go on to make clear that nations rise and fall under God's sovereign hand. Thus, there is no valid analogy between what is owed to God and what is owed to Caesar, nor is Jesus enunciating a "two spheres" approach, much less a "separation of church and state." There is only one sphere when God is in the mix, and it all belongs to God, and we are but stewards of God's property in God's world. It is from reflecting on this sort of logic that some have concluded that Jesus is being entirely ironic here: give back to Caesar his worthless pieces of self-congratulatory metal. God alone is God, and to God alone belong divine honors. On this showing, the saying, far from being a counsel of submission to earthly rulers, is more like a comment on their insignificance compared to the inbreaking dominion of God. Whether or not one paid the tribute neither helped nor hindered the incoming of that reign on earth. Perhaps Jesus might even have thought it a religious duty to hand back to Caesar his "unrighteous mammon."

Notice that Jesus is prepared to handle these coins, which must count against the notion that he was a Zealot. Zealots would have nothing to do at all with such unclean graven images. The image that mattered was the one that each human being bears, each created in God's image (Gen 1:27), and whoever is created in that image owes only God ultimate fealty. When the kingdom is coming, lesser duties to human officials, though allowable, pale into relative insignificance. The big issue that Jews should have been concerned with was that God was coming to town in the person of Jesus, and they had some accounting to do with God. Far less important was whether the tax collector was coming to town on behalf of Caesar.

Paying the Temple Tax: Matthew 17:24-27

Here is a good place to say something about the well-known story of the coin in the fish's mouth, found in Matthew 17:24-27. This story often is confused with the one just discussed, but it should not be, as it deals with a separate matter, the issue of the temple tax, a matter in which a tax collector such as Matthew might well have had a personal interest. The story is set appropriately because Jesus and the disciples are on their last journey to Jerusalem and the temple, and even more apropos, they are doing so in spring, when this tax was due to be paid (Josephus, *Ant.* 3.8.2; *m. Šeqal.* 1:1). Note that this story is about an encounter not with Pharisees or Sadducees but rather with tax collectors, and Jesus' desire not to offend them is noteworthy and striking. Here Jesus appears as a loyal Jew who, though he apparently thinks that he is exempt from being obligated to pay this tax, does it so as not to cause unnecessary offense.

Notice how the story begins with Peter saying that Jesus does indeed pay this tax. Since the end of the Maccabean era adult males throughout the empire had paid this tax, based on Exodus 30:13-16, which speaks of a half-shekel tax that all adult males, rich or poor, are to pay to fund the sacrifice "to atone for your lives." The story begins back at Jesus' home base, Capernaum and opens with a question being asked of Peter: "Does your teacher not pay the temple tax?" This probably reflects the tense atmosphere in Galilee, where there was some resistance to paying taxes to a Judean institution set up by an unpopular Idumean king whose son was now dominating Galilee. What needs to be stressed at this point is that the temple tax was not viewed as mandatory, and so it was a true litmus text of Jewish loyalty. This story must have arisen from an actual occurrence in the life of Jesus, since after the demise of the temple in A.D. 70 there would be little or no point to making up such a tale. In the evangelist's day the issue was whether one would pay the two drachmas to Caesar, as the temple tax was redirected after the fall of the temple.

When Peter enters the house in Capernaum, Jesus asks Peter a question: "What do you think, Simon? From whom do the kings of the earth collect duty and taxes, from their own sons or from others?" The answer, of course, is "from others," and Jesus presses the point by stressing, "So then the sons are free [i.e., exempt]." Notice the analogy being drawn between God the Great King and human kings. The idea is that the sons and daughters of God should not have to pay taxes to their king, who is God.

At first blush, this seems to be referring to Jews in general not having to pay such a tax. But then we have to ask who the "others" are here. Surely they cannot be non-Jews. This in turn means that Jesus apparently means by "sons" of the Great King those who have a special relationship with God through his ministry, while the "others" are other Jews who should be paying this tax. The implied conclusion is that the disciples of Jesus are exempt from the burden of being obligated to pay taxes to their Father (cf., e.g., Mt 5:16, 48; 6:1; 23:9). Here we have a very clear example of the surprising authority that Jesus believed he exercised over a commandment of Torah (in this case, Ex 30:13-14). Once again this reflects his eschatological mindset, which assumes that a new set of arrangements and a new covenant are breaking into Jewish life. In point of fact, there often were exemptions from head taxes for special groups, so Jesus is drawing on a known precedent. For example, the Persians exempted the Jews from tribute (1 Esd 4:49-50), just as Nero exempted the Greeks (Plutarch, *Mor.* 568A). What is also interesting about this teaching is that it implies that Jesus' claim to royalty comes not from his being son of David, a title that he never uses of himself, but rather from his being Son of God.

We might have expected the story to end with Jesus telling Peter to take some money out of the common fund carried by one of the disciples and pay the tax. Instead, Jesus tells Peter to go fishing! Jesus does not want to unnecessarily offend the officials, although he does not see himself as theologically obligated to pay the temple tax. Equally interesting is that Jesus the prophet says that Peter will catch a fish with a four-drachma (or full Tyrian shekel) coin in its mouth, which will cover Peter and him as far as the temple tax is concerned. Here, then, Jesus provides a living example of relying on the providence of God.

Oddly enough, the story does not conclude by saying that Peter did as he was ordered. In fact, it comes to a screaming halt with no proper conclusion. Was Jesus kidding? Is this aphoristic humor? It is possible. But whether the fishing expedition actually transpired or not, this tells us some important things about Jesus' views of such religious obligations. Clearly, he does not think that his disciples are so obligated. And this leads to another important conclusion. Although Jesus does reaffirm that the scribes and Pharisees should be tithing, even tithing their spices (Mt 23:23), he says nothing of the kind to his own disciples. Instead, he presents them with the example of the widow's mite (Mk 12:38-44 par.) to urge them to give self-sacrificially.

What we should conclude from the story in Matthew 17:24-27 is that Jesus does not assume that his disciples are necessarily required to fulfill Pentateuchal demands about money or giving. Nor is tithing mandated anywhere else in the New Testament. It does seem clear from Matthew 17:24-27 that Jesus thinks that there are duties incumbent on other Jews that are not incumbent on his own newly formed eschatological community of sons and daughters of God. They, after all, have given up most everything to follow him, and as we saw, when the rich man refuses to do this, Jesus explains that such a person will have difficulty entering the dominion of God. Clearly enough, Jesus is not an early advocate of the "prosperity gospel."

Summary

The ethics of Jesus when it comes to the issue of wealth and its accumulation can be summed up in a few key sentences: (1) Money is not only not the be-all and end-all of existence; it is a clear and present danger to a fallen person's soul and spiritual life. (2) Money can be called "unrighteous mammon" or, as we might say, "filthy lucre." Jesus' gravest concern about it is that it becomes the master of those who think that they have mastered it, and human beings are not made so that they can serve two masters. In other words, money can prompt idolatry, not in the sense that people bow down and worship the money itself, but rather in the sense that it becomes the object of one's ultimate desires, concerns or trust. (3) The followers of Jesus should live with a fundamental trust in God, who will take care of the basic necessities in life. God knows what is really needed, but even the basic necessities are not supposed to be the primary thing that one seeks in life. One is to seek first God and God's divine saving reign in one's life, and these other things will be added, as God is sovereign and loving. (4) There is no problem with doing one's religious or civic duty when it comes to taxes, tribute money, or tolls, but one's ultimate loyalty must be to God. One must render to God, not to other human beings, the worship and service due only to God. (5) The basic principle of giving enunciated for Jesus' followers is sacrificial giving, not tithing, the latter being a practice for those under the Mosaic covenant, not the new one.

The more one analyzes what Jesus says about money or resources in general, the more clear it becomes how much of a sectarian Jew Jesus was. He believed that his own band of disciples was living under the dawning of a new era in human history as the divine saving reign of God broke into the lives of early Jews. And new occasions teach new duties, with some aspects of the law intensified, some aspects nullified, and some new teaching added in to boot. What Jesus wanted was neither a temple, nor a territory, nor a Torah-centered religion, but rather a God-centered one. God is spirit, and those who worship God truly do so anywhere and everywhere that worship in spirit and in truth transpires. Jesus' followers were seen as sons and daughters of the Great King in a special sense. This raises interesting questions about Jesus' views on health and purity laws and other ritual aspects of the Mosaic code as well as on issues of life and death, to which we now turn.

THE ETHICS OF RITUAL PURITY AND THE LAW

Perhaps the easiest place to start this discussion is with the reminder that Jesus intimated in his teaching on marriage and divorce that various Mosaic rulings were set up due to the hardness of the human heart. Jesus contrasts such rulings with the original intent or creation design of God in Mark 10:2-12 // Matthew 19:3-12. It should not surprise us, then, that Jesus might think the same thing of other aspects of the rules of purity and health or life and death in the Holiness Code and elsewhere in the Old Testament. As it turns out, this expectation is justified. Jesus is even prepared to say that food does not make a person clean or unclean, and that honoring father and mother is superseded by the importance of coming and following him, and that killing is not an option for his followers, and they must not only turn the other cheek but also love their enemies and pray for their persecutors. Nothing was more radical than Jesus' ethic of nonviolence and nonresistance. We will examine these interrelated topics seriatim.

Oaths

A good place to start is with what Jesus says about oaths, in contrast to what Moses says. In the Old Testament oaths were permitted as long as they were not irreverent or false (see Ex 20:7; Lev 19:12; Num 30:3-15; Deut 23:21-23; Ps 50:14; Zech 8:17; Wis 14:28-31). Psalm 50:14 may especially be in the background of Matthew 5:33-37, for it reads "Sacrifice thank offerings to God, fulfill your vows/oaths to the Most High." It is important to note too that James the brother of Jesus did not miss the radical thrust of the teaching here, for he reiterates it at James 5:12. Furthermore, in Matthew 26:63-64 Jesus refuses entirely to speak under oath and simply says to the high priest,

"You have said so." The whole point of swearing an oath is to vouchsafe for the truthfulness of something that one has said, but Jesus is calling for such a high standard of verbal integrity that oaths become quite unnecessary. He is calling for total honesty in every situation. One's yes always means yes, and one's no always means no. This part of the teaching about yes and no suggests that Jesus is mainly concerned about promissory oaths—an oath by which one promises to do something in the future.

There is no indication here that Jesus is mainly exercised about excessive swearing of oaths about even trivial matters (contrast Philo, *Decalogue* 92). Jesus suggests that the taking of oaths is in vain anyway, since only God can truly promise, with 100 percent guarantee of coming through, to do something in the future, since mere mortals never can control all the necessary circumstances. Matthew 5:37 provides a very serious judgment: anything that goes beyond yes or no is from the devil. No swearing on a stack of Bibles! Why? Because anything that goes beyond yes or no is a form of exaggeration, a lie, coming from the father of lies. Notice the reference to Jerusalem being the city of the Great King, presumably referring to God (or himself?), since there was no king in Judea at that time.

A further implementation of this teaching is found in Mark 7:11, where there are Jews who are declaring or promising *corban* ("dedicated," as the word actually means) to the temple certain resources, and when their parents need help, they do not help them because they claim to have already sworn an oath dedicating those resources in another direction. The net effect of Jesus' teaching on oaths is that he wants a new era of nothing but truth-telling, without exaggeration, an age when oaths would no longer be necessary at all. Clearly, he thinks that as God's salvation breaks into history during his ministry, now is the time for the change of praxis in this regard, regardless of what Moses previously permitted. It is true, of course, that being more strict than Moses is not a violation of Moses. Going above and beyond Moses does not necessarily imply going against Moses. But some of the "going beyond" of Jesus' ministry does in fact require going in a totally new direction. One such case involves what Jesus has to say about matters of ritual purity.

Jesus' Ritual Purity

Let us be clear that we have absolutely no stories of Jesus visiting a *mikvah* (ritual bath) or urging his own immediate disciples to do so. This contrasts rather drastically with what we read about the members of the Qumran community, who seem to use a *mikvah* almost daily for one sort of uncleanness or another. Furthermore, as John 4:1-2 tells us, Jesus' disciples did baptize some people, but Jesus himself baptized no one. As far as we know, Jesus, although certainly he endorsed the ministry of his cousin John as valid and even submitted to baptism at his hands, never baptized anyone. In addition, there were complaints about Jesus on the purity front: the Pharisees were upset that Jesus' disciples did not properly wash their hands before eating and that Jesus dined with the unclean—tax collectors and notorious sinners. Notice, for example, in Luke 7:36-50 the typical reaction of a Pharisee to Jesus being touched by a sinful woman.

Jesus had no problems with touching or being touched by unclean persons, ranging from women with a flow of blood, to men and women possessed by demons, to men and women with a fever or some other illness, and even to corpses. In Luke 7:14 Jesus touches the bier on which the corpse of a son of the widow of Nain lay. Nothing is said about Jesus cleansing himself thereafter. It is true, however, that Jesus told various people whom he had healed of disease to visit the local priest or authority to obtain the official attestation of cleanliness and wholeness that allowed a person to reenter normal Jewish society (Mk 1:40-45). Sometimes Jesus also commanded the ill or the blind to go and wash so that they could participate in their own healing (Jn 9:6-7), but again, Jesus is not involved in a water ritual even in these cases, either during or thereafter.

Jesus' Teaching on Ritual Purity in Mark 7

In light of all this, what we find in Mark 7:1-23 is no surprise, and this controversial text calls for an extended discussion because in it, according to Mark himself, Jesus declares all foods clean. Before we do the detailed examination, one further point needs to be made. If it was so clear that Jesus was this radical during his ministry, why did the disciples not understand this? If it was so clear that Jesus had set aside the rules about clean and unclean, why do we have episodes such as the one about Peter and Cornelius (Acts 10)?

The answer to such questions is not as difficult as some would make it. The disciples did not fully understand a great deal of the radical teaching of Jesus when he first uttered it. Indeed, they did not fully understand it until well after his death and resurrection in various cases (see, e.g., Jn 2:22). Such is the way things are with creative and radical thinkers. Very few people believed Galileo's theory of a heliocentric solar system or Einstein's theory of relativity at first. It was not that those people did not at least partially understand such views; they simply did not believe it. In the case of the disciples, their reaction would likely have been, "Alright, that is what he said, but surely he did not mean that!" It is difficult to let go of a powerful mental paradigm that one has spent a lifetime living by. Bearing this in mind, we turn to Mark 7:1-23.

Mark 7 begins with what appears to be an official delegation of Pharisees and some scribes from Jerusalem coming to investigate what Jesus is doing. Yet the bone is picked with Jesus' disciples, who eat with "common" or unclean hands, by which is meant unwashed and thus ritually unclean hands. The issue, however, really has to do with Jesus, who is seen as responsible for the behavior of his followers. It was Pharisaic practice to wash diligently before eating. In order to understand the Pharisees, one must recognize that they attempted to apply the Levitical laws for the cleanness of priests to everyone (see Ex 30:19; 40:13). In a sense, they believed in a real priesthood of all believers, and therefore all Jews were called to priestly cleanness. Mark 7:3 is an editorial remark, of which this section has several. The one in this verse must not be taken too literally, since many Jews in fact did not follow such strict hygenic rules, some because their trade did not permit it (e.g., tanners of hides). In the second half of the verse we are told that this amounted to a keeping of the traditions of the elders. Mark does not say that it is a keeping of Torah. Instead, he sees it as a matter of the oral traditions that the Pharisees had added to the Torah or used to particularize or expand the Torah. Strictly speaking, the washing of hands was required only before the breaking of bread. The practice involved washing with a handful of water.

Mark 7:4 refers to the practice followed after the purchase of food at the marketplace. Mark says that once they have bought food, the Pharisees will not eat unless they wash. This leads to a comment on how the Pharisees also practice the washing of wine pots, vessels, copper utensils, and, according to some manuscripts (A, D, W, et al.), beds. It is easier to see how the reading with "beds" might have been omitted than added at a later date. The point of the washing is to remove uncleanness, and uncleanness could be found on a bed due either to menstrual blood or semen or human waste. Jesus is then asked why his disciples do not follow the halakah that the Pharisees follow.[20]

At Mark 7:6 Jesus responds with a stinging rebuke, quoting a prophecy from Isaiah 29:13. This is the only occurrence in Mark of the word *hypokritēs* ("hypocrite") used of anyone, though it frequently crops up in Matthew. The contrast in the quotation involves those who give lip service to God but

---

[20]There are other similar discussions recognizing that Jews practiced hand-washing. See, for example, *Letter of Aristeas* 305-306.

whose hearts are far removed from him. Their worship is in vain because they teach as divine doctrine the commandments of human beings. Doubtless, it is the latter part of the quotation on which Jesus is focusing. The point of the quotation seems to be this: the Pharisees, in their concern for external observance, substituted the observances for heart religion, which amounted to substituting the traditions of human beings for God's Word.

The danger was that mere human traditions or interpretations of God's Word would be taken as the Word itself, and one would be categorized as a bad Jew if one did not follow this halakah. Thus, Jesus accuses them of neglecting the actual commandments of God in order to keep their own commandments. This amounted to more than just neglect; it amounted to annulling the commandment of God. What happens in such cases is that the law has been separated from God himself and has become the real authority. Thus, ironically, the law becomes an obstacle to a real encounter with God because the means has been mistaken for the end. Sometimes humans of various religious traditions, including the followers of Jesus, have been able to hide behind legal observance and assume that this establishes their righteousness and God's indebtedness to them.

Jesus then proceeds to give an example that justifies his charge against his interlocutors involving the matter of *corban*. What is important here is that Jesus is affirming the essence of a Mosaic commandment at the expense of legislation that vitiated something that was at the heart of the law: honoring parents. In this case, it appears that Jesus is attacking the misuse of the practice of making something *corban* to someone.

Jesus reminds his listeners that they are to honor both father and mother, which may be especially significant because some early Jewish teachers said the father was to be honored more than the mother (see *m. Ker.* 6:9). The word *honor* often was taken in early Judaism to indicate the provision of financial support (cf. Prov 28:24). Notice that Jesus also asserts the negative form of the commandment to honor, saying that the one who does the opposite of honoring by speaking evil of one's parents should be executed. It is truly hard to imagine a more strongly worded way of enforcing the obligations of children to their parents, especially of dependent parents.

In Jesus' era it was indeed possible to declare by means of a vow, using the term *corban* (which means "dedicated"), that one's parents were proscribed from benefiting from some piece of property or material asset because it had been set aside for other purposes (e.g., dedication to the temple treasury). But in fact this procedure had come to be used in Jesus' day to simply place property out of the reach of parental use, without the pious intent to set it aside for some religious purpose. Indeed, the term *corban* may already have begun to have the force of an imprecation in Jesus' day, which would explain the reference to cursing one's parents in this text.

Furthermore, there is the problem that oaths were taken so seriously in Jesus' social setting that it was difficult if not impossible to repent of something said using an oath, even if it was said in haste or in a moment of anger (see, e.g., Mk 6:23). Some early Jewish teachers believed that if one broke an oath, one's life would be forfeit and indeed one would stand in danger of the judgment of God on the last day (Philo, *Hypothetica* 7.3-5). Thus, Jesus complains, "You do not *permit* them to do anything for father or mother." The duty to fulfill a vow had been allowed to take precedent over the duty to parents. Jesus takes the opposite view, strongly affirming the traditional obligation to honor parents, including providing them with financial support and removing obstacles to doing so. Notice also that Jesus elsewhere warned against taking oaths at all, perhaps precisely because in an honor-shame culture it was next to impossible to take it back or renege on an oath, even if it was a shot fired in anger (see Mt 5:33-37).

It is entirely possible that the *corban* pericope originally belonged in some other context, as Mark 7:14-23 seems to follow smoothly from the material in Mark 7:1-8, providing Jesus' response to the original question about his disciples' lack of hand-washing. Mark, then, will have grouped material from several controversies together. Jesus makes clear here that what his disciples did was neither an accident nor a result of laxness; rather, it was grounded in principle. In Mark 7:15 Jesus states unequivocally, "There is nothing outside a person that by going in can defile. Only those things that come from the heart defile." Taken in a straightforward manner, this statement means that Jesus saw a significant portion of the Levitical law code as no longer applicable now that God's divine saving activity, his eschatological dominion, was breaking into human history. Jesus' approach to holiness was not going to focus on the ritual part of the holiness code.

One might say that both the Jesus movement and the Pharisaic movement were holiness movements, but they disagreed on the proper approach to creating a holy people of God. Mark understands well the implications of what Jesus is saying, but he assumes that his audience or some part of it may not understand, and so he inserts the editorial remark "Thus he declared all foods clean" (Mk 7:19). This remark likely intimates that Mark assumes that a significant portion of his audience will not understand the legal niceties of Jewish disputes about clean and unclean. In other words, this surely suggests that Mark assumes that his audience is mostly Gentile and not even God-fearers who knew the law. Jesus, then, is not merely declaring Pharisaic halakah defunct or invalid; he is declaring at least some portions of Leviticus obsolete as well. When all is said and done, Jesus believes that what defiles a person is not physical things but rather moral attitudes.

Although the majority of commentators have concluded that Mark 7:15 likely goes back to Jesus in some form, the dispute over what form shows no sign of abating. In one important monograph, Roger Booth argues that the tradition history of Mark 7 suggests that in its original form Mark 7:15 involves a relative, not an absolute, contrast. Thus, what Jesus actually said was "There is nothing outside a person which *cultically* defiles him as much as the things coming from a man *ethically* defile him."[21] There are several problems with this conclusion. (1) This certainly is not how Mark understands the saying, for his parenthetical editorial comment indicates that he assumes that an absolute contrast is made. "Thus he declares all things clean" would in fact be a false conclusion if Booth is right about the original sense of the saying. (2) The contrast in the saying seems to be between that which enters a person from without and that which comes forth from within the person, not between two different kinds of defilement. (3) Although a relative reading of the contrast is possible, one would expect some sort of signal in the context that "not . . . but" means "not so much . . . but." In other words, one would expect some sort of contextual signal that a relative comparison rather than a real contrast is meant. Such signals are entirely lacking in the context; indeed, the editorial remark of the evangelist points in the opposite direction. The criterion of double dissimilarity also suggests the authenticity of the more radical reading of this saying.

Precisely because of some of the above sorts of considerations, James Dunn takes a different tack in approaching this radical saying.[22] His view is that indeed this is a radical saying in its present form, but that the original form of the saying was otherwise.[23] He urges that the Matthean form of the saying

---

[21]Roger P. Booth, *Jesus and the Laws of Purity: Tradition History and Legal History in Mark 7* (JSNTSup 13; Sheffield: JSOT Press, 1986), p. 214.

[22]James D. G. Dunn, *Jesus, Paul, and the Law: Studies in Mark and Galatians* (Louisville: Westminster John Knox, 1990), pp. 37-60.

[23]Dunn rightly critiques Booth's conclusion that Jesus' original saying was simply about cultic impurity. If that were the case, it is hard to understand how the early church ever could have adopted the viewpoint expressed by Mark himself.

("What goes into your mouth does not make you 'unclean,' but what comes
out of your mouth, that is what makes you 'unclean'" [Mt 15:11]) is likely
closer to what Jesus actually said, in which case the original contrast was between what one eats and what one says. The food laws would be a subset of
the larger body of Levitical laws about impurity, and Jesus would simply be
declaring obsolete some of the food laws. Dunn also reckons with the possibility that the *ou . . . alla* ("not . . . but") structure involves a "dialectial ne-
gation" meaning "More important than ritual impurity is moral impurity."[24]
Despite such reasoning, Dunn in the same discussion later admits, "But the
radical character of a saying which set inward purity antithetically against
ritual purity is fully of a piece with Jesus' teaching as a whole. Jesus is generally remembered as one whose teaching on the law, and on human relations
as governed by the law, was characteristically searching and radical in one
degree or another."[25] I quite agree with this conclusion, in which case it is
perfectly possible that the Markan rather than the Matthean form of this saying is more likely to be original.[26]

There are four other problems with Dunn's reasoning. First, the appeal
to putative oral tradition that Matthew might have used to present an earlier
form of Jesus' saying than that found in Matthew's Markan source is an argument from silence. It is possible, but there is no good reason to think that
it is true, not least because Matthew takes over more than 90 percent of his
Markan source in the material that they share, including over 50 percent of
Mark's exact words. Second, Matthew's dependence on, and softening of,
the harsh edges of his Markan source is too well known to need much demonstration (e.g., compare the cases where, reporting Jesus' words, Mark has
"Have you no faith?" but Matthew has "You of little faith," and Mark has
"Why do you call me good?" but Matthew has "Why do you ask me about
the good?"). Third, is it really more probable that Mark and his community
took a more radical stance on ritual impurity than Jesus did? Why should
Mark's community need Mark's parenthetical explanation about declaring all
foods clean if they themselves already held such a view or Mark had already

[24]See Dunn, *Jesus, Paul, and the Law*, p. 51.
[25]Ibid., p. 52.
[26]At the very least, Jesus is challenging the notion that all commandments of the law should be
    treated as equally important. Jesus therefore stands in the prophetic tradition that speaks of that
    which is more central or more important among the commandments (see, e.g., Jer 7:22-23; Hos
    6:6). In other words, Jesus is not contrasting mere human tradition with the law. His hermeneutic
    is more radical than that.

taught them such a tradition? Would a largely Gentile congregation really be arguing about food laws in the 60s or 70s? Fourth, Matthew's more traditional Jewish portrait of Jesus as a sage and upholder of a good deal of the law is clearly a redactional agenda of the evangelist.[27]

Another way to attempt to blunt the radical character of Mark 7:15 as an utterance of Jesus is to suggest that Jesus is speaking not programmatically but rather prophetically. He is not abrogating or even reinterpreting the law, he is simply summoning God's people to do God's will from the whole person. Robert Guelich concludes, "Instead of attacking the ritual or ceremonial law of purity, Jesus calls for total purity, the sanctification of the whole person, as anticipated for the age of salvation."[28] If this conclusion is correct, it is hard to understand why the Pharisees might ever be depicted as disagreeing with Jesus, for they too were concerned with the purity of the whole person and not just with ritual purity. Equally, this conclusion completely fails to grasp the fact that Jesus was perceived as having negated some of the law or as having taken the law into his own hands and changed things.

Jesus' ministry is consistently portrayed in the Gospels as arising out of a context of social controversy, indeed a variety of controversies. Furthermore, the eschatological tenor of Jesus' teaching is ignored by Guelich's conclusion. Jesus believed that the eschatological reign of God was already breaking into human history through his ministry, and that new occasions taught new duties. New wine could not be poured into old wineskins. A major difference between the holiness movement known as Pharisaism and the holiness movement that was the Jesus movement was not so much the goal (both wanted God's people to be holy unto the Lord) but rather the means by which this was to be achieved. One followed a program of Levitical reform, applying even laws previously just meant for priests to all Jews. The other taught that God himself was already intervening and changing people from the inside out through Jesus' ministry, and thus the gospel according to Leviticus was a message that had had its day and was no longer appropriate to the times.

In short, the various attempts to whittle off the hard edges of Jesus' teaching should be resisted. The more difficult and even offensive the saying, the more likely it is that the church did not invent it, for even after the split between the synagogue and the church the evidence shows that the church was

---

[27]See Ben Witherington III, *Jesus the Sage: The Pilgrimage of Wisdom* (Minneapolis: Fortress, 1994), pp. 335-68.

[28]Robert A. Guelich, *Mark 1–8:26* (WBC 34A; Dallas: Word, 1989), p. 376.

still interested in sharing the gospel with Jews. The odds are that the radical Markan Jesus is closer to the original historical figure than is the less offensive Jesus whom we find in the later Gospels of Matthew and Luke.

At Mark 7:17 we have the motif of in-house teaching for the disciples (cf. Mk 4:1-34). Again at Mark 7:18 the disciples are critiqued for their lack of understanding. Food only goes into the stomach and then passes on into the latrine. David Young observes,

> Jesus' point is that food, which enters a person, is not "dirty"; i.e. people do not eat physically dirty things. Instead, it is one's excretion which is considered "dirty"; what comes out of a person is what is unclean. The simple point of the comparison is the contrast between the "cleanness" of food versus the "filthiness" of excretion. The actual interpretation of the comparison will be given in the following verses.[29]

The sorts of things that do defile a person are listed in Mark 7:21-22. Here the heart is seen as the source and center of human action, determining its character. This catalogue of vices is thoroughly Jewish and traditional. Here we have thirteen items listed (cf. the similar list in 1QS IV, 9-11): evil thoughts, sexual immoralities, thefts, murders, adulteries, envies, malicious acts (note the plurals), deceit, lewdness, the evil eye (cf. Deut 15:9), blasphemy, arrogance, folly. It could be argued that this list of vices is based roughly on the Decalogue, although the "evil eye" concept would be an exception.

The idea of the "evil eye" is well known in earlier Jewish literature (e.g., Deut 28:54; Sir. 14:8-9; Wis 4:12) and is common in the papyri as well (e.g., P.Oxy. 2.292[12] and P.Oxy. 6.930[23]). The concept is that certain persons (or animals, demons, gods), by looking at someone, have the power to cast an evil spell or cause something bad to happen. It was believed that the eye is the window on the heart or soul and the channel through which one's thoughts, desires and intentions could be conveyed. This concept was connected chiefly with envy, jealousy, greed or stinginess (see Plutarch, *Quaest. conv.* 680C-683B). In Mark's first-century world there was considerable fear of the evil eye, and people used curses, amulets and spitting to ward it off, which was seen as a form of sorcery.

Notice that some of these things are attitudes, and some are attitudes

---

[29]David M. Young, "Whoever Has Ears to Ear: The Discourses of Jesus in Mark as Primary Rhetoric of the Greco-Roman Period" (Ph.D. diss.; Vanderbilt University, 1994), p. 262.

that issue in actions with the focus on the deed. Jesus did not bifurcate attitudes and actions or suggest that only one or the other mattered. He could never have said, "It's the thought that counts." Both attitudes and actions counted, and both manifested one's orientation. Jesus, in his own way, heightens the demand for purity beyond what the Pharisees expected, but his approach involves strict moral purity. Personal sin, not physical impurity, is what now defiles, rendering the person unfit for fellowship with God or other humans. Finally, Joel Marcus suggests that Mark presents Jesus' radical teaching here as performative in nature, which is to say that "Jesus in our passage is not just holding a mirror up to nature, depicting what has always been the case, but actually *changing things* by his apocalyptic pronouncement that all foods are (now) clean."[30] Such a pronouncement is not unlike what we find in Genesis 9:3, where before the Mosaic law but after the flood all animals could be eaten.

Mark 7 presents various quandries for those who do not live in a culture where there are strong ritual boundaries. Nevertheless, every culture has its own concepts of what amounts to dirt and what amounts to dirty. "Dirt" has been defined by the cultural anthropologists as "matter that is out of place." Similarly, becoming unclean amounts to a process whereby something or someone clean comes into contact with something out of bounds or out of place—for example, a living person touching a dead person, or a healthy person touching a sick person. The sick and the dead are seen as persons on the margin of society and in some cases out of bounds all together. An outcast is by definition someone who has been placed or has stepped outside the circle of the clean, the acceptable, the normal. At the root of this entire way of thinking is the basic concept that the abnormal is aberrant and therefore must be defined as unclean or inappropriate. Only in this way can the normal know what normalcy is.

From the perspective of the Hebrew way of thinking, at the root of all this is the belief that God demands perfection—perfect sacrifices, perfect behavior, entire holiness of his children. There is also a theology of creation that says that God made everything very good, and any person or thing that is no longer in that condition has strayed from God's intended purpose for such a person or thing. Thus, anything imperfect is seen as unclean, even in some cases unholy if the issue is moral imperfection. In this context, the discussion by Jesus in Mark 7 begins to make a good deal of sense. Jesus is suggesting

---

[30]Joel Marcus, *Mark 1–8* (AB 27A; New York: Doubleday, 2000), p. 457.

that the world is not, in itself, the zone of contamination, and therefore food, flesh, trees, and other objects per se are not unclean. Rather, the zone of contamination has been contracted to the sinful human heart, and what comes out of that is or can be very unclean. Herein we can begin to understand the differing strategies of Jesus and the Pharisees. Both he and they were leading holiness movements.

Jesus and the Pharisees

The Pharisees' view of how to right the ship of Israel was to truly create a priesthood of all believers. Everyone needed to live by the rules previously reserved for Levitical priests. Jesus took a very different tack. His view was that everyone needed to be transformed from the inside out. Israel needed a heart transplant, a new heart, before it could receive new marching orders. The Pharisees' solution placed the emphasis on a new degree of rigor in orthopraxy, whereas Jesus placed the emphasis on human character transformation. Both were concerned with deeds as well as attitudes, but Jesus believed that the kingdom was coming in and God was actually changing people, which the Pharisees apparently did not believe. Jesus taught that it was God's activity, not human activity, much less human tradition, that was the starting point for the blueprint for the new people of God. Paul understood this, which is why in his anthropological remarks he concentrates so much on the transformation or renewal of the mind, the transformation of the heart through the pouring out of God's love, and the like.[31]

I am not saying that the Pharisees were unconcerned with matters of the heart or were mere formalists.[32] They certainly were concerned with such inward things, but they did not believe that a messianic fix was required, they did not believe that a miraculous transformation of the human heart from without was required, and very few of them seem to have believed that Jesus was the only physician who could cure the disease.

The good news involves the transformation of the mind but also the healing of the body. It also involves the leaving behind of some cherished traditions, and often the greatest force of opposition to renewal is not the evils of this world but rather a clinging to past goods. It has been often said that the good is often the worst enemy of the best, and it is so in this case. It was no bad thing for God's people to set themselves apart and strive to be scrupu-

---

[31]On which, see pp. 619-31 below.

[32]Remember Shammai's famous "one-legged" Torah summary (see b. Šabb. 31a). Sometimes one hears of a focus on the great commandment of love or something like the Golden Rule.

lous about the observance of the law, even the ritual law, in order to be holy before God. But when God has done a new work of grace, the old becomes obsolescent. In the dawning eschatological age, when God comes to reign in the lives of his people, it is God in person, not merely the doing of rituals, that purifies the people of God. By the same token, since God can indwell the human life, it is those internal things that dwell in the heart that need to be dealt with, and only God's power and cleansing force, not ritual purification, can deal with such internal matters. A question posed by Macbeth, "Canst thou not minister to a mind diseased?" is appropriate at this juncture, and the answer is "the God who takes up residence in the midst of his people can." One must distinguish between adherence to tradition and obedience to God. Tradition in itself is not necessarily a bad thing, but following it is no substitute for obedience to the heart of the gospel.

A person prepared to challenge other people's eating and cleaning habits and purity rituals is a person who does not necessarily relate ritual purity to health and healing. It seems very clear indeed from a variety of Jesus' teachings that he did not think that sickness, deformity, disability, or disaster could always be linked directly to a particular individual's personal sins or even that the sins of that individual's forebears (see, e.g., Jn 9:1-3; cf. Lk 13:1-5). Jesus indeed did come that people might have life and have it abundantly, and he does not necessarily associate rules of ritual purity with holiness or even cleanness in the most essential sense of purity of heart. Holiness of life comes from holiness of heart, not from ritual practices, though such practices can express that inner purity in a symbolic form. Jesus emphasized the things that made for real life: spiritual transformation of the heart, reception of the good news about healing and wholeness and the Jubilee, celebration of the work of God in fellowship meals, forgiveness of sins and other wrongs, love, mercy and compassion as the heart of obedience to God. Of a piece with this ethic is the ethic of Jesus in regard to violence. At this juncture, we need to look at that ethic.

Jesus and Violence

When Jesus reaffirms the commandment "You shall not kill," not surprisingly he intensifies and surpasses it. In his hands, the commandment does not merely proscribe premeditated murder; it insists that one do no bodily harm at all to others. That we are on the right track with this interpretation is supported by Romans 12–13, where Paul disallows any sort of revenge, and in the same breath he urges the love ethic of Jesus and overcoming evil with good. It is im-

portant to bear in mind from the outset of this part of our discussion that there
is a difference between the use of force and the use of lethal force, between
the use of one's strength or power and the use of violence. Jesus is not totally
opposed to the use of force, as his action in the cleansing the temple shows, but
notice that he entirely avoids any bodily harm to other human beings. This
distinction is an important one and must be kept steadily in view as we consider the matter of nonviolence. "Nonviolence" does not mean "nonforce."

Jesus, in affirming the greatest commandment of all, closely links the
keeping that commandment to love with entering the eschatological dominion of God. The story is found in Mark 12:28-34 (cf. Mt 22:34-40; Lk
10:25-28). There was in early Judaism a great deal of dispute about how to
rank the 613 commandments (248 positive commands, 365 prohibitions) in
the Hebrew Scriptures in terms of importance, and even more debate as to
which of these commandments was paramount and so could be used as a
hermeneutical tool to interpret the rest.

Jesus' Summary of the Law

Thus, the question the scribe raises in Mark 12:28 is not a merely hypothetical
one (unlike the question raised by the Sadducees); it is an inquiry about the
"first" commandment. Jesus responds with the Shema (Deut 6:4-5), which is
perhaps as close as one can get to a Jewish confession of faith. It was the morning prayer for every good Jew from at least the second century B.C. Notice too
that Jesus combines Deuteronomy 6:5 and Leviticus 19:18, which also had
precedent in early Jewish circles.[33] Mark 12:30 has the additional phrase "and
with all your mind," which is not in the Hebrew original. It is interesting
that Mark 12:31 mentions "these," but then the word "commandment" is in
the singular. Possibly, Mark wants us to think that for Jesus, these two commandments are integrally related, love of God and of neighbor being two
expressions of the same basic impulse. On the other hand, we could translate
"another commandment is not greater than these."

Jesus' summary of the law should be compared to that of Hillel (40 B.C.–
A.D. 10): "What you yourself hate, do not do to your neighbor" (b. Šabb.
31a).[34] The scribe is impressed with Jesus' insistence on God's oneness and on

---

[33]See Testament of Issachar 5:2; 7:6; Testament of Daniel 5:3; Testament of Reuben 6:9. See Jay B. Stern,
"Jesus' Citation of Dt 6:5 and Lv 19:18 in the Light of Jewish Tradition," CBQ 28 (1966): 312-
16.

[34]Compare the story about Rabbi Akiba (d. A.D. 135), who died a martyr's death while reciting the
Shema and stated, "To love your neighbor as yourself—this is the fundamental principle of the
Torah" (see y. Ned. 9:4).

the centrality of love. It is striking that this is the only example in the Gospels where a scribe actually agrees with Jesus. He pushes the matter a bit further by referring to the prophetic notion that God prefers loving actions more than any religious rite—whole burnt offerings or regular sacrifices (cf. 1 Sam 15:22; Jer 7:22; Hos 6:6). Jesus saw that the man answered intelligently or wisely and tells him he is not far from the dominion of God. Notice that the scribe had assumed that what was being discussed was the heart of the law, but Jesus' perspective on the law, as on everything else, was eschatologically colored, such that he sees the discussion as being about the requirements for entering the eschatological realm of God or to live therein.[35]

Notice too that the scribe's positive response does not mean that he is now a disciple. He must come and follow Jesus and recognize him, not just his teaching. Still, the man's openness to Jesus' teaching is a good sign. In describing the scribe's response in this fashion, Mark once again indicates the authority of Jesus' teaching, something that Mark normally does by saying that Jesus silenced his opponents (cf. Mk 11:33; 12:12, 17, 27). The end result, however, is the same: "After that no one dared to ask him any question" (Mk 12:34). In fact, the word order in the Greek text makes the closure of this pericope emphatic: "No one, anymore, was daring to question him." As far as Mark is concerned, the last word on Jesus' ethic is love of God and neighbor. And I submit that it is Jesus' working out of this ethic that we find in other love sayings and situations in the ministry of Jesus that we should now review.

The Ethic of Love

The first port of call is the material in Matthew 5:38-48 about nonresistance, nonretaliation, and love of enemy. If we needed any proof that Jesus' enjoinders in the Sermon of the Mount make no allowances for hardness of the human heart, these verses make that quite apparent. Rather, they presuppose the new situation now that the dominion is breaking into human history. The *lex talionis*, "law of the tooth," assumes a vengeful, dog-eat-dog world, and it simply attempts to limit vengeance to only an eye for an eye, a life for a life and so on.

---

[35]On Jesus' hermeneutic and the love commandment, see Victor P. Furnish, *The Love Command in the New Testament* (Nashville: Abingdon, 1972). Note also this observation by Painter: "From one perspective, all the detailed laws, of which there were over six hundred prohibitions and commands, were taken to be expressions of the way two principles of love towards God and neighbour were to be fulfilled. Alternatively, the two principles of love can be taken as the true meaning of all the commandments. From this point of view the love principles become the test of the applicability of the numerous specific commandments. The latter seems to be the understanding advocated by Mark" (*Mark's Gospel*, p. 160).

Jesus asks his disciples to think outside of the reciprocity or payback box. They needed to think of what they ought to do, not merely what was legal to do. Clearly enough, this is the ethics of a special community responding to God's saving activity in Jesus, a community that recognizes the binding authority of Jesus' teaching, superseding various forms of former teachings whether in the Torah or in the oral traditions of early Judaism. The "But I say to you . . ." independent authority of Jesus must have seemed surprising in tradition-bound early Judaism. Jesus uses no footnotes, cites no former teachers, relies on no one else's interpretations. There can be little doubt that Jesus' teaching in this section is at odds with the essence of what we find in Exodus 21:24; Leviticus 24:20; Deuteronomy 19:21.

In Matthew 5:39 Jesus urges that the evildoer be responded to not in kind but rather in kindness. This is a proactive rather than reactive response. The slap with the back of the hand on the right cheek was an honor challenge, meant to shame the recipient of the slap into responding. It was a considerable insult in Jesus' world, and to not respond in kind was to publicly humiliate oneself. Luke 6:29 turns this into a response to violence in general, whereas it is actually a response to a specific kind of use of force. The saying in Matthew, using the verb *anthistēmi* ("to take action against"), may envision the harmed individual taking the offender to court for damages. Thus, we have counsel here not to take legal action against the offender, and then in Matthew 5:40 we have the corollary: if someone seeks to sue you and take your shirt, then give your outer garment as well. This advice is especially remarkable in light of what is suggested in Exodus 22:25-26 and Deuteronomy 24:12-13, where we learn that the outer garment belongs inalienably to its original owner. Jesus is setting up a new ethic for his own community, not merely recycling an old one. Probably, Matthew 5:40 is referring to an attempt to forestall legal action, and it may well be that this advice presupposes a social situation where the prosecuting disciple was of higher social status and would likely win a court case, being able to afford an advocate, unlike a fisherman (cf. the parable of the persistent widow in Lk 18:1-8).

In Matthew 5:41-42 are three different illustrations of the one principle that one ought to do good to one's neighbor or even one's enemy regardless of their behavior. The fundamental principle generating this ethic is unconditional love, not the reciprocity spin cycle. Impressment was a regular Roman army practice whereby someone would be compelled to carry a load or do a duty under orders from a soldier, such as Simon of Cyrene did for Jesus

(Mt 27:32), but here Jesus is suggesting that one ought to do more than what was required, going the extra mile. One acts on the basis of kindness and love and of one's preexisting ethical commitments. One does not just respond naturally or as required in a situation. Disciples are to respond in a helpful way even to those who have no power over them, giving to a beggar or a borrower generously. One gives without thought of return and not merely out of a sense of duty. One gives ultimately because that is the character of the biblical God and of Jesus, and it is therefore the expected character of Jesus' followers. And here we see a clear example where ethics is viewed as the mirror image of theology. Self-sacrifice replaces self-interest as the basis of ethics in the kingdom because it is assumed that Jesus has indeed established a new eschatological situation.

Matthew 5:43 begins with a partial quotation of Leviticus 19:18 (cf. Mt 19:19), leaving out the "as yourself" portion. That is followed by the quotation of a saying that is, as far as I can tell, unprecedented in earlier Jewish literature: "Hate your enemy." There is something like this in 1QS I, 3-4, 9-10; IX, 21-22, which speak of hating the sons of darkness and loving the sons of light, but perhaps Jesus is referring to the Zealot preaching and ethic here. If so, Jesus is referring to behavior that is not determined by kinship or prior commitments of reciprocity. Proverbs 25:21 speaks of showing hospitality to an enemy, but Jesus takes it to another level. The disciple must love indiscriminately just as the heavenly Father makes his blessed rain and sun fall down on the evil and the good. This clearly is a love that goes beyond covenant or in-group love.

In Matthew 5:46 an interesting but offensive comparison is made: if you love only those who love you, how are you any different from despised tax collectors or pagans? Even they love those who love them. Observant Jews would be offended to be equated with these two groups because of only following reciprocity when it comes to love. Matthew 5:48 must not be isolated from this surprising context. To love unconditionally as the Father loves is to be complete or perfect as the Father is. This sort of love arises only out of a new and whole relationship with God. Deuteronomy 18:13 may be in the background here, which refers to being blameless, or perhaps Leviticus 19:2, where the believer is told to be holy as God is holy, but more is meant here than blameless or just holy behavior. Instead, a positive concept of self-sacrificial love is in view. Not flawless moral character but wholehearted love, imitating God's, is envisioned. Jesus is talking about behavior, not feelings or experiences, when he discourses on love here, and it is behavior that is commanded of all the disciples, not just the spiritually advanced ones. To whom more is given in this new eschatological situation, where God's salvation is at work, more is required. Clearly, an ethic of love, even toward enemies, even praying for them, and nonresistance to the use of force against oneself is enunciated here. And Jesus practiced what he preached when he was abused and taken captive in Gethsemane and thereafter. But is there evidence elsewhere that Jesus thought that violence might be warranted in certain circumstances?

Sometimes people point to either Jesus' action in the temple or his cursing of the fig tree as evidence that some degree of violence might be permissible in certain situations. The problem with these examples is that both of the actions described are directed not against human beings but rather against animals or trees. So these texts will not do to make the case. Are there other texts?

What about Luke 22:36-38, where Jesus seems to advise the disciples to obtain a weapon? Again, context is king here. Remember that this is the same Jesus who advised that those who live by the sword will die by the sword (Mt 26:52), and who immediately put a stop to Peter's violence against the high priest's slave and indeed reversed its effects by healing the slave's ear (Lk 22:49-50; Jn 18:10-11). So what is the meaning of this little story, taking into account the larger context of Jesus' teaching? The key is Luke 22:37, where Jesus quotes Isaiah 53:12: "He was numbered with the transgressors." Jesus is telling the disciples that they must fulfill their role as transgressors of what he has taught them. They must play the part of those who do exactly the opposite of what Jesus taught them in the Sermon on the Mount. The disciples become transgressors by seeking out weapons and then planning to use them. That much is perfectly clear from the context, for the disciples then go on to say, "Look, Lord, here are two swords," showing that they already have such weapons. Jesus replies, "That is enough [of this nonsense]," registering his disgust at the fact that they are already transgressing his principles of nonviolence (Lk 22:38).

A careful look at the context brings several more things to light. Jesus refers to the fact that previously he had sent the disciples out without purse, bag or sandals. Now the situation is different. Now the story of Jesus is about to come to a climax and fulfillment, including the prophecy "He was numbered with the transgressors," which here in Luke is clearly linked with the disciples' behavior and Jesus' directives. Who are the transgressors among whom he is numbered in the garden of Gethsemane? What is the context here? Clearly, it is his disciples, who are seen as revolutionaries just like Jesus and therefore as dangerous. Jesus wants them to play their part in the drama so that he will indeed be seen as dangerous and be arrested. It is irrelevant that the disciples fail to understand that he is not urging them to protect him or themselves. He has already said that they will run away, be scattered. And when they do try to use force to protect him or to oppose his captors, he puts an immediate stop to it and then goes the extra mile by healing the slave's ear (see Lk 22:49-50; Jn 18:10-11). Clearly, Jesus knew that two swords would not be enough to hold off a Roman legion or the temple police, so we must take his response as highly ironic, not as straightforward.

When the disciples show Jesus two swords, he either means ironically "Oh, that will be plenty," or more likely, as I have suggested, he means "That will be enough of this nonsense." Either way, there is absolutely no endorsement here by Jesus of his followers using weapons. Carrying weapons makes them fulfill the role of transgressors, as the citation of Isaiah 53:12 makes evident. There is no endorsement of violence against any human beings anywhere in the teaching of Jesus. In fact, there is just the opposite: he teaches that violence only begets violence, leading ultimately to the death of the one who wields the sword, and so instead love of enemy is called for, which is at the other end of the spectrum of responses to hatred and violence. It is no surprise that Jesus was the inspiration of people such as Mohandas Ghandi and Martin Luther King Jr. Both men had a profound grasp of the heart of the ethic of Jesus: love and nonviolence. But was Jesus also the inspiration and influential source of the ethics of New Testament writers?

THE IMPACT OF JESUS' ETHIC ON HIS DISCIPLES

The study of the influence of Jesus' ethical teaching on the ethics of the New Testament writers themselves has not received as much scholarly attention as it should. Part of the problem is that too many scholars have wanted to say that if one does not find clear quotations from Jesus, one cannot be sure of influence, but surely this is to narrow the scope of inquiry too much. The real issue is whether or not we find the ethical ideas and practices of Jesus in the writings of the New Testament authors.

For a start, one has to say that of course the four evangelists reflect this influence; otherwise, they would not have conveyed so much of his ethical teachings. The Fourth Gospel contains much less of these teachings of Jesus, but nonetheless it has some in the farewell discourses. A close examination of this teaching shows that the evangelists seem to have emphasized the more distinctive teachings of Jesus, which made him stand out from the Pharisees and Sadducees, hence all the debates. When the normal material comes up, such as the Ten Commandments or the greatest commandment, Jesus sounds mostly conventional, except that he does not reaffirm the Sabbath law. And when the purity issues come up, he sounds very unconventional indeed at various points. His eschatological orientation seems similar to some of the things we find at Qumran, and yet that made them ratchet up the purity observances, but not so in Jesus' case.

It cannot simply be the heightened eschatology that formed Jesus' perspective on things. It seems clear enough that some of it comes from his own self-understanding of who he was, as well as what time it was, theologically speaking. The Gospel writers are faithful to record debates about Levirate marriage, *corban*, the temple tax, and the like, which are unlikely to have been of much relevance or much of an issue in the Christian audiences they were addressing, with the possible exception of Matthew's audience in Capernaum or perhaps Antioch.

This tells us that we may be reasonably sure that they were not given to retrojecting later Christian ethical concerns back into the mouth of Jesus. Had that happened, we would have expected material on circumcision, Gentile entrance requirements, food offered to idols, various sort of sexual aberrations mentioned by Paul, and the like. We might also have expected more direct comments on the relationship of a follower of Jesus to governing authorities. This gives us confidence that the ethic that we find in the Gospels ultimately comes from Jesus. But again, do we have echoes of it outside the Gospels themselves? The answer is yes.

As I have shown at length in the first volume of the present study, if we start with Jesus' brother James, we find some twenty echoes from the Matthean form of the Sermon on the Mount (and I am not counting echoes from elsewhere in the teaching of Jesus). Clearly, Jesus' brother learned this material, presumably after Easter, and reused it in his own ways for the Diaspora Jewish Christians whom he sought to persuade. This sends a signal that the Sermon on the Mount material was seen as crucial. The concern for the poor, the concern to curb one's tongue, the attempt to deconstruct social hierarchies, and a plethora of other practical concerns ranging from prayer, to fasting, to not storing up treasures on earth, to avoiding oaths were seen as applicable to a wide range of audiences. I will say more on this in the next chapter when we examine the ethics of documents written for Jewish Christians. Perhaps especially telling is that even in a book such as Hebrews or Revelation or 1 Peter we do not lose the ethic of nonviolence and non-resistance, the ethic of being prepared to be persecuted and prosecuted and perhaps even executed.

The call to be prepared to suffer and die is clear in various places in these documents, especially when the alternative is seen as apostasy (e.g., Hebrews and 1 John). Furthermore, the strong stress on love of God and the believing community and on the avoidance of revenge is noteworthy. Revelation, although it is the book that perhaps most dwells on God's judgment on human sin, has the strongest stress on leaving justice entirely in God's hands, for vengeance is God's. There is no call to arms or resistance or fighting other humans anywhere in the New Testament. The battle is with powers and principalities when we hear a call to take up arms in the New Testament (see, e.g., Rom 13; Eph 6).

Even more remarkable is how Paul, in writing to audiences mainly composed of Gentiles, believes that the ethic of Jesus about marriage, divorce, singleness, leaving justice in God's hands, loving enemies, not enforcing ritual purity requirements, not requiring Sabbath observance—in short, most of the gamut of Jesus' ethic—is reapplied to a very different audience: very Hellenized and Romanized Gentiles. Obviously, Paul thought that the core ethic of Jesus, which distinguished him in various respects from other early Jews, had legs and traveled well across ethnic and cultural boundaries; even the teaching on love of enemies is preached to the largely Gentile audience in Rome in Romans 12.

And we could examine Acts as well and see the Jesus ethic in play in the depiction of the Jerusalem community, its generosity and concern for the poor, its excoriation of greed and deception whether from an Ananias and Sapphira or a Simon Magus, its display of love among members, its prayer life, its evangelistic orientation.

In short, even a cursory glance shows that the influence of the ethic of Jesus on the writers of the New Testament is wide and deep, even though Jesus is only occasionally directly quoted. This may be because the authors could assume that the audience knew the sayings of Jesus on various matters. But we need now to explore in some depth the ethical material found in the New

Testament that does not come from Jesus himself but rather in some cases is based in the ethic of Jesus and in some cases responds in a fresh way to new and different situations.

If we were to identify a controlling metaphor for all of Jesus' ethic, it would be cruciform, or self-sacrificial, love in light of the new eschatological situation. This is the baseline that explains all of the ways Jesus altered the standing ethic of early Judaism in fresh directions, from the alterations in the purity code to the practice of nonviolence. Loving one's enemy excludes doing them bodily harm, much less killing them. Jesus extended the ethical implications of the love ethic to an extravagant extent and then demonstrated what it looked like in the last week of his life, leaving a reminder to the disciples that they should be prepared to follow in his footsteps. They had already been taught to pick up their own crosses and follow him, but he got to Golgotha before they did.

The reason for so much emphasis in Jesus' teaching on a new view of marriage, divorce, children, and family is that in Jesus' teaching the family of faith that follows the mandate to live in a cruciform pattern is the primary family, and the dictates of the physical family do not take precedent over it. The physical family must serve not sever the family of faith, and in the new eschatological situation if one is not prepared to set one's priorities in this way, then Jesus says that he comes to bring not peace but rather the sword of the division to physical families. For Jesus, the normal preoccupations of the physical family, the preservation of life and limb and health in general, the building of wealth, the storing up of resources for the future and the expanding of one's personal property, the practice of marrying and having children, could no longer be the primary order of the day.

The final divine saving activity of God was breaking into human history, and new occasions teach new priorities, new duties. It could even lead some to be called to be single, a eunuch, for the sake of the kingdom, as Jesus himself was. Nothing spoke louder of the new eschatological situation in the teaching of Jesus than nonviolence, the leaving of family behind (or eschewing marriage altogether), and the living by a new, more rigorous holiness code. This bespoke the ethic of loving God wholeheartedly without distractions, loving neighbor genuinely without reciprocity, rancor or retaliation, loving enemy without reservations, and even being willing to say, "Father, forgive them, for they know not what they do." In the end, it is love and forgiveness that break the cycle of violence and allow broken human relationships to heal or be repaired. This was the kingdom ethic that Jesus espoused and the credo he lived by, for he believed that God's final saving activity was transforming humans into new creatures who could indeed live by such a credo, and when others saw them doing it, they got a glimpse of the coming kingdom.

Several years ago, in western Pennsylvania, there was a terrible slaughter of Amish school children by a crazed gunman who ended the madness by taking his own life. The Amish did not respond as the world would have or would have expected them to do. Instead of responding in kind, they responded in love, going to the family of the man and telling them that they forgave the man, and that they wished his family no harm and not even that they move out of the area. In fact, they helped the family mourn their own loss. And then the Amish buried their children and mourned them and went on with their radical Christian lives.

This uncommon grace, this outrageous forgiveness, seemed inexplicable to the media. Indeed, it seemed wrong to many. Does not an attitude such as these Amish people displayed just encourage more violence against innocents? Is not a forceful response necessary as a deterrent? Inquiring minds wanted to know. The world had just gotten a glimpse of kingdom ethics, indeed of the kingdom come on earth, and some found it stunning, some found it outrageous, and some found it beautiful beyond belief.

"All those who would come after me," said Jesus, "must take up their cross and follow me." One thing about carrying a heavy cross: it requires that you lay down everything else to pick it up, including laying down your weapons, desire to retaliate, grudges, unwillingness to forgive, lack of love for neighbor, much less for enemy. Only a transformed heart can lead to transfigured behavior of this fashion. Jesus knew this, and so he came to change human beings from the inside out, for he believed that the eschatological day foreseen by Isaiah, indeed the Jubilee Year, was coming and had now arrived when his lambs would lie down with the lions and either be led to slaughter or lead lions to long to become lambs tended by the tender good shepherd.[36]

---

[36]This conclusion presupposes much of what I argued for about the theology and ethic of Jesus in the first volume of the present work rather than here. It therefore is a conclusion to the treatments of Jesus' theology and ethic in both volumes.

10

ETHICS FOR JEWISH CHRISTIANS

Matthew, John, James, Jude, Hebrews, 1-3 John, 1 Peter, Revelation

Matthew is both creating an ordered symbolic world, in which Jesus possesses all authority in heaven and on earth, and defending it against rival world-views. The way in which Matthew constructs that world may be seen in his representation of Jesus as teacher, his account of discipleship as community formation, and his adaptation of eschatology as a warrant for ethics.

RICHARD HAYS[1]

In order to understand the rationale for grouping these New Testament books together in this chapter, one may well wish to consult once more the Venn diagram presented earlier.[2] When the subject is Christian ethics largely for Jewish Christians, one ignores the larger context of early Judaism and its ethics at one's peril. In particular, the interface between a sapiential way of thinking about life and ethics is important, as well as an eschatological way of thinking about life. Also, the earlier intersection of apocalyptic and wisdom thinking in the Jewish world needs to be taken into account.

Some cautionary words are in order as well. Some scholars have made the mistake of assuming that wisdom ethics is all about general maxims, universal proverbs, or the like—the most generic sort of ethical advice that one can give. As a result, New Testament ethical material is compared to maxims, proverbs, aphorisms, and apodictic statements in Greco-Roman literature, including Cynic literature.

---

[1]Richard B. Hays, *The Moral Vision of the New Testament: Community, Cross, New Creation* (San Francisco: HarperSanFrancisco, 1996), p. 94.
[2]See p. 63 above.

Generally speaking, such an approach is not all that helpful, for several reasons: (1) Even when sayings or materials from the larger Greco-Roman thought world are incorporated into the ethical data base of these New Testament writings, they are taken over and reshaped to serve different purposes for specific Christian communities. The citation of, say, an Egyptian proverb or a Cretan aphorism must be interpreted in light of the context into which it is inserted and of the rhetorical purpose it is meant to serve. It does not stand like an alien body in an ethical miscellany. (2) The eschatological worldview that suffuses all the New Testament absolutely shapes the character of the ethical advice given throughout these documents, and there is no comparable eschatological context for the ethics of Diogenes, Seneca, Epictetus, or others. In other words, the Jewish thought world into which such material is inserted shapes the way the material is used and should be viewed. (3) Much of the wisdom material in the New Testament is revelatory and even counterorder, not just conventional. By this I mean that most of it is wisdom that cannot be derived simply by examining nature or human nature. We do not find James or Jude or Matthew saying what "Solomon" says when he exhorts, "Go to the anthill and learn." No, this is new wisdom that comes as part and parcel of a revelation from God. As James puts it, "If any of you lacks wisdom, you should ask God, who generously gives to all without finding fault, and it will be given to you" (Jas 1:5). This presupposes a particular kind of intimate relationship with the biblical God such that one is prepared to receive such wisdom, which comes down from above. One has to be spiritually attuned to do that, not merely be intelligent. (4) The ethics promulgated by all these authors is not general ethics for just anyone but rather, as I have said, ethics for a specific community, the disciples of Jesus. And in this chapter we are looking even more specifically at the ethics offered primarily to Jewish Christians.

This does not mean that such ethics would not be applicable to a wider Christian audience as well, but much of the ethical discourse we find in this material presupposes four things: (1) a knowledge of the Old Testament and its ethics; (2) a knowledge of the teaching Jesus; (3) an understanding of how wisdom ethics works; (4) an understanding of the eschatological context in which all of this is spoken. The world has changed, the eschatological clock is ticking, the form of this world is passing away, and only by means of revelation and salvation can one become wise and know how to respond. What counts as wisdom in the shadow of the eschaton (e.g., a sense of detachment from the world, the flesh, and the devil) would not necessarily look like wisdom to those who were not part of this community and did not buy into an eschatological worldview.

One of the problems in dealing with New Testament ethics is that generally speaking, people start with Paul and do not get much further. This is a mistake on many levels. Many of the New Testament books were written primarily to and for Jewish Christians, and the Gentile mission came along after the Jewish Christian witness was well underway. Though at least some of Paul's letters are chronologically our earliest New Testament documents, he is clearly dependent on the earlier witness of the Jewish Christians in Jerusalem, including on ethical matters. For example, 1 Corinthians 8–10 presupposes the decree of James (Acts 15:13-21) when it comes to the issue of food offered to idols and whether and where one should eat it. Perhaps, then, it is best to examine the material written for Jewish Christians first. I will save the material written primarily for Gentile Christians (the Pauline material, Mark, Luke-Acts, 2 Peter) for the next two chapters. It is wise, I believe, to begin with an extensive look at the material from James, for he became head of the home church of all Jewish Christians in Jerusalem.

JAMES: ADAPTING THE ETHICAL LEGACY OF JESUS

Not surprisingly, the material closest to Jesus ethically, though more limited in topics addressed, is the sermon of James. James has a variety of concerns, but underlying all that he says is his concern that the community reflect the love, hospitality, sacrifice, and equality that ought to characterize a Christian community and, according to Acts 2:43-47; 4:32-37, did characterize the community to which James belonged in Jerusalem. Let us consider some of James' sagacious teaching, addressing first the issue of his indebtedness to his brother and to other Jewish wisdom sources.

In my study of James done some fifteen years ago, I concluded that James the book was mostly conventional wisdom of a generic sort, perhaps written to an audience in Antioch in the form of a circular letter. Since then, I have rethought and revised these conclusions somewhat. For one thing, the use of Jesus' sayings in this document is anything but a mere reiteration of conventional Jewish sapiential material. Instead, it reflects a combination of conventional and counterorder wisdom for a particular subset of the Christian community, Jewish Christians. As such, it is addressed to Jewish Christians throughout the empire but outside of Israel rather than just in Antioch or Asia Minor. Of course, there is traditional Jewish wisdom material here about the taming of the tongue, but it is juxtaposed with Jesus' own critique of wealth and the wealthy, and that is what makes this document so remarkable. Like the teaching of Jesus, it offers something old and something new drawn forth from the resource of Jewish wisdom material. Here it will be useful to set out a brief list of comparative texts both from the LXX and the Jesus tradition insofar as they have echoes in James.

Table 10.1. Echoes of the LXX in James

Prov 3:34	Jas 4:6
Prov 10:12	Jas 5:20
Prov 11:18	Jas 3:18
Sir 15:11-20	Jas 1:12-18
Sir 19:6-12; 20:4-7, 17-19; 35:5-10; 38:13-26	Jas 3 in general

More extensive are the parallels with the Matthean form of the Q sayings of Jesus we find in the Sermon on the Mount.[3]

Table 10.2. Echoes of the Jesus Tradition in James

Mt 5:11-12 // Lk 6:22-23	Jas 1:2
Mt 5:48	Jas 1:4
Mt 7:7	Jas 1:5
Mt 7:11	Jas 1:17
Mt 7:24 // Lk 6:46-47	Jas 1:22
Mt 7:26 // Lk 6:49	Jas 1:23
Mt 5:3, 5 // Lk 6:20	Jas 2:5
Mt 5:18-19 (cf. Lk 3:9)	Jas 2:10
Mt 5:21-22	Jas 2:11
Mt 5:7 // Lk 6:36	Jas 2:13
Mt 7:16-18 // Lk 6:43-44	Jas 3:12
Mt 5:9	Jas 3:18
Mt 7:7-8	Jas 4:2-3
Mt 6:24 // Lk 16:13	Jas 4:4
Mt 5:8	Jas 4:8
Mt 5:4 // Lk 6:25	Jas 4:9
Mt 7:1-2 // Lk 6:37-38	Jas 4:11
Mt 6:19-21 // Lk 12:33	Jas 5:2-3
Mt 7:1 // Lk 6:37	Jas 5:6
Mt 5:11-12 // Lk 6:23	Jas 5:10
Mt 5:34-37	Jas 5:12

---

[3]This is laid out convincingly and discussed in Patrick J. Hartin, *James and the "Q" Sayings of Jesus* (JSNTSup 47; Sheffield: JSOT Press, 1991), pp. 144-45. For my earlier work on James see *Jesus the Sage: The Pilgrimage of Wisdom* (Minneapolis: Fortress Press, 1994), pp. 236-47.

Peter Davids was right to conclude on the basis of this evidence that "while James ultimately has wisdom material as his background, this is refracted . . . through the pre-gospel Jesus tradition."[4] These parallels rule out the earlier suggestions that this was not originally a Christian document or was not very Christian in character. To the contrary, as Wesley Wachob has argued in detail, James seems to have come from the same community, or one allied to it, that produced the pre-Matthean Sermon on the Mount.[5] When analyzing these parallels more closely, we notice several things: (1) James rarely cites the saying of Jesus directly; rather, he weaves various ideas, themes and phrases into his own discourse; (2) this material is then presented as the teaching of James, not the sayings of Jesus, though one may suspect that the audience would recognize the echoes; (3) it does not appear that Matthew is drawing on James or vice versa, but rather that both are drawing on common source material; (4) this in turn suggests, though does not prove, that the Matthean form of the sayings of Jesus is closer to the original form than the Lukan form.[6] If this is correct, then it seems to follow that the Matthean portrait of Jesus is closer to real life than the Lukan one in regard to the ethical teaching in particular, though it has to be said that Luke is right on target in stressing Jesus' concern for the poor. James shares that concern, no doubt in part because of his own experiences in the Jerusalem church in the 40s and 50s. A bit more about the social ethos out of which James wrote will help at this juncture.

James's Social Setting

First, we need to keep in mind the likely marginalized status of Jewish Christians in Jerusalem. There had already been the jailing of some of its members (James Zebedee and Peter) in the 40s, and the execution of at least one of them (James Zebedee during the reign of Herod Agrippa I in the early 40s). Second, there was the issue of regular food shortage sometimes created by a famine crisis in Egypt, sometimes by other factors, which led to a real food shortage crisis in Israel and elsewhere in the eastern part of the empire. This in turn had led to James's plea with Paul to remember the poor (those most hard hit by such crises [see Gal 2:10]), something that Paul was eager to do

---

[4]Peter H. Davids, "The Epistle of James in Modern Debate," *ANRW* 25.5 (1988): 3638.

[5]Wesley H. Wachob, *The Voice of Jesus in the Social Rhetoric of James* (SNTSMS 106; Cambridge: Cambridge University Press, 2000).

[6]On this, see Ben Witherington III, *Matthew* (SHBC; Macon, Ga.: Smyth & Helwys, 2006), pp. 3-33.

to alleviate a difficult social situation in the Jerusalem church. This is why Paul took up the collections he did in his predominantly Gentile churches in various locales, collections that in fact were not brought to Jerusalem until A.D. 58. This reminds us that there was still need to address this issue as late as A.D. 58. In fact, things may have gotten worse in the 50s because another famine struck Egypt in the mid-50s.

Jewish Christians in Jerusalem may have found it difficult to get work because the temple was the primary employer in town (construction was still ongoing in the 50s) and because the tensions between non-Christian Jews and Jewish Christians continued to surface. We must also take seriously what Acts 2:42-47; 4:32–5:11; 6:1-2 suggest about this Christian community: there had been attempts at communitarianism, not unlike that found at Qumran, to make sure that the poor, widows and orphans who were Christians had the basic necessities of life. Under the social circumstances described in these chapters in Acts, and given the various external pressures, including famine and persecution, likely to put this community in an even more precarious state, it is no surprise that James takes a very strong stance on the issue of wealth and poverty, particularly as these phenomena existed in the community. James had been sensitized to these problems in his own church, and naturally he wanted to make sure that other Jewish congregations of Jesus' followers were likewise doing their duty by the poor and not showing partiality to the rich, which could ruin the ethos and *koinōnia* of those communities.

In addition to all this, William Brosend is right to stress that

> the letter of James was written at a time and in a place of considerable social and political tumult and of considerable socio-economic stratification. . . . In Jerusalem and Judea, Samaria and Galilee this general climate was exacerbated by political and religious conflict between ruling parties and classes, and a fairly long list of very undistinguished appointments by Rome. . . . By contemporary standards there was an extreme concentration of wealth among the ruling elite (2%-3% of the population), a small class of retainers, a small merchant class, and the vast majority of the population surviving as peasants, peasant artisans, and slaves. Within Judea, Samaria, and Galilee the latter grouping may have accounted for 85% or more of the population, with most of the arable land controlled by only a few.[7]

---

[7]William F. Brosend II, *James and Jude* (NCamBC; Cambridge: Cambridge University Press, 2004), p. 31.

In an environment of such social stratification and economic distress for the many, such strident remarks made about the wealthy come as no surprise.

We must take seriously the fact that James is addressing Christians some distance away, which is why he chooses typical but known examples of the problems to illustrate the social praxis that he wants to instill in these congregations. We should not expect, since this is an encyclical, that James is addressing some particular problem of a specific region or church. Notice too his assumption that he has authority over all these largely Jewish congregations. He assumes that the charitable and communal practices (as outlined in Acts 2–6) of the parent church in Jerusalem should be emulated by the other Jewish Christian congregations in the Diaspora. Partiality to the rich was always a deadly thing because it created stratification in a congregation, relegating some to second-class status. This ruined the *koinōnia* of such a small community. It is correct to conclude that James is referring to the economically poor and rich in various places in his sermon, not just to the spiritually poor or rich, though surely actual poverty and wealth have their spiritual effects and consequences.

The social function of this document is to reinforce the socializing process for Jews who have recently become Christians and due to pressure, persecution, or hardship are wavering in their faith. In order for the group to continue to exist as a distinct entity, separate from Judaism, certain boundaries for the in group needed to be clearly defined over against the larger culture and, to a lesser degree, over against the Jewish subculture. The paraenesis in James presents a group ethic designed to maintain rather clear boundaries between the in group and the out group. What the document implies is that the Jews who have converted to Christianity were in fact quite Hellenized Jews who struggled with conforming to the ethos of the larger culture and needed to be drawn back to a more Jewish and sapiential ethical lifestyle. The author is deeply concerned with issues of moral purity, and he addresses this concern by indicating ways to control speech, limit behavior and properly relate to others. This is the very sort of minority ethic that other Jews, such as the authors of Wisdom of Solomon and Sirach, set out to help Jews to survive in a hostile and foreign environment.[8]

John Elliott, developing this insight, shows the considerable concern in James for the wholeness and holiness of the community, which is a concern stressed when there is worry about pollution or infiltration of worldly values

---

[8]See Witherington, *Jesus the Sage,* p. 246.

or ideas or behavior. It is not surprising in such circumstances that James would use cultic language about purity and pollution to reinforce the boundaries of the community. Here the issue is orthopraxy rather than orthodoxy, which makes this sermon in some respects different from 1 John. The document is

> written at the point when, from the author's sense of the situation, cultural plurality and social-economic disequilibrium among the believers had become the seed-bed for discrimination of social classes and the currying of favor from wealthy and powerful patrons . . . litigation and dishonoring of the poor (2.6-7) and their neglect (2.13, 14-16), exploitation, and oppression by the wealthy who defraud their laborers, stockpile harvests, and kill the righteous (4.13–5.6); members pursuing their own selfish interests at the cost of their fellows and social cohesion (1.14-15; 4.1-10), brothers speaking evil of and passing judgment upon brothers (4.11-12; 5.9); personal doubt and instability of commitment (1.6-8; 4.8); duplicity in speech (3.1-12); inconsistency between words and action (1.22-24; 2.1-26; 5.12) suffering leads to a loss of patience and hope (1.2, 12-15; 5.7-11); and even apostasy and defection from the community (5.19-20). . . . The community and its members were undergoing an erosion of integrity and cohesion at both the personal and the social levels of life.[9]

We may suspect that the situation was not that drastic in every instance, since this is an encyclical document, but clearly enough James wants to nip in the bud tendencies that lead to the disintegration of Jewish Christian communities. He does this not simply by criticizing various sins, but on the positive side by attempting to inculcate an ethic that he had seen exhibited in the Jerusalem community as described in Acts 2–6. There is one further implication of the social analysis of James: "James reflects the social realities and outlook appropriate to a sect in the early stages of its life."[10]

James's Theological Ethics

It is important to say at the outset that it is a mistake to see the material in this discourse simply as paraenesis or as hortatory in character. It would be better to call it "theological ethics," for it is grounded in a certain view of God and divine activity. God is the one who sends wisdom, gives every good gift, including perseverance, and is the model of rectitude; not a shadow of a doubt or of any behavior that could be called questionable can be predicated of God. It becomes clear from James 1 that by and large, the author is serv-

---

[9]J. H. Elliott, "The Epistle of James in Rhetorical and Social Scientific Perspective: Holiness-Wholeness and Patterns of Replication," *BTB* 23 (1993): 75.
[10]Johnson, *The Letter of James* (AB 37A; New York: Doubleday, 1995), p. 119.

ing up not commonsense wisdom but rather revelatory wisdom, wisdom that comes by revelation and presupposes a particular view of God and the divine activity that enables human beings to be their best selves. These things need to be kept in mind throughout the study of this homily.

The revelatory wisdom of James 1. The discourse proper opens in James 1:2 with the astounding command to "consider it all joy," including all the trials and suffering. The Greek perhaps is better rendered as "consider it entirely as joy" because the phrase should be taken adverbially, or it could be rendered as "pure joy." But what is meant by "joy" here? Clearly enough, it cannot be seen as synonymous with pleasure *(hēdonē)* or even happiness *(eudaimonia)*, for this joy exists even in the midst of trials, temptations and suffering. Joy is repeatedly said to characterize the experience of early Christians (e.g., Acts 13:52; Rom 14:17; 15:13; 2 Cor 1:15; 2:3; Gal 5:22; Phil 1:4; Col 1:11; 1 Pet 1:8; 1 John 1:4; 2 John 12).[11] According to various of these texts, Christian joy is a work of the Spirit, not a result of one's circumstances.

In James 1:2 joy involves mental calculation or reckoning, as the verb *hē-geomai* indicates. But how does one reckon even suffering as joy? Texts such as John 16:20-22; 2 Corinthians 7:4; 1 Thessalonians 1:6; Hebrews 10:34 make clear that suffering and joy are compatible from a Christian point of view. I suggest that here James is talking about the joy of the Lord, which in Pauline letters is said to be part of the fruit of the work of the Spirit within the believer. This seems to refer to the sense of contentment that comes from the assurance of and delight in God's presence in one's life regardless of circumstances, a presence that often is most evident to the believer precisely in the time of greatest distress.

These opening verses have close parallels in at least two other places in the New Testament: Romans 5:2b-5; 1 Peter 1:6-7. We may note that 1 Peter is verbally closer to James than Paul is, though the thought of Paul is closer to James and corresponds at several points, as Paul speaks of suffering producing endurance and endurance producing character. It may be that Peter has read James and is attempting to say something similar, but Paul is likely independent. This suggests that all three may be drawing on some common early Christian material, possibly even from Jesus (cf. Mt 5:11-12). What we have here is an example of rhetorical *gradatio*—a set of stair steps building to a climax by the use of repetition and interlinking of phrases by key words. We should read James 1:2-4 as follows: "Count it as utter [or 'supreme'] cause for

---

[11]Ibid., 177.

rejoicing, my brothers and sisters, when you fall into various trials, knowing that the means of testing your faith results in steadfastness [or 'staying power']. But let steadfastness come to its culmination [or 'let steadfastness have its complete effect'], so that you will be perfect and wholly complete, not lacking anything."

What is the end product of this testing (if one passes the test)? James 1:4 indicates that this testing and the resulting strengthening of one's steadfastness is a process that one must allow to complete its perfect(ing) work. We are talking not about testing to see if a person has faith, but rather about testing existing faith so as to strengthen it. The term translated "perfect" or "complete" *(teleios)* here is eschatological, and we are seeing here what the end product will be by the time Christ returns: we will be perfected. The idea of becoming perfect and complete implies that things are in process, adding to that completeness so that in the end one lacks nothing necessary to stand before the judge (cf. James 5:8-9). Thus, the Christian life is to be seen not only as a having of faith, but also a persevering and improving in character so that a "fully formed uprightness" results. We may call this "progressive sanctification," to use a theological term.

Here we are talking not about an experience of instantaneous perfection but rather about a perfecting process. Equally, we are not talking only about growing up in the faith. James is talking about single-minded loyalty and unmixed motives. This is the work that God is working in believers as they work out their salvation with fear and trembling (to borrow Paul's way of putting in Phil 2:12). "Endurance, the growing capacity to experience disappointment and challenge with grace, courage, and resolve, is an outgrowth of faith, and itself yields maturity and completion, *telos* (perfection). Part of the subversive wisdom at the heart of James' ideology is the conviction that perfection is the goal, and trials are a part of the journey toward it."[12] How very different this is from the notion that suffering or even bad health is always a telltale indication of lack of faith. James, to the contrary, seems to see such trials as part and parcel of every Christian's journey.

James 1:5-8 tells us something about both God and humans, what God willingly gives, and what humans can receive if they do so in faith. Several general features of the text call for notice. In James 1:7 *kyrios* surely refers to God, not Christ, as James 1:5 makes clear. James alternates between using *kyrios* ("Lord") of Christ (as in Jas 1:1) and of God (Jas 4:15; 5:10, 11). For

---

[12]Brosend, *James and Jude*, p. 38.

James, *sophia* ("wisdom") seems to function like the Spirit does in Paul's letters. It is wisdom that gives one the illumination and the strength to stand the test. It is wisdom that is the special gift of God to believers. As we know from the Old Testament, wisdom sometimes was personified, and here in James wisdom, which is a gift of the Spirit, is treated and spoken of almost as if it were wisdom doing the Spirit's job. Wisdom also is viewed by James as the fundamental thing lacking that one should ask of God, and in a sense this homily seeks to remedy that problem by providing godly wisdom to the hearers. To see trials and afflictions in the light that James does and wants his audience to see requires indeed a wisdom from above. Here it is apropos to consider Wisdom of Solomon 7:7, where the king prays and says, "Therefore I prayed, and understanding was given to me; I called upon God, and the spirit of wisdom came to me."

In James 1:5-8 we also gain a clearer sense of what perfection amounts to in James's view. It means being fully equipped with the wisdom (not just knowledge, but know-how, steadfastness) to withstand whatever trials or tribulations may come. It is not unlike Paul's image of the Christian who has put on the full armor of God (see Eph 6:10-20). It entails a person lacking nothing in what is needed to deal with life's slings and arrows. Thus, the focus is not on moral purity per se but rather on having an equipped and complete character, which of course involves moral uprightness and integrity. Here God is contrasted with the waverer. God is single-minded and impartial and gives without making the receiver feel belittled. God gives without reservation, unconditionally. To receive it requires an unconditional, totally trusting response.

James is a firm believer that as one's heart is, so will be one's life and actions. There is an echo in these verses of Wisdom of Solomon 9:6: "Even someone who is perfect/mature *[teleios]* among human beings will be regarded as nothing without wisdom that comes from God." The theme of testing and enduring testing on the basis of divinely given wisdom is shared in these texts. James certainly stands in this tradition, but he freely modifies it to suit the new set of circumstances after the Christ-event. In general, James should be seen as a person who has drunk deeply from the well of various sorts of sapiential material—from the Old Testament, from Sirach and Wisdom of Solomon, and from his brother—and has formulated his own teaching while being indebted to all these sources.

There is likely an echo of Matthew 7:7 in James 1:5. In both cases the subject is prayer and the same verb for "ask" is used, but James takes this idea in a particular direction: asking God for something specific, wisdom. James also portrays the character of God more vividly. God's manner of giving is *haplōs*, which can be rendered in various ways. The word is found only here in the New Testament, and in classical Greek it has the sense of "simply, plainly." It probably is right to see here a contrast of God with the double-minded person. God is singled-minded; God does not hesitate to give, and God does so without reproach and with generosity, giving to "all" (in this case, probably all believers is meant). Likewise in James 1:6-7 we likely have an echo of Mark 11:23 about how those who doubt in their heart will not receive what is prayed for. It appears that the believer's asking for help must be single-minded and pure, analogous to God's single-minded desire to help and give wisdom.

"Arguably the most important theme in James is his concern that Christians display spiritual integrity: singleness of intent combined with blamelessness in actions."[13] Integrity in word and deed is what James is after. One should say what one means, and one should act in such a way to be as good as one's word. It is no accident that the beginning and the end of this discourse involve a discussion of prayer and its importance and efficacy if one asks in faith. Prayer is the clear sign that one is living by faith and depending on God not only for the answers but also for the practical help to get through the trials of life. Lack of prayer is a sign of doubting and spiritual instability, a lack of dependence on God. And this brings us to a crucial point already hinted at: the ethics of the New Testament presupposes a deep and abiding relationship with and reliance on God, as one's prayer life shows. This clearly is not an ethic for anyone and everyone; it is an ethic that presupposes a devout person reliant on God.

In James 1:9-11 the author introduces another of his main topics: the poor and the rich. James 1:9 plays on the contrast between pride *(kauchasthō)* and the humble *(ho tapeinos)*. It is quite clear from the contrast with *plousios* in James 1:10 that the humble are the "humble poor" and the proud are the rich, whereas in Proverbs 3:34 the contrast of the humble is simply with the arrogant, who may or may not be rich. James's concern is with inappropriate sorts of boasting (Jas 3:14; 4:16), but not all boasting is ruled out. This is not surprising, for in the wisdom tradition boasting in the Lord is seen as a good thing. It is interesting that in the New Testament, outside of James

---

[13]Douglas J. Moo, *The Letter of James* (PNTC; Grand Rapids: Eerdmans, 2000), p. 59.

and one reference in Hebrews 3:6, only Paul has anything to say directly about boasting, and Paul too suggests that there are things to boast about, in particular that which comes from the Lord and is done by the Lord, not that which comes from one's self. Behind all such discussions stands Jeremiah 9:23-24: "Thus says the LORD: 'Let not the wise man boast of his wisdom, or the strong man boast of his strength, or the rich man boast of his riches, but let him who boasts, boast about this: that he understands and knows me.'"

What is unclear is whether both the poor and the rich here are envisioned as Christians or whether we should see a hard contrast here between "the believers" and "the rich." In either case, James is not talking solely about one's character with his use of *tapeinos* here but rather about one's economic and social position. Nonetheless, paradoxically, the poor person has something to boast about in his or her humble condition.

Various problems arise in this passage. Who are those rich people? Are they rich Christians or the rich in general? Much will depend on what one makes of James 2:1-7; 5:1-6. It is difficult to imagine James 5:1-6 being said of a person who is truly a Christian; however, there is the rub. Quite clearly in James 2:2 the author is talking about wealthy people who come to a Christian meeting. It seems unlikely that he would be speaking about the rich in general, because as James 1:1 indicates, he is addressing those who are part of the believing community, whom James can address directly (Jas 5:1). James refrains from explicitly calling them "brothers" in James 1:9-11, though it may be implied by the parallel with James 1:9. Thus, on the whole it does appear that James is referring to wealthy Christians, and not only are they being called to account, but also the community will be called to account for giving them special treatment or benefits. The parallel structure here favors the conclusion that the rich are envisioned as being within the community. This in turn means that the "lowly position" of rich Christians is a reference to their social stigma for identifying themselves with Christ and his people.

Nonetheless, James is profoundly dissatisfied with the behavior of these persons toward poor Christians and warns if they do not shape up, they will face God's final judgment. In this, James sounds much like an Old Testament prophet, excoriating the "fat cows" (cf. Amos 4:1) who are among and associate with and claim allegiance to Israel and Israel's God. The contrast in the letter between confession and lifestyle as the mark of someone not truly Christian draws specifically on the example of the rich (Jas 2:14-17). James therefore is mainly speaking about and to those wealthy ones who claim faith but do not live out its implications. However, there may be a reference to rich visitors to the congregation in James 2.

James 1:10 is somewhat difficult to decipher. Should we supply "boast" and make it parallel to James 1:9? Is the verse about the rich Christians being robbed or disenfranchised by persecutors when or after they converted, or is it about the rich having an attitude of self-abasement and engaging in self-effacing living because they know that they must pass away someday and cannot take it with them? Clearly, the rich are not to "glory" in their riches, for they are of no lasting value. Wealth can pass away in an instant; indeed, while the rich are on the move to make more money, they are seen as wasting away. We must see *en tē tapeinōsei* (Jas 1:10) as parallel to *en tō hypsei* (Jas 1:9), so it is a reference to a humble position, not a humble attitude. It is doubtful that James is being sarcastic: "lest the rich boast about his degradation" (i.e., filthy riches). Rather, the point is that the rich person should boast in voluntarily assuming a lower position and more humble circumstances by using riches to help the poor, whereas the poor are relatively better off not facing the temptation of riches; they know they are not self-sufficient and must rely on God for everything.

In his description of the transitoriness and ephemeral value of wealth, James is sounding a traditional sapiential note (cf. Job 24:24; 27:21; Ps 49:16-20). In James 1:11 the word *kausōn* may refer to the scorching west wind but may equally well refer to burning heat. It is interesting that almost every single one of James analogies drawn from nature are also found in the teaching of Jesus: the surging of the sea (Lk 21:25), the flowers of the field (Mt 6:28), the burning of wood (Jn 15:6) the birds of the air (Mt 6:26; 8:20), the fountain of sweet water (Jn 4:10-14), the fig tree (Mt 7:16), the vine (Jn 15:1-5), the moth and the rust (Mt 6:19), and the rain (Mt 5:45). Like earlier sages, Jesus and James believed that wisdom could be gained from close examination of nature, including human nature. Not only do these analogies suit a resident of Israel very well, but also they show the intellectual tradition in which Jesus and James stand. We certainly are right to hear echoes of Psalm 103:15-16 and Isaiah 40:6-8 here. But tellingly, in both cases it is revealed wisdom from God that most gives guidance to Jesus' followers.

Finally, at the end of James 1:11 *en tais poreiais* may mean "in his travels" or "as he goes through life" or even "as he goes about his business," and the second translation might parallel the end of James 1:8. As it turns out, both poverty and wealth are tests of character, trials to be endured and properly responded to. In James 1:9-11 we have echoes of remarks not only of Jesus about transitoriness, using flowers or grass to illustrate, but also of Psalms and Isaiah 40 (see Ps 103:15; Is 40:6-8; Lk 14:11; 18:14; and especially Mt 6:30 par.). Not only is wealth fleeting, but so also is life, and so both may be compared to grass or wildflowers. It is not clear whether we should read what is said here in light of James 4:13–5:9, which clearly makes eschatological reference to the judgment coming when the Lord returns. In view of the fact that we are meant to see this exordium as a preview of coming attractions, I think that the eschatological overtones must be given their due here, all the more so when the very next verse offers up a very Jesus-like eschatological beatitude promising the crown of eternal life. The language of "reversal" in this passage functions much like Jesus' use of it: counterorder wisdom and ethics are what is appropriate in an eschatological situation. The point of the lengthy analogy between the rich and their money and the beautiful flower that wilts and is destroyed is that judgment is coming upon such persons who boast in that sort of status. Isaiah 40:7 certainly lurks in the background here.

James 1:12-18, though a new subsection, bears a rather clear relationship to the material in James 1:2-11, involving offering some correlative ideas, with James 1:12 serving as something of a hinge between what has come before and what comes afterwards. Brosend puts it this way:

> The blessing on the one who endures temptations recalls the "consider it nothing but joy" in the face of "trials of any kind" in vs. 2. The "doubter" of vss. 6-8 anticipates the wrong understanding of temptation in vss. 13-15. The "perfecting of faith" climax is mirrored in reverse by the elaborate climax, from temptation to death in vss. 14-15. The giving of wisdom from the God "who gives to all generously and ungrudgingly" anticipates the "giving of every perfect gift" in vs. 17.[14]

To this, one can add that God's giving of wisdom anticipates the statement about God giving birth to humans through the word of truth.

> The basic dynamic of the passage is clear: (1) the experience of testing naturally calls one to ask about its source; (2) do not think it comes from God, for God is not tempted and tempts not; (3) instead we are tempted by our desires, which if followed lead to death; (4) the unchanging God, on the contrary, gives good things, above all, gives us birth. The interplay of question and answer, temptation and blessing, human desire and divine purpose, birth and death make this a lively and complex passage.[15]

[14]Brosend, *James and Jude*, p. 44.
[15]Ibid., pp. 46-47.

This sort of reasoning reflects the long-standing Jewish sapiential tradition in which the real wisdom that matters is a gift from God (Prov 2:6; Sir 51:17; Wis 8:21; 9:17; 4Q185), and God is seen as being generous for lavishing such wisdom on fallen human beings (Sir 1:9-10).

The word *makarios*, which begins James 1:12, immediately reminds us of the beatitudes in the Sermon on the Mount. Some have translated the term "happy," but in fact this term is not simply a synonym for *eudaimonia* (on the distinction, see Aristotle, *Eth. nic.* 1101A), and in the biblical tradition the term is applied to a person in right relationship with God (see in the LXX, e.g., Deut 33:29; Ps 1:1; 2:12; 31:1), and so the translation "blessed" is best.[16] James says, "Blessed is the man who stands up to the test, because when he has been approved, he will receive the crown of [eternal] life that God has promised to his beloved." Previously, we were told that one could fall into a trial or test, and here we see the converse: standing up under it. Here the author's focus is on eschatological, not temporal, rewards; that is, the one who persevered and is approved receives eternal life, the ultimate blessing, which God himself promised to his beloved children. The use of *stephanos* ("crown") may be drawing on the image of the crown of victory bestowed on the winner of a race, which was a laurel wreath, not a metal crown (see Herodotus, *Hist.* 8.26; Rev 2:9-10).

If James 1:12 was about those who pass the test, James 1:13 is about those about to fail it and are in need of a stern warning. Here we see James using a diatribe form, as we find at length in James 2. There seems to be an echo in James 1:13 of Sirach 15:11-12: "Do not say, 'It was the Lord's doing that I fell away'; for God does not do what he hates. Do not say, 'It was he who led me astray'; for he has no need of the sinful." There is perhaps an especially good reason why James would draw on Sirach and the Wisdom of Solomon in his address to Jewish Christians in the Diaspora: those books, at least in their Greek form, came from the Diaspora and were the popular literature of such Jewish persons.

James wishes to establish that it is quite inexcusable to cast God as the source of one's temptations. Not only is God immune to temptation and thus never conceives or does evil, but also, being perfectly good, he tempts no one. One might naturally expect the writer to go on to talk about Satan, the tempter, but instead he places the responsibility for sin and its source on fallen human nature. James is not trying to tell us what the ultimate source of evil is, though he denies that it is God.

---

[16]Johnson, *Letter of James*, p. 187.

In James 1:14 we have the metaphors of hunting and fishing applied to temptation. One is lured or drawn in by the bait on the hook or is enticed and entrapped by the bait in the net. Philo makes a similar use of this metaphor: "There is no single thing that does not yield to the enticement of pleasure, and gets caught and dragged along in her entangling nets" (*Agriculture* 103). Obviously, temptation can be quite appealing, otherwise it would not be very tempting. When desire conceives of evil, it gives birth to sin, but it is sin that leads to death.[17]

Here we have the *gradatio* in reverse, spiraling downward to a negative climax. Temptation is brought by desire; desire, once it conceives, gives birth to sin; sin, when fully grown, gives birth to death. Put in linear fashion: conception leads to birth, which leads to growth, which leads to death. Some behavior gives birth to life, while other behavior gives birth to death. James offers up a sapiential paradox by drawing on the birth imagery here to describe the process that leads to death and in James 1:18 by contrasting the process that God initiates by which believers become firstfruits of the (new) creation with this process that leads to death. Desire itself is not sin, but if it is wrongly directed, sin is not only conceivable but conceived. Douglas Moo is right to add, "Christian maturity is not indicated by the infrequency of temptation but by the infrequency of succumbing to temptation."[18] He is also right that here we probably have echoes of the discussion of the "loose woman" in Proverbs 5–9. Possibly also Matthew 5 is in the background here.

James 1:16-18 continues on a more positive note. If God does not tempt us or send temptations, what does he send? The answer is good gifts. The imagery here draws on Genesis and the first creation. Note the plural "lights" in James 1:17, and that in the Genesis narrative only the sun and the moon are called "lights" in this fashion. Calling God "the Father of lights" is a distinctive way of referring to God, and all the more so when, having called God Father, James, in the next verse, turns around and says that God gives birth to people through the Word. The text also adds that God made the stars. If this is the background here, then we can make some sense out of the second part of James 1:17. The sunlight that we receive varies in its amount or at least in

---

[17]Some scholars have thought that James reflects the early Jewish notion of the *yetzer hara* and the *yetzer tov* in each person—the inclination toward evil or toward good. But James says nothing about an inclination to do good that is inherent in persons, and it is evil desire, not inclinations, at issue here. But see Joel Marcus, "The Evil Inclination in the Epistle of James," *CBQ* 44 (1982): 607-21

[18]Moo, *Letter of James*, p. 76.

its intensity depending on the time of year. Unlike that phenomenon, God and his light neither change nor vary. The moon is always going through various phases that are like shadows covering parts of the light and changing it. God, however, is not so. Nothing overshadows or changes God, and when God wills to do something, it happens.

In this case, what God wills is the new creation that takes place through the word of truth—that is, the gospel of redemption. The result is that believers are already a sort of firstfruits of God's new creation. Rather than being dead, they are already reborn and part of a new world. Obviously, here we may think of various Pauline texts with similar ideas (e.g., 1 Cor 15:20-25; 2 Cor 5:17-18). Perhaps James knew of Paul's teaching on these matters and varied the imagery to suit his purposes. This exordium to this sermon nicely makes emotional contact with the audience and sets up and introduces most of the main themes that follow. What we learn along the way is that God is the wellspring of wisdom and all that is good, whereas the human heart is the wellspring of wickedness, just as Jesus suggested in Mark 7. Notice that James, like the other New Testament writers, places the moral responsibility for sin, or giving way to temptation, squarely on the shoulders of the believer. Even if Satan is said to be the tempter, he is not ultimately blamed for human misbehavior. And James is particularly concerned with Christian misbehavior, which he believes by the wisdom and grace of God can be avoided.

There is a great deal of repetition of ethical topics and themes in James, and we have examined several already, but we need to focus on one more major part of the discussion: the issues raised at the end of James 1 and in James 2. Here once again, in James 1:19, we hear an echo of the earlier Jewish wisdom tradition, specifically Sirach 5:11: "Be quick to hear, but deliberate in answering. If you have understanding, answer your neighbor; but if not, put your hand over your mouth"; also Proverbs 29:11: "A fool gives full vent to anger, but the wise quietly holds it back."

In James 1:20 *orgē* may refer to the eschatological justice or retribution of God that will fall on the world at the end. This would comport with James 5:9 (God's impending judgment) and with the idea of being saved by the word (i.e., saved from the wrath) in James 1:21. The other possibility is that human anger does not produce the type of righteous action that reflects God's standard, but this seems a less likely interpretation because this letter is thoroughly eschatological to begin with, but more importantly because more likely in the background here is the Sermon on the Mount, where Jesus condemns angry and malicious words and tells those who speak such they are liable to Gehenna (see Mt 5:22). This verse is important also because here the language of "righteous/righteousness" *(dikaios/dikaiosynē)* is introduced into the discourse and will become a major theme (see Jas 2:23-24; 3:18; 5:6, 16).

Note *andros* (*anēr*, "man") in James 1:20. It is possible that here James is specifically exhorting males who were mouthing off, perhaps thinking that their anger was godly or righteous. In support of this conclusion is that it was almost always men who would speak in synagogue and other Jewish public meetings. There are also ancient texts suggesting that anger was more associated with men than women (see Longinus, *On the Sublime* 32). James, however, is speaking here not against righteous indignation but against rather ordinary anger or malice toward another, and perhaps James the sage realized that men especially have a problem with properly expressing their anger, but perhaps we should see *anēr* as equivalent to *anthrōpos* here as it seems to be in other cases in James (cf. Jas 1:8, 12, 20, 23). In any case, there is probably an echo here of Proverbs 17:27, which connects speaking with anger: "A man of knowledge uses words with restraint, and a man of understanding is even-tempered" (cf. Sir 1:22-24). The connection is the propensity of the quick-tempered person to speak too quickly and in an ill-advised manner. James is likely reflecting on sayings of Jesus such as Matthew 5:20, which speaks of his followers' righteousness exceeding that of the Pharisees and scribes, and James probably is not prohibiting righteous anger here, for

> wisdom sayings are notorious for the use of apparently absolute assertions in order to make a general "proverbial point". . . . So we can assume that James intends us to read his warning as a general truth that applies in most cases: human anger is not usually pleasing to God, leading as it does to all kinds of sins. That it can never be pleasing to God would be an interpretation that is insensitive to the [sapiential] style in which James writes.[19]

Here we may sense a contrast between anger/wrath and righteousness. But what does the phrase "righteousness of God" actually refer to here? Is it a descriptor of God's character such as we find in James 1:17? That is possible. Or does this phrase build on James 1:19 and refer to what God expects of Christians, that they manifest in their behavior the righteousness of God? Or is this a reference to God's righteous verdict that he proclaims or to a right standing that God gives, as in justification? The problem with this last

---

[19]Ibid., p. 84.

suggestion is that James is addressing those who are already Jewish Christians, and he is not discussing what happened to them at the point of their conversions. It is right to take note of the verb *ergazomai* here as referring to something humans "produce" or "work." The context indicates that James is talking about human behavior, and so we should see an objective genitive here: the righteousness that God requires believers to work out instead of manifesting their own all-too-human anger, just as God is working his own righteous character into them. This interpretation comports completely with what follows, which speaks of the Word of God implanted in the inner self (and within the community) that saves the person.

James 1:21 draws a conclusion on the basis of James 1:19-20. "Therefore," because anger (including condemning, cursing, even cursing one's oppression) will not bring about God's final judgment, one should be slow to vent or express anger. Instead of such speaking, Christians are to clean out their ears and listen. The word *ryparia* used in a metaphorical sense can mean "moral filth" or even "avarice" (cf. *ryparos* in Jas 2:2; *rypos* 1 Pet 3:21), but it literally refers to ear wax. The context does not favor the purely metaphorical sense, for the context involves hearing and receiving the word. There may be a connection between what is said here and the flow of the discussion in 1 Peter 1:23–2:2, since both passages refer to new birth through the word followed by an exhortation to get rid of evil behavior and embrace the word. The word is to be received either with meekness or with good will. The word *emphytos* surely means "implanted" here because one cannot receive something that is "innate," nor does "ingrafted" quite fit here (see Herodotus, *Hist.* 9.94; *Barn.* 1:2; 9:9). The point is that the word gets so deeply rooted that it becomes a part of one's very being and is able to save the person (cf. Jesus' metaphor of the seed sown in Mk 4:1-20 par.). Salvation here is seen as future; that is, salvation on the day of judgment and this future sense of salvation are also seen at James 2:12; 4:12; 5:15, 20.

The word *psychē* means not "soul' here but rather "self" or even "life." The New Testament authors show no interest in saving only some part of a person but instead wish to save the whole person, and that is what the word means here: "your self, your being, you." No radical dualism is in evidence here. Meekness is said to be the means of cleaning out one's malice. The word *praytēs* may echo the reference to lowliness in James 1:9 but in any case is an important descriptor of both Christ's and a Christian's character (cf. Mt 11:28-30; Gal 5:22-23). It is no accident that many of the character trait lists in the New Testament include virtues that were not seen as virtues in the Greco-Roman world, and meekness, which was seen as weakness by most non-Jews in that world, is one of them. This is one of the examples where Christian character and conduct are meant to model themselves on the distinctive or at least characteristic traits of Jesus.

It is possible that we should see James 1:22-25 as simply a further development of what precedes; that is, "When I say 'receive the word,' I mean do it, not just listen to it." In any event, the section begins with a charitable assumption that they are indeed doing the word. Notice that James 1:22 probably means "But continue to be doers of the word, and not just listeners, deceiving yourselves."

We may ask, "Deceiving themselves about what?" To judge from James 1:21 and what follows, it probably refers to deceiving oneself about salvation or at least about the authenticity of Christian life. Note how orthodoxy that is not coupled with orthopraxy and real fruit in God does not impress James. As James 2:19 says, even the demons believe all the right doctrines, but it does them little good. Here is a salutary lesson against those who pride themselves on their orthodoxy but have so spiritualized and allegorized the gospel's demands that they do not take seriously the cost of discipleship and the demand for deeds of compassion and righteousness. As Brosend so aptly puts it, "when all is said, all is not done."[20] It is worthwhile stressing that Paul says something closely similar in Romans 2:13: "It is not those who hear the law who are righteous in God's sight, but it is those who obey the law who will be declared righteous."

James 1:23-25 raises a host of questions. Obviously, we are dealing with a metaphorical sapiential comparison, so we must not press the text too far. The point of the comparison seems to be the transitoriness of the mirror image's effect and the transitoriness of the effect of hearing without doing. The contrast is between seeing but forgetting to heed what one has seen and seeing and doing, not between the two forms of looking and what can be seen in each mirror. As Davids says, "the momentariness and lack of real effect is the point of the parable, not a comparison with a different type of mirror or a different way of seeing."[21] Thus, there is no need to see any developed contrast between fallible human mirrors, made of copper and bronze and

---

[20]Brosend, *James and Jude*, p. 51.
[21]Peter H. Davids, *The Epistle of James: A Commentary on the Greek Text* (NIGTC; Grand Rapids: Eerdmans, 1982), p. 98.

giving a mediocre likeness even when polished, and God's law as the mirror of the soul. The word *epilēsmonē* in James 1:25 is an interesting one, meaning "forgetfulness." This word occurs nowhere else in the New Testament, but we find it in Sirach 11:27, which says that the afflictions of an hour cause forgetfulness of pleasure. The point is that a "hearer of forgetfulness" is the antithesis of a "doer of the word." Another possible echo of Sirach, this time Sirach 19:20, is found in the use of *poiēsis* in James 1:25 to refer to a "doing" of the law. In Sirach it is said that in all wisdom there is a "doing" of the law, using the same term.

Luke Timothy Johnson does an excellent job of showing how the image of looking into a mirror as a metaphor of moral improvement (with the mirror sometimes signifying the distance between image and reality) was common in the Greco-Roman world and furthermore how looking into the law as into a mirror is an image found in earlier Jewish Wisdom literature (see especially Wis 7:26).[22] One of the keys to understanding the use of the metaphor in James 1:25 is that in the case of the law, the Greek verb for "look" is not the same one used in the phrase about looking into the mirror in James 1:24. Here we have *parakyptō*, which has the sense of leaning over or stooping down to peer into or to gaze intently at or to ponder hard what one is looking at (cf. Lk 24:12; Jn 20:5; and especially 1 Pet 1:12). The transitory glance, however clearly it may have taken in the image, stands in contrast with deep reflection.

The crux of the matter is the identity of the law in James 1:25. Is it the Mosaic law? Is it Christian teaching that is a new law? Is it some combination of both? Looking into the mirror, seeing one's own image, and forgetting is one thing, and looking into the law, seeing God's character, remembering, and doing is another. We should recall that mirrors were far from perfect in antiquity (see 1 Cor 13:12), and James is hardly going to say that the law, which he calls perfect, is like an inexact image in a bronze mirror. The analogy is between a person looking into two different things and then either not acting on what is seen or acting on it appropriately. The law is not identified as a mirror here. An analogy is, after all, a comparison between two largely unlike things that in some specific way are alike.

There are only five uses of the term *logos* in James, except for the incidental use in James 3:2, where it refers to speaking, and all are clustered here in

---

[22]Luke Timothy Johnson, "The Mirror of Remembrance (James 1:22-25)," *CBQ* 50 (1988): 632-45.

James 1 (Jas 1:18, 21, 22, 23). Indeed, this term helps to link the exordium and the proposition of this discourse. If "Be doers of the word" is so essential to James's discourse, why is it that he ceases talking about the *logos* here in the first chapter? Brosend suggests, "It appears that as James's argument unfolds, *logos* is replaced by *nomos* (law), which is first found at 1:25, and that for James the two terms are in many ways synonymous."[23] Let us see if this suggestion makes sense.

First, note that James 1:22 speaks of the "word." Whatever *nomos* means in James 1:25, it is likely to be the same thing as the "word" in James 1:22 in view of both the content and the context of these verses. Second, we have seen how Jesus' teaching underlies much of this letter; surely, that cannot be excluded from this saying about word or law. Third, this law is said to be not a yoke but rather a giver of liberty. Fourth, in James 2:8-12. the author defines this law in part: it is a law from God, a royal law. It must at least involve the Old Testament love commandment and at least parts of the Decalogue. However, just as obviously, it must include that Christian paraenesis and teaching of Jesus which James has already used to exhort his audience. Thus, for James, "law" means not just the Old Testament law or Jesus' teaching or even Christian ethics, but all three. This comports with the use of *logos* in a broad sense, such as we have in James 1. Moreover, James sees Jesus' law as a "new law" that gives freedom, unlike the old law by itself. There may be a contrast in James 1:25 between this perfect law and what had been given before.

This law is new in part because it is implanted in the believer; it does not just exhort a person from outside, and it becomes so deeply rooted in the believer that the doing of it is freedom and a freely chosen act, not a mere duty or compulsion. Here we may compare God's intent to "write the law on the hearts" of his people (Jer 31:33). This law, if divine, gives freedom. God's word, if implanted, is able to save and does not to kill. However, we must note that James is not saying that obedience saves a person. God's word and grace do that.

James is addressing those who already are Christians and is giving them kingdom ethics, what God requires of them after the new birth and on the way to final salvation. James therefore is not at variance with Paul, who also talks about Christian ethics as the "law of Christ" and relates freedom and obedience to God's word or law in Galatians 5:13-14. In short, James's perspective is like that of his brother Jesus and is not to be radically contrasted

---

[23]Brosend, *James and Jude*, p. 53.

with Paul's view. The Old Testament law must be reinterpreted in light of what God has done in Jesus. This means that some of it is fulfilled and no longer applicable. Some of it is retained and reaffirmed. Some of it is expanded or radicalized, and some new commandments are offered as well.

Some of the old law's central teaching is reemphasized, stressed and made central to the new ethic, such as the law of love or the love commandment. Some of it has added to it various new things, including the law's new role in a believer's life, so that it all could be called a "new law" or a "perfect law of liberty." In James 1:25 eschatological blessing appears to be in view, not temporal blessing. A doer of God's word will be blessed instead of cursed on that day which is coming. Here, Moo's conclusions are worth quoting:

> The "law" of vs. 25 must be substantially equivalent to the "word" of vv. 22-23. Yet that "word" must be closely related to, if not identical to, the "word of truth" through which men and women are regenerated to salvation (v. 18). Taken together, these points suggest that James's "law" does not refer to the law of Moses as such, but to the law of Moses as interpreted and supplemented by Christ. Perhaps then, the addition of the word "perfect" connotes the law in its eschatological, "perfected" form, while the qualification "that gives freedom" refers to the new covenant promise of the law written on the heart (Jer 31:31-34 . . .), accompanied by a work of the Spirit enabling obedience to that law for the first time.[24]

There is, however, one further point to stress. Whenever there is a new covenant, not just an old one renewed, it will have at least some new provisions and stipulations, while it may reiterate some of the old ones as well. The eschatological covenant is neither a mere renewal nor a mere fulfillment of any previous ones. It, and its "law," have no built-in obsolescence; it is "perfect," as James says (but see Ps 18:8 LXX [19:7 ET]). This law gives freedom, which is the very opposite of what Paul says about the Mosaic law's effect on fallen human beings.

Is it too much to think that James, like Paul, believed that the eschatological law had been given by Christ with the new covenant, so that which Paul calls the "law of Christ" in Galatians James calls the "royal/perfect law"? Perhaps not, but in any case, Martin Luther's old contrasts between Paul's view of "the law" and James' view clearly were mistaken. Both James and Paul argued for obedience to this new law, whether one calls it the "perfect

---

[24]Moo, *Letter of James*, p. 94.

law" or the "law of Christ." Of course, both were indebted to Jesus, who associated blessedness with hearing the word of God or his own words and keeping or doing them (Mt 7:24; Lk 11:28). Thus, although commentators go too far who say that when we see "law" in James, we shoud read read "gospel," they are on the right track, for James is talking about the "law" or commandments portion of the new covenant.

We have seen James's initial presentation of his major themes, so now we look at the transitional verses James 1:26-27, which lead us to the first major exposition of a theme. Davids observes,

> The final section of this introductory chapter sums up what has preceded and bridges between it and chap. 2. The subject has been true Christianity, and three marks stand out: (a) a true Christian must control his tongue (1:19-21, but also chap. 3 and with it the wisdom sayings, 1:5-8), (b) he must engage in charity, which was certainly the teaching of Jesus (1:22-25, 9-11; chap. 2), and (c) such a one must resist temptation, i.e. the world (1:2-4, 12:15; chap. 4). The summary first states (a) negatively, then (b) and (c) positively.[25]

The term *thrēskos* (unique to James) likely refers to religious observance—rites and rituals, prayer and fasting, the elements of worship and devotional practice—whereas *thrēskeia* refers more generically to religion in its cultic aspects (see Wis 14:18, 27; 4 Macc 5:7, 13; Acts 26:5), something that is re-inforced by the further use of the term *aspilos*, meaning "undefiled, spotless" (cf. 1 Tim 6:14). James is saying that all these religious practices are futile if not accompanied by a bridled tongue, by helping orphans and widows when bereaved and in need, and by keeping away from the evil aspects of the world that can taint one's faith and life. Religious observance without ethical practice is a matter of deceiving oneself in one's own heart; it is an exercise in futility. Here James is simply reiterating an Old Testament refrain about caring for the marginalized in one's community (cf. Ex 22:22; Deut 26:12; Is 1:17; Jer 22:3; Zech 7:10; Tob 1:8; Sir 35:16; 2 Esdras 2:20-21). The warning here against self-deception is apt, especially for Jews in a Greco-Roman environment such as the Diaspora, where religion was regularly associated with correct and exacting performance of religious ritual and not necessarily with various codes of ethical conduct. Of course, there were both Jews and pagans who insisted that proper cultic worship be accompanied by proper behavior, but this connection was not always made or obvious in pagan religion.

---

[25]Davids, *Epistle of James*, pp. 100-101.

Here the tongue is depicted as a runaway horse needing to be reined in lest it do damage. Note how James 1:26 picks up on what is said in James 1:19. "Pure and undefiled" in James 1:27 are two ways of saying the same thing from a positive and negative viewpoint. The phrase "God and Father" as applied to God is typical of Paul and early Christian usage, not just of James. The point is that God is a father to the fatherless and so should the audience be. Here James surely has in mind Psalm 68:5, where God is said to be a father to the fatherless and a defender of widows. These concerns would be especially urgent in a highly patriarchal world, where property was largely controlled and passed from male to male, and a person without a father or husband was in severe jeopardy of poverty and destitution.

The ethics of impartiality in James 2:1-13. James 2:1-13, the first of the two major sections of this chapter, deals with the matter of showing partiality, especially vis-à-vis the rich and the poor. In the background is the idea that God is no respecter of persons, with the implication that neither should his people be. The author is picking up earlier discussions in sapiential literature that speak against favoritism and stress God's impartiality (see, e.g., Sir 7:6-7; 35:10-18). James addresses his audience as "my brothers" once more, so we may be sure that he considered them to be Christians. However, from James's point of view, they are Christians under construction and requiring instruction.

Notice once again the typical structure in James 2:1 in the author'a direct address ("my brothers"), followed by an imperative, followed by illustrations and explanations. James then begins with his proposition for this rhetorical subunit, what he intends to demonstrate in what follows. The issue is showing favoritism or partiality, and what he intends to prove is that partiality and faith in the glorious Lord Jesus are incompatible. That some Christians would exhibit both together is unacceptable and reprehensible because it amounts to a violation of the love commandment. The word *doxa* ("glory") in James 2:1 must be seen as qualifying the whole list of Jesus' names. The phrasing of Jesus' name here is awkward and reads literally "of the Lord our Jesus Christ of the glory." The point is that Christians have faith in an exalted Lord who will one day return and judge. As Davids says, "Thus those who hold 'the faith of our glorious Lord' with partiality are not debasing just any belief, but rather a faith-commitment in the one exalted Lord Jesus whose glory will be fully revealed in eschatological judgment. As the tone implies, this is no matter for casualness or trifling; final judgment is at stake."[26] The word "glory"

---

[26]Ibid., p. 107.

here probably has eschatological overtones.

A further important point about this crucial thesis statement of this part of the argument is that the key phrase reads literally "keep/hold the faith of the Lord." Although regularly rendered "faith in the Lord," that is not exactly what James says, and if that was what he meant, he could have used the prepositional phrase beginning with *en* ("in"). This in turn may well suggest that Jesus is seen as the exemplar here of impartiality, and believers are to keep the "faith of the Lord" (i.e., his trustworthy and faithful ways) by modeling themselves on his behavior. In a stratified world of showing or giving face to one person or another who was thought to be of higher status or more honorable, James and Jesus deconstructed this practice of "sucking up" to the well-heeled.

It is significant that here the phrase *en prosōpolēmpsiais* can be translated "with your acts of favoritism" and involves a term that literally means "receiving face" *(prosōpolēmpsia)*, to which we may compare Leviticus 19:15 LXX: "You shall not render an unjust judgment; you shall not receive/give face *[lēmpsē prosōpon]* to the poor or defer to the great: with justice you shall judge your neighbor."[27] This urges that one must be impartial to all and not show any favoritism to the poor or the rich. The phrase suggests that there are those who make judgments on the basis of "face," the outward appearance of someone, just as we might talk about the "face value" of something.

But is James suggesting, against the text in Leviticus, that one should show partiality to, or a "preferential option" for, the poor? Actually, he is not. He is saying that one should not show favoritism to the rich, which is then unfair to the poor, nor should one slight the poor and so dishonor them. All persons should be treated fairly regardless of socioeconomic status. Of course, one can argue that since there is imbalance in a fallen world full of self-centered, acquisitive persons, God is concerned about balancing the scales, about justice for all, and in a fallen world this may appear to be partiality for the poor. Divine and human advocacy for the poor is necessary just to overcome the inequities experienced by the poor. This, I think, is what James has in mind, and it is in accord with what Leviticus says about impartiality.

James 2:2 is more difficult and moves into a hypothetical though possible example of showing partiality. We know that it is likely a hypothetical example because it is a conditional clause using *ean* plus the subjunctive, and thus

---

[27]One could argue that since Leviticus 19:15, on love of neighbor, is nearby this text, James is doing an exposition of this whole portion of Leviticus at least at the outset of his discourse here.

the author sees it as a "more probable future condition." A definite possibility, to be avoided, is in mind, but not something already plaguing the audience. Here we have a proof from example with the punch line coming in James 2:4 that proves the point: being partial and having faith in or faithfulness to the example of Christ are inconsistent because it makes a person a partial judge of other persons, indeed of other Christians. What sort of gathering, then, is implied in these verses? Is it the Jewish synagogue, the Christian church or some sort of Christian law court?

Against the first option (Jewish synagogue), even though the word *synagōgē* is used, James implies that his Christian audience has some control over what is happening when visitors enter this meeting, and he says "your assembly," which surely implies a Christian one. The word *synagōgē* is found elsewhere in early Christian literature of the church (see Ign. *Pol.* 4:2; cf. *episynagōgē* in Heb 10:25; *synagō* in *Did.* 14:1; 16:2). Yet, as James 5:14 shows, James is perfectly capable of using the term *ekklēsia* of the Christian gathering.

Against the third option (Christian law court), not only does James use a different word for "law court" in this passage (*kritērion* [Jas 2:6]), but also there is evidence for visitors (1 Cor 14:23) and also for well-to-do people becoming members of the Christian community, including the Jewish Christian community in Jerusalem (see, e.g., Acts 4:34–5:11). Nor is 1 Corinthians 6:1-8 an entirely apt parallel, since Paul says that they are in fact going to pagan law courts but argues for them to settle disputes within the Christian community. This implies there was no such church law court when Paul was writing in the 50s. That James says "your" *synagōgē* here rules out it being a pagan court. It probably is a mistake to read later Jewish law court traditions back into the text here. For instance, *b. Šebu.* 31a says, "How do we know that, if two come to court, one clothed in rags and the other in fine raiment worth a hundred manehs, they should say to him, 'Either dress like him, or dress him like you'?"

It is likely that the second option is correct: James is speaking of a Christian worship assembly. If it was like Jewish worship in a small building or home, some might have to stand and others sit. It is evident from later sources that visitors were allowed in and ushered to a spot, a duty that deacons later had. It was Jewish custom to have special and honored places in the synagogue for special people and benefactors (cf. Mt 23:6; Mk 12:30; Lk 11:43, 20, 46). It would not be at all surprising if Jewish Christians carried this custom over. Both the poor and the wealthy examples here are likely viewed as visitors, since both are directed as to where to sit. Thus, we are dealing with a hypothetical but possible situation, and not one that involves a law court. Nothing is said in the telling of this tale about why the rich person and the poor person came into the "assembly," and the partiality issue is raised not in regard to their behavior but rather that of the one seating them, which implies a judgment on the Christian usher's part. The *ean gar* ("for if") makes it entirely unlikely that James is alluding to a notorious event that has already happened in the community, and after all, *synagōgē* is not used elsewhere in the New Testament to refer to a law court.

James, however, finds this behavior unacceptable. The contrast between the rich and the poor persons perhaps is played up a bit, but the wearing of gold rings and fine clothes was widely practiced among the well-to-do Jews and Gentiles in first-century culture, and the description of the poor person as wearing shabby, dirty clothes perhaps indicates a beggar.[28] It is possible that the reference to a person wearing a gold ring indicates a person of equestrian rank and so a potential benefactor to the congregation. James 2:3 makes quite clear that the believer who is seating these visitors is judging them purely by appearance, which often leads to partiality. "The rich person is invited to sit rather than to stand, to proximity rather than to distance, to comfort or prestige rather than to discomfort and dishonor."[29] The relevant verb here, *epiblepō*, can have the sense of "to look upon with favor," as is clearly the case in Luke 1:48; 9:38, which contain the two other uses of the term in the New Testament (cf. in the LXX Ps 12:4 [13:3 ET]; 24:16 [25:16 ET]; 32:13 [33:13 ET]; 68:17 [69:16 ET]). Notice also that the verb is in the plural, suggesting that this sort of favoritism involved more than one Christian usher or leader. The second part of James 2:3 has the phrase "sit at my feet," which sometimes is a technical expression for "be my disciple," but that is not likely meant here (cf. Lk 10:39).

Various commentators take *en heautois* in James 2:4 to imply that the visitors are Christians. This is not a necessary inference, since the focus is on the one showing partiality and what is going on from the angle of the one seating these persons. Obviously, things can go on among the brothers and sisters that involve visitors and various non-Christians. The problem is that

---

[28]This is not necessarily the case. I have encountered many people poorly clad and malodorous in mosques and churches in the Middle East, but this does not mean that all of them are beggars. It has as much to do with the climate as anything else.

[29]Johnson, *Letter of James*, pp. 222-23.

the Christians who are welcoming the visitors are showing partiality, which is unacceptable regardless of what status the visitors have insofar as believing or honor is concerned. When the visitors are with the believers, they are considered part of the worshiping group. The partiality is happening in Christian worship, which is the last place it should happen, for worship is supposed to be where God is perfectly glorified and people are treated as God treats them. Judging by appearances (Jas 2:3) is judging by a false and all-too-human standard of judgment (Jas 2:4). Here it probably is right to hear echoes of the teaching of Jesus in parables such as those found in Luke 14:7-14; 16:19-31, which feature the dynamics of the dramatic contrast of rich and poor and how they are treated in this life, and in the former parable we also hear about places of honor at a gathering.

James 2:5 begins another thought, and here we have a statement about the poor followed by two about the rich. There are three rhetorical questions, all of which expect the answer "yes" from the audience. The function of such questions is to force the audience to answer the questions for themselves, but to do so in a way that coheres with the conclusion that James wants them to draw. Partiality to the rich is bad for the poor and makes no sense because the rich are oppressors of Christians. The three questions serve as a way of amplifying the point that partiality is inconsistent with Christian faith, with the most disturbing question left for last as a climax.

The idea of God showing special concern for the poor is well known from the Old Testament (see, e.g., Deut 16:3; 26:7). Jesus too, in Luke 6:20, picks up the idea of the election of the poor, and we find similar thoughts coming from Paul (e.g., God's choice of the weak and lowly [1 Cor 1:26-29]). Here it seems to mean that God chose the poor for the historical purpose of shaming the rich. James 2:5 speaks of the poor who are poor from the world's point of view but rich in what really matters, faith, and what comes through faith, the status of being inheritors of the kingdom. It does not follow from this that James "romanticizes" poverty; and even more to the point, by "poor" James really means economically poor, not merely "poor in spirit." In fact, he will suggest that spiritually these folks are far from poor; indeed, they are rich. Here *plousios* refers to their being rich in the realm of faith. It is not implied that they had more or more abundant faith in comparison to others; no comparison is made. It is quite clear that the kingdom mentioned here is viewed as future; it is what God has promised to those who love him, a promise not yet fulfilled.

The social dimensions of the poverty must not be overlooked, even if James does share some ideas about the "pious poor." The poverty spoken of is both physical and spiritual, as is the wealth, but no one person in the contrasting example embodies both kinds of wealth or poverty. The poor in question are believers; they may be rich in faith, but this does not give permission for other Christians to treat their physical poverty as if it did not matter. Alfred Plummer sums up things well:

> He does not say or imply that the poor man is promised salvation on account of his poverty, or that his poverty is in any way meritorious. . . . He is spared the peril of trusting in riches, which is so terrible a snare to the wealthy. He has greater opportunities of the virtues which make man Christlike, and fewer occasions of falling into those sins which separate him most fatally from Christ. But opportunities are not virtues, and poverty is not salvation.[30]

Notice also that the poor as described here are said to be heirs of the kingdom. This is the only reference to the *basileia* in James, and it seems to be used in its eschatological sense of something that one inherits or enters in the future, not the present.

In James 2:6 the verb *atimazō* means "to dishonor, show disrespect" to those whom God has especially showered favor upon. Paul shares a similar view about shaming those who have nothing, and the social context that presupposes disunity and favoritism in the assembly is also similar (see 1 Cor 11:22). This is a very unwise course of action, and James 2:12 indicates that the perpetrators are accountable for such actions on judgment day. The standard of judgment is the "law of liberty"—that is, the new law of Christ, which combines something old and something new.

Playing up to the rich makes no sense on another score. Generally speaking, it is the rich who were oppressing believers and having them hauled off to court. James may have some particular incident in mind, but the remarks seem to be generalizations here. Thus, we have irony: the church is oppressing that one poor fellow who came in, while the rich oppress "you," the church as a collective whole. What sense, then, does their behavior make in light of God's word and standards? In James 2:7 the rich are labeled as blasphemers; they are blaspheming Jesus' good name, perhaps because they profess to be pious while their deeds are impious. And if we did not get the point already that James believes that Jesus embodies the glorious presence

---

[30]Alfred Plummer, *St. James and St. Jude* (London: A & C Black, 1969), p. 125.

and nature of God from James 2:1, this verse makes it clear. If Christ's name can be blasphemed, it is a divine name. The second part of James 2:7 may refer to the name of Jesus being called over believers at baptism, but James's interests lie in their current behavior.

James 2:8 presents a problem: should we translate *nomos basilikos* as "royal/sovereign law" or as "supreme law" and see James labeling the love command as the essence of the law? Victor Furnish probably is correct in his understanding of the drift of James' thought:

> Even if you keep all the (other) commandments of the law, but, by showing partiality to the rich, neglect the one commandment to love your neighbor (the poor brother), then you are in fact guilty under the whole law. Thus, if we take into consideration this continuation of the argument, it would appear that the commandment of Leviticus 19:18 is regarded as one among many which are to be kept by the faithful Christian.[31]

If this is right, we probably should translate the phrase in question as "royal law." What may be decisive is that *nomos* is used for a collective body of law, not just an individual commandment, and so we find in James 2:8, 11 selections from it. Thus, even if we translate it as "supreme law" (cf. "perfect law" in Jas 1:25), it refers to the law as a whole, the law of Christ. One should compare Galatians 5:14, where Paul in fact says that this particular commandment sums up the law. I suggest that a more careful scrutiny of what Paul and James say about the law as it applies to Christians shows that they have similar views on this subject.[32]

James 2:8 makes evident that perhaps the most serious problem with showing favoritism is that it is a blatant violation of the great love commandment to love neighbor as self. But why is the law here called "royal" (cf. the use of *basilikos* in Jn 4:46, 49; Acts 12:20-21)? Possibly there is a connection with the use of "kingdom" *(basileia)* language in James 2:5. This might mean the law pertaining to the eschatological kingdom of God. But recall that Jesus identified the dual love commandments as the first and greatest commandment (see

---

[31]Victor P. Furnish, *The Love Command in the New Testament* (Nashville: Abingdon, 1972), p. 179.
[32]Here we must make a distinction between what Paul says about the outmoded and obsolescent Mosaic covenant and what he says about the law of Christ, which is not simply a reiteration of the Mosaic law but does include some commandments from it. If in fact James includes within the royal and perfect law his own and Jesus' teachings, then he too is not simply talking about a reiteration or reinterpretation of the Mosaic law. On Paul's view, see Ben Witherington III, *Grace in Galatia: A Commentary on St. Paul's Letter to the Galatians* (Grand Rapids: Eerdmans, 1998), pp. 341-56.

Mt 22:37-40). This suggests that "royal" might refer to the commandment of King Jesus, the one that he particularly emphasized and said normed the way all other commandments should be interpreted and applied.

James 2:9 makes the point in as drastic a fashion as possible: playing favorites is not just unacceptable to James; it is a sin against God, a sin that brings to the perpetrator conviction under the law as a transgressor. To show partiality is to fail to love the poor neighbor, and to fail at that is to violate the whole law. One does not have to violate all the commandments in order to be a lawbreaker. But the conceptual idea here is this: the law is one because God, who is one, gave it to believers. It is God's Word. James here is offering a short form of a syllogism, an enthymeme, which requires that one supply the missing premise, in this case the minor premise. In full form it would look like this:

Major premise: Whoever keeps the whole law but fails in one point has not kept it.

Minor premise: Showing partiality is a failure to keep a part of the law.

Conclusion: If you show partiality, you are a transgressor of the whole law.

James 2:11 provides a second enthymeme, which makes the same point a slightly different way:

Major premise: God, who said, "Do not commit adultery," also said, "Do not kill."

Minor premise: If you break any individual command, you break the law, since they are all from one source.

Conclusion: If you do not commit adultery but do kill, you still have become a transgressor of the whole law.

Notice that James 2:11 has the phrase "he who said," which indicates that the author saw the law as God's very words—God spoke it. There is no higher endorsement for the law. Paul also expresses the unity of the law in Galatians 5:3, as does Jesus in Matthew 5:18-19; 23:23. Being under the law obligates one to obey the whole law (Rom 2:13). To draw an analogy: it is like one who drops a single drop of food coloring in a glass of water; all the water is affected. One sin taints the whole character, and one sin means that *the* law, not just *a* law, has been broken. The remedy is not stated here, but obviously it is not to ignore the law.

Notice also that James mentions prohibitions first against adultery and then against murder from the Decalogue. It is instructive that Paul highlights these same two prohibitions as representative examples in Romans 13:9 (cf. Lk 18:20). Was there perhaps a common Christian ethical code grounded in the Old Testament, the teaching of Jesus, and some Christian instructions from the apostles that both James and Paul knew and adhered to? For certain, this code, if it existed, did not just involve the Mosaic law as reinterpreted by Jesus, not least because Jesus added his own imperatives, some of which were at variance with what the Mosaic covenant demanded. The ultimate sanction for behavior was that it was what God explicitly stated was the divine will.

James 2:13 perhaps draws on the teaching of Jesus in the Sermon on the Mount again, in particular Matthew 5:7, "Blessed are the merciful, for they will be shown mercy," or Matthew 6:12, "Forgive us our debts, as we forgive our debtors." James, however, turns the beatitude into its converse to make his point. The theme of mercy is common in Wisdom literature (see Sir 27:30–28:7). The believer's status before God at the last judgment is indeed affected by the life that he or she lives after conversion. Paul too knows of the idea of salvation by faith, coupled with a judgment of the believer's deeds (see 2 Cor 5:10). There also comes a point, apparently, where the disjunction of profession and practice is such that one's salvation is in jeopardy; the good tree will produce good fruit, and if it does not, it may be judged to be not a good tree after all, no matter what label is put on it. Judgment without mercy means severe, unrestrained judgment—the full wrath of God.

The second part of James 2:13 perhaps involves the quotation of a proverb meant to give hope: "Mercy triumphs over/overrides judgment." God, of course, looks on human hearts and as well as human lives. In fact, we could render this maxim as "Mercy boasts over judgment," or as we might say, "Mercy has the bragging rights over judgment" in God's way of viewing things. God expects complete loyalty and obedience. Obviously, there are times when humans are unable to do what they intend to do, whether something internal or external prevents it in a fallen world and dealing with fallen people. Those who do strive to do God's will and still fall short have both repentance and the mercy of God to fall back on; otherwise, no one would stand on the day of judgment (see 1 Cor 3:13-14). But more than this, James would have us know that if believers are merciful instead of judgmental, they are mirroring the character of God and fulfilling an essential requirement of the royal law. James's rhetoric certainly will be seen as countercultural by the dominant culture that surrounds the various Jewish Christian communities being addressed. Thus, one of the social functions of the rhetoric of this homily is to help the audience to establish proper boundaries with the world. But is James also trying to stake out a separate domain for Jewish Christians and distinguish those communities from the largely Gentile Pauline ones? Is James taking aim at Paul and his theology and ethics? Several preliminary remarks are needed.

James is not talking about how one comes to Christ or receives initial justification or salvation. Even when he uses the language of "righteousness," it is final vindication or justification at the eschaton to which he is referring. He is addressing those who are already Christians about how they should live. At the same time, Paul is equally clear that postconversion behavior can affect whether one is vindicated in the end, at the final judgment. Both James and Paul are quite sure that moral apostasy is possible and a real danger for the Christian. They are also in agreement that obedience and working out one's salvation after initial salvation is not optional for the Christian.

Faith and works in James 2:14-26. We also must not see James 2:14-26 as a direct response to what we find in Galatians (or Romans, for that matter). As Plummer says,

> Had St. James been intending to give the true meaning of either or both of these statements by St. Paul [Rom 3:28; Gal 2:15-16], in order to correct or obviate misunderstanding, he would not have worded his exposition in such a way that it would be possible for a hasty reader to suppose that he was contradicting the Apostle of the Gentiles instead of merely explaining him. He takes no pains to show that while St. Paul speaks of works of the law, . . . he himself is speaking of good works generally, which Paul no less than himself regarded as a necessary accompaniment and outcome of living faith. . . . It is most improbable that if he had been alluding to the teaching of St. Paul, St. James would have selected the unity of the Godhead as the article of faith held by the barren Christian. He would have taken faith in Christ as his example.[33]

This last point, about James's stress on the oneness of God, is right, and it shows, among other things, that James surely is speaking to Jews in this homily, in this case Jews who follow Jesus, who took monotheism for granted and indeed as the great earmark of their profession, distinguishing them from all others in the Diaspora.

---

[33]Plummer, *St. James and St. Jude,* pp. 142, 152. See his telling exposition of Luther's own comments, where he shows that if Luther himself were consistent, he would have seen that Paul, equally with James, believes that faith without works is dead (ibid., pp. 147-48).

Furthermore, both Abraham and Rahab were favorite topics of discussion when it came to the matter of faith and works in early Judaism. The texts of Wisdom of Solomon 10:5, Sirach 44:20 and 1 Maccabees 2:52 should be consulted, and we may also mention Hebrews 11:17 and Matthew 1:5 from the Christian writings. James's discussion of Abraham is closer to the earlier Jewish one than to the later Pauline one, for the good reason that not only does James focus on the binding of Isaac story, but also he stresses that Abraham is an example of faith that manifests itself in action, in obedience to God. James is pursuing the same line of discourse found in Matthew 12:37: a person is vindicated or even "justified" or accounted righteous as a result of what he or she has done or said. This is a different matter than the discussion of the basis of initial justification or salvation. Clearly enough, James is more likely drawing on the earlier Jewish discussion of these figures of faith than on the later Pauline one. And, once and for all, we must note that when Paul speaks of works of the Mosaic law, in fulfillment of the Mosaic covenant, he is talking about something very different than James's discussion of works that come forth from and express Christian faith. "James and Paul simply do not mean the same thing when they write of 'works,' and interpreters who write as if they did distort the thought of both."[34]

All of this, however, does not rule out the possibility that James is dealing with some issues raised by Jewish Christians from what they have heard, and perhaps misunderstood, about the teaching of Paul in its early stages in the early 50s, when there were in fact Judaizers from Jerusalem going behind Paul in Antioch, Galatia and perhaps elsewhere trying to add observance of the Mosaic covenant to the Pauline gospel even for Gentile Christians.

It may also be said that both James and Paul were concerned about what later came to be called "dead orthodoxy"—faith without its living expression in good works. While it may be true that "'faith without works' spares individuals the embarrassment of radical disruptions in their lives and relationships,"[35] both Paul and James were all about radical disruptions in the lifestyles to which people had previously become accustomed. Here James is busy deconstructing various prevailing social customs and habits and offering up in sacrifice various sacred cows, but Paul did the same thing in his own way.[36]

---

[34]Brosend, *James and Jude*, p. 81.
[35]Pheme Perkins, *First and Second Peter, James, and Jude* (IBC; Louisville: John Knox Press, 1995), p. 13.
[36]This sort of strongly worded statement may suggest that James is not offering an initial salvo here to an audience that he has never addressed before. Instead, this reads more like the kind of critique

Sharyn Dowd suggests that "James is using Paul's vocabulary but not his dictionary,"[37] which is clever but not quite right. Both authors are drawing on previous Jewish usages of this sort of vocabulary, and when one considers even just the Abraham stories in Genesis 12–22, one discovers a range of meaning of the term *faith* as well as on the importance of obedient deeds, not to mention possibilities for the range of meaning of the *ṣaddīq* language. Yet there is some force in the point that Dowd makes when she says,

> Paul never uses *pistis/pisteuō* to mean a mental agreement with a theological construct that has no implications for behavior. In fact, he never uses a *hoti* clause after the noun. . . . But even more important is the fact that Paul would have been incapable of constructing a sentence analogous with James 2:19 in which correct faith is attributed to demons. In Paul's writings the subject of *pisteuein/echein pistin* is always one for whom "Jesus is Lord" (Rom 10:9), a confession only possible under the influence of the Holy Spirit (1 Cor 12:3). The fact that James can speak of the "faith" of demons shows he knows a use of the term that is foreign to Paul's thinking.[38]

The problem with this point is twofold. First, it very well may be that the person speaking is the interlocutor, not James. James perhaps is being accused of believing that God is one just as the demons do. Second, James also thinks that purely mental or even verbal faith is dead faith or useless faith, not real living Christian faith. However, what Dowd's argument provides further support for is the contention that in fact James does not know Paul's letters and the common way Paul expresses such matters.

I am convinced that we may assume that Paul and James knew something of each other's "gospel," both from personal conversation and hearsay but not from reading each other's letters. And I think it right to conclude with Brosend, "It is probably true that Paul and James did not think or worry about each other nearly as much as interpreters of James think and worry about Paul but about as much as interpreters of Paul worry about James. . . . The history of interpreting James using Paul as the measuring rod always inhibits appreciation of James."[39]

It would be hard to overestimate how strongly the issue of faith and works

---

we find in 1 Corinthians, where Paul has had a relationship with the audience for some time, has written to them before, and is pulling no punches in his critique.

[37]Sharyn Dowd, "Faith That Works: James 2:14-26," *RevExp* 97 (2000): 202.

[38]Ibid.

[39]Brosend, *James and Jude*, pp. 79-80.

and salvation is stressed here. Nineteen of the twenty uses of "faith, to have faith" *(pistis, pisteuō)* in James occur in James 2:14-26, as do twelve of the fifteen uses of "work" *(ergon)* and one of the five uses of "to save" *(sōzō)*. Thus, twenty-two of the words in this brief passage (217 total Greek words) are these three words, some 12 percent of the passage.[40]

James begins in James 2:14 by asking his Christian audience whether a faith without works is useful or useless. The nature of the conditional sentence here shows that he thinks that this question might well arise. The second remark is also a question: "Is your faith able to save you?" This is a rhetorical question to which the answer implied is no, if by "faith" is meant that type of faith which James is attacking. Here James has broadened the previous discussion to the more expansive topic of faith and works. Crucial to understanding this verse is recognizing the use of the anaphoric definite article before the word "faith." The question should be translated "Is that sort of faith able to save you?"

Notice that the discussion here has moved on from talking about visitors to the assembly of faith to "brothers and sisters" (one of the few New Testament uses of *adelphē* ["sister'] in a nonphysical sense).[41] At issue here Christian treatment of fellow Christians. There follows a little parable in James 2:15-16, also begun by *ean* ("if"), indicating a condition that is future but probable. Certainly, there were plenty of destitute Christians in the first century needing aid from the community.

James points to a poorly clad and hungry brother or sister. The word *gymnos* need not imply someone being naked but rather refers to someone inadequately or shabbily clothed. This person is indigent, not even having enough food for today.[42] The response in James 2:16 is meant to seem shaky and shallow. It sounds pleasant enough, even concerned in a superficial way: "I hope you are well fed and clothed." But in fact this is an anti-Christian and unloving response that is unacceptable. Beneath the surface is the idea that deeds of mercy are not an option but rather are an obligation for those who profess and have real faith.

"Go in peace" is what the person says to the indigent person, a stereotyped parting formula that often meant no more than "goodbye," though it could have the fuller sense of "blessings" (cf. Gen 15:15; Ex 4:18; Judg 16:6; 1 Sam

---

[40]Ibid., pp. 72-73.

[41]Ibid., p. 73.

[42]On *hē ephēmeros trophē* as daily sustenance, compare Matthew 6:11; Luke 11:3. The phrase probably is an echo of the Lord's Prayer.

20:42; Mk 5:34; Lk 7:50). It appears also that we should translate the verbs in *thermainesthe kai chortazesthe* in James 2:16 as middles, not passives, in which case it means "Warm yourself" and "Feed yourself," not "Be warmed" "Be filled" as a sort of wish. If this is correct, the speaker in question is being very callous indeed, juxtaposing warm words with cold deeds. This person, like so many others since, is saying, in effect, "Pull yourself up by your bootstraps" or "Do it yourself." Quite clearly, what was being asked for was not some luxury item but rather the necessities of the body, clothing and daily bread, but even so, the person in question did not even give these. As Johnson says, "It is not the form of the statement [depart in peace], but its functioning as a religious cover for the failure to act."[43]

To this behavior James rejoins, "If you say you have faith and fail to help, of what use is it? What good does it do you or anyone else?" Possibly, in James 2:17 we should translate *kai* as "even" and read "So [or 'in the same way'] even faith, if it does not have works, is dead by itself." James thus has made two key points: (1) living faith necessarily entails good deeds; (2) faith and works are so integrally related that faith by itself, unaccompanied by works, is useless or dead. Peter Davids summarizes well:

> For James, then, there is no such thing as a true and living faith which does not produce works, for the only true faith is a "faith working through love" (Gal. 5:6 . . .). Works are not an "added extra" any more than breath is an "added extra" to a living body. The so-called faith which fails to produce works (the works to be produced are charity, not the "works of the law" such as circumcision against which Paul inveighs) is simply not "saving faith."[44]

Thus far we have no problems understanding James's meaning, but the rest of the chapter has many difficulties. First, there is the problem of the identity of "someone" *(tis)* in James 2:18. Is it someone who agrees with James? Is it James's imaginary interlocutor? Who is this "someone" who says, "You have faith, and I have works"? Where do the words from this someone cease and James's words return? Throughout James 2:18-20 the opponent starts the debate, and the "you" is James or his ally. James has his imaginary opponent accuse him of being a "faith without works" person, whereas the speaker takes the supposedly higher ground of touting his works.

The proper rhetorical order of protocol is that the first person to speak in

---

[43]Johnson, *Letter of James*, p. 239.
[44]Davids, *Epistle of James*, p. 122.

such a debate should first present proofs and only then rebut the arguments of
the opponent (see Aristotle, *Rhet.* 3.17.1418b.14). This is what happens here,
and rebuttal comes only after the opponent has stated his view in the first part
of James 2:18. But in fact the opponent is taking a reactionary and defensive
posture here—"I have works, while you have faith"—thereby apparently assuming a place in the positive category as a person of Jewish orthopraxy,
while James has only orthodoxy on his side, mere faith. But James's position is that the two things cannot be divorced, while the opponent suggests
that they can be. Thus, he accuses James of mere faith and so, in effect, of
hypocrisy. The examples that James will cite prove the point that real faith
works—the two go together.

The evidence of the diatribal form, along with the "you foolish person"
of James 2:20, suggests strongly that when at James 2:18a James says, "But
someone will say," he is turning to the argument of his opponent. The problem here is not the grammatical structure but rather the train of thought.
Perhaps here James envisions two believers hypothetically debating, and then
he interjects a rebuttal at James 2:18b. The problem here is very clear. This
"person" is still dichotomizing faith and works, as if they could be separate
gifts of different Christians. The argument would be "Works are alright,
but that is not my gift" (or vice versa). To this sort of dichotomizing James
responds, "Show me a person with faith but without works, and I will show
you my faith by my works."

To the believer who merely takes pride in right belief (and clearly in James
2:18-19 faith means something else than what it usually means for James, not
trust in or active dependence on God, but rather mere belief that God exists)
James says, "So you say that you believe that God is one. Good for you! However, so do demons, and they are shuddering in their belief, fearing the wrath
of God to come. A lot of good that faith did them!" The sarcasm in James
2:19 is hard to miss. The demons are the ultimate example of faith divorced
from praxis, right confession divorced from right living.

The phrase "God is One" has its background in the basic Jewish confession, the Shema: "Hear, O Israel, the LORD our God is one" (Deut 6:4). The
point here is the unity of God's being and also his uniqueness, and also of
course that he is the one true God. Here James is stressing essential matters
and probably is implying "You believe in the unity of God; you ought also
to believe and practice the unity of faith and works." The reference to the
demons existing and believing is also characteristic of what we find in the

Gospels (cf. Mk 1:24; 5:7). The demons were perfectly orthodox and perfectly lost, and this makes their condition so much worse than the unbeliever who rejects the truth about God.

In James 2:20 James becomes even more sarcastic: "So, do you want evidence, you empty-headed one, that faith without works is useless/without profit *[argos]*?" And then James turns to the Scriptures. Another way of translating *argos* here is "workless"; faith without works is workless, or, as I would prefer to put it, faith without works will not work. The two examples from Scripture that James cites were very standard examples of true faith among the Jews. He is choosing the most stellar example (Abraham) and, in some ways, the most scandalous example (Rahab the harlot). James knows how much Abraham was idolized in the Jewish tradition. For example, *Jubilees* 23:10 says, "Abraham was perfect in all his deeds with the Lord, and well-pleasing in righteousness all the days of his life." Sirach 44:19 says, "No one has been found like Abraham in glory." More important is 1 Maccabees 2:51-52, which says that Abraham was reckoned righteous not on the basis of his faith but rather as result of passing the test and remaining faithful and obedient when asked to sacrifice his son. Clearly, James does not push his use of the exemplary Abraham to these extremes, but he stands in the tradition of seeing Abraham as the *exemplum* par excellence. It is of more than passing interest that the use made of Genesis 22 here is closely similar to the use made in Hebrews 11:17-19, which says that it was by faith that Abraham, when tested, brought forth Isaac and offered his son. This may suggest that there were some standard interpretations of the key Old Testament figures that circulated in Jewish Christian circles.

James refers to two separate texts in Genesis: the promise in Genesis 15:6 and the offering of Isaac in Genesis 22:12-16. As often happens in midrashic exegesis, here the two texts are combined. James is stressing that it was on the basis of Abraham's obedient offering of Isaac—his deed of obedience— that *edikaiōthē*, "he was justified/vindicated." Principally, James is thinking of Genesis 22:16, where God promises his blessing as a result of Abraham having done what he did. This may be compared to the word of blessing in Genesis 15:6. It is possible that this one climactic example of obedient faith may be a shorthand reference to all ten of the tests that Abraham passed that led to this conclusion of vindication. In any event, in James 2:22 the verb *synērgei* should be seen as an iterative imperfect, which implies that faith was working along with works at the same time side by side; or put another way, it implies that these two things coexisted in Abraham's life over a period of time. Davids ably shows the Jewish train of James's thought here.

> But there is a larger issue because even in Genesis 15, Abraham's believing entailed ensuing obedience—he did what the Lord told him in going to Canaan, in bringing his son for sacrifice, and in so many other ways. His was not a faith separated from works of obedience. His point is that *even* in the case of believing Abraham, his works were essential as an expression of faith. In what sense was he vindicated? His trust in God was vindicated for he dared to offer his son trusting God to provide or take care of the situation. If this is what James takes *edikaiōthē* to mean, it is very different from Paul's notions. Abraham trusts in God that he already had been . . . [relating to] . . . or was vindicated when he offered Isaac, and there was divine intervention. In a real sense, faith was made perfect by his trusting obedience.
>
> So James can go on to say, "You see that faith cooperates with his works, and by works his faith was perfected. The two go together hand in hand, works perfecting faith, which is by implication imperfect without it." The concept of righteousness here at least in vs. 21 seems to be Jewish, not "counted righteous" or considered righteous but declared to *be* righteous, that is—*is* righteous by means of deeds. Abraham's belief was belief in action.[45]

The point of James's argument, then, has nothing to do with a forensic declaration of justification; the argument is simply that Abraham did have faith, which here, unlike other places in James, means monotheistic belief. For this, Abraham was famous in Jewish tradition, but he also had deeds flowing from that faith. Thus, James is not dealing with works of the law as a means to become saved or as an entrance requirement. Notice that he never speaks of "works of the law." He is dealing with the conduct of those who already believe. He is talking about the perfection of faith in its working out through good works. "Work out your salvation with fear and trembling" was how Paul put it in Philippians 2:12, or better, in Galatians 5:6 Paul speaks of faith working itself out through love, while James speaks of faith coming to mature expression or its perfect end or goal in works. These two ideas are closely similar.

This still leaves us with the difficulty of James 2:24, a statement that Paul never would have made in this fashion. However, if, as we should, we take the vindication in James 2:24 as referring to that final verdict of God on one's deeds and life work, then even Paul can be said to have agreed. Even

---

[45]Ibid., pp. 127-28.

he speaks of a final justification/vindication that is dependent on what believers do in the interim (see Gal 5:5 and what follows it).[46] It is this final vindication or acquittal that is in view here. Paul would agree that one cannot be righteous on that last day without there having been some good deeds between the new birth and that last day in the spiritual pilgrimage. Thus, James 2:24b only apparently contradicts Paul, not least because although Paul thought that faith did indeed get one into the body of Christ, not even he thought that faith alone kept one there.

James mentions, as a secondary and more daring example intended to illustrate the same ideas (*homoiōs* ["similarly"] makes this clear), Rahab, who entertained the Hebrew spies and chucked them out (*ekbalousa* ["cast out"]) the back window when the enemy approached. The point here is that if everyone from Abraham to Rahab received final vindication because of faith and works, so too will the followers of Jesus. Rahab's faith is not mentioned, but it was widely recognized by early Jews.[47] We may also think that the rhetorical strategy here involves forestalling the objection "But I am not a towering figure of faith like Abraham!" to which the proper reply is "Well, at least you could follow the example set by Rahab!" The last example, then, removes all excuse for doing nothing and shames the audience into action. Finally, one can also suggest that since both Abraham and Rahab are examples of those who exercised faith and hospitality, which contrasts nicely with the first example in this section of James 2, where no hospitality is shown to the poor, this may in part explain why these two historical examples are cited here.

James probably knew of the Jewish traditions that suggested that perhaps Rahab had converted, married Joshua and become a good Jewish mother of priests, and is said even to be the foremother of Jeremiah and Ezekiel. Rahab was, of course, mainly celebrated for her hospitality to the Jewish spies, but even in later Christian texts she becamse an example of faith (see *1 Clem.* 12:7).

After these illustrations we do well to ask once more, "Does James necessarily show a knowledge of Paul's letters here?" I think not, and Davids

---

[46]It is a mistake to think that "final justification" refers to being declared innocent or to acquittal here. Rather, it has to do with God's recognition that someone has behaved in a way that can be called "right" or "righteous," and at the last judgment those acts are vindicated to be righteous.

[47]For evidence, see the exposition of this passage in Ben Witherington III, *Letters and Homilies for Jewish Christians: A Socio-Rhetorical Commentary on Hebrews, James, and Jude* (Downers Grove, Ill.: IVP Academic, 2007), pp. 479-81.

shows how even the common words are not found in the same context, nor do they have the same content.[48] James is not dealing at all with the question "On what basis do Gentiles get to enter the community of faith?" Rather, the question is "What is the nature of the faith, true Christianity?" Does it necessarily entail deeds of mercy? It is, of course, possible that James got wind of some sort of perverted or garbled Pauline summary that had been heard by his audience, but even this is not a necessary assumption. Jews were fascinated with Genesis 22 and the story of Abraham, and much of the common terminology is to be explained by both James and Paul drawing on the same Old Testament text, possibly both relying on the LXX version. Therefore, I think that we must reject James Dunn's conclusion:

> The most striking passage in James is 2:14-26, his polemic against the doctrine of faith without works. This seems to be directed against the Pauline expression of the gospel, or more precisely, against those who have seized on Paul's slogan, "justification by *faith* (*alone*)." It was Paul who first expressed the gospel in this way (particularly Rom 3:28); so the view which James attacks certainly goes back to Paul. That Paul's argument *is* in view is also indicated by the fact that James in effect refutes the Pauline exegesis of Genesis 15:6: "Abraham believed God and it was reckoned to him as righteousness." This, affirms James, was "fulfilled" in Abraham's *work*, not in his faith—that is, not in "faith alone" (contrast Rom 4:3-22, particularly vv. 3-8; Gal 3:2-7).[49]

I have gone into considerable detail in this discussion of James's sapiential ethics for the very good reason that James often is seen as the sore thumb that sticks out in the canon and does not fit with the ethics of Paul and others. I have shown how deeply indebted James is to earlier Wisdom literature, including the sagacious teachings of his own brother, and it seems fair to say also that James is not busily correcting Paul in this sermon, though he may be correcting some misunderstandings based on what had been heard in Jewish Christian communities in the Diaspora about Paul's teachings.

The ethical rigor of James is matched by the ethical demands that Paul made on his converts, and neither man sees proper behavior as an optional added extra in the Christian life. Both authors have much to say about the implementation of the Christian ethic of love, and both believe that one must work out one's salvation with fear and trembling, which certainly involves

---

[48]Davids, *Epistle of James*, p. 131.
[49]James D. G. Dunn, *Unity and Diversity in the New Testament: An Inquiry into the Character of Earliest Christianity*, 2nd ed. (Philadelphia: Westminster, 1984), p. 251.

deeds of piety and charity. Equally, both are deeply indebted to the ethic of Jesus found in the Sermon on the Mount and are quite keen to apply it to their own audiences. That they do so in somewhat differing ways may be because James is addressing Jewish Christians, whereas Paul is largely addressing Gentiles. Both focus on what can be called "character ethics," and both affirm that it is the perfect, holy, just, merciful, loving character of God that should be reflected in the believer's life. Finally, both affirm that there is a law for Christians that they must keep, whether it is called the "perfect law" or the "law of Christ," and it involves some portions of the Old Testament, some teachings of Jesus, and some new apostolic teachings.

Although James and Paul stand on opposite sides of my Venn diagram, a close examination of their thought shows that the two men shared a common love for and focus on the christological epicenter of Christian faith and its ethical implications, and that they could well have reached across the divide and given each other the right hand of fellowship. In fact, as Galatians 1–2 indicates, they did do this, indicating an awareness that they shared the same ideational thought world and beliefs about many things even though they sometimes told their theological stories differently and drew out the implications of those stories differently because of their different audiences. I have deliberately spent more time in detailed exegesis on James in this chapter because, as I said, his sermon often is seen as the sore thumb that sticks out from the New Testament hand, especially from the Pauline part of that hand. As it turns out, without that thumb the hand could not do very useful work, and the necessity of having a faith that works is a significant part of what James contributes to the score of the New Testament oratorio.

HEBREWS: EXHORTATION BASED ON EXPOSITION

Whatever else one can say about the author of Hebrews, he most certainly was an adept exegete. Unfortunately, scholars have gotten too mesmerized by the exposition of the Old Testament in Hebrews, with its profound theological reflections, and they have tended to treat the exhortation sections in Hebrews as afterthoughts or somehow less important. The truth of the matter is quite the opposite. The expositions of text are intended to support, undergird and lead to certain ethical conclusions, as the main aim of the sermon called "Hebrews" is to prevent the audience from committing apostasy. In other words, everything in this document serves a larger ethical aim or end. There are in some cases theological reasons why there has been neglect of the ethics in Hebrews (and other New Testament documents); it is believed to be of less importance than the theology and having nothing to do with the salvation of the person's in question. This conclusion the authors of the New Testament, and before them Jesus, would have soundly rejected. Let us consider for a moment how important the ethical sections are in Hebrews by examining the structure of the homily.

The sermon begins with a comparison of the Son and angels (Heb 1:1-14), which is followed by paraenesis (Heb 2:1-4) and then a return to the comparison with angels (Heb 2:5-18). Then comes a comparison of Moses and Christ (Heb 3:1-6) and even lengthier paraenesis (Heb 3:7–4:16), then a comparison of Aaron and Christ (Heb 5:1-10) and yet more paraenesis (Heb 5:11–6:20), then a comparison of Melchizedek/Christ and the Levitical priesthood (Heb 7:1–8:3) and a comparison of the first covenant and the new covenant (Heb 8:4–10:18) and a very long paraenesis (Heb 10:19-39). This is followed by an exposition on what faith and faithfulness really look like (Heb 11:1–12:3) and then an exhortation to accept the discipline that comes from suffering (Heb 12:4-17). Next comes a tale of two theophanies that serves as the climax of the discourse, and then finally there is a mixture of the two, leading to an epistolary conclusion containing yet more exhortations, and the discourse as a whole is labeled as an ethical exhortation (Heb 13:1-25).

This *synkrisis*/paraenesis alternation encourages the audience to progress in moral conduct by remaining faithful to the greater revelation in Jesus Christ and emulating the models of its Scriptures, and also it warns the audience of the greater judgment to befall those who are unfaithful to the greater revelation. In fact, the exigence or problem that drives this sermon is the danger of apostasy, of not continuing on a Christian path of life. The theology provides the vital foundation for the ethical exhortations that follow each major theological segment, but the emphasis, by end stress, is on the behavioral issue.

The author's rhetorical strategy in picking texts and discussing theological topics is motivated not by his intellectual curiosity about messianism or a christological reading of the Old Testament. Rather, he chooses and deals with Psalms 8; 95; 110 (and perhaps 40); Jeremiah 31; Habakkuk 2; Proverbs 3 because they help make the case that the inadequacy or ineffectiveness, or "partial and piecemeal," character of previous revelation and covenants is self-attested in the Old Testament. But that is only the negative side of the persuasion going on in this rhetorical masterpiece with carefully selected inartificial proofs from the Old Testament. Other texts are brought in to support the positive side of the argument, which is that the good things said in the Old Testament to be yet to come are now realized only in Christ, and faithfulness is required if these eschatological promises are to be realized in the lives of those who follow Christ. Thus, it can be said of Hebrews, "Theology is the handmaiden of paraenesis in this 'word of exhortation,' as the author himself describes it."[50] It is no accident that at the end of the discourse the author clearly calls the whole thing "a word of exhortation" (Heb 13:22). But what is said in those ethical subsections of the discourse? As it turns out, there is a repetition of several themes, to which we now turn.

The initial thrust of the exhortation is sounded already in Hebrews 2:1: everyone, including the author, must pay very close attention to what they have heard and learned "lest we drift away." Punishment is coming if we "neglect so great a salvation." The theme of remaining faithful and avoiding apostasy could hardly be more clearly announced in Hebrews 2:1-4. Turning to Hebrews 3:7–4:16, we hear (1) that we should not harden our heart and not have a sinful, unbelieving heart; (2) that "we have come to share in Christ, if only we hold firmly to the end our original conviction" (Heb 3:14), followed by the example of the generation wandering in the wilderness as a warning that the consequence of unbelief is missing out on God's rest; (3) that we must not fall short; (4) that we should make every effort "to enter that rest, so that no one will perish" (Heb 4:11); (5) that we should "hold firmly to our confession" of faith (Heb 4:14); (6) that we should draw near to the throne of grace to receive mercy and grace "in our time of need" (Heb 4:16).

Then, in Hebrews 6:1-12 the author becomes explicit about what is needed. The audience needs to move beyond the elementary teachings that include both theological and ethical and practical matters (repentance, faith, water rituals, laying on of hands, resurrection, eternal judgment). The surprising remark that has huge ethical force is the warning that if a person who has become a Christian and been saved then falls away, it is impossible to renew that person to repentance. Even allowing for the rhetorical character of this stern warning, we see by it that the author does believe that Christians can throw away the gift of salvation by repudiating their faith in Christ, thereby crucifying Christ afresh.

Clearly, the most important exhortation comes in Hebrews 10:19-39,

---

[50]John Walters, "The Rhetorical Arrangement of Hebrews," *AsTJ* 51 (1996): 63. Here I follow and am indebted to the compelling argument that Walters makes.

where the audience is told to draw near to God in faith with a heart and conscience cleansed by the blood of Jesus. They are also urged to hold unswervingly to their hope, to spur on one another to good deeds (to be defined more particularly a little later), and to not give up on meeting together for worship and fellowship. A reiteration of something said in Hebrews 6 comes in Hebrews 10:26-39: "If we deliberately keep on sinning after we have received the knowledge of the truth, no sacrifice for sin is left, but only a fearsome prospect of judgment. . . . It is a dreadful thing to fall into the hands of the living God." There is a reminder of suffering, enduring insults, confiscation of property, persecution. The audience is urged once more to not shrink back and perish but rather to believe and be saved (seen as something that happens in the future [Heb 10:39]). Then Hebrews 11, the "hall of faith" chapter, reinforces the need for faithfulness, perseverance, steadfastness unto death. The author acknowledges that it is a struggle, even a struggle against sin, particularly the sin of apostasy (Heb 12:4), and so he is able to remind the audience that they have not yet resisted to the point of shedding blood. Suffering or hardship is seen as something used by God for character formation or discipline. When there are difficulties in persevering, it is easy to become too self-protective and not help one another run the good race, and so at Hebrews 12:12-13 the author encourages the strong to pave the way for the lame and the weak.

At Hebrews 12:14-17 there are brief exhortations: (1) live in peace with one another; (2) let no one fall short of the goal; (3) do not allow bitterness and strife to grow up in the community that is under pressure; (4) keep sexual immorality out of the community. These exhortations are so brief and formulaic that we must assume them to be incidental warnings about things that the author thinks might crop up in a community that is in a distressed state. What he is much more concerned about is the issue of falling away, wilting before the finish line, apostasy. Notice too that right at the end of Hebrews 12 the author urges one and all to devote themselves to proper worship of God and Christ. This is of ethical significance because the main problem for the audience is the possibility of apostasy.

The equally brief exhortations in Hebrews 13 break little new ground. There is a call for hospitality and for love of the brothers and sisters. There is a reminder about visiting those in prison and keeping the marriage bed undefiled. There is an exhortation to live free from the love of money, which does strike a new, albeit brief, note. The audience is urged to support and have confidence in their leaders, avoid strange teachings (not more specifically defined), and remember that they have a high priest, altar, and sacrifice that eclipse all others, so they must be prepared to sacrifice their lives as Jesus did and also be prepared to offer a sacrifice of praise.

Taken as a whole, the paraenesis in Hebrews seems much more general in character than what we find in James, with the exception of the constant stress on avoiding apostasy and persevering in the Christian faith. We should not take this to mean that the author is not serious about the various repeated exhortations about marriage, sexual conduct, hospitality, worship, and the like. It is just that these issues obviously are less urgent than the greater concern about abandoning the faith. Here a brief comment on Jude is in order.

Clearly enough, Jude is concerned about false teachers who also are guilty, in his view, of sexual immorality, not to mention bilking congregations for their own profit. They are shepherds who fleece the sheep rather than feeding them. They are grumblers about others, boasters about themselves, and flatterers of the audience. The real ethical concern, since this is not a discourse directed to the false teachers, is that the audience not be naïve and gullible, not be taken in by the likes of these false teachers, not believe their campaign promises, not give them access to the accepting and loving context of in-house fellowship, where they could do damage at the heart of the community. In Jude 20 the opposite of this is said to be building themselves up in their faith, strengthening and being merciful with doubters, and rescuing the perishing. Notice that the discourse ends with a reassuring doxology to the one who is able to keep them from stumbling. As it is for the author of Hebrews, so too this is a concern for Jude, especially since, unlike in Hebrews, which has no evidence of a struggle with false teachers, Jude's community is "under the influence" of such teachers; hence comes all the strong polemical rhetoric to paint the false teachers in as dark a color as possible to ward off their being embraced by Jude's Jewish Christian audience.

It is striking, and worth stressing at this point that in none of the Jewish Christian documents being examined in this chapter is there any discussion or debate about circumcision, unlike what we find in several of Paul's letters. Besides being a clue to the nature of the audience (they are already Jews), it also tells us that in some respects these authors did not have the same ethical concerns that Paul, Luke and the author of 2 Peter had. It appears that none of the Jewish Christian authors of these documents agreed with the hardline Judaizing (Pharisaic) Christians mentioned in Acts 15 and Galatians that all

Christians needed to be circumcised and keep the Mosaic law. Indeed, the author of Hebrews provides a rationale for why even Jewish Christians need not feel obligated to do that: a new and better covenant is now in force, and the Mosaic one has become old and obsolete. But is Matthew an exception to this rule? Let us see.

MATTHEW: WISDOM FOR JEWISH CHRISTIANS

Matthew's Gospel is written to a pedagogically serious community of Jewish Christians. We know this not only because the author presents an image of Jesus the teacher or sage, but also because he presents himself as a scribe whose job is to preserve, transmit, and interpret the Jesus tradition in light of the Old Testament (see Mt 13:52). He collects the new and the old together, as a scribe trained for the kingdom of heaven. Various scholars have rightly seen Matthew's Gospel as something of a teacher's training manual, helping them to fulfill the Great Commission to make disciples by means of baptizing and teaching them "to obey everything I have commanded you" (Mt 28:18-20).

Richard Hays rightly notices and stresses that the ethic enunciated in Matthew is an ethic for a specific community, the *ekklēsia* of Jesus' followers.[51] More specifically, this community is to be a holiness community—a light to the world, known for its outstanding moral character and good works. "The church is a demonstration plot in which God's will can be exhibited. For that reason, the righteousness of Jesus' disciples must exceed that of the scribes and Pharisees; otherwise the church will not be a compelling paradigm of the kingdom that Jesus proclaimed."[52] The meek and merciful and mourning and the pure in heart are those who characterize this community, but also the peacemakers. This community is not supposed to use violence to advance its credo. "Community members are to put away anger, lust, violence, hypocrisy, pride and materialism. In place of these self-asserting and self-preserving behaviors, they are to love their enemies, keep their promises . . . , forgive freely as they have been forgiven by God, give alms in secret, and trust God to provide for their material needs."[53]

Matthew makes evident that speech and actions are manifestations of what

---

[51]Hays, *Moral Vision of the New Testament*, p. 97.
[52]Ibid.
[53]Ibid., p. 98.

is in the heart, and transformation of the heart is ultimately what the ethics of this Gospel is pointing to and is the presupposition on which it is grounded. As Matthew 7:15-20 suggests, good trees bear good fruit, and bad trees bear bad fruit (cf. Mt 12:33-34). But where does this inner good character come from? Clearly, one source is the transforming grace of Jesus, but in fact this Gospel puts stress on something else: good character comes from training in righteousness by way of good teaching, such as one finds in this Gospel. What is interesting is that Matthew is more concerned with community formation and its relationship to Jesus' wisdom than with the cultivation of a bunch of wise and virtuous individuals. Presumably, since even in Matthew there is not a commandment for all occasions, the author believes that if one educates the habits of the heart well, then the right sort of "improvisation" will result when a new situation arises.[54]

Hays, in his study of Matthew's ethics, points out how Matthew inserts into his Markan source material an emphasis on "mercy rather than sacrifice" as what God desires, citing Hosea 6:6 twice over (Mt 9:10-13; 12:1-8). Notice in the second case that Jesus is said to be greater than the temple, just as his ethic of mercy is seen to be greater than the ethic of sacrifice and forgiveness in the temple. Emphasis is placed in the teaching of Jesus on the weightier matters of the law—mercy, justice, and faith (Mt 23:23). Jesus' yoke is easier than Torah's yoke not just because he is Wisdom come in the flesh, but also because of this emphasis on the weightier matters of the law. Notice how Matthew 22:40 suggests that all the law hangs on the two love commandments (the Shema of Deuteronomy 6:5 plus Leviticus 19:18). At a minimum, this seems to mean that all the other commandments must be evaluated, interpreted, and normed by these two.

How is this ethic manifested in practice? As Hays suggests, it is manifested in a readiness to forgive, to be reconciled, to work for restoration and healing.[55] This is especially clear in Matthew 18:1-35. The parable in Matthew 18:12-14 about the recovery of the one lost sheep shows the direction of the ethic, which is toward mercy and restoration, even presumably after expulsion due to unrepentant behavior. Are there warrants that reinforce this ethic in Matthew's community? Yes, there are two: (1) the living presence of Jesus is said to be with the community whenever two or more are gathered together; (2) the eschatological judgment. Both God and Christ are watching,

---

[54]On which, see pp. 489-93 above.
[55]Hays, *Moral Vision of the New Testament*, p. 101.

and eschatological judgment is coming, starting first with the household of God. This is linked to the return of Christ at some undetermined time in the future. We need to keep in mind, however, that there is a context of humility, concern for restoring the lost, concern for the weak in faith or the little ones as well that make evident that the function of the eschatology is not to thunder condemnation on a beleaguered community but rather to remind them of ultimate accountability for their behavior.

In Matthew's Gospel, then, we find norms, specific implementations of those norms in commandments and wise advice, and eschatological and christological warrants to back them up. There is a moral vision of holiness for the community set in motion in this Gospel, but this is also set within the context of the commandments to love God and one another and of mercy and forgiveness.

How this all comports with and compares to what we find in the other wisdom Gospel, John, we will attend to shortly, but we must give close attention to the Sermon on the Mount at this juncture, without doubt the most influential body of ethical teaching in the New Testament. Our concern here is not to answer source-critical questions about which bits go back to Jesus and which more reflect Matthean (or Q) editing; rather, it is the ethical impact of the Sermon on the Mount as a unit. Oddly enough, this material always stands in danger of either being overemphasized or, due to its high degree of familiarity, underemphasized. As one commentator observed, Matthew 5–7 has been, perhaps more than any other New Testament passage, dramatized, secularized, universalized, criticized, psychologized, politicized and radicalized.[56]

What has come to be known as the Sermon on the Mount is better identified as Wisdom from the Mount for Learners (i.e., disciples). It consists mainly of some of Jesus' most memorable wisdom teaching and sapiential sayings or aphorisms. In fact, in Matthew 5–7 we have a virtual compendium of the usual standing topics that the sages discussed, as a comparison with Proverbs 1–6 or Sirach will show. Here Jesus offers beatitudes and colorful metaphors inculcating good works; Torah is viewed as an expression of wisdom and righteousness (cf. Sir 24); practical teaching is offered on self-control in regard to the tongue (controlling anger, oaths, judging others) and to sexual expression; exhortations are given to love enemies (emulating God), give alms, pray and fast; instructions are provided about the dangers of wealth and

---

[56]Clarence Bauman, *The Sermon on the Mount: The Modern Quest for Its Meaning* (Macon, Ga.: Mercer University Press, 1985), p. 62.

divided loyalties and about the problems of health and subsistence, to which is added appeals to wisdom from nature, meant to reduce anxieties, and to keeping the golden rule, following the narrow path, which involves integrity in both word and deed.

The difference between this and the earlier wisdom material in Proverbs or Sirach is that Jesus offers both conventional and counterorder wisdom, and more specifically the eschatological content and character of this wisdom are evident right from the start, where beatitudes are offered, but the blessing is not realized until the kingdom comes on earth as it is in heaven. Nevertheless, there is a tension in the teaching because throughout it is assumed that the kingdom is already beginning to break into human history, and therefore there is an "already and not yet" character to the instructions just as there is to the kingdom itself.[57]

What is new about this ethic is the counterorder wisdom about no oaths, no retaliation at all, loving enemies, and strong warnings against the accumulation of wealth and its inherent dangers to one's spiritual and everlasting life. Equally stunning is the teaching on the goodness or viability of remaining unmarried. Traditional Jewish wisdom sought to teach people practically so that they could learn to be healthy, wealthy and wise in worldly ways. Jesus does not simply baptize such agendas and call them good; indeed, he warns how such agendas can damage one's relationship with God and one's eternal future. This evangelist is right to stress that much of this counterorder and counterordinary wisdom is revelatory wisdom from above, not something that one would naturally deduce by studying nature or human nature. John Updike understands quite well the revolutionary character of this Matthean discourse:

> Two worlds are colliding; amazement prevails. Jesus' healing and preaching go together in the Gospel accounts, and his preaching is a healing of a sort, for it banishes worldly anxiety; it overthrows the commonsense and materially verifiable rules that, like the money changers in the temple, dominate the world with their practicality. Jesus declares an inversion of the world's order, whereby . . . the poor in Spirit shall possess the Kingdom of Heaven. This Kingdom is the hope and pain of Christianity; it is obtained against the grain, through the denial of instinct and social wisdom and through faith in the unseen. Using natural metaphors as effortlessly as an author quoting his own works, Jesus disclaims Nature and its rules of survival. Nature's way, obvious

---

[57]On all of this and for much more detail, see Witherington, *Matthew*, pp. 113-77.

and broad, leads to death; the other way is narrow and difficult: "Come in by
the narrow gate. . . ."

Christ's preaching threatens men, the virtuous even more than the wicked,
with a radical transformation of value whereby the rich and pious are damned
and harlots and tax collectors are rather more acceptable.[58]

One of the things that makes this ethical teaching radical is not merely
how demanding it is, at various junctures intensifying previous edicts of
God's law, but that it seeks to deal with the roots of the human problem,
within the human heart itself. This is not entirely a surprise, for the promise
of the new covenant in Jeremiah 31 was that God's law would be embedded
in the interior of a person's being, thus obviating the need for reminders of
what ethical rectitude means or, for that matter, what it is to know God and
his will. Thus, for example, Jesus adds odd things after quoting the edict
against adultery from the Decalogue, such as, "I say unto you that if a man
even so much as looks with desire at a woman so that she is led astray into
adultery, then he is guilty of adultery." Here Jesus is suggesting that the root
of the problem is not the alluring woman, something traditionally warned
against in ancient Wisdom literature (see Prov 1–8), but rather the lust that
resides in the male heart.

Jesus' ethic is not about external conformity to external standards but
rather about dousing the fires of lust and anger and hatred and bigotry. But
how is a fallen person to accomplish this? This is where revelatory wisdom
presupposes that a person can and must be born again, must turn and become
as a child and start over down the right and more narrow path into the kingdom, taking the path less traveled. Jesus calls his followers to a righteousness
that exceeds that of the Pharisees, not because he has a penchant for utopian
dreams and ethical schemas, but because he believes that "a change is coming" to transform human lives and human society as God's divine saving
activity breaks into the human sphere. And so the old prayer "Give what
you command, Lord, and command whatsoever you will" is an appropriate
response to this wisdom material. It is neither law nor ethical ideal per se but
rather gospel indicating that God is transforming persons, and to whom more
is now given in the eschatological age more is required.

And herein lies the key to what Jesus says about not one jot or tittle of the
law passing away until all is fulfilled (Mt 5:17-18). The word *plēroō* ("fulfill")

---

[58]John Updike, "The Gospel According to Saint Matthew," in *Incarnation: Contemporary Writers on the New Testament*, ed. Alfred Corn (New York: Viking Press, 1990), pp. 8-9.

is the key term, indicating that all of Scripture, even the law, is being viewed as prophecy that is now being fulfilled in the eschatological age, now that the kingdom is coming. The law is being fulfilled, it is also being intensified, modified and radicalized, and in some cases it is said to have been fulfilled already (and thus has become obsolete). But until all of it is fulfilled, it will still stand as a sentinel, bearing witness to God's high ethical standards.

John Wesley understood the eschatological spirit of this ethic. He urged that when Jesus says, "You shall love your enemies," we should see this not merely as a command but rather as a covered promise, a way of God's saying, "As you become conformed to the image of your Master, you will learn to love your enemies." God enables what he demands, and so the function of the demands was not, as Luther thought, either just to drive one to despair or to distraction or even merely to the limits of one's self and so to the gospel, though certainly the ethical rigor spoken of would drive a disciple back to Christ for grace, explanation, strength. No, the function of the ethic was to paint a picture of what the disciple must and will become as he or she is conformed to the image of God—being holy as God is holy, loving as God loves, and so on. It paints a picture of what happens when the disciple is fully conformed to the image of the Son and so finally is able to enter, inherit and obtain the perfect kingdom one day when Christ returns, the dead in Christ are raised, faith becomes sight, hope is realized, and we become truly like the one whom we admire and thus partakers of the divine nature.

The Gospel of John and 1 John: The Ethics of the Beloved Disciple

> For readers seeking ethical themes, the Gospel of John is a puzzling text. It contains almost none of the specific moral teaching found in the synoptics: no instruction here about violence or possessions or divorce. Jesus is represented in John not as a teacher but as a relentless revealer of a single metaphysical secret: that Jesus himself is the one who has come from God to bring life. He offers minimal moral instruction for the community of his disciples. There are repeated injunctions to the community to keep Jesus' commandments (14:15, 21; 15:10; cf. 1 John 2:3-6), but, remarkably, the actual content of these commandments is never spelled out in the text. If we had only the Fourth Gospel in the New Testament canon, it would be difficult indeed to basis any specific Christian ethic on the teaching of Jesus.[59]

---

[59]Hays, *Moral Vision of the New Testament*, p. 138.

Here Hays speaks for many in this assessment of the Johannine ethic, and he is mostly correct. In John, Jesus is indeed the revealer; in fact, he is Wisdom come in the flesh, not merely a wise teacher or sage. And the wisdom is truly christocentrically focused on the person of Jesus himself. Nowhere is the Old Testament cited as some moral norm. Jesus does not merely give God's wisdom; he is Wisdom, the secret of the divine plan to save the world. If we are to find ethics in this Gospel, we will need to turn to what Jesus says to his community directly in the farewell discourses (Jn 13–17). It is no accident that it is in these chapters that we hear about keeping commandments. Jesus leaves an ethical mandate for his disciples to follow in these discourses, but what does it consist of?

Some scholars have seen the ethic enunciated especially in John 13–17 and 1 John as too insular or sectarian in character. It has been noticed that love in these sources refers to love of God or of one's fellow believer. Nothing is said of love of neighbor in general, much less of one's enemy. The radical character of the love ethic in the Synoptics seems to have gone missing. However, this could simply be a matter of focus rather than a change of ethic.

The Johannine community, clearly enough from Revelation 2–3, is under duress and persecution, and some have been martyred along the way. Under these circumstances it is no surprise to find documents focused on helping the community to survive and remain unified, standing against the inroads of false teachings and rejection in the synagogues and elsewhere. It probably is no coincidence that the only two New Testament documents that talk explicitly and polemicially about expulsion from the synagogue are the Fourth Gospel (see Jn 9:22; 12:42; 16:2) and the book of Revelation. The Johannine community is made up of mostly Jewish Christians who, in order to survive hostility from without, need to strengthen their in group and boundary-defining ethic. This is what we find going on in the Gospel and the Letters of John as well as in Revelation.

Besides the more explicitly ethical material in John 13–17, there are indeed ethical hints along the way in the Fourth Gospel. For example, in John 10:1-30 there is the reassurance that Jesus is the good shepherd who is perfectly capable of protecting his sheep, and we have the promise that no one can snatch those sheep out of his hands. This, however, does not preclude the sheep from voluntarily defecting, as Judas did, and so in John 15:1-8 we have the repeated exhortations to the disciples to keep on abiding in Jesus, not least because "If they persecuted me, they will persecute you" (see Jn 15:18-21). It is no accident that Jesus ends the farewell discourses by praying that God will protect his flock from the Evil One. The world or milieu of the Johannine community is dark and dangerous for all Christians, but perhaps especially so for Jewish Christians because the synagogues seemed to see them as apostate Jews. How, then, should Christians respond to such an environment?

Both in the Fourth Gospel and in 1 John the answer is the same. They should follow the example of Jesus, who loved his followers to the end. Abiding in Jesus is demonstrated by walking as Jesus walked (1 Jn 2:5-6), which entails loving one another in the same fashion that Jesus loved them all (Jn 13:34). Paradoxically, it is this filial love for each other that is said to be the witness that demonstrates to one and all that they are disciples of Jesus (Jn 13:35). What does self-sacrificial love actually look like? It looks like the enacted parable of foot washing; the disciples are called upon to wash one another's feet because even Jesus did this for them. Since foot washing was the ultimate menial and dirty task left to the servants, taking the form and role of a servant and doing this shows the extent of one's self-humbling love. Love not only covers a multitude of sins, but also it cleans a multitude of sinners and heals wounds.

In the Fourth Gospel there is a "new" commandment given to the disciples. Here we do not have the reiteration of the Shema or even the command to neighborly love. Instead, we are told that the disciples are to love one another as Jesus has loved them (Jn 13:34-35). Christ, the paradigm and paragon of love, shows that loving involves not just humiliating forms of service; it can and does also entail being willing to lay down one's life for one's friends. Jesus therefore shows his love to his disciples by giving his life for them. "Thus Jesus' death is depicted by John, in a manner closely analogous to Pauline thought, as an act of self-sacrificial love that establishes the cruciform life as the norm for the discipleship. Those within the community may be called upon literally to lay down their lives for one another."[60]

Is this just a pious saying indicating that disciples should be ready to lay down their life for one another (by definition, a once-in-a-lifetime possibility), or is there a practical, everyday component to this ethic as well? The latter is suggested by 1 John 3:11-18. Laying down one's life for one another is said to entail asking oneself the question "How does God's love abide in anyone who has the world's goods and sees a brother or sister in need and yet refuses help?" This question should sound familiar in light of what we

---

[60]Ibid., p. 145.

saw in James 2.[61] The Johannine ethic, then, is not all norms and no specifics for application. Furthermore, the ethic does not allow the disciple in the Johannine community to love God and not realize that there is a connection between that and the treatment of their brothers and sisters in Christ. This is made emphatic in 1 John 4:20-21: anyone who claims to love God and yet hates a brother or a sister is a liar. Piety without purity and filial love is not seen as a viable form of piety.

But it is not enough to know whom to love and how to love. One also needs to know what not to love: the fallen world and the things of the world (including the flesh and the devil, pride in riches [1 Jn 2:15-16]). One also needs to keep in mind the fact that Jesus' kingdom, though in the world, is not of the world. There is a sectarian and otherworldly character to the Johannine ethic in part because God's reign or saving activity has an otherworldly source, and more importantly is not mediated through human institutions or rulers, be they Jewish or Roman. God deals directly with people through Jesus, who is portrayed as "the way" in this Johannine tradition.

One of the interesting aspects of the Fourth Gospel is its teaching about the Advocate *(paraklētos)*, the Holy Spirit. The disciples are told that during the ministry period that they will not yet be able to understand all that Jesus would like to teach them. The *paraklētos* is said to be the one who will come to the disciples and lead them into all truth and presumably provide moral guidance as well. Does this explain the rather generic nature of the love commands in this Gospel? Presumably not, because John 2:22 suggests that part of the function of the Spirit was to remind the audience about some of the concrete things that Jesus taught during the ministry. How, then, do we interpret a text such as 1 John 2:21-27, where the author says that the audience already knows the truth, and he is simply reminding them of it? Furthermore, it says that the anointing within them or in their midst is such that no one needs to teach them. I suggest that what we are dealing with is a Johannine community that, unlike Matthew's, is not at the level of needing initial ethical catechesis (cf. Heb 6:1-4), but rather is at a level of moral discourse where dealing with the more fundamental baseline of the ethics—love, abiding, and trust—was a sufficient motivator and clarifier for the audience. The author was satisfied with their level of understanding of Jesus' wisdom, as enshrined in places such as the Sermon on the Mount, and was dealing with the underlying basis and empowerer for such an ethic, namely, the Spirit, who pours

---

[61]See pp. 521-39 above.

God's love into the believer's heart, a love that casts out all fear and enables love in action, not to mention godly improvisation on the basic theme and teachings already received.

Also accounting for the form of the material in John 14–17 and 1 John is its sapiential character. The author deliberately couches things in terms that could be universalized and focuses not so much on specific advice as on the ethical norm of love and some of its implications. If these documents are written to those who have been Christians for some time, it is understandable that simple reminders about the norms might suffice. There would be enough elders in the community (see 1 John 2–3) to help them know how to "improvise" on the basis of the norms. Hays puts it this way: "The specific behavior that issues from union with Jesus need not be spelled out in detail, for those who abide in Jesus will intuitively know what is right and do it."[62]

We can see this at work in a text such as 1 John 3:4-10, which boldly says that no one abiding in Jesus sins. That is, those who abide in him know consciously, through the enlightenment of the Spirit, the difference between right and wrong, and if they continually abide in Jesus, they will not commit willful acts of sin. But even if they do, 1 John 2:1 reassures them that they have an advocate with the Father, not the Spirit within them (who is Jesus' advocate on earth) but rather Christ the righteous one in heaven. Perhaps in the end it was enough of an ethical challenge to call the audience to love as Jesus loved. One could spend a lifetime trying to live out of and up to that challenge, and if all behavior was normed by it, then Jesus would be exemplified in human conduct and God would be glorified. If the ethic is more assumed than spelled out in the Gospel of John, things become somewhat more concrete as we turn to Revelation.

REVELATION: ETHICS FOR A PERSECUTED MINORITY

Recently I had occasion to be the external examiner on a dissertation whose thesis is that the whole book of Revelation is paraenetic in character. It is an interesting thesis, and one of its important points is that the recounting of the visions has two ethical purposes: (1) to urge perseverance in the face of persecution and even potential martyrdom; (2) to urge leaving "vengeance" or justice in the hands of God rather than responding in kind to abuse, physical harm and the like. I believe that this thesis is correct. Despite all the *Sturm und Drang* of Revelation 6–19, with the horsemen of the apocalypse leading the

---

[62]Hays, *Moral Vision of the New Testament*, p. 153.

charge and the rider on the white horse (Jesus) bringing up the rear and concluding the acts of judgment upon the earth, a close examination of the book of Revelation from an ethical point of view shows clearly enough that its essential message is this: God is in charge, so leave the administering of justice on the earth to him, and trust that he will vindicate you on earth beyond your wildest imaginings, including in a millennium and then beyond that in a new earth that has merged with a new heaven when the heavenly Jerusalem comes down. In other words, despite all the rhetoric we hear these days about Armageddon in the Middle East, what Revelation actually tells us is that it will not be a matter of human armies battling it out in the end. Instead, it will be a matter of Jesus pronouncing the benediction on all such hostile forces after the millennium, and they will receive summary justice. Within the context of this general ethical character of Revelation, we need to consider several crucial themes as they are manifested especially in Revelation 2–3.

Comfort for the Afflicted and Hope for the Future in Revelation 2–3

It has become almost a commonplace to argue that early Christianity was in general sectarian in character and world-negating in the balance. There is a good deal of truth in this observation, and the phrase "conversionist sect" does correctly convey something about the early Christian movement, which so focused on evangelism. One could also speak about John's attempt at creating a millenarian sect, and certainly his work has been used to further such an undertaking. But it is important to maintain a certain sense of historical balance when one is making use of such terminology. For one thing, the letters that begin Revelation reflect that John thinks that various of his converts or communities are not sectarian enough. In his view, they have compromised too much with the world and the social milieu of Asia Minor, and they need to do a better job of disengaging from their pagan environment. At Laodicea there may even have been collaboration with Roman religion, even the emperor cult in some form.

Nevertheless, we must keep in mind that before there was ever a Roman presence in Asia Minor, this entire region was thoroughly Hellenized, and the values of Hellenistic culture were such that within the polis considerable diversity of religion and religious views could be accommodated. Before Christians were ever present in this region, there had been many Jews and Jewish communities that found ways to acclimate to their surroundings without giving up the distinctives of their Jewish identity. To the extent that the Christian communities that John addresses had grown out of Jewish communities, they had already had some practice in dealing with the issues of accommodation and de-enculturation.

For example, many Jews participated in guilds and associations in this region, and such groups had a religious dimension. Many of them also participated in the activities that transpired in the gymnasiums. It should be no surprise that some early Christians in the region did so as well. The environment was inherently religiously syncretistic, and John's appeals to stricter boundaries with other religions would have gone against the very grain and nature of that society. Part of the problem that John faced was that various of the guilds and associations to which his converts likely belonged had taken up the honoring of the emperor during their meetings. Depending on what form this honoring of the emperor took, John's exhortations might be taken to mean dissociation from the guild itself, which would be very costly in a place where one could not very easily practice one's trade unless one "joined the union." Thus, John's sectarian stance probably was a minority opinion among Christians in the cities of Asia Minor. If all or most of his audience shared it, there was little need for some of his exhortations and many of his visionary accounts about the beast and other things.

Revelation 2–3 constitutes a highly structured epistolary section of this work that picks up some of the elements in the vision in Revelation 1. In view of their dependence on ideas in Revelation 1, it is most unlikely that these letters were independent and later incorporated into the document. "Since both the messages and the following visions aim at prophetic exhortation, the messages may not be divided from the so-called apocalyptic visions but must be understood as an integral part of the author's overall visionary rhetorical composition."[63] An excellent case can be made for seeing these letters as being like prophetic letters in the Old Testament (see 2 Chron 21:12-15; Jer 29; cf. *2 Bar.* 77:17-19; 78-87; Ep Jer 1), and to some degree like Old Testament oracles (see Is 13–23; Jer 46–51; Ezek 25–32; Amos 1–2).

The rhetoric involved in these letters is deliberative in character and highly emotive in nature. By recounting his visions, John is attempting to make a very vivid impression on his audience, so as to stir their emotions with the ultimate aim of their heeding his exhortations given in these letters. In other words, the visions in the main are meant to serve the purpose of amplifying or making vivid or reinforcing the exhortations. This must be kept steadily

---

[63]Elisabeth Schüssler Fiorenza, *Revelation: Vision of a Just World* (PC; Minneapolis: Fortress, 1991), p. 47.

in view when considering the function and purposes of Revelation.

The structure of these letters is as follows:

1. Address to the angel of the particular church in question

2. The "thus says" *(tade legei)* formula indicating prophetic communication ultimately from the Lord himself

3. A description of the one sending the message, drawing on descriptions found in Revelation 1

4. A word of commendation for a church's good qualities, if appropriate

5. The formula "But I have one thing against you" followed by a description of the fault and an exhortation to repent

6. Indication of judgment or consequences of not following the exhortation

7. Gospel-like conclusion: "Let anyone who has ears hear what the Spirit is saying to the churches"

8. Promise of what the conqueror or victor will receive from Christ for conquering

The primary function of this material, and indeed the book as a whole, is to offer an exhortation for the sake of behavior modification and to comfort the afflicted and give them hope for the future, all the while afflicting the comfortable in Laodicea and elsewhere. Bearing these things in mind, we can look at the individual letters one by one.

Without question, Ephesus was the most important city of those that John addressed, and it is appropriate that it was addressed first. John is mostly addressing those who have been Christians for some time and whose initial enthusiasm has waned. Notice at Revelation 2:1 the image of power: the Christ is one who not only holds the stars (i.e., angels) of the churches in his hand but also walks in the midst of the lamp stands, which symbolize the churches (see Rev 1:20). This is not an image of simple comfort, for in this case Christ is coming to inspect this church and exhort it. Notice that John is likely referring to a pre-parousia judgment of Christ that is coming now, before all the events described in Revelation 4–22 transpire. It is the invisible Christ who already walks among the churches and inspects them and calls them into account in the present. His work always involves redemptive judgment, or in this case beatitude follows correction of behavior.

The Ephesian church is praised for its works, which include endurance and intolerance for that which is evil or false. They have put to the test some false apostles and found them wanting. This seems to be in the past, while the trouble with the Nicolaitans seems to be a present matter. Note that nothing is said about true apostles existing or doing the inspection and correction. John obviously agrees that the Ephesian church's endurance and perseverance and discernment about falsity are good things, but the concern for holiness and truth apparently has not been balanced with compassion and love. The Ephesians are said to have left their first love.

The word used for "love" here is *agapē*, and so the reference could be either to the love of God or to the love of fellow believers or, more broadly, fellow human beings. But the mention of "first" love suggests priorities, and the context favors the suggestion that brotherly/sisterly love is mainly in view here. This is confirmed by what Christ tells them to go back and do: works of love for each other. Perhaps, in their zeal for orthodoxy or orthopraxy, they have lost their ability to distinguish between hating the sin and loving the sinner. Unless they do as they are told, Christ will come and take away their lamp stand, their source of spiritual light and life. The point is that without love, the church loses its status as the church.

At Revelation 2:6 we are told of something that Christ himself hates: the deeds of the Nicolaitans. We have no reference to this group outside the book of Revelation, and it is difficult to know the nature of their error. If their name gives any clue, they were the "victory people" or perhaps "conquerors of people" (combining *nikē* and *laos*). We do know that their error affected more than one of these churches. The "victory people" may be contrasted with those who are said to conquer. It may be of some significant that in Revelation 2:7 "churches" (plural) are mentioned. Although these words are addressed particularly to the Ephesians, they are meant for all these churches to hear and heed. In other words, we are dealing with circular letters.

The promise at the end of this first letter is drawn from Genesis. The one who conquers will be given to eat from the tree of life, which is in the paradise of God. In apocalyptic literature the tree of life is regularly the reward for the righteous, following judgment (see *1 En.* 24:4–25:6; *2 En.* 8:3; *T. Levi* 18:11;). Quite clearly, this paradise must be seen as otherworldly. There is a real question as to whether *ho nikōn* ("the one who conquers") should be seen as referring only to martyrs or to all believers who are faithful to the end. If we compare Revelation 3:20-21, we probably should not see this as a technical term for "martyr" here or elsewhere in Revelation, though it would include martyrs.

Turning to the letter to Smyrna, we note that the phrase used to describe Christ in Revelation 2:8 is quite appropriate and fits the content of the message that follows, for he is said not only to be the first and the last, but also to be the one who died and came back to life. This is especially germane when we read of the suffering going on in the church in Smyrna (Rev 2:9). Furthermore, the congregation is said to be in poverty, and yet, in a nonmaterial way, they are said to be rich. This is quite the opposite of what is later said of the Laodicean church. The city of Smyrna had both strong ties to Rome and a large Jewish population, which made it doubly difficult for Christians. It is possible that the reason for the poverty of the Christians here and elsewhere was the guild system. In order to work at a particular trade, one had to be a member of a guild, which required participation in various pagan religious ceremonies. It was the second city in the region in preeminence after Ephesus and was the second allowed to have the imperial cult (Tacitus, *Ann.* 4.55-56).

It is difficult to know whether or not to take Revelation 2:9 literally. It is clear that John blames at least some Jews connected with the synagogue for what has happened to the Christians in Smyrna. He says that these troublemakers "call themselves Jews, but are not." Indeed, they are quite the opposite. It is unlikely that he means that Satan was actually worshiped in their synagogue; rather, their action in persecuting the chuch was "of the devil." Probably also implied here is the sentiment also found in Romans 9:6: not all who are of Abraham's seed are true Jews. John tells the Smyrnaeans not to fear what they are about to suffer. Apparently, more persecutions or perhaps Roman trials are in view, and so is being cast into jail. But imprisonment in the Roman world was only a temporary expedient until one's case was heard and the issue was resolved legally. We must bear in mind that we have the independent testimonies of both Paul's letters and Acts that Jews sometimes brought Christians before the Roman authorities (see Acts 18), as did pagans. But whatever human agencies were involved, John clearly places the ultimate blame on Satan. He is the one who casts them into prison.

Revelation 2:10 probably is not to be seen as a literal reference to ten days of suffering. More likely it means just a definite short period of time. In any case, the Christians are told that if they will just be faithful unto death, Christ will reward them with the crown of life (i.e., eternal life [cf. 1 Cor 9:25; Jas 1:12]), which will prevent them from experiencing the second death. Probably, the crown in view is the laurel wreath won and worn by victors at the Olympic and other Greek games. Pausanias says that Smyrna was famous for such games.

The letter to Smyrna is basically the only one that seems to address with any clarity the relationship of Christians to the world outside the Christian community. The references to Jewish harrassment, suffering, potential imprisonment and death indicate a distressing situation for Christians. The letter to Pergamum mentions the death of a Christian (Rev 2:13), and the letter to Philadelphia mentions Jewish harassment and perseverance despite pressure to recant one's Christian beliefs (Rev 3:8-10). This brings up a crucial point. It is a mistake to overlook the fact that the only references to the wider Roman Asian milieu are to the repression of Christians. These letters contain only one full comment (Rev 2:8-11) and two passing references (Rev 2:13; 3:8-10) to any kind of external issues; all three passages refer to Christian suffering. It is a large mistake to underestimate the context of persecution in which the book of Revelation was written.

Beginning at Revelation 2:12 is the message to the church in Pergamum. Immediately we have the image of Christ as judge, coming with his sharp, two-edged sword. This forewarns us that the message to Pergamum is likely to be strongly negative. Pergamum was the capital city of the region and, like Corinth and Athens, had a huge acropolis on which sat various temples, such as those to Athena and Zeus. There was also a famous temple on the plain below the acropolis for the god Asclepios, the god of healing (see Pausanias, *Descr.* 2.26.9). At the very top of the city's acropolis was an imposing altar to Zeus "the Savior." This sculpture also included images of snakes, so perhaps this is what John is alluding to when he refers to the throne of Satan. It was not just Christians but also Jews who saw this city as such a center of false religion that it was destined for destruction (*Sib. Or.* 5:119). Pergamum was also famous for its library of two hundred thousand volumes. Here, above all, the church was likely to clash with the dictates of Hellenistic culture and the imperial cult. "Satan's throne" could refer to the altar to Zeus, which was visible for miles around, but a more likely suggestion is that the worship of the emperor is in view, for worship of a mere mortal would be seen by a monotheist such as John as an abomination that could only be prompted by Satan. The antagonism toward Rome in this document makes this conjecture quite plausible, and this identification seems to be confirmed by what we find in Revelation 13:2; 16:10.

The Christians in this town are commended for holding on to the faith even in the days when Antipas "my witness" was killed for his faith. It is striking that Antipas is given the same title as Jesus, "the faithful witness," which suggests that the translation "the faithful martyr" is close to the mark. Against this group of Christians Jesus has more than one complaint. In particular, there is the problem of some of the audience holding to the teaching of Balaam. This is not likely the person's real name, but it is given because of the character of his actions (see Num 22–24). John sees him as a false prophet leading God's people astray to immorality and idolatry (cf. Num 31:16). Here we have the association of "idol food" with fornication, an association that is not mere chance. Many take the term "fornication" as a metaphor for idolatry.

I have argued elsewhere at length that the term *eidōlothytos*, wherever it is found in early Christian literature, refers to meat sacrificed and then eaten in the presence of an idol, which is to say within a pagan temple (cf. 1 Cor 8–10; Acts 15).[64] Whether John has in mind sex with sacred prostitutes (which would mean that here *porneia* is used in its technical and root sense) or, more likely, the sexual dalliance that went on at dinner parties held in the temple precincts is uncertain. In either case, John is warning against going to pagan temples and participating in what happens there.

It is unclear whether Revelation 2:15 is telling us that there were Nicolaitans in Pergamum as well or whether the Nicolaitan heresy involved dining and fraternizing in pagan temples. Perhaps the Nicolaitans were high-status Christians who believed that a certain amount of compromise with the dominant culture was acceptable. They could have argued, "Even the Romans do not really believe that the emperor is a god, so why not just go along and have a good living as a member of a guild?" They might also have been dualists like some of the Corinthians (see 1 Cor 8–10), arguing that what one did with the body did not affect one's spiritual condition and status. It is correct to say that the complaint against Balaam is a complaint against syncretism, the luring of Christians into participation in pagan cults. In the early second century there is clear evidence that when Romans discovered that Christians refused to eat meat offered to idols, they dealt with this in stern ways because such a practice could affect not only Christians but also others whom they proselytized (Pliny, *Ep.* 10.96).

The people of Pergamum are called to repent or else Christ will come and attack them with the sword of his mouth, (i.e., his word of judgment). To those who conquer is offered not idol food but rather hidden manna (i.e., bread that is not currently visible, and that comes from heaven). Here is the

---

[64]Ben Witherington III, "Not So Idle Thoughts about *Eidolothuton*," *TynBul* 44 (1993): 237-54.

promise of a much more lasting and satisfying fellowship than one could ever get at a pagan feast, drawing on Jewish messianic traditions about the repeat of the manna miracle in the messianic kingdom (*2 Bar.* 29:4-8). Also on offer is a white pebble with one's new name inscribed on it, which no one knows except the one taking it. Perhaps this is an allusion to the white pebble used in antiquity for admission to some feasts or the one used to vote acquittal in a trial. Here we perhaps should see these stones as the engraved invitation to the messianic banquet. As with an Oscar award, no one knows the name of the winning person on the card, except the one holding the card. The new name implies a new identity, and in this case it implies being someone special in the kingdom. Christians did not have to compromise on earth by socializing with pagans in temples when they had a much better engraved invitation to a much better banquet.

At the outset of the message to Thyatira in Revelation 2:18 we have the one and only reference in this book to Jesus as the Son of God. It is used here probably because of the quotation of Psalm 2:9 at Revelation 2:26-27. The eyes of flaming fire and the feet of bronze are mentioned, picking up on the vision in Revelation 1. The image is of one who sees all, penetrating right to the heart. The bronze feet suggest stability and firmness. Thyatira was a relatively unimportant city of merchants and artisans, and so it was full of trade guilds. Here too there would have been considerable economic pressure on Christians.

The Christians of Thyatira are highly commended in Revelation 2:19 for their love, faith, service and endurance. They were just the opposite of the Ephesians, for the Thyatirans are commended for their latter works being greater than their former ones. Yet this church, perhaps out of love, had tolerated aberration in the form of a prophetess, here called "Jezebel." The suggestion is that this woman was leading them astray into idolatry and immorality, just like the ancient queen of Israel (see 1 Kings 18–19; 2 Kings 9:22). In Revelation 2:20 we hear mention of the same sin previously referred to in Revelation 2:14. This woman was given time and opportunity to repent. She did not, and the result is that Christ has cast her into a sick bed. She has been plagued with some sort of illness that causes suffering. John certainly believes that, on occasion, there is a connection not merely between sickness and sin, but between sickness and judgment, the former being a result of the latter. It is not clear from Revelation 2:22 whether literal adultery characterizes Jezebel's followers, but this is possible. The great suffering was inflicted in hopes of repentance, not because Christ wants even Jezebel to undergo final judgment at the eschaton.

Revelation 2:23 uses the idiom "to kill unto death" *(apoktenō en thanatō)*, which seems to mean "to kill with a pestilence or with suffering" (cf. Ezek 33:27 with Rev 6:8, where death equals pestilence). In Revelation 2:23 Jesus is called "he who searches minds and hearts." He knows all our motives. Strikingly, the first word, *nephros*, literally means "kidney," which was seen as the seat of affections, much as we would use the term *heart*. And the second word, *kardia* ("heart"), here has a sense closer to what we mean by "mind," the rational faculty or intellect. We are told that Christ gives to each according to his or her works. There is indeed a judgment of Christian works, with rewards and punishment accruing according to the evaluation. It appears that the heresy in question in this case involved some sort of promise to know the deep things of God, which actually turned out to be the deep things of Satan. Real necromancy or Satan worship is unlikely to be meant here.

The faithful Christians are to hold fast to their faith until Christ comes. To the victors goes the highest possible honor: power over the Gentile nations, the ability to rule them with absolute power. Thus, a share in Christ's worldwide sovereignty is envisioned. But when would this transpire? John suggests that it will happen in the millennium (see Rev 20). In addition, Revelation 2:28 promises the gift of the morning star. This probably should not be associated with Revelation 22:16. The "morning star" refers to Venus, which to the Romans was the symbol of victory and sovereignty. The point is that Christians will obtain such things not through pagan rituals or by following pagan teaching but rather from Christ, who holds the universe in his hand.

"Jesus' oracle to Ephesus challenges a loveless church; his oracle to Smyrna encourages a persecuted church; his oracle to Pergamum addresses both persecution and compromise; but Jesus' word to Sardis summons a sleeping church to wake up."[65] This message is the most strongly negative of the seven. This church in Sardis had the reputation of being alive, but really it was dead. This was a town living basically on past historical prestige, having been the location where the famous King Croesus had lived. It was destroyed in the huge A.D. 17 earthquake, which racked the region. It was indebted to Rome for its rebuilding. According to Josephus, this city had a substantial Jewish population (*Ant.* 14.259-261; 16.166, 171).

The church in this city had passed on from its better days. Revelation 3:2,

---

[65]Craig S. Keener, *Revelation* (NIVAC: Grand Rapids: Zondervan, 2000), p. 142.

however, suggests that there was a flicker that could be rekindled. None of their works were perfectly acceptable to God. The verb *plēroō* can also mean "to complete," which would suggest that Sardis had never finished the work it was called to in the first place. The first part of the verse probably should be translated "strengthen those who remain but are at the point of death." This seems to refer to the real possibility of martyrdom. Revelation 3:3 is important because it speaks of Jesus' coming as a thief if the Sardisians did not become watchful about their behavior. The image here likely goes back to the original parable of Jesus, and the image is reused where the subject is the parousia (cf. Lk 12:39-40; 1 Thess 5:2-8; 2 Pet 3:10). Here is more evidence, if more is needed, that all the New Testament writers shared the same christocentric narrative thought world, where Christ is the one who changes the story line, whether the issue is redemption or judgment. The elaboration in the second half of Revelation 3:3 suggests that it is the timing that will be surprising. While the reference here could be to the parousia, it is more likely to the invisible coming of Christ to judge this particular church in the present. This image would have been especially striking to the Sardisians because twice in their history they had fallen prey to devastating sneak attacks due to their lack of diligence or alertness.

At Revelation 3:4 we hear of a few who have not defiled their garments. White garments are mentioned seven times in this book as a symbol of purity and holiness. In a city of garment workers, this promise was especially meaningful. The soiled garment in a city famous for its dyed garments and fancy clothing products would be antithetical to their civic pride. We know that in Asia Minor a soiled garment often prohibited a person from participating in an act of worship. The promise to those who are steadfast is a garment of absolute white, and that their names will not be blotted out of the book of life. In the Old Testament the phrase "book of life" refers to earthly life (cf. Ex 32:32; Ps 69:28; Is 4:3), but in the New Testament it refers to eternal life. The image suggests that it is possible to be in such a book and then to be blotted out of it due to one's unacceptable beliefs and practices. The victor will be acknowledged in the highest throne room of all, before God and his angelic entourage. Here we learn a crucial point about our author's moral vision of Christianity. He believes that apostasy is possible, and that although good behavior cannot in itself save a person, nevertheless committing either moral or intellectual apostasy after conversion is possible and leads to the erasure of one's name from the book of life. In this our author's theology does not differ from what we found in Hebrews, with its stress on persevering and avoiding falling short of the kingdom goal. This in turn means that in both these books human behavior of Christians after conversion can affect their eternal status.

Philadephia was a city dedicated to Hellenistic culture and known as "little Athens" because of its many temples. It was in the midst of a vineyard region, and so Bacchus was its favorite deity. It is interesting that only here is the description of Christ not drawn from the vision recorded in Revelation 1. We are told that Christ has the key of David and also the power to open so that no one can shut, and vice versa. Isaiah 22:22 is in the background here, and what is meant is that Christ has the key to the royal household, which in this case means to the new Jerusalem. In all likelihood, the open door mentioned in Revelation 3:8 is in reference to the door into the heavenly city or royal and heavenly mansion. At least a few Christians here have kept Christ's word and not denied his name. Here too, as at Smyrna, the problem is related to the synagogue, and, in an abrupt turn around from older Jewish expectations, we are told that these so-called Jews will worship at the feet of the faithful Christians. Revelation 3:10 sounds congenial to dispensationalism at first. Christ will keep the faithful from the hour of trial that will come upon the whole earth. This is followed by the words "I will come quickly." Notice, however, that the author says nothing about taking the Christians out of the world; rather, he speaks of Christ coming and protecting Christians.[66]

In this message it seems clear that the author has begun to speak of the final eschatological events and not just what "now is." Instead of being a pillar of pagan society, the victor will become a pillar in God's temple, with the most crucial of all things inscribed (i.e., impressed upon and so identified with the believer): God's name, Jesus' name and the name of the new city. The victor now belongs to God and is a part of the heavenly city (see Rev 6:9-11). As Mitchell Reddish observes, Christ is offering the Philadelphians a place of honor and security in the very presence of God. "Now those who kept 'the name' will be inscribed with the name."[67]

The message to the church at Laodicea begins at Revelation 3:14, where Christ is called both "the Amen" (as God is at Is 65:16) and "the beginning of God's creation," an explicit reference to Christ's preexistence. It is pos-

---

[66]"To keep them from the coming trials does not mean the church will be exempt from the difficulties. Rather, this is a promise of Christ's abiding presence with the church that will strengthen and sustain it regardless of the trials ahead" (Mitchell Reddish, *Revelation* [SHBC; Macon, Ga.: Smyth & Helwys, 2000], p. 76).

[67]Ibid., p. 78.

sible that the author knew of the letter sent to Colossae and Laodicea and is reflecting his knowledge of Colossians 1–2 here. The town of Laodicea was well known for several things, notably its banks and its famous medical school (Strabo, *Geogr.* 12.8.20). John clearly knows some of the social and religious particulars about each of these seven cities. The weakness of the city was its lack of a good water supply (Strabo, *Geogr.* 13.4.14). Six miles away, Hierapolis had its hot medicinal springs, and there was also pure water in Colossae. Just across from Laodicea the hot springs went over limestone cliffs and became lukewarm and brackish. Anyone drinking this water would spit it out. Here the imagery seems pointedly directed toward the audience's life situation. There is no commendation at all for Laodicea. The Laodiceans are faulted for being neither hot nor cold. They claim to be rich and have no needs, but the ultimate result of complacency and status quo thinking is a loss of all real self-knowledge. The Laodiceans have in fact become poor and na-ked, spiritually speaking, and only Christ can apply the necessary ointment, the white garment, the necessary spiritual currency to do them real good. He will reprove and discipline the ones whom he loves. Yet, even with people such as the Laodiceans, Christ does not give up.

Notice that this church, which he cannot commend, he still calls to repen-tance, and we hear the famous words about standing at the door and knock-ing. But each individual must respond. The victor gets to have both ongoing fellowship with Christ and even to sit with him on his throne. Finally, we should note the use of the rhetorical device of irony in this letter. Things are not as they appear in Laodicea, and John points out the incongruity through ironical words and images. The encouragement of this last little epistle is that the Master makes house calls even to recalcitrant or self-satisfied Christians, seeking to continue to have fellowship with them, but those followers must let Jesus in if the previous level of intimacy with Christ is to be regained. Herein we see not only the extent of the love of Christ, who seeks and saves even backsliding Christians, but also the ethical response required if a Chris-tian is to continue in fellowship with Christ.

As we consider the social situation described in these brief epistles, we dis-cover several pertinent facts. First, the social fabrics of the churches differed. Some could be predominantly poor, while others might have a goodly num-ber of high-status Christians. The variety in the exhortations reflects these social differences. Second, there are both internal and external problems plaguing these churches. The internal problems involve prophetic figures other than John who may have been the ones who filled the power vacuum when John was exiled. There was also the problem of the relationships with the synagogues. Finally, there were the larger social issues of how to relate to pagan culture, and especially its religious culture, including the emperor cult. In this pagan society Christians are being marginalized and persecuted for their faith. It seems clear that John believes that, in his absence, things have gone awry in these churches, and only the strongest possible sort of exhortations may help to right these ships. Some congregations are seen as being in better shape than others, but none are without difficulties.

The Sectarian and Communitarian Ethics of Revelation

Revelation is a book about justice and God's sovereignty even in the face of the evidence of great evil on the loose in the world. One of the things that one certainly can do with the materials in Revelation 2–3 is reflect on the sort of problems that arise when a church has been in existence for a good period of time. How does one deal with complacency, lack of zeal, self-centered behavior, and, most of all, too much accommodation to the secular culture outside the church?

The sociological literature has a good deal to say about millenarian sects and their attempts to build firm boundaries around their community. This is difficult to do in a cosmopolitan urban setting, and all the more so when one is a member of an evangelistic religion. One of John's problems is that he is dealing with churches that do not seem to have strong indigenous leadership structures. Indeed, they seem to be far too susceptible to false apostles and false prophets. John would like to create a "high group" sense of identity or community among his audiences, but there seems to be little leadership on the ground to which he can appeal for assistance in this group formation.

Notice John's attempt to instill certain accountability factors into the churches' lives by making ethical demands in the context of eschatological warnings about Christ and coming judgment, both imminent and more remote. The thing to bear in mind about millenarian sects such as John is trying to nurture is that they do not simply look for heavenly compensation for earthly deprivation. Instead, they expect matters to be rectified on earth in due course in the millennium when the Lord returns. It is no accident that the saints under the altar in heaven in Revelation 6:10-11 are crying out "How long?" and are given robes while they have to continue to wait. They too have not reached the eschaton. Rectification, however, comes not by a call to arms but rather through prayer for divine intervention. John's vision of how justice is finally done is theocratic, not bureaucratic. It is not surprising that when addressing a tiny minority, one does not set forth a major social program of societal reform, especially when one believes that God in Christ will intervene both imminently and on the more distant horizon. Craig Keener points out that the only two churches unequivocally commended are the churches of Smyrna and Philadephia, which is to say the churches that had or were experiencing suffering. "Suffering has a way of reminding us which things in life really matter, forcing us to depend radically on God, and thus purifying our obedience to God's will."[68] As we soon will see, the author of 1 Peter would simply pronounce the amen to that statement.

One of the major functions that Revelation serves for the Christian community is as a warning against too great an assimilation into the dominant non-Christian culture. In this sense, Revelation certainly is sectarian literature. John writes to those who are being oppressed, but some of them certainly are not on the margins of society. Indeed, some of the audience are in grave danger of entering into a societal pattern that involves the worship of the emperor, among other idolatries.

In order to avoid such idolatries, a strong sense of group identity is necessary, especially when it comes to avoiding ethical aberrations.

> The gospel is never for individuals but always for a people. Sin fragments us, separates us, and sentences us to solitary confinement. Gospel restores us, unites us, and sets us in community. The life of faith revealed and nurtured in the biblical narratives is highly personal but never merely individual: always there is a family, a tribe, a nation—church. . . . A believing community is the context for the life of faith. . . . Love cannot exist in isolation: away from others, love bloats into pride. Grace cannot be received privately: cut off from others, it is perverted into greed. Hope cannot develop in solitude: separated from the community, it goes to seed in the form of fantasies.[69]

There are in fact very few documents in the New Testament written to individuals. It is primarily the church as a corporate entity that is addressed. The book of Revelation is especially not intended primarily for private devotion and private readings. Especially with an esoteric book such as this, private readings are more likely to be wrong than right because few if any modern Christians live in the world of Jewish apocalyptic prophecy. It is precisely isolation from the sociohistorical context in which this material was

---

[68]Keener, *Revelation*, p. 120.
[69]Eugene H. Peterson, *Reversed Thunder: The Revelation of John and the Praying Imagination* (San Francisco: HarperSanFrancisco, 1988), pp. 42-43.

written that has led to such misuse of this book. But it is also true that this book was not intended to be read by those with mere idle curiosity about the future. It was meant to be read in the context of Christian faith, and it was meant to be obeyed, not merely studied.

This brings us to another crucial point for our study of New Testament ethics. All of the ethical advice given in the New Testament is directed toward communities, with the exception of a few of the letters of the New Testament (1-2 Timothy, Titus, 3 John). The assumption is that the community is the locus in which these ethics will be reinforced, and it is not simply left to the private efforts of isolated individual Christians. Apostasy was always a lurking danger under societal pressure, but it became a much less serious danger when the community stuck together, its members were accountable to one another, loved each other and would not willingly let individual members go astray. That accountability was laid not just on the shoulders of the community leaders but rather on all members in these seven churches of Revelation. A sectarian group ethic is to be enforced by the group as a whole. They understood that if they did not hang together, in an environment of persecution they certainly would hang separately.

These observations in turn bring up a crucial point for modern readings of this material: in a radically individualistic culture such as we have in the West, the tendency is to see this material as a call to a commitment to ethical heroism and individual virtue by the most devout individual Christians. Thereby the ethic becomes more utopian and less realistic. But this is entirely the wrong way to read the ethical material of the New Testament, which is communal to the core and presupposes a strong sense of a closely knit group identity. If there is no such community in place, it can be no surprise that there is no such ethic exhibited in one or another group of modern Christians, and all the more so when the call in Revelation is to swim against the predominant cultural stream, following an ethic of nonviolence, nonresistance, perseverance in suffering, and preparation for martyrdom if need be. This brings us to our last port of call in this chapter, the ethics of 1 Peter.

1 Peter: The Ethics of Suffering Servants

Submitting to the Authority of the Suffering Servant in 1 Peter 1–3
If the book of Revelation is the book of the martyrs, 1 Peter is the book that most embodies a theology of suffering for the sake of Christ—imitating the suffering servant. From the very outset of 1 Peter we are told that Christians

have been saved and sanctified for the sake of obedience to Jesus (1 Pet 1:2). Suffering is mentioned at the outset also as something that refines and purifies the faith of the saints, thus proving its genuineness.

The actual opening exhortation does not come until 1 Peter 1:13-15, where there is a call for alertness and, more importantly, to be holy because God is holy. This brings something crucial to light already. The character of God is to be replicated on a lesser scale by the character of the believer. And herein lies one of the more crucial hinge motifs in New Testament ethics; theology and ethics are linked in this respect. God's moral character, more particularly as it is manifested in Christ, is to be replicated in the believer (who is sanctified for the sake of obedience) so that the believer can imitate the self-sacrificial behavior of Christ. There is a further consideration. If a holy God is going to dwell in the midst of his people, they also need to be holy to come into his presence (cf., e.g., Is 6; 1 Jn 1:6-7).

Indeed, Christian ethics can be summed up in the notion that we are to become what God already is, at least in regard to character—holy, loving, merciful, and so forth. We must become true image bearers. This is quite impossible without the grace of God enabling the believer to approximate the character and deeds of God. The word *conduct* here and elsewhere in this discourse refers to public conduct. Notice the reference to "all" conduct being conformed to God. Peter has no interest in constructing an isolationist sect; indeed, he is interested in their public witness for the gospel's sake. In the question of whether Peter is constructing an ethic that seeks to make Christians stand out from the pagan crowd or blend in, the answer is that this ethic is mostly of the former nature, but at the same time Peter wants them, for the sake of the witness, to do what they can to "seek the welfare of the city" and be good citizens and neighbors. It is noteworthy that if indeed Peter's audience is mostly Jews (and I think they are), then the use of Leviticus repeatedly in this discourse will come as no surprise. What is a surprise is that Peter no longer thinks that the ritual purity portions of Leviticus are incumbent on the audience, for now there is a new covenant that does not mean a mere renewal of the old one. Only some of the moral stipulations of the old covenant are carried over into the new, as Peter himself learned through a vision (see Acts 10).

But something else remarkable happens in this opening chapter. We are told in 1 Peter 1:22 that the audience has purified themselves by obeying the truth. Obedience as a means of sanctification appears to be mentioned only here in the New Testament, but it exposes something that the author is trying to get at: there is an integral connection between being and doing, such that doing affects the being. The converse is also true. Sanctification enables good behavior, but obedient behavior also purifies the believer. And this is not all. Peter says that now that they have in fact purified themselves by obedience to the truth in order that they may have sincere love for each other, they should love each other deeply, from a pure heart. This is possible because they have been born again or born of God. This birth and the sanctifying process that follows it do not immediately solve all moral dilemmas, and so the audience is told in 1 Peter 2:1 that as Christians, they must purge themselves of all malice, deceit, hypocrisy, envy and slander. In 1 Peter 2:11 the author speaks of sinful desires that war against the believer's spirit, so he is under no delusions that the audience is already perfect in every way.

The ethic in 1 Peter has a concern for the public witness that moral or virtuous behavior can make to pagans. Their good deeds should be visible to those outside the community and so be a good witness. This document does not have the same sectarian feel as the Johannine material, in the sense that it is not as inwardly directed or absorbed. And this brings us to the section of 1 Peter that requires more detailed comment, for it deals at length with an ethic of submission to authority figures, beginning with the discussion of submission to governing authorities in 1 Peter 2:13.

By the middle of the second chapter of 1 Peter we have arrived at the heart of the discourse and argumentation, with all the more general and preparatory discussion left behind. It becomes clear that Peter is especially concerned about two sticky subjects, submission to authority and suffering, and how one can endure both of these conditions in a manner that is in accord with Christian holiness. Submission was the easier of the two subjects to address in Peter's world, and so he tackles it first under the broader rubric of ways one can live an honorable life, being a good witness and doing good to others. He will leave the more difficult subject of suffering for his third argument, which begins at 1 Peter 3:13, but as is typical of rhetorical arguments there is some overlap, for already in 1 Peter 3:9 we hear the message of no retaliation to persecution, pressure and slander.

Peter is concerned that the audience not merely avoid bad behavior but actually, to the extent they are able, seek the good of their city or town by doing good deeds and even blessing those who misuse them. Peter sees this as a response modeled on the way Jesus handled such situations. Doing good and being exemplary neighbors are seen as a missionary strategy to win over some nonbelievers. This suggests that we should see the so-called household code material in this section of the discourse as pragmatic advice that is part of a missionary or evangelistic strategy. In other words, it should not be seen as Peter's attempt to reinforce the patriarchal structure of society as a matter of principle.

As 1 Peter 3:1 suggests, actively resisting and despising the structures of society makes it more difficult to win over pagans, which is the prime mandate. Peter recognizes that they do have the freedom to behave otherwise (see 1 Pet 2:16), but it is a bad witness in the heated and hostile situation in which they seem to live, where pressure, abuse and persecution are not unusual. Peter is trying to create neither an isolationist sect nor an accommodationist one. There is a delicate balance, a tightrope that he wants the audience to walk: they are to be in the world, do good to the world, convert the pagan world, but they are to do so without being of the world and being assimilated to the dominant values and moral lifestyle of that world. The line is drawn on the basis of theology and ethics and also of good evangelistic strategy.

What we will notice about the so-called household code in this argument is that in crucial respects it is unlike the ones found in Colossians and Ephesians. Two points can be mentioned here because this affects the way we hear Peter's advice. First, Peter is concerned with the social interface between Christians and non-Christians as it transpires both in society and in the household. He is dealing with a mixed society and religiously mixed households. This is why the symmetry or mutuality so striking in the household codes in Colossians and Ephesians is absent here.

There is only one pair addressed, husband and wife, and the husband gets exactly one verse worth of attention (1 Pet 3:7). Otherwise, Christian slaves are addressed but not masters, the discussion of parents and children is omitted altogether, and the duty of all Christians but not that of rulers is discussed. And in fact, the discussion of one's duties to rulers and all those in authority is discussed first and sets the tone for what follows. This is because Peter is focusing on Christian duties to those outside the Christian community, even if they live in the same household as the Christian. Thus, I strongly underline that we do not have a discussion in 1 Peter of the "Christian household," unlike what we find in Colossians and Ephesians. And of course the discussion of duty to rulers can hardly be called part of a household code or duty. The rhetorical rubric being used to bind all this together is Christians' duties to non-Christians, and "1 Peter alone makes his readers' civic obligations the framework in which to present their more specific duties within the household."[70]

But second, in this document the only being to whom Christians are called to offer absolute and unconditional obedience is God. Bear in mind again 1 Peter 2:16, where Peter assumes and stresses that his audience is free to respond properly or to not respond properly to these exhortations. Here he is referring not to political or social freedom but rather to spiritual freedom that comes through new birth in Christ and frees one from bondage to sin, darkness, ignorance and paganism (1 Pet 1:14; 2:9). They can cooperate with their rulers, masters, and spouses or not. Peter is urging cooperation "for the sake of the Lord"—that is, because of the witness to these non-Christians to whom they are relating.

Unconditional and unquestioned "obedience" *(hypakoē)* is reserved for the Christian's relationship to God in Christ (see 1 Pet 1:2, 14, 22). Since Peter under no circumstances would advise Christians to compromise their faith or obedience to God in order to comply with some lesser authority figure, we should see the verb *hypotassō* here when applied to one's relationship to a non-Christian ruler, master or husband (see 1 Pet 2:18; 3:1, 5; cf. 1 Pet 5:5) as meaning something closer to "to defer" or "to respect" rather than "to submit" or "to subject."[71] This leads to the further necessary point that *ktisis* in 1 Peter 2:13 should be allowed to have the same meaning it has elsewhere in the New Testament (cf., e.g., Mk 16:15; Rom 8:20-21; Col 1:15, 23), "creature, creation." Peter is not calling for Christian submission to every creature on the planet, and note that the examples that follow of the emperor or governor are people, not institutions. Instead, Peter is inculcating the need to show respect and deference to all other human beings, starting from the top of that hierarchial society and moving on down. Peter has modified the instructions found in Proverbs 24:21 LXX on this subject. "Fear" is reserved now for God alone, but the ruler is to be honored (see 1 Pet 2:17).

Thus, as Ramsey Michaels concludes, "'Defer to every creature' simply anticpates the command with which v 17 begins: 'show respect for everyone.'"[72] The rhetorical effect of this reading of the argument is that it turns out to be far more profoundly Christian and far less conventional than

---

[70]J. Ramsey Michaels, *1 Peter* (WBC 49; Waco, Tex.: Word, 1988), p. 122.
[71]Ibid., p. 124.
[72]Ibid.

is often imagined, nor is it baptizing the existing social structures and calling them good. What it calls for is Christians to act as Christians on the basis of first Christian principles in all their relationships, whether in the household or in society, especially when they are relating to pagans for the sake of the Lord and the witness.

In some ways the most impressive and surprising move of this particular argument is the use of Christ as a paradigm for the behavior of household servants (and others). Of course, Christ as exemplar is common enough, but here only is the "servant" Christ seen as specifically the model of behavior for Christian household servants.

Of importance at this juncture is that the example here is used for paraenetic purposes, and that the example chosen is a historical one, indeed the most important historical one for this audience, which considerably strengthens the force of the example to its maximum potential, especially because of the authority of the example over the audience. In the midst of this surprising example there is a dramatic play on the verb *pherō* ("bear, carry"). In 1 Peter 2:19 the household servant is exhorted to "bear up under the pain," while in 1 Peter 2:24 it says that "Christ bore our sins in his body." This links the experiences of the believer and Christ, but without identifying the two. Only Christ suffered for other's sins and made atonement, and Peter indicates the distinction by using the prefix *hypo-* with *pherō* in the former verse and *ana-* with *pherō* in the latter verse. The ultimate irony of this argument that makes it a tour de force is that then the household servants become the examples for the whole community of how they should respond to society. The last shall indeed be first.

Here David Balch helpfully reminds us that slaves were expected to take the religion of their masters; thus, when a slave became a Christian, there was a problem on this front, and Peter is suggesting that household servants should give no offense other than the offense of their faith.[73] The same applies to wives as well, as Plutarch shows (*Mor.* 140D; 144D-E). The wife was supposed to worship her husband's gods. What, then, was she to do if she became a Christian? Peter's advice is that in other respects she is to defer to her husband and so be a good witness to him.

> Peter's advice is, unlike Plutarch's, . . . not for wives to abandon the worship of Christ, but for them to continue Christian living so as to win their husbands over to the Christian faith. The summons is not to acculturation to Greco-

---

[73]David L. Balch, *Let Wives Be Submissive: The Domestic Code in 1 Peter* (SBLMS 26; Chico, Calif.: Scholars Press, 1981), pp. 68-75.

Roman society, but to [creative] adaptation to its domestic realities and norms.
Thus will the Christian mission advance in a home despite a mixture there of
religious beliefs.[74]

Were Peter simply an accomodationist to Greco-Roman norms, he never
would have encouraged women and slaves to live out and be loyal to their
Christian faith in clear violation of the normal patriarchal expectations of the
day. The insistence on no religious accommodation to the master or husband
is quite revolutionary.

Near the end of this remarkable piece of argumentation comes the appeal
to a second paradigm, Sarah, as an example for women. Sarah is presented as
a model of deference to one's husband, but if we recognize what is happening
with the use of the Old Testament here, we see a bit of tongue in cheek. In
Genesis 18:12 LXX Sarah calls Abraham "lord," but she is being somewhat
facetious. The context is not deference but rather "incredulous amusement
at the announcement of her future child bearing."[75] Here Peter says that the
wife must hope only in God (honoring only God as God), but she must respect her husband as Sarah did. Notice, however, that although Peter refers
to Sarah obeying and calling Abraham "master," what he asks of Christian
women is "doing good and not fearing intimidation."

What has happened here? Sarah becomes a general example of respecting one's spouse, but the Christian wife is not called to follow her example
exactly. Instead, she is to do good and not be cowed or act on the basis of intimidation. In other words, her behavior should be guided by positive Christian principles of honor and respect, not be grounded in fear-based or craven
behavior. This goes well beyond what Sarah modeled in that Old Testament
story. Doing "the good" here suggests there are women capable of benefactions, and Peter would rather have them do that than spend their money on
jewelry and luxurious apparel. They are to dress modestly. Perhaps the reference to fear has to do with concerns about verbal or physical abuse based on
the wife's newly found religion, but Peter does not say so.

Peter ends this argument with the longest Old Testament quotation in this
entire discourse, and it is clear from the word "finally" in 1 Peter 3:8, which
introduces the conclusion of the argument, that he is summing up. This conclusion shows that he is most concerned with inculcating nonretaliation (a

[74]Barth L. Campbell, *Honor, Shame, and the Rhetoric of 1 Peter* (SBLDS 160; Atlanta: Scholars Press, 1998), p. 148.
[75]Ibid., p. 159.

counterintuitive virtue that distinguished Christians), kindness in behavior toward non-Christians, and brotherly/sisterly love and concord within the fellowship of Christ. Thus, in this entire argument Peter is concerned with both internal behavior in the community and the interface between Christians and society. We now need to consider this material in more detail.

Having enunciated the principle about good Christian behavior in 1 Peter 2:11-12, the author begins in 1 Peter 2:13 what we may identify as the duty or social code section of the document, where deference or possibly submission to rulers, masters and husbands is urged. This is seen as one manifestation of good and godly Christian conduct. Leonard Goppelt is exactly right that we must recognize the differences between what is going on here and what we find in the so-called household codes in Colossians and Ephesians. The focus here is not primarily on Christians relationships within the household structure. Rather, "1 Peter has in mind individual Christians in the institutions of a non-Christian society that discriminates against them."[76] Thus, Peter starts with the largest institution, government, then moves down to the largest economic unit, slave labor, and then finally to the smallest unit of society, marriage and family. Compared to Ephesians and Colossians, "in 1 Peter the sequence is reversed, moving from the civil order surrounding all society to the smallest unit, marriage."[77]

In other words, Peter is dealing with the interface between individual Christian lives and pagan society. Why, then, concentrate on the subordinate member in certain relationships? Because "for them the tie to non-Christians is especially problematic. The relationship of children to parents is left out since Christian children of non-Christian parents would be hardly thinkable in the situation at hand."[78] The atmosphere or ethos out of which this teaching comes is one of threat, slander, persecution, danger to the community, not from within but at the interface with larger society. What is given, then, is advice about conduct under such circumstances, with the desire to keep the community intact and continuing in its witness to the world, all the while minimizing the causes for abuse of Christians. Equally, we may notice the difference between what is going on here and what we find in Romans 13, written at an earlier time in Nero's reign. Here there is no hint of suggesting

---

[76]Leonhard Goppelt, *A Commentary on 1 Peter*, ed. Ferdinand Hahn, trans. John E. Alsup (Grand Rapids: Eerdmans, 1993), p. 164.
[77]Ibid.
[78]Ibid., p. 165.

that God has set up the Roman system or given it the divine imprimatur. The emperor is treated as a subset of the class called "all human creatures," a not-so-subtle critique of the growing importance of the emperor cult in the regions addressed. There is some similarity of vocabulary between what we find here and Romans 13, but the arguments and emphases go in different directions and do not suggest literary dependence one way or the other. The differences between the two texts are significant, particularly in 1 Peter: (1) there is no mention of taxes; (2) there is no reference to divine wrath; (3) there is no reference to governing officials being God's servants; (4) the discussion of fear is in relationship to God, not governors.

The first segment of this paragraph deals with rulers directly, but probably we should see 1 Peter 2:13 as a general introduction to this section paralleling 1 Peter 2:17a, "show honor/respect to all." Sometimes 1 Peter 2:13a is translated so as to have the author encouraging submission to "human institutions," but this will hardly do, because *ktisis* in the Bible refers to creation or its human element, creatures. In fact, the notion that *ktisis* here refers to "human institutions" has no basis in all of Greek literature, and all the examples that follow are human individuals—emperors, proconsuls, masters. Thus, we must translate the clause as "defer/be subordinate to every human being" for the Word's sake. It is possible that Peter says "every creature" here to emphasize that even the emperor is just a creature, just another human being, and in principle one shows him no more respect or deference than one would show to other human beings. It may be of some significance that Peter uses the word "king" *(basileus)* here rather than "emperor." This was the preferred term in the Greek-speaking east, particularly in Anatolia. One other corollary is worth mentioning. If Peter says, "Subject yourself/show deference and respect to every human creature" (as I think he does), this exhortation is hardly gender specific either in its object or in its performer. All Christians are to do this, and the object of this behavior is all other human beings. Thus, this does indeed parallel closely what is said in 1 Peter 2:17a.

What does this deference or submission amount to? Obviously, it does not amount to doing anything that contravenes God's will, for the believer is called to do it for God's sake (cf. Rom 13:1-7; 1 Tim 2:1-3; Tit 3:1-3). Here *kyrios* ("Lord") probably refers to God the Father, not Jesus, as the one who created human beings. If "Lord" referred to Jesus here, the implication would be "Do this as a witness for Christ." More likely it means "Do this because these are creatures that God made, and you are to serve and witness to them."

The verb *hypotagēte* is in the aorist, meaning "start deferring/ subordinating" and is an action taken up voluntarily by people whom the Lord has set free. The verb *hypotassō* has the literal sense of ordering oneself under another or under a group of others, in this case governing officials. It is found nowhere in classical Greek, and only 1 Chronicles 29:23-24 LXX is of relevance when the subject is deference or submission to governing authorities.

Notice that "obey" is not used for this relationship but rather is reserved for one's relationship with God (1 Pet 1:2, 14, 22). The Christian is always to do God's will (1 Pet 2:15) because God never asks of his creatures something immoral or inappropriate. But in fact here it appears that "God's will" refers to the doing of good, not the divine ordering of government. All of these exhortations are in fact grounded on the premise that Christians are free (1 Pet 2:16) in themselves to be a good Christian witness or not, to defer to governing authorities or not. With this background, we can now examine things in a bit more detail.

Note that 1 Peter 2:14 is somewhat ambiguous. Are the "governors" *(hēgemōn)* sent by God, or does this actually refer to their being sent by the emperor as governors and proconsuls to the various provinces? Since 1 Peter 2:13-14 is part of one sentence, the latter option is more likely. It is the emperor who has sent these governors to the provinces to administer justice. A good example of this very language is provided by Josephus, who reports that the Judean Jews asked to be freed from the rule of Herod Archelaus and "be made subject *[hypotassesthai]* to the governors sent there" (Ant. 17.314).

What about the phrase "the will of God," which follows in 1 Peter 2:15? Does it refer to the divine authority of the governors and the king? Apparenlty not, since it seems to go with what follows (see below). This being the case, Peter, possibly unlike Paul in Romans 13, does not speak of the divine authority of these rulers. They are simply creatures to be honored and respected and deferred to but not feared, revered and obeyed unconditionally as God is. This posture is interesting and stands somewhere between what Paul wrote about government in Romans 13 and what the author of Revelation thinks about the emperor and his minions after considerable persecution.

If Peter wrote this letter (as I believe he did), what follows is notable because Nero was indeed a perverse emperor, or perhaps we should say that he did some perverse things to some Christians in the period following the fire in A.D. 64. Peter may be writing at the very inception of all this before Nero's true character came fully to light. Emperors (kings) were supreme, but even governors probably are seen by Peter as sent by God for administering a basic system of reward and punishment (note the passive voice of "are sent" in 1 Pet 2:14). This is, of course, the basic function of any government—to maintain law and order and to judge justly.

The word *houtōs* begins 1 Peter 2:15, and this may look back to what has just been said. A government offering of rewards and punishments for good and bad conduct is God's will. But it may also refer to what follows; that is, God's will is that Christians silence the calumnies of foolish and ignorant people by doing what is good and right. There is a good possibility that here Peter is referring to some Christians' ability to "do the good." Bruce Winter has shown that this phrase normally refers to benefactions, the doing of civic good. What would this entail? "Benefactions included supplying grains in times of necessity by diverting the grain-carrying ships to the city, forcing down the price by selling it in the market below the asking rate, erecting public buildings or adorning old buildings with marble revetments such as in Corinth, refurbishing the theatre, widening roads, helping in the construction of public utilities, going on embassies to gain privileges for the city, and helping in the city in times of civil upheaval."[79] We must bear in mind that this entire region, both then and now, often experienced earthquakes and the accompanying devastation. Christians had frequent opportunities to help towns and cities overcome adversity in this region.

If Winter is right, as I believe he is, this tells us, as does the discussion of women's clothing, that there were some rather high-status Christians among the audience of this circular document. The reference to the "do-gooders" in 1 Peter 2:14-15 must signify more than just those who obey the law and act as expected. If the Christians of Asia Minor were to work for the public good, the official commendations that they would receive would silence criticisms from their accusers.

Peter recognizes Christians' freedom ultimately from the world (1 Pet 2:16), for they are sons and daughters of the kingdom (cf. Mt 17:26). But, he says, they must not use this freedom as a pretext or "cloak" or "guise" to do evil; rather, they must act as God's servants, be his witnesses to the world, and serve the government and people whom God placed in the world (cf. Gal 5:13). Various moralists of the age spoke of inner freedom and stated that it was something even a slave could have. Epicetetus, a Stoic and a former slave,

---

[79]Bruce W. Winter, *Seek the Welfare of the City: Christians as Benefactors and Citizens* (Grand Rapids: Eerdmans, 1994), p. 37.

says, "He is free who lives as he wills, who is subject neither to compulsion, nor hindrance, nor force, whose choices are unhampered, whose desires attain their end, whose aversions do not fall into what they would avoid" (*Diatr.* 4.1.1-2). On this basis he goes on to discuss how a slave can be more free (of the impulse of the passions) than the master. Christians do their service and civic duty not because they are earthly citizens but rather because they must serve God, who ordained the state and governors. Christians serve them in obedience to God, and of course whenever the two conflict, Christians must serve God alone. We should not see this material as lightly Christianized Greco-Roman ethics.

In 1 Peter 2:17 we have a general summary statement preceding the ensuing section. Believers are called to honor or respect everyone, which includes slaves, who had little or no honor and no rights in society, but they must go beyond that in special brotherly/sisterly affection for Christians. The term *adelphotēs* ("brotherhood") is rare, and it occurs again at 1 Peter 5:9 (cf. 1 Pet 5:13) but not elsewhere in the New Testament, nor is it normally used of "spiritual" kinship outside Christian literature. We do find this unusual term in *1 Clement* 2:4 and *Shepherd of Hermas* 38:10, which suggests that it was used in the Roman church to describe the relationship between Christians. Peter may have inaugurated this usage, based on what he learned from Jesus about the concept of the family of faith. Brotherly/sisterly affection, of course, must be done in the context of reverence for God. Notice that Peter concludes with "show honor to the emperor." He does not insist that believers love the emperor in the same way they love fellow Christians, but he does call them to honor and respect him. Notice too that Peter does not insist that Christians agree with everything that the ruler says, but they should submit to his rule.

We also note that God alone is said to be the object of fear or reverence *(phobeomai)*. Not even slaves are called to reverence their earthly masters, but only to serve them. As Paul Achtemeier puts it, "The concluding verse of this section thus establishes a hierarchy of values and allegiances: all people, including the emperor, are to be shown due honor and respect; fellow Christians are to be regarded as members of one's own family and shown appropriate love; God alone is to be shown reverence."[80] The structure here is that of a chiasm, with external relationships referred to in the "honor" clauses at the beginning and end and internal relations (love the Christian family and revere God) referred to in the middle.

---

[80]Paul J. Achtemeier, *1 Peter* (Hermeneia; Minneapolis: Fortress, 1996), p. 188.

Various people, at various times, have been deeply disturbed by the apparent selling out of the gospel in an attempt to live peacefully in a fallen world. Nowhere has this issue been more seriously and severely debated than in the context of the New Testament passages on slavery. How, it is asked, could someone such as Paul and Peter, who affirm that God has set people free from the effects of sin, have acquiesced to the reprehensible institution of slavery? This is a serious question deserving a serious answer, though any answer will be partial at best. The discussion about slaves take place within the larger context of the discussion about social relations and duties in those relationships. There is a tension in this material admirably described by John Elliott:

> Where respect for authority and order is possible without compromise of one's loyalty to God, this respect ("honor" and "subordination") is appropriate. Where, however, adaptation to societal values and norms endangers exclusive commitment to God, Christ, and the brotherhood and obliterates the distinctive identity and boundaries of the Christian community, Christians are to stand fast and resist the encroachments of society, behind which stands the Devil (5:8-9). Keeping open the channels of communication between believers and nonbelievers is not to be confused with advocacy of social assimilation. . . . Contacts between believers and nonbelievers are to be utilized as an opportunity for demonstrating the honorable character of the Christians and their God and are essential for recruitment to the Christian faith.[81]

Even a slave can model Christlikeness; indeed, in some respects especially a slave can do so.

We begin by observing that here we are dealing with the *oiketai*, the household or domestic slaves, in relationship to non-Christian masters (cf. 1 Tim 6:1-2; Ignatius, *Pol.* 4:3). The focus here is quite narrow and specific. Furthermore, it is noteworthy that slaves are addressed at all in these Christian codes, because in the Greco-Roman codes they were not addressed. Here they are treated as persons capable of moral discernment, which is the opposite end of the spectrum from classical theory, which treated them simply as living property lacking the essential qualifications of humanity. Peter is a sensible enough pastor to help his charges make the best of a bad situation, trying to alleviate the problem while figuring out what would be the best witness to the non-Christian involved in the situation.

A general exhortation begins 1 Peter 2:18, as was the case with 1 Peter 2:13. All household slaves are to submit to the master of the house whether he is

---

[81]John H. Elliott, *1 Peter* (AB 37B; New York: Doubleday, 2000), p. 510.

good and considerate or harsh ("crooked" is the literal meaning of *skolios*; cf. NET: "perverse"). This submission is to be offered in all respect, regardless of the treatment one receives in response. It therefore is a matter of principle and of being proactive rather than reactive, but it is also a witnessing tactic, as we will see. Notice that Peter recognizes that there is such a thing as unjust treatment of slaves, whereas Aristotle thought that no true injustice could be done to them, since they were property. Peter, by contrast, views them and wants them treated as persons, persons capable of a relationship with God and of moral decision-making.

There is debate about the referent of the phrase "in all fear." It could refer to fear of God (on *phobos*, see in the LXX, e.g., Gen 31:42, 53; Ex 20:20; Neh 5:9; Prov 1:7, 2), but the natural reference is to *despotais* ("masters") in the clause that follows. Still, 1 Peter 2:17 may suggest otherwise. At the start of 1 Peter 2:19 is the phrase "for this is *charis*," which probably means "a credit to you" or "commendable"; it does not likely mean "grace" here as it does elsewhere in the New Testament. Peter then speaks in terms of a real condition: "If you bear grief, suffering unjustly, this is to your credit" (*ei* plus the present-tense verb indicates a real condition, not a hypothetical one). The phrase *dia syneidēsin theou* is a difficult one. Does it mean (1) "through the conscience of God" (a literal rendering); (2) "through consciousness or awareness of God"; (3) "through common knowledge of God"? In favor of the first option is that elsewhere in the New Testament and in 1 Peter 3:16, 21 the word *syneidēsis* usually means "conscience." But the problem is that Peter cannot be talking about God's conscience here, and that is normally how one would have to construe the genitive here. The argument can go either way at this point, but perhaps the second and third options, which amount to "being conscious of God" (i.e., "being aware that God is taking note of your behavior"), offer the most likely rendering. The advice to slaves is actually advice to all Christians: all should be prepared to endure unjust suffering.

Peter goes on to say that certainly there is no glory in suffering quietly when you deserve a beating, having done wrong. Creditable or grace-filled *(charis)* behavior in God's eyes is when one suffers for or with the doing of what is right. The focus is on doing right here, not on developing a martyr complex or seeking out suffering. Here is advice on how to bear suffering if it does come, even if it is unjust punishment. Peter assumes this to be really happening (*ei* plus the verb). Such patience and suffering, even if wrong, is

what Christians (not just slaves) are called to. The context may suggest that
he is simply talking about suffering "in house," at the hands of one's master.
Here, really for the first time, Peter begins to broach the subject of suffering,
which is to be a major theme throughout the rest of the discourse. Twelve
of the forty-two New Testament occurrences of *paschō* ("to suffer") occur
in 1 Peter (1 Pet 2:19, 20, 21, 23; 3:14, 17, 18; 4:1 [2x], 15, 19; 5:10), as do
four of the sixteen New Testament occurrences of the cognate noun *pathēma*
(1 Pet 1:11; 4:13; 5:1, 9). It is quite obvious that the Christian response to
suffering is a major concern for Peter.

Not accidentally or incidentally, grace *(charis)* is also a major concern in
1 Peter. Goppelt remarks, "No other New Testament document appropriates
this technical term as densely and in a similarly broad variety of usage as does
1 Peter."[82] It begins at the very outset of the letter in 1 Peter 1:2, where the
author prays that grace be upon the addressees. The God of this discourse
is called the "God of all grace" (1 Pet 5:10), even to the extent of bringing
the believer to the eschatological finish line, where grace is once more encountered (1 Pet 1:13). This grace bestows new life in the first place (1 Pet
3:7), is given to the humble (1 Pet 5:5), and becomes the essence of what is
proclaimed in the gospel message (1 Pet 1:10). It is interesting that only in
1 Peter, outside of the Pauline corpus, do we have the mention and discussion
of *charismata* ("gifts" [1 Pet 4:10]). In sum, Peter has a full-orbed theology of
grace comparable to that of Paul.

Peter does not mention slaves by name here. This is advice for all household
members, including slaves. They must remember that Christ suffered for them,
leaving an example so that believers might follow in his footsteps. Here Peter
sees Christ's suffering as vicarious. It is "for us." This may indicate just for the
benefit of believers, but as we will see, it is also Peter's view that Christ's suffering was in place of us, as a substitute. Notice that the call for slaves to imitate
Christ here becomes a general call for all Christians in 1 Peter 3:9.

In 1 Peter 2:21-25 we have something of a meditation on Isaiah 53:4-12
LXX. Scholars have debated whether here Peter is taking over some source,
but probably the poetic diction of Isaiah 53 has inspired the more exalted
prose of this little paragraph. This meditation is framed by references to the
believer's conversion (1 Pet 2:21, 25). At 1 Peter 2:22 is a direct quotation
Isaiah 53:9b LXX, and there are clear allusions to Isaiah 53:4, 12b in 1 Peter
2:24 (e.g., "he bore our sins"); 1 Peter 2:23 then can be seen as a reformula-

---

[82]Goppelt, *1 Peter*, p. 200.

tion of Isaiah 53:9 about the silence of the sheep before their slaughterers, making it applicable to the experience of persecuted Christians. We can also point directly to 1 Peter 2:24, with its quotation "by whose wounds you have been healed" (Is 53:5b), but note the shift from Isaiah's first-person plural to the second-person plural.

Notice that Peter does not follow the order of the narrative in Isaiah 53, and here the result of Christ's passion is healing of sinners. The reference to shepherd and sheep probably echoes Isaiah 53:5-6, but there is also another intertextual echo here that rounds out the brief passage, this one to Ezekiel 34:5-16, the promise about God the shepherd looking after his sheep. In this case it is Christ who is the shepherd (1 Pet 2:25). What is striking is that the passage thus ends with an allusion to a word of comfort to resident alien Jews in Babylon now applied to Peter's resident alien Jewish Christians in Anatolia. We are now prepared to look at these crucial verses in some detail, bearing in mind what Howard Marshall says about its importance: "Here, then, is the fundamental theological statement of the basis of the Christian life in terms of the death of Jesus. It becomes obvious . . . that Christ cannot be an example of suffering for us to follow unless he is first of all the Savior whose sufferings were endured on our behalf."[83]

There is something quite interesting about this meditation that we should note at the outset. This is the only place in the New Testament where Isaiah 53 is so explicitly referred to the death of Jesus as a way of explaining that death. We perhaps owe to Peter himself the insight that Christ's passion is specifically referred to in Isaiah 53. Of the six direct quotations of Isaiah 53 in the New Testament (Mt 8:17; Lk 22:37; Jn 12:38; Acts 8:32-33; Rom 10:16; 15:12), only two are used in reference to Jesus in particular (here and Acts 8:32-33). In Acts 8:32-33 there is no actual meditation as there is here on Jesus and the relating of this passage to Jesus and his sacrifice. "We are thus indebted to the apostle Peter alone for his distinctive Christological use of the Suffering Servant passage to interpret the significance of the suffering and death of Jesus. The Suffering Servant Christology may even have originated with Peter, possibly based on Jesus' teaching."[84]

In 1 Peter 2:21 the author uses some interesting language to describe the example of Christ. First, there is the term *hypogrammos*, which refers to the exact pattern of alphabetic letters, impressed on a wax tablet, which children

---

[83]I. Howard Marshall, *1 Peter* (IVPNTC; Downers Grove, Ill.: InterVarsity Press, 1991), p. 91.
[84]Karen H. Jobes, *1 Peter* (BECNT; Grand Rapids: Baker Academic, 2005), p. 193.

copied or traced so as to learn their letters. The patterns of the letters were impressed into the wax so that the children could copy them, learning how to form their ABC's (cf. 2 Macc 2:28; Clement of Alexandria, *Strom.* 5.8.49; *1 Clem.* 5:7; 16:17; 33:8). Second, there is the word "steps" in this verse. The image is of walking behind someone and literally following in that person's footsteps (cf. Philo, *Virtues* 64). Notice that the author uses an intensified verb, *epakoloutheō*, thus the meaning "follow closely as a disciple" (cf. *akoloutheō* in Rev 14:4, where the redeemed "follow" the Lamb).

The essence of ancient education was following good models, imitating or copying them, and repetition to the point of memorization. The most basic idea here is the patient endurance of unjust suffering, of which Christ is the model. Nothing is said here about seeking martyrdom or suffering, nor even about suffering being the will of God for the audience's life. Peter is saying that if suffering comes, let it be for a just cause and therefore be an unjust form of suffering, not the sort that amounts to punishment for wrongs done. Finally, we should also note that the verb *paschō* sometimes has specific reference to the death of Christ, not merely his preliminary suffering (see Lk 22:15; 24:26, 46; Acts 1:3; 3:18; 17:3; Heb 9:26; 13:12), though it can also refer to the sufferings leading up to the death (Mk 8:31; but cf. Heb 2:18; 5:8, where it refers to Christ's suffering of temptation or in the garden of Gethsemane). In 1 Peter Christians not only have sufferings for which the same terminology is used (1 Pet 5:9-10), but also they participate in Christ's sufferings in some sense (1 Pet 4:13). The paralleling of Christ's story and the story of the audience can be seen in this light: just as Christ suffered in the past, so now believers suffer in the present, and just as Christ was glorified thereafter, so also believers one day will be glorified. In the meantime, the pattern of Christ that believers are to follow is (1) avoid committing sin; (2) do not retaliate; (3) bear with abuse and injustice; (4) recognize in Christ's death a healing.

In 1 Peter 2:22 the author mentions the sinlessness of Christ. Here indeed was unjust suffering. Jesus had done no wrong, and yet he experienced the punishment reserved for the worst slaves and individuals. Here and in 1 Peter 2:23-25 the author is quoting and alluding to Isaiah 53. Christ is seen in light of the suffering servant. Jesus' response was not only to not retaliate, but also to rest his case in the hands of the one truly fair judge, God. The implication is that Christians should do likewise. Peter is saying, "Act as Christ did, on Christian principles, not in response to un-Christian persecution. Do not react in a way that vitiates your Christian life and witness." One of the most interesting aspects of this teaching and use of Isaiah 53 is that it implies that Jesus' teaching about not resisting the one who is evil (Mt 5:39) perhaps was derived from his own reflections on Isaiah 53, but here it is also used as the basis for the disciple's code of conduct (cf. 1 Pet 3:9).

Peter's view of the atonement is seen in some depth in 1 Peter 2:24. Christ took up the cross or bore on the cross in his own body our sins—that is, the punishment for our sins. The phrase "in his body" stresses Christ's humanity. He was truly human, and redemption came through a real historical person. He suffered too, he suffered unjustly, he suffered for those who deserved to suffer as sinners. Here sins may be seen as a burden that Christ lifts from human beings. Since Isaiah 53 is likely in the background here, it also is likely that the implied idea is that Christ bore the punishment for human sins in their stead. Thus, here we have substitutionary atonement by the suffering servant. It is also implied that Jesus takes away human sins; that is, he heals us. To what end? Not only so that human beings might experience redemption, but also so that they may die to sin and live to righteousness, as Christ himself died for sin and lived in righteousness. Christ's death, if one accepts it, requires a willingness to go and sin no more lest one crucify Christ afresh by further sins. Thus, theology necessarily leads to ethics in 1 Peter. To accept Christ means to agree to follow in his righteous footsteps and not to crucify him afresh by sinning again.

At the end of 1 Peter 2:24 we read, "By his wounds/welts we are healed of our sin sickness." The word *mōlōps* means "welt," referring to the marks on the body of one who has been whipped, such as a slave (cf. Is 53:5 LXX). Recall that in Philippians 2 Jesus is said to be a suffering slave, and he received a slave's final punishment, crucifixion. What better way to encourage Christian slaves than to say in fact that Jesus voluntarily became a slave for their sake? "He knows what you go through. He has been there too." Sin is also seen here as a disease that affects one's whole person—desires, thought patterns and so on—not just one's behavior. It is a deadly cancer of which one must be healed lest one be lost.

In 1 Peter 3:1-7 we come to the conclusion of Peter's social code or the household ethics section of it. In 1 Peter 2:13–3:7 we are dealing with material common to the early Christian church, not Peter's invention, as a glance at 1 Corinthians 14; 1 Timothy 2; Ephesians 5–6; Titus 2; 1 Peter; Colossians 3–4 will show. There is an especially close correspondence between 1 Peter

3:3-5 and 1 Timothy 2:9-15 in terms of both vocabulary and substance. We should compare the advice about women's adornments in 1 Peter 3:3 to 1 Timothy 2:9, the call for women's quietness in 1 Peter 3:4 to 1 Timothy 2:11-12, and the use of *kosmeō* ("to adorn") in 1 Peter 3:5 to the use of *kosmeō* and *kosmios* ("well ordered") in 1 Timothy 2:9.

How do we account for this? It is possible to argue for some sort of literary dependency, but it is far more likely that both authors are drawing on some standard early Christian teaching. If so, it provides us with more explanation for the unity of New Testament ethics: all the New Testament writers approved of and drew on the same ethical source material, both Jewish and Christian, both scriptural and otherwise. Peter adopts and adapts this basic Christian teaching to his situation of Christians being persecuted while seeking that they may continue to bear witness to their non-Christian family members and neighbors. This raises the question of how much this material is to be seen as prudential or tactical and situational and how much as a matter of principle for Peter.

David Balch's comments are worth quoting at length:

> Close attention to the text of the household duty code in 1 Peter in its Greco-Roman context enables further specification of the socio-religious situation in which the code functioned. The general situation was . . . [this]: Greco-Roman society suspected and criticized foreign religions. Many of the Christians addressed by the author had rejected traditional religion (1:18b), and the author exhorted Christians to the kind of behavior that would silence the negative reactions which such conversions generated (2:11-12, 15). The stress on "harmony" in the conclusion of the code (3:8) reveals that the author was especially concerned about divided households: many masters and husbands were still pagans, while some slaves and wives had converted to Christianity. In these divided houses, the harmony demanded by the Hellenistic moralists had been disturbed, which was judged to be a negative reflection on the new religion. The author exhorts his readers to make a "defense" (3:15) by reassuring the masters and husbands, perhaps even the governor, that they are obedient slaves and wives, just as the culture expected them to be. Christians are not to exacerbate the situation by meddling in others' domestic affairs (4:15). The readers are warned that governors punish insubordinate persons but are reassured that the authorities praise those who accept their role in the socio-political system (2:14).
>
> The household duty code addressed by the author to this situation is adapted from the Aristotelian topos "concerning household management." He modi-

fied the form by addressing the persons in those roles where tension was focused: slaves and wives. As was traditional in certain strands of Platonic and Neopythagorean literature, the author exhorted wives to be submissive. He silently passed over the Greco-Roman expectation that such submission would include worship of the gods of the husband and master. Some of the husbands had not converted, and given the cultural assumptions of that society, they were probably among those persons slandering the converts. The author exhorted the women to submissive, gentle, quiet, chaste behavior, which might gain the husbands for Christ. They were to take Sarah for their model, who was submissive to Abraham, in whose house God had made "peace," and who led Abraham to a higher vision of God. Whatever domestic, social, or political developments might occur, the wives were not to be terrified (3:6). . . .

The code is paraenetic; it is addressed to Christians, not outsiders. But it was not adopted because eschatological hopes had faded and Christians felt more at home in society. Rather, the code has an apologetic function in the historical context; the paraenesis is given in light of outside criticism. Persons in Roman society were alienated and threatened by some of their slaves and wives who had converted to the new, despised religion, so they were accusing the converts of impiety, immorality, and insubordination. As a defense, the author of 1 Peter encouraged the slaves and wives to play the social roles which Aristotle had outlined; this, he hoped, would shame those who were reviling their good behavior (3:16; 2:12). The conduct of the slaves was not expected to convert masters. However, the author hoped that the wives would convert their husbands by laudable behavior.[85]

In my view, this assessment largely accounts for the occasion of this section but does not entirely do justice to its function. What Peter advises here is indeed a matter of principle for him. Thus, for instance, submission to governors is simply positive Christian teaching. It is not merely because persecution loomed, but it is seen as good missionary practice. Further, part of the point of citing the example of Sarah in 1 Peter 3:6 is that this pattern of behavior has a biblical basis, not merely a basis in contemporary culture. Peter is urging these women to conform to the type, and the implication is that the basic behavioral model or conduct or mode of relationship has not changed and should not change.

In addition, it is not the case that Peter is dealing exclusively with mixed marriages, where tensions obviously exist. He says in 1 Peter 3:1, referring to husbands, that some disbelieve (disobey), not all. Thus, he cannot simply be

---

[85]Balch, *Let Wives Be Submissive*, pp. 108-9.

telling Christian women how to behave toward non-Christian mates, although
that is the central thrust of 1 Peter 3:1-2. A woman's actions are to be taken
within the context of the "pure reverence of God," not merely because it will
prevent abuse by non-Christians. Christian women are to stand on their principles and not be intimidated by hostile mates (cf. the end of 1 Pet 3:6).

Thus, we must conclude the following: (1) this material is a specific application of general Christian social teaching about submission or deference;
(2) this material is occasioned by Christians being persecuted and partially
addresses the tension between Christians and non-Christians, but its advice is
of value and relevance to a wider context as well; (3) not only is such behavior
to be based on matters of Christian respect and holiness principles, but also
the failure to behave in the way described can interfere with one's relationship to God through prayer (1 Pet 3:7b); (4) there is also a missionary motive
to at least some of the behavior. It is not all a matter of apologetics, and it
certainly is not primarily a matter of accommodation to society in general.
Rather, it is a Christian adaptation of the social structures to make it possible
for Christians to continue to practice their religion, which included bearing
witness and being a good citizen. One more thing can be said. Probably some
distinction is being made between a Christian marriage and a mixed marriage in terms of the relationship between husband and wife. The Christian
husband is expected to honor the women in his household and to see them,
or at least the wife, as coheirs of the grace of life. "So necessary is this second
admonition that for the Christian man to ignore it is to have God ignore him:
the prayers of a Christian husband and head of a household who acts otherwise will be ignored by God."[86] In other words, it is incorrect to see here a
fall from the high-water mark of equality in Galatians 3:28.

At 1 Peter 3:1 the term *homoiōs* ("similarly") indicates a new subsection
of the household code. Peter is not saying that women are just like slaves and
must defer and submit like them, but rather that there is a general pattern of
orderliness and deference that has similarities with all these cases, whether it
be all believers respecting and deferring to rulers or all household members
respecting and deferring to the head of the household. We must stress here
that this is in-house advice. Peter is not talking in general about women
submitting to men; here, within the structure of the house or home, wives
and husbands are the sole focus. This is especially clear from the use here of
the word *idios*, which means "one's own." Family relationships were a vital

---

[86]Achtemeier, *1 Peter*, p. 209.

part of early Christianity. Peter wishes them to be seen within the context of the wider Christian family and allow Christian principles and behavior to structure the situation in the physical family, not vice versa. This, then, is not merely an acquiescence to cultural norms for prudential or other reasons; rather, it is the Christianization of non-Christian institutions by changing the Christian individuals and their behavior in these institutions.[87] Indeed, as we saw when we examined Jesus' ethical teachings earlier, it is a matter of following the lead provided by Jesus himself.

We can say with some assurance that women in Anatolia (i.e., the provinces mentioned in 1 Pet 1:1-2) had opportunities to engage in private businesses, serve in some public offices, assume prominent roles in religious cults, run their own households, have some property rights and gain some education to a degree not possible in Peter's native setting, the Holy Land.[88] What "respect" and "defer" to one's husband normally was understood to mean in these provinces would have been something less restrictive than in other settings, and since Peter apparently had been to these regions, he would have known this. What amounted to respectable behavior in one social setting would have been different from what that entailed in others. This is why 1 Peter 3:1-2 suggests that wives are primarily to defer because of the Christian influence that it will give them. In other words, this advice is, to an important degree, pragmatic and missional in concept. The wives are to win over their husbands without a word. It is tremendously significant that there were wives in Peter's audiences who did not practice the religion of their mate or perhaps of their parents. This tells us something about the freedom that at least some women had in these areas.

Notice that Peter starts with wives here, as he did with slaves before, and before that those being ruled. His subject is submission or deference, perhaps because this was where problems were arising, as Balch suggests, but also because this was where guidance was needed. Peter does not say, "Husbands, counsel your wives to submit," or vice versa. This must be an individual and willing action of the party involved, not enforced subordination. Here the verb *hypotassō* is in participial form used like an imperative *(hypotassomenai)*, but perhaps not with the full force of an imperative, as Balch says: "The

---

[87]For a more extended discussion of women in the Greco-Roman world, see Ben Witherington III, *Women in the Earliest Churches* (SNTSMS 59; Cambridge: Cambridge University Press, 1988), pp. 1-23.

[88]See ibid., chap. 1.

participle never attained the full strength of an imperative but rather had the character of describing what should be."[89] The form is mild and passive and may be seen as reflexive here: not "submit," but "you should defer/submit yourselves." But to whom is this voluntary serving to be rendered? The answer given is "your own husband" (cf. 1 Cor 14:34). Peter does not extrapolate this act to include all husbands or all men.

The motive for submission in the case of a mixed marriage is at least in part so that if some husbands "disbelieve the word," the wives can win them "without a word." There is a play on *logos* ("word"). In the first instance, it refers to gospel, and in the second instance it refers to a spoken word or possibly verbal propaganda. The definite article stands before the first reference to distinguish it from the second. The verb *kerdainō* ("to win, gain") has a clear missionary sense (cf. Mt 18:15; 1 Cor 9:22).

Thus, the paradigm of silent, irreproachable, deferential conduct is seen as a total witness to a possibly irritated husband who perhaps had already grown tired of hearing about Jesus. The wife acts in fear of God—that is, with proper awe and morality and due respect for all authority that God has ordained, including the head of the household.

I emphasize at this juncture that Peter's advice here runs directly against the flow of normal household advice regarding religion. Consider, for example, this from Plutarch:

> A wife ought not to make friends on her own, but to enjoy her husband's friends in common with him. The gods are the first and most important friends. Therefore it is becoming for a wife to worship and know only the gods that her husband believes in, and to shut the front door tight upon all peculiar rituals and outlandish superstitions [read: "Eastern religions such as Judaism and Christianity and the worship of Isis and Serapis"]. For with no god do secret rites performed by a woman find any favor. . . . Since some [men] . . . cannot well endure the sight of scarlet and purple clothes, while others are annoyed by cymbals and drums, what terrible hardship is it for women to refrain from such [religious] things, and not disquiet or irritate their husbands, but live with them in constant gentleness. (*Mor.* 140D; 144 D-E)

According to Plutarch, religion is the preeminent thing in which a wife should follow her husband's lead, and certainly she should refrain from trying to influence her husband to join some pernicious Eastern *superstitio*. Peter advises just the opposite. He wants wives to win their husbands to the Christian

---

[89]Balch, *Let Wives Be Submissive*, p. 97.

faith. A wife's practice of a nontraditional religion would have been seen as an act of rebellion by many a husband and as a violation of the social order. Furthermore, a wife who persisted in attending Christian worship could bring shame upon her husband if his friends and neighbors found out. Then too, Peter himself could be accused of usurping the role of the husband by daring to give imperatives to slaves and wives in these religiously mixed homes. Therefore, since there is to be no compromise on religion, they must find other forms of behavior that please their mates—for example, how they dress. But there is no escaping that the uncompromising stand on religion could be seen as unsettling at the least and subversive at the most.

What follows in 1 Peter 3:3 is a very typical contrast between outward and inward beauty, a common enough subject for pagan writers. The point here is that character, not appearance, is what really matters to God and is also what will be likely to win people to Christ. A woman who simply dresses like other well-to-do women will appear no different from other people, whereas a woman who chooses a simple appearance, reserved demeanor and pure behavior will attract attention. To do the latter is to get attention in the right way, and it might lead some to ask, "Why is she different?" This section is very similar to 1 Timothy 2 and implies that there were some well-to-do women already involved in Christianity who had money for such clothes and hairdos. It is possible, though not certain, that Peter wants Christian women to avoid ostentatious outward appearance because this is also how *hetaerae* ("companions")[90] and prostitutes often dressed in Hellenistic style. Consider, for example, this Neo-Pythagorean advice:

> The temperate, freeborn woman must live with her legal husband adorned with modesty, clad in a neat, simple, white dress. . . . She must avoid clothing that is either entirely purple or is streaked with purple and gold, for that kind of dress is worn by *hetaerae* when they stalk the masses of men. . . . You should have a blush on your cheeks as a sign of modesty instead of rouge, and should wear nobility, decorum, and temperance instead of gold and emeralds. (Pseudo-Melista, *Letter to Kleareta* 160-162)

If such is in view here in 1 Peter, this type of dress might be associated with immoral behavior and be a bad witness suggesting that the Christian

---

[90]"Companions" were women who accompanied prominent men to social and public functions, particularly in sections of the empire where it was deemed immodest for the wife to go to the theater or to gladiatorial contests.

wife was either immoral or too worldly (cf. *1 En.* 8:1; Philo, *Virtues* 39-40). It is quite clear that women in Asia Minor, Greece, Rome, and Egypt had more freedom and access to money than Jewish women in the Holy Land had, and so Peter probably is dealing with a real case, not a hypothetical one. Braided hair, gold jewelry, and fine clothes refer to the refined apparel and coiffures of the elite, especially if they wove jewels into the hair.[91] Notice too that Peter in no way councils divorce in the case of a mixed marriage, but rather, as Paul urges, "you may win him to Christ by staying" (see 1 Corinthians 7:12-16).

In 1 Peter 3:4 the author stresses the contrast: develop and be beautiful in "the hidden person of the heart" (*ho kryptos tēs kardias anthrōpos* [cf. Rom 2:15; 2 Cor 4:16; Eph 3:17]). In the background here is the idea that God looks upon the heart, not the outward appearance, and that this generally is what matters. The phrase may mean "the inner person who dwells in the heart" or "the unseen person, the heart" if the genitive phrase is in apposition, but probably the former. The focus is on the whole person, as determined from the heart. What is really of lasting and imperishable or even "immortal" (the literal meaning of *aphthartos*) value is a gentle and quiet spirit, which Jesus himself is said to have modeled (Mt 11:29; 21:5). This surely can refer only to the human spirit and is not a reference to a part of one's being, for it refers to one's disposition, frame of mind, way of relating to and dealing with the outer world. It is a quality of character, not an anatomical part. Three things indicate that this is not a reference to the Holy Spirit: (1) the context refers to human behavior; (2) the model that follows, Sarah, had not received the Holy Spirit; (3) the Spirit in the New Testament is hardly quiet, but rather is dynamic, and the Spirit inspires words, not hinders them. Interestingly, this positive character trait is described as imperishable. The point is that, unlike outward beauty, it cannot fade away. Peter stresses that this is what pleases God; it is precious to him.

The author then speaks in 1 Peter 3:5 of holy women of the Old Testament. Here "holy" may mean morally upright, or just chosen by God, or both, but in any case the phrase "holy women" is unique in the canon. Peter cites but one example, and probably he has in mind Isaiah 51:2, "Look to Abraham your father, and to Sarah who gave you birth," as well as Genesis 18:1-15 LXX (cf. Gen 12; 20, where she is also prominent). However, it is not just the Old Testament texts, but also the intertestamental literature,

---

[91]See Witherington, *Women in the Earliest Churches*, pp. 120-22.

about Sarah that may lie in the background here. Thus, for instance, in *Testament of Abraham* (*T. Ab.* A 5:12-13; A 6:2, 4, 5, 8; A 15: 4) Sarah appears as an example of good deeds and fearlessness, and she is called the "mother of the elect." Sarah, in a whimsical mood, calls Abraham "master," and this is conventional terminology of respect meaning "sir" or referring to him as head of the household. It need not imply more here. Peter is simply trying to insist on respect even for non-Christian husbands. It is perhaps fair to say that Peter relies more on the portrait of Sarah in *Testament of Abraham*, where she appears as a rather conventional Hellenistic woman addressing her husband as "master," than on the less submissive portrait of her in Genesis.

It is hard to say what Peter has in mind when he says, "She obeyed Abraham." It could mean that she followed his directions even when she was told to say that Abraham was her brother (Gen 12:10-20), or more likely that she obeyed him in preparing a meal on the spot when he requested it (Gen 18:1-8). Notice that although Sarah follows her husband's religion, Peter does not suggest that a Christian wife should obey her pagan husband in the matter of following his religion, which was normally expected; the family would believe as the head of the household did. This is why in 1 Peter 3:7 Peter addresses husbands and assumes that all Christian husbands have Christian wives in Anatolia. They are all coheirs of grace. The danger was that Christian wives in a mixed marriage could lose heart or become intimidated, perhaps due to persecution or verbal abuse. Peter insists that a Christian wife should stick to her guns and live as Sarah did, doing good, trusting God, and hoping in God.

It may be in 1 Peter 3:7 that Peter intends only that Christian husbands should respect their wives, remembering that they are the "weaker vessel." It has been suggested, however, that "live with/cohabit according to knowledge" *(synoikeō kata gnōsin)* is a euphemism that refers to fulfilling one's conjugal duty in regard to sexual intercourse (cf. Gen 20:3 [of Abraham and Sarah]; Deut 22:3; 24:1; 25:5; Is 62:5; Sir 25:8), in which case 1 Corinthians 7 gives a commentary here. Probably, however, it involves all of their interaction, including sexual intercourse. Least likely is the view that "according to knowledge" means knowing that God is watching. Showing respect or honor to one's wife is vital and is indeed a means of the husband serving and submitting to his wife and her needs, just as *timē* in reference to the emperor refers to the form of submission (see 1 Pet 2:13, 17). This advice was necessary because men were likely to take the social code about women being subordinate to mean more than it ought to mean in a Christian context.

The use of the term *skeuos* is controversial. Does it mean "body" or "vessel" or "person"? It has been argued that "vessel" implies that the woman is an object, indeed a sex object, and this is degrading. However, since Peter says "weaker *skeuos*," he is implying that the husband is also a *skeuos*, and so no such implication can be drawn here. The clause literally reads, "as with a weaker vessel, a feminine one." Probably the reference is to woman as physically weaker. It certainly is not a reference to woman as morally, spiritually, or intellectually inferior, since Peter goes on to say that she is coheir of the grace of life.

Too often in pagan remarks about women and the household derogatory comments are made about women and their inferiority to men. For example, *Letter of Aristeas* 250 says, "The female sex is bold, positively active for something which it desires, easily liable to change its mind because of poor reasoning powers, and of naturally weak constitution." Peter's remarks are restrained by comparison. So *skeuos* in 1 Peter 3:7 probably means "person," with a special emphasis on the frail mortal form. In 1 Thessalonians 4:4 *skeuos* likely also refers to one's wife, not one's own physical body.[92] In addition, there is material of relevance where women call themselves "those of weaker nature" (see *CPR* 15 from Hermopolis; P.Oxy. 1 [1898] 71, col. 2 [303]). Peter, then, is simply talking about a physical weakness, as is especially clear from his use of the word *skeuos*, which never occurs in these inscriptions that are talking about either a weak "nature" or a weak social position.

Peter is saying that women, equally with men, stand before God as fully heirs of God's grace, kingdom, salvation and eternal life. There is no higher privilege. If that will govern our thinking, and we are called to have the attitude that God has, as Peter insists, there can be no denigrating of females or relegating them to an inferior place in life on the basis of this text. We see here the reformation, though not the outright abolition, of patriarchal culture, as also is the case with Paul. Finally, Peter points out that unless a husband acts with full respect for his wife, it will hinder his prayers. That is, his relationship with God is intertwined with his love and respect for his fellow humans, especially his wife. One relationship affects the other. Here it is probably only the husband's prayers that are in view, since 1 Peter 3:1 begins with *hoi andres*.[93]

---

[92]See Ben Witherington III, *1 and 2 Thessalonians: A Socio-Rhetorical Commentary* (Grand Rapids: Eerdmans, 2006), pp. 109-18.

[93]Two detailed studies about early Christian families and household and also about the family of

This argument concludes in 1 Peter 3:8-12 (note how 1 Pet 3:8 begins with *to de telos* ["finally"]) with a return to the themes involving Christian character enunciated earlier (cf. especially 1 Pet 2:23 with 1 Pet 3:9). There is considerable verbal similarity between what we find here and Romans 12:10-17, suggesting that there was an early Christian ethical tradition shared rather widely, and close examination also suggests that it was in various respects grounded in the ethic of the Sermon on the Mount (cf. *Did.* 1:3; Pol. *Phil.* 2:2). Notice also that the citation of Psalm 34 functions to provide further backing from the sacred text for the ethic of Jesus. In other words, the ethic is not derived by Peter from the psalm, but rather is bolstered and supported by the use of the psalm. And this is the same psalm that Peter previously used to urge the audience to taste and see that the Lord is good.

Here Peter returns to a general exhortation to all his audience and concludes by quoting from a source that he often has in mind, Psalm 34. We may also note that Proverbs 3–4 are also often in the background here. Peter calls Christians to harmony, to all be "of one mind" (*homophrōn*, in its only New Tesament occurrence; cf. Phil 2:2), and to have genuine compassion for one another (*sympathēs*, whence the English word *sympathy*, meaning "suffering with" [cf. Rom 12:15; 1 Cor 12:26; Heb 4:15; 10:34]). Goppelt aptly comments that what results from harmony is "not uniformity but unanimity."[94]

The Greek word *tapeinophrōn* is interesting because it has a unique meaning in Christian contexts. In pagan contexts it is a derogatory term meaning something like "base-minded, ignoble, low, mean," and often it was applied to slaves and their behavior. But Peter sees it as a virtue. It expresses a character directly modeled on Christ and "humbling oneself." Ernest Best adds "a humble mind" (cf. Eph 4:2; Phil 2:3-8; 1 Pet 5:5-6). "This represents a new quality of life which was introduced by Christianity into the Hellenistic world. In classical Greek the underlying word possessed the sense 'base,' 'mean'; in the Christian faith it obtained a new meaning and signified a new virtue 'humility.'"[95] John Elliott is right to add, "In the highly competitive and stratified world of Greco-Roman antiquity, only those of degraded social status were 'humble' and humility was regarded as a sign of weakness and shame, an inability to defend one's

---

faith should be consulted: David L. Balch and Carolyn Osiek, *Families in the New Testament World: Households and House Churches* (Louisville: Westminster John Knox, 1997); Joseph H. Hellerman, *The Ancient Church as Family* (Minneapolis: Fortress, 2001).

[94]Goppelt, *1 Peter*, p. 233.

[95]Ernest Best, *1 Peter* (Edinburgh: T & T Clark, 2004), p. 129.

honor. Thus the high value placed on humility by Israelites and Christians is remarkable."[96]

Notice that this virtue is expected of all believers. They are all called to be servants. Humility comes not from a low opinion of self but rather from a high opinion of God, realizing how much believers owe God and are dependent on God. This is real humility, not false modesty, that Christ calls believers to, and it involves deeds of service, not a craven attitude that denigrates self. This first verse of the summation seems to refer primarily if not exclusively to behavior among Christians themselves. Peter may be remembering what it was like early on in the Jerusalem church (cf. Acts 2:42-47; 4:32-37). In 1 Peter 3:9 we have a repetition of the theme of nonretaliation found in 1 Peter 2:23. Retaliation is a natural and normal response, but it is not a Christian response. Rather, we are to bless those who curse us, so that we might inherit a blessing (cf. Lk 6:28a; 1 Cor 4:12). This teaching here is closest to what we find in Luke 6:27-28.

Here we see the influence of early Christian teaching (cf. Mt 5:12; 25:31-46; Rom 15) and the teaching of Jesus, which was widely known and used in the early church. Notice in 1 Peter 3:9b how a believer's inheritance of a blessing is contingent on that believer giving a blessing through certain forms of behavior. Again the connection between ethics and grace is clearly seen. The receiving cannot be isolated from the giving. It is not clear what this "blessing" to be inherited is. It could be a reference to longer life on earth in view of the psalm that follows this verse, but it could look forward to final salvation. If it is the latter, it is important to note that an inheritance is not something that one earns by good deeds.

Peter's quotation of Psalm 34 in 1 Peter 3:10-12 modifies the psalm in several ways: (1) He omits Psalm 34:16, which discusses the destruction of the evildoers or their "remembrance." Quoting that verse probably would have upset Christians with pagan mates or friends, which would not help. (2) He smooths out the awkward LXX reading. (3) The original reference to length of life on this earth may have been altered to a love of and longing for eternal life here. "Wishing love of life" seems to imply something that the author does not have (cf. 1 Pet 3:9, which speaks of a coming blessing). (4) There is a change from questions to statements. This is but a part of a larger pattern of use of Psalm 34, as we can see from the following comparison:

---

[96]Elliott, *1 Peter*, p. 605.

Table 10.3. The Use of Psalm 34 in 1 Peter

Ps 34:1	1 Pet 1:3
Ps 34:4	1 Pet 1:17
Ps 34:5	1 Pet 2:6
Ps 34:7	1 Pet 1:17
Ps 34:9, 11	1 Pet 2:17
Ps 34:17	1 Pet 3:12
Ps 34:19	1 Pet 1:6
Ps 34:22	1 Pet 1:18; 2:16

What we notice here is that in this discourse Peter is not sequentially working through this psalm, nor is he expositing it; rather, he uses the text sometimes to reinforce what he is saying and sometimes to obtain the biblical vocabulary to speak meaningfully to the audience (implicitly drawing an analogy between the suffering that they are going through and that of the righteous sufferer spoken of in the psalm). Many of these echoes and allusions would have been lost on a formerly pagan audience, though some God-fearers may have picked up an echo here and there. The use of the text is remarkably skillful and subtle at points, and it also reflects sensitivity to the text's original sense and context. The elegant and allusive use of Psalm 34 is another small pointer toward the audience being primarily Jewish Christians and perhaps a few God-fearers, but not former pagans.

Believers are to cease evil speech, deceit and malevolence, and on the positive side they are to do "the good," actively work for and seek peace (in the Christian community but perhaps elsewhere as well, thus fulfilling Mt 5:9 [cf. Rom 12:18]). Then in 1 Peter 3:12 we are told why: God's eyes and ears are on believers, attending to them and listening to their prayers, but his face is set against evildoers. Anyone who wants prayers heard (cf. 1 Pet 3:7) must hear and do God's will; anyone who does not do so will be opposing, and opposed by, God. Thus, we have come back full circle to 1 Peter 2:12, and we can see how intentionally and carefully Peter's rhetoric has been crafted here to convey, reinforce, and make persuasive his message in a rhetoric-saturated environment.

Concluding Thoughts on the Ethics of 1 Peter

I have lingered for a considerable period of time in the Petrine ethical vineyard for the very good reason that many have thought it to have produced a lot of sour grapes, which sets modern teeth on edge. However, when 1 Peter is rightly interpreted, this need not be the case. Peter is not baptizing either patriarchal or slave culture and simply calling it good. He is addressing an existing and ongoing social reality and trying to ameliorate the harsher effects of that reality on his audience, especially on its more vulnerable members. Equally clearly, he is mission-minded, and some of his advice has to do with behavior that might help a wife or a slave to win husband or master to Christ. Most remarkable is the paralleling of the suffering and humility of Christ with that of the slave.

Peter is concerned with the interface between the church and the world and with bearing a good witness to and in that world. Yet this does not cause him to compromise essential elements in the ethic that he inherited from the Old Testament and from Jesus, including the remarkable ethic of love and humility, a good deal of which was foreign to the wider culture. Wives are esteemed as coheirs of grace, slaves are treated as persons with consciences who can make their own moral judgments, and all Christians are expected to show respect and honor toward all other creatures on earth, including authority figures. Peter, unlike Paul in Romans 13, does not provide a warrant based on the notion that all governmental officials derive their authority/power ultimately from God. We will have occasion to explore that teaching in the next chapter. Here it is sufficient to note the intertwining of theology and ethics in 1 Peter 1–3.

Ethics turns out to be the emulation of the behavior of God in Christ to a considerable extent. As such, it is viewed as an essential expression of true faith and something that has a bearing on final salvation or the future inheritance of the kingdom. If theology is about the character and behavior of God, then Christian ethics is about the character and behavior of believers in response to God, relying on the grace of God, the power of God's Spirit, and the need to obey God, being holy as God is holy, loving as God is loving, and merciful as Christ is merciful. What is especially telling about the Petrine ethic is that Peter believes that such obedient behavior in itself helps to sanctify the saint. In other words, sanctification is not solely a work of God in the inner life of a Christian; it is also something Christians must cooperate with and make some contribution to. This is similar to the Paul dictum that believers must work out their salvation with fear and trembling as God is working in them.

SUMMARY

The nexus between theology and ethics is an important subject to discuss, and I will address it later in this study. Here it is sufficient to say that Peter reminds us that salvation is not just about theology or what God does for us; it is also about what God empowers us by grace to do and indeed requires us to do if we are to be saved to the uttermost. It is not just about God's holiness; it is about ours as well, which is possible only by the inward work of the purifying and empowering Spirit. And most importantly, the love ethic is not just about receiving God's love poured into our hearts; it is about our obedience to the great commandment to love God and neighbor wholeheartedly. In other words, ethics, keeping God's commandment, is not just an act of gratitude for what God has done; it is a necessary response to what God has enabled us to do. Faith without works, without love, without mercy, without obedience is dead and saves no one. This is made very clear indeed in more than one of the documents addressed largely to Jewish Christians that we have examined in this chapter. It remains to be seen if the ethical advice to Gentile Christians, to which we will turn next, has a similar flavor, fervor, and flair.

What is the engine that drives the train of the Jewish Christian ethics explored in this chapter? It is the transformed heart or inner person, or as Peter calls it, the "inner person of the heart," by means of what James calls the "implanted word." All the authors studied in this chapter offer a rigorist ethic based on the belief not only that human beings can change, but also in Christ they can and do become new creatures graced and enabled to manifest new attitudes, desires, virtues, and patterns of behavior. The Christian experience of Christ is seen as transformative of the inner person, beginning to be molded in the image of the Master. At the same time, the ethic is pragmatic in that time and again these authors show themselves to be sensitive to the delicate and difficult situations that Christians often faced in a pagan world. The authors' advice meets their audiences where they are, but then it leads them in paths of righteousness because the authors believe that "the one who is within you is great than those forces in the world" (1 Jn 4:4).

Here I must remark on the ethical seriousness of the literature investigated thus far, and how the Jewish Christian writers seem not only to be drawing on common source material but also using it in similar ways. There is a constant concern about pressure from the outside world, whether from pagan or Jewish sources, and its attempt to squeeze Christians into a non-Christian mold or to paint them into a sectarian and unsociable corner. An evangelistic religion needs to avoid such pigeonholing if it seeks to be winsome and win some. We see evidence in this material of what is nonnegotiable for Christians: their faith in Christ. They are to give no offense but the gospel, but they are not to compromise on the latter. The boundaries of the community are christologically drawn, both in a theological and an ethical sense. In the theological sense, Christians cannot involve themselves in syncretism. Their allegiance must be wholehearted and, as James says, undivided. In the ethical sense, Christ models and provides the pattern for Christians in terms of self-sacrificial love and humility. A religion that makes a virtue out of traits normally associated only with slaves, all the while not endorsing but rather seeking to reform slavery, is a remarkable one indeed.

Finally, the ethical seriousness of the material examined in this chapter certainly and absolutely can be attributed in part not only to the authors' desire that their audiences please God, nor only to the eschatological clock heard ticking on the wall since the Christ-event, but also to the authors' belief that apostasy is possible, that faith without works is dead, and that final salvation or justification is affected by one's behavior between new birth and new body. These ethics do not merely have theological presuppositions; they are theological in character, not least because they come from a God who wants his moral character replicated in his people. And surprisingly enough, often the most exalted and remarkable theology is used in service of simple ethical exhortations, as we find in Hebrews, whereas we might have expected it always to be the other way around. But then in the end, this should not surprise us. The authors of all these documents cut their teeth in early Judaism, where the emphasis on orthopraxy was to the fore and often eclipsed an emphasis on orthodoxy.

What we have seen in this chapter is a remarkable harmony in these diverse witnesses, remembering that harmony involves not uniformity (they do not always say the same things, and when they do say the same things, they say them in different ways) but rather unanimity. All of them are in agreement in their focus on Christ, the emulation of his example, the following of his teachings and the belief that he will help them in their journeys, however arduous. Their ethics are christological and christotelic because they believe that there is a christophoric change ongoing in the believer's life. We must see if things look different when we turn to the Jewish apostle to the Gentiles and to others who exhorted such an audience for Christ's sake.

11

ETHICS FOR GENTILE CHRISTIANS
PART ONE
Paul's Letters

If there is no integral relationship between Paul's ethics and his theology,
the normative status of his particular ethical teaching is tenuous. . . .
Theology is for Paul never merely a speculative exercise; it is always a
tool for constructing community.

RICHARD HAYS[1]

On the face of it, early Christians had a daunting challenge to get pagans to become Christians. Christianity was rightly perceived to be some form of Judaism or at least an offshoot of Judaism, and anti-Semitism was a prejudice nursed and nurtured throughout the Roman Empire, even in the popular Roman literature and drama of the day. Jews had been expelled from Rome in A.D. 49 and before that had faced angry mobs in various cities, not least Alexandria. And perhaps most remarkable of all, the lead apostle to the Gentiles had chosen to focus on a message that many, perhaps most, Gentiles would have found not merely implausible but absurd. Preaching Christ crucified and risen when crucifixion was only valorized negatively and resurrection was rejected as an implausible way of viewing immortality, Paul defied the odds and won many Gentiles to Christ. But what is seldom discussed is that however mentally challenging, if not offensive, the theology of early Christianity was for pagans, various aspects of its ethic would have been seen as at least as daunting and doubtful.

On the one hand, Christians were completely committed to evangelizing Gentiles. Galatians 1–2 recounts that even the pillar apostles in Jerusalem

---

[1]Richard B. Hays, *The Moral Vision of the New Testament: Community, Cross, New Creation* (San Francisco: HarperSanFrancisco, 1996), p. 18.

agreed with Paul about this. But at the same time, early Christianity was committed not just to a religion of theological thought and of religious experience, but also to a rigorous, some would say rigid, Jewish ethic. Only so could the boundaries of both belief and behavior be made clear. Sociologically, there was the difficulty with this ethic that while the apostles wanted somewhat porous boundaries into the various Christian communities, wanted a welcoming and hospitable approach to strangers, touting *philoxenia* (literally, "love of strangers," but it had come to mean "real hospitality" to them), wanted to fulfill the commission from Jesus to make disciples far and wide, they also wanted to demand that disciples live by a code of ethics that most Gentiles would have found too demanding, when it was not just too strange. Who wanted to become a servant or slave anyway? Belief and experience were the basis for a new form of behavior, and indeed the creation of a new community of disciples certainly was needed to reinforce these new patterns of behavior. The ethic of early Christianity was not an ethic for individual moral athletes or for Cynic philosophers acting in splendid isolation. It was an ethic for a community to practice together.

It is customary to point out that the demanding ethic found in the New Testament is an in-group ethic, an ethic for a specific community, an ethic required of entrants only after they had come to believe that Jesus is the risen Lord. It certainly was not an ethic that anyone was trying or could try to impose on non-Christians, whether Jews or Gentiles. And some aspects of this ethic, when carefully adhered to, would make this community stand out like a sore thumb in some ways, but apparently it also made that community incredibly winsome in other ways, particularly because of its love ethic and the great generosity and kindness that characterized the early Christian cell groups (see Acts 2:43-47; 4:32-37). In this chapter we will examine perhaps the earliest attempt to do ethics for Gentile believers: Pauline ethics. Here, as we saw in the last chapter, we will find that the nexus between belief and behavior, between theology and ethics, is very close, and at the heart of both is Christ the paragon and paradigm, the trailblazer and finisher of faith and faithfulness who calls for "the obedience of faith."

PAUL'S ETHICAL TEACHING: A GENERAL INTRODUCTION

There are advantages and disadvantages to beginning a discussion of the ethics of the New Testament with Paul. One can argue that chronologically, his documents are the earliest New Testament documents, and that would be correct in regard to some of them. However, Paul came late to the Jesus movement, was not part of his following during the lifetime of Jesus, and was not all that well accepted in some Jewish and Jewish Christian quarters after his radical about face on the road to Damascus. This is why I began the discussion in the preceding chapter with the earlier advocates of Jesus—James, Jude, Peter, Matthew, the Beloved Disciple, those who actually had personal contact with Jesus and heard at least some of his teachings. We branched out, looking at Hebrews and Revelation as well which sprung from the same Jewish Christian tradition.

And not only did Paul get a late start with the Jesus movement, but also we learn along the way that he was indebted to what he had been taught by Peter, James and John during his visits to Jerusalem, and we see evidence of this in places such as 1 Corinthians 7; 15; Romans 12–13. Paul is not entirely ignorant or innocent of the Jesus tradition; indeed, he is indebted to it in various ways. And we must keep constantly in mind that Paul's major missionary focus was Gentiles, an audience very different from the original audience or community of Jesus.

Were we to judge early Christian ethics on the basis of Pauline ethics, there would be some considerable gaps in our knowledge, and we would find facets and features of Pauline ethics that worked well only with Gentiles and were not universally applicable. It is doubtful that there were many devout Jewish converts to the Jesus movement who were sorely tempted to go dine at pagan temples and engage in the sexual dalliances that went on there. Nor were many Jewish men considering living and having intercourse with their father's wife. My point is simply this: especially when it comes to ethics, it matters who the audience is. Thus, we will study the ethical material served up to Gentiles by Paul, Luke, Mark, and others in this chapter and the next.

If the most influential figure for early Jewish Christian ethics was Jesus himself, both his teaching and the pattern of his life, one could argue that the same is true for Christian ethics for Gentiles. However, it is Paul himself and his take on the Christ-event and Jesus' teachings that most shaped the ethics for these communities. Mark, Luke, and the author of Hebrews are indebted to Paul, and the author of 2 Peter knows very well how widely influential Paul's letters had become at the end of the first century. Even those who mainly addressed Jews, such as Peter or Apollos (especially if he is the author of Hebrews, as I think is likely), were heavily indebted to Paul not only in terms of theology, but also in terms of some of the ethical thinking. Paul was the first great theologian and ethicist of the church, even with his late start and his missional focus on Gentiles. He cast a huge shadow in many directions. It thus behooves us to spend considerable time on the Pauline ethical material. And there is another reason to do so: no ethical material in the New Testament is more nuanced and complex, more debated and discussed, or has had a larger ongoing impact on the church than Paul's material. For all these reasons, it is also important to spend some extra time in this chapter in dialogue with other scholars who have insights into this Pauline material and not just investigating texts directly.

PAUL AND THE ETHICAL IMPERATIVE

We live in a world where there is nothing so permanent as change, especially when it comes to what are seen as acceptable norms for human behavior in Western society.[2] Perhaps this is in part why, when it comes to searching for Paul the ancient ethicist, there are so many different proposals for how to analyze the data and no general satisfaction with any of the proposals. Some recent developments, especially in terms of sociological analysis, are helping us get a clearer picture of what the historical Paul had in mind by his exhortations.

It has become a commonplace in Pauline studies to say that the imperative is built upon the indicative. To put it another way, what God has done in Christ and in the believer is seen as the basis for the exhortations and the means that makes obedience possible. If all of theology can be said to be grace, then all of ethics is the response of a grateful heart. This is a truism, but it is insufficient to explain the matter.[3] Since God's saving work through Christ is eschatological in character, it is clear enough that Paul's ethic also has an eschatological cast and framework, as believers live between the "already" of what has been done in Christ and the "not yet" of what remains to be accomplished of the divine salvific work. It is right to stress the close connection between Paul's theology (including his Christology and eschatology) and his ethics, but in my view, Richard Hays goes too far in saying, "There is no meaningful distinction between theology and ethics in Paul's thought, because Paul's theology is

---

[2]Some of what follows is found in another form in Ben Witherington III, *The Paul Quest: The Renewed Search for the Jew of Tarsus* (Downers Grove, Ill.: InterVarsity Press, 1998).

[3]See Victor P. Furnish, *Theology and Ethics in Paul* (Nashville: Abingdon, 1968). For a survey of scholarly treatments of Pauline ethics in the period 1964-1994, see Wendell L. Willis, "Bibliography: Pauline Ethics, 1964-1994," in *Theology and Ethics in Paul and His Interpreters: Essays in Honor of Victor Paul Furnish*, ed. Eugene H. Lovering Jr. and Jerry L. Sumney (Nashville: Abingdon, 1996), pp. 306-18.

fundamentally an account of God's work of transforming his people into the image of Christ."[4] Surely distinctions between Pauline theology and ethics are both possible and pertinent, but at the same time, and this is in the main the burden of what Hays is saying, connections are both necessary and crucial.[5] We will return to this whole matter of the transformation into Christ's image. Here it will suffice to say that when Paul says to his converts, "Behave," he does not simply mean, "Believe," and vice versa.[6]

The Social Character of Paul's Ethics

One of the more important insights in recent research on Paul's ethics, especially that by Richard Hays and Wayne Meeks, is that Paul offers a community-based and community-directed ethic.[7] Even when Paul comments on things such as governing officials (Rom 13), he does so not to address or exhort such officials but rather to exhort his fellow Christians about how they should behave in relationship to those officials. We look in vain in Paul's letters for moral discourses that Paul might offer to the pagan world. Paul's belief and strategy are that change must come "in house," and that ethical demands work in community only where there can be discipline and sanctions and where norms can and should be acknowledged.

The social character and the social basis of Paul's ethical exhortation need to be kept firmly in view. Meeks urges us to inquire about the social character and moral ethos of Paul's communities. Two important things can be said on this front.

First, Paul is well aware that he is dealing with Christians who are only partially socialized into their new moral community. As 1 Corinthians shows in abundance, many of the Corinthians are still doing the things that they had always done: frequenting prostitutes, going to court to gain advantages over one another, attending meals at idol temples, following the usual rules of social stratification at meals in homes, even when those meals are supposed to be Christian meals that include the Lord's Supper ceremony. In such a situation Paul's moral task is to more thoroughly integrate belief and behavior, showing how certain kinds of behaviors are inconsistent with Christian be-

---

[4]Hays, *Moral Vision of the New Testament*, p. 46.

[5]For a compact summary of his views, see Richard B. Hays, "The Role of Scripture in Paul's Ethics," in Lovering and Sumney, *Theology and Ethics in Paul*, pp. 30-47.

[6]And Hays rightly recognizes this point.

[7]Hays, *Moral Vision of the New Testament*; Wayne A. Meeks, *The Moral World of the First Christians* (Philadelphia: Westminster, 1986); *The Origins of Christian Morality: The First Two Centuries* (New Haven: Yale University Press, 1993).

606   NEW TESTAMENT THEOLOGY AND ETHICS

liefs ("You cannot partake of the table of demons and the table of the Lord" [1 Cor 10:21]; "You cannot be one flesh with a prostitute while being one spirit with the Lord and his body" [1 Cor 6:16-17]).

But did Paul in fact simply adopt an ethical strategy based on the already existing structure of the Greco-Roman household and then apply those notions to the body of Christ? This, in essence, is the argument of Gerd Theissen, who says that Paul sought to overcome social divisions in Corinth through an ethic of "love patriarchalism."[8] There are major problems with this assessment. If this was Paul's strategy in Corinth, we might expect to see some sort of household code, or vestiges of it, being applied to the Corinthian situation. Apart from a text such as 1 Corinthians 14:33b-35, there is very little attempt to connect the household with behavior in the family of faith. Furthermore, as we will see later in this chapter, when Paul does offer Christianized versions of household codes and applies them to his churches, he reforms those codes and modifies and mitigates some of their more patriarchal features.[9] He neither simply adopts such codes nor even merely adapts them and tries to soften their harshness by exhorting everyone to mutual love. The patriarchal family was not the model for the Christian community. The Christian community, led by apostles, prophets, teachers and others, met in homes, and that community led to a reform of the view of family and family structure. Women were allowed to use their gifts and serve as Pauline coworkers. They, as well as men, were encouraged to remain single if they had the gift for it. The new reality in Christ was shaping both the view of the Christian community and the physical family within that community.

Second, Rodney Stark points out how the high regard that Christians had for life, and the high ratio of women to men participating in early Christianity compared to other first-century religions, made for some interesting situations. Christians had a high regard for life, and in general they were opposed to infanticide and abortion, the former of which especially targeted females.[10] The high regard for life in general, including the lives of female infants, girls and women in early Christianity, and the high number of female converts led to the condition where "Christian women enjoyed a favorable sex ratio, . . . [which] resulted in Christian women's enjoying superior status in compari-

---

[8]Gerd Theissen, *The Social Setting of Pauline Christianity: Essays on Corinth*, ed. and trans. John H. Schütz (Philadelphia: Fortress, 1982), p. 2.

[9]See pp. 645-82 below.

[10]Paul's mandate in Galatians 5:20 to avoid *pharmakeia* may in fact refer to abortion-producing drugs.

son with their pagan counterparts."[11] Another crucial factor affecting female status and roles in the body of Christ was Paul's argument that women need not be married (1 Cor 7). This in turn gave them fuller opportunities to serve the Lord as some of Paul's coworkers (see, e.g., Rom 16:1, 3, 6, 12, 15; Phil 4:2-3). It is telling that Stark notes that as Christianity became more acceptable in the empire and moved toward becoming the dominant religion there, with more and more men joining the faith, the favorable sex ratio for Christian women declined, and the roles open to them became far more limited.[12] In other words, what limited the roles of women in the body of Christ was not Paul's love patriarchialism but rather the later patriarchal takeover of the church and its leadership structure.

I suggest that one of the keys to understanding Paul's ethics is recognizing his distinctions between the family of faith and the physical family and also his distinctive ways of exhorting each group without simply amalgamating the two. As a text such as Ephesians 5:21–6:9 suggests, the direction of ethical influence moved from the primary family (the family of faith) to the secondary family, with the physical family being normed and reformed in the context of the Christian community or family of faith. This process is very much in evidence also in Philemon, where Paul argues that Onesimus now must be seen as a brother and so as more than a slave. His Christian status should lead to his emancipation from the traditional family role of household slave. Paul by no means simply Christianized or baptized the Greco-Roman household structure, nor did he take his cues from that structure when he exhorted the body of Christ. For Paul, the role of the Spirit was too determinative in the body to allow for such an ethical move. Roles and functions in the body would be determined largely by gifts and graces, plus the social factor of who had the resources and venue to provide a safe, private haven for Christian meetings. The evidence suggests that even in this regard, women, like men, took the lead in hosting the church (cf. 1 Cor 16:15, 19 with Rom 16:1-3, 12; Acts 16:11-15).

In the wake of the work of E. P. Sanders, considerable stress has been placed on the Jewish character of Paul's ethics.[13] This stress is not new, and

---

[11]Rodney Stark, *The Rise of Christianity: A Sociologist Reconsiders History* (Princeton, N.J.: Princeton University Press, 1996), p. 101. See also Ben Witherington III, *Women in the Earliest Churches* (SNTSMS 59; Cambridge: Cambridge University Press, 1988), chap. 1.

[12]Stark, *Rise of Christianity*, p. 108.

[13]See E. P. Sanders, *Paul and Palestinian Judaism: A Comparison of Patterns of Religion* (Philadephia: Fortress, 1977) (note particularly the discussions about "staying in"); *Paul, the Law, and the Jewish People* (Philadelphia: Fortress, 1983).

it is even more strongly reiterated by Brian Rosner.[14] Rosner's approach is to argue that Paul stands clearly within the matrix of pre-Christian Judaism in his ethics, exegesis and understanding of covenantal community. There is a great deal of truth in this approach. Paul is far more indebted to his Jewish heritage in ethics than to the ethics of Aristotle or other influential luminaries of the Greco-Roman world. But there are at least four problems with this approach: (1) it does not account for Paul's approach to the Mosaic law; (2) it does not account for Paul's new covenant theology; (3) it does not take into account the christocentric essence of Paul's ethic; (4) it does not take into account Victor Furnish's careful survey of texts where Paul does cite Scripture in his ethical arguments, about which Furnish concluded, "Paul never quotes the Old Testament *in extenso* for the purpose of developing a pattern of conduct. . . . [It is] never casuistically interpreted or elaborated. . . . There is no evidence which indicates that the apostle regarded [the Old Testament] as in any sense a source book for detailed moral instruction or even a manual of ethical norms."[15] At its heart, Paul's ethic is about the imitation of Christ, not the reiteration of Torah. As Hays puts it, "Paul seeks to commend his normative moral teachings on the basis of the gospel itself: right behavior is understood as 'the fruit of the Spirit.'"[16]

I differ with Hays, however, when he concludes that for Paul, moral judgment is always a matter of discerning God's will rather than obeying a law. Paul is perfectly capable of insisting on obedience to a particular norm. But when dealing with a mature Christian, Paul is able and more apt to appeal for the use of wise Christian judgment and even improvisation according to the needs of the situation. Even then, he would not want such Christians to forget the commandments while discerning God's will. Thus, when Hays says, "Ethics would not be a matter of casuistry, not a matter of reasoning through rules and principles, but of hearing the word of God and responding in imaginative freedom to embody God's righteousness,"[17] he is speaking not of how Paul actually addresses or deals with his converts but rather to some extent how ideally Paul might like to have done so. He would have been grateful not to

---

[14]See Brian S. Rosner, *Paul, Scripture and Ethics: A Study of 1 Corinthians 5–7* (AGJU 22; Leiden: Brill, 1994).

[15]Furnish, *Theology and Ethics in Paul*, p. 33. Few are convinced by the arguments of Peter Tomson that Paul's ethics are deeply grounded in rabbinic traditions of halakic scriptural interpretation (*Paul and the Jewish Law: Halakha in the Letters of the Apostle to the Gentiles* [CRINT 3/1; Minneapolis: Fortress, 1990]).

[16]Hays, "Role of Scripture in Paul's Ethics," p. 31.

[17]Ibid., p. 47.

issue commands and instead to simply witness the fruit of the Spirit produced in Christian life and the voluntary following of the Christ paradigm and the thinking on virtuous things. Consider, for example, how Paul says in Philemon 8-21 that although he could command Philemon to do the right thing, he prefers to persuade him (even though, tongue in cheek, he goes on to say "confident of your obedience . . ."). If all had been positive striving, "against which there is no law," Paul perhaps would have eschewed making demands or issuing imperatives or pointing out commandments. But alas, this was far from the case, and in view of the ongoing struggle between flesh and Spirit, ethics does necessarily (and did for Paul) entail enunciating principles and norms. The law of Christ was not just a paradigm or human model; it also involved specific commandments, such as the one to love as Christ loved. Ethical improvisation did not rule out imperatives when needed in Paul's communities.

Paul and the Law

In regard to Paul's view of the law, here I will simply stress that a failure to see that Paul is essentially a sectarian person who is drawing on his heritage for a new social situation and community can lead to fundamental misunderstandings. The absence of an exhortation to observe the Sabbath or be circumcised is more telling than the presence of various Old Testament maxims and norms. This "selectivity" augurs a new situation where one is no longer under and obligated to the law, which is consistently seen and referred to by Paul as a whole (seen clearly in Gal 5:3).

Furthermore, in Galatians 4 Paul clearly enough has a theology of multiple covenants, and as Galatians 3–4 and 2 Corinthians 3 make evident, this means that he does not see Christians as under the law or Mosaic covenant or obliged to observe it, precisely because Christians are part of the new covenant community. The ethical material from the old covenant used by Paul he uses because he believes that it is now part of the "law of Christ," meant for the new covenant community. Paul's ethic is grounded in the new eschatological situation inaugurated by Christ, and the issue must be not what is the source of this or that piece of ethical material, for Paul uses both Jewish and pagan material (e.g., compare the last three virtues in the list in Phil 4:8, the end of the fruit of the Spirit in Gal 5:17, and the Aristotelean epithet "against which there is no law"), but rather how he uses this material and to what end. The purpose or end of using such material is to give shape or contour to the new life in Christ, and Paul is capable of drawing on all sorts of ethical material to accomplish that aim.

In short, some of the Old Testament material is norm because it is seen as consistent with, or an extrapolation of, the life and teaching of Christ, the ultimate ethical litmus test. Paul means by "the law of Christ" that ethical teaching which reflects the character and mandates of Christ, even when it also included the portions of Old Testament law that Christ reaffirmed, and later apostolic ethics that was seen as a natural extension of the teaching of Christ and the reaffirmed Old Testament mandates. Even the love commandment is stressed not because it is in the Mosaic law but rather because Christ adopted this as part of his own teaching for his followers. The old law and commandments are simply fulfilled in Christ and in his community, the eschatological community in which the prophecies, promises and mandates of the old covenant come true. The new law is applied to the eschatological community of Christ as norm and imperative.

This new law, this new set of ethical imperatives, differs in some very fundamental ways from the Mosaic law. For example, the material in Romans 12:14-21 offers an ethic of nonresistance and indeed of truly loving and blessing one's enemy. This stands in contrast to the *lex talionis* of the Mosaic covenant and shows clearly how Christians are no longer under such a law even in some of its moral as well as its ritual dimensions.

Where does this new ethic come from? It is the character and example of Christ, which Christians are regularly exhorted by Paul to follow. The story of Christ, entailing both his life and teaching, norms the story of Christians, including Paul's own story. Also, Paul believes that the Holy Spirit is busy conforming Christians to the image of Christ, not to the image of the Old Testament saints, even including the life and teachings of Moses. The work of God in the believer tends to the same aim as the work and ethical striving of the believer: conformity to the image of Christ. Walking in step with the Spirit means moving in the shadow of Christ and working out that christoform shape that the Spirit is working in. Thus, the law of Christ includes (1) those portions of the Mosaic law reinscribed in the new covenant by Jesus and others; (2) the new teaching and example of Christ; (3) the apostolic teaching of Paul and others as they expand on and expound the first two items. At this juncture, some discussion of Hays's recent unfolding of Paul's moral vision is in order.

Paul's Theological Framework for his Ethics

Hays is quite right that one of the main reasons we find Paul's ethics both allusive and elusive is that he is writing to communities with which he has already been having an ongoing discussion, including a discussion about ethical matters. Paul can presume a certain understanding of the context and content of these discussions in these communities. Equally helpful is Hays's critique of the older approaches of Martin Dibelius and Hans Dieter Betz, who see Paul simply offering general ethical maxims rather than a specifically Christian ethics grounded in theology. Were that the case, the normative status of Paul's ethics would become tenuous. "When the Christian gospel moves in time or space to a different culture, one could presumably substitute a different set of cultural norms without difficulty."[18] The fundamental connection between belief and behavior for Paul is seen from the fact that he regularly uses his theologizing to shape the behavior of his community (see Phil 2:4-11). Certain fundamental theological convictions undergird and guide the development of his ethical remarks. One can see how Paul's ethics work and why they take the form they do by asking certain fundamental questions, questions that N. T. Wright suggests will illuminate the situation.

Paul's eschatological ethics. The first question is, "What time is it?"[19] Paul's answer is that the church lives in the eschatological age, lives at the time when the ends and fulfillment of all ages and all biblical prophecies and promises are coming to fruition (1 Cor 10:11). The church lives during a time when the form of this world is passing away, and there is no point in simply living according to its ways and mandates (1 Cor 7:31). The church is living in the fullness of time, when the Messiah, born under the law, has come and redeemed from that law various Jewish Christians such as Paul (Gal 4:4-5). Under these circumstances it makes no sense for a Christian to submit to the Mosaic law, for that law is obsolete now that Christ and his teaching and the presence of the Spirit have come. The law was intended as a guardian for God's people in a bygone age. The benefits promised by the law are now available through faith in Christ, and the essence of what the law required is fulfilled in Christ's life and death and, in another sense and to a lesser degree, in the life of Christians who love and bear one another's burdens. Yet in Paul's hands, the Old Testament, as Scripture, is still a source not just for some specific norms or ethical teaching but also a source of narratives that provide paradigms and types—examples of positive and negative behavior. Paul is able to make this hermeneutical move not because he believes that

---

[18]Hays, *Moral Vision of the New Testament*, p. 18.
[19]See N. T. Wright, *Jesus and the Victory of God*, vol. 2 of *Christians Origins and the Question of God* (Minneapolis: Fortress, 1996).

his converts are or should be under the law covenant, but rather because, being the sectarian person he is, he identifies his own community of Jew and Gentile united in Christ as the continuation of Israel, and therefore it is appropriate for it to draw on Israel's scriptural heritage even in the new age and as part of the norms of the new covenant.[20]

It is also germane to bear in mind that Paul's answer to the question "What time is it?" is that the believer lives between the advents, between already and not yet, between the beginning and the completion of being conformed to Christ's image. There is indeed a dialectical tension in the Christian life between now and not yet, especially because the "now" has thus far only affected the believer in the spirit and mind, while the "not yet" is experienced in the still fallen condition of the body (2 Cor 4:16-18). The believer is caught in a tug of war between inwardly being a new person experiencing the renewal of mind and spirit, pulled in that direction by the internal workings of the Holy Spirit, and outwardly having to deal with desires and inclinations to sin called "flesh," with the not yet perfected body being the weak link in the Christian's armor.

The eschatological "not yet" does not lead to a radical interim ethic for Paul, useless for a later age that knows Christ did not come back in the first century. Rather, the possible imminence of the Lord's appearing leads, interestingly enough, to the exhortation to let him find disciples doing what they ought to be doing anyway, while keeping one eye on the horizon. Like Gideon's warriors, they must continue to do the necessary daily tasks of drinking from the well of life, but with weapons in hand and eyes on the horizon (1 Thess 3:6-13; cf. Judg 7:4-8). This orientation leads to heightened ethical concern, not a neglect of such concerns. Preparation for what is to come does not mean neglect of what is at hand, but it does place the latter in the proper eschatological perspective. Hays observes,

> The eschatological perspective allows Paul to counsel a high tolerance for ambiguity. Suffering and joy are present together, and the church should expect this paradoxical condition to persist until the parousia. Nonetheless, the promise of God's ultimate making right of all things allows the community to live faithfully and confidently no matter how bad things may look at present.[21]

---

[20]Hays is right that Paul is not a supersessionist, if by that we mean one who believes that a new community simply replaces the old. Yet Paul does believe that the church is the legitimate development of true Israel and therefore the locus where God's promises are being fulfilled and the place where God's word should be heard and applied.

[21]Hays, "Role of Scripture in Paul's Ethics," p. 26.

Furthermore, the "church community is God's eschatological beachhead, the place where the power of God has invaded the world. All Paul's ethical judgments are worked out in this context . . . [thus] . . . he is sharply critical not only of the old age that is passing away but also those who claim unqualified participation already in the new age."[22] Clearly, then, the context or framework for Paul's ethical remarks is eschatological.

Pauline ethics as imitation of Christ. The second question is "Who or what provides the ethical paradigm?" The answer to this question is not the law but rather Christ, and in particular Christ in his humble, loving, self-sacrifical lifestyle, in his death on the cross, in his resurrection. Christ's own teaching is brought into the discussion chiefly to flesh out or give further concreteness to these motifs (see Rom 12). Thus, the cross is at the heart of what undergirds and shapes Paul's ethics. "For Paul, Jesus' death on the cross is an act of loving self-sacrificial obedience that becomes paradigmatic for the obedience of all who are in Christ."[23] This is not to be taken to mean that Paul simply sees the death of Christ as an ethical example. No, for Paul, Christ's death is a unique and unrepeatable event insofar as it provides reconciliation and redemption for humankind. The cross has both theological significance and ethical implications. An excellent example of how the cross works as ethical example is seen in Philippians 2:4-11. Just as Christ suffered obediently to the point of death, so the Philippians should stand firm in the gospel, even should it cost them their lives (Phil 1:27-30; 2:12). "The twin themes of conformity to Christ's death and imitation of Christ are foundational elements of Paul's vision of the moral life (. . . see Rom 6:1-14; 8:17, 29-30; 15:1-7; 1 Cor 10:23–11:1; 2 Cor 4:7-15; 12:9-10; Gal 2:19-20; 5:24; 6:14)."[24] But notice that, amazingly, Philippians 2:5-11 even suggests that the believer can learn to think through ethical dilemmas just as Christ did ("Have this mind in yourself that also was in Christ Jesus . . .").

Another excellent example of how the Christ paradigm works is in Romans 15:1-13. Here Paul exhorts the strong to accept the weak for the sake of building up the community, following the example of Christ. Notice how the character of Christ's work is explained by a quotation of Psalm 69:9 (Rom 15:3). Paul then adds that Christ's welcoming of Jews and Gentiles (prefigured in various Scriptures: Ps 18:49; Deut 32:43; Ps 117:1; Is 11:10) is the paradigm, and so the Roman Christians likewise should welcome one

---

[22]Ibid., p. 27.
[23]Ibid.
[24]Ibid., p. 31.

another (Rom 15:7). Christ was not one who pleased himself but rather who sought to serve and welcome others. Perhaps the most striking rhetorical move in this passage is that Christ is portrayed as the speaker in these quotations from the psalms (Rom 15:3, 9). What is not clear here is whether Paul is following the historical example of Christ, who used the psalms and other Old Testament texts to exegete his own experience (see, e.g., Mk 14:34; 15:34), or is making a hermeneutical move in which the (preexistent) Son of God is seen as the speaking and praying voice that originally spoke these texts. I tend to think that we are dealing with the former rather than the latter phenomenon, but the latter cannot be ruled out, for Paul clearly believes in the preexistence of the Christ (see 1 Cor 10:4).

Further confirmation of the centrality of the Christ paradigm is seen in the phrase "the faith/faithfulness of Christ." As Hays rightly stresses, this phrase is a sort of summary allusion to the story of Christ's obedience even unto death on the cross. We should consider a series of texts in this connection: Romans 3:22, 26; Galatians 2:16, 20, 3:16; Philippians 3:9. The question that Romans 3:22 raises is "Where is the righteousness of God chiefly manifested?" Is it chiefly manifested in the obedience of Christ unto death, in his faithfulness to fulfill God's will for his life, or is it chiefly manifested in the Christian's faith? The answer, if we are talking about the objective means of God manifesting his righteousness, must be the former rather than the latter. Paul, then, is saying here that God justifies or sets right those who live out of and trust in Christ's faithfulness even unto death, which is (as Rom 3:26c makes clear) of course an act of faith.[25]

Philippians 3:9 is quite similar in form to Romans 3:22. It may be rendered somewhat literally thus: "and be found in him, not having my own righteousness, the [sort that comes] from the law, but [that which comes] through the faithfulness of Christ, the from-God righteousness based upon faith." As with Romans 3:22-26, we are not dealing with an either-or proposition. The text refers to both the faithfulness of Christ and the faith of the believer. Here the very last phrase refers to the believer's faith. But when Paul wishes to discuss the objective means through which righteousness is made available to human beings, he contrasts the righteousness that comes from the law with the righteousness that comes through the saving acts of Christ. As in Romans 3:22, the *dia* ("through") clause refers to something that hap-

---

[25]For a fuller exposition of these key texts, see See Ben Witherington III, *Paul's Narrative Thought World: The Tapestry of Tragedy and Triumph* (Louisville: Westminster John Knox, 1994), pp. 268-72.

pened in and through Jesus' life, not through believers. The Judaizers were enemies not of subjective Christian faith but rather of the notion that the cross of Christ is both the means of right standing with God and the pattern for Christian life, as opposed to the law (Phil 4:18). What, then, does it mean to "gain Christ and be found in him"? It means to be incorporated into the story of Christ and so gain the benefits of his death and resurrection.[26] Paul's life, the life of the believer arises out of the story of Christ and the events that made the proclaiming of that gospel possible.

In Galatians 2:16-20 the issue again is how one obtains right standing or the righteousness that comes from God. Is it by works of the law or through the faith/fulness of Jesus Christ? Of course, in Galatians 2:16b Paul makes clear that this benefit comes to those who believe in Christ. But Galatians 2:16a and Galatians 2:16b should not be seen as examples of a redundancy. Paul speaks of both the objective and subjective means of obtaining such right standing: the faithfulness of Christ and the believer's reception by faith of the benefits of Christ's faithfulness. Notice Galatians 2:20. Here Paul says that he has been crucified with Christ, and that Christ lives in him. This means that the story of Christ is recapitulated in his own life, but there is also a sense in which he has been grafted into the story of Christ so that he gets the benefit of Christ's death and resurrection. Galatians 3:22 goes on to make clear that the Abrahamic promises are conveyable to the believer because of and through the faithfulness of Christ. One must have faith in Christ's faithful act.

The term *pistis*, which can mean both "faith" and "faithful/ness" is crucial for Paul. It is the key term by which he links the story of Christ and the story of Christians. Christ is a paradigm of faithful living. Because of his faithful act of dying for sin, believers can die to sin; because he was raised, believers can arise and live in newness of life. His faithfulness unto death can also be emulated by Christians under pressure and persecution. In gaining Christ, the believer not only has gained the benefits of the story of his life and death but also has been grafted into that story in the sense that by analogy the pattern is repeated in the believer's life. Christ's death as both experience and pattern norms the life of Christians, guides them along to the path to greater Christlikeness. These texts show the very close connection between theology and ethics, between Christology and paraenesis in the life of the believer.

---

[26]The narrative framework that provides the final warrant for Paul's ethical guidance is larger than Christ's story; it involves the scriptural stories that came before that of Christ. It is just that in Paul's view, with the story of Christ one has come to the heart and turning point of the entire narrative.

Steps for living the ethical life. The third question is as important as the first two: "How, then, should believers live?" The answer to this question has three dimensions: (1) imitate Christ, follow and fulfill the law/normative pattern of Christ and his teaching; (2) walk in the Spirit, and do not fulfill the works of the flesh; (3) live as a community in unity. There are theological/cognitive, experiential and social dimensions to the Christian life. It is of critical importance to realize that in all three of these dimensions there is an element of both experience and behavior. By the internal work of the Holy Spirit the believer is being conformed to the image of Christ at the same time he or she is seeking to imitate Christ. By the internal work of the Holy Spirit fruit is being produced in the Christian life that the believer is then called upon to actively manifest in behavior and relationships. By the internal work of the Spirit the believer has been joined to the body of Christ, but also he or she must act and behave in such a way that that body is served not severed, unified not divided.

Hays notes three "warrants" for obedience that are inherent parts of Paul's Gospel: (1) through union with Christ believers undergo transformation that should cause them to "walk in newness of life"; (2) because God has liberated believers from sin's power, they should transfer their allegiance to the one who liberated them; (3) because the Spirit is at work in the community of faith, the fruit of the Spirit should be exhibited in the community's life.[27] Notice the trinitarian character of these warrants. Pauline ethics is grounded in God or, better said, in the divine saving activity that is part of the divine-human encounter. This produces new creatures with a new inward source of life, power and character formation, the Holy Spirit. The theological grounding of Paul's ethics also makes quite clear that his ethics are not simply ad hoc in character. Although Paul tailors how he expresses himself to address the particular ethical situation of his converts, the substance of this ethical material comes from a deep, preexisting well.

The flip side of the positive warrants is the negative sanctions, and the major form of that is exclusion from the final fellowship with God in Christ in the kingdom. It is crucial to note that Paul offers these sorts of warnings to those whom he considers to be Christians. Sometimes the sanction involves Christians being saved but enduring the judgment of their earthly works (see 1 Cor 3:10-15; Gal 6:7-9). It appears to be seen as fortunate that the judge in the case of Christians will be Christ, to whom they must give

---

[27]Hays, "Role of Scripture in Paul's Ethics," p. 39.

an account of their behavior. Notice the progression in 2 Corinthians 5:9-10: "We make it our aim to please God. For all of us must appear before the judgment seat of Christ and receive recompense for the deeds done in the body, whether good or evil." Yet at times Paul trots out the ultimate sanction: the danger of exclusion from the kingdom of God, apparently for major and habitual sin that neither ceased nor was repented of (see 1 Cor 6:9-11; Gal 5:19-21). Since the warning is addressed to Christians, it appears certain that Paul believes in the possibility of apostasy, either theological or ethical in character. One is not eternally secure until one is securely in eternity. However, Paul is not talking about "losing" one's salvation. He is talking about deliberately, through acts of rebellion, throwing it away. This possibility, however unlikely in any particular instance, has the effect of inculcating moral earnestness. It is true enough that good works cannot get someone into the kingdom, but apparently habitual bad ones could, in the end, keep out someone who began as a Christian.

The Social Character of Paul's Ethics Revisited
In the end, it is right to stress the social dimension to much of Paul's ethical teaching. Its aim or goal is not just to enhance personal virtue or one's relationship with Christ. Indeed, as is especially clear from Paul's discussion of the gifts of the Spirit in 1 Corinthians 14, personal benefit is only a by-product of building up the community, edifying others and glorifying God. One is given such gifts for the common good.

Notice, for example, how we tend to misread a text such as Philippians 2:12-13. Modern Western individualists have tended to see this as an exhortation to individuals to get on with earnest moral striving. This, however, overlooks that Paul is addressing not an individual but rather the group (as the plurals in the Greek syntax show). Paul is saying, "Together, as a community, work out your own salvation with fear and trembling." The community, not the closet, is the context, the workshop, where salvation is worked out, expressed, and manifested in deeds of piety and charity. The image of the race and disciplined effort striving toward the goal suggests that Paul believes that progress, even moral progress, is possible in the Christian life (Phil 3:12-14). Paul is not an early advocate of *simul justus et peccator* ("simultaneously righteous and sinful"), if by the second half of that equation one means that progressive sanctification, victory over sin, growth, positive development in the Christian life, and obedience to the Lord's commands are not fully possible over the course of a Christian life. It is a major mistake to think that Paul

presents Romans 7:14-25 as the story of the Christian life. The tension in the
Christian life is not between old person and new person but rather between
flesh and Holy Spirit.[28] Walk in the Spirit, says Paul, and you will not indulge
the works of the flesh. Such statements do not prove Paul to be an optimist or
an idealist in regard to human nature as it is; they simply prove that he truly
believes in the transforming power of God's grace operating in the believer
by means of the Holy Spirit.

Paul does his ethics as a member of a community and directs his remarks
to that community. Even his ethic of moral athleticism presupposes flexing
one's muscles in a context where there is not only "moral" support from
the sidelines but also actual team play en route to the goal line. Paul indeed
believes that people become what they admire, and so he holds up examples
and paradigms for his converts to follow, chiefly that of Christ. It is this
paradigm, and the fleshing out of it in the teaching of Christ and apostolic
Christians, that Paul calls the "law of Christ." Paul certainly was not averse
to commanding things, but he preferred to persuade. He was not reluctant to
urge good works, working out the community's shared salvation by means of
piety and charity. He was not chiefly concerned with the problems of legal-
ism versus libertinism or alien righteousness versus works righteousness in
his Christian manifesto of freedom, the letter to the Galatians. Instead, his
concern was of a salvation-historical nature. One ought not to impose or demand obedience to an obsolescent covenant and its law on anyone now that
a new covenant has been inaugurated by Christ.

Believers needed to remember what time it was, to recognize that they
stood between the "already" and the "not yet," between the beginning of
the new age and its consummation, between new birth and new body, and
so they wrestled with being in the tension between flesh and Spirit. Paul's
ethics of freedom still allows a place for patterns, models, norms, and even
commands when necessary. It allows for the law of Christ to replace the
Mosaic law. It allows for the exhortation that habitual serious sin may keep
someone who presently is a Christian from entering the final kingdom of

---

[28]I disagree with the suggestion that the old person/new person metaphor is simply parallel to the
flesh/Spirit metaphor. By this I mean that the old person/new person metaphor refers to what
happens to a person at conversion, not to the ongoing battle in the Christian's life with the "flesh."
"Flesh," which refers to the sinful inclination still resident in a Christian's fallen human body, is
not indicating the same thing as "old person," which refers to the person controlled by, and under
the lordship of, the old orientation and old self. This is why "flesh" in the moral sense should not
be translated "sin nature." Christians, though they do have sinful inclinations and temptations, do
not have a sin nature controlling their will and behavior.

God. It allows for improvisation when no rule exists. Ethics for Paul, then, was community-based and community-oriented, christoform in character and trajectory, involving both models and norms, both warrants and sanctions, and grounded from start to finish in Paul's narrative thought world, especially in the story of Christ and God's people. There was neither the time nor the need to retrace steps to Sinai, for a clear path had been blazed by the pioneer, the Risen One, that had both clear boundaries and direction leading into the final dominion of God. One had only to follow his lead and in his footsteps, all the while remembering his instructions, and all would be well.

PAULINE ANTHROPOLOGY AND PAULINE ETHICS

Paul had some basic assumptions about the Christian individual and the Christian community. About the former, Paul says that anyone who is in Christ is a new creature/creation; the old has passed away. The text of 2 Corinthians 5:16-21 is a crucial one. It shows that Paul believes in a significant transformation of a person at conversion. This conversion involves not just one's worldview or one's position in the eyes of God; it involves one's will, emotions, thoughts and ultimately behavior. Paul stresses in Romans 7–8 that the law of sin and death no longer rules the Christian life, for believers have been set free by the Holy Spirit, and the ruling principle in their life is a very different one: the law or rule of the Spirit, who gives life (cf. Rom 7:5-6 with Rom 8:1-4). This in turn means that the descriptions given in Romans 7:7-25 are descriptions of fallen humanity outside of the Christian life and community. They are descriptions of Adam and his fallen race, from a Christian point of view.[29] This does not mean that Paul believes that at conversion a person becomes morally perfect. He is quite happy to talk about a tension in the Christian life between sinful inclinations and the leading of the Spirit, as Galatians 5 shows. The point, however, is that while sin remains, it no longer reigns in the believer's life, for the believer is indeed a new creation empowered by the indwelling Holy Spirit. Christ, not sin, is Lord in the believer's life, and so Paul can speak of a way to deal with temptations without inevitably succumbing to them (1 Cor 10).

It is unfortunate that so many Protestant readings of Paul have badly misunderstood Pauline ethics precisely because they misunderstood Pauline anthropology. This brings us back to 2 Corinthians 5:16-21. Hays remarks,

---

[29]See Ben Witherington III and Darlene Hyatt, *Paul's Letter to the Romans: A Socio-Rhetorical Commentary* (Grand Rapids: Eerdmans, 2004), pp. 179-206.

This eschatological transformation of the community explains Paul's extraordinary affirmation that the purpose of God's reconciling work in Christ is "that we might become the righteousness of God" (5:21). He does not say "that we might *know about* the righteousness of God," nor "that we might *believe* in the righteousness of God," nor even "that we might *receive* the righteousness of God." Instead the church is to *become* the righteousness of God: where the church embodies in its life together the world-reconciling love of Jesus Christ, the new creation is manifest. The church incarnates the righteousness of God.[30]

This is precisely correct. As Paul affirms in 1 Thessalonians 4, the will of God for the believer is their sanctification, that they live holy lives, morally upright lives, here and now. Furthermore, Paul believes that Christians have been empowered to do so, empowered to overcome their weaknesses and sinful inclinations. And indeed, Paul believes that they must do so.[31]

Although Paul does not tell us clearly when a Christian may have crossed the line on the road to ruin, he certainly believes that behavior affects eternal destiny. Grossly immoral behavior by a Christian, if insisted upon and persisted in, will result in the perpetrator committing moral apostasy and being disallowed from entering or obtaining the kingdom in the future (see 1 Cor 6:9-11; cf. Gal 5:19-21). Paul stresses in 1 Corinthians 6:11 that since Christians have been washed and sanctified and set right at and after conversion, that they can and must reject all such immoral behavior. The inner purifying process and the indwelling Spirit mean that sinning is not a legitimate option for Christians, and that they have the resources to overcome temptation, and indeed they are not that kind of person any more; they are new creatures, and so they must not behave like fallen ones. What all of this means is that when Paul urges certain courses of ethical behavior, he is ethically serious. He is not just vaguely hoping that his addressees might approximate what he urges; he believes that obedience can and must flow forth from genuine faith.

---

[30]Hays, *Moral Vision of the New Testament*, p. 24.

[31]See, in Kent E. Brower and Andy Johnson, eds., *Holiness and Ecclesiology in the New Testament* (Grand Rapids: Eerdmans, 2007), the following essays: Michael J. Gorman, "'You Shall Be Cruciform for I Am Cruciform': Paul's Trinitarian Reconstruction of Holiness," pp. 148-66; Peter Oakes, "Made Holy by the Holy Spirit: Holiness and Ecclesiology in Romans," pp. 167-183; Bruce W. Winter, "Carnal Conduct and Sanctification in 1 Corinthians: *Simul sanctus et peccator?*" pp. 184-200; J. Ayodeji Adewuya, "The People of God in a Pluralistic Society: Holiness in 2 Corinthians," pp. 201-18; Troy W. Martin, "Circumcision in Galatia and the Holiness of God's Ecclesiae," pp. 219-37; George Lyons, "Church and Holiness in Ephesians," pp. 238-56; J. Ross Wagner, "Working Out Salvation: Holiness and Community in Philippians," pp. 257-74; Andy Johnson, "The Sanctification of the Imagination in 1 Thessalonians," pp. 275-92.

And here is where we should carefully note that obedience is different from perfect performance or perfect conformity to what is commanded. By this I mean that the individual Christian is not the master of all circumstances.

For example, when, as Paul urges, one Christian makes every effort to bear the burdens of a fellow Christian, the outcome of that course of behavior is not entirely in the initiator's hands. Things can intervene. The burdened person might reject the helper's offer. The helper might collapse under the weight of the shared burden. Health problems might prevent the the helper from successfully completing the task. This is why in some forms of Christian's ethics there is a discussion about intentions, even perfect intentions. Intentions are important, but they are not the only crucial factor when it comes to ethics. Behavior is at the heart of the matter. The issue, then, is a matter of good intentions plus a good-faith effort to comply with a commandment or the standard of good Christian behavior to the extent that this is within one's capacity and control to accomplish the end desired. Failure to completely comply or obey can come through no fault of the Christian in question, which is why we hear about judging things on the basis of justice/righteousness tempered with mercy.

However, lest we get the impression that Paul is urging each individual Christian to become an isolated moral athlete trudging along toward the kingdom, we need to stress again that his ethic is not for isolated individuals but rather is for a community. Indeed, even what Paul says about conversion, salvation, and sanctification is communal in nature, and so we should not be surprised that Paul is stressing a team effort when he calls for certain kinds of behavior and accountability. The community must be disciplined and exercise ethical discipline. Let us consider briefly a couple of texts of relevance that make clear the communal nature of how Paul views both salvation and ethics: 1 Corinthians 12:13; Philippians 2:12-13.

In 1 Corinthians 12:13 Paul says that "we" (i.e., we Christians) were all baptized by one Spirit into one body, and all were given the same Spirit from which to drink. This extended water metaphor is important. Conversion is into a body of believers, the body of Christ, not into an isolated relationship with Christ. In addition, every Christian is morally responsible for his or her behavior, because each one has been given the resource of the Holy Spirit, which gives life, sanctifies, empowers, illumines and so on. This brings us to Philippians 2:12-13

As we noted earlier, in Philippians 2:12-13 Paul is addressing not an individual but rather the group (note the plurals in the Greek syntax). Thus, we could offer a Southern-style translation here: "Y'all work out y'all's salvation with fear and trembling, for it is God who works in the midst of y'all to will and to act in order to fulfill his good purpose." Had we backed up to the beginning of Philippians 2:12, we would have heard "As y'all have always obeyed, . . . continue to work out y'all's salvation." In other words, working out one's salvation and obedience go to together, hand in glove. In fact, working out one's salvation, which involves both willing and behavior, is a form of obedience. Progressive sanctification empowers ongoing obedience. And there is no hint whatsoever that salvation means something different here than it means elsewhere in Paul's letters.

This furthermore makes very clear that behavior affects salvation, and equally these verses remind us that theology and ethics go together and are intertwined in Paul's thought, just as we saw was the case when we examined the ethics of James, Peter, the Beloved Disciple, and others in the preceding chapter. Salvation in Paul's theology has three tenses: "I have been saved" (conversion), "I am working out my salvation" (sanctification, progressive or otherwise), and "I will be saved." In the case of the latter two, although human behavior does not cause final salvation, it can affect the outcome. In this context it is easy to see why there is an urgency to Paul's ethical appeals. There is more at stake than just revving up the troops to be good witnesses and be grateful for the gift of salvation.

It will be useful at this point to look at some selected ethical topics in some detail, probing in more depth Paul's anthropology and its implications for human behavior and relationships. Once one has read carefully through 1 Corinthians 5:1-8; 6:14-20, it becomes apparent that Paul has some different notions about human beings and human nature than do the vast majority of modern persons. To be sure, one could almost ignore Paul saying "Though absent in body, I am present in spirit" (1 Cor 5:3) as a pure metaphor meaning something like "I am thinking about you," but what then about "Hand this man over to Satan for the destruction of the flesh, so his spirit may be saved at the day of the Lord" (1 Cor 5:5)? Both texts contrast flesh or body with the human spirit (rather than the Holy Spirit), but what are we to make of this?

Even more puzzling is Paul's diatribe against visiting a prostitute in 1 Corinthians 6:14-20, where Paul in fact insists, "Do you not know that your bodies are members of Christ?" (even though later he will say, "Anyone united to the Lord becomes one spirit with him" [1 Cor 6:17]), and, even more amazingly, "Should I take the members of Christ and make them members of a prostitute?" (1 Cor 6:15). Is Paul really saying that the Christian individual's body is actually connected in some way to the body of Christ and therefore to Christ, such that frequenting of a prostitute could actually result in Christ, through one of his members, being coupled with a prostitute? This seems to be the logic of the argument, and if so, we will need a refresher in first-century anthropology to make sense of either of these texts. We will return to these texts at the very end of this section, once we have had occasion first to survey some of Paul's key anthropological terms.

The English cleric and poet John Donne once said, "I am a little world made cunningly of elements, and an angelic sprite" (*Divine Meditations* 5). It must be said that for Paul, human anthropology is never discussed in the abstract, and indeed the subject always is colored by the fact that he believes that outside of Christ "sin reigns in your mortal bodies" (Rom 6:12; cf. Rom 6:6, 17). For Paul, sin entered the human race with Adam and has been present and bedeviling humans and human nature ever since. Paul was not an early advocate of the "I'm okay, you're okay" school of thinking about human nature. In the apostle's mind, no humans are born sinless or blameless, for human nature as we now find it is sinful (Rom 3:9). If God is the source of life, and if sin separates a person from God, then sin's ultimate consequence is death. Sin, like death, affects the entire person. With this backdrop, we can make some sense of Paul's anthropological terms, but we do well to bear in mind throughout that Paul is not interested in mere anthropology; his is a theologically, not medically, oriented evaluation of human nature.

Not surprisingly, there has long been interest in Paul's anthropological discussions. Indeed, the dominant discussion of the whole matter that set the agenda for all subsequent efforts, the work of Rudolf Bultmann, in effect approaches the whole of Paul's thought through his anthropological remarks.[32] I agree that Paul's anthropological remarks are crucial, but I would not see them as the key to his entire thought world, nor would I urge that they are the starting point for understanding that thought world.

Bultmann brought to his discussion of Paul's anthropological terms certain assumptions about human nature that were highly influenced not merely by the "introspective consciousness of the West,"[33] but more particularly by

---

[32]See Rudolf Bultmann, *Theology of the New Testament*, vol. 1 (New York: Scribner, 1951).
[33]A phrase we owe to Krister Stendahl.

philosophical existentialism, a tradition indebted to various people ranging
from Kierkegaard to Sartre. Bultmann in fact uses existentialism as something of a hermeneutical key to unlock the Pauline mysteries for modern
human beings or, better said, to contemporize Paul's discussion to make it
a dialogue partner with modern Western society, which is highly fixated
on the psychological dimension of the individual. This leads to certain key
Bultmannian slogans that are meant to encapsulate Paul's thought, such as
"Become what you already are," which assumes that ancients were as identity
conscious as moderns are.

Not surprisingly, in his Lutheran environment Bultmann interprets, for
example, the term *sarx* ("flesh") not as the lower, sensual part of the self but
rather as the whole self, oriented toward itself, setting itself up as independent
from God and therefore truly self-centered (in short, Luther's and Pascal's
"the heart turned in upon itself"). Bultmann also interpreted the term *sōma*
("body") as a description not of the outer physical part of a human being
but rather as a term that describes the whole person (a person does not *have*
a body but rather *is* a body).[34] He is rightly critiqued by Robert Gundry on
these points, who shows that even just at the exegetical level, such an interpretation of Paul's use of *sōma* (and *sarx*) cannot not pass muster.[35]

The upshot of recent scholarly discussion of older views of Paul's anthropological views for those who are questing for the historical Paul today is
that we must be very wary of discussions of Paul's anthropological terms that
(1) disregard sociological and anthropological data about ancient persons, or
(2) approach the Pauline anthropological terms in purely modern terms using
modern psychological or philosophical categories to "contemporize" Paul, or
(3) simply assume that Paul's terminology can be analyzed from a theological
point of view with no attention paid to ancient theories of human personality. I propose to analyze a few of Paul's terms in the context of both his Jewish
background and his audience's Greco-Roman foreground.

For Paul, the term *kardia* ("heart") means much the same as it meant for
the Old Testament writers. The heart is seen neither simply as a pump that
sends blood throughout the body nor merely as the locale of human feelings
but rather as the control center of human personality—the seat of thought,

[34]Bultmann, *Theology of the New Testament*, pp. 232-48. For the famous quotation about the body
see, pp. 192-94.
[35]Robert H. Gundry, *Sōma in Biblical Theology: With Emphasis on Pauline Anthropology* (SNTSMS 29;
Cambridge: Cambridge University Press, 1976).

will and affections. The heart can be either good or bad (Rom 10:8). In Romans 1:21 we find that the "heart" is the place where thinking happens (in fact, here many translations render *kardia* as "mind"), but in Romans 1:24 it is associated with lusts and desires. Romans 1:21 also indicates that all persons outside of Christ experience a heart that is darkened. In Romans 2:5 we hear about spiritual hardening of the arteries, and by contrast in Romans 2:29 we hear that circumcision of the heart has to do with the heart's disposition, the cutting away of the calloused or hardened tissue. The heart furthermore is said to be the locale of good desires and even belief (Rom 10:1, 10), and in fact it is said to be the place where the Spirit resides in the human life (2 Cor 1:22). From the flexibility of Paul's use of *kardia* we must conclude that he is not discussing the physical organ in the human body, and so he uses the term metaphorically, and furthermore it appears that the heart is an instrument of one's ego or personality and so can be either good or bad depending on the a person's condition.

The term *nous* ("mind") is used in rather similar fashion. It too is an instrument of the entire person and so can be the tool of either the flesh or the Spirit. It probably is a mistake to think that Paul sees "mind" (reasoning faculty, storehouse of knowledge [1 Cor 14:14-19]) as simply the higher side of human personality, with flesh being the lower or more animalistic side, because Paul can speak of a fleshly mind or "the mind of his flesh" (Col 2:18). The point of this last text is that the mind can be carnal, not merely made of flesh. The near synonym to *nous* is *phronēma* ("mind"), and it too can be said to be carnal (Rom 8:6-7).[36]

A revealing passage is Romans 7:22-25. In Romans 7:23, 25 mind is contrasted with flesh. Flesh in this text is associated with sin that dwells in one's members. Mind in this context is associated with the inner self or conscience, attempting to serve the law of God. We must conclude that this passage suggests that mind involves the inner being, the self, conscience, and is seen here as a good thing as opposed to flesh, which involves sinful desires grounded in one's fallen physical nature. A conscious orientation that follows this fallen nature is what Paul is referring to by a "fleshly mind" or a "mind set on the flesh." There is a very real sense in which Paul thinks that the mind is the key to one's orientation; hence he can discuss the renewal of the mind in Christ (Rom 12:2).

---

[36]On these two terms, see James D. G. Dunn, *The Theology of Paul the Apostle* (Grand Rapids: Eerdmans, 1997), pp. 73-75.

Though sparingly, Paul does use the term *pneuma* of the human spirit. In 1 Corinthians 14:14 (cf. 1 Cor 14:32) he speaks of "my spirit," and in the very next verse spirit and mind are contrasted. Surely 2 Corinthians 7:1 must also be a reference to the human spirit, as the text refers to defilers of the flesh and the spirit. "Spirit" seems to refer to the suprarational or noncognitive aspects of human experience—in short, that which goes beyond the flesh. Dale Martin provides some reason to rethink the notion that Paul means something immaterial by *pneuma*. For one thing, the term *pneuma* also means "wind" or "air," which certainly was not viewed as nonmaterial in antiquity. "For most ancient theorists, *pneuma* is a kind of 'stuff' that is the agent of perception, motion and life itself; it pervades other forms of stuff and, together with those other forms, constitutes the self."[37] It may be that this is the case with Paul as well. Among other things, this would mean that when Paul talks about a "spiritual body" in 1 Corinthians 15:44-49, he is not talking about a nonmaterial body. He would either be referring to a body made out of the stuff known as *pneuma* or be talking about a body completely empowered by the Holy Spirit, probably the latter.

It is clear enough from a text such as 1 Corinthians 2:11-12, where Paul parallels the human spirit and the Holy Spirit, that although he sees the two in similar ways, they are clearly distinguishable (the Holy Spirit needs no salvation [see 1 Cor 5:5]). The Holy Spirit does not inherently dwell within a human person; that happens only through faith in Christ. Paul's references to the human spirit are sparse, but those to the Holy Spirit are plentiful. From this James Dunn correctly concludes, "For Paul the gospel is not about an innate spirituality awaiting release, but about the divine Spirit acting upon and in a person from without. . . . [But the human] spirit is evidently that dimension of the human person by means of which the person relates most directly to God."[38] Of course, Paul can use *pneuma* metaphorically (e.g., the spirit of slavery or of adoption [Rom 8:15]). In Romans 11:8 the term seems to refer to an attitude or orientation of stupor.

Paul also uses the term *psychē* sparingly, even if we include the cognate *psychikos*. It is clear enough that "soul" is not a good translation for this term when found in the Pauline corpus. For example, in Romans 13:1 it simply

---

[37]Dale B. Martin, *The Corinthian Body* (New Haven: Yale University Press, 1995) p. 21. Compare, for example, Dio Chrysostom, who says that *pneuma* is the substance sucked in by people for nourishment (*Dei cogn.* 30).
[38]Dunn, *Theology of Paul the Apostle*, pp. 76-77.

means every "living person." In Romans 1, where *psychē* is used in its Old Testament sense, it simply means life or self, as in 1 Corinthians 15:45, where Adam is said to be a living "being" (a living *psychē*). Similarly, in Romans 16:4 Paul uses *psychē* to speak of those who risked their "lives" (cf. Phil 2:30). At times the term is simply synonymous with "human being" (Rom 2:9; cf. Rom 13:1). Some have used 1 Thessalonians 5:23 to suggest that Paul had a trichotomous view of human nature (body, soul, spirit), but this is highly unlikely. Here *psychē* probably refers to the natural life principle that animates the body.

The term *psychikos* is an adjective used by Paul in its normal sense of "physical" or "natural"—in other words, just the opposite of "soul." It stands on the side of the unspiritual rather than the spiritual (see 1 Cor 2:14; 15:44, 46). The *psychikos* person is someone without the Holy Spirit and thus living on the basis of natural life and natural life principles alone. Paul's use of the term *psychē* shows quite clearly that it is inadequate to read his anthropological terms purely from the perspective of the Greco-Roman philosophical dualism separating body and soul. Paul's usage is far closer to the Hebrew concept of the *nepeš*, which ranges in meaning from "life breath" (the natural animating principle) to "human being animated by life breath" (a living *nepeš* = a living person). For Paul, the human spirit and the human heart, not the human *psychē*, represent the ultimate depths of the human personality.

It is true enough that there is a certain limited anthropological dualism in Paul's letters. We hear of spirit versus the mind, or spirit versus the flesh, or even spirit versus the body. This sort of terminology raises the question about the "inner person/outer person" terminology (see, e.g., 2 Cor 4) and the "old person/new person" terminology. In Romans 7:22-23 the innermost self is either identified or closely associated with the mind. Paul does not see the body as the prison house of the soul, nor does he denigrate the physical body. Since Paul was a Jew with a strong creation theology based on Genesis 1–2, we would not have expected the latter in any case. Paul is not simply adopting the Hellenistic contrast between inner person and outer person, for he also adapts the terminology for his own purposes. For example, in 2 Corinthians 4:16 it is the inner person who is being renewed (cf. Rom 12:2). The inner person, then, cannot simply be identified with the "new creature in Christ" or the "new person"; rather, the "inner person" refers to the mind and/or the human spirit, both of which need renewal, being part of fallen human nature. The phrase "old person" or "old nature" is repeatedly said by

Paul to be what has been crucified and put off at the point of conversion (see Rom 6:6; Col 3:9; Eph 4:22).

This in turn means that the outer person must be seen as the physical body subject to disease, decay and death. The inner person has to do with the nonphysical (though not necessarily nonmaterial) aspects of human personality. The human mind or spirit or heart is revived in conversion, but the body is not (Eph 3:16). This internal revival is what is meant by being a "new creature" or by "putting on the new creation" (Col 3:10; Eph 4:24). It is interesting that this limited dualism nonetheless does not lead Paul to a view where the body is seen as evil, as the real problem, with the mind being seen as good, as the higher nature. Paul is perfectly capable of talking about carnal minds or defiled spirits.

In fact, the body is caught in the middle of a struggle between the inner person and sin reigning there in the case of the nonbeliever (Rom 7) and between the flesh and the Holy Spirit in the believer (Gal 5:16-26). The new creation in principle involves the whole person (body, mind, spirit, heart), but until the day of resurrection, the body does not experience the renewal or new creation. Even miracles are not seen as any sort of permanent renewal of the body, and no doubt this is why Paul refers little to such healing miracles. It would be inappropriate to understand miracles as new creation in the body, when resurrection provides a lasting form of newness in the flesh, though one could say that miracles provide a foreshadowing and foretaste of the bodily resurrection. But in the main, Paul emphasizes the opposite about the body in the here and now: it is wasting away (2 Cor 4–5).

What of Paul's use of the terms *sōma* ("body") and *sarx* ("flesh")? Paul can use both of these terms to refer to an individual's physical body or nature. Notice the rapid succession of synonyms in Romans 7:23-25: "my members," "this body," "my flesh." It is also the case that Paul can use *sōma* in a more metaphorical way. As we might speak of a body of beliefs, Paul speaks of a principle ("body") or proneness or inclination to evil or sin (Rom 8:4-13). Furthermore, there is also clearly a metaphorical use of the term *sarx* in a text such as Romans 7:5, where we hear that believers no longer live in the flesh. Obviously, this does mean that believers have shed their skin; rather, it refers to not living according to or being controlled by one's sinful inclinations or desires (see Rom 8:9). Christians, then, are those who do not walk according to the flesh, which is to say, do not live and act on the basis of sinful inclinations and desires. Living according to the flesh involves setting one's mind on fleshly things (Rom 8:5). Paul does not see the physical flesh as evil in itself, but he does see it as easy prey for sinful desires, hence the surprising phrase applied to Christ, who appeared "in the likeness of sinful flesh" (Rom 8:3). Flesh is also weak because it has needs and strong desires. Sin is seen as clearly more powerful than either the physical flesh or, for that matter, the human mind, unless renewed in Christ. Sin in a fallen person can stifle even the best intentions (Rom 7:22-23). "Flesh" is perhaps the most obvious evidence of the self-centered, self-indulgent nature of a fallen person. Often, fallen persons do not even see their sinful inclinations as either wrong or as self-destructive.

The term *sōma* can be used simply of the human physical body (1 Cor 15:34-39; 2 Cor 5:8), but can it also refer to the whole person, for instance in 1 Corinthians 6:12-20? We cannot radically separate body from personhood and human spirit in this life; nevertheless, even in 1 Corinthians 6:12-20 Paul is not saying that the *sōma is* the whole person even. Rather, how one uses one's body affects the whole person. The physical body, being the weak link in the human armor, can be dominated by sinful desires and even destroyed by them (Rom 6:6). This domination is what has been cut off or circumcised in Christ. Although sin remains, it does not reign in the life of the believer. Notice the progression in Romans 6:6: the old self has been crucified with the result that the body of sin (i.e. the body as dominated by sin) might be destroyed. The speaker in Romans 7:14-25 does not wish to be delivered from the self, or even from the body per se, but rather from the physical body as it is dominated by sin and as it is heading for both spiritual and physical death.

Paul does not think of his converts as isolated individuals who then as an aggregate make up the body of Christ, like individual billiard balls make up a rack when all of them are placed within the triangularly shaped arranging device. For Paul, Christians are actually spiritually a part of each other and spiritually united to Christ the head through their own corporate existence. When it comes to the body of Christ, the whole is greater than the sum of the parts. There is an interactive dimension and interconnectedness between individuals and with the living Christ in heaven. This is why what happens to and with the microcosmic body of the individual Christian can affect not only the macrocosmic body of Christ but also, in some sense, even Christ himself (see discussion on 1 Cor 6:15 below).

Jerome Neyrey rightly stresses that the human body was seen as a microcosm of the larger community. Getting rid of pollution in the community had as a parallel dealing with pollution in an individual's body. So, for example, if a community had been violated by an enemy and damaged or destroyed, one would find individuals going through ritual cleansing of their own bodies, particularly of the orifices, to rid themselves of the effects of pollution. Pollution of the individual could lead to or be part of pollution of the community and vice versa, and necessary cleansing of the community could require cleansing of all its individuals. In a world where knowledge of communicable diseases was far from prevalent and knowledge of microscopic bacteria and viruses was unknown, the ancients nevertheless believed firmly in the interconnectedness and interactive nature of individual and community and took environmental factors affecting human life far more seriously than some moderns do.[39]

This leads us to Paul's paradigmatic statement about the moral struggle of the Christian life, Galatians 5:16-25.[40] Notice that the tension in the Christian life is said to be not between the human spirit and the human flesh but rather between the Holy Spirit and the flesh, with the latter having primarily a metaphorical sense, though of course it entails deeds done in and by the body. It is not the flesh as merely flesh that goads a person to sin; it is the flesh as sinful inclination that does this. Notice that all the works of the flesh listed in Galatians 5:19 are negative, which would not be the case were he talking just about works of the body or merely physical activities. "Flesh," then, is not just mortal frailty but rather is a perverse inclination. Here and elsewhere it is a major mistake to see Paul as an ascetic of some sort. This text reminds us that there is an eschatological tension between the leading of the Spirit in the Christian life and the goading of the flesh. The Holy Spirit is pulling in one direction, the sinful inclinations in another. Literally, the text speaks of the Spirit "desiring" against the flesh and vice versa (Gal 5:17).

This means that there is a major difference between Galatians 5:16-25 and Romans 7:7-25. "In Romans 7:7-25 the power of indwelling sin *prevents* the person existing under the law from fulfilling the divine law in which his inmost self delights; the 'law of sin' in his members wages war against the 'law of the mind' (Rom 7:22f.), and at this stage no mention is made of the Spirit, whereas the conflict in the present [Galatians] text is between flesh

---

[39]See Jerome H. Neyrey, *Paul, in Other Words: A Cultural Reading of His Letters* (Louisville: Westminster John Knox, 1990), chap. 5.

[40]On this, see Ben Witherington III, *Grace in Galatia: A Commentary on St. Paul's Letter to the Galatians* (Grand Rapids: Eerdmans, 1998), pp. 389-413.

and Spirit."[41] Galatians 5:16 is properly translated "Walk by the Spirit, and you will not fulfill the desires of the flesh." A means of victory over sinful inclinations is stressed here. In Romans 7 we hear the cry of one who cannot do what, in his mind, he would like to do. In Galatians 5 the battle is real but not hopeless. If Christians live and act according to the leading of the Spirit, they will not be fulfilling fleshly desires. This implies that the Christian must actively will and do the good, but it also implies that such willing and doing is quite possible. Submitting to the Spirit repeatedly leads to liberation from such desires and inclination. Indeed, submitting to the Spirit leads to character formation in the image of Christ, such that love, joy, peace, patience, kindness, and the like come to characterize one's life.

But here again we are confronted with the fact that the Christian is enmeshed in a social network. The Christian has a relationship with God, and in particular with the Holy Spirit, who dwells both within the individual mortal vessel and in the midst of the community as a whole (cf. 1 Cor 3:16-17 with 1 Cor 6:19). The Christian is unable to manifest the fruit of the Spirit apart from a relationship with the Holy Spirit or apart from drawing on the resources of the Spirit within one's own life and within the life of the Christian community. Individual Christian life, then, is that in which one is thoroughly dependent on God in the person of the Holy Spirit and on one's brothers and sisters as the body of Christ just to be a Christian at all. It not just a matter of the individual's relationship to Jesus Christ, for even that relationship is mediated to a large degree through the body of Christ, of which Christ is the head. The corporate identity is primary, the individual identity is derived from it.

THE BODY OF CHRIST IN 1 CORINTHIANS 5-6

Having completed this all too brief survey of Pauline anthropological terms, we return to 1 Corinthians 5-6. Modern readers of these chapters find themselves in a conceptual world vastly different from their own. It is clear that Paul's primary concern in these chapters is the moral purity of the body of Christ and protecting it from pollution. This pollution can happen when a church member sins within the community or goes outside of it to sin. The analogy is drawn with leaven and dough, with leaven being rotten matter that might pollute the dough. Paul will demand that the Corinthian Chris-

---

[41]F. F. Bruce, *The Epistle to the Galatians: A Commentary on the Greek Text* (NIGTC; Grand Rapids: Eerdmans, 1982), p. 244.

tians cleanse the body of Christ by expelling the polluting agent. According to Dale Martin, what we see here is a "modified sectarianism."

> Although [Paul] insists on maintaining firm boundaries between those inside and outside the church, socially those boundaries are permeable. Paul is not afraid that social contact between a Christian and a non-Christian will pollute the church but he does think that the disguised presence within the church of a representative from the outside, from the "cosmos" that should be "out there," threatens the whole body. The body of Christ is not polluted by mere contact with the cosmos, but it may be polluted if its boundaries are permeated and an element of the cosmos gains entry into the body.[42]

This explanation raises some questions about 1 Corinthians 5—6. What does Paul mean by being "present in spirit"? Since 1 Corinthians was to be read in worship and acted upon by the congregation, it appears that Paul sees himself as present by proxy in his letter. He has expressed his heart in the letter, and when it is properly delivered, his spirit-filled words will come alive, and they will be with the congregation, speaking to them and their situation directly. Paul meanwhile will be praying fervently for the good effect of this letter, even praying in the Spirit (glossolalia?). Something of this sort seems to capture the essence of 1 Corinthians 5:3. By his words Paul has already passed judgment on this offender. Paul believes that when his words are read, "my spirit is present with the power of our Lord Jesus." Like Jesus' healing words spoken at a distance for the daughter of the Syrophoencian woman, Paul believes that he is present by extension through his words, and that they have the power of the omnipresent Christ behind them.

How, then, will Satan destroy the "flesh" of this man? One might reason that Satan would be more likely to encourage than destroy sinful inclinations. Could Paul really be talking about the death of this man? This is quite possible, especially since he refers to the saving of the man's "spirit" only at the Day of the Lord. Or is he? Martin suggests that "saving of the spirit" at the Day of the Lord could refer to the saving of the "spirit" of the congregation rather than the individual.[43] This is quite possible. It is also possible, however, that Paul has in mind the ultimate salvation of the man in question, after this sort of shock therapy and shaming had been administered to him.

Since there was only one Christian group in Corinth, this sort of expulsion might very well move to repentance an offender who wished to continue

---

[42]Martin, *Corinthian Body*, p. 170.
[43]Ibid., pp. 170-75.

to be a Christian, and there is also the parallel practice at Qumran (cf. Leviticus) whereby such persons were expelled as sinners who belonged "outside the camp." Perhaps Paul hoped for repentance on the near horizon, but at least ultimately repentance before death so that the salvation of the man's self, his spirit, could come to pass. In other words, church discipline was necessary for the health of the church but also if there was to be hope of salvation for the man. It was not punitive but rather intended to bring health both to the body and the individual offender. His sinful inclinations must be doused. Finally, this approach might well work if indeed the woman involved had been a part of and remained in the community. In any event, we do indeed see in this text a very clear example of Paul as a sectarian person drawing careful moral boundaries around his community.[44] We see a Paul quite ready to exercise church discipline and believing that the good of the community is more important than the social well-being of the individual, even though the expulsion was also seen as done for the sake of the individual. Paul is a collectivist. He is quite prepared to upset the status quo and ruffle various elite feathers to maintain a body of Christ that has moral integrity.

We must now consider briefly 1 Corinthians 6:12-20. This text affirms certain truths about the individual body of the believer. Whereas the congregation as a body is spoken of in 1 Corinthians 5 (see 1 Cor 3:16-17), the end of this passage in 1 Corinthians 6 refers to the body of an individual Christian being a temple in which the Holy Spirit is meant to dwell. There is some sort of connection, spiritually, between the microcosmic body of the individual believer and the macrocosmic body of Christ, such that when an individual believer couples with a prostitute, he unites the member of Christ with a harlot, and so the body of Christ is polluted. The believer is not only a member of the body of Christ but also of one spirit with the Lord by being connected to the body of Christ.

Sharing a one-flesh union with a prostitute pollutes not only one's own spirit but also one's relationships, both with the Lord and with Christ's people. There is a spiritual bond created between two human beings who couple, and this bond can pollute the already extant bond that one has with the Lord and with his people. Indeed, it can cause spiritual alienation from both Christ and the body and so ultimately cause spiritual death. The situation seems similar to that described in 1 Corinthians 5, although the terminology varies a bit. In both cases we hear about bodies and spirits on the personal and microcos-

---

[44]Ibid.

mic level and bodies and the Spirit on the macrocosmic level. Evidently, Paul thinks that these terms are far more than metaphors. He assumes that there are real spiritual fellowships, connections, unions, pollution.

To be in Christ means a good deal more than to simply be in an association or society; it is to be spiritually linked with Christ and his body. This means that what one does with one's own body, linked as it is to one's spirit, also affects the body and, ultimately, the Lord. Here we have very clear proof, if any more were needed, that Paul did not believe in the concept of radical individualism, much less the private character of one's relationship with Christ. One is joined to Christ only in connection with being joined to Christ's body, and so "No man is an island, entire of itself, every man is a piece of the continent, a part of the main. If a clod be washed away from Europe, Europe is the less. . . . Any man's death diminishes me, for I am a part of mankind. . . . Therefore do not seek to know for whom the bell tolls, it tolls for thee" (John Donne, *Meditation XVII*). Pollution of the body is possible only if there is real spiritual *koinōnia* and union between the members of the body, as well as between the members and the head, Christ himself. Herein lies a clear picture of how deeply embedded Paul sees himself and others in the collective entity known as the body of Christ. They are but limbs of the larger entity, not like individual units within a box. Paul the anthropologist turns out to be Paul the ecclesiologist as well. This leads us to an exploration of Paul's views of body life insofar as it affects the religious roles and status of women and men.

PAUL'S VIEW OF THE BODY AND THE RELIGIOUS ROLES OF WOMEN AND MEN

In antiquity an advocate was a person who represented others sometimes in a legal dispute, sometimes in a business negotiation, sometimes in a series of negotiations during wartime, sometimes before an assembly promoting some particular group's cause. Paul was such an advocate, and although in his public preaching he was an apologist for the gospel discoursing with mostly nonbelievers, in his letters his audience was his own converts and his fellow Christians. Yet we still find him over and over again attempting to persuade these converts to do or be one thing or another. This is because his converts thus far had only caught a slight case of Christianity, they were only partially socialized, and what was required was for them to work out the implications of the gospel for their daily life and practices, for their beliefs and behavior. In a real sense, Paul was like contemporary advocates for various minority groups that deserve rightful recognition and fair treatment in society. Paul's advocacy was primarily on behalf of women, slaves, and whichever ethnic group in a particular locale was more likely to be neglected, taken advantage of, or discriminated against. What we will discover in this section is that Paul is an advocate not just of new individuals but of a new society known as the "body of Christ," where the problems of prejudice, hatred, bigotry, discrimination are overcome, and not only so, but the problems of fear of the unknown and the dark powers are overcome by faith and light.

Human nature, according to Paul, consists of body and spirit, or body and mind, and a natural animating principle. For the Christian, however, there is a further factor, the Holy Spirit, and that Spirit can renew the mind, purify the spirit, even heal the body. The Spirit is such a major factor that Paul believes not only that a person can be better, be a person who manifests the character of Christ or the fruit of the Spirit, but also that a person can do better. A person can have victory over sinful inclinations, a person can use his or her gifts and graces for the glory of God. But a person can do any of this only in the context of the community of God, the body of Christ. A new person has to be a part of a new creation in order to have a context to be all that he or she can be. The person must be embedded in a particular people. So what does it really mean to be "in Christ," and how is that different from being a part of any other group in the Greco-Roman world?

Paul gives us a clue of his real vision of Christian community by following the *via negativa*, defining that community by what it is not. We know that this was a significant matter for Paul, for he says the same thing, with a few variations, to four separate groups of converts: first to the Galatians, then to the Corinthians, then to the Romans, and finally to the Colossians. What is interesting about this is that Paul himself did not found the latter two of these churches. I present this teaching here in parallel columns.

Table 11.1. Paul's *via negativa* Definition of Christian Community

Galatians 3:28	1 Corinthians 12:13	Romans 10:12	Colossians 3:11
Not any Jew or Greek, not any slave or free, not any male and female; for you are all one person in Christ.	In one Spirit we were all baptized into one body, Jews or Greeks, slaves or free.	For there is not a distinction between Jew and Greek, for the same [is] Lord of all.	Not any Greek and Jew, circumcised and uncircumcised, barbarian, Scythian, slvae, free, but Christ is all in all.

The male/female pair occurs only in Galatians, and the slave/free pair shows up in Galatians, Corinthians, and Colossians, but the one pair com-

mon to all four texts is the Jew/Greek pair, which probably from the Pauline
point of view was the most significant of the three pairs. I have dealt at length
with Galatians 3:28 elsewhere,[45] so here I will mainly summarize what I have
said there. What is crucial for us about these texts is neither their source nor
how some of these pairs were used elsewhere and in later contexts but rather
how Paul is using them in his letters. The earliest of the texts, the one from
Galatians, is the fullest and in most ways the most revealing.

Notice that the Galatians text deals with ethnic, social and sexual divisions in society; in other words, it is rather comprehensive. The basic idea
is that all that divided Paul's society could be united in Christ. These basic
markers used by people to determine identity and status in Paul's world were
no longer to do so. What was to determine identity and status was Christ
and whether one was in his body. Notice how Colossians 3:11 puts it: Christ
is everything and in everyone in his body. He is the definer of his people.
Romans 10:12 insists that there is no distinction between Jew and Greek,
not because of anything inherent in them but rather because the same Lord
is Lord of them all. It has been suggested, especially on the basis of Galatians
3:28, that here we are dealing with a baptismal formula, which may well be
correct. This view can be strongly supported from the 1 Corinthians 12:13
form of this saying.[46] The point, then, is the identity and boundary markers
left behind when one was baptized, which are then replaced by one's new
identity in Christ. Especially the end of Galatians 3:28 makes clear what
a collectivist vision of a Christian identity Paul has. The formula does not
say merely that all are united in Christ; it says that all become one person in
Christ.[47] If we ask which person and take a clue from the masculine form of

---

[45]See Ben Witherington III, "Rite and Rights for Women—Galatians 3:28," *NTS* 27 (1981): 593-
604.

[46]This particular version of the formula also makes clear as the others do not that Paul is talking not
just about adherence or joining but rather about a spiritual transaction in which the Holy Spirit
unites one with or immerses one in Christ's body and then becomes the resident inward resource
providing ongoing spiritual life and guidance for the believer. It is interesting that Paul uses the
language of water baptism here but does not specifically mention the rite. This is probably because, as 1 Corinthians 1:14-15 shows, Paul believed that conversion, the spiritual transformation,
was what was crucial. Initiation was not absolutely necessary, though perhaps ideally the rite and
the reality ought to go closely together. In other words, the spiritual transaction, not the water
rite, is what joins one to the body of Christ, though doubtless the two could and sometimes did
come together in close sequence or even simultaneously. On this topic, see Ben Witherington III,
Troubled Waters: The Real New Testament Theology of Baptism (Waco, Tex.: Baylor University Press,
2007).

[47]The masculine form of the word "one" in the Greek makes clear that Paul is talking not about one
thing, force, or union but rather about one person.

the word "one" in the Greek, the answer surely must be Christ himself or, better said, the extension of him on earth known as his body. Jews, Gentiles, slaves, free, women, men—all have become part of the one body of the person Christ, and Christ now defines who they are. They are Christians, those who model, manifest, make known, follow the Christ.[48]

There is, however, one peculiar feature about Galatians 3:28. Paul goes out of his way to break up what would otherwise be a threefold "or" parallelism when he says of the last pair "no male *and* female." Some commentators simply ignore this change, and some simply say that Paul is quoting Genesis 1:27 but draw no conclusions from this fact. I suggest two possible meanings of this change: (1) Paul is denying that there is any androgyny in Christ. Christ is not the creator of an androgynous person representing him on earth. This would be in response to those who suggested such a thing, for there were indeed even early Jewish traditions, mentioned by Philo, for example, that suggested that the original Adam was both male and female. The point here would be that the final "person" would not be like that, whatever one might think of the first Adam.[49] (2) Another possibility takes more seriously the allusion to Genesis 1:27-28 lxx and suggests that Paul is saying that in Christ there is no necessary coupling of male and female. In other words, the Genesis mandate to be fruitful and multiply, connected as it is to the male/female division of humanity, is no longer required of humanity, or at least of those in Christ. It is even possible that some of the Judaizers in Galatia had suggested that since women could not be circumcised, the way for them to become full members of the Christian community was to marry a circumcised Christian male. Paul, as we know from 1 Corinthians 7, not only was prepared to say that Christians need not marry but even says that singleness, if it is one's gift and calling from God, is preferable because it leaves more time for the things of the Lord.

If either of these two theories is correct, it means that Paul is not at all

---

[48]Is Paul then an advocate of some sort of "leveling" or "sameness" that ignores or even destroys particularity? No, he is not. Look at Romans 9–11 and how Paul still affirms and is proud of being a Jew and says that it has many benefits. What Paul is saying, however, is that one's ongoing particularity has been transcended or transformed such that it is not the most defining part of who one is. What is more defining and crucial is being a new creature in Christ; indeed, it is the latter that allows one to have a permanent relationship with God and with Christ's body. From a soteriological point of view, the old distinctions are transcended by the new identity. From a sociological point of view, they still exist and have some benefits.

[49]On these issues, see Wayne A. Meeks, "The Image of the Androgyne: Some Uses of a Symbol in Earliest Christianity," *HR* 13 (1974): 165-208.

suggesting that sexual differences disappear or are unimportant in Christ, and judging from texts such as 1 Corinthians 11, we certainly would not conclude that such was Paul's position. What Paul is denying is that the ethnic differences or the social relationships of slave and free, male and female, are constitutive of the body of Christ and its identity; rather, all are members of the one body as brothers and sisters in Christ. This is the fundamental reality in Christ. One's ethnic origins, one's social condition, one's marital status neither adds to nor subtracts from that reality and the status that it conveys.

The one factor that Colossians 3:11 adds to this discussion is that it makes evident that even non-Greek-speaking persons (the *barbaroi*) and those at the edge of the empire who were much feared (Scythians) could be in Christ and would have the same status as everyone else in Christ. Christ would provide an all-encompassing identity for the human race, and no group would be excluded. It may also be added that the conclusion of this verse no doubt echoes the emphasis in the hymnic material in Colossians 1:16-20. "It is precisely because of the cosmic scope of Christ's work, including above all his act of reconciliation (1:20), that such internal divisions and ways of categorizing peoples and individuals have ceased to have meaning as determinants of Christian self-perception, conduct and relationships. . . . If 'Christ is everything and in everything,' then nothing can diminish or disparage the standing of any one human in relationship to another or to God."[50] Here once again we have the very clear concept of an ancient collectivist culture that suggests that the group defines the identity of the individuals in it, not the other way around.

Yet we need to ask whether this is simply some sort of ideal or if in fact it involved a social program. Did Paul really advocate the breaking down of these barriers in Christ and the revaluation of basic social values in the Christian community? Was he really an advocate for new roles for slaves, Gentiles and women? The answer is yes, as we will see, but there is a reason why Paul believed that such a new vision of the humankind could in fact be implemented.

The work of Christ had set those in Christ free from the powers and principalities, free from the customs and older traditions, free from the elementary principles of the universe, free from the pagan national deities and emperor cult, and free from the reign of sin within the human heart. All the things that enslaved the person had been dealt with through Christ's death and resurrection and his sending of the Spirit. Although these enslaving forces had not ceased to exist, in community and in Christ there was freedom to be all that one was called and meant to be. Galatians 3:28 is not just a manifesto or a goal; it is something that Paul saw as coming to pass, at least in part, in the here and now. Already there really was a new community, and this meant new roles and opportunities for Gentiles and Jews, slaves and free, men and women were now possible in Christ.

We can see this new agenda already working itself out in, for instance, the roles that people such as Titus and other Gentiles were being allowed to play in the body of Christ and as part of the group of Paul's coworkers. Paul valued the service of the slave Onesimus as a newly found brother and coworker in Christ, and because of his understanding of the implications of Onesimus's conversion, Paul made the case to Philemon for the manumission of Onesimus.[51] Clearly, social change of status and roles within the new people of God was envisioned by Paul for such persons. What, then, can we say about Paul's view of women and their roles?

There are several key points and clues along the way. The teaching of Galatians 3:28 as amplified in 1 Corinthians 7 makes clear that Christians, both women and men, were not obligated to marry. This in itself meant that women could assume roles other than wife and mother in the Christian community. What roles do we find them playing in Paul's letters? It is clear enough that some women were among Paul's coworkers in ministry. This is evident from texts such as Philippians 4:2-3. Paul would hardly settle a private squabble in such a public letter, but a struggle between two coworkers and leaders in Philippi was another matter. Then there is Romans 16:1, where we hear about Phoebe the deacon of the church at Cenchreae near Corinth, who also seems to be the bearer of Paul's letter to Rome. The term *diakonos* applied to Phoebe is the same one that Paul uses of his own ministerial role (1 Cor 3:5; 2 Cor 3:6). Phoebe also is seen as a benefactor or possibly even a supervising leader, depending on how one renders *prostatis* in Romans 16:2. Equally clear are the references to Priscilla and Aquila, a husband/wife ministerial team repeatedly presented as Paul's coworkers for the gospel (Rom 16:3-4; 1 Cor 16:9 [note the church in their house]). And we hear of Andronicus and Junia, who are said to be prominent among the apostles (Rom

---

[51]See Ben Witherington III, *The Letters to Philemon, the Colossians, and the Ephesians: A Socio-Rhetorical Commentary* (Grand Rapids: Eerdmans, 2007).

16:7). This is most naturally taken to mean that both are apostles.[52]

The foregoing aforementioned texts raise serious doubts about whether Paul deserves the chauvinist label that some have applied to him. One of the main exponents of this view is Antoinette Clark Wire. She presents Paul as a repressive figure who has as his main opponents in Corinth the Corinthian women prophets.[53] This view fails not only because Paul more often criticizes men in 1 Corinthians (see, e.g, 1 Cor 5–6; 8–10), but also because 1 Corinthians 11:2-16 would be entirely pointless if Paul in fact was attempting to prevent rather than authorize women to speak in Christian worship. Furthermore, Paul also corrects the men in 1 Corinthians 11:2-16. Yet Wire follows the lead of other earlier feminist interpreters of Paul's discussions of women with head coverings in Corinth, such as Elisabeth Schüssler Fiorenza. Fiorenza's argument is even less plausible, for she recognizes that Paul had women as some of his coworkers in ministry.[54] It is interesting that some of the same arguments show up in the cases being argued by Wayne Grudem and others who see Paul taking a strongly traditional patriarchal view of women and their roles.[55]

On the other end of the spectrum are those who in essence see Paul as very much a feminist. The strategy of these scholars, such as William Walker, is to suggest that texts such as 1 Corinthians 11:2-16 and 1 Corinthians 14:33b-36 are interpolations,[56] or that they are post-Pauline or have been badly misunderstood, as with the readings by Alan Padgett and by Richard Clark Kroeger and Catherine Clark Kroeger.[57] Missing from all these discussions is

---

[52]For recent helpful studies along these lines, see Bruce W. Winter, *Roman Wives, Roman Widows: The Appearance of New Women and the Pauline Communities* (Grand Rapids: Eerdmans, 2003); E. J. Epp and B. R. Gaventa, *Junia: The First Woman Apostle*, (Minneapolis: Augsburg Fortress Press, 2005).

[53]Antoinette Clark Wire, *The Corinthian Women Prophets: A Reconstruction through Paul's Rhetoric* (Minneapolis: Fortress, 1990).

[54]See Elisabeth Schüssler Fiorenza, "Women in the Pre-Pauline and Pauline Churches," *USQR* 33 (1978): 153-66; *In Memory of Her: A Feminist Theological Reconstruction of Christian Origins* (New York: Crossroad, 1985), pp. 170-80.

[55]See Wayne A. Grudem, *The Gift of Prophecy in 1 Corinthians* (Washington, D.C.: University Press of America, 1982); "Does *kephale* Mean 'Source' or 'Authority Over' in Greek Literature? A Survey of 2,336 Examples," *TJ* 6 (1985): 38-59; George W. Knight, *The New Testament Teaching on the Role Relationship of Men and Women* (Grand Rapids: Baker, 1977).

[56]See William O. Walker, "The Burden of Proof in Identifying Interpolations in the Pauline Letters," *NTS* 33 (1987): 610-18. See the convincing refutation by Jerome Murphy-O'Connor, "1 Corinthians 11:2-16 Once Again," *CBQ* 50 (1988): 265-74.

[57]Alan Padgett, "The Pauline Rationale for Submission: Biblical Feminism and the *Hina* Clauses of Titus 2:1-10," *EvQ* 59 (1987): 39-52; Richard Clark Kroeger and Catherine Clark Kroeger, *I Suffer Not a Woman: Rethinking 1 Timothy 2:11-15 in Light of Ancient Evidence* (Grand Rapids: Baker, 1992).

the fact that Paul was pragmatic and worked with social structures and networks as he found them, seeking to reform them within the context of the Christian community.

It is not just Paul's position, but the direction or trajectory of his remarks when assessed against the context in which he was operating, that is crucial. The categories "chauvinist" and "feminist" are anachronistic if we are looking for the historical Paul and his views on this subject. Paul plays the societal cards that he is dealt, but he seeks to slip some new cards into the deck, all the while rewriting the rules for those who play the game in his communities. The cards that Paul was dealt show that he operated in a strongly patriarchal culture that often had highly schematized roles for men and women. It is hardly surprising under these circumstances that when he discusses household management, he bears witness to the preexisting patriarchal structure of the home or to the male/female distinctions that often existed in forms of dress and in ritual practices. But the crucial question is this: "What does Paul do with these preexisting structures and customs?" Does he simply endorse them, or does he modify them, and if he modifies them, what is the direction or aim or effect of his remarks? How would they have been heard in his own culture and time? In other words, if we are to rightly decide whether Paul was a reformer or a traditionalist in regard to women and their roles, we must assess the social effect of his remarks in his own culture, not in ours.

Elsewhere I have compiled considerable evidence about women in the Pauline churches that indicates that Paul was indeed open to women playing a variety of roles in the church,[58] but inevitably the discussion usually comes down to texts such as 1 Corinthians 11:2-16; 14:33b-36; 1 Timothy 2 (for those who think that this last text comes from Paul). I suggest that whatever 1 Corinthians 14:33b-36 (which says that women should keep silence as even the law says) means, if it is not an interpolation, it cannot entail any sort of absolute censorship of women speaking in worship, because if that were the case, 1 Corinthians 11:2-16 would make no sense. In 1 Corinthians 11:2-16 we have a series of arguments meant to make clear under what conditions women and men could pray and prophecy during worship. There is no point to such arguments if in fact such activities are forbidden by the apostle. Had Paul wanted to prevent women from speaking in worship altogether, he could have spared himself the tortuous path that he trods to make his point

---

[58]See Witherington, *Women in the Earliest Churches*, pp. 76-127 and the notes. See also Hays, *Moral Vision of the New Testament*, pp. 52-60.

in 1 Corinthians 11. He could have simply said, "There will be no praying or prophesying by women—period."

Another point of importance about this text is that prophecy in Paul's view is the sort of speech that Paul himself offers to his own converts time and again. It is not something that can readily be distinguished in importance from teaching and preaching, and in any case, in terms of the list of church functionaries, Paul ranks those who prophesy right behind apostles (1 Cor 12:27, 29). In short, one cannot argue that women's prophesying is somehow a less important, or less enduring, or less official one than teaching or preaching. Notice that preachers and evangelists are not even listed in 1 Corinthians 12:27-30. In view of all this, one must also recognize that whatever the limitations involved in 1 Corinthians 14:33b-36 or even in 1 Timothy 2, these texts cannot be interpreted to refer to an absolute silencing of women in church. Instead, they must be indicative of corrections, made by the apostle to the Gentiles, to specific abuses of the legitimate gifts that women had and were expected to use.

Finally, it is worth adding that Paul's advocacy of women praying and prophesying in worship does not mean that he was the equivalent of a modern egalitarian who denied that gender makes any difference in the body of Christ.[59] He was an ancient person who in his own day would have been seen as working toward what we today would call a more egalitarian position. Nevertheless, Paul believes that symbolic representations of the goodness and reality of sexual differentiation should be maintained. This is the point of the whole argument about head coverings and, in the case of men, lack of head coverings. There is a reason for this.

Not ethnic differences, such as that between Gentile or Jew, or social differences, such as that between slave and free, but only gender differences are mentioned in the creation narrative as being connected to, grounded in and definitive of the image of God (Gen 1:27). In Paul's view, sexual differences, unlike these other differences, are not part of human fallenness but rather are a part of God's original good plan for humankind. Thus, although the image of God as male and female needs to be renewed in Christ, it does not need to be replaced or obliterated by some sort of androgynous identity. This theology of creation order about the goodness of gender differences makes explicable why Paul takes the stance that he does on homosexuality in Romans 1 and elsewhere.

---

[59]See Hays, *Moral Vision of the New Testmanent*, pp. 52-55; P. B. Payne, *Man and Woman: One in Christ* (Grand Rapids: Zondervan, 2009).

Furthermore, Paul would not have subscribed to the modern theory that human personality can be abstracted from one's gendered existence. He would not have seen humanness as some neutral core of being that can be distinguished from one's maleness or femaleness. To be truly human is to be male and female in the image of God. Thus, Paul looks for a way that both men and women can use the spiritual gifts given to them by God and at the same time indicate and affirm the goodness of the image of God as male and female in worship. To his credit, Paul finds a creative way of doing this that does not involve simply endorsing an older Jewish or Greco-Roman head-covering custom; he creates a new one for Christians.[60] Paul is no advocate of minimalism or abstinence in regard to women's roles in worship, but at the same time he is perfectly prepared to speak about a difference between a man and woman having to do with issues of headship and glory.

In Paul's understanding, equality has to do with both men and women being created in the image of God. It does not have to do with absolute sameness of nature, sameness in symbolic worship apparatus, sameness in all purposes for which one was created, sameness in all human tasks.[61] Indeed, for Paul, it is precisely difference and the insufficiency of each sex by itself that make both male and female important and necessary. Were men and women identical, there would be redundancy, and reproduction would be impossible or unnecessary. Neither man nor woman completely represents the image of God; that image is both male and female.

Thus once more I stress that it is no accident that Paul says in Galatians 3:28 "no male *and* female," breaking up the "or" parallelism. Men and women do not have to be coupled in Christ. Women do not need to be joined to men to be in Christ. Androgyny is the not the goal or the reality in Christ. Indeed, if we must insist on a "oneness" encompassing all, it is the collectivist vision of oneness involving the identity of Christ himself, which transcends and transforms all human identities, both male and female. The "one person" in "all are one person in Christ" is Christ himself. That is, Christian identity in the most important sense is determined by one who transcends and transforms us, Christ. Christian identity is not just about being all that we can be as individuals; rather, it is about becoming more and more Christlike as one

---

[60]See Ben Witherington III, *Conflict and Community in Corinth: A Socio-Rhetorical Commentary on 1 and 2 Corinthians* (Grand Rapids: Eerdmans, 1995), pp. 231-40.

[61]For example, note Paul's emphasis in 1 Corinthians 11 on men always coming forth from women ever since the reverse of this process characterized the creation of the first woman. The roles are not seen as interchangeable at any one point in time.

is molded by him. This transformation takes place not in isolation but rather in the context of being part of Christ's body.

David Horrell provides further evidence of Paul's radical social agendas as he instructed and constructed the body of Christ.[62] In a careful analysis of 1 Corinthians, Horrell shows how Paul seeks to systematically deconstruct the system of social stratification that had been brought by those of higher social status into the body of Christ and was affecting how that body was functioning. He puts the matter thus:

> Paul's criticism of the socially strong, coupled with the absence of any explicit demand for the subordination of weaker social groups, should surely lead us to question the appropriateness of the term love-patriarchialism as a summary of the social ethos of Paul's teaching in 1 Corinthians. . . .
>
> In 1 Corinthians he particularly attacks the socially prominent members of the community, requiring that their behaviour change, and demonstrating that God's way of achieving unity is to elect and honour the lowly and to call the strong to self-lowering. . . . While it is true . . . that Paul does not legitimate the dominant *social* order—on the contrary he undermines and inverts it—he does legitimate an ecclesiastical hierarchy in which he is at the top (at least in relation to the Corinthians). He outlines a hierarchy of leading functions (12.28-30), calls for submission to particular leaders (16.16), and presents himself as the Corinthians' only father—a position from which he is able (and willing) to threaten them with punishment (4.14-21).[63]

Here, by referring to "love-patriarchalism," Horrell is reacting to the term coined by Gerd Theissen to characterize Paul's vision of how the body of Christ ought to operate. By this term Theissen meant to suggest that the harsh aspects of the existing patriarchal social structures were ameliorated by the appeal to the dominant ones to love and respect the weaker members of the body of Christ, without significantly changing those structures. I agree with Horrell that this is an inadequate assessment of Paul's social strategy, an underestimation of the radicality of his social program.

Horrell demonstrates at some length that when Paul prohibits going to idol temples or taking fellow Christians to court, or criticizes sexual immorality, or insists on equal sharing at the Lord's Supper, or advocates Christian

---

[62]David G. Horrell, *The Social Ethos of the Corinthian Correspondence: Interests and Ideology from 1 Corinthians to 1 Clement* (SNTW; Edinburgh: T & T Clark, 1996).

[63]Ibid., pp. 196-97. It is important to add, however, that the hierarchy that Paul is talking about is an inverted one in the sense that it has a cruciform and servant character demanded of the leaders, modeling such behavior for the followers.

slaves taking the opportunity to be free if it presents itself, he was taking away the privileges of the social elite, in particular elite males in the congregation. At the same time, Paul's siding with the weak and inculcating an ethic of self-sacrificial service and a focus on Christ crucified, which is antithetical to any ordinary sort of self-glorification or self-aggrandizing activities, create a very different ethos in the Christian community from that which existed in the world. And yet, as Horrell rightly points out, this social critique did not mean that Paul was advocating a nonhierarchial vision of church leadership. The basis of this hierarchy was not gender or social status or race but rather one's call and gifts. Paul was no supporter of the world's social status quo being maintained in Christ, but at the same time he was no Quaker in his vision of the structuring of that body. Paul undoubtedly will continue to seem an enigma to those who do not see how social, sexual and racial egalitarianism and hierarchial church structure can be spoken of in the same breath. But what actually is Paul trying to accomplish in his household codes? We turn to them at this juncture.

PAUL AND THE HOUSEHOLD CODES

The Colossian Household Code (Colossians 3:18–4:1)

There has been no end of debate about these household codes, and since the one in Colossians seems to be one of the earliest forms of the code, a great deal of debate has centered there.[64] Roughly speaking, the discussion of the code has fallen into two parts: discussion of its content and of its form. John Barclay is right that "there is no precise analogy to the form and theme of the Colossian code, although one can point to many sources that discuss the theme of household relationships and a few texts (both Jewish and non-Jewish) in which such relationships are viewed from both sides."[65]

Some scholars suspect that this sort of code (and the one in Ephesians and perhaps also the one in 1 Peter) was constructed to counter a revolutionary

---

[64]The debate rages on. See Richard E. DeMaris, *The Colossians Controversy: Wisdom in Dispute at Colossae* (JSNTSup 96; Sheffield: JSOT Press, 1994); Clinton E. Arnold, *The Colossian Syncretism: The Interface between Christianity and Folk Belief at Colossae* (WUNT 2/77; Tubingen: Mohr Siebeck, 1995); Troy W. Martin, *By Philosophy and Empty Deceit: Colossians as Response to a Cynic Critique* (JSNTSup 118; Sheffield: Sheffield Academic Press, 1996). What all these studies have in common is too much mirror reading when it comes to trying to figure out the Colossian error and what therefore Paul is opposing. The least plausible of these three studies is that of Martin, who wants to insist that it was a purely Hellenistic philosophy that Paul was opposing.

[65]John M. G. Barclay, *Colossians and Philemon* (NTG; Sheffield: Sheffield Academic Press, 1997), p. 70. Note his further remark there: "It would be safer to say that the Colossian code has no exact formal antecedent."

spirit among Hellenistic Christians, particularly slaves and women,[66] or that
it was apologetical in character, countering the notion that Christians were
social radicals.[67] The problem with both of these suggestions is that they account neither for the exhortations to parents and children nor for the fact
that the Colossian code is directed to those who are already Christians in
Colossae and is directed to the whole household. Equally unconvincing is
the suggestion that there is nothing profoundly Christian or especially radical
about these household codes, as if they merely baptize the status quo and call
it good. To the contrary, when we compare this material either to the ancient
discussion of household management in Aristotle and other sources or to the
Stoic or Greco-Roman codes, we are astonished not only by the Christian elements but also by the social engineering being undertaken to limit the abuse
of power by the head of the household, using Christian rationales to equalize
and personalize as well as Christianize the relationship between that head
and the rest of the family. The fact is that in most of the parallel literature we
do not find the exhortation to heads of households to love their wives, or to
refrain from breaking the spirit of their children, or to treat their slaves with
some equity and justice.[68]

Thus, although what we find here may not be totally unique (most of it
is found in bits and pieces elsewhere), it certainly is distinctive of a Christian
approach to these interrelationships. As Horrell notes, what we find here is
the attempt to embed the Christian faith and its ethical values in the social
structures that already exist.[69] N. T. Wright puts the matter well:

> It is . . . extremely unlikely that Paul, having warned the young Christians
> against conforming their lives to the present world, would now require just
> that of them after all. Nor does he. The Stoics (who provide some of the closest
> parallels to these household lists) based their teaching on the law of nature: this
> is the way the world is, so this is how you must live in harmony with it. Paul
> bases his on the law of the *new* nature: Christ releases you to be truly human,

---

[66]James E. Crouch, *The Origin and Intention of the Colossian Haustafel* (FRLANT 109; Gottingen:
Vandenhoeck & Ruprecht, 1972).

[67]David L. Balch, *Let Wives Be Submissive: The Domestic Code in 1 Peter* (SBLMS 26; Chico, Calif.:
Scholars Press, 1981).

[68]In fact, the head of the household is rarely addressed in such codes at all. But see Seneca, *Epistu-
lae morales* 94.1. Notice how Seneca says that the proper philosophy will "advise how a husband
should conduct himself toward his wife, or how a father should bring up his children, or how a
master should rule his slaves." Here there are no matched pairs of advice, but only a focus on the
head of the household. See also Dionysius of Halicarnassus, *Antquitates romanae* 2.25.4–2.26.4.

[69]Horrell, *Social Ethos of the Corinthian Correspondence*.

and you must now learn to express your true self, according to the divine pattern, not in self-assertion but in self-giving.[70]

The attempt to see this code as an effort to stabilize the Pauline community in the post-Pauline situation and demonstrate that it was a supporter of the conventional cultural household codes and traditional virtues ignores the profound Christianizing of this material and the way it goes against the flow of the culture. It also goes against various aspects of traditional Jewish wisdom, which did seek to repristinize patriarchy (compare the attitude toward women's roles in Sirach and in Josephus, *Ag. Ap.* 2.24-30).

Here is the juncture at which to address the question of why we find this sort of advice given to slaves and masters if in fact Paul was arguing for the manumission of a slave in Philemon and indeed was arguing on the basis of the principle that those who are brothers and sisters should not be or be treated as slaves. Or to strengthen the point even more, 1 Corinthians 7 quite clearly says not only that Christians should not become slaves, but also that they should avail themselves of the opportunity for freedom if presented to them. Why, then, is Colossians different?

There are at least six factors of importance in the Colossian situation. (1) Paul is addressing an existing situation of Christian households that have slaves, and clearly he is trying to minimize the possibility for abusive or un-Christian behavior by either master or slave (or others). He is regulating an existing condition, not endorsing the institution of slavery. Limiting rather than licensing the situation is the ethical move that Paul is trying to make. The same applies to his comments about the patriarchal family structure. (2) Paul is not addressing a personal convert or a close friend here; indeed, he is addressing a group of Christians who are not his converts and whom, as far as we know, he has never addressed in a letter before. There are different levels of moral discourse to choose from, depending on one's audience. If the goal is damage control, such as here, which is believed to be all that can be accomplished on this first occasion of discourse, it is understandable that Paul does not fire all of his guns on this occasion when it comes to the institutions of slavery and patriarchy. This is Paul's opening gambit with the Colossians on these subjects, not his last word with them, and it must be judged in that light. (3) Even in the form in which this household code appears here, it is already a matter of swimming upstream, as we will see, going against

---

[70]N. T. Wright, *Colossians and Philemon* (TNTC: Grand Rapids: Eerdmans, 1986), p. 147.

the flow of much of the cultural assumptions about slavery and patriarchy. (4) The household code must not be abstracted from its present literary context and analyzed on its own, as is so often done, if the goal is to see what Paul is driving at in the use of this material. In evaluating this material, we must consider not only the larger social context but also the immediate literary or exegetical context. When what comes immediately before the code is taken into account, it is quite obvious that Paul expects all household members to behave in accordance with Christian virtues and not continue or go back to old patterns of behavior in their family relationships. The general ethic enunciated in Colossians 3:5-17 prepares for and undergirds the advice given in Colossians 3:18–4:1. If the ruling principles that guide conduct are love, peace, forgiveness, respect and a recognition that in Christ even social relationships such as slave and master or husband and wife have been relativized and transformed (Col 3:11), then a reforming and refashioning of the household relationships is not just possible but is required. Paul is not offering suggestions in the household code; he is exhorting by means of imperatives. Notice too how each exhortation is tied to the person in question's relationship with the Lord. Even the household ethic and its living out is christocentric. (5) The trajectory of the remarks in this household code is as important as the advice actually given. This becomes clearer when we examine the parallel household code in Ephesians 5–6, where Paul has put even more Christian leaven into the dough of household relationships. (6) Understanding this material and judging it fairly is a matter of asking the right questions. There are three questions to be asked about this material: How does it compare to the standard advice given in the culture about household relationships? Where is this advice heading? What would the social situation look like if all the ethical advice given in and around these codes was followed faithfully?

In regard to this last issue, we have the helpful analysis by Harold Van Broekhoven.[71] Van Broekhoven applies the group grid form of social analysis to Colossians with telling results. He finds Paul inculcating a high-grid, high-group situation, by which is meant that the author is trying to draw clear boundaries around the community, though without turning it into an isolationist group or sect. There is also an attempt to clarify the profile of role definitions (high grid). "There is both affirmation of group boundaries and a conformity to generally accepted social structures. The vice-virtue lists help define boundaries and internal cohesion while the house-table rules de-

---

[71]Harold Van Broekhoven, "The Social Profiles in the Colossian Debate," *JSNT* 66 (1997): 73-90.

fine structure. The writer, and his coworkers, exemplify a personal identity shaped by group loyalty *and* a strong internalized sense of role."[72] Van Broekhoven rightly adds that the philosophy that Paul is opposing here seems to be not merely ascetical, but stresses individualism as opposed to group bonding experiences.

As Mary Douglas points out, in a high-grid but low-group situation the individual is left to his or her own devices and tends to trust to know-how, individualistic religious practices, the power of rules and even magic or intermediary beings.[73] High-grid, low-group communities try to fend off or control cosmic forces and define themselves over against the society. These descriptors certainly are reflected in the philosophy that Paul seems to be criticizing. Against introversion and individualist tendencies, Paul's task was "to socialize the church to become a harmonious, caring, stable community with some concern for the social and cultural world of his time. His own self-denial, mentioned in 1:24, serves as a counterpoint to that more self-serving asceticism of the rivals."[74] There is, then, some modeling involved as well as the exhortations in trying to form the community in Colossae. That Paul is willing to attempt this sort of moral suasion says something about the apostolic authority that he presumes to have, even over those who were not directly converted by him.

In terms of the social provenance of the Colossian household code, George Cannon surely is right in suggesting that this code may well reflect a situation in which women and slaves held considerable expectations that their treatment in the home would be different if the situation was a Christian one.[75] After all, in this very letter we find Colossians 3:11, which echoes Galatians 3:28. But then, is this code trying to damp down their enthusiasm for more freedom and less restrictions? Probably not, since what Paul actually says is an attempt not to put women or slaves or even children in their place but rather to make sure that they behave like Christians in the social roles that they already are and always have been playing. There is no evidence that Paul is trying to stifle a feminist or slave revolution in the church in Colossae. Quite the contrary, Paul is trying to Christianize a difficult and possibly abusive situation on his first occasion of addressing the Colossians and so help the

---

[72]Ibid., p. 79.

[73]Mary Douglas, *Natural Symbols: Explorations in Cosmology* (New York: Pantheon, 1982), p. 144.

[74]Van Broekhoven, "Social Profiles in the Colossian Debate," p. 89.

[75]George E. Cannon, *The Use of Traditional Materials in Colossians* (Macon, Ga.: Mercer University Press, 1983), p. 131.

subordinate members of the household not merely survive but have a more Christian environment in which to operate. It must be kept squarely in view that what most distinguishes this household code from those in the pagan or Jewish worlds in general is that Paul is giving strong limiting exhortations to the superordinate person in the family: the husband, father, master. In non-Christian household codes it is almost always only the subordinate members of the household who get such exhortations. What is new about the code here, then, is the Christian limitations place on the head of household. That is what would stand out to a contemporary of Paul upon hearing his discourse for the first time.

Three structural elements in this household code should be kept in mind. First, the subordinate member of a given relationship is addressed first (wives, children, slaves), but always in tandem with the head of the household being exhorted. In fact, the head of the household gets three sets of exhortations, whereas everyone else only gets one. Second, each exhortation consists of an address and admonition, and in some cases a motive or reason for the exhortation, sometimes a specifically Christian one. Third, the groups are arranged in order from the most intimate relationship to the least intimate (wives/husbands; children/parents; slaves/masters). There is an attempt at comprehensiveness here. The head of the household must play three roles and therefore is given three sets of exhortations with limitations.[76]

Women are addressed first in Colossians 3:18, and here the term *gynē* surely means "wife." This in turn means that here Paul is not attempting to address the general issue of the relationship of all Christian women to all Christian men. Nor is there any reason to think that he is merely commenting on behavior in Christian worship. What is said to the wife applies only in her relationship to her husband. Nothing is said about how she should relate to her father, her brother, her cousins, her friends, male leaders in the congregations, or men in general. This code focuses on a specific narrow social context. Here and throughout this code all the members of the family are addressed as morally responsible individuals capable of hearing and heeding on their own the exhortation being given. Furthermore, here, unlike in 1 Corinthians 7, Paul does not seem to be addressing religiously mixed marriages. Paul is addressing homes where all members of the family are assumed

---

[76]For Jewish treatment of the household relationships, see Philo, *On the Decalogue* 165-167; Josephus, *Against Apion* 199-210; Sirach 7:19-28. Doubtless this tradition has affected what is being done in this Christian code as well.

to be Christians and therefore can be exhorted by him.

The verb *hypotassō* is critical here. We find it in the present tense, middle voice, which can then be translated "submit yourselves." Paul does not tell the husbands to subordinate their wives or even to exhort their wives to be subordinate. The exhortation goes directly to the wife, and it is incumbent on her to subordinate herself. This verb was not widely used in other Greek literature that deals with marriage, although Plutarch, a little after the time of Paul, does use it (*Conj. praec.* 142E). Since this verb is used also of Christ's relationship to God the Father (1 Cor 15:28) and of believers' relationships to one another (Eph 5:21), surely it does not imply the ontological inferiority of the submitter to the one submitted to, nor is the submission grounded in gender, for there is no gender issue or relationship between Christ and the Father or between all Christians in general. Rather, it has to do with the nature of a relationship between two persons. It may also have more to do with following the example of Christ, who humbled himself and took a lower place. In other words, in a Christian context the verb *hypotassō* has to do with humility and service as modeled by Christ, who even served the lost as well as believers. Notice too that we are not told in practical terms how this submission to one's husband actually is to be manifested. Paul seems to assume that his audience knows what is implied, and he is assuming that the love command undergirds and norms how this behavior will play out.

The interesting phrase *hōs anēken* modifies the exhortation to wives, and it in turn is further modified by the phrase "in the Lord." Here the verb *anēkō* is in the imperfect and a literal rendering of the whole clause is "as was fitting in the Lord." This form of the verb is found neither in classical nor Stoic forms of discussions about what is fitting. The point seems to be that this action has been customary Christian behavior before and in the present. Submission is a normal and expected part of a close Christian relationship. Conformity to Christ, not to society or to what is natural," is at issue. Here the motive for the behavior is not missionary, as it is in 1 Peter 3:1, for here Paul is addressing a fully Christian household.[77] Not only is a new reason given for this behavior, but also it seems to be implied that a new model, the Lord, is to be used by which one measures or models one's conduct. The parallel exhortation to the husband in Colossians 3:19 involves the characteristic Christian virtue of *agapē* (here expressed with the verb *agapaō*, "to love"). This verb *agapaō* is not used in the discussion of the household duties of the husband

---

[77]On which, see pp. 602-4 above.

in Hellenistic literature, and so it is by no means a conventional exhortation being repeated here. It is not, however, a uniquely Christian word either, though it is a term that most often characterizes the Christian ethic. Interestingly, wives are never exhorted to love their husbands in these Christian household codes in the New Testament. It is fair to assume that Paul thinks that these husbands especially need this exhortation.[78]

This is followed by a negative corollary to the positive exhortation that shows clearly that Paul is trying to limit bad behavior by the head of the household. The Greek clause (*mē pikrainesthe pros autas*) can be translated "do not be sharp with them" or "do not be embittered against them." The husband's action and his anger must be limited by love. As a Christian, he is not free to do as he pleases with his wife. It is telling to contrast what is said on this subject by Ben Sira, who always takes the side of the husband and father in these matters, with the views of Paul (see Sir 25–26; 30:1-13; 42:9-14). This comparison reveals that Ben Sira is trying to reinforce a patriarchal authority structure, but Paul is not. Instead, Paul is trying to ameliorate the harm that such an existing structure does and can do. John Chrysostom grasped the spirit of what Paul was trying to accomplish in these exhortations to husband and wife: "Observe again that Paul has exhorted husbands and wives to reciprocity. . . . From being loved, the wife too becomes loving; and from her being submissive, the husband learns to yield" (*Hom. Col.* 10).

At Colossians 3:20 children (male and female) are exhorted to obey their parents in everything. The phrase *kata panta* ("in everything") is comprehensive in scope and will be used again of slaves in Colossians 3:22. The difference between *hypokouō* used here of children and *hypotassō* used of wives in Colossians 3:18 seems to be that whereas the former term always indicates obedience, the latter term only sometimes does so (see 1 Pet 3:5-6).[79] Notice that *hypokouō* is in the active imperative, which suggests absolute or unquestioned obedience, in contrast to the form of the verb used of wives, which is in the middle voice. "Again here Paul mentions submission and love. And he did not say 'Love your children,' for this would have been unnecessary, seeing that nature itself causes us to do so. Rather he corrected what needed correction; that the love shown in this case should be much stronger, because the

---

[78]We often hear claims that *agapaō* always refers to Godlike love, but there are places in the New Testament where it is used of more self-regarding or unworthy forms of love (see Jn 3:19; 2 Tim 4:10; 2 Pet 2:15; 1 Jn 2:15).

[79]See the discussion of this text on pp. 592-94 above.

obedience commanded is greater" (John Chrysostom, *Hom. Col.* 10). The parallel Hellenistic codes speaking of children honoring rather than obeying parents, which suggests that we should not see the Christian code as a mere adaptation of the Hellenistic household codes. In addition to the phrase "in everything" is the further qualification "for this is pleasing in the Lord." These children are directly addressed, which suggests their presence in the worship service to hear the presentation of this discourse.

We should note that this way of putting things is what one would expect in a deliberative exhortation, where what is "pleasing" or "proper" *(euarestos)* is a major issue. Notice the difference in Ephesians 6:1-2, where the issue is what is right and honorable. This leads to an important observation: besides the Christianizing of the advice, another factor that accounts for differences between this code and the one in Ephesians is the question of the rhetorical species of the discourse. Paul modifies the code in one way or another to suit the rhetorical species he is dealing with in a given discourse. Ephesians is epideictic rhetoric strengthening accepted values. Colossians is deliberative rhetoric urging a change of belief or behavior, to some extent. We should also note that since Paul has the Christian family here in view, he is likely assuming that Christian parents would not demand something of their children that is contrary to Christian teaching. The same applies in the situation of husband and wife. Here, as previously in Colossians 3:18, the phrase "in the Lord" may mean "in the Christian community," which is indwelt by Christ.

Colossians 3:21 begins with *pateres*, which, though it could refer to both parents, probably means "fathers" here. The father is exhorted not to provoke his children and so break their spirits or make them despondent. Notice that the stress is on the father's responsibility and duties, and unlike Ephesians 6:4, there is nothing about the positive duty to train or bring up the children. C. F. D. Moule remarks, "The sensitive understanding of children, with the realization that they might become discouraged and lose heart . . . is a striking feature in this new chapter in social history."[80]

There is a notable contrast here with the fact that the head of a Roman household and even in some cases in Hellenistic Judaism had nearly unlimited authority to do as he pleased with his children. Consider the reminder in Dionysius of Halicarnassus of how the *patria potestas* still continued when the child was an adult: "The law-giver of the Romans gave virtually full power

---

[80]C. F. D. Moule, *The Epistles to the Colossians and Philemon* (CGTC; Cambridge: Cambridge University Press, 1968), p. 129.

to the father over his son, whether he thought it proper to imprison him, to scourge him, to put him in chains and keep him at work in the fields, or to put him to death; and this was so even though the son was already engaged in public affairs, even though he was numbered among the highest magistrates, and even though he was celebrated for his zeal for the commonwealth" (*Ant. Rom.* 2.26.4). In fact, the father even got the children if there was a divorce. The code in Colossians certainly is going against the flow of the culture in several respects. I have used the example from the Roman situation because it more nearly approximates the situation in Asia than does the situation under Jewish law, as it is clear that Paul is dealing mainly with Gentiles in this discourse.

Paul, then, is quite specifically limiting that authority and privilege. He does not exhort the father to exercise his authority over the children, nor does he urge the father to discipline them. What we see throughout this household code is an attempt to rein in the authority and behavior of the head of the household, making it more nearly Christian in character, which is a deliberate modification of the existing patriarchal household structure.

By far the longest single exhortation in this code comes in Colossians 3:22-25, the direct address to slaves, who, like the children, are treated as responsible members of the congregation. In light of Colossians 3:11, they are seen as equal members, persons of equal sacred worth in the church, and Colossians 3:22-25 should be read in light of that earlier verse. Like the exhortation to children, the imperatives here begin with the command to obey in everything. The assumption must be, especially in light of Colossians 4:1, that Christian masters will be treating slaves fairly and properly. In Colossians 3:22 masters are called "lords according to the flesh," with the implicit distinction from *the* Lord.

The slave is exhorted to labor wholeheartedly and to do so not just when the master is watching so as to curry favor by feigning diligence. Paul apparently is dealing with a trait that was assumed to be commonplace: sloth on the part of the unsupervised slave. The clause at the end of Colossians 3:22 could refer to the slave's "lord according to the flesh," mentioned at the beginning of the verse, but more likely it is another example of the Christianizing of this material with the implication that a Christian slave should always work with the recognition that God is always watching, and so it should be done "in the fear of the Lord," being concerned about the Lord's evaluation of conduct rather than fear of reprisal from the master. Colossians 3:23

further supports this interpretation. All work should be done from the heart and "as to the Lord, not as to human beings." This is interesting because it removes the usual motivation for human behavior and places the conduct strictly on the basis of Christian motivation. The approval that one should seek is not human approval but rather that of God, and the evaluation that one should be concerned about is that of the Lord, not lords. The real reason and encouragement for such advice are given in Colossians 3:24.

Slaves in the Greco-Roman world received a *peculium*, a small amount of funds on a regular basis that eventually they could use to pay the price of manumission if that was going to be allowed by the master. Although technically a slave could not inherit any property (slave were considered to be living property), this *peculium* was, in a sense, the slave's inheritance money, and it could be used once freedom was attained or put toward the price of manumission. So here Paul speaks of a different sort of inheritance, one that the slave should be confident of receiving from the Lord. Notice that the inheritance is called a "reward" or "repayment."

Since Paul is addressing Christian slaves, it is clear enough that he is not referring to initial salvation as a reward. Rather, it is the same sort of reward that Jesus promises to believers for good conduct during their believing lives. This line of thinking does indicate, however, that Paul believes that there will be rewards (lesser and greater) in the eschatological state based on one's behavior in this life (cf. 1 Cor 3:10-15). This is followed by the intriguing remark that in fact the slave belongs to or is enslaved to the Lord Christ.

The reference to Christ leads into Colossians 3:25, where the identity of the wrongdoer and the behavior is unclear. Is this a promise that Christ, who does not play favorites, will deal with unfair masters in due course and so Christian slaves should not misbehave if mistreated? This certainly is possible in light of Colossians 4:1. On the other hand, it could be that the slave is being warned about unrighteous conduct being repaid in the eschatological age, just as righteous conduct will be rewarded.

It is appropriate to ponder whether this extended exhortation to slaves is instigated by the Onesimus situation in an attempt to head off further illegal behavior by slaves in Colossae. This certainly is possible. The net effect of this advice is to place the conduct of slaves under the light of divine scrutiny and to help them think this way about it, with extra emphasis on working hard and wholeheartedly at what they do, knowing that their real lord to whom they are bound and even "enslaved" is Jesus, who died for them and set them free already from their sins and bad behavior. Note that traditional discussions of household management do not address slaves directly, but here they are addressed directly as both members of the household and members of the house church. There are also some five references to Christ as Lord in this section involving slaves and masters to make very clear that there has been a thorough overhaul of the way that relationship should be envisioned and what motivates proper behavior when both parties are Christians. This contrasts drastically with the usual ways slaves were motivated to work hard (e.g., holding out rewards such as praise, food, better clothing [see Xenophon, *Oec.* 13.9-12]). Finally, we may note regarding slaves' service to the Lord Christ in Colossians 3:24 that the verb *douleuete* can be indicative, "you are serving," or imperative, "serve."

Colossians 4:1 concludes the argument with a word for the masters. The stress is on Christian "lords" also having a Lord in heaven to whom they are answerable for their conduct. Again conduct is to be guided or modified because of the watchful eye of Christ.

> This notion that the masters of the household have a master over themselves is quite different from other discussions of the household in antiquity. . . . The writer does not say that in the slave/master relationship the master represents Christ, but the relationship within the ancient household that demonstrates both the possession of all believers by their Lord and their obligation to this Lord is that of slaves to their master. For this reason, it is the one that receives the most attention as a paradigm for the motivation that should inform all members of the household and that is summed up in the command of 3:24b: "Serve the Lord Christ."[81]

It is this last clause of the code that clearly relativizes the position and power of the master within the Christian community.

Masters are not to cheat their slaves but rather should provide them with what is right and fair. This is diametrically opposed to what Aristotle says when he remarks that the issue of justice is not raised in regard to slaves; there can be no injustice involved in the way one treats mere property (*Eth. nic.* 5.1134b). Compared to Aristotle, what Paul is saying here is revolutionary. As Wright observes, this way of discussing things would have sounded odd, for what it suggests is that "slaves too are human beings with rights. To talk of 'justice' and 'equality' in relation to slaves would sound extraordinary

---

[81]Andrew T. Lincoln, "The Letter to the Colossians," in *The New Interpreter's Bible*, ed. Leander E. Keck (Nashville: Abingdon, 1994–2004), 11:657.

to most slave-owners of the ancient world."[82] Thus, even if to our ears this advice sounds rather conventional or even conservative and commonplace, it was not so in Paul's day.

The term *isotēs* in Colossians 4:1 is a striking one that was used in earlier Greek democracy and law to speak of equality. Aristotle in fact defines justice as "a state productive of equality *[isotēs]* or distributive of what is equal" (*Top.* 6.5). So could Paul really be saying that masters should treat their slaves on the basis of "equality"? Dunn says that the idea of equality of slave and master "in law" was impossible at this time.[83] However, Paul is talking not about in law but rather about in the community. I submit that in light of Colossians 3:11, this is precisely what Paul means, and here we have a principle that, like what we find in Philemon, would lead to the demise of slavery among Christians. It must be remembered that Paul believed in some of the democratic ideals of old Greece. He calls his community an *ekklēsia*, which is a place where free persons should assemble and discuss the matters of importance and make decisions.[84] Also, he uses the ancient art of persuasion rhetoric, and persuasion is the opposite of strong-arm tactics or dictatorial approaches. Persuasion is a form of treating others with respect as free individuals capable of making their own decisions and judgments. Equality in Christ, like freedom in Christ, was a notion precious to Paul to which he returned early, late, and in between in his writings (cf. Gal 3:28; 1 Cor 12:13; Col 3:11).[85]

Paul already, on this the first occasion of addressing the Colossians, has been pushing the envelope of their thinking so that they will consider all subordinate members of the household, even slaves, as persons having rights, including the right to fair and equal treatment. Even more to the point, there is to be the recognition that they are Christian persons, and the head of the household, as a Christian, must alter conduct in his relationship with all three sets of persons (wife, children, slaves) so that the Lord will be pleased with his conduct. It is this curtailing and Christianizing of the head of the household's rights and privileges and roles that especially stands out in these exhortations as Paul, even in his first address to the Colossians, attempts to transform the character of Christian household relationships by ameliorating the harsh

---

[82]Wright, *Colossians and Philemon*, p. 151.

[83]Dunn, *Epistles to the Colossians and to Philemon*, p. 260.

[84]Does Paul's use of *ekklēsia* merely reflect the influence of the LXX on his vocabulary? I doubt it, for in this passage Paul shows remarkable sensitivity to how words would be understood by Gentile Christians, many of whom had no knowledge of the LXX.

[85]See Dunn, *Epistles to the Colossians and to Philemon*, p. 223.

edges of the existing institutions of slavery and patriarchy. But how much further was Paul prepared to push things when he had a closer relationship with an audience? This we can see in Ephesians 5:21–6:9.

The Ephesian Household Code (Ephesians 5:21–6:9)

In Ephesians 5:21–6:9 the more general principles enunciated in Ephesians 4:1–5:20 are applied to a more specific situation, the Christian home. Unlike what we find in 1 Corinthians 7, here Paul does not address the situation of a religiously mixed marriage, and so all members of the household are addressed directly in this climax of the paraenesis. What we are dealing with here is second-order moral discourse, a form of discourse that goes beyond what one would say to an audience of Christians on the first occasion of addressing them. Many of the differences between the household code in Colossians 3–4 and what we find here can largely be explained on this basis. The sort of discourse found in Colossians 3–4 is presumed to be already familiar to the audience, and so here the discussion of ethics within the Christian family is taken a step further.

This becomes apparent especially when one considers not only the detailed analogy between husband and wife as compared to Christ and the church but also the way that Paul contextualizes the code by introducing it with Ephesians 5:21, which gives a whole different look to the exhortation about submission within marriage. As I said previously, the trajectory and contextualizing of the argument is as important as the details of what Paul says. This argument is an attempt to provide a significant equalizing of relationships within Christian marriage, altering the usual character and direction of a patriarchal marriage situation. Another factor that shapes the Ephesian version of the household code is that the theme of the unity of the church and unity in the church comes into play and helps shape the discussion here of household relationships, mainly by the suggestion that if the Christ/church models are followed by household members, there will be harmony in the household that then becomes an example of the unity of the house church.

The rhetorical force of this argument depends on several factors, not all of which are usually recognized. (1) Paul is presupposing an already extant assent to the basics of the household code as outlined in Colossians 3–4. Paul is not introducing entirely new material here, though he will offer some new rhetorical rationales and build on what has been assented to in the past. It is the continuation of a conversation, not its first salvo. (2) Paul will offer supplementary motivation and argumentation of such a self-explanatory and uncontroversial character (e.g., we all take care of our own body, we should love in analogous fashion to the way Christ loves) that it will produce ready assent. (3) The emphasis on the behavior modification required of the head of the household (who is exhorted three separate times, receiving the bulk of the exhortations, because of his three different roles as husband, parent, master), especially in loving and acting in a Christian manner with family members, has the rhetorical effect of setting up a trajectory or momentum in a direction of a more egalitarian approach to the marital situation. This trajectory can be seen not only by comparing Ephesians 5:21–6:9 with Colossians 3–4, but even more so by comparing the Ephesians passage with other household codes of the era (e.g., Hierocles, *On Duties*). (4) Here the concentration is on the husband/wife relationship, whereas in Colossians it is on the master/slave relationship. This may be because of the circular nature of this document, so that the relationship most commonly in evidence in the audience is given the most attention. The rhetorical effect of this, however, is to focus on the constituting unit of the household (husband and wife) and especially on the way the husband's actions need to mirror Christ's actions well.

Whereas in Colossians the husband is told to not be embittered with his wife, that exhortation here is omitted and is replaced by the extended analogy about Christ and the church. If the audience was already familiar with Colossians, this change would have been readily apparent and striking. Then too, equally striking is the call for mutual submission as the heading for the discussion in Ephesians 5:21, which changes the character of the entire exhortation. Now it is not just wives and other traditionally subordinate members of the household who are to freely submit; so too is the husband. This is why Andrew Lincoln concludes, "All in all, this writer's treatment of the first part of the household code should probably be judged as more thoroughly Christian than that of Colossians."[86] There is no reason to assume that Paul is drawing on any additional sources other than Colossians in this treatment of the household code, whatever sources he may have relied on in composing the Colossian code, and so we are dealing with rhetorical amplification of a known source (the 117 words in Colossians becomes 324 in Ephesians).

Finally, it is asking the wrong question to ponder whether Paul is mainly concerned with the husband/wife relationship here or the Christ/church relationship. The latter relationship is the context for understanding and norming the former relationship when one is dealing with the Christian family. So

---

[86]Andrew T. Lincoln, *Ephesians* (WBC 42; Dallas: Word, 1990), p. 355.

Paul is concerned with both relationships, and in particular he is concerned with how the Christ/church relationship provides a pattern for behavior within the marriage. Marriage is seen as such a fundamental relationship that it in fact terminates or at least relativizes the relationship that husband and wife previously had with their parents. It is unnecessary to go into great detail about the Ephesian household code, since it involves so much repetition from the Colossian one, except that we do need to examine how it is set up in its first several verses.

Ephesians 5:21 is a transitional verse directed to all members of the audience, as is shown by the use of the masculine participle *hypotassomenoi*. The participle could be taken as an imperative, but since it is dependent on the preceding verb "be filled," it probably should not be taken in this fashion, or one could say that it has an imperatival sense as the verb to be supplied in Ephesians 5:22 but serves as a participle in Ephesians 5:21. The verb *hypotassō* appears in Greek literature rather late, and in the active sense it refers to arranging or placing something under something else, and in the middle or reflexive voice it refers to ordering or arranging oneself under something or someone. Most often in earlier literature it refers to submitting to, surrendering to, or humbling oneself before God (cf., in the LXX, Ps 36:7 [37:7 ET]; 61:2, 6 [62:1, 5 ET]; 2 Macc 9:12).

In Paul's writings the verb *hypotassō* is used to refer to the subordination of Christ to God, of believers to one another, of spirits to Christian prophets, and of wives, children and slaves to the head of the household (see 1 Cor 15:28; 14:32; Col 3:18; Eph 5:21). The term does usually carry an overtone of authority and the submission of one's self to authority. Ephesians 5:21 verse calls for mutual submission of all Christians to each other, and although not specifically directed to marital partners, it certainly includes them. Humble service to one another is what Paul has in mind (cf. Phil 2:1-5). It builds on Ephesians 4:2-3, which spoke of bearing with one another in love, which demonstrates the mutuality involved. More importantly, since Ephesians 5:22 is elliptical, whatever "submission" means in Ephesians 5:21, it also means in that next verse; that is, it is not a gender-specific activity. Indeed, it would be better to take Ephesians 5:21 as the heading for what follows in the exhortations to husband and wife, in which case what is described in Ephesians 5:22-33 is how, given their differing roles, husband and wife will submit to and serve one another. Ephesians 5:22–33, then, qualifies and explains the transitional remark insofar as it applies to husbands and wives.

That Paul, in what follows, will deal only with a representative sampling of relationships in regard to what submission looks like is clear enough. For example, he does not deal with any relationships outside the household structure (e.g., the submission of soldiers to their commander, or citizens to their ruler), and even within the household he does not discuss the relationships of extended family, such as the widowed mother of the family head to the man in question. In other words, the household code is not meant to be comprehensive in scope, only providing representative examples. If we are puzzling about how mutual submission and hierarchically arranged relationships can go together and not be incompatible, Lincoln provides some helpful remarks:

> There is an interesting parallel in 1 Peter 5:5, where the exhortation "you that are younger be subject to the elders" is followed immediately by the further appeal "clothe yourselves, all of you, with humility toward one another." The latter admonition was not meant to cancel out the former. Rather, the writer holds that there is a general sense in which elders are to serve their flock, including its younger element, in a submissive attitude, but that mutuality goes along with a hierarchical view of roles.[87]

Just so, and it may be added that putting the Spirit and Christ into the mix as exemplars changes the very nature and character of such hierarchical relationships.

The phrase "in the fear of Christ" in Ephesians 5:21 likewise bears witness to the connection with what follows because immediately in Ephesians 5:22 we hear about wives fearing, a note repeated in Ephesians 5:33, and of slaves fearing in Ephesians 6:5. The phrase in Ephesians 5:21 probably should be compared to 2 Corinthians 5:11, in which case what is meant is that one's present conduct will be reviewed one day by Christ when he sits for final judgment. In other words, we likely have an eschatological sanction applied in several places in this household code, including in its heading in Ephesians 5:21. This does not remove, but rather adds, to the notion that what is meant is a proper respect and reverence for Christ. Ephesians 5:21 is meant to qualify and indeed prevent a reading of the material that follows as intending to demand some sort of absolute unilateral submission. Paul, by placing this verse here, is critiquing the normal understanding of household relationships where only certain members of the household are doing the submitting or serving. Not in the Christian church, says Paul, where everyone should sub-

---

[87]Ibid., p. 366.

mit to and serve everyone else out of reverence for Christ. Since Ephesians 5:21 is dependent on Ephesians 5:18, what is suggested is not that mutual submission is a natural thing but rather is something that can and does happen when someone is filled with the Spirit and so led by God in his or her behavior. As G. B. Caird observes, "What he does is to require that the code of subordination shall be properly baptized with the spirit of Christ. The whole passage is an excellent illustration of the general ethical principle . . . that the Spirit-filled man must and can discern the will of God within the limitations imposed by a defective social order."[88]

It is interesting that Paul chooses, both in the Colossian and in the Ephesian household codes, to address the subordinate members of the household first and then the head of the household. And furthermore, he chooses to give the head much more of an exhortation, at least in his discussion of husband/ wife relationships, than he does the subordinate member in the relationship. This suggests that he is not merely repeating previous advice.

Elsewhere I have dealt at length with the Pauline household codes and their social setting.[89] Here a couple of things need to be revisited. First, the Christian modification of the household code in this discourse makes clear that Paul is not interested in modifications meant to mollify the concerns of outsiders about Christianity and the meetings in its house churches. There is no evidence of an apologetical motif or character to this material (cf. 1 Pet 3), for even the quotations from the Old Testament do not stand alone but rather are set in the context of the more explicitly Christian terms of the discussion. There was, in any case, no Old Testament discussion about husbands and wives such as we find here.

Second, there is still no evidence of a fixed household code in the Greco-Roman or the Jewish world that might have been adopted and adapted by Paul. There certainly are ethical discussions about household duties and relationships, but still we have no evidence of a fixed table. As I have said before, it is not that impressive that various authors before, during and after New Testament times discuss the patriarchal household and in particular the

---

[88]G. B. Caird, *Paul's Letters from Prison: Ephesians, Philippians, Colossians, Philemon* (NCIB/NT 9; London: Oxford University Press, 1976), p. 88.

[89]See Ben Witherington III, *The Letters to Philemon, the Colossians, and the Ephesians: A Socio-Rhetorical Commentary on the Captivity Epistles* (Grand Rapids: Eerdmans, 2007). The most recent helpful overview and comparison of all the New Testament household codes is Johannes Woyke, *Die neutestamentlichen Haustafeln: Ein kritischer und konstruktiver Forschungsüberblick* (SBS 184; Stuttgart: Katholisches Bibelwerk, 2000).

duties of its subordinate members to the head of the household. This is not surprising, nor does it establish some sort of evidence of literary dependency between the New Testament material and what came before. The patriarchal family structure was pervasive and often included extended family such as domestic servants. "The fact that various authors over a wide period of time discuss precisely these three groups and usually manifest a patriarchal orientation does not demonstrate a chain of literary dependency."[90] What it does demonstrate is the stability and continuity of the patriarchal family structure from the time of Aristotle until well after New Testament times. Carolyn Osiek is right to point out that the Greco-Roman discussion is about how the master of the house should manage and exercise authority in his household; he is to rule his slaves like a despot, his children like a king, his wife like a rational being but one without inherent authority (Aristotle, *Pol.* 1259a37; 1260a9). The Christian household codes, however, "are not about how *he* should act authoritatively but benevolently and how *he* should require everyone to treat him with respect."[91] Notice also there is no discussion in the New Testament about how the *pater familias* should manage his finances, quite unlike the discussion in Aristotle and elsewhere. In short, the Christian code is about everyone in the household and treats everyone as moral agents, even the children. It is not all about the head of the household any more.

We should also keep in mind that a list of whom one has duties to, especially if the duties are not explicated (as they are not by Epictetus), is not the same thing as a table of exhortations and duties. What the Greco-Roman evidence shows is a more restrictive approach especially to women's roles than what we find in Ephesians. This is also true of the early Jewish evidence. Philo, for example, says that wives must be in servitude to their husbands, as if they were slaves (*Hypothetica* 7.3-6). Josephus speaks of the need for the wife to be obedient (*Ag. Ap.* 2.199), but he does not use the term *hypotassō*. In fact, the use of *hypotassō* as Paul uses it here of all believers in relationship to each other, as well as of the relationship of wife to husband, seems to have no precedent in the literature. Pseudo-Callisthenes, in his *Historia Alexandri Magni*, does use this term of the wife submitting to her husband (1.22.4), but the earliest manuscript of that document dates to A.D. 300, and in any case is it unlikely to have influenced Paul. Paul's contemporary Plutarch, from a time slightly later, uses this term (*Conj. praec.*

---

[90]Witherington, *Women in the Earliest Churches*, p. 44.
[91]Carolyn Osiek, "The Ephesian Household Code," *TBT* 36 (1998): 361.

33), but this also could not have influenced Paul's discussion.

Especially noteworthy in the Greco-Roman literature is the absence in all such discussions of imperatives or lists of social duties in reciprocal pairs, much less of an exhortation to husbands to love their wives. David Verner probably is correct that the schema that sets apart the Christian code involves (1) an address to a particular social group within the household, (2) an imperative (3) often with an appropriate object, (4) an amplification of the imperative, usually in the form of a prepositional phrase, and (5) a reason clause providing theological warrant or sanction or motivation.[92]

What about the suggestion that the household codes reflect a sort of retrenchment and backing off from the gospel of freedom that Paul preached (Gal 3:28) in an attempt to restrict overly liberated women, slaves, or minors? This explanation makes little sense of the character and trajectory of the Ephesian household code in particular, set as it is in the context of a call for mutual submission and for loving self-sacrifice by the husband/father/ master, which was uncharacteristic of the advice given in the Greco-Roman setting. Pheme Perkins puts it this way: "This ethic describes a well-ordered Christian household independent of the views or actions of outsiders."[93] I do not think that Ephesians manifests the life of an introversionist sect, but I do agree that this code is not conditioned by what might be thought to be acceptable to pagan outsiders who were neighbors. There is far too much evidence in Ephesians of drawing a strong line between pagan immorality and Christian behavior to think that this code was trying to be particularly sensitive to the world's reaction to the Christian household. Rather, Paul is trying to model household relationships on the servantlike and self-sacrificial relationship of Christ to his church. The advice given here would not make the believers invisible in the midst of the larger culture; instead, it would make Christian homes stand out as witnesses to Christ and his love and self-sacrifice. The husband probably would have been seen as somewhat restricted or compromised by the advice given here. This advice is not part of a defensive strategy vis-à-vis the world and its opinions; rather, it is taking a step beyond the Colossian code to socialize the Christians so that they are more evidently distinctive from the culture, standing out as light and as thoroughly

---

[92]David C. Verner, *The Household of God: The Social World of the Pastoral Epistles* (SBLDS 71; Chico, Calif.: Scholars Press, 1983), pp. 86-87. The clearest of the distinctives is the series of exhortations to various groups.

[93]Pheme Perkins, *Ephesians* (ANTC; Nashville: Abingdon, 1997), p. 140.

Christian. The code does not reflect a defensive or apologetic quality, as though the church were trying either to blend in with the existing cultural standards or to defend its distinctiveness. To the contrary, the code is a bold and positive attempt to modify the existing structure.

There seems to be reasonably clear evidence, as I have suggested, that the Ephesian code is an amplification of the Colossian code, not a critique of it. The two codes share some 70 words in common even though the Ephesian code has 207 more words than the 117 of the Colossian code. That is, only 47 words from the Colossian code do not recur in Ephesians. Both the Colossian and the Ephesian household tables have this order of address: wives then husbands, children then fathers, slaves then masters. The only clear evidence of a major source (i.e., another code) that the Ephesian code is dependent on is Colossians. There is also evidence of the use of such traditional material as quotations from the Old Testament and perhaps commonplaces as well. It cannot be said that this code simply arises out of earlier Hellenistic Jewish discussions about the household because first, it is far too christologically shaped in places (the christological element is not a mere add on, after the fact), and second, not only does the code seek to ameliorate the harsher effects of patriarchy, but also it sets a different course by setting the discussion in a more egalitarian context and then stressing the Christian duties of the head of the household. This is nothing like what we find in Philo or Josephus or the writings of Jesus ben Sira.

Since the material in this household code is attempting to regulate and Christianize an existing institution, we should not see it as an implicit critique of asceticism or the validity of remaining single in Christ. Such a suggestion forgets in any case that the very chapter that makes the case for the *charisma* of singleness (1 Cor 7) is also the chapter that argues that each man should have his own wife and vice versa. It is wrong, then, to radically distinguish what is said in 1 Corinthians 7 and what is said here. Nothing here suggests that Paul would not still prefer singleness for various of his converts. Nor is there anything here to suggest that we should read this text as part of the later Christian attempt to develop endogamy rules that in effect do help to turn the Christian community into an introversionist sect with very rigid boundaries. We have not gotten to the situation that we find with Ignatius of Antioch, who says that the bishop must approve a Christian's choice of mate (Ign. *Pol.* 5:1-2). No, this discourse is still talking about exposing the deeds of darkness and being light to those around who might be watching. If these imperatives in Ephesians were enacted, not only would it be noticeable to the neighbors, but also it might well be appealing especially to the subordinate members of other families who would recognize the ethos of love that characterizes the relationships, and in particular the actions of the head of the household. The advice here is not significantly different from the earliest advice found in the Pauline letters about marriage (1 Thess 4:4-5) in regard to the issue of the way Christian marriage practices should be distinctive from pagan ones. The emphasis on holiness in that text is echoed here.

It is especially a misreading of the trajectory of Ephesians 5:21–6:9 to suggest that the main purpose of this text is to provide a theological justification for the subordination of wives, children, and slaves to the head of the household. Nor, contrary to Verner, is the household code here an attempt to correct the liberationist thrust of Galatians 3:28.[94] It is quite true that Paul does not appear here in the guise of a modern feminist. He still discusses the headship of the man in the family. However, that headship has been transformed by the model of Christ. It is precisely the Christian aspects added to this code in a more dramatic way than in the Colossian code that show where the argument is leading, as does the setting of the discussion in the context of Ephesians 5:21, where all are submitting to one another. In other words, if anything is the primary purpose of this code, it is to both ameliorate the harsher effects of patriarchy and to guide the head of the household into a new conception of his roles that Christianizes his conduct in various ways and so turns marriage into more of a partnership and turns household management more into a matter of actualizing biblical principles about love of neighbor and honoring others.

If the code is set in the context of mutual submission, and Christ is given as the example of loving self-sacrifice, and nowhere in this code is the head of the household told to subordinate or to command subordination of the other household members and so "order" his household (contrast *1 Clem.* 1:3; 21:6-9; Pol. *Phil.* 4:2), then it cannot be said that this code simply repristinates the existing patriarchal order of things with gender-specific subordination of the female but no similar expectations of the male head of the household. Clearly, the loving self-sacrifice of the husband is depicted as the same sort of subordination, the same sort of stepping down and serving others, that Christ engaged in, and if Christ is the model of subordination and service, not only in his relationship to the Father but also in the way he chooses to serve his

---

[94]Verner, *Household of God*, p. 109. Galatians 3:28 says nothing about parents or children.

church, then there is nothing particularly patriarchal about the concept here. Instead, subordination has been broadened to describe the relationship of all Christians to each other, including all relationships within the Christian household. In fact, what this household code suggests is that all members of the household are also members of the church and are expected to behave according to Christian standards.

It is also noteworthy that neither here nor elsewhere does Paul connect his discussions of the household with discussions about a Christian's relationships with external authority figures such as rulers and emperors (contrast 1 Pet 2:13–3:7). For Paul, the household is dealt with as an in-house matter, not as part of the larger agenda of the ordering of society in general. In fact, the aims and functions of this household code are quite modest. It confines itself to discussing relationships within the Christian family, and even then it does not discuss all of those relationships. For example, nothing is said about relationships between children or between slaves. Nothing is said about relationships with extended family members who may have dwelt in the household (e.g., the widowed mother of the husband, the freedman living on the estate). Nor is anything said about the relationships between Christian households. There is nothing here about the hospitality that a household should offer to strangers or even to fellow believers. Nor does the code deal with problematic situations, such as a battered wife or a beaten slave, or with the problems caused by masters selling off one member of a slave family, particularly if it is the husband or the wife.

This code does not seek to be all things to all persons and situations. It has instead a rhetorical purpose of setting the Christian tone for the household by commenting on a representative sampling of the relationships in the household and showing what a more Christian model of domestic life might and should look like. Whatever sources Paul uses here, he has made them his own. As Rudolf Schnackenburg remarks, "In his enrichment of the existent exhortation for husband and wife in their marriage by the ecclesiological motif, and his inclusion of Christian spouses in the relationship between Christ and the Church, [Paul] has created instruction on Christian marriage which, in spite of possible external influences, must be regarded as his own work and consequently must first be declared to be such and appreciated as such."[95]

As I said in an earlier discussion of this code, we have here an analogy drawn between the relationship of husband and wife and the relationship

---

[95]Rudolf Schnackenburg, *Ephesians*, trans. Helen Heron (Edinburgh: T & T Clark, 1991), p. 244.

of Christ and the church.[96] It is not an identity statement, so not everything predicated of Christ and the church can also be predicated of husband and wife, and vice versa. One of the clearest signs that we are dealing with a somewhat loose analogy is that Christ and the church are seen as bridegroom and bride, but they are compared to those who are already married. Accordingly, one must not press the analogy beyond its obvious points of contact, the love of Christ and the love of husband for wife, which entails self-sacrifice and self-giving, submission of the wife and of the church, headship of the husband and of Christ, and provision and care for the wife like Christ's provision and care for the church. This means that the material in Ephesians 5:26-27, which describes Christ's sanctifying work and effect on the church, probably should not be pressed to suggest that this is the effect of the Christian husband on the wife, although in light of 1 Corinthians 7:14, this is not impossible.

The flow of thought here is from husband and wife to a more detailed reflection on Christ and the church, and then back again. The husband is not called or seen as the savior of the wife, and so what is said in Ephesians 5:23c, 26a-27c seems to be comments reserved for the Christ/church relationship. It should also be said that the direction of influence between these two pairs of relationships is not one way. The language and even the imagery of betrothal in Paul's day influence the description of Christ's relationship to the church, but it is also clear from Ephesians 5:25c that Christ's action for the church affects the way Paul describes the role of the headship of the husband. Furthermore, the submissive and reverent response of church to Christ conditions how Paul describes the relationship of wife to husband. Although Ephesians 5:31a shows that Paul is well aware of the story of Adam and Eve, his advice here draws more from the pattern of the relationship of Christ and the church. If in Colossians we see first-order moral discourse in the form of a first attempt to give a Christian shape to the Christian family relationships, here we see the discussion and effort taken a step further. A few more details of the opening verses make this clear.

Notice immediately about Ephesians 5:22 that the wife is called upon first and is called upon to subordinate herself (*hypotassomenoi*, middle/passive participle carried over from Eph 5:21). Nothing is said about the husband demanding subordination or being given instructions to pass on to his wife, unlike what we find in *1 Clement* 1:3; 21:6. Rather, each member of the house-

---

hold, even the children and the slaves, is addressed as a responsible moral agent capable of hearing and heeding these exhortations. This is not, then, advice given to the head of the household to use. Each person is addressed in turn. The word *idiois* in Ephesians 5:22 is important because it indicates that here husbands and wives, not men and women in general, are in view, and that the subject is family behavior, not the submission of women to men or church leaders in worship. Had Paul meant that all females are to be submissive to all males, he would have used the adjectives *thēlys* ("female") and *arsēn* ("male"), as he does in Galatians 3:28, rather than the nouns *gynē* ("woman, wife") and *anēr* ("man, husband"). Neither worship nor the relationship of women to male church leaders is discussed here. Of course, the term "her own" also implies a clear endorsement of monogamy, which becomes even more clear when Paul cites Genesis 2:24 in Ephesians 5:31.

The phrase "as to the Lord" should be compared to that in Colossians 3:18, "as is fitting in the Lord." Here the analogy in the two relationships is stressed by the way things are worded. It is possible that the phrase could even be read to mean "as to a lord," in which case an analogy with Christ is not in view (cf. 1 Pet 3:6), but we would have expected *hōs tois kyriois* were that the case. Probably all that is meant is that the subordination of wife to husband is in some ways like the subordination that she offers to Christ. Since only Christ is her savior, it cannot be said to be in all respects like her relationship to Christ. Possibly we should see Ephesians 5:24b as giving clearer explanation: the wife should submit in "all things" to her husband just as she does to Christ, which seems to mean in all areas of the relationship. Of course, it is assumed that the husband will act as he should, modeling himself on Christ, and that he will not ask of his wife anything that Christ would not have wanted him to ask. Clearly, the context is assumed to be not just a superficially Christian one, but one where actual Christian behavior is being practiced. Robert Wall says too much in claiming that spiritual hierarchy involving Christ dismantles the social hierarchy, but what Paul says does reconfigure and revise that social hierarchy and put it under Christian constraints.[97] The wife's relationship to her husband is set within the context of her relationship with the Lord, which also means that this marriage relationship has a vertical component because Christ is involved in the marriage as well as in the individual lives of the partners.

Paul does not envision or deal with a situation in which the husband might

---

[97]Robert W. Wall, "Wifely Submission in the Context of Ephesians," *CSR* 17 (1988): 272-85.

ask something not in accord with Christian love, faith or ethics.[98] Paul clearly is dealing in general terms and with broad strokes, but this is what one would expect in a circular homily of an epideictic sort. Notice that the point of comparison has to do with roles voluntarily assumed, not with a comparison of natures. Headship or subordination is a role that one assumes in relationship to another and is to be characterized in both cases by loving and self-sacrificial behavior, which is in any case a form of submission. Proper exercise of authority should not be seen as tyranny, nor should proper submission be seen as an indication of inferiority of any sort. "Christ is not depicted as a supreme example of male superiority over women. Rather the 'husband's' function as 'head' is modeled after (and limited by) the measure of Christ's headship. Thus, not an absolute, but only a very qualified role as 'head' is attributed to man. I Cor 11:3 makes this explicit by the sequence in which Christ's and the husband's headship are given: the 'head of every husband is Christ, the head of a wife is her husband.'"[99] Notice too that Paul never commands the husband to exercise his headship. This section of the discourse has nothing to do with cracking the whip in order to enforce the subordination of women, as there is no indication in this discourse of any particular problems in the ordering of Christian relationships.

The crucial term in Ephesians 5:23 is *kephalē*, a term already found in Ephesians 1:22-23; 4:15 applied to Christ. The point of using the term here is to say something about the character of an ongoing relationship. The question of the origins of women is not at issue here, and so the translation "source" is inappropriate in this context. It is possible that Paul has taken the phrase "head of the household" (see Aristotle, *Pol.* 1255B) and applied the notion specifically to the husband's relationship with his wife, but it is also possible that he derives it from his usage of the term as applied in various contexts to Christ. There is no clear evidence from the Greco-Roman literature of the period that the husband was seen as the head of the wife and the wife the husband's body. The conjecture of a christological source for the use of "head" for the husband gains legs from the fact that Paul mentions the headship of

---

[98]Notice too, as Caird says, that Paul does not appeal to the natural order of things or to prevailing social custom or cultural values; rather, he appeals to the model of how one relates to Christ. "In this way the demands of social custom can be transformed by being treated as service *to the Lord*" (*Paul's Letters from Prison*, p. 88). Lincoln notes that this is an ideal picture, and the possibility of a conflict between submitting to Christ and to the husband is not even considered. "So in this writer's vision of Christian marriage what is called for from wives is complete subordination to complete love" (*Ephesians*, p. 373).

[99]Markus Barth, *Ephesians 4–6* (AB 34A; Garden City, N.Y.: Doubleday, 1974), p. 614.

the husband only in contexts where he also mentions the headship of Christ (here, and see 1 Cor 11:3-16). Christ, then, is being said to have authority over his bride, to which the church responds by submitting to that authority. Here the rationale (*hoti*, "because") for submission of the wife is given: her husband is her head.

The *hōs* in Ephesians 5:23 probably suggests an analogous view of the husband's headship. The imagery itself, however, does not indicate how this headship is to be exercised. Ephesians 5:25 suggests that it means that the husband is to "go ahead" or take the lead or initiative in active loving and self-sacrificial service as Christ has done in relationship to the church. "Head," then, means "head servant" and refers to a sort of servant leadership (cf. Lk 22:25-27). If Christ, the one who lovingly offered himself as a sacrifice, is the model of headship, then general patriarchy and the assumptions of a patriarchal culture are not providing the model or the way it is to be enacted. The last clause of Ephesians 5:23, "and he himself is its Savior," makes evident that the analogy should not be pressed and does not include many aspects of the two sets of relationships. The emphatic "he himself" and the adversative *alla* that begins the next verse make clear that Christ alone is in view. Here the husband is not being identified as the wife's savior.

Ephesians 5:23 is the only place in the New Testament where we find the phrase "savior of the body" *(sōtēr tou sōmatos)*. Its meaning seems to be that Christ is the protector, sanctifier, healer, even rescuer of the body. This is different from the notion of Christ as Savior of the world, which has to do with conversion and the initial change into a new person. Above all, though, this phrase makes clear that this text is saying nothing about the husband being the savior of the wife or even being the spiritual leader of the family. Christ in fact fulfills both those roles. We may note also how the father's relationship to his children is likewise further normed in a Christian way.

The exhortations to fathers and children in Ephesians 6:1-4 are given more of a Judeo-Christian foundation in several ways than what we find in Colossians. There is the phrase "in the Lord" in Ephesians 6:1. Unlike Colossians 3:20, which simply speaks of duty in the Lord, here the phrase qualifies either "parents" or the verb "obey." In either case, the point is that such obedience presupposes a Christian context where parents will not abuse their children or their children's loyalty and subordinate position. Paul, then, says nothing here about children obeying non-Christian parents. Once again in Ephesians 5–6, as in Colossians 3–4, the advice given assumes a Christian household, not a situation involving a religiously mixed marriage.

Ephesians 6:2 provides an Old Testament support for the first exhortation. Exodus 20:12 says that children should honor their parents so that they will live long in the land. This is modified here in a significant way such that the inducement is said to be "so that it may be well with you and you may live long on the earth." The latter is identified as a promise from God, and the exhortation as a divine commandment. There probably are no ominous overtones here that misbehavior could lead to the death of the child, but that is not impossible in view of what follows in Ephesians 6:4: "Fathers, do not provoke your children to anger, but bring them up in the discipline and instruction of the Lord."

Instead of exercising the *patria potesta* in some arbitrary fashion when children get unruly, the father should take the time to give his children Christian instruction and correction. Here again we see Paul trying to limit the powers of the head of the household and to require the husband to act in a Christian manner and not merely in accord with what the culture allowed or encouraged.

The obligation for fathers to instruct their children was known in the Greco-Roman world, of course, but especially in large houses it was left to a slave guardian of the child (the *paidagōgos*), or to the wife, or even to the older children.[100] Paul, then, is adding or emphasizing extra responsibilities rather than extra privileges for the traditional head of the household. He must assume the tasks of religious instruction with his children.

Summary

What do we learn from a close scrutiny of Colossians 3–4 and Ephesians 5–6 about Paul's views on Christian husbands, wives and children? We learn that although Paul begins with the traditional family structure where he finds it, by no means does he simply baptize the existing patriarchal status quo. Indeed, he works to Christianize all of these relationships and to eliminate the possibility of abuse in a patriarchal family situation. He also, while using traditional terms, redefines the notions of headship and submission. Submission is done in the context of understanding that all Christians should submit to one another and serve one another out of reverence for Christ. In other words, it is not simply something that a wife should do in relationship to her husband. Paul has eliminated the notion that gender alone determines who

---

[100]See the discussion of the *paidagōgos* in Witherington, *Grace in Galatia*, pp. 262-71.

should submit. Headship is redefined in light of the way Christ was the head servant of the church. The sacrificial behavior of Christ, even to the point of dying for the church, sets up the paradigm for how headship should be exercised in the Christian family. Thus, what stands out about this material, and what makes it something that Paul's own audience would have seen as different, is not the way Paul uses familiar terms and concepts but rather the way he modifies those terms and concepts. The direction in which Paul's modifications are tending, in view of the background, is as crucial as what he actually says.

PAUL'S VIEWS ON SLAVERY

This leads us to the thorny issue of Paul's views on slavery, which I must address here, adding some further details to what was discussed in the section on the Colossian household code.[101] There is no question that the Roman Empire was able to exist and expand in large measure because of slave labor. The enslaving of provincials and "barbarians" was a growth industry in the first century A.D. There are even some estimates suggesting that at the height of the empire as much as 85 percent of the people dwelling therein were slaves. This surely is far too high. A better guess would be 50 percent for some parts of the empire, particularly in Rome of the first century, if we are counting both slaves and former slaves (freedmen and freedwomen). A reasonable estimate of those who in a particular year were actually slaves during the period of the middle of the first century A.D. is about 33 percent. Whatever the exact figure might be, it was an enormous number of people, and these people drove the economic engine of the empire, which depended radically on manual labor.

The more territory the Romans captured, the more prisoners they took and so the more they sold into slavery. Although it may surprise us, many people sold themselves into slavery in order to gain a stable economic situation or a decent living. Many also were not that keen on manumission when they found out the cost of being a free and independent person. One inscription on the tomb of a freed slave says, "Slavery was never unkind to me" (*CIL* 13.7119). Most of the slaves in Paul's days came from the eastern end of the Roman Empire, including some Jews. Jews were viewed as good workers and a stable group of people, so Jewish slaves had been settled in various key cities

---

[101]The basic study on this topic is Henneke Güzlow, *Christentum und Sklaverei in den ersten drei Jahrhunderten* (Bonn: Habelt, 1969). The best survey in English is Thomas Wiedemann, *Greek and Roman Slavery* (Baltimore: Johns Hopkins University, 1981).

in the empire, including Antioch and Corinth (see Philo, *Embassy* 281-282, on the Jewish colony in Corinth). Paul, as a Jew from the eastern end of the empire, surely was in a position to know something about slavery in his day. For instance, Paul would have known well that the Torah had specific laws meant to protect slaves from mistreatment, but that Roman laws were far less strict or concerned about such matters.

Slaves, by legal definition, were "living property," as Aristotle had once defined them, and as such had no legal rights. They were basically subject to the will and whims of their owners. There is, however, during the early empire considerable evidence of slaves being allowed to save their money and buy themselves out of slavery. Furthermore, during the reign of Claudius in the 40s and 50s, Seneca says that slaves had a great Saturnalia,[102] not only because many were gaining their freedom, but also because many, through thrift and good business practices, were rising higher in society even without manumission (Seneca *Apol.* 3.12; see also *Ben.* 28.5-7, where he complains about a free man running off to pay an obligatory social call on a wealthy slave). It must be remembered that many of the slaves in the empire were not rustics and formerly had been well-off and well-educated members of their own cities or tribes. These sorts of persons often were sold into slavery and became estate managers or slave guardians and tutors of a wealthy master's children.

People in the modern West, because of Southern antebellum slavery, typically think of slaves on plantations or in largely agricultural settings, or perhaps as indentured servants in wealthy homes in a bygone era in Europe. It is clear that the slaves whom Paul discusses would have been closer to a domestic servant than to a plantation worker, for Paul always and only discusses slaves in the context of discussing the household. Thus, although we could say a good deal about slaves in the Roman mines, or slaves building major structures or roads in the empire, or even slaves as civil servants throughout the empire, including the famous imperial slaves, some of whom Paul seems to encountered and converted while in Rome (see Phil 4:22 [though they may have been Christians before Paul arrived]), we would be missing the focus of Paul's discussion to do so. His concern is with slaves in the home situation, particularly in urban homes.

We therefore must envision Paul meeting household servants, slaves who were artisans, business persons, pedagogues and the like. If it is true that Paul

---

[102]The Saturnalia was the annual festival in which people would reverse roles, with the slaves becoming masters, and vice versa.

converted several entire households in the various cities where he visited, it is quite plausible that there were some slaves among the first converts—for example, in Roman colony cities such as Philippi (the households of Lydia and of the jailer [Acts 16]) or Corinth (the household of Stephanas [1 Cor 16:15]). It is not surprising, then, that Paul feels called upon to deal with this subject in several of his letters (1 Corinthians, Colossians, Philemon, Ephesians). It is especially unremarkable that he should do so when writing to the Corinthians, since Corinth was the great central clearinghouse for the slave trade in the empire. Conservative estimates about that city in the A.D. 50s strongly suggest that at least one-third of the population were slaves of one kind or another, and this estimate may well be too conservative.[103]

If we canvass ancient evidence and attitudes about slavery, we learn the following: (1) no ancient government, not even a Jewish one, sought to abolish slavery; (2) no former slaves who later became writers ever attacked the institution; (3) slave revolts appear to have been aimed not at abolishing the institution but rather at protesting abuses or seeking to become masters instead of slaves, even in the case of the Spartacus revolt;[104] (4) poor free workers were more likely to be abused than slaves because owners who mistreated slaves stood to take a financial loss; (5) unlike in the American South just prior to the Civil War, in the first century A.D. manumission of slaves was so common that Augustus set up laws to restrict the practice. It is interesting that we have evidence that it became a regular practice of Christians to purchase the freedom of some of their slave church members (see *1 Clem.* 55:2; Ign. *Pol.* 4:3; *Herm.* 38:10; 114:2-3). None of this negates the pernicious character of the institution itself, but it is important that we view in its proper historical context.

The discussion of what Paul says begins quite properly with 1 Corinthians 7:21-23. It is correct to say that Roman law did not allow slaves to choose freedom, as if they were master of their own fate. Whatever Paul means in 1 Corinthians 7:21, he cannot be saying, "If you have a chance to choose freedom, do not avail yourself of it." Slaves could work hard, save their money (*peculium*, their nest egg) and then make a strong case for freedom, but they could not force the issue. It was not the slave's choice, but rather the master's. Furthermore, it appears that the slave had no right to refuse manumission if

---

[103]See Witherington, *Conflict and Community in Corinth*, pp. 181-85.
[104]See S. Scott Bartchy, *Mallon Chrēsai: First-Century Slavery and the Interpretation of 1 Corinthinas 7:21* (SBLDS 11; Missoula, Mont.: Scholars Press, 1973), pp. 60-65.

the owner was determined to carry it out.

Manumission could take several forms. There was sacral manumission in which either the slave or some proxy purchased the freedom in a temple in the name of a deity. The deity was seen as the mediator of the transaction. More commonly, a master would stipulate in a will that a slave was to be freed upon the master's death. Manumission could also be readily performed before a magistrate or even informally in a ceremony before friends. What ensued thereafter is interesting.

> When a Roman manumitted his slave, [the slave] would (if the correct formalities had been observed) attain restricted citizenship status, extending even to the right to inherit his patron's estate. There is evidence that the feeling that a loyal domestic servant ought automatically to be granted freedom and civic rights after a number of years was so widespread that the "model" of slavery as a process of integration [into free society] may be useful here. . . . Roman jurists recognised a slave's right to use his *peculium* to buy himself free from his owner.[105]

What all this means is that although Paul has stated as a general principle that it is alright for people to remain in their present social status and situation when they come to Christ, (social status neither commending a person to God nor condemning a person before God), in 1 Corinthians 7:21 he is making an exception to such a rule. He is saying, "If indeed you are to become free, by all means make use of it." Although social status or position is of no major importance and certainly has no eternal significance in Christ (see Gal 3:28), Paul understands that some social conditions are far better than others, especially if one wishes to serve the Lord. Those advantageous social conditions would include being a free person and being a single person, as a close study of 1 Corinthians 7 shows. Paul, however, does not want his converts to evaluate themselves on the basis of society's values.

In fact there is a real sense in which in Christ there is a complete transvaluation or reversal of values. A Christian slave is already the Lord's freedman or freedwoman if we are talking about sin, and yet the free or freed person in Christ is the Lord's servant and the servant of fellow believers. In Christ something like a Saturnalia happens. A close study of "slavery" language as used metaphorically by Paul shows that he is prepared to use this language in a positive manner to refer to his own tasks and condition and that of other

---

[105]Wiedemann, *Greek and Roman Slavery*, p. 3.

Christians as well. As Dale Martin has shown, to some extent this language can even be used to describe a certain leadership style, one that we would call "servant leadership."[106] We therefore must be able to distinguish between the metaphorical use of "slavery" language and what Paul actually says about the social institution itself.

Clearly enough from 1 Corinthians 7:23, Paul is opposed to the trend of people, particularly Christians, selling themselves into slavery to support their family or to pay off debts. There was no point, in Paul's view, in making that sort of change. One of the major themes of 1 Corinthians 7 is that one should not change one's social condition just because one has become a Christian. No social status of any kind prevents conversion or being a Christian, and therefore this sort of social change is not required when there is a spiritual change in one's life. Yet when it was possible to do both, change spiritually and socially, in a positive way, one can and should take advantage of such an opportunity.

Paul does see slavery as making things more difficult for the Christian, and so in 1 Corinthians 7:21-23 he advises taking opportunities for freedom when they arise. His general tendency in this chapter is to minimize social status and its weight, but Paul understands that in reality not all social conditions are the same. Social status and standing become a significant issue if the gospel and its advancement in an individual's life or that of a family or church are impeded.

Paul's feelings about slavery certainly are made a bit clearer in the letter to Philemon, where Paul pleads for Onesimus's manumission. Unlike in 1 Corinthians 7, where Paul does not address masters, in this gem of a letter Paul's feelings about the responsibility of Christian masters become much clearer. Paul does not violate or go outside Roman law, but he does do some rather powerful rhetorical arm-twisting to accomplish his aims. He does set forth in Philemon a principle (all persons in Christ, of whatever social status, are brothers and sisters) that eventually led to a situation where it became clear that slavery and Christianity, with its views about human dignity, freedom and serving only the one Master, are basically two incompatible institutions.[107] When Paul tells Philemon to treat Onesimus "no longer as a slave, but rather more than a slave, a brother in Christ," he has crossed the line into new ethical territory. The radical implications of

---

[106]Dale B. Martin, *Slavery as Salvation: The Metaphor of Slavery in Pauline Christianity* (New Haven: Yale University Press, 1990).

[107]See Moule, *Epistles to the Colossians and Philemon*, pp. 11-14.

what Paul says in Philemon were not immediately understood. Indeed, in many quarters and for many centuries they were not understood at all. This brings us back once more to the household codes, particularly Colossians 3:22–4:1 and Ephesians 6:5-9.

The somewhat lengthy advice to slaves, coupled with the brief advice to masters, in Colossians and Ephesians must not be read in isolation from what Paul already said in 1 Corinthians and Philemon. This is especially so because in all likelihood Colossians was written and delivered at the same time as Philemon and in part at least to the same audience. It also must not be read in isolation from Colossians 3:11, where Paul says that in Christ there is no slave or free any more than there is any Greek or Jew. All are one and have the same status in Christ.

The first point, then, to be made about Colossians 3:22–4:1 is that Paul places the behavior of both slaves and masters in the context of their relationship to the Lord. The slave should serve as if serving the Lord, and the master always should act cognizant of having a Master in heaven. The idea is that both slaves and masters should be on their best behavior, indeed on their best Christian behavior, because the Lord not only is watching, but also is preparing for final judgment, with its rewards and punishments. The slave needs to know that there is such a thing as an eternal reward for the years of good and godly service. It has not been for naught, nor has it been done just for the earthly master.

It is important to keep steadily in view throughout this passage that Paul is assuming that both masters and slaves in this situation are Christians, otherwise the Christian sanctions and exhortations that he gives to each in turn are pointless. Thus, when Paul says, "Slaves, obey your earthly masters in everything . . . fearing the Lord" (which is to say, knowing that he is watching and evaluating things), he is assuming a Christian context, with Christians acting in a Christian fashion, always knowing that the Lord will hold one accountable for one's actions. Notice too that Paul does not direct the masters to tell the slaves to obey; rather, he addresses the slaves directly as persons in Christ.

The key hinge verse of the Colossian code's slavery section is Colossians 3:25, where Paul warns that the wrongdoer will be punished, and that there will be no partiality. This final clause surely is linked with Colossians 3:2 and provides a sanction to make sure that the Christian slaves will do their best in their work. Yet it is probable that it also prepares for what follows in the very next verse, for there Paul says, "Masters, treat your slaves justly and fairly, knowing you have a master [and a judge] in heaven" (Col 4:1). God indeed will not be partial or show favoritism to the master any more than to the slave if they do wrong. Indeed, the biblical principle enunciated elsewhere is that God will require more of those to whom more rights and responsibilities have been given (see Lk 12:48).

What are we to make of this teaching? It must be seen for what it is. Paul is not baptizing the institution of slavery, much less trying to make it easier for masters to take advantage of their slaves because of their Christian faith. Indeed, if anything, he is trying to limit the power of the master by employing the notion of Christ as master and judge of all as a sanction. Instead, he is concerned that even in all too fallen relationships persons should act in a Christian fashion and so be good witnesses to one and all. He is trying to inject the leaven of the gospel into this situation so that relationships between slaves and masters might improve, indeed, so that they might treat each other not just as fellow human beings but as brothers and sisters in Christ. This leads us to Ephesians 6:5-9.

It is interesting to study this text in parallel with the one we have just examined, especially at certain key points.

Table 11.2. Slavery in Colossians 3:22-41 and Ephesians 6:5-9

Colossians 3:22–4:1	Ephesians 6:5-9
Slaves, obey your earthly masters in everything,	Slaves, obey your earthly masters
not only while being watched and in order to please them, but wholeheartedly, fearing the Lord.	with fear and trembling, in singleness of heart, as you obey Christ, not only while being watched, and in order to please them, but as slaves of Christ.
Whatever your task, put yourselves into it, as done for the Lord and not for your masters,	Render service with enthusiasm, as to the Lord and not to men and women,
since you know that from the Lord you will receive the inheritance as your reward; you serve the Lord Christ.	knowing that whatever good we do, we will receive the same again from the Lord, whether we are slaves or free.
For the wrongdoer will be paid back for whatever wrong has been done, and there is no partiality.	And masters, do the same to them.
Masters, treat your slaves justly and fairly, for you know that you also have a Master in heaven.	Stop threatening them, for you know that both of you have the same Master in heaven, and with him there is no partiality.

Even on a cursory examination of the parallels it seems reasonably clear that there is some sort of relationship here, possibly literary, between these portions of the documents. On the whole, it probably is the correct judgment that the Ephesian text is the later of the two and is dependent on the Colossian one, unless both were composed at the same time for different purposes and different audiences.

The Ephesian version of the code is somewhat more demanding of the master than the Colossian one is. For example, not only is the "no partiality" clause clearly placed with the exhortation to the master in Ephesians (where as it is directly connected to the end of the slave exhortation in Colossians), but also there is the explicit command for masters to stop threatening their slaves. Furthermore, in Ephesians 6:9 we have the command for reciprocity between masters and slaves. In this case it is directed at the master and may mean not merely that they too are to have the same attitude as the slaves about seeing their work as being done unto the Lord, but that they are to serve their slaves with the same enthusiasm as their slaves serve them. Or at the very least, masters are to do good to their slaves as they are having it done unto them by their slaves.[108]

Once again in this household code we see Paul's attempt to reform and modify an existing societal structure and ameliorate the harm done by such structures to both the subordinate and superordinate persons in that social relationship. Paul is not trying to gild the lily or provide a Christian rationale for the indefensible. He is clear enough about the humanity of all involved, the impartiality of God toward all involved, and the equality in Christ and the equal obligation to serve one another as we would the Lord in whatever set of relationships we find ourselves. The emphasis once again must be placed on the way Paul modifies the traditional advice about slaves and masters. Andrew Lincoln puts it well:

> What is perhaps most striking about the codes of Colossians and Ephesians, however, is that slaves are addressed not simply as members of the household but as full members of the church. Nor is it simply, as in some other societies or cults, that there was no distinction between masters and slaves in the ritual activities, but these codes reflect the life of a community in which, despite the differences in their duties, both slaves and free can equally fully practice their faith in everyday life.[109]

---

[108]Lincoln probably is wrong to deny that the focus here is on reciprocal doing rather than just having the same attitude about the doing (*Ephesians*, p. 423). "Do the same to them" seems to be a reasonably clear call to action.

[109]Ibid., p. 419.

Here we are a long way from Aristotle's or Plutarch's advice on household management.

The overlap between household and house church is important for understanding Paul's advice given in the household codes. Christian religion in the first century as a worshiping and fellowshiping phenomenon was virtually confined to houses, and as such would have been seen in the Greco-Roman world as an extension of the religion of and in the household. Paul clearly believed that "in house" and "in community" Christianity could make a difference in the first-century world. Change could come in households, not only in individual lives but also in the social networks that existed in the extended family. Relationships, not just individuals, were expected to change. What we are seeing in these household codes is the way Paul was trying to change and so Christianize the household.

As I have stressed elsewhere, apart from the proclamation to all and sundry, Paul's basic strategy for social and spiritual change of the world was to put the leaven of the gospel into the structure of the Christian community, and as a subset of that into the structure of the Christian household and let it do its work over the course of time. The community was to be a witness to all. This focus on the community was for the most part in lieu of placing the leaven directly into secular society.[110] Paul believed in living a true Christian life and letting the implications of that bring reformation to the patriarchal and slave society in which he lived. He insisted that Christians live out their new freedom in Christ as brothers and sisters and as equals (see Gal 3:28). Colossians 3:11 and Galatians 3:28 were not merely slogans without social and spiritual implications, but the implications were played out "in Christ," which meant "in community," which in turn meant "in house" and "in households." By being a new community, a model of how the new creation changes things, a good witness was being borne about a new worldview.

Paul was no mere baptizer of the status quo, nor was he one who believed in taking up arms to resist evil. He was both a realist and in some ways a radical. He would show respect for the existing structures of society, government, family and business, but he would not encourage any of his converts to serve them in some idolatrous fashion. He recognized that the structures were fallen in character and indeed could even be demonized if a truly wicked person became emperor, governor, owner, or parent. But he also believed that government, family, and work were, in the first place, good

---

[110]See Witherington, *Conflict and Community in Corinth*, p. 185.

gifts from God. Paul retained his theocratic worldview throughout his life. In his view, all true or genuine authority and power comes from God. The emperor and his minions rule by permission and empowerment from God. The emperor himself is not God. Even the devil is *God's* devil, and God finally will exercise his sovereignty over him as well. In fact, the decisive victory over the powers of darkness had already been won by Christ on the cross.

Paul was not shy about criticizing these social structures when it was needful, but since he saw them as part of the form of this world, which is passing away, he did not spend most of his time in engagement with such matters. It was better to place the emphasis on the new creation as it was coming into expression in the Christian community and in the Christian household. Yet this necessarily entailed working on reforming the structures within the Christian household and house church. The spiritual roles and realities involved in ministry and the social structures were all part of one larger whole.

Paul, the Authorities, and Pacifism

Here, finally, is the place to discuss what Paul says about submission to those outside the Christian household or church structure. In all likelihood, Romans was written by Paul sometime during the last five years of the 50s. This means that it was written while Nero was emperor, though during a period before he declined into tyranny and the persecution of Christians, which did not happen until at least seven or eight years later. Paul's comments, then, must be taken in this sort of context, when by and large the emperor and the government might be judged by Christians to be acting as it ought to do.

The next thing to be stressed about this text is that it says absolutely nothing about Christians participating in government activities such as war, police actions and the like. Christians were not rulers during this period of time, and furthermore, the Roman government was not a participatory democracy. Even soldiers were not enlisted by means of a lottery of citizens. In short, this text is about pagan rulers and their right to govern and bear the sword for some purposes. The text says nothing about a Christian's right, much less their duty, to bear arms.[111]

We note first that Romans 13:1 directs these comments to every living person *(pasa psychē)*, which in this case likely refers in particular to every Roman Christian whom Paul is now addressing. It may be the case

---

[111]On all of this, see John Howard Yoder, *The Politics of Jesus: vicit Agnus noster* (Grand Rapids: Eerdmans, 1972), pp. 193-214.

that Paul is addressing a situation where some Christians were thinking of rebelling against the Roman authorities, especially in view of the burgeoning growth of the emperor cult. There may even be a very specific crisis in Rome that has prompted this exhortation. Tacitus (*Ann.* 13.50-51) tells us that in A.D. 58, due to numerous complaints about *publicani* engaging in unscrupulous tax farming practices (i.e., the collecting of indirect taxes), Nero contemplated abolishing all indirect taxation. In due course he was persuaded by senators simply to post and strictly enforce the regulations for taxation. It is possible that shortly before this time, when the taxes were most excessive and oppressive, various Roman Gentiles Christians were uneasy about these matters.

The key verb here, *hypotassō* ("to submit"), is the same verb we found applied to relationships within the body of Christ in Colossians 3–4 and Ephesians 5–6. This verb is not identical with *hypakouō* ("to obey"), as can be seen in the differing subjects to which these two verbs are applied in Colossians 3–4. Submitting to the governing authorities, which among other things means recognizing that they have a God-given authority, is not quite the same as obeying them. In other words, this text would not rule out civil disobedience, while still respecting the government's authority, if, for instance, the government required the worship of the emperor. The reason given in Romans 13:1 for this submission is that there is no human "power" *(exousia)* except from God. The existing authorities are so by God. It is quite possible that here the participle *tetagmenai* (from *tassō* ["appoint, establish"]), when coupled with *exousia*, refers to prominent Roman officials.

One intriguing way of reading Paul's discussion here of the powers that be is offered by Walter Wink. His view is that whenever Paul discusses such powers, he means both the human powers and the supernatural powers that influence, guide and use them. Wink is right that in various places in the New Testament a relationship is seen between human and supernatural forces or authorities, but we cannot simply assume that when one is spoken of, the other is also always meant or implied. Nothing in Romans 13:1-7 suggests that Paul is talking about the supernatural "powers behind the throne," other than the very clear connection that he makes between God and these ordained human authorities. It is true that elsewhere Paul sometimes uses *exousia* in a negative sense to refer to malign angelic forces, but this hardly suits the context here, and in any case Paul would not council submission to such forces.[112] Not all new views of the historical Paul and his thought world are plausible ones.

Paul's discussion, then, is not just about submitting to the emperor, but also to lesser governing authorities. This point must be kept clearly in mind, for as we will see, it appears that Paul may have tax officials particularly in view. On a broader front, the point will be that God raises up and deposes all rulers, but this by no means implies an endorsement of all policies of human governments.

Romans 13:2 draws a conclusion on the basis of the preceding verse. If it is true that such authorities are God-ordained and God-endowed, then those who resist them resist God's ordering, and the end result is that one will incur legal judgment. Paul goes on to add in Romans 13:3 that rulers *(archontes)* are a terror not to good works but rather to evil ones. The assumption here is that the officials are working properly and justice is being done. Paul then asks, "Do you wish to not fear the authorities?" "Fine" he says, "then do what is good, and instead of judgment you will actually receive praise from the authorities. They are servants of God for the good of all, including Christians" (Rom 13:3-4). Note that *archōn* was a term regularly used of local or municipal officials. Anyone who does what is evil should be afraid precisely because these officials do not wear and bear the sword for nothing. The authority who "executes wrath" on the wrongdoer is acting as the servant of God.

We should note that here Paul is not offering a discourse on capital punishment. Were he discussing that subject, we would have expected him to say something about crucifixion or beheading at this juncture. There is, however, nothing here to rule out that Paul may have agreed in principle that the governing authorities have the right to use lethal force to maintain order. Nonetheless, the focus here is on curbing resistance or evildoing. Paul could have used other terms had he wanted to speak about capital punishment. In view of Romans 13:6-7, it is possible that Paul already has in mind the tax police, who wore the Roman short sword, but we cannot be sure. I suspect that Paul is talking in general terms up through Romans 13:5 and then turns to a specific illustration, perhaps a very germane one for Roman Christians,

---

[112]This is characteristic of Walter Wink's treatment of this material in *Naming the Powers: The Language of Power in the New Testament* (Philadelphia: Fortress, 1984), pp. 6-47. He does not adequately distinguish between supernatural and natural powers. On this text, see especially pp. 45-47. For a much more balanced treatment of this whole subject which makes clear that both Jesus and Paul believe that the existing governing authorities derived their power and authority from God See Christopher Bryan, *Render to Caesar* (Oxford: Oxford University Press, 2005).

in Romans 13:6-7. Tax police would be but one good illustration of a governing authority's right to wear and bear the sword.

Romans 13:5 rounds out the more general discussion and stresses two reasons why one should have a healthy respect for the governing authorities. First, one should do so because of the real possibility of being subject to lethal force. Second, one should do so because of Christian conscience. Here "conscience" *(syneidēsis)* probably does not focus on guilty feelings but rather refers to prudence, critical realism, being wise as serpents and innocent as doves. Here we see Paul the realist, who does not wish Christians to come to harm and counsels what amounts to Christian wisdom.

Romans 13:6 begins "because of this," which seems to have the preceding verse in view. Because of wise critical reflection on one's situation, one should also pay tribute, by which is meant taxes and customs fees. It must be kept in mind that Jews, and presumably Jewish Christians, had some exemption from some taxes. In particular, they were allowed to pay taxes into their own temple in Jerusalem in lieu of some Roman taxes, since as monotheists they would not contribute to funds spent on pagan religion or the emperor cult. This was the cause of no end of irritation and anger on the part of Romans who had to pay such taxes directly (see Cicero, *Flacc.* 28.67; Tacitus, *Ann.* 5.5.1; Josephus, *Ant.* 16.45, 160-61). There was also the further problem that Roman citizens were exempt from such taxes, which left ordinary Roman Gentiles bearing the burden of them. In this situation it is understandable why Paul might have to exhort his mostly Gentile audience in Rome not only to respect Jews, whom God had not forsaken (see Rom 9–11), but also to pay their taxes as a sign of respect to the God-ordained authority.

Paul actually says in Romans 13:6 that tax collectors not only are public servants but also are servants of God engaged in this very task of making sure that proper tribute money is paid. Romans 13:7 may have an echo of Mark 12:17. There are two technical terms used here. *Phoros* corresponds to *tributum*—direct taxes from which Roman citizens likely would be exempt. *Telos* refers to *vectigalia*—direct taxes referring in the first place to rents from government properties, but also to customs duties, death duties, and taxes on the sale of slaves.[113] Christians, then, should owe no one anything. Taxes and proper honor should be given to all to whom it is due.

What does this teaching tell us about the historical Paul? It makes quite clear

---

[113]See James D. G. Dunn, *Romans 9–16* (AB 38B; Dallas: Word, 1988), pp. 766-67.

that Paul was no revolutionary. This passage should not be seen, however, as a Pauline manifesto suggesting that Christians should obey the government in all things. To submit is not the same as to blindly obey. Paul is suggesting a policy of critical realism, to avoid clashes with governing authorities, and also to avoid the charge that Christians are subversive because they will not pay taxes. These were not incidental matters, for Paul would have known about the expulsion of Jews from Rome a few years before this letter was written (A.D. 49), and to judge from Acts 18, this involved Jewish Christians as well. Christians in Rome were in a somewhat precarious position, and so Paul is counseling a form of political quietism and nonresistance.[114]

In some ways, this pragmatic approach is to be expected of one who was a Roman citizen, one who had benefited in various ways from the order that governing authorities could bring to various situations. Like most ancient persons, Paul takes for granted that governing authorities have their authority from God. Since the primary group in which he is embedded is the Christian community, he is trying to do what he can to protect that community from harm or governmental intrusion. Paul is a community-oriented person whose values are community preservation over personal privilege.

Paul could have claimed exemption from various of these taxes, but he says nothing about such a thing here. Of more interest to us are his views about Christians and the use of force. We will see that Paul says something very different about the behavior that is appropriate for Christian believers than about the behavior that is appropriate for governing officials. In doing so, he shows both his critical realism and his radical character. Let us examine the immediately preceding text, Romans 12:14-21.

As far as I know, in the first century A.D. pacificism was not considered a live option by any significant group of persons, except perhaps by various of the followers of Jesus. Paul, a sectarian person, had not simply brought over into Christianity all the ethical values that he had upheld as a Pharisee. There is nothing in the Pauline corpus about "an eye for an eye" or the like, even if the *lex talionis* was intended to limit rather than license revenge or retaliation. We may take it as virtually certain that since Paul admits that he was a persecutor of Christians, he was indeed prepared to, and had no qualms of conscience about, using force to make Jewish Christians conform to a par-

---

[114]It should be seen that nonresistance is not the same as passive resistance to authority. The Amish are an example of nonresistance, whereas Martin Luther King's and Mohandas Ghandi's civil rights tactics are examples of passive resistance.

ticular form of Jewish orthopraxy and/or orthodoxy. Wherever Paul got the ideas we find expressed in Romans 12:14-21, they did not likely come from either the Old Testament (although see 2 Kings 6:8-23; Is 11; 23; 65–66), nor were they the values that Paul derived from Pharisaism. Indeed, it is the mark of sectarians that although the new thing, the new agenda, the new beliefs are central and determinative of faith and symbolic universe, they will bring in elements of the old belief system and reconfigure them, using them in new ways to support the new faith posture. We see this very procedure in Romans 12:14-21.

This passage is important not least because it addresses how Christians are to deal with those outside the community, having already said a good deal earlier in the chapter about dealing with those inside the Christian community. It is in this context that Paul goes on in Romans 13:1-7 to talk about how to respond to "official outsiders," governing officials, who might be contacting and engaging them. In short, Romans 13:1-7 should not be read apart from what has already been said about Christian behavior in the preceding chapter, especially the end of that chapter. The gist of the teaching in Romans 12:14-21 is that nonretaliation is the proper response of a Christian being attacked, and that one is actually to make a positive effort to love one's enemies and do good to and for them as a response to all hostile acts (see Rom 12:14, 17, 19, 21). As Dunn observes, this stress on doing good to those who have done harm is repeated four times, buttressed by Scripture (Rom 12:20) and given the place of emphasis at the beginning and the end of the passage (Rom 12:14, 21).[115] Paul indeed seems to take for granted that persecution and acts of malice have been happening and will happen to Christians in Rome, and he wants to stress that although they cannot prevent such actions, they can choose how to respond to them. The teaching here is far from hypothetical. Paul outlines a battle plan for responding to persecution in a Christian manner. The former persecutor will advocate a form of pacifism, drawing in part on the teaching of his Master as well as on Jewish Wisdom literature and the Pentateuch.

The echo of the Jesus tradition is particularly strong at Romans 12:14, but since that is the theme verse for the whole section, its importance goes beyond this verse. In fact, Paul uses all his sources here allusively, assuming the authority of it all, but that which sets the agenda is the Jesus teaching (see below on Rom 12:14, 18). No doubt Jesus' personal example is also what is

---

[115]Dunn, *Romans 9–16*, p. 755.

setting the agenda here, as well as Paul's own following of that example (see 1 Cor 4:12). Paul is one who believed as a Christian that one must take every thought and action captive so as to obey Christ, obeying both his teaching and his example (see 2 Cor 10:5).

This subsection begins with a beatitude in Romans 12:14. Blessing someone was a matter of desiring God to bestow favor as opposed to desiring God to blight or punish, which is what cursing was for. Paul's words here are close to the Q saying of Jesus found in Luke 6:27-28 with a variant in Matthew 5:44. The Lukan form is closest: "Love your enemies, and bless those who curse you." In fact, nowhere else in the New Testament other than in Luke 6:28 and Romans 12:14 do we find this specific contrast between cursing and blessing, and this must point strongly to the conclusion that Paul is indeed drawing on the Jesus tradition. This teaching comports neither with the Jewish (and Old Testament) idea that God would curse those who curse God's people nor with Greco-Roman notions of appropriate response to attacks and curses.

In Romans 12:17 Paul says, "Repay no one evil for evil." This can be said to be a strong qualification of the law of retaliation in the Old Testament, which is somewhat close to earlier Jewish ideas (see Prov 20:22; 24:29; *Jos. Asen.* 23:9; 28:5; note also the "Do not return good with evil" exhortation in Prov 17:13). Romans 12:18 adds that if at all possible, Christians should live at peace with everyone. Paul is not advocating a quiet and peaceable life at all costs, in particular not at the cost of compromising their faith. This is quietism not as an ultimate good but rather as part of the larger strategy of nonretaliation.

Romans 12:19 says explicitly, "Do not take revenge yourselves, beloved, but give place for wrath." Here "wrath" presumably refers to God's wrath, though it is not impossible in view of Romans 13:4 that Paul has in mind the governing authorities as executors of God's justice. Paul, as Romans 1:18 shows, believed that God's wrath was already being revealed against ungodliness prior to the final judgment. Paul then quotes, in some form, Deuteronomy 32:25, the point being that since God will make sure that justice is done one way or another, sooner or later, Christians must not take matters, or weapons, into their own hands.

Indeed far from taking vengeance, the proper response is just the opposite. Here again Paul is quoting the Old Testament, in this case the LXX form of Proverbs 25:21-22. The point of the saying is that Christians should respond to hostility with hospitality, to hatred with kindness. It is improbable that this saying is used by Paul to mean "Do kindness to your enemies so that their guilt will be even greater and their punishment more severe." It is possible, however, that Paul means that responding in Christlike fashion may produce repentance, remorse, a seared conscience, and so in fact do some spiritual good to enemies.

Roman 12:21 continues on in this same train of thought about not being negatively reactive but rather being a proactive person, one who acts even in negative situations in a Christlike manner. One should not be overwhelmed by evil and simply become resigned to it; rather one should overcome the bad with the good. This nicely brings us back to Romans 12:14 and rounds off this section of Paul's instructions. The present-tense verbs here indicate the inculcating of an ongoing approach that Christians should adopt, even when under persecution.

We see from the verses that frame this section, Romans 12:14, 21, that Paul is not simply counseling quietism but rather a positive program of good works by Christians, even to their enemies. Not only should they not retaliate or take revenge, but also they are to do the very opposite: love their enemies. For Paul, this is not simply good strategy or tactics for an imperiled minority; rather, it is what Paul takes to be proper Christian conduct, a proper way to follow the example of Christ and his teaching. Thus, although there is a pragmatic dimension to the quietism or pacifism, Paul does not want his converts just to be peaceful and not resist; he wants them to do deeds of love on an ongoing basis even to enemies. Again, this constitutes a social program, not just a survival tactic. As such, it entails a radical ethic that no other known extant community in the first century was advocating. It is still today an ethic that is rare even in the so-called Christian West. Paul was not merely ahead of his time, he was ahead of all our times, living in the shadow of Christ and in the light of the coming eschaton.

In closing this section, I reiterate what I said earlier in this study when talking about Jesus. There is a difference between a use of force, a use of violence, and a use of lethal force. Clearly, Jesus used force, but not against any human being, in his cleansing of the temple. Thus, it is violence and lethal force that these sorts of teachings rule out as un-Christian behavior. I take this to mean that Christians should not serve in public capacities where they might have to use either of those two things. This does not mean that they cannot be good citizens in other ways (e.g., firefighters, medics, chaplains), nor that they should not intervene when a child, family member, or neighbor is being harmed, nor that they should not use force that does no violence or bodily harm to resolve a dangerous situation. And clearly, the ethic of Christ calls Christians to be proactive and be prepared to give up their lives to save the lives of others. None of these principles and practices, however, require or warrant the use of excessive force. What Jesus and Paul are urging is that Christians actually trust God and his human ambassadors in such situations. They are to "give place for wrath" rather than take matters into their own hands.

But why? Why this ethic for the followers of Jesus? I suspect that it is intended to foreshadow the ethic of the coming kingdom, when all swords will be beaten into plowshares. In other words, this is an eschatological ethic, an ethic that gives a glimpse of kingdom come, when the lion will lie down with the lamb without planning to have lamb chops! Christians are supposed to live not out of the old world, whose form is passing away, but rather out of the new one that is breaking into the old one. They are meant to be ensigns of eternity and of Christlikeness in their behavior. Between new birth and new body a new orientation applies when it comes to Christians giving or taking life. They are to be givers, not takers. They are to be totally prolife because they are the witnesses for the one who said, "I have come that they may have life, and have it abundantly" (Jn 10:10).

PAUL ON SINGLENESS AND MARRIAGE

We have already had occasion to explore much about Paul's views on marriage through the study of the household codes, but there are some dimensions of his ethic not covered in such material, and so as this chapter draws to a close, I want to point out a few things about 1 Corinthians 7 and what it tells us about Paul's views of singleness and marriage. Since I have discussed this topic at length elsewhere, here I will simply reiterate several of the most crucial points for Paul's ethics.[116]

As with much of 1 Corinthians, Paul is dealing with problems and indeed is even answering queries from a confused congregation that has written to him. Part of understanding what Paul is saying involves recognizing when he is quoting his audience and when he is giving his own views. In 1 Corinthians 7:1 he begins, "Concerning the things which you wrote . . ." and then immediately quotes one of the Corinthians' own slogans, "It is good for a

---

[116]See Witherington, *Women in the Earliest Churches*.

man not to touch a woman." This is not Paul's view; indeed, he will severely qualify this view in the very next verse, contrasting his own view, "But because of sexual immorality. . . ." It is not Paul who is the ascetic here, but some of his converts in Corinth are, as is especially clear from the question that pops up later in the chapter about those who want to keep their fiancée a virgin but still get married. So we must bear in mind that Paul is responding in shorthand to various off-kilter Corinthian views about which that he has received oral and written reports.

First, it should be stressed that the household codes make evident that Paul does not see marriage simply as a prophylactic against immorality. It is clear from 1 Corinthians 7:2 that he sees that as one of the virtues of marriage, but by no means the only one. Second, Paul says that "each man" should have his own wife, and "each woman" her own husband, which clearly implies that he expects most of the audience to be or get married. He has no problems with that. What he does believe, however, is that it requires a *charisma*, a grace gift, to be married, and so marriage should not be assumed to be for every Christian. This gift has not been given to some, and in view of the travails of marriage, and also the eschatological situation, Paul wishes that more could be unmarried, as he is, but he is under no illusions that the majority of the audience will or should follow such a course of action.

In 1 Corinthians 7:2-4 we get some of the most egalitarian teaching on marriage anywhere in the New Testament or, for that matter, in the ancient world. Men and women are viewed as equals and as mutually dependent. Even more surprising is the remark that the husband's body belongs exclusively to the wife, and vice versa. Here Paul is eliminating the sexual double standard, for although wives were indeed expected to be chaste except in relationship to their husbands, Gentiles in general did not expect that of husbands. Indeed, there is even evidence that husbands were encouraged in some cases to frequent prostitutes when they were itching for sex, presumably to prevent their wives from having more pregnancies.[117] Paul will have none of this sort of nonsense. No doubt it will have come as a revelation to various Corinthian men that "your body belongs exclusively to your wife." Throughout Paul's marital teaching the usual upshot is that men's presumed rights in that patriarchal and pagan culture are attenuated rather severely in one way or another.

In 1 Corinthians 7:5 Paul stresses that husband and wife are not to stop

---

[117]On this, see ibid., chaps. 1-2.

conjugating the verb "to love" except perhaps for a time of prayer, but thereafter they are to come back together again and give each other their conjugal rights. There is a special danger for a married person, accustomed to sexual sharing, being abstinent for too long and thus becoming subject to temptation from Satan, says Paul. And this brings up a crucial point.

When Paul speaks of a concession in 1 Corinthians 7:6, the concession is the time apart from having sex with one another, not the time together. In other words, Paul is not "conceding" marriage here (as this text sometimes was interpreted by ascetics in the Middle Ages especially); rather, he is conceding temporary abstinence for prayer, not commanding it, much less advising it for married folks. Then in 1 Corinthians 7:7 Paul expresses a wish that all persons could be as unencumbered as he is so that they could be singularly focused on serving the Lord. In all likelihood, Paul is speaking either as a widower or as a person who, though he had been married as a Pharisee before his conversion, lost his wife and family through the conversion, after which he was shunned. In any case, he speaks now as someone who is single and probably has been so for a long time, but he also speaks as one who knows the burdens and responsibilities of marriage. And this is precisely why in 1 Corinthians 7:8 he suggests to the unmarried and widows that if possible, it would be good for them to remain as they are, but if they have a strong desire to get married, that certainly is no problem or sin, but he would have them marry in the Lord. He says that getting married is a good thing, but being single is even better. Spoken like a true apostle, with his thoughts on mission and with one eye on the eschatological horizon!

Paul follows the ethic of Jesus when it comes to divorce. Indeed, in 1 Corinthians 7:12 he quotes the Lord's teaching, found in Mark 10:2-12, that says that those whom God has joined together should not divorce. That Paul is thinking of a Christian couple is clear from what follows, for he goes on to add that if a Christian spouse is married to a non-Christian one and the latter wishes to depart or separate (i.e., divorce), such a relationship can be dissolved without disobedience to Christ's teachings. However, Paul encourages the Christian spouse to stay in the relationship because the Christian partner is not defiled by the relationship with a pagan, and indeed the influence goes in the opposite direction: the non-Christian spouse receives a spiritual or sanctifying benefit, and the children of such a religiously mixed marriage are still clean, holy, perhaps set apart for God, if that is what *hagios* means here. Clearly, Paul does not think that Christians need to end relationships with non-Christians for religious reasons. It is possible that Paul is allowing the dissolution of the mixed-marriage relationship if one of the partners has become a Christian subsequent to marrying and cannot manage to both remain married and remain Christian. The latter is more crucial, in Paul's view.

The teaching that follows about engaged couples, though debated, at least clearly suggests that Paul does not want anyone practicing ascetical marriages, but he is fine with the idea that someone who is merely engaged need not consummate the relationship by going forward into marriage and sexual sharing. We need to bear in mind that although this teaching might not seem strange to us, it was strange in Paul's world, where engagement was seen as a sort of binding legal contract, indeed was seen as the first act of marriage, leading inevitably to the consummation and marital union of the couple's relationship. Paul thinks that this need not be the case. Paul clearly also makes evident that a Christian can be a Christian in any sort of social relationship, whether married or single, whether slave or free, and so on. Therefore, it is not needful to change one's relational status in order to become or be a Christian. However, Paul does say that the slave who has the opportunity to gain freedom certainly should seize that opportunity. The contrast between what he says about the marital relationship and the slave situation is striking and shows what Paul's real opinions are about the institution of slavery in contrast to the holy and good institution of marriage.

Were we to go on and examine 1 Corinthians 8–10, which immediately follows this discussion, we would see clearly that while Paul is prepared to lay down the law (namely, the law of Christ) when it comes to some fundamental relationships and behaviors, he also makes plenty of room for improvisation in regard to "things indifferent"—what one eats, wears and the like. So many of life's day-to-day decisions Paul feels no need to give imperatives about. Instead, he expects his audience to be cultivating the mind of Christ and figuring out what they should do in order to serve and edify the church (see 1 Cor 12) and to serve and glorify the Lord. They are indeed to emulate Christ, and they even are called in 1 Corinthians 11:1 to be imitators of the Paul, who imitates or follows the example of Christ. The imperatives provide the broad boundaries of the community, within which there is plenty of freedom for its members to make morally responsible choices about many things not specifically mandated or prohibited; this they do by knowing the teachings of Christ and his apostles, listening to one's Spirit-informed and sanctified conscience, and following good Christian examples. Paul's ethic does not provide a rule for every occasion for the very good reason that Christians who are maturing in Christ eventually grow to a point where they do not need to be constantly told what to do. They have gained critical judgment in Christ and can figure it out for themselves, knowing that the will of God for their lives is always their sanctification in any and all relationships and in any and all situations (see 1 Thess 4).

Summary

We have roamed far and wide in exploring Paul's ethic in this chapter, and yet we have barely scratched the surface. Apart perhaps from Jesus, Paul is the only figure in the New Testament for whom we have enough data to be able to assess the scope, arc, and trajectory of the ethic in question. Yet still, on some issues Paul is tantalizingly brief—for example, Christian pacifism and the Christian's relationship to governing authorities. He is in fact far more preoccupied with the in-house (versus the public sphere) relationships of Christians both in the physical family and in the family of faith. Paul has no problems at all issuing imperatives, though when there is time and opportunity, he much prefers to persuade his audience to do the right thing. He is willing to talk about a Christian ethical code, called the "law of Christ," which, as we saw, involves some carryover from the Old Testament, some of the teaching and example of Jesus (which involved that carryover material in part), and the new apostolic teaching.

But at the same time, Paul is no casuist. He does not believe that there is a rule for every occasion, nor does he believe that there should be. Indeed, he believes that Christians should grow up and learn to make moral choices and decisions without having to be told what to do all the time. There are matters of ethical indifference, choices that become ethically charged only if they have a bad effect on one's neighbor or fellow believer. There is room for improvisation and for taking account of individual conscience, but there are also clear and absolute ethical norms, and they do not just amount to some vague notion of "doing the loving thing." As the many imperatives in Paul's letters show, love has a concrete shape as far as he is concerned. It looks remarkably like the teaching and life of Christ, for it is cruciform in pattern, eschatological in sanction, and Spirit-empowered and community-oriented always.

Paul has much against him in trying to reform the existing patriarchal and slave-driven culture in house. He must, and does, begin with his converts where he finds them, and he tries to lead them into more equitable, free, and gracious relationships modeled on the way Christ treated all people. Watching him inject the gospel leaven into those existing fallen relationships and institutions in stages, as he grew closer to his people and they grew up in the Lord, is both inspiring and challenging, presenting us with an image of a Christlike pastor at work. Paul never should be seen as someone who simply baptized the best of the larger cultural values and called them good, but he was quite ready to adopt and adapt virtue lists and facets of the culture that he saw as consistent with the Christian ethic. Paul knew how to avoid majoring in minors, nor could anyone accuse him of neglecting the more important moral issues of his day. He even addressed some taboo subjects such as slavery, and he shows the way to help people be treated "no longer as slaves, but as brothers and sisters." Anyone who can talk about equality between a master and a slave, or can say that the husband's body belongs exclusively to the wife, or can suggest that children are moral agents just like adults is bold indeed.

The shadow of the Pauline ethic has been understandably long and deep, even to this day. We do well at this juncture, then, to examine a representative sampling of the ethics offered to largely Gentile Christians by other New Testament writers and see if we find that Pauline shadow looming large or if instead it is the "shadow of the Galilean" that most dominates the landscape. Thus, to Mark, Luke and the author of 2 Peter we turn for our final chapter on New Testament ethics.

12

ETHICS FOR GENTILE CHRISTIANS
PART TWO

Mark, Luke, 2 Peter

Stories form our values and moral sensibilities in . . . indirect and complex ways, teaching us how to see the world, what to fear, and what to hope for; stories offer us nuanced models of behavior, both wise and foolish, courageous and cowardly, faithful and faithless.

RICHARD HAYS[1]

When a narrator is telling a story, it is always hard to know whether the thrust of that story is "Go and do likewise" or "Go and do otherwise." For one thing, you have to have a sense of the writer's larger value system to be able to assess the matter. More than that, you have to be able to tease your own mind into active thought to puzzle out the ethical sense of what is being said, or as Amos Wilder once put it, "The road to a moral judgment is by way of the imagination."[2] It is not enough to attend to the specifically didactic passages in Mark or Luke in order to assess the ethical potential of a Gospel or Acts. One must look for consistent patterns of behavior that appear to be endorsed, or at least positive repeated patterns, and the same applies for the negative side of the equation. Nor is it enough to focus on the distinctive material in one or another Gospel, though certainly that is a clue to the moral judgments of the author. What matters in analyzing a Gospel or Acts is not how much the evangelist contributed to the discussion that is unique or distinctive but rather, as Richard Hays says, how, overall, the evangelist

---

[1]Richard B. Hays, *The Moral Vision of the New Testament: Community, Cross, New Creation* (San Francisco: HarperSanFrancisco, 1996), p. 73.
[2]Amos N. Wilder, *Early Christian Rhetoric: The Language of the Gospel* (Cambridge, Mass.: Harvard University Press, 1971), p. 60.

portrays the behavior and praxis of being a disciple—what it does and does not look like.[3]

One of the questions that must be asked is "What is the relationship between the Christology of the book and its ethics?" That is, to what degree is the pattern of Jesus' own behavior seen as the pattern for the behavior of disciples? To what degree are disciples called to take up their own crosses and follow the road that Jesus is treading? Furthermore, there is the question of the intertwining of being and doing, such that when we discover Jesus' identity in these Gospels and affirm it as good news, "we are not just making a theological affirmation about Jesus' identity; we are choosing our own identity as well."[4]

But this whole approach presents a problem, especially when we are dealing with Mark, because as even the casual student of Mark will know, it is not easy to pin down who exactly Jesus is. Is he the Jewish messiah? Yes, but he prefers to use the enigmatic title "Son of Man," and he speaks of the Son of Man being destined for suffering. Is he the Son of God. Yes, but contrary to the usual pagan notions about sons of the gods, this one gets himself crucified, and even before that happens he has beckoned his disciples to travel the same road to Golgotha. Is this some sort of ethical agenda that involves a lust for martyrdom or a death wish? Exactly what does it mean that we only realize who Jesus really is as the Son of God on the cross, and we only truly realize who we are as disciples when we take up our crosses and follow him? These are the sorts of questions that we never get to if we simply analyze Mark 10 or the other obviously ethical passages in Mark's Gospel. Luke, to be sure, is much less apocalyptic and opaque than Mark about these matters, but the same sorts of issues arise in his Gospel, as we will see. Bearing these sorts of things in mind, we need to look briefly at these two Gospels, Mark and then Luke, which likely were written largely for Gentile Christian audiences. Here we do not need to revisit what has already been said in the chapter on Jesus about the ethics in these Gospels. Here we will focus on somewhat broader and narratological concerns.

MARK: THE APOCALYPTIC ETHICS OF THE COMING SON OF MAN

Scholars have long pondered why it is that Mark focuses on Jesus as the Son of Man rather than on other, more conventional titles. The answer to this

---

[3]Hays, *Moral Vision of the New Testament*, p. 74.
[4]Ibid., p. 79.

question seems to be that Mark has taken an apocalyptic approach to his entire telling of this Gospel, and so he focuses on the enigmatic figure from Daniel 7 who comes on the clouds and is given the authority to judge the world and rule forever. In Mark's way of telling the story, the truth dawns on the disciples only by means of revelations from God. Indeed, in this Gospel Jesus himself has his identity confirmed to him by a revelation from God at his baptism at the outset of the story. When the world is stark and dark, discipleship requires extra light from above to illumine the path that a disciple must tread.

In his analysis of the Markan ethical material, Hays focuses on the central section of the Gospel, Mark 8:27–10:45, where there are three passion predictions that the Son of Man must suffer, be killed and arise, followed in each case by protest and/or misunderstanding on the part of the disciples (Mk 8:32-33; 9:33-34; 10:35-41), which in turn is followed by corrective teaching about Christology and discipleship (Mk 8:34–9:1; 9:35-37; 10:42-45). The essential question that a disciple should be asking is not "Can we have the seats of honor on Jesus' right and left when he comes into his glory?" but rather "Are we able to drink the cup and be baptized with the baptism of suffering and even death that Jesus is about to undergo?" (Mk 10:37-41).

Jesus then seizes the moment to impress on the disciples that he is bidding them to come and die if need be, following him unto death. He seeks to produce an attitude correction by indicating thereafter that he is among them not as one who came to be served but rather who came to serve and give his life a ransom for the many (Mk 10:42-45). Lest we think that this is just all about Christology, Jesus reminds them of how the Gentiles lord it over one another and adds, "But it is not so among you; but whoever wishes to become great among you must be your servant, and whoever wishes to be first among you must be slave of all" (Mk 10:43-44). The behavior of the Christ, then, provides the paradigm for the behavior of the Christians. In other words, "To be Jesus' follower is to share his vocation of suffering servanthood, renouncing the world's lust for power. Among 'Gentiles' domination and self-assertion are the rule, but in the new community of Jesus' followers, another logic is at work."[5]

Of course, the disciples glibly say that they can be baptized with the baptism that Jesus is about to undergo, and then there are other protestations of loyalty and faithfulness in the passion narrative, all of which ring hollow,

---

[5]Ibid., p. 82.

for one disciple betrays Jesus, another who swore he would never deny or
desert Jesus does so, and then all the male disciples desert Jesus in the garden of Gethsemane. Mark is not imbued with a large dose of confidence in
the native potential of human beings, even disciples, to successfully follow
Jesus even unto death.[6] Yet the call to discipleship keeps ringing forth in
this Gospel. "There is not the slightest hint in this Gospel that the requirements of God must be prudentially tailored or 'realistically' limited because
of human weakness. Rather, the demand for self-sacrificial discipleship is
uncompromising."[7] This is all the more startling when one notes that this
Gospel never talks about the empowerment of the Spirit to help one obey
or endure. Only in Mark 13:9-11 is there a promise that the Spirit will help
a disciple bear witness when put on trial. How is obedience possible under
such trying circumstances, especially when the demands of discipleship are
so broad and the gate into the kingdom is so narrow? The answer that the
disciples are given to the question "Who then can be saved?" is that for mortals it is impossible, but for God all things are possible (Mk 10:17-31). The
rigors of discipleship are described in this same passage as entailing giving up
goods, families, land and material security. Doubtless there were many like
the rich young man who just could not tear himself away from such things.
Although Jesus promises that when such sacrifices are made, one gains brothers and sisters and family and fields (but with persecutions), he is not talking
about a quid pro quo, because every time the disciples fall into the trap of
calculating their everlasting rewards for being Jesus' disciples, they receive a
stern corrective (Mk 9:33-35; 10:35-45). "The norm for discipleship is defined by the cross."[8]

Lest we think that it is all divine drudgery to which Mark is calling disciples, there is also his teaching about love in Mark 12:28-34, where the heart
of the law is seen as the law of the heart—loving God with one's whole heart
and loving neighbor as self. Although we might expect a connection to be
made between such love and the self-sacrifice called for in this Gospel, Mark
does not make the connection explicit. Here, taking up the cross is not called
an act of love, but only an act of obedience.

As Hays recognizes, ethics is done in the shadow of the eschatological

---

[6]One cannot help but wonder if this reflects in some measure on Mark's painful assessment of his
own failures as a disciple on the first missionary journey with Paul.
[7]Hays, *Moral Vision of the New Testament*, pp. 82-83.
[8]Ibid., p. 84.

realities that are breaking into human history during the era of Jesus' ministry and thereafter. What is most interesting about the eschatological tenor of Mark is that he is quite specifically not urging an interim ethic in view of the short timetable until the return of Christ. To the contrary, he emphasizes that the timing of the second coming is unknown (Mk 13:32), and therefore the ethical response is that one must continue to emulate the behavior of the Master and do what one is called to do, without focusing on the horizon, whether near or far. It is a big mistake to lump together everything that is said in the apocalyptic discourse in Mark 13, as if the author was suggesting that all those events would transpire in the run up to the destruction of the temple in A.D. 70. There is instead an A-B-A-B pattern to the material there, with the A sections referring to signs on the earth that do indeed transpire in the events leading up to the temple's destruction, while the B events involve cosmic signs that augur the return of Christ, and they are simply said to transpire "sometime after these things" (i.e., the preliminary eschatological events and the destruction of the temple). Nor do we have a theme of "necessary imminence" elsewhere in Mark.

The promise of Mark 9:1 is the promise of a parousia preview in the transfiguration, not to be confused with the promise in Mark 13:30, which refers to the forty-year period of eschatological events leading up to the destruction of the temple.[9] It is the transfiguration that some standing there would soon see, a parousia preview, not the parousia itself that is commented on in Mark 9:1. Notice the presence of Moses and Elijah, who would not show up again at Jesus' resurrection, but whom Jesus probably envisioned would be present at the eschaton at the messianic banquet after the resurrection of the righteous.

It is hard to doubt that many scholars, while rightly focusing on the *theologia crucis* emphasis in Mark, have been misled about the ethics of Mark due not only to a misreading of Mark 13[10] but also to a misperception about the ending of this Gospel. In all likelihood, this Gospel did not originally end at Mark 16:8. The attempts to remedy the mutilated ending of Mark by not one, but two, different groups of second-century scribes (including the ones who produced the Freer Logion) show very clearly that they did not believe that Mark would end an ancient biography of Jesus in such a terse and un-

---

[9]I have argued for this at length in my Mark commentary: Ben Witherington III, *The Gospel of Mark: A Socio-Rhetorical Commentary* (Grand Rapids: Eerdmans, 2001).

[10]See ibid., pp. 340–50.

satisfying manner. Neither did Matthew, who probably provides us with the original ending of Mark in Matthew 28:8-10 as well as Matthew 28:16-20 in some form, since he so religiously copied and followed Mark's passion and resurrection narrative up to that point.[11]

Nor should we see the eschatological fervor of Mark's Gospel as suggesting that the day of following commandments or rules has come and gone. Indeed, the eschatological situation ups the ante in terms of the degree of ethical rigor required. It is just that the commandments that one must follow as a disciple are not simply identical in toto with those followed before Jesus came. New occasions teach new duties, especially new eschatological occasions. The disciples are warned to beware of the leaven of the Pharisees and Herodians, not the leaven of the gospel.

Hays is right to stress that Mark's Gospel suggests that the new eschatological situation has changed things. The world is now a "world torn open by God"; from the rending of the heavens in Mark 1 to the rending of the temple veil in Mark 15, God has invaded the mundane sphere in the person of Jesus and his actions, and new and intensified responses are required. As Isaiah 64:1 puts it, God has indeed torn open the heavens and come down, and things can never be business as usual thereafter, especially since God has mounted his climactic campaign against the forces of evil in the person of Jesus. There can be no more concessions to evil, no more concessions to hardness of heart now that the divine saving reign of God is coming on earth.

In other words, the Markan ethic is grounded in what God has already done in Jesus and is now doing, not primarily in what God has yet to do, which only provides a further eschatological sanction for those ethics. The new wine has burst the old wineskins, and there is no going on in the old ways, much less any going back to them. But equally, the new wine is just being poured, and the messianic banquet has not yet transpired. The disciples are betwixt and between the "already" and the "not yet" of the kingdom. The disciples should expect surprising reversals along the way; indeed, they are exhibit A that the last, least and lost are becoming the first, most, and found as the dominion dawns.

This whole schema shows that Mark's Gospel is indeed about reversal of expectations but also reversal of understanding of what power really looks like and how it ought to be wielded. As Hays rightly puts it,

---

[11]On the ending of Mark as being mutilated or lost, see N. Clayton Croy, *The Mutilation of Mark's Gospel* (Nashville: Abingdon, 2003).

Mark's Gospel *redefines the nature of power and the value of suffering.* Because Jesus uses power to serve rather than to be served, authentic power is shown forth paradoxically in the cross. Those who exercise power to dominate others, to kill and oppress, are shown not only as villains but also, surprisingly, as pawns of forces beyond their control. . . . On the other hand, Jesus' apparently powerless passion becomes the true expression of the power of God. Suffering is portrayed as meaningful and necessary in the mysterious working of God's will. . . . A suffering community will find in Mark's story encouragement and validation of their struggle.[12]

In the context of this framework, how should we view the more specific ethical teachings found in Mark's Gospel?

In the first place, it seems clear from Mark 7 that Mark is laboring under the problem that his audience knows little about early Judaism when it comes to the particulars about Pharisaic rules about purity or, for that matter, Old Testament rules about the same. You can tell a good deal about a text from its parenthetical insertions by the author. In Mark 7:3-4, 19 we have two such insertions. The first explains to Mark's Roman Gentile audience about how the Pharisees and all the Jews do not eat without first performing ceremonial cleansing. The second explains that Jesus, by what he said in Mark 7:15-18, was making a radical declaration that all foods are now clean. That this has to be explained suggests that Mark thought that the metaphorical saying in Mark 7:15 might not be clear to some in the audience.

The long and short of the material in this chapter is that it makes clear how, in Mark's view, Jesus was a very radical Jew indeed and, not surprisingly, was at odds with the Pharisees because of how he allowed his disciples to behave and how he himself behaved in regard to issues of clean and unclean. This would include issues of food and also of clean and unclean persons. This material is interestingly juxtaposed with the story about the Syrophonecian woman and her ailing daughter that also deals with food of a sort as well as with an unclean person. Jesus responds to the woman's request by saying that the Jews have a right to his help "first" (implying that it is not wrong for Gentiles to seek it thereafter). There is, then, an emphasis on Jewish priority when it comes to benefiting from Jesus, and so Mark's audience is reminded that they are like the Syrophoenician woman. No food or ritual purity laws will be imposed on them, but they must accept that the gospel is for the Jew first and then also for the Gentiles. And notice that there is

---

[12]Hays, *Moral Vision of the New Testament,* p. 90.

absolutely no example in this or any Gospel of Jesus going through a *mikvah* or a ritual purification rite, unless one count's John's baptism, which in any case was not intended for ritual cleansing. Jesus is bothered neither by the touch of an unclean person with a flow of blood nor by his own willful touching of corpse.

But Jesus' approach to the Sabbath is equally radical. Not only is he prepared to heal on the Sabbath, even when it was not a necessity, but also he insists that the Sabbath was made for the benefit of human beings, not vice versa (Mk 3:27), and he claims to have unique authority over it, being the Lord of the Sabbath. All of this radical reorienting of early Judaism's priority and ethics gets Jesus in hot water over and over, and already in Mark 3:6 we hear about a plot to do him in because of some of his actions and teachings. In that same chapter Jesus enunciates the principle that the family of faith has a higher priority than the physical family (Mk 3:31-35). Indeed, Jesus says that his family is whoever does the will of God, and this teaching would not have resonated very well in early Judaism, especially when he says it at the expense of the claims of his immediate physical family on him. Somewhat paradoxically, Jesus does affirm the need to honor one's parents and to not deprive them of needed help by employing the legerdemain of oaths (*corban*), but apparently not at the expense of the priorities of the kingdom.

The Jesus of Mark's Gospel takes a very strict approach to the issues of marriage, divorce, and the treatment of children in Mark 10. Especially interesting is the unique verse Mark 10:12, which speaks of a wife divorcing her husband, a very rare occurrence indeed in the Holy Land, except in the case of a few elites such as Herodias and Herod Philip. The ethical upshot of the "no divorce" teaching, which Paul also knows (1 Cor 7), is that women are provided with more security in their marital situations, as are the children and extended family. The male privilege of divorce is taken from them if they are members of Jesus' community. We must always keep clearly in mind that Mark is enunciating an in-house ethic. The high value that Jesus places on children, seen in Mark 9–10, and the suggestion that even adults need in some way to be like them if they are to enter the eschatological dominion of God in the future, further reflect his concern about the typically marginalized in a highly patriarchal culture.

What is especially intriguing in Mark is that this portrait of Jesus the Jewish social radical is built up over many chapters, but in Mark 12 we are made to know that this did not mean that Jesus was a political radical or revolutionary, for he allows the paying of the imperial tax but qualifies it by saying that divine honors should only be given to God, not to the emperor. Although this would not have satisfied the Zealots, it would have suggested to Jesus' disciples that respect for governing authorities is an acceptable part of being a disciple, respect even for pagan emperors claiming divine honors. This comports with the advice in Romans 13 and 1 Peter 2, which is equally unrevolutionary.

This suggests that Jesus intended his action in the temple to be making a religious and prophetic statement about the coming doom on Herod's temple, not a political statement calling for the violent overthrow of the "temple domination" system. Judgment of such corruption was to be left in the hands of God. Jesus makes this emphatically clear in the garden of Gethsemane when he says to the authorities who have come to seize him, "Am I leading a rebellion that you come out with swords and clubs to capture me? Every day I was with you teaching in the temple courts, and you did not arrest me" (Mk 14:48-49). What is interesting about this response is that it immediately follows the report about someone standing near who cuts off an ear of the high priest's slave. Apparently, Jesus' words are as much a critique of his followers as of his captors. Jesus is prepared to die for what he believes about himself and the kingdom, not kill for it. The ethic of suffering love and nonviolence is more muted in this Gospel than in others, but it is present. Mark carries forward the ethic of Jesus, applying it now to his Gentile audience without diminution of its intensity of demand and command. We have no reason at all to see in this Gospel the idea of leaving commandments behind in the service of a Jesus who proclaimed only norms of love and mercy. Mark's Jesus is as demanding as that of any other Gospel, and in fact Mark's Jesus is harder on the disciples when they show no faith or fail. The ethic of the kingdom involves both norms or principles and commandments about behavior.

But it is not simply a renewal of the ethics of Torah, for in some case it goes against what Torah had said. The old Mosaic permissions due to hardness of heart fall by the wayside with the dawning of the dominion and the new wine of the gospel. It is God who is repeatedly said to make salvation and a higher form of obedience possible. That Jesus is a social radical is nevertheless seen clearly in the Markan pericopes about Sabbath healing (and eating), and what is especially telling about this is that we find the same pattern probably independently in the Fourth Gospel, where Jesus also deliberately heals on the Sabbath. I suggest that this reflects Jesus' eschatological consciousness and ethic; the Year of Jubilee has dawned, and so it is time for the beginning of the restoration of all things. Thus, what better day to give people rest from what ails them than on the Sabbath? Notions of work and rest are redefined in the light of the inbreaking dominion of God. This sort of approach to the Sabbath may well explain what we find in a text such as Romans 14:5-9, where Paul says believers should make up their own minds about the Sabbath or which day to honor the Lord on. In other words, Paul clearly picked up on the radical tenor of Jesus' ethic and how he came to make all things new, even the approach to the Sabbath.

It cannot have been an easy thing, or for that matter an easy sell, for Mark to persuade Roman, largely Gentile, Christians to embrace the intense ethical demands of Jesus. This in part may explain why Mark has so much less of Jesus' teaching than we find in Matthew and Luke. It would have been hard enough to get them to embrace the eschatological framework for Jesus' ethics, never mind the Sermon on the Mount. So it is that Mark intersperses in his narrative only a few major blocks of teaching in Mark 4; 10; 13. Otherwise, he is satisfied to let the narrative do the teaching and talking, indirectly.

What ethical teaching we do find in Mark reveals a Jesus who was an apocalyptic sage of sorts who perhaps would have been found intriguing in his intensity, not least because he seemed to be critiquing fellow Jews. Mark can clarify for his Gentiles the more technical debates that Jesus engaged in, and the upshot of texts such as Mark 7 would be that Gentiles need not be concerned with food laws and the Sabbath. The overall ethical impression would have been that Jesus was in various ways enunciating a new and challenging ethic with eschatological sanctions, and one that even Gentiles could and should embrace. If they, like the centurion in Mark 15:39, had already pronounced Jesus to be the Son of God, they needed to ponder what it meant to repent because for God's dominion (rather than Caesar's) was at hand. Whose kingdom ethic would they serve: the Prince of Peace's or the ruler who offered the *pax Romana*? We have seen how Mark handles the ethic of Jesus, but how would Luke handle the ethic of both Jesus and his followers? Would he ameliorate the tendencies that he found in Mark, or would he intensify them?

Luke–Acts: The Ethics of the Salvation Historian

There is a great deal more material to work with in Luke's ethics than in Mark's. For one thing, Luke's Gospel is the longest, and it includes most of that good Q teaching material found in Matthew but not in Mark. For another thing, we have the whole second volume to reckon with in Acts. And there is a third factor seldom considered. Luke is a careful historian, striving hard not to be anachronistic. It is possibile with Luke-Acts to see the difference between the earliest Christian ethics as found in Acts and the ethics of Jesus, who is, after all, directing all his remarks to Jews, particularly the pre-Christians who were his disciples. As it turns out, Luke assumes that there is more continuity than discontinuity between these two sources of ethics.

Luke operates as a Hellenistic historian, but as one who writes in the Jewish tradition, by which I mean that he sees his work as a continuation of the biblical saga of salvation history. He makes this quite clear at the outset not only by his Hellenistic prologue (Lk 1:1-4), but also by beginning his story not with Jesus but rather with the family of John the Baptizer (Lk 1:5-25). By writing in a self-consciously Septuagintal style, particularly in Luke 1–2, Luke intends for his audience to see that he is writing in a biblical mode about historic events worthy of being contained in Scripture. His is a story of the relating of how Old Testament promises were coming to fruition in the age in which he wrote—the lifetime of Jesus and thirty some years thereafter.

Perhaps the most important of these promises as far as Luke's second volume was concerned was the promise of God through Joel the prophet that God's Spirit would be poured out on all flesh. Luke has been quite rightly called the "theologian of the Holy Spirit," but he could just as well be called the "ethicist of the Holy Spirit" too. And since there is indeed a strong correlation between the portrayal of Jesus in Luke and his moral vision of how things ought to be in the community of Jesus, especially in the case of the church leaders, we must pay close attention to what Luke is telling us.

We should begin with the programmatic and inaugural sermon of Jesus (according to Luke), which speaks of a man empowered by the Spirit of God who comes to Nazareth and proclaims that the promises of God made through Isaiah are being fulfilled by him in their hearing (see Lk 4:16-30). He quotes Isaiah 61:1-2 and Isaiah 58:6 and thereby presents himself as the servant of God come to help the blind see, the lame walk and the deaf hear, not to mention to proclaim good news to the poor.

There is, as Hays observes, a close linkage between Jesus, who received the Spirit at baptism and therefore and thereby became the Anointed One of God, and his being the servant who fulfills the promises of Isaiah. This in one sense is Luke's contribution to the christological discussion, this combination

of motifs.[13] Jesus, then, presents himself as the liberator of the captives and
the one who comes to see that justice is done. He is also the one who comes
to proclaim that the Year of Jubilee has begun, complete with remission of
debts and sins.[14] A good microsummary of the Lukan portrait of Jesus in the
Gospel is, interestingly enough, found in Acts 10:38: "God anointed Jesus of
Nazareth with the Holy Spirit and with power; . . . he went about doing good
and healing all who were oppressed by the devil, for God was with him."

One of the dimensions of this portrait often commented on is the universalism of the gospel: Jesus is not just the savior of Israel, he is in fact the
savior of the world (see Luke 2:11 on the term *savior* applied to Jesus), and
the extension of the grace of Jesus beyond Israel is foreshadowed in various
ways already in Luke's Gospel. But Luke's stress in his Gospel is to show the
universalization of the Gospel up and down the social scale (from the last,
least and lost to the first, most and found), while in Acts we see the horizontal
universalization as the gospel is taken throughout the Mediterranean crescent
and the Roman Empire.

Although Jesus is not presented as the lawgiver like Moses in Luke-Acts,
he is presented as the prophetic figure that Moses spoke about (Acts 3:22-25).
He was viewed as the litmus test; how one reacted to this prophet like Moses
determined where one stood with God. The job of this prophet was to turn
God's people away from their wicked ways, and if they did not listen, then
they were rooted out of God's people. This, it will be seen, is an essentially
ethical view of Jesus' mission, and in fact from Luke's point of view even
Jesus' miracles are more than acts of compassion; they are warnings that the
kingdom has arrived, and so the nation must repent. The journeying motif
that exists in the central section of Luke's Gospel (Jesus has set his face like a
flint to go up to Jerusalem) suggests that Jesus fulfills Israel's role of journeying to the holy place, and it is surely no accident that Jesus' death and resurrection is called an "exodus" *(exodos)* in Luke's telling of the transfiguration
story (Lk 9:31). Jesus is both the prophet like Moses and God's wandering
people gone right.

A categorization of Luke's portrayal of Jesus' death involves two terms:
innocence and ignorance. Jesus is the innocent and righteous sufferer who
is wrongly executed, while the Jewish authorities are said to have acted in
ignorance. Pilate declares Jesus innocent three times (Lk 23:4, 13-15, 22),

---

[13]See ibid., p. 116.
[14]On which, see pp. 169-74 above.

as does a bandit once on an adjacent cross (Lk 23:40-41). It does appear that Luke is concerned that Theophilus realize that the Roman authorities did not see Jesus as deserving of crucifixion. This is especially punctuated when the Roman centurion declares that Jesus died as a righteous man (Lk 23:47), a clear modification of the parallel in Mark 15:39.

Hays stresses that Jesus is portrayed in line with what we find in Wisdom of Solomon 2:12-20 about the righteous one of God suffering at the hands of the wicked.[15] Acts 3:13-15; 7:51-52 are used to support this reading of the evidence. But it must not be overlooked that Jesus presented himself in Luke 4 as the righteous Isaianic servant of God, and probably we should see Isaiah 53:11 in the background of the centurion's declaration about the crucified Jesus. The point is that Luke is using both of these sources to paint a picture of Jesus as the righteous sufferer or martyr, Jesus the servant of God who dies for his people. The pattern of the end of Jesus' life is replicated in the pattern of the death of the first Christian martyr, Stephen (Acts 7), who cites the precedent of how they treated Jesus. This strongly suggests that Luke sees the pattern of the disciple's life as replicating the pattern of Jesus' life.

And how should a disciple respond to such abuse? One must assume that just as Jesus forgave his tormentors (Lk 23:4), so his followers must forgive theirs. And just as Jesus did not respond to violence with violence but instead commended his spirit into God's hands (alluding to Ps 31:5), so too does Stephen, the paradigmatic Christian martyr. As Hays stresses, this sort of tour de force rereading of the significance of a crucifixion (or a stoning) such that it shows the righteousness rather than the wickedness of the executed person was needful if Jesus' death was to be seen as redeeming, much less as a paradigm for Christian behavior.[16]

Luke is all about continuity between the church and its behavior, and Christ and his behavior. Indeed, as Acts 1:1 suggests, Luke sees the work of the church in its ministry of preaching, teaching, and healing as a continuation of what Jesus began to do and teach. Thus, Luke begins the story of the church much like he began the story of the ministry of Jesus, with the Spirit falling on the parties in question (cf. Lk 3:21-22; Acts 2:1-13). The promise of power from on high (Lk 24:49) is fulfilled by the coming of the Spirit, without which the disciples would have no unction to function or to emulate and continue Christ's ministry.

---

[15]Hays, *Moral Vision of the New Testament*, pp. 119-23.
[16]Ibid., p. 120.

One thing that becomes clear from an examination of the influence of the Old Testament on Luke is that he tends to view things through the lens of Isaiah and Deuteronomy. This includes both Jesus and the early church, including their ethical behavior. Thus, as Hays points out, it is probable that Deuteronomy 15:4-8 is being echoed in the descriptions of the Jerusalem Christian community.[17] That text speaks clearly: "There will be no one in need among you, because the LORD is sure to bless you in the land. . . . If there is anyone among you in need, a member of your community, . . . do not be hard-hearted or tightfisted toward your needy neighbor. You should rather open your hand willingly, lending enough to meet the need, whatever it might be." This indeed seems a proper background to "all things in common," "no one in need," and "no one claimed private ownership of property" in the summaries in Acts 2:44-47; 4:32-35. Ethically, the original church was committed to taking care of its own, the ones who were in need. This kind of material suggests that while Theophilus probably was a Gentile, as was Luke, he was also a God-fearer like Luke. This would make the story of Cornelius in Acts 10 all the more ethically cogent for Luke's patron.

There can be no doubt that issues of wealth and poverty are a major concern throughout Luke-Acts, and it is equally clear that what one does with one's possessions is seen as a clear ensign of the nature of one's relationship (or lack thereof) with God. Remember that it is Luke who has the beatitudes that speak of the poor and the hungry being blessed, and who has the parable about the rich man and Lazarus. It is Luke who balances the story of the rich young ruler with the story of repentant Zacchaeus (which shows that Luke is not expecting total divestment by everyone), and who further expands upon the matter in Acts 5 when he tells of the escapades of Ananias and Sapphira. Hays makes the telling point about the parable of the rich man and Lazarus that Jesus himself says that if people are so hard-hearted that they will not listen to the word of God, then neither will they pay any mind to the work of God, even if God raises someone like Jesus from the dead.[18] Opposed to the hard hearts and skinflints are the glad and generous hearts of Acts 2:46 who share with all, a sure sign that great grace was upon them. The power of the gospel not merely preached and heard but lived out in community is seen to be the most powerful witness of all.

To say that Luke portrays the Jesus movement as countercultural to some

---

[17]Ibid., pp. 123-25.
[18]Ibid., p. 124.

degrce is true enough, if the culture in mind is early Judaism of the Pharisaic, Sadducean, or Qumranite sort. But what about how Luke portrays Christianity in comparison to the Greco-Roman culture and, in particular, its political culture? This is more difficult to assess.

There was a sense that any monotheist, just by being such, was upsetting the apple cart of a polytheistic world, and in particular monotheists would upset the growing practice of the emperor cult when it became a community-wide and community-defining event in various cities around the empire in the mid-to-late first century A.D. In their own way, the Romans had accommodated Jewish monotheism by letting Jews practice their own religion. This issue came up in Judaism when the question of tribute money paid to Caesar or to a temple honoring Caesar was raised, not least because it was paid with coins bearing images of Caesar. Jesus, even in Luke's Gospel, had something to say about this, and it amounted to a call to realize that Caesar was one person and God was another, and divine honors belonged only to God. This need not be seen as revolutionary by the Romans, unless it led to a refusal to pay one's taxes. But Jesus suggested no such thing.

Nor do we get a clear answer to the question "In Luke's view, how revolutionary was the Jesus movement?" by examining texts such as Acts 5:17-42. Of course, if there was a clear line drawn in the sand, such that a Jew or a Christian had to choose between obeying the God of the Bible and obeying the local human authority (whether Jewish or Roman), there was no choice but to obey God. But in fact that sort of clear-cut choice was not in play most of the time. Jews or Christians might be seen as antisocial for not going to the feast at the emperor's temple and as "atheistic" for not worshiping the traditional Greco-Roman gods, but this did not prevent them from becoming citizens of various cities in thc empire, and even being viewed as good citizens in various places and in various ways. Indeed, there are even cases where pagans, as part of their patronage in general of the religious institutions of their city, helped to fund the building of a synagogue here and there.

So the question becomes, "Are the Thessalonians being alarmist when they speak of the violation of Caesar's decrees by the Christians, and we hear of Christians turning the world upside down, or should we take these accusations by pagans seriously?" (see Acts 17:6-7). At least two things can be concluded from a close examination of Acts 17:6-7. First, the Christians were seen as subversive for preaching King Jesus and his kingdom, which would indeed be a violation of the decree of Caesar against making predictions of coming kings in the cities of the empire. Second, the charge of upsetting the *stasis,* or stability, of the city had to do with upsetting the rota of religious celebrations and festivals. If Paul had indeed preached a turning away from idols (i.e., pagan gods and statues) in that city, that could have been seen as destabilizing.

One gets the sense that in Thessalonica the officials perceived more clearly than in other places what would happen if Christianity became a major religious force in that city. For one thing, it would be bad for the economy (cf. the silversmiths in Ephesus [Acts 19:23-27]), and for another thing, it might interrupt the flow of patronage from Rome if it was known that the emperor cult was not being well served. What is remarkable, however, is that Luke does not make more of this incident. It comes and it goes in the larger narrative, and one gets the sense that Luke is telling Theophilus that if one has no objections to long-standing Judaism and its religious peculiarities, then Christianity should not be seen as subversive either. This is one reason why Luke portrays Paul as a Roman citizen in various places in his account in Acts.

In any case, we would have to say that Luke does not institute a revolutionary view of Jesus' ethic in regard to governments and taxes, but the line was drawn when it came to worshiping false gods or emperors, and obeying God rather than human authorities when there was a clear conflict. Otherwise, Christians are portrayed as those who ought to be good citizens in various ways, including being good neighbors. This is understandable. There should be no offense but the offense of this monotheistic gospel about Jesus and his saving activity. And it should be noted that the critique of the emperor cult is never directly made in Luke-Acts; it is only implicit in the exclusivity of the religious claims of the Christian faith itself.[19] Luke, like other New Testament writers, sees the leaven of the gospel working through preaching to the public and through groups of Christians being a Christian community that preserves its own in-house ethic and values. The world is being changed by the scandal of gospel preaching, not by more nefarious means.

It has been noted often and rightly that Luke tends to de-eschatologize various of the sayings and teachings of Jesus. It is not that Luke ceases to affirm the second coming, but rather that there is no "imminence" language in Luke-Acts. Indeed, quite the opposite. The Lukan Jesus, having been asked if he would now restore the kingdom to Israel, leaves this parting shot with his

---

[19]But see ibid., pp. 126-28.

disciples before he ascends: "It is not for you to know the times and periods that the Father has set by his own authority. But you will receive power when the Spirit comes upon you, and you will be my witnesses" (Acts 1:7-8). In other words, there is to be no theological weather forecasting; the Spirit is coming soon, so they are to get on with the proclamation of the eschatological good news about what is already true since Jesus came.

The focus is on the mission now, the growth of the Word and the church across the empire now and discipleship now, for it is only Luke's Jesus who says, "All who would become my followers must deny themselves and take up their cross *daily* and follow me" (Lk 9:23). This implies an ongoing daily commitment, not a one-time self-denying or death-defying act. Luke believes that the church already lives in the eschatological age when the Spirit has been poured out on all the believers, and they all have an obligation to witness. Luke's second volume really is more the Acts of the Holy Spirit than the Acts of the Apostles, most of whom, other than Peter and Paul, get no more than a passing mention in Acts. What Luke is most concerned to show is that the reversals promised by Jesus in his inaugural sermon continued to happen, and this meant good news for the poor, for women, for tax collectors, for the ill and in general for those on the margins of society. But it also made for good news for the well-to-do, not just for the ne'er-do-wells. They had a chance to share, to give back as Zacchaeus did, to take care of those in need with a glad and generous heart.

The ethical ethos of Luke-Acts is that Luke tells his audience that they are part of an ongoing saga of salvation history, with a remarkable pedigree, and recent exciting and crucial events in the life and ministry of Jesus. In antiquity, "new religion" was a term of opprobrium; a *superstitio* was not viewed as a good thing. Luke, by showing that the theology and ethics of the Christ and his followers are a continuation of the Old Testament story, indeed a fulfillment of its promises, gave Christians a context in which they could have a clear moral vision of who they are and whose they are. They were not practicing a completely new religion but rather were fulfilling the dreams of an old one, one that promised a community where glad hearts would gladly share good news and sustenance of other sorts so that there would be no one in need in that community. Luke has no interest in constructing an isolationist sect; he wants to build a world-transforming community that welcomes one and all with open arms. As Hays puts it, "Luke's deep confidence in God's providence imparts to the story a positive, robust, *world-affirming* character. . . . The church in Luke-Acts is not a defensive community withdrawing from an evil world; instead, it acts boldly on the stage of public affairs, commending the gospel in reasoned terms to all persons of goodwill and expecting an open-minded response."[20]

If there is in general a more urbane quality to Luke-Acts than Mark or John, for instance, we then must wonder about the specific ethical teachings of this two-volume text. Will Luke yield to the temptation to compromise the intense demands of Jesus? The answer is an emphatic no. Not only is there the demand for daily self-denial and cross-bearing as the marks of discipleship, but also there is the repeated call for strenuous generosity until it helps the poor, the captives, the possessed and so on. Liberation comes in many forms, and Luke goes out of his way to show how it comes to numerous women, ranging from Mary the mother of Jesus, to Joanna the high-status wife of Chuza, to Lydia, to Priscilla and many others. This is hardly a bourgeois ethic of liberation or even an expression of noblesse oblige.[21]

It is not men liberating women; it is the Holy Spirit, who overshadows Mary, exorcises the demons out of the Magdalene, sets free Joanna from the wickedness of Herod's palace, empowers the mother of John Mark to host the Jerusalem community, propels Tabitha to make garments for the poor, enables Lydia to courageously allow the church to find its home in her home in Philippi, prompts leading women in Thessalonica to embrace the gospel, leads Priscilla and her husband Aquila to plant churches in Corinth, Ephesus and perhaps Rome, all the while instructing the great Christian orator Apollos on the issue of baptism. And much more could be said. No, the repeated stress on the liberation of women by the Spirit from whatever was bewitching, bothering, bewildering, or holding them down is a major theme in Luke-Acts. And to that end, we should notice that the Lukan Jesus, though he says little about marriage or divorce, does say this: "Anyone who divorces his wife and marries another woman commits adultery, and the man who marries a divorced woman commits adultery" (Lk 16:18). This hardly sounds like a compromise with either the early Jewish or the Greco-Roman world. And its net effect was to give married women more security in their marriages. Notice that in this saying only the man's capacity to divorce or marry is addressed.

---

[20]Ibid., p. 134.
[21]See Ben Witherington III, *Women in the Earliest Churches* (SNTSMS 59; Cambridge: Cambridge University Press, 1988).

One of the interesting questions that Acts raises is whether the leaders of the parent church in Jerusalem felt that they could and should give moral guidelines to Gentiles converts outside *'ereṣ yiśrā'ēl* ("land of Israel"). In order to answer this question we need to examine the so-called apostolic decree in Acts 15. In fact, we find the essence of this decree in three places (Acts 15:20, 29; 21:25 [Luke is apt to say really important things three times]). I have dealt elsewhere with the text-critical issue that leads to the conclusion that the earliest reading is *"eidōlothytos*, blood, things strangled, and *porneia."*[22] The term *eidōlothytos* occurs some 112 times in early Jewish literature. All but two of these occurrences are found in Christian literature, and I have shown that even 4 Maccabees 5:2 and *Sibylline Oracles* 2:96 are likely to be Christian interpolations. In short, it appears that *eidōlothytos* is an early Christian polemical term, and its meaning should be determined by the context in which it appears. Clearly enough, the term comes from a monotheistic Jew, or in this case a Jewish Christian, perhaps from James himself originally, since all the other examples are likely later.

I suggest that the term *eidōlothytos* is the negative counterpart to the term *corban* used in early Judaism. *Corban* refers to something dedicated or given to the true God in the temple, whereas *eidōlothytos* refers to something dedicated to a false god, something sacrificed and dedicated to what a Jew would call an idol. Its parallel in the Greek world is *theothytos*, something dedicated to a god and so the food of the gods, just as *hierothytos* refers to something dedicated in a temple. It must be stressed that with all these terms the issue is primarily one of venue, not merely menu. All these terms refer to something dedicated in a temple, and in the case of *eidōlothytos* in a pagan temple.

Thus, the social context of this decree is critical. The proper question to ask about this list is this: Where would you find these four items—things dedicated to an idol, blood, things strangled, and sexual immorality—all in one place? Clearly, they would be found in a pagan temple and at a temple feast following the sacrifice. Pagan sacrificers did not follow the Jewish rules about draining all the blood from the meat. Pagan sacrificers also were known to take small birds and strangle them up next to the statues of the god so as to squeeze the life breath out of the bird and into the deity, thereby further animating the deity through its statue, which was seen as a contact point with the god.

---

[22]See Ben Witherington III, *The Acts of the Apostles: A Socio-Rhetorical Commentary* (Grand Rapids: Eerdmans, 1998), pp. 460-61.

We can see how early Jews thought about the activities that went on in pagan temples from 2 Maccabees 6:4-5 and the account of what Antiochus Epiphanes even did to desecrate the Jerusalem temple: "For the temple was filled with debauchery and reveling by the Gentiles, who dallied with prostitutes and had intercourse with women within the sacred precincts, and besides brought in things for sacrifice that were unfit. The altar was covered with abominable offerings that were forbidden by the laws" (NRSV). And here we get to the gist of it. James speaks in Acts 15:20 about the abominations of idols. It is no accident that James directs his decree specifically to Gentiles, not to Jewish Christians in the Diaspora. Like what we find in 2 Maccabees 6, James assumes that idolatry and immorality happen regularly in the context of a pagan temple feast, and he wants Gentile Christians to stay completely away from such temptations. Indeed, he thinks that this especially will be a bad witness to Jews in the Diaspora synagogues, "where Moses is preached week by week."

What is the very core of the law of Moses? The Ten Commandments. And what did they in essence require? No idolatry and no immorality. Thus, we must conclude that James is not imposing food laws on Gentiles. The issue is their attendance at pagan idol feasts where these four things could be found in one place. Since Jews especially associated all that was worst about pagan culture with the sacrifices and dinners within pagan temples, James is banning Gentile Christians from attending such feasts. This will improve the moral image of Christians when they are witnessing about James's brother in the synagogues in those cities. In other words, it will make clear that Christians are not pagans and do not worship false gods or commit immorality.

Did anyone listen to and try to implement this decree after James sent out the letter to the Pauline, largely Gentile congregations in the Diaspora? Yes, and we see Paul doing his best to implement this decree in 1 Corinthians 8–10. His Corinthian converts must stay away from the "table of demons" (1 Cor 10:21), but it does not matter if the meat that they buy at the public market has come from the pagan temple. That should raise no issue of conscience. The issue is the social and moral context in which it is eaten. The issue is moral venue, not menu. And this brings up an important point about Acts. Luke is striving hard to show that despite the differences between Jewish and Gentile Christians, that there was an essential theological and ethical unity to early Christianity. Here in Acts 15 we find James, Peter, Barnabas, and Paul agreeing on the decision that James made. It is the unnamed Judaizing Pharisaic Christians present (see Acts 15:1-3), not the luminaries, who are gnashing their teeth and are unsatisfied with the compromise. And this was a decision that, according to James, "seemed good to the Holy Spirit and to us" (Acts 15:28). Circumcision and the Mosaic law would not be imposed on Gentiles, but they would be expected to honor the heart of the law by avoiding idolatry and immorality by completely forsaking pagan temples and their feasts.

This does not mean that Luke fails to recognize and portray some differences between James and Paul. James is portrayed as a Torah-true Jew throughout. Paul is portrayed as one who can be the Jew to the Jew (see, e.g., Acts 21) but also the Gentile to the Gentile. In other words, just as his letters suggest (see 1 Cor 9:19-23), Paul did not think that even Jewish Christians were required to keep the Mosaic Law any more, for they were under a new covenant. It is unclear whether James believed that this was necessary for prudential reasons (to be a good witness to Jews, since he lived in a predominantly Jewish milieu) or believed it as a matter of principle. What is interesting is to reflect on whether James realized that the prohibition of idolatry and immorality at the heart of the Mosaic code is the negative counterpart of saying "Love the true God with all your heart, and love your neighbor properly as you love yourself."

Notice that nothing is said in the letter of James to Jewish Christians in the Diaspora about keeping Sabbath or food laws, though perhaps he thought that such exhortations were not needed when he wrote that missive. In short, I suggest that the Lukan portrayal of early Christianity is far closer to the mark of reality than our later attempts to pit James off against Paul as dueling apostles. I do not think that Luke gilds the lily or presents an idealistic portrait of early Christianity. He certainly presents a stylized one, but he is telling the truth as he sees it. And I believe he ought to have known, given that he was a sometime companion of Paul and likely met James and other Jerusalem Christians when he went to Jerusalem with Paul at the end of the third missionary journey. What is clear enough is that Luke is very exercised to show the moral seriousness of early Christianity.

And to what end is all this ethical seriousness and rigor? Acts 2:42-47; 4:32-37 tell us that it is all about the creation of a different community, a community that models the love, joy, and self-sacrificial service of the Christ himself and continues the work that he began to do and the teachings that he began to give. There was no gap between Jesus and his teaching and ministry and that of the early church, but only a continuation. In Luke's view it would be silly to say, as one New Testament scholar (Alfred Loisy) once did, that "Jesus preached the kingdom, and the church showed up." Jesus preached the divine eschatological saving activity of God, and in Luke's view this created a community of the saved that came to be called a Christian community of everyone from the last, least, and lost to the first, most, and found. This was a community of Jews and Gentiles; a community led by women and men; a community empowered by God's Spirit to dream big dreams and attempt great things for God; a community that was missionally minded but communally focused and nurturing; a community that swept across the empire in thirty short years from Jerusalem to Rome and indeed was on the way to turning the Greco-Roman world upside down by a peaceful revolution, a nonviolent social rearrangement. All this did not come by the ancient equivalent of storming the Bastille, or dumping tea in Boston harbor, or reforming governments; it came by the scandalous preaching that God already ruled it all and desired to save us all. And only God deserved the worship, the God of and in Jesus Christ.

Human authorities were to be respected, accepted and submitted to if they made lawful and just demands, but only God was to be served and worshiped. And happily, Luke leaves the door open in Acts 28, leaves the story unfinished, suggesting to his audience that the story of salvation history is still a work in progress. The church did not need an interim ethic in such a circumstance; rather, it needed a stable, life-giving, liberating, uncompromising one on which the church could rely in all generations. The moral vision that Luke casts is greater than the sum of its parts, and it affirms that the future is as bright as the promises and power and work of God because the eschatological Spirit has come, and nothing could remain the same after that—nothing. God had unleashed a juggernaut on the world when Jesus came, followed by the Holy Spirit. The world would never again be the same.

As we come to the end of this subsection, we should ask whether we see something of a Pauline shadow in the Gospels of two men who at one time were traveling companions of Paul. The answer, if we are thinking of ethics, is yes, but only to a degree, and it is hard to tell whether the influence ultimately comes from Jesus or from Jesus through Paul to these two men. Luke, for example, does present a "to the Jew first and also to the Gentile" approach to gospel preaching and teaching when Paul appears on the stage, and this comports well with what we find in Romans 1 and elsewhere when Paul describes the mandate. Luke also is rightly said to stress the universalization of the gospel to one and all, and in this respect too he may show some debt to Paul. His focus on ministry to and with women is matched by that we find in Paul's letters. His respect for governing authorities is matched by Romans 13:1-7, but at the same time it is right to say that Luke understands that the gospel means social change, though not violent revolution, just as Paul saw. Paul's urgent concern about the collection for the poor and starving saints in Jerusalem is matched by the agenda of the first Christian church as described in Acts 2:42-47; 4:32-37. We could go on. If Luke is the evangelist of the Holy Spirit, Paul is the Spirit's apostle. But we do not find in Luke-Acts the profound theology of the cross to the degree that we find it in Paul's writings. A theology of suffering love, however, is clear enough from Luke's Gospel portrayal of the death of Jesus, who even forgives his tormentors from the cross (Lk 23:34), and from the juxtaposition of the story of Stephen, which reiterates this suffering and forgiving love (Acts 6:8–7:60), with the citation of Isaiah 53 immediately thereafter in the story of Philip and the Ethipoian eunuch (Acts 8:26-40). But we must turn to Mark's Gospel to find a robust theology of the cross as a substitutionary atoning force.

If Luke alters the eschatological teaching of Jesus a bit (in the sense of downplaying future eschatology) and damps down the apocalyptic fervor, Mark, by contrast, presents Jesus the apocalyptic seer, and that apocalyptic tenor of things certainly resonates with the eschatological drumbeat of Paul. Paul, like the Markan Jesus, is seen in the letters as one who receives visions and late words of revelation from on high. This affects the ethics of both sources in about the same way: all human institutions and striving have been relativized in the light of the inbreaking dominion of God. Human salvation will come by apocalyptic means; indeed, it will come through a cross. The cross of Christ is indeed central to both Paul's ethic and Mark's (note the three passion predictions in Mk 8:31; 9:31; 10:33-34, climaxing with a fourth in Mk 10:45). Discipleship is about taking up the cross and following Jesus' example, and preaching is seen to have at its heart Christ, and him crucified. For disciples, suffering is not to be avoided; rather, it is to be embraced as a badge of courage and honor and as a sign that one is following the right pilgrim way, as Jesus did to Golgotha. Rewards come only through and beyond the cross; suffering on this side of death fills up the messianic suffering or at least exhibits it to another audience. Neither Mark nor Paul confines the stigma of the stigmata to the Christ. And yet paradoxically, amazingly, suffering love is seen as that which demonstrates to the world that God's power is at work, indeed is made perfect in human weakness, and is sufficient even for apostles and their labors. Triumph comes through apparent tragedy, and the blood of the martyrs is the seed of the church.

I suggest that both Mark and Luke are indebted to Paul in differing ways, to a degree only slightly less than they are indebted to Jesus and the Jesus tradition. Indeed, they tend to look at Jesus and the Jesus tradition through Pauline eyes to some extent and have configured their writings accordingly. And perhaps this is why it is not hard to see the unity of New Testament theology and ethics when we compare these two evangelists and Paul, even in the midst of the obvious differences of emphasis, interests, and genre. It is decidedly "this same Jesus" whom all of them proclaim, and it is "this same path" (called by Luke "the way of the Lord") of disciplined discipleship in a cruciform and christological shape that they hold out for their audiences to follow. The Gentile world would have found in these Gospels a reinforcement of various things that they had already learned from Paul, not the least of which was that there was no going back to being a part of Pharisaic Judaism, only a going forward to being a Jewish sectarian and eschatological offshoot of the parent faith. Not the Mosaic covenant, but rather the daunting new one, was to be embraced, but its ethical challenges would be no less daunting than what Moses offered. And we can hear the voice of these men say, "Would you have expected God to expect less of those to whom he has given more?"

The call of the gospel is not a call to the abandonment or neglect of ethical rigor; rather, it is a call to a renewal and intensification of that rigor by grace and through faith. It is a call to holiness of heart and life. It is a call to recognize that those created in the image of God and recreated through the work of Christ and the actions of the Spirit are to reflect the moral character of God on earth and so be lights to the world, bearing witness to the existence and very nature of a glorious God. This, as we will see in the next section, is what the last New Testament writer meant by calling Christians "partakers of the divine nature."

2 Peter: Ethics for All Christian Converts at the End of the Apostolic Age

Unfortunately 2 Peter has been trivialized and even vilified by some modern scholars, completely without warrant. When it comes to the issue of ethics,

2 Peter has a lot more to add to the discussion besides polemics against false teachers. For one thing, the author has a rather developed Christian anthropology that provides a basis for his ethical remarks. Here at the outset of this part of the discussion we must consider 2 Peter 1:3-11 in considerable detail, not least because this provided the fodder for later church fathers to develop the notion of *theosis,* among other things. Indeed, 2 Peter could be seen as a brief exposition on Christian virtues.

Before talking about Christians manifesting virtues, the author quite rightly must focus on the work of God in the lives of the audience. "These verses make the God who is known by Christians the source of the highest good that ancient moral philosophy could imagine, actual participation in the divine nature itself."[23] The section 2 Peter 1:3-4 is not merely transitional but rather is foundational for the ethical summary of the preaching in 2 Peter 1:5-11. In 2 Peter 1:3 the author stresses that God's power has already bestowed on believers everything necessary for "godly living" (a hendiadys; more literally, "life and piety"). The implication is that no additional information from false teachers is wanted or needed. This power to do God's will and live a godly life came to believers through knowledge of the one who called them. This presumably refers to Christ, and possibly, if we ask what lured them to Christ, it may be answered that they were called and attracted to him by his uniquely excellent glory (another hendiadys; literally, "glory and excellence"). This paves the way for the reference to the transfiguration in 2 Peter 1:16-18. In any case, here *glory* refers to Christ in his incarnation. In the transfiguration we see in Christ the presence and qualities of God.

It is somewhat difficult to decipher the grammar of 2 Peter 1:4. What does *di hōn,* which begins the verse, refer to? The most natural and nearest antecedent is "his own glory and excellence." The point could be that through Christ's manifestation and witness God has given believers these great and precious promises. Elsewhere in 2 Peter these promises are clearly seen to be fulfilled at the eschaton (see 2 Pet 3:4, 9, 13), and this may be the case here as well. The last portion of 2 Peter 1:4 is one of the most discussed segments of the letter. Here we are told the result (or purpose) of receiving the great and precious promises: (1) believers are able to escape the ways of the world; (2) they become sharers in the divine nature. We will examine these two in order.

---

[23]Pheme Perkins, *First and Second Peter, James, and Jude* (IBC; Louisville: John Knox Press, 1995), p. 168.

Richard Bauckham suggests that "having escaped the corruption in the world on account of desire" refers to escaping from human mortality.[24] This, however, may be doubted precisely because of the phrase *en epithymia* ("because of sinful desire"). This could be a reference to the Genesis story, which may imply that mortality entered the world as a result of the original sin. However, it could just as easily be a reference to how moral corruption entered the world through the original sin, and indeed this better fits with the context here, which discusses moral corruption. Further, *apophygontes* is an aorist participle (in the New Testament the verb *apopheugō* is found only in 2 Pet 1:4; 2:18, 20 [cf. Sir 22:22]). The most likely translation is "escaped," and this means that the author is talking about an event in the past, not the future. Fred Craddock comments, "The conversion from this life to the next is not achieved simply by dying and therefore passing from mortality to immortality. Rather the change is moral and ethical."[25] This point must be insisted on because the "corruption" *(phthora)* is not the world itself but rather moral corruption, which the believer is to flee. To be sure, sinful desire leads to corruption, which in turn leads to destruction, but the corruption and the destruction of the world (or of the individual physical existence) are not identical here. As Craddock says, "It is the knowledge of God as revealed in Jesus Christ and not simply a funeral which provides 'entry into the eternal kingdom.'"[26] Further, the common Hellenistic expectation was that there indeed was a way to become a participant in the "divine nature" at least in part here and now. Thus, Michael Green points out how it was commonly expected that one could enter into such a nature:

> Rival pagan schoolmen asserted that you escaped from the toils of *corruption (phthora)* by becoming *participants in the divine nature* either by *nomos* ("law-keeping") or by *phusis* ("nature"). Peter takes up their language, and replies that it is by sheer grace. Did the false teachers . . . suggest that their adherents became more godlike as they escaped the trammels of the material world? Far from it, says Peter. Participation in the divine nature is the starting-point, not the goal, of Christian living. He writes to those who have *escaped* from the seductive allegiance to society at odds with God.[27]

---

[24]Richard Bauckham, *2 Peter and Jude* (WBC 50; Waco, Tex.: Word, 1983), pp. 179-80.

[25]Fred B. Craddock, *First and Second Peter, and Jude* (WestBC; Westminster John Knox, 1995), p. 98.

[26]Ibid.

[27]Michael Green, *The Second Epistle General of Peter, and the General Epistle of Jude*, 2nd ed. (TNTC; Grand Rapids: Eerdmans, 1987), p. 73.

In principle, this is not much different from when Paul talks about how the work of the Spirit in the believer is such that the ruling principle of the Spirit of life has overcome the rule of sin and death in the believer's nature (Rom 8:2), thus making him or her a new creature in Christ (2 Cor 5:17). Plutarch, by contrast, laments that humans feel the passion for immortality, which is a quality of God that they cannot really share, far more than the passion for God's moral excellence, which is within their reach (*Arist.* 6).

Thus, we must reject Bauckham's view of what is escaped from and when participation in the divine nature begins. He is right, however, in regard to what participating in the divine nature means: (1) it involves union with God, not divination of the human; (2) it involves a work of grace in believers so that they can become Godlike in character. It means, then, that participation in eternal life and eternal goodness eventually involves everlasting life and an incorruptible body, but it must be observed that, strictly speaking, participation in the divine nature can have nothing to do with a resurrection body.[28] Even Christ's divine nature never took on human flesh; rather, Christ had two natures, divine and human, as the God-man. To be like God or Christ in divine nature can have nothing to do with escaping physical mortality. We may compare, for example, Wisdom of Solomon 2:23: "God created humans for incorruption and made them in the image of his own eternity."

In the Christian way of viewing this, immortality or everlasting life in its positive sense is not an inherent property of the soul but rather is a gift obtained when one is saved, and it is fully realized at the eschaton. Notice that the author says that this divine nature is something that believers share; we are "sharers" *(koinōnoi)* in it. It is not the individual believer's private possession; it is something shared with other believers. The concept of the spiritual union of believers in Christ may be behind this terminology.

General confirmation of this view is found in 2 Peter 1:9, which refers to the "cleansing from sins long ago." It is this sort of corruption that the author has in view. Whereas in Greco-Roman thought participation in the divine nature meant things ranging from immortality even to apotheosis and entering the Elysian fields, in 2 Peter it has an ethical dimension: one participates in the holiness of God and thereby is enabled to act ethically.[29]

---

[28]Against Bauckham, *2 Peter and Jude*, pp. 190-91.

[29]See James M. Starr, *Sharers in Divine Nature: 2 Peter 1:4 in Its Hellenistic Context* (ConBNT 33; Stockholm: Almquist & Wiksell, 2000); Craddock, *First and Second Peter, and Jude*, p. 98.

A person is not merely saved to serve; a person is saved to be virtuous and model the character of Christ. What is most interesting about the way the author talks about this is that he uses cultural buzzwords that were a familiar part of the ethical discourse in the Greco-Roman world, but he uses them in an entirely Christian manner to talk about how real change in human nature happens through the grace of God in Christ. This is not an example of "inculturation" of the gospel; on the contrary, it is an example of "plundering the Egyptians" or, to borrow Paul's metaphor, taking every sort of moral thought or virtuous idea captive for Christ (cf. 2 Cor 10:5).

Here it certainly is possible to compare at length the language of piety and virtue in the Pastoral Letters, where a similar ethical vocabulary appears and is used to similar ethical effect. Virtue is seen not merely as desirable but also as possible for Christians in these sources, and it is inculcated at length. I suggest that the language of Hellenistic virtues shows up in 2 Peter for the same reason it shows up in the Pastoral Letters. The audience is assumed to know that this language is part of the common currency of their discourse about ethics, and Paul and the author of 2 Peter choose to use it at length. We also should note that Luke, who likely was involved with the Pastoral Letters,[30] sees, like the author of 2 Peter, enough overlap in the language of virtue from the general culture to reaudience it and reuse it with Christians, who are called to *eusebeia* ("piety") as well as purity.

In 2 Peter, as in James and the Fourth Gospel, the word *kosmos* signifies the world as organized by human beings against God, referring to its influences and fallenness. Thus, the author of 2 Peter is talking not about the good material (natural) existence that God created but rather about the bad society that human beings have perpetuated in the world. The latter is what Christians escape at conversion. Sinful human desires led to this state, beginning with the original sin. But believers are no longer slaves to, nor should they be active partakers in, the world in its sinfulness. This will be the author's point as he continues to write. Notice the "already and not yet" perspective: we have already received great promises, but we are now only partial sharers in what we may receive through those promises. Hence the need for ethical exhortation here. Although some see Christianity as essentially about a conversion experience that guarantees eternal life regardless of one's subsequent

---

[30]On which, see Ben Witherington III, *Letters and Homilies for Hellenized Christians*, vol. 1, *A Socio-Rhetorical Commentary on Titus, 1-2 Timothy, and 1-3 John* (Downers Grove, Ill.: IVP Academic, 2006).

behavior—"an initial spasm followed by chronic inertia"[31]—the author will have none of it. Real faith works; it produces not only godly character but also behavior that glorifies God and indeed behavior that is part of the sanctifying and saving process of the believer.

At 2 Peter 1:5 we head even further into Hellenistic language and Asiatic Greek. It is rather grandiose, like a Rubens work of art. It is precisely because Christians have escaped corruption that they must go on avoiding it, and it is precisely because they are in part partaking in the divine nature that they must be very zealous and make every effort to add every positive Christian virtue to their arsenal.

We need to note several things about the developing and interlocked catalogue of virtues here before exploring individual points. First, Bauckham has correctly shown that the list in 2 Peter 1:5-7 is an amalgam of Christian and pagan Hellenistic terms.[32] There may indeed be an intentional development from the foundational starting point, faith, to the ultimate goal and end of all Christian behavior, love. Interestingly, *epichorēgeō*, the verb in 2 Peter 1:5 translated "to supply, provide, add," is related to the words *choros* ("chorus") and *chorēgeō* ("to make provision for a chorus"). It is almost as if the author is saying "direct the chorus of your Christian life" or "orchestrate your Christian life" in the following way.[33] Here we should set this rhetorical device in its larger context because virtue catalogues were characteristic of this ancient world, since it was an honor-shame culture.

The rhetorical device being used in this virtue catalogue is a sorites, or *gradatio*, providing us with an ascending chain of virtues that leads to a climax, in this case to the supreme virtue, Christian love. This device involves repetition, something near to the heart of Asiatic rhetoricians, and it takes the form A-B, B-C, C-D and so on. Chains of virtues were not uncommon in Hellenistic and Stoic philosophy in this era (see Seneca, *Ep.* 85.2; Maximus of Tyre, *Diss.* 16.3b), nor were vice lists. The other New Testament example of this sort of rhetorical construction using virtues is found in Romans 5:3-5, which is similar enough to the *gradatio* in 2 Peter 1:5-7 that one may wonder if the author of 2 Peter knew of the one in Romans. In later Christian literature, *Acts of Peter* II.1:2 is quite similar and probably is

---

[31]James Moffatt, *The General Epistles: James, Peter, and Judas* (Garden City, N.Y.: Doubleday, Doran, 1928), p. 181.

[32]Bauckham, *2 Peter and Jude*, pp. 174-75.

[33]Craddock, *First and Second Peter, and Jude*, p. 100.

based on 2 Peter 1:5-7 (see also *Barn.* 2:2-3; *1 Clem.* 62:2). We should also compare the list in 2 Peter 1:5-7 to Philippians 4:8, with which it shares the characteristic of having a mixture of Hellenistic and more Christian virtues. And like 2 Corinthians 8:7, the list in 1 Peter 1:5-7 begins with faith and ends with Christian love.

We must keep in mind that in some cases in this list the author has taken terms that are prominent in Hellenistic lists, terms such as *gnōsis* ("knowledge"), which sometimes was listed either first or last to indicate its preeminence, but here it is in the middle of the pack. Faith and love are more important. Notice also that some words, such as *pistis* ("faith"), occur in the pagan lists, but with the very different meaning of "loyalty" or even "faithfulness." The list in 2 Peter 1:5-7, then, has something old, something new, and something borrowed but transformed into another concept. Craddock rightly adds that it would have been striking to the ancients to have a list with both mutual affection between brothers and sisters *(philadelphia)* and some other kind of love *(agapē)* listed, as is the case here. "But that is just the point: mutual affection, reciprocal love, pertains to life in the church, to the fellowship. Beyond that, however, is love, *agapē*. Love does not require reciprocity; it includes the stranger, and even the enemy."[34] There are early Jewish chainlink lists of virtues as well, the most similar in form of which is from Rabbi Phineas ben Jair (ca. A.D. 90):

> Zeal leads to cleanliness, and cleanliness leads to purity, and purity leads to self-restraint, and self-restraint leads to sanctity, and sanctity leads to humility, and humility leads to the fear of sin, and the fear of sin leads to piety, and piety leads to the Holy Spirit, and the Holy Spirit leads to the resurrection of the dead. (*m. Soṭah* 9:15).[35]

In some ways, this list is just the opposite of the one in 2 Peter 1:5-7, which presupposes that the audience already has the Holy Spirit, who is helping produce these virtues in the believer. Notice too that ritual purity is not an issue at all in the list in 2 Peter 1:5-7. We may also compare the near contemporary list found in *Herm.* 34:4, but there, unlike here in 2 Peter, it is a list of vices that have a snowballing effect, with one engendering the next (e.g., foolishness produces bitterness). Bauckham points to *Herm.* 16:7, which does use the sorites form and begins with faith and ends with love. *Shepherd*

---

[34]Ibid., p. 101.
[35]To this we may want to compare Wisdom of Solomon 6:17-20, which moves from wisdom to a kingdom.

of Hermas lists seven virtues, and 2 Peter lists eight. But again, in *Shepherd of Hermas* one virtue produces the next, which, despite Bauckham's argument, does not seem to be the case here in 2 Peter.[36]

What is not at all clear is whether Bauckham is right in translating the key verb in 2 Peter 1:5, *epichorēgeō*, as "to produce," thus indicating that each virtue is the means of producing the next. There are various problems with this view. The basic idea of this verb is that someone or something supplies, furnishes, provides, or makes possible something originally. For example, it was used of a financial backer of a Greek chorus and drama.[37] This person was a provider, not a producer. Furthermore, in 1 Peter 4:11 the basic form of this verb, *chorēgeō*, means "to supply, provide"—God provides strength. In 2 Corinthians 9:10 the idea is the same: God supplies; and this verse uses both forms of the verb, with and without the *epi-* prefix. Notice in 2 Corinthians 9:10 that "supplies" is supplemented with "and will increase." The idea here is one of providing and adding to, but not producing. Theophilus uses *epichorēgeō* to mean "to add further supplies" or "to provide more than was expected" (*Autol.* 73B). Here in 2 Peter, to "supply" further means to "add more." It is not at all clear how some of these virtues could be said to be produced by the preceding virtue, but it is not difficult to see how one could be added to the next. We must not confuse the interlocking rhetorical structure with a chain of dependent causes or ideas.

All of these qualities are things that Christians should add to their arsenal. There is a general progression here from faith through knowledge to affection to love; however, this is not because one virtue is produced by another, but rather because the author has the foundational virtue first and the greatest or climactic virtue last. As Norman Hillyer says, "Believers . . . must be lavish in the time and effort they put into developing their Christian lives—not being satisfied with getting by on the minimum, but striving like the *chorēgos* [patron or financial backer of the drama] of old to achieve the finest and most attractive production."[38]

What especially makes 2 Peter 1:5-7 stand out is that even more than in the Philippian list (see Phil 4:8), the author chooses to use terms that were more directly accessible to those who knew the buzzwords of Hellenistic

[36]Bauckham, *2 Peter and Jude*, pp. 175-76.
[37]See Norman Hillyer, *1 and 2 Peter, Jude* (NIBC; Peabody, Mass.: Hendrickson, 1992), p. 164.
[38]Ibid.

moral philosophy: *aretē*,[39] *enkrateia*,[40] *eusebeia, philadelphia*.[41] The terms more characteristic of Christian moral discourse were *pistis*, in the sense of "faith, trust"; *hypomonē*, in the sense of "endurance, hope"; and *agapē*. It is telling that both in 2 Peter and in Paul's writings, including the Pastoral Letters, although the pagan virtues are incorporated into the list, the more Christian virtues receive emphasis.

J. Daryl Charles makes the point that what the author of 2 Peter is doing is linking the theological virtues to the natural ones, the ones admired and manifested in the wider culture.[42] He sums up as follows:

> Whereas the acquisition of virtue in pagan ethics is an absolute good and the highest human goal, for the Christian it is evidence of deeper theological realities. . . . Because God through Christ has made provision for the ethical life—and this *abundantly*—does not mean that there is no cooperation in the ethical enterprise. To the contrary, the readers have a necessary part to play: 'For this reason make every effort to supply . . . ' Arranged in pairs and then distinguished for rhetorically stylized effect, the virtues build upon faith [*pistis*] and culminate in love [*agapē*]. The purpose of the catalog is its demarcation of exemplary—and by implication, unacceptable—behavior. . . . At bottom, Christians are to live a life *worthy* of their calling.[43]

We are dealing with an effort at character building or character formation. So formed, the audience will be better able to judge the behavior (and pedagogy) of the false teachers (who are a part of some Christian communities) for what it is. Indeed, the author immediately helps the audience to see the contrast, for in 2 Peter 1:8-9 we have a contrast between the audience and the blind, or at least nearsighted, guides. One of the evidences of the author's considerable rhetorical skill is that he is able to integrate, adopt, and adapt other people's material into his discourse without interrupting the flow of the discourse. He knows how to make the material his own, and he also knows when to treat a sacred tradition carefully, as in his use of the testimony of Peter, without giving it an extreme makeover. What emerges from this entire first chapter is that the character of Christians is to be like the character of

---

[39]Compare Philippians 4:8; 1 Peter 2:9.

[40]Said by Xenophon to be the foundation of all virtues (*Mem.* 1.5.4).

[41]See Daniel J. Harrington, *Jude and 2 Peter* (SP 15; Collegeville, Minn.: Liturgical Press, 2003), p. 248.

[42]See J. Daryl Charles, *Virtue Amidst Vice: The Catalogue of Virtues in 2 Peter 1* (JSNTSup 150; Sheffield : Sheffield Academic Press, 1997), pp. 126-52.

[43]Ibid., p. 157.

Christ, and being praiseworthy will result in honor and glory as they become sharers in the divine nature.

Perhaps we should cap this discussion beginning with the apt commentary of Ignatius: "The beginning is faith and the end is love, and when the two are joined in unity, it is God" (Ign. *Eph.* 14:1). A sorites tends to climax in the supreme virtue or vice, which in 2 Peter 1:5-7 is *agapē*, and it may be implied that this virtue encompasses and crowns all the rest, being the context out of which the rest are manifested and the manner of their manifestation. We can say of this text what often is said of the ode to love in 1 Corinthians 13: it aptly describes Jesus' character. It was the character and ethic of Jesus that caused authors as diverse as Paul in the Pastoral Letters and the author of 2 Peter to preach virtue ethics with a strong emphasis on the more distinctive Christian virtues highlighted: faith, love, hope, humility, perseverance and the like. At the same time these virtues were being emphasized, other virtues familiar in the Greco-Roman world, such as piety and loyalty, were reaffirmed, showing that becoming like Christ, becoming a disciple, meant the affirming of all that was good, true and beautiful; or as Paul says in Philippians 4:8, whatever is true, honorable, just, lovely and virtuous should be praised and practiced by Christians. Becoming a Christian did not involve an absolute renunciation of everything that characterized the Greco-Roman world. It was believed that Christ's Spirit enabled the believer to model Christlike behavior and so attract the onlooker to Christ. Here it will be helpful to review what the author of 2 Peter thinks that real Christian virtue and character should look like.

Pistis ("faith") appears to be the basic trust in God through Christ or belief in the gospel that results in such trust, not a reference to some body of doctrines. *Aretē* often is used in Hellenistic lists, meaning "virtue" or perhaps "excellence," the proper fulfillment of anything (cf. Phil 4:8). In Hellenistic thought it involves the achievement of human excellence, not obedience to God. *Gnōsis* ("knowledge") is mentioned next and possibly should be distinguished from *epignōsis* (cf. 2 Pet 1:2-3), which could mean for the author "that fundamental knowledge of God in Christ which makes a person a Christian."[44] Possibly, though, *gnōsis* here refers to the practical wisdom necessary for Christian living and progressively acquired. *Enkrateia* means "self-control," another characteristic Hellenistic virtue (see Aristotle, *Eth. nic.* 7.1-11), which usually is taken to signify reason winning out over pas-

---

[44]Bauckham, *2 Peter and Jude*, p. 186.

sion. Here the term is particularly appropriate in view of the apparent antinomianism or libertinism of the false teachers. *Hypomonē* means "steadfastness" and may refer to endurance under pressure or persecution, but here it may be allied to endurance in a Christian way despite temptation. *Eusebeia* is yet another characteristic Hellenistic virtue. Literally, it means "good worship," but it normally has the broader sense of "piety" or "godliness," and in a pagan context it refers to giving the gods their due in respect and in sacrifice and perhaps also to some extent in living a life of virtue. In a Christian context it refers to the godliness that necessarily entails honoring God both in worship and in one's behavior. *Philadelphia*, meaning "brotherly/sisterly affection," occurs elsewhere in ethical lists only in 1 Peter 3:8 (in adjectival form, *philadelphos*), and perhaps the author was led to include it here as a result of his knowledge of Petrine teaching. It is not to be confused with *agapē*, a more distinctively Christian virtue. Green notes,

> The crown of Christian "advance" (to return to the martial metaphor of the Stoic *prokopē* on which this list of qualities seems to be modelled) is *love*. "The greatest of these is love" (1 Cor. 13:13). This word *agapē* is one which Christians to all intents and purposes coined, to denote the attitude which God has shown himself to have to us, and requires from us towards himself. In friendship *(philia)* the partners seek mutual solace; in sexual love *(erōs)* mutual satisfaction. In both cases these feelings are aroused because of what the loved one is. With *agapē* it is the reverse. God's *agapē* is evoked not by what we are, but by what he is. It has its origin in the agent, not in the object. It is not that we are lovable, but that he is love. This *agapē* might be defined as a deliberate desire for the highest good of the one loved, which shows itself in sacrificial action for that person's good. That is what God did for us (Jn. 3:16). That is what he wants us to do (1 Jn. 3:16). That is what he is prepared to achieve in us (Rom 5:5).[45]

This conclusion must be tempered somewhat because *agapē* is used in the LXX, for example in Song of Songs, for sexual love. There is, then, more overlap in these terms, particularly between *agapē* and brotherly/sisterly love than one might expect. The borrowing from pagan virtue lists bespeaks a desire to use the language of the common culture of the audience but also makes clear that "Christian ethics cannot be totally discontinuous with the moral ideals of non-Christian society."[46] Of course here they are invested with Christian

---

[45]Green, *Second Epistle General of Peter*, p. 80.
[46]Bauckham, *2 Peter and Jude*, p. 187.

context and content. It is made clear by 2 Peter 1:8 that Christians not only should have these virtues but also should increase in them. They cannot be seen as static qualities or permanent possessions once given.

The Christian life of witness, insists the author, leads neither to idleness nor fruitlessness (perhaps a litotes, a way of affirming something by negating its opposite, here using two terms for emphasis). The point of 2 Peter 1:8 is that the believer's initial knowledge *(epignōsis)* of Christ leads not to indolence but rather to activity, not to spiritual bareness but rather to a fruitful life of Christian virtue (as exhibited in the qualities/activities listed in 2 Pet 1:5-7). It is not sufficient to simply have an initial knowledge (or experience) of Christ. Without Christian virtue and behavior, a person is *typhlos* and *myōpazōn*. It is unclear whether or not these are two ways of saying the same thing. The former word normally means "blind," and the latter means "nearsighted." However, Asiatic rhetoric is fond of redundancy, saying the same thing in two slightly different ways. On the surface of it, these terms might seem to contradict one another. One might ask, "How can someone who is blind be nearsighted?" Presumably what is meant is a person being blind to spiritual or heavenly things because of a shortsighted focus on earthly things. "This makes excellent sense in view of the immorality and earthiness of the false teachers."[47] The word *myōpazōn* per se does not imply willful blindness, but it does have the basic sense of squinting to block out the bright light. To deny the need for a virtuous life and progressive sanctification is to be oblivious to the cleansing that took place at the point of one's conversion, cleansing of the effects of one's preconversion sins. This probably is a reference not to the effect of water baptism but rather to the effect of regeneration spoken of in "baptism" language, as is so frequent in the New Testament.[48] Possibly the false teachers assumed that their freedom in God's grace was freedom to do as they pleased. Such a notion ignores the fact that God's converting grace was intended to save and cleanse believers from sin, not save them so that they could sin all the more without fear of judgment or with impunity (cf. Rom 6:1-4).

In 2 Peter 1:10 the author addresses the matter of election and human responsibility. After being converted, one cannot just rest on God's laurels and assume "once saved, always saved" regardless of one's postconversion

---

[47]Green, *Second Epistle General of Peter*, p. 82.
[48]See Ben Witheringtom III, *Troubled Waters: The Real New Testament Theology of Baptism* (Waco, Tex.: Baylor University Press, 2007), pp. 5-55.

conduct. Rather, the author says, believers must strive to make their calling and election firm or steadfast—in other words, to make it stand up. The verb *spoudazō* carries the sense of "to make every effort, be exceedingly zealous," picking up the same idea from 2 Peter 1:5. As Galatians 5:21 stresses, the ethical fruits of election are necessary not only to prove or demonstrate one's election and calling but also to obtain final salvation. Green rightly says,

> Election comes from God alone—but man's behaviour is the proof or disproof of it. Though "good works" (gratuitously read here by some MSS) are possible only through the appropriation of God's gracious aid, they are absolutely necessary, and fairly and squarely our responsibility. Hence the use of the middle voice, *poieisthai*, "make sure for yourself." Christian calling and Christian living go together. It seems that the false teachers boasted of their divine calling and election, while making that an "excuse for every kind of license, as though they had permission to sin with impunity because they are predestined to righteousness" (Calvin).[49]

Only by such working out of salvation do believers make their election steadfast, certain, sure. The second part of 2 Peter 1:10 simply stresses that those who are working out their salvation will never stumble so as to fall—that is, to fail to see the goal of final salvation. Here the author probably is not referring to some immunity to sinning, even for those who are zealously striving to be immune, but he is talking about an assurance that they will not ultimately lose out on eschatological salvation as long as they are making their calling and election firm. Even with all such efforts, the eternal kingdom (here seen as something that we enter at the last day) is still to be seen as something that God, in the end, gives believers out of his grace (richly afforded).

Christian behavior is a necessary but not sufficient condition to enter that kingdom, to obtain final salvation. It is necessary because, in a negative sense, without Christian living we will not obtain it, but insufficient because we will still fall short of the goal without God's grace and mercy being added to even our best efforts. The word *eisodos* (2 Pet 1:11) is the opposite of "exodus" and refers to a triumphal entry at the eschaton into the kingdom of Jesus. It is even translated "welcome" in the NIV. This seems to be a reference to the messianic kingdom that precedes the final kingdom of God on earth (see, e.g., Mt 13:41; 16:28; Lk 1:33; 22:29-30; 23:42; Jn 18:36; 1 Cor 15:20-28; Col 1:13; 2 Tim 4:1, 18; Heb 1:8; Rev 11:15). It is clear enough that the

---

[49]Green, *Second Epistle General of Peter*, p. 83.

author reflects the very same sort of eschatology, eagerly looking forward to the parousia, that we find in the earliest New Testament material in Paul's letters. It is the false teachers, not the author of 2 Peter, who feel as though the clock has run out on such hopes in the latter part of the first century A.D. Bauckham rightly adds,

> In this passage the author provides a kind of miniature "farewell sermon" of Peter's, summarizing Peter's definite teaching as he would wish it to be remembered after his death. Although the substance of the passage is no doubt faithful to the historical Peter's message, its form and terminology must be attributed to the author, whose distinctive way of expressing the Christian faith is very evident in these verses. Following the path already pioneered by Hellenistic Judaism, he employs Hellenistic religious ideas and language to interpret the gospel in terms appropriate to his Hellenistic environment. At the same time he gives these borrowings a definitely Christian context which determines their meaning.[50]

Can the essence of the ethics of Jesus and the earliest Christians really be "translated" into the Greco-Roman idiom without losing something significant in the translation? Clearly, the author of 2 Peter believed that the answer to this question is yes. He believed in dramatic change in human nature by means of salvation, but he also believed that progressive sanctification was necessary thereafter, and that this happened only by the Christian making every effort to add one virtue to another, cultivating a moral way of living and acting. In addition, he believed that beyond this cleansing process there was still final salvation to be obtained at the end of it all; human good behavior is not a sufficient condition for entering the kingdom, but it is a necessary one. Although the author does not deal with questions such as how much sin in the Christian's life would earn a disqualification, he is able to point to the false teachers as examples of those who have gone much too far, have committed apostasy, and whose example must be shunned at all costs. Notice that it is not just the sexual immorality that upsets the author when it comes to the false teachers; it is also their heresies or false beliefs, particularly about the eschaton and the return of Christ.

Writing in the 90s, the author believed that the church needed a warning against those who had abandoned the original gospel and its eschatological sanction. But what sort of eschatological sanction for behavior does he

---

[50]Bauckham, *2 Peter and Jude*, p. 192.

provide? While it can be said of Paul and the earliest Christians that they believed "We do not know when Christ will come, but it could be at any time, even soon, so be prepared," it can be said of the author of 2 Peter that he is prepared to state, "We do not know when Christ will come. It could be a long time, so be prepared to wait, for one day is as a thousand years with God, but also a thousand years is as one day." This is a different kind of eschatological sanction. The sanction comes from the reality of the future event, not its timing. For Paul, the possible imminence of Christ's return adds some extra potency to ethical enjoinders (see, e.g., Rom 13:11-14). The author of 2 Peter has not given up on either imminence or eschatology, and apparently he weighs the two possibilities, short versus long, about equally. He compensates for this by his spectacular description of the demise of the current cosmos, presenting his audience with a sort of rhetorical sound and light show in 2 Peter 3:8-13 to dazzle them with a picture of the end.

SUMMARY

From first to last in the New Testament, ethics and eschatology go hand in hand, and the eschatological sanction, though it takes a variety of forms in different texts, is not hard to find in all these texts. This gives a certain bite and hard edge to the ethics as well. They are grounded in the eschatological things that have already happened—the coming of Christ, his death, resurrection and sending of the Spirit, the consequent transformation of the believer's inner life by the Spirit (see Rom 5)—but they gain added urgency by the reminder that the clock is ticking, and one should remember that the big day is coming when Jesus returns to judge the earth. One could identify this sort of ethics as one that stands between the "already" and the "not yet," based in what now is, hoping for and anticipating the horizon and believing fervently that in the end God will bring all matters to a proper and just closure. And this in turn is precisely why Christians need not and should not try to take the matter of justice into their own hands. Vengeance belongs to God, and he will repay at the parousia. Instead, Christians must focus their lives not on justice but on mercy, not on vindication but on love, not on self-justification but on self-sacrifice, not on accruing merit but on exhibiting virtue, not on currying favor but on doing favors, not on earning grace but on being gracious, like Christ.

Following the Christ paradigm becomes possible because of the presence of the Spirit bestowing grace on and in the believer, and also because that paradigm not only leads to glory but also leaves the vindication to God, who is rich in mercy. It was God who raised Jesus from the dead; it will be God who raises the believers. They do not need to engage in honor challenges, they do not need to make a name for themselves, they do not need to get caught up in the reciprocity spin cycle. They can simply concentrate on being like Christ, for God has already made them his children through conversion, and glory is promised in the bargain.

It is a signal mistake not to realize that Christian ethics is not merely authorized by and enabled by Christian theology, but is the logical extension of it, indeed the necessary expression of the working out in a life of what God has worked into that life. The only ethics that we have in the New Testament is theological ethics, and when the pattern of Christ's behavior, taking up a cross, is held up as the pattern for Christian behavior, then ethics is modeled on theology, human behavior on God's.

And so 2 Peter is the perfect place to end this discussion of New Testament ethics, for this author bravely talks about our sharing in the divine nature. Indeed, he believes that without that sharing, there can be no truly Christian and ethical behavior, no Christlike behavior. The very moral character of God is meant to be replicated in the life of the believer. As God is holy, so we are called to be holy. As God is loving, so we are called to be loving. As God is rich in mercy, so we are called to be merciful.

It is therefore never enough to merely talk about theology of and in the New Testament. Nor is it enough to see ethics as a mere afterthought or footnote in the narrative of salvation. Divine action calls forth, indeed demands, a human response. Both are necessary for salvation. This is not because the human response itself saves a person; it is necessary but never sufficient for final salvation. A person could behave impeccably as a Christian, and God still would not be obligated to save that person in the end, since resurrection never is earned but rather is a gift from God. But it is because God has decided not to save us without our freely participating in his work that he has chosen to include our behavior in the process. There is no justification for overemphasizing justification as if it were the be-all and end-all of salvation. It is, rather, only the beginning of the miracle.

I am convinced that one's view of salvation and salvation history affects, if not dictates, one's view of the relationship of theology and ethics, including one's view of the character and importance of ethical behavior as part of the means of sanctification. But how does all of this affect the way we view the relationship of theology and ethics in the Old Testament and in the New Testament? We will explore that issue a bit in the final chapter. Here it is sufficient to say that the ethical DNA of the various New Testament books is similar enough in its christological and eschatological character to be recognizably from the same family of thought, from the family of faith called "Christian," a small sectarian offshoot of early Judaism. The ethical seriousness of all these writers is unquestionable. None of them are purveyors of cheap grace, nor do any of them minimize the importance of behavior as well as belief for pleasing God, and as being necessary, where there is time and opportunity, if one is to be "saved to the uttermost." And all of them—all of them—believe that God, through Christ and the Spirit, is saving people, not merely converting them but also conforming them to the image of God's Son and thereby renewing the effaced but not erased indelible image of God in every human being. Thereby, Christ will not merely inherit all things in the end, but he will have a host of brothers and sisters who, in character, look remarkably like their Master.

Final Surmises and Synopsis

At the outset of this study, I suggested that what explains the relationship between theology and ethics in the New Testament is the concept of the image of God. I need to say a bit more about this as this study draws to a close.

The concept of human beings created in the image of God is a theme announced in the very first chapter of the Bible at Genesis 1:26-27. What is too seldom noticed about this is that the Hebrew word ṣelem is the standard word in the ancient Near East for "idol."

> When a polytheist from the ancient world set out to make an earthly representative of their deity (understood as the incarnation of that which could not be fully incarnated, a lifeless object that must be animated by the deity) that polytheist fashioned a ṣelem. When the language of Genesis 1:26-27 is combined with the images of Genesis 2:7, we see that Yahweh is presenting himself to us as a divine craftsman, who is making an idol of/for himself, which he himself must animate. And that idol is us. Within the worldview of the ancient Near East the message here is clear: we are the nearest representation of Yahweh that exists.[51]

---

[51]Sandra L. Richter, *The Epic of Eden: A Christian Entry into the Old Testament* (Downers Grove, Ill.: InterVarsity Press, 2008), p. 107.

This is exactly correct. Human beings are supposed to be the "image" or "reflection" of the character of God on earth. God is holy, and so should we be. God is love, and so should we be. God is light, and so should we be. God is merciful, and so should we be. God is righteous, and so should we be. We were created to be the mirror image of God on earth, reflecting the divine character, but also engaging in the divine tasks, in a lesser and approximate sort of way. For example, the Genesis mandate for the creation order is for human beings to be fruitful and multiply, to fill the earth and subdue it (Gen 1:28), and that is exactly what God is depicted as doing in the first chapter of the Bible. We are called to be minicreators, minirulers over all other creatures great and small, just as God is. Ethics in a prefallen world is nothing more than fulfilling the original command of God and thereby truly mirroring his character and activity.

But what happens when human beings choose to be autonomous rather than obedient? What happens when human beings choose to decide what amounts to good and evil on their own rather than to obey the one prohibition that God gave Adam and Eve, which delineated what was evil and thus what was good (the latter being trusting God and obeying God)? Then, of course, the mirror cracks. Then humans no longer truly and adequately mirror the character of God, for there is no evil in God, no shadow of turning; God is not temptable or contemptible, nor does God tempt anyone. Now the relationship between theology and ethics changes. The image has been effaced but not erased, but it must be restored, renewed, redeemed if the character of God is again to shine forth in his "image." Now ethics involves countering the effects of the fall, not just offering positive commandments to be fulfilled. And much has to be said against sin, which previously did not need to be spelled out in detail. Theology remains the description of God and his divine character, God and his divine activity, but now a part of that activity is a reclamation project called "salvation." Ethics becomes the description of how the image of God ought to look, what it ought to do to once more to reflect the character of a righteous, holy, loving God on earth, not what it is of and by itself.

The fall of humankind severs the inherent link between God and humankind as image bearer and thereby severs the original connection between theology and ethics. Now the middle term between theology and ethics becomes making human beings new creatures in Christ. Now the middle term between God and his creatures actually becomes the God-man, Jesus, the mediator of the restored relationship, and what is interesting about this is that redemption means being conformed to the image of God's Son rather than that of the Father or the Spirit. Now image-bearing means Christlikeness. How does this differ from simply Godlikeness?

To begin with, being conformed to the image of Christ means taking up one's cross and following Jesus. In other words, we are being conformed to the image of the incarnate Jesus in his earthly mission; we are saved to become servants like Jesus. We are saved to mirror his self-sacrificial life while on earth. We are saved to be more than rulers or conquerors; we are saved to be, like Jesus, redeemers and reclaimers and restorers of the last, least and lost. This is so because the new Eden does not immediately show up just because there are some new creatures in Christ. We are called to extend God's work of redemption as far as the curse is found, as far as disease, decay and death reign, as far as lostness prevails. The mandate of the original creation order to fill the earth and subdue it takes a back seat to the mandate of the new creation order, the Great Commission, whereby we are commanded to make disciples of all peoples, baptizing and teaching them. The reason the Bible is the story of salvation history, not merely of creation maintenance or fulfillment, is that the whole of creation is groaning, looking forward to the day of its redemption, and that redemption must happen for the image bearers first, before there is a renewal of the earth at the resurrection (see Rom 8:18-25).

Without this story in mind, when people try to do theology without doing ethics, they are ignoring the inherent connection between the two, which was part of the divine assignment, the divine design, in the first place; we are supposed to be and bear the image of God on earth, bear witness to the divine character, activity, and plan. All of us are meant to be witnesses to the character and plan of God. We mirror the character and activity of God when we become and behave like God.

This does not amount to our becoming "God" or even "as gods"; rather, it amounts to our fulfilling the divine plan for the image bearer. An image of a deity is not a deity. It is a representation. And even when God animates the image or restores the image, the most that can be said is that "we become partakers of the divine nature," by which is meant that we have both the life of God in the inner being of our human being and the character of God reflected in our character, words and deeds. The creature remains the creature, and the Creator remains the Creator, even at the eschaton. Indeed, especially at the eschaton is this obvious, for the goal is not just the salvation of humankind but rather doxology—the restoration of true worship of God. And worship is an act that makes clearer than anything else that God is God, and human beings are definitely not God.

In order to make clear the enormous amount of ground covered in this study, I relied on several focal images beyond the indelible image. The first of these was the image of the oratorio. This analogy was meant to make clear that the unity of the New Testament is a unity in diversity, a diversity that sings in harmony. I spoke of Jesus, the great soloist, and the New Testament writers as singers of a masterpiece, an oratorio about the Master. We should not see this masterpiece as a monotone oratorio in which all sing exactly the same notes a capella. To the contrary, although all of them are singing recognizably the same musical piece, each one is singing a different or individual part. Each has a distinctive role to play, part to sing, and sometimes they are singing in a major key, and sometimes they are singing in a minor key, so sometimes there is dissonance and sometimes assonance, but it is always part of one larger musical work that will resolve into perfect harmony and a grand conclusion in the end. It is more like Beethoven's Ninth Symphony, with its four different movements that goes through various major and minor changes, than it is like a simple folk song with no harmony, sung in the key of C major. There is complexity and diversity to the singing in the New Testament, and we do it no justice if we try to reduce it to something banal like "Mary had a little lamb" (perhaps a Passover one?).

We should not make the mistake when the New Testament singers are "doubling"—that is, singing exactly the same notes (e.g., when Matthew and Luke talk about virginal conception in their birth narratives)—that therein lies the whole of the unity of the New Testament. The unity lies not in their singing about Jesus with exactly the same notes but rather in the fact that all of them are recognizably singing about this same Jesus. And this Jesus had many faces; he was a person who fit no one formula and could not be confined to any one pigeonhole. The unity of the New Testament is in its magnificent obsession with the Christ, its loving description of the person and works of Christ, its worship of the Christ. Indeed, its theologizing about the Christ often, indeed to a large extent, seems to have been born in the worship of the Christ, whom the New Testament writers had difficulty praising highly enough, finding terms exalted enough to describe the God-man.

Like an oratorio, the unity of the New Testament is additive. One part is added to another, which is added to another and another, until one gets the full effect of the harmony, of the chord progressions, of the various themes and movements of the piece. Accordingly, I have taken an additive approach, first pointing to the shared symbolic universe of Jesus and the New Testament writers, then pointing out their shared narrative thought world (some of which I have rehearsed again above), then beginning to work through the "score" to delineate each writer's contribution to the oratorio. Of course, along the way I have pointed out the "harmonic convergences" of the singers, but without ignoring or underplaying the rich, complex, beautiful diversity of the witnesses. Who would want to leave out the author of Hebrews' remarkable solo about Christ as our heavenly high priest just because neither Jesus nor the other New Testament singers present this theme? Who would want to omit the discussion of the virginal conception just because only Matthew and Luke sing about Jesus' origins in those terms? Who would want to neglect the profound depths of Paul's presentation in Romans 12, where he calls us all to present ourselves as living sacrifices and calls this our true worship of God just because no one else speaks quite this way about our ethical response to God?

Like a great oratorio, the unity of the piece and its ultimate harmony emerge only as one listens intently to the whole of the piece from start to finish and listens intently to all the details and the variations. I make no apology for the length of this volume. Such length is necessary in order to present, examine and discuss the full score of the theology and ethics of the New Testament. With some singers, such as Paul, who are prominent soloists in this oratorio, we were able to see how their part played out over the course of a considerable amount of material and through several movements. With other singers, such as Jude, we needed to focus on seeing a brief but telling contribution. Yet all of these witnesses are in the canon for a reason, and they deserve to be heard and not neglected. The theology and ethics of the New Testament are not footnotes to Paul or the evangelists. This is an ensemble piece, and because of previous neglect in this regard, I have spent more time in the present study on some of the witnesses too often deemed minor rather than major witnesses. Like a conductor conducting a symphony more slowly to help the audience hear and savor all the parts and to bring out some of the lesser-known parts so that their contributions could be heard and appreciated, I have approached the New Testament oratorio so as to recognize it as a classic, a masterpiece performed many times, and it was unnecessary simply to imitate previous performances of this masterpiece in previous works on the theology or ethics of the New Testament.

A third crucial image meant to show the unity of the New Testament was the Venn diagram that appears early in the present volume (see fig. 12.1).

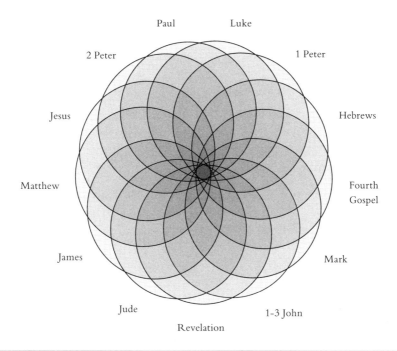

Figure 12.1. Thought World of the New Testament

What we should note here about this diagram is its depiction of Christ and of reflection on Christ as the central unity of the New Testament—not this or that theological theme, such as the glory of God, but rather the person and work of the Christ. But here I need to add something remarkable that I realized after having worked through the whole New Testament. Notice that although I was able to divide the witnesses into those largely addressing Jews and those largely addressing Gentiles, there is an enormous amount of over-lap in the message. Paul and the author of Hebrews have much in common in both theology and ethics. Jude and 2 Peter share many of the same themes; indeed, the author of 2 Peter recycles much of Jude. The point is that these writers clearly share the same gospel, the same theological and ethical orien-tation, despite some differences, including some of them addressing mainly Jews and some of them addressing mainly Gentiles. The social networks were close in early Christianity, and the apostolic witness was influential throughout these churches. Indeed, the entire New Testament can be said to go back to the witness of about eight or so of the original eyewitnesses or their co-workers.[52] In light of this historical reality, the unity of the New Testament is not a surprise. It was important that a growing evangelistic group with a distinctive and indeed controversial message get its story straight from the outset lest people have difficulty believing that "these things are true." Here it will be useful to present a brief synopsis of the various chapters in this particular volume (the reader may also want to consult the synopsis of the first volume at the beginning of this one). The first volume concentrated on the individual witnesses, and this focuses on the collective New Testament witness about theology and ethics.

First, here is the table of contents for the main chapters of the present volume:

---

[52]See Ben Witherington III, *What Have They Done with Jesus? Beyond Strange Theories and Bad History; Why We Can Trust the Bible* (San Francisco: HarperSanFrancisco, 2006).

Notice that after some preliminary methodological considerations, I sought first to point out the shared symbolic universe and narrative thought world of the New Testament writers. All of them were Jews or God-fearers, with the possible exception of the author of 2 Peter (I think it likely that Luke was a Gentile God-fearer), and so this shared christocentric, monotheistic worldview is no surprise. And the author of 2 Peter simply recycles the earlier materials of Peter and Jude with a nod in the direction of Paul. He is not trying to do something new.

This means that there is no purely Gentile theology or ethics in the New Testament. By this I mean that all of it is Jewish in origin and character, even when it addresses Gentiles. Of course, some concessions are made and there is some adopting and adapting of Hellenistic ideas and virtues into the discussion in various places in the New Testament, but even this is done from a profoundly Jewish Christian point of view. There can be no compromise on monotheism (to do so would result in idolatry) or on the strict ethical codes of the Old Testament. This is why James stresses that even Gentiles must stay out of pagan temples and away from violations of the heart of the Mosaic law, the Ten Commandments (Acts 15:13-29); that is, they must avoid idolatry and immorality lest the witness of Christ to Jews be compromised.

Throughout the New Testament we see clear evidence of a reliance on the Scriptures by the Jewish people. Indeed, those Scriptures are the only written source that all the New Testament authors draw on repeatedly as inspired, authoritative, and truthful. Their symbolic universe and narrative thought world have been chiefly shaped by two things: the Old Testament and the Christ-event and its various impacts on them personally. The coherence of the message and person of Jesus with the message of the New Testament writers is not difficult to fathom when we realize that all them were Jews (again, with two possible exceptions) who both held to the sacred Scriptures and conceived of the new eschatological situation brought about by Jesus in much the same way he did, and they viewed Jesus in a way that comported with what he actually said and did and implied about himself.

Because the New Testament is a christocentric collection of books, we focused first on a survey of what the various writers had to say about christological matters. Here we found a profound harmonic convergence of the witnesses, perhaps more so on this subject than on any other. All of these witnesses view Jesus as both truly human and truly divine. They were not satisfied with saying that Jesus was just a great prophet, sage, miracle-worker, or teacher, although they do mention those things. Nor were they satisfied even to simply say he was a son of David like King David, a king of that sort. Even when they thought about things messianic, they agreed that Jesus far exceeded all the previous early Jewish expectations about the messiah, not least in his dying and rising, but also in his more than merely mortal character. In other words, they agreed that both the person and the works of Jesus had to be talked about in exalted terms because Easter had revealed who Jesus truly was and what he was about. He was a man of many faces, many roles—prophet, priest, king, Son of Man, Son of God, Lord, healer, exorcist, Savior.

After focusing on the christological material in the New Testament, we moved on, again using an additive approach (adding one witness's contribution to another), to examine the New Testament consensus about the Father and the Spirit. I stressed repeatedly throughout the discussion that all the New Testament writers manifest the christological reformulation of monotheism and speak of Father, Son, and Spirit as distinguishable persons united as the one God. I stressed especially how they view the Spirit as a person, not merely as a power or presence or force from God. The raw stuff, the basic material for trinitarian thinking, is found in the New Testament, although it is not yet the case that anyone is using the word "Trinity," nor are they even yet using the term *theos* ("God") to refer to the Trinity. In the New Testament *theos* is used overwhelmingly of the Father, but also in seven very different places involving multiple witnesses it is used of the Son, both early and late in the New Testament period. There is no evolutionary spiral of Christology to be found in the New Testament. Some of the most profound Christology is some of the earliest, in Paul's writings and in the christological hymns. One of the more interesting facets to the discussion about the Father is that the use of the term "Father" by Jewish Christians comes primarily not from their general Jewish heritage but rather from Jesus' own "Abba" language, and it reflects the special relationship between Jesus and the Father, such that we have the phrase "the Father of our

Lord Jesus Christ," whom Christians can call "Father" only because of being "in Christ," being his disciple. This has nothing to do with patriarchy and everything to do with the intimate relationship that Jesus had with God the Father, which he bequeathed to us.

The final major theological chapter dealt with soteriology in its eschatological context. I discussed at length how the New Testament writers use the language of "election," "salvation," and the like to express God's call and plan to redeem humankind. I stressed that it is not God's plan or desire for any to perish and showed how the New Testament writers make this clear in various different ways. I stressed that although there are many images of the death of Christ in the New Testament, the image of penal substitution should not be neglected, ignored, or dismissed, not least because it tells us much about the character of the righteous and merciful God who cannot pass over sin forever and must deal with it in order to have a renewed relationship with his people. I stressed that the concepts of election and salvation are distinguishable, and the former is collectivist in character: persons are elect in Israel in the Old Testament and in Christ in the New Testament. Salvation happens by grace through faith, and importantly, salvation has three tenses, involving conversion (new birth), sanctification, and glorification (resurrection). Until one goes through all three phases of salvation, one is not fully conformed to the image of God's Son and is not saved to the uttermost. I spent some time on eschatology in this connection, but since I had dealt with it at some length in the first volume of the present work and elsewhere,[53] I did not dwell on that matter. Suffice it to say that the New Testament writers have great expectations in connection with the return of Christ, the resurrection of believers, the kingdom coming on earth, and the new heaven and new earth, but expectations do not degenerate into calculations or prognostications in the hands of the New Testament writers. We are to live in hope and by faith, knowing that God has revealed enough about the future to give us hope, but not so much that we have no need to continue to live by faith and be faithful. This is why I have emphasized the repeated warnings about the apostasy of true believers in the New Testament.

During this life, the possibility of apostasy is mentioned by Paul, the Beloved Disciple, the author of Hebrews, and John of Patmos. Indeed, the theme of apostasy is one of the ethical themes that comes up most often in the New

---

[53]See Ben Witherington III, *Jesus, Paul, and the End of the World: A Comparative Study in New Testament Eschatology* (Downers Grove, Ill.: InterVarsity Press, 1992).

Testament. One is not eternally secure until one is securely in eternity. Short of that, there can be assurance of things hoped for, but the assurance is given to those who continue to walk in the Spirit and do not indulge the flesh. And herein lies an important point. Ethics is not just the response of a grateful heart to God's grace, although that is true; ethics is the working out of one's salvation with fear and trembling, so indeed the believer has something to do with his or her own sanctification and going on toward glorification. This fact made the connection between theology and ethics clearer, and as we saw, the New Testament has no ethics other than theological ethics. Theology and ethics can be distinguished as what God does and what we do, or as what God is and what we ought to be and do, but in the end these topics belong together and coinhere. Christian experience, or salvation, is the middle term between theology and ethics, subjectively speaking, just as being in the image of God is the middle term, objectively speaking.

Our exploration of the ethical discussions of the New Testament writers showed the great influence of the teaching and example of Jesus in various places in the canon. Of course the imitation of Christ presupposes knowing the story of Christ, so the theology and ethics come together in this way as well. In particular, themes from the Sermon on the Mount crop up in diverse places such as in the letter of James or Paul's letters. I spent considerable time showing the convergence of James and Paul in regard to ethics. Both of them affirm a version of the law of Christ, or what James calls the "royal law," which consists of (1) the example and teachings of Christ; (2) those portions of the ethics of the Old Testament that are reaffirmed in and by Christ; (3) the apostolic teachings that extrapolate or develop the first two items. The phrase "faith works" best describes the nature of living faith in Christ. We are not merely to have faith in Christ, we are to emulate his faithfulness, even unto death on the cross. This is what it means to have "the mind of Christ" and so the behavior of Christ, who came not to be served but to serve. But when we follow the teachings of Jesus as presented in Matthew 5–7, this commits us to an ethic of nonviolence, of nonretaliation, of loving enemies, of forgiving those who wrong us. We are called to be active pacifists—that is, not only abstainers from violence but also active lovers of friend, neighbor, stranger and even enemy. We are not to be overcome with evil or by evil, but rather we are to overcome evil with good. This is an ethic that has one eye on the eschatological horizon, believing that we must take God seriously when he says, "Vengeance is mine, I will repay," and so leave the matter of justice in the hands of God and perhaps also in the hands of those whom he has appointed to administer justice on the earth. The ethic of the New Testament is an ethic for the Christian community, which only Christ's followers can follow, enabled by grace and the power of the Spirit. It is not an ethic that can be imposed on unsaved persons. It is an ethic that presupposes the salvation of those on whom the imperatives fall. The ethical imperative is built on the salvific indicative.

Here, for the sake of clarity, I should reiterate a few things stated along the way. As I said in an earlier work, *The Problem with Evangelical Theology*,[54] it is precisely in our distinctives that the various evangelical and orthodox (both Catholic and Orthodox) theologies are exegetically weakest, and this ought to tell us something. The theology of sinless perfection, the theology of eternal security and divine predetermination, the theology of necessary second blessing and necessary glossolalia, the theology of sacramental salvation, the theology of continued human priesthoods and patriarchal privileges in both the family and the family of faith, the theology of rapture and two peoples of God, the theology of one particular denomination or church having a lock on God's truth, the theology of Marian sinlessness and childlessness (other than Jesus)—all these shipwreck on the hard rocks of the New Testament and the theological and ethical expositions of the New Testament writers.

If we focus on what the New Testament actually says, we will stick to our story, which has a christological core both theologically and ethically, and make the main thing the main thing: Christ, the Alpha and Omega. We should stand fast on the Great Commission, realizing that there is a world that can and should be saved, and God desires for all of it to be saved. We should be broad where the New Testament is broad, and narrow where it is narrow, which means that all true Christians everywhere, of whatever ecclesiological body, are part of the body of Christ and should be welcomed as brothers and sisters. We should affirm that God's Word is truthful and trustworthy in all the things that it intends to teach us, and it is no accident that we are told, in that great affirmation about the plenary inspiration of the Old Testament (2 Tim 3:16), that the Word of God is intended for, among other things, training in righteousness, not for a belief that righteousness is all imputed instead of imparted, that it is all God's doing and no part of our working out of our salvation. Ours is a high calling: to be image bearers, renewed and be-

---

[54]Ben Witherington III, *The Problem with Evangelical Theology: Testing the Exegetical Foundations of Calvinism, Dispensationalism, and Wesleyanism* (Waco, Tex.: Baylor University Press, 2005).

ing renewed in the image of God's Son. The goal is that when people look at us, they see the character of our Savior, the character of our God. The goal is for us to be winsome enough to win some, to be Christlike enough to truly be and act like Christ. May it be so. I certainly believe that God's grace is sufficient to make it so, for he is the potter who can remold even these fragile and cracked earthen vessels into a new and perfected form.

In many great musical works there is a coda in which some final things are attended to. The present work is no different. In the final chapter I will say some things about moving forward toward biblical theology and about the role that New Testament theology must play in such an enterprise.

CODA

Integrating the Old and New Testament Thought Worlds and Moving Forward to Biblical Theology

When the author walks on to the stage, the play is over.

C. S. LEWIS[1]

In using narrative, our New Testament writers were following in the tradition of the Old Testament, where God consistently reveals himself in what he does—in creation, in history, and in what is said and done by his prophets.

MORNA HOOKER[2]

DIFFERENTIATING THE OLD TESTAMENT AND THE NEW TESTAMENT THOUGHT WORLDS

Although it is possible at this juncture to discuss the relationship of the Old Testament to the New Testament, that subject belongs in a discussion of the canon, which is not the focus of this study, and in any case I addressed it somewhat in the first volume of the present work.[3] Here our interest is the relationship of Old Testament theology and ethics to the theology and ethics

---

[1]C. S. Lewis, *Mere Christianity* (New York: Harper, 2001 [1952]), p. 65.

[2]Morna Hooker, "The Nature of New Testament Theology," in *The Nature of New Testament Theology: Essays in Honour of Robert Morgan*, ed. Christopher Rowland and Christopher Tuckett (Oxford: Blackwell, 2006), p. 90. Her argument is essentially the same one that I am making here for narrative being the larger rubric in which one can best understand New Testament theology and ethics.

[3]See Ben Witherington III, *The Individual Witnesses*, vol. 1 of *The Indelible Image: The Theological and Ethical Thought World of the New Testament* (Downers Grove, Ill.: IVP Academic, 2009), pp. 46-51.

that we find in the New Testament. The reason for this distinction is simple: the documents of the New Testament existed in the New Testament era and are expressions of the thought world of that era, long before there was a New Testament canon. The thought world of the New Testament speakers and writers was enormously influenced by the thought world exhibited in many books now found in the Old Testament, although certainly they were also profoundly influenced by intertestamental Jewish literature and thought.

I say "many" books because some books of the Old Testament seem to have exerted little or no influence on the early Christians. An obvious example is the book of Esther, which seems to have made no impact at all, and perhaps this is not surprising, since the Old Testament canon was not fully closed in the New Testament era, and one of the debated books was Esther. In fact, several of the books that later made up the third part of Tanak, the Writings, are missing in action in the New Testament, as are various other Old Testament books (e.g., Nehemiah). And it is not simply that they are not quoted; they are not even alluded to. It therefore is better, on the whole, to talk about the influence not of particular books, although we could do that (the most heavily cited in the New Testament are Isaiah and Psalms), but rather of the influence of the thought world.

And here we note a remarkable fact. The Old Testament, taken as a whole, has precious little to say about the afterlife and only somewhat more about eschatology. And indeed, it is mostly the very latest Old Testament books, including especially the more apocalyptic prophets, that have anything of consequence to say on this subject; and sometimes, even when talking about the Yom Yahweh, they are talking not about some final eschatological judgment on the world but rather about a temporal judgment on Israel or the nations after which there can be redemption for God's people and further mundane life.

By comparison, the thought world of the New Testament writers is overwhelmingly eschatological in character. In this respect, the New Testament thought world is far more like the thought world of some of the intertestamental Jewish literature than that of the Old Testament. Of course, this could be said to create a problem for canonical theologians, at least for those who want to limit the discussion within the parameters of what is found in the Old Testament and the New Testament. But there are red flags right within various New Testament books against taking this sort of approach as well.

For example, the little document called "Jude" clearly draws on extracanonical material from the *Enoch* literature and probably from *Apocalypse of Moses* as well. And then we have Paul, who shows the influence of *Wisdom of Solomon*, and James, who draws on *Sirach*. Thus, we can focus on the relationship between the thought worlds of the Old Testament and the New Testament, but we should not limit ourselves to that discussion, not least because important ideas such as bodily resurrection of the dead, although they did not germinate in the intertestamental period, certainly gestated in that period. When it comes to the Old Testament itself, the concept of resurrection is barely mentioned, in Daniel 12:1-2 and as a metaphor in Ezekiel (and see Is 26:19). Put simply, some of the concepts most crucial and determinative for the early Christian thinkers are almost absent from the Old Testament. Christian theology and ethics could never be done purely on the basis of the careful interpretation of the Old Testament.

And indeed, some scholars have asked probing questions about whether one can even talk about a unified Old Testament thought world, not least because the material found there was produced and edited over an incredibly long period of time, in various places, in different countries, in exile and in the Holy Land, and much of the literature is anonymous, or at least we do not know who actually finally wrote it down. In any case, the concept of books did not exist in the Old Testament era in the same way it did in the first century A.D. By contrast, the gestation period of the New Testament is tiny, the social networks are much more closely knit, and we know a good deal about various of the New Testament authors, including that they either were, or were in touch with, the original eyewitnesses of the events that came to be called the "good news." Then too, all the writers shared something vital in common: a vibrant faith in a recently crucified and risen savior named "Jesus."

There was no singular sort of experience like the Christ-event, not even the exodus and Sinai events, that generated the faith of all the Israelites. In some ways, then, it is unfair to compare the Old Testament and New Testament thought worlds, and in any case the Old Testament thought world reflects a long period of development with some remarkable changes in and after the exile in regard to afterlife theology. We must talk in terms of progressive revelation when dealing with the Old Testament thought world. It is not at all clear that we need to do that with the New Testament thought world. And then too, if we are going to speak at all about biblical theology and ethics, the narratological necessities dictate that we talk about an ongoing tale that has a beginning, a middle, a climax, and an end. The Old Testament does not include the last two elements of the story, although especially its prophetic corpus sometimes foreshadows and foretells it.

Some will ask why is it so important to consider the theology and the ethics in the Bible in a processive and progressive manner. One answer is that we cannot judge the meaning of a story and the character of its actors before we get to the end. Consider for a moment the example of J. R. R. Tolkien's great trilogy, *The Lord of the Rings*. We cannot tell whether Frodo will have the necessary character to do what is required with the ring until we near the end of the story. Up to that point, we do not know whether he will pass the test. Or even more tellingly, we cannot tell whether Gollum is going to end up being an adversary or an assistant in the process of saving the Shire and the world until right near the end. And what of Gandalf? Will he return in time or at all to help the human race ward off evil? We do not know until many hundreds of pages into the story. The Bible involves a similar, even more grand, epic story from creation through fall through various acts of redemption to the final new creation. Viewing the whole story from the end changes the way we look at the character of God, the character of God's people, how human history will play out, the nature of redemption, and a host of other subjects. The truth is that we do not fully know God and the divine character sufficiently for eternal salvation before Jesus turns up to reveal it. We do not fully understand the depths of human depravity until Jesus shows up and dies on the cross to reveal and overcome it. We do not fully understand the importance of creation to God's eternal plan until we hear near the end that God's plan is that all of fallen creation be renewed and restored, and that the resurrection of Jesus will be the harbinger and indeed catalyst of the final stage of redemption for human beings themselves.

THE NECESSITY OF A NARRATOLOGICAL APPROACH TO NEW TESTAMENT THEOLOGY AND ETHICS

It is precisely because biblical history is told in the Bible as an ongoing story that a narratological approach to theology and ethics is not merely useful but actually is required to fully understand what is being claimed and taught. The first question to ask about any theological or ethical remark in the Bible is "Where in the story do we find it?" Is it near the outset, or is it in the middle or toward the end? During the administration of which covenant was this or that teaching given? Most fundamentally, does this or that theological or ethical remark come before or after the Christ-event? Does this point in the story reflect the partial revelations of the earlier period or the fuller revelation that comes in and after the Christ-event?

These are the right sorts of questions to ask when we are thinking about the theology and ethics found in the Bible, and this is precisely why we cannot do biblical theology in a manner that treats the Old Testament as if it provides as full a revelation of God's character, plan, and people as does the New Testament. It does not, nor did the New Testament writers think that it did, even though it was the only Bible that they had. They believed that they were the people on whom the ends of the ages had come, and they believed that in fact the author of this whole story had finally stepped out onto the stage in person to bring in the final chapters and explain the meaning of it all.

With this reminder about the narratological framework and nature of the thought world that we are dealing with, it is appropriate to say some final things about some of the major symbols in the symbolic universe that generated that sort of thought world and story, but first we must note that we have now found a clue or two as to why the early church completely rejected the so-called Gnostic Gospels when considering what eventually would be their canonical texts.

The first reason is that the canonical Gospels do indeed focus heavily on the passion and death of Christ; indeed, each of them can be viewed as a passion narrative with a long introduction. By contrast, the Gnostic Gospels place no focus on the death of Jesus, and indeed they actually avoid doing so. They see no great theological significance in that event, or really any other similar event, which depends on historical reality and particularity.

Equally important, as Luke Timothy Johnson says, "None of the Gnostic Gospels take the form of narrative. Rather, they focus entirely on Jesus as revealer, and take the form of discrete sayings . . . with no narrative framework (*Gospel of Thomas*), or revelatory discourses in response to questions (*Gospel of Mary, Dialogue of the Savior*). Two of the most important Gnostic Gospels (*Gospel of Truth, Gospel of Philip*) take the form of teaching *about* Jesus rather than any sort of story."[4] In other words, the sensibilities and symbolic universe that formed those documents are very different from those Jewish ones that formed our canonical Gospels. In fact, it is not an overstatement to say that most of the Gnostic texts reject the God of the Old Testament altogether, the God of material creation.

---

[4]Luke Timothy Johnson, "Does a Theology of the Canonical Gospels Make Sense?" in Rowland and Tuckett, eds., *Nature of New Testament Theology*, p. 103.

Johnson puts it this way: "Insofar as the God of Israel is the God who creates the material world, the Gnostic texts resist that God. A Gnostic sensibility that finds the world to be a corpse and blessedness in detachment and solitariness (see the Coptic *Gospel of Thomas*) is far both from the sensibility of Torah and of the canonical Gospels."[5] All the writers of the New Testament probably were Jews or God-fearers,[6] not Marcionites or Gnostics, and so we would expect them to devalue neither the Old Testament thought world nor the Old Testament vision of God and creation, and they do not disappoint us in this regard. The changes that we find between the Old Testament and the New Testament symbol systems are christologically, ecclesiologically, and eschatologically engendered, but all of those categories (the discussions of a messiah, of God's people, of the future in connection with the messiah and God's people) are Jewish and must be seen as a further development of Old Testament and early Jewish thinking on such subjects in a particular direction in the light of the Christ-event.

THE NARRATIVE THOUGHT WORLD OF THE OLD TESTAMENT AND ITS RELEVANCE TO CHRISTIAN THOUGHT

At the center of the Old Testament symbolic universe and narrative thought world lies a singular God, Yahweh. Scholars have come to call what they find in the Old Testament "ethical monotheism," and this is an appropriate label. Yahweh, the God of the Bible, is a hands-on deity constantly involved in the affairs of the world and his people, and he is constantly making demands of them in regard to their behavior especially, but also in regard to their beliefs. The Shema frequently is seen as the core credo of the Old Testament God: "Hear, O Israel, the LORD our God is one" (Deut. 6:4). Here "one" presumably means "as opposed to many gods." In other words, this is a statement against polytheism, not about the composition or complexity of the biblical God.[7]

What was believed about this God can be deduced fairly easily from a close reading of the Pentateuch and the first few Historical Books. As the only real God in the cosmos, the biblical God was believed to be the creator of all things and all beings. No other being or thing existed before this God decided to create the universe and all that is within it. This view stands in

---

[5]Ibid., p. 105.
[6]The author of 2 Peter may be an exception to this rule, but Luke probably was a Gentile God-fearer.
[7]On which, see Richard Bauckham, *Jesus and the God of Israel: God Crucified and Other Studies on the New Testament's Christology of Divine Identity* (Grand Rapids: Eerdmans, 2008).

stark contrast to other ancient Near Eastern views about how the universe was created out of a struggle between various deities. The Old Testament writers will have none of that. There is only one God, and there is only one universe, which was created by this God and reflects the divine character. The way this is expressed in the beginning chapters of the Bible is that God created all things and made them *tôb* ("good"), indeed made them *tôb mĕʾōd* ("very good"). A good God made a good creation and good creatures to fill it.

This idea of monotheism created enormous problems when it came to the issue of the origins of evil—the study of theodicy. Polytheism could always explain that evil came about through one or another of the bad deities or through cosmic struggle, but monotheism could not go that route. Some other explanation for evil had to be suggested. What is most interesting in Genesis 1–3 is that we are not told where evil comes from; it simply lurks in the presence of the snake in the garden. It appears that the Old Testament writers were much more interested in talking about how to cope with evil than in debating its source.

However, the Old Testament writers did repeatedly emphasize that the one and only God was not evil, had no dark side, no shadow of turning, nor did this God do evil things. The blame for the "fall," as it came to be called, is placed solely on human beings, not on God for making defective merchandise. This pattern of thought is seen not only in various places in the Old Testament but also in the New Testament. As Paul puts it, Adam is the head of the human race, and as a result all of us have sinned and died in Adam, and it is also true that all of us, on our own, have sinned and fallen short of the glory of God (see Rom 3:23; 5:12-21; 1 Cor 15:20-28, 42-50). Not once in the Bible is there a discussion about some flaw or ethical defect in God. The blame for the human malaise is always placed at the door of human beings, however much they may have been beguiled or bamboozled by the powers of darkness in the universe. God is holy, just, and good and is not responsible for sin and evil.

This raises questions about the sovereignty of God, and the Old Testament does indeed repeatedly insist that God is almighty. Sometimes this takes the form of insisting that God is the maker and ruler of the universe, but more frequently, since the Old Testament is the story of God's dealings with a fallen and imperfect people, it takes the form of insisting that God is almighty to save or rescue his people. God will not willingly let them go down the path of ruin and self-destruction (cf. Gen 6 with Hos 11). At the very heart of the Pentateuch is the story of the exodus and Sinai events, which becomes the paradigm and indeed the litmus test of the character of God—Yahweh is a redeemer God, who rescues his people time and time again. This brings into the picture God's love, compassion and mercy, for there is no suggestion in such stories, not even in Exodus, that these people earned God's favor and deserved to be rescued and therefore that a righteous God was obligated to extricate them (see Ex 34:6-7).

True enough, it is stressed that the Hebrews were victims of horrible oppression, but there is no suggestion in these stories that God rescued them because their character was so much better than that of the Egyptians (see Deut 7:7-8). Indeed, as the traditions of the wilderness wanderings that followed were to demonstrate, these people had some severe issues in regard to both their behavior and their beliefs about the true God. Golden calves and immorality came as neither a total accident nor a total surprise from these people. In other words, although God was just in punishing the Egyptians, he was also gracious in rescuing the Hebrews. And here we come upon a crucial point.

Salvation in the Old Testament is, almost exclusively, a this-worldly proposition. It is something that God does in space and time to rescue, redeem, restore and aid the return of his people to their rightful place or condition or character. There is in fact hardly anything of a doctrine of heaven in the Old Testament (although occasionally an Enoch or an Elijah gets "beamed up" into the living presence of God), and so whatever justice or redemption that happens must happen in the here and now, in space and time. To be sure, in the later and apocalyptic prophecies we begin to see an afterlife or at least a theology of new creation, as in Second and Third Isaiah, Ezekiel and Daniel, but clearly enough Sheol is the dominant concept of the afterlife in most of the Old Testament. But nowhere, apparently, do we find any New Testamentwriters who merely conjure with Sheol after death for anyone.[8]

---

[8]On Old Testament eschatology and apocalyptic, see Bill T. Arnold, "Old Testament Eschatology and the Rise of Apocalypticism," in *The Oxford Handbook of Eschatology*, ed. Jerry L. Walls (New York: Oxford University Press, 2007), pp. 23-39. This excellent survey of the relevant data shows that there is some eschatological and apocalyptic material in the Old Testament, particularly in the later prophetic material, and it demonstrates that there is a connection between the earlier promises of God about land, monarchy, and the like and their final fulfillment in a this-worldly restoration or balancing of the scales of justice. This conclusion is seen not as a natural development of historical processes but rather as a result of divine intervention, whether in connection with the Day of the Lord or by some other means. See also Ben Witherington III, *Jesus the Seer: The Progress*

There is considerable insistence in the Old Testament on God's holiness and righteous character. This, of course, is one reason why we talk about ethical monotheism. The biblical God is not running around committing immoral acts or, like various pagan deities, attempting to mate with mere mortals. Notably, when we have a story such as Genesis 6:1-4, in which angels (called "sons of God") come down from above and violate the creation order by mating with mortals, the heavens break loose and a flood judgment comes upon the earth. The biblical God will not tolerate, never mind perpetrate, a breach of the creation order, much less blur the line between Creator and creature in this regard. Thus, when we hear God say, "Be holy, for I am holy" (e.g., Lev 11:44), we are beginning to get to the root of the matter in terms of the Old Testament symbolic universe. God is one, and God is holy, and God's people should be both one and holy as well.[9]

And here is where I say that just as theology and ethics are bound up in the character of God and one could talk about the theological story of an ethical God acting ethically, so also theology and ethics are intertwined in what is expected of God's people. The character of God is to be reflected in the behavior (and belief) of God's people. Put another way, when one knows and believes in the true character of the biblical God and has experienced God acting "in character" on behalf of his people, the only appropriate response is to mirror that character in one's own community and life. "Be holy, for I am holy" is a mandate not merely to set oneself apart from the behavior patterns of the larger culture but rather to model oneself on the divine character. And interestingly, such imitation is never seen to violate the distinction between Creator and creature or to lead to a human being's apotheosis. It is the voice of the snake, not of God, that promises, "You shall be as gods." Yet it must be stressed that the primeval story insists that human beings are created in the image of God, created with a capacity for a special relationship with God, and thus in some ways the story of salvation history throughout the Bible is the story of God's efforts to bring about the renewal of that indelible but effaced image. Only so could human beings once more be said to be, as in Psalm 8:5, "a little less than God" (or at least than the angels, depending on how one reads *ʾĕlōhîm* in this verse).

---

of Prophecy (Peabody, Mass.: Hendrickson, 1999). What Arnold, quite rightly, does not say or suggest is that in the Old Testament this conclusion of things is closely or regularly linked to a human messianic figure intervening or returning.

[9]Here the reader will profit from reviewing the critique of Francis Watson's view of such matters and biblical theology in general in Witherington, *Individual Witnesses*, pp. 32-40.

A further feature of the Old Testament thought world that strongly shapes its contours is the notion of covenant. The God of the Bible is a God who cuts covenants with both individuals, such as Noah or Abraham, and also with a whole group of people—a chosen people. Covenants are agreements, and the biblical ones mostly take the form of covenants between suzerain and vassal, not parity treaties. Yahweh dictates the terms in these covenants, and they contain not only stipulations but also sanctions involving blessing and curse. They are ratified by a sacrifice and also have a covenant sign, such as circumcision or even a rainbow. It would be hard to overestimate the importance of covenant in the relationship between God and his people as described in the Old Testament. God made demands, not only ritualistic but also ethical, of his people in a fashion similar to an ancient dowry or betrothal agreement. To fail to live up to the stipulations resulted in the curse sanctions being enacted on God's people.

And this brings up another crucial point. God's people, either individually or collectively, are not immune to judgment. Their chosenness does not exempt them from God's justice; indeed, judgment, according to the Old Testament, begins with the household of God. It is a singular mistake to muddle up the concept of chosenness or election and the concept of salvation. As we have noted, the Old Testament has very little to say about "everlasting life," and when it speaks of "chosenness," it does so not in terms of eternal benefits to particular individuals.

Indeed, chosenness in the Old Testament normally has to do with God picking someone or some group for a specific historical purpose, such as the choice of Cyrus to release God's people from exile in Babylon. But even when the concept is applied collectively to Israel, it normally has the sense that God has chosen this people to be a light to the nations, bearing witness to God's character and demands, and to be a blessing to the nations (e.g., the promises to Abraham). Election, then, has historical purposes in the Old Testament, and little or nothing is said about personal eternal fringe benefits. The corollary of this should be clear: later Christian concepts of election and salvation (especially as blended together into one idea) ought not to be read back into the Old Testament willy nilly. When dealing with the relationship of the Old Testament thought world to the New Testament thought world, one must have a sense of progressive revelation and the progress of a developing understanding of concepts such as election and salvation. Missional election, however, is a concept carried over into the New Testament.

THE NECESSITY OF PROGRESSIVE REVELATION

This brings us to another important, indeed crucial, point. Biblical or canonical theology and ethics, if they are even going to be attempted, should not be done in an ahistorical manner, as if the Bible could be treated flatly as a thesaurus of theological and ethical ideas in which "salvation" in Exodus means exactly the same thing as "saved by grace through faith in Christ" means in Ephesians. If there is no sense of or sensitivity to the way ideas develop over time and concepts are modified and change across the biblical witness, if there is no sense of understanding of progressive revelation, then attempts at biblical or canonical theology and ethics should be forsaken because such attempts will run roughshod over the historical character and givenness of these wonderful texts. Don Carson makes this helpful observation: "Precisely because God's self-disclosure has taken place over time, New Testament theology, as part of the larger discipline of biblical theology, is committed to understanding the constitutive documents within the temporal framework. In this respect, New Testament theology differs widely in emphasis from systematic theology, which tends to ask atemporal questions of the biblical texts, thereby eliciting atemporal answers."[10] But is systematic theology a legitimate exercise? If we denude New Testament theology of its historical givenness, is such an exercise possible without serious distortion and transformation of the New Testament material into something other than it was intended to be and to say?

It is true that the same God is revealed in the Old Testament and the New Testament, but it is not true that God's Old Testament people and New Testament people had the same level of understanding or even the same understanding of that God. This is made quite clear by comparing the Shema with its Christian modification in 1 Corinthians 8:6: Christians refer the term "God" to the Father and the term "Lord" to a different person, Jesus, yet paradoxically, they do not deny the oneness of God. What one could say is that these various witnesses had compatible understandings of God.

As the author of Hebrews reminds us in Hebrews 1:1-2, the revelation was partial and piecemeal in the Old Testament era, but now God has revealed himself fully in his Son. This means that any biblical or canonical theology worth the paper it is written on will have a clear sense of development, of before and after, of partially and more fully revealed, of promise/prophecy and

---

[10]D. A. Carson, "New Testament Theology," in *Dictionary of the Later New Testament and Its Developments*, ed. R. P. Martin and P. H. Davids (Downers Grove, Ill.: InterVarsity Press, 1997), p. 808.

fulfillment, and of typology. In other words, we must have a historical way of thinking about these theological and ethical concepts and their development, and we must conjure with the fact that some things that God revealed to and demanded of his people in one era were either partial or took account of what Jesus calls "the hardness of the human heart." This is what it means to think in a self-consciously Christian manner about the Old Testament, to think christologically and ecclesiologically about it, to think historically about it.

From the Christian point of view, Christ is both the climax of all God's revelation to humankind and the hermeneutical key to understanding all of what has come before, which was only preparatory for the coming of the Christ. This is not to say that God's love for Israel was mere prolegomena for what was to follow. Indeed not. It is to say, however, that God always had in mind to save the world through the Jewish messiah, so God's love for Israel was not the end of the story or an end in itself; rather, it was the means by which Israel could come to fulfill its destiny in the person of Jesus, who would be the light of the world.

If a former Pharisee such as Paul can say of the Mosaic law that it was only a "childminder" *(paidagōgos)* of God's people until Christ came, and when Christ came, God's people reached their majority and moved beyond the childminder or guardian and so on to a new covenant, then we know that it will not suffice either to say that the new covenant is just the old one renewed or to assume that the continuity with what came before is dominant and the new elements in the new covenant are subdominant. The whole discussion about the obsolescence of the Mosaic covenant in Galatians and Hebrews prevents us from overstressing the continuity and underplaying the radical new character of the new covenant in so many ways, both theologically and ethically.

I frankly state that I, as a Christian, assume the truth of the New Testament witness, and I assume also that the hermeneutic of the New Testament writers and their way of viewing and handling the Old Testament constitute the way Christians should attempt to view it today, namely, eschatologically, viewing what has come before in the light of the inbreaking kingdom, the coming of the Messiah and the like. And what that meant was not merely "new occasions teach new duties (and ethics)"; it meant a new understanding of God, reenvisioned in the light of the significance of the Christ-event.

Christ cannot be found under every rock of the Old Testament. Indeed, he cannot be found under many, for there are few messianic texts in the Old

Testament. A generous estimate sees about 5 percent of the Old Testament having to do with messianism, the longing for a future and more perfect ruler for God's people. So when I say that we must read the Old Testament in the light of the Christ-event, what I mean is not that we read Christ back into the Old Testament at various junctures without a clear leading from the Old Testament or New Testament itself (thus, e.g., Christ is not the angel of the Lord, there was no incarnation of Christ before the incarnation), but rather that we have the strong sense that that whole era was preparatory for the coming of the Christ to earth so that "when the time had fully come, God sent forth his Son" (Gal 4:4).[11] We can learn much about the first person of the Trinity from the Old Testament itself, but not much about the second and third persons of the Trinity; those two persons do not come fully to light until and after the Christ-event. This way of studying the Bible not only prevents Christian anachronism; it allows us to read the Old Testament with our Jewish friends with profit and respect for the historical givenness and character of that text. After all, the Old Testament was the Word of God for Jews before it ever became part of the Christian Bible.

When a covenant's stipulations were broken in antiquity (and here we are talking about a suzerain/vassal treaty), then it was entirely up to the ruler to decide what to do next, besides exact the curse sanctions of the original treaty that had to be put into play once the law had been broken. If the ruler decided to relate in a positive way with a people again, then a new covenant would have to be drawn up, and various of the ideas, stipulations, and sanctions of the new covenant could be a repetition to one degree or another of various of the previous ones. For example, honoring parents is affirmed in both the Mosaic law and in the law of Christ (the imperatives that Christ gives). The reason why Christians obey such an imperative is that it is in the new covenant, not that it was once in an old one, as if the old one was still continuing.

When a new covenant is cut, the old one becomes obsolete, if we are talking about the same two parties doing the covenanting. In fact, when the curse sanction of a covenant is enacted, that covenant is over.[12] In the New

---

[11]Similarly, Howard Marshall stresses, "The concept of a *threefoldness* in God is simply not present in the Old Testament" ("The Development of Doctrine," in *Beyond the Bible: Moving from Scripture to Theology*, with Kevin J. Vanhoozer and Stanley E. Porter [Grand Rapids: Baker Academic, 2004], p. 49).

[12]Nowhere does the Old Testament state anything to the effect that the Abrahamic covenant makes the Noachic one obsolete or defunct. However, such a statement was unnecessary because the Noachic covenant was not with the forebear of Israel, Abraham. It was a covenant with Noah and his family and also with the earth. The Abrahamic covenant was the beginning of covenants with

Testament some of the authors seem to see the death of Jesus as absorbing the curse sanction against sin in God's people from the previous covenants and thus as the end of that covenant. In Colossians Paul even calls Jesus' death a "circumcision," associating it with the covenant sign, and Mark, with his rending of the veil of the temple, signals the end of an era of God's presence located in what was becoming, so to speak, the temple of doom. And one more thing: were it the case that election equals eternal salvation in the New Testament, how do we explain the fact that Jesus, the one person whom God did not need to save from fallenness, is the one person viewed as the Elect One in Ephesians and elsewhere in the New Testament? Election and salvation, it turns out, are two different but related concepts in both Testaments, but in no instance should we assume that the former idea simply implies eternal salvation.

A useful line of questioning involves God's sovereignty as depicted in the Old Testament. How does the Old Testament depict the way God exercises that sovereignty? Does the Old Testament suggest either that God so controls everything that nothing contrary to his will ever happens or that everything that does happen is part of his plan? Certainly, the answer to that question must be no. God is not the ultimate author of sin, and the Old Testament nowhere suggests such a view. One test case can be considered by reflecting on how God relates to his own people. There is no more poignant depiction of this than in Hosea 11:1-11:

> When Israel was a child, I loved him, and out of Egypt I called my son. The more I called them, the more they went from me; they kept sacrificing to the Baals, and offering incense to idols. Yet it was I who taught Ephraim to walk, I took them up in my arms; but they did not know that I healed them. I led them with cords of human kindness, with bands of love. I was to them like those who lift infants to their cheeks. I bent down to them and fed them. They shall return to the land of Egypt, and Assyria shall be their king, because they have refused to return to me. The sword rages in their cities, it consumes their oracle-priests, and devours because of their schemes. My people are bent on turning away from me. To the Most High they call, but he does not raise them up at all.
>
> How can I give you up, Ephraim? How can I hand you over, O Israel? How can I make you like Admah? How can I treat you like Zeboiim? My heart

---

those who would come to be called "Hebrews," and the Noachic covenant was not. This is why, for instance, Paul says nothing about the Noachic covenant but must talk about the Abrahamic and Mosaic ones.

recoils within me; my compassion grows warm and tender. I will not execute my fierce anger; I will not again destroy Ephraim; for I am God and no mortal, the Holy One in your midst, and I will not come in wrath. They shall go after the LORD, who roars like a lion; when he roars, his children shall come trembling from the west. They shall come trembling like birds from Egypt, and like doves from the land of Assyria; and I will return them to their homes, says the LORD. (NRSV)

What should we conclude from this poignant prophetic poem? In this poem God is depicted as a parent who calls his children, but they do not automatically or always respond in the way God desires. They continue to behave sinfully over and over again, and with moral consequences as well, such as being overcome by their enemies. But God, like a spurned parent, will not give up on Israel. God keeps calling them from exile and does not express his wrath against Israel's sin. Rather, God roars like a mighty lion, and his cubs finally recognize the sound of his voice and come running back to their parent.

I submit that this reveals a great deal about God's character. It reveals that God, who has the power to simply organize all things and all the behavior of his people in a preordained way, chooses instead to relate to his children in love and by means of love. He calls them back, he does not compel or predetermine them to come back. There is something about a love relationship that could not be predetermined anyway. Love can be freely given and freely received only between personal beings. Love cannot be coerced, compelled or even just predetermined. And Yahweh had decided not to act like some humans would to compel a response or to destroy those who do not respond according to the desired script. The power of contrary choice has been given to God's people, and they do not always respond as they ought to do.

But even more impressively, God has chosen to relate to his people in a loving manner, wooing and winning their response. This picture of God comports with texts such as John 3:16-17, which tells us that God's heart is big, and that he does not desire (and has not predetermined) that anyone should perish. It comports with texts such as 1 Timothy 2:1-6, which tell us that not only did Jesus die as a ransom for all the world, but also God desires that all people come to a knowledge of the truth and be saved. Thus, accordingly, the concepts of election and salvation look different when we understand that this is the character of the gracious biblical God, and that his modus operandi is much as we find it to be in places such Hosea 11:1-11 and 1 Timothy 2:1-6.

This brings us to a crucial point. The Old Testament says very little about the coming messiah, and yet on almost every page of the New Testament Jesus takes center stage. I suggest that there could be no clearer proof that we are not dealing merely with the gestation of religious ideas over time. New Testament theology is not merely a natural development of Old Testament theology, though there is considerable overlap, and the same can be said about the ethics in the New Testament compared to the ethics in the Old Testament.

Something happened in space and time to change the thought world of the early Jews who ended up writing books of the New Testament. That something was the coming of the historical Jesus and the impact that he had on these Jews. To study New Testament theology and ethics and leave Jesus out of the equation or relegate him and his teaching to a presupposition for, or addendum to, New Testament thought is a huge mistake, and I have attempted to avoid that mistake in these volumes.

The person, work, teaching, and impact of Jesus are the chief reasons for the differences between the Old Testament and New Testament thought worlds. Of course, the New Testament writers, so to speak, pick up the Jesus ball and run with it in several different creative directions, but it is Jesus who is the catalyst for all that is going on theologically and ethically in the New Testament. This is why, in my view, it is beyond comprehension that anyone would attempt to examine New Testament theology or ethics and leave Jesus and the Jesus tradition out of consideration or treat it last, as Caird does, as if it had little impact on figures such as Paul, James, and Peter, and as if they were simply doing theologies all on their own after the fact, politely ignoring the teachings and life of their founder. True, it is a challenge to show the relationship between the thought world of Jesus and that of his followers, but it is not impossible, as I have tried to show in this study.

Relating the Old Testament and the New Testament Thought Worlds

Another Venn diagram may help us conceptualize both the relationship and the overlap between the thought worlds of the Old Testament and the New Testament (see fig. 13.1).

This purely symmetrical representation of the relationship is a bit lopsided

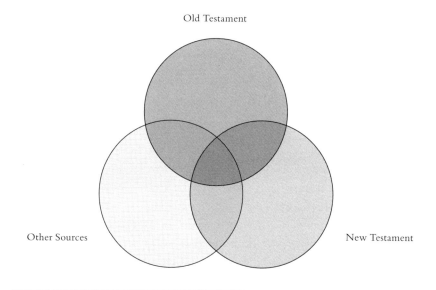

Figure 13.1. Thought World of the Old and New Testaments and Other Sources

if we are talking about the historical realities of the situation. The overlap between the Old Testament and the New Testament thought worlds is greater than the overlap between those of the Old Testament and the ancient Near East or between those of the New Testament and the Greco-Roman milieu, but still we get the picture. The overlap between the Old Testament and the New Testament symbolic universes is considerable, but it does not consist of a majority of the material that we find in the New Testament, precisely because so much of the New Testament is generated out of the Christ-event, which of course affected none of the Old Testament writers.

Or again, the overlap between the Old Testament and the ancient Near Eastern thought worlds is considerable, as is the overlap between those of the New Testament and the Greco-Roman milieu (in both theology and ethics), but it is less than the overlap between the Old Testament and New Testament. What lies at the very center of the diagram, where all the circles intersect? The answer is, of course, the profound concern for both some form of God-talk or religion and some form of ethical norms related to the God-talk. Both the biblical monotheistic culture and the polytheistic culture were profoundly concerned with the divine and its influence on the world of humanity and intensely interested in what sort of behavior and belief satisfied the divine demands on human life. In all of these cultures priests, temples, and sacrifices were at the heart of the divine-human exchange. Christianity offered something new in suggesting that the time had arrived where literal temples and sacrifices, and the priests who attended them, were no longer necessary. God had been propitiated once and for all, and sin had been expiated once and for all, and a people had been delivered once and for all, and this changed the whole concept of religious life and what amounted to true piety.

Furthermore, there would be no more talk of a monarchial succession of kings. Jesus is the final monarch, who would have no successors; he is the Son of Man, who would personally rule forever in a forever kingdom (Dan 7:13-14). And last but not least, there would not be a mere holy land. Christians were not worried at all about a doctrine of the land or a particular holy place, for Christ was coming back to reign over the entire earth. No doctrines of Torah, temple, or territory would be reaffirmed in their original senses in the new covenant, and yet this did not mean that there was an abandonment of the concept of laws and norms, or of temples or priests, or of a reign upon the earth.

What changes is that all these concepts are now processed through the Christ-event and its implications. It will be the law of Christ, the people as his sanctuary/temple/dwelling, and Christ's return to rule the whole earth that will be the transmutation found in the New Testament. What is interesting about this transformation is that it has both spiritual and eschatological dimensions. Clearly enough, it was believed that Jesus would literally come back and literally reign upon the earth, though he would not be rebuilding any temples. The sacred zone would extend throughout the earth, and worship in spirit and truth anywhere would be true worship. Yet also, all believers, male and female, can be said to be already, here and now, enlisted in Christ's new priesthood, and they can indeed offer spiritual sacrifices of self and praise to God, all the while viewing their own bodies and the body of Christ as temples, the places were Christ dwells.

It cannot be emphasized enough that the Christian movement truly was something radical in this regard in the eyes of a Greco-Roman person, for it placed far more emphasis on belief and ethical behavior and far less emphasis on rituals performed correctly as being at the heart of the religion. It also promised far fewer this-worldly benefits and far more afterlife benefits, though most of them involve this world in its final transformed state. Salvation in the New Testament is often spoken of in terms of the final state of affairs, and not merely as some form of current healing, help, rescue, or deliverance, though it could begin with such things, sometimes at conversion. In other words, when the language of "God" and "salvation" changes not merely in an eschatological direction but also in a christological direction, then we are dealing with a profound refocusing of the symbol system.

In 1977 James Dunn wrote an important book entitled *Unity and Diversity in the New Testament: An Inquiry into the Character of Earliest Christianity.*[13] Its essential thesis is that a range of diversity is found within the New Testament canon. This is, of course, true. But what is less well emphasized in Dunn's study is the profound unity that is also shared by the New Testament documents, especially when it comes to Jesus. But one more point of importance is this: the diversity found in the New Testament is not divergence or what might be called "dueling theological banjos." Diversity, yes; differences, yes; radical disagreements and contradictions, no. There is a unity that does not amount to uniformity; it is a unity in harmony, not a monotone unity.

Thus, we do not have one author saying that Jesus is the Son of Man, and another saying that he is not. We do not have one author saying that Jesus is the divine Son of God, and another saying that he is not. We do not have one author saying that the kingdom is breaking in, and others saying that it is not. We do not have one author saying that Gentiles must keep all of the Mosaic law, and another saying that they must not. The degree of diversity is not nearly so great as Dunn wants to make it, and the degree of unity is more profound than he seems to allow. There is a reason for this. The authors of the New Testament are, as we have noted, part of a small minority sect that is well connected and highly networked such that there was a basic agreement on many things in terms of theology and ethics, especially about the gospel and Jesus. There is already manifest in the New Testament a shared proto-orthodoxy about a variety of subjects, not least the importance of Jesus for salvation. We have no Marcionite or Gnostic authors of New Testament books not because of the later orthodoxy of the fourth century, when the canonizing of the New Testament became finalized; rather, it is because there were no such Christian writers or groups in the New Testament era, or if there were, they were treated as false teachers even then (see 1-3 John), and their writings were not shared among the Christian communities. More particularly, there were no apostles or original disciples of Jesus of such persuasions.

In short, we should expect no more diversity within the New Testament

---

[13]A second edition was published in 1990, and a third edition in 2006 (London: SCM Press).

documents than we might find among the community documents at Qumran (by which I mean their original documents, not merely their library books). All of the New Testament is written by Jews who were part of this movement, with the possible exception of Luke, who seems likely to have been a God-fearer, and perhaps the author of 2 Peter. In any case, all of the New Testament books are written from a committed Jewish Christian perspective. The range of opinion on matters of right belief is not great, nor is the range of opinion on most ethical issues. The range of opinion on matters of orthopraxy is somewhat more diverse.

NEW TESTAMENT THEOLOGY AND ETHICS IN LIGHT OF POSTMODERN EPISTEMOLOGY

In a provocative essay Leander Keck suggests that tracing a history of ideas and their development is not really doing theology. He puts it this way:

> NT theology *as theology* cannot be pursued simply by extending, correcting or refining the history of early Christian theologies, even when limited to those in the NT. Rather, NT theology proper is a historically informed theological discipline that asks its own questions and answers them in its own way. Appropriately, the historian of early Christian thought looks for origins (especially the origin of Christology) and sequences, infers influences, and emphasizes differences in order to reconstruct the past; the historically informed NT theologian looks for logical relationships between the ideas generated by root premises in order to grasp the subject matter of the NT. Each discipline has its own integrity and value, each complements the other. . . .
>
> New Testament theology makes explicit the *rationale* of the Gospel (the salvific import of the Jesus-event) and its various expressed logical, moral and communal entailments in the NT as a whole. Moreover, because the theology of the NT is not simply "there" waiting to be exposed like a vein of ore, every statement of NT theology is an interpretive construct by an interpreter who is as historically conditioned as the texts.[14]

It is interesting that in fact Rudolf Bultmann critiqued the *religions-geschichtliche* ("history of religions") approach a long time ago. He said that the great mistake of the *religionsgeschichtliche* school of thought, and indeed of historical criticism in his day, was "tearing apart the act of thinking from the act of living and hence . . . [there was] a failure to recognize the intent of

---

[14]Leander E. Keck, "Paul in New Testament Theology: Some Preliminary Remarks," in Rowland and Tuckett, eds., *Nature of New Testament Theology*, p. 110.

theological utterances."[15] It is not that often that I find myself agreeing with Bultmann, but he is absolutely right that it is a mistake to divide history and social context on the one hand from theology and ethics on the other. This is why I have insisted on identifying what is happening in the New Testament as theologizing and ethicizing into particular historical contexts, speaking in particular ways. The incarnational nature of the expressions and thoughts must not be avoided or ignored. When Paul says, "If Christ is not raised, your faith is futile, and you are still in your sins" (1 Cor 15:17), it is perfectly clear that he believes that historical events are what generate much of the gospel theology, and properly interpreting those events is in fact what theologizing is all about.

If Keck were right, then only a minority of the material in the two volumes of the present work could be said to involve the task of doing New Testament theology. Even when I have compared and synthesized data in this study, showing harmonic convergences and the like, what I have not done is a task that I would think belongs to a systematic theologian, not a New Testament theologian, namely, making explicit the rationale of the gospel or, for that matter, comparing concepts such as the virginal conception and the incarnation and asking about their relationship to each other. I did not look for logical relationships between such ideas, though certainly I am interested in the ideas themselves.

New Testament theology, as described by Keck, is not a matter of pursuing the historical task of simply presenting the various theologizing efforts in the New Testament texts. It is an after-the-fact, indeed an after-the-canonical-fact, enterprise that the New Testament writers did not and could not have undertaken in their own day because, of course, they did not have a New Testament staring them in the face. The present study has been an examination of the theologizing and ethicizing *in the texts*, with some comparing and contrasting. I have not engaged in *doing* a theology of the New Testament texts collectively after the fact and trying to figure out rationales, logic and the like. Furthermore, there is a difference between showing the compatibility or convergences between discrete witnesses and creating a whole called "New Testament theology" out of all the witnesses. The latter is always an after-the-fact product and perhaps will most reflect the emphases and tendencies of the compiler and synthesizer of the project, at least more so than an attempt to allow the various New Testament writers to speak for themselves. There is

---

[15]Rudolf Bultmann, *Theology of the New Testament*, vol. 2 (New York: Scribner), pp. 250-51.

nothing wrong with such an enterprise, but what I have done in the present study should be seen as the sort of prerequisite before undertaking it.

Reader-Response Theory and the Meaning of the New Testament Texts

This brings us to some concluding thoughts about language theory.[16] One effect of reader-response criticism and the radical epistemology and hermeneutics that often undergird it is that it is perfectly possible to sever the nexus between what a text meant then and what it means now and never feel the pain. What happens is that "the meaning of the text today," say, a theological or ethical meaning, becomes something that the text could not possibly have meant in its original historical setting, and this is not seen as a problem. A meaning is read into the text with impunity because it is assumed that "meaning is in the eye of the beholder."

As we saw earlier, Philip Esler is quite right to criticize the fallacy of overplaying the notion of "intentional fallacy,"[17] and I stress that it is deadly to the enterprise of doing New Testament theology or ethics or of theology or ethics on the basis of the New Testament. Those who no longer much care what the original authors had in mind and meant in their original historical settings are simply using the New Testament as a springboard for their own ideas. With such an ahistorical approach and set of presuppositions, there is no control over the ways the Bible can be used, and the result is often a sort of strip mining of the text to serve all sorts of modern agendas and notions.

And here too is where a high view of the revelatory character of Scripture ought to play a role. If you believe that the Bible is the living Word of God and is, as such, something that a believer should submit to the authority of, and if you believe that it was possible for God to clearly and faithfully reveal his truth through the writers of the New Testament in those ancient languages and cultures, then surely you cannot place yourself as a creator or interpreter of meaning on the same plane with the writers of the New Testament, much less assume that what they originally said and meant is somehow irrelevant to your quest to find your own personal meaning in these texts for yourself. Surely, it ought to be a matter of conforming one's own thoughts and ideas to the normative ones found in the text of Scripture itself, and this necessarily

---

[16]On this matter, see pp. 53-57 in the prolegomena above.
[17]On which, see pp. 13-28 above.

implies that the text has a latent and inherent meaning that is making a claim on us. Perhaps part of the problem is that when New Testament theology is severed from New Testament ethics, then the voice of the ethical claims of the text on us, which ought to guide our conduct as Christian interpreters, is muted if not completely silenced.

I stress the dictum "What the text meant then is still what it means today," though certainly it may have various different significances and applications for us than it had for the original writers and hearers. It is not our job to tell the text what it does or ought to mean today. It is our job to listen, learn, and apply God's truth to our lives with as little intrusion as possible from our own modern and nonbiblical assumptions and concepts and with no intrusion from antibiblical ideas and concepts, such as some of the Gnostic ones. All of this implies that the careful historical study of the text in its original contexts is not merely a necessary prerequisite to understanding the theologizing and ethicizing of the New Testament writers. It must be part and parcel of making sense of the New Testament text and then doing theologizing or ethicizing in dependency on the spirit of that text.

On various of these matters I have discovered that G. B. Caird said, some time ago and in much better prose, some of the things that I have been trying to say in the last few paragraphs, so it will be useful to let him speak for himself:

> If God speaks through the writers of Scripture, He speaks not only through their lips but through their minds. He does not indulge in double-talk, allowing Isaiah or Paul to mean one thing by what they say, while He Himself means another. If there is anything that distinguishes Christianity from all other religions and philosophies it is this: Christianity in the first instance is neither a set of doctrines nor a way of life, but a gospel; *and a gospel means news about historical events, attested by reliable witnesses, and having at its centre a historical person.* Whenever Christians have attempted to give to the scriptures a sense other than the plain sense intended by those who wrote them, Christianity has been in danger of running out into the sands of Gnosticism. And the danger is at its greatest when dogma or philosophical presuppositions are allowed to take control of exegesis.
>
> One example may be given. In recent years theologians have been much tempted to welcome the attempts by literary critics and structuralists to persuade us that a text, once launched into the world, attains an existence of its own and can accumulate new meanings which are quite independent of the original intention of the author. Every verse of Scripture must yield some sense acceptable to the reader. For many this is the hope of the future. But against all

such Gadarene precipitations into the Dark Ages it must be asserted that such critics, whether they are studying a literary masterpiece or a book of the Bible, ought to be aware that *perhaps they are in touch with a creative mind considerably more profound and percipient than their own.* What right have they to assume that the glimpses of meaning which have occurred to them were hidden from the author? . . . Only in so far as we are able to suppress our temptations to intellectual and spiritual superiority are we likely to be able to listen accurately to what [a biblical writer] has to say.

Language is in essence a medium of communication. *If the hearer takes words in a sense not intended by the speaker, that is not an enlargement of meaning but a breakdown of communication.* This claim applies to all uses of language, but it is especially apposite where a claim of revelation is involved. Certainly anyone, when reading a text of Scripture, may have a bright idea which is independent of the author's intention, but which comes upon the reader with all the force and persuasiveness of revealed truth. *But when that happens it is the reader's idea, not the meaning of what he or she was reading; and any authority which we may attach to the text is irrelevant to the question of the truth or validity of the reader's idea.*[18]

To this I am inclined to simply add a hearty "Amen!" Interpreting the New Testament is not like taking a Rorschach test, where one is looking at an ink blot in the hope that some form or meaning will emerge. Were the Bible like that, it would not be like looking at a revelation at all; it would be like frantically peering into a dark cloud of unknowing.

Perhaps in the end the whole problem has to do with looking without first listening. It was Jesus who urged, "Let those with two good ears hear." Listening and learning require silence, the stilling of the active mind, concentration, and allowing the speaker to have his or her say before pondering the meaning of it. Listening and learning do not, in the first instance, require looking intently into texts with one's own modern predilections, prejudices and presuppositions firmly in place and thus clearly in the way of hearing someone else's point of view, especially an ancient one.

If the Bible is, as I believe, the living Word of God, then when we conjure with the meaning of this text, we are not merely in touch with the writings of a bunch of long-dead saints with whom we may still have some *koinōnia,* by which I mean communion or sharing in common. We are in touch with the

---

[18]G. B. Caird, *New Testament Theology,* compl. and ed. L. D. Hurst (Oxford: Oxford University Press, 1994), pp. 422-23 (second, third, and fourth of italics mine). For me there is a certain irony and poignancy to quoting Caird, as originally I was accepted to go and work with him at Oxford, but I got a better offer at Durham and studied with C. K. Barrett and C. E. B. Cranfield. I have often wondered how I would have viewed New Testament theology had I studied with Caird.

very mind of the living God, who in fact is still around to define and defend the meaning of the text by means of his Holy Spirit, who not incidentally is said to lead the believer into all truth (Jn 16:13). Between listening intently to the text and listening to the still small voice of the Spirit, who is still speaking to the churches, there is a better than average chance of hearing at least some of the meaning of the text. And what we may well hear in the first instance is "What I said is still what I am saying, and what I meant is still what I mean." There is a reason for this. God in Christ told the truth in the first place, and it requires no improvements. What it requires, then, is the recognition that historical study is the incarnational door into theological and ethical understanding. What it requires is learning and applying the truth to our own lives, and in that context doing theology and ethics on the basis of those still potent biblical witnesses. What it requires is not only a spirit of inquiry and curiosity but also a posture of submission. And if we can manage to do that, we may hope to hear the final approbation "Well done, good and faithful servant, inherit the kingdom."

A fine theologian at St. Andrews, Trevor Hart, helps us to see how in our encounter with the Word we can be taken up into the grand narrative of redemption and allow our own story to be decisively shaped by that narrative:

> It is precisely here that moral conviction of the truth of this story, and hence its authority, is rooted. God speaks. He convinces us that things between himself and the human race are in reality much as they are in the [biblical] story. We are drawn into the world of the text precisely as we are drawn into a relationship with its central character. As this happens, we find ourselves confronted by many of the same realities and experiences as are narrated in the text. Suddenly sin, grace, reconciliation, the power of God's Spirit, the risen Christ and so on are not mere elements in a narrative world, but constituent parts of our own world, players and factors to be taken into consideration in our daily living and in our attempts to make sense of our own situation.[19]

Moving Beyond the Bible to Later Theological Formulations

This brings us to another and rather daunting topic. What about going beyond the Bible? What about the incomplete ideas in the New Testament canon that point us beyond themselves? This question will always be raised somewhat tentatively by those who have taken seriously the Reformation notion of *sola scriptura*. But even the strongest advocates of that position agreed

---

[19]Trevor A. Hart, *Faith Thinking: The Dynamics of Christian Theology* (Downers Grove, Ill.: InterVarsity Press, 1995), pp. 161-62.

in the end that this notion allowed for the spinning out of the logical implications of nodal ideas in the New Testament and the pursuing of trajectories already embarked upon in the New Testament. And this enterprise, in my view, must be undertaken. A few examples must suffice.

There is no full-blown doctrine of the Trinity worked out in the New Testament itself. The ideas are there in numerous places (in a variety of witnesses Jesus is identified as God; in Hebrews the Spirit and Christ, like the Father, are said to speak as God; various doxologies, baptismal formulae and brief credos are trinitarian in character), but the full spelling out of the idea of the Trinity is not to be found in the New Testament. However, so important is the idea of God to the symbol system inaugurated in the New Testament era that it seems not only inevitable but also required that more be said. Of course, this "more" needs to comport with what actually is said or implied in the biblical text. And sometimes that did not happen.

In the Nicean and Chalcedonian formulae much of worth is hammered out, but also, unfortunately, there was the importation of ideas from Greek philosophy that needed more scrutiny than they received—for example, the ideas of immutability and impassability. It must be remembered that the Council of Nicea took place before there was a canon of the New Testament, and so the ideas in that creed were not normed at the time by the measuring rod of the New Testament. For example, a closer examination of what the New Testament means by statements such as "Jesus Christ is the same yesterday, today, and forever" (Heb 13:8) could have helped those discussions.

The New Testament does not affirm that no change happened to God at the juncture of the incarnation. It affirms that a human nature was added to the divine nature of the preexistent Son of God. This certainly is not a negligible change. Indeed, it is so important that one could say that there was no Jesus (the name of a human being) before the incarnation, though of course the Son of God existed before then. As it applies to God in the New Testament, "immutability" simply means that God's character is constant and does not change and thus is reliable. This is the sense of the statement "Jesus Christ is the same yesterday, today, and forever" in Hebrews 13:8. And as for "impassability," something similar can be said. The God of the Bible does have emotions, and they do vary from time to time. The God of the Bible is not the God of Stoicism, though I would hasten to add that the New Testament does not suggest that God has "irrational passions" or is controlled by some sort of merely emotive state. Nevertheless, the love and righteous anger of the biblical God must be accounted for, and a strict notion of impassability does not help in such an endeavor.

A second example has to do with what the New Testament says about men and women in the order of redemption, which is not viewed as simply a perfecting of the flaws incurred from the fall. It is clear enough in the "household code" texts in the New Testament that Paul and Peter, and presumably other New Testament writers, were pursuing a trajectory of change in the way women were viewed and treated, change from the dominant patriarchal system that was in place everywhere. The theologizing about the headship of the husband in 1 Corinthians 11 and the household codes was intended not to assert the husband's authority against liberationist tendencies but rather to restrict and Christianize the use of that already existing system of authority in relationship to all the subordinate members of the household, including wives.

This is especially clear in 1 Corinthians 11, where Paul's elaborate argument has the function of authorizing women to pray and prophesy in worship as long as the "head" issue is properly addressed. As I pointed out earlier, the failure to recognize the levels of ethical discourse especially in Paul's letters has led to all sorts of erroneous conclusions about his views on both women and slaves. The letter to Philemon shows clearly that the Pauline logic is heading toward the liberation of slaves, for the very good reason that once someone becomes a Christian brother (or sister), that person should no longer be viewed or treated by other Christians as a slave.

Similarly, Ephesians 5:21 quite deliberately goes beyond what we find in Colossians 3–4 by urging mutual submission of all Christians to each other. In that context, the submission of wives to husbands and the self-sacrificial love of wives by husbands simply illustrate the broader principle enunciated in Ephesians 5:21, a principle that is not gender specific. In short, it is not enough to assess the position of Paul's remarks, for we must also take into account the direction of the remarks, which is countercultural and goes against the flow of the patriarchal worldview that was regnant in those ancient cultures.

A third example is the most obvious one, but it must be hiding in plain sight because many theologians never refer to it. It is impossible to talk about New Testament theology or ethics at all without a clearly delineated concept of the New Testament and its limits. This means that although we can begin to see the preservation of sacred apostolic texts and the first steps of the canonizing process during the New Testament era, we apparently do not have such a defined collection in that era itself. The motto *sola scriptura* presupposes a canon, but that in turn requires that one allow the apostolic developments to play out to their conclusion well beyond the apostolic era.

Likewise, it is impossible to talk about a doctrine of Holy Scripture without a canon, but that too requires that we take into account the historical processes set in motion in the New Testament but not coming to a climax until several centuries later. In other words, not only are the lines between sacred tradition and Scripture rather fuzzy during the period of the first through fourth centuries A.D. (not least because what counted as apostolic and authoritative was still being debated in this period), but also the doctrine of the inspiration and authority and truth claims of those sources had yet to be fully fleshed out—although, as I have argued at length elsewhere, we do have New Testament texts that begin to discuss the matter.[20] In other words, development beyond the teachings in the books written in the New Testament era was not merely inevitable, it was necessary.

This means in turn that any sort of *sola scriptura* doctrine that does not take into account the trajectories of change and development already set in motion in books written by New Testament authors is ignoring or resisting the meaning and direction of the remarks in the texts of what was to become the New Testament. This being the case, evangelicals would do well to tone down the rhetoric about how the Bible is the final authority for Protestants while tradition seems to be the final authority for Catholics. Both must reckon with some combination of Scripture and tradition, and they do so de facto anyway.

The question then becomes "Is there enough guidance and provision of examples in the New Testament books to help us to know what orthodoxy and orthopraxy ought to look like?" My answer to this question is yes. There is already a concept, call it "proto-orthodoxy" or "proto-orthopraxy," that is in play and defining boundaries in the New Testament era before there is a New Testament canon. Orthodoxy neither waited for nor was initially dependent on the existence of a New Testament canon to define and defend itself. Indeed, christological orthodoxy in an apostolic vein was hammered out before the closing of the New Testament canon. There was a *regula fidei* before there was a *regula canona*.

And this brings us to another critical point. The final authority at councils such as Nicea lay with the logical outworkings of apostolic truth, in this case mainly about Jesus. It was the job of the council to articulate and make

---

[20]See Ben Witherington III, *The Living Word of God: Rethinking the Theology of the Bible* (Waco, Tex.: Baylor University Press, 2008).

plain what the apostles had in mind.[21] The genuine apostolic witness had authority because it told the truth about Jesus. It did not, in the first instance, have authority because it was found in an authorized collection of books or because it came from what one group or another deemed the proper church. Neither the canon nor the church was the final authority; the true apostolic witness that led to the formation of them both played that role. Put another way, the buck stopped with the gospel. It had the final authority over church and council and creed alike, and it led to the recognition, not the formation, of the New Testament canon, a process of discerning what preserved the original and true apostolic witness and what did not.

In a recent helpful study entitled *Beyond the Bible*, Howard Marshall, in dialogue with Kevin Vanhoozer and Stanley Porter, discusses at length the issue named in the book's title.[22] I will dialogue with them in the following paragraphs. Early on in the study Marshall raises the issue of what I will call "the ethical basis of New Testament theology"—that is, the necessity of truth-telling in order for a text to have authority over its audience. He puts it this way: "What makes the Bible different from other books for us, of course, is that it is *Scripture*, which signifies (among other things) that it possesses authority over its readers, *speaking in the language of truth and command.*"[23]

The authority of the text comes from its truth-telling about the nature of reality, what is the case about reality, and also what it means and signifies. Marshall stresses in addition that the apostles claimed an authority for what they said and also wrote, not just for the specific audience for whom they spoke and wrote and for the specific occasion into which they spoke and wrote, but more widely. He suggests that at least some of them, such as Paul or Luke, seem to have been clearly conscious of producing something akin to Scripture. I would put the matter a bit differently: they were cognizant of producing the living Word of God, which in due course was to become canonical Scripture. This is quite clear in a text such as 1 Corinthians 7, where Paul not only says that he is passing on a mandate that is a mandate "in all the churches" (1 Cor 7:17 [all his churches?]) but also stresses that he has the Spirit of God and is speaking God's Word on this subject (1 Cor 7:40 [cf. 1 Cor 14:37]).

---

[21]See the fascinating study by Ramsay MacMullen, *Voting about God in Early Church Councils* (New Haven: Yale University Press, 2006).

[22]I. Howard Marshall, with Kevin J. Vanhoozer and Stanley E. Porter, *Beyond the Bible: Moving from Scripture to Theology* (Grand Rapids: Baker Academic, 2004).

[23]Ibid., p. 13 (second italics mine); see also especially p. 14 n. 6.

As I have stressed in another study, the concept of inspiration and authority is not something applied to the texts after the fact because they are canonical; rather, they become part of the Bible because they are inspired and are telling the truth about something. Marshall goes on to plead that it is especially incumbent on those who have a high view of Scripture, such as evangelicals, to provide some kind of reasoned, careful, principled approach to the development of doctrine from, but going beyond, Scripture.[24] He then adds that he has looked in vain to find such an approach. Each person seems to do, as the book of Judges might have put it, "what is right in his own eyes." We perhaps could point to the Catholic magesterium as an example of how such a thing could be done in a disciplined way, but there is no Protestant equivalent to that group, and even if evangelicals formed such a group, it is extremely unlikely that it would ever be allowed to have any sort of authority over various Protestant denominations in regard to doctrine or ethics.

Marshall then suggests that we can look to the New Testament itself for guidelines as to how doctrine can and should be developed out of and going beyond the New Testament itself. For example, he points to what happens to the Jesus tradition in the Fourth Gospel, which he agrees is a faithful representation of what Jesus really meant and taught but is written up freely in the evangelist's own distinctive manner.[25] This suggests some freedom in regard to the form of the way biblical truth is conveyed, though care must be taken in regard to the substance of that truth lest the new form distort, misrepresent, or betray the original content.

Marshall then asks what happens to the process of the development of doctrine and praxis initiated in the New Testament books themselves once there is a canon, a measuring rod, in place. "Here, an important distinction must be made between the production of further Scriptures, which is ruled out by the creation of a canon as a closed list, and the development of doctrine and practice on the basis of those canonical writings. *The closing of the canon is not incompatible with the non-closing of the interpretation of that canon.*"[26] I agree with this in principle. However, I want to stress that although the need for further interpretation of the text is always there, interpretation and the development of doctrine or praxis are not the same thing.

Marshall then proceeds to helpfully suggest that the development of doc-

---

[24]Ibid., p. 45.
[25]Ibid., p. 51.
[26]Ibid., p. 54.

trine and praxis beyond the canon requires three things: (1) a clear and profound grasp of the apostolic deposit and its meaning; (2) a mind so nurtured on Scripture and in Christ that one thinks in ways that are naturally coherent with what Scripture teaches; (3) a regular seeking of and listening to the guidance of the Spirit (and of God in general) and submission to it.[27] Marshall suggests that it is precisely these three things that we find working in the lives of the New Testament authors themselves, and presumably we would require the same sort of things to be in place if we are to faithfully develop doctrine and praxis.

Marshall rightly sees getting Christology right as perhaps the most essential part of the discernment process. He proposes three principles of guidance for interpretation and then draws seven conclusions. The principles are these: (1) the early Christian reading of the Old Testament took place in light of the new covenant inaugurated by Jesus, and so Christians ever since should be reading the Old Testament in a similar way; (2) the teaching of Jesus must be understood in light of his death and resurrection and of the later apostolic teaching; (3) the teachings of the apostles took place on the basis of a combination of interpreting the Word (in light of the Christ-event) and on the basis of insights given by the Spirit.[28]

The seven points that Marshall believes he has established are these: (1) The later documents (in the canon) need not necessarily be more mature than the earlier ones, even though in general there is a development in doctrine throughout the Bible that leads to greater diversity and maturity of expression. For example, the high Christology in Paul's writings is early, whereas some of the post-Pauline writings do not reflect as high a Christology (e.g., Luke-Acts). (2) There is an incompleteness in Scripture, seen in, for example, its lack of dealing with later questions (e.g., modes and recipients of baptism), which means that doctrine can and must develop beyond Scripture. (3) We need to have a concept of both progressive revelation and the totality of revelation so that the meaning of texts will be seen in light of the larger context, and particularly the earlier texts must be read in light of the later ones in the New Testament. (4) Nevertheless, there is a continuity throughout the process because the God of the Old Testament is the same as the God of the New Testament, and the teaching of Jesus stands in continuity with both Old Testament teaching and the later apostolic teachings. (5) The development is controlled (and in fact prompted) by the shift from the

---

[27]Ibid., p. 71.
[28]Ibid., p. 77.

old covenant to the new covenant, and from the limnal period during Jesus' ministry to the period of the early church, and by the facing of new situations and new errors. (6) Development in doctrine and praxis is inevitable after the closing of the canon and must be in continuity with the faith once given to God's people and be in accord with "the mind of Christ." (7) We must continue to affirm the supreme authority of Scripture while recognizing that Scripture continually needs fresh interpretation and application.[29] There is much to commend in all these conclusions, and I find myself in fundamental agreement with them.

In his response to what he humorously calls "the Marshall plan," Kevin Vanhoozer makes various helpful suggestions and critiques. First, Vanhoozer stresses that the quest for meaning precedes the assessment of a statement's truth. "One cannot make a judgment as to a text's truth until one has first determined what it is saying/claiming."[30] This is precisely why he stresses that understanding the genre of Scripture is crucial to determining its meaning and thus to assessing its truth content. In addition, he sees as helpful Marshall's intuition to look for principles of development within Scripture as a basis or model for doing the development of theology and praxis beyond Scripture. In my view, Vanhoozer is right in calling into question a loose use of the phrase "going beyond" Scripture. What exactly does this phrase mean? "More than" need not mean "other than," and a change of wording does not necessarily connote a value added to a nodal concept in Scripture. How do we go beyond Scripture without going against it? Some will cautiously say that we should be able to make explicit what is implicit in Scripture. This amounts to little more than clarification of what is said or implied in Scripture. Few would object to this concept of going beyond Scripture.

But then Vanhoozer takes up the issue of pursuing redemptive trajectories thought to be found in Scripture and pursuing them beyond the bounds that Scripture takes such trajectories. He rightly queries whether we have the right to assume that we are further down the track along the trajectory and hence can see better where it was going than the biblical writers did. "Can one decide what counts as redemptive movement without pretending to stand at the end of the process, without claiming to know what kind of

[29]Ibid., pp. 78-79.
[30]Kevin J. Vanhoozer, "Into the Great 'Beyond': A Theologian's Response to the Marshall Plan," in Marshall, *Beyond the Bible*, p. 83.

eschatological world the Spirit is creating?"[31] Recognizing that Vanhoozer has put his finger on a potential problem, I still suggest that if there are clear intimations or statements in Scripture itself as to where things ought to go in a best-case scenario, then we have an obligation to do our best to see them through to that end. Two examples must suffice.

There are plenty of Pauline texts, such as Galatians 3:28; Ephesians 5:21; 1 Corinthians 7; 11, in which it becomes readily apparently that Paul is pushing the envelope in regard to balancing or equalizing relationships between males and females in Christ while affirming the reality and goodness of gender differences. There is also a text such as Philemon, which provides a serious critique of the institution of slavery within the context of the Christian community. What do we make of these sorts of texts, which clearly go beyond other New Testament texts such as the household codes in Colossians 3–4?

Some degree of sophistication about recognizing levels of moral discourse needs to be developed. Colossians is Paul's opening salvo with an audience that he did not convert, and in this regard it is rather like Romans. Ephesians is second-order moral discourse written to some of the same audience in the same region as an encyclical and taking certain things in the Colossian household code a step further. Philemon is third-order moral discourse, a discussion between friends or intimates, and it pushes the envelope in regard to slavery even further. If there is clear evidence of a trajectory within the canon itself, then it should be evident that Paul, in this case, would be best pleased if we followed this trajectory to its logical conclusions. The trajectory of discussion within Scripture norms and guides how to pursue the trajectory beyond Scripture. Indeed, I maintain that the evidence of a trajectory within Scripture requires that we pursue the implications of the fullest or furthest developments of the concepts and praxis that we find there.[32]

Vanhoozer goes on to argue,

> Doctrine directs the church to speak and act in new situations (e.g., "beyond the Bible") biblically by cultivating what I will call "the mind of the canon." That to which theologians must attend in Scripture is not the words and concepts so much as the *patterns of judgment*. Christian doctrine describes a pattern of judgment present in the biblical texts. . . . *The same judgment can be rendered in a variety of conceptual terms.* . . .

---

[31]Ibid., p. 91.

[32]See Ben Witherington III, *The Letters to Philemon, the Colossians, and the Ephesians: A Socio-Rhetorical Commentary on the Captivity Epistles* (Grand Rapids: Eerdmans, 2007).

We move from Bible to doctrine not by systematizing Scripture's concepts, nor by extracting (e.g., decontextualizing) principles, but rather by discerning and continuing a pattern of judgment rendered in a variety of linguistic, literary, and conceptual forms.[33]

This is very helpful, but when Vanhoozer turns around and says that what is predicated about Christ in the Nicean formula is the same as what is predicated of Christ in Philippians 2:5-11, I am puzzled. No, Nicea goes well beyond and, perhaps in some limited respects, against the conception of Christ in that Christ hymn. That Vanhoozer does not see this is disturbing. I would like to have heard more from him on his concepts of covenant, progressive revelation and canonical Christ-centered interpretation, but that is a conversation for another day. What is said here is meant only to further the ongoing discussion, not to draw definitive conclusions.

Where, then, does this leave us in the discussion of the relationship of New Testament theology and ethics to those found in patristic sources, to the later canonical and biblical theology of various sorts, and finally to much later systematic theology ranging from Aquinas to Barth and beyond? My answer is that New Testament theology and ethics should take pride of place in evaluating the validity of all subsequent theologizing and ethicizing of whatever sort. Stated negatively, the New Testament must be allowed to dictate the proper terms of the discussion about apostolic truth, not some later theological construct or category. This is why I have resisted using systematic categories (justification, sanctification, etc.) to group the data in this study.

The categories for the discussion of the New Testament data should, if at all possible, arise from the texts of the New Testament themselves, and later theological systems, be they Protestant or Catholic, need to be constantly checked against and normed by the apostolic witness. The later systems should not be allowed to define what orthodoxy or orthopraxy must look like and how we must approach the New Testament. Instead, such systems must be put through the refiner's fire of the apostolic witness found in the New Testament over and over again. If their substance cannot be either found in the New Testament documents or be shown to be a clear and logical development thereof, so much the worse for their substance. If even the earliest creeds should be constantly checked against the New Testament witnesses, all the more so should later confessions (Westminster, Augsburg, Trent, Dordt),

---

[33]Vanhoozer, "Into the Great 'Beyond,'" p. 93.

however noble in diction and character.

Confessions, for good or ill, seem often to major in ideas or at least feature as distinctive ideas things that can be debated as to whether or not one can even find them in the Bible. Here are several examples: (1) not merely the fallenness of all human beings, but their "total depravity" outside the saving grace of Christ; (2) the predetermination by God of some to be lost for all eternity, come what may, do what they will; (3) the "perfection" of the Christian in this lifetime and prior to the return of Christ; (4) the perpetual virginity of Mary. We could name many others.

If we use these sorts of distinctive ideas as a grid through which to read the New Testament and by which to determine what is orthodoxy or orthopraxy, much less who is a true Christian and who is not, we are clearly a long way from the substance and the spirit of the New Testament witnesses themselves, who wanted us to focus on Christ, him crucified and raised, and the salvation message to be spread abroad to the world. I do not say that confessions are inherently a bad thing. I do say that they need to be far better grounded in the substance of the New Testament itself than they have been heretofore.

It was the great merit of Karl Barth's work that he truly and profoundly wrestled with the details in the New Testament text in order to come to exegetical and theological and ethical conclusions.[34] Any Christian systematic theology ought to do so. But herein lies the problem: few systematicians are also able exegetes of the New Testament (and the converse is true). Who is sufficient for such a cross-disciplinary task? And perhaps equally problematic, systematicians are, generally speaking, not historians either. They have difficulties dealing with the historical givenness of the New Testament texts without reducing them to a pile of doctrines, principles, propositions or the like.

Alas, the same could be said of many biblical theologians who, in order to synthesize the necessary data, reduce it to ahistorical categories time and again. And then we have the further problems with canonical theologians who want to treat the Old Testament in such an ahistorical manner that it becomes a sort of second Christian source of information about Christ and other subjects that are actually not much, or not directly, addressed before the

---

[34]James Mead quotes Barth as saying that while we need to give close consideration to the "differences between then and now, there and here" when we interpret the Bible, in the end such "investigation can only be to demonstrate that these differences are, in fact, purely trivial" (*Biblical Theology: Issues, Methods, and Themes* [Louisville: Westminster John Knox, 2007], p. 258 n. 151). Really?

New Testament period itself. How do we remedy these problems?

My suggestion, though it may seem overly simplistic, is the best one I know of. Exegetes and systematicians and canonical and biblical theologians need to do a better job of spending time together, talking to each other, and even working together on scholarly projects. Can it be done? In fact it can, as has been demonstrated, with interesting results, by recent conferences at St. Andrews University in which both exegetes and theologians were invited to study John and Hebrews. We live in an age of overspecialization, which results in scholars being rather lopsided, with overdeveloped skills and knowledge in their own fields and underdeveloped understanding of other disciplines and the relationship of New Testament studies to them. We have miles to go before we understand each other, never mind miles to go before we can truly work together on understanding Christian orthodoxy and orthopraxy.

The Unity of the New Testament

In *The Problem with Evangelical Theology* one of the main points I stressed repeatedly is that the problem with evangelical theologies of various sorts is, paradoxically enough, that they are not biblical enough, and even more to the point, they become unbiblical at the precise junctures where they try to say something distinctive from the things that all orthodox Christians basically agree on.

For example, the theologies of predetermination and perfection do have a claim to some basis in the New Testament text, but upon further review, it turns out that the biblical texts mean something other than what Calvinists and Arminians thought. The New Testament does not talk about fully "perfected" sinless Christians short of the resurrection and full conformity to the image of Christ, nor does it talk about certain individuals being predetermined to be saved in the first place. Furthermore, the concept of election in and of Christ in the New Testament cuts against all sorts of individualistic readings of the language of election and salvation. Christ is the Elect One, who needed no saving, and we are elect and saved insofar as we are in Christ. This does not explain how one gets "into Christ" in the first place, which is usually said to be "by grace through faith."

Or again, the distinctive idea of the rapture in dispensational theology turns out to be an exaggeration based on what 1 Thessalonians 4:13-18 does say: the dead in Christ will rise to meet and greet the Lord in the air when as he comes to rule the earth for good and all. However, meeting the Lord in the air does not equal rapture into heaven during a tribulation. Indeed, there is no text in the New Testament that has that sort of escape clause. Even the "left behind" texts in Matthew 24:40–41 and elsewhere make clear that being "taken away" refers to being taken away for judgment, as in the Noachic flood, whereas being "left behind" when the judgment comes is a consummation devoutly to be wished. And against all forms of Protestant "eternal security" arguments stands the apostasy texts found throughout the New Testament, in sources as diverse as 1 John, Hebrews, and the Pastoral Letters.

Then we have the problem with pentecostal views because Acts 2:1-13 has nothing to do with glossolalia or a second definitive work of grace in the believer called the "baptism of the Spirit." And the discussion in 1 Corinthians 12 absolutely rules out the notion that the gift of speaking in tongues is the required initial evidence that a person is filled with the Spirit. Indeed, one could even say that the very notion of getting more of the Spirit over time (as if the Spirit could be quantified and then doled out in portions) results from a defective way of looking at the Spirit as some sort of power or force rather than as a whole person. One can no more have a little bit of the Spirit in one's life than one can be a little bit pregnant (cf. Jn 3:34). When the Spirit comes into a person's life, it is the Spirit as a whole person who comes in, not just the power of the Spirit. I could go on in this vein, but what I am pointing out is that the distinctives of evangelical theology are no more immune to criticism on the basis of the biblical text than are the distinctives of Catholic or Orthodox theology. These are the things that divide us, and as it turns out, they are the least biblical parts of our own thought worlds.

In short, the New Testament is innocent of our later theological agendas and buzzwords and categories, whether we think of patristic theology or Thomist theology or Lutheran theology or Calvinist theology or Wesleyan theology or dispensational theology or pentecostal theology. Perhaps it is time for each of us to be more self-critical of our own theological distinctives and ask what the New Testament truly suggests that makes us uncomfortable when it comes to those ideas. Here is a rule of thumb: do not resort to exegetical gymnastics to explain a text or whittle off the hard edges of the texts that make you squirm when it comes to your own theological distinctives. It may be precisely those texts that you most need to hear and heed and to conform your theology to. That warning I give to myself first of all.

Let us then for a moment, instead of reading the New Testament through the lens of later theologies and ethical agendas, evangelical or otherwise, ask what is it that unifies New Testament theology and ethics and binds the New Testament together. For those who have followed the discussion this far, it will come as no surprise when I say that the unifier is Christ—his person, work, and words. This unifies not only the theologies within the New Testament but also the ethics within the New Testament. Not the theme of God's sovereignty and electing grace, or the theme of God's glory, or the theme of justification, or the theme of the manifestations of the Spirit, or the theme of end-time prophecy (including a rapture), or the theme of God's kingdom unites all this diverse literature. No, it is the person, work, and words of Jesus.

Consider how this is so. Question: Who or what caused the reconfiguration of the meaning of the very term *God* in the early Jewish Christians symbolic universe? Answer: It was the Christ and the Christ-event, which led to a christological reformulation of monotheism. Question: Who or what changed the story or brought the narrative thought world of early Jewish Christianity to its proper climax and denouement? Answer: It was the Christ and the Christ-event. Question: Who or what prompted the theologizing and ethicizing found in the New Testament? Answer: It was the Christ and the Christ-event—his person, words, and works. Question: Who or what caused a change in the soteriology of these early Jewish Christians? Answer: It was the Christ and the Christ-event—more specifically, Christ crucified and risen. Question: Who or what changed the eschatology of the earliest Jewish Christians? Answer: It was the Christ and the Christ-event, accompanied by the divine saving activity called "the kingdom." Question: Who or what changed these early Jewish Christians' views about the Mosaic covenant and its ethic? Answer: It was the Christ and the Christ-event, including his teachings about a new covenant with a new ethic.

Even when we are dealing with a figure as creative as Paul, it is perfectly clear that the person, work, and teachings of Christ are what Paul intends to base his theologizing and ethicizing on, including things as different as his ethic of marriage and divorce, his ethic of nonviolence and respect for the state, his theology of the coming kingdom and return of the thief in the night, and a host of other subjects. Christ is not merely a great shadow hovering behind and over the writings and writers of the New Testament; he and his work and words are their constant preoccupation. Christ's ethic of nonviolence, cross-bearing, and self-sacrifice, even if need be unto death, permeates the teachings of figures as diverse as Paul, Peter, and John of Patmos and derives from both the story and the words of Jesus.

Of course, Christ is not the subject of every theological and ethical discourse and discussion in the New Testament, but his person, words, and work guide, guard, and even goad all those discussion into quite specific "Christian" and christological directions. Christ is the basis, the focus, the Alpha and Omega of New Testament thought, such that even the long tale of salvation history suddenly condenses to the story of Jesus when he walks on the stage of human history. And what a story it is: a God who so lavishly loves not merely "his people" or "the elect," though that is true enough, but the world that he sends his Son to save the world, not condemn it.

Christ is not merely the fulcrum of change in the world; he is the anvil on which that change is wrought, and he is the one who brings it about through his own willing and free self-sacrifice. Christ is the one who forces us to see God as he really is—God in his great glory as a holy and loving self-sacrificial being, not a self-centered, self-indulgent, narcissistic deity. Indeed, the nodal ways that the Trinity is revealed in the New Testament point to the relational character of the Trinity and how the Father loves the Son, the Son loves and serves the Father, the Spirit serves both the Father and the Son, and so on. Even within the Godhead, then, the terms of discourse make clear that God's love is other-directed, directed in the first instance toward other persons in the Godhead and then toward the world in all its multiplicity.

As I draw this section to a close, I return to the focal point with which it began: the indelible image. All human beings are created in the image of God, and all Christians are re-created in the image of Christ for good works. As Christians, we are meant to represent and reflect the holy, just, merciful, loving, blessed character of God in our lives. Theology and ethics are related through the middle term of Christian experience as God reproduces his character in us through a process of salvation that enables us to act "in character," a character that reflects God's own pure and moral character. We are to become, on a lesser scale, what we admire and emulate, but the good news is that God is working in us to will and to do, to conform us to the image of his Son. God is working into us what we must work out, but in the end God must intervene again, not merely at conversion or along the way in the Christian life, but in the end by means of resurrection, which has nothing to do with human striving. Both initial salvation and final salvation are overwhelmingly acts of God. Salvation is indeed by grace, otherwise it would never happen at all. It was not and is not a human self-help program.

However, behavior in the Christian life does indeed affect the sanctification process either positively or negatively. God has called us to participate in our own sanctification, so that the indelible image of God in humankind might truly shine forth both in this life and in the one to come. God is holy, and he expects his people to be so. God is loving, and he expects his people to be so. God is just, and he expects his people to be so. God is merciful and forgiving, and he expects his people to be so. God implanted his image in humankind, but after the fall it is restored and renewed through Christ so that we reflect the divine character both by God working in us (sanctification) and by our working out our salvation with fear and trembling (ethics). Ethics, then, entails both being like God in moral character and acting consistently in accordance with that "being."

It is my hope that this two-volume study, which is far from complete or perfect, will serve as a catalyst for some person or persons being able to more fully produce a "theology of the New Testament" or an "ethics of the New Testament" that is thoroughly grounded in the text itself, some person or persons willing to take the risk of developing its ideas beyond the confines of the canon in directions that the apostolic witness suggests. This will be the first step toward providing a base line for discussion of canonical or biblical theology in general. It will also be a first tentative step in the direction of the systematicians of theology. We have much to learn from each other. If this study furthers that process, I am content. *Christos aneste; sola Deo gloria.*

CRITICAL REFLECTIONS ON SOME RECENT ATTEMPTS AT BIBLICAL THEOLOGY

Since there actually have been some rather well-received attempts at doing biblical theology of late, it will be helpful to evaluate them here, especially because we also now have a careful and helpful textbook on biblical theology written by James Mead. My approach in this "coda" is first to examine some of the things that Mead brings to light and then to apply those insights to the analysis of two important works, Sandra Richter's *The Epic of Eden* and Charles Scobie's *The Ways of Our God*.[35] I need to stress from the outset that Richter is not claiming to do a full-dress biblical theology; she is an Old Testament scholar doing the important work of trying to get Christians to

---

[35]James K. Mead, *Biblical Theology: Issues, Methods, and Themes* (Louisville: Westminster John Knox, 2007); Sandra L. Richter, *The Epic of Eden: A Christian Entry into the Old Testament* (Downers Grove, Ill.: IVP Academic, (2008); Charles H. H. Scobie, *The Ways of Our God: An Approach to Biblical Theology* (Grand Rapids: Eerdmans, 2003).

embrace the first two-thirds of their canon as part of "their story" instead of being Marcionites. Nevertheless, since she is operating with an overarching schema of biblical theology, which she derives in large measure from a significant biblical theologian, Meredith Kline (who taught both of us), her work deserves to be treated in this portion of our study.

Frank Mead

Toward the end of his excellent book Frank Mead presents a definition of biblical theology as follows:

> Biblical theology seeks to identify and understand the Bible's theological message and themes, as well as how the Bible witnesses to those themes and to whom and by whom it declares that message. The outcome of such investigation will lead us to hear what the Bible says about God's being, words, and actions; about God's relationship to all of creation, especially humankind; and about the implications this divine-human encounter has for relationships between human beings.[36]

What is immediately noticeable about this definition is that it is so generic that it leaves the issue of Christology entirely unmentioned. It is a theocentric definition without being a christocentric one. I doubt that the writers of the New Testament would have been satisfied with this definition, but it points to a crucial factor: biblical theology that reads the theology of the Bible from front to back is bound to come up with a definition like this so that the whole canonical witness can be taken into account under one rubric. If, however, one starts with the New Testament and reads the Bible from back to front before reading it from front to back, and one interprets the Old Testament christologically just as the New Testament authors did, the definition will look different.

Mead adds this summary at the very end of his study:

> The biblical canon consists of a family of writers—individuals who are related to each other by virtue of a shared history, culture, and belief system. But, like all families, these members are unique individuals who bring their own knowledge understanding, experiences, and concerns to their task. They do not adopt the same perspective on every issue, but they nonetheless share a common calling to give voice to God's character, words, and actions, as well as to the relationship humans have with this God and with one another. Bibli-

---

[36]Mead, *Biblical Theology*, p. 242.

cal theology is the exciting task of listening to their conversation, discovering their similarities and differences, understanding their deepest convictions, and making connections with them that bring to life the Bible's message for each and every generation.[37]

Missing from both these statements is any sort of theology of revelation or inspiration, any sort of consideration of the divine author as well as the human authors. I submit once again, as I did at the outset of the present volume, that to presuppose a theology and ethic of the New Testament, to say nothing of the whole Bible, is to presuppose some sort of unity to these diverse documents and that this unity is grounded in God and in the inspiration that God gave these writers to write. In other words, I do not think that the unity results simply from all these authors belonging to a "family of writers." Nor do I think it fair to say, if we are including the Old Testament, that all of the writers were "conversation partners." The latter phrase is more nearly true of the New Testament writers, writing over a much shorter period of time and with close social networks in their minority sect.

Mead wants to suggest that when we get to the point of canonizing these books, what happened was a finalizing of the problem of their unity and diversity, which has been with us ever after. To some extent he is right about this, as he is right that if there is going to be an attempt at real biblical theology, then the relationship between the Old Testament and the New Testament becomes perhaps the crucial issue. James Barr, who always has challenging thoughts about such matters, hits the nail on the head when he says, "Perhaps the New Testament sees itself not as the completion of tradition coming right up to its own time, but as the fulfillment of an ancient scripture."[38] In my view, that is how the New Testament writers viewed what they were saying, doing, and writing. Of course, this is more evident in some New Testament texts than others (e.g,. Matthew, with its fulfillment citations), but that mentality seems evident right to the end of the canon in 2 Peter.

The New Testament writers wrote as those who fervently believed that they were living in the eschatological age after the climactic Christ-event and awaiting the consummation. Because of all this, I insist that any definition of biblical theology that omits Christ and a concept of revelation, including

---

[37]Ibid., p. 247.
[38]James Barr, *The Concept of Biblical Theology: An Old Testament Perspective* (Minneapolis: Fortress, 1999), p. 366.

progressive revelation, and does not work with a historical hermeneutic that is consonant with the one used by the New Testament writers, a hermeneutic that talks about typology, about the progress of salvation history, about the fulfillment of ancient hopes and dreams and promises and prophecies, will not, at the end of the day, be a Christian biblical theology, or at least it will not be an adequate one.

And none of these desiderata just listed controvert what John Goldingay is getting at when he says that the Old Testament "antedates Jesus and never mentions him."[39] This is true enough. The crucial question is, however, Does the Old Testament provide types, foreshadowings, prophecies and promises of the one who is the final great king, prophet and priest? The answer to this surely is yes. We can make that affirmation without violating the historical particularity of those Old Testament texts. To not make this affirmation is in fact to imply that the New Testament authors' reading of the Old Testament is simply wrong. I am not prepared to go there. To not make this affirmation is, when all is said and done, to not do biblical theology as the New Testament writers would have wanted it to be done.

At the same time, I agree with Mead when he says, "Nothing in the New Testament authorizes biblical theologians to work backward from the New to the Old and pour a developed Christology or Trinitarian theology into every messianic reference or text about the spirit."[40] Fair enough, emphasis on the word "developed," and so we learn that it is hard to strike the right balance in the endeavor of trying to do and to discern a biblical theology.[41]

There are, then, more and less helpful Christological readings of the Old Testament, and certainly one that is unwarranted is the reading into the Old Testament of Jesus himself—for example, in the guise of the angel of the Lord, or on the assumption that there is a clandestine trinitarianism lurking in the Old Testament books that goes beyond the notion that God, though one, is a complex being. There was no incarnation before the incarnation; even that New Testament doctrine is historically grounded in a particular point in time. I am much happier with Frank Matera's approach and his conclusion that "the New Testament writings witness in diverse ways to an overarching narrative of revelation, redemption, life in community, new moral

---

[39]John Goldingay, *Old Testament Theology*, vol. 1 (Downers Grove, Ill.: InterVarsity Press, 2003), p. 26.

[40]Mead, *Biblical Theology*, p. 175.

[41]See the proper cautionary remarks of Brent A. Strawn, "And These Three Are One: A Trinitarian Critique of Christological Approaches to the Old Testament," *PRSt* 31 (2004): 191-210.

life, and eschatological hope, all of which are rooted in the story of Israel, Jesus, and the church."[42]

Let us focus for a moment on the word *narrative*. I suggest that there is definitely something of a narrative unity to the Bible. We see this most clearly in the New Testament and in some of the latter parts of the Old Testament, but the whole is bound together as a tale of creation, fall and redemption, an epic that goes from Eden to the new Jerusalem, a salvation-history saga about God's relationship with humankind and his choosing a people to help him in the process of redeeming humankind. This is why it is critical to assess the narrative thought world of the writers of the Bible, including the writers of the New Testament. To be sure, narrative is a dominant genre of literature in the Bible, but we need to ask why this is so. George Stroup has put his finger on it. It is not just because narrative is the means by which individuals and communities tend to make sense of life's experiences, though certainly that is true, but also because "the faith of Jews and Christians is radically this-worldly and historical."[43] Exactly!

Thus, when we think of key theological ideas such as cross/atonement, resurrection, and the like, we need to ask about what part of the larger story they are explaining. We must ask, "Where do they fit into the story?" not "Where do they fit in my linear or systematic theological schema?" We also must ask, "What is the function of such ideas within the given story and the larger narrative thought world?" A narrative approach to biblical theology is as necessary as the recognition that such theology is historically grounded, and so both a historical approach and a narrative approach to biblical theology are required. This leads me to interact at this point with Sandra Richter, who very much wants to see biblical theology from start to finish in terms of a salvation history articulated by means of a grand narrative.

Sandra Richter

Sandra Richter is nothing if not forthright in throwing down the gauntlet in her book *The Epic of Eden*. The Bible, she says, is the story of redemption, but lest we think that her study will be all narratology and no history, she also stresses at the outset that when one opens the Bible, one discovers that "the God of history has chosen to reveal himself through a specific human cul-

---

[42]Frank J. Matera, "New Testament Theology: History, Method, Identity," *CBQ* 67 (2005): 16.
[43]George Stroup, *The Promise of Narrative Theology: Recovering the Gospel in the Church* (Eugene, Ore.: Wipf & Stock, 1997), pp. 145-46.

ture. To be more accurate, he chose to reveal himself in several incarnations of the same culture."[44] This does not lead her to suggest that God had canonized a particular culture and called it good, nor does she suggest that God should do so, but she does want to insist that the eternal truths about God's character and plan are mediated through a very specific cultural vehicle, and since, as she likes to put it, context is king, one cannot strip the enduring content from the context without distortion. Words, after all, have meanings only in specific contexts, and the same can be said of stories.

The culture out of which the Old Testament came was, as Richter puts it, patriarchal, patrilineal, and patrilocal. By this she means that the primary sense of identity or belonging in such a culture moved in ever widening circles, starting with one's association with the patriarch (the oldest living male of the clan) and his household, then one's larger clan, then one's tribe, and finally one's "nation." Most important was one's association with that innermost circle, the inner sanctum of the "father's household" where an extended family lived. The reason for repeated Old Testament demands to care for widows and orphans is precisely because they lacked the necessary connections and protections of the father's household. By contrast, there is the firstborn son, who, since he will be the next patriarch of the clan, gets a double portion of the inheritance of his father. Richter sees as evidence that God critiques every culture, including these ancient patriarchal ones, the fact that in various key stories, including those of Jacob and David, God chooses the younger son, not the firstborn, to lead God's people. This must have irked the "old man" of the clan on various occasions. Richter also takes Genesis 2:24 to be a critique of the patriarchal culture, for normally it is the wife who does the leaving and cleaving.[45] But according to Genesis 2:24, the husband is to do this, thereby making plain that his relationship with his wife, not his relationship with his father, is his most important relationship going forward. In other words, Richter sees a pattern of critique of the fallen human culture and its conventions, even in the more ancient narratives in the Old Testament.[46] In my view, she is right that Adam and Eve are indeed presented as coequal partners in Eden in Genesis 1–2, and I suggest that this

---

[44]Richter, *Epic of Eden*, p. 23.

[45]Ibid., p. 38.

[46]Richter (ibid., p. 39) gives an interesting reading of John 14:1-2, where Jesus talks about going back to his father's house and preparing room for his disciples to join him there. The imagery is of the patrilocal home, and we are being told that we will be welcomed not into our own heavenly mansion but rather into the household of the Father by his only begotten Son.

means that patriarchy is viewed in Genesis 3 as a result of the fall, for as the curse statement shows, to love and to cherish degenerates into a desire to dominate (see Gen 3:16).

At the same time, Richter shows in detail that the term *redemption* in the Old Testament conjures up a very specific set of ideas involving the patriarch of a clan who puts his own resources on the line to ransom a family member driven to the margins of society (see the story of Naomi, Ruth, and Boaz), or someone taken captive by enemies against whom the captive is defenseless (see the story of Lot and Abraham), or someone who becomes enmeshed in a sinful life and cannot get free of it (see the story of Gomer and Hosea). Thus, Richter urges,

> Yahweh is presenting himself as the patriarch of the clan who has announced his intent to redeem his lost family members. Not only has he agreed to pay whatever ransom is required, but he has sent the most cherished member of his household to accomplish his intent—his firstborn son. And not only is the firstborn coming to seek and save the lost, but he is coming to share his inheritance with these who have squandered everything they have been given. His goal? To restore the lost family members to the *bêt ʾāb* [household of the father] so that where he is, they may be also. This is why we speak of each other as *brother* and *sister*, why we know God as *Father*, why we call ourselves *the household of faith*. God is beyond human gender and our relationship to him beyond blood, but the tale of redemptive history comes to us in the language of a patriarchal society.[47]

Not only so, but understanding that social and historical context is key to understanding the use of the term *redeem* in those texts and, by extension, in various places in the New Testament. What Richter in essence is arguing is that to understand the lexicon of the New Testament, we must read it in light of the lexicon and context of the Old Testament. I agree with this to some extent, but this sort of reading forward into the New Testament has its limits, as Richter acknowledges. What she also is arguing is that God prepared for the way he would relate to all of us through his Son by means of the various ways he related to Israel in the Old Testament. If one understands the latter, one is far more likely to understand the nuances of the New Testament story as well. The language is culturally conditioned, and one needs to know the culture to understand it, but God's redemptive plan transcends one particular culture or cultural conditioning.

Although Richter's book is intended not to be a full-scale biblical the-

---

[47]Ibid., p. 45.

ology study but rather, as its subtitle suggests, to help Christians reclaim the Old Testament, she is addressing biblical theological matters, and so her presentation merits close scrutiny. The organizing principle for her biblical theology that binds the whole together is the familiar notion of covenant, and not just any sort of covenant, but mainly the type of covenant between suzerain and vassal, and even more specifically the form which that took in the second millennium B.C., containing both the historical prologue in which the overlord listed the benefits that the vassal or servant nation had already received and the curse and blessings sanctions.

Richter sees this as a crucial rubric for analyzing what is going on when the Sinai covenant involving Yahweh and Moses is described in the Pentateuch, not least because she takes the inclusion of the historical prologue ("I am the God who delivered you up out of bondage in Egypt") as evidence that even the Mosaic covenant was one of grace, to which Israel must respond with obedience. This differs from the analysis of some scholars who distinguish a largely promissory covenant (e.g., Abrahamic covenant) from a law covenant (Mosaic covenant), which would explain why Paul so clearly contrasts the two covenants instead of seeing the Abrahamic covenant as leading to or even fulfilled in the Mosaic one (Gal 3–4). Paul draws a link between the Abrahamic covenant and the new covenant, but not between the Mosaic covenant and the new covenant. In any event, she has made her point that one concept or rubric that can be used to unite the whole of biblical theology is the concept of a covenant between an overlord and a servant (or servant people), a covenant that is confirmed or inaugurated by a sacrifice and by oaths and involves a historical prologue rehearsing past benefits, stipulations and curse and blessing sanctions. With this rubric one can analyze in some detail the way God chose to relate to his people through various covenants and eras.

Richter further clarifies her view, arguing that we can tag the various Old Testament covenants with key Old Testament figures—Adam, Noah, Abraham, Moses, David. The other interesting note that Richter emphasizes is that in a patriarchal world where people had no obligations to those not within their patriarchal circle, clan, tribe, or national group, covenants were a way of creating a family sort of relationship, complete with family obligations between two parties that were not family. There is a technical term for this legal fiction, *fictive kinship*. Is this, however, the sort of sociological concept that we should use to analyze why Jesus says that whoever does his will is his brother or sister (Mk 3:31-35)? I think not and neither does Richter. Her point is that this concept made possible certain forms of covenanting, and she is right on this point.

Richter understands a text such as Genesis 15 to be showing the very character of God, who himself passes between the pieces of the sacrificial animal to demonstrate to and reassure Abraham that he will keep his promises, he will be faithful and demonstrate covenant love, even when the human party failed from time to time. She sees this as a foreshadowing of Christ, who presented himself as a sacrifice that inaugurated the new covenant.[48] The important point here is that Richter sees in the Old Testament a deliberate pattern of divine behavior revealed in covenanting that foreshadows and prepares for the ultimate covenant, the new covenant. She wants to read the biblical narrative from start to finish, but she allows that none of it makes total sense without the climax in the new covenant. I will say more about this in a moment, but here it is enough to say that such a front-to-back reading of the canon is a necessary but insufficient way to explain New Testament theology, as Richter, I believe, in the end would agree.

Such a reading is inadequate because the New Testament writers do not see the new covenant as simply a renewal of any of the old covenants, nor do they see the various Old Testament covenants as simply one covenant in many administrations. This is clear not only in the use of "covenants" (plural) in Romans 9:4 and Galatians 4:24 but also in the way Paul says in Romans 10:4 that Christ is the end of the Mosaic covenant ("end of the law") and the author of Hebrews says that the new covenant has made obsolete any and all of the old covenants (e.g., Heb 8:13 [see also 2 Cor 3:4-18]). In fact, in Paul's theology it is in Christ that the promises to Abraham are said to be fulfilled and his inheritance is now brokered to a larger Jewish and Gentile audience. Paul also says quite explicitly that the Mosaic covenant was a temporary one until the Redeemer should come (Gal 4). I will say a bit more on this shortly.

Even just from the point of view of the sort of ancient covenants about which Richter is talking, when a suzerain/vassal covenant was broken by the servant, the overlord was under no obligation to adhere to what was originally promised if the servant remained loyal and kept the covenant. Nor was the overlord even obligated to continue the covenant. Instead, what often happened was that the curse sanctions were applied to the offending vassal

---

[48]Ibid., pp. 78-79.

and the vassal's people, and that would be the end of the covenant with that vassal. Clearly, the analogues with ancient Near Eastern covenants, though helpful, can be pressed only so far, precisely because the God of the Bible was a different sort of sovereign with a different and more gracious character than, for example, one of the Hittite or especially the Assyrian kings. Richter clarifies this:

> To take this further, in reality very few suzerains upheld their end of the bar-gain even if the vassal *was* loyal. So I would never claim that the secular image of the suzerain is the ultimate reflection of God's actions in redemption . . . but suzerain is a critically important metaphor, mostly because it is the one God chooses. I see the covenant as a metaphor in the drama of redemption much like the metaphor of parent. You would be hard-pressed to find a parent who parents as God does. But you would be more hard-pressed to understand God's metaphor if you'd never seen a parent at all.[49]

But the various old covenants and the Hittite suzerain/vassal covenants had this in common: they could be brought to an end by a serious violation, followed by curse sanctions. They were not perpetual covenants if seriously violated, unless the sovereign chose to forgo the curse sanctions and the end-ing of the relationship, which seldom was seen as a smart political move be-cause one would appear inept, weak, or even not keeping one's oath in regard to the curse sanctions. This would not do in an honor-shame culture.

In an interesting and telling exegetical move, Richter reads the story of the creation of humankind in God's image as evidence of the pluriform nature of the deity. She says, "Note the deliberative plural: 'Let us make . . . in our image . . . male and female he created them' (Gen 1:26-27). It seems that the plurality of humanity (male and female in relationship) reflects the plurality of the original; and humanity, like deity, is created to live in relationship."[50] I take "let us make" as a reference to God speaking to the heavenly council of angels, and Richter discusses this possibility later in the book. Richter is right that the fact that the image of God in humankind is "male and female" and so the plural in Genesis 1 does suggest that if the image truly reflects the origi-nal, then God too is pluriform in some way. This in turn makes better sense of the New Testament teaching about Christians being conformed to the im-age of the Son (Rom 8:28-30), a particular member of the Trinity.

In addition, Richter takes Genesis 3:15 and the promise to Eve that her

---

[49]Sandra L. Richter, e-mail to the author, January 20, 2009.
[50]Richter, *Epic of Eden*, p. 107.

descendant will crush the head of the serpent as a foreshadowing of the role of Christ in his cosmic battle with Satan.[51] Further, she sees the sabbatical pattern of the week—six days of work, one of rest—as revealing that our lives are not meant to be all work. Humans are made for both work and rest, both labor and worship. She sees the expulsion of Adam and Eve from Eden as their being driven from God's presence. They were no longer fit for either a perfect creation or a perfect relationship with God. There were to be labor pains for both Adam and Eve, though in different senses. She adds, "When we ask the salvation question, what we are really asking is, what did the First Adam lose? And when we answer the salvation question, what we are really attempting to articulate is, what did the Second Adam (i.e., Jesus) buy back?"[52] In other words, she sees the Genesis stories as foundational for understanding redemption and what human life ultimately was to be restored to. She follows the lead of Paul in the way she puts together the pieces of the tale of creation, fall, and redemption.

There is more, however. Richter emphasizes the cosmic effects of Adam's sin: the whole world fell with Adam, not just humanity. The irony, as she puts it, is that although humans were created to subdue the earth, now a fallen, rotting earth will subdue each one of us when we die, are laid to rest, and become fertilizer. The earth creature (which is what "Adam" means) will be swallowed up by the earth that it has corrupted, which is poetic justice if there ever was any.

How would God begin to effect reconciliation with his estranged and fallen children? Richter sees one major stage as the establishment of the tabernacle as a place for God to dwell in the midst of his people, noting Exodus 25:8: "Let them construct a sanctuary for me, that I may dwell among them." But this would be an isolated spot, and unlike Eden, this sanctuary would not be for human habitation; indeed, only priests would be able to enter into the divine presence. Otherwise, human beings had to stay in the outer court where the sacrifices would be made. In an interesting move, Richter sees the reference to the angels on the curtains shielding the holy of holies as being like the cherubim who fenced off Eden to prevent reentry by the fallen Adam and Eve. And further, she sees the cherubim on the mercy seat on top of the ark of the covenant as protecting God from defilement (and, I would add, perhaps also the priests from God's deadly powerful presence, for a fallen per-

---

[51]Ibid., p. 110.
[52]Ibid., p. 118.

son cannot come close to the holy God without serious consequences).[53] God is envisioned as sitting above the cherubim with the ark as his footstool. The tabernacle, then, like the later temple, has Eden motifs in it meant to remind and turn the heart of the believer back toward Eden.[54] But that is not all. The next port of call is Ezekiel 47, part of Ezekiel's vision of the restored temple. She focuses on Ezekiel 47:8-12, where we are told about a river that flows forth from the throne room of the holy of holies and goes out and transforms the Dead Sea into a living sea; but more tellingly, this river produces everlasting trees that continually bear fruit and support life. She sees in this an echo of the tree of life in Eden.[55] Not surprisingly, she connects this to the material in Revelation 21–22, stressing that there is no temple in the new earth because there is no reason to house God or fence God off from a no longer fallen world or fallen humanity. The outpost of God in a fallen world, tabernacle, or temple, has become the whole, but not without a return to Eden.

Richter acknowledges that the final vision is of a city, the new Jerusalem, and there is nothing about a city in Genesis 1–2, though the city in Revelation 21–22 certainly has a garden. She also stresses that there are no cherubim in the new Jerusalem, as there is no need to protect the ruler or, for that matter, those ruled. But why, according to this same book of Revelation, are there angels in heaven in the new Jerusalem above worshiping God? This question is especially pressing because John's vision is that heaven in the form of the new Jerusalem will come down and effect a merger with earth. If there are angels in heaven, where the new Jerusalem now is (see, e.g., Gal 4:24-26), then it is reasonable to expect them to be in the new Jerusalem on earth as well. Richter's explanation is that although angels and cherubim are both in the general category of divine beings, the cherubim are of a different class than ordinary angels. She says that angels and cherubim are not equated in the Old Testament.

More convincing is her comment that the essential plot line of the Bible, after Genesis 3, is "How do we get Adam back into Eden?" The bulk of the Bible is seen as the tale of the rescue plan to accomplish that intent. All God ever wanted was for those created in his image to dwell forever in his presence in a holy paradise, enjoying him forever. Richter rightly stresses that the finish line in the Bible is never "dying and going to heaven." Instead, it is

---

[53]Ibid., pp. 120-23.
[54]Ibid., p. 126.
[55]Ibid., p. 127.

heading for the new Eden, the new Jerusalem, which transpires after Christ returns, the dead are raised and the kingdoms of this world become the kingdom of God once and for all. This is unsurprising, since human beings are earth creatures—flesh and bone. It follows that a material place would need to be the finish line for this sort of creature. We are not angels. Thus heaven comes down, and there is a return to Eden for the earth creature in the end.

Richter then seeks to make sense of God's making a series of covenants leading up to the new one. She says, in effect, that redemption is presented to us as a series of steps, a series of covenanting acts, with Noah, Abraham, Moses, David and finally the new covenant. She argues that in God's design all of what had to be accomplished would not be accomplished in one fell swoop. The goal is to have the people of God dwelling in the place of God enjoying the presence of God. The Noachic covenant reestablished contact between God and humankind and speaks to all of creation. The Abrahamic covenant reestablished the relationship such that there is a people of God dwelling in God's place (the Holy Land). The Mosaic covenant began to reestablish the last bit of the equation, God dwelling in the midst of his people. This covenant typologically fulfills the promises to Abraham, but only typologically.[56] The Davidic covenant then added "the capstone of a human leader whose first ambition is to lead his people in their service to God. David is, in essence, the ideal vassal."[57] He becomes the prototype of the Messiah/Christ.

The covenanting progression moves from a covenant with one man (Noah), to one family (Abraham), to one people or nation (Israel), to all people (the church). "Each of the stages in the story brings ʾAdām one step closer to full deliverance; each serves to reeducate humanity as to who the God of Eden was and is."[58] In Richter's vision, the fall had such devastating intensive and extensive effects on Adam and all of creation that the redemption plan took several stages, climaxing in Jesus and the new covenant but not complete until the new Jerusalem at the eschaton. It is clear that for Richter, Romans 5:12-21 is perhaps the most crucial of New Testament texts for her overall schema of biblical theology. Jesus is Adam gone right, the one who was born sinless like Adam but, unlike Adam, resisted temptations. She summarizes thus:

> When [Jesus] chose to participate in the crucifixion by taking the wrath of God upon himself on our behalf, he did two things. One, he proved that the

---

[56]Ibid., p. 131.
[57]Ibid., p. 132.
[58]Ibid.

first Adam could have succeeded in his charge. Two, he bore in his own body the curse of Eden, so that the children of Adam would not have to. And when Jesus *rose* from the grave, he *defeated* death; he eradicated the curse of Eden. And because Jesus was both human and God, his death and resurrection was of such a nature that it could be vicariously applied to all of Adam's children.[59]

Richter's reconstruction raises two important questions. First, was redemption really delivered in stages, covenant by covenant, or only by Christ in the new covenant. Second, if redemption was delivered only by Christ in the new covenant, why the need for all those other covenants? Why not just go from the first Adam to the last Adam and spare the world millennia of misery? In response to the first question she says, "This of course is a complex question. Redemption is presented to us 'stage by stage' in the biblical narrative, but we are also told that Christ was slain before the foundation of the world (Rev 13:8) . . . so there are in actuality no stages."[60]

In terms of Richter's modus operandi, one tool in her arsenal is what typically is called "catchword connection." So, for example, the use of the term *tēbat* ("ark") for the vessel that Moses is placed in when he is set loose in the Nile is seen as "an obvious and intentional association with Noah's *tēbat*."[61] I am not so sure that the connection is obvious, because as far as I can see, *tēbat* is not a technical term. Richter has a very high view of Scripture, and she assumes that nothing is there by accident or chance. I agree that this is so, but the use of catchword connections between texts that otherwise have no connection can easily lead to overreading. There is no flooding of the Nile when Moses is put into it, and he is rescued not from water but rather from a death edict by a wicked human being. The mere presence of water in the two texts is not enough to warrant pressing an analogy. I agree, however, that in view of the Hebrews' fear of the chaos waters and the story of the flood, it is an obvious connection to see in Revelation 21:1 the final defeat of a formidable foe, the sea, that had often troubled humankind, including Noah, Moses and the Israelites at the Red Sea, Jonah, and others.

More promising is Richter's belief that typology is the basic hermeneutic that helps us relate the Old Testament to the New Testament, the old covenants to the new one. As she points out, a typology involves two sets of historical events, persons, institutions or even places that are compared

---

[59]Ibid., pp. 134-35.
[60]Sandra L. Richter, e-mail to the author, January 20, 2009.
[61]Richter, *Epic of Eden*, p. 146.

in some way. The underlying idea is that God's character is consistent, and so God acts in ways in earlier eras of salvation history that foreshadow the way he acts in later eras. But Richter wants to stress that "a type operates upon the principle of limited fulfillment."[62] She draws an analogy between a model airplane and a real one. Both are planes, both can fly, but the model plane cannot carry the same freight as the real one. So she sees the comparison of the first Adam and the last Adam as a form of typology, or the comparison of circumcision and baptism as a form of typology, or we could suggest Melchizedek and Christ as an example of a typology focusing on someone who is a priest. Typology, unless the comparison is between two persons, events, places or institutions within the Old Testament, is an exercise in cross-Testament biblical theology, which is precisely what Richter is doing in her book. If the New Testament did not exist, no one would ever guess that Adam or circumcision or the priesthood was a mere foreshadowing type. In other words, this is reading the Old Testament in light of its fulfillment in the New Testament, a fulfillment that transpires in various ways. The undercurrent of Richter's presentation is that the events, institutions, and persons in the Old Testament are preparatory for what we find in the New Testament, prefiguring and preparing for them. Again, this is a specifically Christian theological way of reading the Old Testament, a way that many Jews would find objectionable because they do not accept the New Testament as the further adventures of Yahweh—hence the subtitle of Richter's book, *A Christian Entry into the Old Testament*.

Regarding the tabernacle, Richter takes it not merely as the sign but as the evidence that God had taken up residence with his people once more; however, "the double-edged sword of the tabernacle was the truth that God was once again with *'Adām*, but *'Adām* was still separated from God."[63] Hereby it was made clear that Israel had not been cleansed from all sin, and atonement was still needed to be made repeatedly clean, and even then only the high priest, once a year, could dare to venture into the presence of God without risking death (see Lev 16:2). Richter stresses that what is going on in the Old Testament is not mere shadowboxing or play acting or symbol. She puts it this way: "Important as we think about the nature of types and typology is the fact that the tabernacle did provide some level of atonement for God's people (Lev 1:1-4; 4:35). It was real. It was effective. It was historical. But

---

[62]Ibid., p. 179.
[63]Ibid., p. 182.

like all types, it provided *limited* atonement."[64]

But what is the function of an inadequate type that does not really, or at least not fully, do the job that it is meant to do? Richter's answer is that it has a pedagogical function as much as anything else, and thus in fact it does do what God intended it to do. Because of the type, all God's people are educated in the need for atonement, the need for mediation and a mediator, the need for a final and ultimate sacrifice. And the mission of atonement is necessary so that God can and will permanently dwell with his people. Again, this is a Christian reading of these Old Testament institutions, an exercise in biblical theology that wishes to preserve some viability, some unction in the antetype while still insisting that the type is where the real, complete, final, fulfilling action is. By this means, the Old Testament is recovered partly for Christians as a pedagogical tool that helps them understand the nature of God and the New Testament.

Richter goes on to suggest that what Hebrews 10 and various Pauline texts indicate is that the Old Testament law, though a good and godly thing, could not enable fallen persons to keep it. The law only foreshadowed and instructed about the good things yet to come in Christ, but until God came and dwelled within his people individually, not just in their midst, their hearts of stone would not be transformed into hearts of flesh, and Jeremiah 31:31-33 would not be fulfilled and fleshed out. At a crucial juncture in her argument Richter follows the suggestion of Scott Hafemann and others that the new covenant is not really a "new" covenant that has a "new" law, since the problem was not with the law of God but rather with the people of God, and so Jeremiah 31 is indeed talking about the Mosaic law being renewed and applied to God's new covenant people.[65]

The problem with this suggestion is that it fails to do justice to what Paul actually says about the Mosaic law in 2 Corinthians 3, Romans 10, Galatians 3–4, and elsewhere, never mind what the author of Hebrews says. According to Paul, the Mosaic law was not a mere tutor. A *paidagōgos* (see Gal 3:24) is a slave guardian, and there are problems with such guardians if they overstay their time period. Their job was only to help the child of a well-to-do person rehearse lessons after school and to keep the child in bounds and safe in transit from home to school and back again. The *paidagōgos* definitely was not the primary educator or tutor.

---

[64]Ibid.
[65]Ibid., p. 186.

Paul is quite clear that when Christ came, he came to redeem people out from under the Mosaic law because there were problems with this law, not in intent but in effect. First, the Mosaic law was impotent. It could not enable fallen persons to keep it, and so as Paul says that the effect of this law was to turn sin into trespass and condemn the fallen person. It ended up being death-dealing rather than life-giving, though of course that was not the intent of the law, which was good in itself. Second, as the author of Hebrews stresses, the Mosaic law was unable in any way to cause new birth or transform hearts. It could only produce outward change at best, hence the need for the covenant that Jeremiah had in mind. The problem with the Hafemann approach to biblical theology is that it overemphasizes the continuity between various of the old covenants and the new one, specifically when it comes to the matter of law.

In any case, Paul indicates in Galatians 6 that there is a new sheriff in town when Jesus appears, and he offers a new law, the law of Christ (discussed at length in this two-volume study). Richter concludes her discussion of the Mosaic law by suggesting that in fact Jesus, in his critique of the Pharisees and Saducees, probably is partly critiquing Jewish halakah or haggadah, those traditions of the Pharisees built up to erect a fence around the law. I think that there is some truth to this, but it is not the full picture. Jesus believes that he lives in the eschatological age of fulfillment, and both the Old Testament law and the prophets are being fulfilled in him, and once fulfilled, they become obsolete. Of course, the law and the prophets remain, and should remain, until all is fulfilled, not least because they are still valuable for training in righteousness (as 2 Tim 3:16 puts it), but laws no longer need to be obeyed once they have been fulfilled, their purpose has been served, and their usefulness has been completed.

But talking about fulfillment is different from suggesting that Jesus repristinizes the old covenant or the old law, and Richter is careful not to suggest the latter. Jesus acts in relationship to that law with the sovereign freedom of one who came to give a new law; sometimes he reaffirms old commandments, sometimes he intensifies them, sometimes he offers entirely new commandments, sometimes he abolishes old commandments. This is because he is indeed inaugurating a truly new covenant, not merely renewing an old one. This is also why Paul speaks of "covenants" (plural) and sees the new covenant as the replacement for the Mosaic one and as the fulfillment of the Abrahamic one.

Richter recognizes the difficulties that I have been pointing out, and in a supplemental clarifying discussion at the end of her study she says that she is not certain how things should be adjudicated (though she is sure that the old "ritual/political law is abrogated, moral law of Moses is continued" distinction does not work). She tentatively suggests,

> And for all the Mosaic law, be it superseded or not, we need to recognize that we can (and must) still learn a great deal about the character of God through these laws, even if we can no longer directly apply them to ourselves in this new covenant. So rather than thinking in terms of the Mosaic law being obsolete *except* for what Jesus maintains (as has been the predominant view), perhaps we should begin to think in terms of the law being in force except for what Jesus repeals.[66]

The problem with this suggestion is it leaves Christians obligated to an awful lot of Old Testament laws that are not reaffirmed in the New Testament—for example, laws about tithing. It is better and safer to say that Christians are obligated to obey only those portions of the law reaffirmed in the New Testament.

The final piece of the Old Testament puzzle is put in place by the Davidic covenant, for here, in texts such as 2 Samuel 7, we see the beginnings of messianism, the promise of a kingly dynasty in the shoot from the stump of Jesse. What is needed is a human but royal representative who not only leads but also stands as mediator between God and his people.[67] From here it is easy to see a straight line to Jesus, who is presented in the very first chapter in the New Testament as the son of David but also as the son of Abraham.

Having gotten up a considerable head of Old Testament steam, connecting the six covenants with six key figures (the last, of course, with Jesus), Richter brings the full weight of this paradigm to bear on her interpretation of Jesus when she says,

> Jesus is prophet, priest, and king. He is the last Adam who defeats Eden's curse; the second Noah commissioned to save God's people from the coming flood of his wrath [see 1 Pet 3:18-22]; the seed of Abraham; the new lawgiver who stands upon the mountain and amazes his audience by the authority with which he speaks; and he is the heir of David.[68]

Looking for other connections with the Old Testament, Richter presents John the Baptizer as the last prophet of the Mosaic line, who nevertheless

---

[66]Ibid., 228-29.
[67]Ibid., p. 190.
[68]Ibid., p. 217.

uses the sign of the new covenant to identify the new king, who is promptly anointed by God, not by the prophet, and God makes the coronation announcement to the king, calling him "son" (see 2 Sam 7).[69] Here she sees a period of overlap between the old covenant and the new covenant. The problem with this interpretation of the baptism of Jesus is that later in the New Testament it is made clear that John's baptism of repentance is not the sign of the new covenant, and those who have received it need rebaptism (see Acts 18–19). Equally interesting, though debatable, is her connection of the tongues as of fire and the wind in Acts 2 with Exodus 40 and 1 Kings 8, pointing out how the tabernacle and temple were inaugurated with cloud, fire, and wind. Her point is that God has come in person to dwell "in" his people who become his temple or tabernacle.[70] The point of all this is to make the case for the Old Testament being the Christian's story. I would put it rather differently. The Old Testament is not our story, since Christians are not Jews, but it is a story into which, as Paul puts it, we Gentiles have been grafted through our Jewish messiah, Jesus, when we came to be "in Christ." We are not by nature the children of Abraham, but we have become his adopted heirs through Christ, the seed of Abraham.

Richter's approach to biblical theology has many merits. Unlike too many Christian attempts at this, she in no way neglects the Old Testament (which one would not expect anyway, since she is a Old Testament scholar). If anything in her book is given too slender a treatment, it is a reckoning with the New Testament and the way the New Testament reconfigures the nature of the discussion of theology and ethics, but then again, the book is intended to be a Christian entry into the Old Testament, not a full biblical theology. She is to be commended also for neither compromising nor neglecting the historical nature and givenness of the Old Testament text in her theologizing. She neither allegorizes the Old Testament nor readily overreads Christian concepts back into the Old Testament. She confines herself to patterns, word connections, and typologies that do not vitiate the historical character and development of the story of God and his people.

Also commendable is the way she skillfully presents a narrative theology that encompasses the entire canon, not merely by talking about creation, fall and redemption, but by giving good and detailed discussion of all the Old Testament covenants. Much more discussion of the new covenant, es-

---

[69]Ibid., p. 214.
[70]Ibid., p. 222.

pecially regarding the continuity and discontinuity between the various old covenants and the new one, would have been useful, but surely that is a task for a further study.

I would have liked at least a recognition that what the New Testament writers mean by "salvation" is rather different from what is meant by "redemption" in the Old Testament. Although the two Testaments often share vocabulary, they are operating with different lexicons and meanings at various points, not least because the Old Testament says precious little about a theology of the afterlife and even less about a theology of the other world, and also because the cultural context of Jesus is, in important ways, quite different from that of the previous five covenants and major covenant figures. Richter does recognize that what "kingdom" means when Jesus says that it has come in his ministry is something very different from what "kingdom" meant on the lips of a Saul, David, or Solomon. Those kings were not envisioning God ruling directly, but the dominion of God that Jesus has in mind indeed involves the direct divine saving activity of God from above, transforming people from the inside out and re-creating the people of God, almost from scratch.

Richter's book is a very good beginning for a genuine biblical theology. In many ways it is the most clear, succinct, and helpful attempt that I have encountered, and it gives me hope that biblical theology can be done in responsible and helpful ways by Christians. I find nothing major lacking in the way Richter reads the canon from front to back. What is lacking is a more profound reading of the canon from back to front, for the New Testament writers reasoned over and over again from solution to plight, not the other way around. By this I mean that once they had fully grasped the surprising nature of salvation through the advent, death and resurrection of the Son of Man (something that early Jews certainly were not looking for), they had to go back and reread their Scriptures with new and more christological lenses. It changed the way they evaluated all those Old Testament covenants and even changed the way they viewed major figures such as Adam, Abraham, Moses, and David.

Perhaps only when there is a cooperative venture between Old Testament and New Testament scholars will a biblical theology emerge that does full justice to the need to read the canon front to back and at the same time eschatologically and so back to front, the latter being, in my view, the more crucial hermeneutical move. Indeed, the back-to-front reading is the hermeneutical move that we see the New Testament writers making again and again. All told, however, Richter has done us a great service in reminding us of the epic of Eden and how we need to get there by going forward to the end, not by going backwards to the garden paradise.

Charles Scobie

For me, reading the work of Charles Scobie is a cautionary tale because too few people have been willing to undertake the long journey through his study on biblical theology, *The Ways of Our God*—some one thousand pages. In some ways it is appropriate that we end this long odyssey with a discussion of his work, which really is the only full-dress, comprehensive biblical theology available these days that is conversant with most of the relevant literature and approaches the subject with a critical rigor to produce competent results. Providentially, Scobie writes in a very readable manner, and so it is not difficult to understand what he is trying to convey. This one volume, which was completed after Scobie retired, reflects the good fruit of a lifetime of studying and teaching the Bible. Scobie is a New Testament scholar with a great love for the Old Testament, and his approach to biblical theology is characterized by deep thought and a real grasping and grappling with the nettle. His is a thematic rather than narratological approach to biblical theology. He says that "the main goal of biblical theology is to hear the two different voices of Old Testament and New Testament in their canonical integrity, yet also to understand them as both witnesses to the one divine reality of Jesus Christ."[71]

This comports with his understanding that biblical theology is not merely a theology based on the Bible; rather, it is theology contained in the Bible and, more specifically, is "the ordered study of what the Bible has to say about God and his relationship to the world and to humankind."[72] Scobie approaches biblical theology as an intermediate discipline "lying between the historical study of Scripture and the appropriation of the biblical message in the life and work of the Church, including the preaching of the Word."[73] This is an interesting approach, since biblical theology typically is seen as the middle term between biblical studies and something like systematic theology, and it reflects Scobie's profound concern that biblical theology be done for the sake of the church. I suggest that it can be done for both the academy and

---

[71]Scobie, *Ways of Our God*, p. xi.
[72]Ibid., pp. 4–5.
[73]Ibid., p. xi.

the church, and also that biblical theology needs to be done as a basis for, and in dialogue with, systematic theology or else we will continue to have the problem of systematic theology being done in a way that fails to do justice to the historical and exegetical particulars of the biblical text.

Scobie begins his study by stating his conviction that biblical theology must be based only on the canonical text of Scripture. He allows that extrabiblical sources can help us understand biblical theology, but he, like Brevard Childs, is doing a form of canonical theology. In this regard, he pays less attention to the sort of ancient Near Eastern material that Sandra Richter finds crucial for understanding and more attention to detailed exegesis of particular biblical texts. As both Scobie and Frank Mead have noted, the study of and construction of a biblical theology is a modern preoccupation. Indeed, the expression "biblical theology" does not even show up until W. J. Christmann uses it in 1629.[74] Scobie is fully cognizant of the history of the discussion of this subject since that time, and he is unpersuaded by the naysayers who maintain that the Bible is too diverse a corpus of literature for anyone to be able to find a singular biblical theology within it.

Scobie is indebted to Brevard Childs in his approach in that he too believes that biblical theology must concentrate on the final form of the text, not what is behind the text. One of the problems with this approach is that the Bible comes from many different historical contexts, and the meanings of the words in the Bible are conditioned by those contexts, not merely by the immediate literary context in a particular biblical book, or even by the larger literary context of the Bible as a whole, but by the larger historical, religious, social, and rhetorical contexts. To focus on apparent biblical themes to the neglect of hearing these various texts in their various contexts always runs the risk of stripping out the real nuances and contextual dimensions of the theologizing that is being done into specific contexts.

To his credit, Scobie does not skimp on the contextual exegetical study of the Bible on the way to his presentation of biblical theology. At the same time, he knows that the fundamental presupposition to doing biblical theology at all is a high view of Scripture and a conviction that it is God's Word and so has a unity to it. The presuppositions of Scobie's study include "belief that the Bible conveys a divine revelation, that the word of God in Scripture constitutes the norm of Christian faith and life, and that all the varied material of the OT and NT can in some way be related to the plan and purpose of

---

[74]Ibid., p. 3.

the one God of the whole Bible."[75] It becomes obvious, the further one reads into Scobie's magnum opus, that he clearly sees biblical theology not as the summing up of Old Testament theology plus New Testament theology but rather as a much more synthetic project of creating a theology of the whole canon.[76] The question is whether this can be accomplished without denuding the Old Testament and New Testament theologies of their distinctive characters and contributions. Scobie's answer is this: "What is maintained here is that [biblical theology] can *both* do justice to the OT *and* hold that, in the context of the canon, the NT is its continuation and fulfillment."[77] This hints to some degree at his approach, which assumes more continuity than discontinuity between the Testaments and their respective theologies.

Scobie is right as well that the Jewish approach to Tanak, which focuses on the "T" (Torah/law) portion of the canon, differs considerably from the Christian approach to the Old Testament, which generally focuses on the salvation history, beginning with creation, fall, and then the long chronicling of God's rescue operation with his people. "The addition of the NT of course shifts the central focus of God's revelation away from the Torah to the Christ event witnessed to primarily in the Gospels. The whole OT is now seen as preparing for and pointing to this event."[78] The very arrangement of the Old Testament books by Christians in an order different from the one used by Jews is a theological move that helps make the point that the biblical center of gravity has shifted in the canon.

Scobie places the approaches to biblical theology in three categories: systematic, historical, and thematic. He clearly favors the last of these. He recognizes that there are problems with all three approaches, and in fact the thematic approach is a relatively new one, whereas the oldest of the three is the systematic approach, which began with and after the Reformation (e.g., Melanchthon).[79] He admits that it is relatively easy to come up with a central or focal theme of the New Testament—Christ or, more broadly, Christol-

---

[75]Ibid., p. 47.

[76]Ibid., p. 59.

[77]Ibid., p. 60.

[78]Ibid., p. 68.

[79]Scobie critiques the first two approaches, saying, "A systematic approach, based on categories imported from dogmatic theology, is to be rejected as tending to a certain degree to distort biblical thought, and as failing to deal adequately with all aspects of the biblical material. A historical approach tracing the development of biblical thought period by period or book by book is of course valuable, but it belongs rather to the kind of historical study of the Bible that is presupposed by, rather than part of, an 'intermediate [biblical theology]'" (ibid., p. 87).

ogy—but more difficult to do so for the Old Testament, with some scholars contending that Old Testament theology has no center or focal point. Walther Eichrodt used the concept of covenant as his organizing principle in arranging the main themes of the Old Testament (cf. the work of Richter discussed in the preceding section). But Scobie says that "'covenant' is not an all-pervasive theme in the Old Testament, and parts of the outline [of Eichrodt] are linked with it in an artificial way," and that "covenant is even less a pervasive theme in the NT than it is in the Old."[80] He is absolutely right about this, but at least this theme is mentioned in both Testaments, whereas the phrase "kingdom of God," which has been used as a thematic rubric for doing biblical theology, is not found anywhere directly in the Old Testament (though the idea is present in, e.g., Dan 7) and is a dominant theme in the New Testament only in the Synoptic Gospels. Scobie complains, "It is difficult to understand the obsession with finding one single theme or 'center' for OT or NT theology, and more so for an entire [biblical theology]. . . . An approach that recognizes several themes would appear to be more productive."[81] Still, efforts are being made to find one overarching key theme. For example, Richter appears to be unique in focusing on the theme of Eden while using the organizing device of the covenants.

According to Scobie, it is the task of biblical theology to explore the relationship between the Old Testament and New Testament, and so it is no surprise that the theme on which he focuses, promise and fulfillment, necessarily spans the two Testaments and is not to be fully found in either singular Testament.[82] This might almost be identified as a theology that unites the two Testaments rather than describes the Old Testament and New Testament theologies found in the two.

Scobie thinks that the theme of salvation history, if taken as the major theme of the Bible, is inadequate, not least because not only does salvation in the New Testament sense of conversion to Christ not occur in the Old Testament, but also, even more broadly, redemption usually indicates something "less spiritual" in the Old Testament than it does in the New Testament. He cautions,

> Scripture is concerned not just with God's relation with his chosen people,
> but with his relation to the whole world that he has created and to all human-

---

[80]Ibid., p. 86.
[81]Ibid., p. 87.
[82]Ibid., p. 88.

kind. . . . The relation of God to his people does not just involve "salvation"; . . . it is also a history of disobedience and hence of judgment. The significance of salvation history for the NT is a matter of dispute, though it can be eliminated only by ignoring Luke-Acts.[83]

Brevard Childs provides a helpful cautionary word at this juncture when he says that the task of biblical theology, like that of the Old Testament, is "not to Christianize the Old Testament by identifying it with the New Testament witness, but to hear its own theological testimony to the God of Israel whom the church confesses also to worship."[84]

In describing his own approach, Scobie emphasizes,

The structure that is proposed here is one in which the major themes of OT and NT are *correlated* with each other. Minor themes are then grouped around the major ones. Extensive study of key biblical themes again and again reveals a common pattern in the way these themes are developed within Scripture.[85]

One of the basic organizing principles will be the use of typology, seeing Old Testament events, persons, and institutions as patterns, examples and foreshadowings of New Testament ones, and thus one looks for both theological and historical correspondence, with the usual assumption that the type is grander and a fulfillment of the antetype.

One of the helpful distinctions made in Scobie's study is the one between promise and predictive prophecy. Chris Wright describes the difference as follows:

Imagine in the last century a father promises his young son a horse of his own when he comes of age! In the meantime cars are invented. On his twenty-first birthday, his father therefore gives him a car instead. The promise is fulfilled, because the substantive meaning of the promise was a personally owned means of transport. It would be pointless to say it would only be fulfilled if the son gets a horse as well, or later. That would be to take the original promise as a mere prediction which will have "failed" unless it is literally honoured.[86]

The point of this illustration is clear: promise is a broader category than

---

[83]Ibid., p. 90.
[84]Brevard S. Childs, *Old Testament Theology in a Canonical Context* (Philadelphia: Fortress, 1986), p. 9.
[85]Scobie, *Ways of Our God*, p. 91.
[86]Chris Wright, "A Christian Approach to Old Testament Prophecy Concerning Israel," in *Jerusalem: Past and Present in the Purposes of God*, ed. Peter W. L. Walker (Cambridge: Tyndale House, 1992), p. 5.

predictive prophecy, and its fulfillment need not take an absolutely literal or exact form. This, presumably, is why Scobie chooses the category of promise and fulfillment as his unifying theme, not least because, as Paul says, in Christ all sorts of and every one of God's promises are a yes (2 Cor 1:20). Scobie sees the "already and not yet" character of fulfillment in both Testaments as a clue that promise and fulfillment is something that can be said of both Testaments in isolation but also together, presumably with the New Testament being more about fulfillment and the Old Testament more about promise and prophecy. Scobie claims that this theme or structuring device is not imposed on the text but rather arises out of the text.

With this rubric Scobie then identifies four master themes: (1) God's order (both the creation order and the historical and eschatological order); (2) God's servant (whether prophet, priest, king, or even Israel, and culminating in the suffering servant Christ, the ultimate mediator between God and humankind); (3) God's people (including subthemes such as covenant or election, land, city, worship); (4) God's way (piety, spirituality, ethics, ethos). This last category is Scobie's attempt to do justice to the overwhelmingly large amount of paraenetic material in both Testaments, and here he stresses the connection between theology and ethics, following Childs, who says, "The Old Testament's portrayal of ethical behaviour is inseparable from its total message respecting Israel, that is to say, from its theological content."[87] The present study has validated this statement as being just as true for the New Testament as it is for the Old Testament. The only ethics that we have in the New Testament are theological ethics; the two things are intimately intertwined, and Scobie wisely sees and affirms this truth.

Scobie's four themes are viewed as proclaimed or declared and promised in the Old Testament, partially fulfilled there, and then further fulfilled in the New Testament era, but all of them await the eschatological consummation for their complete fulfillment. What is promised in the Old Testament, then, is a new order, a new servant, a new people and a new way, and all of these are partially fulfilled in and through the Christ-event, but they await the consummation for the full completion of what was promised. Thus, the Old Testament and New Testament eras share the characteristic of being "already and not yet."

Here we get a glimpse of what is fundamentally wrong with Scobie's ap-

---

[87]Brevard S. Childs, *Biblical Theology of the Old and New Testaments: Theological Reflection on the Christian Bible* (Minneapolis: Fortress, 1993), p. 676.

proach. Even if we grant all the above, it leaves out of consideration what precipitated the need for such promises: the fall. And furthermore, it is not the creation order, but rather the fallen creation order, that needs redeeming. My point is this: without the narratological scheme, which is tripartite (creation, fall, redemption), we cannot do justice either to the narrative flow of the Testaments or to the two dramatic events that precede the need for promise and fulfillment and indeed for salvation history.

There is the further problem that certainly one could debate the clustering of various of the subthemes within the four major themes. The four major themes are quite generic and defined too broadly, and they become catchalls for all sorts of ideas, not because there is no connection between, say, God's people as a theme and worship as a theme, but rather because this heuristic device does not allow us to see that various of these so-called subthemes are connected to the other major themes as well.

Furthermore, even when one is dealing with a large theme like the people of God, we must ask where we are in the story in order to meaningfully talk about that topic. In the New Testament era, Paul defines the people of God as Jew and Gentile united in Christ. This definition will hardly work for the Old Testament people of God. In other words, I am unconvinced that this sort of schematized and carefully categorized thematic approach is as helpful as the narratological one. In the end, a thematic approach is just another form of a topical approach, however carefully one has coordinated subthemes under the headings of major themes, and as such, it bears considerable resemblance to the old systematic categorization of ideas and topics, even though Scobie does not operate with purely soteriological categories (justification, sanctification, glorification) or some of the other schemas that old-school systematic theology uses to sort the biblical data.

The Bible, of course, does not organize itself thematically (or topically), and the real deficiency of this sort of approach is in ignoring not only where in the story this or that theme appears, but also how differently it is treated in an earlier phase of the story from a later phase. There is also the danger of ignoring the genre of material in which an idea occurs and how that changes the nature of the discussion and the theme. For example, a promise in a covenant document is one thing (that is a legally binding contract), but a conditional promise in an apocalyptic letter from John of Patmos to his converts, contingent on their believing and behaving more properly, is another thing. Some promises are conditional, some are not. The promises in a covenant may well be taken literally ("If you disobey me, you will die"), whereas the images, ideas, and themes in a document of apocalyptic prophecy are not meant to be taken literally. In Revelation 12 there is no real dragon to chase around a real woman in a real wilderness, but the promise of spiritual protection conveyed in this apocalyptic visionary story form certainly is real.

What we find in Scobie's study is a massive amount of carefully sifted data, fully conversant with the history and the current state of scholarly discussion on that data. Texts are helpfully exegeted and interpreted, and indeed the study is well written and is done in a way that not only makes it accessible to a wide audience but also often gives it a helpful pastoral dimension. However, reading Scobie's book is somewhat like reading a biblical theology dictionary with a pastoral heart on this or that topic and then following the related topics listed at the end of the article for further elucidation and connections. This is helpful, but it is perhaps not the best way to connect the dots of biblical theology. The great promise (and fulfillment!) of Scobie's study is that he shows that there are a lot of intricate connections between the two Testaments and between various themes found in each Testament. The "not yet" of Scobie's study is showing both why this or that theme appears where it does in the story and why the theme modulates and changes as the biblical story develops, climaxes, and heads for an eschatological conclusion.

In closing, I suggest that we consider these carefully chosen words by Frank Mead about the problems with thematic approaches to biblical theology:

> First, the sheer number and diversity of themes that biblical theologians have identified and discussed makes it difficult to do justice to the breadth and depth of the Bible's theology. Even if one limited the scope only to the proposed "centers" or major themes, the amount of material would be quite large indeed. . . . Second, the multiplicity of methods also affects the choice and arrangement of the themes. . . . Third, the relationship of the testaments becomes acute when we address biblical themes, because very important categories do not easily carry over between the Old and the New Testaments. For example, the messianic identity of Jesus, the nature of the resurrection, and the worldwide scope of the church's mission are significant in the New Testament message, but where should they be considered in relation to Old Testament themes?[88]

Where indeed? Perhaps after all the correlation of themes into slots, however clarifying in some ways, is not, at the end of the day, the best way to do biblical theology.

---

[88]Mead, *Biblical Theology*, p. 170.

George Herbert, the great English cleric and metaphysical poet, wrote a sonnet entitled "The Holy Scriptures." It reads in part,

Ladies, look here; this is the thankfull glasse,
That mends the lookers eyes: this is the well
That washes what it shows. Who can indeare
Thy praise too much? thou art heav'ns Lidger here,
Working against the states of death and hell. . . .
Oh that I knew how all thy lights combine,
And the configurations of their glorie!
Seeing not only how each verse doth shine,
But all the constellation of the storie. . . .
Such are thy secrets, which my life makes good,
And comments on thee: for in ev'ry thing
Thy words do finde me out, and parallels bring,
And in another make me understood.

It is a consummation devoutly to be wished that we might see the full constellation of the biblical story, but as of yet we are only pilgrims on the way to such a capacious vision, and biblical theology may well help us get there, but as for now, it has "miles to go . . . and promises to keep," as Robert Frost once said. In the meanwhile, we must apply the whole of the biblical text to ourselves and the whole of ourselves to the biblical text, as Johannes Bengel insisted. And when we do this, we repeatedly discover that the biblical text uncovers and discovers us, or as Herbert more eloquently puts it, "Thy words do finde me out, and parallels bring / And in another make me understood."

Lord, may we understand not only your Word but also ourselves in the light of your Word, written and incarnate, and so become what we admire, mirrors of Christ, bearers of the indelible and restored image. Amen.

Subject Index

Scripture Index

Finding the Textbook You Need

The IVP Academic Textbook Selector
is an online tool for instantly finding the IVP books
suitable for over 250 courses across 24 disciplines.

www.ivpress.com/academic/